I0199640

Presented to
by

ECHOTA
PLATE I

HISTORY
OF THE
CHEROKEE INDIANS
AND
Their Legends and Folk Lore.

With a

New Added Index

By
EMMET STARR

New Added Index By
JEFF BOWEN

JANAWAY PUBLISHING
Santa Maria, California

History of the Cherokee Indians and Their Legends and Folk Lore.
With a New Added Index

Published by:

Janaway Publishing, Inc.
732 Kelsey Ct.
Santa Maria, California 93454
(805) 925-1038
www.JanawayGenealogy.com

2018

ISBN: 978-1-59641-414-3

Made in the United States of America

PREFACE.

This humble effort is attempted for the purpose of perpetuating some of the facts relative to the Cherokee tribe, that might otherwise be lost. The object has been to make it as near a personal history and biography of as many Cherokees as possible.

Without the assistance of the magnanimous, wholesoul membership of the nation, the work would not have been possible and for that reason I wish to thank each and every member, for their hearty collaboration and express my regret that the work has not the merit with which many others might have invested it.

Emmet Starr.

Claremore, Okla.
December 12, 1921.

Contents

ECHOTA
PLATE II

HON. ROBT. L. OWEN

O. H. P. BREWER

Oliver Hazard Perry Brewer, the son of Lieutenant Colonel Oliver Hazard Perry and Delilah (Vann) Brewer, was born in Canadian District on March 15, 1871. A member of the senior class at the Male Seminary he was expelled about a couple of months before graduation day for condemning the action of the principal of that school in unmercifully beating one of the smaller boys. Brewer then attended Arkansas University and graduated on December 6, 1893. He was elected Senator from Canadian District on August 5, 1901. Elected a member of the Cherokee National School Board and chosen as its president in November, 1903. A democrat, he was elected delegate to the Oklahoma State Constitutional Convention from District Number Seventy-seven on November 6, 1906. Appointed postmaster of Muskogee in 1917.

GRADUATES OF THE CHEROKEE NATIONAL FEMALE SEMINARY 1903

D. M. FAULKNER

(SEQUOYAH)

CHEROKEE CAPITOL

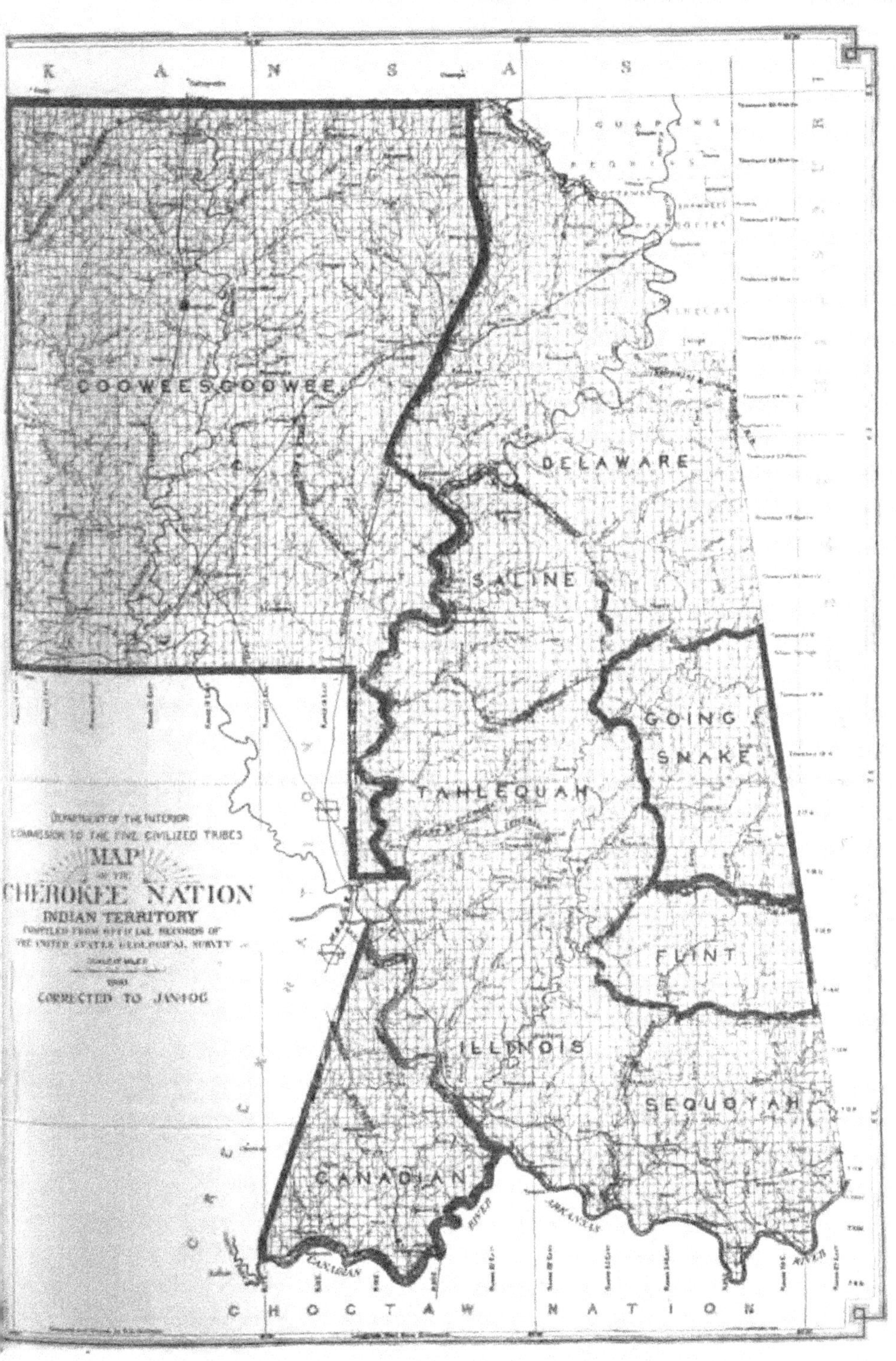
K A N S A S
COOWEESCOOWEE
DELAWARE
SALINE
GOING
SNAKE
TAHLEQUAH
FLINT
ILLINOIS
SEQUOYAH
CANADIAN
DEPARTMENT OF THE INTERIOR
COMMISSION TO THE FIVE CIVILIZED TRIBES
MAP
CHEROKEE NATION
INDIAN TERRITORY
CORRECTED TO JAN 1-06
C H O C T A W N A T I O N

CHEROKEE ALPHABET.

CHARACTERS SYSTEMATICALLY ARRANGED WITH THE SOUNDS

Ꭰ		Ꭱ		Ꭲ		Ꭳ	Ꭴ	Ꭵ
a		e		i		o	oo	v
Ꭶ	Ꭷ	Ꭸ		Ꭹ		Ꭺ	Ꭻ	Ꭼ
ga	ka	ge		gi		go	gu	gv
Ꭽ		Ꭾ		Ꭿ		Ꮀ	Ꮁ	Ꮂ
ha		he		hi		ho	hu	hv
Ꮃ		Ꮄ		Ꮅ		Ꮆ	Ꮇ	Ꮈ
la		le		li		lo	lu	lv
Ꮉ		Ꮊ		Ꮋ		Ꮌ	Ꮍ	
ma		me		mi		mo	mu	
Ꮎ	Ꮏ	Ꮑ	Ꮐ	Ꮒ		Ꮓ	Ꮔ	Ꮕ
na	hna	ne	nah	ni		no	nu	nv
Ꮖ		Ꮗ		Ꮘ		Ꮙ	Ꮚ	Ꮛ
qua		que		qui		quo	quu	quv
Ꮝ	Ꮜ	Ꮞ		Ꮟ		Ꮠ	Ꮡ	Ꮢ
s	sa	se		si		so	su	sv
Ꮣ	Ꮤ	Ꮥ	Ꮦ	Ꮧ	Ꮨ	Ꮩ	Ꮪ	Ꮫ
da	ta	de	t	di	ti	do	du	dv
Ꮬ	Ꮭ	Ꮮ		Ꮯ		Ꮰ	Ꮱ	Ꮲ
dla	tla	tle		cle		tlo	tlu	tlv
Ꮳ		Ꮴ		Ꮵ		Ꮶ	Ꮷ	Ꮸ
tsa		tse		tsi		tso	tsu	tsv
Ꮹ		Ꮺ		Ꮻ		Ꮼ	Ꮽ	Ꮾ
wa		we		wi		wo	wu	wv
Ꮿ		Ᏸ		Ᏹ		Ᏺ	Ᏻ	Ᏼ
ya		ye		yi		yo	yu	yv

SOUNDS REPRESENTED BY VOWELS

A as a in father, or short as a in rival.
E as a in hate, or short as e in met.
I as i in pique, or short as i in pin.
O as o in note, but as approaching to aw in law.
U as oo in moon, or short as u in pull.
V as u in but, nasalized.

CONSONANT SOUNDS.

G, is sounded hard approaching to k; sometimes before e, i, u and v, its sound is k. D has a sound between the English d and t; sometimes, before o, u, and v its sound is t; when written before l and s the same analogy prevails.

All other letters as in English.

Syllables beginning with g, except ga have sometimes the power of k; syllables when written with tl, except tla sometimes vary to dla.

HISTORY OF THE CHEROKEE INDIANS

CHAPTER I

Origin, Religion, First Civilization, Early Wars

FOR four hundred years the question: "From whence came the Indian?" has been a recurrent problem. Four centuries of quest and investigation have not brought the solution nearer and it's sanest answer of today is conjecture.

Every person, who has made an extended study of Indians either as a tribe or as a race, has naturally evolved some idea of their possible origin and this is very often based on tribal migration legends.

At some ancient period, so remote that even legend does not note it, the earth most probably came so ear the sphere of influence of some other planet, that it momentarily swung out of its solar trend, causing a cataclysm that instantly transforme dthe zones so suddenly that the giant mammoths were frozen as they stood, to be later incased in great masses of ice and preserved so well that as it melted away from their bodies the flesh was so fresh that it was eaten by dogs and other animals.

The immense glaciers were left in the temperate and possibly the torrid zones. As to whether any land was raised at that time there is a question, but there is very little doubt that much of the land connecting northern Europe and America was submerged, leaving only Greenland, Iceland and a few other elevated portions above sea level. The flora and fossil remains indicate a previous continuity and the charts of the ocean bed show a well defined plateau at only a comparatively shallow depth extending from Labrador to Norway.

These seismic and climatic convulsions most probably very nearly destroyed the cave dwellers of what had been the united continent of Euromerica, but on account of their peculiar hardiness a few survived to repopulate the riven continent.

Aeons later, so late that even the historians of the early civilizations were able to gather bits of legends concerning it, the fabled continent of Atlantis, lying west of Spain and possibly joining southern Europe or Northern Africa with South or Central America, sank with its mythical civilization and possibly leaving parts of a homogenous people in America, North Africa and Eurasia.

Other people possibly came to western America from Asia and the South Sea Islands. As the people became more numerous they commenced to migrate. The Cherokees, with the soft accents of the underhills, which was obviously the mother dialect, were evidently from a southern country, for the pleasant fluent languages always come from a southern people in contradistinction from the harsher tones of the north. This tribe moved gradually to the north and east as is evidenced by mounds in Iowa, Illinois, Ohio, Virginia and Tennessee that have been explored and showed artifactuary and thhnic composition almost identical and peculiar to known early Cherokee customs and handicraft. In each of these the well known crematory marks of this tribe were found; the charred post at the apex of the mound, to which the victim had been bound. The hardened saucer like clay deposit with the ashes, charred bones and fire marks, one above another, as the mound had been added to. Among the mortuary remains near the center and base of the mounds of these regions were found monitor pipes that were identical with those described by Adair as having been made and used by the Cherokees in the eighteenth century.

In the center of a mound at Etowah, Georgia and on the surface of the ground were found two copper plates. This territory was known to have been inhabited by the Cherokees since 1540. The only known similar designs to these are those of Central America, Yucatan and the Levant.

An intertribal tradition details that the Cherokees got as far east as Delaware River before they were stopped by the warlike Iroquois confederacy, although they had been in contact with that tribe of northern origin so long that each of the tribes had imbibed many words in common.

The Cherokees most probably preceded by several hundred years the Muskogees in their exodus from Mexico and swung in a wider circle, crossing the Mississippi River many miles north of the mouth of the Missouri River as is indicated by the mounds. All of the northern mounds are so built that the structure indicates they were built by other poplee. The Muskogees claim that when they came to the "black grass country" they crossed the Mississippi. This probably has reference to the frost line.

The Cherokees came so suddenly and unexpectedly into the coastland that the Senecas and many other tribes thought that they came from the earth, and called them "cave men" or "the people that came from a hole in the ground." The ancient Delawares, who called themselves "Lenni Lenape" or "The People," called the Cherokees, "Allegans." The Cherokees were known to the Shawnees, another Algonquin tribe, as the Keetoowhas. The Shawnees called the Muskogees, "Swamp People" or "Humaskogi" and this foreign name was slightly changed and adopted by the Muskogees when they formed their confederacy, but the Muskogees changed the word to Emmussuk, of Medicine, referring to the "black wash" and ogee, meaning confederacy or the confederacy of those who drank the black wash, a stringent emmenagogue and chologague for purification purposes immediately preceding the green corn dance and on other stated occasions. The Muskogees were probably driven out of Mexico by the Aztecs, Toltecs or some other of the northwestern tribal invasions of the ninth or preceding centuries. This is evidenced by the customs and devices that were long retained by the Creeks.

The Cherokees were forced back from the vicinity of the Great Lakes and Atlantic by assailants, led by the valorous Iroquois, until they reached the southern Appalachian mountains, where they held all enemies at bay and created a neutral strip extending north to Ohio river, on which no tribe or warrior dared settle with impunity.

When the early missionaries came among the Cherokees, they were astonished at the similarity of the religious traditions of the Cherokees to the biblical accounts. In recounting the religious views of the Cherokees, they stated that from time immemorial the tribe had been divided in sentiment. That while the greater part had been idolatrous, worshiping the sun, moon, stars and other gods; a small portion denied that system and taught that there were three beings above, who created all things and will judge all men. That they fixed the time and manner of death. Their names were: U-ha-he-ta-qua, the great head of all power; A-ta-no-ti and U-squa-hu-la. These three beings were said to be always unanimous in thought and action and always will be. They sit on three white seats above and are the only objects to which worship and prayers should be directed. The Angels are their messengers and come down to earth to attend to the affairs of men.

They claimed that Yehowa was the name of a great king. He was a man and yet a spirit, a great and glorious being. His name was never to be spoken in common talk. This great king commanded them to rest every seventh day. They were told not to work on this day and that they should devote it to talking about God[1].

Yehowa created the world in seven days at Nu-ta-te-qua or the first new moon of autumn, with the fruits all ripe[2]. God made the first man of red clay and he was an Indian, and made woman of one of his ribs.[3] All people were Indians or red people before the flood. They had preachers and prophets who taught the people to obey God and their parents. They warned the people of the approaching flood, but said that the world would only be destroyed by water once, and that later it would be destroyed by fire, when God would send a shower of pitch and then a shower of fire which would burn up everything. They also taught that after death the good and the bad would be separated, the good would take a path that would lead to happiness, where it would always be light, but the bad would be urged along another path which would lead to a deep chasm over which lay a pole with a dog at each end. They would be urged on to this pole and the dogs, by moving it, would throw them off into the gulf of fire beneath. But if they got over they would be transfixed with red hot bars of iron and thus be tormented forever.[4]

A little before the flood men grew worse and worse. At length God sent a messenger from above to warn the people of the flood unless they turned from their wickedness. God then told a man to make a house that would swim, take his family and some of the different kinds of animals into it[5]. The rain commenced and continued for forty days and forty nights, while the water at the same time gushed out of the ground, so that as much came up as came down from the clouds[6].

The house was raised upon the waters and borne away. At length the man sent out a raven, and after some time, sent a dove, which came back with a leaf in her mouth. Soon after this the man found the house was resting on dry ground on the top of a mountain. This being in the spring of the year the family and all the animals left the house and the family descended to the botton of the mountain and commenced their farming operations[7].

The Cherokees detailed to the missionaries parallels to practically every one of the stories of the Bible. They called Abraham, Aquahami; Moses was called Wasi. These accounts were so circumstantial that many investigators were led to believe that the Cherokees were of Semitic origin. But it is palpable that they had been told these stories by Priber during his short stay among them and that they had forgotten their origin within seventy years and attributed it to legends that had descended from the mythical Kutani and their primal religion. On account of the fact that the Cherokees thought that the missionaries were bringing back to them their old religion, it was a comparatively easy task to convert them from a tribe of savages to a Christian nation within the comparatively short period of thirty years. When they were converted, they, at the behest of the missionaries cast aside every vestige of their ancient customs to such an extent that not any of their mythology has ever been preserved, even among those of the tribe that speak the Cherokee language preferably.

On May 10, 1540, De Soto, according to the historiographer, "a gentleman of Elvas," entered the province of Chelaque, which was most probably one of the Underhill settlements, as the use of the sound of the letter "l" was universal with them in preference to the letter "r" which was occasionally used by the Overhills, notably in the word oochera in contradistinction to oochela, as used by the Underhills. After traveling a northward course through their country he came to Xualla, probably Qualla, and then turning westward the Spaniards traversed the entire Cherokee country, visiting Canasauga on the way.

In the decade of 1666-1676 an exploring party sent out from Appomattox by Sir William Berkeley, Governor of Virginia, came to some abandoned fields and settlements located on a river flowing to the westward when their Indian guides refused to proceed, alleging that not far away dwelt a powerful tribe that never suffered strangers who discovered their towns to return alive[1]. This was in the vicinity of the Cherokees, and was thought to allude to them.

Alexander Dougherty, a Virginia trader, was the first white man to marry a Cherokee, the date was 1690.[2] The Cherokees in concert with the Muskogee towns of Alabama, Abekas and Conchartys were said to have been in league to attack the French in 1708 but probably did not do so.

Two hundred and eighteen Cherokees accompanied the colonists under Colonel Barnwell in 1712 in the subjugation of the Tuscaroras, an Iroquoian tribe that lived adjacent to and southeast of the Cherokees. Following the success of this expedition, the tribe then moved northward and joined the Iroquoian confederacy on the Great Lakes. Three years later the Cherokees joined the Yamassees, Appalachians and Creeks against the colonists, but they were defeated and the Yamassees and Appalachian tribes were destroyed.

In January 1716 the Cherokees killed the Frenchmen de Ramsey and de Longueie, the latter being a member of the illustrious de Moyne family that founded Biloxi and New Orleans and furnished the first two governors of Louisiana, both of whom were the paternal uncles of young de Longueil, whose father was Governor of Canada. In reprisal for the death of his son, the Governor induced the Iroquois to attack and burn two of the Cherokee towns.

The estimated population of the Cherokee country in 1715 was eleven thousand, in 1735 fifteen thousand. In 1738 the ravages of smallpox which was a hitherto unknown disease with them, reduced their number by one half, later reports gave their population for 1875, 19,717; 1880, 21,920; 1890, 28,000; 1900, 32,376 and 1910, 38,300.

De Iberville established Biloxi as the capital of Louisiana in 1699, it was moved to Mobile in 1702, which was fortified nine years later, and was finally transferred to New Orleans in 1718. Fort Toulouse, among the Creeks, Fort Rosalie among the Natchez and other fortified stations among the Chickasaws and Choctaws were established with the consent of those tribes by the French in 1714 or earlier, and four years later the ambitious promotions of Law threatened to found a formidable French colony in the lower Mississippi valley. Of all the tribes east of the great river only the Cherokees remained friendly to the English and in order to counteract the French influence, Governor Nicholson of South Carolina concluded a treaty of peace and commerce with them in 1721 by which their boundaries were defined. This was their first treaty with the whites.

In 1729, Sir Alexander Cumming, of England, was led, by a dream of his wife's, to undertake a voyage to America with the object of visiting the Cherokees. He sailed on September 13th, arrived at Charlestown on December 5th, and on March 11, 1730 began his journey to the Cherokee country. At Keowee, three hundred miles from Charlestown and which was the first important location on the road, locally called the trace from Charlestown to the Cherokee nation, he met Ludovic Grant, a Scotch trader from Tellico, who had lived there since 1720, had married a Cherokee woman and spoke their language. He informed Grant that he wanted to visit the Cherokees and prevailed on him to accompany him on the trip. They stopped at the residence of Joseph Baker, a trader at Keowee and that evening attended a meeting of the headmen at the townhouse, where the Indians met every night. Sir Alexander made the first of his stereotyped addresses in which he stated "that he was one of the Great King George's children but was not sent either by the Great King or any of his Governors—that he was no public person and only came for his own private satisfaction to see their country, and that he would drink the King's health hoping that all persons would pledge him, which he accordingly did upon his knee desiring those present to follow his example. He carried with him into the townhouse, his gun, cutlass and a pair of pistols; upon one of the traders telling him that the Indians never came there armed and that they did not like to see others do so, he answered, with a wild look, that his intention was, "if any of the Indians had refused the King's health I would have taken a brand from out the fire, that burns in the middle of the room and set fire to the house. I would have guarded the door and put to death every one that endeavored to make his escape, so that they might have all been consumed in the flames."[1]

On the next morning he departed from Keowee on a trip of over one hundred and fifty miles into the center of the nation, during which time he never stopped for more than one night at a place. When any of the Cherokees met him, they would, as was their custom, shake hands with him, upon which he would take down their names in a note book, saying that he had made a "friend of him."

Sir Alexander was told of the ceremonies that were used in making a "beloved man," or ouka; of which there were many in the nation, the word was ordinarily translated into English as "king" and the cap of red or yellow dyed opossum skin was generally spoken of as a crown. When Sir Alexander arrived at Neguasse he expressed a desire to see one of the crowns and upon being shown one, requested that he be allowed to take it to England and present it to the King. In an article in the London Daily Journal of October 8, 1730, he made claims to have been made a chief of the tribe and that he was further allowed to name Mogtog of Tellico as their emperor. He told the Indians he would soon return to England and that if any of them would like to accompany him he would take them. Seven Cherokees signified their willingness to go, two of whom were Attacullaculla and Oconostota. They arrived at Charlestown on April 13, 1730 and on June 5th they landed at Dover, England, on the English man-of-war Fox. On the 22nd they were presented to the King. Sir Alexander laid the opossum skin "crown" at his feet and the Indians added four scalps and eagle tail feathers to the tribute. This audience developed the real reason of his activities which were to follow in, a degree, the machinations of Crozat and Law in France. Among his schemes, was one for paying off eighty millions of the national debt by settling three million Jewish families in the Cherokee mountains to cultivate the land, and for relieving the American colonies from taxation by establishing numerous banks and a local currency, but he could find no one who would take his schemes seriously. In a letter from South Carolina bearing date of June 12th and published in the Edinburgh Weekly Journal of September 16, 1830 Sir Alexander was accused of having defrauded the settlers out of large sums of money and other property by means of fictitious promissory notes. He did not answer these charges and his chimera collapsed. The Indian delegation was loaded with presents by the government and returned to Charlestown.

The Principal Chiefs of the Cherokees have been: 1736 Moytog; Attacullaculla, died 1778; Oconostota, died 1785; Tassel, killed in July 1788· Hanging Neaughe, Blackfox; Pathkiller; William Hicks, was chief for only one year, 1827; John Ross 1828 to 1866; William Potter Ross, Reverend Lewis Downing, William Potter Ross, Reverend Ochalata, Dennis Wolf Bushyhead. Joel Bryan Mayes, Thomas Mitchell Buffington, Colonel Johnson Harris. Samuel Houston Mayes, Thomas Mitchell Buffington and William Charles Rogers. The Principal Chiefs of the Westeren Cherokees were, consecutively: John Bowles 1795-1813; Takatoka 1813-1818; Tahlonteeskee, John Jolly, John Brown and John Rogers. The latter was deposed in 1839 and his valuable property at Grand Saline was confiscated by Chief John Ross. John Rogers was the grandfather of William Charles Rogers, the last Chief of the Cherokees.

Governor Glenn of South Carolina concluded a treaty with the Cherokees on November 24, 1855 by which that colony acquired five million five hundred twenty six thousand four hundred acres and the right to construct and garrison three forts in the Cherokee country, and soon afterwards the Governor built Fort Prince George within gunshot of Keowee and Fort Moore, one hundred and seventy miles further down on Keowee River. A treaty of alliance was made in 1756 between the Cherokees, Catawbas and North Carolina. During this year the Earl of London having been appointed commander in chief of the British forces in the American colonies, sent Major Andrew Lewis to build the third fort in the Cherokee nation. He located it on the Tennessee River within five miles of Echauta, the capital of the nation. The English translation of Echauta is "place of rest." The English ordinarily spelled the name Chota. This fort was named London in honor of the Earl. It was garrisoned with two Scotch companies under Captains Paul Demere and John Stuart and was over one hundred and fifty miles from the nearest white settlenent.

General Braddock marching to attack Fort Duquense with a well equipped army of more than two thousand regulars and the famous Virginia Militia was met in ambush on the Monongahela River by seventy-two French regulars, two hundred and fifty Canadian volunteers and six hundred thirty seven Indians under Captain Marie de Beauyeu and ingloriously defeated. The French had already ingratiated themselves with all of the western Indians except the Cherokees and the effect of Braddock's defeat was to encourage the Indians to scour the frontier in large and small bodies, killing, burning and destroying. The tide of emigration that had for several years steadily flowed westward over the Alleghenies commenced to rapidly recede. During this time Colonel George Washington wrote to his former employer, Lord Fairfax, that three hundred and fifty wagons had crossed one ford of the Monocacy River, eastbound, within three days. Colonels William Byrd and Peter Randolph were deputed by the Colony of Virginia in November 1755 to treat with the Cherokees for their active cooperation; as Colonel George Washington expressed it "without Indians we will be unable to cope with the cruel foes of our country."[1]

Major Andrew Lewis had led a company of Cherokees in an attack on the Shawnees, who were allies of the French and while on their return a party of them was entertained by a back settler in Augusta County, Virginia and when they had taken their leave, some of his friends, whom he had placed in ambush for that purpose, fired upon and killed several of them. Those who escaped arrived in their towns just as Byrd and Randolph were on the point of concluding their treaty.[2] Great excitement ensued, and but for the devotion of Silonee and the wisdom and tact of Attacullaculla, the treaty would not only have been defeated, but the commissioners themselves would have been killed.

Attacullaculla hastened to apprise the commissioners of their danger, warning them to stay within their tent, and on no account to appear abroad. Silonee saved the lives of the commissioners by standing in their tent door and telling a body of warriors that before they got to the commissioners they would have to kill him, as Colonel Byrd was his friend. In addressing the council Attacullaculla expressed the indignation that they all felt at the treachery of the Virginians and declared he would have full satisfaction for the blood of his countrymen. "Let us not, however" he added, "violate our faith, or the laws of hospitality, by imbruing our hands in the blood of those who are now in our power; they came to cement a perpetual alliance with us. Let us carry them back to their own settlement; conduct them safely to their confines; and then take up the hatchet and endeavor to exterminate the whole race of them."[1] A treaty of alliance was finally concluded.

For three years the Cherokees adhered to their promise made in the treaty and defended the western frontier, rendered every aid possible to the settlers and when General Forbes assembled his levies to attack the French a large number of Cherokees joined him at Winchester, Virginia.[2] Dr. John Forbes, a Scotch physician, who had been serving in the Canadian service as a lieutenant colonel was promoted to a brigadier generalship by James Abercromby, the new British commander in chief, early in 1758. General Forbes was a strict disciplinarian who profited much by correcting many of the military mistakes of Braddock. He was domineering, petulant and at that time in such bad health that he had to be carried on a litter, and died in March 1759. He did not understand the irregular but effective mode of warfare as practiced by his Cherokee allies and his irritable complaints and continuous insults, even to the magnanimous Attacullaculla, caused the Cherokees to quit his command on November 15, 1758, ten days before his reduction of Fort Duquesne. On the nineteenth the General ordered that they be intercepted, their horses, guns and ammunition be taken from them and if they protested they should be stripped of everything except their breech clouts and then escorted back to their nation, to prevent them from reprisals. Thus the only tribe that had been faithful allies of the English for the last thirty seven years, after having been driven from the army by the continuous petty insults of the commander, was offered this last indignity and this, by the orders of the general must be executed by Colonel Byrd[2] whose life had been saved in 1755 by Attacullaculla, who was on this latter occasion the commander of the Cherokees.

In addition to this, the colonial Indian affairs of the army which was under the "control of Edmund Atkin, Indian Agent,"[1] were so badly managed that, instead of receiving the encouragement their services and bravery merited, they were met by what they considered injustice, neglect and contempt. At one time ten of them were imprisoned on suspicion of being spies in the French interest; another party, after having undergone the perils and privations of their long march, went into action in their destitute condition, behaved nobly and rendered valuable service to the colony; but on returning with their trophies of honor, found neither agent nor interpreter to reward or thank them; nor any one who could tell them why they were thus neglected. But for the intervention and kind treatment of Colonel George Washington, they must have returned to their nation, fired with just resentment, if not open war, against their allies."[1]

The Cherokees were attacked as they were returning from Forbes' camp by some of the back settlers, the very same people that they had gratuitously protected, but the settlers did not discriminate between friendly Indians and enemy Indians, but set upon and killed twelve or more of the unsuspecting Cherokees, alleging that they had stolen some of their horses.

The young warriors clamored for war but the old chiefs persuaded them to wait until they had asked satisfaction from the colonies, in accordance with treaty stipulations. They sought reparation and satisfaction from Virginia, then North Carolina and afterwards South Carolina, but in vain. War, their only alternative, began. Among others, two soldiers of the garrison at Fort London, who were out hunting, were killed. Governor Lyttleton, of South Carolina mobilized the colonial militia in the vicinity of the Congarees to march against the Cherokees. Oconostota and thirty one other chiefs visited the Governor at Charlestown in an attempt to settle affairs. He told them that he would make his demands known only when he had reached their country, and if they were not granted he would take satisfaction by force of arms; that they must follow his army back to the nation. Upon Oconostota arising to protest, the Governor forced him to be seated and would not allow him to utter a word. The chiefs were forced to march behind the army to the Congarees where they were made prisoners, taken to Fort Prince George and shut up in a room that was scarcely large enough for the accommodation of six persons.

The Governor's military ire cooled in proportion to the distance that he got from Charlestown. When he arrived at Fort Prince George, he sent for Attacullaculla, the known friend of the English and upon that chief's arrival he insolently demanded the twenty-four Cherokees who had been accused of killing whites. Attacullaculla promised to do whatever he could in their delivery and asked that some of the prisoners be freed so that they might assist in the endeavor. Oconostota and seven others were accordingly liberated and the others, although they had gone as peace envoys were detained.

Two of the Indians that had been demanded were brought in and exchanged for two of the imprisoned chiefs; and an agreement was entered into on December 26, 1859 that the others would be delivered, but they had fled and could not be apprehended. Despairing of being able to rescue the prisoners by any other means Oconostota asked the commander of Fort Prince George for a conference and Captain Cotymore, Lieutenant Dogherty, Ensign Bill and their interpreter, Foster, met him on February 16, 1760, the parties being on opposite banks of the Savannah River. At a signal from Oconostota some warriors who had been hidden near him, fired and wounded all four of the party from the fort, the Captain being so severely wounded that he died two or three days later. The Indians stormed the fort but were repulsed and the twenty-two hostages were killed.

War, with all of its dreaded consequences was now on, and the back settlers appealed in vain to Governor Nicholson. Colonel Montgomery, who was later Earl Eglington was dispatched from New York to Charlestown from whence he marched against the Cherokees, raised the seige in May 1760 that Oconostota was conducting against Fort Prince George, and on June 27, 1760, he destroyed Etchoe, which had been deserted by its inhabitants, but on account of the incessant attacks it became necessary for him to retreat and in doing so he had to destroy and abandon all of his surplus supplies in order to expedite his progress. He reached Charlestown and sailed for New York.[1]

At the same time that Oconostota attacked Fort Prince George, Willinawa threw a strong cordon around Fort London. Manned by two companies of Scotch highlanders, the Fort mounted twelve cannon and was amply supplied with ammunition. Runners were sent to Virginia and South Carolina, but the former was not able to reach their destination on account of the distance, and the defense of the latter was centered in the fleeing, harassed Montgomery, and when his forces were safely away. Oconostota assumed the command of the investment of Fort London. Courageous, active and vigilant, he had the unaccounable reputation of having never lost a man in battle? Rations became shorter and shorter, and despite the fact that the Cherokee wives of many of the soldiers dared death in taking food to their husbands, the garrison was soon reduced to horse flesh. In this extremity Captain Stuart, the junior commander, whose wife was Süsannah Emory, the quarter blood granddaughter of the Scotch trader Ludovic Grant, and who spoke the Cherokee language fluently, was known to them on account of his great shock of blond hair as Oonotota or Bushyhead asked for and had a conference with the Cherokee Chiefs at the townhouse of Etchauta, and agreed on the following articles of capitulation:

"That the garrison of Fort London march out with their arms and drums. each soldier having as much powder and ball as their officers shall think necessary for their march, and all the baggage they may choose to carry· that the garrison be permitted to march to Virginia or Fort Prince George, as the commanding officer may think proper, unmolested; and that a number of Indians be appointed to escort them, and hunt for provisions during their march; that such soldiers that are lame or by sickness disabled from marching, be received into the Indian towns and kindly used until they recover, and then be allowed to return to Fort Prince George; that the Indians do provide for the garrison as many horses as they conveniently can for their march, agreeing with the officers and soldiers for payment; that the fort, great guns, powder, ball and spare arms be delivered to the Indians without fraud or further delay, on the day appointed for the march of the troops."

This agreement was signed by Captain Paul Demere representing the garrison and by Oconostota and Cunigacatgoae for the Indians.[1]

The Fort was evacuated on August 7, 1760, the garrison under the escort of Oconostota and Outacite started for Fort Prince George and encamped that evening on Tellico Plains after having travelled some fifteen miles. Noticing that his escort was gradually leaving him, Captain Demere posted sentries, who came in early in the morning and reported that Indians painted for war were quietly approaching in large numbers. Hardly had he formed his men when a volley was fired into their ranks, killing Captain Demere, three of his officers and about twenty-six men. The attack continued with war whoops and an incessant rattle of guns from all quarters. The rest of the men were either killed outright or captured and returned to Fort London. After the soldiers left, the Indians found that the British had, contrary to agreement, buried much of their powder and equipment. This breach of faith incensed them and was the primary reason for the Tellico Plains attack.

As soon as Attacullaculla heard that Captain Stuart had been returned to Fort London with the other prisoners, he hastened there and purchased him, giving in exchange his arms and all of his clothing except his breech clout. He took his prisoner to Captain Demere's house, which he had appropriated and entertained him. Oconostota was anxious to renew the investment of Fort Prince George and proposed that Captain Stuart be compelled to operate the artillery that they had captured, against the fort. Captain Stuart appealed to Attacullaculla to save him from this fratricidal position. The Chief stated that he was going on a hunt and that he intended taking his prisoner with him. As soon as they were safely in the northern hunting grounds and outside the Cherokee settlements they turned eastward to Virginia, where Attaculaculla delivered Captain Stuart to his friends and retraced his way to Fort London.

Attacullaculla was a small, slender man, distinguished as an orator and diplomat instead of being a great warrior. The word attacullaculla is translated as a pole or reed slightly stuck in the earth and leaning; or leaning stick.

Captain John Stuart was born in Scotland in the early part of the eighteenth century and died at Pensacola, Florida, February 21, 1779.

The assembly of South Carolina tendered Captain Stuart a vote of thanks, together with a reward of 1500 pounds for his heroic defense of Fort London and he was later appointed British Superintendent of Indian Affairs South of the Ohio River.

Fort Prince George was strengthened. In January 1761 Lieutenant Colonel James Grant, who had succeeded to the command of Colonel Montgomery's Highland Scotch regiment arrived at Charlestown and went into winter quarters. By the accession of Provincial Militia, Choctaw and Chickasaw allies his command was brought up to twenty-six hundred men. They arrived at Fort Prince George on May 27, 1761, when they were met by Attacullaculla who plead the cause of his people and begged Colonel Grant to delay his march until he could return to the nation and attempt to bring about peace.

Colonel Grant refused to listen to him and started from Fort Prince George on June 7th. After a rapid march he reached a gap in the mountains, where he detailed Lieutenant Francis Marion, who later played such an important part in the revolution, with thirty men to reconnoiter. Scarcely had this advance force entered the gap before they were enfiladed and twenty-one of the men fell at the first discharge. The battle lasted for about three hours with a loss of about sixty men killed on each side and the Cherokees were defeated. For a month more Colonel Grant devastated the middle Cherokee settlements, burned every habitation and destroyed all crops. Driven to distress the Cherokees made a treaty of peace with the South Carolinians in September 1761 and another with the Virginians on November 9, 1761 For fifteen years peace reigned in the Cherokee nation, but on May 9, 1776, circular letters were sent out by the British Superintendent, Stuart, to the Cherokees and Tories asking them to fall on and destroy the western American settlers. The Cherokees at first demurred but finally acceded to the wishes of King George, as they understood that he was the head of the English. It was hard for them to understand how one part of any people could fight others of their own nationality. But at last many of the young warriors listened to the persuasive Stuart, who had been their friend and agent for some ten years.

It was agreed to make a simultaneous attack on the western settlers. For this purpose the Cherokees were to furnish seven hundred warriors to be divided into three bodies. One of these under Dragging Canoe was to attack the Holston settlements, the second contingent under Abraham of Chilhowee was to destroy the Watuga settlements and Raven (Colonah) was to march against Carters Valley. The attack was to be made on the morning of July 21, 1776. But as soon as she was certain that the preparations were in earnest Mrs. Nancy Ward, the Ghigan or the beloved woman of the Cherokees, who was living at Chota dispatched William Thomas, a white trader and William Fawling, an eighth blood Cherokee and a son of Rim and Elizabeth (Emory) Fawling to apprise the settlers of their danger. Hastily assembling they were ready to meet the advance of the British allies which included warriors and Tories. The little army from the Holston settlement met Dragging Canoe's contingent at Long Island on July 20, 1776 and after a short skirmish in which thirteen Cherokees were left dead on the field, Dragging Canoe withdrew his forces.

On the next morning at sunrise, Abraham attacked Fort Watauga, which was garrisoned by forty men under Captain James Robertson and Lieutenant John Seiver and this post was invested for twenty days but the Indians were finally compelled to retire. On account of the repulse of Dragging Canoe and Abraham and the further fact that he found the citizens of Carter's Valley forted up, Raven failed to make the concerted attack.

"Upon the whole, the Indian invasion was a failure, owing to the timely warning of Nancy Ward, and the concentration of the inhabitants in forts built in consequence of the information she conveyed. If the well guarded secret of the Indian campaign had not been disclosed, and they had been permitted to steal upon the defenseless backwoodsmen, who, in fancied security, had remained scattered over the extensive frontiers, every soul of them would have been swept from the borders of Tennessee."[1]

Isaac Thomas' services were recognized and rewarded by the Virginia legislature. Mrs. William Bean, the mother of the first white child born in Tennessee, and Samuel Moore, a boy, were captured at the attack on Fort Watauga. They were taken back to the Cherokee nation where the boy was burned at the stake and a like punishment was being meted to Mrs. Bean, who was tied to a stake on the top of the mound that stood in the center of Etsauta, the fagots were piled around her and the frenzied savages were gloating over their chance to also sacrifice their second. Defeat had whetted their remorseless appetites, but just as the torch was about to be applied, the Ghigan exercising her prerogatives approached the pyre, pronounced the pardon of Mrs. Bean, cut the strands that bound her and took her to her home, kept her until it was safe to send her under the escort of her brother Longfellow and her son Firekiller, to her home and husband. Chief Tassel said afterward that Moore was the only white person that was ever burned by the Cherokees.

In retaliation for the Cherokee attacks North Carolina sent twenty-four hundred men under Colonel Griffith Rutherford against the Cherokees, two hundred Georgians under Captain Jack, eighteen hundred and sixty South Carolinians and two thousand Virginians under Colonel William Christian attacked and destroyed most of the nation; destroyed their crops, appropriated their property and burned fifty of their towns and reduced the people to dire destitution. Etsauta, the home of Attacullaculla and Ghigau was spared from destruction by Colonel Christian, the commander of the Virginia forces. A treaty of peace was concluded with the South Carolinians and Georgians at De Witt's Corner on May 20, 1777, and exactly two months later another with Virginia and North Carolina at Long Island of the Holston. By these two treaties they ceded five million two hundred sixty four thousand acres. Outacita, Young Tassel and Dragging Canoe did not attend either of these treaties and the latter chief withdrew with many implacable young warriors and established the five Chicamauga towns, east of the present city of Chattanooga. Dragging Canoe was at this time a stalwart, subtle and daring warrior of about twenty four years of age. Outacita was at this time seventy-five years old, discontented, he moved to the Chicamauga settlements but on account of his age was not active in their affairs. Young Tassel was a half blood English-Cherokee who was later known as John Watts. He settled in the vicinity of the Chicamaugas, but did not join them. Chief Attacullaculla died in 1778 and was succeeded by Oconostota. The Chicamauga towns flourished and became the headquarters of the British authority south of the Ohio. The British agent Colonel Brown and subagent John McDonald were established there. McDonald's store became the British commissary. Many warriors from that community prepared to join Governor Henry Hamilton in a general attack on the western frontier, but the Governor was arrested on February 25, 1779 by Colonel George Rogers Clark and the Chicamaugas decided to attack the Holston settlement, but in the meantime James Robertson who was located at Etsauta as the first American Cherokee agent had ascertained their moves and with a force of five hundred men attacked and destroyed the eleven Chicamauga towns by way of the Tennessee. Among other property destroyed was one granary of twenty thousand bushels of corn. Upon hearing of this destruction the Cherokee warriors retraced their way to their devastated homes.

The lull that followed this destruction enabled the Transylvania troops to furnish many expert riflemen to the American forces at Kings Mountain, where the tide of war was changed in favor of the young republic. It also gave the Chicamaugas time to remobilize their forces for another general attack, but this was thwarted by a counter attack by Colonel John Sevier in the winter of 1780-81 in which he destroyed the Overhill towns and those on the Hiwassee River. In the summer of 1781 a treaty of peace was concluded with the Overhills. For a third time in three years the western settlements of the Cherokees were over run and ruined, this time by Colonel Sevier, in September, 1782.

Conditions were not any longer tenable for the impoverished Chicamaugas, within the Cherokee settlements, so they moved about forty-five miles westward and established the Five Lower towns of: Running Water, Chicamauga, Nickajack, Crow and Lookout Mountain, forming a strategic point for the assembling of Chicamaugas, Tories, Shawnees and Creeks. Oconostota resigned the Chieftaincy on account of old age in 1782 and was succeded by Tassel. Oconostota died in 1785. The English interpretation of his name was pounded ground hog, or popularly called "ground hog sausage." Fifty-five years before his death he had, as a young chief, visited England, and for that reason was most probably born about the beginning of the eighteenth century.

THE LAMENT OF THE CHEROKEE

By John Howard Payne, Author of Home, Sweet Home.

O, soft falls the dew, on the twilight descending,
And night over the distant forest is bending
And night over the distant forest is bending
Like the storm spirit, dark, o'er the tremulous main.
But midnight enshrouded my lone heart in its dwelling,
A tumult of woe in my bosom is swelling
And a tear unbefitting the warrior is telling
That hope has abandoned the brave Cherokee.

Can a tree that is torn from its root by the fountain,
The pride of the valley; green, spreading and fair,
Can it flourish, removed to the rock of the mountain,
Unwarmed by the sun and unwatered by care?
Though vesper be kind, her sweet dews in bestowing,
No life giving brook in its shadows is flowing.
And when the chill winds of the desert are blowing,
So droops the transplanted and lone Cherokee.

Sacred graves of my sires; and I left you forever?
How melted my heart when I bade you adieu;
Shall joy light the face of the Indian? Ah, never;
While memory sad has the power to renew.
As flies the fleet deer when the blood hound is started,
So fled winged hope from the poor broken hearted;
Oh, could she have turned ere forever departing,
And beckoned with smiles to her sad Cherokee.

Is it the low wind through the wet willows rushing,
That fills with wild numbers my listening ear?
Or is it some hermit rill in the solitude gushing,
The strange playing minstrel, whose music I hear?
'Tis the voice of my father, slow, solemnly stealing,
I see his dim form by yon meteor, kneeling
To the God of the White Man, the Christian, appealing,
He prays for the foe of the dark Cherokee.

Great Spirit of Good, whose abode is in Heaven,
Whose wampum of peace is the bow in the sky,
Wilt thou give to the wants of the clamorous ravens,
Yet turn a deaf ear to my piteous cry?
O'er the ruins of home, o'er my heart's desolation;
No more shalt thou hear my unblest lamentation;
For death's dark encounter, I make preparation;
He hears the last groan of the wild Cherokee.

CHAPTER II

Trouble with the Chicamaugas, Attack at Knoxville, Mussel Shoals Massacre, Removal to Arkansas, First Printed Laws.

The first treaty between the United States and the Cherokees was made at Hopewell on the Keowee River on November 28, 1875, between "Benjamin Hawkins, Andrew Pickens, Joseph Martin and Lachlan McIntosh, Commissioners Plenipotentiary of the United States and the Headmen and Warriors of all the Cherokees." The Commissioners were among the most distinguished men of the southern part of the republic. Pickens and McIntosh had been brigadier generals of militia in the revolution; Martin and Hawkins had held honorable positions both in military and civil life. Both parties agreed to restore all prisoners. The Cherokees acknowledged the exclusive protection and authority of the United States. Boundary lines were to be definitely marked, peace declared and the Cherokees should have a right to a delegate to Congress.

The belligerency of the Chicamaugas was practically unimpeded, although Dragging Canoe died at Running Water on about the first of March 1792 and was succeeded as town chief by John Bowles, an auburn haired, blue eyed, half blood Scotch Cherokee aged about thirty-two years. Tassel, head chief of the Cherokees and a well known friend of the whites, with his son and two others was invited to the headquarters of Mayor James Hubbert in 1788. They came unarmed, under a flag of truce and promise of protection although they were not at war. As soon as they were within his lines, Habbert had them conveyed to a vacant house and placing a tomahawk in the hands of a young man whose parents had been killed by a marauding band of Cherokees, told him to kill all of the visiting Cherokees, which he did while the Mayor stood guard at the door. This is the only instance of a head chief of the Cherokees being killed, either while in office or later, excepting the murder of Richard Fields, the Texas Cherokee Chief. Tassel was the uncle of John Watts, Tahlonteeskee and Unakateehee. Scolacutta or Hanging Maugh succeeded Tassel as head chief of the Cherokees.

A treaty was made by Governor William Blount and the Cherokees on Holston River on July 2, 1791. It was practically a reiteration of the treaty of 1785, but granted the Cherokees an annuity of one thousand dollars, and on February 17, of the next year a supplementary treaty was made at Philadelphia increasing the annuity to fifteen hundred dollars. This was raised to five thousand per annum on June 26, 1794.

While Dragging Canoe was succeeded by John Bowles as town chief of Running Water, his succession to the leadership of the Chicamaugas passed by an election by that band to John Watts in the latter part of March 1792 and two months later, on Sunday, May 21st, the Chicamaugas met Governor Blount at Coyateehee in the nation, where elaborate plans had been made by them to receive and honor him. A ball play was held the following day and was succeeded by a council in which Watts and the Cherokees again pledged fealty to the United States. Watts promised that he would visit Governor

Blount, ten days later, stay a few days with him and then accompany him on a mission to the Choctaws and Chickasaws.

On the day after the departure of the Governor, Watts went to Toquo, where a courier delivered a letter to Watts, from William Panton, a wealthy Scotch merchant at Pensacola, where he had fled from Georgia after his property in that province had been confiscated and destroyed because he was a tory. The letter invited Watts and such other friends as he cared to bring, especially Tahlonteeskee, to visit him and the Spanish Governor O'Neal at his establishment at Pensacola, where they would be given many presents.

Taking letters of introduction from John McDonald of Chicamauga, late Assistant British Superintendent of Indian Afairs; Watts, Tahlonteeskee and a son of the late Dragging Canoe set out for Pensacola. On arriving there they were flattered and shown every attention, then were reminded of the perfidious death of Tassel. They were assured of the fact that neither English nor Spaniards ever coveted their hunting grounds but that the settlers were continually encroaching upon them. They were given pack loads of arms, ammunition and presents and told they might have as much ammunition and arms as they needed to get satisfaction for the death of their kinsman, Tassel.

On their return to the nation, Watts issued a call to the Chicamaugas to meet at his residence at Wills Valley on the following green corn dance date, which was in August. On their assembling, Watts laid before them the proposition of Panton, and while this was bitterly opposed by Bloody Fellow, it gained almost unanimous approval. The war party started out three days later against the Cumberland settlements, but hearing that Unakateehee had arrived at the mouth of Lookout Creek, with a load of whiskey, they had it brought to Willston where they drank and feasted for several days and were delayed some ten days longer, debating modes and plans of attack. Tahlonteeskee went forward to reconnoiter the Kentucky and Cumberland roads, but only encountered some travelers, killing one of them. Middlestriker of Willstown with fifty-five warriors prepared an ambush near Crab Orchard on the Walton road, where on September 23, 1792 he attacked Captain Samuel Handley, who was captured by Arthur Coody and later liberated.

General James Robertson, commander of the Tennessee troops, dispatched on September 25th, Clayton and Jonathan Gee, two of his most trusted spies to locate the Cherokees, but they were met by George Fields and John Walker on a like errand for Watts, and killed. Fields as a captain and Walker, a major of the Cherokee auxilliaries rendered good account of themselves with the Americans under General Andrew Jackson at the battle of Horseshoe Bend in 1814.

Watts command of about one hundred and sixty seven Cherokees, thirty Shawnees from Running Water under Shawnee Warrior and eighty three Creeks under Talotiskee of Broken Arrow got near enough to Buchanan's Station to hear the lowing of the cows on the evening of the thirtieth of September, where it became necessary to have another conference, as Talotiskee and Doublehead wished to attack that station, which was small and Watts had planned to attack Nashville, which was only four miles further and was the largest station in this vicinity. The adherents of the former proposition were successful and the attack was made near midnight. After a fierce melee of several hours it became apparent that General Robertson was approaching from Nashville and the Indians withdrew. Kiachatalee of Nickajack, Shawnee Warrior of Running Water and Talotiskee of Broken Arrow were killed and seven Cherokees were wounded, three of whom later died from the effects of their wounds. John Watts and Unakateehee were among those wounded, but both survived. No casualties occurred to those in the blockhouse.

On June 12, 1793, a delegation had gathered at Hanging Maugh's preparing to proceed to Philadelphia in compliance with an invitation from the President transmitted to them by Governor Blount, the Governor had already gone ahead, on the seventh of the month to make preparations for their coming and had delegated John McKee to accompany them. Watts, Doublehead and several other prominent Cherokees were some who had come to see the delegates off. Without warning, a company of whites under Captain John Beard, who had been hunting the slayers of Thomas Gillum and his son James, appeared at Maugh's residence and began firing promiscuously, killing about twelve and wounding many others, including Hanging Maugh, his wife and daughter and Elizabeth, the daughter of Nancy Ward. Upon the repeated requests of the Cherokees, Captain Beard was tried before a court martial but was acquitted.

Finding that the protection that had been promised them by treaties was of no effect, the Cherokees again commenced to prepare for retaliation and the settlers for defense. Knoxville had a garrison of forty men. General Sevier with a force of four hundred mounted was at Ish's Station, across the river from Knoxville, Campbell's Station, fifteen miles west of Knoxville, one of the strongest posts on the border was well guarded and Cavitt's Station, half way between Knoxville and Campbell's Station contained people, three of whom were gun men. John Watts with one thousand warriors crossed Tennessee River below the mouth of Holston on the evening of September 24, 1793 and marched all night intending to surprise Knoxville at daylight but on account of the bickering of Doublehead and others who wished to attack instead of avoid the small stations on the way they arrived near Cavitt's Station at the time that Watts had planned to reach Knoxville. An assault was made on that Station. Alexander Cavitt was killed and five Indians were killed or wounded. A parley was then held in which the people of the Station surrendered on the promise of protection, but they were brutally murdered by the intractable Doublehead. The Indians, knowing that their plans were known, then recrossed the Tennessee.

General Sevier with about seven hundred men pursued the hostiles, who were both Creeks and Cherokees and came up with them at the mouth of Etowah River on October 17, 1793 where after a spirited engagement of only a few minutes in which less than ten men were killed, the Indians abandoned the field. After this skirmish the middle towns were at peace with the settlers although daring leaders of the Chicamaugas, either single or with small bands kept up desultory depredations until Major James Ore destroyed Nickajack and Running Water on September 13, 1794 and put an end to the Cherokee war.

In June 1794 some emigrants who were on their way down Tennessee River to the western settlements were attacked at Mussel Shoals. John Bowles and all of his men were killed. "After this bloody tragedy, which is known as the Mussel Shoals Massacre, the whole party of Cherokees went aboard the boats, descended the Tennessee, Ohio and Mississippi to the Mouth of the St. Francis River. There they placed all the white women and children in one boat, granted to each of the married ladies a female servant, put on board an ample stock of provisions and four strong and able black men and let them descend the Mississippi to New Orleans, the place of their destination. With one of these ladies I afterward became acquainted. At her residence I have frequently domiciled when visiting New Orleans, and found her, though a widow, truly a mother in Israel. She was to New Orleans what Mrs. Isabella Graham was to New York. It was from her lips that I received the foregoing particulars. She often spoke of the kindness and courtesy with which she and all the white ladies and children were treated by Bowl and his party.

But to return to my narrative, after the departure of the boat for New Orleans, the Bowl and his party ran the other boats, with their contents of goods, servants, etc., a few miles up the St. Francis River to await the issue of the affair. They feared that their conduct at the Mussel Shoals would be regarded by our government as a violation of the treaty of amity, and as a renewal of hostility. As soon as the massacre of Mussel Shoals was known to the Cherokees in their towns they convened a general council, and in a memorial to the United States government, declared that they had no part in the tragedy; that they wished to be at peace with the United States and that they would do all in their power to aid the United States in bringing them to justice. They sent for Bowl and his party to return and submit to a trial for taking the lives of white citizens of the United States. When this whole matter was investigated by the government of the United States the Cherokees were fully justified and the property confiscated and declared by treaty to belong justly to the perpetrators of the Mussel Shoals Massacre."

The Cherokees had been settling in the St. Francis country for at least forty years, as Lieutenant Governor Couzat reported to Governor Amazoga on December 10, 1775 that the Cherokees had driven the miners away from Mine La Motte, fifteen leagues from St. Genevieve.[1]

"The course pursued by the Cherokee council toward the refugees tended to alienate their minds from their people in the home of their fathers, and made them less reluctant to remain in their new homes west of the Mississippi Added to this, the abundance of game, the fertility of the soil and the blandness of the climate, soon made them prefer their homes here to those where they had resided in the east. Other parties who crossed the Mississippi for the purpose of hunting and trapping, when they saw the prosperity of the original refugees, joined them.

Louisiana was delivered to the United States government at St. Louis on March 10, 1804 and all of that portion lying north of the thirty-fifth parallel was constituted, on March 8, 1805, the Territory of Louisiana.

During the month of December 1811, the great siesmatic disturbances of the St. Francis River country, in which the Cherokees were located, caused much of this territory to be submerged; while subterranean rumbling and roaring continued for many years. Fearing that this country was under the ban of the Great Spirit, the Cherokees moved en masse to a new location between the Arkansas and White Rivers.[1]

On June 4, 1812 the Congress of the United States created the Territory of Missouri and on the succeeding thirty first day of December, the County of Arkansas, Territory of Missouri, was created, embracing practically the present state of Arkansas, and during the following year Lawrence County was constituted from that portion of Arkansas County lying north of the mouth of Little Red River. Thus it will be seen that the Cherokee settlement was successively within the Spanish province of Louisiana, Territory of Louisiana, Territory of Missouri and the Counties of Arkansas and Lawrence, Territory of Missouri. During all of which time they had been settlers without warrant of title to their habitations and it was not until the ratificaion of the United States-Cherokee treaty of of July 8, 1817, that they were confirmed in their rights to their homes.

In 1813 a considerable accession was made to their number by voluntary emigration from the old nation and they became so numerous that the United States sent Samuel Treat to be their agent in the St. Francis country and he accompanied them to their new location between the Arkansas and White Rivers; he was succeeded in 1813 by William L. Lovely.[3]

The rights of the Western Cherokees to their lands in Arkansas was confirmed by the treaty of 1817, at Turkeytown in which the government agreed to give the Arkansas Cherokees as much land "acre for acre" between the Arkansas and White Rivers as they would cede of their domain in the east. besides paying the emigrants that might thereafter move, for their improvements, transport them to their new homes, subsist them for twelve months after their arrival, besides other perquisites and valuable considerations. The result of this treaty was a considerable emigration from the east to the west in the years 1818 and 1819. From that time until their union by the treaty of 1835, which was not effected, in fact, until 1839, the Arkansas Cherokees were estimated at one-third of the whole tribe.

In the opening of 1819 Thomas Nuttall, the naturalist, ascended the Arkansas River, and gave the following of the Western Cherokees, as he found them: "Both banks of the river as we proceeded were lined with the houses and fences of the Cherokee, and although their dress was a mixture of indigenous and European taste, yet in their homes, which were decently furnished, and in their farms, which were well fenced and stocked, we perceived a happy approach toward civilization. Their numerous families, also, well fed and clothed, argue a propitious progress in their population. Their superior industry, either as hunters or farmers, proves the value of property among them, and they are no longer strangers to avarice and the distinctions created by wealth. Some of them are possessed of property to the amount of many thousands of dollars, have houses handsomely and conveniently furnished, and their tables are spread with our dainties and luxuries."

The capital of the Cherokee Nation West from 1813 to 1824 was at Takatoka's village; from 1824 to 1828 it was at Piney, on Piney Creek; from

1828 to 1838 at Tahlonteeskee on the south side and near the mouth of the Illinois River and for a short time in 1839 at Takatoka or Double Springs on Fourteen Mile Creek.

By the provisions of a treaty between the United States and the Osage Indians on June 2nd, 1825, the latter ceded to the United Sates all of their land lying " east of a line to be drawn from the head sources of the Kansas River southwardly through Rock Saline." This was afterwards marked as the hundredth meridian, thus becoming automatically the western boundary line of Arkansas.

It being the policy of the United States to settle all of the Indians that were located within the organized States and Territories in the extreme western uncharted lands of the government and the Cherokees wishing to escape the oppression and inconvenience of being located in a small narrow reservation where they were continually hampered and disturbed, they exchanged their lands in the Territory of Arkansas for a like amount lying west of the old line of Arkansas. In accordance with this treaty the Western Cherokees moved to their new territory in 1828-29.

Bowles' village was between Shoal and Petit Jean Creeks, on the south side of the Arkansas River, and consequently not within the territory ceded to the Cherokees by the treaty of 1817. On account of this fact and also to gratify a general wish of his townsmen to locate within Spanish territory, where they thought they would find such pleasant surroundings as they had encountered in the vicinity of New Madrid in southeast Missouri, but they did not stop to remember that while that had been Spanish territory, that their neighbors and officers had been Frenchmen. But nevertheless the sixty families of Bowles' town moved to and located in Texas in the winter of 1819-20. They were shortly afterwards joined by Richard Fields (Grant 1^1 1^2 3^3 2^4) a man of striking personality, of considerable intelligence and although he spoke the English language fluently and preferably, he was not able to sign his name. From the time that he joined them until his death, he was untiring in his efforts to obtain a title for the Cherokees, to the land on which they resided. A title to these lands were obtained from the Republic of Texas, by treaty on February 23, 1836. They were driven from this land on July 16. 1839 by the entire army of the Republic of Texas, commanded by Brigadier General Kelsey H. Douglas, who was accompanied by Vice and Acting Governor David G. Burnett, Secretary of War Albert Sidney Johnson and Adjutant General Hugh McLeod, thus making the Republic responsible for their acts.

Three plats of land, each a mile square were set aside by the provisions of article two of the treaty of Tellico, of October 25, 1805, ostensibly for government purposes, but in reality, as shown by a second article of the treaty for Doublehead and Tahlonteeskee as a bribe for their support in making the treaty. Tahlonteeskee disposed of his two allotments and joined the Cherokees in Arkansas, where he became principal chief. Doublehead stayed in the Eastern Cherokee Nation where he dared the scorn of his neighbors. In the summer of 1807, a great ball play was held on Hiwassee River, attended by more than a thousand Cherokees, after the close of the game, a chief named Bonepolisher upbraided Doublehead for his perfidy and Doublehead drew his revolver and killed him. During the evening, Doublehead who had been drinking entered a tavern where he encountered John Rogers, (Grant 1^1 1^2 2^3) Ridge (Ridge 1^1 1^2) and Alexander Sanders (Sanders 1^1 2^2). Rogers commenced to berate him for his crime. Doublehead said to him: "You are a white man and live by sufferance among us, hush and let me alone or I will kill you." Doublehead snapped his pistol at him, some one extinguished the light, a shot was fired and when the lamp was relighted Doublehead was lying on the floor with a large wound in his lower jaw. Doublehead was then taken to a neighbor's loft but was found and killed by Sanders, who was accompanied by Ridge.[1].

The progress of a people is best exemplified by their efforts to establish equal rights for all of their people and their printed laws are the best index to their advancement. The first printed law of the Cherokees was:

LAWS OF THE CHEROKEE NATION

Resolved by the Chiefs and Warriors in a National Council assembled. That it shall be, and is hereby authorized, for the regulating parties to be organized to consist of six men in each company; one Captain, one Lieutenant and four privates, to continue in service for the term of one year, whose duties it shall be to suppress horse stealing and robbery of other property within their respective bounds, who shall be paid out of the National annuity, at the rates of fifty dollars to each Captain, forty toeach Lieutenant, and thirty dollars to each of the privates; and to give their protection to children as heirs to their father's property, and to the widow's share whom he may have had children by or cohabited with, as his wife, at the time of his decease, and in case a father shall leave or will any property to a child at the time of his decease, which he may have had by another woman, then, his present wife shall be entitled to receive any such property as may be left by him or them, when substantiated by two or one disinterested witnesses.

Be it resolved by the Council aforesaid, When any person or persons which may or shall be charged with stealing a horse, and upon conviction by one or two witnesses, he, she, or they, shall be punished with one hundred stripes on the bare back, and the punishment to be in proportion for stealing property of less value; and should the accused person or persons raise up with arms in his or their hands, as guns, axes, spears and knives, in opposition to the regulating company, or should they kill him or them, the blood of him or them shall not be required of any of the persons belonging to the regulators from the clan the person so killed belonged to.

Accepted.—BLACK FOX, Principal Chief,
PATHKILLER, Sec'd.
TOOCHALAR.

CHAS. HICKS, Sec'y to Council.

Brooms Town, 11th Sept. 1808.

Be it known, That this day, the various clans or tribes which compose the Cherokee Nation, have unanimously passed an act of oblivion for all lives for which they may have been indebted, one to the other, and have mutually agreed that after this evening the aforesaid act shall become binding upon every clan or tribe; and the aforesaid clans or tribes, have also agreed that if, in future, any life should be lost without malice intended, the innocent aggressor shall not be accounted guilty.

Be it known, also, That should it happen that brother, forgetting his natural affection, should raise his hand in anger and kill his brother, he shall be accounted guilty of murder and suffer accordingly, and if a man has a horse stolen, and overtakes the thief, and should his anger be so great as to cause him to kill him, let his blood remain on his own conscience, but no satisfaction shall be demanded for his life from his relatives or the clan he may belong to.

By order of the seven clans.

TURTLE AT HOME,
Speaker of the Council.
Approved—BLACK FOX, Principal Chief,
PATH KILLER, Sec'd.
TOOCHALER.

In the war between the United States and the Creeks in 1814 a large body of Cherokees volunteered to assist the army led by Generals Andrew Jackson and John Coffie. Among the officers were Colonel John Lowry, Major George Lowry, Major Ridge, Major John Walker, Captain George Fields, Captain Alexander Sanders, Captain John Rogers, Adjutant John Ross and private Charles Reese. In the crucial battle of Horse Shoe Bend in which the Creeks were strongly barricaded behind cypress log ramparts and were holding their own against the frontal attacks, a detachment of Cherokees came up on the opposite side of the river, Charles Reese swam across and towed a canoe to his associates, the canoe load of warriors crossed the stream and each one got a canoe. In this manner the Cherokees landed in the back part of the bend, attacked the Creeks from the rear. In attempting to repel this assault the Creeks so weakened their front that a breach was made nearly annihilating the belligerent Creek forces. From that day Andrew Jackson became increasingly popular. Historians carefully refrain from giving the Cherokees mention or credit for a part in this combat and Reese's family received a silver mounted rifle as acknowledgement for his actions, three years after his death.

An act of the Cherokee Council that served as a substitute for a constitution was as follows:

Whereas, fifty-four towns and villages have convened in order to deliberate and consider on the situation of our Nation, in the disposition of our common property of lands, without the unanimous consent of the members of Council, and in order to obviate the evil consequences resulting in such course, we have unanimously adopted the following form for the future government of our Nation.

ART. 1st. It is unanimously agreed that there shall be thirteen members elected as a Standing Committee for the term of two years, at the end of which term they shall be either re-elected or others; and in consequence of the death or resignation of any of said Committee, our head Chiefs shall elect another to fill the vacancy.

ART. 2d. The affairs of the Cherokee Nation shall be committed to the care of the Standing Committee; but the acts of this body shall not be binding on the Nation in our common property and without the unanimous consent of the members and Chiefs of the Council, which they shall present for their acceptance or dissent.

ART. 3d. The authority and claim of our common property shall cease with the person or persons who shall think proper to remove themselves without the Cherokee Nation.

ART. 4th. The improvements and labors of our people by the mother's side shall be inviolate during the time of their occupancy.

ART. 5th. This Committee shall settle with the Agency for our annual stipend, and report their proceedings to the members and Chiefs in Council, but the friendly communications between our head Chiefs and the Agency shall remain free and open.

ART. 6th. The above articles for our government, may be amended at our electoral term, and the Committee is hereby required to be governed by the above articles, and the Chief and Warriors in Council, unanimously pledge themselves to observe strictly the contents of the above articles.—Whereunto we have set our hands and seals at Amoah, this 6th day of May, one thousand eight hundred and seventeen.

Approved in Council, on the day and date above written.

EHNAUTAUNAUEH,

Speaker of the Council

Approved of the within government by the head Chief,

PATHKILLER.

A. McCoy, Sec'y to the Council.

CHAS. HICKS.

Unanimously agreed, That schoolmasters, blacksmiths, millers, salt petre and gun powder manufacturers, ferrymen and turnpike keepers, and mechanics are hereby privileged to reside in the Cherokee Nation under the following conditions, viz:

Their employers procuring a permit from the National Committee and Council for them and becoming responsible for their good conduct and behavior, and subject to removal for misdemeanor; and further agree, that blacksmiths, millers, ferrymen and turnpike keepers, are privileged to improve and cultivate twelve acres of ground for the support of themselves and families, should they please to do so.

JNO. ROSS, Pres't. Nat'l. Com.

A. McCOY, Cl'k. Nat'l. Com.

In Committee, New Town, Oct. 26th, 1819.

On July 8, 1817, a treaty was made with the United States, the main feature of which was the exchange of land east of the Mississippi for land in Arkansas, so that the Western Cherokees might have title to their homes. On February 27, 1919 another treaty was made confirming the treaty of 1817 and providing for the basis of the Cherokee National school fund. The Eastern Cherokee Nation was divided into eight districts by:

New Town, Cherokee Nation, October 20th, 1820.

Resolved by the National Committee and Council, That the Cherokee Nation shall be laid off into eight districts, and that a council house shall be established in each district for the purpose of holding councils to administer justice in all causes and complaints that may be brought forward for trial, ana one circuit judge, to have jurisdiction over two districts, to associate with the district judges in determining all causes agreeable to the National laws, and the marshals to execute the decisions of the judges in their respective districts, and the District Councils to be held in the spring and fall seasons, and one company of lighthorse to accompany each circuit judge on his official duties, in his respective districts, and to execute such punishment on thieves as the Judges and Council shall decide, agreeably to law, and it shall be the duty of the marshals to collect all debts, and shall be entitled to eight per cent for the same; and the Nation to defray the expenses of each District Council, and in case of opposition to the marshals in execution of their duty, they shall be justifiable in protectingtheir persons from injury in the same manner as is provided for the National lighthorse by law.

By order of the National Committee.

JNO. ROSS, Pres't. N. Com.
Approved—PATH KILLER (X) his mark.
CHAS. R. HICKS.

A. McCOY, Clerk.

and the undated act

Resolved by the National Committee and Council, That the Cherokee Nation be organized and laid off in Districts, and to be bounded as follows:

1st. The first District shall be called by the name of Chickamaugee, and be bounded as follows: beginning at the mouth of Aumuchee creek, on Oostennallah river, thence north in a straight course to a spring branch between the Island and Rackoon village, thence a straight course over the Lookout Mountain, where the heads of Will's and Lookout creeks opposes against each other on the Blue Ridge, thence a straight course to the main source of Rackoon creek, and down the same into the Tennessee river, and up said river to the mouth of Ooletiwah creek, and up said creek to take the most southeastern fork, thence a southern course to the mouth of Sugar Creek, intc the Cannasawgee river, and down the said river to its confluence with the Oostenallah river, and down the same to the place of beginning.

2d. The second District shall be called by the name of Challoogee, and be bounded as follows; beginning on the mouth of Rackoon creek, in the Tennessee River, and down the said river to the boundary line, commonly called Coffee's line, and along said line where it strikes Will's Creek, and down the said creek to its confluence with the Coosa river, and thence embracing the boundary line between the Cherokees and Creeks, run by Wm. McIntosh and other Cherokee Commissioners by their respective Nations, running south eastwardly to its intersection with Chinubee's trace, and along said trace leading eastwardly by Avery Vann's place, including his plantation, and thence on said trace to where it crosses the Etowah river to its confluence with Oostannallah river, and up said river to the mouth of Aumuchee creek, and to be bounded by the first District.

3d. The third District shall be called by the name of Coosawatee, and bounded as follows: beginning at the widow Fool's ferry, on Ooostannallah river, where the Alabama road crosses it, along said wagon road eastwardly leading towards Etowah town to a large creek above Thomas Pettit's plantation, near to the Sixes, and said creek, northeastward, to its source; thence a straight course to the head of Talloney creek, up which the Federal road leads, thence a straight course to the Red Bank creek, near Cartikee village; thence a straight course to the head source of Potatoe Mine creek; thence a straight course to the most southern head source of Cannasawagee river; thence a northwestern course to Cannasawgee river, to strike opposite the mouth of Sugar Creek, into the Cannasawgee river, and to be bounded by the first and second Districts.

4th. The fourth District shall be called by the name of Amoah, and be the third District strikes the said source; thence eastwardly a straight course bounded as follows: beginning at the head source of Cannasawgee river, where to Spring Town, above Hiwassee Old Town; thence to the boundary line run by Col Houston, where it crosses Sloan creek;—thence westwardly along said line to the Hiwassee river;—thence down said river into the Tennessee river, and down the same to the mouth of Oolatiwah creek, and to be bounded by the first and third Districts.

5th. The fifth District shall be called by the name of Hickory Log, and shall be bounded as follows: beginning at the head of Potatoe Mine Creek, on the Blue Ridge to where Cheewostoyeh path crosses said ridge, and along said path to the head branch of Frog Town creek, and down the same to its confluence with Tahsantee; thence down Chestotee river; thence down the same into the Chattahoochee river; and down the same to the shallow wagon ford on said river; above the standing Peach Tree; thence westward along said wagon road leading to ——— Town to where it crosses Little river, a fork of the Etowah river, and down the same to its confluence with Etowah river, and down the same in a direct course to a large Creek, and up said creek to where the road crosses it to the opposite side, and to be bounded by the third District.

6th. The sixth District shall be called by the name of Etowah, and be bounded as follows: beginning on the Chattahoochee river, at the shallow wagon ford on said river, and down the same to the Buzzard Roost, where the Creek and Cherokee boundary line intersects the said river; thence along said boundary line westward, to where it intersects Chinubees trace, and to be bounded by the fifth and third districts, leaving Thomas Pettit's family in Etowah District.

7th. The seventh District shall be called by the name of Tahquohee, and be bounded as follows: beginning where Col. Houston's boundary line crosses Slare's creek, thence along said boundary line south-eastwardly, to the Unicoy turnpike road, and along said road to where it crosses the Hiwasee river, in the Valley Towns; thence a straight course to head source of Coosa creek, on the Blue Ridge above Cheewostoyĕh, and along said Ridge eastwardly, where the Unicoy turnpike road crosses it and thence a direct course to the head source of Persimon creek; thence down the same to the confluence of Tahsantee, and with the Frog Town creek; and to be bounded by the third, the fourth and fifth Districts.

8th. The eighth District shall be called by the name of Aquohee, and be bounded as follows: beginning where the seventh District intersects the Blue Ridge, where the Unicoy turnpike road crosses the same; thence eastwardly along said ridge to the Standing Man, to Col. Houston's boundary line, thence along said line to the confluence of Nauteyalee, and Little Tennessee river; thence down the same to Tallassee village, thence along said boundary line westwardly, to where it intersects the Unicoy turnpike road; and to be bounded by the Seventh District; and that each District shall hold their respective Councils or Courts, on the following days:

The first Mondays in May and September, for Chicamaugee District; and on the

First Mondays in May and September for Coosewatee District; and the
Second Mondays in May and September, for Amoah District; and on the
First Mondays in May and September, for Hickory Log District; and the
Second Mondays in May and September, for Etowah District, and on the
First Mondays in May and September for Aquohee District; and on the
Second Mondays in May and September, for Tauquohee District; and each of the Councils or Courts shall sit five days for the transaction of business at each term.

By order of the Committee and Council.

CHAS. R. HICHS,

The above act was passed before October 25, 1820, as other acts relating to the officers of the several districts were passed on that and subsequent dates. Gambling and drinking were restricted by

New Town, Cherokee Nation, November 8th, 1822.

Whereas, the great variety of vices emanating from dissipation, particularly from intoxication and gaming at cards, which are so prevalent at all public places, the National Committee and Council, seeking the true interest and happiness of their people, have maturely taken this growing evil into their serious consideration, and being fully convinced that no nation of people can prosper and flourish, or become magnanimous in character, the basis of whose laws are not found upon virtue and justice; therefore, to suppress, as much as possible, those demoralizing habits which were introduced by foreign agency,

Resolved by the National Committee, That any person or persons, whatsoever, who shall bring ardent spirits within three miles of the General Council House, or to any of the court houses within the several Districts during the general Council, or the sitting of the courts, and dispose of the same so as to intoxicate any person or persons whatsoever, the person or persons so offending, shall forfeit his or their whiskey, the same to be destroyed; and be it further

Resolved, That gaming at cards is hereby strictly forbidden, and that any person or persons whomsoever, who shall game at cards in the Cherokee

Nation, such person or persons, so offending, shall forfeit and pay a fine of twenty-five dollars, and further, any person or persons whatsoever, who may or shall be found playing cards at any house or camp, or in the woods within three miles of the general Council House, or any of the court houses of the several Districts during the session of the General Council, or setting of the District Courts, such person or persons, so offending, shall forfeit and pay a fine of fifty dollars each for every such offense, and that any person or persons whatsoever, who shall bring into the Cherokee Nation and dispose of playing cards, such person or persons, being convicted before any of the Judges, Marshals, or light horse, shall pay a fine of twenty-five dollars for every pack of cards so sold; and it shall be the duty of the several Judges, Marshals and light horse companies, to take cognizance of such offenses and to enforce the above resolution; and

And be it further resolved, That all fines collected from persons violating the above resolution, the money so collected shall be paid into the national treasury. To take effect and be in full force from and after the first day of January next.

By order of the National Committee.

JNO. ROSS, Pres't. N. Com.

Approved—PATH KILLER (X) his mark.

A. McCOY, Clerk of Com.

ELIJAH HICKS, clerk of Coun'l.

Miscegenation was penalized by:

New Town, Cherokee Nation, November 11th, 1824

Resolved by the National Committee and Council, That intermarriages between negro slaves and indians, or white, shall not be lawful, and any person or persons, permitting and approbating his, her or their negro slaves, to intermarry with Indians or whites, he or she or they, so offending shall pay a fine of fifty dollars, one half for the benefit of the Cherokee Nation; and

Be if further resolved, That any male Indian or white man marrying a negro woman slave, he or they shall be punished with fifty-nine stripes on the bare back, and any Indian or white woman, marrying a negro man slave, shall be punished with twenty-five stripes on her or their bare back.

By order of the National Committee.

JNO. ROSS, Pres't. N. Com.

Approved—PATH KILLER (X) his mark.

A. McCOY, Clerk of Com.

ELIJAH HICKS, clerk of Coun'l.

New Town, Cherokee Nation, November 11th, 1824

Resolved by the National Committee and Council, That it shall not be lawful for negro slaves to possess property in horses, cattle or hogs, and that those slaves now possessing property of that description, be required to dispose of the same in twelve months from this date, under the penalty of confiscation.

and any property so confiscated, shall be sold for the benefit of the Cherokee Nation.

By order of the National Committee.

JNO. ROSS, Pres't. N. Com.

Approved—PATH KILLER (X) his mark.

A. McCOY, clerk of Com.

Another step towards a constitution was:

For the better security of the common property of the Cherokee Nation, and for the protection of the rights and privileges of the Cherokee people, We, the undersigned members of the Committee and Council, in legislative Council convened, have established, and by these presents do hereby declare, the following articles as a fixed and irrevocable principle, by which the Cherokee Nation shall be governed. These articles may be amended or modified, by a concurrence of two-thirds of the members of the Committee and Council in legislative Council convened; viz:

ART 1st. The lands within the sovereign limits of the Cherokee nation, as defined by treaties, are, and shall be, the common property of the Nation. The improvements made thereon and in the possession of the citizens of the Nation, are the exclusive and indefeasible property of the citizens respectively who made, or may rightfully be in possession of them.

ART. 2d. The annuities arising from treaties with the U. States, and the revenue arising out of tax laws, shall be funded in the National Treasury, and be the public property of the Nation.

ART. 3d. The legislative Council of the Nation shall alone possess the legal power to manage and dispose of, in any manner by law, the public property of the Nation, Provided, nothing shall be construed in this article, so as to extend that right and power to dispossess or divest the citizens of the Nation of their just rights to the houses, farms and other improvements in their possession.

ART. 4th. The Principal Chiefs of the Nation shall in no wise hold any treaties, or dispose of public property in any manner, without the express authority of the legislative Council in Session.

ART. 5th. The members of Committee and Council, during the recess of the legislative Council, shall possess no authority or power to convene Councils in their respective districts, or to act officially on any matters, excepting expressly authorized or delegated by the legislative Council in session.

ART. 6th. The citizens of the Nation, possessing exclusive and indefeasible rights to their respective improvements, as expressed in the first article, shall possess no right or power to dispose of their improvements to citizens of the United States, under such penalties, as may be prescribed by law in such cases.

ART 7th. The several courts of justice in the Nation shall have no cognizance of any case transpiring previous to the organization of courts by law, and which case may have been acted upon by the chiefs in council, under the then existing custom and usage of the Nation, excepting there may be an express law embracing the case.

ART 8th. The two Principal Chiefs of the Nation, shall not, jointly or Separately, have the power of arresting the judgment of either of the courts or of the legal acts of the National Committee and Council, but that the judiciary of the Nation shall be independent and their decisions final and conclusive, Provided, always, That they act in conformity to the foregoing principles or articles, and the acknowledged laws of the Nation.

Done in Legislative Council, at New Town, this 15th day of June, 1825.

JNO. ROSS, Pres't. N. Com.
MAJOR RIDGE, Speaker of Council,
Approved—PATH KILLER (X) his mark.

New Echota was established as the capital by the four following acts:

New Town, Cherokee Nation, November 12th 1825.

Resolved by the National Committee and Council, That one hundred town lots, of one acre square, be laid off on the Oostenallah river, commencing below the mouth of the creek, nearly opposite the mouth of Caunausauga river. The public square to embrace two acres of ground, which town shall be known and called Echota; there shall be a main street of sixty feet and the other streets shall be fifty feet wide.

Be it further resolved, That the lots, when laid off, be sold to the highest bidder. The purchasers right shall merely be occupancy, and transferrable only to lawful citizens of the Cherokee Nation, and the proceeds arising from the sales of the lots shall be appropriated for the benefit of the public buildings in said town; and

Be it further resolved, That three commissioners be appointed to superintend the laying off the aforesaid lots, marking and numbering the same, and to act as chain carrier, and a surveyor to be employed to run off the lots and streets according to the plan prescribed. The lots to be commenced running off on the second Monday in February next, and all the ground lying within the following bounds, not embraced by the lots, shall remain vacant as commons for the convenience of the town; viz: beginning at the mouth of Caunausauga, and up said creek to the mouth of the dry branch to the point of the ridges, and thence in a circle round along said ridges, by the place occupied by Crying Wolf, thence to the river.

JNO. ROSS, Pres't. N. Com.
MAJOR RIDGE, Speaker.
Approved—PATH KILLER, (X) his mark.
CH. R. HICKS.

A. McCOY, clerk of Com.
E. BOUDINOTT, Clerk N. Council.

New Town, Cherokee Nation, November 12th, 1825

Judge Martin, George Saunders and Walter S. Adair, are elected commissioners to superintend the laying off the lots in the town of Echota.

By order. JNO. ROSS, Pres't N. Com.

A. McCOY, clerk of Com.

Echota, Cherokee Nation, November 12th. 1825.

The subject of improvements made, and now occupied by individuals, on the public ground selected for the jurisdiction of the town of Echota, have been taken up by the National Committee. The question arising is, whether the Nation is bound to pay for any such improvements made by individuals since the site has been selected by the Nation for the establishment of a town as the seat of government. The decision of the Committee on this question is, that the Nation is not bound to make compensation for any such improvements, but in order to extend indulgence toward Alex. McCoy and E. Hicks, who are now within said bounds, and are in possession of dwelling houses of some value, it is hereby agreed and

Resolved by the National Committee and Council, That should the dwelling houses of the aforesaid McCoy and Hicks fall with lots which are to be laid off, they shall have the preference of occupancy to said lots, Provided they pay for the same at the rate which any other lot of equal value and advantageously situated may sell for; it is further agreed and admitted, that the improvement lately occupied by War Club, and the one now in the possession of Crying Wolf shall be paid for at the public expense; agreeably to the valuation made by W. Hicks, Geo. Saunders and Jos. Crutchfield.

JNO. ROSS, Pres't. N. Com.
MAJOR RIDGE, Speaker.
Approved—PATH KILLER (X) his mark.
CH. R. HICKS.

A. McCOY, clerk Com.
E. BOUDINOTT, Clerk N. Council.

Echota, Cherokee Nation, November 14th, 1825.

Alexander McCoy is hereby authorized and permitted to cultivate and raise a crop the ensuing year, in the field lying on the river below the ferry, and also the one lately owned by the War Club, on the river below the mouth of the spring branch, which improvements belong to the public, and lie within the town of Echota; Provided, said McCoy does not suffer the stakes to be removed which are to separate the town lots, to be laid off in said fields, and that said McCoy surrender possession of those fields to the public on or before the second Monday in October next.

JNO. ROSS, Pres't. N. Com.
MAJOR RIDGE, Speaker.
Approved—PATH KILLER (X) his mark.
CH. R. HICKS.

A. McCOY, clerk Com.
E. BOUDINOTT, clerk Coun'l.

Provisions were made for the selection of delegates for a constitutional convention by:

Whereas, the General Council of the Cherokee Nation, now in session, having taken into consideration the subject of adopting a constitution for the future Government of said Nation, and after mature deliberation, it is deemed expedient that a Convention be called, and in order that the wishes of the people of the several Districts may be fairly represented on this all important subject,

It is hereby resolved by the National Committee and Council, That the persons hereinafter named be, and they are hereby nominated and recommended to the people of their respective districts as candidates to run an election for seats in the Convention; and three out of the ten in each District who shall get the highest number of votes shall be elected; and for the convenience of the people in giving their votes, three precincts in each District are selected, and superintendents and clerks to the election are chosen; and no person but a free male citizen who is full grown shall be entitled to a vote: and each voter shall be entitled to vote for three of the candidates herein nominated in their respective Districts, and no vote by proxy shall be admitted; and that all the votes shall be given in viva voce; and in case of death, sickness or other incident which may occur to prevent all or any of the superintendents from attending at the several precincts to which they are chosen, the people of the respective precincts shall make a selection to fill such vacancies. And in case of similar incident occurring to any of the members elect, the person receiving the next highest number of votes shall supply the vacancy.

In Chicamauga District, John Ross, Richard Taylor, John Baldridge, Jas Brown, Sleeping Rabbit, John Benge, Nathaniel Hicks, Sicketowee, Jas. Starr and Daniel McCoy, are nominated and recommended as candidates; and the election in the first precinct shall be held at or near Hick's mill, and Charles R. Hicks, and Archibald Fields, are chosen superintendents, and Leonard Hicks, clerk. The election in the second precinct shall be held at or near Hunter Langley's in Lookout Valley, and James Lowrey and Robert Vann are chosen superintendents, and John Candy, clerk. The election in the third precinct shall be held in the Court House, and Joseph Coodey and William S. Coodey, are chosen superintendents and Robert Fields, Clerk.

In Chattanooga District, George Lowrey, Samuel Gunter, Andrew Ross, David Vann, David Brown, Spirit, The Bark, Salecooke, Edward Gunter and John Brown, are nominated and recommended as candidates; and the election in the first precinct in this District shall be held at or near Edward Gunter's school house in Creek Path valley, and Alexander Gilbreath and Dempsey Fields are chosen superintendents, and John Gunter, clerk. The election in the second precinct shall be held at or near Laugh at Mush's house, in Wills valley, and William Chamberlin and Martin McIntosh are chosen superintendents and George Lowrey, Jr., clerk. The election in the third precinct shall be held at the court house, and Charles Vann and James M'Intosh are chosen superintendents, and Thomas Wilson, clerk.

In Coosawaytee District, John Martin, W. S. Adair, Elias Boudinott, Joseph Vann, John Ridge, William Hicks, Elijah Hicks, John Saunders, Kelechulah and Alex McCoy, are nominated and recommended as candidates. The election in the first precinct in this District shall be held at or near William Hick's house on Ooukillokee creek, and Edward Adair and G. W. Adair are chosen superintendents and Stand Watie, clerk. The election in the second precinct shall be held at Elechaye, and George Saunders and Robert Saunders, are chosen superintendents, and James Saunders, clerk. The election in the third precinct shall be held at the court house, and George Harlin and William Thompson are chosen superintendents, and Jos. M. Lynch, clerk

In Amohee District, The Hair, Lewis Ross, Thos. Foreman, John Walker, Jr., Going Snake, George Fields, James Bigbey, Deer-in-water, John M'Intosh, and Thomas Fields are nominated and recommended as candidates. The election in the first precinct in this District shall be held at or near Kalsowee's house at Long Savannah, and Wm. Blythe and John Fields, are chosen superintendents and Ezekiel Fields, clerk. The election in the second precinct shall be held at or near Bridge Maker's house, at Ahmohee Town, and Ezekiel Starr and Michael Helterbrand, are chosen superintendents, and James M'Nair, clerk. The election in the third precinct shall be held at the court house, and David M'Nair and James M'Daniel, are chosen superintendents and T. W. Ross, clerk.

In Hickory Log District, James Daniel, George Still, Woman Killer, Robert Rogers, Moses Parris, John Duncan, Moses Downing, George Ward, Tahquoh, and Sam Downing, are nominated and recommended as candidates. The election in the first precinct in this District, shall be held at or near George Welch's house, at the Cross Roads, and A. Hutson and E. Duncan, are chosen superintendents, and Joshua Buffington, Clerk. The election in the second precinct shall be held at or near Big Savannah, and John Downing and E. M'Laughlin, are chosen superintendents, and John Daniel, clerk. The election in the third precinct shall be held at the court house, and John Wright and Ellis Harlin, are chosen superintendents, and Moses Daniel, clerk.

In Hightower District, George M. Waters, Joseph Vann, Alexander Saunders, John Beamer, Walking Stick, Richard Rowe, The Feather, Old Field, Te-nah-la-wee-stah, and Thomas Pettit, are nominated and recommended as candidates. The election in the first precinct in this District shall be held at or near the Old Turkey's house, and Tahchi-see and John Harris, are chosen superintendents, and John Sanders, clerk. The election in the third precinct shall be held at the court house. and Charles Moore and W. Thompson, are chosen superintendents, and Joseph Phillips, clerk

In Tahquohee District, Chuwalookee, George Owen, Too-nah-na-lah, Wm. Bowlin, Chips, Ooclen-not-tah, Soo-wa-keee, Sour John, The Tough, and Charles, are nominated and recommended as candidates. The election in the first precinct in this District, shall be held at or near Nahtahyalee, and A. M' Daniel and Metoy, are chosen superintendents, and Thomas, clerk. The election in the second precinct shall be held at or near The Spirit's house, and Benjamin Timson and Edward Timson, are chosen superintendents, and J. D. Wofford, clerk.

In Aquohee District, Sitewake, Bald Town George, Richard Walker, John Timson, Allbone, Robin, (Judge Walker's son-in-law) Ahtoheeskee, Kunsenee, Samuel Ward, and Kalkalloskee, are nominated and recommended as candidates. The election in the first precinct in this District, shall be held at or near Tasquittee, and Thompson and Dick Downing, are chosen superintendents, and William Reid, clerk. The election in the second precinct shall be held at or near Samuel Ward's house, and Isaac Tucker and John Bighead, are chosen superintendents, and David England, clerk. The election at the third precinct shall be held at the court house, and Whirlwind and Bear Conjurer, are chosen superintendents, and Rev. E. Jones, clerk.

Be it further resolved, That the election at the several places herein selected for each District, shall be held on the Saturday previous to the commencement of the Courts for May Term next, and a return of all the votes given shall be made to the superintendents of the election at the court house on the Monday following, being the first day of court, with a certificate of the polls, signed by the superintendents and clerks, and after all the votes being collected and rendered in, the three candidates having the highest number of votes shall be duly elected, and the superintendents and clerks at the court house, shall give to each of the members elected a certificate. And in case there shall be an equal number of votes between any of the third candidates, the members of the Convention shall give them the casting vote, and that the superintendents shall, before entering upon their duties, take an oath for the faithful performance of their trusts; and that the members so elected shall, on the 4th day of July next, meet at Echota and form a convention, and proceed to adopt a Constitution for the Government of the Cherokee Nation.

Be it further resolved, That the principles which shall be established in the Constitution, to be adopted by the Convention, shall not in any degree go to destroy the rights and liberties of the free citizens of this Nation, nor to effect or impair the fundamental principles and laws, by which the Nation is now governed, and that the General Council to be convened in the fall of 1827 shall be held under the present existing authorities; Provided nevertheless, that nothing shall be so construed in this last clause so as to invalidate or prevent the Constitution, adopted by the Convention, from going into effect after the aforesaid next General Council.

New Echota, 13th October, 1826.

JNO. ROSS, Pres't. N. Com.
MAJOR RIDGE, Speaker.
Approved—PATH KILLER (X) his mark.

JOHN ROSS
1827-1866

From an old painting

CHAPTER III

Convention of Delegates, Constitution is Adopted

The elected delegates met and formed the following constitution:

CONSTITUTION OF THE CHEROKEE NATION

Formed by a Convention of Delegates From the Several Districts, at New Echota, July, 1827

We, the Representatives of the people of the Cherokee Nation, in Convention assembled, in order to establish justice, ensure tranquillity, promote our common welfare, and secure to ourselves and our posterity the blessings of liberty; acknowledging with humility and gratitude the goodness of the sovereign Ruler of the Universe, in offering us an opportunity so favorable to the design, and imploring His aid and direction in its accomplishment, do ordain and establish this Constitution for the Government of the Cherokee Nation.

Article 1.—Sec. 1.—The boundaries of this Nation, embracing the lands solemnly guaranteed and reserved forever to the Cherokee Nation by the Treaties concluded with the United States, are as follows, and shall forever hereafter remain unalterably the same, to-wit:

Beginning on the north bank of Tennessee river at the upper part of the Chickasaw old field, thence along the main channel of said river, including all the islands therein, to the mouth of the Hiwassee river, thence up the main channel of said river, including islands, to the first hill which closes in on said river about two miles above Hiwassee Old Town, thence along the ridge which divides the waters of the Hiwassee and Little Tillico, to the Tennesse river at Tallassee, thence along the main channel, including islands, to the junction of the Cowee and Nanteyalee, thence along the ridge in the fork of said river, to the top of the blue ridge, thence along the blue ridge to the Unicoy Turnpike road, thence by a straight line to the main source of the Chestatee, thence along its main channel, including islands, to the Chattahoochy, and thence down the same to the Creek boundary at Buzzard Roost, thence along the boundary line which separates this and the Creek Nation, to a point on the Coosa river opposite the mouth of Wills Creek, thence down along the south bank of the same to a point opposite Fort Strother, thence up the river to the mouth of Wills Creek, thence up along the east bank of said creek to the west branch thereof, and up the same to its source, and thence along the ridge which separates the Tombeccee and Tennessee waters to a point on the top of said ridge, thence due north to Camp Coffee on Tennessee river, which is opposite the Chickasaw Island, thence to the place of beginning.

Sec. 2—The sovereignty and Jurisdiction of this Government shall extend over the country within the boundaries above described, and the lands therein are, and shall remain, the common property of the Nation; but the improvements made thereon, and in the possession of the citizens of the Nation, are the exclusive and indefeasible property of the citizens respectively who made; or may rightfully be in possession of them; Provided ,that the citizens of the Nation, possessing exclusive and indefeasible right to their respective improvements, as expressed in this article, shall possess no right nor power to dispose of their improvements in any manner whatever to the United States, mdividual states, nor individual citizens thereof; and that whenever any such citizen or citizens shall remove with their effects out of the limits of this Nation, and become citizens of any other Goverment, all their rights and privileges as citizens of this Nation shall cease; Provided nevertheless, That the Legislature shall have power to re-admit by law to all the rights of citizenship, any such person or persons, who may at any time desire to return to the Nation on their memorializing the General Council for such readmission. Moreover, the Legislature shall have power to adopt such laws and regulations, as its wisdom may deem expedient and proper, to prevent the citizens from monopolizing improvements with the view of speculation.

Article II.—Sec. 1.—The power of this government shall be divided into three distinct departments; the Legislative, the Executive, and Judicial.

Sec. 2—No person or persons belonging to one of these Departments shall exercise any of the powers properly belonging to either of the others, except in the cases hereinafter expressly directed or permitted.

ARTICLE III—Sec. 1.—The Legislative power shall be vested in two distinct branches; a Committee and a Council, each to have a negative on the other, and both to be styled the General Council of the Cherokee Nation; and the style of their acts and laws shall be.

"Resolved by the Committee and Council, in General Council convened."

Sec. 2. The Cherokee Nation, as laid off into eight Districts, shall so remain.

Sec. 3—The Committee shall consist of two members from each District, and the Council shall consist of three members from each District, to be chosen by the qualified electors of their respective Districts, for two years; and the elections to be held in every District on the First Monday in August for the year 1828, and every succeeding two years thereafter; and the General Council shall be held once a year, to be convened on the second Monday of October in each year, at New Echota.

Sec. 4—No perosn shall be eligible to a seat in the General Council, but a free Cherokee male citizen, who shall have attained the age of twenty-five years. The descendants of Cherokee men by all free women, except the African race, whose parents may have been living together as man and wife, according to the customs and laws of this Nation, shall be entitled to all the rights and privileges of this nation, as well as the posterity of Cherokee women by all free men. No person who is of negro or mulatto parentage, either by the father or mother side, shall be eligible to hold any office of profit, honor or trust under this Government.

Sec. 5—The electors and members of the General Council shall, in all cases except those of treason, felony, or breach of the peace, be privileged from arrest during their attendance at election, and at the General Council, and in going to, and returning from the same.

Sec. 6—In all elections by the people, the electors shall vote viva voce. Electors for members to the General Council for 1828, shall be held at the places of holding the several courts, and at the other two precincts in each District which are designated by the law under which the members of this Convention were elected; and the District Judges shall superintend the elections within the pricincts of their respective Court Houses, and the Marshals and Sheriffs shall superintend within the precincts which may be assigned them by the Circuit Judges of their respective Districts, together with one other person who shall be appointed by the Circuit Judges for each precinct within their respective Districts; and the Circuit Judges shall also appoint a clerk to each precinct.—The superintendents and clerks shall, on the Wednesday morning succeeding the election, assemble at their respective Court Houses and proceed to examine and ascertain the true state of the polls, and shall issue to each member, duly elected, a certificate, and also make an official return of the state of the polls of election to the Principal Chief, and it shall be the duty of the Sheriffs to deliver the same to the Executive; Provided nevertheless, The General Council shall have power after the election of 1828, to regulate by law the precincts and superintendents and clerks of elections in the several Distircts.

Sec. 7.—All free male citizens, (excepting negroes and descendants of white and Indian men by negro women who may have been set free,) who shall have attained to the age of eighteen years, shall be equally entitled to vote at all public elections.

Sec. 8.—Each house of the General Council shall judge of the qualifications and returns of its own members.

Sec. 9—Each house of the General Council may determine the rules of its proceedings, punish a member for disorderly behavior, and with the concurrence of two thirds, expel a member; but not a second time for the same cause.

Sec. 10—Each house of the General Council, when assembled shall choose its own officers; a majority of each house shall constitute a quorum to do business, but a smaller number may adjourn from day to day and compel the attendance of absent members in such manner and under such penalty as each house may prescribe.

Sec. 11.—The members of the Committee shall each receive from the public Treasury a compensation for their services which shall be two dollars and fifty cents per day during their attendance at the General Council; and the members of the Council shall each receive two dollars per day for their services during their attendance at the General Council:—Provided, that the same may be increased or diminished by law, but no alteration shall make effect during the period of service of the members of the General Council, by whom such alteration shall have been made.

Sec. 12.—The General Council shall regulate by law, by whom and in what manner, writs of elections shall be issued to fill the vacancies which may happen in either branch thereof.

Sec. 13.—Each member of the General Council before he takes his seat shall take the following oath or affirmation, to-wit:

"I, A. B., do solemnly swear, (or affirm, as the case may be,) that I

have not obtained my election by bribery, treats or any undue and unlawful means used by myself, or others by my desire or approbation, for that purpose; that I consider myself constitutionally qualified as a member of
and that, on all questions and measures which may come before me, I will so give my vote, and so conduct myself, as may in my judgment, appear most conducive to the interest and prosperity of this Nation; and that I will bear true faith and allegiance to the same; and to the utmost of my ability and power observe, conform to, support and defend the Constitution thereof."

Sec. 14.—No person who may be convicted of felony before any court of this Nation, shall be eligible to any office or appointment of honor, profit or trust within this Nation.

Sec. 15.—The General Council shall have power to make all laws and regulations, which they shall deem necessary and proper for the good of the Nation, which shall not be contrary to this Constitution.

Sec. 16.—It shall be the duty of the General Council to pass such laws as may be necessary and proper, to decide differences by arbitrators to be appointed by the parties, who may choose that summary mode of adjustment.

Sec. 17.—No power of suspending the laws of this Nation shall be exercised, unless by the Legislature or its authority.

Sec. 18.—No retrospective law, nor any law, impairing the obligations of contracts shall be passed.

Sec. 19.—The legislature shall have power to make laws for laying and collecting taxes, for the purpose of raising a revenue.

Sec. 20.—All bills making appropriations shall originate in the Committee, but the Council may propose amendments or reject the same.

Sec. 21.—All other bills may originate in either house, subject to the concurrence of rejection of the other.

Sec. 22.—All acknowledged Treaties shall be the Supreme law of the land.

Sec. 23.—The General Council shall have the sole power of deciding on the construction of all Treaty stipulations.

Sec. 24.—The Council shall have the sole power of impeaching.

Sec. 25.—Any impeachments shall be tried by the Committee;—when sitting for that purpose, the members shall be upon oath or affirmation; and no person shall be convicted without the concurrence of two thirds of the members present.

Sec. 26.—The Principal Chief, assistant principal Chief, and all civil officers, under this Nation, shall be liable to impeachment for any misdemeanor in office, but Judgment, in such cases, shall not extend further than removal from office, and disqualification to hold any office of honor, trust or profit, under this Nation. The party whether convicted or acquitted, shall nevertheless, be liable to indictment, trial, judgment and punishment, according to law.

ARTICLE IV.—Sec. 1. The Supreme Executive Power of this Nation shall be vested in a Principal Chief, who shall be chosen by the General Council, and shall hold his office four years; to be elected as follows,—The General

Council by a joint vote, shall, at their second annual session, after the rising of this Convention, and at every fourth annual session thereafter, on the second day after the House shall be organized, and competent to proceed to business, elect a Principal Chief.

Sec. 2.—No person, except a natural born citizen, shall be eligible to the office of Principal Chief; neither shall any person be eligible to that office, who shall not have attained to the age of thirty-five years.

Sec. 3.—There shall also be chosen at the same time, by the General Council, in the same manner for four years, an assistant Principal Chief.

Sec. 4.—In case of the removal of the Principal Chief from office, or his death, resignation, or inability to discharge the powers and duties of the said office, the same shall devolve on the assistant principal Chief, until the inability be removed, or the vacancy filled by the General Council.

Sec. 5.—The General Council may, by law, provide for the case of removal, death, resignation or inability of both the Principal and assistant Principal Chiefs, declaring what officer shall then act as Principal Chief, until the disability be removed, or a Principal Chief shall be elected.

Sec. 6.—The Principal Chief, shall, at stated times, receive for their services,—a compensation—which shall neither be increased nor diminished during the period for which they shall have been elected; and they shall not receive, within that period, any other emolument from the Cherokee Nation, or any other government.

Sec. 7.—Before the Principal Chief enters on the execution of his office, he shall take the following oath, or affirmation; "I do solemnly swear (or affirm) that I will faithfully execute the office of Principal Chief of the Cherokee Nation, and will; to the best of my ability, preserve, protect and defend, the Constitution of the Cherokee Nation."

Sec. 8.—He may, on extraordinary occasions, convene the General Council at the Seat of Government.

Sec. 9.—He shall from time to time give to the General Council information of the State of the Government, and recommend to their consideration such measures as he may think expedient.

Sec. 10.—He shall take care that the laws be faithfully executed.

Sec. 11.—It shall be his duty to visit the different districts, at least once in two years, to inform himself of the general condition of the Country.

Sec. 12.—The assistant Principal Chief shall, by virtue of his office, aid and advise the Principal Chief in the Administration of the Government, at all times during his continuance in office.

Sec. 13.—Vacancies that may happen in offices, the appointment of which is vested in the General Council, shall be filled by the Principal Chief, during the recess of the General Council, by granting Commissions which shall expire at the end of the Session.

Sec. 14.—Every Bill which shall have passed both Houses of the General Council, shall, before it becomes a law, be presented to the Principal Chief of the Cherokee Nation. If he approves, he shall sign it, but if not, he shall return it, with his objections, to that house in which it shall have originated, who shall enter the objections at large on their journals, and proceed to reconsider it. If, after such reconsideration, two thirds of that House shall agree to pass the bill, it shall be sent, together with the objections, to the other house, by which it shall likewise be reconsidered, and if approved by two thirds of that house, it shall become a law. If any bill shall not be returned by the Principal Chief within five days (Sundays excepted) after it shall have been presented to him, the same shall be a law, in like manner as if he signed it; unless the General Council by their adjournment prevent its return, in which case it shall be a law, unless sent back within three days after their next meeting.

Sec. 15.—Members of the General Council and all officers, Executive and Judicial, shall be bound by oath to support the Constitution of this Nation, and to perform the duties of their respective offices with fidelity.

Sec. 16.—In case of disagreement between the two houses with respect to the time of adjournment, the Principal Chief shall have the power to adjourn the General Council to such a time as he thinks proper, provided, it be not to a period beyond the next Constitutional meeting of the same.

Sec. 17.—The Principal Chief shall, during the sitting of the General Council, attend to the Seat of Government.

Sec. 18.—There shall be a Council to consist of three men to be appointed by the joint vote of both Houses, to advise the Principal Chief in the Executive part of the Government, whom the Principal Chief shall have full power, at his descretion, to assemble; and he, together with the assistant Principal Chief, and the Counsellors, or a majority of them may, from time to time, hold and keep a Council for ordering and directing the affairs of the Nation according to law.

Sec. 19.—The members of the Council shall be chosen for the term of one year.

Sec. 20.—The resolutions and advice of the Council shall be recorded in a register and signed by the members agreeing thereto, which may be called for by either house of the General Council; and any counsellor may enter his dissent to the resolution of the majority.

Sec. 21.—The Treasurer of the Cherokee Nation shall be chosen by the joint vote of both Houses of the General Council for the term of two years.

Sec. 22.—The Treasurer shall, before entering on the duties of his office, give bond to the Nation with sureties to the satisfaction of the Legislature, for the faithful discharge of his trust.

Sec. 23.—No money shall be drawn from the Treasury, but by warrant from the Principal Chief, and in consequence of appropriations made by law.

Sec. 25.—It shall be the duty of the Treasurer to receive all public monies, and to make a regular statement and account of the receipts and expenditures of all public monies at the annual Session of the General Council.

ARTICLE V.—Sec. 1.—The Judicial Powers shall be vested in a Supreme Court, and such Circuit and Inferior Courts, as the General Council may, from time to time ordain and establish.

Sec. 2.—The Supreme Court shall consist of three Judges, any two of whom shall be a quorum.

Sec. 3.—The Judges of each shall hold their Commissions for four years, but any of them may be removed from office on the address of two thirds of each house of the General Council to the Principal Chief, for that purpose.

Sec. 4.—The Judges of the Supreme and Circuit Courts shall, at stated times, receive a compensation, which shall not be diminished during their continuance in office, but they shall receive no fees or perquisites of office, nor hold any other office of profit or any other power.

Sec. 5.—No person shall be appointed a Judge of any of the Courts before he shall have attained to the age of thirty years, nor shall any person continue to execute the duties of any of the said offices after he shall have attained to the age of seventy years.

Sec. 6.—The Judges of the Supreme and Circuit Courts shall be appointed by a joint vote of both houses of the General Council.

Sc. 7.—There shall be appointed in each District, under the Legislative authority, as many Justices of the Peace as it may be deemed the public good requires, whose powers, duties and duration in office, shall be clearly designated.

Sec. 8.—The Judges of the Supreme Court and Circuit Courts shall have complete criminal Jurisdiction in such cases and in such manner as may be pointed out by law.

Sec. 9.—Each Court shall choose its own Clerks for the term of four years; but such Clerks shall not continue in office unless their qualifications shall be adjudged and approved of by the Judges of the Supreme Court, and they shall be removable for breach of good behaviour at any time, by the Judges of their respective courts.

Sec. 10.—No Judge shall sit on trial of any cause, where the parties shall be connected with him by affinity or consanguinity, except by consent of the parties. In case all the Judges of the Supreme Court shall be interested in the event of any cause, or related to all, or either of the parties, the Legislature may provide by law for the selection of three men of good character and knowledge, for the determination thereof, who shall be especially commissioned by the Principal Chief for the case.

Sec. 11.—All writs and other process shall run in the name of the Cherokee Nation, and bear test, and be signed by the respective clerks.

Sec. 12.—Indictments shall conclude, "against the peace and dignity of the Cherokee Nation."

Sec. 13.—The Supreme Court shall hold its session annually at the seat of Government to be convened on the second Monday of October in each year.

Sec. 14.—In all criminal prosecutions, the accused shall have the right of being heard, of demanding the nature and cause of the accusation against him, of meeting the witnesses face to face, of having compulsory process for obtaining witnesses in his favor; and in prosecutions by indictment or information, a speedy public trial by an impartial jury of the vicinage; nor shall he be compelled to give evidence against himself.

Sec. 15.—The people shall be secure in their persons, houses, papers and possessions, from unreasonable seizures and searches, and no warrants to search any place or to seize any person or things, shall be issued without describing them as nearly as may be, nor without good cause, supported by oath, or affirmation. All prisoners shall be bailable by sufficient security unless for capital offenses, where the proof is evident, or presumption great.

ARTICLE VI.—Sec. 1.—Whereas, the ministers of the Gospel are, by their profession, dedicated to the service of God and the care of souls, and ought not to be diverted from the great duty of their function, therefore, no minister of the Gospel, or public preacher of any religious persuasion, whilst he continues in the exercise of his pastoral functions, shall be eligible to the office of Principal Chief, or a seat in either house of the General Council.

Sec. 2.—No person who denies the being of a God, or a future state of rewards and punishment, shall hold any office in the civil department of this Nation.

Sec. 3.—The free exercise of religious worship, and serving God without distinction shall forever be allowed within this Nation; Provided, That this liberty of conscience shall not be so constructed as to excuse acts of licentiousness, or justify practices inconsistent with the peace or safety of this Nation.

Sec. 4.—Whenever the General Council shall determine the expediency of appointing delegates or other Agents for the purpose of transacting business with the Government of the United States; the power to recommend, and by the advice and consent of the Committee, shall appoint and commission such delegates or public agents accordingly, and all matters of interest touching the rights of the citizens of this Nation, which may require the attention of the government of the United States, the Principal Chief shall keep up a friendly correspondence with that Government, through the medium of its proper officers.

Sec. 5.—All commissions shall be in the name and by the authority of the Cherokee Nation, and be sealed with the seal of the Nation, and signed by the Principal Chief.

The Principal Chief shall make use of his private seal until a National seal shall be provided.

Sec. 6.—A Sheriff shall be elected in each District by the qualified electors thereof, who shall hold his office for the term of two years, unless sooner removed. Should a vacancy occur subsequent to an election, it shall be filled by the Principal Chief as in other cases, and the person so appointed shall continue in office until the next general election, when such vacancy shall be filled by the qualified electors, and the Sheriff then elected shall continue in office for two years.

Sec. 7.—There shall be a Marshal appointed by a joint vote of both houses of the General Council, for the term of four years, whose compensation and duties shall be regulated by law, and whose jurisdiction shall extend over the Cherokee Nation.

Sec. 8.—No person shall for the same offense be twice put in jeopardy of life or limb, nor shall any person's property be taken or applied to public use without his consent; Provided, That nothing in this clause shall be so construed as to impair the right and power of the General Council to lay and collect taxes. All courts shall be open, and every person for an injury done him in his property, person or reputation, shall have remedy by due course of law.

Sec. 9—The right of trial by jury shall remain inviolate.

Sec. 10—Religion, morality and knowledge being necessary to good government, the preservation of Liberty, and the happiness of mankind, schools and the means of education shall forever be encouraged in this Nation.

Sec. 11—The appointment of all officers, not otherwise directed by this Constitution shall be vested in the Legislature.

Sec. 12—All laws in force in this nation at the passing of this Constitution, shall so continue until altered or repealed by the Legislature, except where they are temporary, in which case they shall expire at the times respectively limited for their duration; if not continued by an act of the Legislature.

Sec. 13—The General Council may at any time propose such amendments to this Constitution as two-thirds of each house shall deem expedient; and the Principal Chief shall issue a proclamation, directing all the civil officers of the several Districts to promulgate the same as extensively as possible within their respective Districts, at least nine months previous to the next general election, and if at the first session of the General Council after such general election, two thirds of each house shall, by yeas and nays, ratify such proposed amendments they shall be valid to all intents and purposes, as part of the Constitution; Provided, That such proposed amendments shall be read on three several days, in each house as well when the same are proposed as when they are ratified.

Done in Convention at New Echota, this twenty-sixth day of July, in the year of our Lord, one thousand eight hundred and twenty-seven; In testimony whereof, we hae each of us, hereunto subscribed our names.

JNO. ROSS, Pres't Con.

Jno. Baldrige, Geo. Lowrey, Jno. Brown, Edward Gunter, John Martin, Joseph Vann, Kelechulee, Lewis Ross, Thomas Foreman, Hair Conrad, James Daniel, John Duncan, Joseph Vann, Thomas Petitt John Beamer, Ooclenota, Wm. Boling, John Timson, Situwaukee, Richard Walker,

A. McCOY, Sec'y to Con.

The emigration of Cherokees to Arkansas met with strenuous objections as may be evidenced by the following acts of council:

"Resolved by the National Committee and Council, That any person or persons, whatsoever, who shall choose to emigrate to the Arkansas country, and shall sell the possessions he or they may be in possession of, to any person or persons whatsoever, he or they, so disposing of their improvements shall forfeit and pay unto the Cherokee Nation the sum of one hundred and fifty dollars; and be it further

"Resolved, That any person or persons whatsoever, who shall purchase any improvements from any person or persons so emigrating, he or they, so offending shall also forfeit and pay a fine of one hundred and fifty dollars to the Nation, to be collected by the marshal of the district. By order of the National Committee.

JONH ROSS, Pres. National Committee.
ALEXANDER McCOY, Clerk National Committee.

Approved: October 27th, 1821.

His
PATH x KILLER.
Mark

Chas. R. Hicks.[1]

Resolved by the National Committee and Council, in General Council Convened, That from and after the passage of this act, if any citizen of the Nation shall bind themselves by enrollment or otherwise as emigrants to Arkansas, or for the purpose of removing out of the jurisdictional limits of the Nation, he, she or they so enrolling or binding themselves, shall forfeit thereby all the rights and privileges he, she or they may have previously thereto claimed or enjoyed as citizens of this Nation and shall be viewed in the same light as others not entitled to citizenship, and treated accordingly.

Be it further resolved, That if any person or persons, citizens of this Nation, shall sell or dispose of his, her or their improvements to any person or persons so enrolled or otherwise bound as above mentioned, he, she or they, shall be viewed as having disposed of his, her or their improvements to a citizen of the United States, and shall be ineligible to hold any office of honor, profit or trust in this Nation, and upon conviction thereof, before any of the circuit courts of the several districts, be fined in a sum not less than one thousand dollars, nor exceeding two thousand dollars, and be punished with one hundred lashes.

Be it further resolved, In order to prevent any person from screening him, her or them from the penalties above prescribed by pretending to have sold or disposed of his, her or their improvements to a lawful citizen and not an emigrant, all citizens of this Nation who may hereafter buy, sell or dispose of in any manner their improvements to each other, be, and they are hereby required, the disposer as well as the purchaser of such improvements, to make affidavit, to be filed in the clerk's office of the district, before any of the District Judges of Clerks of the several courts, that he, she or they did not dispose of or transfer, purchase or obtain any improvement for the purpose of having it valued by the United States commissioners or agents, or were not acting as agents or emigrants in making such purchase or transfer, and in case any such person or persons shall fail to comply with this requirement, such person or persons shall, upon conviction before any of the Circuit Courts of the Nation, pay a fine of not less than one dollar, nor exceeding two hundred dollars, for every offense so committed.

Be it further resolved, That if any citizen or citizens of this Nation shall dispose of or transfer his, her or their improvements without complying with the requirements of the third section of this act, and the person or persons to whom the sale or transfer of such improvements may be made, should thereafter by enrollment or otherwise become an emigrant or emigrants, and shall get said improvement or improvements valued by the agents of the General Government, within thirty days after such purchase or transfer shall have been made, or at any time whilst the disposer continues to remain in possession of the same, then, in that case, the person or persons who may have so disposed of or transferred the improvements as aforesaid shall be subject to the same penalty prescribed in the second section of this act, for disposing of improvements to emigrants.

Be it further resolved, That any person or persons, whosoever, who have bound themselves together by enrollment or otherwise as emigrants under the treaty of 1828, with the Arkansas Cherokees, or who have had, or intend to have their improvements valued by the agents of the General Government, and do not remove out of the jurisdictional limits of this Nation within fifteen days after the passage of this act, they shall be viewed and treated as intruders in the same manner as those who may become emigrants hereafter.

Be it further Resolved, That the Principal Chief of the Nation be, and he is hereby authorized, by and with the advice of the executive councillors, to order the aprehension of any intruders within the limits of the Nation. to be delivered over to the agents of the United States for the Cherokees, to be prosecuted under the intercourse laws of the United States, or to expel or punish them as they please.

Approved: JOHN ROSS,
Principal Chief, Cherokee Nation.

New Echota, Octoger 31, 1829.

Encroachments on the Cherokee Nation in Arkansas were increasingly troublesome and on May 28, 1828 the following treaty was made by the delegation at Washington:

WILLIAM P. ROSS
Chief, August, 1866, to November, 1867
November 11, 1872, to November, 1875

CHAPTER IV

Proclamation May 28, 1828

TREATY WITH THE WESTERN CHEROKEE, 1828.

May 6, 1828. 7 Stat. 311. Proclamation, May 28, 1828. Articles of a Convention, concluded at the City of Washington this sixth day of May, in the year of our Lord one thousand eight hundred and twenty-eight, between James Barbour, Secretary of War, being especially authorized therefor by the President of the United States, and the undersigned, Chiefs and Head Men of the Cherokee Nation of Indians, West of the Mississippi, they being duly authorized and empowered by their Nation.

Object of the Treaty. Whereas, it being the anxious desire of the Government of the United States to secure to the Cherokee nation of Indians, as well as those now living within the limits of the Territory of Arkansas, as those of their friends and brothers who reside in States East of the Mississippi, and who may wish to join their brothers of the West, a permanent home, and which shall, under the most solemn guarantee of the United States, be, and remain, theirs forever—a home that shall never, in all future time, be embarrassed by having extended around it lines, or placed over it the jurisdiction of a Territory or State, nor be pressed upon by the extension, in any way, of any of the limits of any existing Territory or State; and, Whereas, the present location of the Cherokees in Arkansas being unfavorable to their present repose, and tending, as the past demonstrates, to their future degradation and misery; and the Cherokees being anxious to avoid such consequences, and yet not questioning their right to their lands in Arkansas, as secured to them by Treaty, and resting also upon the pledges given them by the President of the United States, and the Secretary of War, of March 1818, and 8th October, 1821, in regard to the outlet to the West, and as may be seen on referring to the records of the War Department, still being anxious to secure a permanent home, and to free themselves, and their posterity, from an embarrassing connection with the Territory of Arkansas, and guard themselves from such connections in future; and, Whereas, it being important, not to the Cherokees only, but also to the Choctaws, and in regard also to the question which may be agitated in the future respecting the location of the latter, as well as the former, within the limits of the Territory or State of Arkansas, as the case may be, and their removal therefrom; and to avoid the cost which may attend negotiations to rid the Territory or State of Arkansas whenever it may become a State, of either, or both of those Tribes, the parties hereto do hereby conclude the following Articles, viz:

Western Boundary of Arkansas Defined. Art. 1. The Western boundary of Arkansas shall be, and the same is, hereby defined, viz: A line shall be run, commencing on Red River, at the point where the Eastern Choctaw line strikes said River, and run due North with said line to the River Arkansas,

Territory Guaranteed to Cherokees by United States. Art. 2. The United States agree to possess the Cherokees, and to guarantee it to them forthence in a direct line to the South West corner of Missouri.

ever, and that guarantee is hereby solemnly pledged, of seven million acres of land, to be bounded as follows, viz: Commencing at that point on Arkansas River where the Eastern Choctaw boundary line strikes said River, and running thence with the Western boundary line of Missouri till it crosses the waters of Neasho, generally called Grand River, thence due west to a point from which a due South course will strike the present North West corner of Arkansas Territory, thence continuing due South, on and with the present Western boundary line of the Territory to the main branch of Arkansas River, thence down said River to its junction with the Canadian River, and thence up and between the said Rivers Arkansas and Canadian, to a point at which a line running North and South from River to River, will give the aforesaid seven millions of acres. In addition to the seven millions of acres thus provided for, and bounded, the United States further guarantee to the Cherokee Nation a perpetual outlet, West, and a free and unmolested use of all the Country lying West of the Western boundary of the above described limits, and as far West as the sovereignty of the United States, and their right of soil extend.

United States to Run the Lines. Art. 3. The United States agree to have the lines of the above cession run without delay, say not later than the first of October next, and to remove, immediately after the running of the Eastern line from the Arkansas River to the South West corner of Missouri, all white persons from the West to the East of said line, and also all others, should there be any there, who may be unacceptable to the Cherokees, so that no obstacles arising out of the presence of a white population, or a population of any other sort, shall exist to annoy the Cherokees— and also to keep all such from the West of said line in future.

Persons to Be Appointed to Value Cherokee Improvements. Art. 4. The United States moreover agree to appoint suitable persons whose duty it shall be, in conjunction with the Agent, to value all such improvements as the Cherokees may abandon in their removal from their present homes to the District of Country as ceded in the second Article of this agreement, and to pay for the same immediately after the assessment is made, and the amount ascertained. It is further agreed, that the property and improvements connected with the agency, shall be sold under the direction of the Agent, and the proceeds of the same applied to aid in the erection, in the country to which the Cherokees are going, of a Grist, and Saw Mill, for their use. The aforesaid property and improvements are thus defined: Commence at the Arkansas River opposite William Stinnetts, and run due North one mile, thence due East to a point from which a due South line to the Arkansas River would include the Chalybeate, or Mineral Spring, attached to or near the present residence of the Agent, and thence up said River (Arkansas) to the place of beginning

Further Agreement. Art. 5. It is further agreed, that the United States, in consideration of the inconvenience and trouble attending the removal, and on account of the reduced value of a great portion of the lands herein ceded to the Cherokees, as compared with that of those in Arkansas which were made theirs by the Treaty of 1817, and the Convention of 1819, will pay to the Cherokees, immediately after their removal which shall be within fourteen months of the date of this agreement, the sum of fifty thousand dollars; also an annuity for three years, of two thousand dollars, toward defraying the cost and trouble which may attend upon going after and recovering their stock which may stray into the Territory in quest of the pastures from which they may be driven—also, eight thousand seven hundred and sixty dollars, for spoil-ations committed on them, (the Cherokees,) which sum will be in full of all demands of the kind up to this date, as well as those against the Osages, as those against citizens of the United States—this being the amount of the claims for said spoilations, as rendered by the Cherokees, and which are believed to be correctly and fairly stated.—Also, one thousand two hundred dollars for the use of Thomas Graves, a Cherokee Chief, for losses sustained in his property, and for personal suffering endured by him when confined as a prisoner on a criminal, but false accusation; also, five hundred dollars for the use of George Guess, another Cherokee, for the great benefits he has conferred upon the Cherokee people, in the beneficial results they are now experiencing from the use of the Alphabet discovered by him, to whom also, in consideration of his relinquishing a valuable saline, the privilege is hereby given to locate and occupy another saline on Lee's Creek. It is further agreed by the United States, to pay two thousand dollars, annually, to the Cherokees, for ten years, to be expended under the direction of the President of the United States in the education of their children, in their own country, in letters and the mechanic arts; also, one thousand dollars towards the purchase of a Printing Press and Types to aid the Cherokees in the progress of education, and to benefit and enlighten them as a people, in their own, and our language. It is agreed further that the expense incurred other than that paid by the United States in the erection of the buildings and improvements, so far as that may have been paid by the benevolent society who has been, and yet is, engaged in instructing the Cherokee children, shall be paid to the society, it being the undersanding that the amount shall be expended in the erection of other buildings and improvements, for like purposes, in the country herein ceded to the Cherokees. The United States relinquish their claim due by the Cherokees to the late United States Factory, provided the same does not exceed three thousand five hundred dollars.

Further Agreement. Art. 6. It is moreover agreed by the United States, whenever the Cherokees may desire it, to give them a set of plain laws, suited to their condition—also, when they may wish to lay off their lands, and own them individually, a surveyor shall be sent to make the surveys at the cost of the United States.

Cherokees to Surrender Lands in Arkansas Within Fourteen Months. Art. 7. The Chiefs and Head Men of the Cherokee Nation, aforesaid, for and in consideration of the foregoing stipulations and provisions, do hereby agree, in the name and behalf of their Nation, to give up, and they do hereby surrender to the United States, and agree to leave the same within fourteen months, as herein before stipulated, all the lands to which they are entitled in Arkansas, and which were secured to them by the Treaty of 8th January, 1817, and the Convention of the 27th February, 1819.

Cost of Emigration, etc., to be Borne By the United States. Art. 8. The Cherokee Nation, West of the Mississippi having, by this agreement, freed themselves from the harassing and ruinous effects consequent upon a location amidst a white population, and secured to their posterity, under the solemn sanction of the guarantee of the United States, as continued in this agreement. a large extent of unembarrassed country; and that their Brothers yet remaining in the States may be induced to join them and enjoy the repose and blessings of such a State in the future, it is further agreed, on the part of the United States, that to each Head of a Cherokee family now residing within the chartered limits of Georgia, or of either of the States, East of the Mississippi, who may desire to remove West, shall be given, on enrolling himself for emigration, a good Rifle, a Blanket, and Kettle, and five pounds of Tobacco: (and to each member of his family one Blanket,) also, a just compensation for the property he may abandon, to be assessed by persons to be appointed by the President of the United States. The cost of the emigration of all such shall also be borne by the United States, and good and suitable ways opened, and provisions procured for their comfort, accommodation, and support, by the way, and provisions for twelve months after their arrival at the Agency; and to each person, or head of a family, if he take along with him four persons. shall be paid immediately on his arriving at the Agency and reporting himself and his family or followers, as emigrants and permanent settlers, in addition to the above, provided he and they shall have emigrated from within the Chartered limits of the State of Georgia, the sum of fifty dollars, and this sum in proportion to any greater or less number that may accompany him from within the aforesaid Chartered limits of the State of Georgia.

A Certain Tract of Land To Be Reserved for the Benefit of the United States. Art. 9. It is understood and agreed by the parties to this Convention, that a Tract of Land, two miles wide and six miles lond, shall be, and the same is hereby, reserved for the use and benefit of the United States, for the accommodation of the military force which is now, or which may hereafter be, stationed at Fort Gibson, on the Neasho, or Grand River, to commence on said River half a mile below the aforesaid Fort, and to run thence due East two miles, thence Northwardly six miles, to a point which shall be two miles distant from the River aforesaid, thence due West to the said River, and down it to the place of beginning. And the Cherokees agree that the United States shall have and possess the right of establishing a road through their country for the purpose of having a free and unmolested way to and from said Fort.

Capt. J. Rogers to be Paid in Full for Property Lost in the Service of United States. Art. 10. It is agreed that Captain James Rogers, in consideration of his having lost a horse in the service of the United States, and for services rendered by him to the United States, shall be paid, in full for the above, and all other claims for losses and services, the sum of Five Hundred Dollars.

Art. 11. This Treaty to be binding on the contracting parties so soon as it is ratified by the President of the United States, by and with the advice and consent of the Senate.

Done at the place, and on the day and year above written.

James Barbour. [L. S.]
Black Fox, his x mark, [L. S.]
Thomas Graves, his x mark, [L. S.]
George Guess,* [L. S.]
Thomas Maw,* [L. S.]
George Marvis,* [L. S.]
John Looney,* [L. S.]
John Rogers, [L. S.]
J. W. Flawey, counsellor of Del. [L .S.]
Chiefs of the delegation.

Witnesses:

Thos. L. McKenney,
James Rogers, interpreter,
D. Kurtz,
H. Miller,
Thomas Murray,
D. Brown, secretary Cherokee delegation,
Pierye Pierya,
E. W. Duval, United States agent, etc.

Ratified with the following proviso:

"Provided, nevertheless, that the said convention shall not be so construed as to extend the northern boundary of he 'perpetual outlet west' provided for and guaranteed in the second article of said convention, north of the thirty-sixth degree of north latitude, or so as to interfere with the lands assigned, or to be assigned west of the Mississippi river, to the Creek Indians who have emigrated, or may emigrate, from the States of Georgia and Alabama, under the provisions of any treaty or treaties heretofore concluded between the United Sates and the Creek tribe of Indians; and provided further. That nothing in the said convention shall be construed to cede or assign to the Cherokees any lands heretofore ceded or assigned to any tribe or tribes of Indians, by any treaty now existing and in force, with any such tribe or tribes."

Department of War,
31st May, 1828.

To the Hon. Henry Clay,
Secretary of State:

Sir: I have the honor to transmit, herewith, the acceptance of the terms, by the Cherokees, upon which the recent convention with them was ratified. You will have the goodness to cause the same to be attached to the treaty, and published with it.

I have the honor to be, very respectfully, your obedient servant,

Sam'l. L. Southard.

To the Secretary of War,
Washington City:

Council Room, Williamson's Hotel,
Washington, May 31st, 1828

Sir: The undersigned, chiefs of the Cherokee Nation, west of the Mississippi, for and in behalf of said nation, hereby agree to, and accept of, the terms upon which the Senate of the United States ratified the convention, concluded at Washington on the sixth day of May, 1828, between the United States and said nation.

In testimony whereof, they hereunto subscribe their names and affix their seals.

Thomas Graves, his x mark, [L. S.]
George Maw, his x mark, [L. S.]
George Guess, his x mark, [L. S.]
Thomas Marvis, his x mark, [L. S.]
John Rogers.

Signed and sealed in the presence of—

E. W. Duval, United States agent, etc.
Thomas Murray,
James Rogers, interpreter.

The inaccuracies of this treaty were corrected by:

TREATY WITH THE WESTERN CHEROKEE, 1833.

Articles of agreement and convention made and concluded at Fort Gibson, on the Arkansas river on the fourteenth day of February one thousand eight hundred and thirty-three, by and between Montfort Stokes, Henry L. Ellsworth and John F. Schermerhorn duly appointed Commissioners on the part of the United States and the undersigned Chiefs and Head-men of the Cherokee nation of Indians west of the Mississippi, they being duly authorized and empowered by their nation.

Preamble. Whereas articles of convention were concluded at the city of Washington, on the sixth day of May, one thousand eight hundred and twenty-eight, between James Barbour, Secretary of War, being specially authorized therefor by the President of the United States, and the chiefs and head men of the Cherokee nation of Indians west of the Mississippi, which articles of convention were duly ratified. And whereas it was agreed by the second article of said convention as follows "That the United States agree to possess the Cherokees, and to guarantee it to them forever, and that guarantee is solemnly pledged, of seven millions of acres of land, said land to be bound as follows, viz, commencing at a point on Arkansas river, where the eastern Choctaw boundary line strikes said river, and running thence with the western line of Arkansas Territory to the southwest corner of Missouri, and thence with the western boundary line of Missouri till it crosses the waters of Neosho, generally called Grand river, thence due west, to a point from which a due south course will strike the present northwest corner of Arkansas Territory, thence continuing due south on and with the present boundary line on the west of said Territory, to the main branch of Arkansas river, thence down said river to its junction with the Canadian, and thence up, and between said rivers Arkansas and Canadian to a point at which a line, running north and south, from river to river, will give the aforesaid seven millions of acres, thus provided for and bounded. The United States further guarantees to the Cherokee nation a perpetual outlet west, and a free and unmolested use of all the country lying west of the western boundary of the above-described limits; and as far west, as the sovereignty of the United States and their right of soil extend. And whereas there was to said articles of convention and agreement, the following proviso viz. "Provided nevertheless, that said convention, shall not be construed, as to extend the northern boundary of said perpetual outlet west, provided for and guaranteed in the second article of said convention, north of the thirty-sixth degree of north latitude, or so as to interfere with the lands assigned or to be assigned, west of the Mississippi river, to the Creek Indians who have emigrated, or may emigrate, from the States of Georgia and Alabama, under the provision of any treaty, or treaties, heretofore concluded, between the United States, and the Creek tribe of Indians—and provided further, that nothing in said convention, shall be construed, to cede, or assign, to the Cherokees any lands heretofore ceded, or assigned, to any tribe, or tribes of Indians, by any treaty now existing and in force, with any such tribe or tribes. And whereas,it appears from the Creek treaty, made with the United States, by the Creek nation, dated twenty-fourth day of January eighteen hundred and twenty-six, at the city of Washington; that they had the right to select, a part of the country described within the boundaries mentioned above in said Cherokee articles of agreement—and whereas, both the Cherokee and Creek nations of Indians west of the Mississippi, anxious to have their boundaries settled in an amicable manner, have met each other in council, and, after full deliberation mutually agreed upon the boundary lines between them—Now therefore, the United States on one part, and the chief and head-men of the Cherokee nation of Indians west of the Mississippi on the other part, agree as follows:

Land granted to the Cherokees; Further guaranty. Art. 1. The United States agree to possess the Cherokees, and to guarantee it to them forever, and that guarantee is hereby pledged, of seven millions of acres of land, to be bounded as follows viz: Beginning at a point on the old western territorial line of Arkansas Territory, being twenty-five miles north from the point, where the Territorial line crosses Arkansas river—thence running from said north point, south, on the said Territorial line, to the place where said Territorial line crosses the Verdigris river—thence down said Verdigris river to the Arkansas river—thence down said Arkansas to a point, where a stone is placed opposite to the east or lower bank of Grand river at its junction with the Arkansas—thence running south, forty-four degrees west, one mile—thence in a straignh line to a point four miles northerly from the mouth of the north fork of the Canadian—thence along the said four miles line to the Canadian—thence down the Canadian to the Arkansas—thence, down the Arkansas, to that point on the Arkansas, where the eastern Choctaw boundary strikes, said river; and running thence with the western line of Arkansas Territory as now defined, to the southern corner of Missouri—thence along the western Missouri line, to the land assigned the Senecas to Grand river; thence up said Grand river, as far as the south line of the Osage reservation, extended if necessary—thence up and between said south

Osage line, extended west if necessary and a line drawn due west, from the point of beginning, to a certain distance west, at which, a line running north and south, from said Osage line, to said due west line, will make seven millions of acres within the whole described boundaries. In addition to the seven millions of acres of land, thus provided for, and bounded, the United States, further guarantee to the Cherokee nation, a perpetual outlet to the west and a free and unmolested use of all the country lying west, of the western boundary of said seven millions of acres, as far west as the sovereignty of the United States and their right of soil extend—Provided however, that if the saline, or salt plain, on the great western prairie, shall fall within said limits prescribed for said outlet, the right is reserved to the United States to permit other tribes of red men, to get salt on said plain in common with the Cherokees—and letters patent shall be issued by the United States as soon as practicable for the land hereby guaranteed.

Quit claim to the United States of former grant. Art. 2. The Cherokee nation hereby relinquish and quit claim to the United States all the right, interest and title which the Cheerokees have, or claim to have in and to all the land ceded, or claimed to have been ceded to said Cheerokee nation by said treaty of sixth of May one thousand eight hundred and twenty-eight, and not embraced within the limits or boundaries fixed in this present supplementary treaty or articles of convention and agreement.

Sixth article of treaty of May 6, 1828, annulled. Art. 3. The Cherokee nation, having particularly requested the United States to annul and cancel the sixth article of said treaty of sixth May, one thousand eight hundred and twenty-eight, the United States, agree to cancel the same, and the same is hereby annulled—Said sixth article referred to, is in the following words—"It is moreover agreed by the United States, when the Cherokees may desire it, to give them a plain set of laws, suited to their condition—also when they may wish to lay off their lands and own them individually, a surveyor shall be sent to survey them at the expense of the United States.

Blacksmith and other workmen, materials and shops. Art. 4. In consideration of the establishment of new boundaries in part, for the lands ceded to said Cherokee nation, and in view of the improvement of said nation, the United States will cause to be erected, on land now guaranteed to the said nation, four blacksmith shops, one wagon maker shop, one wheelwright shop, and the necessary tools and implements furnished for the same; together with one ton of iron, and two hundred and fifty pounds of steel, for each of said blacksmith shops,to be worked up, for the benefit of the poorer class of red men, belonging to the Cherokee nation—And the United States, will employ four blacksmiths, one wagon-maker, and one wheelwright, to work in said shops respectively, for the benefit of said Cherokee nation; and said materials shall be furnished annually and said services continued. so long as the president may deem proper—And said United States, will cause to be erected on said lands, for the benefit of said Cherokees, eight patent railway corn mills, in lieu of the mills to be erected according to the stipulation of the fourth article of said treaty, of sixth May, one thousand eight hundred twenty-eight, from the avails of the sale of the old agency.

This supplementary to a former treaty. Art. 5. These articles of agreement and convention are to be considered supplementary, to the treaty before mentioned between the United States and the Cherokee nation west of the Mississippi dated sixth of May one thousand eight hundred and twenty-eight, and not to vary the rights of the parties to said treaty, any further, than said treaty is inconsistent with the provisions of this treaty, now concluded, or these articles of convention or agreement.

One mile square for the agency. Art. 6. It is further agreed by the Cheerokee nation, that one mile square shall be reserved and set apart from the lands hereby guaranteed, for the accommodation of the Cherokee agency: and the location of the same shall be designated by the Cherokee nation, in conjunction with the agent of the Government of the United States.

Treaty binding when ratified. Art. 7. This treaty, or articles of convention, after the same have been ratified, by the President and Senate shall be obligatory on the United States and said Cherokee nation.

In testimony whereof, the said Montfort Stokes, Henry L. Ellsworth, and John F. Schermerhorn, commissioners as aforesaid, and the chiefs and head men of the Cherokee nation aforesaid, have hereunto set our hands, at Fort Gibson on the Arkansas river, on the 14th day of February, one thousand eight hundred and thirty-three.

Montfort Stokes,
J. F. Schermerhorn,
Black Coat, his x mark,
Henry L. Ellsworth,
John Jolly, his x mark,
Walter Weller,
Principal chiefs:

John Rogers, President Commissioners.
Glass, president council.
Signed, sealed, and delivered in our presence:

S. C. Stambaugh, secretary commissioners,
M. Arbuckle, colonel Seventh Infantry,
Wilson Nesbitt,
Peter A. Carns,
Wm. Thornton, clerk committee.
Charles Webber, clerk council.
Geo. Vashon, agent Cherokees west,
Jno. Campbell, agent Creeks,
Alexander Brown, his x mark,
Jno Hambly,
Interpreters,
N. Young, major U. S. Army,
W. Seawell, lieutenant Seventh Infantry,

The Cherokees had always been an agricultural people and for that reason were more attached to their homes than are town dwellers. They had passed an act in May, 1825, imposing a death penalty on anyone who should propose the sale or exchange of their lands, and although the boundaries and acreage of their reservation was not satisfactory to anyone they were much displeased with the action of the delegation and many threats were made against them. The entire Arkansas Cherokee nation moved in the winter of 1828-9 to their new western home. Tohlonteeskee, or Deep Creek, a southern branch of Illinois river, section sixteen, township twelve north, range twenty-one east, was created the capitol and the nation was divided into four districts.

THE CIRCUIT COURTS.

Sec. 1. Be it further enacted, That there shall be established two judicial circuits, and one Judge elected to each circuit.

The following division of the Nation into four Districts shall continue until otherwise altered by law, to wit:

1. Neosho District.—Commencing at the line of Washington county where the Saline road crosses the same, and following said road to the head of Spring creek; thence down the same to Grand river; thence down Grand river to the Arkansas, and thence along the western boundary of the Nation, including all the country north and west of the above line.

2. Salisaw District.—Beginning at the line of Washington county near Wilson's store, where the wagon road crosses the same by Jack Bean's; thence along said road by Chas. Vann's down the Salisaw to the crossing of the creek by Dr. Palmer's; thence, south, to the top of the mountain, and along the top of the same to a point opposite John L. McCoy's; thence to the crossing of the Salisaw by the military road, and along said road to Grand river.

3. Illinois District.—Commencing at the mouth of Salisaw creek, and running up the same to the military road; thence along said road to Grand river, and down the same to the Arkansas, including all the country west of this line and the Arkansas.

4. Lees Creek District.—Including all the country lying south and east of the above described lines.

The Northern circuit shall be composed of Neosho and Salisaw Districts; and the Southern of Illinois and Lee's Creek District. And the following places are designated in each District for holding courts, viz:

In Neosho District, at Sitewake's Village on Spavinaw.

In Salisaw District, at Tahlequah.

In Illinois District, at Tah-lon-tuskee.

In Lees Creek District, at George Guess'.

The Judges shall hold their respective courts in Neosho and Illinois Districts, on the first Monday in May and September, and for Salisaw and Lee's Creek Districts, on the second Monday in May and September.

Sec. 4. The Circuit Court shall have complete jurisdiction, in all criminal matters, and also in civil cases where the amount at issue is not less than one hundred dollars; but may also try and decide suits, when the amount is less than one hundred and over twenty-five dollars, provided such suit has been brought by appeal from the District Court; and all decisions where the sum does not exceed one hundred dollars, shall be final; but if above that amount, an appeal may be granted to the Supreme Court, if moved for before the adjournment of such court; and in the trial of all cases, the Clerk shall write out in full the testimony which may be given by witnesses of both parties. And in the event of an appeal to the Supreme Court, such written testimony, with the proceedings and decisions of the court, being certified to by the Clerk, sealed and marked on the outside, with the nature of the case and the names of the parties, they shall be transmitted by the Sheriff of the District, directed to the Chief Justice. And the party, so appealing to the Supreme Court, shall be required to enter into bond with security, to the satisfaction of the Court, for the maintenance of said suit and payment of all costs.

This jurisdictional division was in vogue and it was succeeded by:

An Act to Organize the Nation into Eight Districts and for Holding Elections.

Be it enacted by the National Council, That the following divisions of the Nation into eight Districts, shall continue until altered by law—to wit:

I.

Skin Bayou District.

Commencing at the mouth of Salisaw Creek, thence up the same to a point where the Rogue's Path crosses; thence along said path to Bear Meat's old place; thence on a direct line to the two Knobs or Peaks, running between the same, to the nearest point of the State line; thence south along said line to the Arkansas river, and up the same to the place of beginning.

II.

Illinois District.

Commencing at the point where the Rogue's Path crosses Salisaw Creek; thence on a direct line to Big Bear's (Allen Gafford's) on Elk Creek, and down said creek to its junction with Illinois river; thence crossing Short Mountain to Eli Harlin's, (including said Harlin in the District;) thence along the road by Joseph Coodey's and Dennis Biggs' to Grand River, at Fort Gibson; thence on the main road to the ferry on the Verdigris river, down the same to the Arkansas river; thence down said river to the mouth of Salisaw Creek, and up the same to the place of beginning.

III.

Canadian District.

Commencing at the junction of the Arkansas and Canadian rivers; thence up the Canadian to the Creek boundary; thence along the said boundary to the Arkansas river, and down the same to the place of beginning.

IV.

Flint District.

Commencing at the point where the Rogue's Path crosses the Salisaw creek; thence along the line of Illinois District to the Illinois river; thence up said river to the mouth of Caney creek, and up said creek to Buffington's, thence along the main old road to the crossing of the south branch of the Barren Fork of Illinois; thence up said creek to the State line, and along said line to the line of Skin Bayou District; thence west along said District line to the place of beginning.

V.

Going Snake District.

Commencing on Caney creek at Fawn's Camp on the right, and following the path leading to Thos. F. Taylor's until the same forks on the mountain; thence along the right hand old path (leaving said Taylor's to the left,) to Dick Sanders' on the Barren Fork; thence along the road to James McDaniel's on Big Illinois; thence along the road or path leading to the Grand Saline, to Spring creek, thence up said creek to the crossing of the Washington county wagon road, at Gore's old cabin, following said road to Flint creek, then up said creek to the State line; then south along said line to Flint District, and along the same to the place of beginning.

VI.

Tahlequah District.

Commencing at Fawn's Camp on Caney Creek, and following the line of Going Snake District to Spring creek; thence down said creek to Grand river, and down the same to Fort Gibson; thence along the line of Illinois District to the Illinois river; thence up said river to Caney creek, and up the same to the place of beginning.

VII.

Delaware District.

Commencing at the point on Spring Creek where Going Snake and Tahlequah Districts corner; thence to the nearest source of Little Saline Creek, and down the same to its junction with Big Saline Creek; thence on a direct line to Grand river at the mouth of Spavinaw creek; thence up said river to the termination of the Cherokee territory, and including all of the country east of the above described line to the State line and north of Going Snake District

VIII.

Saline District.

Commencing at the north-west corner of Delaware District; thence south along the western line of the said District to Tahlequah District on Spring creek; thence down said creek to Grand river, and along the same to Fort Gibson, including all the country west not embraced in any of the before described Districts.

Be it further enacted, That the election of two members of the National Committee, and three members of the Council, and one Sheriff for each District, shall be held on the first Monday in August, 1841:—and all free male citizens, who shall have attained to the age of eighteen years, shall be equally entitled to vote in the District of which they may be residents; and every voter shall name the person for whom he votes.

Be it further enacted. That there shall be two superintendents at each precinct, to preside over the elections, who shall appoint a clerk, whose duty it shall be to make a list of all candidates, and register the name of each voter, stating the candidate for whom each vote is given.

In the event that any persons hereinafter named as superintendents, are unable or refuse to serve as such, then the people assembled to vote may choose others to fill such vacancies as may occur. The register or list of votes polled at each precinct shall be certified by the superintendents and clerk, and on the following day after the election, the superintendents shall assemble at the first named precincts in this act, in each District, and count all votes legally given, and issue a written certificate of election to each candidate, who shall have received the highest number of votes. The certified register of votes shall then be sealed up, and transmitted to the Principal Chief, marked, "Election returns for —— District."

The following places are designated as precincts in the several Districts·

1. For Skin Bayou District.—First precinct at the present place of holding Courts:—George Lowrey, jr., and Michael Waters, superintendents. Second precinct at Little Jno. Rogers':—G. W. Gunter and John Rogers, superintendents.

2. Flint District.—First precinct at George Chambers' Camp Ground:—George Chambers and Andrew Ross, superintendents. Second precinct at Broken Canoe's:—Ezekial Starr and George Still, superintendents.

3. Illinois District.—First precinct at Moses Smith's:—John Brewer and Richard Ratcliff, superintendents. Second precinct at Cat Fields:—Archibald Fields and Alexander Foreman, superintendents.

4. Canadian District.—First precinct at James Thorn's:—Joseph Vann and John Thorn, superintendents. Second precinct at George Chisholm's:—Dutch and David Foreman, superintendents.

5. Going Snake District.—First precinct at Hair Conrad's:—Hair Conrad and Samuel Foreman, superintendents. Second precinct at Rising Fawn's in Piney Woods)—Geo. Starr, John Harnage, superintendents.

6. Tahlequah District.—First precinct at Tahlequah:—Stephen Foreman and David Carter, superintendents. Second precinct at William Campbell's:—Thomas Wilson and Thigh Walker, superintendents.

7. Delaware District.—First precinct at J. Buffington's:—Richard Taylor and William Wilson, superintendents. Second precinct at Johnson Fields':—James D. Wofford and Hiram Landrum, superintendents.

8. Saline District.—First precinct at the Grand Saline:—Nicholas M'Nair and Brice Martin, superintendents. Second precinct at West's Saline:—David Vann and Bluford West, superintendents.

The superintendents and clerks shall be required to take the following oath:—"You do solemnly swear that you will conduct the election according to the provisions of the act passed Nov. 4th, 1840."

Approved—JNO. ROSS.

Tahlequah, Nov. 4th, 1840.

The jurisdiction of Delaware District was extended over the "Neutral Land" by:

An Act Annexing a Tract Called 800,000 Acres of Land, to Delaware District.

Be it enacted by the National Council, That this section of country ceded to the Cherokees by the Treaty of 1835, and known as the "eight hundred thousand acre tract," be, and the same is hereby attached to Delaware District, and shall henceforth form a part of said District.

Tahlequah, Dec. 1st, 1846.

Approved—JNO. ROSS.

The name of Skin Bayou District was derived from the local stream, which had been named by the early courier de bois. It was changed by:

An Act Changing the Name of Skin Bayou District.

Be it enacted by the National Council, That the name of Skin Bayou District be, and the same is hereby changed, and that the said District shall be called from and after the passage of this act, Se-quo-yah; and so much of the act passed November 4th, 1840, as militates against this act be and the same is hereby repealed.

Tahlequah, November 4th, 1851.

Approved—JNO. ROSS.

Cooweescoowee District was constituted in 1856 by:

An Act Organizing Cooweescoowee District

Be it enacted by the National Council, That all that portion of the territory belonging to the Cherokee people, within the following boundary, be and is hereby organized into a District, to be known as Cooweescoowee District, with all the immunities and corporate capacities of other districts of this Nation, towit: Commencing at the cornerstone of the Creek Nation, a few miles north or northwest of old Union Mission; running thence a due east course until it strikes the Missouri road, running west of Neosho or Grand River; then along said road to about one mile northward of the crossing of Rock Creek; then along a certain trail known as Mathis' tract, until said trace strikes the northern boundary line of the Cherokee country; then westward along said line, and following the boundary line of the Cherokee outlet west to the point of beginning.

Be it further enacted, That the precincts for holding elections shall be and are placed at the following localities:

1. At the Sulphur spring on Dog Creek, near Jim McNair's cow-pen.
2. At the White Spring.
3. At the Yellow Spring.
4. At or near Dick Duck's.

The court house of Cooweescoowee District from 1856 to December 7, 1867, was on Bird Creek in the eastern part of Osage county and was located by:

An Act to Amend an Act entitled "An Act Relative to the Court House in Cooweescoowee District."

Be it enacted by the National Council, That the act in relation to building a court house in Cooweescoowee District, passed December 7, 1867, be so amended as to require the District Judge to have said court house built at the Sulphur Springs, on the waters of Dog Creek, near Jesse Henry's, in said District, instead of the place designated in said act, "Clermont's Mounds."

JOHN YOUNG, Speaker of Council.

Concurred in—PIG SMITH, President of the Senate.

Presented and approved, 24th November, 1868.

LEWIS DOWNING, Principal Chief of the Cherokee Nation.

Tahlequah, C. N., Nov. 13, 1868.

The Eastern Cherokees enacted earlier election laws but the following was in a fuller and more perfect form:

Resolved by the Committee and Council, in General Council Convened, That the elections to be holden hereafter in the several Districts for members of the General Council, Sheriffs and Constables, shall be held at the following precincts until otherwise altered by the General Council, viz: Chickamauga District: The first precinct to be at the Court House, the second at Hunter Langly's in Lookout Valley; third at Hick's Mill and the fourth at Kah-noh-cloo's. Chattooga District. First precinct at the Court House, second at Ah-ne-lah-ka-yah's in Turkey Town, third at James Fields', Turnip Mountain, fourth at Laugh-at-mush's, Will's Valley, fifth at Edward Gunter's in Creek Path, and sixth at Raccoon Town, at Little Turtle's house. Coosawatee District: First at the Court House, and the third at Ellijay. Ahmohee District: First at the Court House, second at Squires in Long Savannah, third at Chee-squah-ne-ta's, fourth at Swimmers, Highwassee Old Town. Hickory Log District: First at the Court House, second at the old Court House, third at or near Big Savannah. Hightower District: First at the Court House, second at Pipes Spring, third at Yon-nah-oo-woh-yee's. Tahquohee District: First at the Court House, second at Choowalookee's, third at Oowatee's, fourth at Skenah Town, fifth at Beach Town. Aquohee District: First at the Court House, second at Lame Dick's, third at Highwassee Town, fourth at widow Nettle Carriers', fifth at Chee-yoh-ee.

Be it further Resolved, That two superintendents and one clerk shall be appointed to take the votes at each precinct, and it shall be the duty of the Circuit Judges respectively to make such appointments while on their Judicial Circuit last preceding the general elections for members of the General Council, and shall notify the managers and clerks of their appointment, by the Sheriff of the District, and in case either of the Circuit Judges shall fail to hold his courts agreeably to law, or any of the managers or clerks shall refuse to act, the District Judge shall be authorized to fill such vacancies; and in case any shall fail to attend on the day of the election, the voters shall be allowed to choose some suitable person or persons to act in his or their stead.

Be it further Resolved, That the clerks shall particularly take down the names of all persons voting and for whom they may vote; and the managers and clerks shall meet at the court house in their respective Districts on the Wednesday succeeding the election, then and there to count the votes and issue a certificate to each member elect, of his constitutional election.

Be it further Resolved, That the managers and clerks while acting shall be upon oath, and shall not be entitled to receive any compensation from the National Treasury for their services.

New Echota, 2d Nov., 1829.

Approved—JNO. ROSS.

The first comprehensive election law of the "Old Settler" Cherokees was:

An Act Respecting Elections.

Resolved by the Committee and Council, in General Council Convened, That from and after this date, the members of the National Committee and

Council, and the officers (Judges and Light-horse) of the Cherokee Nation, shall be elected by a vote of the people, given in at their respective precincts in each District, and for which purpose it is hereby

Further Resolved, That the people of the Cherokee Nation shall meet at their respective precincts in each District once in two years, on the second Monday in July, and proceed to elect by vote, two memebrs of the National Committee and two members of the National Council, which members shall be elected to serve two years from the date of their election; and there shall be also elected at the same time and place two District Judges and two National Light-horse to serve two years from the date of their election, whose duties it shall be to serve in their respective Districts as set forth by law.

Resolved Further, That all elections under the law as herein above speci-specific purposes, shall be superintended by the Judges of the same District, and each candidate for the above named offices shall make known to the Judges superintending the elections, which office they design to run for; and it shall be the duty of the Judges to have this distinctly understood by the people before voting, after which they can proceed to vote, one at a time by calling the names of such candidates which they judge are the best qualified to fill the office running for, and after all the people present have voted, the Judges shall count out publicly the number of votes given to each one of the candidates took up for the same office, and such candidates as have thereby gained the highest number of votes for the different offices shall thereby be considered duly and lawfully elected to the respective offices for which they were candidates and run for. And it shall be the duty of the Judges as before required under section third to give each member thus elected to the National Committee and Council, Judges and Light-horse, a certificate of their election, which shall be their voucher to the National Council of such members, Judges and Light-horse having been duly elected according to law.

Resolved Further, That all elections under the law as herein above specified for the purpose of electing members to the National Committee and Council, Judges and Light-horse shall be and are hereby required to be held at the following named places in each District: That is the precinct or place for holding elections under the law; that in Lees Creek District, shall be at the present residence of Little Charles, of Skin Bayou; that in Sallisaw District at Fox's residence on Sallisaw Creek; that in Illinois District at the National Council House (Tah-lon-tee-skee) and that in Neosho District at John Drew's residence on Bayou Menard.

Tah-lon-tee-skee, May 10, 1834.

Approved—JOHN JOLLY, Prin'l. Chief.

At various subsequent dates the election laws were changed to conform with the progress of the Cherokee Nation, but they always adhered to the viva voci method of voting, recorded by a clerk from each party, judges of election supervising the work of the opposing party clerk, all parties except the voter being kept at a distance of fifty feet from the polls by regularly appointed supervisors or guards. Council met before 1867 on the first Monday of October and after 1867 on the first Monday of November of each year, the regular session lasting four weeks. Elections were held on the first Monday of August of odd numbered years.

It had become apparent to many Cherokees that their retention of their homes and institutions east of the Mississippi river was of but short duration John Ross was in favor of selling their lands for twenty million dollars but the government steadfastly refused to pay more than five million for it. Conditions were becoming more untenable each year and as a consequence the great mass of the people were becoming more and more impoverished. Many of the wealthier Cherokees had and were moving west at their own expense. The minority seeing the hopeless condition of their people, within the limits of Georgia, Tennessee, Alabama and North Carolina, concluded the folllowing treaty:

LEWIS DOWNING
Chief—November, 1867, to November, 1875.

CHAPTER V

Treaty With The Cherokee, 1835

Dec. 29, 1835. 7 Stat., 478. Proclamation, May 23, 1836. Article of a treaty, concluded at New Echota in the State of Georgia on the 29th day of Dec. 1835 by General William Carroll and John F. Schermerhorn commissioners on the part of the United States and the Chiefs, Head Men and People of the Cherokee tribe of Indians.

Preamble . Whereas the Cherokees are anxious to make arrangements with the Government of the United States whereby the difficulties they have experienced by a residence within the settled parts of the United States under the jurisdiction and laws of the State Governments may be terminated and adjusted; and with a view to reuniting their people in one body and securing a permanent home for themselves and their posterity in the country selected by their forefathers without the territorial limits of the State sovereignties, and where they can establish and enjoy a government of their choice and perpetuate such a state of society as may be most consonant with the views, habits and conditions; and as may tend to their individual comfort and their advancement in civilization.

And whereas a delegation of the Cherokee nation composed of Messrs. John Ross, Richard Taylor, Danl. McCoy, Samuel Gunter and William Rogers with full power and authority to conclude a treaty with the United States did on the 28th day of February 1835 stipulate and agree with the Government of the United States to submit to the Senate to fix the amount which should be allowed the Cherokees for their claims and for a cession of their lands east of the Mississippi river, and did agree to abide by the award of the Senate of the United States themselves to recommend the same to their people for their final determination.

And whereas on such submission the Senate advised "that a sum not exceeding five millions of dollars be paid to the Cherokee Indians for all their possessions east of the Mississippi river."

And whereas this delegation after said award of the Senate had been made, were called upon to submit propositions as to its disposition to be arranged in a treaty which they refused to do, but insisted that the same "should be referred to their nation and there in general council to deliberate and determine on the subject to ensure harmony and good feeling among themselves."

And whereas a certain other delegation composed of John Ridge, Elias Boudinot, Archilla Smith, S. W. Bell, John West, Wm. A. Davis and Ezekiel West, who represented the portion of the nation in favor of emigration to the Cherokee country west of the Mississippi entered into propositions for a treaty with John F. Schermerhorn commissioner on the part of the United States which were to be submitted to their nation for their final action and determination:

And whereas the Cherokee people, at their last October council at Red

Clay, fully authorized and empowered a delegation or committee of twenty persons of their nation to enter into and conclude a treaty with the United States commissioner then present, at that place or elsewhere and as the people had good reason to believe that a treaty would then and there be made or at a subsejuent council at New Echota which the commissioners it was well known and understood, were authorized and instructed to convene for said purpose; and since the said delegation have gone on to Washington city, with a view to close negotiations there. as stated by them notwithstanding they were officially informed by the United States commissioner that they would not be received by the President of the United States; and that the Government would transact no business of this nature with them, and that if a treaty was made it must be done here in the nation, where the delegation at Washington last winter urged that it should be done for the purpose of promoting peace and harmony among the people; and since these facts have also been corroborated to us by a communication recently received by the commissioner from the Government of the United States and read and explained to the people in open council and therefore believing said delegation can effect nothing and since our difficulties are daily increasing and our situation is rendered more and more precarious, uncertain and insecure in consequence of the legislation of the States; and seeing no effectual way of relief, but in accepting the liberal overtures of the United States.

And whereas Gen. William Carroll and John F. Schemerhorn were appointed commissioners on the part of the United States, with full power and authority to conclude a treaty with the Cherokees east and were directed by the President to convene the people of the nation in general council at New Echota and to submit said propositions to them with power and authority to vary the same so as to meet the views of the Cherokees in reference to its details.

And whereas the said commissioners did appoint and notify a general council of the nation to convene at New Echota on the 21st day of December 1835; and informed them that the commissioners would be prepared to make a treaty with the Cherokee people who should assemble there and those who did not come they should conclude gave their assent and sanction to whatever should be transacted at this council and the people having met in council according to said notice.

Therefore the following articles of a treaty are agreed upon and concluded between William Carroll and John F. Schermerhorn commissioners on the part of the United States and the chiefs and head men and people of the Cherokee nation in general council assembled this 29th day of Dec. 1835.

Cherckees Relinquish to United States all Their Lands East of The Mississippi.

Article 1. The Cherokee nation hereby cede, relinquish and convey to the United States all the lands owned, claimed or possessed by them east of the Mississippi river, and hereby release all their claims upon the United States for spoliations of every kind for and in consideration of the sum of five millions of dollars to be expended, paid and invested in the manner stipulated and agreed upon in the following articles. But as a question has arisen between the commissioners and the Cherokees whether the Senate in their resolution by which they advised "that a sum not exceeding five millions of dollars be paid to the Cherokee Indians for all their lands and possessions east of the Mississippi river" have included and made any allowance or consideration for claims for spoliations it is therefore agreed on the part of the United States that this question shall be again submitted to the Senate for their consideration and decision and if no allowance was made for spoliations that then an additional sum of three hundred thousand dollars be allowed for the same.

Treaty of May, 1828, and Feb., 1833, Referred to. Art .2. Whereas by the treaty of May 6th 1828 and the supplementary treaty thereto of Feb. 14th 1833 with the Cherokees west of the Mississippi the United States granted and secured to be conveyed by patent, to the Cherokee nation of Indians the following tract of country "Beginning at a point on the old western territorial line of Arkansas Territory beginning twenty-five miles north from the point where the territorial line crosses Arkansas river, thence running from said north point south on the said territorial line where the said territorial line crosses Verdigris river; thence down said Verdigris river to the Arkansas River, thence down said Arkansas to a point where a stone is placed oppposite the east or lower bank of Grand river at its junction with the Arkansas; thence running south forty-five degrees and west one mile; thence in a straight line to a point four miles northerly, from the mouth of the north fork of the Canadian; thence along the said four mile line to the Canadian; thence down the Canadian to the Arkansas; thence down the Arkansas where the eastern Choctaw boundary strikes said river and running thence with the western line of Arkansas Territory as now defined, to the southwest corner of Missouri; thence along the western Missouri line to the land assigned the Senecas; thence on the south line of the Senecas to Grand river as far as the south line of the Osage reservation, extended if necessary; thence up and between said south Osage line extended west if necessary, and a line drawn due west from the point of beginning to a certain distance west, at which a line running north and south from said Osage line to said due west line will make seven millions of acres within the whole described boundaries. In addition to the seven millions of acres of land thus provided for and bounded, the United States further guaranty to the Cherokee nation a perpetual outlet west, and a free and unmolested use of all the country west of the western boundary of seven millions of acres, as far west as the sovereignty of the United States and their right of soil extend:

Proviso. Provided however: That if the saline or salt plain on the western prairie shall fall within said limits prescribed for the said outlet, the right is reserved to the United States to permit other tribes of red men to get salt on said plain in common with the Cherokees; And letters patent shall be issued by the United States as soon as practicable for the land hereby guaranteed."

Additional Land Conveyed to The Nation, Etc. And whereas it is apprehended by the Cherokees that in the above cession there is not contained sufficient quantity of land for the accommodation of the whole nation on their removal west of the Mississippi the United States in consideration of the sum of five hundred thousand dollars therefore hereby covenant and agree to convey to the said Indians, and their descendants by patent, in fee simple the following additional tract of land situated between the west line of the State of Missouri and the Osage reservation beginning at the Southeast corner of the same and running north along the east line of the Osage lands fifty miles to the northeast corner thereof; and thence east to the west line of the State of Missouri; thence with said line south fifty miles; thence west to the place of beginning; estimated to contain eight hundred thousand acres of land; but it is expressly understood that if any of the lands assigned the Quapaws shall fall within the aforesaid bounds the same shall be reserved and excepted out of the lands above granted and a pro rata reduction shall be made in the price to be allowed to the United States for the same by the Cherokees.

Further Agreement. 1830, ch. 148. Right to Establish Forts, Etc. Article 3. The United States also agrees that the lands above ceded by the treaty of Feb. 14, 1833, including the outlet, and those ceded by this treaty shall all be included in one patent executed to the Cherokee nation of Indians by the President of the United States according to the provisions of the act of May 28, 1830. It is, however, agreed that the military reservation at Fort Gibson shall be held by the United States. But should the United States abandon said post and have no further use for the same it shall revert to the Cherokee nation. The United States shall always have the right to make and establish such post and military roads and forts in any part of the Cherokee country, as they may deem proper for the interest and protection of the same and the free use of as much land, timber, fuel and materials of all kinds for the construction and support of the same as may be necessary; provided that if the private rights of individuals are interfered with, a just compensation therefore shall be made.

Osage Titles to Reservations to be Extinguished. Article 4. The United States also stipulate and agree to extinguish for the benefit of the Cherokees the title to the reservations within their country made in the Osage treaty of 1825 to certain half-breeds and for this purpose they hereby agree to pay the persons to whom the same belongs or have been assigned or to their agents or guardians whenever they shall execute after the ratification of this treaty a satisfactory conveyance for the same, to the United States, the sum of fifteen thousand dollars according to a schedule accompanying this treaty of the relative value of the several reservations.

Missionary Reservations to be Paid For. And whereas these several treaties between the United States and the Osage Indians, the Union and Harmony Missionary reservations which were established for their benefit are now situated within the country ceded by them to the United States; the former being situated in the Cherokee country and the latter in the State of Missouri. It is therefore agreed that the United States shall pay the American Board of Commissioners for Foreign Missions for the improvements on the same what they shall be appraised by Capt.

Geo. Vashon Cherokee, sub-agent Abraham Redfield and A. P. Chouteau or such persons as the President of the United States shall appoint and the money allowed for the same shall be expended in schools among the Osages and improving their condition. It is understood that the United States are to pay the amount allowed for the reservations in this article and not the Cherokees.

Land Permanently Ceded to the Nation. Article 5. The United States hereby covenant and agree that the lands ceded to the Cherokee nation in the foregoing article shall, in no future time without their consent, be included within the terriorial limits or jurisdiction of any State or Territory. But they shall secure to the Cherokee nation the right by their national councils to make and carry into effect all such laws as they may deem necessary for the government and protection of the persons and property within their own country belonging to their people or such persons as have connected themselves with them: provided always that they shall not be inconsistent with the constitution of the United States and such acts of Congress as have been or may be passed regulating trade and intercourse with the Indians; and also, that they shall not be considered as extending to such citizenship and army of the United States as may travel or reside in the Indian country by permission according to the laws and regulations established by the Government of the same.

Peace to be Preserved. Art. 6. Perpetual peace and friendship shall exist between the citizens of the United States and the Cherokee Indians. The United States agree to protect the Cherokee nation from domestic strife and foreign enemies and against internecine wars between the several tribes. The Cherokees shall endeavor to preserve and maintain the peace of the country and not make war upon their neighbors they shall also be protected against interruption and intrusion from citizens of the United States, who may attempt to settle in the country without their consent; and all such persons shall be removed from the same by order of the President of the United States. But this is not intended to prevent the residence among them of useful farmers mechanics and teachers for the instruction of Indians according to treaty stipulations.

Congress May Allow a Delegate From the Cherokee Nation. Article 7. great progress in civilization and deeming it important that every proper and laudable inducement be offered to their people to improve their condition as well as guard and secure in the most effectual manner the rights guaranteed to them in this treaty, and with a view to illustrate the liberal and enlarged policy of the Government of the United States towards the Indians in their removal beyond the territorial limits of the States, it is stipulated that they shall be entitled to a delegate in the House of Representatives of the United States whenever Congress shall make provisions for the same.

Expenses of Removal to be Paid by United States. Article 8. The United States also agree and stipulate to remove the Cherokees to their new homes and to subsist them one year after their arrival there and that a sufficient number of steamboats and barge-wagons shall be furnished to remove them comfortably, and so as not to endanger their health, and that a physician well supplied with medicines shall accompany each detachment of emigrants removed by the Government. Such persons and families as in the opinion of the emigrating agent are capable of subsisting and removing themselves shall be permitted to do so; and they shall be allowed in full for all claims for the same twenty dollars for each member of their family; and in lieu of their one year's rations they shall be paid the sum of thirty-three dollars and thirty-three cents if they prefer it.

Such Cherokees also as reside at present out of the nation and shall remove with them in two years west of the Mississippi shall be entitled to allowance for removal and subsistence as above provided.

Agents to Value Improvements Made by Cherokees. Article 9. The United States agree to appoint suitable agents who shall make a just and fair valuation of all such improvements now in the possession of the Cherokees as add any value to the lands; and also of the ferries owned by them, according to their net income; and such improvements and ferries from which they have been dispossessed in a lawful manner or under any existing law of the State where the same may be situated.

The just debts of the Indians shall be paid out of any monies due them for their improvements and claims; and they shall also be furnished at the discretion of the President of the United States with a sufficient sum to enable them to obtain the necessary means to remove themselves to their new homes, and the balance of their dues shall be paid them at the Cherokee agency west of the Mississippi. The Missionary establishments shall also be valued and appraised in a like manner and the amount of them paid over by the United States to the treasurers of the respective missionary societies by whom they have been established and improved in order to enable them to erect such buildings and make such improvements among the Cherokees west of the Mississippi as they may deem necessary for their benefit. Such teacherrs at present among the Cherokees as this council may select and designate shall be removed west of the Mississippi with the Cherokee nation and on the same terms allowed to them.

The President to make investments in productive stock. Article 10. The President of the United States shall invest in some safe and most productive public stocks of the country for the benefit of the whole Cherokee nation who have removed or shall remove to the lands assigned by this treaty to the Cherokee nation west of the Mississippi the following sums as a permanent fund for the purposes hereinafter specified and pay over the net income of the same annually to such persons as shall be authorized or appointed by the Cherokee nation to receive the same and their receipt shall be full discharge for the amount paid to them viz: the sum of two hundred thousand dollars in addition to the present annuity of the nation to constitute a general fund the interest of which shall be applied annually by the council of the nation to such purposes as they may deem best for the general good of their people. The sum of fifty thousand dollars to constitute an orphans' fund the annual income of which shall be expended towards the support and education of such orphan children as are destitute of the means of subsistence. The sum of one hundred and fifty thousand dollars in addition to the present school fund of the nation shall constitute a permanent school fund, the interest of which shall be applied annually by the council of the nation for the support of common schools and such a literary institution of a higher order as may be established in the Indian country. And in order to secure as far as possible the true and beneficial application of the orphans' and school fund the council of the Cherokee nation when required by the President of the United States shall make a report of the application of those funds and he shall at all times have the right if the funds have been misapplied to correct any abuse of them and direct the manner of their application for the purposes for which they were intended. The council of the nation may by giving two years' notice of their intention withdraw their funds by and with the consent of the President and Senate of the United States, and invest them in such manner as they may deem most proper for their interest. The United States also agree and stipulate to pay the just debts and claims against the Cherokee nation held by the citizens of the same and also the just claims of citizens of the United States for services rendered to the nation and the sum of sixty thousand dollars is appropriated for this purpose but no claims against individual persons of the nation shall be allowed and paid by the nation. The sum of three hundred thousand dollars is hereby set apart to pay and liquidate the just claims of the Cherokees upon the United States for spoliations of every kind, that have not been already satisfied under former treaties.

Commutation of school fund. Article 11. The Cherokee nation of Indians believing it will be for the interest of their people to have all their funds and annuities under their own direction and future disposition hereby agree to commute their permanent annuity of ten thousand dollars for the sum of two hundred and fourteen thousand dolllars, the same to be invested by the President of the United States as a part of the general fund of the nation; and their present school fund amounting to about fifty thousand dollars shall constitute a part of permanent school fund of the nation.

Provision respecting Cherokees averse to removal. Article 12. Those individuals and families of the Cherokee nation that are averse to a removal to the Cherokee country west of the Mississippi and are desirous to become citizens of the States where they reside and such as are qualified to take care of themselves and their property shall be entitled to receive their due portion of all the personal benefits accruing under this treaty for their claims, improvements and per capita; as soon as an appropriation is made for this treaty.

Such heads of Cherokee families as are desirous to reside within the States of North Carolina, Tennessee and Alabama subject to the laws of the same; and who are qualified or calculated to become useful citizens shall be entitled, on the certificate of the commissioners to a preemption right to one hundred and sixty acres of land or one quarter section at the minimum Congress price; so as to include the present buildings or improvements of those who now reside there and such as do not live there at present shall be permitted to locate within two years any lands not already occupied by persons entitled to pre-emption privileges under this treaty and if two or more families live on the same quarter section and they desire to continue their residence in these States and are qualified as above they shall, on receiving their pre-emption certificate be entitled to the right of pre-emption to such lands as they may select not already taken by any person entitled to them under this treaty.

It is stipulated and agreed between the United States and the Cherokee people that John Ross, James Starr, George Hicks, John Gunter, George Chambers, John Ridge, Elias Boudinot, George Sanders, John Martin, William Rogers, Roman Nose Situwake and John Timpson shall be a committee on the part of the Cherokees to recommend such persons for the privilege of preemption rights as may be deemed entitled to the same under the above articles and to select the missionaries who shall be removed with the nation; and that they be hereby fully empowered and authorized to transact all business on the part of the Indians which may arise in carrying into effect the provisions of this treaty and settling the same with the United States. If any of the persons above mentioned should decline acting or be removed by death; the vacancies shall be filled by the committee themselves.

It is also understood and agreed that the sum of one hundred thousand dollars shall be expended by the commissioners in such manner as the committee may deem best for the benefit of the poorer class of Cherokees as shall remove west or have removed west and are entitled to the benefits of this treaty. The same to be delivered at the Cherokee agency west as soon after the removal of the nation as possible.

Settlement of claims for former reservations. Article 13. In order to make a final settlement of all the claims of the Cherokees for reservations granted under former treaties to any individuals belonging to the nation by the United States it is therefore hereby stipulated and agreed and expressly understood by the parties of this treaty—that all the Cherokees and their heirs and descendants to whom any reservations have been made under any former treaties with the United States, and who have not sold or conveyed the same by deed or otherwise and who in the opinion of the commissioners have complied with the terms on which the reservations were granted as far as practicable in the several cases; and which reservations have since been sold by the United States shall constitute a just claim against the United States and the original reservee or their heirs or descendants shall be entitled to receive the present value thereof from the United States as unimproved lands. And all such reservations as have not been sold by the United States and where the terms on which the reservations were made in the opinion of the commissioners have been complied with as far as practicable, they or their heirs or descendants shall be entitled to the same. They are hereby granted and confirmed to them—and also all persons who were entitled to reservations under the treaty of 1817 and who as far as practicable in the opinion of the commissioners, have complied with the stipulations of said treaty, although by the treaty of 1819 such reservations were included in the unceded lands belonging to the Cherokee nation are hereby confirmed to them and they shall be entitled to receive a grant for the same. And all such reservees as were obliged by the laws of the States in which their reservations were situated, to abandon the same or purchase them from the States shall be deemed to have a just claim against the United States for the amount by them paid to the States with inerest thereon for such reservations and if obliged to abandon the same, to the present value of such reservations as unimproved lands but in all cases where the reservees have sold their reservations or any part thereof and conveyed the same by deed or otherwise and have been paid for the same, they their heirs or descendants or their assigns shall not be considered as having any claims upon the United States under the article of the treaty nor be entitled to receive any compensation for the lands thus disposed of. It is expressly understood by the parties of this treaty that the amount to be allowed for reservations under this article shall not be deducted out of the consideration money allowed to the Cherokees for their claims for spoliations and the cession of their lands; but the same is to be paid for independently by the United States as it is only a just fulfillment of former treaty stipulations.

Pensions to certain warriors. Article 14. It is also agreed on the part of the United States that such warriors of the Cherokee nation as were engaged on the side of the United States in the late war with Great Britain and the southern tribes of Indians, and who were wounded in such service shall be entitled to such pensions as shall be allowed them by the Congress of the United States to commence from the period of disability.

Funds to be divided among the Indians. Article 15. It is expressly understood and agreed between the parties to this treaty that after deducting the amount which shall be actually expended for the payment for improvements, ferries, claims, for spoliations, removal subsistence and debts and claims upon the Cherokee nation and for the additional quantity of lands and goods for the poorer class of Cherokees and the several sums to be invested for the general national funds; provided for in several articles of this treaty the balance whatever the same may be shall be equally divided between all the people belonging to the Cherokee nation east according to the census just completed; and such Cherokees as have removed west since June 1833 who are entitled by the terms of their enrollment and removal to all the benefits resulting from the final treaty between the United States and the Cherokees east they shall also be paid for their improvements according to their approved value before their removal where fraud has not already been shown in their valuation.

Indians to remove in two years. Article 16. It is hereby stiplated and agreed by the Cherokees that they shall remove to their new homes within two years from the ratification of this treaty and that during such time the United States shall protect and defend them in their possessions and property and free use and occupation of the same and such persons as have been dispossessed of their improvements and houses; and for which no grant has actually issued previously to the enactment of the law of the State of Georgia, of December 1835 to regulate Indian occupancy shall be again put in possession and placed in the same situation and condition, in reference to the laws of the State of Georgia, as the Indians that have not been dispossessed; and if this is not done, and the people left unprotected, then the United States shall pay the several Cherokees for their losses and damages sustained by them in consequence thereof. And it is also stipulated and agreed that the public buildings and improvements on which they are situated at New Echota for which no grant has been actually made previously to the passage of the above recited act if not occupied by the Cherokee people shall be reserved for the public and free use of the United States and the Cherokee Indians for the purpose of settling and closing all the Indian business arising under this treaty between the commissioners of claims and the Indians.

The United States, and the several States interested in the Cherokee lands shall immediately proceed to survey the lands ceded by this treaty; but it is expressly agreed and understood between the parties that the agency buildings and that tract of land surveyed and laid off for the use of Colonel R. J. Meigs Indian agent or heretofore enjoyed and occupied by his successors in office shall continue subject to the use and occupancy of the United States, or such agents as may be engaged especially superintending the removal of the tribe.

Commissioners to settle claims. Article 17. All the claims arising under or provided for in the several articles of this treaty, shall be examined and adjudicated by such commissioners as shall be appointed by the United States by and with the advice and consent of the Senate of the United States for that purpose and their decision shall be final and on their certificate of the amount due the several claimants they shall be paid by the United States. All stipulations in former treaties which have not been superseded or annulled by this shall continue in full force and virtue.

United States to make advances for provisions, clothing, etc. Article 18. Whereas in consequence of the unsettled affairs of the Cherokee people and the early frosts, their crops are insufficient to support their families and great distress is likely to ensue and whereas the nation will not, until after their removal be able advantageously to expend the income of the permanent funds of the nation it is therefore agreed that the annuities of the nation which may accrue under this treaty for two years, the time fixed for their removal shall be expended in provisions and clothing for the benefit of the poorer class of the nation; and the United States hereby agree to advance the sum for that purpose as soon after the ratification of this treaty as an appropriation for the same shall be made. It is however not intended in this article to interfere with that part of the annuities due the Cherokees west by the treaty of 1819.

Treaty Binding When Ratified. Article 19. This treaty after the same shall be ratified by the President and Senate of the United States shall be obligatory on the contracing paries.

Article 20. [Supplemental article. Stricken out by Senate.]

In testimony whereof, the commissioners and the chiefs, head men, and people whose names are hereunto annexed, being duly authorized by the people in general council assembled, have affixed their hands and seals for themselves ,and in behalf of the Cherokee nation.

I have examined the foregoing treaty, and although not present when it was made, I approve its provisions generally, and therefore sign it.

Wm. Carroll,
J. F. Schermerhorn.

Major Ridge, his x mark; James Foster, his x mark; Test-ta-esky, his x mark; Charles Moore, his x mark; George Chambers, his x mark; Tah-yeske, his x mark; Archilla Smith, his x mark; Andrew Ross; William Lassley; Cae-te-hee, his x mark; Te-gah-e-ske, his x mark; Robert Rogers; John Gunter; John A. Bell; Charles F. Foreman; William Rogers; George W. Adair; Elias Boudinot; James Starr, his x mark; Jesse Half-breed, his x mark [L. S.]

Signed and sealed in presence of—

Western B. Thomas, secretary; Ben F. Currey, special agent; M. Wolfe Batman, first lieutenant, sixth U. S. Infantry, disbursing agent; John L. Hooper, lieutenant, fourth Infantry; C. M. Hitchcock, M. D., assistant surgeon, U. S. A.; G. W. Currey; Wm. H. Underwood; Cornelius D. Terhune; John W. Underwood.

In compliance with instructions of the council at New Echota, we sign this treaty.

Stand Watie,
John Ridge.

March 1, 1836.
Witnesses:

Elbert Herring, Alexander H. Everett, John Robb, D. Kurtz, Wm. Y. Hansell, Samuel J. Potts, John Litle, S. Rockwell.

Dec. 31, 1835. 7 Stat., 487. Whereas the western Cherokees have appointed a delegation to visit the eastern Cherokees to assure them of the friendly disposition of their people and their desire that the nation should again be united as one people and to urge upon them the expediency of accepting the overtures of the Government; and that, on their removal they may be assured of a hearty welcome and an equal participation with them in all the benefits and privileges of the Cherokee country west and the undersigned two of said delegation being the only delegates in the nation from the west at the signing and sealing of the treaty lately concluded at New Echota between their eastern brethren and the United States; and having fully understood the provisions of the same they agree to it in behalf of the western Cherokees. But it is expressly understood that nothing in this treaty shall affect any claim of the western Cherokees on the United States.

In testimony wehereof, we have, this 31st day of December, 1835, hereunto set our hands and seals.

James Rogers,
John Smith.
Delegates from the western Cherokees.

Test:

Ben. F. Curry, special agent.
M. W. Batman, first lieutenant, Sixth Infantry.
Jno. L. Hooper, lieutenant, Fourth Infantry.
Elias Boudinot.

Schedule and estimated value of the Osage half-breed reservations within the territory ceded to the Cherokees west of the Mississippi, (referred to in article 5 on the foregoing treaty,) viz:

Augustus Clamont one section	$6,000
James " " "	1,000
Paul " " "	1,300
Henry " " "	800
Anthony " " "	1,800
Rosalie " " "	1,800
Emilia D., of Mihanga	1,000
Emilia D, of Shemianga	1,300
	$15,000

I hereby certify that the above schedule is the estimated value of the Osage reservations; as made out and agreed upon with Col. A. P. Choteau who represented himself as the agent or guardian of the above reservees.

J. F. Schermerhorn.

March 14, 1835.

March 1, 1836. 7 Stat., 488. Proclamation, May 23, 1836. Supplementary article to a treaty concluded at New Echota, Georgia, December 29, 1835, between the United States and Cherokee people.

Whereas the undersigned were authorized at the general meeting of the Cherokee people held at New Echota as above stated, to make and assent to such alterations in the preceding treaty as might be thought necessary, and whereas the President of the United States has expressed his determination not to allow any pre-emptions or reservations his desire being that the whole Cherokee people should remove together and establish themselves in the country provided for them west of the Mississippi river.

Preemption rights declared void. Article 1. It is therefore agreed that all the pre-emption rights and reservations provided for in article 12 and 13 shall be and are hereby relinquished and declared void.

Article 2. Whereas the Cherokee people have supposed that the sum of five millions of dollars fixed by the Senate in their resolution of —— day of

March, 1835, as the value of the Cherokee lands and possessions east of the Mississippi river was not intended to include the amount which may be required to remove them, nor the value of certain claims which many of their people had against citizens of the United States, which suggestion has been confirmed by the opinion expressed to the War Department by some of the Senators who voted upon the question and whereas the President is willing that this subject should be referred to the Senate for their consideration and if it was not intended by the Senate that the above-mentioned sum of five millions of dollars should include the objects herein specified that in that case such further provision should be made therefor as might appear to the Senate to be just.

Allowance in lieu of preemptions, etc. Article 3. It is therefore agreed that the sum of six hundred thousand dollars shall be and the same is hereby allowed to the Cherokee people to include the expense of their removal, and all claims of every nature and description against the Government of the United States not herein otherwise expressly provided for, and to be in lieu of the said reservations and pre-emptions and of the sum of three hundred thousand dollars for spoliations described in the 1st article of the above-mentioned treaty. This sum if six hundred thousand dollars shall be applied and distributed agreeably to the provisions of the said treaty, and any surplus which may remain after removal and payment of the claims so ascertained shall be turned over and belong to the education fund.

But it is expressly understood that the subject of this article is merely referred hereby to the consideration of the Senate and if they shall approve the same then this supplement shall remain part of the treaty.

Provisions for agency reservations not to interfere, etc. Article 4. It is also understood that the provisions in article 16, for the agency reservation is not intended to interfere with the occupant right of any Cherokees should their improvement fall within the same.

It is also understood and agreed, that the one hundred thousand dollars appropriated in article 12 for the poorer class of Cherokees and intended as a set-off to the pre-emption rights shall now be transferred from the funds of the nation and added to the general national fund of four hundred thousand dollars.

Expense of negotiations to be defrayed by the United States. Article 5. The necessary expenses attaching the negotiations of the aforesaid treaty and supplement and also of such persons of the delegation as may sign the same shall be defrayed by the United States.

In testimony whereof, John F. Schermerhorn, commissioner on the part of the United States, and the undersigned delegation have hereunto set their hands and seals, this first day of March, in the year one thousand eight hundred and thirty-six.

J. F. Schermerhorn.

Major Ridge, his x mark; James Foster, his x mark; Tah-ye-ske, his x mark; Long Shell Turtle, his x mark; ohn Fields, his x mark; George Welch, his x mark; Andrew Ross; William Rogers; John Gunter; John A. Bell; Jos. A. Foreman; Robert Sanders; Elias Boudinot; Johnson Rogers; James Starr, his x mark; Stand Watie; John Ridge; James Rogers; John Smith, his x mark, [L. S.]

Witnesses: Elbert Herring, Thos. Glascock, Alexander H. Everett, Jno. Garland, Major, U. S. Army, C. A. Harris, John Robb, Wm. Y. Hansell. Saml. J. Potts, S. Rockwell.

Chief Ross strenuously objected to it. Slowly and tediously the United States labored to its fulfillment. Emigration officers backed by an army which was at first under General John E. Wool and later under General Winfield, two of the most humane officers of the army were dispatched to the Cherokee nation to superintend the imigration.

Chief Ross was informed of the unalterable intention of the government, by the following communication:

"War Department, March 24, 1837.

Gentlemen: Your memorial of the 16th instant, addressed to the President of the United States, has been laid before him; and I now proceed to communicate to you his decision upon the proposition you have submitted.

The treaty concluded at New Echota, on the 29th of December, 1835, has been ratified, according to the forms prescribed by the constitution and it is the duty of the Executive to carry into effect all its stipulations, in a spirit of liberal justice. The considerations to which you have invited the attention of the President were brought to the notice of the Senate, before they advised its confirmation, and of the House of Representatives, before they made appropriations therein provided for. Their final action must be regarded as the judgment of these branches of the Government, upon the degree of weight to which they were entitled. It remains for the Executive to fulfill the treaty, as the supreme law of the land.

Your second and third propositions, therefore, it is considered, cannot be acceded to, as they involve an admission that the treaty of 1835 is an incomplete instrument. To your first proposition I can only answer as the Department has already assured you, that any measure suggested by you will receive a candid examination, if it be not inconsistent with, or in contravention of, the provisions of the existing treaty.

Very respectfully,

Your most obedient servant,

J. R. Poinsett.

Messrs. John Ross, R. Taylor, James Brown, Samuel Hunter, John Benger, George Sanders, John Looney, Aaron Price, William Dutch and Wm. S. Coody, Eastern and Western Cherokees.

Washington."

Chief Ross exerted his influence among his people against the idea of emigration until July 1838. If a member of the council died, resigned, was expelled or removed west, his place in the body was filled by appointment by Chief Ross.

"Proposition of Cherokee delegation to General Scott.

Amohe District, Aquohee Camp,

July 23, 1838.

Sir: In respectfully presenting for your consideration the following suggestions in relation to the removal of the Cherokee people to the West, it may be proper very briefly to advert to certain facts which have an important bearing on the subject.

It is known to you, sir, that the undersigned, delegates of the Cherokee nation, submitted to the honorable Secretary of War the project of a treaty, on the basis of a removal of the Cherokee nation from all "the lands now occupied by them eastward of the Mississippi" and on terms the most of which the honorable Secretary expresses himself as "not unwilling to grant." The present condition of the Cherokee people is such, that all disputes as to the time of emigration are set at rest. Being already severed from their homes and their property—their persons being under the absolute control of the commanding general and being altogether dependent on the benevolence and humanity of that high officer for the suspension of their transportation to the West at a season and under circumstances in which sickenss and death were to be apprehended to an alarming extent, all inducements to prolong their stay in this country are taken away; and, however strong their attachment to the homes of their fathers may be, their interest and their wishes now are only to depart as early as may be consistent with their safety, which will appear from the following extract from their proceedings on the subject:

Resolved by the national committee and council and people of the Cherokee Nation, in general council assembled, That it is the decided sense and desire of this general council that the whole business of the emigration of our people shall be undertaken by the nation; and the delegation are hereby advised to negotiate the necessary arrangements with the commanding general for that purpose.

In conformity, therefore, with the wishes of our people, and with the fact that the delegation has been referred by the honorable Secretary of War to conclude the negotiation, in relation to emigration, with the commanding general in the Cherokee country, we beg leave, therefore, very respectfullly to propose:

That the Cherokee nation will undertake the whole business of removing their people to the West of the Mississippi;

That the emigration shall commence at the time stipulated in a pledge given to you by our people, as a condition of the suspension of their transportation until the sickly season should pass away, unless prevented by some cause which shall appear reasonable to yourself;

That the per capita expense of removal be based on the calculation of one wagon and team, and six riding, being required for fifteen persons;

That the Cherokees shall have the selection of physicians and other persons as may be required for the safe and comfortable conducting of the several detachments to the place of destination, their compensation to be paid by the United States.

We have the honor to be your obedient servants,

John Ross.
Elijah Hicks,
Edward Gunter,
Samuel Gunter,
Situwakee,
White Path,
Richard Taylor.

Major General Winfield Scott,
U. S. Army, Commanding, etc."

General Scott acceded to the proposition of the Cherokee delegation on July 25, 1838 with the understanding that the Cherokees take every precaution to get all of the Cherokees except certain ones that had been allowed to stay and become citizens of the States and such of the treaty party as might object to removal under the superintendence of Ross and his associates[1]. The arrangement was finally concurred in on the 27th of July, [2] and General Scott fixed the date for the departure of the first contingent on the first day of September 3. On July 31st the committee submitted an estimate of transportation for each thousand emigrants, distance eight hundred miles at eighty days travel, with twenty persons to the wagon:

Fifty wagons and teams at a daily expense of $350. including forage	$28,000.
Returning, seven dollars for each twenty miles	14,000
250 extra horses, at 40 cents each per day	8,000.
Ferriages, etc.	1,000.
80,000 rations at 16 cents each	12,800.
Conductor, at five dollars per day	400
Assistant conductor at three dollars per day	240.
Physician at five dollars per day	400.
Returning $15. for every hundred miles	120.
Commissary at $2.50 per day	200.
Assistant commissary at $2.00 per day	160.
Wagon master, at $2.50 per day	200.
Assistant wagon master, at $2.00 per day	160.
Interpreter, at $2.50 per day	200.
Total	$65,880.

"Cherokee Agency, August 1, 1838.

Gentlemen: In your note of yesterday, you estimate that $65,880. will be the necessary cost of every thousand Cherokees emigrated by land from this to their new country.

As I have already stated to some of you in conversation, I think the estimate an extravagant one.

Take the principal item, or basis of your calculation; one wagon and five saddle horses for every twenty souls.

I have already consented, with a view to lighten the movement by land, that all the sick, the crippled and superannuated of the nation should be left at the depots until the rivers be again navigable for steamboats. All heavy articles of property, not wanted on the road may wait for the same mode of conveyance.

Deducting the persons just mentioned, I am confident that it will be found that among every thousand individuals, taken in families, without selection, there are at least 500 strong men, women, boys and girls not only capable of marching twelve or fifteen miles a day, but to whom the exercise would be beneficial, and another hundred able to go on foot half that distance daily. There would then be left according to your basis, only four hundred and fifty individuals, most of them children, to ride, and children are light. The 250 saddle horses or ponies would accommodate as many riders; leaving but 200 souls to be steadily transported in fifty wagons, or only four to a wagon.

Now, the wagons are large, and each drawn by five or six horses, (as must be presumed from your high estimate of seven dollars for each wagon going and returning) it strikes me that one such team and five horses ought to accommodate, on the route, thirty or thirty-five emigrants including subsistence for a day or two, from depot to depot.

I repeat, that I do not absolutely reject or cut down your estimate (which I think also too high) in putting down the rations at sixteen cents each. The whole expense of the emigration is to be paid out of appropriations already made by Congress, the general surplus of which is to go to the Cherokee nation in various forms; therefore, they have a direct interest in conducting the movement as economically as comfort will permit. Nevertheless, for the reasons stated, I wish the several items of the estimate submitted be reconsidered.

I remain, gentlemen, yours respectfully,

Winfield Scott.

Messrs. J. Ross, E. Hicks, J. Brown and others, agents, etc."[1]

CHARLES THOMPSON
Chief, November, 1875, to November, 1879.

CHAPTER VI

The Emmigration From Georgia. Cost Detachment. Resolutions of Protest. Political Differences. Civil War Averted.

Under the provisions of the treaty of 1835 and the congressional acts to carry it into effect the Cherokee Nation was entitled to $6,537,634. By the treaty $600,000 were set aside from this amount to defray the expenses of removal[3]. The detachments were placed under the following conductors:

No.	Conductor	Started	Arrived west	Days on road
No. 1.	Hair Conrad	August 28, 1838	January 17, 1838	143
2.	Elijah Hicks	Sept. 1, 1838	January 4, 1839	126
3.	Rev. Jesse Bushyhead	Sept. 3, 1838	February 27, 1839	178
4.	John Bengi	Sept. 28, 1838	January 11, 1839	106
5.	Situwakee	Sept. 7, 1838	February 2, 1839	149
6.	Captain Old Field	Sept. 24, 1838	February 23, 1839	153
7	Moses Daniel	Sept. 20, 1838	March 2, 1839	164
8.	Choowalooka	Sept. 14, 1838	March 1, 1839	162
9.	James Brown	Sept. 10, 1838	March 5, 1839	177
10.	George Hicks	Sept. 7, 1838	March 14, 1839	189
11.	Richard Taylor	Sept. 20, 1838	March 24, 1839	186
12.	Peter Hildebrand	Oct. 23, 1838	March 25, 1839	154[4]
13.	John Drew	Dec. 5, 1838	March 18, 1839	104[2]

The number of emigrants turned over to each conductor was kept by Captain Page of the United States army and Captain Stephenson of the United States army made the official report of those that were mustered out in the west.

No.	Page's	Stephenson's	Ross'	Births	Deaths	Descrtions	Accessions
1	710	654	729	9	54	24	14
2	859	744	858	5	34		
3	846	898	950	6	38	148	171
4	1079	1132	1200	3	33		
5	1205	1033	1250	5	71		
6	841	921	983	19	57	10	6
7	1031	924	1035	6	48		
8	1120	970	1150				
9	745	717	850	3	34		
10	1031	1039	1118				
11	897	942	1029	15	55		
12	1449	1311	1766				
13		219	231				
Totals	10813	11494	13149	71	424	182	191

The original contract for removal was at the rate of $65.88 per capita, to which was added by agreement, a proportion of three pounds of soap to every hundred rations, at fifteen cents per pound[3] making the cost of the removal of each individual $66.24[4]. On this basis, Captain Page, as dis- as "Superintending Agent of the Cherokee Nation for Cherokee Removal"[5] bursing agent of the government paid on November 13, 1838 to John Ross $776,393.98[6].

General Scott agreed to the proposal of Chief Ross that if the estimated eighty days were found in any instance a longer period than was necessary for emigration of any detachment that the difference should be refunded by Chief Ross to General Scott and if a longer time should be required by any of the detachments that Chief Ross should be paid proportionately for the contract of August 1, 1838 was merely an estimate subject to the later agreement and accordingly filed a claim for an additional $486,939.50[7]. This claim was refused by Secretary of War, Poinsett and President Van Buren, but was allowed and paid by John Bell, Secretary of War under John Tyler on September 6, 1841[8], just one week before he relinquished the office. This second award brought the amount that Chief Ross received for the removal to $1,263,338.38 or at the rate of $103.25 per head[1]. This amount was deducted from the sum that the Cherokees received for their land east of the Mississippi River under the provisions of the treaty of 1835[2].

The number of wagons and teams with each of the detachments, were:

	Wagons and teams	Riding horses	Collected for return of wagons and teams
No. 1.	36	288	$10080.
2.	43	344	12040.
3.	48	334	13440.
5.	62	436	17360.
4.	60	480	16800.
6.	49	392	13720.
7.	52	415	14560.
8.	58	462	16240.
9.	42	338	11760.
10.	56	448	15680.
11.	51	358	14280.
12.	88	705	24640.[5]

Before leaving the Eastern Cherokee Nation, the following resolution was passed by their council. In the light of later happenings, this act is of prime importance, as it shows the spirit of the emigrants.

"Whereas, the title of the Cherokee people to their lands is the most ancient, pure, and absolute, known to man; its date is beyond the reach of human record; its validity confirmed and illustrated by possession and enjoyment, antecedent to all pretense of claim by any other portion of the human race:

And whereas, the free consent of the Cherokee people is indispensable to a valid transfer of the Cherokee title; and whereas, the said Cherokee people have, neither by themselves nor their representatives, given such consent; It follows, that the original title and ownership of said lands still rest in the Cherokee Nation, unimpaired and absolute:

Resolved, therefore, by the Committee and Council and People of the Cherokee Nation in General Council assembled, that the whole Cherokee territory, as described in the first article of the treaty of 1819 between the United States and the Cherokee Nation, and, also, in the constitution of the Cherokee Nation, still remains the rightful and undoubted property of the said Cherokee Nation; and that all damages and losses, direct or indirect, resulting from the enforcement of the alleged stipulations of the pretended treaty of New Echota, are in justice and equity, chargeable to the account of the United States.

And whereas, the Cherokee people have existed as a distinct national community, in the possession and exercise of the appropriate and essential attributes of sovereignty, for a period extending into antiquity beyond the dates and records and memory of man:

And whereas, these attributes, with the rights and franchises which they involve, have never been relinquished by the Cherokee people; but are now in full force and virtue:

And whereas, the natural, political, and moral relations subsisting among the citizens of the Cherokee Nation, toward each other and towards the body politic, cannot, in reason and justice, be dissolved by the expulsion of the nation from its own territory by the power of the United States Government:

Resolved, therefore, by the National Committee and Council and People of the Cherokee Nation in General Council assembled, that the inherent sovereignty of the Cherokee Nation, together with the constitution, laws, and usages, of the same, are, and, by the authority aforesaid, are hereby declared to be, in full force and virtue, and shall continue so to be in perpetuity, subject to such modifications as the general welfare may render expedient.

Resolved, further, That the Cherokee people, in consenting to an investigation of their individual claims, and receiving payment upon them, and for their improvements, do not intend that it shall be so construed as yielding or giving their sanction or approval to the pretended treaty of 1835; nor as compromising, in any manner, their just claim against the United States hereafter, for a full and satisfactory indemnification for their country and for all individual losses and injuries.

Be it further resolved, That the principal chief be, and he is hereby, authorized to select and appoint such persons as he may deem necessary and suitable, for the purpose of collecting and registering all individual claims against the United States, with the proofs, and report to him their proceedings as they progress.

RICHARD TAYLOR,
President of the National Committee.
GOING SNAKE,
Speaker of the Council.

Captain Broom, Katetah,
Toonowee, Richard Foreman

Samuel Foreman,	William,
Howester,	Beaver Carrier,
Samuel Christy,	Kotaquasker.

Signed by a committee in behalf of the whole people.

Aquohee Camp, August 1, 1838[1].

Upon arriving in the western Cherokee Nation Chief John Ross settled at Park Hill. Many of the emigrants camped in the vicinity of his residence, the earliest written communication from this camp which was known as "Camp Illinois," was dated April 23, 1839[1]. The emigrants camped at this place in large numbers through the spring and summer of that year.

The following letter was written by Chief Ross to the western Cherokees. "Friends: Through the mysterious dispensations of Providence, we have been permitted to meet in general council on the border of the great plains of the West. Although many of us have, for a series of years past, been separated, yet we have not and cannot lose sight of the fact, that we are all of the household of the Cherokee family, and of one blood. We have already met, shook hands, and conversed together. In recognizing and embracing each other as countrymen, friends and relations, let us kindle our social fire, and take measures for cementing our reunion as a nation, by establishing the basis for a government suited to the condition and wants of the whole people, whereby wholesome laws may be enacted and administered for the security and protection of property, life, and other sacred rights, of the community. Our meeting, on this occasion, is full of interest, and is of peculiar importance to the welfare of our people. I trust, therefore, that harmony and good understanding will continue to prevail, and that the questions which may come up for consideration will be maturely weighed previous to a final decision.

The following letter was sent to the Chiefs of the Western Cherokees.

Friends: On the 8th of December, 1836, I had the satisfaction, with other delegates who were associated with me, of meeting our Western brethren in council, held at Toluntcesky, and submitting before them the proceedings of the Cherokee Nation, east, in general council held at Red Clay on the 28th September, 1836, and of receiving the unanimous approval of the council of the western Cherokee to the same; and also being associated with a delegation appointed by them for the purpose of co-operating and uniting with us in a joint effort to negotiate a treaty with the United States, for the best interests of the whole Cherokee people. The joint proceedings of these delegations, and the result of the mission, have been fully made known to you. Since that period, the eastern Cherokees have done no act to compromise or detract from any of the sentiments expressed in relation to those matters. But after the seizure and captivity of the whole Cherokee people east, by the military power of the United States Government, a set of resolutions was adopted in general council expressive of their sentiments, and reaffirming all their previous acts in relation to the rights and interests of the nation. From these facts, it will be clearly seen that the great body of the people who have recently been removed into this country, emigrated in their national character, with all the attributes, from time immemorial, which belonged to them as a distinct community, and which they have never surrendered; and, although being compelled by the strong arm of power to come here, yet, in doing so, they have not trespassed or infringed upon any of the rights and privileges of the people are equal. Notwithstanding the late emigrants received in their national capacity, and constitute a large majority, yet there is no intention nor desire on the part of their representatives to propose or require any thing but what may be strictly equitable and just, and satisfactory to the people. Being persuaded that these feelings will be fully reciprocated, I trust the subject matter of this council will be referred to the respective representatives of the eastern and western people; and that, in their joint deliberations, we may speedily come to some satisfactory conclusion for the permanent reunion and welfare of our nation. Without referring in detail to our acknowledged treaties, and other documentary facts to show, I will conclude by remarking that there are great interests of a public and private character yet to be adjusted with the Government of the United States, and which can only be secured by a just and amicable course on the part of our nation. The injuries and losses sustained by the nation from the whites, in violation of treaty stipulations; holds a strong claim on the justice of the people and Government of the United States, which it is to be hoped will, in the end, be remunerated. The tenure of the soil on which we now stand, and the relations which shall hereafter exist between our nation and the United States, are questions of the first magnitude, and necessary to be understood and clearly defined by a general compact, for the security and protection of the permanent welfare and happiness of our nation. Let us never forget this self-evident truth; that a house divided against itself, cannot stand; or, united we stand, divided we fall.

JOHN ROSS.

June 10, 1839."[1]

It will be noticed that Chief Ross did not address this letter to any one, and in that manner evaded a written recognition of the western Cherokee officers and that he did not append to his signature the customary "Principal Chief" and thereby palliated differences.

By stating "a set of resolutions was adopted in general council expressive of their sentiments, and reaffirming all their previous acts in relation to the rights and interests of the nation. From these facts, it will be clearly seen that the great body of the people who have recently been removed into this country, emigrated in their national character, with all the attributes, from time immemorial, which belonged to them as a distinct community, and which they have never surrendered." Reference was made to the act in the old nation, at Aquohee on August 1, 1838. This act was unknown to the western Cherokees, but was published at Washington in H. R. Doc. No. 129 subsequent to March 12, 1840 after which time it became, for the first time, accessible to the western Cherokees. The purport of the preceding article obscured by "they have not trespassed or infringed upon any of the rights and privileges of those who were here previous to themselves," caused the following correspondence to be issued by President Vann of the National Council (Western).

"Takattokah, June 11, 1839.

The national council is unable to act understandingly upon the propositions of our brother emigrants from the eastern Cherokee Nation. The subject seems to have been too ambiguously presented by them to be understood what their views and real wishes are.. The national council respectfully request that the chiefs would ask Messrs Ross and Lowry to state, in writing, what they really wish and desire, and to give them in as plain and simple manner as possible, in order that no misconstruction can be had upon the subject. After which, the council will act upon it according to your request, and, if possible, to the satisfaction of our brothers.

A. M. VANN, President National Council.
WM. THORNTON, Clerk.

Messrs. John Brown, John Looney and John Rogers,
Chiefs Cherokee Nation.

We hand this to Messrs. Ross and Lowry, and hope the request of the council will be complied with as soon as convenient.

John Brown,
John Looney,
John Rogers.

"Council Ground, June 13, 1839.

Gentlemen: From the note which you sent us, it appears that you have been requested to ask us, to state in writing what we really wish and desire.

We take pleasure to state distinctly, that we desire to see the eastern and western Cherokees become united, and again live as one people, and our sincere wish is, that this desirable and important object may be harmoniously accomplished, to the satisfaction and permanent welfare of the whole Cherokee people.

The representatives of the eastern Cherokees have this day had this important subject under consideration, and have adopted a set of resolutions in reference to it, based upon the strict rules of equity and justice, which we take pleasure in laying before you, with the hope that it may also be adopted by the representatives of the western Cherokees.

We are, gentlemen, your obedient servants,

George Lowry, John Ross,
Chiefs of the Eastern Cherokees.

Messrs, John Brown, John Looney and John Rogers,
Chiefs of the Western Cherokees."

"Takattokah, June 13, 1839.

Whereas, the people of the Cherokee Nation east, having been captured and ejected from the land of their fathers by the strong arm of the military power of the United States Government, and forced to remove west of the river Mississippi:

And, whereas, previous to the commencement of the emigration, measures were adopted in general council of the whole nation on the 31st of July and August 1st, 1838, wherein the sentiments, rights, and interests of the Cherokee people were fully expressed and asserted; and, whereas, under these proceedings the removal took place, and the late emigrants arrived in this country and settled among those of their brethren (who had previously emigrated) on lands which had been exchanged for, with the United States, by the Cherokee Nation, for lands east of the river Mississippi; and, whereas, the reunion of the people, and the adoption of a code of laws for their future government are essential to the peace and welfare of the whole Nation; and, it being agreed upon, that the eastern and western Cherokees henceforward be united as a body politic, and shall establish a government west of the river Mississippi, to be designated the Cherokee Nation; therefore,

Be it resolved, by the Committee and Council of the eastern and western Cherokees, in General Council assembled, that the three chiefs of the eastern and western Cherokees each, to-wit: John Ross, George Lowry and Edward Gunter, on the part of the Eastern Cherokees and John Brown, John Looney and John Rogers, on the part of the Western Cherokees, are hereby authorized and required to associate with themselves three other persons, to be selected by them from their respective council or committee, and who shall form a select joint committee; for the purpose of revising and drafting a code of laws for the government of the Cherokee Nation, and they be and are hereby required to lay the same before the general council of the nation to be held at Takattokah on the —— day of ———, 1839; and which, when approved, shall be immediately submitted to the people for their acceptance.

Be it further resolved, that the respective laws and authorities of the Eastern and Western Cherokees shall continue to be exercised and enforced among themselves until repealed, and the new government which may be adopted, shall be organized and take effect, and that in all matters touching the public interest of the nation with the Government of the United States and the Indian nations, the chiefs and representatives of the nation shall act understandingly and jointly in reference to the same, as well also, in the passage of any new laws which may be adopted in council after this date affecting the rights, interests, and welfare of the people.

Members of the Committee:

Richard Taylor, President Nat. Com.; Daniel McCoy; Hair Conrad; Thomas Foreman; George Still; Richard Fields; G. W. Gunter; James Hawkins; Old Field; Chu-noo-las-kee; William Proctor; George Hicks; Nah-hoo-lah; J. D. Wofford.

Members of Council:

Going Snake, Speaker; Situwakee; Soft Shell Turtle; Bean Stick; Tah-quoh; John Watts; James Spears; Money Crier; Charles; John Keyes; John Otterlifter; Small Back; Bark; Young Squirrel; Hunter Langley; Walter Downing; Walking Stick; Te-nah-lay-we-stah; Peter.

Takattokah, June 14, 1839.

Gentlemen: The National Council has taken up your proposition of June 13, 1839, and given them due consideration. You state that your wishes are to unite the people. As to that matter, it is believed by the National Council that the two people have already been united. Our chiefs have met their brother emigrants, and made them welcome in the country; they are, thereby, made partakers of all the existing laws in the country, enjoy all its benefits; and are, in every respect, the same as ourselves. Since our chiefs have made them welcome, they have come to the chiefs and taken them by the hand, and expressed great satisfaction with the manner in which they have been received. This is sufficient to justify the belief that the people are, in general, very well satisfied; consequently, the National Council cannot justify the course of keeping up the uniting question, merely to protract a debate, when the uniting of the people has already been fully and satisfactorily accomplished.

As it respects your wishes for your original laws. created beyond the Mississippi, to be brought here, brought to life, and to have full force in this Nation, it is believed by the National Council that such an admission is, and would be, entirely repugnant to the government and laws of the Cherokee, Nation which would thereby create great dissatisfaction among the people. To admit two distinct laws or governments in the same country, and for the government of the same people, is something never known to to be admitted in any country, or even asked for by any people.

A. M. Vann,
President National Committee.
Wm. Thornton, Clerk.

Messrs. Ross and Lowry will please receive this as an answer to their propositions.

Respectfully yours,
John Brown,
John Looney,
John Rogers,
Chiefs of the Cherokee Nation.

Messrs. John Ross and George Lowry." [1]

"To the Committee and Council of the Eastern Cherokees

Council Grounds, June 15, 1839.

Gentlemen: Your proceedings of the 13th instant have been submitted before our Western brethren, as will be seen from the accompanying copy of a letter which we addressed to them; and the result of their deliberation on the subject will be found in the copy of a letter receivd from them, bearing date of the 14th instant,, herewith annexed.

You will no doubt feel the regret and surprise that we do, in relation to the singular views entertained and expressed by the signers of this letter.

We deem it our duty to lay before you, at this time, the joint resolutions which were adopted by you, and approved by the people east of the Mississippi on the 21st of July and 1st of August 1838; and you, who are the immediate representative of the people, and as guardians of their rights, understanding their interests, and knowing their sentiments, it is your bounden duty to obey their will when clearly and publicly expressed by themselves; therefore, should we fail in our representative capacity to come to any satisfactory or definite understanding with those who represent our brethren, in the adoption of measures for reuniting the people under some provisional arrangements for the establishing a new government, it will become your duty to consult the feelings and sentiments of the people, and to take steps for ascertaining their will in reference to this important subject.

Respectfully submitted,
John Ross,
George Lowry.

Messrs. Rd. Taylor, President Committee and
Going Snake, Speaker of Council.'"[1]

The two councils still met at Takatoka, although the meeting places were quite a distance apart and the deliberations of each were absolutely distinct from the other. Upon receiving the above given communication from the Western Cherokee council through Chiefs Ross and Lowry the Eastern Cherokee council answered with:

"Council Grounds, July 19, 1839.

The National Committee and Council of the Eastern Cherokees having had under consideration the communication from those of the Western Cherokees, cannot but express their regret at the course pursued by their western brethren, as well as the views entertained by them on a question so important and so indispensable to the welfare of the great Cherokee family as the reunion of the two Nations.

To the assertions made in that communication, that, "It is believed by the National Committee that the two people have already been united," we are compelled to refuse our assent.

That the ancient integrity of the Eastern Nation should be dissolved, and her existence annihilated without discussion, without conditions, and without action of any kind, is utterly inconceivable; and the rejection by the representatives of our western brethren, of the reasonable proposition to unite the two nations on the basis of the strictest rules of justice and equality, is an act equally unlooked for and surprising. Therefore,

Resolved, that the declarations of the general council of the nation, at Aquohee Camp, on the first day of August, 1838, in reference to attributes of sovereignty, derived from our fathers, be, and they are hereby, reasserted and confirmed.

Resolved, That the proceedings of the committee and council be forthwith laid before the people, that their sense may be had upon the subject.

Richard Taylor,
President National Committee.
Going Snake,
Speaker National Council.
John Ross,
George Lowry."

A call was issued on June 20th for a "general council" of the people of the eastern and western Cherokees to met at the national council at Illinois Camp Grounds on Monday the 31st day of July, 1839." It was signed by George Guess and Captain Bushyhead. On the twenty-first the following notice was sent to Agent Stokes.

"Takattokah Council Ground.
June 21, 1839.

Sir: We deem it our duty to address you on this occasion, for the purpose of communicating the result of this general council. You are aware that the objects for which it was convened were to effect a union of the eastern and western Cherokees and to take measures for remodeling their government and laws so as to meet the exigencies of both branches of the Cherokee family, and to provide equally for the tranquility and permanent welfare of the whole people. But we regret to say that the reasonable propositions submitted to the consideration of the representatives of our western brethren have not been received by them in a manner compatible with the wishes of the whole people. They require the unconditional submission of the whole body of the people, who have lately arrived, to laws and regulations, in the making of which they have had no voice. The attempt of a small minority to enforce thier will over a great majority contrary to their wishes appears to us to be a course so repugnant to reason and propriety, that it cannot fail to disturb the peace of the community, and to operate injuriously to the best interests of the nation. We are not without hopes, however, that everything will yet be amicably settled. The sense of the people who form a branch of this general council, has been expressed on the subject. They deem it essential to the welfare of the nation that the desired union should be formed, and equal and wholesome laws established, by which the general prosperity and happiness of the country may be proomted; and to carry their wishes into effect, they have called a national convention of the eastern and western Cherokees, to meet at Illinois Camp Ground, on Monday, July 1, 1839.

Under these circumstances, we feel it due to the interests of the late emigrants, as well as to all concerned, to request, through your official authority, that no disbursements of moneys due to those whom we represent, nor any other business of a public character affecting their rights be made or transacted by the agent of the Government with any other Cherokee authority than the undersigned, until a reunion of the people shall be effected.

We have the honor to be, sir, very rsepectfully your friends and brothers,

John Ross, Principal Chief,
Richard Taylor, President National Com.

George W. Gunter, George Hicks, Thomas Foreman, Hair Conrad, George Hicks, William Proctor, James Hawkins, James D. Wofford, George Still, Old Field, Nah-hoolah, Chu-noo-lu-hus-kee, Culsaltehee.

Governor M. Stokes,
United States Agent.'"

Three men had been mainly instrumental in making the treaty of 1835. They were Major Ridge, a full blood Cherokee of the Deer clan, born at Hiwassee in 1771. When still a young man he adopted the manner of living of the white man, mastered their language and became a well educated man. This course was at that time very unpopular, as the great mass of the Cherokees were stil full bloods and very jealous of their old customs and any full blood that would attempt in any way to take up the ways of the backwoods provincials was certain to incur the scorn of his tribesmen. But by sheer force of character, integrity and worth he gradualy forced himself to a high place in the nation. He had been president of the committee and was a major of the Cherokee allies of the Americans in the Creek war of 1814. His son, John Ridge, aged about forty years, had been educated in Cornwall, Connecticut, and had returned to the Cherokee nation in 1822. He was a close observer, a brilliant and convincing orator. The third of this trio was Elias Boudinot, born in 1804. He was the son of Oowatie, the interpretation of whose name was the ancient or revered. Oowatie was a full brother of Major Ridge. Killakeena or Buck (male deer) Oowatie or as they were later known as Watie, while on his way to school at Cornwall, where he attended with his cousin John Ridge, met in Philadelphia, Elias Boudinot of New Jersey, a signer of the national constitution and one of the most prominent men of his day. On account of some favor that he conferred, the boy Buck Watie adopted the name of his benefactor. Boudinot like his uncle and cousin had early ascended to high places in the councils of the nation and the three men seeing the hopeless condition of their exploited people in the east had made the treaty of 1835 that secured to the Cherokee Nation a splendid home in the west. Men of keen discernment, eloquent and fearless they were publicists to be dreaded.

Before daylight on the morning of Saturday, June 22, 1839 the home of John Ridge, near the northwest corner of Arkansas, was surrounded, entered and he was dragged into the yard where two men held his arms while others of their party stabbed him repeatedly and then severed his jugular vein. A few hours later during the same morning while his father, Major Ridge, was traveling southward along the Cherokee Nation—Arkansas line road, he was fired on by an ambushed party and killed. This was some twenty-five or thirty miles from the scene of the meurder of the son. At about the same time as the killing of Major Ridge, Elias Boudinot was shingling a new house near his residence and withing two miles of the residence of Chief John Ross. Three Cherokees appeared and requested medicine of a sick child of one of the party. Mr. Boudinot had studied medicine so that he could give gratuitous services and medicines to the needy. He started with them to get the required treatment when one of the three stepping behind struck him in the spine with a bowie knife and his groan was the signal for the others to dispatch him with tomahawks. The place of his death was about thirty miles from the murder of Major Ridge and fifty miles from the assassination of John Ridge. Immediately after his death, Mrs. Boudinot sent word by Rufus McWilliams to Stand Watie and Watie sent his slave, Mike, to inform John Adair Bell, and in this manner those two escaped mobs that hunted them. Three days later a party that was hunting Stan Watie, searched the house of Rev. Samuel A. Worcester in their quest

Chief Ross notified General Arbuckle on the twenty-second of the killing of Elias Boudinot and that Mrs. Boudinot had informed him that Stan

Watie had determined on raising a company of men for the purpose of taking Ross' life. He further wrote "I trust that you will deem it expedient forthwith to interpose and prevent the effusion of innocent blood, by executing your authority, in order that an unbiased investigation might be had in the matter."[1] General Arbuckle invited Chief Ross to the post at Fort Gibson if he still thought that there was any danger, he also invited Chiefs Brown. Looney and Rogers to come to the post by the twenty-fifth so that they might concert action to avoid civil strife.[2] Chief Ross on the twenty-third asked that a detachment of troops be sent to protect him.[3]

"Headquarters, Ind. Dept W. Division.
Fort Gibson, June 24, 1839.

Dear Sir: A number of friends of Messrs Ridge and Boudinot are here. I have advised them of your desire to have a full investigation of the late murders committed in your nation. This, they declare, is all they desire; and they have requested me to say to you that they expect that you will take immediate measures to have the murderers apprehended and brought to trial, agreeably to the laws of the Cherokee Nation. Justice to you requires that I should state to you that they have informed me that they have heard that some of the murderers are now at your house. If this is the case, I must believe that you are not apprized of the fact; and if, on inquiry, the report made to me on this subject is correct, the troops sent out will take charge of them if turned over, and convey them in safety to this post. I hope you will avail yourself of the opportunity of the command to visit this post, as I expect the chiefs named to you in my letter of the 23rd ultimo will be here this evening or early tomorrow morning.

I am, sir, with much respect, your obedient servant,
M. Arbuckle,
Brevet Brig. General, U. S. A.

John Ross, Esq.
Principal Chief of the Emigrant Cherokees, Illinois."

Chief Ross on account of the disturbed condition of affairs which caused bodies of men to congregate for protection or reprisal, both among the eastern and western Cherokees, refused to attend the proposed meeting at Fort Gibson except that he be allowed to bring a large body guard of emigrant Cherokees with him.

Fort Gibson, June 28, 1839.

Friends and Brothers: We the undersigned, principal chiefs of the Cherokee Nation, having been invited to this post by General Arbuckle, the commandant of the United States troops in this quarter, to take into consideration matters of the greatest importance to the peace and prosperity of our nation. We have met here in accordance with that invitation.

We have received information that three of our people, or three Cherokees who had been received as citizens of our nation, have been killed, and, it is believed, by some of the late emigrants. This has caused us much sorrow and distress. And we learn, further, that other Cherokees are threatened with death wholly or principally for their political acts. This is not all we have to complain of, as it would appear from a communication made by John Ross and other principal men of the late emigrants to General Stokes, Cherokee Agent, under date of the 21st June, that the late emigrants have called what they denominate a convention of the Cherokee Nation, on Monday, the 1st day of July next, to establish a government for the Cherokee Nation, without the least notice having been given to the undersigned. It must be apparent to Mr. John Ross, and to those who have called this meeting, that these proceedings are altogether irregular; and we feel ourselves bound to protest against all acts that may be passed by the said nominal convention of the Cherokee Nation, that may have the effect to impair the free and undisturbed authority of said Nation as it existed and was in force before the arrival of the late emigrants, all of whom have been received as friends and as citizens of the present Cherokee Nation, and allowed fully to participate and enjoy all the privileges and benefits thereby secured to the Cherokee people. It is believed that this kind and just treatment on our part would have been received in the spirit in which it was offered; and that, if our present form of government was not altogether satisfactory to our brethren late in the east, they would, at an early period, have an opportunity of having a share in that government, when the desired changes might be made.

The undersigned wish nothing but peace and friendship from their brothers late from the east; but, as it appears they are not satisfied, and that mischief has already taken place, the undersigned, in the hope and wish to spare the futher shedding of Cherokee blood, will agree to meet their eastern brethren upon the following terms:

That no individual of the Cherokee Nation shall be killed hereafter for their former political acts or opinions; that a convention of the Cherokee Nation shall be held at Fort Gibson, in which both parties shall be equally represented; and that the said convention shall have power to remodel the government of the Cherokee Nation.

The undersigned do not wish to dictate, or arbitrarily to determine, the number of which this proposed convention shall consist; but they believe that sixteen men from each party, of good understanding and approved character, would be a sufficient number to form a convention calculated to harmonize and reunite the whole Cherokee people; and that they have power to elect a president.

If these propositions are acceeded to, it is the sincere belief of the undersigned that it will tend to the reestablishment of peace and confidence in the Cherokee Nation, and greatly promote the happiness and prosperity of the people. If these just and reasonable propositions shall be accepted by our eastern brethren, we shall be much gratified; but if they are disregarded, and an appeal to arms be determined on, however much we may deplore the shedding of more Cherokee blood, and the disasters of such a conflict, we and our friends must meet it, as men unwilling to surrender our own rights, or to invade the rights of others.

If we shall have the good fortune to hear that these propositions, however uncalled for, are accepted by our eastern friends, we further propose, that the convention meet at Fort Gibson, on the twenty-fifth day of July next, and proceed to consider and decide upon the important matters confided to them.

The undersigned regard it as a respect due to themselves. and to the Cherokee people, distinctly to state to the principal men of the late emigrants, that they are not insensible of the indignity offered to the Cherokee government and themselves by the late outrages and acts which have been committed in the Cherokee Nation by the late emigrants, and could not, for any other motive than that given, as the thought of making a further concession to them, which they do not conceive they are in justice entitled to.

John Smith, his x mark, John Rogers,
John Looney, his x mark, John Brown,
Executive Council.

Witnesses:

M. Stokes, Agent for Cherokees,
S. G. Simmons, 1st Lieut. 7th Infantry.

John Ross, Esq..

And other chiefs and principal men of the emigrant Cherokees."[1]

Fort Gibson, June 29, 1839.

Gentlemen: We have the pleasure of enclosing, herewith, a communication to you from the chiefs of the Cherokee Nation, which we hope will be acceptable to you and your people who have arrived here of late from the east; as a compliance with the propositions now made to the late emigrants will, at an early period, enable them to enjoy a full participation in the government of the Cherokee Nation, when such alterations in the government can be made as will secure justice to the whole nation.

If the proposition now made to you by the old settlers be rejected, we can scarcely doubt that serious difficulties and misfortunes will happen to the Cherokee people at an early period, which we hope you will cordially assist us to prevent. We have done all we could with the chiefs and others here to induce them to make the accompanying proposition to you, which we hope and believe you ought to accept, and that you should, without delay, take measures to prevent the further effusion of Cherokee blood. A report was received here yesterday that a party of Cherokees are now ranging through the country about Honey creek, with the object of killing three Cherokees; two of them for former political offenses, and the other, as it is supposed, for an offense of a personal nature.

We believe that two governments cannot exist in the Cherokee Nation without producing a civil war, and are of the opinion that the government that existed before the arrival of the late emigrants should continue until it is changed in a regular and peaceable manner. We hope that you will take the proposition of the chiefs into consideration, and make an early decision, as some of the chiefs and others will remain here until they know the result.

We are, gentlemen, with much respect, your obedient servants,

M. Arbuckles, Brevet. Brig. General, U. S. A.
M. Stokes, Agent for Cherokees.

John Ross Esq. and other Chiefs,
or Principal Men of the late emigrant Cherokees."[1]

"Park Hill, June 30, 1839.

Gentlemen: Yours, with the accompanying communication, by Captain McCall, has been duly received, and is under serious consideration.

We perfectly concide with your judgment that two governments cannot and ought not, to exist in the Cherokee Nation any longer than arrangements can be made for uniting the two communities; and, in conformity with these views, we have used our best endeavors to bring about this desirable event, in a manner which might be satisfactory to all parties and by which all rights might be provided for, and the peace and well being of the Cherokees permanently secured.

We claimed no jurisdiction over our western brethren, nor can we, consistent with the responsibilities with which our constitutents have invested us, recognize their jurisdiction over us. We claim to stand on equal ground; we ask for no concessions, nor for any admissions which would be humiliating in the slightest degree. We have no wish to trample on their laws, nor disregard their rights. And, as proof that we entertained no such disposition, we have not availed ourselves of the advantage of superior numbers in our intercourses with them.

When they refused to mingle councils with us, for free conversation on our affairs, and requested that our wishes might be reduced to writing, we offered to meet them on equal ground. But our just and reasonable overtures were unconditionally rejected by them, and our communication treated with contempt. We have no disposition, however, to stand upon punctilios; but what are we to understand by the proposition now made (and even these, rigorous as they are, it appears, are yielded with reluctance, through your influence and at your instance.) Is it required that the late emigrants relinquish all their rights, and appear before the western chiefs in the attitude of suppliants? If such be their wish, and we are compelled to say that we do not believe our brethren, the western people, have the least desire to reduce us to so abject a condition. Indeed, they have expressed their sentiments; and, in the exercise of their inalienable and indefeasible rights, have appointed a national convention for Monday, July 1, 1839; and, for ourselves, we are unable to perceive any irregularity in their proceedings; they formed an integral branch of the late general council. Their acts were perfectly legitimate, and we cannot assume the responsibility of protesting against them, or of declaring them invalid.

It appears to us that the western chiefs, in their communication, blend questions which, in their nature, are altogether separate and distinct, and, in so doing, have fallen into glaring inconsistencies. While the eastern Cherokees are denied recognition in the character of a political community, and their representatives are by the western chiefs stripped of their official relations to the people, it would seem somewhat out of character to lay on the shoulders of these private individuals the burden of controlling the ebulition of the public feeling, and stopping the effusion of Cherokee blood. Regardless, however, of this inconsistency, we feel forward to use our influence and exert our utmost efforts to stay the hand of violence, and restore tranquility with the least possible delay.

We have thought it proper to say this much in advance, by Captain McCall, the subject being still under serious consideration. Entertaining the hope that all excitement may be allayed, and a satisfactory accommodation speedily effected.

We have the honor to be, gentlemen, your obedient servants,
John Ross, George Lowry, Edward Gunter, Lewis Ross.
In behalf of the eastern Cherokees.

Brig. Gen. M. Arbuckle,
United States Army and
His Excellency, Governor M. Stokes,
United States Agent."

P. S. Of the report of a party of Cherokees, "ranging through the country at Honey creek with the object of killing three Cherokees," we have heard nothing, except what is contained in your letter. But we beg you to be assured that no pains, on our part, shall be spared to put a stop to all such proceedings."

In answer to the letter of the western Cherokees inviting them to a conference to be held at Fort Gibson on the twenty-fifth day of July the eastern Cherokees reiterated their invitation to the western Cherokees to attend the convention to be held at Camp Illinois on July 1, 1839.[2] Chief Ross informed William Armstrong, Superintendent of Indian Affairs, on June 30th that armed men were congregated in his vicinity "for the sole purpose of acting on the defensive."[3] The convention was convened at the Illinois Camp ground on August 1, 1839. Two thousand Cherokees were in attendance including five old settlers: George Guess, Tobacco Will, David Melton, Looney Price and William Shory Coody.[4] Invitations were sent to the Old Settler chiefs on the second and fifth day of the month to attend and participate. But the fate of the Ridges and Boudinot and the large body of armed emigrants at the convention was not reassuring to free speech and action.

"In National Convention,
Illinois Camp ground, July 12, 1839.

Sir: We deem it proper to report further to you, for your information, the proceedings of the national convention in reference to the late excitement.

In order effectually to stop the further effusion of blood, the convention has, by decree, buried all past grievances in oblivion, on the sole condition of the parties giving assurance to maintain the peace in future.

Measures have been taken to inform those persons who claimed protection at the fort of these proceedings so that the collecting their friends to secure themselves from violence is rendered altogether needless.

These provisions, which are in exact conformity with your wishes as well as with our own, will prove to you our determination to prevent mischief and to promote peace.

We have the honor to be, sir, your friends and obedient, humble servants,
George Lowry, President, George Guess, Vice President,
Elijah Hicks, Secretary, John Ross.
By order of the National Convention.
Brevet Brig. Gen. M. Arbuckle,
United States Army, Commanding."[1]

It was required by this act that the prominent treaty men to which it related should appear at the Illinois Council ground, confess their sorrow for having signed the treaty of 1835 and pledge themselves to live peaceably, upon which event they would be permitted to live, but would be inelegible to hold office in the nation of five years.[1] This act was abrogated on January 16, 1840.[2]

Amnesty to the murderers of Boudinot and the Ridges was granted by:

"Know all men by these presents, that, in order to stop the further effusion of blood, to calm the present unhappy excitement, and to restore peace and harmony and confidence in the community, we, the people of the eastern and western Cherokees in national convention assembled, in our name, and by the authority and the exercise of our plenary powers, do ordain and decree, and by these presents it is ordained and decreed accordingly, that a full, free pardon and amnesty be, and is hereby granted to all persons, citizens of the eastern and western Cherokee nation, who may be chargeable with the act of murder or homicide, committed on the person of any Cherokee previously to the passage of this decree, whether the same may have been committed within the limits of the eastern or western Cherokee country or elsewhere. And by the authority aforesaid, we do further ordain and decree, that all persons so chargeable are, and by these presents are declared to be, fully exempted, released, and discharged from all liability to prosecution, punishment, or disabilities of any kind whatever, on the aforesaid account; and that they be restored to the confidence and favor of the community, and to the enjoyment and protection, and benefits of the laws, to all intents and purposes, as if the act or acts for which they stand chargeable had not been committed.

Given under our hands, at Illinois camp ground, this 10th day of July 1839. By order of the national convention.[1]

The following act of union between the eastern and western Cherokees was signed on August 12, 1839.

DENNIS B. BUSHYHEAD
November, 1879, to January, 1888

CHAPTER VII

Act of Union Between The Eastern And Western Cherokees

Whereas our Fathers have existed, as a separate and distinct Nation, in the possession and exercise of the essential and appropriate attributes of sovereignty from a period extending into antiquity, beyond the records and memory of man: And Whereas these attributes, with the rights and franchises which they involve, remain still in full force and virtue, as do also the national and social relations of the Cherokee people to each other and to the body politic, excepting in those particulars which have grown out of the provisions of the treaties of 1817 and 1819 between the United States and the Cherokee Nation, under which a portion of our people removed to this country and became a separate community: But the force of the circumstances having recently compelled the body of the Eastern Cherokees to remove to this country, thus bringing together again the two branches of the ancient Cherokee family, it has become essential to the general welfare that a union should be formed, and a system of government matured, adapted to their present condtion, and providing equally for the protection of each individual in the enjoyment of all his rights:

Therefore we, the people composing the Eastern and Western Cherokee Nation, in National Convention assembled, by virtue of our original and unalienable rights, do hereby solemnly and mutually agree to form ourselves into one body politic, under the style and title of the Cherokee Nation.

In view of the union now formed, and for the purpose of making satisfactory adjustments of all unsettled business which may have arisen before the consummation of this union, we agree that such business shall be settled according to the provisions of the respective laws under which it originated, and the Courts of the Cherokee Nation shall be governed in their decisions accordingly. Also, that the delegation authorized by the Eastern Cherokees to make arrangements with Major General Scott for their removal to this country shall continue in charge of the business, with their present powers, until it shall be finally closed. And also that all rights and title to public Cherokee lands on the east or west of the river Mississippi, with all their public interests which may have vested in either branch of the Cherokee family, whether inherited from our Fathers or derived from any other source, shall henceforward vest entire and unimpaired in the Cherokee Nation, as constituted by this union.

Given under our hands, at Illinois Camp-ground, this 12th day of July, 1839.

By order of the National Convention:

GEORGE LOWRY,
President of the Eastern Cherokees,
GEORGE GUESS, his x mark,

Eastern Cherokees: R. Taylor, V. P.; James Brown, V. P.; Te-ke-chulas-kee, V P.; George Hicks; John Benge; Thomas Foreman; Archibald Campbell; Jesse Bushyhead; Lewis Ross; Edward Gunter; Te-nah-la-we-stah;

Stephen Foreman; Daniel McCoy. By order of the National Convention.

JOHN ROSS, Principal Chief Eastern Cherokees.

GOING SNAKE, Speaker of Council.

Western Cherokees: Tobacco Will, V. P.; David Melton, V. P.; John Drew, V. P.; George Brewer; Thomas Candy; Moses Parris; James Campbell; Loony Riley; Charles Gourd; Lewis Melton; Young Wolf; Charles Coodey; Ah-sto-la-ta; Jack Spears; Looney Price. By order of the National Convention.

August 23, 1839. JOHN LOONEY, His x mark.

Acting Principal Chief Western Cherokees.

The foregoing instrument was read, considered, and approved by us this 23d day of August, 1839.

Aaron Price, Major Pullum, Young Elders, Deer Track, Young Puppy, Turtle Fields, July, The Eagle, The Crying Buffalo and a great number of respectable Old Settlers and late Emigrants, too numerous to be copied.

It being determined that a constitution should be made for the inchoate government, men were selected by its sponsors, from those at the Illinois Camp ground, including as many western Cherokees as could be induced to sign it; their number being less than two dozen out of a total of eight thousand.[2] The constitution as drafted by William Shory Coody, was accepted by the Convention:

Constitution of The Cherokee Nation.

The Eastern and Western Cherokees having again re-united, and become one body politic, under the style and title of the Cherokee Nation: Therefore,

We, the people of the Cherokee Nation, in National Convntion assembled, in order to establish justice, insure tranquility, promote the common welfare, and secure to ourselves and our posterity the blessings of freedom—acknowledging, with humility and gratitude, the goodness of the Sovereign Ruler of the Universe in permitting us so to do, and imploring His aid and guidance in its accomplishment—do ordain and establish this Constitution for the government of the Cherokee Nation.

Article I.

Sec. 1. The boundary of the Cherokee Nation shall be that described in the treaty of 1833 between the United States and Western Cherokees, subject to such extension as may be made in the adjustment of the unfinished business with the United States.

Sec. 2. The lands of the Cherokee Nation shall remain common property; but the improvements made thereon, and in the possession of the citizens of the Nation, are the exclusive and indefeasible property of the citizens respectively who made, or may rightfully be in possession of them: Provided, That the citizens of the Nation possessing exclusive and indefeasible right to their improvements, as expressed in this article, shall possess no right or power to dispose of their improvements, in any manner whatever, to the United States, individual States, or to individual citizens thereof; and that, whenever any citizen shall remove with his effects out of the limits of this Nation, and become a citizen of any other Government, all his rights and privileges as a citizen of this Nation shall cease: Provided, nevertheless, That the National Council shall have power to re-admit, by law, to all the rights of citizenship, any such person or persons who may, at any time, desire to return to the Nation, on memorializing the National Council for such readmission.

Article II.

Sec. 1. The power of the Government shall be divided into three distinct departments—the Legislative, the Executive, and the Judicial.

Sec. 2. No person or persons belonging to one of these departments shall exercise any of the powers properly belonging to either of the others, except in the cases hereinafter expressly directed or permitted.

Article III.

Sec. 1. The Legislative power shall be vested in two distinct branches —a National Committee, and Council; and the style of their acts shall be— Be it enacted by the National Council.

Sec. 2. The National Council shall make provision, by law, for laying off the Cherokee Nation into eight Districts; and if subsequently it should be deemed expedient, one or two may be added thereto.

Sec. 3. The National Committee shall consist of two members from each District, and the Council shall consist of three members from each District, to be chosen by the qualified electors in their respective Districts for two years; the elections to be held in the respective Districts every two years, at such times and place as may be directed by law.

The National Council shall, after the present year, be held annually, to be convened on the first Monday in October, at such place as may be designated by the National Council, or, in case of emergency, by the Principal Chief.

Sec. 4. Before the Districts shall be laid off, any election which may take place shall be by general vote of the electors throughout the Nation for all offices to be elected.

The first election for all the officers of the Government—Chiefs, Executive Council, members of the National Council, Judges and Sheriffs— shall be held at Tah-le-quah before the rising of this Convention; and the term of service of all officers elected previous to the first Monday in October 1839, shall be extended to embrace, in addition to the regular constitutional term, the time intervening from their election to the first Monday in October, 1839.

Sec. 5. No person shall be eligible to a seat in the National Council but a free Cherokee male citizen who shall have attained to the age of twenty-five years.

The descendants of Cherokee men by free women except the African race, whose parents may have been living together as man and wife, according to the customs and laws of this nation, shall be entitled to all the rights and privileges of this Nation, as well as the posterity of Cherokee women by all free men. No person who is of negro or mulatto parentage, either by the father or mother's side, shall be eligible to hold any office of profit, honor, or trust under this Government.

Sec. 6. The electors and members of the National Council shall in all cases, except those of treason, felony, or breach of the peace, be privileged from arrest during their attendance at elections, and at the National Council. in going to and returning.

Sec. 7. In all elections by the people, the electors shall vote viva voce.

All free male citizens, who shall have attained to the age of eighteen years shall be equally entitled to vote at all public elections.

Sec. 8. Each branch of the National Council shall judge of the qualifications and returns of its own members; and determine the rules of its proceedings; punish a member for disorderly behaviour, and, with the concurrence of two thirds, expel a member; but not a second time for the same offence.

Sec. 9. Each branch of the National Council, when assembled, shall choose its own officers; a majority of each shall constitute a quorum to do business, but a smaller number may adjourn from day to day and compel the attendance of absent members in such manner and under such penalty as each branch may prescribe.

Sec. 10. The members of the National Council, shall each receive from the public Treasury a compensation for their services which shall be three dollars per day during their attendance at the National Council; and the members of the Council shall each receive three dollars per day for their services during their attendance at the National Council, provided that the same may be increased or diminished by law, but no alteration shall take effect during the period of service of the members of the National Council by whom such alteration may have been made.

Sec. 11. The National Council shall regulate by law by whom and in what manner, writs of elections shall be issued to fill the vacancies which may happen in either branch thereof.

Sec. 12. Each member of the National Council, before he takes his seat, shall take the following oath, or affirmation: I, A. B. do solemnly swear (or affirm, as the case may be,) that I have not obtained my election by bribery, treats, or any undue and unlawful means used by myself or others by my desire or approbation for that purpose; that I consider myself constitutionally qualified as a member of ——, and that on all questions and measures which may come before me I will so give my vote and so conduct myself as in my judgment shall appear most conducive to the interest and prosperity of this Nation, and I will bear true faith and allegiance to the same, and to the utmost of my ability and power observe, conform to, support and defend the Constitution thereof.

Sec. 13. No person who may be convicted of felony shall be eligible to any office or appointment of honor, profit, or trust within this Nation.

Sec. 14. The National Council shall have the power to make all laws and regulations which they shall deem necessary and proper for the good of the Nation, which shall not be contrary to this Constitution.

Sec. 15. It shall be the duty of the National Council to pass such laws as may be necessary and proper to decide differences by arbitration, to be appointed by the parties, who may choose that summary mode of adjustment.

Sec. 16. No power of suspending the laws of this Nation shall be exercised, unless by the National Council or its authority.

Sec. 17. No retrospective law, nor any law impairing the obligation of contracts, shall be passed.

Sec. 18. The National Council shall have power to make laws for laying and collecting taxes, for the purpose of raising a revenue.

Sec. 19. All bills making appropriations shall originate in the National Committee, but the Council may propose amendments or reject the same; all other bills may originate in either branch, subject to the concurrence or rejection of the other.

Sec. 20. All acknowledged treaties shall be the supreme laws of the land, and the National Council shall have the sole power of deciding on the construction of all treaty stipulations.

Sec. 21. The Council shall have the sole power of impeaching. All impeachments shall be tried by the National Committee. When setting for that purpose the member shall be upon oath or affirmation; and no person shall be convicted without the concurrence of two-thirds of the members present.

Sec. 22. The Principal Chief, assistant Principal Chief, and all civil officers shall be liable to impeachment for misdemeanor in office; but judgment in such cases shall not be extended further than removal from office and disqualification to hold an office of honor, trust, or profit under the Government of this Nation.

The party, whether convicted or acquitted, shall, nevertheless, be liable to indictment, trial, judgment and punishment according to law.

Article IV.

Sec. 1. The Supreme Executive Power of this Nation shall be vested in a Principal Chief, who shall be styled the Principal Chief of the Cherokee Nation.

The Principal Chief shall hold his office for the term of four years; and shall be elected by the qualified electors on the same day and at the places where they shall respectively vote for members of the National Council.

The returns of the election for Principal Chief shall be sealed up and directed to the President of the National Committee, who shall open and publish them in the presence of the National Council assembled. The person having the highest number of votes shall be Principal Chief; but if two or more shall be equal and highest in votes, one of them shall be chosen by joint vote of both branches of the Council. The manner of determining contested elections shall be directed by law.

Sec. 2. No person except a natural born citizen shall be eligible to the office of Principal Chief; neither shall any person be eligible to that office who shall not have attained to the age of thirty-five years.

Sec. 3. There shall also be chosen at the same time by the qualified electors in the same manner for four years, an assistant Principal Chief, who shall have attained to the age of thirty-five years.

Sec. 4. In case of the removal of the Principal Chief from office, or of his death or resignation, or inability to discharge the powers and duties of the said office, the same shall devolve on the assistant Principal Chief until the disability be removed or the vacancy filled by the National Council.

Sec. 5. The National Council may by law provide for the case of removal, death, resignation, or disability of both the Principal and assistant Principal Chief, declaring what officer shall then act as Principal Chief until the disability be removed or a Principal Chief shall be elected.

Sec. 6. The Principal Chief and assistant Principal Chief shall, at stated times, receive for their services a compensation which shall neither be increased nor diminished during the period for which they shall have been elected; and they shall not receive within that period any other emolument from the Cherokee Nation or any other Government.

Sec. 7. Before the Principal Chief enters on the execution of his office, he shall take the following oath or affirmation:

"I do solemnly swear, or affirm, that I will faithfully execute the duties of Principal Chief of the Cherokee Nation, and will, to the best of my ability, preserve, protect, and defend the Constitution of the Cherokee Nation."

Sec. 8. He may, on extraordinary occasions, convene the National Council at the seat of Government.

Sec. 9. He shall from time to time, give to the National Council information of the state of the Government, and recommend to their consideration such measures as he may deem expedient.

Sec. 10. He shall take care that the laws be faithfully executed.

Sec. 11. It shall be his duty to visit the different districts at least once in two years, to inform himself of the general condition of the country.

Sec. 12. The Assistant Principal Chief shall, by virtue of his office, aid and advise the Principal Chief in the administration of the government at all times during his continuance in office.

Sec. 13. Vacancies that may occur in offices, the appointment of which is vested in the National Council, shall be filled by the Principal Chief during the recess of the National Council by granting commissions which shall expire at the end of the next session thereof.

Sec. 14. Every bill which shall pass both branches of the National Council shall, before it becomes a law, be presented to the Principal Chief; if he approves, he shall sign it; but if not, he shall return it, with his objections to that branch in which it may have originated, who shall enter the objections at large on their journals and proceed to reconsider it; if, after such reconsideration, two-thirds of that branch shall agree to pass the bill, it shall be sent, together with the objections, to the other branch, by which it shall likewise be reconsidered. and, if approved by two-thirds of that branch, it shall become a law. If any bill shall not be returned by the Principal Chief within five days (Sundays excepted), after the same has been presented to him, it shall become a law in like manner as if he had signed it, unless the National Council, by their adjournment, prevent its return, in which case it shall be a law, unless sent back within three days after their next meeting.

Sec. 15. Members of the National Council, and all officers, executive and judicial, shall be bound by oath to support the Constitution of this Nation, and to perform the duties of their respective offices with fidelity.

Sec. 16. In case of disagreement between the two branches of the National Council with respect to the time of adjournment, the Principal Chief shall have power to adjourn the same to such time as he may deem proper; provided, it be not a period beyond the next constitutional meeting thereof.

Sec. 17. The Principal Chief shall, during the session of the National Council, attend at the seat of government.

Sec. 18. There shall be a council composed of five persons, to be appointed by the National Council, whom the Principal Chief shall have full power at his discretion to assemble; he, together with the Assistant Principal Chief and the counselors, or a majority of them, may, from time to time, hold and keep a council for ordering and directing the affairs of the Nation according to law; provided, the National Council shall have power to reduce the number, if deemed expedient, after the first term of service, to a number not less than three.

Sec. 19. The members or the executive council shall be chosen for the term of two years.

Sec. 20. The resolutions and advice of the council shall be recorded in a register, and signed by the members agreeing thereto, which may be called for by either branch of the National Council; and any counselor may enter his dissent to the majority.

Sec. 21. The Treasurer of the Cherokee Nation shall be chosen by a joint vote of both branches of the National Council for the term of four years.

Sec. 22. The Treasurer shall, before entering on the duties of his office, give bond to the Nation, with sureties, to the satisfaction of the National Council, for the faithful discharge of his trust.

Sec. 23. No money shall be drawn from the Treasury but by warrant from the Principal Chief, and in consequence of appropriations made by law.

Sec. 24. It shall be the duty of the Treasurer to receive all public moneys, and to make a regular statement and account of the receipts and expenditures of all public moneys at the annual session of the National Council.

Article V.

Section 1. The judicial powers shall be vested in a Supreme Court, and such circuit and inferior courts as the National Council may, from time to time, ordain and establish.

Sec. 2. The Judges of the Supreme and Circuit courts shall hold their commissions for the term of four years, but any of them may be removed from office on the address of two-thirds of each branch of the National Council to the Principal Chief for that purpose.

Sec. 3. The Judges of the Supreme and Circuit courts shall, at stated times, receive a compensation which shall not be diminished during their continuance in office, but they shall receive no fees or perquisites of office, nor hold any other office of profit or trust under the government of this Nation, or any other power.

Sec. 4. No person shall be appointed a judge of any of the courts until he shall have attained the age of thirty years.
elected by the National Council, and there shall be appointed in each district

Sec. 5. The Judges of the Supreme and Circuit courts shall be as many Justices of the Peace as it may be deemed expedient for the public good, whose powers, duties, and duration in office shall be clearly designated by law.

Sec. 6. The Judges of the Supreme Court and of the Circuit Courts shall have complete criminal juridiction in such cases, and in such manner as may be pointed out by law.

Sec. 7. No Judge shall sit on trial of any cause when the parties are connected [with him] by affinity or consanguinity, except by consent of the parties. In case all the Judges of the Supreme Court shall be interested in the issue of any case, or related to all or either of the parties, the National Council may provide by law for the selection of a suitable number of persons of good character and knowledge, for the determination thereof, and who shall be specially commissioned for the adjudication of such cases by the Principal Chief.

Sec. 8. All writs and other process shall run "In the Name of the Cherokee Nation," and bear test and be signed by the respective clerks.

Sec. 9. Indictments shall conclude—"Against the Peace and Dignity of the Cherokee Nation."

Sec. 10. The Supreme Court shall, after the present year, hold its session annually at the seat of government, to be convened on the first Monday of October in each year.

Sec. 11. In all criminal prosecutions the accused shall have the right of being heard; of demanding the nature and cause of the accusation; of meeting the witnesses face to face; of having compulsory process for obtaining witnesses in his or their favor; and in prosecutions by indictment or information, a speedy public trial, by an impartial jury of the vicinage; nor shall the accused be compelled to give evidence against himself.

Sec. 12. The people shall be secure in their persons, houses, papers, and possessions from unreasonable seizures and searches, and no warrant to search any place, or to seize any person or thing, shall issue, without describing them as nearly as may be, nor without good cause, supported by oath or affirmation.

Sec. 13. All persons shall be bailable by sufficient securities, unless for capital offenses, where the proof is evident or presumption great.

Article VI.

Section 1. No person who denies the being of a God or future state of reward and punishment, shall hold any office in the civil department in this Nation.

Sec. 2. The free exercise of religious worship, and serving God without distinction, shall forever be enjoyed within the limits of this Nation; provided, that this liberty of consicence shall not be so construed as to excuse acts of licentiousness, or justify practices inconsistent with the peace or safety of this Nation.

Sec. 3. When the National Council shall determine the expediency of appointing delegates, or other public agents, for the purpose of transacting business with the government of the United States, the Principal Chief shall recommend, and by the advice and consent of the National Committee, appoint and commission such delegates or public agents accordingly. On all matters of interest, touching the rights of the citizens of this Nation, which may require the attention of the United States government, the Principal Chief shall keep up a friendly correspondence with that government through the medium of its proper officers.

Sec. 4. All commissions shall be "In the Name and by the Authority of the Cherokee Nation," and be sealed with the seal of the Nation, and signed by the Principal Chief. The Principal Chief shall make use of his private seal until a National seal shall be provided.

Sec. 5. A sheriff shall be elected in each district by the qualified electors thereof, who shall hold his office two years, unless sooner removed. Should a vacancy occur subsequent to an election, it shall be filled by the Principal Chief, as in other cases, and the person so appointed shall continue in office until the next regular election.

Sec. 6. No person shall, for the same offense, be twice put in jeopardy of life or limb; nor shall the property of any person be taken and applied to public use without a just and fair compensation; provided, that nothing in this clause shall be so construed as to impair the right and power of the National Council to lay and collect taxes.

Sec. 7. The right of trial by jury shall remain inviolate, and every person, for injury sustained in person, property, or reputation, shall have remedy by due course of law.

Sec. 8. The appointment of all officers, not otherwise directed by this Constitution, shall be vested in the National Council.

Sec. 9. Religion, mortality and knowledge being necessary to good government, the preservation of liberty, and the happiness of mankind, schools and the means of education shall forever be encouraged in this Nation.

Sec. 10. The National Council may propose such amendments to this Constitution as two-thirds of each branch may deem expedient, and the Principal Chief shall issue a proclamation, directing all civil officers of the several districts to promulgate the same as extensively as possible within their respective districts at least six months previous to the next general election. And if, at the first session of the National Council, after such general election, two-thirds of each branch shall, by ayes and noes, ratify such proposed amendments, they shall be valid to all intent and purposes as parts of this Constitution; provided, that such proposed amendments shall be read on three several days in each branch, as well when the same are proposed, as when they are ratified.

Done in convention at Tahlequah, Cherokee Nation, this sixth day of September, 1839.

GEORGE LOWRY, President of the National Convention.

Hair Conrad, his x mark; John Benge, his x mark; Archibald Campbell, his x mark; Thomas Candy; John Drew; George Guess, his x mark; Walter Scott Adair; Young Elders, his x mark; Will Shorey Coodey; Thomas Foreman: Richard Taylor; Thomas Fox Taylor; O-kan-sto-tah Logan, his x mark; James Spears, his x mark; John Spears; Stephen Foreman; Young Glass, his x mark; Looney Price; Tobacco Will, his x mark; Major Pullum, his x mark; Moses Parris; George Washington Gunter; Kench Logan, his x mark; Young Wolf; Joseph Martin Lynch; Sal-la-tee-skee Watts, his x mark; George Brewer, his x mark; Joshua Buffington; Jesse Bushyhead: Jesse Russell; John Fletcher Boot, his x mark; Crying Buffalo, his x mark; Bark Flute, his x mark; Oo-la-yo-a, his x mark; Soft Shell Turtle, his x mark; Edward Gunter; Daniel Colston, his x mark; Lewis Ross; George Hicks; Tah-lah-see-nee, his x mark; James Brown; Charles Coodey; Riley Keys; Daniel McCoy; Lewis Melton.

PROCLAMATION AND AMENDMENTS TO THE CONSTITUTION

Adopted November 26, 1886. Proclamation by the Principal Chief.

Whereas, The National Council adopted certain amendments to the Constitution of the Cherokee Nation and submitted the same to a general convention of the people of the Cherokee Nation, called at Tahlequah, on the 26th day of November, A. D. 1866, and which said amendments, with the preamble thereto attached. were in the following words, to-wit:

Whereas, By the treaty executed at Washington, on the 19th day of July, A. D. 1866, between the United States and the Cherokee Nation, through its delegation, ratified by the Senate and officially promulgated by the Presidents of the United States. August 11, 1866. certain things were agreed to between the parties to said treaty, involving changes in the Constitution of the Cherokee Nation, which changes cannot be accomplished by the usual mode; and

Whereas, It is the desire of the people and government of the Cherokee Nation to carry out in good faith all of its obligations, to the end that law and order be preserved and the institutions of their government maintained; therefore,

Be it resolved by the National Council, That the following amendments to the Constitution of the Cherokee Nation be submitted to a convention of the Cherokee people. to assemble at Tahlequah, on the twenty-sixth (26th) day of November, A. D. 1866, under the proclamation hereunto annexed, be ratified by said convention, then they shall be officially published, and declared by the Principal Chief to be, and shall constitute a part, or parts, of the Constitution of the Cherokee Nation.

AMENDMENTS

AMENDMENTS TO ARTICLE I.

Section 1. The boundary of the Cherokee Nation shall be that described in the treaty of 1833, between the United States and the Western Cherokees, subject to such modifications as may be made necessary by the 17th article of the treaty concluded at Washington City on the 19th day of July, 1866, between the United States and the Cherokee Nation.

Sec. 2. The lands of the Cherokee Nation shall remain common property until the National Council shall request the survey and allotment of the same, in accordance with the provisions of Article 20 of the treaty of 19th of July, 1866, beween the United States and the Cherokee Nation.

AMENDMENTS TO ARTICLE III.

Section 1. The Upper House of the National Council, known as the National Committee, shall be hereafter known and styled the Senate of the Cherokee Nation, and shall consist of two Senators for every district in the Cherokee Nation.

Sec. 2. The Council shall consist of two members from each district, and when a district shall have to exceed two hundred voters, it shall have an additional member, and for every additional two hundred voters in said district, upwards of four hundred, it shall have an additional member; provided, that when any district shall have less than one hundred voters according to the census, it shall still be entitled to one representative.

Sec. 3. In order to ascertain and fix the representation to the Council, provided for above, shall be made before the first day of June, and shall gov- taken, as soon as practicable, a census of the population of the Cherokee Nation, according to districts. A second census shall be taken in like manner in the year 1870, and each ten years thereafter, and the National Council shall regularly apportion representation among the several districts, as provided in the preceding section, agreeably to such census. The first apportionment, provided for above, shall be made before the first day of June, and shall govern the election to be held on the first Monday in August, 1867.

Sec. 4. The National Council shall, after the present year, be held annually, to be convened on the first Monday in November, at such place as may be designated by the National Council, or in case of emergency, by the Principal Chief.

Sec. 5. No person shall be eligible to a seat in the National Council but a male citizen of the Cherokee Nation who shall have attained to the age of twenty-five years, and who shall have been a bona fide resident of the district in which he may be elected, at least six months immediately preceding such election. All native born Cherokees, all Indians, and whites legally members of the Nation by adoption, and all freedmen who have been liberated by voluntary act of their former owners or by law, as well as free colored persons who were in the country at the commencement of the rebellion, and are now residents therein, or who may return within six months from the 19th day of July, 1866, and their descendants, who reside within the limits of the Cherokee Nation, shall be taken, and deemed to be, citizens of the Cherokee Nation.

Sec. 6. The members of the National Council shall each receive from the public treasury a compensation for their services, which shall be three dollars per day, during their attendance at the National Council upon any regular session, not exceeding thirty days; provided, that the per diem allowance may be increased or diminished by law; but no alteration shall take effect during the period of service of the members of the National Council, by whom such alteration may have been made.

Sec. 7. All male citizens, who have attained the age of eighteen years, shall be deemed qualified electors of the Cherokee Nation, and there shall be no restrictions by law, save such as are required for persons convicted of crime, or for such limit as to residence, not exceeding six months in the district where the vote is offered, as may be required by census or registration.

AMENDMENTS TO ARTICLE V.

Section 1. The Supreme Court shall consist of three judges, who shall be elected by the National Council, and whose duties, jurisdiction, and compensation, shall be defined by law, in the manner prescribed by the Constitution. The National Council, at its annual session in 1867, shall elect one of the Supreme Judges for three years, one for two years, and one for one year, and at each annual session of the National Council thereafter, shall elect one Supreme Judge, whose official term shall be three years.

Sec. 2. The judges of the Circuit Court shall hereafter be elected by the people, for the term of four years, and shall have the same jurisdiction, discharge the same duties, and be compensated in the same manner as is now provided for by the Constitution. There shall be elected in like manner in and for each district as many judges as it may be deemed expedient for the public good, whose powers, duties and duration in office shall be clearly designated by law.

AMENDMENTS TO ARTICLE VII.

Section 1. Neither slavery nor involuntary servitude, shall ever hereafter exist in the Cherokee Nation, otherwise than in the punishment of crime, whereof the party shall have been duly convicted; and any provision of the Constitution of the Cherokee Nation conflicting with the foregoing section, is hereby annulled.

Sec. 2. The persons now holding office shall continue therein, except as may be otherwise expressly provided by law for Canadian district, until their successors be commissioned in November, 1867.

Tahlequah, Cherokee Nation, November 26, 1866.

SMITH CHRISTIE,
President of National Committee.

Concurred: WRITER,
Speaker of Council.

Approved: WILL P. ROSS.

At a general convention of the people of the Cherokee Nation, held at Tahlequah, Cherokee Nation, on the 28th day of November, A. D. 1866. for the purpose of taking into consideration the foregoing amendments to the Constitution of the Cherokee Nation; and, whereof, Riley Keys, Chief Justice of the Supreme Court, was chosen President, and Budd Gritts, Secretary; the said amendments to the Constitution of the Cherokee Nation were read, considered and severally approved and adopted by the Cherokee people.

In testimony whereof, the President and Secretary of said convention have subscribed the same at Tahlequah, Cherokee Nation, on this the 28th day of November, A. D. 1866.

RILEY KEYS,
President of the Convention.

BUDD GRITTS,
Secretary.

And, Whereas, The foregoing amendments to the Constitution were duly submitted to the said general convention of the Cherokee people, and were severally read, considered, and adopted on the 28th day of November, A. D. 1866; now,

Therefore, Be it known that I, William P. Ross, Principal Chief of the Cherokee Nation, do issue this, my proclamation, declaring said amendments to be a part of the Constitution of the Cherokee Nation.

In testimony whereof, I have hereunto subscribed my name, this the 7th day of December, A. D. 1866.

WILL P. ROSS,
Principal Chief.

The constitution was generally accepted by the nation on January 16, 1839[3] and October 26, 1840.

Fort Gibson, September 28, 1839.

Sir: We have been required by instructions from the War Department to arrest and bring to trial the murderers of the Ridges and Boudinot. Although we have the names of several of the individuals charged, yet, as you are the chief of the emigrant Cherokees, by some of whom we have no doubt these murders were perpertrated, we therefor deem it proper to apprize you of this order. We believe that you can have the prsons charged delivered at this post, without resorting to other means, which it is our wish to avoid. Should we be disappointed in our expectations in this particular, the military force of the United States will be employed in carrying out the instructions of the War Department. In the meantime, we expect and require of you that no violence or disability whatever be imposed on the treaty party in consequence of the treaty of 1835, which has received the sanction of the Government of the United States.

We extremely regret the unfortunate events to which we have referred; and also that no union has taken place beetween the eastern Cherokees, of whom you are the acknowledged head, and John Brown, principal chief of the western Cherokees. An early reply to this communication is requested.

Respectfully, your very obedient servants,
M. Arbuckle,
Brevet Brig. General, U. S. A.
Wm. Armstrong,
Acting Superintendent, W. T.

John Ross,
Principal Chief of the emigrant Cherokees.

"Tahlequah, Cherokee Nation
September, 30, 1839.

Gentlemen: Your communication of the 28th instant, came duly to hand by express.

You appraise me of having received "instructions from the War Department to arrest and bring to trial the murderers of Ridges and Boudinot," and express expectations "that I will arrest the persons charged, and deliver them over to the military post at Fort Gibson without resorting to other means." I hold myself at all times in readiness, so far as I may be concerned, to comply with the established regulations between the United States and the Cherokee Nation, and for all offenses which may be committed by individual Cherokees, and over which the United States may have proper jurisdiction, and their courts cognizance assuredly, I could not in duty to the Nation and to myself, but exercise all necessary and proper efforts to sustain and preserve unimpaired the confidence and friendship of both parties. You cannot be otherwise than fully impressed with the fact that there exists in this country a feeling decidedly friendly to the Government and people of the United States, and no wish or attempt to cause innovation in the plain and well understood method of communication and intercourse. In relation to the particular subject of " arrest and trial" of which you speak, I am wholly at a loss to conjecture by what right or sound policy the Cherokee people are to be deprived of the exercise of their own legislate authority over acts of one Indian against another. An authority founded upon natural as well as conventional rights. I cannot conceive how, if the persons charged be Cherokees, they have violated either treaty stipulation or act of Congress, that they should be held answerable to the courts of the United States, and the miltary force employed for their arrest. Any effort directed to that purpose is depreciated as calculated to disquiet the country, to weaken the confidence of the people in their exertions to allay excitement and the enjoyment of some respite from the difficulties and embarrassments which have so long distressed them.

None of the persons charged with the act you instructed upon are known me; some of them may be of the late emigrants, or all for ought I know; nor do I feel that it is again necessary for me to review the subject among the people, when you are doubtless appraised that they themselves, in convention, considered and disposed of the matter in a manner satisfactory to the whole people. You express regret "that no union has taken place between th eeastern Cherokees and John Brown, principal chief of the western Cherokees." This may be true to some extent, yet it is equally true that a union has been formed between the eastern and western Cherokee people. To that union, if it has pleased some to withhold their approbation, and among them John Brown, still the people acted for themselves. They are the acknowledged source of power in this country, and their original acts require not the sanction of any chief to accredit it with authority. Many of the old settlers, who could not attend in person, forwarded their names to be enrolled upon that act.

Although the fact may not have been formally announced to you, yet it was believed that you were informed of the adoption of a constitution for the government of the Cherokee Nation, in accordance with the act of union. Elections have also taken place under its provisions for officers, etc., and the national council, composed both of old settlers and emigrants, without, however, any distinction, are now about to terminate its session, having been engaged in passing such laws as were required for the security and protection of the persons and property of the people.

Fro mthese facts, I trust that you will be fully convinced of the earnest desire of the Cherokees to preserve and maintain the peace and friendship which have so long subsisted between them and the citizens of the United States.

I have the honor to be, gentlemen, very respectfully, your obedient servant,

John Ross, Principal Chief.

Brevet Brigadier General M. Arbuckle, U. S. A.
Captain William Armstrong,
Acting Superintendent, W. T. Fort Gibson."[1]

After a little more desultory correspondence, the matter of prosecution for the murderers, was dropped.

The public school system of the Cherokee Nation was inaugurated in 1842. In the spring of that year Sequoyah started to the southwest in search of a Cherokee settlement in the neighborhood of the Rio Grande. He died at San Fernando in August 1843. The Cherokee Advocate, a weekly newspaper, owned and operated by the Nation and its oficial organ, published volume one, number one at Tahlequah on September 25, 1844.[2]

Chief Ross married on September 2, 1844, Mary Brown Stapler a native of Delaware. On account of the widespread dissatisfaction among the treaty party and old settlers, a delegation of fifty-four of their leaders left the Cherokee Nation for southwest Texas on September 1, 1845. They found a settlement of sixty-three Cherokees on the bank of Brazos river, at the mouth of Basky Creek. These Cherokees were from Monclovis, Mexico. While on this trip Charles Reese died. The delegation returned to Ft. Gibson on January 19, 1846, not being able to find a home in the west.

The residence of Return Jonathan Meigs, son-in-law of Chief John Ross was burned by Thomas Starr and his band on the night of November 2, 1845 Mr. Meigs, who lived within three miles of his father-in-law, was an estimable citizen and this act was a part of the feud that had been raged uninterruptedly since 1839. On the ninth of the month, thirty-two men rode up to the home of James Starr, father of Thomas, and shot him to death. He was one of the signers of the treaty of 1835 and a member of the first elected Cherokee committee (senate) from 1841 to 1843. No prosecution followed this murder.

Delegations from the emigrant, treaty party and old settlers divisions of the Cherokee Nation visited Washington in the summer of 1846 where they in conjunction with representatives of the United States, concluded a treaty for the purpose of establishing national tranquility and arriving at a more equitable adjustment of their vested rights:

JOEL B. MAYES
Chief—January 1888, to December, 1891

CHAPTER VIII

Treaty With The Cherokees 1846. Schools Established. Old Settler Payments. Keetoowah Society Organized. Organization of Military Companies. Cherokees Enter The Civil War. General Waite Surrenders.

Aug. 6, 1846. 9 Stat., 871. Ratified Aug. 8, 1846. Proclaimed Aug. 17, 1846. Articles of a treaty made and concluded at Washington, in the District of Columbia, between the United States of America, by three commissioners, Edmund Burke, William Armstrong, and Albion K. Parris; and John Ross, principal chief of the Cherokee Nation; David Vann, William S. Coody, Richard Taylor, T. H. Walker, Clement V. McNair, Stephen Foreman, John Drew, and Richard Fields, delegates duly appointed by the regularly constituted authorities of the Cherokee Nation; George W. Adair, John A. Bell, Stand Watie, Joseph M. Lynch, John Huss, and Brice Martin, a delegation appointed by, and representing that portion of the Cherokee tribe of Indians known and recognized as the "Treaty Party;" John Brown, Captain Dutch, John L. McCoy, Richard Drew, anad Ellis Phillips, delegates appointed by and representing, that portion of the Cherokee Tribe of Indians known and recognized as "Western Cherokees," or "Old Settlers."

Preamble. Whereas serious difficulties have, for a considerable time past, existed between the different portions of the people constituting and recognized as the Cherokee Nation of Indians, which it is desirable should be speedily settled, so that peace and harmony may be restored among them, and whereas certain claims exist on the part of the Cherokee Nation, and portions of the Cherokee people, against the United States; Therefore, with a view to the final and amicable settlement of the difficulties and claims before mentioned, it is mutually agreed by the several parties to this convention as follows, viz:

Lands Occupied by Cherokee Nation to be Secured to Whole People and a Patent to be Issued. 1830, Ch. 148. Article 1. That the land now occupied by the Cherokee Nation shall be secured to the whole Cherokee people for their common use and benefit; and a patent shall be issued for the same, including the eight hundred thousand acres purchased, together with the outlet west, promised by the United States, in conformity with the provisions relating thereto, contained in the third article of the treaty of 1835, and in the third section of the act of Congress, approved May twenty-eighth, 1830, which authorizes the President of the United States, in making exchanges of lands with the Indian tribes, "to assure the tribe or nation with which the exchange is made, that the United States will forever secure and guarantee to them, and their heirs or successors, the country so exchanged with them; and if they prefer it, that the United States will cause a patent or grant to be made and executed to them for the same: Provided, always, That such lands shall revert to the United States if the Indians become extinct or abandon the same.

Reversion to be in United States. All Difficulties and Disputes Adjusted, and a General Amnesty Declared. Laws to be Passed for Equal Protection, and for the Security of Life, Liberty, and Property. No One to be Punished for any Crime, Except on Conviction by a Jury. Article 2. All differences heretofore existing between the several parties of the Cherokee Nation are hererby settled and adjusted, and shall, as far as possible, be forgotten and forever buried in oblivion. All party distinctions shall cease, except so far as they may be necessary to carry out this convention or treaty. A general amnesty is hereby declared. All offences and crimes committed by a citizen or citizens of the Cherokee Nation against the nation, or against an individual or individuals, are hereby pardoned. All Cherokees who are now out of the nation are invited and earnestly requested to return to their homes, where they may live in peace, assured that they shall not be prosecuted for any offence heretofore committed against the Cherokee Nation, or any individual thereof. And this pardon and amnesty shall eextend to all who may now be out of the nation, and who shall return thereto on or before 1st day of December next. The several parties agree to unite in enforcing the laws against all future offenders. Laws shall be passed for equal protection, and for the sucurity of life, liberty, and property; and full authority shall be given by law to all or any portion of the Cherokee people, peaceably to assemble and petition their own government, or the Government of the United States, for the redress of grievances, and to discuss their rights. All armed police, light horse, and other military organizations, shall be abolished, and the laws enforced by the civil authority alone.

No one shall be punished for any crime or misdemeanor except on conviction by a jury of his country, and the sentence of a court duly authorized by law to take cognizance of the offence. And it is further agreed, all fugitives from justice, except those included in the general amnesty herein stipulated, seeking refuge in the territory of the United States, shall be delivered up by the authorities of the United States to the Cherokee Nation for trial and punishment.

Certain Claims Paid out of the $5,000,000 Fund to be Reimbursed by the United States. Article 3. Whereas certain claims have been allowed by the several boards of commissioners heretofore appointed under the treaty of 1835, for rents, under the name of improvements and spoliations, and for property of which the Indians were dispossessed, provided for under the 16th article of the treaty of 1835; and whereas the said claims have been paid out of the $5,000,000 fund; and whereas said claims were not justly chargeable to that fund, but were to be paid by the United States, the said United States agree to re-imburse the said fund the amount thus charged to said fund, and the same shall form a part of the aggregate amount to be distributed to the Cherokee people, as provided in the 9th article of this treaty; and whereas a further amount has been allowed for reservations under the provisions of the 13th article of the treaty of 1835, by said commissioners, and has been paid out of the said fund, and which said sums were properly chargeable to, and should have been paid by, the United States, the said United States further agree to re-imburse the amounts thus paid for reservations to said fund; and whereas the expense of making the treaty of New Echota were also paid out of said fund, when they should have been borne by the United States, the United States agree to re-imburse the same, and also to re-imburse all other sums paid to any agent of the government, and improperly charged to said fund; and the same also shall form a part of the aggregate amount to be distributed to the Cherokee people, as provided in the 9th article of this treaty.

Provision for the Equitable Interest of the Western Cherokees in Lands Ceded by Treaty of 1828. How the Value of Said Interest Shall be Ascertained. Release by Western Cherokees to United States. Article 4. And whereas it has been decided by the board of commissioners recently appointed by the President of the United States to examine and adjust the claims and difficulties existing against and between the Cherokees themselves, that under the provisions of the treaty of 1828, as well as in conformity with the general policy of the United States in relation to the Indian tribes, and the Cherokee Nation in particular, that that portion of the Cherokee people known as the "Old Settlers," or "Western Cherokees," had no exclusive title to the territory ceded in that treaty, but that the same was intended for the use of, and to be the home for, the whole nation, including as well that portion then east as that portion then west of the Mississippi; and whereas the said board of commissioners further decided that, inasmuch as the territory before mentioned became the common property of the Whole Cherokee Nation by the operation of the treaty of 1828, the Cherokees then west of the Mississippi, by the equitable operation of the same treaty, acquired a common interest in the lands occupied by the Cherokees east of the Mississippi river, as well as in those occupied by themselves west of that river, which interest should have been provided for in the treaty of 1835, but which was not, except in so far as they, as a constituent portion of the nation, retained, in proportion to their number, a common interest in the country west of the Mississippi, and in the general funds of the nation; and therefore they have an equal claim upon the United States for the value of that interest, whatever it may be. Now, in order to ascertain the value of that interest, it is agreed that the following principle shall be adopted, viz: All the investments and expenditures which are properly chargeable upon the sums granted in the treaty of 1835, amounting in the whole to five millions six hundred thousand dollars, (which investments and expenditures are particularly enumerated in the 15th article of the treaty of 1835,) to be first deducted from said aggregate sum, thus ascertaining the residuum or amount which would, under such marshalling of accounts, be left for per capita distribution among the Cherokees emigrating under the treaty of 1835, excluding all extravagant and improper expenditures, and then allow to the Old Settlers (or Western Cherokees) a sum equal to one third part of said residuum, to be distributed per capita to each individual of said party of "Old Settlers," or "Western Cherokees." It is further agreed that, so far as the Western Cherokees are concerned, in estimating the expense of removal and subsistence of an Eastern Cherokee, to be charged to the aggregate fund of five million six hundred thousand dollars above mentioned, the sum of removal and subsistence stipulated in the 8th article of the treaty of 1835, as commutation money in those cases in which the parties entitled to it removed themselves, shall be adopted. And as it affects the settlement with the Western Cherokees, there shall be no deduction from the fund before mentioned in consideration of any payments which may hereafter be made out of said fund; and it is hereby further understood and agreed, that the principle above defined shall embrace all those Cherokees west of the Mississippi. who emigrated prior to the treaty of 1835.

In consideraion of the foregoing stipulation on the part of the United States, the "Western Cherokees," or "Old Settlers," hereby release and quitclaim to the United States all right, title, interest, or claim they may have to a common property in the Cherokee lands east of the Mississippi River, and to exclusive ownership of the lands ceded to them by the treaty of 1833 west of the Mississippi, including the outlet west, consenting and agreeing that the said land, together with the eight hundred thousand acres ceded to the Cherokees by the treaty of 1835, shall be and remain the common property of the whole Cherokee people, themselves included.

Per Capita Allowance for Western Cherokees to be Held in Trust by United States, etc. Not Assignable. Committee of Five From "Old Settlers." Article 5. It is mutually agreed that the per capita allowance to be given to the "Western Cherokees,' or "Old Settlers, upon the principle above stated, shall be held in trust by the Government of the United States, and paid out to each individual belonging to that party or head of family, or his legal representatives. And it is further agreed that the per capita allowance to be paid as aforesaid shall not be assignable, but shall be paid directly to the persons entitled to it, or to his heirs or legal representatives, by the agent of the United States, authorized to make such payments.

And it is further agreed that a committee of five persons shall be appointed by the President of the United States, from the party of "Old Settlers,' whose duty it shall be, in conjunction with an agent of the United States, to ascertain what persons are entitled to the per capita allowance provided for in this and the preceding article.

Indemnity for "Treaty Party." Provisions for Heirs of Major Ridge, John Ridge, and Elias Boudinot. Proviso. Article 6. And whereas many of that portion of the Cherokee people known and designated as the "Treaty Party" have suffered losses and incurred expenses in consequence of the treaty of 1835, therefore, to indemnify the treaty party, the United States agree to pay to the said treaty party the sum of one hundred and fifteen thousand dollars, of which the sum of five thousand shall be paid by the United States to the heirs or legal representatives of Major Ridge, the sum of five thousand dollars to the heirs or legal representatives of John Ridge, and the sum of five thousand dollars to the heirs or legal representatives of Elias Boudinot, and the balance, being the sum of one hundred thousand dollars, which shall be paid by the United States, in such amounts and to such persons as may be certified by a committee to be appointed by the treaty party, and which committee shall consist of not exceeding five persons, and approved by an agent of the United States, to be entitled to receive the same for losses and damages sustained by them, or by those of whom they are the heirs or legal representatives: Provided, That out of said balance of one hundred thousand dollars. the present delegation of the treaty party may receive the sum of twenty-five thousand dollars, to be by them applied to the payment of claims and other expenses. And it is further provided that, if the said sum of one hundred thousand dollars should not be sufficient to pay all the claims allowed for losses and damages, that then the same shall be paid to said claimants pro rata, and which payments shall be in full of all claims and losses of the said treaty party.

Values of Salines to be Ascertained and Paid to Individuals Dispossessed of Them. Article 7. The value of all salines which were the private property of individuals of the Western Cherokees, and of which they were dispossessed, provided there be any such, shall be ascertained by the United States agent, and a commissioner to be appointed by the Cherokee authorities; and, should they be unable to agree, they shall select an umpire, whose decision shall be final; and the several amounts found due shall be paid by the Cherokee Nation, or the salines returned to their respective owners.

Payment for a Printing Press, Arms, etc. Article 8. The United States agree to pay to the Cherokee Nation the sum of two thousand dollars for a printing-press, materials, and other property destroyed at that time; the sum of five thousand dollars to be equally divided among all those whose arms were taken from them previous to their removal West by order of an officer of the United States; and the further sum of twenty thousand dollars, in lieu of all claims of the Cherokee Nation, as a nation, prior to the treaty of 1835, except all lands reserved, by treaties heretofore made, for school funds.

A Fair and Just Settlement of all Moneys Due the Cherokees Under the Treaty of 1835 to be Made. Article 9. The United States agree to make a fair settlement of all moneys due to the Cherokees, and subject to the per capita division under the treaty of 29th December, 1835, which said settlement shall exhibit all money properly expended under said treaty, and shall embrace all sums paid for improvements, ferries, spoliations, removal, and subsistence, and commutation therefor, debts and claims upon the Cherokee Nation of Indians, for the additional quantity of land ceded to said nation; and the several sums provided in the several articles of the treaty, to be invested as the general funds of the nation; and also all sums which may be hereafter properly allowed and paid under the provisions of the treaty of 1835. The aggregate of which said several sums shall be deducted from the sum of six-millions six hundred and forty-seven thousand and sixty-seven dollars, and the balance thus found to be due shall be paid over, per capita, in equal amounts, to all those individuals, heads of families, or their legal representatives, entitled to receive the same under the treaty of 1835, and the supplement of 1836, being all those Cherokees residing east at the date of said treaty and the supplement thereto.

Rights Under Treaty of Aug. 1, 1835, Not Affected. Article 10. It is expressly agreed that nothing in the foregoing treaty contained shall be construed as in any manner to take away or abridge any rights or claims which the Cherokees now residing in States east of the Mississippi River had, or may have, under the treaty of 1835 and the supplement thereto.

Certain Questions to be Submitted to Senate of United States. Article 11. Whereas the Cherokee delegates contend that the amount expended for the one year's subsistence, after their arrival in the west, of the Eastern Cherokees, is not properly chargeable to the treaty fund: it is hereby agreed that that question shall be submitted to the Senate of the United States for its decision, which shall decide whether the subsistence shall be borne by the United States or the Cherokee funds, and if by the Cherokees, then to say, whether the subsistence shall be charged at a greater rate than thirty-three, 33-100 dollars per head; and also the question, whether the Cherokee Nation be allowed interest on whatever sum may be found to be due the nation, and from what date and at what rate per annum.

Article 12. [Stricken out.]

Article 13. This treaty, after the same shall be ratified by the President and Senate of the United States, shall be obligatory on the contracting parties

In testimony whereof, the said Edmund Burke, William Armstrong, and Albion K. Parris, Commissioners as aforesaid, and the several delegations aforesaid, and the Cherokee nation and people, have hereunto set their hands and seals, at Washington aforesaid,this sixth day of August, in the year of our Lord one thousand eight hundred and forty-six.

Edmound Burke. Wm. Armstrong. Albion K. Parris.

Delegation of the Government Party:

Jno. Ross, Wm. S. Coody, R. Taylor, C. V. McNair, Stephen Foreman, John Drew, Richard Fields.

Delegation of the Treaty Party: Geo. W. Adair, J. A. Bell, S. Watie, Joseph M. Lynch, John Huss, Brice Martin (by J. M. Lynch, his attorney).

Delegation of the Old Settlers: Jno. Brown, Wm. Dutch, John L. McCoy, Richard Drew, Ellis F. Phillips.

(To each of the names of the Indians a seal is affixed.)

In presence of—

Joseph Bryan, of Alabama.
Geo. W. Paschal.
John P. Wolf, (Secretary of Board.)
W. S. Adair.
Jno. F. Wheeler.

On November 12, 1847 an act was passed by the national council for the establishment of the two national high schools, the Male and Female Seminaries, the two distinctive tribal schools that were thenceforth to be the pride of the nation and its most inportant factors in producing solidarity and patriotic instinct. Large sums were diverted and well spent for their maintainance, instead of being used for inervating payments. The only payments made to the Cherokees thereafter, were old settlers and emigrant payments of

1851 and 1852,		
1875,		10.60
1880,	"Bread money"	16.55
1883.	"Grass money," rent from Cherokee outlet	15.50
1886,		15.95
1890,		13.76
1894,	From sale of the outlet	365.70
1896,	Old Settlers	159.10
1902,	Destitute. $5.00 to single persons and $4.00 each to members of families	
1910,	Emigrants	133.19
1912,		$15.00
1914,		$12.00
1916,	Final disbursement	3.30

The Cherokees that fled to the mountains in 1838 congregated in western North Carolina where according to a roll made in 1849 by J. C. Mullay, federal census taker they numbered two thousand one hundred thirty three. They were placed on a reservation, called Qualla, where they still reside.

Fort Gibson was abandoned by the United States on June 23, 1857, and its buildings were formally transferred to the Cherokee Nation on the ninth day of September.

The Keetoowha society was originated among the Cherokees by Reverends Evan and John B. Jones in 1859. It is a secret society for the purpose of protecting national and community interests and for the fuller development of the nobler qualities of individualism. It has always been especially active in upbuilding the religious and patriotic instincts of its members, and is the only lodge in the United States whose principal emblem is the United States flag. During the civil war its insigna was a couple of pins crossed on the left coat lapel, and for that reason its members were known as "Pin Indians."

Early in 1861, Stand Watie organized a company to cooperate with the confederacy. Watie became the Captain; Buzzard, First Lieutenant; Wilson Suagee, Second Lieutenant; Charles Edwin Watie, Third Lieutenant and Henry Forrester, Orderly Sergeant. Their service was in Delaware District and Neutral Land which was a legal part of that district. Other companys having been formed they met near Fort Wayne on July 12, 1861 and formed the Cherokee Mounted Rifle regiment and elected the following officers: Colonel Stand Watie; Lieutenant Colonel, Thomas Fox Taylor[1]; Major, Elias Cornelius Boudinot; Adjutant, Charles E. Watie; Quarter Master, George Washington Adair[2]; Commissary, Joseph McMinn Starr, Sr.; Surgeons, Drs. Walter Thompson Adair and William Davis Polson; Chaplain, C. M. Slover; Sergeant Major, George West[3] and Joseph Franklin Thompson.

It has been impossible to obtain a roster of the several companies, but a fragmentary list of them, is:

Company A. Captain Buzzard; First Lt. Wilson Suagee, Second Lt.

Charles E. Watie, Third Lt. Dumplin O'Fields, Orderly Sergeant Henry Forrester. Privates: Lucien Burr Bell, Vann Ward, John Ketcher, Alfred Pigeon, Logan Pigeon, Jack Pigeon, Stand Suagee, Archibald Ballard, Edmond Duncan Carey, Olcut Moore, David Moore, John Moore, Jesse Pigeon, Daniel Squirrel, David Suagee, Charles Huss, Joseph Summerfield, Saladin Waite, Charles Lowrey, Thomas Jefferson Woodall, Ned Moore and Jack Squirrel.

Company B. Captain Robert Calvin Parks, First Lt. Ephriam Vann, Second Lt. Martin Buzzardflopper and Walker A. Daniel, Third Lt. Reese Candy. Privates: David Burkett, James Burkett, James Leon Butler, Red Bird Harris, William Harris, George Harlan, Fishtail, Mitchell Harlan, Cabbage Vann, Coon Vann, Yartunnah Vann, Joseph Vann, Alexander McCoy Rider and Thomas Jefferson Parks.

Company C. Captains Daniel Ross Coody, O. H. P. Brewer and Thomas Fox Brewer, First Lt. O. H. P. Brewer and Thomas Fox Brewer, Second Lts. Richard Crossland and William Snow Brewer, Third Lt. Reliford Beck, Orderly Sergeant Joseph Absalom Scales. Privates: James McDaniel Keyes, William Keys, Charles H. Campbell, Robert Taylor Hanks, James Ore, John Joshua Patrick, Wiliam V. Shepherd, Jesse Bean Burgess, John Walker Starr, John W. Jordan, Moses Nivens, John Nivens, Johnson Vann, Perry Andre Riley, George Lowrey, John A. Sevier, John Linder, Emory Ogden Linder McCoy Smith, Julius Caesar Linder, Russell Bean, Frank Smith, Samuel ("Buster") Smith, John Gunter Lipe[1], Thomas Stoneroad, Lorenzo D. Chambus,

"Written in the autograph album of Miss Victoria Hicks, who later married DeWitt Clinton Lipe, are these verses:

"To Miss Vic.

I stand at the portal and knock,
And tearfully, prayerfully wait.
O! who will unfasten the lock,
And open the beautiful gate?

Forever and ever and ever,
Must I linger and suffer alone?
Are there none that are able to sever,
The fetters that keep me from home?

My spirit is lonely and weary,
I long for the beautiful streets.
The world is so chilly and dreary,
And bleeding and torn are my feet.

Tahlequah, Cherokee Nation.
February 27th, 1861. J. G. Lipe."

John Gunter Lipe, Samuel ("Buster") Smith, John Nivens and ——— Parris were killed at the same time as was their commander Lt. Col. Thomas Fox Taylor, on Greenleaf Bayon, July 21, 1862.

Charles Drew, John Calhoun Sturdivant, Martin Butler Sturdivant, Archibald Lovett, John Lovett, Bruce Brown, Richard Neal, Frank Pettit, Clinton

Osmund, Richard Boggs, Gideon Reynolds, George Reynolds, Michael Hildebrand, Reese Hildebrand, Richard Brewer, Almon Martin, John Ferguson, William Patrick, Wilborn Vickery, Ellis Starr, James Hood, Benjamin Lafew, Pleasant Bean, Simpson G. Bennett, John Calhoun West, William M. West, James Polk West, Samuel Benge, George Yates, William Vann, William Harris, Michael Spaniard, John Q. Hayes, Surry Eaton Beck, William Beavert, George Kirk, William Beatty, Ellis Beck, Weatherford Beck, Jeffrey Beck, John Porter, Allen Latta, Diver Latta, Rider Whitekiller, Jolly Thornton, William Edwin Brown, Hugh Montgomery McPherson, George Elders, John Rogers, David Hicks, Wilson Boggs, Charles Kirk, Andrew Spaniard, Johnson Sosa, John Tinker, Henry Clay Starr, Johnson Riley, David R. Vann, Stephen Hildebrand, Joseph Martin Hildebrand, Charles Webber, Solomon Hosmer, John Coody, Henry Vann, Daniel Webster Vann, Marcellus Nivens, Joseph Riley, John McLain, James Starr, Lafayette Catron, William Lucas, Noah Scott and Sterling Scott.

Company D. Captain James Madison Bell, First Lt. Joseph Martin Lynch, Second Lt. John A. Raper, Third Lt. Pinson England, Orderly Sergeant Hugh Montgomery Adair. Privates: Lewis Ross Kell, Watie Lafabre, Proctor Landrum, Robert McDaniel, David Moore, Dumplin O'Fields, Johnson O'Fields, Kiowa Ratliff, Joseph Rogers, Napoleon Rogers, John Tinney, Thomas Tinney, Reuben R. Tyner, Hill Wilkinson, Moses Williams, Franklin Wright, John Talala Kell, Bear Timpson, John Adams, Walter Adair West, David McLaughlin, Saladin Watie, Charles Webber, Daniel Webster Vann, Benjamin Franklin Adair, William Penn Adair, David Jarrette Bell, George Bell, John Bell, James Brower, Arseenee, Gesseau Chouteau, Charles Coats, John Coats, Thomas Cox, Chuwalooka, Virgil Crawford, David Davis, Archibald Elliott, George W. Elliott, Walter Elliott, Martin England, Mitchell England, Henry Freshower, Joseph Freshower, Wallace Freshower, Daniel O'Conner Kell and Joseph Kell.

Company E. Captain Joseph Franklin Thompson, First Lt. Thomas Jefferson McGee, Second Lt. Stand Wawaseet, Third Lt. William Y. H. Foreman, Orderly Sergeant William Adolphus Daniel. Privates: Thompson Fields, Morrison Shoeboots, Stephen Walker, Joshua Daniel, Thomas Daniel, Ansel Green, Runabout Shoemaker, Chuwanosky, Alexander Beamer, Charles Hillian, E. G. Holcomb, Oliver Morris, Vann Ward, George M. Ward, Joseph Bledsoe, Lorenzo Bledsoe, Thomas Bledsoe, Isaac Dick, David McGee, John Shields, William Shields, Lewis Glenn, David Denton, Jack Caldwell, Boot, Moses Buck, Ross Thomas Carey, Caleb Conner, Colston, Corntassel, Broom Cramp, Harry Cramp, Ned Cramp, Riddle Cramp, John Martin Daniel, Marmaduke Daniel, John Davis, Nicholas Deerhead, John Doghead, John Duck, William Eckridge, L. L. Farley, John Fawling, Grasshopper, Stephen Gray Garbarina Hawk, John Hensley, Elam, Richard Fields, Dr. Charles H. Preston, George Fields, George Washington Fields, Ezekiah ("Bud") Fields, Ezekiah Fields, Albert Morris, John R. McGee, Albert McGee, Albert McGee, Tee-ge-ski, Daniel Miller, George Washington Trout, Oo-ni-quan-na, Jackson Jones, Stand Smith, Richard Pheasant, W. A. Kincade, James Burkett, Bee Marshall, John Marshall, James Horsefly, Ned Jailer, Drewry Jones,

James Jones, John Jones, Wilborn Jones, Charles Lisenbe, Washington Lisenbe, Eli Lisenbe, Andrew Miller, John Martin Miller, Joseph Gambold Miller, Thomas Miller, Mouse, Henry Nightkiller, Rock Shirt, James Rogers, Saltface, Lewis Rogers, William Rogers, Rottenman, Flea Smith, Joseph Smith, Stand Smith, Thomas Smith, Shell, Looney Tiger, Bear Timson, Wawaseet, William Webster Weir, Waseeter, James Waseeter, Womankiller, Charles Lowry, Ellis Dick, Luke Blevins, Samuel Palmer, Samuel Bright, Michael Condon, Dusky Rattlinggourd, William Conner Sr., William Conner, Jr., James Humphrey, George Frayser, Leander McGee, Samuel Steele, Elias Reader, Joseph Henry, Thomas Hadley, John Matthis, Joseph Rogers, Hill Wilkerson and David Pogue.

Company F. Not known.

Company G. Captains George Harlan Starr, Alexander Wofford and Ephriam Martin Adair, First Lts. Jonh Gott, John R. Wright, Ephriam Martin Adair and Joseph McMinn Starr Jr., Second Lts. Alexander Wofford, Ezekial Starr and Joseph Martin Lynch, Third Lts. Thomas Wilkerson, Andrew Cummings Johnson and Mark Bean, Orderly Sergeant —— Root, John Henry Danenburg and John R. Vann. Privates: Andrew Alberty, Jesse Clinton Alberty, Cornelius Bean, Mark Bean, William Bean, Releford Beck, Joseph Beck, Samuel E. Beck, James Blake, Jesse Adair, John Alexander, Jonathan Buffington, John W. Bumgarner, James Carselowry, Cornelius Clyne, Joel M. B. Clyne, William Collins, Virgil Crawford, Charles Crittenden, Wellington Crittenden, John Henry Danenburg, William Danenburg, John Denton, William Henry Drew, George Washington Crittenden, James Crittenden, Ignacious Few, Elias Gourd Foreman, George Gott, William Gott, John Griffin, John Brown ("Oce") Harlan, Erastus J. Howland, John Bean Johnson, Andrew Cummings Johnson, Kell, James Morgan, Calvin Sanders, David Sanders, Watson Sanders, William Sanders, John Sexton, John Scott, Samuel Sixkiller, Joseph Smallwood, John Smith, Lewis Stansel, Martin Butler Sturdivant, Ezekiah Taylor, John Thornton, William H. Thornton, Timothy Trott, Walter Duncan West, Stephen Whitmire, Benjamin C. Wilborn, Harrison Williams, Robert Wofford, John Martin, Charles W. Starr, James Starr, Joseph McMinn Starr, Jr., Walter Adair Starr, Benjamin Fisher, William Eubanks, Jeremiah Horn, George Noisywater, Johnson Watts, William Lafayette Trott, Andrew Reese, George Reese, Murray Reese, Caleb Wright, Hugh Montgomery Adair, Benjamin Franklin Adair, James Adair, Jesse M. Adair, John Bell Adair, George Washington Adair, Oscar Fitzaland Adair, Rufus Bell Adair, George Alberty, Joshua Alberty, John Alberty, Bailey Bacon, John Ellis Bean, Joseph McMinn Bean, James Lafayette Bigby, Thomas W. Bigby, David McLaughlin Beck, John Beck, James Bell, John Bell, Benjamin Jackson Bigby, William Edwin Brown, George Byers, Nicholas Byers, James Chandler, George George, James Choate, James Collins, William Collins, Harry Crittenden, William Daniel, George Davis, John Davis, William Henry Davis, James Devine, Harlin Eaton, Richard Eaton, Samuel Foreman, Thomas Gallagher, Benjamin Franklin Goss, Dennis Gonzales, John Griffin, Oliver Hogg, Philip Inlow, Sylvester Inlow, James Johnson, Shade Kagle, Jesse Killian, James R. Lamar, Gatz Lewis, Joseph Martin

Lynch, Richard Mayes, John Walker Mayfield, Alfred Miller, Joshua Morgan, Lone Morgan, Mark Morgan, George Reese, Charles Sanders, George Seabolt, Jeremiah Seabolt, Charles Washington Starr, Ellis Starr, James Starr, Allison Woodville Timberlake and John Vickery.

Company H. Captain John Thompson Mayes, First Lt. Daniel McKizzick, Second Lt. William Catterson, Third Lt. William H. Hendron, Orderly Sergeant John Stewart. Privates: William Ballard, George Buffington, Frank Conseen, Michael Davis, Maxwell Dixon, Green Graham, J. B. Graham, John Graham, John Golston, Matthew Golston, Benjamin Harmon, James Harmon, Murphy Harmon, W. A. Y. Hastings, Joseph Hazlett, William Hazlett, Joel Bryan Mayes, William Henry Mayes, John Phillips, Sooter Phillips, William Phillips, John Rogers Stover, James Tucker, John West, James Wilson, George W. Snardy, Charles Webber, John Hogan and John L. Davis.

Company I. Captains George W. Johnson and Bluford West Alberty, First Lts. James Benge and David McNair Faulkner, Second Lts. David McNair Faulkner and John Martin Bell, Third Lts. David McNair Faulkner, Orderly Sergeants William Myers and William Eubanks. Privates: Isaac Sanders, Thomas Pettit, John Faulkner, Wilson Sanders, John Stansil, Lewis Stansil, Buck Few, L. D. Chambers, Lewis Robards, Watt Downing, Shorey Pack, John Seminole, Robert Sanders, James Colby, Andrew Waters, John Walker Mayfield, Alexander McCoy Rider, William R. Foreman, William Eubanks, Charles Foreman, Joshua Sanders, Cornelius Sanders, Berry Price, John Price, John Hinman, Seven Fields, John Vanita, Josephus Simco, Bose Simco, George W. Alberty, William Butler, Cicero M. Cunningham, Charles A. Fargo, John Bell Adair, John Brown Harlan, Jesse Clinton Alberty, William McCracken, Lock Langley, Walter Scott Agnew, Joel McDaniel, Robert McDaniel, Samuel Foreman, Richard Pate, Cornelius Clyne, James Trott or Badger, Creek Pigeon, Creek Liver, Robert Waters, Amos Price John Gafford, Jesse Gafford, George Smoker, John H. Baugh and Joseph Wyatt.

Company K. Captain John Spears, First Lt. ——Foster, Second Lt. Lewis Weaver, Third Lt. Thomas Wilkerson. Privates: John W. Bumgarner, Samuel Hair, John Hair and Joseph Vann.

Company L. Captain James Thompson.

Shortly after the formation of the First Cherokee Mounted Rifles: Joel Mayes Byran organized and became Major of Bryan's Battalion. The letters of the companies are not known, but the companies were probably:

Captain C. C. Waters, First Lt. Jasper Wilkerson, Second Lt. James Chambers Yeargain, Third Lt. Daniel Herron, Orderly Sergeant Mal Banks Privates: David Copeland, George Sullivan, Henry Ward, William Ward, Lewis Baker, Wallace Brown, John Banks, George Banks, George Buchanan, Jefferson Cordell, Charles Baker, John Baker, Frank Davis, John Edwards, Samuel Gamble, Augustus Gailey, Joseph Gailey, Lucien Gailey, Warren Gailey, Randolph Gallion, William Clark, William Grinder, Caleb Gillett David Holt, George Holt, Henry Holt, William Latta, Matthew Latta, Henry Lukens, Alexander McCall, James Patton, Henderson Rotrammel, Henry

Rotrammel, James Rotrammel, John Rotrammel, Wilson Rotrammel, George Russell, Joseph Shelton, P. N. Thomas, Samuel Shelton, Monroe Smith, Robert Vinyard, George De Shields Ward and William Wilkerson.

Captain John R. Harden and First Lt. William Hendron. Private: Jacob M. Hiser.

Captain William Shannon.

On August 31, 1862 the First Cherokee Mounted Volunteers was organized with Stand Watie as Colonel, Lieutenant Colonel Robert Calvin Parks, Major Joseph Franklin Thompson, Quartermaster John Lynch Adair, Surgeon Dr. William J. Dupree, Chaplain John Harrell.

The Second Cherokee Mounted Volunteers was organized several months later under Colonel William Penn Adair, Lieutenant Colonel James Madison Bell and later, O. H. P. Brewer, Major Porter Hammock succeeded by John R. Harden, Quartermaster Joel Bryan Mayes, Commissary C. S. Lynch, Surgeon Dr. Waldemar Lindsley and Chaplain John Harrell. Shortly after the organization of the Second Cherokee Mounted Volunteers Moses Frye organized a battalion and became its Major, he was succeeded by Joseph Absalom Scales.

It has been impossible to identify the companies with the above given regiments and batalions, but fragmentary rosters are as follows:

Captain John W. ("Scoy") Brown, became demented and succeeded by E. G. Smith and later by John Gunter Scrimsher. First Lts. E. G. Smith, John Gunter Scrimsher and Dempsey Handle. Second Lt. Dempsey Handle, and Dumplin O'Fields, Third Lt. William Parrott, Orderly Sergeants John Anthony Foreman and Clark Charlesworth Lipe. Privates: John Chambers Jr., Joseph Chambers, George Davis, Deerham, Richard Fool, William Fool, Looney Hicks, Hogshooter, Jack Justice, Watie Lafabre, Talet Morgan, Johnson O'Fields, Tetenahi, Henry Covel, John Kickup, Joseph Turnover and George Runabout. In calling the roll orderly sergeant Lipe always finished with "Kickup, Turnover and Runabout."

Captain James Leon Butler, First Lt. Clement Vann Rogers, Second Lt. John Talala Kell, Third Lt. William Henry Mayes. Privates: Lucien Burr Bell, Daniel O'Conner Kell, Joseph Kell, Lewis Ross Kell, Robert Due Knight, Thomas Rogers Knight, James L. McLaughlin, Thomas McLaughlin, Thomas Lewis Rogers, Rogers Stover, Saladin Watie, Robert Fite, Henry Shaw, Joseph Landrum, Calvin Miller, Bevelly Bean Hickey, Bailey Bacon Thomas Bacon, John Calhoun West, William M. West, George West, John Gunter Scrimsher, Robert Mann, Rufus Montezuma Morgan, Calvin Jones Hanks, Talet Morgan, Benjamin Franklin Adair, Green Parris, Charles H. Campbell, Robert Taylor Hanks, John Chambers Jr. and Maxwell Chambers. Butler's company was probably in the organization at Ft. Wayne in July, 1861.

Captain Benjamin Wisner Carter, First Lt. Richard Carter, Second Lt. Johnson Fields, Third Lt. Catcher Teehee. Privates: Seaborn F. Tyner, Reuben Bartley Tyner, Abraham Woodall, Ezekial Bolin, Walter Bolin, Simon Boynton, John Ross Carter, Charles Coody, Millard Filmore, Joseph Freshower Joseph Hedricks, William Hedricks, Isaac Keys, Looney Keys.

Monroe Keys, Samuel H. Keys, Samuel Houston Mayes, Worcester McCoy, Lewis Clark Ramsey, Randolph Riley, Samuel A. Riley, Antoine Rogers, Andrew Tyner, Daniel Teehee, George Teehee, John Teehee and Thomas Teehee. Possibly a company of the First Cherokee Mounted Volunteers.

Captain John Childers', First Lt. Samuel Lee and Second Lt. Ellis Sanders'. This was probably a company of Frye's Battallion.

Captain John Porum Davis, First Lt. Charles Drew, Second Lt. James Christopher McCoy, Third Lt. John Q. Hayes, Orderly Sergeant Richard Neal, Second Sergeant John Evans, Third Sgt. Teesee Guess, Fourth Sgt. Samuel Campbell, Fifth Sergeant Heavy Butler, First Corporal George Downing, Second Corp. John Poorbear, Third Corp. Albert P. Shepherd, Fourth Corp. Thomas O. Bowles. Privates: George Arnold, Joe Ashes, James Applegate, George Bowles, James Bowles, Johnson Bowles, Samuel Bowles, Badger, Johnson Baldridge, David Barberry, Isaac W. Bertholf, Robin Bob, John Butterfield, Cahlahhoola, Chunarchur, Crane, David Davis, Small Dirt, David Downing, Edward Downing, Joseph Downing, Benjamin Ellis, Lafayette Ellis, Stand Foreman, Flyingaway, Buck Girty, Simon Girty, Buffalo Garves, James Griffin, William Griffin, David Harris, Nathan Hicks, Walter Jackson, John Kettle, Allen Latta, Hercules T. Martin, John Miller, George Morris, Daniel McCoy, W. S. McCoy, David McLaughlin, Oolskunee, Oowalooka, Joseph Ore, Satanka, Joseph Shepherd, William Shepherd, George Smoker, Splitnose, Ellis Starr, Ezekial Starr, George Starr, Tobacco John, James Starr, James Starr, George Sunshine, Allison Woodville Timberlake, David Vann, Jesse Vann, Monkey Vann, Yartunnah Vann, Thomas Watts and Reuben Williams.

Captain William Eckridge First Lt. Thomas Jefferson McGee, Second Lt. Lewis Rogers, Third Lt. Albert McGee, Orderly Sergeant Dr. Charles H. Preston. Privates: David Bashears, Elap, George Broughill, David Burkett, John Beamer, Joseph Bledsoe, Lorenzo Bledsoe, John Caldwell, Ellis Dick, Isaac Dick, Dick Duck, John Duck, Ezekial ("Bud") Fields, Ezekial Fields, George Washington Fields, George Fields, Henry Fields, Matthew Fields, Thompson Fields, George Frazier, John Brown Harlan, Samuel G. Heffington, Scott Hunt, Calvin Jackson, Harvey Jackson, Benjamin King, Samuel Kinkade, Charles Lisenbe, Washington Lisenbe, Bee Marshall, John Mathis, David A. McGee, John McMurtrey, Solomon Moore, Oliver Morris, Wilson Muskrat, David Pogue, George Raper, John L. Rogers, Joseph Rogers, Shotpouch, Frank Simms, William Stover, Ticanooly, George Washington Trout, George Washington Walker, Vann Ward, Hill Wilkerson and Albert Morris. This company was probably first, a part of Bryan's Battallion and later (Co. D?) of the Second Cherokee Mounted Volunteers.

Captain John W. Fagan.

Captain Richard Fields, First Lt. Moses Edwards, Second Lt. Bevelly Bean Hickey, Orderly Sergeant Coon Vann. Privates: George ("Buckskin") Waters, Sunday Hogtoter, Benjamin Fisher, Hogstoter, George Waters, Yartunna Proctor, Tetenahi, Benjamin King, Dreadfulwater, Lorenzo D. Chambers, John Quincy A. Smith, William Henry Mayes, Robert Mc-

Lemore and Thomas Henry Still.

Captain Alexander Foreman.

Captain Roswell W. Lee, First Lts. Henry Forrester and J. W. Gregg, Second Lts. William Taylor and Riley Wise Lindsey, Orderly Sergeants John Reese, Taylor Clark and John R. Vann. Privates: Lee Silk, Thomas Peter, Brush, Charles Hicks, Rider Cloud, William Crane, William Womack, John Polk, Robert Barnard, James Brower, McCoy Smith, George W. Alberty, Arseena, Samuel Benge, Alonzo Bledsoe, Thomas Bigby, James Crittenden, John Doghead, J. Hilary Clark, John Campeau, Richard Hurd, John Marshall Isaac Proctor, Ootlenowi, Ice Nitts, William Phillips, James Seymour, Ketcher Solomon, Bailey Bacon, John Bacon, William Taylor, J. Riley Baker, Cap Edwards, William Walker and William Deadrick. This was an artillery company. They got their battery; three twelve pound howitzers and a 2.25 pound brass rifle, early in 1863. One twelve pounder lost in Elk Creek after the battle of Honey Springs and found by the federals while searching for dead. Three other guns were added but their sources not known. One gun bursted by over charging at the capture of the Steamer J. R. Williams on June 15, 1864 and the others were surrendered to the United States at the close of the war.

Captain Moses C. Frye, First Lt. John Childers, Second Lt. William Alexander and John Edward Gunter, Third Lt. William Barnes. Privates: Charles A. Fargo, Isaac Sanders, John Price, Thomas Jefferson Carter, Samuel Candy and Ellis Sanders. This is probably the same company that was commanded by John Childers after Captain Frye organized and became Major of the battalion.

Captain Samuel Gunter, First Lt. William Alexander, Second Lt. Calvin Jones Hanks, Third Lt. Rufus Bell Adair, Orderly Sergeant Robert Taylor Hanks. Privates: Felix N. Witt, John Bell Adair, Samuel Candy, John Edward Gunter, Stephen N. Carlile, George Washington Fields, Charles Jones, Matthew Jones, James Ussrey, Philip Ussrey, Tobe Ussrey, Lock Langley, John Price, Allen Matthis, William McCracken, Robert Alexander, John Poorbear, John Candy, Henderson Holt, John Gafford, George Smoker, John Lafayette Brown, David Ussrey, William Ussrey, John H. Shanks, Charles Harmon, Buck Elmo, Jefferson Eldridge, George Yates, Moses Edwards, Seven Fields, Bertie Simmons, Keekee Gunter, Jesse Gafford, Jolly Colwell, Samuel Wheeler, Moses Holt, Joseph Perdue, John Perdue, John Frazell, John Gonzales, Snake Puppy, William Johnson and Benjamin Johnson.

Captain Charles Holt, First Lts. Montgomery Morgan and Squire Baldridge, Second Lts. John D. Alberty and Jack Miller, Orderly Sergeants James Reed and Coon Vann. Privates: Stephen N. Carlile, Charles Jones, James Ussrey, George Reese, Stephen Whitmire, George ("Buckskin") Waters, Samuel Payne, John Marshall, Little Leach, Charles Hicks, Arseena Vann, Abraham Lincoln, J. L. McCorkle and William Lowrey.

Captain Richard O'Fields, First Lt. Johnson O'Fields.

Captains Thomas Jefferson Parks and John W. Fagan, First Lt. John

W. Fagan. Privates: John Pinkney Chandler, Aaron Head Beck and Releford Beck.

Captain Clement Vann Rogers, First Lt. Joseph Martin Lynch, Second Lt. Thomas Lewis Rogers, Third Lt. Henry Chambers, Orderly Sergeant Robert McDaniel. Privates: Richard Griffin, Daniel Webster Vann, Napoleon Bonapart Rogers, Isaac Howell, John Hair, John W. Bumgarner, Caleb Wright, Virgil Crawford, Joseph Rogers, Antoine Rogers, Maxwell Chambers, Joseph Martin Hildebrand, Hilary Clark, Thomas Hubbard, Wilkerson Hubbard, Reuben Finley, Moses McDaniel, James Beavert, Lemuel Smith, John O'Reiley and Joseph H. Bennett.

Captain Joseph Smallwood.

Captain John M. Smith, First Lt. Edward Foreman, Second Lt. Heman Lincoln Foreman, Third Lt. Martin Buzzardflopper, Orderly Sergeant Looney Tiger. Privates: Richard L. Martin, John Palmer, Moses Williams and Nelson McDaniel.

Captain John W. T. Spencer, First Lt. Robert McDaniel, Second Lt. James Beavert, Third Lt. Randolph Coker, Orderly Sergeant Daniel Webster Vann. Privates: Houston Allen, John Bell, John Boot, James Cannon, Virgil Crawford, David Cogswell, Archibald Elliott, George W. Elliott, James Elliott, Walter Elliott, Jefferson Gage, John Griffin, Alexander Gordon, Wiley McNair Guilliams, William Hicks, Daniel O'Conner Kell, Joseph Kell, Richard L. Martin, Nelson McDaniel, David McLaughlin, Ezekial McLaughlin, John McNulty, John McPherson, John Palmer, John Poorbear, James Benjamin Franklin Rogers, James Spencer, Napoleon Bonapart Rogers, Claybourne Taylor, Andrew Townsend, Reuben R. Tyner, Bryan Ward, James Ward, John Ward, James Williams, John Williams, Moses Williams, John Witt and William McCracken.

Captain James Stewart, First Lt. ———Catterson, Second Lt. George W. Snardy, Third Lt. Newton Swinney, Orderly Sergeant John Anderson. Privates: James Brower, Frank Bryan, Jack Bryan, Samuel Bryan, John Burns, John Campeau, John Campbell, Thomas Coffelt, John Crabtree, Thomas Eby, Charles Edmondson, N. B. Edmondson, George Washington Elliott, J. William Gregg, Daniel O'Conner Kell, Joseph Kell, Alexander L. Martin, Napoleon B. McCreary, John Nance, M. P. Snider, John Stotts, Joseph Lynch Thompson, George Wagoner, Walter Adair West and James Yost.

Captains William Taylor and William Eubanks, First Lt. William Eubanks, Second Lt. George Reese, Third Lt. John Alexander.

Captain Hugh Tinnon, First Lt. Jeter Thompson Cunningham, Second Lt. William Evans, Third Lt. Joseph Ingle, Orderly Sergeant Patrick Patton. Privates: Hugh Abercrombie, Charles Barney, Henry Baumister, John Bradshaw, John Brickey, William Brickey, Mitchell Blevins, Ransom Blevins Thompson Blevins, John Abercrombie, Lafayette Abercrombie, Freeman Authur, John Chastain, Chuwanosky, Henry Coats, John Coats, James Coleman, William Compton, Alexander Copeland, Austin Copeland, Andrew Countryman, George Countryman, John Countryman, Samuel Countryman, David Denton, Jack Dickey, Edward Evans, Lewis Fair, James Sanford

Fields, Moses Fields, Robert Francis, Henry Gates, William Green, Richard Holland, William Howell, John Ingle, Thomas Ingle, John Isbell, Columbus Isbell, Chapman Johnson, Thomas Johnson, Elijah Keith, John Keith, Thomas Keywood, William Keywood, Thomas King, Samuel Kirkpatrick, Henrry Louks, P. G. Lynch, Charles McFadden, Tella McFadden, Thomas McFadden, Samuel McPhail, Marshall McSpadden, John O'Bryan, Shipman Reed, John Rhea, John Rogers, Samuel C. Sager, John Smith, Elisha Stover, Rogers Stover, John Calhoun Sturdivant, Zimerhew Thomas, James Tinnon, William Tinnon, Stephen Walker, David White, James White and Marion White.

Captain John Shepherd Vann, First Lt. Walker Carey. Private Calvin Jones Hanks.

Captain Charles E. Watie, First Lt. Wilson Suagee, Second Lt. Samuel Mush, Third Lt. John Maw. Privates: John Ketcher, Alfred Pigeon, Logan Pigeon, Jack Pigeon, Stand Suagee and Ezekial Beck.

Captain Erastus Howland, First Lt. ———Knight, Second Lt. ——— Boone, Third Lt. Antoine LaHay. Privates: Heman Lincoln Foreman, Alexander McCoy Rider and Riley J. Keys.

Captain William H. Turner, First Lt. Antoine LaHay, Second Lt. Return Jonathan Foreman, William W. Bark, Orderly Sergeant Jacob Markham. Privates: Amos Foreman, Squataleechee, William Cochran, Carter Daniel Markham, George Foreman, Lewis Cochran, John Cochran, Henry Blalock, George Arseena, J. P. Blackstone, Joseph Bledsoe, Littlebird, Samuel Cochran, Charles Cochran Sr., Charles Cochran Jr., John S. Coats, Wilson Cordery, Thomas Cordery, James Davis Sr., James Davis Jr., W. A. Dennison, Jackson Foreman, Looney Downing, Thomas Harvingston, George W. Kirk, John Inlow, Charles Jumper, Robert Kanard, John LaHay, John Mosley, John Martin Miller, Andrew Miller, Washington Miller, Robert J. Mann, Wilson Muskrat, James Proctor, Nelson Proctor, Johnson Thomas, Thomas C. Thomas, James Winifield, Ulrich Waldron, Samuel Wisner, James Wortham, John O'Reilly, Charles Hillen and William C. Daniel.

Governor Rector of Arkansas wrote Chief Ross on January 29, 1861 requestng the cooperation of the Cherokees with the Confederacy to which Chief answered avowing neutrality[2]. The Chief by letters of May 17th[3], June 12th[4] and 17[5] and in a proclamation of May 17th reiterated his stand for this principle[6]. On July 12th Stand Watie the political opponent of Chief Ross organized his regiment and shortly afterwards the chief called a general convention of the Cherokees to meet at Tahlequah on August 21st. The Chief again urged neutrality[7] and the convention passed resolutions in keeping with that sentiment[8]. The Chief wrote General McCullough that "we are authorized to form an alliance with the Confederate States, which we are determined to do as early as practicable. This determination may give rise to movements against the Cherokee people upon their northern border. To be prepared for any such emergency, we have deemed it prudent to proceed to organize a regiment of mounted men and tender them for service. They will be raised forthwith, by Colonel John Drew, and if received by you will require to be armed"[9]

Chief Ross appointed the following officers for Drew's regiment: Colonel John Drew, Lieutenant Colonel William Potter Ross, Major Thomas Pegg, Adjutant James S. Vann, Surgeon Dr. Robert D. Ross, Chaplain Lewis Downing. Captains: Co. A, Pickens M. Benge; Co. B, Richard Fields; Co. C John Porum Davis; Co. D, James McDaniel; Co. E, Lewis Ross, succeeded by Newton Hildebrand; Co. F, William W. Alberty; Co. G, Anderson Springston; Co. H, Nicholas Byers Sanders; Co. I, George M. Murrell, succeeded by Jefferson Hicks; Co. K, George Washington Scraper and Co. L, James Vann

A treaty was concluded at Hunters Home, the residence of George M. Murrell on October 7, 1861 between the Confederate States and the Cherokee Nation and two days later Chief Ross delivered his message to the national council:

MESSAGE OF THE PRINCIPAL CHIEF TO THE CHEROKEE NATION.

To the National Committee and Council in National Council convened:

Friends and Fellow-Citizens: Since the last meeting of the National Council events have occurred that will occupy a prominent place in the history of the world. The United States have been dissolved and two governments now exist. Twelve of the states composing the late Union have erected themselves into a government under the style of the Confederate States of America, and, as you know, are now engaged in a war for their independence. The contest thus far has been attended with success almost uninterrupted on their side and marked by brilliant victories. Of its final result there seems to b no grounds for a reasonable doubt. The unanimity and devotion of the people of the Confederate States must sooner or later secure their success over all opposition and result in the establishment of their independence and a recognition of it by the other nations of the earth.

At the beginning of the conflict I felt that the interest of the Cherokee people would be best maintained by remaining quiet and not involving themselves in it prematurely. Our relations had long existed with the United States Government and bound us to amity and peace alike with all the States. Neutrality was proper and wise so long as there remained a reasonable probability that the difficulty between the two sections of the Union would be settled, as a different course would have placed all our rights in jeopardy and might have lead to the sacrifice of the people. But when there was no longer any reason to believe that the Union of the States would be continued there was no cause to hesitate as to the course the Cherokee Nation should pursue. Our geographical position and domestic institutions allied us to the south, while the developments daily made in our vicinity and as to the purposes of the war waged against the Confederate States clearly pointed out the path of our interest.

These conisderations produced a unanimity of sentiment among the people as to the policy adopted by the Cherokee Nation, which was clearly expressed in their general meeting held at Tahlequah on the 21st of August last. A copy of the proceedings of that meeting is submitted for your information.

In accordance with the declarations embodied in the resolutions then adopted the Executive Council deemed it proper to exercise the authority conferred upon them by the people there assembled. Messengers dispatched to General Albert Pike, the distinguished Indian Commissioner of the Confederate States, who having negotiated treaties with the neighboring Indian nations, was then establishing relations between his government and the Comanches and other Indians in the Southwest, who bore a copy of the proceedings of the meeting referred to, and a letter from the executive authorities, proposing on behalf of the nation to enter into a treaty of alliance, defensive and offensive, with the Confederate States.

In the exercise of the same general authority, and to be ready as far as practicable to meet any emergency that might spring up on our northern borddder, it was thought proper to raise a regiment of mounted men and tender its services to General McCullough. The people responded with alacrity to the call, and it is believed the regiment will be found as efficient as any other like number of men. It is now in the service of the Confederate States for the purpose of aiding in defending their homes and the common rights of the Indian nations about us. This regiment is composed of ten full companies, with two reserve companies, and, in addition to the force previously authorized to be raised to operate outside of the Nation by General McCullough, will show that the Cherokee people are ready to do all in their power in defense of the Confederate cause, which has now become our own. And it is to be hoped that our people will spare no means to sustain them, but contribute liberally to supply any want of comfortable clothing for the approaching season.

In years long since past our ancestors undaunted those who would invade their mountain homes beyond the Mississippi. Let not their descendants of the present day be found unworthy of them, or unable to stand by the chivalrous men of the South by whose side they may be called to fight in self-defense. The Cherokee people do not desire to be involved in war, but self-preservation fully justifies them in the course they have adopted, and they will be recreant to themselves if they should not sustain it to the utmost of their humble abilities.

A treaty with the Confederate States has been entered into and is now submitted for your ratification. In view of the circumstances by which we are surrounded and the provisions of the treaty it will be found to be the most important ever negotiated on behalf of the Cherokee Nation, and will mark a new era in its history. Without attempting a recapitulation of all its provisions, some of its distinguishing features may be briefly enumerated.

The relations of the Cherokee Nation are changed from the United to the Confederate States, with guarantees of protection and a recognition in future negotiations only of its constitutional authorities. The metes and boundaries, as defined by patent from the United States, are continued, and a guarantee given for the Neutral Land or a fair consideration in case it should be lost by war or negotiation and an advance thereon to pay the national debt and to meet other contingencies. The payment of all our annuities and security of all our investments are provided for. The jurisdiction of the Cherokee courts over all members of the Nation, whether by birth, marriage, or adoption, is recognized.

Our title to our lands is placed beyond dispute. Our relations with the

Confederate States is that of a ward; theirs to us that of a protectorate, with powers restricted. The district court, with a limited civil and criminal jurisdiction, is admitted into the country instead of being located at Van Buren, as was the United States court. This is perhaps one of the most important provisions of the treaty, and secures to our citizens the great constitutional right of trial by a jury of their own vicinage, and releases them from the petty abuses and vexations of the old system, before a foreign jury and in a foreign country. It gives us a delegate in congress on the same footing with delegates from the Territories, by which our interests can be represented; a right which has long been withheld from the Nation and which has imposed upon it a large expense and a great injustice. It also contains reasonable stipulation in regard to the appointing powers of the Agent and in regard to licensed traders. The Cherokee Nation may be called upon to furnish troops for the defense of the Indian country, but is never to be taxed for the support of any war in which the States may be engaged.

The Cherokee people stand upon new ground. Let us hope that the clouds which overspread the land will be dispersed and that we shall prosper as we have never before done. New avenues of usefulness and distinction will be open to the ingenious youth of the country. Our rights of self-government will be more fully recognized, and our citizens will be no longer dragged off upon flimsy pretexts, to be imprisoned and tried before distant tribunals. No just cause exists for domestic difficulties. Let them be buried with the past and only mutual friendship and harmony be cherished.

Our relations with the neighboring tribes are of the most friendly character. Let us see that the white path which leads from our country to theirs be obstructed by no act of ours, and that it be open to all those with whom we may be brought into intercourse.

Amid the excitement of the times it is to be hoped that the interests of education will not be allowed to suffer and that no interruption be brought into the usual operations of the government. Let its officers continue to discharge their appropriate duties.

As the services of some of your members may be required elsewhere and all unnecessary expense should be avoided, I respectfully recommend that the business of the session be promptly discharged.

John Ross.

Executive Department,
Tahlequah, C. N., October 9, 1861.

On October 28th the council issued the following declaration:

Declaration by the People of the Cherokee Nation of the Causes Which Have Impelled them to Unite Their Fortunes With Those of the Confederate States of America.

When circumstances beyond their control compel one people to sever the ties which have long existed between them and another state or confederacy, and to contract new alliances and establish new relations for the security of their rights and liberties, it is fit that they should publicly declare the reasons by which their action is justified.

The Cherokee people had its origin in the South; its institutions are similar to those of the Southern States, and their interests identical with theirs. Long since it accepted the protection of the United States of America, contracted with them treaties of alliance and friendship, and allowed themselves to be to a great extent governed by their laws.

In peace and war they have been faithful to their engagements with the United States. With much hardship and injustice to complain of, they resorted to no other means than solicitation and argument to obtain redress. Loyal and obedient to the laws and the stipulations of the treaties, they served under the flag of the United States, shared the common dangers, and were entitled to a share in the common glory, to gain which their blood was freely shed on the battlefield.

When the dissentions between the Southern and Northern States culminated in a separation of State after State from the Union they watched the progress of events with anxiety and consternation. While their institutions and the contiguity of their territory to the states of Arkansas, Texas and Missouri made the cause of the seceding States necessarily their own cause, their treaties had been made with the United States, and they felt the utmost reluctance even in appearance to violate their engagements or set at naught the obligations of good faith.

Conscious that they were a people few in numbers compared with either of the contending parties, and that their country might with no considerable force be easily overrun and devasted and desolation and ruin be the result if they took up arms for either side, their authorities determined that no other course was consistent with the dictates of prudence or could secure the safety of heir people and immunity from the horrors of a war waged by an invading enemy than a strict neutrality, and in this decision they were sustained by a majority of the Nation.

That policy was accordingly adopted and faithfully adhered to. Early in the month of June of the present year the authorities of the Nation declined to enter into negotiations for an alliance with the Confederate States, and protested against the occupation of the Cherokee country by their troops, or any other violation of their neutrality. No act was allowed that could be construed by the United States to be a violation of the faith of treaties.

But Providence rules the destinies of nations, and events, by inexorable necessity, overrule human resolutions. The number of the Confederate States increased to eleven, and their government is firmly established and consolidated. Maintaining in the field an army of two hundred thousand men, the war became for them but a succession of victories. Disclaiming any intention to invade the Northern States, they sought only to repel invaders from their own soil and to secure the right of governing themselves. They claimed only the privilege asserted by the Declaration of American Independence, and on which the right of the Northern States themselves to self-government is formed, of altering their form of government when it became no longer tolerable and establishing new forms for the security of their liberties.

Throughout the Confederate States we saw this great revolution effected without violence or suspension of the laws or the closing of the courts. The military power was nowhere placed above the civil authorities. None were seized and imprisoned at the mandate of arbitrary power. All division among the people disappeared, and the determination became unanimous that there should never again be any union with the Northern States. Almost as one man all who were able to bear arms rushed to the defense of an invaded country, and nowhere has it been found necessary to compel men to serve or to enlist mercenaries by the offer of extraordinary bounties.

But in the Northern States the Cherokee people saw with alarm a violated constitution, all civil liberty put in peril, and all rules of civilized warfare and the dictates of common humanity and decency unhesitatingly disregarded. In states which still adhered to the Union a military despotism had displaced the civil power and the laws became silent amid arms. Free speech and almost free thought became a crime. The right of the writ of habeas corpus, guaranteed by the constitution, disappeared at the nod of a Secretary of State or a general of the lowest grade. The mandate of the Chief Justice of the Supreme Court was at naught by the military power and this outrage on common right approved by a President sworn to support the constitution. War on the largest scale was waged, and the immense bodies of troops called into the field in the absence of any law warranting it under the pretense of suppressing unlawful combination of men.

The humanities of war, which even barbarians respect, were no longer thought worthy to be observed. Foreign mercenaries and the scum of the cities and the inmates of prisons were enlisted and organized into brigades and sent into Southern States to aid in subjugating a people struggling for freedom, to burn, to plunder, and to commit the basest of outrages on the women; while the heels of armed tyranny trod upon the necks of Maryland and Missouri, and men of the highest character and position were incarceraated upon suspicion and without process of law, in jails, in forts, and prison ships, and even women were imprisoned by the arbitrary order of a President and Cabinet Ministers; while the press ceased to be free, and the publication of newspapers was suspended and their issues seized and destroyed; the officers and men taken prosiners in the battles were allowed to remain in captivity by the refusal of the Government to consent to an exchange of prisoners; as they had left their dead on more than one field of battle that had witnessed their defeat, to be buried and their wounded to be cared for by southern hands.

Whatever causes the Cherokee people may have had in the past to complain of some of the southern states, they cannot but feel that their interests and destiny are inseparably connected with those of the south. The war now waging is a war of Northern cupidity and fanaticism against the institution of African servitude; against the commercial freedom of the south, and against the political freedom of the states, and its objects are to annihilate the sovereignty of those states and utterly change the nature of the general government.

The Cherokee people and their neighbors were warned before the war commenced that the first object of the party which now holds the powers of government of the United States would be to annul the institution of slavery in the whole Indian country and make it what they term free territory and after a time a free state; and they have been also warned by the fate which has befallen those of their race in Kansas, Nebraska and Oregon that at no distant day they too would be compelled to surrender their country at the demand of Northern rapacity, and be content with an extinct nationality, and with reserves of limited extent for individuals, of which their people would soon be dispoiled by speculators, if not plundered unscrupulously by the state.

Urged by these considerations, the Cherokees, long divided in opinion, became unanimous, and like their brethren, the Creeks, Seminoles, Choctaws, and Chickasaws, determined, by the undivided voice of a General Convention of all the people, held at Tahlequah on the twenty-first day of August, in the present year, to make common cause with the South and share its fortunes.

In now carrying this resolution into effect and consummating a treaty of alliance and friendship with the Confederate States of America the Cherokee people declare that they have been faithful and loyal to their engagements with the United States until, by placing their safety and even their national existence in eminent peril, those States have released them from those engagements.

Menaced by a great danger, they exercise the inalienable right of self defense, and declare themselves a free people, independent of the Northern States of America, and at war with them by their own act. Obeying the dictates of prudence and providing for the general safety and welfare, confident of the rectitude of their intentions and true to the obligations of duty and honor, they accept the issue thus forced upon them, unite their fortunes now and forever with those of the Confederate States, and take up arms for the common cause, and with entire confidence in the justice of that cause and with a firm reliance upon Divine Providence, will resolutely abide the consequences.

THOMAS PEGG,
President of National Committee.

JOSHUA ROSS,
Clerk National Committee.

LACEY MOUSE,
Speaker of Council.

THOMAS B. WOLF,
Clerk of Council.

Approved. JOHN ROSS.

Brigadier General Albert Pike was assigned to the command of the Indian Territory on November 22, 1861. The battle of Bird Creek between Opothleyohola's federal Creek refugees and the confederate forces, including Drew's regiment was fought on December 9th. After the battle of Pea Ridge, in Arkansas on March 6, 1862, the confederate authorities diverted all possible forces and equipment to the east side of the Mississippi. Thus the Cherokee Nation was left with scarcely any protection from their confederate allies. The Cherokees received no pay as soldiers. Funds, ammunitions, artillery, arms, commissary supplies and clothing that had been meant for them was stopped at Fort Smith and Little Rock[1]. During the month of March, Brigadier General Albert Pike paid to Cherokee national treasurer, Lewis Ross, at his brother John Ross' residence at Park Hill, as per the requirements of the late treaty, one hundred and fifty thousand dollars in confederate bills and seventy thousand dollars in gold.

A federal expedition was outfitted at Fort Scott and started to the Cherokee Nation on March 6, 1862. It was designated the "Indian expedition" and was under the command of Colonel William Weer, who wrote from Le Roy, Kansas on the thirteenth of June that "John Ross is undoubtedly with us, and will come out openly when we reach there."[2] The Indian expedition rapidly approached from the north by way of Humboldt, Kansas[3] and Cowskin Prairie[4], Cherokee Nation. Brigadier General Pike had made his headquarters at Camp McCullough near Red River since the battle of Pea Ridge and a Colonel J. J. Clarkson had been appointed as confederate commander in the Cherokee Nation on June 26th, ranking Colonels Watie and Drew, and independent of Brigadier General Pike. His unpicketed camp at Locust Grove was surprised a little before daybreak on July 3 by Colonel Weer. Col. Clarkson and several of his men were captured. Nearly all of Drew's regiment which had been camped on Flat Rock Creek on the west side of Grand River, some twenty miles southwest of Locust Grove, joined the federal forces on Cabin Creek on the third, fourth, fifth and sixth of July. Colonel Drew remained loyal to the confederacy. The Second Indian Home Guards federal service was organized at Cabin Creek on the fifth under Colonel John Ritchey. William A. Phillips became colonel of the Third Indian Home Guards, U. S. A. The Home Guards returned to Flat Rock on the eleventh.

Captain Harris S. Green, of the Sixth Kansas Cavalry, which was a part of the Indian expedition arrived at Chief Ross' on July 15th and Col. Weer occupied Fort Gibson on the same date. Captain Greeno reported that "Chief Ross feels very badly on acount of our not having any forces on this side of the river (Grand) for protection."[1] Over two hundred members of Home Guards regiments were at Chief Ross' at the time and Captain Greeno went through the formality of arresting Chief Ross, Lieutenant Colonel William P. Ross, Major Thomas Pegg, First Lieutenants Anderson Benge and Joseph Chooie, Second Lieutenants Lacey Hawkins, Archibald Scraper, George W. Ross, Third Lieutenants Allen Ross, Joseph Cornsilk and John Shell.

Colonel Weer was arrested at the camp on Cabin Creek by Colonel Frederick Solomon of the Ninth Wisconsin Volunteers on the charge of having conducted the command to a distant station where they were not in communication with the commissary department and practically out of provisions, but the whole affair had the appearance of jealous insubordination, as Colonel Weer was shortly afterwards advanced in rank. The prairies were covered with the cattle of the Cherokees[2] but other food was not to be had locally. But from this date cattle stealing[3] became so popular with the Kansans that before the end of the war cattle became a rare sight in the Nation. Colonel Solomon withdrew his northern forces to Hudson ferry of Grand River, on the Kansas line and the Cherokees were left on Flat Rock Creek, ten miles north of the present city of Wagoner.

Lieutenant Colonel Thomas Fox Taylor and several of his command were killed on Bayou Menard on the morning of July 27th, Chief Ross, with his friends and relatives together with the national records and the two hundred fifty thousand dollars that had been received from the confederate government started north under a federal escort in the afternoon of the same day. They arrived at Fort Scott on August 7, 1862[1]. Notwithstanding the dire distress of most of the Cherokee refugees in southeastern Kansas, Chief Ross, his family and a few relatives, left one week later[2] for Pennsylvania, where they staid during the remainder of the war.

The battle of Fort Wayne was fought on October 22, 1862, the confederates were defeated, their artillery captured and they retired to Canadian River. Fort Davis, opposite Ft. Gibson, was burned by the federals on December 27th.

The First Indian Home Guard regiment was principally Creeks. The Second and Third regiments of this brigade were predominantly Cherokee. The Second had sixty six officers and one thousand eight hundred privates. The Third had fifty two officers and one thousand four hundred thirty seven privates, totaling three thousand three hundred eighty eight men. A fragmentary list of these organizations are: Second Regiment, Colonel John Ritchey, Lt. Colonels David B. Corwin and Frederick W. Schuarte, Surgeon Dr. A. J. Ritchie.

Captain Co. A James McDaniel, First Lt. ———McLain, Second Lt. Walter Long. Privates: Jug Whitepath, West Beamer, Cat, Dick Duck, John McIntosh, John Glass, Hungry, Levi O'Fields, Rocky Mountain, Thomas Potato, Shade, Walter Stop, Swimmer, Joseph Swimmer, Tun-ne-no-lee, Backwater, Wahsosee, Oganiah Weliny.

Captain Co. B Moses Price, First Lt. John M. Hunter, Second Lt. Alexander Hawk, Orderly Sergeant Charles Teehee. Privates: Chu-hi-tla, Walter Downing, Isho-wah-no-ski, Daniel Tucker, William Tucker, Henry White, Tee-coo-ti-gi-ski, Henry Blackfox, Daniel Chopper, Daylight Chopper, Wilson Drum, Lewis Forkedtail, Joseph Fox, Gu-no-hi-du, Oochalata, Oolawate, Archibald Spears, Sweetwater, Redbird Tiger and Wheeler Tiger.

Captain Co. C James H. Bruce. Privates: Samuel Crittenden, Littlebear Bigmush, Thomas McCoy, Mankiller Catcher, Ned Wickett, Chu-hi-sa-ta, Elowe, George Wilson Girty, Jimmy, Dick Gagawi, Bark Prince, Jackson

Prince, Taylor Prince, Squirrel Starr, Eli Tadpole, Tough and James Taylor.

Captain Co. D Archibald Scraper. First Lt. John C. Palmer, Second Lt. Joseph Chooie, Orderly Sergeant Henry Scraper. Privates: Delaware Sixkiller, Canaheela, Crawler, Creek George, Dick Crittenden, John Foster, Goingsnake, Hider, Going to mill, Isaac Hawk, Wilson Lacey, Stephen Oolstoo, George Washington Scraper, Sicooie, Pelican, Sand, Too-cu-ta, Edward Walker, Walter, Whaler Watt and Jack Watt.

Captain Co. E Daniel McCoy Gunter, First Lt. William H. Kendall, Second Lt. Rufus O. Ross, Orderly Sergeant Daniel Ross Hicks. Privates: David Hendricks, James Hair, Charles Harjo, John Riley, Samuel Sanders, Lester Schneider, George Tiesky, Wareagle, Jack Woodard, Loony R. Gourd, John R. Hicks, Charles R. Hicks, Lewis Ross Thornton, William H. Thornton, Robert B. Ross, Lewis Dunbach, Armistead Maxfield, Tarsutta McCoy, Samuel Crossland, George Love, Lewis Hicks, William McCoy, James West, Thornton, Creek Jim Fox, Benjamin Foster, James Foster, Richard Dick, Nicholas Sanders, Jesse Sanders, Eli Sanders, Andrew Cordrey, Jefferson Robertson, Richard Robertson, Wade H. Robertson, John Walker, George W. Gage, Ross Adair and Benjamin Adair.

First Lt. Co. F Arleecher. Privates: Tu-ya-stee-ka, Henry Vann, Walter Hunter, Aaron, Archey, Arneechee, Tom Big, James Bolin, John Baldridge, Archibald Canoe, Thomas Cornsilk, Creek Tulsa, Adam Dirtseller, David Holmes, Johnson, Eli Lowrey, Lovett, Scott Mankiller, Edward Mayfield, Nelson, Plow, Spirit, Su-yo-du, Ta-ka-li-gi-ski, Houston Mayfield and Key Dougherty.

Captain Co. G Bud Gritts. Privates: John Bean, James Beaver, Jumper Blackburn, Bullfrog, George Drum, Askwater, James Vann and Reed Vann.

Captain Co. H Andrew J. Waterhouse. Privates John Wright and Scraper Nicholson.

Captain Co. I Dirtthrower, First Lt. Jesse Henry.

Captain Co. K Springfrog.

Colonel Third Indian Home Guards William A. Phillips, Lieutenant Colonel Lewis Downing, Major John A. Foreman.

Captain Co. A Smith Christy, First Lt. Samuel Houston Benge.

Captains Co. B Isaac Tyner and Alexander C. Spillman, First Lt. Alexander C. Spillman, Second Lt. William Sunday. Privates: John Thompson, Lacey Beartoter, Richard Bearpaw, Harry Cutter, Johnson Dick, Peter Dry, Adam Feeling George, Hungry Dick, Johnson Jug, Jack Rabbit, Johnson Ridge, George Ridge, John Sharp, Sharp, Tom Sunday, George Seven, Smoker, John Starr, Jesse Witch, John Bear, Otterlifter, Waterhunter, Tom Spikebuck, David Conserie, Red Ellis, Eli Goodmoney, Joe F. Reese, Lewis Wolf, Soup, Sulteeska, Wolf Smoke, Hogshooter, Grass and Runabout Puff.

Captain Co. C Nathaniel Fish. Privates: Thompson Bean, George Cooweescoowee, Goback, Wilson Hair, Thomas Suake, Tadpole Crossing, George Weaver, Joseph Butler, Ellis Johnson, William Catcher, Looney McLain, Andrew Nowife, John Riley, Shoe Boots, Tallow Mayes, Lewis Scontihee, George Adams, William Cade, Thomas Hammer, James Hite, Jaybird Raft, Mick Leach, Young Puppy and Jackson Rail.

Captain Co. D Talala. Privates: Dragging Downing, David Horn, Samuel Knight, Charles Pumpkin, Hunter, Runabout Fodder, Samuel Spirit, George Soap, Wiley, Jesse Smoke, Sanders, Blackhaw, Dull Downing, Samuel Henry, John Pickup, Bigtalker, Jack' Double, Alexander Downing, Thomas Hammond, George Hog, Situake, William Sourjohn, Tony and Arch Keener.

Captain Co. E William Webber and Thomas Pegg, First Lt. John S. Hanway, Second Lt. Bear Brown, Orderly Sergeant Robin Crawford. Privates: Jesse Davis, Josiah Stealer, Jim Yohola, George Washington Clark, Crapo, Creek Sam, Sidney Justice, Frank Kerr, John Meigs, Murdoch McLeod, James McTier, Henry Nave, Nicholas B. Woods, DeKinney Waters Salt, John Young, Joseph Young, Roach Young, Thomas Young, Josiah Ridge, Peter Emory, Jumper, James, Misaeala, John Sekeekee, Sunday and James Oowano.

Captain Co. F Huckleberry Downing, First Lt. Andrew W. Robb. Privates: George Brush, Nightkiller, George Rooster, Avery Vann, Drinker Walkingstick, Washington Clay, Aaron, James Beanstick, John Coleman, Jesse Grass, Lacey Hawkins, Jumper, Johnson Jack, Joseph T. Glass, Twist, Waleeska Batt, Dave, John Duck, Nathaniel Ellis, Daniel Foster, James Harris, Squirrel Lowrey, Charles Timberlake, Oochalata, Charles Otter, Dirt Seller, Johnson Situwake, Wahachi and Thicket Baldridge.

Captain Co. G Maxwell Phillips, Second Lt. Carselowry Proctor, Orderly Sergeant Spencer S. Stephens. Privates: Henry Christy, Charles Walkingstick, Little Grimmett, Sold, Tieska Pritchett, Josiah Pigeon, John Walkingstick, Stand, Horace Broom, Runner Catcher, Richard Christy, Doctor, Alex Puppy, Benjamin Sanders, Johnson Shade, Turningabout, Bottom Water and Hawk Fourkiller.

Captain Co. H. Simon Snell, First Lt. Harmon Scott, Second Lt. Basil G. McCrea. Privates: Jackson Bird, Rider Foreman, Moses Sixkiller, Long Charley, Leaf, Youngwolf Sixkiller, Thomas Starr, Pheasant Tanner, Elijah, Crying Wolf, Johnson Geesky, George Hildebrand, Wasody Stop and Joseph Butler.

Captain Co. I Whitecatcher, First Lt. Charles Brown, Second Lt. William Sunday. Privates: Stephen Spears, Silas Ross, George W. Ross, Allen Ross, Michael Hildebrand, John Smith, James Burns, James Shelton and John L. Springston.

Captain Co. K James Vann.

Captain Co. L Solomon Kaufman, First Lt. Redbird Sixkiller, Second Lt. Jules C. Cayot, Orderly Sergeant William H. Hendricks. Privates: Ezekial Proctor, James Chambers, Aaron Goingwolf, John Hendricks, Isaac Glass, William Hendricks Jr., Benjamin Haney, Jesse Bushyhead and Samuel Sixkiller. This was an artillery company.

Captain Co. M Henry S. Anderson.

Ft. Gibson was occupied on April 8, 1863 by the First, Second and Third Indian Home Guards, four companies of Kansas cavalry and Hopkins battery, aggregating three thousand one hundred fifty men. They threw up some earthworks above the site of the old post and called it Fort Blount in honor of Major General James G. Blunt U. S. V., then in command of Kansas and Indian Territory. On May twentieth a sortie was made on the fort by a small detachment of Watie's command which captured all of the mules and most of the horses belonging to the garrison.

The battle of Honey Springs was fought on July seventeenth. The powder used by the confederates had been bought in Mexico and would hardly eject the bullet from the rifle and consequently they were defeated Colonel Watie led an expedition to Tahlequah, where he burned the capitol buildings on October 28th and on the following day he burned Chief Ross' house at Park Hill.

It was the policy of both armies to place the supreme command with White men, on the theory that the Indian would not make a good general commander. During the earlier years of the war when conditions were more favorable, Generals Pike, Steele, Maxey and Cooper commanded the Indian Territory. After the tide of war had turned decidedly in favor of the Union, when Forts Smith and Gibson were in the hands of the federals Stand Watie was made a brigadier general of the confederate army and in command of the Cherokee brigade and practically independent of Brigadier General Cooper. On the fifteenth of June 1864 General Watie captured at Pheasants Bluff on Arkansas River the steamboat J. R. Williams, laden with supplies for Ft. Gibson. On September nineteenth he in conjunction with Brigadier General Richard M. Ganoe captured at Cabin Creek a military train of three hundred wagons, loaded with commissary supplies valued at over one million dollars, enroute from Ft. Scott, Kansas to Fort Gibson.

General Watie surrendered, by the following articles:

THE TREATY.

"Treaty stipulations made and entered into this 23rd day of June 1865 near Doaksville Choctaw Nation between Sent. Colonel A. C. Mathews and W. H. Vance U. S. Vol. commissioners appointed by Major General Herron U. S. A. on part of the military authorities of the United States and Brig. General Stand Watie Governor and Principal Chief of that part of the Cherokee Nation lately allied with Confederate States in acts of hostilities against the Government of the United States as follows towit:

"ARTICLE I. All acts of hostilities on the part of both armies having ceased by virtue of a convention entered into on the 26th day of May 1865 between Major General E. R. S. Cantry U. S. A. comdg. Mil. Division West Miss. and General E. Kirby Smith C. S. A. Comdg. Trans. Miss Department The Indians of the Cherokee Nation here represented lately allied with the Confederate States in acts of hostilities against the Government of the United States.

"Do agree at once to return to their respective homes and there remain at peace with United States, and offer no indignities whatever against the whites or Indians of the various tribes who have been friendly to or engaged in the service of the United States during the war.

"ARTICLE II. It is stipulated by the undersigned commissioners on part of the United States, that so long as the Indians aforesaid observe the provisions of article first of this agreement, they shall be protected by the United States authorities in their person and property, not only from encroachment on the part of the whites, but also from the Indians who have been engaged in the service of the United States.

"ARTICLE III. The above articles of agreement to remain and be in force and effect until the meeting of the Grand Council to meet at Armstrong Academy, Choctaw Nation on the 1st day of September A. D. 1865 and until such time as the preceedings of said Grand Council shall be ratified by the proper authorities both of the Cherokee Nation and the United States.

"In testimony whereof the said Lieut. Col. A. C. Mathews and adjutant W. H. Vance commissioners on part of the United States and Brig. General Stand Watie Governor and Principal Chief of the Cherokee Nation have hereunto set their hands and seals.

Signed. A. C. Mathews, Sent. Col.
W. H. Vance, Adjr.
Commissioners.

Stand Watie Brig. Genl. Governor and Principal Chief Cherokee Nation.

The old agency site of the Arkansas Cherokees was sold by the federal Cherokee delegates:

Transfer of 3400 acres of land, more or less. Situated in Township 7 Range 21, State of Arkansas. Said land being the former agency and residue of the tract disposed of by Cherokees by treaty of 1828.

Know all men by these presents, that, whereas the Cherokee Nation owns a tract of land in the state of Arkansas, known as the Cherokee reservation lying in township No. 7, range 21, west of the fifth principal meridian, and containing three thousand four hundred (3400) acres more or less, and all which is occupied or claimed by squatters and others claiming title adverse to the said Nation, under color of various titles. And whereas it is provided by the 4th article of the treaty between the United States and the Cherokee Nation, of May 6th 1838, said tract shall be sold under the direction of the agent of the Cherokee Nation. And whereas the Cherokee Nation by its delegation hereto duly authorized have sold said lands to John Brown Wright, of the city of Washington, and have received in payment therefor the sum of five thousand dollars which they agree shall be applied by the Nation to the use named in said treaty and amendments thereto. Said sale having been made by direction and with the approval of Justin Harlin the agent appointed by the United States for the Cherokee Nation. Now therefore the said Cherokee Nation by its delegation hereto fully authorized to do hereby request the Secretary of the Interior to cause a patent to be issued for the said John Brown Wright for the said land and do release the United States from all liability for said land or its proceed.

Witness our hands this, 10th day of May A. D. 1866.

Daniel H. Ross, White Catcher, I. H. Benge, James McDaniel, Smith Christie, J. B. Jones.

City of Washington, District of Columbia. I, Justin Harlin agent of the United States for the Cherokee Nation do hereby approve of and consent to the above sale, which was made by my direction this tenth day of May, 1866.

J. HARLIN, U. S. Indian Agent.

C. J. HARRIS
Chief—December 23, 1891, to November, 1895

S. H. MAYES
Chief—November, 1895, to November, 1899

CHAPTER IX

Treaty With The Cherokee 1866. Delawares Acquire Full Rights. Shawnees Adopted by Cherokees. Land Sold to Osages. Officers Salaries Fixed. Land Donation to Masons. Lodges.

The United States and Cherokees concluded the following treaty:

TREATY WITH THE CHEROKEE, 1866.

July 19, 1866. 14 Stats., 799. Ratified July 27, 1866. Proclaimed Aug 11, 1866. Articles of agreement and convention at the city of Washington on the nineteenth day of July, in the year of our Lord one thousand eight hundred and sixty-six, between the United States, represented by Dennis N. Cooley, Commissioner of Indian Affairs, [and] Elijah Sells, superintendent of Indian affairs for the southern superintendency, and the Cherokee Nation of Indians, represented by its delegates, James McDaniel, Smith Christie, White Catcher, S. H. Benge, J. B. Jones, and Daniel H. Ross—John Ross, principal chief of the Cherokees, being too unwell to join these negotiations.

Preamble. [Whereas existing treaties between the United States and the Cherokee Nation are deemed to be insufficient, the said contracting parties agree as follows, viz:

Pretended Treaty Declared Void. Article 1. The pretended treaty made with the so-called Confederate States by the Cherokee Nation on the seventh day of October, eighteen hundred and sixty-one, and repudiated by the national council of the Cherokee Nation on the eighteenth day of February, eighteen hundred and sixty-three declared to be void.]

Amnesty. Article 2. Amnesty is hereby declared by the United States and the Cherokee Nation for all crimes and misdemeanors committed by one Cherokee on the person or property of another Cherokee, or of a citizen of the United States, prior to the fourth day of July, eighteen hundred and sixty-six; and no right of action arising out of wrongs committed in aid or in suppression of the rebellion shall be prosecuted or maintained in the courts of the United States or in the courts of the Cherokee Nation.

But the Cherokee Nation stipulate and agree to deliver up to the United States, or their duly authorized agent, any or all public property, particularly ordnance, ordnance stores, arms of all kinds, and quartermaster's stores, in their possession or control, which belonged to the United States or the so-called Confederate States, without any reservation.

Confiscation Laws Repealed and Former Owners Restored to Their Rights. Article 3. [The confiscation laws of the Cherokee Nation shall be repealed, and the same, and all sales of farms, and improvements on real estate, made or pretended to be made in pursuance thereof, are hereby agreed and declared to be null and void, and the former owners of such property so sold, their heirs or assigns, shall have the right peaceably to re-occupy their homes, and the purchaser under the confiscation laws, or his heirs or assigns, shall be repaid by the treasurer of the Cherokee Nation from the national funds, the money paid for said property and the cost of permanent improvements on such real estate, made thereon since the confiscation sale;]*** the cost of such improvements to be fixed by a commission, to be composed of one person designated by the Secretary of the Interior and one by the principal chief of the nation, which two may appoint a third in cases of disagreement, which cost so fixed shall be refunded to the national treasurer by the returning Cherokees within three years from the ratification hereof.

Cherokees, Freed Persons, and Free Negroes May Elect to Reside Where. Article 4. All the Cherokees and freed persons who were formerly slaves to any Cherokee, and all free negroes not having been slaves, who resided in the Cherokee Nation prior to June first, eighteen hundred and sixty-one, who may within two years elect not to reside northeast of the Arkansas River and southeast of Grand River, shall have the right to settle in and occupy the Canadian district southwest of the Arkansas River, and also all that tract of country lying northwest of Grand River, and bounded on the southeast by Grand River and west by the Creek reservation to the northeast corner thereof; from thence west on the north line of the Creek reservation to the ninety-sixth degree of west longitude; and thence north on said line of longitude so far that a line due east to Grand River will include a quantity of land equal to one hundred and sixty acres for each person who may so elect to reside in the territory above-described in this article: Provided That that part of said district north of the Arkansas River shall not be set apart until it shall be found that the Canadian district is not sufficiently large to allow one hundred and sixty acres to each person desiring to obtain settlement under the provisions of this article.

Those so Electing to Reside There May Elect Local Officers, Judges etc. Proviso. Article 5. The inhabitants electing to reside in the district described in the preceding article shall have the right to elect all their local officers and judges, and the number of delegates to which by their numbers they may be entitled in any general council to be established in the Indian Territory under the provisions of this treaty, as stated in Article XII, and to control all their local affairs, and to establish all necessary police regulations and rules for the administration of justice in said district, not inconsistent with the constiution of the Cherokee Nation or the laws of the United States; Provided, The Cherokees residing in said district shall enjoy all the rights and privileges of other Cherokees who may elect to settle in said district as hereinbefore provided, and shall hold the same rights and privileges and be subject to the same liabilities as those who elect to settle in said district under the provisions of this treaty; Provided also, That if any such police regulations or rules be adopted which, in the opinion of the President, bear oppressively on any citizen of the nation, he may suspend the same. And all rules or regulations in said district, or in any other district of the nation, discriminating against the citizens of other districts, are prohibited, and shall be void.

Representation in National Council. Unequal Laws. Article 6. The inhabitants of the said district hereinbefore described shall be entitled to representation according to number in the national council, and all laws of the Cherokee Nation shall be uniform throughout said nation. And should any such law, either in its provisions or the manner of its enforcement, in the opinion of the President of the United States, operate unjustly or injuriously in said district, he is hereby authorized and empowered to correct such evil, and to adopt the means necessary to secure the impartial administration of justice, as well as a fair and equitable application and expenditure of the national funds as between the people of this and of every other district in said nation.

Courts. Process. Proviso. Article 7. The United States court to be created in the Indian Territory; and until such court is created therein, the United States district court, the nearest to the Cherokee Nation, shall have exclusive original jurisdiction of all causes, civil and criminal, wherein an inhabitant of the district hereinbefore described shall be a party, and where an inhabitant outside of said district, in the Cherokee Nation, shall be the other party, as plaintiff or defendant in a civil cause, or shall be defendant or prosecutor in a criminal case, and all process isued in said district by any officer of the Cherokee Nation, to be executed on an inhabitant residing outside of said district, to be executed on any inhabitant residing in said district, shall be to all intents and purposes null and void, unless indorsed by the district judge for the district where such process is to be served, and said person, so arrested, shall be held in custody by the officer so arresting him, until he shall be delivered over to the United States marshal, or consent to be tried by the Cherokee court: Provided, That any or all the provisions of this treaty, which make any distinction in rights and remedies between the citizens of any district and the citizens of the rest of the nation, shall be abrogated whenever the President shall have ascertained, by an election duly ordered by him, that a majority of the voters of such district desire them to be abrogated, and he shall have declared such abrogation: And provided further, That no law or regulation, to be hereafter enacted within said Cherokee Nation or any district thereof, prescribing a penalty for its violation, shall take effect or be enforced until after ninety days from the date of its promulgation, either by publication in one or more newspapers of general circulation in said Cherokee Nation, or by posting up copies thereof in the Cherokee and English languages in each district where the same is to take effect, at the usual place of holding district courts.

Licenses to trade not to be granted unless, etc. Article 8. No license to trade in goods, wares, or merchandise shall be granted by the United States to trade in the Cherokee Nation, unless approved by the Cherokee national council, except in the Canadian district, and such other district north of Arkansas River occupied by the so-called southern Cherokees, as provided in Article 4 of this treaty.

Slavery, etc., not to exist. Freedmen. No pay for emancipated slaves. Article 9. The Cherokee Nation having, voluntarily, in February, eighteen hundred and sixty-three, by an act of the national council, forever abolished slavery, hereby covenant and agree that never hereafter shall either slavery or involuntary servitude exist in their nation otherwise than in the punishment of crime, whereof the party shall have been duly convicted, in accordance with laws applicable to all the members of said tribe alike. They further agree that all freedmen who have been liberated by voluntary act of their former owners or by law, as well as all free colored persons who were in the country at the commencement of the rebellion, and are now residents therein, or who may return within six months, and their descendants, shall have all the rights of native Cherokees: Provided, That owners of slaves so emancipated in the Cherokee Nation shall never receive any compensation or pay for the slaves so emancipated.

Farm products may be sold, etc. Article 10. Every Cherokee and freed person resident in the Cherokee Nation shall have the right to sell any products of his farm, including his or her live stock, or any merchandise or manufactured products, and to ship and drive the same to market without restraint, paying any tax thereon which is now or may be levied by the United States on the quantity sold outside of the Indian Territory.

Right of way of railroads. Article 11. The Cherokee Nation hereby grant a right of way not exceeding two hundred feet wide, except at stations, switches, waterstations, or crossing of rivers, where more may be indispensable to the full enjoyment of the franchise herein granted, and then only two hundred additional feet shall be taken, and only for such length as may be absolutely necessary, through all their lands, to any company or corporation which shall be duly authorized by Congress to construct a railroad from any point north to any point south, and from any point east to any point west of, and which may pass through, the Cherokee Nation. Said company or corporation, and their employes and laborers, while constructing and repairing the same, and in operating said road or roads, including all necessary agents on the line, at stations, switches, water tanks, and all others necessary to the successful operation of a railroad, shall be protected in the discharge of their duties, and at all times subject to the Indian intercourse laws, now or which may hereafter be enacted and be in force in the Cherokee Nation.

General Council. Article 12. The Cherokees agree that a general council, consisting of delegates elected by each nation or tribe lawfully residing within the Indian Territory, may be annually convened in said Territory, which council shall be organized in such manner and possess such powers as hereinafter prescribed.

Census. First. After the ratification of this treaty, and as soon as may be deemed practicable by the Secretary of the Interior, and prior to the first session of said council, a census or enumeration of each tribe lawfully resident in said Territory shall be taken under the direction of the Commissioner of Indian Affairs, who for that purpose is hereby authorized to designate and appoint competent persons, whose compensation shall be fixed by the Secretary of the Interior, and paid by the United States.

First general council; how composed. Time and place of first meeting. Session not to exceed thirty days. Special sessions. Second. The first general council shall consist of one member from each tribe, and an additional member for each one thousand Indians, or each fraction of a thousand greater than five hundred, being members of any tribe lawfully resident in said

Territory, and shall be selected by said tribes respectively, who may assent to the establishment of said general council; and if none should be thus formally selected by any nation or tribe so assenting, the said nation or tribe shall be represented in said general council by the chief or chiefs and headmen of said tribes, to be taken in the order of their rank as recognized in tribal usage, in the same number and proportion as above indicated. After the said census shall have been taken and completed, the superintendent of Indian affairs shall publish and declare to each tribe assenting to the establishment of such council the number of members of such coucnil to which they shall be entitled to represent said tribes shall meet at such times and place as he shall approve; but thereafter the time and place of the sessions of said council shall be determined by its action: Provided, That no session in any one year shall exceed the term of thirty days: And provided, That special sessions of said council may be called by the Secretary of the Interior whenever in his judgment the interest of said tribes shall require such special session.

Powers of general council. Laws, when to take effect. Third. Said general council shall have power to legislate upon matters pertaining to the intercourse and relations of the Indian tribes and nations and colonies of freedmen resident in said Territory; the arrest and extradition of criminals and offenders escaping from one tribe to another, or into any community of freedmen; the administration of justice between members of different tribes of said Territory and persons other than Indians and members of said tribes or nations; and the common defence and safety of the nations of said Territory.

Laws, when to take effect. Legislative power may be enlarged. All laws enacted by such council shall take effect at such time as may therein be provided, unless suspended by direction of the President of the United States. No law shall be enacted inconsistent with the Constitution of the United States, or laws of Congress, or existing treaty stipulations with the those above indicated: Provided, however, That the legislative power of such general council may be enlarged by the consent of the national council of each nation or tribe assenting to its establishment, with the approval of the President of the United States.

President of council. Fourth. Said council shall be presided over by such person as may be designated by the Secretary of the Interior.

Secretary of council. Pay. Fifth. The council shall elect a secretary, whose duty it shall be to keep an accurate record of all the proceedings of said council, and who shall transmit a true copy of all such proceedings, duly certified by the presiding officer of such council, to the Secretary of the Interior, and to each tribe or nation represented in said council, immediately after the sessions of said council shall terminate. He shall be paid out of the Treasury of the United States an annual salary of five hundred dollars.

Pay of members of council. Sixth. The members of said council shall be paid by the United States the sum of four dollars per diem during the term actually in attendance on the sessions of said council, and at the rate of four dollars for every twenty miles necessarily traveled by them in going from and returning to their homes, respectively, from said council, to be certified by the secretary and president of the said council.

Courts. Article 13. The Cherokees also agree that a court or courts may be established by the United States in said Territory, with such jurisdiction and organized in such manner as may be prescribed by law: Provided, That the judicial tribunals of the nation shall be allowed to retain exclusive jurisdiction in all civil and criminal cases arising within their country in which members of the nation, by nativity or adopton, shall be the only parties, or where the cause of action shall arise in the Cherokee Nation, except as otherwise provided in this treaty.

Lands for missionary or educational purposes. Not to be sold except for. Proceeds of sale. Article 14. The right to the use and occupancy of a quantity of land not exceeding one hundred and sixty acres, to be selected according to legal subdivisions in one body, and to include their improvements, and not including the improvements of any member of the Cherokee Nation, is hereby granted to every society or denomination which has erected, or which with the consent of the national council may hereafter erect, buildings within the Cherokee country for missionary or educational purposes. But no land thus granted, nor buildings which have been or may be erected with the consent and approval of the Cherokee national council and the Secretary of the Interior. And whenever any such lands or buildings shall be sold or disposed of, the proceeds thereof shall be applied by said society or societies for like purposes within said nation, subject to the approval of the Secretary of the Interior.

The United States may settle civilized Indians in the Cherokee country. How may be made part of Cherokee Nation. Those wishing to preserve tribal organization to have land set off to them. Article 15. The United States may settle any civilized Indians, friendly with the Cherokees and adjacent tribes, within the Cherokee country, on unoccupied lands east of 96°, on such terms as may be agreed upon by any such tribe and the Cherokees, subject to the approval of the President of the United States, which shall be consistent with the following provisions, viz: Should any such tribe or band of Indians settling in said country abandon their tribal organization, there being first paid into the Cherokee national fund a sum of money which shall sustain the same proposition to the then existing national fund that the number of Indians sustain to the whole number of Cherokees then residing in the Cherokee country, they shall be incorporated into and ever after remain a part of the Cherokee Nation, on equal terms in every respect with native citizens. And should any such tribe, thus settling in said country, decide customs, and usages, not inconsistent with the constitution and laws of the Cherokee Nation, they shall have a district of country set off for their use by metes and bounds equal to one hundred and sixty acres, if they should so decide, for each man, woman, and child of said tribe, and shall pay for the same into the national fund such price as may be agreed on by them and the Cherokee Nation, subject to the approval of the President of the United

States, and in cases of disagreement the price to be fixed by the President.

To pay sum into national fund. Limits of places of settlement. And the said tribe thus settled shall also pay into the national fund a sum of money, to be agreed on by the respective parties, not greater in proportion to the whole existing national fund and the probable proceeds of the lands herein ceded or authorized to be ceded or sold than their numbers bear to the whole number of Cherokees then residing in said country, and thence afterwards they shall enjoy all the rights of native Cherokees. But no Indians who have no tribal organizations, or who shall determine to abandon their tribal organizations, shall be permitted to settle east of the 96° of longitude without the consent of the Cherokee national council, or of a delegation duly appointed by it, being first obtained. And no Indians who have and determine to preserve the tribal organizations shall be permitted to settle, as herein provided, east of the 96° of longitude without such consent being first obtained, unless the President of the United States, after a full hearing of the objections offered by said council or delegation to such settlement, shall determine that the objections are insufficient, in which case he may authorize the settlement of such tribe east of the 96° of longitude.

Where the United States may settle friendly Indians. Lands. Article 16. The United States may settle friendly Indinans in any part of the Cherokee country west of 96°, to be taken in a compact form in quantity not exceeding one hundred and sixty acres for each member of each of said tribes thus to be settled; the boundaries of each of said districts to be distinctly marked, and the land conveyed in fee-simple to each of said tribes to be held in common or by their members in severalty as the United States may decide.

Said lands thus disposed of to be paid for to the Cherokee Nation at such price as may be agreed on between the said parties in interest, subject to the approval of the President; and if they should not agree, then the price to be fixed by the President.

Possession and jurisdiction over such lands. The Cherokee Nation to retain the right of possession of and jurisdiction over all of said country west of 96° of longitude until thus sold and occupied, after which their jurisdiction and right of possession to terminate forever as to each of said districts thus sold and occupied.

Cession of lands to the United States in trust. Article 17. The Cherokee Nation hereby cedes, in trust to the United States, the tract of land in the State of Kansas which was sold to the Cherokees by the United States, under the provisions of the second article of the treaty of 1835; and also that strip of the land ceded to the nation by the fourth article of said treaty which is included in the State of Kansas, and the Cherokees consent that said lands may be included in the limits and jurisdiction of the said State.

Lands to be surveyed and appraised. The lands herein ceded shall be surveyed as the public lands of the United States are surveyed, under the direction of the Commissioner of the General Land-Office, and shall be appraised by two disinterested persons, one to be designated by the Cherokee national council and one by the Secretary of the Interior, and, in case of disagreement, by a third person, to be mutually selected by the aforesaid appraisers. The appraisement to be not less than an average of one dollar and a quarter per acre, exclusive of improvements.

May be sold to highest bidder. Improvements. Proviso. And the Secretary of the Interior shall, from time to time, as such surveys and appraisements are approved by him, after due advertisements for sealed bids, sell such lands to the highest bidders for cash, in parcels not exceeding one hundred and sixty acres, and at not less than the appraised value: Provided, That whenever there are improvements of the value of fifty dollars made on the lands not being mineral, and owned and personally occupied by any person for agricultural purposes at the date of the signing hereof, such person so owning, and in person residing on such improvements, shall, after due proof, made under such regulations as the Secretary of the Interior may prescribe, be entitled to buy, at the appraised value, the smallest quantity of land in legal subdivisions which will include his improvements, not exceeding in the aggregate one hundred and sixty acres; the expenses of survey and appraisement to be paid by the Secretary out of the proceeds of sale of said land: Provided, That nothing in this article shall prevent the Secretary of the Interior from selling the whole of said lands not occupied by actual settlers at the date of the ratification of this treaty, not exceeding one hundred and sixty acres to each person entitled to pre-emption under the pre-emption laws of the United States, in a body, to any responsible party, for cash, for a sum not less than one dollar per acre.

Sales by Cherokee of lands in Arkansas. Article 18. That any lands owned by the Cherokees in the State of Arkansas and in States east of the Mississippi may be sold by the Cherokee Nation in such manner as their national council may prescribe, all such sales being first approved by the Secretary of the Interior.

Heads of families. Article 19. All Cherokees being heads of families residing at the date of the ratification of this treaty on any of the lands herein ceded, or authorized to be sold, and desiring to remove to the reserved country, shall be paid by the purchasers of said lands the value of such improvements, to be ascertained and appraised by the commissioners who appraise the lands, subject to the approval of the Secretary of the Interior; and if he shall elect to remain on the land now occupied by him, shall be entitled to receive a patent from the United States in fee-simple for three hundred and twenty acres of land to include his improvements, and thereupon he and his family shall cease to be members of the nation.

And the Secretary of the Interior shall also be authorized to pay the reasonable costs and expenses of the delegates of the southern Cherokees.

The moneys to be paid under this article shall be paid out of the proceeds of the sales of the national lands in Kansas.

Lands reserved to be surveyed and allotted. Article 20. Whenever the Cherokee national council shall request it, the Secretary of the Interior shall cause the country reserved for the Cherokees to be surveyed and allotted among them, at the expense of the United States.

Boundary line to be run and marked. Article 21. It being difficult to learn the precise boundary line between the Cherokee country and the States of Arkansas, Missouri, and Kansas, it is agreed that the United States shall, at its own expense, cause the same to be run as far west as the Arkansas, and marked by permanent and conspicuous monuments, by two commissioners, one of whom shall be designated by the Cherokee national council.

Agent of Cherokees to examine accounts, books, etc. Article 22. The Cherokee national council, or any duly appointed delegation thereof, shall have the privilege to appoint an agent to examine the accounts of the nation with the Government of the United States at such time as they may see proper, and to continue or discharge such agent, and to appoint another, as may be thought best by such council or delegation; and such agent shall have free access to all accounts and books in the executive departments relating to the business of said Cherokee Nation, and an opportunity to examine the same in the presence of the officer having such books in charge.

Funds, how to be invested. Interest, how to be paid. Article 23. All funds now due the nation, or that may hereafter accrue from the sale of their lands by the United States, as hereinbefore provided for, shall be invested in the United States registered stocks at their current value, and the interest on all said funds shall be paid semi-annually on the order of the Cherokee Nation, and shall be applied to the following purposes, to wit: Thirty-five per cent. shall be applied for the support of the common-schools of the nation and educational purposes; fifteen per cent. for the orphan fund, and fifty per cent. for general purposes, including reasonable salaries of district officers; and the Secretary of the Interior, with the approval of the President of the United States, may pay out of the funds due the nation, on the order of the national council or a delegation duly authorized by it, such amount as he may deem necessary to meet outstanding obligations of the Cherokee Nation, caused by the suspension of the payment of their annuities, not to exceed the sum of one hundred and fifty thousand dollars.

Payment to Rev. Evan Jones. Article 24. As a slight testimony for the useful and arduous services of the Rev. Evan Jones, for forty years a missionary in the Cherokee Nation, now a cripple, old and poor, it is agreed that the sum of three thousand dollars be paid to him, under the direction of the Secretary of the Interior, out of any Cherokee fund in or to come into his hands not otherwise appropriated.

Bounties and Arrears for Services as Indian Volunteers; How to be Paid. Artice 25. A large number of the Cherokees who served in the Army of the United States having died, leaving no heirs entitled to receive bounties and arrears of pay on account of such service, it is agreed that all bounties and arrears for service in the regiments of Indian United States volunteers which shall remain unclaimed by any person legally entitled to receive the same for two years from the ratification of this treaty, shall be paid as the national council may direct, to be applied to the foundation and support of an asylum for the education of orphan children, which asylum shall be under the control of the national council, or of such benevolent society as said council may designate, subject to the approval of the Secretary of the Interior.

Possession and Protection Guaranteed. Article 26. The United States guarantee to the people of the Cherokee Nation the quiet and peaceable possession of their country and protection against domestic feuds and insurrections, and against hostile tribes. They shall also be protected against interruptions or intrusion from all unauthorized citizens of the United States of hostilities among the Indian tribes, the United States agree that the party or parties commencing the same shall, so far as practicable, make reparation for the damages done.

Military Posts in Cherokee Nation. Spirituous, etc., Liquors Forbidden Except, etc. Certain Persons Prohibited from Coming into the Nation. Article 27. The United States shall have the right to establish one or more military posts or stations in the Cherokee Nation, as may be deemed necessary for the proper protection of the citizens of the United States lawfully residing therein and the Cherokee and other citizens of the Indian country. But no sutler or other person connected therewith, either in or out of the military organization, shall be permitted to introduce any spirit[u]ous, vinous, or malt liquors into the Cherokee Nation, except the medical department proper, and by them only for strictly medical purposes. And all persons not in the military service of the United States, not citizens of the Cherokee Nation, are to be prohibited from coming into the Cherokee Nation, or remaining in the same, except as herein otherwise provided; and it is the duty of the United States Indian agent for the Cherokees to have such persons, not lawfully residing or sojourning therein, removed from the nation, as they now are, or hereafter may be, required by the Indian intercourse laws of the United States.

Payment for Certain Provisions and Clothing. Article 28. The United States hereby agree to pay for provisions and clothing furnished the army under Appotholehala in the winter of 1861; and 1862, not to exceed the sum of ten thousand dollars, the accounts to be ascertained and settled by the Secretary of the Interior.

Expenses of Cherokee Delegation. Article 29. The sum of ten thousand dollars or so much thereof as may be necessary to pay the expenses of the delegates and representatives of the Cherokees invited by the Government to visit Washington for the purpose of making this treaty, shall be paid by the United States on the ratification of this treaty.

Payment for Certain Losses by Missionaries, etc. Article 30. The United States agree to pay to the proper claimants all losses of property by missionaries or missionary societies, resulting from their being ordered or driven from the country by United States agents, and from their property being taken and occupied or destroyed by United States troops, not exceeding in the aggregate twenty thousand dollars, to be ascertained by the Secretary of the Interior.

Inconsistent Treaty Provisions Annulled. Article 31. All provisions of treaties heretofore ratified and in force, and not inconsistent with the provisions of this treaty, are hereby re-affirmed and declared to be in full force:

and nothing herein shall be construed as an acknowledgment by the United States, or as a relinquishment by the Cherokee Nation of any claims or demands under the guarantees of former treaties, except as herein expressly provided.

Execution. In testimony whereof, the said commissioners on the part of the United States, and the said delegation on the part of the Cherokee Nation, this ninth [nineteenth] day of July, A. D. one thousand eight hundred and sixty-six.

D. N. Cooley, Commissioner of Indian Affairs.
Elijah Sells, Superintendent of Indian Affairs.
Smith Christie,

White Catcher, James McDaniel, S. H. Benge, Danl. H. Ross, J. B. Jones.
Delegates of the Cherokee Nation, appointed by Resolution of the National Council.

In presence of—W. H. Watson, J. W. Wright.

Signatures witnessed by the following-named persons, the following interlineations being made before signing: On page 1st the word "the" interlined, on page 11 the word "the" struck out, and to said page 11 sheet attached requiring publication of laws; and on page 34th the word "ceded" struck out and the words "neutral lands" inserted. Page 47½ added relating to expenses of treaty.

Thomas Ewing, jr.
Wm. A. Phillips,
J. W. Wright.

"No one can fully appreciate the wealth, content and comparative happiness the Cherokees enjoyed before the late rebellion, or very shortly after it was begun, unless he had been here and seen it (which was my case) and no man can believe more than half of the want, misery and destitution of the Cherokee people now. Blackened chimneys of fine houses are now all that is left, fences burned, and farms laid waste. The air of ruin and desolation envelops the whole country. None have wholly escaped. No man can pass through the country without seeing all that I have attempted to describe, and no man can fully appreciate it unless he has seen it.'"

The policy of the Cherokee Nation from its inception until June 30, 1898 was that of strict nonalienation of any land to whites because they realized that if any of their land was so disposed of that it would be an entering wedge to the dissolution of their government. After the practical demolition of their jurisdictional rights by act of congress, they voted to allot their land and discontinue tribal functions.

The Cherokees that had espoused the fortunes of the federal government in 1862, had full control of the government until November 1867 when the southern Cherokees reassumed their place in the body politic as a result ot the Downing coalition success at the polls at the August election.

The Delaware Indians who had been living in Kansas, acquired full rights in the Cherokee Nation, by:

ARTICLES OF AGREEMENT WITH THE DELAWARES.

Made this 8th day of April, A. D. 1867, between the Cherokee Nation, represented by William P. Ross, Principal Chief, Riley Keys and Jesse Bushyhead, delegates, duly authorized parties of the first part, and the Delaware tribe of Indians, represented by John Connor, Principal Chief, Charles Journeycake, Assistant Chief, Isaac Journeycake and John Sarcoxie, delegates, for and on behalf of said Delaware tribe, duly authorized, witnesseth:

Whereas, by the 15th article of a certain treaty between the United States and the Cherokee Nation, ratified August 11, 1866, certain terms were provided, under which friendly Indians might be settled upon unoccupied lands in the Cherokee country, east of the line of 96° of west longitude, the price to be paid for such lands to be agreed on by the Indians to be thus located and the Cherokee Nation, subject to the approval of the President of the United States; and whereas, by a treaty between the United States and the Delaware tribe of Indians, ratified August 10th, 1866, the removal of the said Delawares to the Indian country, south of Kansas, was provided for, and in the 4th article whereof an agreement was made by the United States to sell to the Delawares a tract of land, being part of a tract the cession of which by the Cherokees to the United Staes was then contemplated; and whereas, no such cession of land was made by the Cherokees to the United States, but, in lieu therof, terms were provided as hereinbefore mentioned, under which friendly Indians might be settled upon their lands; and whereas, a full and free conference has been held between the representatives of the Cherokees and the Delawares, in view of the treaties herein referred to, looking to a location of the Delawares upon the Cherokee lands, and their consolidation with said Cherokee Nation: Now, therefore, it is agreed between the parties hereto, subject to the approval of the President of the United States, as follows:

The Cherokees, parties of the first part, for and in consideration of certain payments, and the fulfillment of certain conditions hereinafter mentioned, agree to sell to the Delawares, for their occupancy, a quantity of land east of the line of the 96° west longitude, in the aggregate equal to 160 acres of land for each individual of the Delaware tribe who has been enrolled upon a certain register made February 18, 1867, by the Delaware agent, and on file in the office of Indian affairs, being the list of the Delawares who elect to remove to the "Indian country," to which list may be added, only with the consent of the Delaware Council, the names of such other Delawares as may, within one month after the signing of this agreement, desire to be added thereto; and the selections of the lands to be purchased by the Delawares may be made by said Delaawres in any part of the Cherokee reservation east of said line of 96°, not already selected and in possession of other parties; and in case the Cherokee lands shall hereafter be allotted among the members of said Nation, it is agreed that the aggregate amount of land herein provided for the Delawares, to include their improvements according to the legal subdivisions, when surveys are made (that is to say, 160 acres for each individual,) shall be guaranteed to each Delaware incorporated by these articles into the Cherokee Nation; nor shall the continued ownership and occupancy of said land by any Delaware so registered be interfered with in any manner whatever without his consent, but shall be subject to the same conditions and restrictions as are by the laws of the Cherokee Nation imposed upon the native citizens thereof; provided, that nothing herein shall confer the right to alienate, convey, or dispose of any such lands, except in accordance with the constitution and laws of said Cherokee Nation.

And the said Delawares, parties of the second part, agree that there shall be paid to the said Cherokees, from the Delaware funds, now held or hereafter received by the United States, a sum of money, equal to one dollar per acre, for the whole amount of 160 acres of land, for every individual Delaware who has already been registered upon the aforesaid list, made February 18, 1867, with the additions thereto, heretofore provided for. And the Secretary of the Interior is authorized and requested to sell any United States stocks belonging to the Delawares to procure funds necessary to pay for said lands; but, in case he shall not feel authorized, under existing treaties, to sell such bonds belonging to the Delawares, it is agreed that he may transfer such United States bonds to the Cherokee Nation, at their market value at the date of such transfer. And the said Delawares further agree, that there shall be paid, from their funds, now and hereafter to come into possession of the United States, a sum of money, which shall sustain the same proportion to the existing Cherokee National fund, that the number of Delawares registered as above mentioned, and removing to the Indian country, sustains to the whole number of Cherokees residing in the Cherokee Nation. And, for the purpose of ascertaining such relative numbers, the registers of the Delawares herein referred to, with such additions as may be made within one month from the signing of this agreement, shall be the basis of calculation as to the Delawares; and an accurate census of the Cherokees, residing in the Cherokee Nation, shall be taken, under the laws of that Nation, within four months, and properly certified copies thereof filed in the office of Indian Affairs, which shall be the basis of calculation as to the Cherokees. And, that there may be no doubt hereafter, as to the amount to be contributed to the Cherokee National fund by the Delawares, it is hereby agreed, by the parties hereto, that the whole of the invested funds of the Cherokees, after deducting all just claims thereon, is $678,000. And the Delawares further agree, that in calculating the total amount of said National fund, there shall be added to the said sum of $678,000, the sum of $1,000,000, being the estimated value of the Cherokee neutral lands in Kansas, thus making the whole Cherokee National fund $1,678,000, and this last mentioned sum shall be taken as the basis for calculating the amount which the Delawares are to pay into the common fund; provided, that, as the $678,000 of funds now on hand, belonging to the Cherokees, is chiefly composed of stocks of different values, the Secretary of the Interior may transfer, from the Delawares to the Cherokees, a proper proportion of the stocks now owned by the Delawares, of like grade and value, which transfer shall be in part of the pro rata contribution herein provided for by the Delawares to the funds of the Cherokee Nation; but the balance of the pro rata contribution by the Delawares to said fund, shall be in cash or United States bonds, at their market value. All cash, and all proceeds of stocks, whenever the same may fall due or be sold, received by the Cherokees from the Delawares under this agreement, shall be invested and applied in accordance with the 23d article of the treaty with the Cherokees, of August 11th 1866.

On the fulfillment by the Delawares of the foregoing stipulations, all the members of the tribe, registered as above provided, shall become members of the Cherokee Nation, with the same rights and immunities, and the same participation (and no other) in the national funds, as Native Cherokees, save as hereinbefore provided. And the children hereafter born of such Delawares so incorporated into the Cherokee Nation, shall in all respects be regarded as native Cherokees.

Wm. P. Ross, Principal Chief; Riley Keys; Cherokee Delegation.

John Connor, his x mark, Principal Chief; Charles Journeycake; Isaac Journeycake; John Saxcoxie, his x mark; Delaware Delegation.

Executed and delivered in our presence by the above named delegates of the Cherokee and Delaware Nations, at the city of Washington, in the District of Columbia, the day and year first above written.

Ratified by the National Committee, June 15, 1867.

John G. Pratt, Wm. A. Phillips, Edward S. Menagus, Smith Christie, President National Committee. John Young, Speaker of Council.

Two years later the Shawnees were adopted into the Cherokee Nation, by:

AGREEMENT BETWEEN SHAWNEES AND CHEROKEES, CONCLUDED JUNE 7TH, 1869, APPROVED BY THE PRESIDENT JUNE 9TH, 1869.

Articles of Agreement, made and entered into at Washington, D. C., this seventh day of June, A. D. 1869, by and between H. D. Reese and William P. Adair, duly authorized delegates representing the Cherokee Nation of Indians, having been duly appointed by the National Council of said Cherokees, parties of the first part, and Graham Rogers and Charles Tucker, duly authorized delegates representing the Shawnee tribe of Indians, parties of the second part, witnesseth:

Whereas, It is provided by the fifteenth article of the treaty between the United States and the Cherokee Indians, concluded July 19th, 1866, that the United States may settle any civilized Indians, friendly with the Cherokees and adjacent tribes, within the Cherokee country, on unoccupied lands east of 96°, on such terms as may be agreed upon by any such tribe and the Cherokees, subject to the approval of the President of the United States, which shall be consistent with certain provisions specified in said article; and

Whereas, The Shawnee tribe of Indians are civilized and friendly with the Cherokees and adjacent tribes, and desire to settle within the Cherokee country on unoccupied lands east of 96°.

It is therefore agreed, by the parties hereto, that such settlement may be made upon the following terms and conditions, viz:

That the sum of five thousand dollars belonging to the Shawnee tribe of Indians, and arising under the provisions of treaties between the United States and said Shawnee Indians, as follows, viz:

For permanent annuity for educational purposes, per fourth article treaty, 3d August, 1795, and third article, 10th of May, 1854, one thousand dollars;

For interest, at five per centum, on forty thousand dollars for educational purposes, per third article treaty, 10th May, 1854, one thousand dollars;

For permanent annuity, in specie, for educational purposes, per fourth article treaty, 29th September, 1817, and third article, 10th May, 1854, two thousand dollars; shall be paid annually to the Cherokee Nation of said Indians, and that the annuities and interest, as recited, and the investments upon which the same are based, shall hereafter become and remain the annuities and interest and investment or investments of the Cherokee Nation of Indians, the same as they have been the annuities and interest and investments of the Shawnee tribe of Indians. And that the sum of fifty thousand dollars shall be paid to the said Cherokees, as soon as the same shall be received by the United States, for the said Shawnees, from the sale of the land in the State of Kansas, known as the Absentee Shawnee Lands, in accordance with the resolution of Congress, approved April 7th, 1869, entitled: "A resolution for the relief of settlers upon the Absentee Shawnee Lands in Kansas," and the provisions of the treaty between the United States and the Shawnee Indians, concluded May 10th, 1854, and also that the said Shawnees shall abandon their tribal organization.

And it is further agreed by the parties hereto that in consideration of the said payments and acts agreed upon, as hereinbefore stated, that the said Cherokees will receive the said Shawnees—referring to those now in Kansas, and also to such as properly belong to said tribe who may be at present elsewhere, and including those known as the Absentee Shawnees, now residing in Indian Territory—into the country of the said Cherokees, upon unoccupied lands east of 96°, and that the said Shawnees shall be incorporated into and ever after remain a part of the Cherokee Nation, on equal terms in every respect, and with all the privileges and immunities of native citizens of the said Cherokee Nation; provided, that all of said Shawnees who shall elect to avail themselves of the provisions of this agreement, shall register their names, and permanently locate in the Cherokee country, as herein provided, within two years from the date thereof, otherwise they shall forfeit all rights under this agreement.

In testimony wehereof, the parties hereto have bereunto subscribed their names ,and affixed their seals, on the day and year first above written.

[SEAL.] H. D.REESE.

[SEAL.] WM. P. ADAIR,

Delegates representing the Cherokee Nation of Indians.

[SEAL.] GRAHAM ROGERS,

[SEAL] CHARLES TUCKER

Delegates representing the Shawnee Tribe of Indians.

W. R. IRWIN, H. E. McKEE,
A. N. BLACKLEDGE, JAS. B. ABBOTT.

On June 5, 1872 the Cherokees sold one million five hundred sixty six thousand three hundred eight acres of land lying west of the ninety sixth meridian to the Osages. This automatically formed the western boundary line of the Nation.

The several cessions of land by the Cherokees and amounts received for same, in whole numbers have been:

1900. Apr. 9,

		Acres	Consideration.	
1721		1678720		
1755.	Nov. 24,	5526400		
1768.	Oct. 14,	544000		
1770.	Oct. 18,	5888000		
1772.		500480	$5000.	
1773.	June 1,	672000		
1775.	Mar. 17,	17312000	5000.	
1777.	May 20,	1312640		
1777.	July 20,	3951360		
1783.	May 31,	1056000		
1785.	Nov. 28,	4083840		
1791.	July 2,	2660480	1000.	annuity.
1798.	Oct. 2,	984960	1000.	annuity and 5000.
1804.	Oct. 28,	86400	1000.	annuity and 5000.
1805.	Oct. 25,	5195520	3000.	annuity and 14000.
1805.	Oct. 27,	800	.1600.	
1806.	Jan. 7,	4397440	10000.	
1816.	Mar. 22,	94720		
1816.	Sept. 14,	2197120	65000.	
1817.	July 8,	651520		
1819.	Feb. 27,	3802240		
1828.	May 28,	3020800		
1835.	Dec. 29,	7882240		
1866.	May 10,	3400	In Pope Co. Arkansas.	
1866.	July 19,	1234294	Cherokee and Crawford Cos. Kansas.	
1872.	June 5,	1466167	To the Osages.	
1872.	June 5,	100141	" " Kaws.	
1876.	Apr. 10,	230014	" " Pawnees.	
1878.	May 27,	90710	" " Nez Perces.	
1881.	Mar. 3,	101894	" " Poncas.	
1881.	Mar. 3,	129113	" "Oto-Missouris.	
1893.	Mar. 4,	8144682	Cherokee Outlet.	
1900.	Apr. 9,	4420067	Allotment.	

By the proclamation of King George III on October 7, 1763 a prohibition of private purchase of land was promulgated and the realm became the guardian of the Indians and by subsequent rulings the courts of the United

States have emphasized the relationship of guardian and ward. From 1785 to 1900 over ten million acres have been purchased by treaty from the Cherokees at a proportional rate of about sixty cents an acre and then disposed of it to the settler, for one dollar and twenty five cents per acre.

Steady progress in civil, industrial and educational lines was a marked feature of the Cherokees and they came into the State of Oklahoma with a patriotic impulse and pride of state that is equal to that of any citizen. The following citizens of the Cherokee Nation were elected members of the constitutional convention: James W. Swarts, James Riley Copeland, Clement Vann Rogers, James Turner Edmondson, Albert Sidney Wyly, O. H. P. Brewer, William N. Littlejohn, Charles O. Frye and Rev. Henry Cloud, the latter was a full blood Cherokee who defeated James Brooks Ayers Robertson by a vote of nine hundred fifty eight to eight hundred ninety three. Rev. Cloud was the only Cherokee in his constitutional district. The wife of Thomas J. Leahy of the fifty sixth district was Osage-Cherokee origin. The following Cherokees and Cherokee citizens have represented Oklahoma in the halls of Congress: Senator Robert Latham Owen; Congressmen William Wirt Hastings, James Sanford Davenport, Thomas Albert Chandler and Charles D. Carter, of Chickasaw-Cherokee descent. Hundreds of other Cherokees have held other offices in the state and thereby evinced their fealty to the State.

The salaries of the officers of the Cherokee Nation as fixed by acts of the council on: October 4, 1839, November 23, 1859, November 29, 1866, November 5, 1875 and in 1892 were, with slight variations, as follows:

	1839.	1859.	1866.	1875.	1892.
Principal Chief	$500.	$400.	$900.	$2000.	$1500.
Assistant Chief	300.	200.	600.	1000.	600.
Executive Councilers	3. day	2.	4.	5.	3.50
Supreme Judges	200.	3. d	5.	800.	500.
Clerk Sprm. Court	3.	2.	60.	300.	150.
Circuit Judges	200.	200.	300.	600.	500.*
District Judges	110.	125.	200.	400.	400.
Sheriffs	200.	150.	250.	400.	500.
Clerk Dt. Court	2. d	2.	60.	500.	400.
Juror	1.	.50	1.	2.	2.
Treasurer	500.	400.	500.	1000.	1000.
Clerks of legislature	3.	2.	4.	4.	3.50
Editor Advocate	500.	400.		1000.	400.
Solicitor	100.		150.	400.	400.
Spt. Education	300.		500.		500.
Legislators		2.	4.	5.	3.50
Solicitor General				1000.	800.
High Sheriff				800.	500.
Auditor				500.	300.

*The Circuit judges for the northern and central districts received $500. per year and the judge for the southern district, which embraced only Canadian District received $200.

MASONS AMONG THE CHEROKEES.

Be it enacted by the National Council, That lots Nos. five and six of square No. nineteen, in the town of Tahlequah, be and they are hereby donated to the Cherokee Lodge of Masons and the division of the Sons of Temperance, now in existence at this place, for the purpose of erecting thereon a lodge building, to be held and owned by them and their successors, through such a board of trustees as they may from time to time appoint: Provided, that the said building shall be erected within two years of the date of this act; otherwise the grant hereby made shall be null and void.

Tahlequah, October 30, 1852. JOHN ROSS'.

The above enactment referred to Cherokee Lodge No. 21 of Tahlequah of the Arkansas jurisdiction, the oldest Masonic lodge in the state of Oklahoma. The date of the charter is not known but the officers for the year of 1848 were Walter Scott Adair, W M; Nathan Baron Danenburg, S W; Joseph Coody, J W.[3]

The membership of Cherokee Lodge No. 21 in 1850 was: Nathan Danenburg, W M; Joseph Coody, S W; Walter Scott Adair, J W; Henry Dobson Reese, Secretary; members: David Carter, Charles R. Gourd, Levi Keys, William Potter Ross, John Griffith Harnage, John Walker Candy, Joseph Martin Lynch, Edwin Archer, Thomas Jefferson Parks, John Shepherd Vann, George M. Lavender, Johnson Foreman, James Daniel, Rev. Thomas Bertholf, Rev. J. W. Williams and H. Tament. The lodge was discontinued by the Grand Lodge of Arkansas on November 17, 1868, but they continued until September 5, 1877 when they were chartered under the Grand Lodge of Indian Territory as Cherokee Lodge No. 10, with Henry Dobson Reese, W M; John Ross Vann, S W; John Lynch Adair J W and the following members: William Frederick Rasmus, John Wardell Stapler, William Eubanks, William T. McCoy, Thomas F. Trainor, Johnson Thompson, Joseph Franklin Thompson, Dr. Walter Thompson Adair, Joel Bryan Mayes, Leonidas Dobson, James Latta, Jackson R. Gourd, T. K. B. McSpadden, Philip T. Johnson, Levi Keys, Dr. I. D. Leoser, E. Poe Harris, James Shelton, John Anthony Foreman, George Keys, David Wheeler and John Hildebrand Cookson.

In 1882 John Wardell Stapler was W M; Robert Latham Owen SW; Evans Price Robertson, JW; John Lynch Adair S D; J. B. Gladney, J D; Robert Bruce Ross, Secretary and William Johnston, Treasurer. Members not given above: Bluford West Alberty, John Martin Riley, Richard Martin Benge and Walter N. Evans.

Fort Gibson Lodge No. 35 was chartered by Arkansas on November 5, 1850 with the following officers: W. M. Chapman, W M; M. Rudder, S W; C. DeLano, J. W. and P. Lukenbill, Secretary. The charter of this lodge was discontinued by the Arkansas Grand Lodge on November 6, 1867. It was chartered under the Indian Territory Grand Lodge on November 5, 1878 as Alpha Lodge No. 12. The officers in 1879 were: P. J. Byrne, W M; Henry Clay Meigs, S W; William Thomas, J W; Florian Haradan Wash, S D; Dr. R. B. Howard, Treasurer and William S. Nash, Secretary.

In 1882 Florian H. Nash was W M; Henry C. Meigs S W; Dr. R. B.

Howard J W; Thomas French S D; George O. Sanders S S; William Jackson J S; Connell Rogers, Secretary: William Potter Ross and O. H. P. Brewer were members.

Flint Lodge No. 74 was chartered by the Grand Lodge of Arkansas on November 9, 1853. The officers for 1854 were: John Griffith Harnage W M; R. M. Johnson S W; John Thompson Adair, J W and William Penn Adair, Secretary. The lodge was discontinued by the Arkansas Grand Lodge on August 27, 1867, but this lodge as well as those at Tahlequah and Fort Gibson continued their organizations until they became a part of the Indian Territory Grand Lodge under which this lodge was chartered on March 28, 1876 as Flint Lodge No. 11.

The Grand Lodge of Indian Territory was organized at Caddo on October fifth, 1874 by Muscogee Lodge No. 90 of Eufaula, which became No. 1 of the new jurisdiction; Doaksville Lodge No. 279 of Doaksville, becoming No. 2 and Caddo Lodge No. 311 became No. 3. The old numbers were those of the Arkansas Grand Lodge. After the organization of the Grand Lodge, and following the first convocation, Oklahoma Lodge No. 217 of Boggy Depot applied for membership and was accepted as Oklahoma Lodge No. 4. Vinita Lodge No. 5 of Vinita was chartered on September 8, 1875 with George W. Franklin as W M; John Swain J W; James Blythe, Treasurer; James A. Thompson Secretary and the following were members: William Penn Adair, William W. Buffington, George W. Clark, Joseph Vann Cratchfield, James O. Hall, Benjamin F. Landrum, August Sager, W. F. Tucker and D. H. Tucker. Henry Armstrong, Charles Bluejacket, David Taylor, Robert Taylor and Samuel M. Couch were members in 1876. George W. Franklin was W M; J. T. Cunningham, S W and Henry Eiffort, S D in 1879. Among the members in 1880 were: George W. Franklin, W M; Thomas F. Couch, S W; A. W. Timberlake, J W; J. T. Cunningham, S D; Joseph Lynch Thompson, J D; J. J. Caldwell, Tyler and Ross Carey a member. In 1882 the following names are registered: James M. Tittle, William J. Strange, John C. Hogan, Samuel H. Mayes, Archibald McCoy, Robert Lunday, Surry Eaton Beck and John Henry Covel.

The following citizens of the Cherokee Nation have been Most Worshipped Grand Masters of the Grand Lodge of Indian Territory: Harvey Lindsey, 1882, Florian H. Nash, 1885, 1886 and 1887; Leo. E. Bennett, 1889, 1890, 1891 and 1892 and Wilson O. Bruton in 1904. O'Lonzo Conner was M W G M of the Oklahoma Grand Lodge in 1919. Leo E. Bennett was Grand Treasurer from 1899 to 1917.

T. M. BUFFINGTON
Chief—December 5, 1891, to December 23, 1891
November, 1899, to November, 1903

CHAPTER X

The Texas Cherokee 1820-30. Grant From Mexico. Grant From Texas. Treaties. Expulsion.

By the year of 1812, about one-fourth of the Cherokee Nation east had emigrated to the Arkansas territory between the Arkansas and White Rivers. John Bowles, a chief, and a large number from Running Water Town, on the Mussel Shoals of the Tennessee, had left in the year 1874 and emigrated to the St. Francis River country in southeast Missouri. During the winter of 1811-12 this branch moved to the Arkansas Territory, where they were domiciled until a survey of the Cherokee Nation, Arkansas was made by the United States Government in 1819 in accordance with the provisions of the Treatv of 1817.

Bowles' village was located between Shoal aand Petit Jean Creeks, on the south side of Arkansas River, outside of the stipulated Cherokee Territory, on account of this fact and in compliance with the wishes of his followers to locate in Spanish territory, he, with sixty families, migrated in the winter of 1819-20 to territory that was claimed to have been promised them by the representatives of the Dominion of Spain, on Sabine River and extending from the Angelina to the Trinity Rivers in the Province of Texas.

Settlement was made north of Nacogdoches, then an expanse of waste and ruin, the result of warfare waged between the American and Spanish forces of Long and Perez. The climatic conditions auguring favorable to the pursuits of agriculture, stock-raising and hunting, their numbers were augmented occasionally by recruits from their brethren in Arkansas and other tribes of Indians in the United States.

For one whole year the Cherokees lived in peace and happiness under the roof of the hospitable Spaniard. Whether title to the lands accorded to and occupied by them was by prescription rights, the Indian mode of occupancy or in fee from the Monarch of Spain, is immaterial—they were there: their rights undisputed, under the impression they had a perfected right.

The Mexicans, their authority emanating from the imperial government at Mexico City, becoming dissatisfied with Spanish suzerainty over this portion of Latin America, adopted drastic measures toward throwing off the Spanish yoke.

By the Plan of Iguala, adopted by the revolutionary government of Mexico, 24th February, 1821, the Mexicans published to the world that "all inhabitants of New Spain, without distinction, whether Europeans, Africans or Indians, are citizens of the monarchy, with a right to be employed in any post, according to their merit and virtues", and that "The person and property of every citizen will be respected and protected by the government" The Treaty of Cordova, of the 24th August, 1821, and the Declaration of Independence of the 28th September, 1821, reaffirmed the principles of the Plan of Iguala. Also the decree of the 9th April, 1823, which reaffirmed the three guaranties of the Plan of Iguala, viz:—1. Independence; 2. The Catholic religion; 3. Union of all Mexicans of whatever race. The decree of the 17th September 1822, with a view to give effect to the 12th Article of the Plan of Iguala, declared that classification of the inhabitants with regard to their origin, shall be omitted. The foregoing solemn declarations of the political power of the government, had the affect, necessarily, of investing the Indians with the full privileges of citizenship, as effectually as had the Declaration of Independence of the United States of 1776 of investing all those persons with these privileges, residing in the country at the time.

Under the constitution and laws of Mexico, as a race, no distinction was made between the Indians, as to rights of citizenship and the privileges belonging to it and those of European or Spanish blood. The Mexican Republic from the time of its emancipation from Spain, always dealt most liberally with foreigners, in its anxiety to colonize its vacant lands. Where the grant declared that a citizen of the United States had been naturalized, it was taken for true. Thus, it will be seen during this transitory period in the political affairs of the country, the Cherokees bore the status of full-fledged citizens of the Republic of Mexico, with all the privileges and immunities attached to the other inhabitants thereof. The first evidence of any attempt at acquiring legal title to the lands so occupied since their advent, is adduced by a letter from Richard Fields to James Dill, Alcalde of Nacogdoches, as follows:

"February 1st, 1822.

Dear Sir: I wish to fall at your feet and humbly ask you what must be done with us poor Indians? We have some grants that were given us when we lived under Spanish Government, and we wish you to send us news by the next mail whether they will be reversed or not. And if we were permitted, we will come as soon as possible to present ourselves before you in a manner agreeable to our talents. If we present ourselves in a rough manner, we pray you to right us. Our intentions are good toward the government.

Yours as a Chief of the Cherokee Nation,

Richard Fields."[1]

It appears that this communication went unanswered but was forwarded to the Governor of the Province of Texas at Bexar or San Antonio.

An indisputable title or unquestioned right of occupancy was desired on their part. With this object in view, a delegation repaired to Bexar and on the 8th November, 1822, an agreement was entered into between the Cherokees and Jose Felix Trespalacios, Governor of the Province and acting for the Republic of Mexico.

"Articles of Agreement, made and entered into between Captain Richard (Fields) of the Cherokee Nation, and the Governor of the Province of Texas.

"ARTICLE 1. That the said Captain Richard (Fields) with five others of his tribe, acompanied by Mr. Antonio Mexia and Antonio Wolfe, who act as interpreters, may proceed to Mexico, to treat with his Imperial Majesty, relative to the settlement which said Chief wishes to make for those of his tribe who are already in the territory of Texas, and also for those who are in the United States.

"ART. 2nd. That the other Indians in the city, and who do not accompany the before mentioned, will return to their village in the vicinity of Nacogdoches, and communicate to those who are at said village, the terms of this agreement.

"ART. 3rd. That a party of warriors of said village must be constantly kept on the road leading from the province to the United States, to prevent stolen animals from being carried thither, and to apprehend and punish those evil disposed foreigners, who form assemblages, and abound on the banks of the River Sabine within the territory of Texas.

"ART. 4th. That the Indians who return to their town, will appoint as their chief, the Indian Captain called Kunetand, alias Tong Turqui, to whom a copy of this agreement will be given, for the satisfaction of those of his tribe, and in order that they may fulfill its stipulations.

"ART. 5th. That meanwhile, and until the approval of the Supreme Government is obtained, they may cultivate their lands and sow their crops in free and peaceful possession.

"ART. 6th. That the said Cherokee Indians will become immediately subject to the laws of the Empire, as well as others who tread her soil, and they will also take up arms in defense of the nation, if called upon to do so.

"ART. 7th. That they shall be considered Hispano-Americans, and entitled to all the rights and privileges granted to such, and to the same protection, should it become necessary.

"ART. 8th. That they can immediately commence trade with the other inhabitants of the province, and with the exception of arms and ammunitions of war, with the tribes of savages who may be friendly with us.

"Which agreement, comprising the eight preceeding articles, has been executed in the presence of twenty-two Cherokee Indians of the Baron de Bastrop, who has been pleased to act as interpreter, of two of the Ayuntamiento, and two officers of this Garrison.

Bexar, 8th November, 1822.

Jose Felix Trespalacios, Jose Flores, Nabor Villarreal, Richard Fields, x his mark, El Baron de Bastrop, Manuel Iturri Castillo, Franco de Castanedo."[1]

In pursuance of this agreement Governor Trespalacios addressed the following communication to Don Caspar Lopez Commandant of the Eastern Internal Provinces, sending it by Lieutenant Don Ignacio Ronquillo:

"Captain Richard (Fields) of the Cherokee Nation, with twenty-two more Indians that accompanied him, visited me to ask permission for all belonging to his tribe, to settle upon the lands of this province. After I had been informed myself through foreigners, who are acquainted with this Nation, that it is the most industrious and useful of the tribes in the United States, I entered with said Captain, into an agreement, the original of which I send you. This arrangement provided that Vaptain Richard and six others of his nation, with two interpreters, escorted by Lieutenant Don Ignacio Ronquillo and fifteen men of the Visscayan, shall proceed to your headquarters and, if it meet your approval, thence to the court of the Empire.

"The Cherokee Nation, according to their statement, numbers fifteen thousand souls; but there are within the borders of Texas only one hundred warriors and two hundred women and children. They work for their living, and dress in cotton-cloth, which they themselves manufacture. They raise cattle and horses and use firearms. Many of them understand the English language. In my opinion, they ought to be useful to the Province, for they immediately became subject to its laws, and I believe will succeed in putting a stop to carrying stolen animals to the United States, and in arresting those evil-doers that infest the roads."[1]

From the foregoing agreement and communication, it will be seen that the matter of procuring title was only partially and temporarily realized. While occupation or prescription rights were accorded by the authorities, they were also recognized as Hispano-Americans and were clothed with judicial as well as police powers, pledging their unqualified support in time of war. They were reorganized as agriculturists, manufacturers and stock-raisers and were to apprehend and try offenders against the laws of the Empire.

Not being satisfied with conditions as to land titles, it was their determination to push their claims for a more satisfactory arrangement. Repairing to Saltillo, headquarters of the Commandant General, they were sent, early in December on their way to Mexico City, where they arrived in the Spring of 1823. The conditions of the country were chaotic. The throne of Emperor Iturbide toppled and he was succeeded by Victoria, Bravo and Negrete on March 30th, 1823, who held the reigns of government, exercising a joint regency.

During the progress of affairs, Fields and his fellow-companions were detained, awaiting the decision of the government. The Minister of Relations gave notice that the agreement entered into between Fields and Trespalacios would be recognized, pending the passage of a general colonization law. The Minister of Relations, Lucas Alaman, in the new provisional government, wrote to Don Felipe de la Garza, the successor of Lopez, as Commandant General of the Eastern Internal Provinces, as follows:

"The Supreme Executive Power has been pleased to resolve that Richard Fields, Chief of the Cherokee Tribe of Indians, and his companions, now in this Capitol, may return to their country, and that they be supplied with whatever may be necessary for that purpose. Therefore, Their Supreme Highnesses have directed me to inform you that, although the agreement made on the 8th—November, 1822, between Richard Fields and Colonel Felix Trespalacious, Governor of Texas, remains provisionally in force, you are nevertheless required to be very careful and vigilant in regard to their settlements, endeavoring to bring them towards the interior, and at places least dangerous, not permitting for the present, the entrance of any new families of the Cherokee tribe, until the publication of the General Colonization Law, which will establish the rules and regulations to be observed, although the benefits to arise from it, cannot be extended to them, in relation to all of which, Their Highnesses intent to consult the Sovereign Congress. That while this is effecting, the families already settled, should be well treated, and the other chiefs also, treated with suitable consideration, provided that those already within our territory respect our laws, and are submissive to our authorities; and, finally, Their Highnesses order, that in future neither these Indians, nor any others, be permitted to come to the City of Mexico, but only send their petitions in ample form, for journeys similar to the present are of no benefit and only create unnecessary expense to the state. All of which I communicate to you for your information and fulfillment."

That the delegation regarded their land titles secure, is apparent. They returned home seemingly satisfied with their accomplishments. Victoria, Bravo and Negrete, through their Minister of Relations, had confirmed the then existing contract until such time that a general colonization law was enacted, implying that titles would be more securely vested under such a law.

About a year later, Fields proposed a union of all the Indian tribes in Eastern Texas, proposing to exact a pledge from them, of fidelity to the government. In promulgating this, he gave a summary of his accomplishments in Mexico City and of his plans for the future. On March 6th, 1824, he wrote to the Governor at San Antonio, as follows:

"It was my intention, on my return from Mexico, to present myself at San Antonio, in order that the authorities there might examine the papers which I received from the Superior Government of the Nation; but it was impossible to do so, because a party of Comanches had prepared an ambush on the road. However, I had the good fortune to escape them.

"The Superior Government has granted me in this province, a territory sufficient for me and that part of the tribe of Indians dependent on me to settle on, and also a commission to command all the Indian tribes and nations that are in the four eastern provinces.

"I pray your honor to notify all the Indians within your terirtory, and particularly the Lipans, that on the 4th of July next, I shall, in compliance with the order of the Supreme Government, hold a general council of all the Indian tribes, at my house in the rancheria of the Cherokees, twelve miles west of the Sabine River. At this Council, I shall propose a treaty of peace to all Indians who are willing to submit themselves to the orders of the Government. In case there should be any who may not wish to ratify what I propose, I shall use force of arms to subdue them.

"I beg you to notify the commandant at San Antonio that he shall, for the satisfaction of his people, send some trusted person to aid in the treaty of peace and see how the affair is managed.

"Should it be convenient, have this letter translated and have the authorities send it to Rio Grande and Monclova, in which two places I left copies of the documents from the Superior Government."

The Grand Council took place in pursuance of call, with exception of the date which was changed to August 20th, 1824. All the tribes convened in council at Fields' residence, with the exception of the Comanches and Tonkawas, on whom he proposed to make war.

Closely following these events the 24th January, 1823, the Central Government under Augustine, the first constituted Emperor of Mexico, enacted the Imperial Colonization Law of 1823, which decreed, among other things—"that the Mexican Government will protect the liberty, property and civil rights of all foreigners, etc." This was followed by the National Colonization Law of August 18, 1824, in which it was decreed—"To all who shall see and understand these presents—That the Mexican Nation offers to foreigners, who came to establish themselves within its territory, security for their persons and property, provided, they subject themselves to the laws of the country, etc. "and for this purpose, the legislatures of all the states will, as soon as possible, form colonization laws, or regulations for their respective states, conforming themselves in all things to the constitutional act, general constitution, and the regulations established in this law, etc."

In pursuance of the foregoing, the State of Coahuila and Texas passed a colonization law March 25th, 1825, the first article of which reads:

"All foreigners who, in virtue of the general law of the 18th of August, 1824, which guarantees the security of their persons and property in this republic, shall wish to emigrate to any of the settlements of the State of Coahuila and Texas, are permitted to do so; and the said state invites and calls them." Second. "Those who shall thus emigrate, far from being molested, shall be admitted by the local authorities of said settlements, and permitted by the same to freely engage in any honest pursuit, provided they respect the general laws of the republic, and the laws of the state."

It is noticeable that the provisions of the three consecutive colonization laws, the word "foreigners" and the phrase "those who shall thus emigrate" would apply to those who arrived after their passage, the first, the Imperial; decreed the 4th of January, 1823. For the sake of clearness, it is deemed advisable to reiterate that the Cherokees were Mexican citizens and had been prior to the passage of these laws, as much so as any others who emigrated to Texas and were so made by statute or constitutional enactment.

Possibly, owing to the absence of the locomotive, telegraph and other modes of travel and conveniences of communication, many of the early settlers of Texas did not know of the passage of these laws, or whether the vested rights of the Cherokees were purposely ignored on the part of the authorities of Coahuila and Texas, sitting at Saltilla, made divers and sundries grants of lands. These embraced portions of Cherokee territory, and among the donors were David G. Burnet, Vincente Filisola, Robert Leftwich, Frost Thorn and the Edwards Brothers. This act so incensed the Cherokees, that a council was soon after convened. Peter Ellis Bean reported to Stephen F. Austin that Fields addressed the council substantially as follows:

"In my old days, I traveled two thousand miles to the City of Mexico to beg some lands to settle a poor orphan tribe of Red People, who looked to me for protection. I was promised lands for them after staying one year in Mexico and spending all I had. I then came to my people and waited two years, and then sent Mr. Hunter, after selling my stock to provide him money for his expenses. When he got there, he stated his mission to the government. They said they knew nothing of this Richard Fields and treated him with contempt.

"I am a Red Man and a man of honor and can't be imposed on this way. We will lift up our tomahawks and fight for land with all those friendly tribes that wish land also. If I am beaten, I will resign to fate, and if not, I will hold lands by the force of my red warriors."

John Dunn Hunter, a White man, had come among the Cherokees sometime during the year 1825. Through his intervention, hope was held out that the agitated question of land title would be amicably settled. With this end in view, he was dispatched to Mexico City to plead their cause. He arrived at the seat of government March 19th, 1826 and returned in September, after fruitless attempts at a settlement of title.

Seeing their lands taken possession of by newcomers, their homes and fire-sides so long established, what they considered wrongfully wrested from them, they began to prepare to maintain their holdings peacefully if possible, but by force, if they must. Touching these events, Stephen F. Austin wrote the Commander of Texas September 11, 1826 in part, as follows:

"There is reason to fear that the delay of the measures concerning the peaceable tribes, has disgusted them; and should this be the case, it would be a misfortune, for 100 of the Cherokees are worth more as warriors than 500 Comanches."

Hunter, "pictured in story and glowing language the gloomy alternative, now plainly presented to the Indians, of abandoning their present abodes and returning within the limits of the United States—or preparing to defend themselves against the whole power of the Mexican Government by force of arms. - - - - - - - -"

John G. Purnell wrote to Fields from Saltillo on October 4th, 1825, as follows:

"When I last saw you in my house at Monterey, I little thought in so short a time you would have commenced a war against your American brothers and the Mexican Nation; more particularly a man like yourself who is acquainted with the advantages of civilization. - - - - If your claims for lands were not granted at a time when the government was not firmly established, that should not be a cause of war. Ask and it will be given to you; this nation has always felt friendly inclined toward yours, and I am sure if you cease hostilities they will enter into a treaty with you by which you will obtain more permanent advantages than you can by being at war - - - - ".

On November 10th, 1825, F. Durcy, also of Saltillo, wrote to Francis Grapp, a well-known Indian trader at Natchitoches:

"Knowing the weight of your influence with all the savage nations and also the ascendancy that you have over the character of Mr. Fields, your son-in-law, I think that no one could stop, better than yourself, the great disturbance which is about to be raised by the Indians, whom you understand better than I. I say that you can distinguish yourself for the welfare of humanity in general, in making the savages understand the evils which await them in following the plans of Mr. Fields, and likewise causing Mr. Fields to be spoken to by his brother, who can prevail upon him (le determiner) to abandon a plan which will have no other end than that of destroying himself and all who shall have the misfortune to follow him."

Hunter's mission to Mexico City failed of its purpose. The Edwards brothers, who had been granted territory on which to settle eight hundred families, discovered that their claims of title conflicted with others originating under the Spanish regime. These lands also over-lapped the Cherokee session. They had consumed large sums of money, time, and enormous amount of work in the United States arranging for the introduction of the eight hundred families called for by the terms of the empresario contract with the Mexican government. Finding themselves in dispute over their lands, almost the same as their neighbors, the Cherokees' affairs were rapidly reaching a critical stage in that portion of Texas.

The Edwardses, highly incensed at the prospects of losing their all at one fell swoop, determined to throw off Mexican sovereignty and thus declare Texas a free and independent nation, under the name of the Republic of Fredonia.

Fields and Hunter concluded to confer with this embryo government on future plans. On their arrival at Nacogdoches, they found all excitement and chaos. A compact was entered into by Fields and Hunter, on the part of the Red people, Harmon B. Mayo and Benjamin W. Edwards, as agents of the Committee of Independence, culminating into a Solemn Union, League and Confederation in peace and war to establish and defend their independence against Mexico.

The compact entered into, follows:

"Whereas, The Government of the Mexican United States, have, by repeated insults, treachery and oppression, reduced the White and Red emigrants from the United States of North America, now living in the Province of Texas, within the territory of said government, which they have been deluded by promises solemnly made, and most basely broken, to the dreadful alternative of either submitting their free-born necks to the yoke of the imbecile, unfaithful, and despotic government, miscalled a Republic, or of taking up arms in defense of their inalienable rights and asserting their independence; they—viz: The White emigrants now assembled in the town of Nacogdoches, around the independent standard, on the one part, and the Red emigrants who have espoused the same Holy Cause, on the other, in order to prosecute more speedily and effectually the war of Independence, they have mutually undertaken, to a successful issue, and to bind themselves by the ligaments of reciprocal interests and obligations, have resolved to form a treaty of Union, League and Confederation.

"For this illustrious object, Benjamin W. Edwards and Harmon B. Mayo, Agents of the Committee of Independence, and Richard Fields and John D. Hunter, the agents of the Red people, being respectfully furnished with due powers, have agreed to the following articles:

"1. The above named contracting parties, bind themselves to a solemn Union, League, and Confederation, in peace and war, to establish and defend their mutual independence of the Mexican United States.

"2. The contracting parties guarantee mutually to the extent of their power, the integrity of their respective territories as now agreed upon and described, viz: The territory apportioned to the Red people, shall begin at the Sandy Spring, where Bradley's road takes off from the road leading from Nacogdoches to the Plantation of Joseph Dust; from thence west by the compass, without regard to variation, to the Rio Grande; thence to the head of the Rio Grande; thence with the mountains to the head of the Big Red River; thence north to the boundary of the United States of America; thence with the same line to the mouth of Sulphur Fork; thence in a right line to the beginning.

"The territory apportioned to the White people, shall comprehend all the residue of the Province of Texas, and of such other portions of the Mexican United States, as the contracting parties, by their mutual efforts and resources, may render independent, provided the same shall not extend further west than the Rio Grande.

"3. The contracting parties mutually guarantee the rights of Empresarios to their premium lands only, and the rights of all other individuals, acquired under the Mexican Government and relating or appertaining to the above described territory, provided the said Empresarios and individuals do not forfeit the same by an opposition to the independence of the said territories, or by withdrawing their aid and support to its acomplishment.

It is distinctly understood by the contracting parties, that the territory apportioned to the Red people, is intended as well for the benefit of those tribes now settled in the territory apportioned to the White people, as for those living in the former territory, and that it is incumbent upon the contracting parties for the Red people to offer the said tribes a participation in the same.

"5. It is also mutually agreed by the contracting parties, that every individual, Red or White, who has made improvements within either of the Respective Allied Territories and lives upon the same, shall have a fee simple of a section of land, including his improvement, as well as the protection of the government in which he may reside.

"6. The contracting parties mutually agree, that all roads, navigable streams, and all other channels of conveyance within each Territory, shall be open and free to the use of the inhabitants of the other.

"7. The contracting parties mutualy stipulate that they will direct all their resources to the prosecution of the Heaven-inspired cause which has given birth to this solemn Union, League and Confederation, firmly relying upon their united efforts, and the strong arm of Heaven for success.

"In faith whereof, the Agents of the respective contracting parties hereunto affix their names.

"Done in the town of Nacogdoches, this the twenty-first of December, in the year of our Lord, one thousand eight hundred and twenty-six."

Richard Fields, John D. Hunter, B. W. Edwards, H. B. Mayor.

"We, the Committee of Independence, and the Committee of the Red people, do ratify the above Treaty, and do pledge ourselves to maintain it in good faith.

"Done on the day and date above mentioned.

Richard Fields, John D. Hunter, Ne-Ko-Lake, John Bags, Cuk-To-Keh,

Martin Parmer, President, Hayden Edwards, W. B. Legon, John Sprowl, B. J. Thompson, Jos. A. Huber, B. W. Edwards, H. B. Mayo.

While these things were transpiring in and around Nacogdoches, the Mexicans, with their chief allies Stephen F. Austin and Peter Ellis Bean, were stirring up dissatisfaction among the Fredonians, both Red and White people. To forestall any further preparations on the part of the infant revolutionary government, Bent on 16th—December, arrived with thirty-five Mexican soldiers from San Antonio. On learning of the feelings that pervaded the Fredonians, he retired to a point west of Nacogdoches to await reinforcements, realizing his forces were inadequate to successfully cope with the revolutionary forces. About the 20th of the same month, two hundred strong under Colonel Mateo Ahumada, with banners flying, the glittering of steel and the clanking of arms, marched out of San Antonio, bent on the conquest of Nacogdoches. This contingent was accompanied by Jose Antonio Saucedo, the Political Chief, in full charge of operations.

On January 22nd—1826, Austin addressed the Mexican people in terms, as follows:

"To the Inhabitants of the Colony:

"The persons who were sent on from this colony by the Political Chief and Military Commandant (Austin) to offer peace to the madmen of Nacogdoches, have returned—returned without having affected anything. The olive branch of peace which was held out to them has been insultingly returned, and that party have denounced massacre and desolation to this colony. They are trying to excite all the Northern Indians to murder and plunder, and it appears as though they have no other object than to ruin and plunder this country. They openly threaten us with massacre and the plunder of our property.

"To arms then, my friends and fellow-citizens, and hasten to the standard of our country.

"The first hundred men will march on the 26th. Necessary orders for mustering and other purposes will be issued to commanding officers.

Union and Mexico.

S. F. Austin.

San Felipe de Austin,
January 27th—1827."

The authorities and leading citizens of Austin's Colony lost no time in fomenting dissension in the ranks of the Fredonians. From the capitol of his colony, Austin hurled all the epithets at his command against his liberty-loving American brothers. Writers of Texas history condemn him for the course taken in this instance. A careful perusal of the compact entered into by the Fredonians will not disclose an iota justifying his denunciations in such terms, in his proclamation to the colonists. The compact was to them, what the immortal document of 1776 was to the Americans during the gloomy days of the American Revolution. It was their divorcement from a weak, unstable and vacillating rule. It was the forerunner of the glory of San Jacinto, the climax that thrills the heart of every loyal Texan and freeman throughout christendom. Doomed to failure it was, and the perpetrators suffered the consequences.

Their propaganda was successful. Promises of land and other preferments by Bean and Austin detached large numbers of the Fredonians, leaving the loyal, in a hopeless state. Bowles and Mush, of the Cherokees, were among the detached. Due to their machinations, Fields and Hunter were foully murdered by men of their own people. The Edwards contingent was dispersed and fled to Louisiana, and other portions of the United States. For his services in having Fields and Hunter put out of the way, Bowles was invested with a commission as nominal Colonel in the Mexican army, as was also Peter Ellis Bean. The Fredonia affair was terminated.

Affairs in this portion of Texas were restored to normalcy, with the exception of the mooted question of land titles. To further complicate matters, the legislature made a division of the territory in question between David G. Burnet and Joseph Vehlein.

The Act of April 6th, 1830, prohibiting the further emigration of Americans into Texas, was passed. General Teran, Commandant General of the Eastern Interior States, determined to perfect title in the Cherokees, to lands so long occupied by them, and on August 15th, 1831, wrote to Letona, Governor of Coahuila and Texas:

"In compliance with the promises made by the Supreme Government, to the Cherokee Indians, and with a view to the preservation of peace, with the rude tribes, I caused them to determine upon some fixed spot for their settlement, and having selected it on the head waters of the Trinity, and the banks of the Sabine, I pray your Excellency may be pleased to order that possession be given to them, with the corresponding titles, with the understanding that it will be expedient, that the commissioners be appointed for this purpose, should act in conjunction with Colonel Jose de las Piedras, commanding the military forces on the frontier of Nacogdoches."

Teran's suggestions that title be consummated was universally concurred in by the authorities. March 22, 1832, Governor Letona ordered the political chief to furnish Commissioner Piedras with the necessary documents in due form for that purpose. On the eve of preparations to carry out such orders, he was expelled from Nacogdoches by an uprising of Americans. Soon afterwards, Teran committed suicide and was succeeded in office by Vincente Filisola who held an empresario contract in his own name. This appointment was detrimental to the interests of the Cherokees in the extreme, because his contract embraced a portion of their lands. Governor Letona died of yellow fever and was succeeded by Beramendi.

The attempts on the part of Mexico to grant title, ended with these transactions.

On July 20th, 1833, a delegation headed by Colonel Bowles, repaired to San Antonio and petitioned the Political Chief for title to their lands. They were directed to Monclova, the Capitol of the Province of Coahuila and Texas, where they were given assurance that their claims would receive due consideration. But, inasmuch as David G. Burnet and Vincente Filisola had immatured colonization contracts which were to expire December 21st—1835, all land title, he maintained, must, of necessity, be held in abeyance for the time being. However, on March 10th—1835, the Political Chief wrote the Supreme Government, admonishing the authorities that the Cherokees be not disturbed in their possessions until the central government at Mexico City could finally pass on the question.

On May 12, 1835, the legislature of the state of Coahuila and Texas passed the following resolution:

"Art. 1. In order to secure the peace and tranquility of the state, the government is authorized to select, out of the vacant lands of Texas, that land which may appear most appropriate for the location of the peaceable and civilized Indians which may have been introduced into Texas.

"Art. 2. It shall establish with them a line of defense along the frontier to secure the state against the incursions of barbarous tribes."

This was the last utteranec of the Mexican government in reference to the Cherokee claims.

At the beginning of the disaffection of the Americans, the Committee of Public Safety, the Permanent Council and Consultation, successively, had deemed it just and prudent to arrive at some understanding with the Cherokees and other Indians concerning their land claims.

The state of affairs at this period existing between the Central Government at Mexico City and the State of Coahuila and Texas was exceedinglyl critical. On the 19th of September, 1835, on behalf of the Committee of Safety, Stephen F. Austin addressed the people of Texas in part: "That every district should send members to the General Consultation, with full powers to do whatever may be necessary for the good of the country."

The General Consultation convened on the 16th—October, 1835, but adjourned for want of a quorum. It reassembled at San Felipe de Austin on November 1st, but was unable to dispatch business until the 3rd, when a quorum appeared. Dr. Branch T. Archer of Brazoria, formerly Speaker of the House of Delegates in the Virginia Legislature, was unanimously elected President. This was the third deliberative body authorized on the American plan, superseding the conventions of October 1, 1832, and April 1, 1833. In an elaborate speech to the convention, President Archer reviewed the condition of affairs of the country and recommended plans upon which Texas was to erect autonomy and at the same time contest upon the field of battle for a long-cherished independence. Among other things impressed upon the members of the Consultation, were the need of establishing a provisional Government, with a Governor, Lieutenant Governor and Council to be clothed with Legislative and executive powers; and that "there are several warlike and peaceful tribes of Indians that claim certain portions of our land. Locations have been made within the limits they claim, which has created great dissatisfaction amongst them. Some of the chiefs of those tribes are expected here in a few days, and I deem it expedient to make some equitable arrangement of the matter that will prove satisfactory to them."

On the 7th of November 1835, the Unanimous Declaration of the Consultation was adopted. It declared that "General Lopez de Santa Anna and other military chieftains have, by force of arms, overthrown the federal institutions of Mexico and dissolved the social compact which existed between Texas and other members of the Mexican Confederacy; Now, the good people of Texas, availing themselves of their natural rights, Solemnly Declare—1st. That they have taken up arms in defense of their Rights and Liberties, - - - - -".

In pursuance of this Declaration of Independence, a Plan or Constitution for a Provisional Government was drawn by a committee headed by Henry Smith, reported to that body on November 9th, but was not adopted as the organic act until the 11th, at which time it was enrolled and signed. A provisional Government was thus created, among the prerogatives or duties imposed upon the Governor and Council were to hypothecate the public lands and pledge the public faith for a loan not to exceed one million dollars; to impose and regulate imports and tonnage duties and provide for the collection of the same; treat with the several tribes of Indians in reference to their land titles, and, if possible, to secure their friendship; establish post-offices and post-roads; regulate postal rates and appoint a post-master general; grant pardons and hear admiralty cases.

Adoption of this plan and the election of officers toook place on November 12th, and signed by the fifty-four delegates present on the following day. Henry Smith, opposed by S. F. Austin, was duly elected Provisional Governor, while James W. Robinson of Nacogdoches, was elected Lieutenant Governor.

From the time of the conception of a separation of Texas from Mexico, it was deemed advisable to conciliate the Indian tribes within her borders, and this could best be brought about by entering into a treaty of friendship and neutrality and at the same time guarantee to them title to the lands occupied. The Cherokees were peacefully domiciled in east central Texas and were regarded, and justly so, as agriculturists, manufacturers, stock-raisers and the following of other pursuits that well plaeed them out of the savage or hunter class and compelled the fitting appellation of Civilized Indians. They possessed, as a nation, several hundred soldiers or warriors who were expert riflemen.

On November 13th, 1835, the day of the adoption of the Plans and Powers of the Constitution of the Provisional Government, the following Solemn Declaration was unanimously adopted and signed by the entire body of fifty-four members:

"Be It Solemnly Decreed, That we, the chosen delegates of the Consultation of the people of all Texas, in general convention assembled, solemnly declare that the Cherokee Indians, and their associate bands, twelve tribes in number, agreeable to their last general council in Texas, have derived their just claims to lands included within the bounds hereinafter mentioned from the government of Mexico, from whom we have also derived our rights to the soil by grant and occupancy.

"We solemnly declare that the boundaries of the claims of the said Indians to the land is as follows, to-wit: Lying north of the San Antonio road and the Neches, and west of the Angelina and Sabine Rivers. We solemnly declare that the Governor and General Council, immediately on its organization, shall appoint Commissioners to treat with the said Indians, to establish the definite boundaries of their territory, and secure their confidence and friendship.

"We solemnly declare that we will guarantee to them the peaceful enjoyment of their rights to the lands, as we do our own; we solemnly declare, that all grants, surveys and locations of lands, hereinbefore mentioned, made after the settlements of said Indians, are, and of right ought to be, utterly null and void, and that the Commissioners issuing the same, be and are hereby ordered, immediately to recall and cancel the same, as having been made upon lands already appropriated by the Mexican Government.

"We solemnly declare that it is our sincere desire that the Cherokee Indians, and their associate bands, should remain our friends in peace and war, and if they do so, we pledge the public faith for the support of the foregoing declarations.

"We solemnly declare that they are entitled to our commisseration and protection, as the just owners of the soil, as an unfortunate race of people, that we wish to hold as friends, and treat with justice. Deeply and solemnlly impressed with these sentiments as a mark of sincerity, your committee would respectfully recommend the adoption of the following resolution:

"Resolved, That the members of this convention, now present, sign this Declaration, and pledge the public faith, on the part of the people of Texas.

"Done in Convention at San Felipe de Austin, this 13th day of November, A. D., 1835.

(Signed) B. T. Archer, President,

John A. Wharton, Meriwether W. Smith, Sam Houston, William Menifee, Chas. Wilson, Wm. N. Sigler, James Hodges, Wm. W. Arrington, John Bevil, Wm. S. Fisher, Alex. Thompson, J. G. V. Pierson, D. C. Barrett, R. Jones Jesse Burnam, Lorenzo de Zavala, A. Horton, Edwin Waller, Daniel Parker, Wm. P. Harris, John S. D. Byrom, Wm. Whitaker, A. G. Perry, Albert G. Kellogg, C. C. Dyer, Geo. M. Patrick, J. D. Clements, Claiborne West, Jas. W. Parker, J. S. Lester, Geo. W. Davis, Joseph L. Hood, A. E. C. Johnson, Asa Hoxey, Martin Parmer, Asa Mitchell, L. H. Everett, R. M. Williamson, Phillip Coe, R. R. Royal, John W. Moore, Benj. Fuga, Sam T. Allen, Wyatt Hanks, James W. Robinson, Henry Millard, Jesse Grimes, A. B. Hardin, Wyly Martin, Henry Smith, David A. Macomb, A. Houston, E. Collard.

P. B. Dexter,

Secretary."

Pledging the public faith on the part of the people of Texas, among other things the "Solemn Declaration," after defining the boundaries of the claims of the Cherokees enunciated "that we will guarantee to them the peaceful enjoyment of their rights to their lands, as we do our own, we solemnly declare that all grants, surveys and locations of lands, within the bounds hereinbefore mentioned, made after the settlement of said Indians, are, and of right ought to be, utterly null and void, and the commissioners issuing the same, be and are hereby ordered, immediately to recall and cancel the same, as having been made upon lands already appropriated by the Mexican Government."

After the passage of the Colonization Laws, giving to the respective states the right to make disposition of the vacant lands within their boundaries, it will be remembered that David G. Burnet and others were awarded contracts affecting lands within the boundaries described and partially in the Cherokee Nation.

When the consultation was published to the world, it was the just a little over a month until the date of the expiration of the contracts of Burnet and Fileasola, which fell on December 21, 1835. "And all grants, surveys and locations of lands within the bounds hereinbefore mentioned, made after the settlement of said Indians, are, and of right ought to be, null and void."

As has been said, the Cherokees settled on these lands in the winter of 1819-20, while the contracts of Burnet bear date of December 22, 1826. All the acts of the Consultation were the basic or organic laws of the land and if any act is to be accepted as such, these contracts must ceratinly have been annulled, since their provisions bore directly upon lands already appropriated by the Mexican Government and so recognized by the Consultation and the Provisional Government of Texas. "Language could not be made more plainer or obligatory than was this guarantee to these tribes."

Among the several acts of this body, a Major General who was to be Commander-in-chief of all the Military forces, was elected by that body. Sam Houston was the unanimous choice. His commission follows:

"In the name of the people of Texas, free and sovereign.

"We, reposing special trust and confidence in your patriotism, valor, conduct and fidelity, do by these presents constitute and appoint you to be Major General and Commander-in-chief of the armies of Texas and of all the forces now raised or to be raised by it, and of all others who shall voluntarily offer their services and join the army, for the defense of the constitution and liberty, and for repelling every hostile invasion thereof; and you are hereby vested with full power and authority to act as you shall think best for the good and welfare of the service.

"And we do hereby strictly charge and require all officers and soldiers under your command to be obedient to your orders, and diligent in the exercise of their several duties.

"And we do also enjoin you to be careful in executing the great trust reposed in you, by causing strict discipline and order to be observed in the army and that the soldiers be duly exercised, and provided with all convenient necessaries.

"And you are to regulate your conduct in every respect by the rules and discipline of war adopted by the United States of North America, or such as may be hereafter adopted by this government; and particularly to observe such orders and directions, from time to time, as you shall receive from this or a future government of Texas.

"This commission to continue in force until revoked by this or a future government.

Done at San Felipe de Austin, on the fourteenth day of November, eighteen hundred and thirty-five

Henry Smith,
Governor.

P. B. Dexter, Secretary of
Provisional Government."

On November 14th, the Consultation ceased its labors. Governor Smith immediately convened the Council for the government of the country. Upon the organization of the Council, Governor Smith addressed that body the following letter relative to carrying into effect that portion of the Declaration touching the Cherokee claims:

"San Felipe, December, 18, 1835.

Gentlemen of the Council:

"---------------- --I further have to suggest to you the propriety of appointing the Commissioners on the part of this government to carry into effect the Indian treaty as contemplated by the Convention. I can see no difficulty which can reasonably occur in the appointment of the proper agents on our part, having so many examples and precedents before us. The United States have universally sent their most distinguished military officers to perform such duties, because the Indians generally look up to and respect their authority as coercive and paramount. I would therefore suggest the propriety of appointing General Houston, of the army, and Col. John Forbes of Nocogdoches, who has been already commissioned as one of my aides. The Commissioners would go specially instructed, so that no wrong could be committed either to the government, the Indians, or our individual citizens. All legitimate rights would be respected, and no others. I am aware that we have no right to transcend the superior order, and Declaration made by the convention, and, if I recollect that article right, the outline of external boundaries was demarked within which the Indian tribes alluded to, should be located; but at the same time paying due regard to the legitimate rights on the citizens within the same limits.

"If these Indians have introduced themselves in good faith under the Colonization Laws of the Government, they would be entitled to the benefit of these laws and comply with their conditions. I deem it a duty which we owe them to pay all due respects to their rights and claim their co-operation in the support of them and at the same time not to infringe upon the rights of our countrymen, so far as they have been justly founded.

"These agents going under proper instructions, would be enabled to do right, but not permitted to do wrong, as their negotiations would be subject to investigation and ratification by the government before they became a law.

I am, gentlemen,
Your Obedient Servant,
Henry Smith,
Governor."

Resolution Appointing Commissioners to Treat With the Cherokee Indians, Etc.

"Be It Resolved by the General Council of the Provisional Government of Texas, That Sam Houston, John Forbes and John Cameron, be and they are hereby appointed Commissioners to treat with the Cherokee Indians, and their twelve Associated Bands, under such instructions as may be given them by the Governor and Council ,and should it so happen that all the Commissioners cannot attend, and two of them shall have power to conclude a treaty and report the same to the General Council of the Provisional Government, for its approval and ratification.

"Be It Further Resolved, etc. That said Commissioners be required to hold said treaty so soon as practicable.

"Passed, Dec. 22d, 1835.

James W. Robinson,
Lieut.-Gov. and ex-offico
Pres't. of G. C.

E. M. Pease, Secy. to General Council,
Approved, December 28, 1835.

Henry Smith, Governor.

C. B. Stewart,
Sec'y. to Executive."

Resolution for Instructing Commissioners Appointed to Treat with the Cherokee Indians and Their Associate Bands:

"Be it resolved by the General Council of the Provisional Government of Texas, That Sam Houston, John Forbes and John Cameron, appointed Commissioners to treat with the aforesaid Indians, be and they are hereby instructed, to proceed as soon as practicable, to Nacogdoches, and hold a treaty with the Indians aforesaid, and that they shall in no wise transcend the Declarations made by the Consultation of November last, in any of their articles of treaty.

"Sec. 2. Be it Further Resolved, etc. That they are required in all things to pursue a course of justice and equity toward the Indians, and to protect all honest claims of the whites, agreeably to such laws, compacts or treaties, as the said Indians may have hereto made with the Republic of Mexico, and that the (said) Commissioners be instructed to provide in said treaty with the Indians, that they shall never alienate their lands, either separately or collectively, except to the Government of Texas, and to agree that the said Government will at any time hereafter, purchase all their claims at a fair price and reasonable valuation.

"Sec. 3. Be It Further Resolved, etc., That the Governor be required to give to the Commissioners, such definite and particular instructions, as he may think necessary to carry into effect the object of the foregoing resolutions, together with such additional instructions as will secure the effective co-operation of the Indians at a time when it may be necessary to call all the effective forces of Texas, into the field, and agreeing for their services in a body for a specified time.

"Sec. 4. Be It Further Resolved, etc., That the Commissioners be authorized and empowered to exchange other lands within the limits of Texas, not otherwise appropriated in place of the lands claimed by said Cherokee Indians and their Associated Bands.

"Passed at San Felipe de Austin, Dec. 26, 1835.

James W. Robinson,
Lieut.-Gov. and ex-officio Prest. of G. C.

Henry Smith,
Governor.

E. M. Pease,
Sec'y. of General Council
C. B. Stewart, Sec'y. of Executive.

Treaty Between the Commissioners on Behalf of the Provisional Government of Texas and the Cherokee Indians and Twelve Associated Tribes:

"This treaty this day made and established between Sam Houston and John Forbes, Commissioners on the part of the Provisional Government of Texas, on the one part, and the Cherokees and their associate bands now residing in Texas, of the other part, to-wit: Shawness, Delawares, Kickapoos, Quopaws, Choctaws, Bolupies, Jawanies, Alabomas, Cochaties, Caddoes of the Noches, Tahovcattokes, and Unatuquouous, by the head chiefs and head men and warriors of the Cherokees, as elder brothers and representatives of all other bands, agreeable to their last council. This treaty is made in conformity to the declaration made by the last general consultation at San Felipe and dated the 13th, of November, 1835.

"Article 1. The parties declare that there shall be a firm and lasting peace forever, and that friendly intercourse shall be preserved by the people belonging to both parties.

"Article 2. It is agreed and declared that the before-mentioned tribes or bands shall form one community and that they shall have and possess the lands within the following bounds, to-wit: Lying west of the San Antonio road and beginning on the west at the point where the road crosses the river Angelina and running up said river until it reaches the first large creek below the great Shawnee Village emptying into said river from the northwest; thence running with said creek to its main source, and from thence a due northwest course to the Sabine river, and with said river west, then starting where the San Antonio road crosses the Angelina river, and with the said road to a point where it crosses the Neches River, and thence running up to the east side of said river in a northwest direction.

"Article 4. It is agreed by all parties that the several bands or their tribes named in this treaty shall all remove within the limits or bounds as above described.

"Article 5. It is agreed and declared by the parties aforesaid that the land lying and being within the aforesaid limits, shall never be sold or alienated to any person or persons, power or government whatsoever other than the government of Texas, and the Commissioners on behalf of the Government of Texas, bind themselves to prevent in the future all persons from intruding on said bounds. And it is agreed on the part of the Cherokees, for themselves and their younger brothers, that no other tribes or bands of Indians whatsoever shall settle within the limits aforesaid, but those already named in this treaty and now residing in Texas.

"Article 6. It is declared that no individual person, member of the tribes before named, shall have power to sell or lease land to any person or persons not a member or members of this community of Indians, nor shall any citizen of Texas be allowed to lease or buy land from any Indian or Indians.

"Article 7. That the Indians shall be governed by their own regulations and laws, within their own territory, not contrary to the laws of the Government of Texas. All property stolen from the citizens of Texas, or from the Indians shall be restored to the party from whom it was taken and the offender or offenders shall be punished by the party to whom he or they may belong.

"Article 8. The Government of Texas shall have power to regulate trade and intercourse, but no tax shall be laid oon the trade of the Indians.

"Article 10. The parties to this treaty agree, that as soon as Jack Steel and Samuel Benge shall abandon their improvements without the limits of the before recited tract of country and remove within the same—that they shall be valued and paid for by the Government of Texas—the said Jack Steele and Samuel Benge, having until the month of November, next succeeding from the date of this treaty, allowed them to remove within the limits before described. And all the lands and improvements now occupied by any of the before named bands or tribes not lying within the limits before described, shall belong to the Government of Texas and subject to its disposal.

"Article 11. The parties to this treaty agree, and stipulate that all the bands or tribes, as before recited (except Steele and Benge) shall remove within the before described limits within eight months from the date of this treaty.

"Article 12. The parties to this treaty agree that nothing herein contained shall effect the relations of the neighborhood thereof, until a General Council of the several bands shall take place and the pleasure of the convention of Texas be known.

"Article 13. It is also declared, That all the titles issued to lands not agreeable to the Declaration, of the General Consultation of the people of all Texas, dated the thirteenth day of November, eighteen hundred and thirty-five, within the before recited limits—are declared void—as well as all orders and surveys made in relation to the same.

"Done at Colonel Bowl's Village on the twenty-third day of February eighteen hundred and thirty-six, and the first year of the Provisional Government of Texas.

Signed:

Witness:—Fox (his x mark) Fields, Henry Millard, Joseph Durst, A. Horton, George W. Case, Mathias A. Bingham, George V. Hockley, Sec'y. of Commisssion, Sam Houston, John Forbes, Colonel (his x mark) Bowl, Big (his x mark) Mush, Samuel (his x mark) Benge, Oozovta (his x mark), Corn (his x mark) Tassell.

The (his x mark)Egg, John Bowl, Tunnetee (his x mark).

Commissioners Sam Houston and John Forbes, on the part of the Provisional Government of Texas, reported as follows to the Governor:

Washington, February 29, 1836.

To His Excellency,
Henry Smith, Governor of Texas.
Sir:—

In accordance with a commission issued by your Excellency dated the 26th day of December, 1835, the authorized commissioners, in the absence of John Cameron, Esquire, one of the commissioners named in the above mentioned instrument, most respectfully report: That after sufficient notice being given to the different tribes named in the commission, a treaty was held at the house of John ————————, one of the tribe of Cherokee Indians -------------------------. The Commissioners would also suggest to your Excellency that titles should be granted to such actual settlers as are now within the designated boundaries, and that they should receive a fair remuneration for their improvements and the expenses attendant upon the exchange in lands or other equivalent.

It will also be remembered by your Excellency that the surrender by the Government of the lands to which the Indians may have had any claims is nearly equivalent to that portion now allotted to them and we must respectfully suggest that they should be especially appropriated for the use of the government. They also call your attention to the following remarks, viz: "The state of excitement in which the Indians were first found by your commissioners, rendered it impossible to commence negotiations with them on the day set apart for it. On the day succeeding, the treaty was opened. Some difficulty then ocurred relative to the exchange of lands, which the Commissioners proposed making for those now occupied by them, which was promptly rejected. The boundaries were those established as designated in the treaty alone and that such measures should be adopted by your excellency for their security as may be deemed necessary -------------------. The Commissioners used every exertion to retain that portion of territory for the use of the government, but an adherence to this would have but one effect, viz: that of defeating the treaty altogether."

"Under these circumstances the arrangement was made as now reported in the accompanying treaty. They would also suggest the importance of the salt works to the government and the necessity that they should be kept for the use of the government.

"The Commissioners also endeavored to enlist the chiefs of the different tribes in the cause of the people of Texas and suggested an enrollment of a force from them to act against our common enemy, in reply to which they informed us that the subject had not before been suggested to them, but a general council should be held in the course of the present month, when their determination will be made known.

"The expenses attendant upon the treaty are comparatively light, a statement of which will be furnished to your Excellency.

"All of which is most respectfully submitted.

John Forbes." Sam Houston,

After about sixteen years the ambition of the Cherokees to acquire undisputed title to their lands were at last realized. Their boundaries were definitely established; they were in a national existence, holding their lands in community or in common, living under laws of their own making, executed by their own officers without outside interference, living under the protection of the Government of Texas with one or more agents among them.

Without doubt, the main issue between them and the Spanish and Mexican authorities was that the Cherokees desired their lands in common, which was their method in the United States, while this policy was unknown to the two regimes mentioned and contrary to the Caucasian method of conveying title. However, their settled claims were held in abeyance until finally settled under the terms of the "Solemn Declaration" of November 13, 1835 and the foregoing treaty.

Immediately following the submission of the treaty and report, General Sam Houston repaired to and took command of the army on March 11, 1836.

On March 1, the convention assembled and adopted the Declaration of Independence of Texas. On the following day, same was signed by the fifty-two members present; later six others appeared and signed, making the total fifty-eight. The arrival of Provisional Governor Smith, the Lieutenant Governor and the remnant of the Council and the submission of the following report by the Provisional Governor, marked the closing of the Provisional Government and the institution of a new order:

"To the President and Members of the Convention of the People of Texas

"Gentlemen: Called to the gubernational chair by your suffrages at the last Convention, I deem it a duty to lay before your honorable body a view, or outline of what has transpired since your last meeting, respecting the progress and administration of the government placed under my charge, as created and contemplated by the organic law.

"The Council, which was created to co-operate with me as the devisors of ways and means, having complied with all the duties assigned to them, by the third article of the Organic Law, was adjourned on the 9th of January last, until the 1st of the present month.

"The agents appointed by your body, to the United States, to contract a loan and perform the duties of agents generally, have been dispatched and are now actively employed in the discharge of their functions, in conformity with their instructions: and, while at the City of New Orleans, contracted a loan under certain stipulations, which together with their correspondence on that subject, are herewith submitted for your information ....

"................ Gen. Houston, Col. John Forbes and Dr. Cameron were commissioned on the part of this government to treat with the Cherokee Indians and their associate bands, in conformity with the Declaration of the Convention in November last, who have performed their labors as far as circumstances would permit, which is also submitted to the consideration of your body. Our naval preparations are in a state of forwardness. The schooners of war, Liberty and Invincible, have been placed under the command of efficient officers and are now on duty, and the schooners of war, Independence and Brutus, are daily expected on our coast from New Orleans, which will fill out our navy as contemplated by law. Our agents have also made arrangements for a steamboat, which may soon be expected, calculated to run between New Orleans and our seaports, and operate as circumstances shall direct. Arrangements have been made by law for the organization of the militia; but, with very few exceptions, returns have not been made as was contemplated, so that the plan resorted to seems to have proved ineffectual.

"The military department has been but partially organized, and for want of means, in a pecuniary point of view, the recruiting service has not progressed to any great extent, nor can it be expected ,until that embarassment can be removed.

"Our volunteer army of the frontier has been kept under continual excitement and thrown into confusion owing to the improvident acts of the General Council by the infringements upon the prerogatives of the Commander-in-chief, by passing resolutions, ordinances, and making appointments, etc., which in their practical effect, were calculated in an eminent degree, to thwart everything like systematic organization in that department.

"The offices of auditor and controller of public accounts have some time since been created and filled, but what amount of claims have been passed against the government, I am not advised, as no report has yet been made to my office ;but of one thing I am certain, that many claims have been passed for which the government, in justice, should not be bound or chargeable. The General Council has tenaciously held on to a controlling power over the offices, and forced accounts through them contrary to justice and good faith, and for which evil I have never yet been able to find a remedy; and if such a state of things shall be continued long, the public debt will soon be increased to an amount beyond all reasonable conception.

"With a fervent and anxious desire that your deliberations may be fraught with that unity of feeling and harmony of action so desirable and necessary to quiet and settle the disturbed and distracted interests of the country, and that your final conclusions may answer the full expectations of the people at home and abroad,

"I subscribe myself with sentiments of the highest regard and consideration,

Your obedient servant,

Henry Smith,

Governor."

March 1, 1836.

"Executive Department, Washington,

March 2nd, 1836.

Fellow-Citizens of Texas:

"The enemy are upon us. A strong force surrounds the walls of the Alamo, and threatens the garrison with the sword. Our country imperiously demands the service of every patriotic arm, and longer to continue in a state of apathy will be criminal. Citizens of Texas, descendants of Washington, awake! Arouse yourselves!

"The question is now to be decided, are we now to continue free men, or bow beneath the rod of military despotism? Shall we, without a struggle, sacrifice our fortunes, our liberties and our lives, or shall we imitate the example of our forefathers and hurl destruction on the heads of our oppressors? The eyes of the world are upon us. All friends of liberty and the rights of men are anxious spectators of our conflict, or are enlisted in our cause. Shall we disappoint their hopes and expectations? No! Let us at once fly to arms, march to the battle-field, meet the foe, and give renewed evidence to the world that the arms of freemen, uplifted in defense of liberty are right, are irresistible. Now is the day and now is the hour, when Texas expects every man to do his duty. Let us show ourselves worthy to be free, and we shall be free.

"Henry Smith,
Governor."

Lacking a quorum, the Council met from day to day only to adjourn. on the 11th, General Thos. J. Rusk of Nacogdoches introduced resolutions in the plenary convention, relieving the Governor and Council of the duties conferred upon them by the Consultation of November 3-14, 1835. It now became the duty of the convention to institute a new government.

The convention proceeded with utmost decorum until 16th when by special enactment a government ad interim was created for the republic until a regular government could be provided for. The ad interim government consisted of a President, Vice President and Cabinet. The President was clothed with all but dictatorial powers. On the 17th, a constitution for the republic was adopted and later submitted to the people for ratification or rejection. The convention elected the first President and Vice President.

The last day of the session fell upon March 18, 1836. The government ad interim elected as officers David G. Burnet, President, and for Vice President, Lorenzo de Zavala, the Mexican who espoused the cause of Texas. A full complement of officers was elected ,including the re-election of Sam Houston, as Commander-in-chief. The labors of the convention ended on the 18th, and on the 21st, moved to Harrisburg. Its members thereupon dispersed. Some joined the army while others made haste to reunite with their families to remove them to places of safety.

At the head of the Texas army stationed at Gonzales, General Houston wrote the following letter to Colonel Bowl, Chief of the Cherokee Nation, under date April 13, 1836:

"My Friend Col. Bowl:

I am busy and will only say, how da do, to you! You will get your land as it was promised in our treaty, and you, and all my Red brothers, may rest satisfied that I will always hold you by the hand, and look to you as Brothers and treat you as such!

"You must give my best compliments to my sister, and tell her that I have not worn out the moccasins which she made me; and I hope to see her and you and all my relatives, before they are worn out.

"Our army are all well, and in good spirits. In a little fight the other day several of the Mexicans were killed and none of our men hurt. There are not many of the enemy in the country, and one of our ships took one of the enemy's and took 300 barrels of flour, 250 kegs of powder and much property—and sunk a big warship of the enemy, which had many guns."

The struggle for Texas Independence culminated in the Battle of San Jacinto on April 21st, 1836. With 783 Texans against the army of Mexico, commanded by the President and Dictator, Santa Anna with upwards of 1500 men, General Houston gained a decisive victory, capturing the President and dispersing his army.

While these things were transpiring, the Cherokees were living in quiet and peace on their land in East Texas where they had been domiciled for upwards of seventeen years. True to form, they had been reported to the Prothe Treaty of February 23, 1836. This treaty had been reported to the Provisional Government ,as per instructions, on February 29th, 1836 by General Houston and John Forbes the commissioners. On March the 11th, the Governor Council surrendered all the official documents to the Convention. This treaty and report without doubt were among them. If the government did not avail itself of this opportunity to ratify the treaty as was doubtless the purpose of the Consultation, there appears to be no record of it. However, the Texas Government and army were in a precarious state. The former was moved from place to place for convenience as well as safety, while the army was continually on the march eluding the strong Mexican army, headed by its President, was in pursuit.

The Neutrality, on the part of the Cherokees was sought and obtained at the outset. This was very essential at this stage of affairs, and if it was ever the intention of the government to fail or refuse to ratify the treaty this could not be hazarded at this time.

Under the provisions of the constitution, the government ad interim passed out of existence. An election was held the first Monday in September, 1836 for the purpose of electing a full set of officers. Sam Houston was chosen the first President of the New Republic, while Mirabeau B. Lamar was elected as Vice President. On October 2nd, they were inducted into office at Columbus, the seat of government.

In December, 1836, the Cherokee Treaty was forwarded to the Senate for consideration, President Houston commenting in part, as follows:

" ----------- In considering this treaty you will doubtless bear in mind the very great necessity in conciliating the different tribes of Indians who inhabit portions of our country almost in the center of our settlements as well as those who extend along our border."

No action was taken at this session. At the next session a committee was appointed to investigate the report. A report was made October 12, 1837, about ten months after its first submission to the senate, as follows:

"Resolved by the Senate of the Republic of Texas that they disapprove and utterly refuse to ratify the Treaty or any article thereof, concluded by

Sam Houston and John Forbes on the 23rd day of February, 1836, between the Provisional Gov (ernment) of Texas of the one part and the "Head Chiefs," Head Men and warriors of the Cherokees on the other part Inasmuch as that said treaty was based on false promises that did not exist and that the operation of it would not only be detrimental to the interests of the Republic but would also be a violation of the vested rights of many citizens ------------------------."

During his tenure of office as first President, General Houston made no further attempt to secure its ratification by the Senate. That the failure of the Texas Government to ratify rendered it invalid cannot be accepted as just. In summarizing, it will be seen that the provisions for its making were instituted and carried into effect by the Provisional Government. The same was reported to the Governor and Council and lay dormant during the existence of the government ad interim, but was finally resurrected and placed before the Senate in December, 1836. No action was taken until October 12th, 1837, only to be rejected primarily on the grounds that the treaty "was based on promises that did not exist." This took place during the fourth government of the country, while during the first it was necessary, under the then existing conditions, that the Cherokees be treated with and in the language of Provisional Governor Smith, "the commissioners would go specially instructed, so that no wrong could be committed, etc. ----------." If the "premises did not exist" it certainly must have been presumptuous for the government, at its very incipiency, to so assume an act. The "Solemn Declaration" was published to the world by the Consultation unsolicited by the Cherokees. The treaty commissioners appeared unheralded at the village of Bowles. Houston remarked in his report, "The state of excitement in which the Indians were first found by your Commissioners rendered it impossible to commence negotiations with them, etc. ---------------."

The "Solemn Declaration had been passed, adopted and signed by all of its fifty-four members unsolicited and unbeknown to them. The treaty negotiations were held and concluded on Cherokee soil. That the treaty should have received ratification seems to be the chief argument, especially for the present-day writers to expostulate in endeavoring to justifiy Texas for the expulsion of 1839.

In urging the Council to appoint Commissioners to treat with the Cherokees in conformity to the acts of the Consultation, Provisional Governor, Henry Smith said: "I can see no difficulty which can reasonably occur in the appointment of the proper agents on our part, having so many examples and precedents before us. The United States have universally sent their most distinguished military officers, etc. -----------."

Very little had transpired in the eastern portion of Texas to disturb the tranquility of the Cherokees with the possible exception of Cordova, a Mexican military officer, who attempted to stir up a rebellion against Texas authority. Emissaries Miracle and Flores had been apprehended, and on their person were found dispatches for Mexico City, to the Cherokee authorities, soliciting their aid in a war to recover Texas. If these dispatches ever reached their destination, there is no record of it. Suffice to say, if they did, they fell upon deaf ears, because the Cherokees did not attempt to espouse their cause. After a battle with the Kickapoos, General Rusk discovered the dead body of a Cherokee upon the battle-field and complained to Chief Bowles. The Chief answered his attempt to place any blame on his people by pointing out that the individual was a renegade member of his tribe and that whatever his acts, did not render them a national affair.

Notwithstanding, that, under Article Five of the treaty, the Texas Government bound itself "to prevent in future all persons from intruding within the said bounds," and that such treaty was made in conformity to the "Solemn Declaration," members of the Killough and Wilhouse families were alleged to have met death at the hands of unknown persons within the bounds of the Cherokee Nation. Col. Bowles immediately ordered the bodies delivered to the settlements without Cherokee territory, explaining that roving bands of prairie Indians were responsible for the deeds. The efforts of the Mexican representatives to procure the aid of the Cherokees and the murder of members of the Killough and Wilhouse families seem to constitute the entire grounds on the part of the Texas Government to remove them from their homes so long occupied but no legal cognizance was taken of them—long before any Americans touched Texas soil in quest of a home where peace and happiness might be their lot.

She had obligated herself to perfect a survey of Cherokee territory. To carry this into effect, President Houston, in the latter part of 1838, ordered Alexander Horton to make such survey. The south side, which is marked by the San Aantonio road, was run, but it does not appear any further effort was made on the part of the government to complete the survey. However, suffice it to say the three remaining sides are natural demarcation, namely—The Angelina, Neches and Trinity rivers.

On October 27th, 1838, Col. Bowles wrote Horton, which is indicative of his attitude towards Texas, as follows:

"Mr. Horton:

Dear Sir: I have accomplished my desire in raising my men for to guard and aid you while you are running the line. Insomuch I understand that some of the white people are against it, I am sorry to hear that for we wish to do right ourselves and we hoped that white people wanted to do the same. As for your disputes among yourselves, I have ordered my men to have nothing to do with it. My express orders to my men are to guard you and your property from the enemy.

"I hope that you will be particular with us in consequence of us not understanding your tongue and also we will pay that respect to you. I hope you will let us know when you need us and where and I will be at your service.

"I will detain Gayen till I get a line from you as he may read our writing.

I have twenty-five volunteers to send you.

So nothing more.

Only your friend,

Bowl."

Under the wise and able guidance of President Houston, the government under the new republic was a complete success. Order had been restored within her boundaries, the national debt reduced and, in the main, had well taken her place among the sovereign nations of the earth.

Immediately upon the induction of the second administration under President Mirabeau B. Lamar into power, the policy of exterminating all the Indians in Texas was adopted and closely adhered to as will be seen. Lamar had been private secretary to Governor Troupe of Georgia, during whose administration the Cherokees were forced to abandon the homes occupied by them from time immemorial and seek a place of abode in the wilderness west of the Father of Waters.

Pretext after pretext was sought in order to find some excuse for the sin the government was about to commit upon an innocent people. The act of Cordova appears to have been distorted into the long wished for pretext. This incident was the chance for the Secretary of War to give vent to his feelings against the Cherokees and to further put into effect the policy of extermination. His letter of April 10, 1838, to Col. Bowl, follows:

"The President grants peace to them but is not deceived. They will be permitted to cultivate undisturbed as long as they manifest by their forbearance from all aggressive acts and their friendly conduct the sincerity of their professions or until Congress shall adopt such measures in reference to them as in their wisdom they may deem proper. With a clear view of all matters connected with their feeling and interests it should not surprise the Cherokees to learn that such measures are in progress under the orders of the President as will render abortive any attempt to again disturb the quiet of the frontier nor need it be any cause of alarm to those who intend to act in good faith. All intercourse between the friendly Indians and those at war with Texas must cease. The President directs that you will cause the contents of this communication to be made known to all the chiefs who were present at the council."

A dark and threateninng cloud began to gather and envelop the skies. This portended the great destructive conflagration that was to sweep over the band of the unoffending Cherokees. Major B. C. Waters, early in April 1839, was ordered to construct a military post on the Great Saline within the limits of the Cherokee Nation. Col. Bowles mobilized his forces and ordered Major Waters to retire from Cherokee soil, which he did, considering his forces inadequate to cope with his adversaries. This act of Chief Bowles in protecting his domains from intrusion, aroused the ire of President Lemar. He wrote Col. Bowles as follows:

"You assume to be acting under a treaty negotiated at your village on the twenty-third day of February, 1836, with Commissioners appointed by the Provisional Government of Texas" ----------------.

He concluded: "I, therefore, feel it my duty as the Chief Magistrate of this Republic, to tell you in plain language of sincerity that the Cherokees will never be permitted to establish a permanent and independent jurisdiction in the limits of this government—that the political and fee simple claims which they set up to our territory now occupied by them will never be allowed—and they are permitted to remain where they are only because this government is looking forward to the time when some peaceable arrangement can be made for the removal without the necessity of shedding blood; but that their final removal is contemplated is certain and that it will be friendly negotiating, or by violence of war, must depend on the Cherokees themselves."

If the Mexican government desired to place on foot plans for the recovery of Texas is not a matter of speculation or discussion here. Whether or not they desired the assistance of the Cherokees and other tribes of Indians is not a matter material. There is no evidence that these Indians espoused the Mexican cause or made the slightest effort in that direction while on the other hand, indications are that they were heartily in accord with the Texan authorities. If the Texans, Mexicans or other tribes of Indians desired to trade or carry on intercourse, there was nothing in the treaty with Texas, the "Solemn Declaration," or in their own laws or regulations to prevent it. The main point is, did the Cherokee government actually commit any overt acts of war? Then did the attempts of the Mexican emissaries to gain their support in a war against Texas, constitute cause sufficient for the Texan Government to conclude that a state of war existed between the Cherokee Nation and the Republic of Texas?

Let us pause for a minute and indulge in a retroactive glance into the past. On the first Monday in September, 1838, Mirabeau B. Lamar was elected the second President of the Republic. During the years 1831-32 when the celebrated cases of the Cherokee Nation vs. Georgia and Worcester vs. Georgia were tried in the Supreme Court of the United States, this same Lamar was private secretary to Governor Troupe of that state. To say that the acts referred to were oppressive and unconscionable is not exaggeration to say the least. Why Lamar left Georgia is not known but on his entrance into Texas, he found a well organized state there, governed by a portion of the same people he knew years before in Georgia, enjoying the confidence of the constituted authorities and wielding a large influence over surrounding tribes. His antipathy toward them must have been well matured and reached the point of overflow. That his policy of the complete extermination of the Indians within Texan borders was well known and "that the boundaries of this Republic shall be marked by the sword" was carried out according to schedule as we shall see.

To further the well established policy of his chief, on May 30th, 1839. the acting Secretary of State addressed the following letters to the Texan Minister at Washington:

"Department of State.
Houston, May 30, 1839.

"Hon. Richard G. Dunlap.

Sir: I am requested by the President to transmit you the accompanying documents, marked as in the subjoined schedule, which were recently captured from a party of Mexicans as you will find detailed in the copy of report of Col. Burleson, Secretary of War.

"This government has long been in possession of testimony sufficient to justify them in adopting the most summary and imperative measures towards the Cherokees and other bands of northern Indians, resident in Texas. Their unauthorized emigration and protracted stay in our country has always been a source of disquietude and anxiety to the civilized population and their removal has long been desired. But the President, actuated by feelings of humanity towards a people who have been too much accustomed to profit by and abuse similar indulgence, has been unwilling to resort to force to procure their expulsion, while a hope could be entertained that their withdrawal might be effected by peaceable means. That hope has been founded on the application heretofore made to the Government of the United States relative to this interesting subject. Those applications appear to have been ineffectual thus far, while the humane forbearance on the part of this government toward these intruding Indians, has been productive of many disasters to our frontier settlements, and if longer continued might result in irreparable injury to Texas. The most enduring patience may be exhausted and must yield to the duty of self-preservation, when its exercise evidently gives encouragement and aggravation to the hostile spirit of the offenders. Such is our present condition relative to these immigrant savages; and the President has resolved to put an end to the repeated aggressions of the Cherokees by compelling their departure from our territory. You are at liberty to make known this fact to the government at Washington, and to request that such measures may be seasonably adopted by the government, as will fulfill the provisions of the 33rd article of the treaty entered into between the United States and Mexico on the 5th of April, 1831, and will effectually prevent the return of these savages to our territory.

"Our rights to eject these Indians can scarcely enter into your correspondence with the government of the United States; but should it be incidently alluded to, you will find it clearly suggested in the letter of Mr. Forsythe to Mr. Castillo, Charge de Affairs from Mexico which is transcribed in dispatch No. 42 from your predecessor to this department.

"You will not however solicit an elaborate discussion on this subject or any other connected with the obligations of the United States and Mexico; for a protracted discussion is seldom desirable and may be productive of inconveniences, if not of ill-feeling between parties, which we would very sedulously avoid.

"The President conceives that the government of the United States has frankly and justly acknowledged the rights of Texas to the benefits of that treaty, especially in reference to the 33d—article which has a direct territorial relation to this Republic as now organized; and he cannot imagine that any objection will be raised or difficulty occur on that ground. You will therefore confine your communications, unless constrained to take a wider range, to the fact of the intended expulsion of the Cherokees and such other of the immigrant bands as may prove to have been or may hereafter be implicated in the late atrocious attempt on the part of the Mexican authorities to employ the Indians of the United States in desolating our frontiers.

These machinations have been known to us for some time, but are now so fully developed in relation to the Cherokees that longer forbearance towards them is utterly inconsistent with the first duties of this government. If, in the progress of your correspondence it shall be assumed as has been suggested by the Charge de Affaires here, that the government of the United States is not bound to receive or to restrain those Indians and the ill-advised treaty partially made with them on the 23d day of February, 1836, by Commissioners appointed by the late Provisional Government of Texas, be alleged in support of this position, you can present conclusive refutation of that assumption in the fact that pretended treaty has never been ratified by any competent authority on the part of Texas. On the contrary, when it was first submitted to the Senate of the Republic, which was the only power to confirm it, it was rejected by a decisive vote of that body; and no subsequent action of the government has been had upon it. Indeed should this matter be pressed upon in such terms as to indicate a determination on the part of the government at Washington to avail itself of that treaty, as absolving it from all obligations touching these Indians (which can hardly be possible) you can further disclaim the validity of the treaty on the ground that the Provisional Government itself under whose authority the treaty purports to have been made, was acting without the sphere of any legitimate power and could not in any matter so extraneous to the avowed purpose of its creation as the alienation of a large and valuable portion of territory impose any moral or political obligations upon the independence and separate government of Texas. You will recollect that the Provisional Government passed its brief existence anterior to the Declaration of Independence and was organized under the Mexican Federal Constitution of 1824—that although its organization was in direct violation of that Constitution, and may be considered as partially revolutionary, its assumptions of power were no more obligatory upon the independent government of Texas than they would have been on the Federal Government of Mexico had that government been restored and Texas returned to her previous attitude. By the very constitution of that government, Texas, as such, was incompetent to make treaties. She was but a department of the confederate state of Coahuila and Texas, and in her conjunction state capacity was also precluded from entering into treaties with foreign powers. I suggest this as an ultimate plan of argument to be pursued but not to be restored to except in case of strict necessity. You are aware that the lines designated in the treaty were run by Col. Alex Horton some time in the fall of last year at the instance of General Houston, who was then exercising the functions of this government. This fact, too, may be adduced against you; but you will find no great difficulty of diverting it of any serious consideration by suggesting that the act of Col. Horton was without authority, the President having no right to carry a treaty into effect anterior to or independent of the action of the Senate on such treaty. In this instance the assumed right was exercised in direct contradiction to the adivce of the senate and every act so done was an absolute nullity, and could impose no legal or moral obligation on this government. Should the government of the United States decline to render you any satisfactory assurance concerning the future return to our territory of the Cherokees now about to be ejected from it, this government will be compelled to resort to its own energies; and a protracted war may ensue between Texas and the northern Indians within her borders. We should greatly deprecate such an event, for it cannot escape an ordinary discernment that it would be more than likely to enlist a portion of the original tribes from whom these intruding bands have been recently removed to the west of the Mississippi by the Government of the United States. It is also more than probable that such a contest would involve the Government of the United States in an Indian war of greater magnitude than any they have heretofore sustained.

"It is not intended to impute error to that government in the congregating of so many (sic) tribes of savages on their remote western frontier, for they did so in the exercise of indisputable right. But while we fully acknowledge the abstract right, we cannot but perceive and deeply regret that its practical operation has been already eminently injurious to Texas and may possibly inflict still more serious evils upon her. The migration of several bands of these very tribes, to our territory was a direct and natural consequence of their removal from their ancient habitations and their location in our vicinity by that government. We entertain too profound a confidence in the magnanimity of the government of our fatherland to believe for a moment that they still omit to give to this fact all the consideration that an enlightened sense of propriety could suggest; or that they fail to find in it, additional reasons for observance of the treaty of 5th of April, 1831, heretofore referred to. No government to act on the beneficient principles of Christianity will permit itself to prosecute a course of domestic policy, the evident tendency of which is destructive of the peace and happiness of a neighboring nation. It will either abandon the policy or should its continuance be of paramount importance to its own well-being, it will so modify and restrain its pernicious results that the neighboring people may suffer no serious detriment from it. In previous instructions from this government you will find the Coshatties and the Biloxies mentioned in connection with the Cherokees and other northern tribes. These bands have been too long residents in Texas (I believe they emigrated from the Creeks during the American Revolution) to be included in the list of intruders from the United States. You will not, therefore, press them upon the attention of that government in your future correspondence. The Cherokees, Kickapoos, Delawares, Pottawotomies, Shawnees and Caddoes are the bands that have recently entered our territory, and of whom we complain. The Cherokees, Kickapoos and Caddoes are the most numerous and most obnoxious of these, and it is their recall by the United States which we most ardently desire, and to which we are clearly entitled. - - - - - The President is quite indisposed, but I trust will be about again in a few days.

Very Respectfully,
I have the honor to be,
You Obedient Servant,
David G. Burnet,
Acting Secretary of State."

In order to clarify statements indulged in by the high state officials of the Republic in the foregoing, it is but proper to re-iterate that the first authentic record of Cherokee emigration to Texas was during the winter of 1819-20. The first American, Moses Austin, first saw that country fully ten months afterwards, appearing at San Antonio de Bexar, December 23rd, 1820. Before succeeding in perfecting plans to procure empresario contracts for lands on which to make settlements, death over-took him on June 10th, 1821, while enroute home. His dying injunction was that his son, Stephen F. Austin, proceed with the carrying out of his colonization schemes. Under him, the first white or American settlement was made on New Years Creek, in what is now Washington County, January 1, 1822. The Cherokees permanently settled near Nacogdoches about two years before this first American settlement was started.

These "intruding Indians" were hospitably received by the Spanish authorities and were later happily domiciled under the newly instituted Mexican government, which made them full-fledged citizens.

The statements so oft repeated that the Cherokees were "intruders", and their unwarranted long-stay cannot be founded upon facts, if the legal and historical documents of the country can be taken for true. These, founded upon anything other than truth and justice, cannot be successful in hoodwinking public opinion in the face of indisputable facts. And the term "savages" may best be disposed of by drawing the mantle of charity over the unsettled conditions of the country; that the Republic was no longer in danger of being molested by her civilized Indians within her borders and the Republic of Mexico. The time was ripe, judging from the trend of events, to disposess them of the lands to which they had vested rights and repudiate their own "Solemn Declaration" and Treaty.

Much stress has been placed on the 33rd Article of the Treaty of April 5, 1831, between the United States of America and the United Mexican States.

At the time of the formation of this treaty, the Cherokees were peaceably located on their domains. They were full-fledged Mexican citizens and enjoying all the privileges thereto attached.

The following is an account of the Expulsion by Henderson Yoakum. Judge Yoakum was a citizen of Texas, an able lawyer, and in every way a competent judge of all the circumstances surrounding the transaction. His "History of Texas" quotes verbatim the account, which is found on pages 263-271 Vol II-1856.

"The treachery of Cordova and the warlike demonstrations of the Indians in Eastern Texas in 1838, are already before the reader, and their causes known. The president in his message of the 21st of December, 1838, assumed the position that the immigrant Indian tribes had no legal or equitable claim to any portion of the territory included within the limits of Texas; that the federal government of Mexico neither conceded nor promised them lands or civil rights; that it was not necessary to inquire into the nature and extent of the pledge given to the Cherokees by the Consultation of 1835 and the Treaty of February, 1836, consequent upon it, for the Treaty was never ratified by any competent authority.

In 1822, long before any colonist had settled in Eastern Texas, or any colony contract had been made for that section, the Cherokees immigrated to Texas. They established a village North of Nacogdoches—the town at that time being a waste, lately swept by the forces of Long and Perez.

For fourteen years the Cherokees had occupied this land, holding it in quiet and undisputed possession. They were not intruders on the whites, for they were there first. The Mexican authorities recognized them as an agricultural tribe, with Mexican privileges and Colonel Bean was official agent for them, in common with other tribes. No voice had been raised against their title. It was deemed by all both legal and equitable. To give weight and dignity to this title, the Consultation of November, 1835, at a time when Texas was weak; when a heavy cloud hung over her hopes and her liberties were suspended upon a most unequal and most unjust war, made a very solemn pledge to these Indians, acknowledging their just claim to the lands, setting forth the boundaries thereof, and saying further:

"We solemnly declare that we will guarantee to them the peaceable enjoyment of their rights to their lands, as we do our own. We solemnly declare that all grants, surveys, or locations of lands, within the bounds hereinbefore mentioned, made after the settlement of the said Indians, are, and of right ought to be, utterly null and void."

On the other hand, it was impossible that the Indians should have an independent government within that of Texas. They must necessarily come under the Texan laws as citizens. The great object of many was to get their lands, for they were located in a fine and desirable country. The Texas were the first violators of the pledge of 1835. The ink was scarcely dry on the paper when locators and surveyors were seen in their forests; and this, too, notwithstanding the Consultation, by the decree of November 13, 1835, had ordered such locations and surveys to cease all over Texas.

"But it is useless to dwell further upon the subject. The Cherokees were charged with the plunder and murder of many of the inhabitants residing among them and in their vicinity. The Killough family were cruelly massacred; only three or four escaped, and they were brought into the settlements by the Cherokees, who by their "cunning representations", says the secretary of war, charged these acts upon the prairie Indians, and the treacherous Mexicans. To prevent such occurrences, Major Waters had been ordered with two companies to occupy the Neches Saline, not only to watch the Cherokees, but to cut off their intercourse with the Indians of the prairies. Fowles, the Cherokee Chief, notified Major Waters that he would repel by force such occupation of the Saline. As the Major's force was too small to carry out his orders, he established his post on the west bank of the Neches, out of the Cherokee Territory.

Colonel Burleson, who was then collecting a force on the Colorado to operate against other Indians, was directed to march his troops lower down, so as to be ready on the shortest notice to enter the Cherokee territory. In the meantime government came into possession of the papers of Manuel

Flores, including those to the Chiefs of the Cherokees. On their reception, Burleson was ordered to increase his force to 400 men and march into the Cherokee Nation. He reached the east bank of the Neches on the 14th day of July and about the same time Colonel Landrum's regiment from Eastern Texas arrived there. The Nacogdoches regiment under General Rusk had arrived some days before and taken position near the Cherokee village. The entire force was placed under the command of Brigadier General Douglas. Commissioners had, for some days, been in conference with the Cherokees to effect, if possible, their peaceful removal. The Commissioners offered to pay them for their improvements, but we have no information that any offer was made for the lands. The Indians were required to surrender their gun-locks and remove to their brethren in Arkansas. At noon, on the 15th of July, all further attempts to make a treaty were abandoned and General Douglas was directed to put his troops in motion. The council ground was about five miles below the Indian camp. When the Texans arrived there, the Cherokees had retreated about seven miles farther up the river. They pursued and a company of spies, which first came into sight of them, was fired on. The Indians deployed their forces on the point of a hill, having a ravine and thicket on the left. General Rusk motioned to them to come on; they advanced and fired four or five times, and immediately occupied the ravine and thicket on the left. The main body of Texans coming up in the open prairie now formed, and the action became general. The Texans charged the ravine and advanced up from the left. A portion of the Indians, who were attempting to approach the troops on the left flank, were repulsed. The Cherokees fled when the charge was made, leaving eighteen dead on the ground. The Texans had three killed and five wounded. The engagement commenced a little before sunset and the pursuit ended at night.

On the morning of the 16th, the troops proceeded on the trail made by the Indians the night previous. In the forenoon, they were found strongly posted in a ravine half a mile from the Neches, and seemed eager for a fight. While the Texan advance was dismounting, the Indians commenced the action, killing several horses and one man before their opponents could form, but they were soon driven by the advance into the ravine. The Indians were protected by a ravine and a thicket in the rear, while the Texans had to advance upon them through an open wood and down a hill. The main body coming up was formed, and firing commenced at a distance of a hundred and fifty yards. The Texans kept advancing and firing until within fifty yards of the ravine, when upon a signal, they charged. When they reached the ravine, th Indians fled and retreated into the dense thicket and swamp of the Neches bottom. The charge was gallantly continued into the swamp, but the enemy made no stand. Thus ended the conflict of the 16th. It lasted an hour and a half and was well contested by the Indians. The Texans lost five killed and twenty-seven wounded. The loss of the Cherokees was probably a hundred killed and wounded, and among the former was their distinguished Chief Bowles. In the official report of the action he was styled "the long-dreaded Mexican ally, Colonel Bowles".

The trail of the retreating Cherokees was followed for some days. Several Indian villages were passed, their extensive corn fields cut down and houses burned. On the evening of the 25th, further pursuit being useless, the secretary of war, who accompanied the expedition, directed the troops to be marched to their homes and mustered out of service. "For eighteen months afterward", says an officer in the engagements, "the Indians came back in small parties, and committed fearful depredations upon the lives and property of the people on the frontiers".

In the march of General Douglas, he passed the villages of nearly all the civilized Indians. He says, "the Cherokees, Delawares, Shawnees, Cadoes, Kickapoos, Biloxies, and Cuchies had established during the past spring and summer many villages and cleared and planted extensive fields of corn, beans, peas, etc., preparing evidently for an efficient co-operation with the Mexicans in a war with this country". It was very natural to infer from these agricultural labors, that the Indians were preparing for a war against Texas; but neither their plans nor their crops were permitted to mature. He speaks also of the Indian territory through which he marched and says that in point of richness of soil and the beauty of situation, water and productions, it would vie with the best portions of Texas".

Thus the vexed question with regard to the civilized Indians was settled, and there could be no hindrance to surveyors or settlements on their fine lands. The previous administration had endeavored by treaties and presents to conciliate the frontier Indians; this had pursued a sterner policy. It had, in all conflicts, killed about three hundred warriors, leaving five thousand more all exasperated against Texas and ready to unite with her great enemy against her.

Following the expulsion, the Cherokee National Council assembled at Fort Gibson, Indian Territory, and took action in reference to the Texas Cherokees as evidenced by the following letter written by M. Arbuckle, Commanding 2nd W. Division of the United States Army:

"Headquarters, 2nd W. Division
Fort Gibson, April 28th, 1840.

To His Excellency,
Mirabeau B. Lamar,
President of Texas,
City of Austin.

Sir: I was requested by a Cherokee Council assembled at this Post that the whole of their people now in Texas should immediately return to their nation and thereafter remain in their own Country. I have no doubt the Cherokee people are sincere in the wish they have expressed on the subject; and as many of their people that formerly lived in Texas have returned of late, they hope that the time is not distant when their wishes will be fully accomplished. Under such circumstances they hope your government will not desire to detain any of their people in Texas.

"With respect to the wishes of the Cherokee Nation in relation to some of their people now in Texas, I regard it proper to assure you, that if such of them as may be prisoners, are conveyed out of Texas in the direction of Fort Towson, that the commanding officers of that post will be instructed to issue such quantity of provisions to them as may be necessary to enable them to return to their nation.

"I have the honor to be, sir, with great respect,

Your obedient servant,

M. Arbuckle,

Brevet. Brigr. Gen. U. S. A."

The Texan Secretary of War replied as follows:

"War Department,

City of Austin, 11th June, 1840.

Brevt. Brigadier General,

M. Arbuckle, U. S. A.

Sir: You will please accept the thanks of His Excellency, the President, and of this Department for your communication of date Fort Gibson, April 28th, 1840.

"We have suffered and are still suffering most serious injury from the intrusive advances of the Cherokee people, within the limits of our jurisdiction and territory.

"The position in which we stand to the Cherokee people, within our limits is hostile; we should therefore be greatly pleased to see them returned to their legitimate home, and again united with their own people in the United States.

"The Cherokee prisoners have been dispatched to the post most convenient to our command. An attempt to send them to Fort Towson would have been no less hazardous to them than their escort; our prisoners being exclusively women and children.

"We trust that within thirty days from this date, they will be at Fort Jessup (La.).

"I have the honor to be, with great respect,

Your obt. sub.

B. T. Archer, Secretary of War.

By order of His Excellancy,

The President."

When the expulsion took place, General Houston was in the United States on business. On his return to Nacogdoches, he addressed the citizens in reference to same. On his first attempt to do so, he was met with hisses, catcalls and threats of violence. He at last succeeded in gaining an audience then he proceeded to charge Texas with bad faith on her part and that the expulsion and the killing of the Cherokees on the field of battle was unbecoming a civilized and Christian nation. His commanding figure and eloquence triumphed on this as well as on occasions formerly and afterwards. (Extract from a speech made by Senator Sam Houston, in the United States Senate, January 29-31, 1855).

"I can exemplify to some extent, an impression that I have when I contrast war measures with peace measures. I well remember in 1835, 1836, 1837 and 1838, in Texas, we had peace. The Comanches would come down to the very seaboard in amity and friendship, would repose confidently in our dwellings, would receive some trifling presents and would return home exulting, unless they were maltreated, or their chiefs received indignities. If they did receive such, they were sure to revisit that section of the country as soon as they went home and fall upon the innocent. For the years I have mentioned, in Texas, we had perfect peace, and, mark you, it did not cost the government over $10,000.00 a year. We had no standing army. A new administration came in and the Congress immediately appropriated $1,500,000.00 for the creation of two regular regiments. Those regiments were raised. What was the consequence? The policy had changed in the inauguration of the president. He announced the extermination of the Indians. He marshalled his forces. He made incursions on a friendly tribe who lived in sight of our settlements where the arts of peace were cultivated and pursued by them—by agriculture and other arts, and by exchange and traffic of such productions of the soil as were convenient. They lived by traffic with Nacogdoches. The declaration was made, and it was announced by the cabinet that they would kill off 'Houston's pet Indians'. Well, sir, they killed a very few of them, and my honorable colleague (Senator T. J. Rusk) knows very well, if it had not been for the volunteers they would have licked the regular army—and the Indians said: 'I was not there'. The Cherokees had been very friendly and when Texas was in consternation, and the men and women were fugitives from the myrmidons of Santa Anna, who were sweeping over Texas like a simoon, they had aided our people, and given them succor—and this was the recompense. They were driven from their homes and left desolate. They were driven up among the Comanches. What was the consequence? Every Indian on our borders from the Red River to the Rio Grande took the alarm. They learned that extermination was the cry, and hence it was that the flood of invasion came upon our frontiers and drenched them with blood.

"The policy of extermination was pursued and a massacre of sixteen chiefs at San Antonio, who came in amity for a treaty, took place. This was in 1840. Before this army was raised they had been in the habit of coming down for purposes of peace and commerce. But an army of Indians marched through the settlements to the seaboard, one hundred or one hundred and fifty miles, undetected, I grant you, avoiding the dense settlements, went to Linville upon the tidewater, rifled the stores and slaughtered the men. If there were any, the women were treated with cruelty and their children's brains dashed out against the walls of the peaceful habitations. The exterminating policy brought it on. The country became involved in millions of debt, and the Indians were kept in constant irritation. That was in 1840 and it was not until the year 1843 that intercourse could be had with them through the pipe of peace, the wampum and the evidence of friendship".

On page 57, Volume 1 of his History of Van Zandt County, Texas. Wentworth Manning says: "After the Cherokees had been driven out of East Texas, the fight opened up for the valuable lands formerly occupied by them. The reason for their expulsion became apparent among the pale faced contestants in a mad scramble of possessing the territory from which they were dispossessed was fierce to the Echo."

On page 549, Volume 1, John Henry Brown's History of Texas, says: "The noble Travis, in command at San Antonio, increased his force to one hundred and fifty men and prepared by every means in his power to defend the place to the last. Governor Smith kept couriers in the saddlle dispatching them to the coast, Nacogdoches, San Augustine and elsewhere, with messages urging the people to action. Houston (and Forbes under his instructions) proceeded to treat with the powerful Cherokees and their allies and secure their neutrality—a matter of life and death importance at that hour."

No better evidence can be adduced as to the circumstances surrounding the Expulsion of 1839, than the testimony of Texan statesmen and writers quoted in the foregoing passages. No shadow of doubt can be cast upon the statements of the immortal Houston, Terrell, Yoakum, Brown and others of that day or of Wentworth Manning of Wills Point, Texas, of today. The government, with its regular and volunteer armies, was present on the battle field. The highest state official to the lowest military officer of the armies were present, directing the operations. No other than the renowned Albert Johnston of later Confederate fame, then the Texan Secretary of War was on the field, as well as the Vice President, David G. Burnet, of the Republic, acting president, instead of Lamar, who was absent in the United States.

The Cherokee Nation was, up to the time of the conclusion of the Treaty of February 23, 1836 an integral part of the Republic of Mexico. When Texas threw off the Mexican yoke and inaugurated an independent government under the Convention, termed the Consultation, the Cherokees remained a separate and independent government from Texas and by this "Solemn Declaration" they were so treated.

As has been noted, this body provided for the appointment of Commissioners to negotiate a Treaty with them which was done on February 23, 1836. By its terms, their allegiance was transferred to Texas whereby they became a quasi-independent nation, subject to and existing under the suzerainty of that government.

The unwarranted expulsion of the Texas-Cherokees is one of the world tragedies. "The EPIC is yet to be written."

CHAPTER XI

Public School System Established. National Officials. Male and Female. Seminary Graduates. Eleemosynary Institutions.

Prior to 1842 the educational interests of the Cherokees was in the hands of the missionaries of the Moravian, Presbyterian, Methodist, Congregational and Baptist churches. The United Brethren or Moravians commenced their missionary work among the Cherokees at Spring Place in Georgia in 1801[1]. The American Board of Foreign Mission, maintained by the Presbyterian and Congregational churches entered the field at Brainard in 1817[2]. The Baptists commenced their labors in the western part of North Carolina, during the same year[3] but soon allowed their work to lapse until 1820 in which year Valley Town Mission was founded.[4] In 1824 the Methodists established their first mission in the Cherokee country. Some of the Cherokees most probably attended schools in neighboring provinces and states prior to 1800. Notably, Charles Hicks, a half breed, who as early as 1808 was known to have had a splendid education.[5]

The idea of public and higher schools for the Cherokees was advocated and provided for by the treaty of 1835[6]. The Cherokee negotiators in this treaty were: John Ridge, Elias Boudinot, John West, Archilla Smith, Samuel W. Bell, William A. Davis and Ezekial West.

Section six, article nine of the Cherokee constitution of 1839 is as follows: "Religion, morality and knowledge, being necessary to good government, the preservation of liberty and the happiness of mankind, schools and the means of education, shall forever be encouraged in this Nation." Pursuant to that idea the council enunciated, "Be it enacted by the National Council, That all facilities and means for the promotion of education, by the establishment of schools, and the diffusion of general intelligence among the people shall be afforded by legislation, commensurate with the importance of such objects, and the extent and condition of the public finances; and all schools which may be, and are now in operation in this Nation, shall be subject to such supervision and control of the National Cuncil as may be provided.

Section 2. Be it further enacted, That in future no missionary school or establishment shall be located or erected without permission first being obtained from the National Council for such purpose, and the place designated by law for the same, with such other general regulations as may be deemed necessary and proper, either as conducive to its particular usefulnes or conformity to national rights and interest.

Section 3. Be it further enacted, That in furtherance of the design of this act, a committee of three persons shall be appointed by nomination of the Principal Chief to the National Committee, whose duty it shall be to mature and prepare a system of general education by schools, with such laws for its establishment and promotion as may be necessary; and to report the same to the Principal Chief before the next annual meeting of the National Council, who shall submit such report with his views in relation thereto; said committee shall also visit all the schools in the Nation, examine the plan upon which they are taught, the improvement of pupils, and utility of each, and report such information to the Principal Chief, to be submitted before the National Council.

Tahlequah, 26th, Sept., 1839.

Approved—John Ross.

The time was later extended for another year.[1] On October 2, 1839, the establishment of several missionary schools was authorized.[2]

The interest on the invested school funds of the Cherokees as shown by various Annual Reports of the Commissioners of Indian Affairs, were: 1839, $2,606.90; 1860, $11,848.00; 1870, $29,460.04.

A Superintendent of Education and eleven public schools were provided for by an act of council on November 16, 1841. Two thousand two hundred fifty seven dllars and thirty cents was appropriated to meet the past expenditures for the year of 1842.[4] At the same time five thousand eight hundred dollars was appropriated to support the schools for the year of 1843 and twenty two hundred dollars was set aside to defray the expenses of the orphans attending the public schools.[1] The salary of public school teachers in 1843 was thirty dollars per month.[2]

On December 23, 1843, council authorized the establishment of seven additional public schools, which brought the number up to: Delaware District, three; Saline, two; Going Snake, three; Tahlequah, two; Illinois, two, Canadian, one; Skin Bayou, two and Flint, three. The two school sessions were fixed at five months each, with a winter and summer vacation of one month each. The maximum teachers wage was forty dollars per month.[3]

In the year 1845 there were eighteen public schools in the Cherokee Nation:

Delaware District	Pupils
Tahquoee,	42.
Honey Creek,	47.
Lebanon,	34.
Saline District	
Spring Creek,	35.
Saline,	32.
Going Snake District	
Locust Grove,	27.
Oak Grove,	61.
Evan Jones,[1]	31.
Tahlequah District	
Caney,	43.
Fourteen Mile Creek	21.
Illinois District	
Greenleaf,	23.
Vian,	23.
Canadian District	
Webbers Falls,	36.
Skin Bayou District	

Sweetwater, --------22.
John Benge's, ------29.
Flint District
Honey Hill, ---------57.
James Bigby's ------37.
Clear Springs, -----55.

		Orphans
	655	121
Male	402	71
Female	253	50[1]

An additional public school was located at Muddy Springs in Flint District, one at Peavine on Barren Fork in Going Snake District and one in the Daniel neighborhod in Delaware District by act of council on November 18, 1845.[1] By an act of November 26, 1845 the school on Fourteen Mile Creek was moved to Tahlequah,[2] where this first public school of Tahlequah was opened on March 2, 1846 with Mr. Caleb Covel as teacher.[3] A subscription school had been opened in the town in June 1845 with Miss Nancy Hoyt, as teacher.[4] The Superintendent of Education was given authority in November 1846 to move schools that were insufficiently attended.[5]

Seven thousand five hundred dollars were appropriated to defray the ex-- penses of the public schools for the years 1848 and six hundred dollars were appropriated to pay the expenses of orphans attending the public schools.[6] Thirty dollars each was allowed for the board and clothing of orphans during the schol term. The public school appropriation for 1849 was seven thousand and three hundred six hundred for the orphan fund.[7] An examining board of three members to pass on the qualifications of teachers was created on November 2, 1849.[8]

The public school appropriations for 1850, 1851 and 1852 were seven thousand dollars for each year, the orphan appropriation for 1850 was thirty six hundred dolars and thirty-five hundred for each of the two succeeding years.

The teachers of the several public schools of the Cherokee Nation on September 11, 1858 and August 30, 1859, were:

School	Enrollment	1858	1859
Caney Creek,	70	Mary Buffington Adair,	Sarah E. Walker
Boots Chapel,	67	Sarah Hicks,	Minnie E. Boynton
Pleasant Valley,	50	S. S. Stephens,	S. J. Wolf.
Post Oak Grove,	60	Eliza M. Bushyhead,	James D. Alberty
Requa,	47	Ben W. Trott,	Ben Wisner Carter.
Delaware Town,	41	Thomas W. McGhee,	Heman L. Foreman.
Spavinaw Vale,	46	Joseph Vann,	
Beatties Prairie,	40	William H. Davis,	Moses C. Frye.
Honey Creek,	50	James L. Thompson,	Sarah Ruth Mosley.
Mount Claremore,	39	Nannie Jane Rider,	Nannie Jane Rider.
Baptist Mission,	76	W. P. Upham,	W.P. Upham.
Peavine,	66	Esther Smith,	Esther Smith.
Oak Grove,	57	Lucinda M. Ross,	Lucinda M. Ross.
Muddy Springs,	50	Caroline E. Bushyhead.	Caroline E. Bushyhead

School	Enrollment	1858	1859
Sugar Valley,	52	Martha J. Dameron,	Martha J. Dameron.
Forest Hill,	40	E. Jane Ross,	E. Jane Ross.
Gunter's Prairie,	45	Victoria Susan Hicks,	Jane Bertholf.
Sweet Springs,	41	Sarah E. Walker,	Cynthia T. Frye.
Sallisaw,	48	Moses C. Frye,	Corinne E. Barnes.
Green Leaf,	46	Emma Lowrey Williams,	John G. Scrimsher.
Canadian River,	45	Eliza Holt[1]	
Briartown,			Victoria Susan Hicks.
Clear Creek,			Elizabeth Letitia Bertholf.
Vann's Valley,			Eliza M. Bushyhead.
Falls Creek,			Martha J. Keyes.
Long Prairie,			Susan Ross.
Echo Bend,			Nancy Thompson.
Locust Vale,			George Harlan Starr.
Lee's Creek,			Nannie Holmes.
Arkansas Bottom,			Hugh Montgomery Adair.
Wild Horse,			Eliza Holt.
Webbers, Falls,			Delia Mosley.[2]

Upon the reorganization of the Cherokee Nation after the civil war, thirty-two public schools were provided for. They were to commence on March 1, 1867. The locations were to be:

Delaware District: Delaware Town, Sequoyah's New Place and Snell's.

Saline District: Requa, Cul-car-law-skees and Little Spring Creek.

Going Snake District: Tyners, Rabbit Trap, Barren Fork and Baptist Mission.

Tahlequah District: Tahlequah, Caney and Killermore's.

Illinois District: Fort Gibson, Seabolt's and White Oak Spring.

Canadian District: Webber's Falls, Brier Town and Jimmy Vann's.

Sequoyah District: Joseph Coody's, Lee's Creek and the Court House.

Flint District: Clear Spring, John Glass' and Alexander Scott's.

Cooweescoowee District: Lacey Hawkens on Grand River, John Hatchett's and on Dog Creek.

Two Negro schools to be located by the Superintendent of Education.

Five orphans may be maintained and educated at each of these thirty-two schools at a cost of thirty dollars each per term for board and clothing. The terms shall be from the first Monday in March to until July 15th and from the first Monday in September until the last Friday in January.[1] The Cherokee Nation always maintained free text books and accessories. The school houses were built at the expense of the community and each school had a local board of three directors.

The school previously located at White Springs near Lacey Hawkins' was removed by council in the spring of 1869 to West Point "near the mouth of Dog Creek."[1] By act of November 29, 1869 fourteen thousand eight hundred dollars were appropriated to pay the public school teachers and four thousand twenty dollars as the orphan allowance. The school was removed from the Moravian Mission to Oak Grove in Going Snake District. A school was established at Vian Camp Ground near Joseph Duval's in Illinois District, at Captain Nathaniel Fish's in Tahlequah District, at Contention Spring in Delaware, near Ellis Sanders' in Sequoyah, near Delaware Miller's in Cooweescoowee and a Negro school in Fort Gibson.[2] Ten more schools were provided for on December 10, 1869: Muddy Springs in Flint, Richard Benge's in Illinois on Illinois-Sequoyah line, Falling Pot's in Saline, Black Jack Grove in Canadian, John Rattlinggourd's in Illinois, Peggy Woodall's in Tahlequah, Dick Old Field's in Delaware, Wilson Sittingdown's in Sequoyah and near George Whitmire's in Going Snake. The two Negro schools located by the Superintendent of Education in March 1869 were at Tahlequah and on Fourteen Mile Creek in Tahlequah District.[3]

There were fifty-nine schools in 1871, sixty in 1873 and seventy-five in 1877[4]. The number and efficiency of the public schools gradually grew until there were over one hundred and twenty at the dissolution of the Cherokee Nation. The progress of the Cherokees was due to their excessive pride in their schools, which were never allowed to be under the supervision in any way of the educational authorities of the United States and none of their schools were ever visited by officers or agents of the departmnt of education at Washington, until after June 30, 1898.

Superintendents of Education of the Cherokee Nation.

1841. Rev. Stephen Foreman.[2]
1843. David Carter.
1845. James Madison Payne.[3]
1847. Walter Scott Adair.[4]
1849. Walter Scott Adair.[5]
1851. Rev. Walter Adair Duncan.
1853. Henry Dobson Reese.
1855. Henry Dobson Reese.
1857. Henry Dobson Reese.
1859. Charles Holt Campbell.
1867. Spencer S. Stephens.
1869. Spencer S. Stephens.
1871. Oliver Hazard Perry Brewer.

Boards of Education of the Cherokee Nation.

1873. Spencer S. Stephens.
Rev. Leonidas Dobson.
George S. Mason.
1875. John Ross Vann.[1]
Allison Woodville Timberlake.
William Henry Davis.

Superintendents of Education.

1876. December 9, Oliver Hazard Perry Brewer.

Boards of Education.

1877. November 26, William Potter Ross.
John Lynch Adair, suspended September 10, 1879.
William Henry Davis.

1878. November 25, Lucien Burr Bell.
1879. September 15, Henry Dobson Reese, appointed, vice John L. Adair.
1879. November 3, John Albion Spears, elected, vice John L. Adair.
1879. November 14, John Lynch Adair, reinstated by Council.
1879. November 24, George Wesley Choate, vice William Henry Davis.
1880. November 23, John Lynch Adair, resigned.
1880. November 23, John Albion Spears, elected vice John L. Adair.
1880. November 23, Allison Woodville Timberlake, vice L. B. Bell.
Robert Latham Owen, appointed vice G. W. Choate.
Willia mHenry Davis, appointed vice J. A. Spears.
1881. November. Oliver Hazard Perry Brewer, President, elected.
Robert Latham Owen, Secretary.
Lorenzo Delano Spears.
1882. December 5, Rev. Walter Adair Duncan, President.
1883. Thomas James Adair, Secretary.
1884. William Potter Ross.
1885. November 30, Martin Ross Brown.
William Henry Davis.
Lorenzo Delano Spears.
1886. Robert Taylor Hanks.
188. November, Timothy Brown Hitchcock.
1889. Eli H. Whitmire.

Superintendents of Education.

1890. November 3, Office created.
1890. November 8, William Wirt Hastings.
1891. November, Walter Hampton Jackson.

Boards of Education.

William Vann Carey, President.
Augustus Edward Ivey, Secretary.
Charles Oliver Fry.
William J. McKee.
John Elijah Butler, vice Carey.
1897. November 13, George Washington Mitchell.
1898. November 2, Mark Lee Paden.
1898. Rev. Walter Adair Duncan, President.
Connell Rogers, Secretary.
Rev. Joseph Franklin Thompson.
1898. November 18, Harvey Wirt Courtland Shelton.
Jefferson Thompson Parks.
James Franklin McCullough.
Thomas Carlile.
Theodore Perry.
Stand Watie Woodall, vice McCullough.
Darius Edwin Ward, vice Perry.

Oliver Hazard Perry Brewer, President. Albert Sidney Wyly, Secretary.
Samuel Frazier Parks, vice Carlile Miss Carlotta Archer, vice S. F. Parks.

The proposition for high schools for the Cherokees was proposed by the Cherokee negotiators of the treaty of December 25, 1835[1] but it was not until eleven years later that the tribe felt that they were in financial condition to commence the construction of the necessary buildings.[2]

A year later full regulations were embraced in an act of Council for the establishment and conduct of the two schools.[1] The Female Seminary was located three miles southeast and the Male Seminary one and one half miles southwest of Tahlequah. They were built of brick that was made near the site of each school. Built in a land of fine springs, neither building was located contiguous to a spring. The erection of the replicated buildings began in 1847, the cornerstone of the Female Seminary was laid by Chief Ross on June 21, 1847 and they were finished in 1850. The Male Seminary was opened on May 6, 1851 and the Female Seminary on the following day.

"The seminaries, and in fact, all the schools of the Cherokee Nation, are supported by money, invested in United States registered stocks, from the sale of lands to the United States government. The interest alone of this investment is drawn and used for educational purposes. The boarders are charged a mere nominal sum as an addition to the school fund. The United States government renders no assistance to the Seminaries, Asylum or common schools of the Cherokee Nation, outside of paying interest on money borrowed from the Nation."[3]

The buildings were one hundred eighty-five feet long, one hundred nine feet wide, part two stories and part three stories in height.

Boarders paid at the rate of five dollars per month in advance, or forty-five dollars per school year. That sum paid for board, laundry, lodging, lights, fuel, text books and all necessary supplies, and the pupils had to furnish only their comforts, blankets, linen and toilet articles. Provision was made by the National Council for the acceptance, without any expense to them, of fifty pupils whose parents were not able to pay their tuition and board.[1]

"The Steward purchases all supplies, has the direction and management of the appropriations, collects all board bills and employs all assistance in the domestic department. The Domestic Superintendent has charge of the domestic affairs, secures clothing and supplies for the primaries and other duties. The Medical Superintendent is appointed by the National Council, gives medical and sanitary attention. The Matrons attend the sick, receive the clothing from the laundry, attend its mending and distribution.

Preparatory Department.

First year: Penmanship, Phonetics, Reading, Object Lessons, Grammar, Penmanship, Geography, Geography, Arithmetic.

Second Year: Penmanship, Reading, Object Lessons, Composition, Phonetics, Reading, Arithmetic, Geography.

Third Year: Reading, Object Lessons, Composition Phonetics, Reading, Arithmetic, Geography.

Academic Department.

Freshmen—Ancient languages[1]: Latin, Greek; English: Grammar, Geography; History: U. S. History; Mathematics: Arithmetic, Algebra; Physical Geography, Physiology.

Sophomore—Ancient languages: Caesar, Anabasis; English: Rhetoric; History: English History; Mathematics: Algebra, Geometry; Chemistry, Natural Philosophy.

Junior—Ancient languages: Cicero, Ovid, Trucydides Modern languages: French, German; English: English literature, American literature; Mental Science: Political Economy, Moral Philosophy; Mathematics: Trigonometry, Analytical Geometry; Botany, Geology.

Senior—Ancient languages: Virgil, Livy, Homer; Modern languages: Moliere, Goethe; English: Criticism; Mental Science: Mental Philosophy, Logic; Mathematics: Surveying and Calculus; Astronomy, Zoology.

Daily Programme.

	A. M.		P. M.
Students rise,	5:30	Recitations	2:00-4:00
In Study Hall	6:00- 7:00	Military drill	4:15-4:45
Breakfast and detail	7:00- 8:30	Supper	5:00
Chapel	8:30- 9:00	Study hall	6:45-8:45
Recitations	9:00-12:00	First retiring bell	9:00
Noon	12:00- 2:00	Second retiring bell	9:15

Preparatory Department.

The course of study in this department embraces three years, and prepares students for the Seminary proper. The school is thoroughly graded. Object lessons, compositions, oral, written and other exercises calculated to develop the power of written and oral expresion are given. Ideas of number, form, size and actual measurement precede the more complex arithmetical operations. Map drawing, the use of the excellent maps in the Seminaries and topical exercises render geography practical. The Principal of this department spends an hour each Saturday with the students, assisting them in selecting books from the library.

Seminary Proper.

The course of study embraces four years. The work in this institution is equal to that of the best institutions of the country. This school possesses many advantages over similar institutions, from the fact that teacher and students are together. Teachers instruct and direct, not only in the text book studies but in general reading, in the use of reference books and library work —a thing impossible when students have not libraries and books of reference in their homes or boarding houses. The usual degrees are conferred, upon the completion of courses of study.

Graduates of the Cherokee National Seminary.

February 1855.[1]

Mary Buffington Adair,	Dr. Walter Thompson Adair.
Caroline Elizabeth Bushyhead,	William Robert Quarles.
Charlotte Candy,	William Fields.
Martha Candy,	Joel Bryan Mayes.

Eliza Forester,	Benjamin W. Trott.
Catherine Hastings,	Jenkins Whitesides Maxfield.
Lucy Lowrey Hoyt,	Monroe Calvin Keys.
Amanda McCoy,	Daniel Bushyhead.
Nannie Patrick,	James R. Gourd.
Nannie Rider,	Daniel Ross Hicks.
Sallie Rider,	Samuel King Riley.
Martha Wilson,	Reverend Walter Adair Duncan.

February 1856.

Mary Ellen Adair,	Rev. Joseph Franklin Thompson.
Eliza Missouri Bushyhead,	David R. Vann and Bluford West Alberty.
Elizabeth Annie Duncan,	Isaac Brown Hitchcock.
Victoria Susan Hicks,	DeWitt Clinton Lipe.
Nannie Holmes,	George Washington Benge.
Martha McNair,	Joel Bryan Mayes.
Margaret Lavinia Rogers,	Allison Woodville Timberlake.
Lucinda M. Ross,	Charles Renatus Hicks.
Alabama Elizabeth Scrimsher,	John Lafayette Adair and Dennis Wolf Bushyhead.
Martha Nannie Thompson,	John Ticanooly Adair and Augustus Van Edmondson.
Mary Delilah Vann,	George Drew and Joel Bryan Mayes.
Sallie Josephine Vaught,	George Washington Nave.
Martha Whiting,	Fox.
Emma Lowrey Williams,	George Washington Gunter.

"Cousin Vic."

The time is approaching near
When we shall bid adieu;
To teacher and companions dear,
And breathe the lonely word, adieu.

Many friends we've here found,
Within these favored walls
And sad will be the sound,
When we say farewell, to all.

But may we in friendship, dwell united,
And our lives be love
And meet when hopes are not blighted,
In that happy land above.

Your affectionate cousin,
L(ucinda) M. R(oss.)

Female Seminary
January 17, 1856."

"For Victoria Hicks. The Future.

The past with all its joys and sorrows is gone, with it alone fond memory can converse. The present is busy working its many changes. Yet 'tis to the future that these thoughts will most naturally fly, we involuntarily look there for our greatest pleasure, profit and happiness. Hope comes with her train of fair images and leads us through rich scenes of rapture and delight. And indeed life would be dull, void and bereft of every pleasure, unless there was a plan marked out in the future to fill our bosoms with zeal, and stimulate us to action. But since our human life hangs over accident and misfortune, and since the future must know us ever, the great question is, how shall we meet it, all doubtfully mixed with its pleasures, its delights, its cares and its dangers.

Then, I would say to meet it calmly, and boldly and with a pleasure. Venture not upon it with your own understanding as a guide; peril not such great interests to the dictation of your own reason, but take as a buckler and shield, the wise counsel of Him who marks all changes. In order that the future shall ever find you glorifying in triumph.

Your friend,

J(oel) B. Mayes.

Male Seminary, C. N.
January 29, 1856."

"Life

We can not tell what happiness
What might on earth possess
If in singleness of heart
We would strive to act a proper part.
'Tis true we see the effects of sin
All without and all within.
We long may live a life in vain,
Much good possess, but still complain.
We may appear to other eyes,
To be extremely rich and wise;
But if our hearts are not right,
Life will not be beautiful and bright.
Oh! may our life, day by day,
In love and duty pass away;
And at last when our bodies die,
We may live in that world above the sky;
Where free from sin, death and pain,
The good will meet and love again.

Emma (Lowrey Williams.)

Cherokee Seminary
November 4th, 1855."

January 27, 1879.

Isabel Cobb[1],
Tennessee Vann Steele, Robert Colburn Fuller.

June 27, 1879.

Anna Cora Archer, William Ross Shackelford.

Fannie Blythe, Lemuel Walker Marks.
Elizabeth Dougherty, Ellis Buffington Wright.

July 2, 1880.

Caroline V. Armstrong, Frank M. Overlees.
Nannie Catherine Daniel, Richard Lafayette Fite,
Lillie Maxfield, Claude Hanks McDaniel.
Sallie Clementine Rogers, John Thomas McSpadden.
Sarah Stapler Ross, Samuel Houston Adair.
Margaret Hicks Stapler,
Jeanette Starr, Frances Alexander Billingslea.

June 30, 1881.

Ella Adair, DeWitt Clinton Wilson.
Eleanor Margaret Boudinot, John Henry Nave.
Martha Cobb, Clement George Clarke.
Joanna Coody Rogers, John Calhoun Duncan.

June 28, 1883.

Carlotta Archer[1] and Emma Breedlove.
Mae Washburn,[2] John Carlton Anderson[3].

June 28, 1884.

Mary Ann Elizabeth, Duncan, Harvey Wirt Courtland Shelton.[4]

June 25, 1885.

Oregonia Bell,[5] Spratt Scott,
Florence Anna Caleb,[6] Henry Benton Smith.
Martha Fields, Dr. Philip Donahoo.

May 13, 1886.

Mary Jett Norman, Dr. George Albert McBride.

The Female Seminary was totally destroyed by fire on Sunday, April 10, 1887. The erection of the new seminary building in the north part of Tahlequah began on November 3, 1887. It was finished on April 18, 1889 and dedicated on Tuesday, May 5, 1889.

June 28, 1888.[1]

Rachel Caroline Eaton,[2] James Alexander Burns.
Elizabeth Bushyhead McNair,
Addie Roche Ross. William Henry Norrid.

June 28, 1890.

Charlotte Delilah Hastings Samuel Grant Victor.
Elizabeth Clyde Morris, William Presley Thompson.
Gulielma Ross, James Sanford Davenport.

June 23, 1892.

Sarah Jane Adair, James Augustus Lawrence,
Martha Anna Mayes, Edwin Mooring Pointer,[3]
Florence Wilson McSpadden, Philip Wharton Samuel.

June 29, 1893.

Martha Eulalia Miller, Jackson H. Merchant.

Lulu Mayfield Starr, William Wirt Hastings
Janana Thompson, William Penn Phillips.

June 28, 1894.

Lulu Dale Duckworth, Walter I. Jones.
Mary Llewellyn Morgan, William Lucullus Mayes,
Julia Anna Phillips, James Turner Edmondson,[4]
Georgia Ella Prather, Lee S. Robinson.

June 27, 1895.

Caroline Blair, Richard Henry Smith.
Josephine Crittenden, William Robert Sartain.
Sarah Lulu Foreman, John Gunter Lipe.
Flora Sabrina Lindsey, Charles Golston Watts,[1]
Cora Archer McNair, William Buffington Wyly.
Susie Phillips, Ernest Vivian Scrimsher.

June 26, 1896.

Janana Ballard.

June 25, 1897.

Anna Ballard, Crawford Conner.
Martha Pauline Eaton, James Mooring York,[2]
Cherokee Vashti Edmondson, Robert Bruce Garrett.
Beuna Vista Harris, Bascom Porum Rasmus.
Cora Archer Musgrove, James Herbert Moore.
Gertrude Whitman Rogers, Dr. George Shimoon.
Dora Olive Ward, William Pugh Cunningham.[3]

June 1, 1898.

Lena Carlile, Dr. C. W. Vowell.
Jennie McClellan Foreman. David Jesse Faulkner.
Pixie Alberty Mayes,
Juliette Melvina Scrimsher, Abraham Vandyke Robinson,[1]
Lura Ward, Gilbert Thompson Loux.

June 29, 1899.

Cherokee Cornelia Adair, Junius Brutus Moore.
Lucinda Ballard, William Lee Harlan.
Ella Mae Covel and Alice French.
Nellie May Duncan, Eugene Nixon Williamson.
Lulu Belle James, Robert Lee Huggins.
Grace Phillips, Preston Majors.
Fannie Vann Ross, Walter Ellis Duncan.
Eldee Starr and Mamie Starr.
Mineola Ward, Everett Virgil Allen.

May 25, 1900.

Josephine Barker, Dr. Robert Lee Mitchell.
Mollie Lipe Blackstone, Edward Knippenberger.
Belle Cunningham, Thomas Oscar Graham.
Eugenia Catherine Eubanks, Walter Maecenas Charlesworth.

Mary Elizabeth Gulager,
Bettina Lucile McIntosh,
Jennie Fields Ross,
Aneliza Eulalia Sevier.[1]

George Houston.
Jesse Clifton Cobb.
Edward Foreman Blackstone.

May 30, 1901.

Minnie Benge,[2]
Mary Garrett,
Rosanna Harnage,
Josephine Landrum Howard,
Mary Jane McSpadden,
Juliette Taylor Smtih.
Lelia Alice Maitland Thornton,

Sid Campbell.
Frederick McDaniel.
Andrew Jackson Rogers.
Thomas R. Crookshank.
G. S. MacKey.

May 29, 1902.

Sarah Eleanor Ballard,
Golda Barker.
Beulah Benton Edmondson,
Bertha Lillian Faulkner,
Mary Angeline Rider,
Elizabeth Vann Ross,
Susie Ray Sevier,
Dora Anna Starr,
Clara Estella Tyler,
Genobia Anna Ward,
Lola Llewellyn Ward,

Roy Woods.
Charles V. Knight.
Richard Croker.
Charles Clarence Starr.
Alfred A. Campbell.
Carl Mills.
Lawrence McAllister.
Ewing Markham.
Frank Selman.
Allen Douthitt,
John Black Tinnin.

June 9, 1903.

Laura Effie Duckworth,
Victoria Lipe Foreman,
Caroline Bertha Freeman,
Allie Rhea Garrett,
Janie Stapler Hicks,
Rosa Gazelle Lane.
Virginia Lee Lindsey.
Caroline Quarles McNair,
Elizabeth Peach McSpadden,
Maude Hoyt McSpadden,
Elizabeth Adair Morgan,
Llewellyn Hopewell Morgan,
Sallie Pauline Parris,[1]
Susie Vivian Scott,
Grace Raper Wallace,
Leola Fay Ward,

Guy Boatright.
James Stephenson Kennedy.
Garland Baird.
Dr. John Chisholm Breedlove.
John Griffith Harnage.
James Walker McSpadden.
Jesse Bartley Milam.
Woodley Gail Phillips.
Samuel P. Mathews.
William Everett Foreman.
Rhoderick Dhu Richards.
William Newton.

June 3, 1904.

Lulu Elizabeth Alberty,
Frances Bushyhead.
Eunice Marie Chamberlin,
Clara M. Couch,

John Woodson Conner.
James Knox Gibson.
Frank Edward Nix.

Joseph Alice Crutchfield,
Roxie Cunningham,
Stella Marie Ghormley,
Mary Hampton,
Elizabeth Covel Keys,
Nellie Blackwell Meek,
Amanda Payne Morgan,
Phoeba Montana Rider,

Joseph Oscar Dale.
Dr. Edward B. Reed.
Charles Kay.
Eugene Willard Tiger.

Emerson Elliott.
Frank Rolla Bell.
Jesse Albert Barbre.

June 1, 1905.

Lola Garrett,
Caroline Elizabeth Ghormley,
Mary Holand,
Sallie Jennings,
Mamie Butler Johnson,
Mary Anna Martin,
Ethel Martin,
Maude Rosamond Meigs,
Sallie Mayo Morgan,
Anna Belle Price,
Janie Stapler Ross.
Ethel Corinne Scales,
Anna Elizabeth Skidmore,
Martha Wallace,

Ephriam Monroe Bowers.
Johnson Harris.
Ernest Trenary.
Marion Gibson.
Dr. Francis M. Adams.
Timothy Meigs Walker.
Henry Pierson.
Eustace Adolphus Hill.
Vail Kimsey.
John Casper Lipe.
William Penn Adair.
Charles Inglish.
Andrew Johnson McDaniel.
Miles C. Chastain.

May 31, 1906.

Annie May Balentine,
Ruth Ballard,
Ella Jay Chandler,
Mary Ada Condray
Mary Louise Crafton,
Bird Adair Dameron.
Fannie Adair Danenburg,
Dora Early,
Penelope Adair Faulkner,
Bertha Elizabeth Frellick,
Fannie Etta Holland,
Clyde Horn,
Josephine Meigs,
Ara Ellen Ross,
Charlotte Elizabeth Spears,
Caroline Lucinda Starr,
Edith Lyle Stover,
Joy Lorraine Washburn,

William Potter Ross.
Hardy Frank Fleming.
William Edmonds.
Emmett Barker.
Daniel Baker.
George Pierce Cantrell.
Bancroft C. Kress.
Newell Tucker.
Eugene Gilbert.
Colonel E. Mayes.
Dr. Ulyssus Grant Hall.
Edmond Brigham Arnold.
James K. Blake.
Franklin Gritts Milligan.
George Guinn.
James Robert Wyly.
Edwin Bentley Hunt.
E. P. McCartney.

May 29, 1907.

Lelia Eaton.
Olive Estelle Edmondson,
Allie Johnson and Vera Jones.
May McSpadden,

Cicero Johnson Howard.
Charles Walton Poole.

Zoe McSpadden, Earl Preston Whitehill.
Nola Alice Monroe. Ward C. Crawford and Frederick Oyler

May 27, 1908.

Catherine Crafton, Kline Jordan.
Lucile Freeman, Roy Bearman.
Addie Gravitt and Alice Lynd Gravitt.
Frances Jane Lindsey, Joseph Daniel Hicks.
Ida Lois Lindsey, Jarrette Bell Harlan.
Ada Painter, E. B. Bell[2].
Bertha Reed, Perkins.
Ida Whetzell, Grover Tinnin.

May 27, 1909.

Gladys Mildred Anderson
Sallie Martha Bledsoe, L. C. Freeman.
Narcissa Brown, James Edward Wells.
Electa Crittenden.
Minnie Berkely Feland, Frederick McKinney.
Anna Victoria Hanes, E. Dickerson.
Clara Elizabeth Melton, Marcus Grover Cox.
Ella Quatie Richards, Frederick Albert Dedman.
Anna Laura Turner, Homer F. Gilliland.
Lena Norene Ward, Joseph Tryon Attenberry.

The Female Seminary building, which is two hundred and ninety two feet in length and three stories high, was sold to the state of Oklahoma.

Graduates from the Cherokee National Male Seminary.

February 1855[1].

Charles Holt Campbell, Lucy Lowrey.
Jonathan Riley, Mary Jack nee Gunter.
Joshua Ross, Muskogee Yargee.
Ready Taylor and David Lucullus Vann

February 1856.

William W. Campbell, Pauline Holt, Nannie Holt and Emeline Stegall nee McKnight.
William Henry Davis, Eliza Lowrey.
Jeremiah Everett Foreman. Celeste Stidham.
Moses C. Frye.
Joel Bryan Mayes, Martha McNair, Martha Candy and Mary Delilah Drew nee Vann.

October 1856.

Benjamin Wisner Carter, Nannie Elliott and Serena Guy.
Spencer Seago Stephens, Sarah Hicks.
Allison Woodville Timberlake, Margaret Lavinia Rogers.

The Male Seminary was closed on October 20, 1856 on account of lack of funds. The Female Seminary was also closed at the end of the regular fall term. Neither of these schools were opened again until after the civil war.

1882.

Harvey Wirt Courtland Shelton,	Mary Anna Elizabeth Duncan.
George Andrew Williams,	Cora Gregg nee Hogg.

June 26, 1884.

William Wirt Hastings,	Lulu Mayfield Starr,
Jefferson Thompson Parks,	Ruth Etta Duncan,
William Presley Thompson,	Elizabeth Clyde Morris.

June 25, 1885.

William Henry Clark,	Lilla Flournoy,
James William Duncan,	Lucinda Buffington.
William Elliott,	
Walter Adair Frye,	Eliza Jane Blair.
Jesse Stephen Lamar,	Emma Dale Simms.
Samuel W. Mills,	

May 14, 1886.

Thomas Brewer French,	Delilah Nave.
Walter Hampton Jackson,	Cherokee Brewer.
Samuel Houston Mayes,	Florence Nicodemus.
Paul Rogers,	
Lewis Wolf Ross,	Mary French.
Henry Benton Smith,	Florence Anna Caleb.
Archibald Spears,	Caroline Mary Boudinot.
John Shepherd Thornton,	Cynthia Pettit.
Thomas William Triplett,	Elizabeth Bushyhead.
Charles Edward Vann,	Ada Raymond.
John Rogers Hastings,	Elizabeth Victoria Shelton.

June 30, 1887.

Jesse Crary Bushyhead,	Fay Ione Reynolds.
Stand Watie Mayfield,	Amanda Caroline Thompson.
Mark Lee Paden,	Mary Louvinia Starr and Sarah Nix
Robert Parris,	Edith LaRue.
Lewis Right[1],	
John Otto Rogers,	Cora Archer Hicks.
Charles McClellan Ross,	Tommie Scruggs and Susie Morris.
Elizur Butler Sanders,	Elizabeth Downing.
Simon Ross Walkingstick,	Rebecca Osborn and
John R. Welch,	
Walter Duncan West,	Leona Scraper.

June 28, 1888.

James Austin Clark.	
Walter Tolbert Duncan,	Anna Stein.
John Thomas Johnson.	
Andrew Jackson Martin,	Anna Belle Morrow.
James Lee Mills and James Carroll Ward.	
James Tandy Musgrove	
Phillips Ross and Emmet Starr.	
Charles Lawrence Saunders.	Zena Pace.

June 27, 1889.

William Arnold, David M. Ingram and John Melvin Lisenbe.
Suake Lewis Miller, Minnie L. Ballard.

December 21, 1890.

William Wallace Ross, Mary Henrietta Moore.
John Caleb Starr, Libbie Belle Zimmerman.
Albert Sidney Wyley[1], Lillian Alexander.

June 23, 1892.

George McLaughlin Hughes, Addie Boudinot nee Foreman.
Richard Napoleon Wallace, Mary Forbes.
Charles Worcester Willey, Janana Sanders.

June 26, 1894.

Daniel Edmond Danenburg, Ruth Meacham.
James Turner Edmondson,[2] Julia Phillips.
Samuel Frazier Parks[3], Alberta Cora Markham,
Rufus Daniel Ross, Tooka Sixkiller and Samantha Parris.

June 23, 1895.

James Frank McCullough, Martha Hampton.
Robert Lee Mitchell, Josephine Barker.

June 24, 1896.

George Alexander Cox, Pearl Hampton.
Joseph Rasmus Danenburg.
George Tolliver Hampton, Fannie Josephine Carr.
Landrum Crittenden Jennings, Janana Benge.
Joseph Johnson Lynch, Georgia Vann.
Edward Butler Smith, Ella Pratt.
Stand Watie Woodall, Madge Paden and

June 25, 1897.

Royal Roger Eubanks, Martha Lelia Morgan and Bessie McCurry
William Charles Ghormley, Elizabeth Foreman.
Clifford Rogers,

June 29, 1898.

John Edgar Buffington,
James Price Evans, Pearl Gillispie.
Robert Wyly Fields.
Joseph Foreman Gladney, Mary Jane Dodson.
Albert Blunt James, Lucinda Miller.
Richard Vance McSpadden, Ermina Essie Foreman.
Thomas Asbury Scott, Daisy Belle Miller.
Homer Lafayette Smith, Alice Velinda Flournoy.
Nathaniel DeWitt Smith, Lucy Martin.

June 30, 1899.

Edward Foreman Blackstone, Aneliza Eulalia Sevier.
Henry Adair Dameron, Zona Lanyon.

John Merrit Eaton, Mary Bond.
John Casper Lipe, Anna Belle Price.
Gilbert Stephen Thompson.

May 24, 1900.

James Milner Crutchfield, Ida Lowrey Bell.
William Richard Harris.
DeWitt Clinton Lipe.
John J. Lovett[1], Margaret Loretta Cookson.

May 31, 1901.

John Walter Adair.
William Henry Balentine[2], Olive Antoine.
Walter Maecenas Charlesworth, Eugenia Catherine Eubanks.
Robert Bruce Garrett, Cherokee Vashti Edmondson.
Walter Duncan Smith,

May 28, 1902.

Francis William Caywood.
George Washington Fields[1], Jennie Lula Glass.
William Clyde Freeman, Clara Lowrey.
George Owen Grant[2], Lilian May Cunningham.
Dennis Bushyhead McNair.
Charles Scott Monroe Elizabeth Terrell.
William Taylor Scott.

June 10, 1903.

Claude Eugene Duncan, Allie Marian Shelton.
James Bascom Johnson[3],
Claude Stephen Mitchell, Fern Hogue.
Rhoderick Dhu Richards, Grace Raper Wallace.
James S. Sanders[4], Minnie Holland.
Eugene Willard Tiger. Mary Hampton.

June 2, 1904.

William Houston Ballard,[1] Anna Buchanan and Saphronia Carr nee Butler.
Andreas Newton Leerskov, Eril Webb.
Houston Bartow Fite
William Daniel Freeman.
William Richard Holland, Minnie Buckner.
William Adair McClellan,
Clarence Bluford Markham, Catherine Oldham.
Felix Hurd Mayes and Charles P. Pettit
Wilson Nivens Smith[2].
Samuel Jesse Starr[3], Nellie Whitmire.
James Oliver Ward.

June 2, 1905.

Jarrette Bell Harlan[1], Ida Lois Lindsey.
John Delancy Gulager,
Joseph Alexander Patterson, Ione Cranston.

May 31, 1906.

Elmer E. Fields.
Allen Boudinot Foster, Aurolla Upchurch.
James B. Markham, Blanche Bruce.
Henry H. Wood[2], Winifred Scott.

May 29, 1907.

Andrew Jackson Brown, Nola LeFlore.
Gunter Duckworth, Pauline Kaho.
Austin Grant Reagan, Grace Wade.
Martin Benge Teehee,
George Marion Tyner, Ethel Marshall.

May 27, 1908.

John Alvis Alberty, Bessie M. Atkins.
Perry Ashbrook Foreman.
Joseph William Garrett.
Andrew Denney Lane, Odeyne Henry.
George Clyde Whitmire. Fannie Dudley.

May 28, 1909.

Leroy A. Byrd and Andrew G. Tiffany
Francis Edmond Chouteau.
John Grover Scales, Ctaherine Whitley.

The Cherokee National Male and Female Seminaries were combined in September 1909 and on March 20, 1910 the Male Seminary building was burned and the senior class for that year had their graduation exercises at the Northeastern State Normal on May 31, 1910. They were:

Elizabeth Dee Bailey, Augustus Chouteau,
Lorena Allen Bean, William Francis Graham.
Oliver Maurice Haynes, Rachel Crouch.
Thomas Herbert McSpadden,
Susie Lowrey Martin, Robert Walker.
Lee Roy Mitchell[2], Ruth Foreman.
Grace Reid, Troy Arrington.

The sum of twenty two hundred dollars was appropriated by the council on December 23, 1842 for the board and clothing of orphan children attending the several public schools of the Cherokee Nation[1]. Most of these children were cared for by relatives or adopted into families where they were generally treated as the children of the household. Th maximum amount fixed for board was one dollar per week[2] and on December 4, 1845 the amount of thirty dollars per annum was fixed as a just compensation for the board and clothing of an orphan, during which time they must attend the regular sessions of the public schools.

This approximation was accepted as equitable and fair until January 26, 1872[3]. Soon after this date the orphan asylum was opened in the Male Seminary building[4]. The establishment of an orphan home school was first considered by an act of Council on December 19, 1842[5] but on account of lack of necessary funds the subject was dismised until November 3, 1848[6] when a committee consisting of the Superintendent of Schools, Richard Taylor and Rev. Stephen Foreman were empowered to negotiate with the authorities of the Methodist Episcopal Church, South for the establishment of an orphanage for the education of the orphans exclusively, Therefore,

Be it enacted by the National Council, That in order to provide for the education and instruction for the destitute orphans of the Nation, upon the manual labor plan, the Superintendent of Public Schools, Messrs. Richard Taylor and Stephen Foreman, Executive Councilors, be and they are hereby appointed as a committee on the part of the Nation to meet a committee on the part of the Methodist Church South, for the purpose of determining upon the most practicable plan of establishing and conducting schools for the benefit of the destitute orphans of both sexes to be located and established separately and apart at two springs on the mountain between Fourteen Mile Creek and Samuel Downing's, at a place where William Sourjohn now lives, and the terms on which said Church will take charge of said schools and conduct the same.

Be it further enacted, That the said Committee, consisting of the Superintendent of Public Schools, Stephen Foreman and Richard Taylor, Executive Councilors, shall report the result of their conference with the Committee on the part of the Methodist Church to the National Council, for their approval or rejection and should the parties enter into an agreement and the same be approved by the National Council, the said committee shall proceed to assess the value of the improvements of the said William Sourjohn with his consent and the value of the same shall be paid out of the Orphan funds.

Be it further enacted, That such substantial buildings of logs as may be necessary for the accommodation of about two hundred pupils of both sex, together with the teachers and mechanics, who may be employed to conduct the said schools, shall be built.

Be it further enacted, That the said Committee be and they are hereby authorized to mature and determine upon the most convenient plan for the building of the aforesaid houses, and to receive proposals and make the necessary contracts for the erection of the same.

Be it further enacted, That the said Committee be and they are hereby authorized to mature and determine upon the most convenient plan for the building of the aforesaid houses, and to receive proposals and make the necessary contracts for the erection of the same.

Be it further enacted, That the aforesaid Committee be and they are hereby further instructed to agree with the Church that should there be any net profit arising from any of the departments of said schools that the same shall be applied to the support of additional scholars.

Be it further enacted, That the Principal Chief be and he is hereby authorized, upon the certificate of said Committee, to issue warrants on the National Treasurer for such sums as may be required to meet any of the contracts to be paid out of the Orphan fund, and not otherwise appropriated.

Tahlequah, November 3, 1848.

Approved—George Lowrey, Acting Principal Chief."

Laws of the Cherokee Nation, 1852, page 182.

"The Committees appointed on the part of the Cherokee Nation and of the Missionary Society of the Methodist Episcopal Church, South to take into consideration the practicability of establishing a Manual Labor School for the benefit of the Orphan Children of the Nation, under the care of the Indian Mission conference of said Church, report the following as the result of their deliberations and agreement.

Article 1. There shall be an Orphan Manual Labor School in the Cherokee Nation, under the patronage of the Missionary Society of the Methodist Episcopal Church, South.

Article 2. The School shall be limited in its commencement from fifty to one hundred children consisting of equal number of children of both sexes, as nearly as possible.

Article 3. The site of said school to be selected by the joint Committee acting on the part of the Nation and the Church.

Article 4. There shall be a board of six Trustees for the Management of the School; three to be appointed by the Nation and three by the Missionary Society of the Methodist Episcopal Church, South.

Article 5. The buildings for the schools with the necessary fixtures and apparatus, the farm, tools, stock animals with all and every expense, including boarding, clothing, medical attendance, etc. to be paid out of the Orphan School Fund of the Nation.

Article 6. The children to be well taken care of boarded, clothed, instructed in all the branches, so far as practicable, of a good English education. The boys shall be instructed in the use of tools and to work on the farm. The girls; spinning, weaving, knitting, sewing, dairying, with all that pertains to household and domestic economy.

Article 7. The children admitted into the school not under six nor over fourteen years of age, and to continue in the same so long as the Board of Trustees may think necessary and profitable.

Article 8. It shall be the duty of the Board of Trustees to examine the accounts of the Institution quarterly, apportion the time for labor and teaching and fix he salaries of the teachers.

Article 9. The number of scholars and the extent of improvements may be enlarged or diminished when the Board of Trustees shall find the same necessary.

Article 10. The Superintendent of said school shall have power to call together the Board of Trustees whenever he shall find the same necessary.

Article 11. The Missionary Society of the Methodist Episcopal Church, South shall furnish the Superintendent and teachers and pay annually to their support the sum of one thousand dollars.

Article 12. This agreement shall go into effect so soon as concurred by the authorities of the Cherokee Nation and the Missionary Society of the Methodist Episcopal Church, South and the proper officers shall have been appointed to superintend and regulate the same.

Article 13. This agreement may be altered or annulled at any time upon the recommendation of the Board of Trustees; due notice being given of the same to the Cherokee National Council and to the Missionary Board of the Methodist Episcopal Church, South.

Article 14. Should there be any net profits arising from the farm, shops etc., the same shall be applied to the benefit of the school.

Article 15. Al speculation, in any way, upon the funds, the property of the Institution, to be carefully guarded against.

The foregoing articles agreed to and concurred in this 10th day of November 1848; by Walter Scott Adair and Richard Taylor.

Committee on the part of the Cherokee Nation.

Thomas Ruble, Thomas Hurlburt and Thomas Bertholf.

Committee on the part of the Missionary Society of the M. E. Church, South.

Be it enacted by the National Council, That the foregoing agreement be, and the same is hereby confirmed and approved and so much of the act passed 3rd day of November 1848, as militates aaginst any of the provisions of said foregoing agreement be and the same is hereby repealed.

And be it further enacted, That should the said Committees select the improvement of any citizen, for the locations of said school, be and they are hereby authorized to purchase the same, and so much of the act passed as above, as authorizes the said Committee to value any such improvement is hereby repealed.

But for some reason it failed of fruition.[1] Another committee was appointed by the council[2] but no report of their deliberations is available.

On November 25, 1871 an act was passed by council providing for the establishment of the "Cherokee Orphan Asylum," which was to be located on an estate of not more than two miles square[3]. The Asylum was opened in the Male Seminary building in 1872. Twenty thousand dollars or so much as may be necessary was appropriated to purchase the location which had already been decided to be the Lewis Ross property at Grand Saline or Grand River, and after further negotiations twenty eight thousand dollars was paid to his heirs.[4] Necessary improvements were made so that the building on completion would accommodate one hundred twenty five pupils, besides the teachers, Superintendent and his family.[1]

Tahlequah, November 10, 1848.

Approved: George Lowrey, Acting Principal Chief."

Laws of the Cherokee Nation, 1852, page 182.

The Superintendents were, consecutively: Rev. Walter Adair Duncan 1872 to 1882; Rev. Joseph Franklin Thompson 1882 to 1894; William Wallace Ross 1894 to 1897; Rev. Joseph Franklin Thompson 1897 to 1901; John Henry Danenburg 1901 to 1902. Danenburg was the last Superintendent under the authority of the Cherokee Nation and he was succeeded under the government supervision by Elias Cornelius Alberty, who was Superintendent at the time, when on Tuesday November 17, 1903 it was accidentally and entirely destroyed by fire. The building and equipment was valued at one hundred thousand dollars, exclusive of land. The faculty at the time of its destruction was: Principal, Robert Bruce Garrett; First Assistant, James Bascom Johnson; Second Asistant, Rhoderick Dhu Richards: Third Asistant, Miss Flora Sabrina Lindsey and Music Teacher, Mrs. Robert Bruce Garrett.[2]

CHAPTER XII

Missionary Activities. First Printing.

When the missionaries commenced work among the Cherokees at the beginning of the nineteenth century they found a condition awaiting them that was never presented to the christian workers by a heathen people. Within less than three quarters of a century before, Christian Priber, ex-jesuit had identified himself with this tribe, became one of them, learned their language, related to them the biblical stories, which the tribesmen had retained and remembered in infinite detail, although they had entirely forgotten Priber and the source of the stories. The sturdy Scotch and English countryman had also insidiously imbued the people with many of their ideas and notions.

Then the missionary came telling the self same Bible stories that the Cherokees had but recently derived from Priber, but in forgetting him they attributed them to an origin from their old religion that had legendarily been destroyed by the Ku-ta-ni. Upon an attempt to tell the story of Abraham, the missionary was almost invariably stopped by Cherokee auditors, who then told the story in, to the missionary, astonishing precision, even giving the personal names with remarkable correctness.

The recently revived New England idea of the evangelization of the non christians furnished a fresh impetus and many zealous workers to many fields that had been dormant, and the missionaries were entirely oblivious of the principal impelling causes of their advantage among this tribe but on account of the success that attended their efforts, they put forth extra exertions to win those who were so appreciative.

The Cherokees were naturally very amenable to a doctrine and belief that was identical with the legends that they thought had come from their primeval ancestry and within three decades became a christian people.

In 1801 James Vann, a wealthy halfbreed Scotch-Cherokee had a commodious two story brick dwelling on Chicamauga Creek in North Georgia and in April of that year Reverends Abraham Steiner and Gottleib Byhan, Moravian missionaries, became his invited guests until they could erect the initial mission buildings at Spring Place, so named on account of the number of springs in the vicinity. During the civil war, long after the missionaries and Indians had moved away, the bloody battle of Missionary Ridge was fought on its site. In 1821, the Moravians established a mission at Ootcalogy, about thirty miles south of Spring Place. Its creator and director was Reverend John Gambold, who had been at Spring Place since 1805. He died on November 6, 1827.

A mission was established in the western Cherokee nation, on Barren Fork, below the mouth of Tyner's Creek, in Adair County. It was moved to Harmony, near Beatty's Prairie, in the early fifties and after the civil war it was moved to Spring Place, on the west side of Illinois River, in the northern part of what is now Cherokee County, Oklahoma.

In 1803, Reverend Gideon Blackburn, a Presbyterian, opened two schools among the Cherokees in the vicinity of the present North Carolina Tennessee line.

He made two trips through the Cherokee country. One of six weeks in 1808 and one of twelve weeks during the succeeding year. Besides acquainting himself with the conditions of the country; he encouraged various industries; especially that of preparing and spinning cotton and wool. This bore rich fruits, in a few years, in the abundance of cloth that was woven and worn by the Cherokees. This cloth became so popular among them that the buckskin garment was a rare sight in the Cherokee country by 1830 and the striped home made hunting shirt, which was really a loose frock coat, trimmed with red yarn fringe, of the Cherokees became as distinctive a mark as was the Scotch tartan.

After the Cherokees came west and became the peacemakers of the plains, this Cherokee hunting shirt became the safest guarantee of life of any emblem that might be exhibited to the hostile Indians between the Mississippi River and Rocky Mountains.

On account of ill-health, Reverend Blackburn gave up his missionary work among the Cherokees in 1810.

In 1816, Reverend Cyrus Kingsbury, a native of Alstead, New Hampshire, visited the Cherokee country, with a view of locating a mission among the tribe. He reported favorably on the proposition and was delegated by the American Board of Commissioners for Foreign Missions, a non denominational organization, composed of Presbyterians and Congregationalists, to erect the necessary buildings.

He arrived at the proposed site, on Chicamauga Creek, on January 13, 1817 and immediately commenced the establishment of Brainard Mission, which was destined to be the precurser of much missionary work among the Cherokees.

On March 7, 1817, Moody Hall, a native of Cornish, New Hampshire and Loring S. Williams of Pownal, Vermont arrived at Brainard. Other missionary accessions to Brainard were Reverend Ard Hoyt of Danbury, Connecticut and Reverend Daniel Sabin Buttrick, on January 3, 1818. The latter was born at Windsor, Massachusetts on August 25, 1879 and died at Dwight Mission on June 8, 1851. On March 10, 1818, Reverend William Chamberlin a native of Newbury, Vermont, arrived at Brainard. He was the affianced husband of Miss Flora, the daughter of Reverend and Mrs. Ard Hoyt and they were married at the mission on March 22, 1818. Their son. Amory Nelson Chamberlin was born at Brainard on November 29, 1821. He had an equally fluent command of both the English and Cherokee languages and on account of his unassuming erudition and purity of character he was loved and respected by all that came in contact with him. He married on December 3, 1846 Dolly Eunice, the eldest daughter of his uncle, Milo Hoyt. Mrs. Chamberlin was the granddaughter of George Lowry, Assistant Chief of the Cherokee Nation. Reverend and Mrs. A. N. Chamberlin, died at their home near Vinita during the month of July 1849. His death preceding hers by about three weeks.

In January 1818, Catherine Brown, aged seventeen, a three quarters blood Cherokee girl, joined the Presbyterian church at Brainard. Two years later she established Creek Path Mission, near her home in Alabama, a hundred miles southwest of Brainard. She died on July 11, 1823.

The mission among the Cherokees being in successful operation, Reverend Kingsbury and Wiliams left the Cherokee mission work for a new field among the Choctaws, about the first of June 1818.

In 1819 Reverend Ard Hoyt was Superintendent of Brainard with Reverend Daniel S. Buttrick, as assistant. The school had sixty pupils that year. One of them, Lydia Lowrey, aged sixteen, daughter of George Lowrey, later Assistant Chief of the Cherokee Nation, joined the Presbyterian Church and was baptised on January 31, 1919. Shortly afterwards she had a dream in which the words came to her so impressively that on arising in the morning she wrote them out as the first hymn written by a Cherokee. She married Milo Hoyt, a son of Reverend Ard Hoyt and they were the ancestors of the Cherokee Hoyts. Mrs. Hoyt died on July 10, 1862. John Arch, "an unpromising looking young man" entered the school this year. He was a full blood Cherokee from western North Carlina. He soon became a good English scholar and interpreter and was noted for his sincere christianity and splendid character. He died at Brainard on June 18, 1825. President James Monroe, accompanied by Major General Edmund P. and Mrs. Gaines, visited Brainard on May 27 and 28, 1819, stopping over night there.

Reverend William Potter and Dr. Elizur Butler, with their families arrived at Brainard on January 10, 1821. In the autumn of 1844, Reverend Henry C. Benson on his way from the Choctaw school at Fort Cobb to Tahlequah to attend the first annual conference of the Methodist church in Indian Territory, which was held at Riley's Chapel, two miles south of Tahlequah from October 23 to 28, 1844, Bishop Thomas A. Morris, presiding, described his visit to Fairfield Mission as follows: "We found Dr. (Elizur) Butler sitting in an arm chair, in a dark room, prepared to spend the night in that position. He was suffering from asthma to such an extent as to render it impossible for him to lie upon a bed and sleep in a recumbent position. For many successive nights he had been compelled to sit alone in his dark chamber while the hours were slowly passing. At the ring of the bell we were admitted, with a brotherly and Christian cordiality that was truly grateful to our hearts at the end of our day's journey. Mrs. B., being indisposed, did not rise; but Miss Esther Smith, the teacher of the Mission school, and two fine Cherokee misses, who were about fourteen years of age, came and, in a few minutes, prepared us a substantial tea.

We were impressed with the good sense and economy which characterized, as far as we could discover, the entire establishment. There were no servants; Mrs. B., Miss Smith and six Cherokee girls who had been received into the family, did the kitchen and chamber work. These girls were not treated as servants, but daughters; they were neat, intelligent and sufficiently comely to pass reputably in any society. The furniture of the mission was plain, yet comfortable; while the table was destitute of every article that might be considered a luxury, the food was good, substantial and of sufficient variety."

John C. Ellsworth arrived at Brainard on November 24, 1821 and on the succeeding nineteenth of December John Vail and Henry Parker arrived.

A grist mill, a saw mill and a blacksmith shop were installed at Brainard during this year. These were for the use of the mission and to accommodate the public. At the end of the year there were eighty seven Cherokee pupils in attendance at Brainard, thirty girls and fifty seven boys.

Mr. Dean, a blacksmith from Vermont, with his wife, arrived in January 1822 and two months later, Ainsworth E. Blunt, a cooper and Sylvester Ellis, a farmer were added to the mission establishment. Blunt was a native of New Hampshire and Ellis of Vermont.

In May 1822, the property of the Mission was valued at $17,390.00. There were eighty Cherokee and two Osage pupils. These Osages, named by missionaries: John Osage Ross and Lydia Carter, had been adopted by the Cherokee after they had killed their parents in the battle of Pasuga or Claremore's Mound, in the present county of Rogers, State of Oklahoma, in Anoya or Strawberry moon of 1818. Lydia died at Mrs. William L. Lovely's in the Western Cherokee nation in the winter of 1823. The boy was taken to New England by General James Miller, the hero of Lundy's Lane, who was the first governor of Arkansas Territory and ex officio Superintendent of Indian Affairs. He was educated and learned the trade of a saddle, harness and trunk maker, he was living in 1835 and possibly has descendants in Massachusetts or New Hampshire that are not aware that they belong to the richest nation in the world, as the Osages enjoy enormous quarterly payments. The battle of Claremore mound was won by the Cherokees but they were not always so fortunate in their fights with the Osages, for in October or November 1816 an entire war party of one hundred Cherokees under their favorite war chief Walk in the Water was killed in a battle with the Osages and their allies on White River, excepting the White men: William Noland, Col. Lynn and L. D. Lafferty, who were captured and later escaped.

On October 12, 1822 Mr. and Mrs. Isaac Proctor of New Hampshire arrived at Brainard and on the thirteenth of the same month Mr. Frederick Ellsworth of Vermont, arrived.

Reverend Samuel Austin Worcester arrived at Brainard on October 21, 1825. He was born at Worcester, Worcester County, Massachusetts on January 19, 1798. Graduated from University of Vermont in 1819 and Andover Seminary in 1823; ordained in Park Street Church, Boston on August 25, 1825 and departed for Brainard six days later. He remained at Brainard as it supervising missionary through 1826. He left the Cherokee Nation some time during the summer of 1827 for Boston to supervise the making of the matrices for the Sequoian syllabary, have the type cast and purchase a printing press for the Nation.

The first printing done from this type was in the December number of 1827 of the Missionary Herald, it being the first to the fifth verses of the first chapter of Genesis. He arrived at New Echota, capital of the Cherokee Nation, on Conasanga River, in Georgia, on November 27, 1827 and immediately commenced the work of translating the Scriptures from Greek to Cherokee. He also systematized the phonetic arrangement of the Cherokee syllabary to the form that it subsequently bore. The printers: Isaac N. Harris and John Foster Wheeler arrived at New Echota on December 23, 1827 and the press arrived about a month later and volume 1, number 1 of the Phoenix appeared on February 21, 1828. Shortly after the issuance of the first copy, John Walker Candy, became an apprentice on the paper. Rev. Worcester was a continuous contributor to the paper and had a great deal of religious literature published from this press. He was arrested by the Georgia militia on July 7, 1831, on the charge of being in the Cherokee Nation, without a permit from Georgia and in violation of an act of the Georgia legislature, bearing date of December 22, 1830.[1] He was sentenced to the penitentiary on September 16, 1831 and was released by the Governor of Georgia on January 14, 1833. He returned to Brainard on March 15,

W. C. ROGERS
Chief—November 1903, to November 1917.

1834. Reverend Worcester's first wife was Miss Anne Orr, a native of Bedford, New Hampshire.

Reverend Worcester procured another press and full complement of Cherokee type and emigrated with them to the Western Cherokee Nation where he first stopped at Dwight and then proceeded to Union Mission, on Grand River, arriving there in the fall of 1835 and set up his press from which he published several religious works both in the Choctaw and Cherokee languages, notably the Cherokee Almanac for the year of 1836. These publications were the pioneers of Oklahoma printing. As he moved to Park Hill on December 2, 1836, it is possible that no Almanac was published for the year 1837, but it was published at the latter place for each consecutive year thereafter, until 1861. Elias Boudinot soon joined him in the work of translating and the mechanical press work was done by his son, John Walker Candy and Edwin Archer. Reverend Worcester's second wife, whom he married at Dwight Mission on April 3, 1841, was Miss Ermina Nash, a native of Cummington, who had begun her missionary work at Creek Path Mission, on November 5, 1825. He died at Park Hill, on April 20, 1859. He and his first wife, nee Ann Orr, a native of Bedford, New Hampshire was buried in the Park Hill cemetery.

Miss Lucy Ames, a native of Groton, Massachusetts arrived at Brainard on November 7, 1827. She married at Hawais Mission on August 14, 1830 Dr. Elizur Butler.

The station at Brainard sustained a great loss by the burning of the principal portion of the Mission buildings on the twelfth of March 1830, including the kitchen, dining hall, school rooms for both departments, lodging rooms for both scholars and family, together with supplies and furniture. The fire was so rapid that not more than fifteen minutes were allowed for awakening and saving the occupants. There were more than fifty children, besides the missionary family.

The missionaries, almost frantic with the responsibility, rushed into and through the burning buildings, almost into the very jaws of death, to see if any of the beloved charge remained unsaved. Then, when the roof had fallen in, a rush was made down to the bank of the beautiful Chickamauga, where the saved ones had been ordered to go. There, in the gray morning twilight the lines were formed, the count was made, and all dropped on their knees and thanked God for deliverance. All were saved."[1]

A mission was established by Reverend Moody Hall on the federal road in Georgia, sixty miles southeast of Brainard, on November 2, 1819[2]. It was at first called Taloney but they later changed to Carmel. The school was opened in May, 1820. There were thirty pupils attending in September, 1821. Reverend and Mrs. John Thompson and Miss Catherine Fuller were attached to the school on January 23, 1822. Reverend Daniel S. Buttrick had charge of the school in 1823. The school was maintained until 1836.

Creek Path Mission was established in April 1920 by Miss Catherine Brown, a three quarters blood Cherokee girl. It was in Alabama, one hundred miles southwest of Brainard. Reverend William Potter was assigned to Creek Path January 19, 1822 and stayed there until July 1837. Dr.

Elizur Butler was attached to Creek Path May 7, 1824 and remained until 1826. Miss Ermina Nash arrived at Creek Path on November 5, 1825 and staid until 1837. There were thirty one pupils at Creek Path in 1828.

Willstown Mission, located in Will's Valley, Alabama was founded March 28, 1823 by Reverend William Chamberlin, who had charge of the mission until 1839. He moved to Illinois and died at Alton on March 14, 1849.

Willstown was so named because it was the home of Will, an auburn haired, halfbreed Cherokee sub-chief.

Reverend and Mrs. Ard Hoyt, the parents of Mrs. Chamberlin, settled at Willstwn on May 22, 1824 and remained there until his death, which occurred on February 18, 1828. Mrs. Hoyt returned north in 1834.

Hawais Mission, originally called Turnip Mountain, in Georgia, was established in 1823 by Mr. John C. Ellsworth. Dr. Elizur Butler was attached to Hawais on May 1, 1826. Mrs. Butler nee Esther Post of South Concord, Connecticut died there on November 21, 1829. Dr. Butler was arrested by Georgia militia on July 7, 1831 for residing in the Cherokee Nation without a permit from Georgia; sentenced to the penitentiary on September 16 of that year and released by the Governor of Georgia on January 14, 1833.

Etowa Mission, improperly pronounced "Hightower" was founded in 1823 by Mr. and Mrs. Isaac Proctor. It was located on Etowa River in Georgia, eighty miles southeast of Brainard and thirty five miles west of Carmel.

Candy's Creek Mission was founded in 1824 by John Vail and William Holland. In 1828 there were thirty Cherokee pupils in this school.

New Echota,[1] the capital of the Cherokee Nation was established by an act of council in 1818. An act providing for the erection of an office for the "Cherokee Phoenix" was enacted on November 15, 1826. New Echota was never used as a mission location, but a church was maintained by the A. B. C. F. M., and a great deal of religious literature was printed on the Phoenix press.

In July 1820, Reverends Cephus Washburn and Alfred Finney accompanied by James Orr and Jacob Hitchcock arrived in the Western Cherokee Nation, Arkansas Territory. Shortly afterward they established Dwight Mission, on the west bank of Illinois Creek, four miles from Arkansas River. It was named in honor of Reverend Timothy Dwight, President of Yale College and the first signatory member of the A. B. C. F. M.

By the first of October 1820 they had erected two "comfortable cabins" and soon afterwards Washburn and Finney returned to Elliott Million, in Mississippi, for their families. They returned to Dwight on May 10, 1821. Miss Ellen Stetson, born March 30, 1873 at Kingston, Massachusetts arrived at Dwight on December 22, 1821 where she died on December 29, 1848.

The missionaries commenced the erection of the school building upon their return to the mission, but before they finished it they ran out of nails and had to go to Union Mission, over two hundred miles distant, to borrow enough to complete the building, which they did and commenced school on January 1, 1822.

In January 1826, the following missionaries were at Dwight: Reverends Washburn and Finney, missionaries; Dr. George L. Weed who afterwards moved to Cincinnati, Ohio, physician and teacher; Jacob Hitchcock, steward; Miss Cynthia Thrall, charge of school; Miss Ellen Stetson, teacher; James Orr, farmer; Samuel Wisner and Asa Hitchcock, mechanics. Reverend and Mrs. Worcester Willey arrived at Dwight on January 31, 1826.

The Western Cherokees exchanged their land in Arkansas for land west of that Territory on May 6, 1828, and by the succeeding spring practically the entire Western nation had moved to their new possession. For that reason it became incumbent on the missionaries to also remove to the Indian Territory. The entire missionary establishment of Dwight Mission was moved to and located on the site of Nicksville, the late county seat of Lovely County, Arkansas, in 1828. The location is in the northern half of section two, township twelve north, range twenty-three east and in the south half of section thirty-four, township thirteen north, range twenty-three east in Sequoyah County, Oklahoma.

Miss Esther Smith, born July 25, 1806, at Harrisburg, N. Y., arrived at Dwight on December 22, 1832. She was transferred to the Mission at the Forks of the Illinois in 1835; to Park Hill Mission in 1836, and back to Dwight in 1838. In 1841 she was transferred to Fairfield, where she continued until her release from the service of the American Board on September 6, 1853. She remained in the Cherokee Nation and taught in the national schools. Just before the Civil war she was teaching at Peavine school, which was about one mile south of the present town of Baron. She remained with the Cherokees during the Civil war and died at Fort Gibson in January, 1865. Her remains being interred in the post burial ground, from whence they were later removed and reburied, by the government contractors, among the unknown dead in the National Cemetery, several years later.[1]

Reverend and Mrs. Jesse Lockwood arrived in Dwight in January, 1834. He died of fever at that Mission on the succeeding eleventh of July. Mrs. Lockwood returned to New England in April, 1835.[1]

On account of the emigration Reverends D. S. Buttrick, William Potter and Elizur Butler came to Dwight from the Old Cherokee nation in 1839.

Mulberry Mission had been established as a branch station to Dwight, on Mulberry Creek in Pope County, Arkansas, and was moved in 1828 to a location some fifteen miles north of Dwight and its name was changed to Fairfield. It was placed under the direction of Dr. Marcus Palmer.

Union Mission, section sixteen, township nineteen north, range nineteen east, in Mayes County, Oklahoma, was established in 1820 by Reverend William F. Vaill of the United Foreign Missionary Society for work among the Osage Indians. A large farm was established in 1822. It was under the direction of Reverend Wiliam B. Montgomery as missionary and George Requa a "superintendent of secular concerns." The location was about four miles from the main mission establishment and run in connection with the school.

The first Protestant conference, in what is now the state of Oklahoma, was held at Union Mission, from November second to the seventh 1822; the sessions being from 5:15 a. m. to 9 p. m. of each day, except the last, which was ended shortly before noon. There were representatives from Union, Dwight and Harmony, which was located on the Maries des Cygnes River in Missouri. Reverend Burton Pixley of Harmony was chosen moderator and Epaphrus Chapman, scribe.

As early as 1823 there were fourteen missions at this place and the property was valued at twenty-four thousand dollars.[1]

Dr. Marcus Palmer was granted a restricted license to preach on November 7, 1825, by a conference that was held at Union.

In January, 1826, the missionaries attached to Union were: Reverend William F. Vaill, missionary; Dr. Marcus Palmer, Physician; Stephen Fuller, Abraham Redfield, John M. Spaulding, Alexander Woodruff and George Requa, assistant missionaries, farmers and mechanics, and seven females. At this time they had twenty-six pupils.

On May 10, 1826, the United Foreign Missionary Society and the American Board of Commissioners for Foreign Affairs were united and continued under the name of the latter organization.

In the fall of 1835 Reverend Samuel A. Worcester located at Union and set up his mission press.

Park Hill Mission was founded in about 1829 by Samuel Newton, late of Osage Mission, in Kansas. He named the Mission "Park Hill" on account of the natural beauty of its surroundings. His residence and mission was at Campbell's Spring,[2] between the later residence of Chief John Ross and Reverend Samuel A. Worcester. The Mission was later moved to a location about a quarter of a mile east of the residence of Reverend Worcester and at the latter place the Mission press was established. Mr. Newton afterwards moved to Washington County, Arkansas, and was postmaster of Boonesborough in 1847.

The "Mission at the Forks of the Illinois" was in operation in 1830 and was perpetuated in the Elm Springs Mission.

Reverend Humphrey Posey, a native of North Carolina, was appointed by the Baptist Board as a missionary to the Cherokees on October 13, 1817.[1] He immediately repaired to the Western part of his own state, where there were living at that time several thousand of this tribe. Having established a few schools, he felt called to do some exploring in the regions West of the Mississippi, doubtless with a view of locating there. His protracted absence caused a loss of interest in the schools and their necessary suspension. On his return, early in 1820, he established a mission station at Valley Town, on Hiwassee River, in the southwest corner of the State and Thomas Dawson was appointed assistant. A farm of eighty acres was cleared, put in cultivation and three houses were built. Shortly after the school started, it had forty pupils.

Evan Jones was born in Brecknockshire, Wales on May 14, 1788. At the age of fifteen he was apprenticed to a linen draper and spent a number of years with him. While there he met Miss Elizabeth Lanigan, who was also working in this store and in course of time she became his wife. The Jones' emigrated to America, reaching Philadelphia early in 1821. Mr. Jones had previously left the formal church of England and joined the Methodists, but during the summer of 1821 he and his wife became members of the "Great Valley Baptist Church,,' near their home. It was under the pastorage of Reverend Thomas Roberts, who, with others, was at that time preparing to enter into a mission to the Cherokees.

A month after the reception of Mr. and Mrs. Jones into the Baptist church, found them members of the missionary band to the Cherokees. Traveling in farm wagons these missionaries arrived at Valley Town in September, 1821. Reverend Roberts took the directing office of Missionary Superintendent and among the other assignments were Isaac Clever, blacksmith; John Farrier, farmer and weaver; Evan Jones, teacher, and it is not known what the other score of people did. The date of the ordination of Evan Jones to the ministry is not known, but we do know that by 1825 he and his family were the only ones of the Great Valley missionary band that still remained with the Cherokee mission work.

A mission was established at Notley, sixteen miles southwest of Valley Town in the summer of 1822. Shortly afterwards another mission was established at Tinsawatee,[2] sixty miles southwest from Valley Town, in Georgia.[1] In 1823 the Baptist missions received their convert in the person of John Timson.[2] In this year they were joined by Reverend and Mr. Duncan O'Bryant, who were assigned to the station of Tinsawatee and shortly afterwards he moved themission from Tinsawatee to Hickory Log, a distance of some ten miles.[3]

Kaneeda, .a full-blood Cherokee, was converted at Hiwassee in 1829, and became the first native Baptist minister among the Cherokees. On account of his character, Reverend Jones gave him the English name of John Wickliffe. He began preaching in 1831 and was ordained in 1833. He died in Saline District on November 22, 1857.[4]

During the time that these Baptist missionaries were prosecuting their work among the full bloods in the eastern part of the Cherokee Nation, Jesse Bushyhead, the son of a prominent family, after having attended school in Tennessee, joined the Baptist church and was baptised in 1830. He returned to the Cherokee Nation and gathered a congregation at Ahmohee, which was in the neighborhood in which his parents resided. It was not until quite a while after he had built up a good church here that he met any of the Baptist missionaries.[1] He was ordained to the ministry on the same day as was John Wickliffe. Reverend Bushyhead had a circuit of two hundred and forty miles in which he was assisted from 1834 to 1838 by Reverend Beaver Carrier, a young Cherokee minister who was later a senator from Saline District.

Reverend Bushyhead was one of the leaders of the Ross party, being at the time of his death on July 17, 1844, Chief Justice of the Cherokee Nation. His disinterestedness in the feudal and political troubles among his people gained for him the pecular distinction of being the only man of any consequence among the Cherokees who habitually traveled among his people in the troubluos period of 1839-46, unarmed, except, as he said, with his Bible.

Aganoyah, a full blood Cherokee, was a contemporary Baptist minister with Bushyhead and Wickliffe.

The Baptist church membership in 1835 in the Cherokee Nation "East" was two hundred and twenty-seven.

Mrs. Elizabeth Lanigan Jones died at Valley Town on February 5, 1831.[2] Reverend Jones' second wife was Miss Pauline Cunningham.

About thirty families from the vicinity of Hickory Log Mission, under the leadership of Reverend O'Bryant, migrated to the Cherokee Nation "West" in 1831, stablishing New Hope Mission o nBarren Fork Creek and about two miles from the Arkansas line. They shortly afterwards added a grist and saw mill. Reverend O'Bryant died in 1834 and was succeeded by Reverend Samuel Aldrich of Cincinnati, Ohio, who died after one year's service and then the mission lapsed.[1]

Other accessions to the missionary working force among the Eastern Cherokees were Leonard and Mrs. Butterfield and Miss Sarah Rayner in 1832 and Chandler Curtis in 1835.

Reverend Bushyhead established a camp near the Arkansas line upon his arrival in 1839, at which rations were issued to needy emigrants and for this ration the camp was locally known as "Bread Town,"[2] but he immediately commenced his religious work here and the location soon became known as Baptist Mission, the name that it justly bears to this day, although the mission was removed to Tahlequah by John B. Jones, in 1867. The Jonses settled at and became a part of Baptist Mission shortly after their arrival in the Western Cherokee Nation.

John Buttrick Jones, son of Reverend Evan and Mrs. Elizabeth Lanigan Jones, was born at Valley Town, North Carolina on December 24, 1824. He was Cherokee interpreter for his father at the age of thirteen. Was baptised by Reverend John Wickliffe in 1844. The Jonses, assisted by Harvey Upham and Mark Tiger, published at Union Mission the Cherokee Message, a monthly missionary publication a part of which was printed in the Cherokee language. Its first issue was in August 1844. Only about fourteen issues were printed.

John B. Jones graduated from the University of Rochester, New York in 1855. He was ordained to the ministry in that city on July 14, 1855 and was married there in October of the same year to Miss Jennie M. Smith. They repaired immediately to the Baptist Mission and entered the missionary work.[1]

Both Evan and his son John B. Jones were men of magnetic and sympathetic presences, splendid acquisitive minds an drare executive abiilties. While the father was perfectly conversant with the Cherokee language, he always used an interpreter when preaching to the Chrokees. The son, having been born in the Cherokee country, rapidly gained a facile and perfect knowledge of the Cherokee language and customs and no man or men were ever able to sway the minds and policies of the full blood Cherokees as did this father and son.

They were the real directors of the Cherokee Nation from 1839 to 1867, through the numerically dominant full bloods, who as a body were always swayed by impulse rather than reason. As ministers of the gospel they were apparently meek and humble, but the sentiments that they powerfully and insiduously engendered among the full bloods were perforce the governmental policies of Chief Ross.

At the same time they almost always courted the good will of the astute and suave Ross, but upon the accession of his nephew, William P. Ross, to the Chieftancy they broke with him and by promoting an aliance, in 1867, between the friends of Lieutenant Colonel, the Reverend Lewis Downing and the ex-Confederate Cherokees, they formed the Downing party, which after this time elected all the Chiefs, except one Dennis W. Bushyhead and he was opposed to his first election by many of the prominent Ross leaders.

The Jones' were the moving and dominant spirits in the inception of the Keetoowha Society in 1859. Its membership was at first practically all full bloods and one of its prime principles was abolitionism which severely affected the Ross family, as many of them were large slave owners. On account of this agitation the Jones were proscribed by the federal and national authorities in 1861 and then became the active negotiators with their full blood friends in persuading them to give up their affiliation with the confederacy in 1862, deserting their Colonel, John Drew and the Ross family. Drew joined the confederates but almost all the Rosses went over to the federal cause.

With hardly an intermission the Baptist educational success has been: Valley Town Mission 1820-39; Baptist Mission 1839-67; Baptist Mission at Tahlequah 1876-85 and because the Cherokee Nation would not make them satisfactory land grants the mission was moved to the Muskogee Nation where its name was changed to Bacom University and has maintained a laudable existence since 1885.

Reverend Evan Jones died in August 1873 and Reverend John Buttrick Jones died on June 13, 1876.

A unique religious observance among the full blood Cherokees is the annual "Baptist Association' which meets at some selected place on the east side of the Grand River in the late summer or early autumn. They come with their entire families and camp for a week, attending church and fraternizing. Their provisions are assembled in a general tent, cooks are allotted for each meal. These cooks are almost universally clean and mistresses of their art. The meals are served to all and without price. The fervor of their worship is a moral stimulus to all who come in contact with them. As beneficient hallowedness seems to permeate the very atmosphere as these people who live close to nature met render their obeisance and thanks to their creator.

The largest of these Baptist Association establishments was described in the Annual Report of the Commissioners of Indian Affairs for 1859 on page 176, as follows: Delawaretown church on September 5, 1859 was a main room eighty by twenty feet, with two side rooms equipped with two stoves and a bell, together with the thirty other buildings which were occupied by the people who came to attend the Association, these were hewn log houses ranging from twelve feet square to fifty by twenty feet and also a comfortable log school house thirty by twenty beet with a good floor, stove and four glazed windows. This was the establilshment of a people nearly all full blood Cherokees, practically all of whom were in moderate circumstances.

The policy of the Methodists was not to build mission establishments. Their work was more along the evangelical lines, primary instruction being subsidiary.

In 1822, at the solicitation of Richard Riley, Reverand Richard Neeley of the Tennessee Methodist Conference, commenced to preach in the Cherokee country. Riley and several others joined the church during this year.[2] Reverends I. W. Sullivan and Ambrose F. Driskill succeeded Neeley.

The first Methodist Mission school was established in the Cherokee country in 1824[3] and during that year John Fletcher Boot was licensed to preach. "He was an orator and simple. He was unaffected, unstudied, graceful and powerful."[4] He died while filling the Canadian District circuit in 1852 or 3.

There were three missions in 1825, four in 1826 and seven in 1827. Truth Fields, a veteran of the Creek war of 1841 was converted in 1826 and licensed to preach during the next year. In 1827 he filled the Coosawatee[5] circuit. He was a signer of the constitution of 1839.

Greenwood LeFlore, Chief of the Choctaws, whose wife was Elizabeth Coody, niece of Chief Ross, was converted and joined the Methodist church in 1827.

In the fall of 1828 the Tennessee conference made the following appointments for the Cherokee Nation:

Superintendent of Missions, Reverend William McMahon.

Wills Valley and Oostanalla, Reverend B. M. Ferran with Joseph Blackbird as interpreter.

Coosawater, Reverend Truth Fields.

Mount Wesley and Ashbury, Reverend Dixon C. McLeod. A mission school attached.

Chatooga, Reverend Greenbury Garrett. A school attached.

Sullacooie, Reverend Nicholas Dutton Scalis.[1] A school attached.

Neeley's Grove, Reverend Allen F. Scraggs. A school attached.

Conasauga, Reverend Thomas J. Elliott. A school attached.

General Missionary to travel through the Nation, Reverend James Jenkins Trott.

Chief John Ross joined the Methodist church and Reverend Richard Neeley died during this year.[2]

COMMISSION APPOINTED BY PERSIDENT CLEVELAND, 1893
Thos. R. Knight Coffee Woodall Darius E. Ward, Sec.
Jas. M. Keys Wm. H. Hendricks, Pres.

CHAPTER XIII

Officers of The Cherokee Nation, September. 9. 1839 to June 30, 1908.

The anomaly of a fully constitutional government with all of the concomitant expenses of executive, legislative, judicial and educational departments; being in existence for fifty-nine years, selfsustaining, without direct personal taxes, would seem at first thought, utopian and impossible. But this was the condition presented by the Cherokee Nation from September 6, 1839[1] to July 1, 1898.[2] A contented and satisfied communal government in which personal land titles were nonexistant; livestock had free range, universally attended free schools with free text books, were the center of each annuities of the tribe was to be paid; two-thirds to the Cherokees living east Education was a shibbolath, extreme poverty unknown and individual efforts were often crowned with affluence.

The permanent funds for the maintenance of the Cherokee Nation was derived from the sale of portions of their tribal lands and had its inception in a provision of an indemnatory article in the United States-Cherokee treaty of October 24, 1804, which provided an annuity to the Cherokee Nation ,of three thousand dollars.

According to the sixth article of the treaty of February 27, 1819 the annuities oft he tribe was to be paid; two-thirds to the Cherokees living east of the Mississippi River and one third to those that had emigrated to Arkansas and were known as Western Cherokees, in accordance with their estimated proportional population.

Article ten of the treaty of December 29, 1835, set aside the following amounts from the five million dollars sale price of the Cherokee lands east of the Mississippi River: two hundred thousand as a general fund, fifty thousand as an orphan fund and one hundred and fifty thousand as a school fund for the Cherokee Nation.

The permanent annuities that had accrued under the provisions of former treaties were commuted for an additional general fund of two hundred and fourteen thousand dollars. Under the provisions of article twelve it was primarily agreed that one hundred thousand dollars should be used to aid indigent parties who had previously emigrated west. This award was rescinded by a supplementary article that added this sum to the general fund.

The apportionment of the disbursement of interest on the national fund was divided under the treaty of July 19, 1866, as follows: General fund, fifty per cent; school fund thirty-five per cent and orphan fund, fifteen per cent.

The general fund was used to meet the expenses of the national government, excepting those of education.

The only official census enumerations available are:

1838 - - 22,500.
1880 - - 21,920.
1890 - - 28,000.

1900 - - 32,376.
1910 - - 38,300.

State bonds purchased and held in trust by the United States for the Cherokees, under authority of the treaty of 1835, as shown by the Report of the Commissioner of Indian Affairs for the year 1839:

		General Fund.
Kentucky	5%	$ 94,000.00.
Tennessee	5%	250,000.00.
Alabama	5%	300,000.00.
Maryland	6%	761.39.
Michigan	6%	64,000.00.
		School Fund.
Maryland	5%	$ 41,138.00
Missouri	5½%	10,000.00.

The interest on their invested funds that were paid to the general fund only as reported by the Commissioner of Indian Affairs in his reports for the following years were given as :

1839 - - $36,085.65.
1850
1860 - - 28,914.93.
1870 - - 53.445.01.
1880 - - 43,430.93.
1890 - - 30,958.31.
1898 - - 71,427.16.

The exact dates of the regular elections of the Cherokee Nation were on the first Monday of August of the odd numbered years, and were as follows:

September	9, 1839	Chief's election.	John Ross, elected
August	2, 1841		
"	7, 1843	" "	" " "
"	4, 1845	" "	" " "
"	2, 1847	" "	" " "
"	6, 1849	" "	" " "
"	4, 1851	" "	" " "
"	1, 1853	" "	" " "
"	6, 1855	" "	" " "
"	3, 1857		Died August
"	1, 1859	" "	" " " 1, 1866
"	5, 1861		
"	5, 1867	" "	Rev. Lewis Downing, elected.
"	2, 1869		
"	7, 1871	" "	Rev. Lewis Downing. Died Nov. 9,
"	4, 1873	" "	1872.
"	2, 1875	" "	Rev. Charles Thompson.
"	5, 1877		
"	4, 1879	" "	Dennis Wolf Bushyhead.
"	1, 1881	" "	

"	6, 1883	"	"	Dennis Wolf Bushyhead.
"	3, 1885			
"	1, 1887	"	"	Joel Bryan Mayes.
"	5, 1889			
"	3, 1891	"	"	Joel Bryan Mayes. Died Dec. 14, 1891.
"	1, 1893			
"	5, 1895	"	"	Samuel Houston Mayes.
"	2, 1897			
"	7, 1899	"	"	and council only. Thomas Mitchell Buffington.
"	5, 1901			council only.
"	3, 1903	"	"	council only. William Charles Rogers.

The courts of the Cherokee Nation were abolished by the act of congress of June 28, 1898, entitled "An Act for the Protection of the People of the Indian Territory and for other purposes," effective July 1, 1898.

Rev. Lewis Downing was Principal Chief from August 1, 1866 to October 18, 1866. William Potter Ross was elected Principal Chief by council in October 19, 1866, vice John Ross, deceased and was elected November 11, 1872 vice Reverend Lewis Downing, deceased. Assistant Chief Henry Chambers having predeceased Chief Joel B. Mayes by four days the succession descnded to Thomas Mitchell Buffington, President of the Senate, who held the office until Colonel Johnson Harris was elected and qualified on December 23, 1893 and Buffington was elected as Delegate to Washington.

William Charles Rogers, the last Chief of the Cherokees was elected in 1903 and under the provisions of the United States-Cherokee agreement made at Muskogee on July 1, 1902 this was the last election in the Cherokee Nation, but he was retained as Principal Chief of the Cherokees until his death on November 8, 1917, in order that he, as the properly authorized representative of the Nation, might sign the deeds transferring the title of the community lands of the Cherokee Nation to the individual allottees of the same.

Oochalata, who spoke very little English, was the son of a full blood Cherokee father and his mother was a white woman who spoke the Cherokee language only. Oochalata owned and operated a good sized mercantile establishment at his home on Spavinaw Creek. On being elected senator from Delaware District in 1867 he thought that he should have an English name and said that as Dr. Jeter Lynch Thompson had been senator for a long time and because he was taking his place he would adopt the name Thompson; and taking the sound of Chala out of his Cherokee name, Oo-cha-la-ta, he called himself Chala or Charles Thompson. For some time before Charles Thompson had been elected Chief, he had been a deacon of the Baptist church and had been acting as the local preacher in the commodious frame church house that he had and maintained. The Baptist church had refused to ordain him, giving as their reason, the fact that he was a lawyer. Shortly after he was elected Chief he was ordained as a Baptist minister.

Chiefs John Ross and his nephew William Potter Ross belonged to the Ross party. Chief Dennis Wolf Bushyhead belonged to the National party which was formed in 1879 and became the successor to the Ross party and all of the other chiefs belonged to the Downing party.

Joseph Vann, who afterwards became a resident of Saline District was elected Assistant Chief on September 9, 1839. On June 26, 1840, Anderson Vann, an "Old Settler" was chosen to succeed his brother Joseph, who resigned as a result of the political compromise of that date. George Lowery who had been sponsor for Sequoyah was elected Assistant Chief in 1843 and 1847. Richard Taylor was elected in 1851. John or "Jack" Spears was elected in 1855. He was a full blood Cherokee; he had been left an orphan at an early age and took his name from a family that adopted him. A splendid intrepreter, he was a popular and able man. Joseph Vann of Saline District was again elected in 1859. Being a confederate sympathizer he was succeeded in the federal Cherokee government by Thomas Pegg in 1862. Pegg was a captain in Drew's confederate regiment, but on joining the federals in 1862 he was elected Major of the Second Indian Home Guards U. S. A. Captain James Vann, a cripple, magnanimous, brave and humane was elected in 1867. Robert Buffington Daniel was elected in 1871 and died on January 16, 1872. Captain James Vann was again elected, by the council on November 23, 1872 vice Daniels. David Rowe was elected in 1875. Colonel William Penn Adair, six foot and two inches in height, magnetic, logical and frankly agreeable, the ablest and most brilliant of all Cherokees, was elected in 1879 and did in Washington, D. C., on October 21, 1880. Rabbit Bunch was elected by council on November 5, 1880 and reelected in 1883. Samuel Smith was elected in 1887. Bunch and Smith were prosperous full bloods, spoke the Cherokee language only and were distinguished orators. Henry Chambers ,a quarter blood or less, noted for his integrity and genial philosophic nature was elected in 1891 and died during an epidemic of influenza on December 10, 1891. Stephen Teehee, a splendid type of the full blood Cherokee was elected by council on December 23, 1891. Reverand George Washington Swimmer, a full blood Cherokee and well to do merchant and farmer was elected in 1895 and 1899. David McNair Faulkner, a half blood Cherokee known best by his seasoned wisdom and earnest integrity. A master Mason in every sense of the term, was elected August 3, 1903. He was retained in the office until June 30, 1914. He died August 2, 1914.

Joseph Vann, George Lowery, Richard Taylor, John Spears were elected by the Ross party. Rabbit Bunch and Henry Chambers belonged to the National party. All of the other Assistant Chiefs were elected by the Downing party.

The constitution of the Cherokee Nation was formed and promulgated near the mouth of the Tahlequah Creek, under a brush harbor but within a few days thereafter the council moved to the present site of Tahliquah and thence forward until the civil war the capitol was at that town, but the location was not fixed specifically by act of council until October 19, 1841 which was as follows: "An Act Establishing the Seat of Government.

Be it enacted by the National Council, That the seat of the Cherokee Government is hereby established at Tahlequah.

Tahlequah, October 19th, 1841.

Approved A. M. Vann, Acting Chief."[1]

The site was at that time a wooded valley with numerous springs, west of and adjacent of Rev. Youngwolf's farm which had up to the spring of 1834 been the home of Blackcoat, Third Chief of the Old Settler Cherokees. It was settled by a band of Natchez before Blackcoat's tenure.

The council passed an act prohibiting the destruction of timber within a quarter of a mile from Tahlequah, on October 4, 1839.[2]

One hundred and sixty acres was platted into town lots and sold in 1844.[1] Taleq, Tillico or Tahlequah had for years been a favorite town name with the Cherokees, although the origin of the name is unknown.

On November 10, 1847, council authorized the National Treasurer to contract for the erection of two hewed log buildings, each to be twenty feet square, a brick chimney, floored and ceiled overhead with plank, each crack to be stopped inside and out with mortar; shingle roof, one door and four windows, one story high and underpinned with stone. One for the use of the committee and the other for the council, to be completed by the first day of October 1848, at a cost not to exceed two hundred and fifty dollars each. Said buildings to be erected on the public square at or near the sites occupied by the cabins that had been used by the committee and council.[2] These buildings were constructed by James Kell who was paid for them by act of council on October 5, 1848.[3] On October 14, 1848 an appropriation of four hundred dollars was made by council to have two buildings similar to the committee and council houses built for offices of the Chief and Treasurer.[4] They were built in a row on the east side of the square and were used as capitol buildings until the civil war when they were burned on Otcober 28, 1863 by Colonel Stand Watie.[1]

Under authority of an act of council of December 9, 1867, the present county court house of Cherokee County, Oklahoma, which was the capitol building of the Cherokee Nation until its dissolution, was built.

According to the provisions of the constitution of 1839 a full complement of officers were elected by that body on or about September 1839.[2]

On account of the vigorous protests of the "Old Settlers" and "Treaty Party," on the unequal representation a new alignment of officers was agreed upon by a joint committee of the factions at Fort Gibson on October 26, 1840.

The only members of this council whose names are available are: Committeemen; Thomas Fox, William Rogers, James Carey, Thomas Lewis Rogers, Captain William Dutch, John Duncan, Bluford West, George Washington Adair, Joseph Lynch Martin, John Drew, Thomas Pegg, Reverend Truth Fields, John Spears, George Washington Gunter, James Spears, Hair Conrad, William Shorey Coody, President of the Senate and Reverend Stephen Foreman, Clerk of the Senate.

Councilors; Ezekeal Starr, William Holt, Lame Glass, Charles Thornton vice William Thornton,[3] Wind, Samuel W. Bell, James Rogers, Lovely Rogers, Rev. Youngwolf, Speaker of Council and David Carter, Clerk of Council.

The committee was provided for by the twenty-two sections of the third article of the constitution of 1839. The first eight districts: Delaware Saline,

Going Snake, Tahlequah, Illinois, Canadian, Skin Bayou and Flint were created by act of council of November 4, 1840. The name of the Committee was changed to the Senate in 1867 but the latter will be used here as a matter of convenience. The Salaries were at first fixed by article three, section ten of the constitution at three dollars per day, subject to change by council.

Senators from Delaware District.

1841. Joseph Martin Lynch and the other one unknown.

1843. Old Fields and Moses Daniel. The latter elected President of the Senate, vice Charles Coody, deceased.

1845. James Kell and Anderson Springston.

1847. James Kell and Robert Buffington Daniel.

1849. James Kell and Lewis W. Hildebrand. The former was elected President of the Senate.

1851. James Kell and Charles Landrum.

1853. James Kell and Charles Landrum. The former was elected President of the Senate.

1855. Dr. Jeter Lynch Thompson and Charles Landrum.

1857. Dr. Jeter Lynch Thompson and Jeffrey Beck.

1895. Dr. Jeter Lynch Thompson and John Daniel.

1861. Unknown.

1867. Charles Thompson and Alexander Hawk.

1869. Charles Thompson and Alexander Hawk.

1871. Charles Thompson and John Landrum.

1873. Charles Thompson and Benjamin Franklin Landrum.

1875. Lewis Ross Kell and Benjamin Franklin Landrum.

1876. February 4th, Moses Ridge, vice Lewis Ross Kell, deceased.

1877. Moses Ridge and Benjamin Franklin Landrum. The latter was elected President of the Senate and died February 18, 1879.

1879. Joseph Dirteater and Walker A. Daniel. Daniel died January 9, 1880.

1880. Noember 6, Aaron Tanner, vice Walker A. Daniel, deceased.

1881. David Dixon Landrum and William Wirt Buffington.

1883. Hiram Terrell Landrum and William Coffee Woodall.

1885. Lucien Burr Bell and William Penn Henderson. The former was elected President of the Senate.

1887. Lucien Burr Bell and Charles Thompson.

1889. Lucien Burr Bell and William Penn Henderson. The former was elected President of the Senate.

1891. Claude Lorraine Washburn and Thomas Mitchell Buffington. The latter was elected President of the Senate.

1893. Claude Lorraine Washburn and Thomas Jefferson Monroe.

1895. William T. Davis and Elias McLeod Landrum[1]. The latter resigned on account of having accepted a position in Tahlequah.

1897. Thomas Jefferson Muskrat and John Rogers Hastings.

1899. Thomas Jefferson Muskrat and John Rogers Hastings.

1901. Thomas Jefferson Muskrat and John Rogers Hastings.

1903. Thomas Jefferson Muskrat and William T. Davis.

Senators from Saline District.

1841. James Vann McNair and Joseph Vann. The latter was elected President of the Senate.

1843. Reverand Beavercarrier and Charles Coody. The latter was elected President of the Senate and died in May 1844.

Ti-se-ski elected, vice Charles Coody, deceased.

1845. Clement Vann McNair and John Chambers.

1847. Clement Vann McNair and Elijah Hicks. The latter was elected President of the Senate.

1849. John Lucien Brown and Joseph Vann.

1851. Robert Daniel Ross and Reverand Lewis Downing.

1853. Dr. Robert Daniel Ross and Thomas Pegg.

1855. Dr. Robert Daniel Ross and Clement Neeley Vann.

1857. Dr. Robert Daniel Ross and Charles Landrum.

1859. Dr. Robert Daniel Ross and Reverend Lewis Downing.

1861. Not known.

1867. Reverend Ooo-you-su-ta and Tog.

1869. Reverend Oo-you-su-ta and William Penn Adair.

1871. Reverend Rope Campbell and William Penn Adair.

1873. Coffee Blackbird and William Penn Adair.

1875. Reverend Rope Campbell and George Washington Clark.

1877. Johnson Downing and Reverend Samuel Smith.

1879. Reverend Ooo-you-su-ta and George Sanders.

1881. Frog Sixkiller and Reverend Samuel Smith.

1883. Frog Sixkiller and Reverend Samuel Smith.

1885. George Sanders and Clark Goingwolf. The latter died December 23, 1886.

1887. March 15, Bird Jones elected, vice Clark Goingwolf, deceased.

1887. Henry Clay Ross and George Sanders.

1889. Henry Clay Ross and Reverend George Washington Swimmer.

1891. Daniel Redbird and George Sanders.

1893. Reverend Samuel Smith and George Sanders.

1895. Reverend Samuel Smith and Drift Hummingbird. The former was elected President of the Senate.

1897. George Sanders and John Reuben Leach.

1899. George Sanders and John Reuben Leach.

1901. Charles Teehee and Henry Clay Ross.

1903. Thomas Smith and Daid Welch Ragsdale.

Senators form Going Snake District.

1841. James Starr and Charles Reese.

1843. Thomas Foreman and Young Glass.

1845. Thomas Foreman and Reverend Lewis Downing.

1847. Jefferson Hair and Dr. John Thornton.

1849. Jefferson Hair and George Washington Scraper.

1851. John Murphy and Thomas Fox Taylor. The latter was elected President of the Senate.

1853. Aaron Wilkerson and James Foster.

1855. Aaron Wilkerson and Thomas Fox Taylor.

1857. George Hicks and Thomas Fox Taylor. The latter was elected President of the Senate.

1859. Aaron Wilkerson and John T. Fosted. The latter was elected President of the Senate. Wilkerson died during this term and Henry Crittenden was elected as his successor.

1861. Not known.

1867. Frog Sixkiller and Bud Gritts. The latter was elected President of the Senate and died on December 1, 1867.

1869. Frog Sixkiller and Archibald Scraper. The latter was elected President of the Senate.

1871. Tail Sixkiller and John Shell.

1873. Tail Sixkiller and Jesse Redbird.

1875. Johnson Robbins and Jesse Redbird.

1877. Johnson Robbins and Ezekial Proctor.

1879. Richard Murrell Wolfe and Adam Feeling.

1881. Johnson Robbins and Adam Feeling.

1883. Johnson Robbins and Joseph McMinn Starr.

1885. John Daniel Buffington and John Gritts.

1887. Eli H. Whitmire and Richard Murrell Wolfe.

1889. Johnson Whitmire and Richard Murrell Wolfe.

1891. Ellis Buffington Alberty and Richard Murrell Wolfe.

-893. Johnson Spade and Richard Murrell Wolfe. The latter was elected President of the Senate.

1895. Simon Ross Walkingstick and Parker Morris.

1897. Simon Ross Walkingstick and Wolf Coon. The latter was elected President of the Senate.

1899. David Hitcher and Ned Bullfrog.

1901. Lincoln England and Wolf Coon.

1903. Ezekial Proctor and Ellis Buffington Alberty.

Senators from Tahlequah District.

1841. Daniel McCoy. Resigned. Other Senator not known.

1842. David Carter, vice Daniel McCoy, resigned.

1843. John Spears and James Sanders.

1845. John Spears and James Sanders.

1847. John Spears and Thomas Fox Taylor.

1849. John Spears and William Potter Ross.

1851. Thomas Pegg and William Potter Ross.

1853. Nicholas Byers Sanders and William Potter Ross.

1855. David Carter and William Potter Ross.

1857. John Thorne and William Potter Ross.

1859. Thomas Pegg and Johnson Foreman.

1861. Thomas Pegg. Elected President of the Senate. Other senator not known.

1867. Allen Ross and Lewis Anderson Ross.

1869. Allen Ross and Lewis Anderson Ross.

1871. Allen Ross and Choo-hoo-sta.

1873. Lewis Anderson Ross and Choo-hoo-sta.
1875. Eli Spears and William H. Hendricks.
1877. Eli Spears and Robert Bruce Ross.
1879. Eli Spears and William H. Hendricks.
1881. Eli Spears and Robert Bruce Ross.
1883. Jesse Sanders and Lacey Hawkins.
1885. Ned Grease and John Albion Spears. The latter died.
1887. May 5, Reverend Evans Price Robinson, vice J. A. Spears, deceased.
1887. William H. Hendricks and Lacey Hawkins. The latter was elected President of the Senate.
1889. William Triplett and John Ross Meigs.
1891. Ned Grease and Caleb Wilson Starr.
1893. George Washington Benge and Robert Bruce Ross.
1895 . William H. Hendricks and Daniel Gritts.
1897 . Skake Manus and Michael Pritchett.
1899. William Thomas Harnage and Colonel Johnson Harris.
1901. Gideon Morgan[2] and George Washington Benge.
1903. William Thomas Harnage and Charles Lawrence Saunders.

Senators from Illinois District.

1841. Moses Parris and Aaron Price.
1843. John Drew and William Drew. The latter resigned in December 1844.
John Brewer elected, vice William Drew, resigned.
1845. Alexander Foreman and Pheasant.
1847. Alexander Foreman and William Drew.
1849. Alexander Foreman and John Drew.
1851. Alexander Foreman and James W. Daniel.
1853. Alexander Foreman and Richard Fields.
1855. Alexander Foreman and James Mackey. The former was elected President of the Senate.
1857. Alexander Foreman and Richard Fields.
1859. John W. Brown and John Brewer.
1861. Not known.
1867. Roach Young and Pig Smith. The latter was elected President the Senate.
1869. Samuel Houston Benge and William Potter Ross.
1871. Samuel Houston Benge and Pig Smith. The latter died October 1, 1871.
William Potter Ross elected, vice Pig Smith, deceased.
1873. Samuel Houston Benge and Daniel Hicks Ross.
1875. Samuel Houston Benge and Roach Young.
1877. Joseph Young and Roach Young.
1879. Samuel Houston Benge and Timothy Meigs Walker. The former was elected President of the Senate, vice John Porum Davis, deceased.
1881. George Oceola Sanders and Roach Young. The latter was elect- of the Senate.

1883. Samuel Houston Benge and Roach Young.
1885. John Hildebrand Cookson and Connell Rogers.[1]
1887. Samuel Houston Benge and Mortor Vann.
1889. William Potter Ross and Roach Young.
1891. Edley Levi Cookson and Martin Van Benge.
1893. Roach Young and Martin Van Benge.
1895. Roach Young and Edley Levi Cookson.
1897. Redbird Smith and Connell Rogers.
1899. Edley Levi Cookson and Connell Rogers.
1901. Edley Levi Cookson and John Lafayette Brown.
1903. Martin Benge and John Lafayette Brown.

Senators from Canadian District.

1841. Captain William Dutch[2] and the other one unknown.

1843. Captain William Dutch and Joseph Tally. Both resigned.

1844. John Shepherd and Nelson Riley, vice Dutch and Talley, resigned.

1845. James Mackey and William Shorey Coody. The latter was elected President of the Senate.

1847. Captain William Dutch and William Shorey Coody. The latter died April 16, 1849.

1849. Josiah Reese and Lightningbug Bowles.

1851. Daid Boggs and Nelson Riley.

1853. David Boggs and Teesee.Guess.

1855. John Drew and Lightningbug Bowles.

1857. John Drew and William Doublehead.

1859. Joseph Abalom Scales and Daniel Coody. The latter died. Oliver H. P. Brewer, vice Daniel Coody, deceased.

1861. Not known.

1867. John Brewer and John Porum Davis.[1]

1869. James Madison Bell and Johnson Foreman.

1871. Richard Fields and Johnson Foreman. The latter died June 28, 1872.

1872. August 22, Levi Toney elected, vice Johnson Foreman, deceased.

1873. Richard Fields and John Porum Davis.

1875. Stephen Hildebrand and John Porum Davis. The latter was elected President of the Senate.

1877. Joseph Martin Lynch and Calvin Jones Hanks. The latter was killed May 15, 1879.

1879. Pleasant Napoleon Blackstone and John Porum Davis. The latter was elected President of the Senate and died during this term of office.

1881. Pleasant Napoleon Blackstone and Colonel Harris.

1883. Abraham Woodall and Colonel Johnson Harris. The latter was elected President of the Senate.

1885. Stand Watie Gray and Colonel Johnson Harris.

1887. Stand Watie Gray and Joseph Martin Lynch.

1889. Stand Watie Gray and Walter Scott Agnew.

1891. James Harris and William McLain.

1893. Stand Watie Gray and Charles Edward Vann.[2]
1895. Henry Clay Lowrey and William Vann.
1897. Henry Clay Lowrey and William Vann.
1899. Henry Clay Lowrey and Wilson Girty.
1901. Henry Clay Lowrey and O. H. P. Brewer. The former died March 20, 1902.
1902. August 7, Robert Emmett West elected vice Henry Clay Lowrey, deceased.
1903. Robert Emmett West and John Jay Sevier.

Senators from Skin Bayou District.

1841. Andrew Sanders and the other one not known.
1843. John Benge and James Brown.
1847. George Washington Gunter and George C. Lowrey. The latter died on October 22, 1848.
1849. George Washington Gunter and Sanders Choate.
1851. November 4. The name of the District was changed by act of council from Skin Bayou to Sequoyah.
1853. Joseph Proctor and Nicholas B. Byers.
1855. Archibald Lowrey and Alexander Alexander.
1857. James Brown anad Daniel Ross Nave.
1859. Picken M. Benge and Daniel Ross Nave.
1861. Not known.
1867. Joseph Coody and Mink Downing.
1869. Joseph Coody and Mink Downing.
1871. William Wilson and Thomas Ross.
1873. George Washington Wilson. The latter was elected President of the Senate.
1875. William Chambers and Bluford Baldridge. The latter died December 18, 1875. Rufus Bell Adair elected, vice Bluford Baldridge, deceased.
1877. Joseph Seabolt and John Childers.
1879. David McNaiir Faulkner and John Childers.
1881. David McNair Faulkner and Chee-chee.
1883. Charles Oliver Frye[3] and Adam Lacey.
1885. Stephen Teehee and John Edward Gunter. The latter resigned and was elected a member of the Citizenship Court.
1887. May 5, Chee-chee elected, vice John E. Gunter, resigned.
1889. David McNair Falkner and Stephen Teehee.
1891. Charles Washington Starr and Charles Augustus Fargo.
1893. John Edward Gunter and Isaac Abraham Jacobs[4].
1895. David McNair Faulkner and Charles Foreman.
1897. John Edward Gunter and James Coleman.
1899. John Edward Gunter and James Coleman.
1901. David McNair Faulkner and Charles Oliver Frye.
1903. George Washington Baldridge and George Bradley.

Senators from Flint District.

1841. Ezekial Starr and the other one not known.

1843. Samuel Downing and Jesse Russell.
1845. James Pritchett and Jesse Russell.
1847. James Pritchett and Jesse Russell.
1849. James Pritchett and Glory.
1851. Jay Hicks and David Sanders.
1853. Reverend Walter Adair Duncan and Samuel Chambers.
1855. William Penn Adair and Richard Fields.
1857. William Penn Adair and William Penn Boudinot.
1859. William Penn Adair and J. A. Johnson.
1861. Not known.
1867. Eli Smith and Walter Christy.
1869. Eli Smith and Keith Wahlaneeta.
1871. Rabbit Bunch and George Keith.
1873. John R. Ross and Johnson Keith.
1875. John R. Ross and Jackson Christy.
1877. John R. Ross and Robert McLemore.
1879. Jackson Christy and John B. Teehee. The latter died and Ned Acorn was elected.
1881. Samuel E. Sanders and Cicero Leonidas Lynch.
1883. Ezekial Eugene Starr and Ned Acorn.
1885. John B. Tulsa and William Young.
1887. David Muskrat and Jackson Christy.
1889. James Christy and Rabbit Bunch.
1891. Ellis West Buffington and Adam Sevenstar.
1893. Ellis Starr and Jackson Christy.
1895. Andrew Taylor Paden and Charles Poorbear.
1897. Jackson Christy and David Muskrat.
1899. Benjamin Gilbreath Fletcher and Charles Scott.
1901. Benjamin Gilbreath Fletcher and Charles Smith.
1903. George Ferguson and Richard Lee Taylor[1].

Senators from Cooweescoowee District.

1857. James McDaniel and Eli Murphy.
1859. John Chambers and Jackson Tyner.
1861. Not known.
1867. James McDaniel and Robin Smith.
1869. James Conner and Robin Smith.
1871. John Chambers and Jesse Thompson.
1873. John Chambers and Jesse Thompson.
1875. Henry Chambers and James Horsefly.
1877. Henry Chambers and DeWitt Clinton Lipe[2].
1879. Clement Vann Rogers[3] and John Gunter Schrimsher.
1881. Clement Vann Rogers and John McIntosh
1883. Clement Vann Rogers and John Gunter Schrimsher.
1885. Samuel Houston Mayes and DeWitt Clinton Lipe. The latter resigned and was elected a member of the Citizenship Court.
1887. May 5, Francis Marion Musgrove elected, vice DeWitt Clinton Lipe, resigned.

1887. John Gunter Scrimsher and Riley Wise Lindsey[4].
1889. William Charles Rogers and Samuel Houston Mayes.
1891. James McDaniel Keys[5] and Joel Lindsey Baugh.
1893. William Edward Sanders[1] and George Washington Mayes[3].
1895. William Charles Rogers and John Thomas Gunter.
1897. John Gunter Scrimsher and Joseph Martin LaHay.
1899. Ellis Buffington Wright and Clement Vann Rogers.
1901. George Washington Mayes and John Franklin[4].
1903. Joseph Martin LaHay and Clement Vann Rogers.

Article three, section nine of the constitution vests the following right: "Each branch of the National Council shall choose its own officers." In accordance with an act of council of October 4, 1839 it was stipulated that "The Clerks of the National Committee and Council shall each receive three dollars per day while in service." The Clerks of the Senate were:

1841. Thomas Fox Taylor.
1843. William Potter Ross.
1845. Elijah Hicks.
1847. Dennis Wolf Bushyhead.
1849. Robert Buffington Daniel.
1851. William Penn Boudinot.
1853. William Penn Boudinot.
1855. William Penn Boudinot.
1857. Daniel McCoy Gunter.
1859. Hercules T. Martin.
1861. Joshua Ross.
1867. Rev. Stephen Foreman.
1869. George Washington Johnson.
1871. George Washington Johnson.
1873. Lucien Burr Bell.
1875. Lucien Burr Bell.
1877. Lucien Burr Bell.
1879. John Leaf Springston.
1881. Daniel Ross Hicks.
1883. John Taylor Drew.
1885. Robert Taylor Hanks.
1887. Marmaduke Daniel.
1889. Andrew Henderson Norwood.
1891. William Presley Thompson, resigned.
1893. Charles Worcester Willey.
1895. Richard Murrell Wolfe.
1897. Richard Murrell Wolfe.
1899. Lucien Burr Bell.
1901. Samuel Frazier Parks, resigned.
Edward Northup Washburn[5].
1903. Joel Lindsey Baugh.

The Council or lower house of the Cherokee legislature was provided for by the third section of article three of the constitution of 1839 and the salaries were at first fixed by article three, section ten at three dollars per day, subject to change by act of council.

Councilors from Delaware District.

1841. Rev. John Huss and the other two unknown.

1843. Goo-la-chi, Chu-wa-chu-kah and Hanging Charles. The latter died and was succeeded by Little Pot.

1845. James D. Wofford, William Tucker and Moses Pott.

1847. Moses Pott, William Tucker and Peter½.

1849. Moses Pott, Laugh at Mush and James V. Hildebrand.

1851. Moses Pott, Laugh at Mush and James V. Hildebrand.

1853. Laugh at Mush, James V. Hildebrand and Stand Watie.

1855. Laugh at Mush, Pelican Tiger and Stand Watie. The latter was elected Speaker of the Council.

1857. Laugh at Mush, Henry Davis and Stand Watie. The latter was elected Speaker of the Council.

1859. Stand Watie, Pelican Tiger and James V. Hildebrand.

1861. Not known.

1867. Daniel Muskrat, Sequoyah Tanner and Aaron Tanner.

1869. Aaron Tanner, Daniel Hilder, William Adolphus Daniel and Jeter Thompson Cunningham.

1871. Daniel Hider, Moses Ridge, William Adolphus Daniel and Josiah Sutteeyah.

1875. Josiah Sutteeyah, Walker A. Daniel, William Coffee Woodall and Aaron Tanner.

1877. Walker A. Daniel, William Coffee Woodall, Jeffrey Beck and Alexander Hawk.

1879. John M. Miller, Thomas Fox Thompson, Rev. Charles Bluejacket[1] and James Tuck Woodall.

1881. William Ballard, Aaron Tanner, Oo-so-wie, John Snell, George Washington Fields and Arleecher Ridge. The latter died.

1882-8-21. Daniel Chopper, vice Arleecher Ridge, deceased.

1883. Daniel Chopper, Benjamin Seth Landrum, John Martin Daniel, Alexander Hawk, Qualatah and George Washington Ward.

1885. Benjamin C. Chouteau, William Howell, John M. Miller, Joseph Lynch Thompson, Benjamin Franklin Lamar and Alexander Hawk. The latter was elected Speaker of Council.

1887. Francis Marion Conner, Joseph Lynch Thompson, John M. Miller, Thomas Bluejacket[2], Samuel Russell and James Sanford Fields.

1889. James Sanford Fields, Benjamin Franklin Lamar, John Hawkins, Simpson Foster Melton, Weatherford Beck and James Madison Monroe. The latter died November 19, 1890 and Beck died earlier in the same year.

1890-10-30. Samuel Nidiffer elected, vice Weatherford Beck[1], deceased.

James Proctor Butler[2] elected, vice James M. Monroe, deceased.

1891. William T. Davis, James Riley Copeland,[3] Rev. Jesse Starr, Ezekial Fields, William Ballard and Samuel Nidiffer.

1893. William T. Davis, James Bonaparte Woodall, Percy L. Walker, Thomas Ballard, Daylight Chopper and James Sanford Fields.

1895. Benjamin Franklin Lamar, William Henry Doherty, John B. Martin, T. Wyman Thompson[4], John M. Miller and William Stover.

1897. James H. Hildebrand, Jefferson Dick, John Hamilton Gibson[5], Samuel Beck, Andrew Hyder and James Landrum McLaughlin. The latter died November 10, 1897.

Benjamin Seth Landrum, vice James L. McLaughlin, deceased.

1899. Edward Northrup Washburn, Lee Bell Smith[6], Johnson Fawling. James Franklin McCullough, Benjamin Cornelius England and James Bonaparte Woodall, John Fawling, Daniel Tananeesie and Andrew Hider. The

1901. George Alexander Cox[7], Joseph Lynch Thompson, James Bonaparte Woodall, John Fawling, Daniel Tananeesie an dAndrew Hider. The latter died.

James Henry Daniel, vice Daniel Hider, deceased.

1903. William Wiley Ward, Johnson Fawling, John Hamilton Gibson. Walter Winchester Breedlove, James H. Hildebrand and Thomas Thomas.

Councilors from Saline District.

1841. Chu-wa-loo-ky, John W. West anad Brice Martin.

1843. Oo-soo-ya-duh, Chu-wa-loo-ky and Fishtail.

1845. Oo-soo-ya-duh, Ka-nee-ta and Standingdeer.

1847. Chu-wa-loo-ky, Willy Too-wa-ly and Standingdeer.

1849. Standingdeer, Springfrog and Whale.

1851. Chu-wa-loo-ky, Jesse Cochran and Sunday.

1853. Rev. Lewis Downing, Springfrog and Standingdeer.

1855. Rev. Lewis Downing, Standingdeer and John Chambers.

1857. Standingdeer, Archibald Vann and Walker.

1859. Charles Wickliffe, Springfrog and Adam Lacey.

1861. Not known.

1867. Stand Whirlwind, Necooie Thompson and Daniel Redbird.

1869. Moses Sixkiller and the other two not known.

1871. Chun-he-ne-tah, Lacey Hawkins and Coffee Blackbird.

1873. Daniel Redbird, Oo-you-su-ta and George Washington Clark.

1875. Oo-you-su-ta, Coffee Blackbird and Lacey Hawkins. The latter was elected Speaker of Council.

1877. Daniel Redbird, Youngwolf and Youngbird.

1881. Johnson Bigacorn, Bird Jones and Benjamin Franklin Adair.

1883. Goingsnake and Oo-you-su-ta.

1883-9-10. Bird Jones. Probably on a tie. He was elected Speaker at Council. Oo-you-su-ta died July 6, 1884.

1885. Johnson Bigacorn, George Washington Swimmer and Frank Consene.

1887. Osceola Powell Benge, William Batt and Frank Consene.

1889. James Wickliffe, Frank Consene and Frog Sixkiller. The latter died in April 1891.

1891. Frank Consene, Wilson Cummings and Eli Batt.

1893. William Batt, Jackson Ross and Bird Jones. The latter was elected Speaker of Council.

1895. Frank Consene, William Batt and Stephen Boney.

1897. Johnson Bigacorn, Jackson Ross and Eli Batt.

1899. Lucullus Rowe, Jesse Drywater and Daniel Squirrel.

1901. William Standingwater, David Hair and Daniel Squirrel.

1903. James Lovely Bumgarner, George Bluford Downing and Cicero Johnson Howard[1].

Councilors from Going Snake District.

1841. Robert Parris and the other two unknown.

1843. De-nah-lah-whi-stah, Sixkiller and William Proctor.

1845. De-nah-lah-whi-stah, Sixkiller and William Proctor.

1847. George Hicks, Sixkiller and Archibald Vann.

1849. John Young, George Hicks and Sixkiller. The latter elected Speaker of Council.

1851. Richard Wilkerson, Sixkiller and William Proctor.

1853. Joseph McMinn Starr, Sixkiller and James Hair.

1855. John T. Foster, John Young and George Washington Scraper.

1857. Too-nah-na-la Foster, George Washington Scraper and John Young.

1859. George Washington Scraper, Cricket Sixkiller and Bird Gritts.

1861. Not known.

1867. Archibald Scraper, Tail Sixkiller and John Shell.

1869. Tail Sixkiller, Corn Silk and John Shell.

1871. Nee-tah-kee-kah, Soldier Sixkiller and Walter Feeling.

1873. Archibald Scraper, Eli Wright, John Wright Alberty and Soldier Sixkiller.

1875. Walter Christy, John Shell, Ellis Hogner and John Williams.

1877. Tail Sixkiller, Charles Augustus Rider, Walter Christy and Cornsilk.

1879. Peacheater Sixkiller, John Sanders, George Washington Crittenden and James Crittenden.

1881. George Washington Crittenden, John Sanders, Tail Sixkiller and John Walkingstick.

1883. George Washington Crittenden, Wolf Coon, Johnson Spade and Joseph Chooie.

1889. Johnson Spade, William Mitchell, Ned Bullfrog and Nelson Terrapin.

1891. John Daniel Buffington, Wolf Coon, Coming Snell and Jefferson Tickaneesky.

1893. Lincoln England, Ned Bullfrog, Thomas Still and Carselowy Terrapin.

1895. Aaron Goingwolf, David Blackfox, William Wolf and Edward D. Foreman.

1897. Lincoln England, Abraham Sixkiller, James Russell and William Wolf.

1899. Lincoln England, John Sanders, Jack Soap and Walter Scott Whitmire.

1901. Francis Clark Adair[1], Benjamin Mocker, John Sanders and Thomas Still.

1903. Thomas Welch, Francis Clark Adair, Edward Adair Clyne' and Alexander Corntassel.

Councilors from Tahlequah District.

1841. John Riley and the other two not known.

1843. John Riley, Archibald Campbell and Hair Conrad. The latter died November 2, 1844. John Riley died February 14, 1845.

1845. Joseph Spears, John Young and Archibald Campbell. The latter was elected Speaker of Council.

1847. Rev. John Fletcher Boot, John Young and Archibald Campbell. The latter was elected Speaker of Council.

1849. Samuel Downing, James Sanders and Joseph Spears.

1851. Daniel Colston, Johnson Keith and Looney Riley. The latter was elected Speaker of Council.

1853. Jesse Sanders, Johnson Keith and John Thorne. The latter was elected Speaker of Council.

1861. Not known.

1867. Peach Watts, Choo-hoo-stah and Osceola Hair.

1869. Nathaniel Fish, Osceola Hair and the other one unknown.

1871. William H. Hendricks, Osceola Hair, Nathaniel Fish, French and Rufus O. Ross.

1873. William H. Hendricks, John Hendricks, Samuel Osage, Rabbit Downing and Columbus Baldridge.

1875. James Shelton, Robert Bruce Ross, Ned Grease, Rabbit Downing and Joseph Brown. The latter a Negro. Rabbit Downing died October 31, 1876.

1876-11-20. Osceola Hair, vice Rabbit Downing, deceased.

1877. William Triplett, Ned Grease, Yartunnah Vann, Osceola Hair and John Hendricks.

1879. Ellis Johnson, Columbus Baldridge, Ned Grease, John Hendricks and Osceola Hair. The latter was elected Speaker of Council.

1881. Osceola Powell Daniel, Osceola Hair, Yartunnah Vann, Bug Tucker and John Parris. The latter died July 26, 1882.

1882-8-21. Samuel Houston Downing, vice John Parris, deceased.

1883. John Proctor, George Swimmer, Bug Tucker, John Hendricks and Ned Grease.

1885. George Downing, Calib Starr Thompson, Thomas Hendricks, Benjamin Kitcher and Hunter Brown. The latter died April 25, 1886.

1886-6-11. Phillip Osage, vice Hunter Brown, deceased.

1887. Mankiller Kitcher, Return Robert Meigs, Johnson Fields, Michael Pritchett and Benjamin Kitcher. The latter died December 8, 1887.

1889. Charles Tehee, Wilkerson Hubbard Parris, Philip Bennett, Daniel Gritts and Osceola Dew.

1891. Daniel Gritts, Thomas Shade, John R. Gourd, Skake Manus and John Hendricks.

1893. Michael Pritchett, Thomas Horn, Rev. Leonidas Dobson, Joseph Downing and Stick Ross. The latter a negro.

1895. Michael Pritchett, Key Ketcher, Return Robert Meigs, David Tipton and Ned Irons. The latter a Negro.

1897. David Downing, Wilkerson Hubbard Parris, Key Ketcher, Boot Pigeon Jack Roberson.

1899. Wilkerson Hubbard Parris, John Franklin Wilson, Joseph Downing, Ross Taylor Daniel and Jesse Pigeon.

1901. Wilkerson Hubbard Parris, Benjamin F. Johnson, Robert Colburn Fuller, Philip Osage and Charles Lawrence Saunders.

1903. Willes Taylor Richards, William Wallace Ross, Noah Parris and Wilkerson Hubbard.

1903-9-21. Ross Taylor Daniel. Elected on this date on account of a tie in the regular election.

Councilors from Illinois District.

1841. Richard Drew, William Drew and Archibald Fields. The latter was elected Speaker of Council.

1843. Richard Drew, Archibald Fields and William Drew. The latter resigned in December 1844 and Archibald Fields died in September 1844.

1844. John Brewer, vice Archibald Fields, deceased.

1845. Robert Lovett, John Brewer and Allen Ratley.

1847. Da-gah-sta-sca, John Brewer and James Mackay.

1849. Pheasant, Allen Ratley and Richard Benge.

1851. Allen Ratley, James Souiekiller and Joseph Duval.

1853. Allen Ratley, John W. Brown and Moses Parris.

1855. John Brewer, George Chambers and Joseph Duval.

1853. Allen Ratley, John W. Brown and Moses Parris.

1855. John Brewer, George Chambers and Joseph Duval.

1857. Ellis Fox Phillips, Edward Smith and Singer Justice.

1859. Allen Ratley, John Boston and George Chambers. The latter died and was succeeded by Diver Glass.

1861. Not known.

1867. John Rogers Duval, Daniel Backbone and John Young. The latter elected Speaker of Council. Daniel Backbone died October 25, 1867.

1867. Joseph Cornsilk vice Daniel Backbone, deceased.

1869. Thomas Fox Brewer and the other two unknown.

1871. Lewis Hicks, Wallace Vann, Robin Crawford and John Rogers Duval. The latter was elected Speaker of Council.

1873. Robin Crawford, John Mussel, Daniel Redbird and John Rogers Duval. The latter was elected Speaker of Council.

1875. William Young, John Mussel, Richard Boggs and John Rogers Duval. The latter two died. Wallace Vann, vice John R. Duval, deceased.

1876-4-3. Daniel Hicks Ross, vice Richard Boggs, deceased.

1877. James Raincrow, William Snow Brewer, Bushyhead Sevier and Wallace Vann.

1879. Simon Girty, Dekinney Waters, George Drum and Henry Clay Starr. The latter died November 16, 1879.

1879-12-4. Joseph Young, vice Henry C. Starr, deceased.

1881. John Hildebrand Cookson, Lawson Runyan, Charles Washington Starr and John Young. The latter died.

1882-8-21. John Bean Johnson, vice John Young, deceased.

1883. John Benge[1], Joseph Topp, Dekinney Waters and Columbus Baldridge.

1883-9-10. John Raincrow.

1885. George Bulleth Foreman, John Walker, Dekinney Waters and Jack Brown.

1887. Lawson Runyan, Redbird Smith, Joseph Topp, John Raincrow and Frank Vann. The latter was a Negro. John Raincrow died and was succeeded by George Mc Daniel.

1889. Redbird Smith, Morgan West, Joseph Tapp, John Glass and George McDaniel. The latter died and was succeeded by Stephen Hildebrand.

1891. Wallace Thornton, Lorenzo Dow Chambers, Wallace Vann, Cabin Miller and Fox Glass.

1893. John Wesley Sharp, Jesse Hair, John Walker, Charles Fodder and George Benge.

1895. John Wesley Sharp, John Stearns, Creek Sam, Charles Bark and Samuel Stidham. The latter was a a Negro.

1897. John Terrell, George Waters, Alexander McCoy, John Thompson and Charles Percival Pierce.

1899. Moses Frye Sanders, Dekinney Waters, George Bulleth Foreman, Richard Martin Walker and Samuel Stephen Sanders.

1901. Richard Martin Walker, Alexander Ballard, Alexander McCoy, Moses Frye Sanders and Martin Van Benge. The latter was elected Speaker of Council.

1903. Samuel Stephen Sanders, Charles Harris Sisson, Walter Scott, William Frank Sanders and Frank Gonzales.

Councilors from Canadian District.

1841. Joseph Talley, Wind and Wrinklesides.

1843. Lightningbug Bowles, Dahlahseenee and Oosoody. Bowles would not qualify and Lewis Riley was elected. Dahlahsunee died October 26, 1844 and Oosoody died November 29, 1844.

1845. Lewis Riley, John Shepherd and Jefferson Nivens.

1847. Lightningbug Bowles, Jacob Thorne and Wiliam Doublehead.

1849. Leggings[1], David Boggs and William Arnold.

1851. Charles Chambers, John Porum Davis and third party unknown.

1853. Leggings, Lightningbug Bowles and Duqulilu Wagon Bowles.

1855. Dempsey Fields, Lightningbug Bowles and Duqulilu Wagon Bowles.

1857. Lightningbug Bowles, William Rees and William Arnold.

1859. Lightningbug Bowles, Cabin Smith and John Porum Davis.

1861. Not known.

1867. James Christopher McCoy, Calvin Jones Hanks and Sanders Choate.

1869. Rev. John Sevier, Charles Drew and other party unknown.

1871. Franklin Gritts, James Christopher McCoy and other party unknown.

1873. Stephen Hildebrand, John Q. Hayes and Franklin Gritts.

1875. Rev. John Sevier, Snake Grity and Thomas Watts.

1877. Rev. John Sevier, Thomas Watts and George Teehee.

1879. Robert Taylor Hanks, Henry Clay Lowrey and James Muskrat.

1881. Robert Taylor Hanks, Thomas Watts, Wilson Girty and Rev. John Sevier. The latter was elected Speaker of Council.

1883. Wilson Girty, Thomas Watts, George Downing and Richard Crossland.

1885. Franklin Gritts, George Downing, Richard Crossland and Henry Clay Lowrey.

1887. Richard Neal, Walter Scott Agnew, Charles Jones and Richard Crossland.

1889. Isaac Groves, Richard Crossland, William Shepherd and William Henry Barker. The latter was elected Speaker of Council.

William Shepherd died January 23, 1890.

1891. Thomas Fox Woodall, Isaac Groves, Thomas Fields and John Dimar Jordan[1].

1893. William Vann, Isaac Groves, John Dimar Jordan and Thomas Watts.

1895. Jesse Bushyhead Raymond, Thomas Jefferson Whisenhunt[2], Duncan Leader and William Billingslea Beck[3].

1897. Jesse Bushyhead Raymond, Thomas Jefferson Whisenhunt, William Billingslea Beck and John Alexander Sevier. The latter died June 5, 1898.

1898-8-8. McCoy Smith, vice John A. Sevier, deceased.

1899. Robert Emmett West[1], McCoy Smith, David Downing and Jesse Bushyhead Raymond. The latter died October 28, 1900.

1900-12-3. James Jay Sevier, vice Jesse B. Raymond, deceased.

1901. James C. Grooves, Walter Scott Agnew, McCoy Smith and John Ross Fields.

1903. John Ross Fields, James C. Groves, Thomas Fox Woodall and Anderson Pierce Lowrey.

Councilors from Skin Bayou District.

1841. John Lowrey McCoy, Sawnee Vann and the other one not known.

1843. Tobacco Will, Hunter Langley and James Madison Payne. The latter was elected Speaker of Council. Hunter Langley died in September, 1844.

1845. James Brown Jr., Oganstota Logan and Young Elders. The latter died October 2, 1845.

1847. Wrinklesides, Nicholas B. Byars and Andrew Sanders.

1849. Youngpuppy, Andrew Sanders and Nicholas Porter.

1851. Andrew Sanders, Thomas Sanders and Nicholas Porter.

The name was changed from Skin Bayou District to Sequoyah District by an act of National Council on November 4, 1851. See page 227, Cherokee Laws of 1852.

Councilors from Sequoyah District.

1853. Black Fox, Dutsasa and Walter Lee.

1855. Dutsasa, Bat Puppy and Step.

1857. Black Fox, William Benge and Samuel Houston Benge.

1859. Crapgrass, Walter Lee and William Benge.

1861. Not known.

1867. Joseph Seabolt, Stephen Teehee and Cheechee.

1869. Richard Benge, John Crossland and David McNair Faulkner.

1871. Richard Benge, Thomas Pettit and Cheechee.

1873. John Blalock, John Childers and John Choate.

1875. Joseph Seabolt, John Walkingstick and Jesse Baldridge. The latter died December 13, 1876.

1877. David McNair Faulkner, Lorenzo Dow Chambers and Columbus Baldridge.

1879. Joseph Starr, Cheechee and Frank Mayo Morgan.

1881. Charles Augustus Fargo, Columbus Benge and Adam Lacey.

1883. Josiah Seabolt, Joseph Starr and William Holt.

1885. William Holt, Josiah Seabolt and Thomas Blair.

1887. Edward Everett Adair, George Washington Gunter and David M. Lee.

1889. Joseph Starr, William Holt and Calvin Fargo.

1891. William Chuculate, Thomas Blair and John Roastingear.

1893. George Washington Swimmer, William Bethel and James Coleman.

1895. Obediah Martin Benge, Isaac Abraham Jacobs[1], and Edward Everett Adair.

1897. James Madison Seabolt, George Chuculate and William Charles Dumont Patton[2].

1899. David Jesse Faulkner[3], James Willoughby Breedlove[4] and John Roastingear.

1901. William Nucholls Littlejohn[5], Andrew Jackson Rogers and Ellis Starr.

1903. Tandy Walker Adair, Daniel Holt and Gideon Jay Patton.

Councilors from Flint District.

1841. Samuel Chambers, Oganstota Logan and one other.

1843. Chu-noo-luh-hus-ky, Bark Flute and David Downing.

1845. Chu-noo-luh-hus-ky, John Key and Bark Flute.

1847. Bark Flute, William Grimmett and George Chambers.

1849. Charles Downing, John Keith and George Chambers.

1851. George Chambers, Charles Downing and Eli Smith.

1853. George Chambers, John Keith and George Blair.

1855. Charles Downing, Ellis Sanders Harlan and John Glass.

1857. Charles Downing, William Griffin and John Glass.

1859. William Griffin, James Vann and Tsa-la-tee-hee.

1861. Not known.

1867. Wah-lah-nee-tah, Alexander Scott and Chicken Christy.

1869. Not known.

1871. Oo-squa-luke, Chicken Christy and Poorbear.

1873. Oo-squa-luke, Chicken Christy and John B. Tulsa.

1875. Charles Poorbear, James Christy and Richard Glory.

1877. Nicholas B. Byers, John Shell and John Batt.

1879. David Muskrat, Charles Sanders and Samuel E. Sanders.

1881. French Rowe, Robert McLemore and James Teehee.

1883. John Justice, Dirtthrower Vann and Sundaychair.

1885. French Rowe, Lewis Cochran and Sundaychair. The latter died.

1885-10-19. Rev. Isaac Sanders, vice Sundaychair, deceased.

1887. Charles Smith, Johnson Simmons and Robert McLemore. The latter died and Taylor Duncan was elected in his stead.

1889. James Christy, Charles Poorbear and James Starr.

1891. Lewis Cochran, John Justice and Candy Adair.

1893. Chulio Liver, George Scott and Rufus Cochran.

1895. Hoolie Sanders, Dirtthrower Vann and Johnson Simmons. The latter was elected Speaker of Council.

1897. Oo-squa-luke, Wiley Bolin and Peter Bird.

1899. Dirtthrower Vann, Andrew Otterlifter and George Deer-in-the-water.

1901. James Starr, George Washington Ferguson and William Taylor.

1903. Thomas Colbert Buffington, Martin Hopper and Thomas Sanders.

Councilors from Cooweescoowee District.

1857. John Chambers, Robin Smith and John Lucien Brown.

1859. Lewis Melton, James Hair and Oo-soo-ya-ta.

1861. Not known.

1867. Jesse Thompson, Writer and John Glass.

1869. Jesse Thompson, John Chambers and Jumper Mills. The latter was elected Speaker of Council.

1871. John Lucien Brown, John Fawling, Hiram Terrell Landrum and Writer.

1873. Hiram Terrell Landrum, Samuel Houston Downing, Joseph Thompson and Thomas Hatchett.

1875. Thomas Hatchett, Looney Riley, Jesse Thompson and Joseph Thompson.

1876-2-28. John Bullette, vice Joseph Thompson, deceased.

1877. William Henry Mayes, William McCracken, Bear Timpson and Jesse Thompson. The latter was elected Speaker of Council.

1879. Rev. Dempsey Fields Coker, George Swannock, William Sunday and John H. Secondyne.

1881. Francis Marion Musgrove, James Horsefly, Joe Parker, William Charles Rogers, Josiah Henry, Johnson Fisher and John R. McNair.

1883. William Charles Rogers, John Young, Washington White, Albert Morris, John Glass, John Martin Thompson and John Lucien Brown. The latter died April 12, 1884.

1884-7-14. Nelson Foreman, vice John L. Brown, deceased.

1885. James Walker, Nelson Foreman, Albert Morris, Austin Lowrey,

Marmaduke Daniel, George Washington Bible and George Washington Mayes[1].

1887. Edward Sunday, William Winter Chambers, James Chambers, George Washington Walker, Arthur Armstrong, Daniel Webster Vann and Henry Rogers. The latter died.

1888-1-24. Francis Marion Musgrove, vice Henry Rogers, deceased.

1889. George Washington Walker, Ezekial Taylor, William Winter Jerry Alberty. The latter a Negro.

1891. John M. Tucker, William Richard Mills, John Ross Carter, Joseph Benson Cobb[2], George Washington Mayes, Alexander Lewis McDaniel and George Washington Clark. The latter was elected Speaker of Council.

1893. Joseph Benson Cobb, Coocoodigesky, Valentine Gray, Samuel Tiblow, Rollin Kirk Adair, John Sarcoxie and James Monroe Crutchfield. The latter died.

1894-9-25. Caldean Ward, vice James M. Crutchfield, deceased.

1895. Jesse Bean Burgess, Daniel Webster Vann, Bluford West Rider, Cyrus Cicero Cornatzer, Job Parker, William Johnstone and John R. Gourd.

1897. John Sanders, Benjamin Hildebrand, George Washington Walker, Josiah Henry, Ellis Buffington Wright and John Ross Mslntosh[1]. The latter was elected Speaker of Council.

1899. Benjamin Hildebrand, Bluford West Starr, Cyrus Cornatzer, Ellis Manchell Eaton, Frederick McDaniel, Edward Alexander Adair and James Sanford Davenport[2]. The latter was elected Speaker of Council. He was the only White man that was in the constitutional succession to the office of Principal Chief of an Indian tribe.

1901. Samuel Houston Mayes, Henry Cirkham Walkey[3], George Pumpkin, William Lafayette Trott[4], Teesee Chambers, Ellis Manchell Eaton and Emmett Starr.

1903. John Zollicoffer Hogan, Virgi lHarvey Adair, John Henry Shufeldt[1], John Young, John Lewis Denbo, Francis Alexander Billingslea and William Joel Walker.

Delaware District was named from a town or settlement of Delaware Indians on the south side of Spavinaw Creek, near Eucha from about 1820 to 1839.

Saline District was named for the salt spring at Grand Saline, one mile east of Salina.

Going Snake District was named for Goingsnake, a noted Cherokee orator and Speaker of Council in 1828.

Tahlequah District was named for the town of Tahlequah, capital of the Cherokee Nation from 1839 to 1898.

Illinois District was named from Illinois River, which was named by the early French "courier du bois."

Canadian District was named from Canadian River. This district always nominated only one ticket for election.

Skin Bayou District was named from the stream of that name. The name was changed to Sequoyah in honor of the inventor of the Cherokee syllabary.

Flint District was named for its predominent geological formation.

Cooweescoowee was Chief John Ross' Cherokee name.

Clerks of the Council.

See Article three, section nine of the constitution for authorization of office and act of Council of October 4, 1839 for salary.

1841. Rev. Jesse Bushyhead.
1843. Jonathan Mulkey.
1845. Rev. David McNair Foreman.
1847. Hercules T. Martin.
1849. Hercules T. Martin.
1851. Thomas B. Wolf.
1853. Thomas B. Wolf.
1855. Hercules T. Martin.
1857. Hercules T. Martin.
1859. Thomas B. Wolf.
1861. Thomas B. Wolf.
1867. Thomas B. Wolf.
1869. Clement Neeley Vann.
1871. Ellis Sanders.
1873. George Osceola Sanders.
1875. Allen Ross.
1877. John Francis Lyon. Resigned.
Daniel Ross Hicks, vice John F. Lyon, resigned.
1879. Daniel Ross Hicks.
1881. Joel Bryan Mayes. Resigned.
Joel B. Mayes, resigned.
1883. Seaborn Cordery.
1885. Clark Charlesworth Lipe.
1887. Richard Baxter Choate.
1889. William Presley Thompson.
1891. Walter Goss Fields.
1893. John Henry Dick.
1895. John Reuben Leach.
1897. William Wallace Ross.
1899. Claude Stull Shelton.
1901. Claude Stull Shelton.
1903. Martin Rowe.

Judges of Delaware District.

Office authorized by the Constitution of 1839.

Salary one hundred dollars per annum. Act of Council October 4, 1839.

Benjamin B. Wisner 1841; James Kill 1843; James V. Hildebrand 1845; David Kell 1847; Peter 1849 and 1851; George Owen 1853 and 1855; Luther Rice 1857 and 1859; Elowie Butler 1867 and 1869; William Coffee Woodall 1871; Unknown 1873; Isaac Turner 1875; Robert Fletcher Wyley 1877, 1879, 1881 and 1883; Joseph Lynch Ward 1885 and 1887; Thomas Mitchell Buffington 1889, having been elected senator he resigned in November 1891 and Dudley H. Tucker was appointed; Joseph Lynch Ward 1891;

Elias McLeod Landrum[1] 1893; Joseph Lynch Ward 1895 and James Bonaparte Woodall in 1897.

Judges of Saline District.

Bluford West 1841; Bird Doublehead 1843 and 1845; John McIntosh 1847; Benjamin B. Wisner 1849; Joseph V. Chugan' 1851; Archibald Vann 1853; Daid Rowe 1855 and 1857; Andrew Ross 1859; Not known 1861; Charles Wickliffe 1867 and 1869; Saturday Vann 1871, suspended; Redbird Sixkiller, June 6, 1872, vice Saturday Vann; Saturday Vann 1873; Elowie 1875; Not known 1877; Coffee Blackbird 1879; George Washington Scraper 1881; Carter Daniel Markham 1883; Henry Clary Ross 1885; Coffee Blackbird 1887, he died January 26, 1888, Charles Wickliffe, appointed vice Coffee Blackbird, deceased, Charles Wickliffe died August 10, 1888, George Feeling appointed August 14, 1888 ice Charles Wickliffe, deceased; David Welch Ragsdale 1889; Henry Clay Ross 1891, 1893 and 1895 and Edward Sylvester Adair 1897.

Judges of Going Snake District.

Joseph McMinn Starr 1841; Moses Downing 1843, he died September 9, 1845; John T. Foster 1845; Benjamin Vann 1847; Eli Murphy 1849; E. G. Smith 1851; Eli Murphy 1853; John D. Paxton 1855; Johnson Reese 1857; Johnson Robbins 1859 and 1867, Wiley Glover Thornton 1869; Henry Crittenden 1871; Johnson Whitmire 1873; Nelson Terrapin 1875; Joseph McMinn Starr 1877; James Lafayette Bigby 1879, 1881 and 1883; Jesse Redbird 1885; John Virgil McPherson 1887; Edward D. Foreman 1889; Adam Lacey 1891; Joseph McMinn Starr 1893, he died and Pleasant H. Holland was appointed; John R. Crittenden 1895, he died in July 1896 and John W. Holland was appointed; Joseph Smallwood 1897.

Judges of Tahlequah District.

David Carter 1841; Riley Keys 1843; Thomas B. Wolf 1845; Moses Hildebrand 1847; David Hildebrand 1849; Thomas Davis 1851 and 1853; Jay Hicks 1855; David Hildebrand 1857; Thomas Davis 1859; Jackson R. Gourd 1867; Unknown 1869; Jackson R. Gourd 1871; James R. Hendricks 1873 and 1875, he was suspended and Henry Dobson Reese, appointed; William H. Turner 1877; Mankiller Ketcher 1879; Lord Wellington Shirley 1881; Osceola Hair[3] 1883; John Wesley Wolf 1885 and 1887; Benjamin King 1889; Lord Wellington Shirley 1891; John Wesley Wolf 1893; Jefferson Robertson 1895 and William Triplett 1897.

Judges of Illinois District.

James Mackay 1841; James Souiekiller 1843 and 1845; John Thompson 1847; Smith Thornton 1849; Unknown 1851; George Washington Gunter 1853; Rev. Walker Carey 1855; James Mackey 1857; James Souiekiller 1859; Unknown 1861; Amos Thornton 1867; Jacob Bushyhead 1869; Amos Thornton 1871 and 1873; George Osceola Sanders 1875 and 1877; Amos Thornton 1879; Timothy Meigs Walker 1881; George Osceola Sanders 1883; John Silversmith 1885, he died and Thomas Ballard was appointed on December 29, 1886. Ballard died March 12, 1887 and George Osceola Sanders was appointed March 23, 1887. Wallace Ratley 1887;

George Bullette Foreman 1889 and 1891, he died July 4, 1892 and Richard Martin Walker was appointed; Edley Levi Cookson 1893; Henry Clay Meigs 1895 and William Thompson 1897.

Judges of Canadian District.

John Brewer 1841; Robert G. Anderson 1843; Nelson Riley; George Washington Campbell 1847; William Reese 1849; Lewis Riley 1851; William Reese 1853; Star Deer in the water 1855; Dempsey Fields 1857; William Doublehead 1859; James Ore 1861; Joseph Martin Hildebrand 1867 and 1869; Abraham Woodall 1871, 1873, 1875, 1877, 1879 and 1881; Stephen Hildebrand 1883 and 1885; Henry Clay Lowrey 1887 and 1889. Herman Johnson Vann 1891 and 1893; Walter Scott Agnew 1895 and Herman Johnson Vann 1897.

Judges of Skin Bayou District.

William Wilson 1841; Michael Waters 1843, he died April 6, 1845. George Washington Gunter 1845; Felix Riley 1847 and 1849; Unknown 1851.

Judges of Sequoyah District.

George Washington Gunter 1853 and 1855; William Wilson 1857; Dah-lah-see-nee Foster 1859; Unknown 1861; Samuel Adair 1867; Ezekial Starr 1869; Franklin Faulkner 1871; Ezekial Starr 1873 and 1875, he died and Franklin Faulkner was appointed; Franklin Faulkner 1877, 1879, 1881 and 1883, he died and John Childers was appointed April 4, 1885; Oscar Fitzaland Adair[1] 1885 and 1887; Isaac Abraham Jacobs 1889 and 1891, he was elected Senator and resigned in November 1893, George Vann was appointed; Lacey Lasley 1893; Andrew Jackson Russell 1895 and 1897.

Judges of Flint District.

Eli Sanders Harlan 1841; Eli Smith 1843; George Washington Candy 1845; Jay Hicks 1847; Thomas Jefferson Pack 1849; Unknown 1851; Eli Sanders Harlan 1853; Samuel Adair 1855 and 1857; Eli Smith 1859; Samuel Adair 1867; Jackson Christy 1869 and 1871; Samuel Adair 1873, 1875 and 1877, he died February 18, 1879 and Jackson Christy was appointed March 24, 1879; Robert Wesley Walker 1879; Benjamin Franklin Paden 1881, John B. Tulsa 1883; Benjamin Franklin Paden 1885, suspended May 7, 1886 and George Cochran, appointed, Benjamin Franklin Paden, reinstated November 11, 1886; John B. Tulsa 1887; Johnson Swimmer 1889; Benjamin Franklin Paden 1891; Charles D. Patterson 1893; R. W. Johnson 1895 and Richard Baxter Choate 1897.

Judges of Cooweescoowee District.

Not known 1855; John Lucien Brown 1857; Charles Coody Rogers 1857; Jackson Tyner 1861; Daniel Ross Hicks 1867 and 1869; Charles Coody Rogers 1871, 1873 and 1875; Clement Vann Rogers 1877; Alexander McCoy Rider 1879; James Cristopher McCoy 1881; John Anthony Foreman 1883; Walter Adair Starr 1885, 1887, 1889 and 1891; John Gunter Scrimsher 1893; Walter Adair Starr 1895 and 1897.

Sheriffs of Delaware District.

Jesse Cochran 1841 and 1843; Choo-wa-chu-kuh 1845; Charles Landrum 1847 and 1849; Jesse Buffington 1851; Choo-wa-chu-kuh 1853; Archibald Ballard 1855 and 1857; suspended and Choo-wa-chu-kuh appointed; Archibald Ballard 1859; Thomas Jefferson McGhee 1867; William Snell 1869; Stand Suagee 1871; John Martin Daniel 1873; James Tincup 1875 and 1877; Andrew Cummings Johnson 1879; David Suagee 1881; Joseph D. Muskrat 1883; Benjamin Seth Landrum 1885; William Penn Henderson 1887; Percy Wyley 1889; Thomas Jefferson Monroe 1891; Thomas Jefferson Muskrat 1893; John Lafayette Dameron 1895 and Benjamin Cornelius England 1897.

Sheriffs of Saline District.

John Lucien Brown 1841, 1843 and 1845; George Cochran 1847; Hiram Terrell Landrum 1849; George Cochran 1851; Jefferson Hicks 1853 and 1855; Joseph V. Clingan 1857 and 1859; George Downing 1867; Backwater 1869; John Leaf Springston 1871, suspended and Frank Consene, appointed; Jackson Rope 1873 and 1875, he died and John Wickliffe, appointed; Henry Clay Ross 1877, 1879 and 1881; Osceola Powell Benge 1883 and 1885; Edward Sylvester Adair 1887; Jesse Sunday 1889, he died and William Smith was appointed February 11, 1890; John North West 1891; Napoleon Bonaparte Rowe 1893; John Henry Ross 1895, he died and George Downing was appointed September 23, 1897; David Ridge 1897, he died and James Lovely Bumgarner was appointed.

Sheriffs of Going Snake District.

George Washington Scraper 1841 and 1843; Benjamin Vann 1845, Aaron Wilkerson 1847 and 1849; Eli Sanders 1851; Cornelius Wright 1853, Eli Sanders 1855; Cornelius Wright 1857; Eli Sanders 1859; Ezekial Proctor 1867; Daniel Webster 1869; John R. Wright 1871, 1873 and 1875; John Walkingstock 1877; Nelson Foreman 1879; George Washington Lee 1881; Andrew Taylor Akin 1883; John Walkingstick 1885; Lincoln England 1887; Benjamin Knight 1889; Thomas Welch 1891; Isaac Walkingstick 1893, killed May 4, 1894 and Ezekial Proctor appointed; John Sanders 1895 and 1897.

Sheriffs of Tahlequah District.

Benjamin Downing 1841 and 1843; Daniel Grasshopper 1845; Nicholas Byars Sanders 1847, 1849 and 1851; Benjamin Downing 1853; Wah-la-neeta 1855; Nicholas Byars Sanders 1857; Brushwood 1859; Eli Spears 1867, 1869 and 1871; Robert Bruce Ross 1873: Henry Clay Barnes 1875, suspended and John Ross Meigs appointed March 18, 1876, Henry Clary Barnes was reinstated by council and again suspended March 17, 1877 and Harrison Williams, appointed; Henry Clay Barnes 1877; Madison Sanders 1879 and 1881; Aaron Turrell 1883 and 1885, he was suspended August 13, 1887 and John Ross Meigs appointed on same day; George Roach 1887; Jay T. Clark 1889; Ezekial Proctor Parris in 1891; Charles Proctor 1893; Leonard Williams 1895, he was suspended and Philip Osage was appointed on March 20, 1897; Andrew Bell Cunningham 1897.

Sheriffs of Illinois District.

Alexander Foreman 1841 and 1843; George Fields 1845; Samuel McDaniel Taylor 1847; Robert Brown 1849; Tatnall Holt Post 1851; Cornsilk 1853; John W. Brown 1855; George Washington Brewer 1857; Martin McCoy 1859; Bear Brown 1867; William Young 1869; Lovely Rogers 1871,

1873 and 1875, he died and Emory Linder was appointed January 5, 1877: Dekinney Waters 1877, he was elected to council and resigned and Edward Adair Walker was appointed on November 3, 1879; Redbird Smith 1879, Samuel McCoy 1881; Thomas R. Gourd 1883; John Lafayette Brown 1885: John Benge' 1887; John Lafayette Brown 1889, 1891 and 1893; Henry Ganoe Adair 1895 and Joseph J. Cookson 1897.

Sheriffs of Canadian District.

James Mackey 1841 and 1843; James Ore 1845; Josiah Reese 1847; John Shepherd Vann 1849; James Starr 1851; Nelson Riley 1853; Joseph M. Reese 1855; John Porum Davis 1857; Charles Drew 1859; Unknown 1861; Charles Drew 1867; John Q. Hayes 1869 and 1871; Stand Watie Gray 1873; Thomas Jefferson Bean 1875 and 1877, he was suspended and Henry Clay Lowrey was appointed April 16, 1879; McCoy Smith, 1879, William Mosley West 1881; Stand Watie Gray 1883, he was suspended and William Vann, appointed June 20, 1884; William Vann 1885, 1887, 1889 and 1891; John Calhoun West 1893; Robert Emmett West 1895 and Thomas Graves 1897.

Sheriffs of Skin Bayou District.

George C. Lowrey 1841, 1843 and 1845; Daniel Ross Nave 1847 and 1849; William Benge 1851.

Sheriffs of Sequoyah District.

Carter Daniel 1853; Bluford Baldridge 1855 and 1857; Bat Puppy; Jesse Baldridge 1867; Rufus Bell Adair 1869; Samuel Gunter 1871, he died and Bluford Baldridge was appointed; Richard Benge 1873; John Edward Gunter 1875 and 1877; Albert M. Johnson 1879 and 1881, he was killed May 5, 1882 and Robert Faulkner was appointed; Thomas Blair 1883, George Washington Baldridge 1885; Thomas Blair 1887; Josiah Seabolt 1889; Robert Czarnikow 1891; John Faulkner 1893; Mitchell Ellis 1895 and George Washington Baldridge 1897.

Sheriffs of Flint District.

William Griffin 1841, 1843 and 1845, he was suspended December 4, 1845; William Foreman 1847; Isaac Proctor 1849; William Chambers 1851; Runabout Scraper 1853, 1855 and 1857; Samuel Adair 1859; Unknown 1861; Jackson Christy 1867; Unknown 1869; John B. Tulsa 1871; Lewis Quinton 1873; Cicero Leonidas Lynch 1875 and 1877; John Bell Adair 1879; Ellis Starr 1881; Thomas Tail 1883 and 1885, he died September 18, 1886 and Charles Smith was appointed; Richard Lee Taylor 1887 and 1889; John Bell Adair 1891; Richard Lee Taylor 1893; Charles Smith 1895 and John Bell Adair 1897.

Sheriffs of Cooweescoowee District.

John W. T. Spencer 1855; John Lucien Brown 1857; Daniel Ross Hicks 1859; Unknown 1861; John Gunter Schrimsher 1867; John W. T. Spencer 1869 and 1871, he was suspended for attempting to destroy election returns and John M. Smith was appointed December 2, 1872; William McCracken 1873 and 1875; John Gunter Scrimsher 1877; Jesse Cochran 1879; Samuel Houston Mayes 1881; Jesse Cochran 1883; William Edward Sanders

1885 and 1887; Edward Alexander Adair 1889; William Edward Sanders 1891; James Tandy Musgrove 1893, he was killed June 3, 1895 and Joel Bryan Cornelius Ward was appointed; Joel Bryan Cornelius Ward 1895 and 1897.

Solicitors of Delaware District.

"Be it enacted by the National Council, That a Solicitor or Attorney be chosen by a joint vote of both houses of the National Council for each District, whose term of service shall be one year; and such Solicitor or Attorney, before he enters on the duties of his office, shall be commissioned by the Principal Chief.

Be it further enacted, That it shall be the duty of such Solicitor or Attorney, to prosecute, in behalf of the Nation, all persons charged with criminal offenses. * * * See Laws of the Cherokee Nation, 1852. Pages 52, 84, 107, 132, 170 and 219. Anderson Springston 1841, 1842, 1843 and 1844, William Wilson 1845 and 1846; Chuwachukah 1847 and 1848; Isaac Newton Hildebrand 1849, 1851 and 1853; Horsefly 1855; Joel Tucker 1857; Isaac Newton Hildebrand 1859; Moses Sixkiller 1867; Unknown 1869; Runabout Six 1871; Lome Seven 1873½; Joseph Dirteater 1875; Dumplin O'-Fields 1877, he died on December 7, 1878 and Samuel Melton was appointed December 25, 1878; Cyrus Cornatzer 1879; Surry Eaton Beck 1881; Joseph Lynch Thompson 1883; Surry Eaton Beck 1885; Charles Ewing Snell 1887 and 1889; James Bonaparte Woodall 1891; Joseph D. Muskrat 1893; James Franklin Crittenden 1895 and Simpson Monroe Melton 1897.

Solicitors of Saline District.

Clement Vann McNair 1841 and 1842; James Shepherd Vann 1843 and 1844; Isaac Springton 1845 and 1846; Black Haw 1847 and 1848; George Cochran 1849; Isaac Dick 1851; Rope Campbell 1853; DeWitt Clinton Duncan 1855; Levi Toney 1857; Rope Campbell 1859; James Smith 1867; Unknown 1869, 1871 and 1873; Fallingpot 1875; George Washington Clark 1877; Tan-yu-nee-sie 1879; James Chuleowa 1881; John Wickliffe 1883 and 1885; Walter Adair West 1887; Millard Filmore Hicks 1889; Jesse Drywater 1891; Rider Fawling 1893; James Keener 1895 and Daniel Squirrel 1897.

Solicitors of Going Snake District.

Unknown 1841, 1842, 1843 and 1844; Joseph A. Foreman 1845 and 1846; James Madison Payne 1847 and 1848; Thomas Johnson 1849; Thomas Wilkerson 1851 and 1853; Gu-le-stu-ee-ski 1855; John Alexander 1857; John Dougherty 1859; Aaron Goingwolf 1867; Unknown 1869, 1871 and 1873; John Gritts 1875, he was suspended and George Washington was appointed August 16, 1876; Unknown 1877; Joseph Smallwood 1879; Ellis Hogner 1881; Joseph Smallwood 1883; David Hitcher 1885; Nick Snip 1887; Samuel England 1889; Mark Bean 1891; David Hitcher 1893; Mark Bean 1895 and Newton Morton 1897.

Solicitors of Tahlequah District.

Leroy Keys 1841 and 1842; Thomas B. Wolfe 1843 and 1844; Henry Dobson Reese 1845 and 1846; Huckleberry 1855; Brushwood 1857; Huckleberry 1859; Nelson Terrapin 1867; Unknown 1869, 1871 and 1873; William Triplett 1875, he was suspended and Henry Dobson Reese was appointed: Lewis Hawkins 1877, he was suspended and Bark Nugen was appointed April 17, 1879; Ezekial Tucker 1879; William Triplett 1881; Daniel Gritts 1883; George Washington Benge 1885; Daniel Gritts 1887; Wilson Sanders 1889; John Henry Dick 1891; Daniel Gritts 1893; Charles Deer in the Water 1895 and 1897.

Solicitors of Illinois District.

Alexander Foreman 1841 and 1842; Daniel Spencer 1843 and 1844; George Washington Parris 1845 and 1846; Robert Brown 1847 and 1848; Tatnall Holt Post 1849; Unknown 1851; James Souiekiller 1853; David Rat 1855; aJmes Souiekiler 1857; John Kickup 1859 and 1867; Unknown 1869; Charles R. Gourd 1871, he resigned and Lewis Ross Thornton was appointed November 13, 1872; Unknown 1873; Joseph Young 1875; Soldier Tolen 1877; Lewis Ross Thornton 1879; Soldier Tolen 1881; Martin Van Benge 1883, 1885, 1887 and 1889; George McDaniel 1891, he was killed and Charles Percival Pierce was appointed July 15, 1893; Edward Adair Walker 1893, 1895 and 1897.

Solicitors of Canadian District.

Lewis Riley 1841 and 1842; David Boggs 1843 and 1844; Robert G. Anderson 1845 and 1846; David Boggs 1847 and 1848; George Washington Campbell 1849; Unknown 1851; Star Deerinthewater 1853; John Porum Davis 1855; Charles R. Gourd 1857; Gah-luh-do-la-duh 1859; Levi Toney 1867; Charles Edwin Watie 1869; Snake Girty 1871; Unknown 1873; William Penn Payne 1875, suspended for incest, John Taylor Drew appointed; Johnson Blythe 1877; he died July 3, 1878 and James Halfbreed appointed, he died January 13, 1879 and Snake Girty was elected February 3, 1879; Robert McDaniel 1879; Isaac C. Groves 1881; Snake Girty 1883: David Downing 1885; James Jay Sevier 1887; Claude Hanks McDaniel 1889 he resigned and William Wilson Harnage was appointed; James Jay Sevier 1891, 1893, 1895 and 1897.

Solicitors of Skin Bayou District.

James Madison Payne 1841 and 1842; Joseph Blackbird 1843 and 1844; Daniel Ross Nave 1845 and 1846; Robert Brown Jr. 1847, 1848 and 1849; Unknown 1851.

Solicitors of Sequoyah District.

Sut-tee-yah 1853 and 1855; Ellis Sanders 1857; Samuel Houston Benge 1859; John Lee 1867; Unknown 1869 and 1871; Rider Swimmer 1873, he died and Lacey Lasley was elected November 12, 1874; Chee-chee 1875, he was suspended and Arthur Austin was appointed in March 1876; Bluford Baldridge 1877, Lacey Lasley, appointed vice Bluford Baldridge and Chee -chee was elected; Lacey Lasley 1879; Robert B. Patton 1881; Bluford Sittingdown 1883; Eli Carselowry 1885; Lacey Lasley 1887; Andrew Jackson Jeremiah 1889; James T. Stewart 1891; Eli Sanders 1893, Jeremiah M. Seabolt appointed August 8, 1895 vice Eli Sanders; Smith Baldridge 1895 and Clement C. Morton 1897.

Solicitors of Flint District.

Ellis Sanders Harlan 1841 and 1842; Brushheap 1843 and 1844; William H. Foreman 1845, 1846, 1847 and 1848; David Sanders 1849; Unknown 1851; Jesse Owen 1853; John Cochran 1855; Jumper Duck 1857; Alexander Dollar 1859; Jesse Redbird 1867; Unknown 1869, 1871 and 1873; Robert McLemore 1875; Yellowbird Adair 1877, he resigned and John Batt was appointed September 15, 1879; John E. Welch 1879 and 1881; David Muskrat 1883; Ellis Starr 1885, 1887 and 1889; Charles Lawrence Saunders 1891; Taylor Duncan 1893; Charles Gettingdown 1895 and James Lee Walker 1897.

Solicitors of Cooweescoowee District.

Unknown 1857 and 1858; Charles Bushyhead 1859; John McIntosh 1867; Unknown 1869, 1871 and 1873; John McIntosh 1875, he was suspended and Josiah Henry was appointed; Rev. Dempsey Fields Coker 1877; James McDaniel Keys 1879; Bryan Ward 1881; James McDaniel Keys 1883; Jese Cochran 1885 and 1887; James Eliott 1889; Elias Cornelius Alberty 1891 and 1893; John Bullette 1895 and James Lincoln Taylor 1897.

District Clerk of Delaware District.

Article V. Section 68 Cherokee Code of 1875, page 55. "There shall be one clerk for each of the several districts of this Nation, who shall be a resident of the district for which he may be elected, and who shall be elected by the qualified ellectors thereof, and commissioned as provided by law." The first election occurred in each District on Janury 21, 1874.

Joseph Miller Ross 1874, 1875, 1877 and 1879; John Henry Covel 1881; Joseph Miller Ross 1883, 1885 and 1887; Robert Emmett Adair 1889; July 29, 1890; aJmes Robert Garrett 1891; William Walter Wright 1893, 1895 and 1897[1]

Clerks of Going Snake District.

Benjamin Franklin Goss 1874 and 1875; Unknown 1877; William Covington Ghormley 1879, 1881 and 1883; John R. Wright 1885, 1887 and 1889, he died April 27, 1890 and James Robert Garrett was appointed July 29 1890; James Robert 1891; William Walter Wright 1893, 1895 and 1897½.

Clerks of Tahlequah District.

Osceola Powell Daniel 1874; Daniel Ross Hicks 1875; Allen Ross 1877, 1879, 1881, 1883, 1885, 1887 and 1889, he died April 21, 1891 and Elias Cornelius Boudinot Jr. was appointed on April 22, 1891; Thomas William Triplett 1891, 1893 and 1895; Benjamin F. Johnson 1897.

Clerks of Illinois District.

George Osceola Sanders 1874; George Washington Benge 1875; Richard Martin Walker 1877 and 1879; Martin Ross Brown 1881; Thomas Jefferson Thornton 1883; Richard Martin Walker 1885; Thomas Jefferson Thornton 1887; Nicholas McNair Thornton 1889 and 1891, he died July 21, 1892 and Bluford Wilson was appointed on July 30, 1892; Henry Clay Meigs 1893; William Thompson 1895 and Andrew Griffin Cookson 1897.

Clerks of Canadian County.

Robert E. Blackstone 1874; Herman Johnson Vann 1875, 1877, 1879 and 1881; John Smith 1883 and 1885; Herman Johnson Vann 1887; Charles Edward Vann 1889 and 1891; George Jennings 1893; ·1895 and

1897.

Clerks of Sequoyah District.

Ready Taylor 1874; Joseph Hall Alexander 1875; Charles Oliver Frye 1877, 1879 and 1881; John Edward Gunter 1883; Edward Everett Adair 1885; Walter Adair Frye 1887; John Harrell Adair 1889; Wilson Otho Bruton 1891; William E. Whitsett 1893; Robert Fargo 1895 and Henry Benge 1897.

Clerks at Flint District.

Unknown 1874; Sanders Choate 1875, he died March 23, 1877 and Samuel Adair Bigby was appointed: Samuel Adair Bigby 1877 and 1879; William Nucholls Littlejohn 1881; George Washington Choate 1883; William J. McKee 1885 and 1887; William Nucholls Littlejohn 1889; Benjamin Gilreath Fletcher 1891; Richard Baxter Choate 1893; John Bell Lynch 1895 and 1897.

Clerks at Cooweescoowee District.

DeWitt Clinton Lipe 1874 and 1875; Clark Charlesworth Lipe 1877 and 1879; John Bullette 1881; Archibald McCoy 1883; William Vann Carey 1885 and 1887; Henry Hardin Trott 1889 and 1891; Joseph Martin LaHay 1893 and 1895; William H. Fry 1897.

Treasurers of the Cherokee Nation.

The office of treasurer was provided for by article four, section twenty one of the constitution, as follows: "The treasurer of the Cherokee Nation shall be chosen by a joint vote of both branches of the National Council for the term of four years." The annual salary was fixed on October 4, 1839 at five hundred dollars[1].

David Vann 1839, 1843, 1847 and 1851; Lewis Ross 1855 and 1859: Springfrog 1867, he died and Clement Neeley Vann was elected in November 1870; Dennis Wolf Bushyhead 1871 and 1875; De Witt Clinton Lipe November 11, 1879; Henry Chambers 1883; Robert Bruce Ross January 19, 1888; Colonel Johnson Harris, November 6, 1891, he was elected Principal Chief on December 23, 1891 and Ezekial Eugene Starr was elected as his successor on the same day; DeWitt Clinton Lipe November 14, 1895; Joseph Martin LaHay, November 17, 1899 and Dr. Jesse Crary Bushyhead 1903.

Supreme Court of the Cherokee Nation.

The powers and prerogatives of the judiciary of the Cherokee Nation is given in the thirteen sections of article five of the constitution and "The Judges of the supreme court shall each be allowed three dollars per day, while in serice in holding court."

1839. John Martin, Chief Justice, Reverend Jesse Bushyhead and four other unknown associates. Elected by Constitutional convention.

1844. Rev. Jesse Bushyhead, Chief Justice, vice John Martin, died October 17, 1840, and Judge Bushyhead died July 17, 1844. George Hicks elected Chief Justice October 11, 1844 vice Bushyhead. Associated Justices. Thomas Pegg, Moses Parris and David Carter. The latter resigned and John Thompson Adair was elected. Rev. Stephen Foreman, elected October 11, 1844.

1847. David McNair Foreman, elected Chief Justice October 3, 1847.

Associate Justices: Joseph Vann, James Sanders, John Thorne, Nichols Byars McNair and John Thompson Adair.

1851. David Carter, Chief Justice. Associate ustices: Lewis W. Hilldebrand, Riley Keys, Rev. Isaac Sanders, Clement Vann McNtir and John Thompson Adair.

1855. Richard Fields, Chief Justice. Associates: Riley Keys, Jesse Russell and Nicholas Byars McNair.

1857. Riley Keys, Chief Justice. Associate Justices: David Carter, John Thompson Adair, Jesse Russell, Thomas Pegg and Louis W. Hildebrand.

1876. John Thompson Adair, Chief Justice. Associate Justices: J. A. Johnson and George Washington Scraper.

1869. John Porum Davis, Chief Justice. Associate Justices: Thomas Teehee and Thomas B. Wolf.

1872. Riley Keys, Chief Justice. Associate Justices: John Shepherd Vann and Redbird Sixkiller.

1875. John Thompson Adair, suspended April 10, 1876, Charles Wickliffe, appointed Chief Justice, then George Washington Scraper appointed Chief Justice, John Landrum, appointed Chief Justice November 10, 1876 and John Thompson Adair was reinstated as Chief Justice by Council on November 18, 1876 and he was again suspenden on October 11, 1877. This was part of the wholesale suspendings at the instance of W. L. G. Miller.

1877. Ephriam Martin Adair, Chief Justice. Associate Justices: Samuel McDaniel Taylor and John Landrum. The latter died November 7, 1880 and George Washington Parks was elected in his place. Rufus Bell Adair was elected Associate Justice in 1880.

1881. Richard Murrell Wolfe was elected in November 1881 vice Rufus Bell Adair, deceased. David Dixon Landrum and O. H. P. Brown were Associate Justices in 1881. Samuel Adair succeeded O. H. P. Brewer.

1882. May 17, Samuel Adair Bigby, elected Chief Justice vice Ephriam Martin Adair, deceased. Joseph Abalom Scales was elected Chief Justice, November 15, 1882. Associate Justices: Joel Bryan Mayes and Samuel Adair Bigby.

John Wright Alberty was elected Chief Jusitce in 1883. John Taylor Drew was one of his Associate Justices. Jackson Christy was elected Chief Justice, March 2, 1885. James McDaniel Keys was elected Chief Justice in November 1885 and Roach Young was one of his Associate Justices. Joseph Absalom Scales succeeded Keys as Chief Justice. John Edward Gunter succeeded Scales as Chief Justice. John Young, Eli H. Whitmire and Bluford West Alberty[1] were Aassociate Justices. John Wickliffe succeeded Gunter as Chief Justice. Associate Justice Samuel Adair Bigby died July 29, 1892 and Jeter Thompson Cunningham was appointed on August 4, 1892. Bluford West Alberty succeeded John Wickliffe as Chief Justice on November 15, 1892. Robert Wesley Walker was elected Justice in November 1893 and the last supreme court elected November 13, 1897 was John McIntosh, Chief Justice, Jesse Redbird and Cicero Leonidas Lynch, Associated Justices.

Circuit Judges, Northwestern Circuit.

Article five, section five of the constitution, specifies "The Judges of the

Supreme and Circuit Courts shall be elected by the National Council." By act of October 4, 1839 "The Circuit Judges shall be allowed each a salary of two hundred dollars per annum." By act of November 28, 1850 stipulated the same salary.

Unknown 1831; Thomas Jefferson Pack 1843, he resigned and Riley Keys elected, vice Pack; Unknown 1845; Thomas B. Wolf 1847; Riley Keys 1849; Thomas Jefferson Pack 1851; Unknown 1853; Samuel McDaniel Taylor 1855 and 1857; Leroy Keys 1859; David Rowe 1867 and 1871; Joel Bryan Mayrs 1875; George Washington Clark 1879 and 1883; George Washington Benge 1887; Hiram Terrell Landrum 1891 and Thomas Mitchell Buffington 1895.

Circuit Judges, Southern Circuit.

John Thorne 1841 and 1843; Unknown 1845; Aaron Hicks 1847; Moses Parris 1849; John Thorne 1851; Unknown 1853; Moses Alberty 1855 and 1857; James Mackey 1859; David Duval 1867; Samuel McDaniel Taylor 1871; John Shepherd Vann 1875, he died May 22, 1876 and Levi Toney was appointed, he died and Robert Taylor Hanks was appointed on May 3, 1876 and was elected August 5, 1878; John Brewer 1879; Joseph Martin Lynch 1883; W. H. Shomake 1887; William Henry Barker 1891 and William McLain in 1895.

Circuit Judges, Middle Circuit.

Timothy Meigs Walker 1867; Jacob Bushyhead 1871, Kinick Sixkiller appointed in 1872 to try Ezekial Proctor; Timothy Meigs Walker 1875; Stephen Teehee 1879; Cicero Leonidas Lynch 1883 and 1887; William Nicholls Littlejohn 1891, he resigned August 26, 1895 and Benjamin Goss was appointed August 27, 1895; Martin Van Benge 1895, he resigned and Charles Harris Sisson was appointed May 1, 1897.

National Medical Board.

Appointed December 27, 1890.

Northern District: Drs. Bartow Francis Fite, Benjamin Franklin Faulkner and Austin Worcester Foreman.

Southern District: Drs. Charles Harris, George Albert M. Bride and William W. Campbell.

Middle District: Drs. Richard Lafayette Fite, George Washington Waters and Walter Thompson Adair.

Executive Councilors.

The office of Executive Councilor was provided for by article four, sections eighteen and nineteen of the Constitution . Number reduced to three on October 9 ,1845. Per diem pay fixed on October 4, 1839 at three dollars and reduced to two dollars on November 28, 1850.

Five unknown 1839; Five unknown 1841; Five unknown 1843; Three unknown 1845; Richard Taylor, Rev. Stephen Foreman and Thomas Foreman 1847; Richard Taylor, Rev. John Fletcher Boot and Archibald Campbell 1849; Unknown 1851; James Brown, Joseph Vann and Archibald Campbell 1853; Joseph Vann, Rev. Stephen Foreman and Archibald Campbell 1855; Joseph Vann, Rev. Walter Adair Duncan and Archibald Campbell 1857; James Brown, John Drew and Daniel Colston 1859; Moses Alberty,

Samuel Smith and Smith Christy 1867, the latter died on November 27, 1867 and Huckleberry Downing was elected in his place; Jesse Henry and two unknown 1869; Jesse Henry died November 25, 1870; Daniel Redbird, James Vann and James Baldridge 1871, the latter died and John Lynch Adair was appointed and Daniel Ross Hicks was elected on November 13, 1872 vice James Baldridge; John T. Beamer and two unknown 1873.

Johnson Spader, John Hildebrand Cookson and James Vann 1875, the latter died and Rabbit Bunch was elected on November 10, 1876. He resigned and Arleicher Ridge was appointed.

Huckleberry Downing, George Downing and John Chambers 1877, the latter two resigned, Stephen Teehee was appointed, vice John Chambers and James Tuck Woodall was appointed, vice George Downing, Jesse Redbird was elected November 29, 1878 vice George Downing and Lewis Rogers of Cabin Creek was elected on the same date vice John Chambers.

Charles Henry Armstrong, Johnson Spade and Daniel Redbird 1879; Coocoodigesky, Johnson Downing and Nelson Terrapin 1881; Johnson Downing, Walter Adair Starr and Adam Feeling 1883; David Muskrat, Daniel Redbird and Ned Christy 1885; William Eubanks, Daniel Redbird and Stout Locust 1887; John Batt, Johnson Downing and George Teehee 1889; the latter died November 24. 1889 and Moses O'Fields was elected November 30. 1889; Aaron Corntassel, George Waters and John Batt 1891; Oosqualuke, David Blackfox and David Tadpole 1893; William Young, Hunter Poorbear and George Sanders 1895; Daniel Watt, John Batt and Jesse Pigeon 1897; Thomas Smith, Walter Goss Fields and George Washington Baldridge 1899; Walter Goss Fields, Samuel Campbell Foster and George Washington Baldridge 1901; George Waters, Samuel Houston Adair and Charles Smith 1903.

Delegates to Washington.

Authorized by article six, section three of the Constitution.

1839. John Ross, William Shorey Coody, Archibald Campbell, George Hicks, Edward Gunter, Richard Taylor, Joseph Martin Lynch, John Looney, Elijah Hicks, Looney Price and Rev Jesse Bushyhead.

1843. John Ross, John Benge, David Vann, Elijah Hicks and William Potter Ross, Secretary.

1845. John Ross, Richard Taylor, John Looney, Carter Walker, Moses Daniel, William Shorey Coody, Joseph Vann, Aaron Price and John Spears.

1846. John Ross, William Potter Ross, Clement Vann McNair and David Vann.

1847. John Ross, Robert Buffington Daniel and Richard Taylor.

1849. John Ross, William Potter Ross, David Vann and John Drew.

1851. John Ross, Joseph Vann, James Kell, Thomas Pegg and Rev. Lewis Downing.

1853. John Ross and John Thompson Adair.

1859. John Ross, John Drew, Pickens M. Benge and Thomas Pegg.

1863. John Ross, Lewis Downing, James M. Daniel and Rev. Evan Jones.[1]

1864. John Ross, Thomas Pegg, George Washington Scraper and Smith Christy.

1866. (Federal Delegates). John Ross, Whitecatcher, Smith Christy, Daniel Hicks Ross, Samuel Houston Benge and John Buttrick Jones. John Ross died August 1, 1866. Whitecatcher died at Pleasant Hill, Missouri, August 17, 1866.

1866. (Southern Cherokee Delegates). John Rollin Ridge, Richard Fields, William Penn Adair, Saladin Watie and Elias Cornelius Boudinot.

1867. Samuel Smith, James McDaniel, Archibald Scraper, Joseph Absalom Scales, Henry Dobson Reese, ohn Porum Davis, William Penn Adair and John Brewer.

1868. John Porum Dais, Henry Dobson Reese, Archibald Scraper, William Penn Adair, Samuel Smith and Lewis Downing.

1869. John Porum Davis, Samuel Smith, Archibald Scraper, Lewis Downing, Clement Neely Vann and Samuel Houston Benge.

1870. Samuel Smith, George Washington Scraper, Lewis Downing, Clement Neely Vann and William Penn Adair.

1871. William Potter Ross, William Penn Adair, Samuel Houston Benge and Clement Neely Vann.

1872. Joseph Vann, William Penn Adair and William Potter Ross.

1873. Rufus O. Ross, William Penn Adair, John Buttrick Jones and William Potter Ross.

1874. Dennis Wolf Bushyhead, Rufus O. Ross, William Penn Adair and John Buttrick Jones.

1875. Rufus O. Ross, Daniel Hicks Ross, John Lynch Adair and William Penn Adair.

1876. William Potter Ross and Hiram Terrell Landrum.

1877. William Penn Adair and Daniel Hicks Ross.

1878. William Penn Adair, William Potter Ross, Samuel Smith and Daniel Hicks Ross.

1879. William Penn Adair, Richard Murrell Wolfe, John Lynch Adair and Rabbit Bunch.

1880. George Sanders and Pleasant Napoleon Blackstone.

1881. Daniel Hicks Ross and Richard Murrell Wolfe.

1882. Robert Bruce Ross and Richard Murrell Wolfe.

1883. Lucien Burr Bell and John Gunter Schrimsher.

1884. Richard Murrell Wolfe and Hiram Terrell Landrum.

1885. William Penn Boudinot, John Chambers and John Schrimsher.

1886. Colonel Johnson Harris and Hiram Terrell Landrum.

1889. Dennis Wolf Bushyhead and John Lynch Adair.

1891. Elias Cornelius Boudinot and Thomas Mitchell Buffington.

1892. William Wirt Hastings and Martin Van Benge.

1895. Colonel Johnson Harris, Roach Young, George Washington Benge and Rev. Joseph Smallwood.

1900. Lucien Burr Bell, Percy Wyly, Benjamin Hildebrand and Jesse Cochran.

The Cherokee Phoenix.

Owned and published by the Cherokee Nation at New Echota, Georgia. Volume 1, Number 1 was issued on February 21, 1882. The last issue Volume 5, Number 52 was issued on May 31, 1834.[1]

Editors of the Cherokee Phoenix.

February 21, 1828, Elias Boudinot resigned August 1, 1832 and Elijah Hicks was immediately appointed by Chief Ross.

Cherokee Advocate

Owned and published by the Cherokee Nation at Tahlequah.

First series; September 26, 1844 to September 28, 1853. Stopped for lack of funds. Second series; April 26, 1870 to December 26, 1874. Entire office destroped by fire. Third series; March 4, 1876 to March 3, 1906. Discontinued by the United States government. A new office was built and entire new press, type and accessories were purchased at the beginning of each series. The full equipment for the third series was purchased for the Nation in St. Louis, Missouri by Assistant Chief David Rowe.

Editors of the Cherokee Advocate.

Elected every two years by National Council.

William Potter Ross 1844; James Shepherd Vann; David Carter; William Penn Boudinot 1870; John Lynch Adair 1873; William Penn Boudinot 1876; George Washington Johnson 1877; Elias Cornelius Boudinot 1879; Daniel Hicks Ross 1881 and 1883; Elias Cornelius Boudinot 1885; William Penn Boudinot 1888; Robert Fleetcher Wyly 1889; Hugh Montgomery Adair 1891; George Oliver Butler 1893; Waddie Hudson 1895; Joseph R. Sequitchie 1879; William Leoser 1899; George Oliver Butler 1901 and Wiley James Melton 1903.

National Auditors.

Authorized by act of Council of November 19, 1851.

William P. Mackey 1851; Unknown 1853, 1855, 1857 and 1859; Charles R. Gourd 1867; Lewis Anderson Ross 1869; Richard Halfbreed[1] 1871 and 1875; Stand Watie Gray 1875; Heman Lincoln Foreman 1877; Connell Rogers 1879; George Washington Benge 1881 and 1883; Lewis Anderson Ross 1884; Samuel D. Love 1888; Isaac Bertholf 1889; Stand Watie Mayfield 1891; Simon Ross Walkingstick 1893; John Calhoun Danenburg 1895; Albert Andrew Taylor 1897 and Thomas Martin Knight 1899.

Townsite Commissioners.

1871. William L. Gordon Miler, Rev. Joseph F. Thompson and J. Woodard Washburn. The latter resigned and John Ross Vann was appointed.

1881. Lucien Burr Bell, James McDaniel Keys and Elizer Butler Sanders.

1884. William Potter Ross, William McCracken and Henry Hardin Trott.

1885. William McCracken and William Henry Drew.

1886. William Henry Drew, Lucien Webster Beffington and Henry Hardin Trott.

1888. Lucien Webster Buffington, Marion Muls and Rollin Kirk Adair.

1890. Lewis Ross Thornton, Nathan Baron Danenburg and Francis Marion Conner.

1892. Ellis Buffington Wright, William Goodlet Nelms and Francis Marion Conner.

1893. Mannie Garrett Butler.

1895. Thomas Albert Chandler.[1]

Committee to Dispose of the Cherokee Outlet.

1891. Joseph Absalom Scales, Elias Cornelius Boudinot, Rev. Joseph Smallwood, Roach Young, George Downing, Thomas Smith and William Triplett.

Committee to negotiate With the Commissioners to the Five Civilized Tribes.

Clement Vann Rogers, Percy Wyly, George Sanders, Wolf Coon, John Edward Gunter and Robert Bruce Ross.

Committee to Build the National Jail.

Riley Keys, John Lynch Adair and John Francis Lyon. The appropriation of six thousand dollars was authorized in November 1873 and the building was to be completed by November 1, 1874.

High Sheriffs of the Cherokee Nation.

This was the title of the jail wardens.

Samuel Sixkiller 1875 and 1877; Robert Mosby French 1879; Charles Washington Starr 1883; John Hawkins 1886, William McCracken 1888, he died and was succeeded by Jesse Bushyhead Mayes; Caleb Wilson Starr George Washington Mayes and John Ellis Duncan.

Attorneys for the Cherokee Naltion Before the Commission to the Five Civilized Tribes, which was acting as a Citizenship Court.

William Wirt Hastings and Charles Percival Pierce.

Solicitor Generals for the Cherokee Nation.

1875. Joseph Absalom Scales.

1877. John Taylor Drew.

Attorney Generals for the Cherokee Nation.

William Wirt Hastings, elected November 25, 1891, Robert Wesley Walker temporarily appointed December 20, 1892. Hastings resumed office; Robert Fletcher Wyly 1897.

Revenue Collector on Alien Property.

Leroy Ladd Crutchfield 1889. He was reappointed as Collector in 1890 but his territory was only Cooweescoowee District to which the Cherokee Outlet was added in 1891. The other collectors appointed in 1890 were: James Jay Sevier for Canadian, Benjamin Franklin Adair for Saline, Blue Housebug for Flint, John W. Holland for Going Snake, Robert J. Thompson for Tahlequah and Robert W. Tittle for Delaware District. Tittle was succeeded in 1891 by Thomas Albert Chandler.

Citizen Courts.

1879. Roach Young, Chairman, William Harnage and George Washington Mayes. Joel Bryan Mayes, clerk and John Francis Lyon, Attorney for the Cherokee Nation.

1881. Alexander Wolf, Thomas Fox Thompson and Thomas Teehee,

Chairman. DeWitt Clinton Duncan, Clerk and Wilson Sanders attorney for the Cherokee Nation.

1886. DeWitt Clinton Lipe, John Edward Gunter and John Thompson Adair, Chairman. Robert Fletcher Wyly, attorney for the Cherokee Nation.

In the period of the war, from July 1862 to November 1867, both the federal and confederate Cherokees maintained a government. The federal government, as well as can be traced is as follows:

Principal Chief: John Ross, he died August 1, 1866 and was succeeded by Lewis Downing.

Assistant Chief: Thomas Pegg and Smith Christy.

Executive Council: Nathaniel Fish, Wareagle and Anderson Springston, elected October 18, 1863. Daniel Hicks Ross, Moses Catcher and Redbird Sixkiller, elected October 5, 1865.

Treasurer: Lewis Ross.

Auditor: Allen Ross and Spencer S. Stephens.

Superintendent of Education: Albert Barnes and Henry Dobson Reese.

Chief Justice: Wiley Glover Thornton; Associate Justices, Riley Keys, Thomas Pegg, James Shelton and Nicholas Byers Sanders. Riley Keys elect-Cihef Justice October 5, 1865.

Judge, Northern Circuit: David Rowe.

Judge, Southern Circuit: Joseph Duval.

Delegates to Washington, elected on Cowskin Prairie, February 20, 1863: Rev. Lewis Downing, James McDaniel and Rev. Evan Jones.

Delegates elected October 18, 1864: John Ross, Thomas Pegg, Smith Christy and George Washington Scraper.

Delegates elected November 3, 1865: Smith Christy, Whitecatcher. Daniel Hicks Ross, Samuel Houston Benge, James McDaniel, John Buttrick Jones and Thomas Pegg.

Committee.

Delaware District:

Saline District: Lewis Downing, Charles Wickliffe and Toostoo.

Going Snake District: Archibald Scraper, Bud Gritts and Redbird Sixkiller.

Tahlequah District: Whitecatcher.

Illinois District: Charles R. Gourd, William Potter Ross and Joshua Ross.

Canadian District: Flute Foxskin.

Sequoyah Districa: Cmith Christy, Cheechee and aJmes Vann, President of Committee.

Flint District: Eli Smith.

Cooweescoowee District: James McDaniel and Robin Smith.

Clerk of Committee: John Buttrick Jones and Robert Bruce Ross.

Council.

Delaware District: Luther Rice, James D. Wofford, Big Robin, Robert Guess, Ezekiel Blackfox and Ben Snail, Speaker of Council.

Saline District: Lacey Mouse, Chuwachukah and Springfrog, Speaker of Council.

Going Snake District: George Washington Scraper, Alexander Love, Eli Sanders, Redbird Sixkiller, Johnson Robbins, and Joe Chooie.

Tahlequah District: Tarcheche and Jack Downing.

Illinois District: Bark Scruggs, Moses Price and John Young, Speaker of Council.

Canadian District: James Hammer and Whitewater.

Sequoyah District:

Flint District: Chalateehee, Walter Christy and Talala.

Cooweescoowee District: Jumper Mills, John Glass, Josiah Stealer and Writer, Speaker of Council.

Clerk of Council: William Scraper and Henry Dobson Reese.

District Judges.

Delaware District: Luther Rice, Oochalata and Johnson Long Charles.

Saline District: George Beamer and Charles Wickliffe.

Going Snake District: Frog Sixkiller and Johnson Robbins.

Tahlequah District: Jackson R. Gourd.

Illinois District: Robin Crawford.

Canadian District: Franklin Gritts and William Doublehead.

Sequoyah District: Mink Downing and George Blair.

Flint District: Johnson Bolin, Chalateehee and Wesley Gritts.

Cooweescoowee District: Stop Sconatee and Daniel Ross Hicks.

Sheriffs.

Delaware District.

Saline District: Samuel Smith.

Going Snake District: Ezekial Proctor.

Tahlequah District: Eli Spears.

Illinois District:

Canadian District: Coming.

Sequoyah District: Jesse Baldridge.

Flint District:

Cooweescoowee District: William Sunday and Dick Duck.

Solicitors.

Delaware District: Allen Tanner and Robert Guess.

Saline District: Alexander Hawk and Isaac Dick.

Going Snake District: John T. Beamer and Aaron Killanigger.

Tahlequah District: Nelson Terrapin and George Pumpkin.

Illinois District: Daniel Backbone and Mussel.

Canadian District: Youngpuppy and Ned Baldridge.

Sequoyah District: Jackenny.

Flint Distirct: Jesse Redbird and Wesley Gritts.

Cooweescoowee District: Jack Gobbler.

The first Confederate Cherokee "convention" was in session for eleven days during August 1862 at Tahlequah; the second and final session was from May 22nd to June 1, 1863 near the mouth of Coody Creek in Canadian District. The officers were:

Principal Chief: Stand Watie.

Assistant Cheif: Samuel McDaniel Taylor.

Members of Convention.

Delaware District: Charles Edwin Watie, L. E. Mush, E. G. Smith died and was succeeded by Lucien Burr Bell.

Saline District: James M. Bell, Joseph Lynch Martin and Dr. Walter Thompson Adair.

Going Snake District: Joseph McMinn Bean, L. Foster, George Harlan Starr, died and was succeeded by George Washington Mayes.

Tahlequah District: Smallwood, W. Benge and Johnson Foreman.

Illinois District: Richard Fields, John Brewer, John W. Brown and Alexander Foreman, President of Convention.

Canadian District: J. A. Scales, Walker Carey and O. H. P. Brewer.

Sequoyah District: Daniel Ross Nave, Moses C. Frye, John Walker Starr, died and was succeeded by Samuel Gunter.

Flint District: Walkingwolf and William Griffin.

Cooweescoowee District: Leroy Keys, Clement V. Rogers and John G. Scrimsher.

William Penn Boudinot, Secretary of Convention; Joel Bryan Mayes Assistant Secretary.

Jack Spears, Executive Councilor.

Elias Cornelius Boudinot, Delegate to the Confederate Congress.

Richard Carter, Judge of Cooweescoowee District.

Lucien Burr Bell, Sheriff of Deleware District.

RUINS OF OLD FEMALE SEMINARY, BURNED IN 1887

CHAPTER XIV

Old Families and Their Genealogy

In order to have a correct understanding of the succeeding genealogical tables, it will be necessary to keep in mind, that;

1.

The numbers to the left of the names denote the place in the family, of the person, following.

a—All numbers under a heading denote brothers or sisters.

b—When the dates of the births of the brothers and sisters are positively known to be consecutive, they are preceded by an OK.

c—The small number to the right, in front of the names, denotes the generation in the family, to which the person following, belongs.

d—A horizontal line between two numbers, show that those above that line are only half brothers and sisters to those below it.

e—A perpendicular line before two or three numbers denote that they are twins or triplets.

f—A transverse line (/) before a name denotes that the person following, is of illegitemate birth.

g—In reading the numbers; read each one separately, giving the last small number at the right, thus; $1^{1}4^{2}10^{3}2^{4}$, should be read, as: one, four, ten two, fourth generation.

2.

The name or names to the right of the first name after the numbers, is that of the husband or wife, or husbands or wives of that person.

3.

All persons dying without issue have an * after their names.

4.

To find the parents of any person; drop the last large number to the right in front of the name, turn back to the preceding generation and find the identical number. To find the grandparents, drop two of the large numbers to the right and turn back two generations and find the identical numbers. Follow the same retrogression to find the other ancestors.

5.

To find the names of the children of any person, add a large number one, to the number in front of the name of the parent, turn to the succeeding generation and find the identical number, thus giving the eldest child, followed by the names of the other brothers and sisters, according to their relative ages.

6.

The serial numbers, to the right of the names, refer to the numbers, indexing the biographical notes on the preceding names.

Explanatory.

Take the following individual family on page ——as an example.

$1^{1}1^{2}3^{3}1^{4}$ Bushyhead. Nannie Foreman.

---

2 Richard Fields. Jennie Buffington, Elizabeth Hicks, Nancy Timberlake nee Brown and ———Grapp. A8
OK 3 George Fields. Nannie Brown and Sarah Cody. A9
4 Lucy Fields. Daniel McCoy and James Harris.
5 John Fields. Elizabeth Wickett.
6 Turtle Fields. Ollie, and Sarah Timberlake. A10
7 Thomas Fields. Nannie Rogers nee Downing.
8 Susannah Fields. George Brewer and Thomas Foreman.
9 John Martin. Nellie McDaniel and Lucy McDaniel. A11
10 Nannie Martin. Jeter Lynch. A12
11 Rachel Martin. Daniel Davis. A13

The $1^1 1^2 3^3 1^4$ is the heading (a) of this family of brothers and sisters.

That the relative ages of the brothers and sisters is correct is indicated by the OK, (b) preceding their names.

That these brothers and sisters are in the fourth generation in this, the Grant family, is shown by the last small number ^{4} to the right of the numbers of the heading (c) and preceding the name of the Bushyhead, the oldest brother.

The horizontal lines (d) between the first and second numbers and be tween the eighth and ninth numbers show that Field's are younger half brothers and sisters of Bushyhead and that they are older half brothers and sisters of the Martins.

The perpendicular line (e) before Thomas and Susannah Fields show that they are twins.

Be careful in reading the numbers as indicated by (f), as; one, one, three, one, fourth generation. Richard Fields' number is $1^1 1^2 3^3 2^4$, George Fields' number is $1^1 1^2 3^3 3^4$ and so on down to the youngest sister, Rachel Martin's number which is one, one, three, eleven, fourth generation.

2.

Nancy Foreman was the wife of Bushyhead.

Richard Fields married Jennie Buffington, Elizabeth Hicks, Nancy Timberlake nee Brown and ——Grapp and the other brothers and sisters married as indicated.

3.

Richard Fields had children by his first three wives, but not by the last, as is indicated by the * after her name.

4.

To find the parents of this individual family, drop the last large and small number (1^4) and turn back to the third generation find the number $1^1 1^2 3^3$ and you will have the names of the parents (Bushyhead's father Captain John Stuart, a British officer). The grandparents of the Bushyhead-Fields-Martin brothers and sisters will be found by dropping the ($3^3 1^4$) from the $1^1 1^2 3^3 1^4$, turning back to the second generation and finding the numbers $1^1 1^2$ are before the names of William Emory and his wife who was the daughter of Ludovic Grant.

5.

To find the names of the children of Susannah Fields who married George Brewer and Thomas Foreman, take her number; $1^{1}1^{2}3^{3}8^{4}$, add one large number one and a small number five to indicate the fifth generation, turn forward until you find her children.

$1^{1}1^{2}3^{3}8^{4}1^{5}$ Aky Brewer. Archibald Foreman.

---

2 Samuel Foreman. Sallie R. Gourd.

OK 3 Nellie Foreman. Adam Bible.

4 Charles Foreman. Annie Seabolt and Thirsey Colvin.

5 William Hicks Foreman. * Mary Sweetwater.

6 Joseph Anthony Foreman. Narcissa Reeves Carey and Lethe Parris.

7 Sallie Foreman. *

8 David McNair Foreman. Sarah Sweetwater, Agnes Foreman Sweetwater and Mary Foreman nee Sweetwater.

9 George Foreman. Elizabeth Fields and Elizabeth Fields.

10 Thomas Foreman. Elizabeth Chicken.

11 Susan Foreman. Samuel Jones and Walter Stopp.

12 James Foreman. *

13 Edward Foreman. Mary Proctor, Sarah Proctor and Jennie Sosa nee Conrad.

14 Elizabeth Foreman. Johnson Proctor and Redbird Sixkiller.

Grant.

1^{1} Ludovic Grant. A1

$1^{1}1^{2}$ Grant. William Emory.

$1^{1}1^{2}1^{3}$ Mary Emory. Rim Fawling and Ezekial Buffington. A2

2 Elizabeth " Robert Due and John Rogers.

OK 3 Susannah " John Stuart, Richard Fields and Joseph Martin.

$1^{1}1^{2}1^{3}1^{4}$ John Fawling. Nannie Vann. A4

2 William "

OK 3 Samuel Martin. Catherine Hildebrand, Charlotte Wickett.

---

4 Elizabeth Buffington. David McLaughlin and Jeremiah C. Towers.

5 Susannah Buffington. Jeffrey Beck and Surry Eaton.

6 Annie Buffington. * James Daniel.

7 Ellis Buffington Catherine Daniel and Lydia Snow nee Wright.

8 Mary Buffington. James Daniel.

9 Thomas Buffington Mary Daniel.

$1^{1}1^{2}2^{3}1^{4}$ Jennie Due. John Rogers. A6

2 Mary Buffington. David Gentry. A5

OK 3 Charles Rogers. Nannie Downing and Rachel Hughes.

4 Aky Rogers. George Hicks and Daniel Vickery.

5 John Rogers. Elizabeth Coody. A7

6 James Rogers. Nannie Coody.

7 Nannie Rogers. Looney Price and Nelson B. Grubbs.

$1^1 1^2 3^3 1^4$ Bushyhead. Nannie Foreman.

---

2 Richard Fields Jennie Buffington, Elizabeth Hicks, Nancy Timberlake nee Brown and —— Grapp. A8

OK 3 George Fields. Nannie Brown and Sarah Coody. A9

4 Lucy Fields. Daniel McCoy and James Harris.

5 John Fields. Ellizabeth Wickett.

6 Turtle Fields. Ollie and Sarah Timberlake. A10

7 Thomas Fields. Nannie Rogers nee Downing.

8 Susannah Fields. George Brewer and Thomas Foreman

---

9 John Martin. Nellie McDaniel and Lucy McDaniel. A11

10 Nannie Martin. Jeter Lynch. A12

11 Rachel Martin. Daniel Davis. A13

$1^1 1^2 1^3 1^4 1^5$ Ruth Fawling. John Shepherd.

$1^1 1^2 1^3 2^4 1^5$ Edmond Fawling. Nellie Lowrey.

$1^1 1^2 1^3 3^4 1^5$ Brice Martin. Naomi Roach.

2 Joseph Martin. Judith Roach.

OK 3 Lucinda Martin. Joseph Spears and William Dennis.

4 Martha Martin. John Ross Daniel.

5 William A. Martin. Nannie Lucas nee Guinn, Necie Wade.

6 John Martin. *

7 Elizabeth Martin. McKenzie Coats.

8 James Martin. Mary Duncan.

9 Ellen Martin. Nathaniel Green Duncan, Joseph Riley and Aaron Merrill.

10 Susie Martin. Noah Lilliard.

---

11 Mary Martin. * Levi Jones.

---

12 George Martin. *

13 Nellie Martin. John Agnew.

$1^1 1^2 1^3 4^4 1^5$ Ezekial Buffington McLaughlin. ——— McDaniel* and Hannah Duncan.

2 Andrew McLaughlin. Maria McDaniel and Elizabeth Landrum.

OK 3 James McLaughlin. *

---

4 Ellis Buffington Towers. Charlotte Eaton.

$1^1 1^2 1^3 5^4 1^5$ Elllis Beck. Charlotte Downing.

2 Joseph Beck. Cynthia Downing.

OK 3 Ezekial Beck. Ruth Hicks.
4 John Beck. Emily Duncan.
5 Jeffrey Beck. Sallie Downing.
6 Pauline Beck. Aaron Downing, James Crittenden, Stephen Hildebrand and James Kesterson.
7 Arie Beck. Joseph A. Sturdivant and Brice Hildebrand.

---

8 Charlotte Eaton. Ellis Buffington Towers.
9 Sinia Eaton. Solomon Denton and Young Charles Gordon Duncan.
10 Richard Eaton. Elizabeth Alberty.
11 Harlin Eaton. * Rebecca Crittenden.
$1^11^21^37^41^5$ James Buffington. Matilda Benge.
2 Ezekiel Buffington. Louisa Newman.
OK 3 Mary Buffington. * Johnson McBreer and Hiram McCreary.
4 Ruth Buffington. * Robert Agnew and William Langford.

---

5 Susie Buffington. Martin Root.
6 Jennie Buffington. Charles Dougherty and John D. Alberty.
7 Clara Buffington. Elllis West and John Wright Alberty.
8 Ellis Buffington. Elizabeth Starr.
9 Elizabeth Buffington. Moses Alberty.
$1^11^21^38^41^5$ Robert Buffington Daniel. Ann Daniel.
2 Ezekial Daniel. Niesa Muskrat.
OK 3 James Daniel. *
4 John M. Daniel. *
5 Susan Daniel. Samuel Knight Weir.
6 Mary Daniel. George Carselowry, Isaac Woodall and Victor Benton.
7 Annie Daniel. Thomas Woodall and Jacob Houston Woodall.
$1^11^21^39^41^5$ Susannah Buffington. Alfred Hudson.
2 Joshua Buffington. Sabra Lynch.
OK 3 Nannie Buffington. * Thomas Fox Taylor.
$1^11^22^31^41^5$ Annie Rogers. John W. Flawey and Thomas Irons.
2 Joseph Rogers. *
OK 3 William Rogers. Nellie May.
4 Tiana Rogers. David Gentry and Samuel Houston.
5 Susannah Rogers. Nicholas Miller.
$1^11^22^32^41^5$ Elizabeth Gentry. Ezekial Williams.
2 Isabel Gentry. *
OK 3 Patience Gentry. *
$1^11^22^33^41^5$ Pleasant Rogers.
2 Eliza Rogers. John Seabolt.

OK 3 Levi Rogers. Margaret Fields.
4 Richard Rogers. * Eliza Lacey.
5 Joseph Rogers. *
6 Charles Rogers. Maria Reynolds.
7 John Rogers. *
8 Elizabeth Rogers. George Whitney Brand.
9 Alzira Rogers. Lewis Fields.
10 Catherine Rogers. * William Elders.
$1^1 1^2 2^3 4^4 1^5$ Aaron Hicks. * Nannie Riley.
2 Nannie Hicks. * John Bickle.

OK 3 Naomi Vickery. Felix Riley.
4 Moses Vickery. Diana Pheasant.
$1^1 1^2 2^3 5^4 1^5$ Cynthia Rogers. Joseph Coker and John Crump.
2 Thomas Lewis Rogers. Ruth Maugh, Ellen Lombard and Lucy Brown.
OK 3 George Washington Rogers. Malinda Scrimsher and Martha England.
4 Charles Coody Rogers. Elizabeth McCorkle, Nannie Coker nee Patton and Jennie Harlan.
5 Nelson Rogers. Rose West and Margaret Scrimsher.
6 Granville Rogers. *
7 Randolph Rogers. *

---

8 Isaac Rogers. Takey Cooley.
$1^1 1^2 2^3 6^4 1^5$ Delilah Rogers. William D. Shaw.
2 Ruth Rogers. Lewis McIntosh.
OK 3 Martha Rogers. Peter Harper and William Armstead.
4 Jefferson Rogers. *
5 William Rogers. *
6 Julia Rogers. James Kell.
7 Elizabeth Rogers. Lewis Riley.
$1^1 1^2 2^3 7^4 1^5$ Moses Price.
2 Alzira Price. Peter May.
OK 3 Looney Price. Coleesta Jolly, Lucinda Phillips and Letitia Coody.

---

4 Nelson Grubb. * Sarah Williams.
$1^1 1^2 3^3 1^4 1^5$ Jesse Bushyhead. Eliza Wilkerson.
2 Isaac Bushyhead. Catherine Ratliff and Ghigau Snaker.
OK 3 George Bushyhead. Guwohida Stofel.
4 Nannie Bushyhead. John Walker and Lewis Hildebrand.
5 Susan C. Bushyhead. Ezekial Lyons and L. P. Harris.
6 Jacob Bushyhead. Nannie McDaniel and Elizabeth Romine.
7 Charles Bushyhead. Pauline Starr and Sallie Miller nee McCoy.
$1^1 1^2 3^3 2^4 1^5$ George Fields. Sallie Daniel.
2 Nannie Fields. William Blythe

OK 3 Elizabeth Fields. William Thompson and John Blagg
4 John Fields. Elizabeth Wells.
5 Ezekial Fields. Mary Ann Sexton.

---

6 Moses Fields. Elizabeth Bigby and Mahala Cadle.
7 Dempsey Fields. Julia Harris.
8 Henry Fields. Hester Ross.

---

9 Lucy Fields. George Hicks.
10 James Fields. Elizabeth Miller.
11 Delilah Fields. James Foreman.
12 Isabel Fields. Dennis Wolf.
$1^1 1^2 3^3 3^4 1^5$ Annie Fields. Bigfeather.

---

2 Johnson Fields. Rebecca Fawn and Elsie Lee.
4 Archibald Fields. Quatie Brown nee Conrad and Elizabet Hicks.
6 Robert Fields. Sallie Murphy.
7 Susie Fields. Richard Taylor.
10 Rachiel Fields. Crawford.

---

3 Richard Fields. Lydia Shorey and Henrietta Ridgeway.
5 Rider Fields. Margaret Bruner, Jennie Huss and Sallie McDaniel.
8 Ruth Fields. John West.
9 Nannie Fields. Richard Ratliff.
11 Dempsey Fields. Annie Claunch.
12 Martha Fields. William Mosley, John Thompson, John O'Bannon and Joseph Riley.
13 John Fields. *
$1^1 1^2 3^3 4^4 1^5$ Nellie McCoy. Charles Reese.
OK 2 Susie McCoy. John McPherson.
3 Sallie McCoy. *
4 Alexander McCoy. Aky Gunter and Sarah Elizabeth Hicks.
5 Daniel McCoy. Margaret Wolf and Littie Boyd Starr nee Chambers.
6 Rory McCoy. *

---

7 Rachel Harris. Archibald Lowrey and Harrison Daley.
8 Nannie McCoy. Walter Scott Adair.
$1^1 1^2 3^3 5^4 1^5$ John Wickett Fields. Susannah Halfbreed.
2 Agnes Fields. Archilla Smtih.
OK 3 Charles Fields. Ollie Rowe and Elizabeth.
4 Richard Fields. * Ghiyoku.
5 James Fields. Lydia Wrinklelside.
6 Tiana Fields. Joseph Swimmer.
7 Tieska Fields. Lydia Vann and Charlotte Rowe.

8 Sarah Fields. Thomas Smith.
9 Elizabeth Fields. Thomas Spencer.
10 George Fields. Rachel Grimmett.

$1^1 1^2 3^3 6^4 1^5$ Sherain Fields. Ghi-yu-nu-nu Looney.
2 Cat Fields. Liti.
OK 3 James Fields. Ga-yo-ka Eagle.
4 Nannie Fields. *
5 Daniel Fields. Jennie Drum and Susannah Eagle.
6 Thomas Fields. Lydia Drum.

$1^1 1^2 3^3 7^4 1^5$ Sarah Elizabeth Fields. James V. Hildebrand.
2 Rachel Jane Fields. William Stiff and Henry H. Hickey.
OK 3 Ruth Fields. Jeremiah Bigelow.
4 Richard F. Fields. Rachel Elizabeth Goss and Minerva Kerr.
5 Margaret Wilson Fields. Robert Mosby French and Daniel Fields.
6 Josiah Foreman Fields. *
7 Caroline Matilda Rogers Fields. William Penn Boudinot.

$1^1 1^2 3^3 8^4 1^5$ Aky Brewer. Archibald Foreman.
2 Samuel Foreman. Sallie R. Gourd.
OK 3 Nellie Foreman. Adam Bible.
4 Charles Foreman. Annie Seabolt and Thirsey Colvin.
5 William Hicks Foreman. * Mary Sweetwater.
6 Joseph Anthony Foreman. Narcissa Reeves Carey and Lethe Parris.
7 Sally Foreman. *
8 David McNair Foreman. Sarah Sweetwater, Agnes Foreman Sweetwater and Mary Foreman nee Sweetwater.

---

9 George Foreman. Elizabeth Fields and Ellizabeth Fields.
10 Thomas Foreman. Elizabeth Chicken.
11 Susan Foreman. Samuel Jones and Walter Stopp.
12 James Foreman. *
13 Edward Foreman. Mary Proctor, Sarah Proctor and Jennie Sosa nee Conrad.
14 Elizabeth Foreman. Johnson Proctor and Redbird Sixkiller.

$1^1 1^2 3^3 9^4 1^5$ Martha Martin. George Washington Adair.
2 Annie Martin. Benjamin Franklin Thompson.
3 Joseph Lynch Martin. Julia Lombard, Sallie Childers, Lucy Rogers, Caroline Garrett and Jennie Harlin.
4 Brice Martin. Sarah Jones.
5 Gabriel Martin. Eliza Webber.
6 Susannah Martin. Clement Vann McNair.
7 Richard Fields Martin. *
8 Ellen Martin. * James Jeremiah Vann.
9 Charlotte Martin. Joseph Martin Lynch.
10 Jennie Martin. John Adair Bell.

11 Eliza Martin. Franklin Adair, Devotion O. Wright and John A. Richards.
12 John Martin. Eliza Vann and Martha Chambers.
13 Nannie Martin. David Bell, William Cunningham and Bluford West Alberty.
14 Cicero Martin. *
15 Rachel Martin. Samuel W. Bell.
16 Pauline Martin. Braxton Nicholson, Levi Sidney, Thomas Landrum and Robert Rogers.

---

17 Amelia Martin. * John B. Duncan.
$1^1 1^2 3^3 10^4 1^5$ Martin Lynch. James Allen Thompson.
2 Sallie Lynch. Jonathan England.
OK 3 Mary Lynch. John Williams.
4 Berilla Lynch. —— Marshall and Lowrey Williams.
5 Sabra Lynch. Joshua Buffington and John Adair Bell.
6 Joseph Martin Lynch. Charlotte Martin.
7 Maria Lynch. Johnson Thompson and Andrew Brown Cunningham.
8 Rachel Lynch. Thomas Benjamin Adair.
$1^1 1^2 3^3 1 1^4 1^5$ Martin Davis. Julia Anna Tate.
2 William Davis. *
OK 3 John Davis. Jennie Saphronia Tate.
4 Lorenzo Dow Davis. Susie Miller.
5 Coleman J. Davis. Eliza Huff.
6 Jeter Davis. *
7 Elias Earl Davis. Amanda Brown.
8 Joseph C. Davis. * Malissa Stallings.
9 Delilah Davis. *
10 Amanda Jane Davis. *
$1^1 1^2 1^3 2^4 1^5 1^6$ Edward Fawling. Margaret Smith.
OK 3 Joseph Fawling. Lydia Brown.
4 Rim Fawling. *
5 Ellis Fawling. Elizabeth Griffin.
6 Elizabeth Fawling. Hiram Moody and Samuel Scharble.
7 James Fawling. *
8 Susie Fawling. Thomas Smith and Isaac Timmons.
$1^1 1^2 1^3 3^4 1^5 1^6$ Samuel Martin. Mary McLaughlin.
$1^1 1^2 1^3 3^4 2^5 1^6$ Mary Martin.
$1^1 1^2 1^3 3^4 3^5 1^6$ Mary Spears. Lewis Duncan.
2 Annie Spears. Wahuska and McKenzie Coats.

OK 3 Elizabeth Dennis. *
4 Martha Dennis. * Isaac Mouse.
5 Margant Dennis. —— Meredith and Thomas Tinney.
6 Benjamin Dennis.

7 Missouri Dennis.
8 Marion Dennis.
9 Caroline Dennis. Fredrick Sykes.
$1^{1}1^{2}1^{3}3^{4}4^{5}1^{6}$ Eliza Annie Daniel. John S. Freeman and Henry Lee Hill Hill.
2 William Adolphus Daniel. Lucy Ann McGhee.
OK 3 Thomas Webster Daniel. * Amanda J. McCreary.
4 Joshua Buffington Daniel. Sallie Clark.
5 John Martin Daniel. Nannie Josephine Watie * and Alice Rebecca Smith.
6 Marmaduke Daniel. A. E. Dumas.
7 Emma Jennie Daniel. Henry Donnelly.
8 Susie Ellen Daniel. Surry Eaton Beck.
$1^{1}1^{2}1^{3}3^{4}5^{5}1^{6}$ John Brice Martin. Lucinda Still.
2 Sarah Jane Martin. Samuel Bryant.
OK 3 Almon Martin. Charlotte Jane Cordery and Sarah Catherine Moore.
4 Mary E. Martin. John McLain and George Still.

---

5 Samuel Martin. *
6 Susie Martin. Peter Tovey.
7 William A. Martin. Mary Still.
8 Rose Martin. *
$1^{1}1^{2}1^{3}3^{4}7^{5}1^{6}$ George Coats. *
2 Charles Coats. Jennie Cope.
OK 3 Mary Coats. *
$1^{1}1^{2}1^{3}3^{4}8^{5}1^{6}$ William Penn Martin. *
2 Charlotte Martin. *
$1^{1}1^{2}1^{3}3^{4}9^{5}1^{6}$ Bluford West Duncan. Samantha Carter nee Lane.
2 Rebecca Jane Duncan. Francis Mariôn Conner.

OK 3 James Thomas Riley. Martha Jane Hillen.

---

4 Oscar Merrell. Mary J. Conner nee Crockett.
$1^{1}1^{2}1^{3}3^{4}10^{5}1^{6}$ Mariamnne Catherine Lillard. Thomas Ballard.
2 Minerva Elizabeth Lillard. John Joshua Patrick.
OK 3 Boliver Decatur Lillard. *
4 Andrew Jackson Lillard. Vada Stiles * and Mary White.
5 Zachariah Taylor Lillard. Ella Patrick.
6 William Lillard. * Elizabeth Raft.
7 Cynthia Lillard. Benjamin Talley.
$1^{1}1^{2}1^{3}3^{4}13^{5}1^{6}$ Walter Scott Agnew. Sarah Seabolt nee Riley and Mary E. Cobb.
2 Charlotte Agnew. Allen Roberts.
OK 3 Margaret Agnew. John S. Spradling and William Coffee Woodall.
4 Cynthia Agnew. Josiah Fields Seabolt.

5 Caroline Agnew. Anderson Landrum Crittenden Jennings and John George Butler.

$1^11^21^34^41^51^6$ Mary McLaughlin. Samuel Martin and George W. Hughes.

2 John McLaughlin. *

OK 3 Ezekial Collins McLaughlin. Susan Harkins and Ellen J. Harkins.

4 Jennie McLaughlin. Ellis McDaniel.

5 David McLaughlin. Frances Reynolds.

$1^11^21^34^42^51^6$ George McLaughlin. Sinia Beck and Sarah Langley.

2 Willliam McLaughlin. Ahoka.

OK 3 Elizabeth McLaughlin. John Calhoun Sturdivant.

---

4 Rebecca Ann McLaughlin. Andrew Jackson Chick.

5 James Landrum McLaughlin. Sarah Ann Smith.

6 Andrew Leonidas McLaughlin. *

7 Joshua Ezekial McLaughlin. Celia Davis, Etta Renfro and Margaret Caroline Inlow.

8 Mary Jane McLaughlin. * Lewis Glenn and William Hendricks.

9 Joseph Frank McLaughlin. Minnie M. Price.

10 Maria Caroline McLaughlin. Jack Jones.

11 Rachiel Susan McLauglin. William Henry Donaldson.

12 Charles Gordon McLaughlin. *

13 Benjamin Peters McLaughlin.

$1^11^21^34^44^51^6$ Mary Elizabeth Towers. *

2 Jeremiah Clinton Towers. *

OK 3 William J. Towers. Theodosia Nicodemus.

4 Charlotte Towers. Jacob U. Alberty.

5 Athena Josephine Towers. Henry Clay Mayes.

6 Susie Towers. Sanders Crittenden.

$1^11^21^35^41^51^6$ Orange Beck. Louisa Tiger and Lethe Parris.

2 Jeffrey Beck. Rachel Muskrat.

OK 3 Susannah Beck. Albert McGhee and Alfred Pigeon.

4 Samuel Beck. Susie Sixkiller, Salina Foreman and Elizabeth Dry.

5 Cynthia Beck. Releford Beck, Henry Mitchell and William Taylor Barton.

$1^11^21^35^42^51^6$ Aaron Headin Beck. Catherine McCreary nee Foreman and Josephine Downing nee Welch.

2 Arie Beck. Andrew Pettit, Archibald Love and Jonathan Riley.

OK 3 Mary Beck. Frank Pettit.

4 Releford Beck. * Cynthia Beck.

5 Wetherford Beck. Sabra Sturdivant.

6 Joseph Beck. *

7 Jeffrey Beck. Mary Ann McLain.

8 Surry Eaton Beck. Julia Hildebrand.

9 Susie Beck. John Pinkney Chandler.

10 Ellis Beck. *

11 Elizabeth Beck. John Riley and John Wilson Howerton.

---

12 Lethe Beck. John Butler, Wellington Crittenden, L. Harrison and Dr. Peter Tabler.

$1^1 1^2 1^3 5^4 3^5 1^6$ Caroline Beck. Matthew Young.

$1^1 1^2 1^3 5^4 4^5 1^6$ William Wilborn Beck. *

2 David McLaughlin Beck. Mary Vickory, Julia ——— and Amanda Hillen.

OK 3 Louisa Beck. John Pinkney Chandler.

4 Martha Beck. *

5 Tabitha Beck. Andrew Freeny.

6 Mary Beck. John Talbert and Henry Clay Freeny.

7 Aaron Headin Beck. *

8 Elizabeth Beck. Daniel Foreman and Rider Cloud.

9 Joseph Beck. *

10 Sinia Beck. Jerimiah Horn and James Murphy.

11 Susie W. Beck. *

12 Sallie Jane Beck. Seaborn G. Mabry.

13 Emily Beck. John Alexander Sevier and Thomas Dyer.

14 John Walter Beck. Cynthia Ragsdale.

$1^1 1^2 1^3 5^4 5^5 1^6$ Mary Beck. Stephen Hildebrand.

2 Ezekial Beck. Martha Sturdivant and Mary Ellen Woodall.

OK 3 John Beck. *

4 Surry Eaton. Margaret McCoy and Sussie Ellen Daniel.

5 Sinia Beck. George McLaughlin.

6 Sabra Ann Beck. George Selvidge and John Parker Collins.

$1^1 1^2 1^3 5^4 7^5 1^6$ John Calhoun Sturdivant. Elizabeth McLaughlin.

2 Martha Sturdivant. Ezekial Beck.

OK 3 Martin Butler Sturdivant. Matilda Barnett.

4 Sabra Sturdivant. Weatherford Beck.

5 Robert Sturdivant. *

---

6 William Ballard. Fannie Ann Myers.

$1^1 1^2 1^3 5^4 8^5 1^6$ Mary Elizabeth Towers. *

2 Jeremiah Clinton Towers. *

OK 3 William F. Towers. Theodosia Nicodemus.

4 Annie Charlotte Towers. Jacob U. Alberty.

5 Athena Josephine Towers. Henry Clay Mayes.

6 Susie Towers. Sanders Crittenden.

$1^1 1^2 1^3 5^4 9^5 1^6$ Eliza Denton. James Abercrombie Duncan.

2 John T. Denton. Margaret Downing, Sallie Shirley and Elizabeth Holt.

OK 3 Amanda Cherokee Duncan. John Talbert Scott.

4 Temperance Duncan. *

5 Millard A. Duncan. *

$1^1 1^2 1^3 5^4 10^5 1^6$ Ellis Manchell Eaton. Mary Frances Alberty.

2 Susie Mary Eaton. Elias Cornelius Alberty.

OK 3 William Henry Eaton. *

4 Walter Richard Eaton. Margaret Mary Musgrove.

$1^1 1^2 1^3 7^4 1^5 1^6$ Ellis Buffington. Martha Copeland.

2 Jennie Buffington. Joseph Gambold Miller.

OK 3 Elizabeth Buffington. Cornelius Wright.

4 Ezekial Buffington. * Martha Thomas nee Copeland.

5 Ruth Ann Buffington. Hindman Booth Hoyt.

6 John Buffington. * Mary Burgess.

MALE SEMINARY

$1^1 1^2 1^3 7^4 2^5 1^6$ Catherine Buffington. Leonidas Holt.

2 Mary Jane Buffington. Jerome Lorenzo Greer.

OK 3 Jonathan L. Buffington. *

4 John Daniel Buffington. Fannie Morris.

5 Ezekial Lafayette Buffington. *

6 Senia Elizabeth Buffington. Samuel Benjamin Ward.

7 Thomas Mitchell Buffington. Susie H. Woodall * and Emma L. Gray.

$1^1 1^2 1^3 7^4 5^5 1^6$ William Root. *

OK 2 Martin T. Root. Lucy Crittenden.

$1^1 1^2 1^3 7^4 6^5 1^6$ Ellis Dougherty. *

2 Eli West Dougherty. Jennie Chinosa Vann.

OK 3 Lydia A. Alberty. *

4 Jacob U. Alberty. Annie Charlotte Towers.

5 Flora Alberty. *

6 John A. Alberty. *

$1^1 1^2 1^3 7^4 7^5 1^6$ Charlotte Belle West. Jacob West Markham and William Lavesque Wilder.

---

2 Bluford West Alberty. Louvina Jane Adair nee Lewis.

OK 3 Ellis Buffington Alberty. * Eugenia Vann.

4 Moses Alberty. Nancy Jane Holland.

5 Joseph Vann Alberty. Nannie Louvenia Akins nee Danenburg.

$1^1 1^2 1^3 7^4 8^5 1^6$ Ezekial Starr Buffington. Annie Scasewater.

2 Jennie Buffington. Samuel Adair and John Bean Johnson.

OK 3 Joshua Buffington. *

4 Ellis West Buffington. Malcena Clementine Fisher and Alice Hanks.

5 Sabina E. Buffington. Rufus Bell Adair.

6 Almenta Buffington. James Scasewater and James Robert Sanders.

$1^1 1^2 1^3 7^4 9^5 1^6$ Clara Eva Alberty. Francis Marion Musgrave.

2 William Henry. *

OK 3 Thomas Buffington Alberty. Julianna Danenburg.

4 George Washington Alberty. Cynthia Musgrove nee Rogers.

5 Ellis Buffington Alberty. Martha Murrell.

6 John Alberty. Norma Adair.

7 Lydia Ann Alberty. *

8 Jacob Alberty. Nevada Jones.

9 Mary Francis Alberty. Ellis Manchell Eaton.

$1^1 1^2 1^3 8^4 1^5 1^6$ Eliza Daniel. John Thomas McSpadden and Frederick W. Strout.

2 Fannie Daniel. Samuel Gunter, Henderson Holt and James Monroe Crutchfield.

OK. 3 Susie Daniel. Daniel O'Conner Kell and Dr. Morris Frazee.

4 Osceola Powell Daniel. Susie Ross, Emma Ross, Flora Riley and Nannie Thompson nee Taylor.

5 Richard T. Daniel. *

6 Walker A. Daniel. * Hester Ketchum.

7 Thomas Fox Daniel. *

8 Robert J. Daniel. *

$1^1 1^2 1^3 8^4 2^5 1^6$ Robert Daniel.

$1^1 1^2 1^3 8^4 5^5 1^6$ Annie Eliza Weir. * Bird Woodard.

2 Webster Wayne Weir. Sabra England.

OK 3 Eudocia Weir. Jordan Clark.

4 Theodore Weir. *

5 Mary Weir. George Washington Fields.

6 Martha Weir. *

$1^1 1^2 1^3 8^4 6^5 1^6$ James Madison Carselowry. Catherine Emory.

---

2 Annie Woodall. * Robert Wingfield.
OK 3 Susie H. Woodall. * Thomas Mitchell Buffington.
4 Jennie Woodall. James Frederick Charlesworth.
111871 Louisa Woodall. Jesse Roberts and William Coble.
2 Mary Ellen Woodall. Ezekial Beck.
OK 3 Charles Woodall. Roxie Ann Morris.

---

4 Emma Woodall. William Penn Thorne.
5 Elizabeth Ethel Woodall. Howe Leonidas Rogers.
$1^{1}1^{2}1^{3}9^{4}1^{5}1^{6}$ Louisa C. Hudson. * Jacob Alberty.
2 Joshua Thomas Buffington Hudson. Sarah Berry.
OK 3 Mary Elizabeth Hudson. Caleb Duncan.
$1^{1}1^{2}1^{3}9^{4}2^{5}1^{6}$ Nannie Buffington. William West Alberty, James Blake and William Lavesque Wilder.

---

2 William Wirt Buffington. Josephine Bell and Caroline Thompson nee McCord.
OK 3 John Ross Buffington. Nannie Bryan.
4 Webster Buffington. *
5 Eliza Buffington. Joseph George Washington Vann.
6 Mary Jane Buffington. Robert Fletcher Wyly.
$1^{1}1^{2}2^{3}1^{4}1^{5}1^{6}$ Elmira Flawey. * ——Farrington.
OK 2 Elsie Flawey. *
$1^{1}1^{2}2^{3}1^{4}3^{5}1^{6}$ Robert Due Rogers. *
2 Jennie Rogers. John D. Alberty.
OK 3 Mary Ann Rogers. Josiah Knight and Valentine Gray.
4 Minerva Rogers. James Augustus Choutau.
5 Musidora Rogers. William West Alberty.
6 Caroline Rogers. John Rufus Wyatt.
$1^{1}1^{2}2^{3}1^{4}4^{5}1^{6}$ Gabriel Gentry. *
2 Joanna Gentry. *
$1^{1}1^{2}2^{3}1^{4}5^{5}1^{6}$ Melzie Miller. *
$1^{1}1^{2}2^{3}2^{4}1^{5}1^{6}$ Mary Williams.
$1^{1}1^{2}2^{3}3^{4}1^{5}1^{6}$ Jennie Rogers. John Willingham.
$1^{1}1^{2}2^{3}3^{4}2^{5}1^{6}$ Joseph Rogers Seabolt. *
2 William Holly Seabolt. Sallie Campbell.
OK 3 John Looney Seabolt. * Jennie Riley.
4 Francis Marion Seabolt. * Eliza Cozens nee Smith.
5 Sallie Seabolt. * Josiah Pigeon.
6 Emeline Seabolt. *
7 David Riley Seabolt. * Sallie Riley.
8 Nannie Catherine Seabolt. George W. Harkins and Ezekial Starr.
9 Martha Seabolt. Joseph Lawrence and George Bark.
$1^{1}1^{2}2^{3}3^{4}3^{5}1^{6}$ James Rogers. Mary Sanders.
$1^{1}1^{2}2^{3}3^{4}6^{5}1^{6}$ Charles Rogers. * Susie Foreman.
OK 2 Elmira Rogers. Timothy Fields.

$1^1 1^2 2^3 3^4 8^5 1^6$ Elizabeth Brand. Theodore Cummings and Solomon Bragg

2 Frances Brand. William Elders.

OK 3 John Rogers. Missouri Emma Quinton.

4 Cynthia Ann Rogers. *

---

5 Margaret Brown. *

$1^1 1^2 2^3 4^4 3^5 1^6$ Nancy Jane Riley. William Rider, Frederick Hill and Charles Wallace.

OK 2 Samuel Riley. *

$1^1 1^2 2^3 4^4 4^5 1^6$ Nelson C. Vickery. Mary L. James.

$1^1 1^2 2^3 5^4 1^5 1^6$ Minerva Coker. Yocum and John Daniel.

2 Dempsey Fields Coker. Eliza Jane Marlow and Elizabeth Sigmon.

OK 3 John Rogers Coker. Annie Hogan.

4 George Coker. Nancy Patton.

5 Randolph Coker. Minerva Foster.

$1^1 1^2 2^3 5^4 2^5 1^6$ Lucy Brown Rogers. Joseph Lynch Martin.

2 Elizabeth Rogers. John W. T. Spencer.

OK 3 Thomas Lewis Rogers. Ellen Coody and Nannie Martin.

4 Rose Ella Rogers. *

5 John Rogers. *

6 Napoleon Bonaparte Rogers. Annie Charlotte Martin and Jennie Martin nee Harlin.

8 Granville Rogers. *

10 Elmira Rogers. Thomas Rodman.

13 Julia Rogers. Martin Payne.

14 Nancy Ellen Rogers. Richard Lewis Martin.

15 Cynthia Rogers. William Due Musgrove and George Washington Alberty.

---

7 Victoria Rogers. Joel McDaniel and Amos Flint.

9 Eliza Rogers. William North West.

| 11 Joseph Rogers. Elizabeth Carpenter.

| 12 Antoine Rogers. Elizabeth Rogers nee Carpenter.

$1^1 1^2 3^3 5^4 3^5 1^6$ John Lewis Rogers and Harriettee Meeks, Margaret Cummings and Sabra Berilla England.

2 William Wilson Rogers. Martha Frazier.

OK 3 Georgia Ann Rogers. Richard Prather.

4 Ella Ann Rogers. *

$1^1 1^2 2^3 5^4 4^5 1^6$ Cynthia Rogers. *

2 Sarah Rogers. *

OK 3 John Benjamin Franklin Rogers. * Annie F. McCoy.

4 William Charles Rogers. Nannie Haynie.

5 Mary Ann Rogers. Reuben Bartley Tyner.

---

6 Joanna Coody Rogers. John Calhoun Duncan.
7 Charles Patton Rogers. *
8 Augustine Rogers. Archibald McCoy.

---

9 Delilah Beatrice Rogers. William Henry McLain.
10 Charles Henry Rogers. Mary V. Brady.
$1^1 1^2 2^3 5^4 5^5 1^6$ Lewis Rogers. Josephine Landrum, Helen Ross and
2 Sarah Rogers. David Vaught, William Wilkerson, Alfred Campbell and J. J. Griggs.
OK 3 Eliza Rogers. Virgil Rogers and Alexander McDaniel.

---

4 Welllington Rogers. Mary Scrimsher, Susie Reed and Dora E. Hicks nee Scovel.
5 Charlotte Rogers. ———Rogers and Patrick Shanahan.
$1^1 1^2 2^3 5^4 8^5 1^6$ George Rogers. * Sallie Colston.
OK 2 Nannie Rogers. * William Reese.
$1^1 1^2 2^3 6^4 1^5 1^6$ Houston Shaw. *
OK 2 Henry Shaw. * Nannie Rhoda Ross nee Stiff.
$1^1 1^2 2^3 6^4 2^5 1^6$ William R. McIntosh.
2 Alexander McIntosh. *
3 "Fisky" McIntosh.
$1^1 1^2 2^3 6^4 3^5 1^6$ Margaret Harper. * Alfred Finney Chisholm.
OK 2 Nannie Harper. Edward Cobb and John M. Burns.
$1^1 1^2 2^3 6^4 6^5 1^6$ Helen Alice Kell. Thomas Fox French.
2 Catherine Delilah Kell. Robert Mosby French.
OK 3 James Kell. *
$1^1 1^2 2^3 6^4 7^6 1^5$ James Riley. * Ida Gustavia Dance.
OK 2 Flora Riley. Osceola Powell Daniel.
$1^1 1^2 2^3 7^4 2^5 1^6$ Elizabeth May. *
2 Rachel May. William Henry Mayes.
OK 3 Laura May. *
$1^1 1^2 2^4 7^5 3^3 1^6$ Joseph Price. Sallie Rogers nee Colston.

---

2 William Shorey Price. *
OK 3 Daniel Coody Price. Mary Ann Jones.
4 Montezuma Price.
5 Millard Filmore Price. *
6 George Murrell Price. Eliza Jane Vinyard nee Roach.
7 Annie F. Price. Otis Saladin Skidmore.
8 Caroline Walker. James Lee Floyd.
$1^1 1^2 3^3 1^4 1^5 1^0$ Jennie Bushyhead. Richard Drew.
2 Dennis Wolf Bushyhead. Elizabeth Alabama Adair nee Scrimsher and Eloise Perry Butler.
OK 3 Daniel Colston Bushyhead. * Amanda McCoy.
4 Charlotte Bushyhead. George Washington Mayes.
5 Edward Wilkerson Bushyhead. * Helen Nicholls nee Corey.
6 Caroline Elizabeth Busheyhead. * William Robert Quarles.

7 Eliza Missouri Bushyhead. * David Rowe Vann and Bluford West Alberty.
8 Jesse Bushyhead. *
9 Nannie Sarah Bushyhead. Dr. Felix Hurd McNair.
$1^{1}1^{2}3^{3}1^{4}2^{5}1^{6}$ Ann Olivia Bushyhead. John Brown Choate.
2 Nancy Abigal Bushyhead. William Watson Walker and Thomas Nathaniel Cropper.
$1^{1}1^{2}3^{3}1^{4}3^{5}1^{6}$ Tip Bushyhead. *
2 Smith Miles Bushyhead. Elizabeth Sixkiller and Nellie Summers.
OK 3 George Wilson Bushyhead. Martha Sixkiller.
$1^{1}1^{2}3^{3}1^{4}4^{5}1^{6}$ Sarah Walker. George Washington Lasley.
OK 2 Eben Walker. Sarah Lasley nee Harlan.
$1^{1}1^{2}3^{3}1^{4}5^{5}1^{6}$ Sarah Lyons. John Dance and Saturday Vann.

---

2 Vivian Harris.
OK 3 Josephine Lyons. *
4 Emma Lyons. John Bradshaw.
5 Flora Harris.
$1^{1}1^{2}3^{3}1^{4}6^{5}1^{6}$ Henry Bushyhead. Sarah Langley and Emma Crittenden.
2 Joseph Bushyhead. Delilah Sixkiller.
OK 3 Lovely Ann Bushyhead. John Beard.
$1^{1}1^{2}3^{3}1^{4}7^{5}1^{6}$ Runabout Bushyhead.
2 Jesse Bushyhead. Sallie Walker and Jennie Snail.
$1^{1}1^{2}3^{3}2^{4}1^{5}1^{6}$ Richard Fields. Mary Wilds.
2 James Fields. Jennie Berry.
OK 3 Nannie Fields. John Crutchfield.
4 Elizabeth Fields. Charles Mograin.
5 Louisa Fields. William Kendall.
6 Mary Ann Fields. George Grimmett.
7 Thomas Monroe Fields. Martha Jane Clingan.
$1^{1}1^{2}3^{3}2^{4}2^{5}1^{6}$ John Blythe. Justine Cadle, Jane Lane nee Harlan and Polina James nee Tucker.
2 Martha Jennie Blythe. Alexander Adam Clingan.
OK 3 William Blythe. Fannie Hammondtree.
4 Elizabeth Blythe. Ira Goddard.
5 Mary Blythe. Andrew Jackson Tucker.
6 Elijah Blythe. Martha Clingan.
7 James Chastine Blythe. Sarah Jemima Rogers and Sarah Matila Kell nee Harlan.
8 Absalom Ellis Blythe. Mary J. Millsap.
9 Nancy Ann Rogers. Archibald Henry and William E. Bean.
10 Joseph Riley Blythe. *
$1^{1}1^{2}3^{3}2^{4}3^{5}1^{6}$ John Thompson. Margaret Fields, Minerva Biggs and Elizabeth Griffin.
2 Charles Thompson. Susie Taylor.
OK 3 Alexander Thompson. Ruth Phillips and Elmira McLain.

$1^1 1^2 3^3 2^4 4^5 1^6$ Martha Fields. Hilliard Rogers.

2 Richard M. Fields. Margaret Ann Wolf.

OK 3 Nannie A. Fields.

4 Mary A. Fields. Louis Mograin.

5 James W. Fields.

6 John R. Fields.

7 Sabra Jane Fields. Robert Donald Foster and John Secrest.

8 Sarah E. Fields. *

$1^1 1^2 3^3 2^4 5^5 1^6$ Delilah Fields. John Scroggins.

2 Jennie Fields. Frank Padgett.

OK 3 Ruth Fields. Isaac Scrimsher.

4 Richard Fields. Elizabeth Blagg.

5 Martha Fields. Jacob Muskrat.

6 George Washington Fields. Mary Melvina Weir, Sarah McGhee and Elizabeth Silversmith.

7 Ezekial Fields. Margaret Weir.

8 Mary Fields. Ellis Dick.

$1^1 1^2 3^3 2^4 6^5 1^6$ Catherine Fields. James Rawles.

2 Mary Jane Fields. James Rawles and William Phillips.

OK 3 James Sanford Fields. Charlotte Stover.

4 Margaret Fields. James Smith.

5 Samuel Igo Fields. Caroline Belvidere Phillips.

6 Martha Emeline Fields. John Ross Simons and Louis Langley Horsley.

7 Sarah Penelope Fields. John Jackson Smith.

8 Laura Victoria Fields. Jacob Yeager.

9 Moses Albert Fields. *

10 Saphronia Fields. Franklin Pierce Milligan.

11 Susie Fields. * William Tweedle.

$1^1 1^2 3^3 2^4 7^5 1^6$ Charles Fields. Nannie Hornet.

2 Daniel Fields. *

3 Elizabeth Fields. Taylor Girty.

4 Sarah Fields. * Charles Thompson.

$1^1 1^2 3^3 2^4 8^5 1^6$ Richard Fields. *

$1^1 1^2 3^3 2^4 9^5 1^6$ Delilah Hicks. * Bryan Ward.

2 Jefferson Hicks. Nannie Lowrey and Margaret Lowrey.

OK 3 Eleanor Ophelia Hicks. Gilbert Wilson.

4 Henry Hicks. *

5 David Hicks. * Elzina Wilson.

6 Frank Hicks. * Celia Baldridge.

7 William Hicks. Priscilla Thompson.

8 Mary Hicks. W. A. Coleman.

$1^1 1^2 3^3 2^4 10^5 1^6$ Martha Fields. * Richard Wofford and Joseph Martin Hildebrand.

2 Andrew Fields. Virginia Doherty.

OK 3 Elmira Fields. James Starr, John Walker Starr and John Joshua Patrick.

$1^1 1^2 3^3 2^4 11^5 1^6$ Susan Henrietta Foreman. Anderson Benge and Henry Harrison.

2 Elizabeth Foreman. Samuel Worcester McCoy.

OK 3 John Foreman. *

4 Margaret Foreman. James Christopher McCoy.

5 Spencer Foreman. *

$1^1 1^2 3^3 2^4 12^5 1^6$ Thomas Wolf. Sarah Nix.

2 Nancy E. Wolf. * Thomas Jefferson Monroe.

OK 3 Margaret Ann Wolf. Richard M. Fields and George Ewers.

4 James Wolf. *

5 Martha Wolf. *

-- $1^1 1^2 3^3 3^4 1^5 1^6$ Washington Lowrey. Jennie.

---

2 Archibald Sixkiller. Charlotte Pettit nee Adair.

3 Thomas Sixkiller.

-- 4 Tire.

---

5 George Bigfeather. Jennie Sanders.

6 Annie Bigfeather. *

7 Hawk Bigfeather. *

---

8 Oolagala. Charlotte Rowe.

$1^1 1^2 3^3 3^4 2^5 1^6$ David Fields. *

OK 2 Elizabeth Fields. *

$1^1 1^2 3^3 3^4 3^5 1^6$ Elizabeth Pack Fields. William Shorey Coody and John Shepherd Vann.

2 Amanda Fields. Major General Delos Bennett Sackett U. S. A.

3 William Fields. Charlotte Candy.

4 Wirt Fields. Sarah Woodard.

---

5 Lucy Fields. Redbird Smith.

6 Richard Fields. Lydia Backbone.

---

7 Letitia M. Fields. James Daniel Wilson.

$1^1 1^2 3^3 3^4 4^5 1^6$ Jennie Fields. Allen Ross.

2 Louisa Fields. James Mackey.

OK 3 George Washington Fields. Elvina McCoy.

4 John Fields. *
5 Sarah Fields. Alexander Foreman.
6 Martha Fields. * Samuel McDaniel Taylor.
$1^{1}1^{2}3^{3}3^{4}5^{5}1^{6}$ Sarah Fields. Jacob Miller.

---

2 Ellen Fields. *
3 Rachel Fields. * Benjamin Fife.
5 Susan Fields. Charles Coody and David Steele.

---

4 Catherine Fields. *
6 Nannie Fields. Lewis Bruner.

---

7 Annie Fields. Archibald Ballard.
$1^{1}1^{2}3^{3}3^{4}6^{5}1^{6}$ Johnson Fields. *Ghigau Teehee and Mary Lowrey.
2 Susie Fields. Catcher Teehee.
OK 3 Cherokee Fields. *

$1^{1}1^{2}3^{3}3^{4}7^{5}1^{6}$ Annie Taylor. Robert Buffington Daniel.
2 Mary Jane Taylor. Dr. Jeter Lynch Thompson.
OK 3 Eliza Christine Taylor. Johnson Thompson.
4 Frances Taylor. James Leon Butler.
5 Louisa Taylor. John Osborn Walker.

$1^{1}1^{2}3^{3}3^{4}8^{5}1^{6}$ William Mosley West. Elizabeth J. Clyne.
2 George Rider West. *

OK 3 Martha West. Jackson Cozens.
4 John Calhoun West. Margaret Elizabeth Hickey.
5 Kiamitia West. Allen Gilbert.
6 James Polk West. Missouri Barnett.
7 Ruth Elizabeth West. Richard Brewer and William Walter Finley.
8 Franklin Pierce West. Mary Ellen Allen nee Brewer.

$1^{1}1^{2}3^{3}3^{4}9^{5}1^{6}$ William Ratliff. Eliza Scales and Martha Crossland.
2 Cherokee Ratliff. George Washington Brewer.
OK 3 Kiowa Ratliff. *

$1^{1}1^{2}3^{3}3^{4}10^{5}1^{6}$ Lacey Wilson. Margaret Johnson.

---

2 Robin Crawford. Annie Boston.
OK 3 Jennie Crawford. * Wildcat.
5 Mary Crawford. William Griffin and Waspeaker.

$1^{1}1^{2}3^{3}3^{4}11^{5}1^{6}$ Mary C. Fields. J. C. Cromwell and James L. Smith.

$1^{1}1^{2}3^{3}3^{4}12^{5}1^{6}$ Sarah Elizabeth Mosley. John Leak Springston.

---

2 Ruth Drew. Joseph Miller Ross.

OK 3 George Fields Drew. *

---

4 Nancy Jane Riley. * Daniel Webster Vann.
6 John Martin Riley. Nannie Ethel Brewer.
5 Richard Fields Riley. * Eliza Webber.
7 Martha C. Riley. John West Markham.
$1^{1}1^{2}3^{3}4^{4}1^{5}1^{6}$ Sallie Reese. James Taylor and ——Redmond.
2 Henry Dobson Reese. * Rachael Wolf and Ellen Keys.
OK 3 Catherine Reese. Thomas Starr.
4 Mary Reese. Frederick Cable and Tatnall Holt Post.
5 Polly Reese. Fields Starr, Matthew Guerin, Oliver Miller.
6 Charles Reese. *
7 John C. Reese. *
8 Eleanor Reese. Charles Lowrey.
9 George Reese. *
10 Margaret Ann Reese. William Coffin Woodall.
11 Rory McCoy Reese. Martha Josephine Griffin.
12 Charlotte Reese. Henry Nave and McDuff Ross.
$1^{1}1^{2}3^{3}4^{4}2^{5}1^{6}$ George Washington McPherson. Elmira Gardenhier.
2 Lucy McPherson. Charles Griffin, John Gordon and Coo-weescoowee.
OK 3 Christine McPherson. Nathan Baron Danenburg.
4 Hugh Montgomery McPherson. Harriette Candy.
5 Alexander McPherson. Charlotte Towers.
6 Elizabeth McPherson. Engevine Coody.
7 Nannie McPherson. William Starr.
8 John Virgil McPherson. Lucinda Painter, Elizabeth Morris and Mary Dawson nee Ragsdale.
9 Silas McPherson. * Minerva Eldridge.
$1^{1}1^{2}3^{3}4^{4}4^{5}1^{6}$ Jorn Lowrey McCoy. Charlotte Ratliff, Emma Bennett and Lucy Jane Adair.

---

2 Lucy McCoy. James Gatlin.

OK 3 Elvina McCoy. George Washington Fields.
4 Mary Ann McCoy. Washington Starr and George Gann.
5 Richard Martin McCoy. Ellen Adair.
6 Araminta McCoy. Bluford West Rider, James Starr, Andrew Sanders and Joseph Tapp.
7 Edward Hicks McCoy. Sallie Swimmer nee Haley.
8 Charles R. McCoy. * Nannie Watts and Arie Ann Massey.
9 Elizabeth McCoy. * Ellis Sanders.
10 Nancy Caroline McCoy. James Lafayette Bigby.
$1^{1}1^{2}3^{3}4^{4}5^{5}1^{6}$ Joseph Rogers McCoy. Mary Hicks.
2 Sallie McCoy. Andrew Miller and Charles Bushyhead.
OK 3 James Christopher McCoy. Jennie Adair, Margaret Fore-

man and Malinda Carey nee Downing.

4 Rory McCoy. *

5 Ruth Emeline McCoy. George Washington Hause and Jerome Newton Kepheart.

6 Samuel Worcester McCoy. Elizabeth Foreman.

7 Mary McCoy. Wiley Vann.

8 Amanda McCoy. * Daniel Bushyhead.

9 Margaret McCoy. * Surry Eaton Beck.

10 Daniel Hicks McCoy. Nannie Davis and Rebecca Fowler.

11 Sabra Buffington McCoy. * John Ross Hicks.

12 John Alexander McCoy. Elizabeth Keys, Jennie Dennis, Annie Coker, Annie Chooie and Margaret Hogan.

---

13 Annie F. McCoy. * John Benjamin Franklin Rogers.

$1^1 1^2 3^3 4^4 7^5 1^6$ James Lowrey. Ellen Pigeon.

---

2 Joseph Perdue. Nannie Keener and Martha Matlock.

OK 3 Rufus Daley. Mary Holman and Missouri Weathersby.

4 Nannie Adair Daley. John Washington Hughes.

$1^1 1^2 3^3 4^4 8^5 1^6$ Elizabeth Neeley Adair. Timothy Meigs Walker.

2 James Warren Adair. Susannah Deborah Bean.

OK 3 Susan Caroline Adair. Robert S. C. Noel and Edwin Dow Allen.

4 Sarah Ann Adair. William Penn Adair.

5 Edward Underwood Adair. *

6 Mary Buffington Adair. Dr. Walter Thompson Adair.

7 Hugh Montgomery Adair. Eliza Jane Hearst, Martha L. Johnson and Phoeba Acena Morris nee Pace.

8 Lucy Fields Adair. Waldemar S. Lindsley.

9 Minerva Cornelia Adair. *

$1^1 1^2 3^3 5^4 1^5 1^6$ Elizabeth Fields. * Stand Watie.

2 Mary Fields. * Rufus McWilliams, John Adair Duncan, Thomas Fleming and Daniel Pinson.

OK 3 John McFerran Fields. Elizabeth Smith.

4 Eliza Fields. John Alexander Watie and Samuel Smith.

5 Timothy Fields. Eliza McIntosh, Polly Fields and Elmira Rogers.

6 Rachel Fields.

7 James Fields. * Dollie Eunice Lowrey.

$1^1 1^2 3^3 5^4 2^5 1^6$ John Smith. * Margaret Hendricks.

2 Rachel Smith. John Rider.

OK 3 Charles Smith. *

4 Elizabeth Smith. John McFerran Fields, Thomas Adkins and George Drum.

5 Samuel Houston Smith. *

6 Eliza Smith. David Grayson, Jackson Cozens and Francis Marion Seabolt.

$1^{1}1^{2}3^{3}5^{4}3^{5}1^{6}$ Catherine Fields. Joseph V. Clingan and Edward Pumpkinpile.
2 Jennie Fields. * John Downing.
OK 3 Susannah Fields. Lacey Hawkins.
4 Lucy Fields. Levi Toney.
5 Elizabeth Fields. * Joseph Raper.
$1^{1}1^{2}3^{3}5^{4}5^{5}1^{6}$ Seven Fields. * Sallie Guess.

OK 2 Tiana Fields. *
$1^{1}1^{2}3^{3}5^{4}6^{5}1^{6}$ Johnson Vann. Margaret Winters.

OK 2 Joseph Swimmer. Sallie Sixkiller.
$1^{1}1^{2}3^{3}5^{4}7^{5}1^{6}$ Jennie Fields. Rufus Bell Adair.

OK 2 Thomas Fields. *
$1^{1}1^{2}3^{3}5^{4}8^{5}1^{6}$ Eli Smith. * Elizabeth Ashhopper.
OK 2 Nannie Smith. *
$1^{1}1^{2}3^{3}5^{4}9^{5}1^{6}$ America Spencer. *
$1^{1}1^{2}3^{3}5^{4}10^{5}1^{6}$ Walter Fields. *
OK 2 George Fields. *
$1^{1}1^{2}3^{3}6^{4}1^{5}1^{6}$ Daniel Fields. Margaret Wilson French nee Fields.
2 Aky Fields. *

---

3 Margaret Fields. * Bearpaw Prince.
$1^{1}1^{2}3^{3}6^{4}2^{5}1^{6}$ Martha Fields. Samuel Smoker.
$1^{1}1^{2}3^{3}6^{4}3^{5}1^{6}$ Ollie Fields. *
$1^{1}1^{2}3^{3}6^{4}5^{5}1^{6}$ Squirrel Fields. Susie Gritts, * and Nannie Bolin.

OK 2 Nannie Fields. *
$1^{1}1^{2}3^{3}6^{4}6^{5}1^{6}$ Sarah Fields. Finney Hicks and Johnson Waters.
$1^{1}1^{2}3^{3}7^{4}1^{5}1^{6}$ James V. Hildebrand. Adelaide Taylor.
2 Elizabeth Hildebrand. * Johnson O'Fields.
OK 3 Jemima Hildebrand. * Matthew Thompson.
4 Martha Hildebrand. James Smart.
5 Ann Eliza Hildebrand. Hugh Miller Howdershell.
$1^{1}1^{2}3^{3}7^{4}2^{5}1^{6}$ Nannie Rhoda Stiff. * Silas Ross, Henry Shaw and Thomas McDaniel.

---

2 Bevelly Bean Hickey. Louise Rolston Kell.
OK 3 Henry French Hickey. *
4 Margaret Elizabeth Hickey. John Calhoun West.
5 Mary Ann Hickey. George Washington Pettit.
6 Thomas Preston Hickey. Lucinda Gott.
7 George Hickey.
$1^{1}1^{2}3^{3}7^{4}3^{5}1^{6}$ Josephine Bigelow. Henry Clay Meigs.
$1^{1}1^{2}3^{3}7^{4}4^{5}1^{6}$ Walter Goss Fields. Ella E. Norris.
2 Nannie E. Fields. Colonel Johnson Harris.

4 Thomas Fields. Sarah Simmons.
5 Joseph Allen Fields. Valera Marsh Little.
6 Margaret Penelope Fields. Thomas Fox Woodall.

---

3 William H. Fields. Fannie C. Doctor.

---

7 Chauncey Fields.
$1^1 1^2 3^3 7^4 5^5 1^6$ Henry French. *
2 Robert Mosby French. Catherine Kell and Janana Thompson.
OK 3 Thomas Fox French. Helen Alice Kell and Nannie Ratliff.
4 Richard Fields French. *
5 Cabel Vaughn French. *
6 Joseph Mason French. Sallie Riley and E. May Elliott.
7 Laura Augusta French. * Lewis Ross.
8 Jefferson Thompson French. Margaret Elizabeth Pennel.
$1^1 1^2 3^3 7^4 7^5 1^6$ Elias Cornelius Boudinot. * Susan Adelaide Foreman.
2 Richard Fields Boudinot. Mary Catherine Treppard.
OK 3 Eleanor Margaret Boudinot. John Henry Meigs.
4 Henry French Boudinot. * Elizabeth Starr.
5 Francis Josiah Boudinot. Annie Stapler Meigs.
6 Caroline Mary Boudinot. Archibald Spears.
$1^1 1^2 3^3 8^4 2^5 1^6$ Nannie Foreman. John T. Foster and Redbird Sixkiller.
2 Sarah Foreman. Benjamin Foster and Elijah Mayfield.
OK 3 Elias Gourd Foreman. Jennie Alberty and Mary Sanders nee Smith.
4 Catherine Foreman. Aaron Crittenden, George Tiesky, Scudders Downing and Nelson Terrapin.
5 Ellis Foreman. Elizabeth Crittenden and Sarah Kelly nee Phillips.
$1^1 1^2 3^3 8^4 3^5 1^6$ Elizabeth Bible. John Anderson.
2 John Bible. Mary Jane Brown.
OK 3 Philip Bible. *
4 Christopher Bible. * Rebecca Jane Sweeten.
$1^1 1^2 3^3 8^4 4^5 1^6$ Minerva Jane Foreman. William Thornton, Alexander Ross and John Childers.
2 Thomas Leroy Foreman. Sue M. Wolfe.
OK 3 William Riley Foreman. Susan Caroline Lattamore.
4 Charles Lafayette Foreman. Susie Sanders and Sarah Ross.
5 Samuel Adair Foreman. Caroline Rebecca Guilliams, Jennie Riley, Ellen Martin and Elizabeth Fowler.

---

6 Ellis Foreman. Margaret Richardson.
7 Edward D. Foreman. Salina Brown.
8 Mary Foreman. William Crowder.
9 Nelson Foreman. Annie Alberty.

Scraper, Annie Scraper and Malinda Centers.

---

2 Robert Foreman. Amanda Teusdale.

OK 3 Salina Foreman. Jesse Barnett.

$1^1 1^2 3^3 8^4 8^5 1^6$ Heman Lincoln Foreman. Mary Boots.

2 Hannah Jane Foreman. Archibald Coody.

OK 3 Margaret Foreman. *

4 Susan Foreman. Simeon Turnbull.

5 Pauline Foreman. *

6 Caroline Foreman. Calvin Beams.

7 Ruth Foreman. * Samuel Beams.

8 John Wickliffe Foreman. *

$1^1 1^2 3^3 8^4 9^5 1^6$ William Shorey Foreman.

$1^1 1^2 3^3 8^4 10^5 1^6$ Frances Flora Foreman. Samuel Sixkiller.

2 Bluford West Foreman. Emeline McCoy Robinson.

OK 3 Eliza Elizabeth Foreman. William Johnston.

$1^1 1^2 3^3 8^4 11^5 1^6$ Elizabeth Jones. Alexander Wolf.

---

2 Sarah Emeline Stopp. Lemon and Sardine.

OK 3 Ophelia Catherine Stopp. John Walkingstick.

$1^1 1^2 3^3 8^4 13^5 1^6$ Stephen Foreman. Maude Elizabeth Hunter.

---

2 Elizabeth Foreman. Yellowhammer Suake.

OK 3 Fannie Foreman. Archibald Turtle.

---

4 Joseph Anthony Foreman. Rachel Hampton.

5 Susie F. Foreman. * George Washington Smith.

6 Thomas Fox Foreman. Ada Vann nee Chandler.

$1^1 1^2 3^3 8^4 14^5 1^6$ Margaret Proctor. Spencer Shelton.

2 Charles Proctor. Louisa Townsend and Eliza Pritchett.

OK 3 Eliza Jane Proctor. William H. Horn.

4 Susan Proctor. James Taylor.

5 Nannie Proctor. Jeremiah Springstead, Benjamin Crittenden, Jeremiah Horn and Alburton Brown.

6 Spencer Proctor. *

7 Mary Proctor. *

$1^1 1^2 3^3 9^4 1^5 1^6$ William Penn Adair. Sarah Ann McNair and Sue McIntosh Drew.

2 Brice Martin Adair. Sarah McNair.

OK 3 Walter Thompson Adair. Mary Buffington Adair, Ruth Markham and Fannie Gray.

4 John Ticanooly Adair. Martha Nannie Thompson.

5 Mary Ellen Adair. Joseph Franklin Thompson.

6 Benjamin Franklin Adair. Mary Delilah McNair.

7 Rachel Jane Adair. Milton Howard McCullough.

8 Cherokee Cornelia Adair. Jesse Bushyhead Mayes.

$1^1 1^2 3^3 9^4 2^5 1^6$ Mary Annie Thompson. Caleb Starr Bean.

2 Wirt Thompson. Marjory Hicks.
OK 3 John Martin Thompson. Louisa McCord.
4 Susan Thompson. * John Tipton Lackens.
5 Martha Thompson. * Benjamin Wilson.
6 Ellen Thompson. John W. Wilson.
7 Isabelle Thompson. Benjamin Wilson and Henry Tucker.
8 Benjamin Franklin Thompson. Annie Harden and Gippie Randall.
9 Cherokee Thompson. Joseph Hall Alexander.
$1^1 1^2 3^3 9^4 3^5 1^6$ Polisha Martin. William Bryant and James Thompson.
2 Alexander Lombard Martin. Emily McAllister, Rachel Hunt Sanders, Caroline Shoop nee Pettit, Margaret Green and Saphronia Ann Quinton.

OK 3 Richard Lewis Martin. Nannie Ellen Rogers and Flora Burnett Cummings nee Rogers.
4 Annie Charlotte Martin. Napoleon Bonaparte Rogers.
6 Cicero Holt Martin. *
7 Susie Emory Martin. George Washington Mayes.
8 Martha Washington Martin. *

---

5 Joanna Martin. Frank Consene.

---

9 Ruth Ellen Martin. James Franklin Benge.
10 John Rogers Martin. Tabitha Louisa West.
11 Hernando DeSoto Martin. Jeanette Birdine Lamb.

---

12 Victoria Rogers Martin. Joseph Robert Rogers.
13 Jessie Beatrice Martin. John Lee Lamb and George Crittenden.
14 Granville Augustus Martin. Lola Mayes.
15 Willie Penn Adair Martin. Edward Cochran.
$1^1 1^2 3^3 9^4 4^5 1^6$ Helen Marr Martin. John LaHay, Samuel Sanders, Frederick Morley and James S. Phelps.
$1^1 1^2 3^3 9^4 5^5 1^6$ William M. Martin. Mary Still, Margaret Bolin and Agnes Bolin.
OK 2 John Walter Martin. Laura Reasoner and Nannie Brackley
$1^1 1^2 3^3 9^4 6^5 1^6$ Martha McNair, Henry Rogers and John Martin Thompson.
OK 2 John Martin McNair. Mary Jane Hale.
$1^1 1^2 3^3 9^4 9^5 1^6$ John Lynch. *
2 Caroline Lynch. James Madison Bell.
OK 3 Jeter Lynch. *
4 Joseph Martin Lynch. Susan Frances Raymond nee Foreman.
5 Cicero Leonidas Lynch. Nannie Bell.
6 William Lynch. *
7 Braxton Bragg Lynch. * Sarah ——.
$1^1 1^2 3^3 9^4 10^5 1^6$ Andromache Bell. Harvey Shelton.
2 Josephine Bell. William Wirt Buffington.

OK 3 Charlotte Bell. James Washington Ivey.

4 Lucien Burr Bell. Sabra Ann Cunningham and Mary Frances Starr.

$1^1 1^2 3^3 9^4 11^5 1^6$ Lucy Jane Adair. John Lowrey McCoy.

2 Nancy Ellen Adair. Samuel Mitchell Couch.

OK 3 Franklin Wright. *

4 Mary Ellen Wright. Marion Walker Couch.

---

5 Joseph A. Richards. Caroline Catherine Kelleams.

$1^1 1^2 3^3 9^4 12^5 1^6$ Arkansas Cherokee Martin. Hiram Terrell Landrum.

---

2 Nannie Martin. Thomas Lewis Rogers and David A. Ware.

OK 3 Luther Martin. *

$1^1 1^2 3^3 9^4 13^5 1^6$ John Martin Bell. Sarah Catherine Harnage.

2 Foster Bell. *

OK 3 Cicero Martin Cunningham. Nannie Bell nee Martin and Sarah A. McCoy.

---

4 Beatrice Alberty. James B. Markham.

$1^1 1^2 3^3 9^4 15^5 1^6$ George Bell. *

2 John Bell. *

OK 3 Eliza Jane Bell. William Henry Mayes.

$1^1 1^2 3^3 9^4 16^5 1^6$ Ann Eliza Nicholson. * Edward W. Byrd.

2 Joseph Nicholson. *

OK 3 Richard Nicholson. *

---

4 Mary Sidney. *

---

5 Benjamin Landrum. Martha Madalene Hyde.

6 Thomas Livingston Landrum. Nannie Rider.

$1^1 1^2 3^3 10^4 1^5 1^6$ Jeter Lynch Thompson. Mary Jane Taylor.

2 William Thompson. *

OK 3 Johnson Thompson. Eliza Christine Taylor.

4 John Martin Thompson. Corinne E. Washburn, Martha Rogers nee McNair and Mary Jane McNair Hale.

5 Matthew Thompson. Sallie Turner Denman, Lucy Ann Clark and Jemima Hildebrand.

6 Rachel Caroline Thompson. Thomas Gillispie Allison.

7 Maria Ann Thompson. Thomas Jefferson Parks.

8 Mary Eliza Thompson. Thomas Gillispie Allison.

9 Sabra Elizabeth Thompson. William Vann and Joseph Ballard.

10 Martha Nannie Thompson. John Ticanooly Adair and Augustus Van Edmondson.

11 Joseph Franklin Thompson. Mary Ellen Adair, Fannie Adair nee Gray and

$1^1 1^2 3^3 10^4 2^5 1^6$ Nannie England.
2 Annie England. Livingston Garrett and Thomas Clark.
OK 3 Joseph England. *
4 Mary England.
5 Martha England. George Washington Rogers.
6 William Lowry England. Rebecca Trott nee Moore.
7 Sabra Berilla England. John Lewis Rogers.
$1^1 1^2 3^3 10^4 3^5 1^6$ Almira Williams. Samuel McDaniel Taylor.
2 Louisa M. Williams. James Ward.
OK 3 Rachel Caroline Williams. George DeShields Kinney.
4 Joseph Lynch Williams. Louisa J. Stover.
$1^1 1^2 3^3 10^4 4^5 1^6$ Cherokee A. Williams. Robert Fletcher Wyly.
$1^1 1^2 3^3 10^4 5^5 1^6$ William Wirt Buffington. Josephine Bell and Caroline Elizabeth Thompson nee McCord.
2 John Ross Buffington. Nannie Bryan.
OK 3 Daniel Webster Buffington. *
4 Eliza Buffington. Joseph George Washington Vann.
5 Mary Jane Buffington. Robert Fletcher Wyly.
$1^1 1^2 3^3 10^4 6^5 1^6$ John Lynch. *
2 Caroline Lynch. James Madison Bell.
OK 3 Jeter Lynch. *
4 Joseph Martin Lynch. Susan Frances Raymond nee Foreman .
5 Cicero Leonidas Lynch. Nannie Bell.
6 William Lynch. *
7 Braxton Bragg Lynch. * Sarah ———.
$1^1 1^2 3^3 10^4 7^5 1^6$ James Franklin Thompson. Caroline Elizabeth McCord.
2 Joseph Lynch Thompson. Frances Kell, Alice Tucker and Miranda King nee Young.

OK 3 Sabra Ann Cunningham. Lucien Burr Bell.
4 Jeter Thompson Cunningham. Keziah Camille Moore.
$1^1 1^2 3^3 10^4 8^5 1^6$ John Lynch Adair. Mary Jane Jeffries.
$1^1 1^2 3^3 11^4 1^5 1^6$ Jennie Davis. William Columbus Patton.
2 Rachel Davis. George Washington Hill.
OK 3 Mary Davis. James Orval Hall.
4 John Davis. Ruth Hall.
5 Theresa Lane Davis. William Little.
6 Martin Davis. *
$1^1 1^2 3^3 11^4 3^5 1^6$ Georgia Ann Davis. Ezekial Jackson Dunagan.
2 Samuel Tate Davis. Lucinda Pitchlynn nee Starr and Belle Wofford.
OK 3 Susannah Davis. * Taylor Connelly.
4 Daniel Davis. Berilla Davis.
5 Cicero Davis. Sidney Whisenhunt.
6 John Davis. Bessie Satterwhite.

7 Jennie Saphronia Davis. Clark Barker Garmany.
8 Robert Lee Davis. Ruth Phillips and Hester May Curry.
$1^1 1^2 3^3 11^4 4^5 1^6$ Daniel Davis. Mary E. Davis.
2 Delilah Davis. Benjamin Davis.
OK 3 Joseph Davis. Martha A. Perry.
4 Hannah Davis. William Corn.
5 Susan Davis.
6 Berilla Davis. Daniel Davis and Newton Satterfield.
7 Lorenzo Davis. Theodosia Whitmire.
8 Miller Davis. Elizabeth Simmons.
9 Elias Earl Davis.
$1^1 1^2 3^3 11^4 5^5 1^6$ William Davis. Malissa Davis.
OK 2 Jennie Davis. Oscar Sites.
$1^1 1^2 3^3 11^4 7^5 1^6$ Lorenzo Dow Davis. Malinda Mabry.
2 Elizabeth Davis. Herman Johnson Vann.
OK 3 John Brown Davis. Lucy Kettle and Jennie Barnhill.
4 Jefferson Davis. * Annie Chastain.

CHEROKEE ORPHAN ASYLUM

TAHLEQUAH.

Written By MRS. LENA HARNAGE ADAIR, of Tahlequah.

Here's to Tahlequah with her wooded hills,
Her sparkling springs and tinkling rills,
Her rocky cliffs by fern o'ergrown,
And her shady nooks by lovers known;
Her maidens fair and cultured dames,
And gifted sons of illustrious names.
He who drinks of these limpid springs;
Though far he may wander, fond memory brings
Sweet thoughts of the village that nestles serene,
So tranquil and lovely—an enchanted scene;
Visions of beauty he will long retain,
And in dreams he will visit Tahlequah again.
About her foothills of the Ozarks arise,
Like a gem surrounded by her setting she lies,
Near by flows the Illinois—a crystal stream,
Brightly the waters o'er its pebbly bed gleam.
He who loves beauty, along its banks may find
Picturesque spots to delight the mind.
You should see Tahlequah in the month of May,
When nature has donned her brightest array,
When incense, borne by the perfumed breeze,
Blows through the snow-white locust trees,
Around the quaint old capital square,
Floats out upon the warm sweet air;
When the emerald sward is decked with flowers
And the birds sing in their leafy bowers,
And the voice of the school children on the street,
Falls upon the air like music sweet.
Here many a family its lineage traces
Back to old England's proudest races,
For many a noble, to hide his head,
In Cromwell's time, to America fled.
They sought the Cherokee, whose open hand
Welcomed them to this wonderland.
And in the days when Freedom's strife
Often endangered the royalist's life,
Over the mountains of Tennesse,
The Tory came to the Cherokee;
For during that period the Indians were loyal
To the British crown and the family royal.
The names that Cherokee history adorn,
Were not assumed, but were proudly borne,
By dscendents of these old English sires,
Who safety sought at the Cherokee camp fires.
The name Talequah to this town was given
By the old Cherokees, when they were driven
From their eastern homes, afar to the west,
Till they reached this spot, "A haven of rest,"
Poor, sorrowing exiles, of their homes bereft,
Grieving for firesides which they had left.
God who takes care of those whom the strong oppress,
And pities them in their sore distress,
Brought it to pass, that the land of the given,
By treaty as sacred and solemn as Heaven,
Was better than that of which they had been despoiled,
Where long years they had lived, and loved and toiled.
Little the white brothers knew of this land
Which they gave to the remnant of this proud band.
Knew naught of the mineral wealth which hides
Its bounteous stores in the mountain sides;
Naught of the verdant fruitful plains,
Nor the varied resources this country contains.
Here the Cherokees rested, their long journew o'er,
And this wildwood was given to be theirs evermore,
Here they made the council-ground,
And here their Kihegas oft were found
In solemn assembly and council grave,
When the laws to govern the nation they gave.
Here Sequoyah, the Cadmus, his alphabet brought,
Which with infinite patience and skill he wrought;
Schools were established to teach the youth,
And churches, to spread Christianity's truth.
Soon the wilderness was made to bloom
As homes were built and dispelled its gloom.
And the town by the little woodland stream
Threw its light afar like a diamond's gleam.
Such was the birth of this historic town,
Which for her beauty is of wide renown,
For her fountains that gush from the rough hillside,
And her halls of learning, the Nation's pride.
Like Athens of old, she is of learning the seat,
So peaceful and quiet, a sylvan retreat;
May contentment and happiness fall to the lot
Of all who dwell here in this romantic spot.

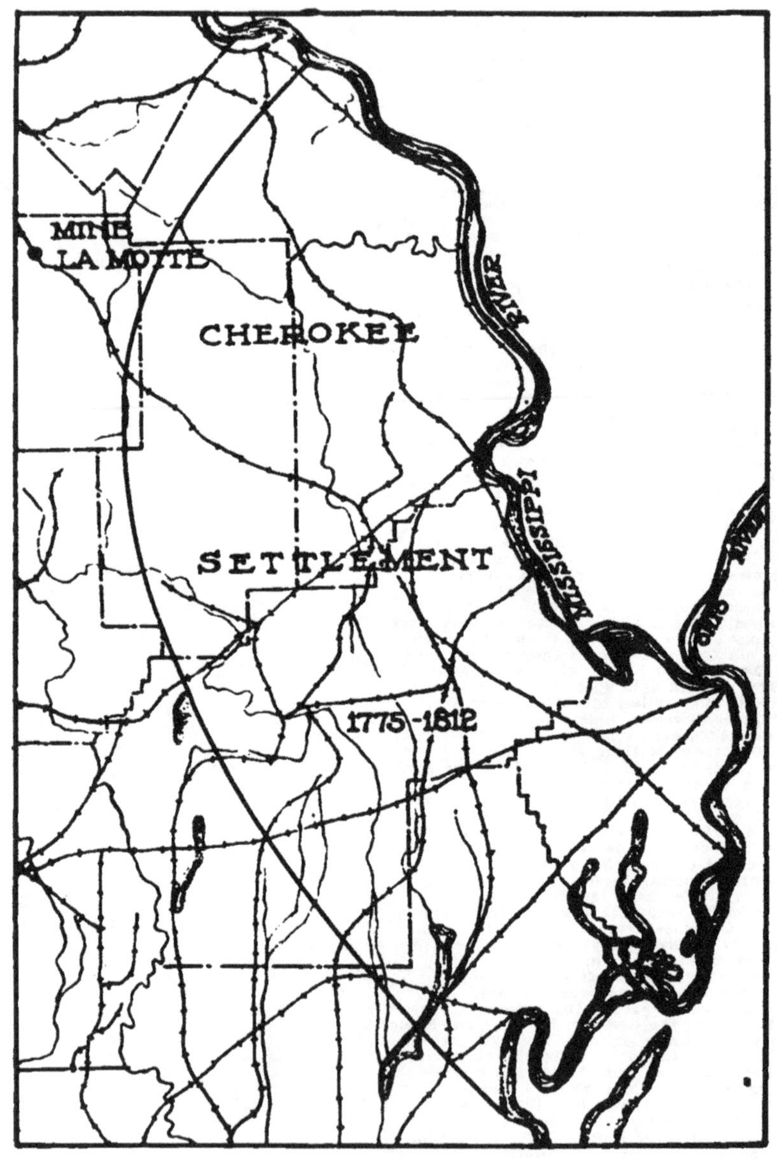
MINE
LA MOTTE
CHEROKEE
SETTLEMENT
1775-1812
MISSISSIPPI
RIVER

CHAPTER XV

Continuation of Old Families

Downing.

1^{1} Major Downing. A14

$1^{1}1^{2}$ George Downing.

2 John Downing. Jennie and Nannie.

3 William Downing.

4 Nannie Downing.

$1^{1}1^{2}1^{3}$ James Downing.

2 Alexander Downing. Oo-go-yo-sti.

3 John Downing. Leah Lovelady.

4 Elizabeth Downing. Stephen Whitmire.

$1^{1}2^{2}1^{3}$ Ollie Downing. *

2 Samuel Downing. Susie Dougherty and Elsie Dougherty.

3 David Downing. Peggy Dougherty.

4 Isaac Downing. *

5 Peggy Downing. Archibald Tuckwa.

6 Nellie Downing. *

7 Moses Downing. Oo-yo-sti or Polly and Lydia.

8 Elizabeth Downing. Galcatcher.

9 Celia Downing. * Ezekial McLaughlin.

10 Jesse Downing. * Chicken.

11 Charlotte Downing. Ellis Beck.

12 William Downing. Elizabeth Dougherty and Elsie Downing.

13 Cynthia Downing. Joseph Beck.

14 James Downing. —— Parris.

15^{3} Catherine Downing. * —— Still.

16 John Downing. Ollie.

17 Sallie Downing. Tadpole.

$1^{1}4^{2}1^{3}$ Thomas Pettit. Catherine.

---

2 James Crittenden. Nancy Hughes and Ko-ta-Ka-ya.

3 Jennie Crittenden. Jack Wright. A15

---

4 Margaret McSwain. Avery Vann.

5 Elizabeth McSwain. David Welch.

$1^{1}1^{2}1^{3}1^{4}$ George Downing.

2 Peacheater Downing.

$1^{1}1^{2}2^{3}1^{4}$ Lethe Downing. Hiram Bright.

2 Annie Downing. Pumpkin or Murphy.

3 Charles Downing. *

4 Scudders Downing. Polly Bean and Catherine Tiesky nee Foreman.

5 John Downing. *

$1^{1}1^{2}3^{3}1^{4}$ Martha Jane Downing. Jackson Smith and Joshua Morgan.

$1^{1}1^{2}4^{3}1^{4}$ George Washington Whitmire. Catherine Wofford and Elizabeth Faught.

OK 2 Jonathan Whitmire. Charlotte Downing and Temperance Holt.

$1^{1}2^{2}2^{3}1^{4}$ Lewis Downing. Lydia Price, Lucinda Griffin and Mary Eyre.

2 John Downing. Jennie Fields.

OK 3 Margaret Downing.

4 Thompson Downing.

---

5 Aaron Downing.

---

6 Samuel Downing.

7 Mary Downing. Charles Dougherty and Charles Crittenden.

---

8 Henry Downing. Jennie Fodder.

$1^{1}2^{2}3^{3}1^{4}$ John Downing. Jennie Clingan.

2 Elizabeth Downing. Richard Turner.

3 George Downing. Elizabeth Consene, Mary Smith and Rosella Downing nee Adair.

4 Rachel Downing. John Smith.

5 Sarah Downing.

6 John Downing.

7 Lydia Downing. John Canoe.

8 Judith Downing. George Still.

9 Thompson Downing. Sallie.

10 Lucinda Downing. Archibald Canoe.

11 Archibald Downing. Josie Craft and Sallie Butler.

$1^{1}2^{2}5^{3}1^{4}$ Benjamin Tuckwa. *

2 Catherine Tuckwa. *

$1^{1}2^{2}7^{3}1^{4}$ Aaron Downing. Susie Beck and Eilzabeth Vann.

4 Celia Downing. Walkingwolf.

5 William Downing. * Aelia Vann.

6 James Downing. Lucinda Woodall and Eliza Parris.

7 Elizabeth Downing. David Tadpole.

8 Judith Downing. eGorge Still.

10 Ambrose Downing. Gatsie Parris and Josephine Welch.

11 John Downing. Rachel Dennis.

12 Catherine Downing. * George Still.

---

2 Cash Downing. * Elizabeth Goodin.

3 Dicey Downing. William Proctor.

---

9 Celia Downing. *

$1^{1}2^{2}8^{3}1^{4}$ Rebecca Galcatcher. James Muskrat.

2 James Galcatcher.

3 Thomas Galcatcher. Peggy and Minnie Vann.

$1^1 2^2 11^3 1^4$ Oran Beck. Louisa Tiger and Letha Parris.

2 Jeffrey Beck. Rachel Muskrat.

OK 3 Susie Beck. Albert McGee and Alfred Pigeon.

4 Samuel Beck. * Susie Sixkiller, Salina Foreman and Elizabeth Dry.

5 Cynthia Beck. Releford Beck, Henry Mitchell and William Taylor Barton.

$1^1 2^2 12^3 1^4$ Sallie Downing. Jeffrey Beck.

2 John Downing. Dennis.

---

3 Susie Downing. John Still.

4 David Downing. Catherine Faught.

$1^1 2^2 13^3 1^4$ Aaron Headin Beck. Catherine McCreary nee Foreman and Josephine Downing. nee Welch.

2 Arie Beck. Andrew Pettit, Archibald Love and Jonathan Riley.

OK 3 Mary Beck. Frank Pettit.

4 Releford Beck. * Cynthia Beck.

5 Weatherford Beck. Sabra Sturdevant.

6 Joseph Beck. *

7 Jeffrey Beck. Mary Ann Harris.

8 Surry Eaton Beck. Julia Ann Hildebrand.

9 Susie Beck. John Pinkney Chandler.

10 Ellis Beck. *

11 Elizabeth Beck. John Riley and John Wilson Howerton.

$1^1 2^2 14^3 1^4$ Edward Downing.

2 James Downing.

3 Locust Downing.

4 Thomas Downing.

5 Mink Downing. Nellie Vann.

6 Dragging Downing.

7 Dooley.

8 Sallie Downing. Thomas Hammer.

$1^1 2^2 15^3 1^4$ Tickaneesky Still. Sallie.

2 Dorcas Still. Ned Still.

3 Aelia Still. Jack Still.

---

4 George Still. Judith Downing and Catherine Downing.

5 Jack Still.

$1^1 2^2 16^3 1^4$ Nannie Downing. Charles Rogers and Thomas Fields.

2 Tarcheche Downing.

3 Caleb Downing.

$1^1 2^2 17^3 1^4$ Nannie Tadpole. Thomas Woodall.

2 David Tadpole. Elizabeth Downing.

---

3 Lucy Still. *

$1^1 4^2 1^3 4^4$ Benjamin Pettit. Peggy Cunnigan.

2 Thomas Pettit. Elsie Hughes.

OK 3 William Pettit. —— and Maria James.

4 Washington Pettit. * Mary Blackbird.

5 Agnes Pettit. Charles Wofford.

6 Elizabeth. Pettit. —— Robbins and William Post.

7 Nannie Pettit. James Humphreys.

$1^1 4^2 2^3 1^4$ Wiliam Crittenden. Malinda House and Louisa Cross.

2 Edward Crittenden. Ghi-goo-ie.

3 Joseph Crittenden.

4 Lydia Crittenden. Samuel Quinton.

5 Lewis Crittenden. Rebecca Shirley and Martha Richardson.

6 Charles Crittenden. Nannie Downing nee ——.

7 Jack Crittenden. Nannie Nugen and Sarah Bolin nee McCabe.

8 Elizabeth Crittenden. Lord Wellington Shirley.

9 Delilah Crittenden. James McDaniel, Richard Glory, Runabout Scraper and William George.

10 Peggy Crittenden.

11 Polly Crittenden. Archibald Vann.

12 Aelie Crittenden. Thomas Butler.

$1^1 4^2 3^3 1^4$ Sallie Wright. Moses Alberty. A16

2 Lydia Wright. Benjamin Snow and Ellis Buffington.

OK 3 Mary Wright. John Alberty.

4 Clarissa Wright. Elijah Phillips. A17

5 William Wright. *

6 Melvina Wright. Thomas Clyne.

7 Rebecca Wright. Joel Mayes Bryan. A18

8 Eli Wright. Nannie Vann.

9 Delilah Wright. Reuben Daniel.

10 Cornelius Wright. Harriette O'Bryan and Elizabeth Buffington.

$1^1 4^2 4^3 1^4$ Joseph Vann. Catherine Rowe and Elizabeth Rowe. A19

2 David Vann. Jennie Chambers and Martha McNair. A20

OK 3 Margaret Vann. David Webber.

4 Andrew M. Vann. Margaret Lasley and Susie Alexander. A21

5 Nannie Vann. John Chambers.

6 Catherine Vann. * John Rogers and William Williams.

7 Mary Vann. William Lasley.

8 Keziah Vann. Robert Webber.

9 Charles Vann. * Eliza West.

10 Clement Vann. *

11 Sallie Vann. Robert Rogers and William Alexander Musgrove.

12 Elizabeth Vann. George West and David Rowe.

13 Eliza Vann. John Martin.

14 Clara Vann. *

15 Jennie Vann. *

$1^1 4^2 5^3 1^4$ Elizabeth Welch. Isaac Ragsdale,—— Nix and Moses Alberty.

2 George Washington Welch. Margaret Jones.

OK 3 Sidney Welch. *

$1^1 1^2 2^3 1^4 1^5$ Charlotte Bright. Joshua Humphrey.

2 Delilah Bright. John W. Bannon.

OK 3 William Bright. Sallie Morton.

4 Samuel Bright. Barsheba Morton.

$1^1 1^2 2^3 2^4 1^5$ Elizabeth Murphy. *

2 Charles Murphy. *

OK 3 Dennis Murphy. Elizabeth Sullicooie.

4 Andrew Murphy. *

5 Thomas Murphy. Nannie and Nellie Gritts nee Manus.

6 James Murphy. Sinia Beck and Martha White.

7 Annie Murphy. *

8 Sallie Murphy. Anderson Gritts and Sulecooya.

$1^1 1^2 2^3 4^4 1^5$ Edward Downing. Jennie —— and Elizabeth Murphy nee Sullecooie.

---

2 Celia Downing. Lewis Cording and Edward Still

OK 3 Rufus Downing.

---

4 William Penn Downing. Nannie J. Walkingstick.

5 Henry Downing. Lydia Ann Walkingstick.

6 David Downing. Martha Wolf.

$1^1 1^2 3^3 1^4 1^5$ Amanda Smith. Alexander Wofford.

2 Mary Smith. Thomas Sanders and Elias Gourd Foreman.

OK 3 Jackson Smith. * Isabel Love nee Eldridge.

---

4 James Morgan. Josephine Clyne.

5 Mark Morgan. Cynthia Smith and Saphronia Taylor nee Griffin.

6 Leean Morgan. * Jeremiah Horn.

7 George Morgan. * Eliza Muskrat.

$1^1 1^2 4^3 1^4 1^5$ Stephen Whitmire. Elizabeth Horn and Quatie Corntassel.

2 Nathaniel Whitmire. *

3 Charlotte Cornelia Whitmire. John R. Wright.

4 Charles Faught Whitmire. Palmyra Phillips.

5 Delilah Whitmire. David Sanders.

6 John Downing Whitmire. Malderine Still and Elizabeth Sanders.

7 Walter Scott Whitmire. Elizabeth Reese and Ethie Russell.

8 Eli H. Whitmire. Mary Wright and Moltcke Boquet.

9 White McClellan Whitmire. Annie Corntassel.

10 Nannie J. Whitmire. Edward Adair Clyne.

11 Margaret C. Whitmire. Joseph M. Easky, Thomas Grider.

12 George Getty Whitmire. Lydia Walkingstick.

$1^1 1^2 4^3 2^4 1^5$ William Whitmire. *

2 Walter Samuel Whitmire. Nannie Bushyhead Wilkerson and Ella Still.

OK 3 Charlotte Whitmire. *

4 George Washington Whitmire. Ida Bailey.

5 Alexander Whitmire.

6 Sarah Jane Whitmire. David Lee Bird.

7 Charles Whitmire.

8 Jonathan Whitmire. Minnie McTier.

9 Henry Whitmire.

$1^1 2^2 2^3 1^4 1^5$ Samuel Houston Downing. Penelope Wolf.

3 Jennie Downing. Charles Kiper.

OK 3 Catherine Downing. Samuel Whirlwind.

---

4 Lewis James Downing. *

5 William Downing. *

$1^1 2^2 2^3 7^4 1^5$ Agnes Dougherty. Black Haw.

2 Sukie Dougherty. William Tutt.

$1^1 2^2 2^3 8^4 1^5$ Nellie Downing. Thomas Lacey.

$1^1 2^2 3^3 1^4 1^5$ James Downing. Emma Sixkiller nee England.

2 Margaret Downing. John J. Hicks.

3 Jinnie Downing. Charles Kiper.

4 Joseph Downing. Nannie Ridge.

5 John Downing.

6 Charlotte Downing. Charles Riper.

7 Walter Downing. Ada Hicks.

8 Agnes Downing. *

9 William Downing.

$1^1 1^2 3^3 2^4 1^5$ Richard Turner. *

2 Jesse Turner. Susie Smith.

3 Nellie Turner. *

4 Ollie Turner. *

5 Rachel Turner. Skilly Vann.

6 Nannie Turner.

7 Jack Turner. Walleuke Houston.

$1^1 2^2 3^3 3^4 1^5$ Susie Downing. Jesse McKnight.

---

2 William Downing.

---

3 Mary Downing.

4 Edward Adair Downing.

5 Elizabeth Downing.

6 Joel Mayes Downing.

7 Lafayette Downing.

$1^{1}2^{2}3^{3}4^{4}1^{5}$ Elizabeth Smith. George Vann.

$1^{1}2^{2}3^{3}7^{4}1^{5}$ Catherine Canoe.

2 John Canoe. Lydia Fields nee Backbone.

3 Archibald Canoe. Elsie Murphy.

$1^{1}2^{2}3^{3}8^{4}1^{5}$ Edward Downing.

2 Samuel Downing.

---

3 Samuel Downing.

4 Sissie Downing.

$1^{1}2^{2}3^{3}9^{4}1^{5}$ Martha Downing. *

2 Polly Downing. Stephen Osage.

3 Lucy Downing.

4 Nannie Downing.

$1^{1}2^{2}3^{3}11^{4}1^{5}$ Polly Downing. Leander Dugger.

---

2 Scott Downing.

3 Brice Downing.

$1^{1}2^{2}7^{3}1^{4}1^{5}$ Moses Downing. *

2 Malinda Downing. Richard Wofford, Walker Carey and James Christopher McCoy.

$1^{1}2^{2}7^{3}3^{4}1^{5}$ Sarah Proctor. Edward Foreman.

2 Elizabeth Proctor. James Kesterson.

3 Ezekial Proctor. Rebecca Mitchell, Margaret Downing and Eliza Chaney nee Welch.

4 Adam Proctor. *

5 Archibald Proctor. *

6 Rachel Proctor. *

7 Nannie Proctor. * Abraham Sixkiller.

$1^{1}2^{2}7^{3}4^{4}1^{5}$ Margaret Walkingwolf. Rider Cloud.

2 Charlotte Walkingwolf. * Tassel.

3 Elizabeth Walkingwolf. * Tassel.

4 Eliza Walkingwolf. * John Lowrey.

3 Elizabeth Walkingwolf. * Tassel.

6 Nannie Walkingwolf. Earbob and Johnson Riley.

$1^{1}2^{2}7^{3}6^{4}1^{5}$ Lucy Downing.

2 Joseph Downing. Agnes Hothouse, Nannie Butler and Aelie Still.

---

3 George Downing. * Eliza Downing.

4 Mary Downing. John Still and Frank Charles Corban.

5 Cynthia Downing. Joseph Vann.

6 Edwin Downing. Elizabeth Still.

7 James Downing. * Aelia Vann.

8 Martha Downing. Bluford Whitmire and George W. Taylor.

9 Malachi Downing. Eliza Vann and Sallie Still.

10 Margaret Downing. George W. Taylor, Richard Crittenden and Benjamin Strickland.

$1^1 2^2 7^3 7^4 1^5$ Joshua Tadpole. *

2 Eli Tadpole. *

3 David Tadpole. Utiyu Vann.

4 Susie Tadpole. * Oceola Woodall.

5 John Tadpole. *

$1^1 2^2 7^3 8^4 1^5$ Mary Still. William Martin.

2 George Still. Agnes Bolin.

3 Aaron Still. *

4 Jesse Still. *

5 Ezekial Still. Mary E. Langley.

$1^1 2^2 7^3 10^4 1^5$ Margaret Downing. Ezekial Proctor.

2 Catherine Downing. William Kell.

OK 3 Elizabeth Downing. George Welch.

$1^1 2^2 7^3 11^4 1^5$ Dennis Downing.

2 Peter Downing. Elsie Hawk.

OK 3 Timothy Downing. * Mary Henson.

4 Elizabeth Downing. Henry Canada Williams and Wade Hampton Williams.

$1^1 2^2 8^3 1^4 1^5$ Annie Muskrat. Henry Schoonover.

2 Jennie Muskrat. Alexander Earbob.

OK 3 Eliza Muskrat. Stephen Morris McDaniel.

4 Calhoun Muskrat. Mollie Toney, Sallie Girty and Susie Davis.

5 Joseph Muskrat. Agnes Standingman.

6 Saphronia Muskrat. Thomas Parker.

7 Noah Muskrat. *

$1^1 2^2 8^3 3^4 1^5$ Charles Galcatcher. Margaret. Budder.

---

2 Lee Galcatcher. Susie Henry nee Foreman.

---

3 Lucy Galcatcher. Roy Gordon and John McFarland.

4 Thomas William Galchatcher. Mary Nicodemus.

$1^2 2^1 11^3 1^4 1^5$ Charlotte Beck. Rowe Smith and Riley Scott.

2 Susie Beck.

$1^1 2^2 11^3 2^4 1^5$ Caroline Beck. William Hughes and Isaac Dougherty.

2 Ani Beck. Joseph Landrum and James Horsefly.

OK 3 Thomas Beck. Sarah Lacey and Eliza DeShane.

$1^1 2^2 11^3 3^4 1^5$ Joanna McGhee. Jeremiah Hanna and John Jones.

2 Lucy Ann McGhee. William Adolphus Daniel, Jason Stilley, James Hudson.

OK 3 Cynthia Ann McGhee. Bluford Sixkiller, George William Talbert and James Welch.

4 Emma Jane McGhee. James Buchanan Smith.

---

5 Webster Halfbreed.

$1^1 2^2 12^3 1^4 1^5$ Mary Beck. Stephen Hildebrand.

2 Ezekial Beck. Martha Sturdivant and Mary Ellen Woodall.

OK 3 John Beck. *

4 Surry Eaton Beck. Margaret McCoy*, Susie Ellen Daniel

5. Sinia Beck. George McLaughlin.

6 Sabra Ann Beck. George Selvidge and John Collins.

$1^1 2^2 12^3 3^4 1^5$ Lucinda Still. Archilla Sanders and John Martin.

2 John Still. Elizabeth Walls.

3 George Still. Mary E. Martin.

4 Elizabeth Still. Edmond Downing and Green Catcher.

5 William Still.

6 Eliza Still. James Barnett.

7 Sallie Still. William Silcox, John Andrew Jackson Lucas.

8 Margaret Still Epp G. Thompson.

9 Catherine Still. James Kizer.

10 James Still. Mary Jones.

$1^1 2^2 12^3 4^4 1^5$ Caroline Downing.

2 William Alexander Downing. Eliza Bright.

OK 3 George Brewer Downing. Arabella Wagoner.

$1^1 2^2 13^3 1^4 1^5$ Richard Beck. Ida A. Martin.

2 John Anthony Beck. Sarah Azilu Carnis.

OK 3 Susie Beck. John W. Carnis.

$1^1 2^2 13^3 2^4 1^5$ Josephine Pettit. Henry Clay Ross.

---

2 Archibald Love. *

OK 3 Joseph Riley. *

$1^1 2^2 13^3 3^4 1^5$ Joanna Pettit. Thomas Dedymus Sanders and William Cooper.

2 Joseph Beck Pettit. Fannie Marsh.

OK 3 Robert Armstrong Pettit. Tennesee Hensley.

4 Amelia Pettit. Lorenzo Spears Lee.

5 Cynthia Pettit. John Shepherd Thornton * and John Lewis Miller.

6 Andrew Jackson Pettit. Ophelia Wickett.

$1^1 2^2 13^3 5^4 1^5$ Joseph Beck.

2 Jeffrey.

OK 3 Harlin Bede Beck.

4 Samuel Beck.

5 Releford D. Beck. Ida Wilson.

6 John Butler Beck.

7 Wetherford Beck.

8 Eula Beck. Jay Hendron.

9 Guy Beck.

$1^{1}2^{2}13^{3}8^{4}1^{5}$ John Beck.

$1^{1}2^{2}13^{3}9^{4}1^{5}$ Ada Chandler. William Heath, William Moore, Luculus Vann, Thomas Fox Foreman and Stephen Sears.

2 John Carson Chandler. Emma Malloy Paden nee Foreman.

OK 3 Samuel Wesley Chandler.

4 Eliza Chandler.

5 David Lorain Chandler.

8 Ella Gray Chandler.

7 Thomas Henry Chandler.

$1^{1}2^{2}13^{3}11^{4}1^{5}$ Ida Riley. John Beck.

---

2 Sarah Josephine Howerton.

OK 3 Weatherford Howton.

4 Olivia Howerton.

5 Sabra A. Howerton.

$1^{1}2^{2}14^{3}5^{4}1^{5}$ Rachel Downing. Thomas Potts and Henry Nugen.

2 Caroline Downing. Josiah Vann and Andrew Jackson Rogers.

3 Lucinda Downing. Sarah Neeley.

4 Elizabeth Downing. Harlan Nakedhead.

$1^{1}2^{2}15^{3}1^{4}1^{5}$ Charles Tickaneesky. Ruth Lee and Susie Easky.

2 Richard Tickeneesky. Susie Easky.

OK 3 Elizabeth Tickaneesky. Benjamin Vann.

4 Moses Tickaneesky. Catawnee and Still nee Walls.

5 Ellis Tickaneesky. Catherine Bolin.

6 Benjamin Tickaneesky. Nancy Hogshooter.

7 Linnie Tickaneesky. Johnson Reed, Aaron Crittenden and —— Woodruff.

8 RebeccaTickaneesky.John Smith and Bark Nugen.

9 John Tickaneesky. Margaret Chambers.

10 Ollie Tickaneesky. * Beanstick.

$1^{1}2^{2}16^{3}1^{4}1^{5}$ Pleasant Rogers.

2 Eliza Rogers. John Seabolt.

OK 3 Sarah Elizabeth Fields. James V. Hildebrand.

4 Rachel Jane Fields. William Stiff and Henry H. Hickey.

5 Ruth Fields. Jeremiah Bigelow.

6 Richard F. Fields. Rachel Elizabeth Goss and Minerva Kerr.

7 Margaret Wilson Fields. Robert Mosby French and Daniel Fields.

8 Josiah Foreman Fields. *

9 Caroline Matilda Rogers Fields. William Penn Boudinot.

$1^{1}2^{2}17^{3}1^{4}1^{5}$ Robert Woodall. Quatie Landrum.

2 Elizabeth Woodall. *

3 Margaret Woodall. Alexander Sanders, John Scott, Hampton Wiliams, Marshal Wagnon and William Brown.

4 Isaac Woodall. Mary Carselowry nee Daniel.
5 aJcob Houston Woodall. Annie Woodall nee Daniel.
6 Lucinda Woodall. James Downing and Thompson Buzzard.
7 Abraham Woodall. Susannah Hendricks.
8 Celia Woodall. Andrew Emory and Joseph Cephas.
9 Thomas Woodall. Annie Daniel.
$1^1 2^2 17^3 2^4 1^5$ Joshua Tadpole.
2 Eli Tadpole.
3 David Tadpole. Utiya Vann.
4 Susie Tadpole. * Osceola Woodall.
5 John Tadpole. Lucinda ———
$1^1 4^2 1^3 1^4 1^5$ Nannie Pettit. Franklin Faulkner.
2 Charles Pettit. Charlotte Sixkiller nee Adair, Sarah Lovett.
OK 3 Agnes Pettit. Patrick Lyman.
4 Delilah Pettit. William Lovett and John Griffin.
5 Thomas Pettit. Nannie E. Sanders, Sarah Swimmer nee Lee, Mary F. Walker, Caroline Timson and Nannie Sanders.
6 Benjamin Pettit. Mary Ann Phillips.
$1^1 4^2 1^3 2^4 1^5$ Moses Pettit. *
2 Delilah Pettit. *
OK 3 Sidney Pettit. Blackhaw Pettit.
4 Levi Pettit. *
5 Nannie Pettit.
$1^1 4^2 1^3 3^4 1^5$ William Zion Pettit. Emily Cookson.
2 Mary Pettit. James C. Fooy, ——Perry and Frank Bethel.
3 Catherine Pettit.
4 Marcus Pettit. *
5 Pleasant Pettit. *

6 Charles Pettit. * Elizabeth Krebs.
7 Samuel Worcester Pettit. Maria Choate.
8 Andrew Pettit. *
9 Ellen Pettit. John Hildebrand.
10 Julia Pettit. John Bean Johnson.
$1^1 4^2 1^3 5^4 1^5$ Charlotte Wofford. James McCracken.
2 Catherine Wofford. James Daniel.
OK 3 John Wofford. Eugenia Carpenter.
4 Robert Wofford. Jennie Bolen nee Wright.
$1^1 4^2 1^3 6^4 1^5$ Joshua Robbins. Nannie Parris and Alzerine Post.

2 Tatnall Holt Post. Mary Reese and Elizabeth Bell nee Phillips.
OK 3 Mary Arminda Post. Jackson Gladney.
4 John Marion Post. *
$1^1 4^2 1^3 7^4 1^5$ Sallie Humphrey. Robert Mitchell.
2 Catherine Humphrey. Bigwood and Charles Pettit.
OK 3 Joshua Humphrey. Catherine Bright and Rachel Thompson.

4 Mary Humphrey. Samuel Quinton and James Collins.
5 Eliza Humphrey. Edward Crittenden.
$1^1 4^2 2^3 1^4 1^5$ Sidney Crittenden. Elijah Phillips.
2 Jennie Crittenden. Amos Richardson.
OK 3 James Crittenden. Margaret Parris.
4 Thomas Crittenden. Nannie Woods.
5 Moses Crittenden. Edith Woods nee Quinton and Margaret Howell.
6 Sarah Crittenden. John Phillips and John Pierce.
7 George Washington. *
8 Lydia Crittenden. Joseph Quinton.

---

9 William Crittenden. Catherine Boydston.
10 Edward Crittenden. *
$1^1 4^2 2^3 2^4 1^5$ Andrew Crittenden.
2 Berry Crittenden.
$1^1 4^2 2^3 3^4 1^5$ Richard Crittenden.
$1^1 4^2 2^3 4^4 1^5$ Nellie Quinton. John Johnson and Joel Kelly.
2 Elizabeth Quinton. Thomas Woods and Moses Crittenden.
OK 3 Jennie Quinton. Levi Robbins.
$1^1 4^2 2^3 5^4 1^5$ Wellington Crittenden.
2 Israel Crittenden. Sallie Shirley, Clara Crittenden and Pamelia Capps.
$1^1 4^2 2^3 7^4 1^5$ Malinda Crittenden. ——— Brannon.
2 James Crittenden. Jennie Hanson.
3 Mary Crittenden. * William J. Sanders, Book Sunday and Silas Harlin.
4 Nannie Crittenden. John Tobacco.
5 Hettie Crittenden. Lewis Weaver.
6 Clement Crittenden. Maria Eve.
7 Delilah Crittenden. Charles Noblett and Henry N. Cook.
8 Hugh Crittenden. Amelia Wederbrock.
9 Thomas Crittenden. *

---

10 Lydia Crittenden. Ellis Harlin.
11 Charles Crittenden.
12 Jack Crittenden.
$1^1 4^2 2^3 8^4 1^5$ Martha Shirley. John Ryan and Nicholas Byers.
14291 Catherine McDaniel. John Price.

---

2 Adeline Glory. John Brock.
$1^1 4^2 2^3 10^4 1^5$ Sarah Glory. Bark Nugen.
$1^2 4^1 2^3 11^4 1^5$ Ephriam Vann. Rebecca Wilson.
2 Sallie Vann. John Towie and William Pigeon.
3 William Vann. *
4 Nellie Vann. William Pumpkin.
5 Elizabeth Vann. *

$1^{1}4^{2}2^{3}12^{4}1^{5}$ Ezekial Hair. Catherine Frenchhawk and Amanda Kanoska.

---

2 Margaret Butler. Alexander Vann and Charles Teehee.

$1^{1}4^{2}3^{3}1^{4}1^{5}$ Nannie Alberty. Bluford West and James Markham.

2 John D. Alberty. Jennie Rogers and Jennie Doroughty nee Buffington.

OK 3 Levi Alberty. Susie Love.

4 Delilah Alberty. Eli Harlan.

5 Amelia Alberty. Thomas Lewis Rider.

6 David Alberty.

7 William West Alberty. Musidora Rogers and Nannie Buffington.

8 Jacob Alberty. Louisa C. Hudson and Elvira Rachford nee Brown.

9 Bluford West Alberty. Nannie Cunningham nee Martin and Eliza Missouri Vann nee Bushyhead. *

$1^{1}4^{2}3^{3}2^{4}1^{5}$ Martha Snow. William Harnage.

2 Susan Buffington. Martin Root.

OK 3 Jennie Buffington. Charles Dougherty, John D. Alberty.

4 Ellis Buffington. Elizabeth Starr.

5 Clara Buffington. Ellis West and John Wright Alberty.

6 Elizabeth Buffington. Moses Alberty.

$1^{1}4^{2}3^{3}3^{4}1^{5}$ Moses Alberty. Elizabeth Buffington.

2 Frances Alberty. Dr. John Thornton and Joshua W. Ellis.

OK 3 John Wright. Clara West nee Buffington and Maria Hildebrand.

4 Cornelius Alberty. Elizabeth Tyner and Ruth Ann Thornton.

5 Elizabeth Alberty. Richard Eaton.

6 Jesse Clinton Alberty. Catherine Collins and Elmira Vann nee Ward.

$1^{1}4^{2}3^{3}4^{4}1^{5}$ John Phillips. Sarah Crittenden.

2 Jefferson Phillips. *

$1^{1}4^{2}3^{3}6^{4}1^{5}$ Catherine Clyne. * Archibald Dellingham, Eli Sanders and John Morgan.

2 John Peter Oliver Clyne. Jennie Adair.

OK 3 Ezekial Clyne. *

4 Wiliam R. P. Clyne. * Catherine Daniel nee Wofford.

5 Eli Clyne. Hannah Few.

6 Joel M. Bryan Clyne. *

7 Thomas Clyne. *

8 Elizabeth J. Clyne. William Mosley West.

9 Cornelius Clyne.

10 Eliza Clyne. George W. Alberty.

$1^{1}4^{2}3^{3}7^{4}1^{5}$ John Copeland Bryan. *

2 Charlotte Elmira Bryan. John Harvey Baugh.

OK 3 Nancy Jane Bryan. John Ross Buffington.

4 Maria Louisa Bryan. Riley Wise Lindsey.

5 Flora Elvina Bryan. Joseph H. Bennett.
6 Rebecca Caroline Bryan. Clement Hayden.
7 Joella Bryan. Columbus Fair Walker.
8 Joel Mayes Bryan. Lydia Ida Dougherty and Margaret Jane Ross.
$1^{1}4^{2}3^{3}8^{4}1^{5}$ John R. Wright. Charlotte Whitmire.
2 Jennie Wright. Lewis Bolin and Robert Wofford.
OK 3 Sallie Elizabeth Wright. Walter Adair West.
4 Cornelius Wright. *
5 Jesse Wright. Frances Wright and Sarah Finia Choate.
6 Anna Eliza Wright. John Gunter Harlin.
7 Alexander Wright. * Mary Lunnie Duncan.
8 Mary Wright. Eli H. Whitmire.
$1^{1}4^{2}3^{3}9^{4}1^{5}$ Sallie Daniel. * John Shepherd.
2 James W. Daniel. Catherine Wofford.
OK 3 Caroline Daniel. Smith Thornton.
4 Carter Daniel. Catherine Benge.
5 Elizabeth Jane Daniel. Charles Sanders.
6 William Daniel. Catherine Brown.
7 Nannie Catherine Daniel. Anderson Springston Wilson and Henry Clay Barnes.
8 Eliza Daniel. *
$1^{1}4^{2}3^{3}10^{4}1^{5}$ Martha J. Wright. James W. Alberty.
2 Nannie Wright. *
OK 3 Caleb Powell Wright. Ruth Ann Collins.
4 Thomas Bolin Wright.
5 Frances Wright. Jesse Wright.

—————

6 Oscar Wright. Nancy Ellen Boydston.

—————

7 Ellis Buffington Wright. Elizabeth Dougherty.
8 William Walter Wright.
$1^{1}4^{2}4^{3}1^{4}1^{5}$ Mary Frances Vann. Edwin Archer.
2 Clarinda Rebecca Vann. John Summers.

—————

OK 3 David Rowe Vann. * Eliza Missouri Bushyhead.
4 Louisa Jane Vann. Dr. Felix Hurd McNair.
5 Jennie Chinosa Vann. Eli West Dougherty.
6 Kiamitia Elizabeth Vann. * Jackson Walker Drake.
$1^{1}4^{2}4^{3}2^{4}1^{5}$ Susan Vann. Oliver Perry Ross.
2 Juliette Lewis Vann. * Devereux Jarrette Bell and Samuel McDaniel Taylor.

—————

OK 3 Clement Neeley Vann. Isadora V. Mackey.
4 Nicholas Byers Vann. *
5 David Lucullus Vann. *
6 Mary Delilah Vann. George Washington Drew and Joel

Bryan Mayes. *

7 Charles Avoy Vann. *

8 Joseph Lewis Vann. Caroline Elizabeth Sixkiller.

9 Martha Elizabeth Vann. Samuel Houston Mayes.

$1^{1}4^{2}4^{3}3^{4}1^{5}$ Jonathan Webber. Nannie Wofford.

$1^{1}4^{2}4^{3}4^{4}1^{5}$ Cynthia Vann. Leroy Starr.

2 William Vann. Louvenia Coster.

$1^{1}4^{2}4^{3}5^{4}1^{5}$ Martha Chambers. John Martin.

2 Calvin Chambers. Margaret Bryan.

OK 3 Catherine Chambers. John Lowrey McCoy and Henry Clay Barnes.

4 Sarah Chambers. Paul Chouteau and Lewis Ross Kell.

$1^{1}4^{2}4^{3}7^{4}1^{5}$ George Washington Lashey. Sarah Walker and Sarah Harlan.

2 Joseph Vann Lasley. Elizabeth Davis and Nannie Perlony Keys nee Harlan.

OK 3 Samuel Lasley. *

$1^{1}4^{2}4^{3}8^{4}1^{5}$ Elsie Webber. Andrew Jackson Griffin.

2 Aky Webber. *Thomas Foreman, Robin Ratliff and James Roach.

OK 3 Margaret Webber. Scott Tyler Cavillier and Edward Crutchfield.

4 Clement Vann Webber. *

5 Eliza Webber. Richard Fields Riley and William M. Hughes.

$1^{1}4^{2}4^{3}11^{4}1^{5}$ Margaret Lavinia Rogers. Allison Woodville Timberlake.

2 Clement Vann Rogers. Mary A. Scrimsher and Mary Bible.

OK 3 Francis Marion Musgrove. Clara Elizabeth Alberty.

4 William Due Musgrove. Cynthia Rogers.

$1^{1}4^{2}4^{3}12^{4}1^{5}$ Napoleon Bonaparte Rowe. Lethe Campbell.

2 Clarinda Vann Rowe. Daniel Webster Vann.

OK 3 David Lucullus Rowe. Eliza Scraper.

4 Margaret L. Rowe. *

5 Joseph Vann Rowe.

$1^{1}4^{2}4^{3}13^{4}1^{5}$ Arkansas Cherokee Martin. Hiram Terrell Landrum.

$1^{1}4^{2}5^{3}1^{4}1^{5}$ Nannie Buffington. William West Alberty, James Blake and William Lavesgue Wilder.

---

2 David Welch Ragsdale. Mary Jane Alberty and Ruth Raper nee Palone.

OK 3 Winnie Jane Ragsdale. Daniel P. Boone.

---

4 Eli Snow Alberty.

5 George Washington Alberty. Eliza Clyne and —Harmon nee

$1^{1}4^{2}5^{3}2^{4}1^{5}$ David Welch. Harriette Elizabeth Smithwick.

2 Lemuel Bruenton Welch. Mary Ann Harris.

OK 3 Sidney Welch. Prince Albert Carnes* and John Wilkey.

4 Diana Welch. Joseph Henry Carnes.

5 Margaret Ann Welch. William Green Ward.
6 George Welch. Nannie Jones.
7 Rosanna Welch. William McCoy.

Ghigau

Descendants of the Ghi-ga-u, commonly called Nancy Ward.

1^{1} Ghi-ga-u. Kingfisher and Bryan Ward. A22
$1^{1}2^{2}$ Catherine. Samuel Candy, John Walker, Ellis Harlan. A23
2 Fivekiller. * Catherine.

OK 3 Elizabeth Ward. Joseph Martin and ———Hughes.
$1^{1}1^{2}1^{3}$ Samuel Candy. Elizabeth West.

---

2 John Walker. Elizabeth Sevier nee Lowrey.
OK 3 Jennie Walker. Charles Fox, ———Taylor and John McIntosh. A53

---

4 Nannie Harlan. Caleb Starr.
5 Sallie Harlan. Jacob West.
6 Ruth Harlan. Joseph Phillips.
7 Elizabeth Harlan. Peter Hildebrand. A25
8 George Harlan. Nannie Sanders, Annie May,* Eliza Riley.*
9 Ezekial Harlan. Hannah Lewis.
10 Susannah Harlan. Otterlifter.
$1^{1}3^{2}1^{3}$ James Martin. *
2 Nannie Martin. Michael Hildebrand.

OK 3 Rachel Hughes. Charles Rogers.
$1^{1}1^{2}1^{3}1^{4}$ Ollie Candy. Hair Conrad.
2 Thomas Candy. Susan Graves, Catherine Gentry nee Drew.
OK 3 George Washington Candy. Elizabeth Hughes Bell and Elizabeth Webber nee Watie.
4 Samuel Candy. *
5 Nannie Candy. John Harlin and Henry Cobb.
6 John Walker Candy. Mary Watie and Electa W. Adams.
$1^{1}1^{2}2^{3}1^{4}$ John Walker. Emily Meigs and Nannie Bushyhead.
OK 2 Carter Walker. Sallie Brewer.
$1^{1}1^{2}3^{3}1^{4}$ Richard Taylor. Ellen McDaniel and Susie Fields.
2 Fox Taylor. Mary Vann and Lucy Otterlifter.
OK 3 Susan Taylor. Samuel Parks.

---

4 Nellie McIntosh. James McDaniel.
$1^{1}1^{2}4^{3}1^{4}$ Mary Pauline Starr. Austin Rider and James Woods.*
2 James Starr. Nelie Maugh and Susie Maugh.
OK 3 Thomas Starr. Nannie Wolf.
4 Ruth Starr. John Bean.
5 Ezekial Starr. Mary Upshaw.
6 Sallie Starr. Jesse Mayfield.

7 George Harlan Starr. Nellie Carr, Nannie Bell and Mary Taylor nee Blackburn.*

8 Joseph McMinn Starr. Delilah Adair.

9 Rachel Starr. * Samuel Lattamore.

10 Nannie Starr. * Samuel Lattamore.

11 Deborah Starr. Richard Newland, William Harvey Sloan.

12 Ellis Starr. * Delilah Johnson.

$1^11^25^31^4$ John West. Ruth Fields.

2 Bluford West. * Nannie Alberty.

3 Eliza West. Leroy Markham.

4 Rosa West. Nelson Rogers.

5 Ellis West. Clara Buffington.

6 George West. * Elizabeth Vann.

7 Ezekial West. *

$1^11^26^31^4$ Sallie Phillips. Robert Beatty.

2 Lucinda Phillips. Looney Price.

OK 3 Ruth Phillips. * Alexander Foreman.

4 John Philips. *

5 Joseph Phillips.

6 Ellis Fox Phillips. * Mary Foreman.

7 Elizabeth Phillips. Edmond Bean,* William Thornton, David Bell* and Tatnall Holt Post.*

8 Martha Phillips. *

$1^11^27^31^4$ Barbara Hildebrand. Hiram Linder.

2 James V. Hildebrand. Sarah Elizabeth Fields.

OK 3 Jennie Hildebrand. John Williams.

4 Catherine Hildebrand. Levi Bailey.

5 John Walker Hildebrand. Eliza Jane White.

6 Ellis Harlan Hildebrand. Sallie Stover and Josephine ——.

7 Lewis W. Hildebrand. Lucy Ratliff.

8 Isaac Newton Hildebrand. Jennie Ratliff.

9 Mary Elizabeth Hildebrand. Daniel Jones Frazier.

10 Minerva Hildebrand. Charles Ratliff, Anderson Reynolds.

$1^11^28^31^4$ Eli Harlan. Delilah Alberty.

2 Ellis Sanders Harlan. Nannie Barnett.

OK 3 Sallie Harlan. Jacob Harnage.

4 Elmira Harlan. Joshua Roach.

$1^11^29^31^4$ David M. Harlan. Lucinda Tucker, Rebecca Welch nee Vannoy and Julia Ann Lane nee Tucker.

2 Eliza Harlan. Samuel Craig.

OK 3 Susan Jane Harlan. James Perry.

$1^11^210^31^4$ Nannie Otterlifter. ———Haynes and David Miller.

2 Alexander Otterlifter. Elsie Sleepingrabbit.

OK 3 Jew Otterlifter.

4 Lucy Otterlifter. Fox Taylor.

5 Diana Otterlifter. Samuel Ballard.

6 Nellie Otterlifter. * Samuel Ballard.
7 Rachel Otterlifter. * Anderson Springston.
8 Elsie Otterlifter. Charles Hoskins, and Daniel Newton McIntosh.
$1^1 3^2 2^3 1^4$ Elizabeth Hildebrand. James Pettit and Robert Armstrong.
2 John Hildebrand. Nicey Russell and Annie Wasp.
OK 3 Jennie Hildebrand. Joseph Cookson.
4 Margaret Hildebrand. John Catron.
5 Delilah Hildebrand. Jesse McLain.
6 Eliza Hildebrand. Joshua Kirkpatrick.
7 Stehen Hildebrand. Mary Potts and Mary Beck.
8 Rachel Hildebrand. Reese T. Mitchell.
9 Nannie Hildebrand. Thomas Horn, George Lovett, Frederick Lovett, Charles Poe and ———Hoskins.
10 Joseph Martin Hildebrand. Lucy Starr, Louvenia Patterson, Elizabeth Gentry, Mary King, Martha Wofford and Mary E. Coyne.
11 Brice Hildebrand. Mary Sturdivant nee Beck and Mary Swimmer.
12 Mary Hildebrand. Isaac Mayfield.
$1^1 3^2 3^3 1^4$ Levi Rogers. Margaret Fields.
2 Richard Rogers. * Eliza Lacey.
OK 3 Joseph Rogers. *
4 Charles Rogers. Maria Colston.
5 John Rogers. *
6 Elizabeth Rogers. George Whitney Brand.
7 Alzira Rogers. Lewis Fields.
8 Catherine Rogers. * William Elders.
$1^1 1^2 1^3 1^4 1^5$ Elizabeth Hair. Daniel Hopkins.
2 Susie Hair. Charles Gourd.
OK 3 Jefferson Hair. Chicooie O'Fields, Eliza Ramsey nee Tyner and Mary Tyner nee Sanders.
4 Diana Hair. Wade Hampton Robinson.
5 John Hair. Lucy Robinson, Annie Sanders, Mary Butler and Lucy Justice.
6 Nannie Hair. *
7 Mary Hair. John Ramsey.
$1^1 1^2 1^3 2^4 1^5$ Jackson Candy.
2 Henry Candy. * Nellie Goings.
OK 3 Reese Candy. Ruth Riley, Jennie Downing* and
4 Thomas Candy. *
5 Elizabeth Candy. David Ballew and Ned Grease.
6 Samuel Candy. Mary Hayden.

---

7 John Candy. Mary Starr and Eliza Fields.
$1^1 1^2 1^3 3^4 1^5$ John Candy. *
2 Maria Candy. *

OK 3 Worcester Candy. *

4 Charlotte Candy. William Fields.

5 Martha Candy. * Joel Bryan Mayes.

6 Juliette Melvina Candy. John Gunter Scrimsher.

$1^11^21^35^41^5$ Ruth Harlin. Robert Turnbull.

2 James Harlin.

OK 3 Candy Harlin. *

4 John T. Harlin.

5 Aenaes Harlin. *

6 Robert Harlin. *

7 Elizabeth Harlin. Joseph T. Medley and William England.

8 Salina Harlin. * ——Beckham.

9 Mary Harlin. * James Giddings.

10 Samuel Harlin. *

$1^11^21^36^41^5$ Harriette Candy. Hugh Montgomery McPherson.

2 Susan Candy. * Henry Lee Hill.

OK 3 Elizabeth Candy. * Hindman Booth Hoyt.

$1^11^22^31^41^5$ Timothy Meigs Walker. Elizabeth Adair.

2 Elizabeth Grace Walker. James Coleman and Pryor Smith.

OK 3 Minerva Jane Walker. James Armstrong Lee and Lorenzo Delano.

4 John Osborn Walker. Lucretia Taylor and Georgianna Wilkins. *

---

6 Ebenezer Walker. Sarah Lasley nee Harlan.

5 Sarah E. Walker. George Washington Lashey.

$1^11^22^32^41^5$ Eliza Walker. * John Adair and James Rogers.

2 John Walker. *

OK 3 Jennie Walker. William Boot.

4 George Washington. Elsie Downing, Rachel Rogers and Mary Jane Davis nee Harlow.

5 Joseph Walker. *

6 Elizabeth Walker. * Joseph Smith.

7 Susie Walker. * John P. Stidham and Henry Sanders.

8 Amanda Walker. James Martin.

9 William Walker. *

$1^11^23^31^41^5$ Thomas Fox Taylor. Nannie Buffington and Mary Blackburn. *

2 Elizabeth Taylor. John Brewer.

OK 3 Samuel McDaniel Taylor. Almira Williams, Martha Fields and Juliette Lewis Bell nee Vann.

---

4 Annie Taylor. Robert Buffington Daniel.

5 Mary Jane Taylor. Dr. Jeter Lynch Thompson.

6 Eliza Christine Taylor. Johnson Thompson.

7 Frances Harvey Taylor. James Leonidas Butler.

8 Lucinda Taylor. John Osborn Walker.

$1^1 1^2 3^3 2^4 1^5$ James Taylor. Sallie Reese.
2 Richard Taylor. *
OK 3 Jennie Taylor. Thomas Jefferson Pack.
4 Nannie Taylor. Levi Timberlake.
5 Susie Taylor. * Charles Thompson.
6 William Taylor. Elizabeth Grimmett and Margaret Halfbreed.

7 Margaret Taylor. *
8 Nellie Taylor. *
9 Charles Taylor. *
10 Nannie Taylor. John Martin and John White.
$1^1 1^2 3^3 3^4 1^5$ Ruth Parks. Dickson Price.
2 Almira Parks. * James Price.
OK 3 Jennie Parks. *John Langley and Joseph Collier.
4 George Washington Parks. Louisa Spriggs.
5 Thomas Jefferson Parks. Mary Ann Thompson.
6 Richard Taylor Parks. Sarah Elizabeth Day and Sarah Elizabeth Grigsby.
7 Calvin Parks. Almira Wilson and Arie Hildebrand.
8 William Parks. *
9 Mary Ann Parks. William Conway Day.
10 Robert Calhoun Parks. Clara Rider.
11 John Ross Parks. *
12 Samuel Parks. * Sarah G. Taylor.
$1^1 1^2 3^3 4^4 1^5$ John McDaniel. *
2 Catherine McDaniel. Lewis Keys.
OK 3 Margaret Ann McDaniel. Bluford West Starr and William Pettit.
4 Samuel McDaniel. *
$1^1 1^2 4^3 1^4 1^5$ Thomas Lewis Rider. Amelia Alberty.
2 Nannie Rider. David Thompson.
OK 3 Elizabeth Rider. John M. Smith.
4 Caleb Starr Rider. Elsie Price.
5 John Rider. Rachel Smith.
6 Ezekial Rider. *
7 Bluford West Rider. *
8 William Rider. *
9 Ellis Rider. *
10 Charles Austin Augustus Rider. Mary Ann Bigby and Sarah Jane Forrest nee Nix.
11 Laura Narcissa Rider. King Fulsom, Byron Boynton and Charles Pritchard.
$1^1 1^2 4^3 2^4 1^5$ Joseph Starr. Nannie Reese and Rachel Guess.
OK 3 Fields Starr. Mary Reese.
4 Washington Starr. Mary Ann McCoy.
8 Samuel Starr. * Laura Davis. --
10 Mary Starr. Andrew Digiesky.

11 Leroy Starr. *
12 Rachel Starr. John Walker Starr.
14 Jennie Starr. John Francis Marion Christie.
16 Caleb Starr. *
18 Lucy Starr. George Washington Adair and William Russell.
19 Sallie Starr. Ephriam Martin Adair.

---

2 Thomas Starr. Catherine Reese.
5 Bean Starr. *
6 James Starr. Araminta Rider nee McCoy, Akie Nelowie and Elmira Starr nee Fields.
7 William Starr. Nannie McPherson.
9 Ellis Starr. * Catherine Justice.
13 John Starr. *
15 Ezekial Starr. * Amanda Terrell, Caroline Smith and Elizabeth Lee nee Smith.
17 Pauline Starr. Charles Bushyhead,* Richard Drew and Samuel Campbell.

---

20 Nannie Starr. Buck Girty and Jug Davis.
$1^11^24^33^41^5$ James Starr. Lettie Boyd Chambers.
2 Ellis Harlan.
OK 3 Richard Taylor Starr. *
4 Nancy Jane Starr. Joseph Chambers.
5 Bluford West Starr. Margaret Ann McDaniel.
$1^11^24^34^41^5$ Margaret Bean. John Gott.
2 Elizabeth Bean. Risden Johnson.
OK 3 Caleb Starr Bean. Mary Ann Thompson.
4 Nannie Bean.
5 Mary Bean. Edward Johnson.
6 Rachel Alzira Bean. Josiah Matthis*.
7 Joseph McMinn Bean. Sarah Finley.
8 Susie Deborah Bean. James Warren Adair.
9 Sarah Emily Bean. Benjamin Franklin Goss.
10 Lucinda Bean. John Harrison Paden.
11 John Ellis Bean. Henrietta Danenburg.
12 Mark Bean. Victoria Texas Wright.
$1^11^24^35^41^6$ Ruth Starr. John Griffith Harnage.
2 Caleb Starr. Lucinda Griffin.
OK 3 Elizabeth Starr. Ellis Buffington.
4 Leroy Starr. Cynthia Vann.
5 Sarah Starr. John Wilson Mayfield.
6 Nannie Starr. * John Ragsdale.
7 Ellis Starr. Susie Dougherty.
8 John Walker Starr. Rachel Starr and Elmira Fields.
9 James Starr. Sarah Byers, Emma Jane Evans nee Rider.

10 Ezekial Starr. Nannie Catherine Harkins nee Seabolt.

11 Mary Jane Starr. * James Johnson.

$1^1 1^2 4^3 6^4 1^5$ Nannie Mayfield. George Harnage.

2 Penelope Mayfield. John Thompson Adair.

OK 3 John Wilson Mayfield. Sarah Starr and Mary Ann Stovall.*

4 Emily Walker Mayfield. John Griffith Harnage.

5 Carter Walker Mayfield. Jennie Blackburn.

6 Elvira Mayfield. Newton Howell and William Henry Barker.

7 Sabina Mayfield. Dr. George Wyche.

8 Victoria Hulda Mayfield. Thomas Henry Still and Robert Gilmore.

$1^1 1^2 4^3 7^4 1^5$ Jennie Starr. George Howard.

---

2 John Walker Starr. *

OK 3 Mary Frances Starr. Lucien Burr Bell.

4 George Colbert Starr. *

5 Ezakial Eugene Starr. Margaret Starr.

6 Joseph Jarrette Starr. *

7 Caleb Ellis Starr. Malderine Elizabeth Adair and Jennie Butler nee.

8 Samuel Jesse Starr. Sarah Ruth McClure.

$1^1 1^2 4^3 8^4 1^5$ Nancy Ann Starr. William Wirt Duncan and Young Charles Gordon Duncan.

2 George Harlan Starr. *

OK 3 Martha Jane Starr. George Washington Crittenden.

4 Joseph McMinn Starr. Sarah Crittenden and Susie Shell.

5 Walter Adair Starr. Ruth Ann Alberty nee Thornton, Ella Elizabeth Christie and Saphronia F. Barrett nee Crutchfield.*

6 Sallie Elizabeth Starr. Frank Howard.

7 Edward Bruce Starr. Rachel Pauline Henry.

9 Caleb Wilson Starr.

$1^1 1^2 4^3 11^4 1^5$ James Newland.

2 Nannie Newland. Nathan Merrell.

OK 3 William Henry Sloan. Nannie Lane and Martha Jones.

4 Samuel Harker Sloan.

5 Edward Estel Sloan. Naomi Ann Cole.

6 John Willis Sloan.

$1^1 1^2 5^3 1^4 1^5$ William Mosley West. Elizabeth J. Clyne.

2 George R. West. *

OK 3 Martha S. West. * Jackson Cozens.

4 John Calhoun West. Margaret Elizabeth Hickey.

5 Kiamitia West. Allen Gilbert.

6 James Polk West. Missouri Barnett.

7 Ruth E. West. Richard Brewer and William Walter Finley.

8 Franklin Pierce West. Nannie Ellis Allen nee Brewer.

$1^1 1^2 5^3 3^4 1^5$ Jacob West Markham. Charlotte Belle West.

2 Carter Daniel Markham. Mary F. Hufaker and Eliza Matthews nee Adair.

OK 3 James B. Markham. Beatrice Alberty.

4 John West Markham. Martha C. Riley, Sallie Jane Daniel.

5 Ruth A. Markham. Dr. Walter Thompson Adair.

$1^1 1^2 5^3 4^4 1^5$ Lewis Rogers. Josephine Landrum, Helen Ross and.

2 Sarah Rogers. David Vaught, William Wilkerson, Albert Campbell and J. J. Griggs.

3 Louisa Rogers. Virgil Rogers and Alexander McDaniel.

$1^1 1^2 5^3 5^4 1^5$ Charlotte Belle West. Jacob West Markham and William Lavesque Wilder.

$1^1 1^2 6^3 1^4 1^5$ William Crawford Beatty. Emeline Parris.

$1^1 1^2 6^3 2^4 1^5$ Joseph Price.

CHEROKEE INSANE ASYLUM

$1^1 1^2 6^3 7^4 1^5$ Ruth Ann Alberty. Cornelius Alberty and Walter Adair Starr.

$1^1 1^2 7^3 1^4 1^5$ Nancy Eveline Linder. George Elders, William Green and Daniel Ross Hicks.

2 Malderine Elizabeth Linder. George Washington Adair.

OK 3 Emory Ogden Linder. Martha Ann Vann.

4 John Ross Linder. Eliza Keziah Pennel.

5 Ann Eliza Linder *Pickens M. Benge, William H. Hendricks

6 Cinderella Linder. * Robert McDaniel.

7 Julius Caesar Linder. * Emma Hildebrand.

$1^1 1^2 7^3 2^4 1^5$ James V. Hildebrand. Adelaide Taylor.

2 Elizabeth Hildebrand. * Johnson O'Fields.

OK 3 Jamima Hildebrand. * Matthew Thompson.

4 Martha Hildebrand. James Smart.

5 Ann Eliza Hildebrand. Hugh Miller Howdershell.

$1^1 1^2 7^3 3^4 1^5$ James Franklin Williams. Mary Jane England.

2 Paralee Williams. John F. Thomas.

OK 3 Johnanna Williams. Jesse Adam Thomas.

$1^1 1^2 7^3 4^4 1^5$ Jennie Bailey. ———Jackson.

2 Savilla Bailey. Yellowbird.

OK 3 Elan Bailey. Johnson O'Fields.

4 Mary Bailey. *

---

5 Louisa Cunnigan. John Charley and George Frederick Private.

$1^1 1^2 7^3 5^4 1^5$ Mary White Hildebrand. Joshua Columbus Hannah.

2 Amelia Eglantine Hildebrand.

OK 3 Eliza Jane Hildebrand. *

4 Emily Cherokee Hildebrand. James Layton Webb.

5 Lawrence William Hildebrand. Eglentine Orr.

6 John Walker Hildebrand. *

$1^1 1^2 7^3 6^4 1^5$ Ellis Hildebrand.

$1^1 1^2 7^3 7^4 1^5$ Annie Hildebrand. William Sweetwater.

2 Ermina Hildebrand. ———Talbert.

OK 3 James H. Hildebrand. Ida Youngbird nee Tunooie.

---

4 Albert Hildebrand. *

5 Charles Hildebrand. *

$1^1 1^2 7^3 8^4 1^5$ John F. Hildebrand. *

2 Sarah Jane Hildebrand. *

OK 3 Emma Hildebrand. * Julius Caesar Linder.

4 Newton Hildebrand. *

5 Lewis W. Hildebrand. *

6 Ida Jane Hildebrand. *

7 Peter Hildebrand. *

$1^1 1^2 7^3 9^4 1^5$ Serena Frazier. * Alfred Pigeon.

2 Rebecca Frazier. *

OK 3 Frances E. Frazier. *

4 Ebenezer Frazier. *

5 Daniel Jones Frazier. Elizabeth Hood.

6 John Frazier. Elizabeth Crapoe nee Boggs.

$1^1 1^2 7^3 10^4 1^5$ Lucy Ratliff. John Nixon Davis.

---

2 John Reynolds. Sallie Pennel.

OK 3 Henry Bowers. *

$1^1 1^2 8^3 1^4 1^5$ George Harlan. Mary McCoy.

2 Sarah Harlan. George Washington Lasley, Ebenezer Walker and Joseph Tackett.

OK 3 Mitchell Harlan. Letitia Victoria Keys.

4 Ezekial Harlan. Rachel Sands.
5 Nancy Perlony Harlan. Riley J. Keys, Joseph Vann Lasley and Joseph Robins.
6 Jennie Harlan. Charles Coody Rogers and Granville Torbett.
$1^1 1^2 8^3 2^4 1^5$ James Ellis Harlan. Margaret Reed and Nancy Ann Gibson nee.
2 Sallie Matilla Harlan. John Poole, George Lane, Lewis Ross Kell, James Chastine Blythe and Charles Chandler.
OK 3 Mary Josephine Harlan. Mitchell Sanders.
4 John Brown Harlan. Mary Ann McGhee.
5 Ruth Jane Harlan. William Writtenberry and Joseph Henry Hunt.
6 Timothy Dwight Harlan. *
7 Emily D. Harlan. George Finley.
$1^1 1^2 8^3 3^4 1^5$ George Harlan Harnage. *
$1^1 1^2 8^3 4^4 1^5$ Emily Roach. Edward Walls and Aaron Crittenden.
2 William Roach. Nannie Lowrey and Eliza Lowrey.
OK 3 Nannie Roach. Lafayette Catron and John Horn.
4 James Roach. *
5 Mary Roach. *
6 George Roach. Nannie Pritchett and Sarah Triplett.
7 John Roach. Nellie Grant.
8 Sarah Roach. Looney Townsend and William Sullivan.
9 Joshua Roach. *
$1^1 1^2 9^3 1^4 1^5$ Jennie Harlan. Garrett Lane and John Blythe.
2 John Harlan. *
OK 3 Napoleon Harlan. Sarah Evaline Blythe.
4 Lucinda Harlan. Thomas Archer and Albert Willard.
5 David Lewis Harlan. Harriette Shoe and Nessie Ann Hardin.
6 Albert Weir Harlan. Sarah Ballard and Matilda Kirby.
7 Lafayette Harlan. Margaret Davis.
8 Murion Harlan. Belle Cue.

---

9 George Washington Harlan. Sarah Jane Cecil.
10 Eliza Harlan. Thomas Cannon and Henry Hardin Trott.
11 Andrew Oliver Harlan. Cora Pearl Richards.
$1^1 1^2 9^3 2^4 1^5$ John Craig. Mary Underwood.
2 Adeline Craig. Henry Clay McDonald and James Bivins.
OK 3 Penelope Craig. Logan Henderson Duncan.
4 William Craig. *
5 Granville Craig. Jennie Means.
6 Louisa Jane Craig. Huff D. Coats.
7 Frank Wallace Craig. Catherine Tetrick.
$1^1 1^2 9^3 3^4 1^5$ Rodolph Leslie Perry. *
2 Hannah Almeda Perry. William B. James.
OK 3 Oliver Valdi Perry. Stacy Eliza Burson.

4 Silas Aepecides Perry. Jennie Albright and Fannie D. Fox nee Cole.

5 Florence Caroline Perry. Leander Bell Smith.

6 Texanna Cherokee Perry. * Samuel M. Ramsey.

7 Ezekial Harlan Perry. Susan Melvina Harvey nee Morrow.

8 Nathan Murion Perry. Fannie Sellers.

9 Sion Marcellus Perry. Lydia Augusta Lumpkin.

$1^{1}1^{2}10^{3}1^{4}1^{5}$ Ezekial Miller. Minerva Cherokee Ward.

OK 2 Andrew Miller. *

$1^{1}1^{2}10^{3}2^{4}1^{5}$ Nannie Otterlifter. George Washington Ross.

2 Elizabeth Otterlifter.

OK 3 Washburn Otterlifter.

$1^{1}1^{2}10^{3}4^{4}1^{5}$ Margaret Taylor. *

2 Nellie Taylor. *

OK 3 Charles Taylor. *

4 Nannie Taylor. John Martin and John White.

$1^{1}1^{2}10^{3}5^{4}1^{5}$ Mary McDaniel. * George Drumgoole.

---

2 Archibald Ballard. Annie Fields.

OK 3 John Ballard. Susie Arthur.

4 Jennie Ballard. Charles Lowrey.

5 Susie Ballard. William Penn Henderson and Hiram Storm.

$1^{1}1^{2}10^{3}8^{4}1^{5}$ Annie Hoskins. Daniel Landrum.

2 Julia Hoskins. James McGhee.

---

3 Orsinoe McIntosh. * Jackson Smith.

$1^{1}3^{2}2^{3}1^{4}1^{5}$ Andrew Pettit. Arie Beck.

2 Minerva Pettit. John Anderson, Lewis Hicks, John Journey, Israel J. Ward, Jesse Russell and Alfred Clark Raymond.

OK 3 William Pettit. Margaret Anne Starr nee McDaniel,* Nannie Tyner and Emma Johnson.

4 Frank Pettit. Nellie Smith and Mary Beck.

---

5 Amelia Ward. William Percival and William Livingston Harris.

$1^{1}3^{2}2^{3}2^{4}1^{5}$ Stephen Hildebrand. Mary Beck, Amanda Hildebrand nee Hair and Jennie Mesenheimer.

---

2 Margaret Hildebrand. *

OK 3 Michael Hildebrand. Sarah Hooks.

4 Chiouke Hildebrand. *

$1^{1}3^{2}2^{3}3^{4}1^{5}$ John Hildebrand Cookson. Elizabeth Adair, Nellie Lyman and Matilda Lawly.

2 Emily Cookson. William Zion Pettit.

OK 3 Elizabeth Cookson. * George Wiggins.

$1^1 3^2 2^3 4^4 1^5$ Caroline Catron. Jesse Sanders.

2 Lafayette Catron. Nannie Roach.

OK 3 Levannah Elizabeth Catron. Thomas Holmes Carlile and Levi Rogers Keys.

$1^1 3^2 2^3 5^4 1^5$ Elvira Jane McLain. *Alexander Thompson and William Hayes.

2 Calvin McLain. Charlotte Martin.

OK 3 Austin McLain. * Melissa Arminda Cordery.

4 Mary Ann McLain. Jefferson Ratliff.

5 Nancy Elmira McLain. Joseph Watkins and James Thomas Morrow.

6 John McLain. Mary Martin and Susannah Moore.

7 Joseph McLain. Martha Scott, Elizabeth Kerr nee Clyne and Lonnie Nelson.

8 Lewis McLain. * Susie Woods.

9 William McLain. Elizabeth Chambers and Elizabeth Horn.

10. Mary Emeline McLain. Francis Marion Scott.

$1^1 3^2 2^3 6^4 1^5$ William Patrick. Elizabeth Fields and Emma A. Beck nee Hayes.

2 Rachel Patrick. Alexander Ballard and Houston De Armond.

OK 3 Nancy Jane Patrick. Noah Lillard and James R. Gourd.

4 Margaret Patrick. Henry Fry, Louis Diena and Henry Morris.

5 John Joshua Patick. Minerva Elizabeth Lillard and Elmira Starr nee Fields.

6 Elias Patrick. *

7 Mary Patrick. John P. Lyman and Calloway Burke.

8 George Washington Patrick. Polina Jane Keys, Nannie C. Langley and Nannie Jenkins.

9 Lucy Patrick. Joseph Heinrichs.

10 Michael K. Patrick. Delilah Cookson and Josephine Hawkins.

$1^1 3^2 2^3 7^4 1^5$ Jennie Hildebrand. William Lucas.

---

2 Julia Ann Hildebrand. Surry Eaton Beck, Nathaniel Wofford, James Barnett and Jasper Bee.

OK 3 Susan Hildebrand. George Washington Mitchell.

$1^1 3^2 2^3 8^4 1^5$ Nannie Mtichell. Charles H. Allen.

2 Jennie Mitchell. *

OK 3 Rebecca Mitchell. Ezekial Proctor.

4 Henry Mitchell. * Cynthia Beck.

5 Louvisa Mitchell. Daniel Anderson, John Lane and Samuel Rounds.

6 Mitchell Hildebrand Mitchell. Margaret Underwood.

7 John Mitchell. Jennie Norris nee Rennecker.

8 William Mitchell. Elizabeth Newton.

9 Franklin Pierce Mitchell. Elizabeth Thompson and Georgia Ann Newton.

10 Eliza Mitchell. George Washington Talbert.

11 Reese T. Mitchell. Nannie Acorn.

$1^{1}3^{2}2^{3}9^{4}1^{5}$ James Lovett. Annie Quinton and Annie Griffin.

2 Annie Lovett. * Houston De Armond.

OK 3 David Lovett. Belle McCutchan.

4 John Lovett. Elizabeth Young nee Tetrincha.

5 Louisa Amanda Lovett. * Houston DeArmond.

---

6 William Irving. Henrietta Oakley nee Fry.

7 Joseph Irving. Minnie Louisa See and Henriette Ann Marlowe.

---

8 Brice Poe. *

$1^{1}3^{2}2^{3}10^{4}1^{5}$ Michael Hildebrand. Amanda Hair.

OK 2 Elizabeth Hildebrand. ——Hurd.

OK 3 Reese Hildebrand. *

4 Josephine Hildebrand. John Meeker.

5 Alice Hildebrand. Charles Antoine Schmidtman and Andrew Cornelius Cordery.

---

6 Effie Hildebrand. William W. Nelson.

$1^{1}3^{2}2^{3}11^{4}1^{5}$ Reese Hildebrand. Lydia Latta.

2 Elizabeth Hildebrand. Thomas Beaver, William Cramp, Andrew Crane and Samuel Campbell.

$1^{1}3^{2}2^{3}12^{4}1^{5}$ Nannie Elizabeth Mayfield. Thomas L. Gaston.

2 Michael Mayfield. Elizabeth Sanders and Ellen Hammonds.

OK 3 Susan Jane Mayfield. Isaac Allison Milligan and Samuel Lee Milligan.

4 John Ross Mayfield. Annie McDaniel and Nellie Phillips.

5 Lillar Mayfield. William Rufus James, John Smith and Robert B. Williams.

6 Joseph Mayfield. Helen Dobson and

7 Isaac H. Mayfield. Sarah McNabney.

8 Rogina Mayfield. Cornelius Willis.

$1^{1}3^{2}3^{3}1^{4}1^{5}$ James Rogers. Mary Sanders.

$1^{1}3^{2}3^{3}4^{4}1^{5}$ Charles Rogers. * Susie Foreman.

OK 2 Elmira Rogers. Timothy Fields.

$1^{1}3^{2}3^{3}6^{4}1^{5}$ Elizabeth Brand. Theodore Cummings and Solomon Bragg.

2 Francis Rogers. William Elders.

OK 3 John Rogers. Missouri Emma Quinton.

4 Cynthia Ann Rogers. *

---

5 Margaret Brown. *

$1^{1}3^{2}3^{3}7^{4}1^{5}$ Elizabeth Fields. William Patrick.

CHAPTER XVI

Continuation of Old Families.

Foreman.

The descendants of Anthony Foreman, a Scotchman who married two full blood Cherokee wives.

1^{1} Anthony Foreman. Susie and Elizabeth. A26

$1^{1}1^{2}$ John Foreman. Nannie Drumgoole nee Doublehead and Ruth Springston.

2 Catherine Foreman. James Bigby.

OK 3 Thomas Foreman. Susannah Brewer nee Fields.

4 Nannie Foreman. Bushyhead.

5 Sallie Foreman. William Hicks.

6 Richard Bark Foreman. ——— and Rachel Seabolt.

———

7 Archibald Foreman. Aky Brewer and Theresa Kerr. A27

8 Elsie Foreman. James Spears.

9 Stephen Foreman. Sallie W. Riley and Ruth Candy nee Riley.

10 Edward Foreman. Minerva Kerr.

11 Mary Foreman. Thomas Barnes.

12 Alexander Foreman. Ruth Phillips * and Sarah Fields.

$1^{1}1^{2}1^{3}$ Richard Foreman. Sallie —— and Dorcas Rattlinggourd.

———

2 John Foreman. Lucretia ——— and Ya-ki-ny.

———

OK 3 James Foreman. Delialh Fields.

4 Elizabeth Foreman. Edley Springton.

———

5 Elizabeth Foreman. John Elliott.

———

6 Johnson Foreman. Elizabeth B. Mann.

$1^{1}2^{2}1^{3}$ Mary Ann Bigby. David Taylor. A28

2 Jennie Bigby. Andrew Taylor.

OK 3 Thomas Wilson Bigby. Margaret Catherine Adair.

4 James Bigby. * Louisa Levi.

5 Elizabeth Bigby. Moses Fields.

6 Wiley Bibgy. Mary McLaughlin and Elnora Nicholson.

7 Sallie Bigby. Leonard Bonaparte Williams.

8 Jackson Bigby. *

9 Susie Bigby. Felix Riley.

10 Malinda Bigby. William Guilliams and Jesse Redman.

$1^{1}3^{2}1^{3}$ Nannie Foreman. Allen Gafford and Martin North.

———

2 Samuel Foreman. Sallie Rattlinggourd.

OK 3 Nellie Foreman. Adam Bibles.

4 Charles Foreman. Annie Seabolt and Thirsey Colvin.

5 William Hicks Foreman. * Mary Sweetwater.

6 Joseph Anthony Foreman. Narcissa Reaves Carey and Lethe Parris.

7 Sallie Foreman. *

8 David McNair Foreman. Sarah Sweetwater, Agnes Foreman Sweetwater and Mary Foreman nee Sweetwater.

9 George Foreman. Elizabeth Fields and Elizabeth Fields.

10 Thomas Foreman. Elizabeth Chicken.

11 Susan Foreman. Samuel Jones and Walter Stopp.

12 James Foreman. *

13 Edward Foreman. Mary Proctor, Sarah Proctor and Jennie Spaniard nee Terrapin.

14 Elizabeth Foreman. Johnson Proctor and Redbird Sixkiller.

$1^{1}4^{2}1^{3}$ Jesse Bushyhead. Eliza Wilkerson.

2 Isaac Bushyhead. Catherine Ratliff and Ghi-ga-u Snake.

OK 3 George Bushyhead. Go-wo-hi-du.

4 Nannie Bushyhead. John Walker and Lewis Hildebrand.

5 Susan C. Bushyhead. Ezekial Lyons and L. P. Harris.

6 Jacob Bushyhead. Nannie McDaniel and Elizabeth Romine nee Riley.

7 Charles Bushyhead. Polly Starr and Sallie Miller nee McCoy.

$1^{1}5^{2}1^{3}$ Eli Hicks. Isabel Miller.

2 Jay Hicks. Catherine Levi.

3 Ruth Hicks. Ezekial Beck and William Rogers.

4 William Hicks. *

5 Carrington Hicks. *

6 Margaret Hicks. Jacob Nicholson.

7 Ella Hicks. Joseph Spears.

8 Abijah Hicks. Hannah Worcester.

9 Anna Hicks. Charles French.

10 Charles Hicks. *

11 John Hicks. *

12 Sarah Hicks. Spencer Seago Stephens.

13 Nannie Hicks. Sebastian Boynton and William A. Reese.

$1^{1}6^{2}1^{3}$ Jennie Foreman. Celle Robbards and Henry Glenn.

---

2 Annie Laura Foreman. Lord Wellington Shirley.

OK 3 Archibald Foreman. Sarah Walkingwolf.

4 Anthony Foreman. *

5 Susan Louella Foreman. David Sanders, John Horn and John Clark Cleveland.

6 Daniel C. Foreman. Elizabeth Beck.

7 Stephen Foreman. Christine Hogeland nee Sands.

8 Catherine Foreman. William McCreary and Aaron Headin Beck.

9 Robert Foreman. *

10 Martha Foreman. * James Allison.

$1^{1}7^{2}1^{3}$ Mary Foreman. Ellis Fox Phillips and William C. Dickson.

2 Minerva Foreman. Amos Thornton and Wallace Vann.

OK 3 Archibald Foreman. *

$1^{1}8^{2}1^{3}$ Nannie Spears. *

2 Eli Spears. Elizabeth Hall.

OK 3 John Spears. Annie Welch.

4 Elizabeth Spears. Charles Dobbins.

5 Mary Ann Spears. William Coody Ross.

6 Elmira Spears. Stephen David.

7 Stephen Spears. Maria Louisa Roberson.

8 Archibald Spears.

---

9 Charles Spears. Mary J. Crockett.

$1^{1}9^{2}1^{3}$ Austin Worcester Foreman. *

2 Ermina Nash Foreman. *

OK 3 Jeremiah Everett Foreman. Celeste Stidham.

4 Susie Elizabeth Foreman. *

5 John Anthony Foreman. Eliza Mary Blythe and Nannie Amanda Smith.

6 Stephen Taylor Foreman. Ada Carter McClellan.

7 Jennie Lind Foreman. Charles McClure McClellan.

8 Archibald Alexander Foreman. * Annie Rucks.

9 Austin Worcester Foreman. Emily Josephine Ridenhour and Margaret Edith George.

---

10 Charles Hodge Foreman. *

11 Flora Elizabeth Foreman. Austin J. Rider.

12 Araminta Ross Foreman.

$1^{1}11^{2}1^{3}$ John Albert Barnes. *

2 Rachel Barnes. Jenkins Whiteside Maxfield.

3 Alexander Foreman Barnes. *

4 Corinne Abigal Barnes. John Nathaniel Taylor.

5 Theresa Elizabeth Barnes. Thomas Ivey.

6 Henry Clay Barnes. Catherine Chambers, Nannie Catherine Wilson nee Daniel and Mary Cornelia Nowlin.

7 Sarah Barnes. * Stephen Hart.

8 Minnie Barnes. Charles Edward Willey.

9 Fannie Barnes. George Washington Benge.

$1^{1}12^{2}1^{8}$ Pierce Butler Foreman. *

2 Edward Foreman. Cherokee Brown and Emma Barnes.

OK 3 George Bullette Foreman. Nannie Elizabeth Garrison.

4 Josephus W. Foreman. *

5 Thomsia Elizabeth Foreman. * Thomas W. Collins.

6 Ermina Cooie Foreman. Robert Preston Vann.

Sequoyah.

1^1 Sequoyah. Sallie and U-ti-yu.

$1^1 1^2$ Teesey Guess. U-ti-yu and Rebecca Bowles. A29

2 George Guess. *

OK 3 Polly Guess. Flying and Thomas Brewer.

4 Richard Guess. *

---

5 E-ya-gu Guess. George Starr.

6 Ooo-loo-tsa Guess. *

7 Gu-u-ne-ki Guess. Sixkiller.

$1^1 1^2 1^3$ George Guess. Girty.

2 Richard Guess. *

OK 3 Joseph Guess. *

---

4 Sallie Guess. William Foster or Tu-noo-ie.

5 Joseph Guess. *

6 Catherine Guess. Joseph Downing.

$1^1 3^2 1^3$ Annie Flying. Joseph Griffin.

$1^1 5^2 1^3$ Joseph Starr. *

$1^1 7^2 1^3$ Araminta Sixkiller.

$1^1 1^2 1^3 1^4$ Mary Guess. George Mitchell and Andrew Russell.

2 Guess.

$1^1 1^2 4^3 1^4$ Susie Foster. Levi Toney.

$1^1 1^2 6^3 1^4$ Nannie Downing. Richard H. Bowles.

2 Lucile Downing. Coggle.

OK 3 Edward Downing.

4 Sequoyah Downing.

5 Maud Downing.

$1^1 3^2 1^3 1^4$ Ti-du-gi-yo-sti.

$1^1 1^2 1^3 1^4 1^5$ George W. Russell. Minnie Holston.

$1^1 1^2 4^3 1^4 1^5$ Calvin Hanks Toney.

2 Cicero Davis Toney.

OK 3 Margaret Toney.

4 Catherine Toney.

5 Sallie Toney.

$1^1 1^2 6^3 1^4 1^5$ Leo Bennett Bowles.

OK 2 Richard Bowles.

$1^1 1^2 6^3 2^4 1^5$ Cecil W. Coggle.

2 Houston Coggle.

Oolootas.

1^1 Oo-loo-tsa, of the Holly clan.

$1^2 1^1$ Ghi-go-ne-li.

$1^1 1^2 1^3$ Nannie. George Lowrey.

2 Ghi-go-ne-li.

$1^{1}1^{2}1^{3}1^{4}$ John Lowrey. Elizabeth Shorey and Ga-ne-lu-gi McLemore.
2 George Lowrey. Lucy Benge. A31
OK 3 Jennie Lowrey. Tah-lon-tee-skee. 32
4 Elizabeth Lowrey. Joseph Sevier and John Walker.
5 Sallie Lowrey.
6 Nellie Lowrey. Edmond Fawling.
7 Aky Lowrey. Arthur Burns.
$1^{1}1^{2}2^{3}1^{4}$ Catherine. John Gunter. A30
2 Polly. Smith.
$1^{1}1^{2}1^{3}1^{4}1^{5}$ Elizabeth Lowrey. William Shorey Pack.

---

2 Jennie Lowrey. Robert Benge.
OK 3 Eliza Lowrey. Martin Benge.
$1^{1}1^{2}1^{3}2^{4}1^{5}$ James Lowrey. Elizabeth McLemore.
2 Susan Lowrey. Andrew Ross.
2 George Lowrey. Elizabeth Baldridge.
4 Lydia Lowrey Milo Hoyt.
5 Rachel Lowrey. David Brown and Nelson Orr.
6 John Lowrey. *
7 Anderson Pierce Lowrey. Mary Nave.

---

8 Archibal Lowrey. Rachel Harris and Delilah Baldridge.

---

9 Washington Lowrey. Jennie

---

10 Charles Lowrey. Jennie Ballard and Ellen Reese.
$1^{1}1^{2}1^{3}3^{4}1^{5}$ George Lovett. Nannie Horn nee Hildebrand and Elizabeth Swimmer.
$1^{1}1^{2}1^{3}4^{4}1^{5}$ Margaret Sevier. Gideon Morgan.
2 Eliza Sevier. W. Templin Ross.

OK 3 John Walker. Emily Meigs and Nannie Bushyhead.
$1^{1}1^{2}1^{3}5^{4}1^{5}$ Tsa-gi-na. Pigeon.

---

2 No-na.

OK 3 Elizabeth.

---

4 Baldridge.

---

5 Switzler Lowrey. Rachel Brownlow.

---

6 Rope Campbell.
$1^{1}1^{2}1^{3}6^{4}1^{5}$ Edward Fowling. * Margaret Smith.
2 Edmond Fawling. Jennie Stanridge.
OK 3 Joseph Fawling. Lydia Brown.

4 Rim Fawling. *
5 Ellis Fawling. Elizabeth Griffin.
6 Elizabeth Fawling. Hiram Moody and Samuel Scharble.
7 James Fawling. *
8 Susie Fawling. Thomas Smith and Isaac Timmons.
$1^{1}1^{2}1^{3}7^{4}1^{5}$ Mary Burns. William Alexander Davis.
OK 2 Elizabeth Burns. Michael Huraker.
$1^{1}1^{2}2^{3}1^{4}1^{5}$ Samuel Gunter. A-yo-ku.
2 Aky Gunter. Alexander McCoy.
OK 3 Martha J. Gunter. Richard Blackurs.
4 Edward Gunter. Elsie McCoy and Letitia Keys.
5 Elizabeth Hunt Gunter. Martin Matthew Scrimsher.
6 John Gunters.
7 Catherine Gunter. James B. Vaught and Oliver Wack Lipe.
$1^{1}1^{2}2^{3}2^{4}1^{5}$ Walter Smith. *
$1^{1}1^{2}1^{3}1^{4}1^{5}1^{6}$ Thomas Jefferson Pack. Jennie Taylor.
OK 2 Cynthia Pack. John Cowart.
$1^{1}1^{2}1^{3}1^{4}2^{5}1^{6}$ Mary Benge. * John Lee.
2 Eliza Benge. Henry Seabolt.
OK 3 John Benge. Caroline Gordon.
4 Robin Benge. *
5 McLemon Benge. Margaret Seabolt.
6 Young Benge. *
7 Pickens Benge. Angeline Franklin.
8 Sarah Benge *
$1^{1}1^{2}1^{3}1^{4}3^{5}1^{6}$ Samuel Houston Benge. Lucy Blair and Nannie Brewster.
2 George Washington Benge. * Nannie Holmes.
OK 3 Obediah Martin Benge. Margaret Blair and Etta ——.
4 Richard Benge. Charlotte Frye.
5 Rhoda Benge. Stephen Teehee.
6 William Benge. Elizabeth Ross.
7 Catherine Benge. George Washington Gunter.
$1^{1}1^{2}1^{3}2^{4}1^{5}1^{6}$ Lucy Lowrey. John W. Brown.
2 William Lowrey. Anohi Bigbullet and Lucy Fourkiller.
OK 3 Charles Lowrey.
4 John Lowrey. Elizabeth Blair.
$1^{1}1^{2}1^{3}2^{4}1^{5}1^{6}$ Oliver Perry Ross. Susie Vann and Elzina Hair nee Goonan.
2 Daniel Ross. Naomi Chisholm and Sarah Halfbreed.
OK 3 Andrew J. Ross. Nannie Otterlefter and Nannie Halfbreed.
4 Samuel Houston Ross. Sarah Grimmett.
5 William Coody Ross. Mary Ann Spears.
6 Joseph Miller Ross. Rachel Drew.
7 Joshua Ross. Muskogee Yargee.
8 Richard Johnson Ross. Elizabeth Stidham.
9 Jennie Pocahontas Ross. John D. Murrell.
$1^{1}1^{2}1^{3}2^{4}3^{5}1^{6}$ Jennie Lowrey. James Brown Choate.

$1^1 1^2 1^3 2^4 4^5 1^6$ Dollie Eunice Hoyt. Amory Nelson Chamberlain.

2 Nancy Ann Hoyt. Hamilton Balentine.

OK 3 Esther Susan Hoyt. James Ward.

4 Hindman Hoyt Hoyt. Ruth Ann Buffington and Elizabeth Candy. *

5 Sarah Hoyt. Richard Hunter.

6 Lucy Lowrey Hoyt. Monroe Calvin Keys.

7 Milo Ard Hoyt. Harriette Washburn nee Folsom.

$1^1 1^2 1^3 2^4 5^5 1^6$ John L. Brown. Ann Schrimsher.

OK 2 Catherine Brown. William Daniel.

$1^1 1^2 1^3 2^4 7^5 1^6$ Daniel Webster Lowrey.

2 Henry Lowrey. Mary Parris and Evaline Evans nee Russell.

OK 3 Lucy Ann Lowrey. Charles Hicks Campbell.

4 Dollie Eunice Lowrey. James Fields, * Thomas Starr and Charles Galloway. *

5 George Lowrey. *

6 Susan Lowrey. Richard Robertson and Jefferson Carter.

7 Eliza Lowrey. William Henry Davis.

9 James Monroe Lowrey. Susie Vickery.

10 Andrew Lowrey. Dora Pinckney nee Bruton.

---

8 Austin Lowrey. Sallie Coker.

$1^1 1^2 1^3 2^4 8^5 1^6$ James Lowrey. Ellen Pigeon.

$1^1 1^2 1^3 2^4 9^5 1^6$ George Lowrey. Elizabeth Proctor.

$1^1 1^2 1^3 2^4 10^5 1^6$ Orsinoe Lowrey. Charles Reese Starr.

2 Lucy Lowrey. *

OK 3 Alice B. Lowrey.

4 Return Johnson Lowrey. Drucilyla Medley.

5 Charles Pickens Lowrey. Laura Rider.

$1^1 1^2 1^3 3^4 1^5 1^6$ James Lovett. Annie Quinton and Annie Griffin.

2 Annie Lovett. * Houston DeArmond.

3 David Lovett. Belle McCutchan.

4 John Lovett. * Elizabeth Young nee Tetincha.

5 Louisa Amanda Lovett. * Houston DeArmond.

---

6 Louisa Lovett. *

7 Eliza Lovett. *

---

8 William Lovett. Susie Crossland and Nannie Pettit.

9 Sarah Lovett. Deertrack Candy.

10 Lucy Lovett. * John Proctor.

11 Susie Lovett. * Joseph Goings.

$1^1 1^2 1^3 4^4 1^5 1^6$ Margaret Ann Ward Morgan. Robert Taylor Hanks and J. Henry Effort.

2 George Washington Morgan. Martha Keziah Mayo.

OK 3 Elizabeth Lowry Morgan. Hugh McDowell McElreath and William C. Eblin.

4 Cherokee America Morgan. Andrew Lewis Rogers.

5 Rufus Montezuma Morgan. * Mary Holt.

6 Amanda Patience Morgan. Frank Fowler and Joseph Absalom Scales.

7 Robert Hanks Morgan. *

$1^1 1^2 1^3 4^4 2^5 1^6$ Andrew Ross. Lucinda Gentry.

2 Samuel Potts Ross.

OK 3 Benjamin Franklin Ross.

4 Joseph Ross. Priscilla Gentry.

5 Margaret Melvina Ross.

6 Hannah Ross. Fin B. Tompkins.

7 Robert Ross.

8 Mary Ann Ross.

$1^1 1^2 1^3 4^4 3^5 1^6$ Timothy Meigs Walker. Elizabeth Neely Adair.

2 Elizabeth Grace Walker. James Coleman and Pryor Smith.

OK 3 Minerva Jane Walker. Armstrong Lea and Lorenzo Delano.

4 John Osborn Walker. Lucinda Taylor and Georgianna Wilkins.

---

5 Sarah E. Walker. George Washington Lasley.

6 Ebenezer Walker. Sarah Lasley nee Harlan.

$1^1 1^2 1^3 5^4 1^5 1^6$ Ellen Pigeon.

2 Lucy Pigeon.

3 Josiah Pigeon.

4 Lucinda Pigeon.

$1^1 1^2 1^3 5^4 2^5 1^6$ John Lowrey McCoy. Charlotte Ratliff, Emma Bennett and Lucy Jane Adair.

---

2 Gu-wo-du-gi-sdi.

3 Gu-yo-ti-hi.

$1^1 1^2 1^3 5^4 3^5 1^6$ Aky.

2 Nellie.

3 Elizabeth.

4 Uwo-no-sdi.

$1^1 1^2 1^3 5^4 4^5 1^6$ Mary Baldridge. Walker Hogner.

2 George Baldridge. *

3 Ewi Baldridge.

4 Ets-wo-ti-sgi Baldridge.

$1^1 1^2 1^3 5^4 5^5 1^6$ Margaret Lowrey. Jefferson Hicks and Wilson Hornet.

2 Edward Lowrey. Rose Welch and Sarah Welch.

OK 3 Samuel Lowrey. *

4 Mary Lowrey. George Foreman and Philip Webster.

5 Nannie Lowrey. * William Roach.

6 Eliza Lowrey. William Roach and William Batt.

$1^1 1^2 1^3 5^4 6^5 1^6$ Sophia Campbell. Jack Fox, Rat and John M. Smith.
2 John Campbell. Lydia Dry.
OK 3 Susie Campbell. * John Brown Wright.
4 Elizabeth Campbell. Henry Clay Ross.
5 Lethe Campbell. Charles Hermann and Napoleon Bonaparte Rowe.
6 Jennie Campbell. John Brown Wright and Levi O'Fields.
7 Hook Campbell. *

---

8 Mary Campbell. Charles Hendricks and Alexander Hendricks.

$1^1 1^2 1^3 6^4 2^5 1^6$ Edmond Fawling. Mary —— and Cass Pippins.
2 Henry Fawling. Adeline Collum and Margaret Wilson.
OK 3 Susan Fawling. John Williams and Hugh Snider.
4 Mary Fawling. Jacob Williams and John Stafford.

$1^1 1^2 1^3 6^4 5^5 1^6$ Alexander Fawling. Susan Dolusky Hensley.
2 Nannie Fawling. Armstead B. Maxwell.
OK 3 Sarah Fawling. —— Kelly and Hollis Lorenzo Chubbuck.
4 George W. Fawling. Sarah Jane Langley, Lena ——, Malinda Isreal and —— Warren.
5 Mary Fawling. James Horton.
6 Lydia Fawling. * Lafayette Guinn.

$1^1 1^2 1^3 6^4 8^5 1^6$ Mary Smith. George Downing.
2 Jennie Smith. Flying.
OK 3 James Smith. Nannie Youngblood.
4 Hiram Smith.
5 Lucy Smith. Isaac Shade.
6 George Smith. Elizabeth Keener.
7 John Smith. Sarah Whitwater.
8 Elizabeth Smith.
9 William Smith.

$1^1 1^2 1^3 7^4 1^5 1^6$ Cynthia Pack Davis. John Thompson Mayes.
2 Laura Cornelia Davis. *
OK 3 Sarah Ophelia Davis. James Allen Mayes.
4 John Lowrey Davis. Harriette Folsom.
5 William Henry Davis. Eliza Lowrey.
6 George Washington Davis. *
7 Mary Elizabeth Davis. Robert Harrison Akin and Theodore Freeland Folsom.

$1^1 1^2 1^3 7^4 2^5 1^6$ Mary Hufaker. Carter Daniel Markham.
OK 2 Cynthia Hufaker. * John R. McNair.

$1^1 1^2 2^3 1^4 1^5 1^6$ George Washington Gunter. Eliza Nave.

$1^1 1^2 2^3 1^4 2^5 1^6$ Lucy McCoy. James Gatlin.

$1^1 1^2 2^3 1^4 3^5 1^6$ Samuel R. Blackburn. Nannie P. Lattamore.
OK 2 Jennie Blackburn. Carter Walker Mayfield.

$1^1 1^2 2^3 1^4 4^5 1^6$ Nannie Gunter. * Wiliam Shipley.

2 Nellie Gunter. Lachlan Beavert.

---

3 Sarah Gunter. John R. Nicholson.

4 James Gunter. *

---

5 Margaret Gunter. Rufus Coody and Madison Coody.

6 Eliza Gunter. Riley Keys, John Alexander Adair and —— Mowry.

8 Daniel McCoy Gunter. *

9 John Gunter. *

10 Catherine Gunter. Daniel Hicks Ross.

11 Martha Gunter. *

---

7 Jennie Gunter. Leroy Keys.

---

12 Elizabeth Gunter. Alexander McCoy Rider.

$1^1 1^2 2^3 1^4 5^5 1^6$ John Gunter Scrimsher. Juliette Melvina Candy.

2 Elizabeth Alabama Scrimsher. John Lafayette Adair and Dennis Wolf Bushyhead.

3 Mary America Scrimsher. Clement Vann Rogers.

4 Sarah Catherine Scrimsher. *

5 Martha Lucretia Scrimsher. Fredrick William Gulager.

$1^1 1^2 2^3 1^4 6^5 1^6$ Nellie Gunter. John We-tu-su-te.

$1^1 1^2 2^3 1^4 7^5 1^6$ Sarah Josephine Vaught. * George Washington Nave and Olney Sevier Morgan.

---

2 Dewitt Clinton Lipe. Victoria Susan Hicks and Mary Elizabeth Archer.

OK 3 Nannie E. Lipe. *

4 John Gunter Lipe. *

5 Jennie Catherine Lipe. Pleasant Napoleon Blackstone.

6 Clark Charlesworth Lipe. Libbie Farmer and Margaret Emma Thompson.

Bowles.

1^1 John Bowles. Jennie, Oo-loo-tsa and Oo-ti-yu. A33

$1^1 1^2$ John Bowles. Jennie.

2 French Bowles. *

OK 3 Nellie Bowles. *

---

4 Lightningbug Bowles. A-yu-su.

5 Tu-noo-ne-ski Bowles. *

6 Du-qu-li-lu- Wagon Bowles. Fannie Davis.

7 Qua-ti-ni Bowles. *

8 Tsa-gi-na Bowles. Bird Tail.

---

9 Rebecca Bowles. Tee-see Guess. A29

10 Samuel Bowles. I-doo-si.

11 Eliza Bowles. John Porum Davis.

12 Nannie Bowles. * George Chisholm.

$1^{1}1^{2}1^{3}$ James Bowles. Eliza Halfbreed.

$1^{1}4^{2}1^{3}$ Joseph Bowles. *

2 Caroline Bowles. *

OK 3 John Bowles. *

4 Jefferson Bowles. *

$1^{1}6^{2}1^{3}$ Johnson Bowles. *

2 Etta Bowles. *

OK 3 Elizabeth Bowles. *

4 Thomas Bowles. *

$1^{1}8^{2}1^{3}$ Gu-de-gi. *

2 Ghi-go-ne-li.

3 Go-yi-ne. *

$1^{1}9^{2}1^{3}$ Sallie Guess. Wiliam Foster.

2 Joseph Guess. *

OK 3 Catherine Guess. Joseph Downing.

$1^{1}10^{2}1^{3}$ George Bowles. *

$1^{1}11^{2}1^{3}$ John Davis. *

$1^{1}1^{2}1^{3}1^{4}$ Minnie Bowles. Elijah Hermogene Lerblance and Orlando Shay.

OK 2 Richard H. Bowles. Bettie Blythe and Nannie Downing.

$1^{1}9^{2}1^{3}1^{4}$ Susie Foster. Levi Toney.

$1^{1}9^{2}3^{3}1^{4}$ Nannie Downing. Richard H. Bowles.

2 Lucile Downing. Coggle.

3 Edward Downing.

4 Sequoyah Downing.

5 Maud Downing.

$1^{1}1^{2}1^{3}1^{4}1^{5}$ Lillian Leblance.

OK 2 Jessie Lamar Shay.

$1^{1}1^{2}1^{3}2^{4}1^{5}$ Thomas Bowles.

---

2 Leo Bennett Bowles.

OK 3 Richard Bowles.

$1^{1}9^{2}1^{3}1^{4}1^{5}$ Calvin Hanks Toney.

2 Cicero Davis Toney.

OK 3 Margaret Toney.

4 Catherine Toney.

5 Sallie Toney.

$1^{1}9^{2}3^{3}1^{4}1^{5}$ Leo Bennett Bowles.

OK 2 Richard Bowles.

$1^{1}9^{2}3^{3}2^{4}1^{5}$ Cicero W. Coggle.

2 Houston Coggle.

CHAPTER XVII

Continuation of Old Families

Sanders.

2 Eli Sanders. Elmira Eldridge, Catherine Dilingham nee Clyne and Lucy Thornton nee Crittenden.

1^{1} Susannah. Mitchell Sanders A34

$1^{1}1^{2}$ George Sanders. Jennie Pritchett.

2 Alexander Sanders. Peggy Sonicooie. A35

OK 3 John Sanders. Dorcas Smith.

4 Andrew Sanders. Mary Brewster.

5 David Sanders. Susie Peacock.

6 Nannie Sanders. George Harlan and Ambrose Harnage. A36

7 Agnes Sanders. Jacob Alberty.

8 Jennie Sanders. William Crittenden.

$1^{1}1^{2}1^{3}$ Elsie Sanders. Maxwell Chambers.

2 Walter Chambers. Sallie and Elizabeth.

OK 3 Samuel Sanders. * Ghi-ga-u Meanman.

4 James Sanders. Dorcas Fields.

5 Nannie Sanders. Joseph Spears.

6 Elizabeth Sanders. *

7 Nicholas Byers Sanders. Sallie Eagle.

8 Jesse Sanders. Caroline Catron.

$1^{1}2^{2}1^{3}$ George Sanders. Elsie ——.

2 Mitchell Sanders. and Polly Overtaker.

3 John Sanders. *

4 Thomas Sanders. Nannie Sonicooie.

5 Jennie Sanders. John Winters.

6 Richard Sanders.

7 Andrew Sanders. Elizabeth Butler nee Puppy and Araminta Starr nee McCoy.

8 Mary Sanders. Isaac Ragsdale.

9 Ellis Sanders. * Elizabeth McCoy.

$1^{1}3^{2}1^{3}$ Agnes Sanders. Isaac Childers.

2 Robert Sanders. Mary McCreary.

OK 3 Alexander Sanders.

4 Isaac Sanders. Jennie Campbell.

5 Benjamin Sanders. Nana and Rachel.

6 David Sanders. Tiana Overtaker.

7 Edward Sanders. Agnes Rattlinggoourd.

8 Elizabeth Sanders. Nathan Childers.

9 Margaret Sanders. John Colwell.

10 Moses Sanders. *

11 Charles Sanders. Elizabeth Jane Daniel.

$1^{1}4^{2}1^{3}$ Thompson Sanders. Nakie Lee.

2 Annie Sanders. William Richardson, Charles Fargo and Eli Sutton.

OK 3 Archibald Sanders. Margaret Taylor and Isabel Eldridge.

4 Betsy Sanders. Hampton Williams.

5 Polly Sanders. Archibald Henry.

$1^1 6^2 1^3$ Eli Harlan. Delilah Alberty.

2 Ellis Sanders Harlan. Nannie Barnett.

OK 3 Sallie Harlan. Jacob Harnage.

4 Elmira Harlan. Joshua Roach.

---

5 William Harnage. Martha Snow.

6 John Griffith Harnage. Ruth Starr and Emily Walker Mayfield .

7 George Harnage. Nannie Mayfield.

8 Andrew Jackson Harnage. *

9 Elizabeth Harnage. John Adair Bell.

$1^1 7^2 1^3$ Johnson Alberty. Catherine Hood.

2 Lydia Alberty. William Crittenden.

OK 3 Sallie Alberty. John Shell.

4 Moses Alberty. Mary Love and Ruth Dougherty.

$1^1 8^2 1^3$ Henry Clay Crittenden. Susie Wolf.

$1^1 1^2 1^3 1^4$ John Chambers. Catherine Seabolt, Amelia Bean and Almira Bean.

2 Robert Chambers. *

3 Lettie Boyd Chambers. James Starr and Daniel McCoy.

4 Henry Chambers. Nannie Hendricks.

5 Joseph Chambers. Nancy Jane Starr.

6 David Chambers. *

7 James Chambers. Catherine Hendricks.

8 William Williams Chambers. Pauline Parris.

$1^1 1^2 2^3 1^4$ Mary Sanders. Leroy Tyner and Jefferson Hair.

2 Thomas Chambers. Mary Smith.

3 John Sanders. Jennie Sanders * and Agnes Crittenden.

4 David Sanders. Delilah Whitmire.

5 Annie Sanders. John Hair.

6 Catherine Sanders. William Brymer.

7 Takie Sanders. *

8 Jennie Sanders. * Silas Ross.

---

9 Susie Sanders. Jesse Wolf and Jack Bean.

$1^1 1^2 4^3 1^4$ Lucinda Jane Sanders. * Levi Keys.

2 George Osceola Sanders. Elizabeth Brewer nee Allen *.

OK 3 William J. Sanders. Elizabeth Hildebrand and Mary Crittenden.

4 Samuel Sanders.

5 James M. Sanders. Catherine Baptiste and Keziah James.

6 Elizabeth Sanders.

7 John M. Sanders. Emma Polk.

$1^1 1^2 5^3 1^4$ George Spears. *

$1^1 1^2 7^3 1^4$ Elizabeth Sanders. William Holt and Fredrick W. Rutherford.

2 Sallie Sanders. *

3 Jennie Sanders. William James Largen.

4 James Sanders. Rachel Christy.

$1^1 1^2 8^3 1^4$ Madison Sanders. Louisa Holland.

2 Margaret Sanders. Thomas Blair.

OK 3 Cynthia Ann Sanders. George Bradley.

4 Elizabeth Sanders. Michael Mayfield.

5 Nicholas Sanders. Mary Tanksley.

6 John Catron Sanders. Sallie Jane Clay.

7 Florence Sanders. James Miller.

$1^1 2^2 1^3 1^4$ Johnson Sanders. Polly Bean.

$1^1 2^2 2^3 1^4$ Jennie Sanders. George Bigfeather.

2 Mary Sanders. James Rogers.

3 David Sanders. Caroline Elk.

$1^1 2^2 4^3 1^4$ Wilson Sanders. Laura Wells Wilkerson.

---

2 Susie Sanders. * Charles Lafayette Foreman.

OK 3 Jerusha Sanders. *

4 Annie Sanders. *

5 Sallie Sanders. *

6 Thomas Jefferson Sanders. Elizabeth Bearpaw.

7 Rachel Sanders. Nicholas Benjamin McNair.

8 William Sanders. *

9 Lewis Sanders. *

$1^1 2^2 5^3 1^4$ Clara Winters. James Ellis.

2 Elizabeth Winters.

OK 3 Peggy Winters. Johnson Vann and Nathaniel Stewart.

4 Mary Winters. Aaron Burr.

$1^1 2^2 6^3 1^4$ John Sanders. *

2 David Sanders. *

$1^1 2^2 7^3 1^4$ John Sanders. Eliza Seabolt nee Starr, Jennie Vann and Adeline Mitchell.

2 Thomas Didymus Sanders. Maria Gaford and Joanna Pettit.

OK 3 Jackson Sanders. *

4 Samuel D. Sanders. Nancy Jane Gafford and Martha Ann Harris.

---

5 Henry Harrison Sanders. Charlotte Stocker nee Starr.

$1^1 2^2 8^3 1^4$ Margaret Ragsdale. *

2 John Ragsdale. Araminta Gunter.

OK 3 Polly Ragsdale. Joseph Dawson and John Virgil McPherson.

4 Ellen Ragsdale. Jasper Chaney.

5 Lucy Ragsdale. Charles D. England.

6 Isaac Harnage Ragsdale. Johanna Johnson.
7 Cynthia Ragsdale. Joseph Hines.
$1^13^21^31^4$ John Childers. Minerva Ross nee Foreman and Nannie Swimmer.
OK 2 Eliza Childers. Sanders Choate.
$1^13^22^31^4$ Ellis Sanders. Martha Jane Brown and Cynthia T. Frye.

---

2 Elizabeth Ann Sanders. John Tommason Duncan.
OK 3 George D. Sanders. *
4 Mitchell Sanders. Mary Josephine Harlan and Mary Roberts.
5 Marion W. Sanders. *
6 Elizur Butler Sanders. Catherine Moore.
7 Samuel E. Sanders. Mary Frye.
8 Esther Sanders. Gaines Clinton Smith.
$1^13^23^31^4$ Archilla Sanders. Lucinda Still.

---

2 John Sanders. Sallie Sequichie, Catherine Henry nee Coocoodigisky and Annie Goss.
$1^13^24^31^4$ Diana Melvina Sanders. John White.
2 Margaret Elizabeth Sanders. Peter Parson and George Washington Boyles.
OK 3 Rachel Hunt Sanders. Alexander Lombard Martin.
4 Mary Ellen Sanders. Joseph Raincrow.
5 Lucy Travennes Sanders. Andrew Nowife and George Waseet.
6 David Edward Sanders. Elsie Ballard and Caroline Ballard nee Romine.
$1^13^25^31^4$ Aaron Sanders. Tiana Chuculate.
2 Oceola Sanders. Nannie Eagle.
3 Nannie Sanders. Youngwolf Vann.

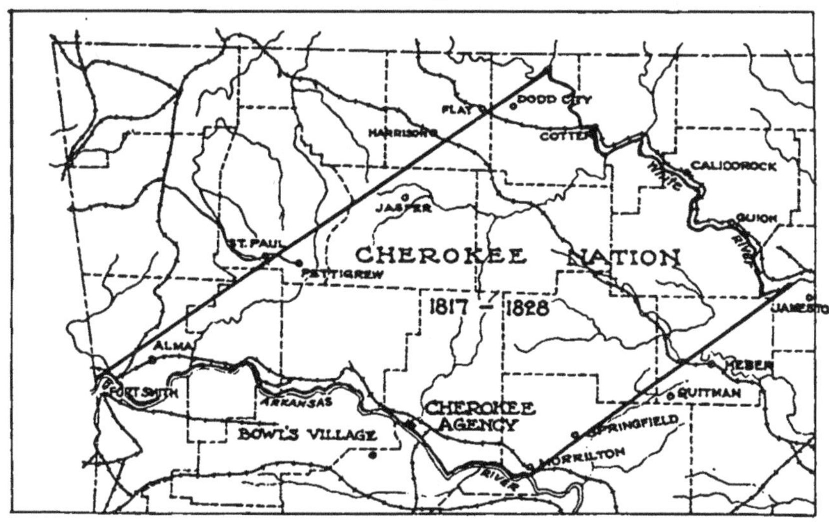

$1^{1}5^{2}1^{3}$ Elizabeth Sanders. *

OK 3 Nannie Sanders John Thompson and Thomas Pettit.

5 David Sanders.

---

4 Neki Sanders.

6 Jolly ("Hoolie") Sanders. Mary Rogers.

7 Burns Sanders. * Lucy Pritchett.

8 Elizabeth Sanders.

9 Agnes Sanders. Alexander Heaven.

10 Jennie Sanders.

11 Thomas Sanders. *

$1^{1}3^{2}6^{3}1^{4}$ Isaac Sanders. Isabel Hampton.

2 Sallie Sanders. * Cornelius Sanders.

OK 3 Charles Sanders. *

$1^{1}3^{2}7^{3}1^{4}$ Elsie Sanders. * Alexander B. Clapp.

$1^{1}3^{2}8^{3}1^{4}$ Samuel Childers. Sarah Bean.

$1^{1}3^{2}9^{3}1^{4}$ John Jolly Colwell. * Cynthia Chaney.

2 Cynthia Colwell. John P. Hall.

OK 3 Nannie Colwell. George Washington Starr.

4 Mary Colwell. Matthew Terrell.

$1^{1}3^{2}11^{3}1^{4}$ Caroline Elizabeth Sanders. George Washington Choate.

2 Martha Jane Sanders. Cornelius Sanders and George Washington Fields.

OK 3 Elizabeth Catherine Sanders. George Washington Choate.

4 William Frank Sanders. Ellen Minerva Flournoy.

$1^{1}4^{2}1^{3}1^{4}$ Mary Sanders. William Thornton and William Wilson.

2 Lucinda Sanders. John Thornton and Lock Langley.

3 Joshua Sanders. Charlotte Ann Adair, Nannie Ragsdale and Mary Quinton.

4 Cornelius Sanders. Sallie Sanders, Sallie Smith and Martha Jane Sanders.

5 William Sanders. *

6 John Sanders. Elizabeth Tiesky* and Nancy Jane Sweat.

$1^{1}4^{2}2^{3}1^{4}$ Elizabeth Richardson. George Washington Doherty, William Patton and Thomas Pettit.

---

2 Charles Augustus Fargo. Narcissa Jacobs and Effie Wilson nee Davis.

OK 3 Calvin Fargo. Susan Margaret McKinney, Delilah Johnson nee Baldridge.

1431 Ruth Thompson. Robert Patton.

---

2 Oscar Dunre Pettit. Emily Faulkner.

OK 3 Amanda Pettit. * Isaac Abraham Jacobs.

$1^{1}5^{2}2^{3}1^{4}$ Thomas Sanders. *

2 John Murphy Sanders. Anna L. Bell.

OK 3 George Sanders. Elizabeth Thornton and Margaret Garner.

4 Frank Sanders. *

5 Alexander Sanders. *

---

6 William Edward Sanders. Sarah Catherine Scrimsher and Etta Jane Scraper.

---

7 Sallie Sanders. *

$1^{1}5^{2}3^{3}1^{4}$ Jennie Sanders. * John Sanders.

2 Polly Sanders. Robert Klaus.

OK 3 Susie Sanders. Henry Cook.

---

4 Boone Sanders. *

$1^{1}5^{2}4^{3}1^{4}$ Mitchell Williams.

OK 2 Richard Murrell Wolfe. Susan Elizabeth Shirley.

$1^{1}5^{2}5^{3}1^{4}$ Rachel Pauline Henry, Edward Bruce Starr, Joseph Vann and Walter Starr Crittenden.

OK 2 Levi James Henry. *

$1^{1}6^{2}1^{3}1^{4}$ George Harlan. Mary McCoy.

2 Sarah Harlan George Washington Lasley, Ebenezer Walker and William Tackett.

3 Mitchell Harlan. Letitia Victoria Keys.

4 Ezekial Harlan. Rachel Sands.

5 Nancy Perlony Harlan. Riley J. Keys, Joseph Vann Lasley and Joseph Robbins.

6 Jennie Harlan. Charles Coody Rogers and Granville Torbett.

$1^{1}6^{2}2^{3}1^{4}$ James Ellis Harlan. Margaret Reed and Nancy Ann Gibson nee Bell.

2 Sallie Matilla Harlan. John Poole, George Lane, Lewis Ross Kell, James Chastine Blythe and Charles Chandler.

OK 3 Mary Josephine Harlan. Mitchell Sanders.

4 John Brown Harlan. Mary Ann McGhee.

5 Ruth Jane Harlan. William Writtenberry and Joseph Henry Hunt.

6 Timothy Dwight Harlan. *

7 Emily D. Harlan. George Finley.

$1^{1}6^{2}3^{3}1^{4}$ George Harlan Harnage. *

$1^{1}6^{2}4^{3}1^{4}$ Emily Roach. Edward Walls and Aaron Crittenden.

2 William Roach. Nannie Lowrey and Eliza Lowrey.

3 Nannie Roach. Lafayette Catron and John Horn.

4 James Roach. *

5 Mary Roach. *

6 George Roach. Nannie Pritchett and Sarah Triplett.

7 John Roach. Nellie Grant.

8 Sarah Roach. Looney Townsend and William Sullivan.
9 Joshua Roach. *
$1^16^25^31^4$ Elizabeth Harnage. Lemuel Murrell and John Lewis Wardlow Williams.
OK 2 Nannie Harnage. Gilbert Wesley Wilson.
$1^16^26^31^4$ Sarah Caroline Harnage. John Martin Bell and Samuel G. Heffington.
2 Ezekial Sanders Starr Harnage.

OK 3 William Thomas Harnage. Mary Rebecca Wyche.
4 Mary Victoria Harnage. William Lucullus Carr.
5 Ida Eugenia Harnage. Jonathan Taylor Ewers and John M. Morse.
6 Loretta Beldora Harnage. John Stringer Scott.
7 Nannie Elvira Harnage. William Boone.
8 John Custis Lee Harnage. Frances Catherine Hunt.
9 Lena Harnage. Thomas James Adair.
$1^16^27^31^4$ John Sanders Harnage. *
2 Sarah Harnage. Charles Henry Bacon.
OK 3 William Wilson Harnage. Jennie Vann.
4 Nannie Sabina Harnage. John Dana Bacon.
$1^16^29^31^4$ Nancy Ann Bell. Quinton Kosciusko Gebson and James Ellis Harlan.
$1^17^21^31^4$ Delilah Alberty.
2 Martha Elizabeth Alberty. Columbus Marion Reeves.
3 Joshua Alberty. *
4 George Alberty. * Elizabeth Faught.
5 Andrew Jackson Alberty. Amanda Folsom nee Dibble.
6 Mary Alberty. *
7 John Alberty. Emily Clay McDonald.
8 Archibald Alberty. Julia A. Peake.
9 Patsy Alberty. Stephen Palone.
$1^17^22^31^4$ James Crittenden. Isabel Doherty.
2 Lucy Crittenden. Smith Thornton and Eli Sanders.
3 Nannie Crittenden. Judge Pathkiller and Stephen Smith.
4 Jacob Crittenden. *
5 Elizabeth Crittenden. Ellis Foreman.
6 Agnes Crittenden. John Sanders.
7 Emily Crittenden. Henry Bushyhead.
8 Benjamin Crittenden. Nannie Proctor and Mary Weaver.
$1^17^23^31^4$ Toas Shell. Jennie Walkingstick.
$1^17^24^31^4$ Annie Alberty. Nelson Foreman.
2 Jennie Alberty. Elias Gourd Foreman.
3 Margaret Alberty. *
4 Catherine Alberty. * Frank Harris.

---

5 Nannie Alberty. James McA. Messer.

$1^18^21^31^4$ Rebecca Crittenden. * Harlin Eaton.

2 Charles Nelson Crittenden. *

OK 3 John Ross Crittenden. Alice Harlin.

4 Mary Crittenden. *

5 Sarah Crittenden. Joseph McMinn Starr.

6 George Washington Crittenden. Martha Jane Starr and Nancy Jane Wilkey.

7 Lucy Crittenden. Martha T. Root.

8 Charlotte Crittenden. * John Gunter Harlin.

9 Henry Clay Crittenden. Mary Susan Morris.

Ridge-Watie

1^1 Oganstota.

11^1 Major Ridge. Susie Wickett. A37

2 Oowatee. Susannah Reese. A37

$1^11^21^3$ John Ridge. Sarah Bird Northrup.

2 Sarah Ridge. George Washington Paschal.

OK 3 Walter Ridge. * Elizabeth.

$1^12^21^3$ Nannie Watie. John Foster Wheeler.

2 Stand Watie. Elizabeth Fields, Isabel Hicks nee Miller, Eleanor Looney and Sallie Caroline Bell. A38

3 Killekeena Watie. Harriette Gold and Delight Sergeant. A37

OK 4 Thomas Black Watie. *

5 Mary Ann Watie. John Walker Candy.

6 John Alexander Watie. Eliza Fields.

7 Elizabeth Watie. Lewis Webber.

8 Charles Edwin Watie. *

$1^11^21^31^4$ John Rollin Ridge. Elizabeth Wilson.

2 Clarinda Ridge. *

OK 3 Herman Ridge. *

4 Susan C. Ridge. J. Woodward Washburn.

5 Aenaes Ridge. Mavia Saunders.

6 Andrew Jackson Ridge. Helen C. Doom.

7 Flora Chamberlin Ridge. William Davis Polson.

$1^11^22^31^4$ George Washington Paschal. Frances Tilley.

2 Ridge Paschal. Virginia Gasman nee Winston.

OK 3 Emily Agnes Paschal. William McNair.

$1^12^21^31^4$ Theodore Frelinghyson Wheeler. *

2 Susan Wheeler. William Wallace Perry.

OK 3 Mary Anna Wheeler. Ethelbert Britton Bright.

4 Harriette Boudinot Wheeler. Argyle Quesenbury.

5 Sarah Paschal Wheeler. Clarence P. Ashbrook and William Goodlet Nelms.

6 John Caldwell Wheeler. Lucilla Greenfield Sandels.

7 William Watie Wheeler. Emma Carnall.

8 Nannie Wheeler. *

$1^12^22^31^4$ Susannah Watie. * Charles Woodall.

---

2 Comisky Watie. *
OK 3 Saladin Ridge Watie. *
4 Solon Watie. * (Cherokee name Wa-ti-ke)
5 Nannie Josephine Watie. * John Martin Daniel.
6 Charlotte Jackoline Watie. *
$1^{1}2^{2}3^{3}1^{4}$ Eleanor Susan Boudinot. Henry J. Church.
2 Mary Harriette Boudinot. * Lyman Case.
OK 3 William Penn Boudinot. Caroline Matilda Rogers Fields.
4 Sarah Parkhill Boudinot. *
5 Elias Cornelius Boudinot. * Clara Corinth Minear.
6 Frank Brinsmade Boudinot. Annie.
$1^{1}2^{2}5^{3}1^{4}$ Harriette Candy. Hugh Montgomery McPherson.
2 Susan Candy. * Henry Lee Hill.
OK 3 Elizabeth Candy. * Hindman Booth Hoyt.
$1^{1}2^{2}6^{3}1^{4}$ Susannah Inez Watie. Thomas Jefferson Bean.
OK 2 Nannie Wheeler Watie. * Lewis Keys.
$1^{1}2^{2}7^{3}1^{4}$ Walter Webber. *
OK 2 Charles Theodore Webber. *

Ward

1^{1} Catherine McDaniel. John Ward. A22
$1^{1}1^{2}$ James Ward. Sidney Redding* and Lucy Haynie.
2 George Ward. Lucy Mayes. A39
OK 3 Samuel Ward. Easter Davis and Sallie Earwood.
4 Elizabeth Ward. Elijah Sutton and John Cox.
5 Susie Ward. William England.
6 Nannie Ward. Thomas Monroe and Stephen Carroll.
7 Bryan Ward. Temperance Stansel.
8 Charles Ward. Nannie Cross, Ruth Hollingsworth and Mary Elvira Hensley.
$1^{1}1^{2}1^{3}$ Catherine Ward. Joseph Keaton.
2 John Ward. *
3 Thomas Carroll Ward. Mary Annie Hicks.
4 Moses Haynie Ward. Elizabeth Lear.
5 Bryan Ward. Martha Kinchlow and Delilah Hicks. *
6 George Ward. Mary Kinchlow and Mary Townsend.
7 Lucy Ward. James Williams.
8 Rosanna Ward. Daniel Tittle.
9 James Ward. Esther Susan Hoyt.
10 Nannie Ward. Caldean Gunter.
$1^{1}2^{2}1^{3}$ Sabrina Ward. Felix Arthur.
2 Charlotte Ward. John Henry Stover.
OK 3 John M. Ward. Narcissa Monroe.
4 James Ward. Louisa M. Williams.
5 Nannie Ward. William Dameron.
6 Martha Ward. John Countryman.
7 Mary Ward. Joseph Henry Clark.

8 Samuel Ward. Louisa England, Laura Spears, Tennessee Howell and Louisa J. Vann.

9 Susie Ward. Joshua Lindsey.

10 Lucy Ann Ward. George Colcher, Matthew Thompson, Robert Howell and Napoleon Bonaparte Luckey.

11 Malinda Josephine Ward. Samuel Elihugh Thornton.

$1^{1}3^{2}1^{3}$ Samuel Ward. Cynthia Annie Wagnon.

---

2 George Howard Ward. Mary Carroll.

OK 3 Martin Ward. Sallie Cooper.

$1^{1}4^{2}1^{3}$ John W. Sutton. Mary Copeland.

2 Harriette Sutton.

OK 3 Henrietta Sutton. ——— Elledge.

4 Loretta Sutton. Youngbird.

5 Catherine Sutton. *

---

6 George Morris. *

$1^{1}5^{2}1^{3}$ Sabra England. William Henderson, Joseph Kirby and John Stover.

2 Matilda England. William Queen.

OK 3 Hepsie Tngland. Jeremiah Roberson.

4 Joseph England. Sabra Cooper, Martha Adams and Mary Brown.

5 Tillman England. *

6 William England. Arminda England and Elizabeth Medley nee Harlin.

7 Chapman England. *

$1^{1}6^{2}1^{3}$ Narcissa Monroe. John M. Ward and Samuel Melton.

2 Simpson Foster Monroe. Rebecca Hopkins.

OK 3 Fincher Monroe. Mary Shields.

4 Lucretia Monroe. James Humphrey, —— McDuff, —— Mulford, James Joleff and William Colwell.

5 Thomas R. Monroe. Saphronia England and Susie Conner.

---

6 Susie Carroll. John Carroll.

7 Annie Carroll. * Hareford.

8 Lucy Jane Carroll. * William Hathaway.

9 Lettie Carroll. *

10 Caroline Carroll. Thompson Fields.

$1^{1}7^{2}1^{3}$ John S. Ward. Jennie Loveless.

2 Mildred Ward. John Woods and Lewis Wilkerson.

3 Martha Ann Ward. Lewis Scrimsher.

4 George Hilmon Ward. Margaret McIntosh.

5 Frances Catherine Ward. James Duncan, ———Marcum and Charles Barney.

$1^{1}8^{2}1^{3}$ Elizabeth Jane Ward. Daniel Newnon McIntosh.

2 Mary Adeline Ward. Wiley Ingram, Martin Vann, Joseph Brown and John A. Richards.

OK 3 William Ward. * Susannah Vann.
4 Minerva Ward. Lewis Clark, John Creason, Eli Stucker and James A. Jackson.

---

5 Matilda Ward.
6 Mary Elvira Ward. John Wesley Holland.
7 Martha Catherine Ward. James Cloud.
8 John Tisdale Ward. Elizabeth Killian.
9 George Washington Ward. Margaret Pinion and
10 Charles Rufus Ward. Catherine Ray and
11 Benjamin Ward. Jennie Ray.
$1^{1}1^{2}1^{3}1^{4}$ Lucy Keaton. Abel Fike Dial.
2 Nannie Keaton. Martin Dial.
OK 3 Martha Keaton. Pinkney Martin.
$1^{1}1^{2}3^{3}1^{4}$ Rose Ann Ward. Bayless Langley, Buck Gear and Newton Martin.
2 John Franklin Ward. Sallie Quixanna Summerhill.
OK 3 Julia Ann Ward. Joseph Newton Thompson.
4 Barbara Alice Ward. Rufus Sidney Steward.
5 James Carroll Ward.
6 George Oscar Ward. Minnie Bullock and Alma Bullock.
7 Thomas Charles Ward.
8 Sarah Catherine Ward. Hutchinson Murphy Roberson.
9 Lucy Ann Ward. Alfred Washington Shelley.
10 Mary Ellen Ward. John William Bradshaw.
11 Daniel Moses Ward. Lydia M. Burke.
$1^{1}1^{2}4^{3}1^{4}$ Thomas Franklin Ward. Elizabeth Ward.
2 James McDaniel Ward. Susie Stepp.
OK 3 Caldean Ward. Nannie E. Griffin.
4 Josephine Ward. Charles Henson Franks.
5 Helen Naomi Ward. Rhoderick Dhu Perry.
6 Joel Bryan Ward. Florence A. Newton.
$1^{1}1^{2}5^{3}1^{4}$ John Ward. *
2 James Ward. *
OK 3 William Jasper Ward. Dora Florence Francis.
4 Mary Elizabeth Ward. Robert William Swim.
5 Nannie Ward. William Jackson.
6 Evaline Ward. Joseph Cephus Bean and ———Grover.
7 Esther Ward. Jack Roberson.
8 Joel Bryan Cornelius Ward. Catherine Mills and Minnie Lowrey.
$1^{1}1^{2}6^{3}1^{4}$ Elizabeth Ward. William Kelly and Tillman Queen.
2 Lucy Ann Ward. Albert Gass.
OK 3 Alexander the Great Ward. Sarah Elizabeth Thomas.
4 Yell Clement Ward. Julia Cynthia Thomas.
5 James Ward.
6 Fannie M. Ward. Robert Andrew Hosey.

7 Martha Jane Ward. Ira Washington Thomas.
8 John Ward. Sallie Blackwood.
9 Caroline Ward. Forest Guilliams.
$1^1 1^2 7^3 1^4$ Nannie Elizabeth Williams. George Washington Eaton.
OK 2 Martha Pauline Williams. Epp G. Thompson.
$1^1 1^2 8^3 1^4$ James Marion Tittle. Annie Henrietta Prather and
2 Amelia Arline Tittle. August Sager.
OK 3 Robert Wooden Tittle. Mary Susie Murry nee Blackburn.
4 Mary Madora Tittle. John Robert Dobkins.
5 Martha Ellen Tittle. Jacob M. Hiser.
6 Susan Jane Tittle. Thomas Tipton Wimer.
$1^1 1^2 9^3 1^4$ Darius Edwin Ward. Sallie Caroline Ritter and Mary Murphy nee Hester.
2 Lydia Ann Ward. William Clifford Chamberlin.
OK 3 Clara Alice Ward.
4 William Wirt Ward. Roxana Stannard.
5 Henry Julian Ward. Emma Luckenback.
$1^1 1^2 10^3 1^4$ Ann Eliza Gunter. John Powell and Burgis Gaithor Chandler.
2 Lavinia Arline Gunter. Lewis Lafayette Duckworth.
OK 3 Lucy Jane Gunter. Dr. Benjamin Franklin Fortner.
4 John Thomas Gunter. Alice Lee Heath.
5 Amanda Olivia Gunter. David Matthew Marrs.
6 Lulu Hazeltine Gunter. William Curtis.
7 Sarah Amnia Gunter. Samuel Frazier.
8 Nannie Augusta Gunter. James Alfrey.
9 Caldean Gunter.
$1^1 2^2 1^3 1^4$ Charlotte Arthur. * Milton Tarrents.
2 Lucy Arthur. Isaac Nidiffer.
OK 3 Sallie Arthur. John Ballard.
4 Nannie Arthur. Jacob Nidiffer.
5 Freeman Arthur. *
6 George Arthur. *
7 Martha Arthur. George Washington Luckey.
$1^1 2^2 2^3 1^4$ Sabrina Stover. Benjamin Large.
2 Nannie Stover. Yancey Dameron.
OK 3 Sallie Stover. * Ellis Hildebrand.
4 George Stover. *
5 Elisha Stover.
6 James Stover.
7 Louisa J. Stover. Joseph Lynch Williams and William Archibald Yell Hastings.
8 Charlotte Stover. James Stanford Fields.
9 Martha Francis Stover. Thomas Stewart Bacon and George Thomas Black.
10 John Rogers Stover.
11 Malinda Rogers Stover. * William Lafayette Trott.

12 Madora Stover. James Campbell Trott.

13 William Riley Stover. Minerva E. Garrison.

$1^1 2^2 3^3 1^4$ George Monroe Ward. Emily Jane Roberts, Amanda Skaggs nee ———, Charlotte Mayes, Mary Ezell and Martha Jane Nidiffer.

2 Nannie Ward. William Hamilton and John Henry Clark

OK 3 Lucy Ward. * Stephen Brown.

$1^1 2^2 4^3 1^4$ Samuel Taylor Ward. Catherine Jane Lear.

2 Joseph Lynch Ward. Alice N. Scott.

OK 3 George De Shields Ward. Eliza Frances Phillips.

4 John Lowrey Ward. Laura Ann Edmondson.

5 William Wyly Ward. Addie Belle Handlin.

6 James Oliver Ward. *

$1^1 2^2 5^3 1^4$ Lucy Jane Dameron. John Anderson Johnson, John Hunt.

2 Martha J. Dameron. * George W. Johnson.

OK 3 Mary Ann Dameron. Lemuel Cowart, R. H. F. Thompson

4 Susan Frances Caroline Dameron. Charles Patterson.

$1^1 2^2 6^3 1^4$ John Marcus Countryman. Belle Hopkins, Esther Blevins nee Ward, Dove Piercefield and Vinita Belle Mayes.

2 George Washington Countryman. Minerva Ballard.

OK 3 Mary Countryman. Ransom Blevins, William Taylor and James Ward.

4 Andrew Jackson Countryman. Clementine Hastings, Rebecca Morris, Rebecca Duncan and Zimerhew Black nee Ward.

5 Lucy Ann Countryman. Samuel McDowell and Caleb Conner.

6 Samuel Countryman. *

7 Malinda Nancy Countryman. Thomas Ballard and George W. Williams.

$1^1 2^2 7^3 1^4$ George Washington Clark. Lydia A. Scraper.

2 James Clark. *

OK 3 Lucy Ann Clark. William Abbott Thompson, Joshua Bertholf Duncan and James Abercrombie Duncan.

4 Louisa Maria Clark. Daniel Young.

5 Ellen Clark. Joseph M. Scraper and Washington Taylor.

6 William Andrew Clark. Lillian Belle Berry.

$1^1 2^2 8^3 1^4$ Valzie Lucy Ward. John Emmett Vann.

---

2 Jeanette Ward. Berry H. Ladd.

3 Minnie Viola Ward. Robert Edward Lee Rogers.

---

4 Nina Ward. William Thomas Byrd.

5 Joseph McCann Ward.

6 Zona Ward. Justis Jones.

7 Hugh Tinnon Ward. Lulu Barlow.

8 Rose Alvin Ward. *

9 Lillie Deloris Ward.

10 Beulah Belle Ward.

11 Delena Ward.

$1^1 2^2 9^3 1^4$ Margaret E. Lindsey. Henry H. Curry.

OK 2 Sabrina Lindsey. Bartley Elam Scott.

$1^1 2^2 11^3 1^4$ George Washington Thornton. Emily Jane Austin and Elizabeth Rebecca McKenzie.

OK 2 Lucy Gertrude Thornton. Samuel Early Aultman.

$1^1 3^2 1^3 1^4$ Mary Ward. Issac Boyce Cornwell, —— Harris and William Lyman.

2 Esther Ward. William Blevins and John Marcus Countryman.

OK 3 Martin Ward. *

4 Burrell Ward. * Jennie Sherrell.

5 James Ward. Margeret Robertson and Mary Ann Taylor nee Countryman.

6 Martha Ward. Frederick Risemon.

7 Cynthia Ward. Henry Benton.

8 Zimerhew Elizabeth Ward. Randolph Black and Andrew Jackson Countryman.

9 Josephine Ward. James Mitchell.

$1^1 3^2 2^3 1^4$ Sallie Ann Ward. James Mitchell.

2 Louisa Jane Ward. Samuel Trout Jackson and Samuel Smith.

OK 3 Van Velt Ward. Elmira Long, Kalena Bradley and Mary Isreal.

4 Amanda Melvina Ward. Jesse Champion Wood.

5 Minerva Cherokee Ward. Ezekial Miller.

6 Martin Cicero Ward. * Sarah Blevins.

7 Samuel Foster Ward. * Malissa Blevins.

8 Mary Ann Ward. William Blevins.

9 Sabra Elizabeth Ward. Ezekial Fields.

$1^1 3^2 3^3 1^4$ Sallie Ann Ward. George Washington McClure.

OK 2 Samuel Benjamin Ward. Sinia Elizabeth Buffington and Amanda Read.

$1^1 4^2 1^3 1^4$ George Sutton. * Mary Malinda Cushman nee Melton and Jennie Reno.

2 William Henry Sutton. Harriette Rozila Raymond.

OK 3 Nancy Ann Sutton. Samuel Cass Glenn.

4 Elizabeth Jane Sutton. John Henry Clark.

5 Alexander Sutton. Sarah Price.

6 John Seaborn Sutton. Minnie F. Walker.

$1^1 5^2 1^3 1^4$ Wiliam Penn Henderson. Susie Ballard and Eliza Marshall nee Condon.

---

2 James McGhee. Julia Hoskins.

OK 3 Matilda Kirby. Albert Weir Harlan.

$1^1 5^2 2^3 1^4$ Martha Cherokee Queen. *

2 Tillman Queen. A. Phillips and Elizabeth Kelly nee Ward.

3 John Queen. *

$1^1 5^2 3^3 1^4$ M. J. Roberson.

2 J. C. Roberson.

3 Samuel H. Roberson.

$1^1 5^2 4^3 1^4$ Susan Ann England. Elias Reeder, John B. Harris and Henry Edmonds.

2 William England. Sarah Mayes.

OK 3 Benjamin Cornelius England. Jincy Jane Ezell.

4 Sabra England. William Webster Weir.

5 Louisa England. David Suagee.

---

6 Martha Adeline England. James Cobb Cowles.

7 Mary Josephine England. Joseph Quinton Buchanan.

8 Viola Jane England. William B. Rains.

$1^1 5^2 6^3 1^4$ Mary Jane England. James Franklin Williams, William Havish and Daniel Bachtel.

---

2 Catherine Indiana Englland. Larkin Goddard and Fleming H. Wasson.

OK 3 Chapman England.

$1^1 6^2 1^3 1^4$ George Monroe Ward. Emily Jane Roberts, Amanda Skaggs nee ———, Charlotte Mayes, Mary Ezell and Martha Jane Nidiffer.

2 Nannie Ward. William Hamilton and John Henry Clark.

OK 3 Lucy Ward. * Stephen Brown.

---

4 Mary Malissa Melton. Harris Alexander, John Cushman, George Sutton and William Dawes.

5 Simpson Foster Melton. Isabelle Murphy nee Graham.

6 Charles Franklin Melton. Elizabeth Robb nee Lindsey.

7 Elizabeth Melton. William M. Toffelmire.

8 Wiley James Milton. Ella Wilkerson.

9 William Thomas Melton. Louisa Beavert and nee Tunnell.

$1^1 6^2 2^3 1^4$ Louisa Monroe. * William Hereford.

2 Ryland Myers Monroe. *

OK 3 Julia Esther Monroe. Treadwell Scott Remson.

4 Narcissus Monroe. Logan Henderson Duncan.

$1^1 6^2 3^3 1^4$ James Madison Monroe. Mary Frances Kelly.

2 Thomas Jefferson Monroe. Florence Vinita Landerdale.

OK 3 Miriam Monroe. Randolph Ballard.

4 Martha Monroe. Addison Allen Roach.

$1^1 6^2 4^3 1^4$ William Humphrey. *

2 John Humphrey. Dora Jackson and Mary Louisa Hoffman.

3 Fannie Humphrey. * William Rogers and Thomas Hooper.
4 Nannie Humphrey. Jackson Blevins.
5 Ellen Humphrey. *
6 David Humphrey. Narcissa Blevins and
7 Malinda Humphrey. Joseph Whipple and John Galligher.
$1^16^25^31^4$ Saphronia Monroe. James H. Hereford.

---

2 Clarinda Susan Monroe. John Calvin Morets and James Ray.
OK 3 William Allen Monroe. *
4 Minerva Sijourney Monroe. William A. Fisk.
5 Ellen Rebecca Monroe. Thomas Clark.
6 Nannie Drucilla Monroe. Luke Harrison.
7 Dora Nettie Monroe.
8 Myrtle Pauline Monroe. Robert L. Sanders.
$1^16^26^31^4$ Hugh Carroll. Lucy Putnam.
OK 2 Fincher Carroll. *
$1^16^210^31^4$ Johnson Thompson Fields. Delilah Cox and Norma Rebecca Hepler nee Robison.
2 Matthew Fields. Margaret V. Trotter.
OK 3 Victoria Fields. John E. Barks.
$1^17^21^31^4$ Eliza Jane Ward. James H. Deems and James Stout. A36

---

2 Charlotte E. Ward. James Lovely Bumgarner.
OK 3 Susie Ward. Edward Gwartney.
4 Margaret M. Ward. Joseph Frank Baker.
5 Delora B. Ward. Henry F. Carter.
6 Joel Ward. Myrtle L. Crance.
7 Queen Victoria Ward. William T. Holt.
8 Elizabeth Ward. R. L. Holt.
$1^17^22^31^4$ Hillman Wilkerson. Mary Brown.
2 Mildred Jane Wilkerson. John Patton.
OK 3 Catherine Wilkerson. * William Woodard.
$1^17^23^31^4$ John Scrimsher.
2 Temperance Scrimsher. James Duncan and George Southerland.
OK 3 Ann Eliza Scrimsher. John Lairy and Elisha Gray.
$1^17^24^31^4$ Sallie Ann Ward. James H. Bendure and Edward Livingston.
2 Mary Jane Ward. James Duncan.
3 Bryan Ward. *
$1^17^25^31^4$ Ruth Rogers. Daniel Webster Rogers.

OK 2 Felix Barney. Mary Joe Arwood.
$1^18^21^31^4$ Albert Gallatin McIntosh. Elizabeth Fisher and Mary Frances Boulton.
2 Lucy McIntosh. Charles Bard.

OK 3 Freeland Buckner McIntosh. Catherine Louisa Archer, Georgia Ann Vann and Catherine Welch.

4 Susie McIntosh. Thomas Harvison.

5 Rowley C. McIntosh. Fannie Adkins.

6 Daniel Newnon McIntosh. Alice Bailey.

$1^{1}8^{2}2^{3}1^{4}$ Louisa Ingram. *

---

2 Charles Brown. Mary Coker.

$1^{1}8^{2}4^{3}1^{4}$ Myrtle Clark. William Stucker and Frank Thompson.

$1^{1}8^{2}5^{3}1^{4}$ Annie Beaver. Benjamin Price and James Walker Gott.

$1^{1}8^{2}6^{3}1^{4}$ Manuel Jefferson Holland. Martha Matilda Pennell and Mary Crittenden Gore.

2 Alfred Benjamin Holland. America Johnson.

OK 3 Sarah Loretta Holland. Isaac Payne.

4 Martha Alice Holland. Robert Wesley Early and John H. Abbott.

5 John Alvin Holland. Rebecca Welch and Margaret J. Brown.

6 Noah Seaborn Holland. Julia Ann Johnson and Mary Holland.

7 Mary Elizabeth Holland. George Gasaway and Thomas J. Jones.

8 Melvina Holland. Richard Willey King.

9 James Adolphus Holland. Laura C. Johnson.

10 Lillie Belle Holland. John H. Gibson.

11 Ida Josephine Holland. James Wesley Halford.

12 William Richard Holland. Minnie Buckner.

$1^{1}8^{2}7^{3}1^{4}$ Charles Cairo Cloud. Mary Jane Townsend nee Horn.

2 Laura Vianna Cloud. William Lemuel Cowart.

OK 3 Robert Littleton Cloud. Lucy Adair.

4 James Loamner Cloud. Sarah J. Townsend.

5 Hallie Etta Cloud. Benjamin Felix McPherson.

6 John Edward Coud.

7 Joseph Henry Cloud. Catherine Christy.

8 George Starr Cloud. Lura———.

9 William Monroe Cloud. Lena Bates.

$1^{1}8^{2}8^{3}1^{4}$ Charles Ward.

$1^{1}8^{2}9^{3}1^{4}$ Mary Keziah Ward.

2 Martha Ward.

3 Annie Ward.

4 John Ward.

5 Charles Ward.

6 Samuel Ward.

7 Martin Ward.

8 Harry Ward.

$1^{1}8^{2}10^{3}1^{4}$ Annie Ward.

$1^{1}8^{2}11^{3}1^{4}$ Martha Ward.

2 Annie Ward.

3 Charles Ward.

Cordery.

1^1 Thomas Cordery. Susannah nee Sonicooie.

1^11^2 Sarah Cordery. John Rogers.

2 Lucy Cordery. Robert Rogers.

OK 3 Nannie Cordery. Parker Collins.

4 Charlotte Cordery. Henry Vickery.

5 David Cordery. Charlotte Goss.

6 Hettie Cordery. Henry Vickery and John Vance.

7 Early Cordery. Charlotte Berryhill.

8 Susan Cordery. John Mosley.

$1^11^21^3$ Robert Rogers. Mary Ann Baptiste and Mary Scott Jones.

2 William Rogers. Mary Vann Neely nee McNair and Louisa Reedy.

OK 3 Johnson K. Rogers. * Octavia Ann Mount.

4 Joseph Rogers. Hannah Foster.

5 Lovely Rogers.

6 Mary Rogers. Nicholas Byers McNair.

7 Jackson Rogers. Sarah G. Blackburn. A42

8 Cynthia Rogers. John Lowe.

9 Annie Chapel Rogers. John Wilson Lenoir.

10 Henry Curtis Rogers. Louisa Jane Thompson nee Blackburn.

11 George Rogers. Polina Phillips.

12 John Pendergrass Rogers. Martha Crawford and Mary Eugenia Eliza Spencer nee Garland.

$1^12^21^3$ Catherine Rogers. Alexander McDaniel.

2 Nannie Rogers. Alexander Jordan and John Anderson.

OK 3 Robert Rogers. Sallie Vann.

4 John Rogers. Hettie Mosely and Catherine Vann.

5 James Rogers. *

$1^13^21^3$ Ira Rogers. Charlotte Wickett.

---

2 Sallie Collins. Charles Harris.

3 Jennie Collins. Charles Harris.

4 Eliza Collins. Bird Harris.

5 Susan Collins. William Harris.

6 Catherine Collins. William Harrison Autry.

7 Mary Collins. *

8 Martha Collins. *

9 Lucinda Collins. Henry Sutton.

10 Nannie Collins. John Mimms.

11 Joseph Collins. Mary Miller.

12 Parker Dickson Collins. Mary Treble.

$1^14^21^3$ Annie Vickery. John Pinder, —— Ratliff, John Forbison and Archibald Wilson.

2 Jennie Vickery. George Freeman.

OK 3 Charles Vickery. Malinda Black.
4 Mary Vickery. Samuel Bennett.
5 Sallie Vickery. Thomas Cordery.
6 John Vickery. Eliza McNulty.
7 Lucy Vickery. Andrew Jackson Cobb.
8 Susie Vickery. Andrew Jackson Cobb.
$1^15^21^3$ Thomas Cordery. Sallie Vickery.
2 Wilson Cordery. Nannie Miller and Nannie Hall.
OK 3 Andrew Cordery. Mary Adair nee Miller.
4 Seaborn Cordery. Margaret Fawling, Catherine McDaniel, Amanda Jane Fulton and Nannie J. Smith.
5 Charlotte Cordery. Unakateehee Rider.
6 Nannie Cordery. Washington Miller, —— Hampton and Lemuel Sanders.
$1^16^21^3$ Wilborn Vickery. *
2 Margaret Vickery. Samuel Bumgarner.
OK 3 Henry Vickery. *

---

4 Richard Early Vance. Mary Sunday nee Burgess.
5 Susannah Vance. William Burgess.
$1^17^21^3$ Nannie Angeline Cordery. Joseph Collins.

---

2 Sarah Ann Cordery. James Fox.
OK 3 David Cordery. *
$1^18^21^3$ Mary Mosley. *
2 Hettie Mosley. John Rogers.
OK 3 Annie Mosley. John P. Stidham.
4 Alfred Mosley. *
5 Delilah Mosley. Charles Fox Taylor.
6 Sarah Ruth Mosley. Lewis Clark Ramsey and Ezekial Taylor.
7 John Mosley. Martha Ramsey.
$1^11^21^31^4$ Charles Rogers. Louisa Nailor.
2 Gilbert Rogers. Mary Ann Shira.
OK 3 William Rogers. *
4 John Howard Rogers. Catherine Marcum nee Ward and Mary Ann Caulk.
5 Sarah Ellen Rogers. Redbird Harris.
6 Robert Emmett Rogers. *
7 Thomas Tipton Rogers. Nannie Elizabeth Brink.

---

8 Jackson Thaddeus Rogers. Mary Jane Owen.
9 Robie Rogers. Sterling Austin.

---

10 George Mitchell Rogers. Elizabeth Rebecca Foster.
$1^11^22^31^4$ Albina McNair Rogers. Anderson Smith Bell.
2 Henry Rogers. Martha McNair.

OK 3 David M. Rogers. Mary Strickland.
4 Robert Nicholas Rogers. Sarah Jones.

---

5 Mary Rogers. James Douglas.
6 Sarah Rogers. Joseph L. Moore.
7 William Rogers. *
8 Augustus Lovely Rogers. Margaret Hallman and Julia A. Petree.
$1^1 1^2 4^3 1^4$ Eliza Mary Rogers. William Harris.
2 Oscar Rogers. Elmira Josephine Bolin and Queen——.
OK 3 Sarah Jemima Rogers. James Chastain Blythe and Frank Skinner.
4 Margaret Caroline Rogers. *
5 John Rogers. *
6 Catherine Rogers. Mansfield Seymore
7 Joseph Ann Rogers. Willis Claybourne Hall
$1^1 1^2 5^3 1^4$ Lovely Rogers.

---

2 Joseph Lovely Rogers. Margaret McCarty.
3 John Cooley Rogers. *
$1^1 1^2 6^3 1^4$ Sarah McNair. Brice Martin Adair.
2 Martha McNair. * Joel Bryan Mayes.
OK 3 Lucullus McNair. Rachel Mayes.
4 John R. McNair. Cynthia Hufaker and Elizabeth Parrott
5 Clement McNair. *
6 Mary Delilah McNair. Benjamin Franklin Adair.
7 Talbert McNair. Nellie Carter.
8 Oscar McNair. *
9 Nicholas Benjamin McNair. Rachel Sanders and Martha E. Jones.
$1^1 1^2 7^3 1^4$ Laura Rogers. Thomas Dunn Beard.
2 Emily Lovely Cherokee Rogers. Nathan Wofford.
OK 3 Sarah Rogers. William Cavender.
4 William Ridge Rogers. Lucy P. Rogers.
$1^1 1^2 8^3 1^4$ Julia P. Lowe. *
2 Sarah Alice Lowe. George Moor.
OK 3 John J. Lowe. Annie Knox.
4 Octavia Lowe. * Jackson Nichols.
$1^1 1^2 9^3 1^4$ Henry Lenoir. *
2 Mary Octavia Lenoir.
OK 3 Thomas Rogers Lenoir. Mary J. Franklin.
4 John Albert Lenoir. Mary Jackson.
5 Sarah Frances Lenoir. Zachariah Taylor Roberts.
6 Cynthia Ann Lenoir. Marion Roberts.
7 Emma Elizabeth Lenoir. Alexander Pearson Roberts.
$1^1 1^2 10^3 1^4$ Mary Kenney Rogers.
2 Catherine Rogers. Isaac Newton Strickland.

OK 3 Lucy P. Rogers. * William Ridge Rogers.

4 Eugenia Overby Rogers. Wiliam Rufus Greer.

5 William Henry Rogers. Margaret Elizabeth McGhee nee Pemberton.

6 Stonewall Jackson Rogers. Fannie Kelly.

$1^1 1^2 11^3 1^4$ Augusta Rogers. Charles Stinson.

2 Levaga Rogers. Isabelle Pulcher.

OK 3 Labrunta Rogers. *

$1^1 1^2 12^3 1^4$ Walter Scott Rogers. Sarah Louisiana Hogue.

---

2 Georgia Cordelia Rogers. Walter Price Bryce, John Warren Pogue and Albert Livingston McAffree.

OK 3 Minnie Isadore Rogers. Albert Wales Thomas and William Philips McBride.

4 Laura Garland Rogers. Presley Bartow Cole.

5 Leona Rogers. Charles Lloyd Stealey.

6 John Mann Rogers.

$1^1 2^2 1^3 1^4$ Lucy McDaniel. *

2 David McDaniel. Emma McCall.

OK 3 Ellis McDaniel. Rachel Bell and Emma McLaughlin.

4 Robert McDaniel. * Cinderella Linder.

5 Catherine McDaniel. Seaborn Cordery, Edward Marsh and Stephen Duncan.

6 Sarah McDaniel. * Robert Klaus.

7 Lewis McDaniel. *

$1^1 2^2 2^3 1^4$ Elizabeth Jordan. Dimar W. Reeves, Benjamin Pope and Hiram Barnes.

2 Andrew Vann Jordan. Sallie Ann Williams.

OK 3 Eliza Jane Jordan. Samuel Houston Hensley.

4 Catherine Jordan. John Ivey.

5 Alexander Jordan. Catherine E. Matthies and Cecilia Rebecca Nichols.

---

6 Robert Anderson. *

7 Richard Anderson. Louisa Dunbar and Julia F. Stanley nee Dunbar.

8 Sarah Anderson. John Wilson.

$1^1 2^2 3^3 1^4$ Margaret Lavinia Rogers. Allison Woodville Timberlake.

OK 2 Clement Vann Rogers. Mary America Scrimsher and Mary Bible.

$1^1 2^2 4^3 1^4$ Nannie Rogers. *

$1^1 3^2 1^3 1^4$ Elizabeth Ann Rogers. George Sullivan.

OK 2 John Rogers. * Catherine Wickett.

3 Nannie Rogers. John McDaniel.

4 Joseph Rogers. Nannie Smith.

5 Emily Rogers. Edley Adair and Louis Dunbach.

6 Ira Rogers. *

$1^1 3^2 2^3 1^4$ Nannie Harris. Willis Cumpton.

2 Parker Collins Harris. Elizabeth Little and Narcissa Little.

OK 3 Thomas Jackson Harris. Martha Bailey.

$1^1 2^2 2^3 1^4$ Mary Narcissa Harris. George Sisson and Jesse Wolf.

2 Martha Elizabeth Harris. William Jackson.

OK 3 Sue Harris. Alfred Mason Gott.

4 Joseph Charles Harris. Emma Jane Walker.

5 Trusle Bird Harris. * Mary Elizabeth Alberty.

$1^1 3^2 5^3 1^4$ Emily Harris. *

2 James S. Harris. Jennie Hunter and Pyrene Strickland.

OK 3 Joseph B. Harris. Beuna Vista Deaver and Rosa B. Chew.

4 Redbird Harris. Sarah Ellen Rogers.

5 William G. Harris. *

6 Charles Harris. Apsilla Bailey.

7 Parker Collins Harris. Mary Angeline Davis.

8 Eliza Jane Savannah Harris. William D. McMakin.

9 Philo Harris. Margaret Hammer nee Smith.

10 John Harris.

11 Colonel Johnson Harris. Nannie E. Fields, Mary Elizabeth Adair and Caroline Alice Collins nee Hall.

$1^1 3^2 6^3 1^4$ Mary Ann Autry. * John H. Shinn.

2 Martha Autry. *

3 Elizabeth Jane Autry. John H. Shinn.

4 Edward Parker Autry. *

5 Christopher Columbus Autry. Mary Jane Jones nee Bridges.

6 Catherine Autry. Robert Jackson King and George Wallace.

7 William Harrison Autry. *

$1^1 3^2 10^3 1^4$ Sarah Ann Mimms.

2 Eliza Mimms. James Hughes.

3 Cenia Mimms. James Hughes.

4 Rennie Mimms. *

5 Laura Mimms.

6 John Mimms.

7 Columbus Mimms.

$1^1 3^2 11^3 1^4$ Parker Collins. Mildred Matthews.

$1^1 3^2 12^3 1^4$ Joseph Boudinot Collins. *

2 Martha Ann Hall Collins. George Grisom McDaniel.

OK 3 Mary Malissa Collins. Robert W. Foster.

4 Thomas Parker Collins. Caroline Alice Hall.

$1^1 4^2 1^3 1^4$ Eli Pindar. *

2 Susie Pindar. William Wharton Chisholm * and William Archibald Foreman.

3 Charles Pindar. *

4 Jefferson Ratliff. Mary Ann McLain.

---

5 John Forbison. *

---

6 Mary Ann Wilson. William V. Shepherd.
7 Samantha Wilson. * Samuel Crossland.
$1^14^22^31^4$ Sarah Charlotte Freeman. *
2 Mary Elizabeth Freeman. John Ross Meigs.
3 Cynthia Louisa Freeman.
OK 4 Salina Keziah Freeman. William Noel Stewart.
5 Henry Benajah Freeman. Elizabeth Goss.
6 Georgianna Freeman. Nathaniel Wofford.
$1^14^23^31^4$ Mary Elizabeth Vickery. David McLaughlin Beck.
2 John Henry Vickery. Mary Doss.
3 Malinda Jane Bennett. Sidney L. Erwin and William James
4 James Newton Vickery. Martha Emma Padgett.
5 Frances Isabelle Vickery.
6 Frank Scott Vickery. Lydia Padgett nee Bettis.
$1^14^24^31^4$ Simpson Clark Bennett. * Emily Kell.
2 Eliza Levisa Bennett. Daniel Ross Coody.
3 Malinda aJne Bennett. Sidney L. Erwin and Wiilliam James Kuhn.
$1^14^25^31^4$ Malissa Arminda Cordery. Austin McLain and William Sanders.
2 David Jackson Cordery. *
OK 3 Andrew Cornelius Cordery. Alice Schmidtman nee Hildebrand and Mary Belle McGeehon.
4 Charlotte Jane Cordery. Almon Martin.
5 Lucy Ann Cordery. *
6 Mary Susan Cordery. * Lewis R. Coody.
$1^14^26^31^4$ Wilborn Vickery.
2 Samuel Vickery.
3 Elsie Jane Vickery. * Henry Clay Lowrey.
4 Henry Vickery.
5 Mary Vickery. Henry R. Collins.
6 John Vickery. Elizabeth J. Quinton.
7 Susan Vickery. James Monroe Lowrey.
$1^14^27^31^4$ Josephine Cobb. Josiah M. Pugh.
2 Josephine Cobb. *
OK 3 Mary Elizabeth Cobb. Walter Scott Agnew.
4 Margaret Charlotte Cobb. George Zufall.
$1^14^28^31^4$ Rufus Benton Cobb. Mary Kell.
2 James Henry Cobb. Alice Chisholm and Ida Still nee Hollingsworth.
3 Edward Cobb. * Nannie Harper.
4 Charles Nathaniel Cobb. *
5 Howell Cobb.

$1^15^21^31^4$ Malissa Arminda Cordery. Austin McLain and William Sanders.

2 David Jackson Cordery. *

OK 3 Andrew Cornelius Cordery. Alice Schmidtman nee Hildebrand and Mary Belle McGeehon.

4 Charlotte Jane Cordery. Almon Martin.

5 Lucy Ann Cordery. *

6 Mary Susan Cordery. * Lewis R. Coody.

$1^15^22^31^4$ Lewis C. Cordery. Eliza Hicks nee Gourd.

2 Thomas Clark Cordery. Amanda Pack and Annie Nunnally.

3 Malderine Cordery. Henry Collins and Samuel Horn.

4 Cornelius Cordery. Sarah Eastman nee Tucker.

5 William Lafayette Cordery. Elizabeth R. Gourd and Jeanette R. Gourd.

6 Anderson Cordery. Laura Isaacs and Susie Hendricks.

---

7 Louisa Cordery. Albert Anderson.

8 Joseph Cordery. Elizabeth Brown.

9 Rosa Cordery. Henry Graham and William Marsh.

$1^15^23^35^4$ Lovely Rogers Cordery. *

---

2 Frances Jane Cordery. Hugh McAffrey.

$1^15^24^31^4$ Seaborn Cordery. *

---

2 Mary Ellen Cordery. Jehn Eve Kelly.

OK 3 Florence Jane Cordery.

4 Maud Cordery.

5 Thomas Jefferson Cordery. Mary E. Fagan nee McCully.

6 James Benjamin Cordery.

---

7 John Wilson Cordery.

8 May Cordery.

9 Sallie Cordery.

10 Charlotte Cordery.

$1^15^25^31^4$ Johnson Rider. *

2 William Rider. Nancy Jane Riley and Louisa Sykes.

OK 3 David Rider. Elizabeth Baldridge and Cynthia Bullock.

4 Nannie Rider. Cyrus Augustus Watkins.

5 Stand Watie Rider. Alice Rush.

6 Charles Rider. Delilah Nivens.

7 Susan Rider. *

$1^15^26^31^4$ Warren Andrew Miller. Mary Elizabeth Crittenden.

2 Mary Miller. Robin Bean.

3 Elizabeth Miller. *

4 Noah Miller. Hester C. Yarborough.

5 Sallie Miller. Henry Hines and M. D. L. Dowell.

6 Martin Miller. Nannie Foreman and Alice Reynolds

---

7 John William Hampton. Vicey Peirce and Louisa Roberts.

$1^1 6^2 2^3 1^4$ John Wise Bumgarner. Susan Priscilla Johnson nee Walker

2 Mary Jane Bumgarner. William Davidson Clingan.

OK 3 James Lovely Bumgarner. Charlotte E. Ward.

4 Margaret Blanche Bumgarner. Dr. Rollin Aaron Burr.

$1^1 6^2 4^3 1^4$ Sue Vance. Alexander Lewis McDaniel.

$1^1 6^2 5^3 1^4$ Elizabeth Burgess. John Wilkerson.

2 Sarah Ann Burgess. John McPherson and William Williams.

OK 3 Hettie Burgess. Rufus Denton.

4 John Bean Burgess. Emma McDaniel nee McCall and Malissa Hogan nee Martin.

5 Jennie Burgess. David Weaver.

6 Cooweescoowee Burgess. Dona Whitman.

$1^1 7^2 1^3 1^4$ Marthena Collins. *

2 Luvenia Collins. Andrew George.

OK 3 Ruth Ann Collins. Caleb Powell Wright.

4 James Bradley Collins. *

5 Joseph Flournoy Collins. *

6 Catherine Collins. Jesse Clinton Alberty.

7 John Parker Collins. Sabra Ann Selvidge nee Beck and Elizabeth Beck nee Davis.

8 Theodosia Collins. *

9 Martha Collins. Henry Beck.

$1^1 7^2 2^3 1^4$ Frank Bowden Cordery. Laura Daylight.

---

2 Jennie Fox. Robert Miller and Amos Anderson.

OK 3 Eliza Fox.

4 Moses Fox.

5 Passie Fox.

6 David Fox.

7 Susie Fox.

8 Lucinda Fox.

$1^1 8^2 2^3 1^4$ Nannie Rogers. *

$1^1 8^2 3^3 1^4$ George Sanford Mosely. Neosho Russell nee Davis.

$1^1 8^2 5^3 1^4$ William Brewer Taylor. *

$1^1 8^2 6^3 1^4$ Susan Elizabeth Ramsey. Joseph Morgan Allton.

$1^1 8^2 7^3 1^4$ Mary Delilah Mosley. *

CHAPTER XVIII

Continuation of Old Families

Daniel.

1^1 Nannie Still Marmaduke Daniel.

$1^2 1^1$ James Daniel. Mary Buffington. See Grant $1^1 1^2 1^3 8^4$

2 Moses Daniel. Martha Tarrant.

3 Catherine Daniel. Ellis Buffington. See Grant $1^1 1^2 1^3 7^4$

4 Mary Daniel. Thomas Buffington and Lewis BlackburnA43.

5 Walker Daniel. *

6 John Ross Daniel. Martha Martin. See Grant $1^1 1^2 1^3 3^4 4^5$

7 Nannie Daniel.

8 Jennie Daniel. * Hiram McCreary.

9 Thomas Daniel. *

$1^1 4^2 1^3$ Susannah Buffington. Alfred Hudson.

2 Joshua Buffington. Elizabeth Welch and Sabra Lynch.

OK 3 Nannie Buffington. * Thomas Fox Taylor.

---

4 Elizabeth Blackburn. Alfred Scudder.

5 Frances H. Blackburn. Madison Hudson and Samuel Weil.

6 Mary Blackburn. Thomas Fox Taylor and George Harlan Starr. *

7 Sarah G. Blackburn. Jackson Rogers. A42

8 Louisa Blackburn. Alfred Thompson and Henry Curtis Rogers.

9 Cynthia Emily Blackburn. John S. Oliver.

10 Martha Catherine Blackburn. William Pierce Nichols.

$1^1 4^2 1^3 1^4$ Louisa C. Hudson. * Jacob Alberty.

2 Joshua Thomas Buffington Hudson. Sarah Berry.

$1^1 4^2 2^3 1^4$ Nannie Buffington. William West Alberty, James Blake and William Levesque Wilder.

---

2 William Wirt Buffington. Josephine Bell and Caroline Thompson nee McCord.

OK 3 John Ross Buffington. Nancy Jane Bryan .

4 Webster Buffington. *

5 Eliza Buffington. Joseph George Washington Vann.

6 Mary Jane Buffington. Robert Fletcher Wyly.

$1^1 4^2 4^3 1^4$ Josephine Helen Scudder. Matthew Bell.

2 Frances Henrietta Scudder. Thomas Allen Warwick.

OK 3 Jacob McCarty Scudder. *

4 Lewis Blackburn Scudder. Malinda Elmira Kelly.

5 William Henry Harrison Scudder. Margaret J. Garmany.

$1^1 4^2 5^3 1^4$ Lewis Blackburn Hudson. Nannie Malinda Williams.

$1^1 4^2 6^3 1^4$ John Martin Taylor. *

$1^2 4^1 7^3 1^4$ Laura Rogers. Thomas Dunn Bard.

2 Emily Lovely Cherokee Rogers. Nathan Wofford.
OK 3 Sarah Rogers. William Cavender.
4 William Ridge Rogers. Lucy P. Rogers.
$1^14^28^31^4$ Mary Kinney Rogers.
2 Catherine Rogers. Isaac Newton Strickland.
OK 3 Lucy P. Rogers. * William Ridge Rogers.
4 Eugene Overby Rogers. William Rufus Greer.
5 William Henry Rogers. Margaret Elizabeth McGee nee Pemberton.
6 Stonewall Jackson Rogers. Fannie Kelly.
$1^14^29^31^4$ Georgia Ann Oliver. William Hamilton.
2 Joshua Oliver. *
OK 3 Albert Gallatin Oliver. Stella Roberson.
4 Homer Oliver. *
$1^14^210^31^4$ Mary Jane Nichols. Nicholas Bittings.
2 Henry Nichols. *
3 Jackson Nichols. Octavia Lowe.
4 Augustus Beauregard Nichols. Alice S. McGhee.
5 Sarah Catherine Nichols. Micajah Pope Haynes.
6 Emma Nichols. *
7 Elizabeth Nichols. *
8 Taylor Osceola Nichols. Laura Stafford.

Chisholm-Wilson

1^1Malinda Wharton. Thomas Chisholm and William Wilson. A44
1^11^2 Jennie Elizabeth Chisholm. Joseph Blagne Lynde and Caswell Wright Bruton.
2 Alfred Finney Chisholm. Margaret Harper.
OK 3 William Wharton Chisholm. Susie Pindar.
4 Narcissa Clark Chisholm. Robert Latham Owen.
5 Emily Walker Wilson. Napoleon Bonaparte Breedlove.
6 William Wilson. * Alice Coody.
$1^11^21^3$ Alice Lynde. William Otway Owen.
2 Caroline Walton Bruton. John Washington Breedlove.
OK 3 Robert Owen Bruton. *
4 Wilson Otho Bruton. Mary L. Goodman.
$1^13^21^3$ Alice Chisholm. James Henry Cobb.
2 Narcissa Chisholm. * Matthew Archer and Frank Taylor.
$1^14^21^31^4$ William Otway Chalmers Owen.
OK 2 Robert Latham Owen. Daisy Hester.
$1^15^21^3$ Lelia Wilson Breedlove. James Senora Stapler.
2 Waller Winchester Breedlove. Priscilla Williams.
OK 3 Emma Maria Breedlove. *
4 Florence Breedlove. Othie Andrew Smith.
5 Jennie Breedlove. *
$1^11^21^31^4$ Robert Otway Owen. Rowena Booth.
2 Jennie Owen. Charles Heald.
OK 3 William Otway Owen. Mary H. Severs.

4 Charles Owen. Pauline Webb.

5 Owen Owen. Cassie Breedlove.

6 Alice Owen.

$1^11^22^31^4$ James Willloughby Breedlove. Mary Beatty Eiffort.

2 William Otway Breedlove. Cecil Watts.

OK 3 John Chisholm Breedlove. Allie Rhea Garrett.

4 Cassie Breedlove. Owen Owen.

5 Wharton Hicks Breedlove. Ordie Boozman.

6 Walton David Breedlove. Ora Walton.

7 Charles Winchester Breedlove. Esther Snyder.

$1^11^24^31^4$ Caswell Bates Bruton. Nina Smith.

OK 2 Robert Otho Bruton. Edith Brownfield.

$1^13^21^31^4$ James Edward Cobb. Sarah C. Morris.

2 Charles Henry Cobb. Addie Watson.

OK 3 Andrew Jackson Cobb. Lucy Watson.

4 William Wharton Cobb.

5 Susannah May Cobb. Roy Zufall.

$1^14^21^31^4$ William Otway Chalmers Owen. Una.

$1^14^22^31^4$ Dorothea Owen. John Hawkins.

$1^15^21^31^4$ Lorena Oklahoma Stapler. Earl Hampton Fleming.

2 Anna Phillips Stapler. Williams Jerrems.

OK 3 Otway Hicks Stapler. * Evelyn Gidney.

4 John Wharton Stapler.

$1^15^24^31^4$ Lee Breedlove Smith.

2 Lelia Lucile Smith.

OK 3 Ruby Emily Smith.

4 Owen Philip Smith.

$1^11^21^31^41^5$ Otway Owen.

OK 2 Owen Owen.

$1^11^22^31^41^5$ Willoughby Walton Breedlove.

2 Jack Thompson Breedlove.

OK 3 William Curtis Breedlove.

$1^11^22^32^41^5$ Bessie Breedlove.

2 William Otway Breedlove.

$1^11^22^33^41^5$ John Chisholm Breedlove.

$1^11^22^35^41^5$ Jane Gail Breedlove.

$1^11^22^36^41^5$ Walton David Breedlove.

$1^11^22^37^41^5$ Signa Gloria Breedlove.

$1^11^24^31^41^5$ Dale Bruton.

2 Joseph Bruton.

OK 3 Wilson Otho Bruton.

$1^14^22^31^41^5$ Owen Hutchins Hawkins.

$1^15^21^31^41^5$ James Stapler Fleming.

2 John Barton Fleming.

3 Anna Eugenia Fleming.

$1^15^21^32^41^5$ Alexander Stapler Jerrems.

Carter

1^{1} Nathaniel Carter.

$1^{1}1^{2}$ Alexander Carter. Nannie.

2 Jennie Carter. Reuben Tyner.

OK 3 David Carter. Jennie Riley. A45

$1^{1}2^{2}1^{3}$ Nathan Tyner. Elizabeth Childers.

2 Mary Tyner. ———Irving, William Riley Butler and John Ramsey.

OK 3 Jackson Tyner. Delilah Seabolt and Letitia Gunter nee Keys.

4 Eliza Tyner. John Ramsey, Jefferson Hair and Samuel Ward.

5 Leroy Tyner. Mary Sanders.

$1^{1}3^{2}1^{3}$ Richard Carter. Nannie Coody.

2 Alexander Carter. *

OK 3 John Ross Carter. * Sarah Rogers.

4 Benjamin Wisner Carter. Nannie Elliott and Serena Josephine Guy.

5 Diana Carter. William Parrott.

6 Sallie F. Carter. Looney Rattlinggourd.

7 Jefferson Carter. Susie Robertson nee Lowrey and Mary Webb.

8 Nannie Carter. James Brown.

9 David Tecumseh Carter. Emma Williams Chambers.

10 Osceola Carter. *

$1^{1}2^{2}1^{3}1^{4}$ Lewis Tyner. Sallie Parris and Ellen White.

2 Alexander Tyner. Catherine Smith and Jennie Cain.

OK 3 Medley Tyner. Nannie Childers.

4 Seaborn Thorn Tyner. Elizabeth Bender and Catherine Sampson nee McLish.

5 Reuben Bartley Tyner. Mary Ann Rogers and Roxie Ann Pierson.

6 Doctor Jayne Tyner.

7 Sarah Jane Tyner. John W. Baker and John Thomas.

$1^{1}2^{2}2^{3}1^{4}$ Eliza Irving. Neeley Denton.

2 Cynthia Irving. Isaac William Keys.

---

3 Ruth Ann Butler. Hugh Russell.

4 William Butler. *

---

5 Mary Ramsey. Schooler Cobb and Calvin L. Kinyon.

$1^{1}2^{2}3^{3}1^{4}$ Reuben R. Tyner. Almira Irons.

2 Elizabeth Tyner. * Edward Melton.

---

3 Nannie Tyner.. William Pettit.

4 Lydia Tyner. Bluford West Rider.

5 George W. Tyner. Mary Shaw and Mary Ann Elder.

6 Fannie Tyner. *
$1^1 2^2 4^3 1^4$ Jennie Ramsey. Isaac William Keys.
2 Lewis Clark Ramsey. Sarah Ruth Mosely.
3 Catherine Ramsey. Cyrus Lawrence, ——Holt, Samuel Keys and Moses Parris.

---

4 Frances Marion Hair. Sarah Watkins.

---

5 Joseph Ward. Malissa York.
6 John Ward. Annie York.
7 Sarah Ward. William Clemens York.
$1^1 2^2 5^3 1^4$ Martha Tyner. Frank Boyd Swift.
$1^1 3^2 1^3 1^4$ James Madison Carter. *
2 Jennie Carter. *
3 Nellie Carter. * Talbert McNair.
4 Richard R. Carter. *
$1^1 3^2 4^3 1^4$ John Elliott Carter. Mary Eliza Heald.

OK 2 Charles David Carter. Ada Gertrude Wilson and Cecile Jones nee Whittington.
$1^1 3^2 5^3 1^4$ Elizabeth Parrott. * John R. McNair.
2 Cynthia Parrott. Dr. Thomas Benton Dickson.
OK 3 Serena Carter Parrott. William Fair McSpadden.
$1^1 3^2 6^3 1^4$ James Gourd.
OK 2 Henry Gourd. Tottie M. Trotter and Sarah Hair.
$1^1 3^2 9^3 1^4$ Minnie Carter. * Stephen Riley Lewis.

Adair

1^1 ——Adair.
$1^1 1^2$ John Adair. Ga-ho-ga and Jennie Kilgore. A47
2 Edward Adair. Elizabeth.
$1^1 1^2 1^3$ Samuel Adair. Margaret Deeson and Edith Pounds.
2 Walter Adair. Rachel Thompson. A48
OK 3 Charlotte Adair. Stephen Ray.
4 Edward Adair. Martha Ritchie.
5 John Adair. *

---

6 James Adair.
7 Thomas Benjamin Adair. Rachel Lynch.
8 Margaret Jane Adair. William Richardson Nicholson.
9 William Henry Adair.
10 Charles Duncan Adair.
11 George Washington Adair.
12 Elbert Earl Adair.
13 Mary Adair.
14 Benjamin Franklin Adair.
15 John Alexander Adair. Eliza Keys nee Gunter.
$1^1 2^2 1^3$ Edward Adair. Nannie Shields and Mary Harnage.

OK 2 Walter Scott Adair. Nannie Harris. A49
$1^1 1^2 1^3 1^4$ Samuel Adair. Mary Hughes.
2 Andrew Adair. Sallie Copeland, Mary Miller, Elsie and Annie Vann.
OK 3 Charlotte Adair. Stephen Ray.
4 Margaret Catherine Adair. Thomas Wilson Bigby.

---

5 Mary Adair. Benjamin Franklin Adair and George W. Gage.
6 Rachel Pounds Adair. James Jenkins Trott.
7 Anna Adair. *
8 John Lafayette Adair. Elizabeth Alabama Scrimsher.
9 Elizabeth Adair. Sterling Scott.
$1^1 1^2 2^3 1^4$ Mary Adair. Thomas Goss.
2 George Washington Adair. Martha Martin.
OK 3 Nannie Adair. Samuel Mayes.
4 Sallie Adair. James Jenkins Trott.
5 John Thompson Adair. Frances E. Thompson and Penelope Mayfield.
$1^1 1^2 3^3 1^4$ John Adair Bell. Jennie Martin, Elizabeth Harnage and Sabra Buffington nee Lynch.
2 Elizabeth Hughes Bell. George Washington Candy.
OK 3 David Bell. Nannie Martin and Elizabeth Thornton nee Phillips. *
4 Samuel W. Bell. Rachel Martin.
5 Nannie Bell. George Harlan Starr.
6 Devereaux Jarrette Bell. * Juliette Lewis Vann.
7 Sallie Caroline Bell. Stand Watie.
8 Charlotte Bell. William J. Dupree.
9 James Madison Bell. Caroline Lynch.
10 Martha J. Bell. Walter Adair Duncan.
$1^1 1^2 4^3 1^4$ Benjamin Franklin Adair. Mary Adair.
2 John Adair. Annie Berry Graham.
OK 3 Narcena Adair. Collins McDonald.
4 Sarah Ann Adair. Calvin Price Guthrie.

---

5 Calvin Adair. Lucinda Miller.
$1^1 1^2 7^3 1^4$ John Lynch Adair. Mary Jane Jeffries.
$1^1 1^2 15^3 1^4$ Benjamin Franklin Adair. Lola Spurlock.
OK 2 Eliza Adair. George Matthews and Carter Daniel Markham.
$1^1 3^2 1^3 1^4$ Delilah Adair. Joseph McMinn Starr.
2 Susie Adair. *

OK 3 Jennie Adair. John Perry Oliver Clyne.
4 Edley Adair. Emily Rogers.
5 Elizabeth Adair. John Hildebrand Cookson.
$1^1 2^2 2^3 1^4$ Elizabeth Neeley Adair. Timothy Meigs Walker.
OK 3 Susan Caroline Adair. Robert S. C. Noel and Edward Dow Allen.

4 Sarah Ann Adair. William Penn Adair.

5 Edward Underwood Adair. *

6 Mary Buffington Adair. Walter Thompson Adair.

7 Hugh Montgomery Adair. Elizabeth Jane Hearst, Martha L. Johnson and Phoeba Acena Morris nee Pace.

8 Lucy Fields Adair. Waldemar S. Lindsley.

9 Minerva Cornelia Adair. *

$1^1 1^2 1^3 1^4 1^5$ George M. Adair. Catherine Fields.

2 Charlotte Adair. Charles Pettit and Archibald Sixkiller.

OK 3 Audelia Adair. Dennis Gonzales.

4 John Bell Adair. Elizabeth Clingan.

$1^1 1^2 1^3 2^4 1^5$ George Washington Adair. Malzenie Elizabeth Linder * and Mary ——.

2 Margaret Adair. Jesse Mayfield and Samuel Adair Bigby.

OK 3 Jennie Adair. * James Christopher McCoy and John Hunt.

4 Samuel Adair. * Jennie Buffington.

5 Collins Adair. *

6 Emily Adair. William Nucholls Littlejohn.

7 Charlotte Ann Adair. Joshua Sanders.

---

8 Ellen Adair. Richard Martin McCoy.

9 Rufus Bell Adair. Jennie Fields and Elizabeth Sabina Buffington.

---

10 Susan Adair. * John Hunt.

11 Catherine Adair. *

14 Malzerine Elizabeth Adair. Caleb Ellis Starr.

---

15 Rosella Adair. John Downing, George Downing and Mitchell Squirrel.

16 Edward Sylvester Adair. Rebecca Baugh and Caroline Boudinot Brewer.

$1^1 1^2 1^3 3^4 1^5$ Margaret Ray. Robert Garvin.

2 Sarah Catherine Ray. James Devine and William Covington Ghormley.

OK 3 Elizabeth Ray. Joshua Bertholf Duncan.

4 Ruth Ray. *

5 Wesley Ray. *

6 Walter Adair Ray. *

7 Andrew Ray. *

$1^1 1^2 1^3 4^4 1^5$ Samuel Adair Bigby. Margaret Mayfield nee Adair.

2 Mary Ann Bigby. Charles Austin Augustus Rider.

OK 3 James Lafayette Bigby. Nannie Caroline McCoy.

4 Charlotte Elizabeth Bigby. Robert Harrison Fletcher.

5 Benjamin Jackson Bigby. *

6 Stephen Foreman Bigby. *

7 Esther Smith Bigby. Harrison Roberts.

8 Thomas Whitfield Bigby. Rebecca Thompson.
9 David Taylor Bigby. Nancy Jane Guilliams.
10 Malinda Jane Bigby.
$1^1 1^2 1^3 5^4 1^5$ Martha Jane Adair. Silas Aiken.
2 Ross Adair. *
OK 3 Mary Elizabeth Adair. *
4 Benjamin Adair. Sarah Guerin.
5 Rachel Ann Adair. James Roe Trippard and Charles L. Bowden.
$1^1 1^2 1^3 6^4 1^5$ Nannie A. Trott. Joseph George Vann.
2 John Ross Trott. Emma A. Clayton.
OK 3 James Campbell Trott. Madora Stover.
4 Timothy Trott. *
5 Elizabeth Trott. *
6 William Lafayette Trott. Malinda Stover * and Louisa Moore.
7 Charlotte Trott. Benjamin Johnson.
8 Henry Harden Trott. Eliza Cannon nee Harlan.
$1^1 1^2 1^3 8^4 1^5$ Levi Adair. Eliza Consene nee Vann.

OK 2 John Martin Adair. Triphena Terrell.
$1^1 1^2 1^3 9^4 1^5$ Stella Ann Adair. George Washington Scott.
OK 2 Maybelle Adair. Martin Van Benge.
$1^1 1^2 2^3 1^4 1^5$ Walter Adair Goss. *
2 Benjamin Franklin Goss. Sarah Emily Bean and Demaris Pace.
OK 3 Rachel Elizabeth Goss. Richard F. Fields.
$1^1 1^2 2^3 2^4 1^5$ William Penn Adair. Sarah Ann Adair and Sue McIntosh Drew.
2 Brice Martin Adair. Sarah McNair.
OK 3 Walter Thompson Adair. Mary Buffington Adair, Ruth A. Markham and Fannie Gray.
4 John Ticanooly Adair. Martha Nannie Thompson.
5 Mary Ellen Adair. Joseph Franklin Thompson.
6 Benjamin Franklin Adair. Mary Delilah McNair.
7 Rachel Jane Adair. Milton Howard McCullough.
8 Cherokee Cornelia Adair. Jesse Bushyhead Mayes.
$1^1 1^2 2^3 3^4 1^5$ George Washington Mayes. Charlotte Bushyhead and Sarah Alice Nicodemus nee Taylor.
2 John Thompson Mayes. Cynthia Pack Davis.
OK 3 Frank A. O. Mayes.
4 James Allen Mayes. Ophelia Davis, Ruth Springston and Annie Foster.
5 Joel Bryan Mayes. *Martha McNair, Martha J. Candy and Mary Drew nee Vann.
6 Walter Adair Mayes. *
7 Rachel Mayes. Lucullus McNair and John W. Petty.

8 William Henry Mayes. Rachel May, Eliza Jane Bell, Martha McNair and Susan Virginia Weir.

9 Richard Taylor Mayes. *

10 Samuel Houston Mayes. Martha Elizabeth Vann and Minnie Harrison nee

11 Wiley B. Mayes. Emma Bonebrake, Margaret Gillis nee McLaughin and Ermina Cherokee Vann.

12 Noel French Mayes. *

$1^1 1^2 2^3 4^4 1^5$ Benjamin Walter Trott. Eliza Forester, Sarah Seabolt nee Campbell and Rebecca Stafford nee Moore.

OK 2 Mary Thompson Trott. John P. Stidham, Mark Tiger and Thomas Howie.

$1^1 1^2 2^3 5^4 1^5$ Jesse Mayfield Adair. *

2 Rachel Louvenia Adair. David McNair Faulkner.

OK 3 Sarah Ruth Adair. Charles Washington Starr.

4 Oscar Fitzaland Adair. Mary Catherine Rider and

5 Edward Everett Adair. Rachel Louvenia Twist.

6 John Harrell Adair. Emma Choate.

7 Samuel Houston Adair. Sarah Stapler Ross.

$1^1 1^2 3^3 1^4 1^5$ Andromache Bell. Harvey Shelton.

2 Maria Josephine Bell. William Wirt Buffington.

OK 3 Charlotte Bell. James W. Ivey.

4 Lucien Burr Bell. Sabra Ann Cunningham and Mary Frances Starr.

---

5 Nannie Bell. Cicero Leonidas Lynch.

---

6 Nancy Ann Bell. Quinton Kosciusko Gibson and James Ellis Harlan.

$1^1 1^2 3^3 2^4 1^5$ John Candy. *

2 Maria Candy. *

OK 3 Worcester Candy. *

4 Charlotte Candy. William Fields.

5 Martha J. Candy. * Joel Bryan Mayes.

6 Juliette Melvina Candy. John Gunter Scrimsher.

$1^1 1^2 3^3 3^4 1^5$ John Francis Bell. *

---

2 John Martin Bell. Sarah Catherine Harnage.

OK 3 Foster Bell. *

$1^1 1^2 3^3 4^4 1^5$ George Bell. *

2 John Bell. *

OK 3 Eliza Jane Bell. William Henry Mayes.

$1^1 1^2 3^3 5^4 1^5$ John Walker Starr. *

2 Mary Frances Starr. Lucien Burr Bell.

OK 3 George Colbert Starr. *

4 Ezekial Eugene Starr. Margaret Starr.

5 Joseph Jarrette Starr. *

6 Caleb Ellis Starr. Malzerine Elizabeth Adair and Jennie Butler nee.
7 Samuel Jesse Starr. Sarah Ruth McClure.
$1^{1}1^{2}3^{3}7^{4}1^{5}$ Saladin Ridge Watie. *
2 Solon Watie. *
OK 3 Nannie Josephine Watie. * John Martin Daniel.
4 Charlotte Jackoline Watie. *
$1^{1}1^{2}3^{3}8^{4}1^{5}$ Emma Dupree. * John C. Gray.
2 William E. Dupree. Fannie Wright.
OK 3 Annie Eugenia Dupree. Dr. Alfred Marshall Clinkscales.
4 Maude Ethel Dupree.
$1^{1}1^{2}3^{3}9^{4}1^{5}$ Caroline Bell. Frank Skinner.
2 Charlotte Bell. * Elijah J. Warren.
OK 3 Delia Palmer Bell. Jefferson Jordan.
4 William Watie Bell. *
$1^{1}1^{2}3^{3}10^{4}1^{5}$ Mariamme Celeste Duncan. * Thomas Everidge Oaks.
2 Anacreon Bell Duncan. *
OK 3 Jarrette Mirini Duncan. Nannie Buffington.
$1^{1}1^{2}4^{3}1^{4}1^{5}$ Martha Jane Adair. Silas Aiken.
2 Ross Adair. *
OK 3 Mary Elizabeth Adair. *
4 Benjamin Adair. Sarah Guerin.
5 Rachel Ann Adair. James Roe Trippard and Charles L. Bowden.
$1^{1}1^{2}4^{3}2^{4}1^{5}$ Mildred Thomas Adair. John Rufus Allison.
2 Virgil Balentine Adair. Talitha Jane Bates.
OK 3 Edward Alexander Adair. Narcissa Malissa Harrison.
4 Margaret Martha Adair. John Christopher Hogan.
5 Narcena Ann Berry Adair. Napoleon Bonaparte Littlejohn.
6 William Pendleton Adair. Julia Frances Allison.
$1^{1}1^{2}4^{3}3^{4}1^{5}$ John Ross McDonald. Sarah Malinda Adair.
2 Mary Ann McDonald. David Wilson Harrison.
OK 3 George Washington McDonald. Sarah Elizabeth Boles nee Jernigan.
4 Martha Caroline McDonald. Levi Anderson Daniel King Wetzel.
5 Andrew Adair McDonald. *
6 Sarah Jane McDonald. John A. Moreland.
7 Emily Clay McDonald. John Alberty.
8 Nannie Missouri McDonald. Joseph Kincaid and Addison D. Reeves.
$1^{1}1^{2}4^{3}4^{4}1^{5}$ Mary Harriette Guthrie. Benjamin Gilreath Fletcher.
2 Loren Philemon Guthrie. Sarah Emma Kelly and Mary Simms.
OK 3 Calvin Price Guthrie. Ruth Collins.
4 Sarah Ann Guthrie. William Kelly.
5 Walter Duncan Guthrie.

6 Florence Azilee Guthrie. Joseph P. Willis.
7 Oscar Guthrie.
$1^1 1^2 4^3 5^4 1^5$ Ephriam Martin Adair. Sallie Starr and Louvenia Jane Lewis.
OK 2 George Washington Adair. Lucy Starr.
$1^1 1^2 7^3 1^4 1^5$ Thomas James Adair. Lena Harnage.
2 Rachel Louisa Adair. Willliam Peters McClellan.
OK 3 Arthur Franklin Adair. Mary Elizabeth Miller.
4 John Lynch Adair. Abbie G. Boardman.
5 Mary Zoe Adair. Claude Stull Shelton.
$1^1 1^2 15^3 1^4 1^5$ Alice Adair.
2 Etta Adair.
OK 3 Olney Morgan Adair.
4 William Penn Adair.
$1^1 1^2 15^3 2^4 1^5$ George Matthews. *

---

2 Fortner Covel Markham.
OK 3 Beatrice Markham.
4 DeWitt Markham.
| 5 David Hogan Markham. Joy Pratt.
| 6 Earl Byrne Markham. Camille Lannom.
7 Lucile Markham.
$1^1 2^2 1^3 1^4 1^5$ Nancy Ann Starr. William Wirt Duncan and Young Charles Gordon Duncan.
2 George Harlan Starr. *
OK 3 Martha Jane Starr. George Washington Crittenden.
4 Joseph McMinn Starr. Sarah Crittenden and Susie Shell.
5 Walter Adair Starr. Ruth Ann Alberty nee Thornton, Ella Elizabeth Christie and Saphronia Barrett nee Crutchfield*
6 Sallie Elizabeth Starr. Frank Howard.
7 Edward Bruce Starr. Rachel Pauline Henry.
8 Clement Vann Starr. *
9 Caleb Wilson Starr.
$1^1 2^2 1^3 3^4 1^5$ Emily Clyne. Frank Howard.
2 Edward Adair Clyne. Nannie J. Whitmire.
OK 3 Elizabeth Clyne. Martin Jackson Bradford.
4 Sallie Clyne.
5 Timothy Walker Clyne. Nora Alice Smith.
6 Ella Clyne. Frank Stapler Howard.
$1^1 2^2 1^3 4^4 1^5$ Ruth Adair. *
2 James Adair. *
$1^1 2^2 1^3 5^4 1^5$ Andrew Griffin Cookson. Mary Jane Carlile.
2 Edley Levi Cookson. Agnes Pettit.
3 Joseph J. Cookson. Eliza Pettit.
4 Delilah Cookson. Michael K. Patrick.
$1^1 2^2 2^3 1^4 1^5$ Emily Walker. John Polk Drake.
2 Nannie Adair Walker. James Albert Coleman.
OK 3 John Walker. Susie Danenburg.

4 Suake Walker. * Mary Delilah Johnson.
5 Richard Martin Walker. Elizabeth Pettit and Edith Smith nee Hicks.
6 Edward Adair Walker. Catherine Deerinthewater.
7 Lowrey Pack Walker. Sarah Brown.
8 Timothy Meigs Walker. *
9 Thomas Hindman Walker. *
$1^1 2^2 2^3 2^4 1^5$ Penelope Adair. Philip T. Johnson.
2 Nannie Ruth Adair. John Pinckney Painter.
OK 3 Mary Lucinda Adair. William Gott.
4 John Walker Adair. Sarah Tula Smith.
5 Margaret Elizabeth Adair. Alfred Estis Holland.
6 Minerva Cornelia Adair. Thomas H. Horn.
7 George Starr Adair. Stella Rhodes.
$1^1 2^2 2^3 3^4 1^5$ Walter Alanson Allen. Frances E. Leatherwood.
$1^1 2^2 2^3 4^4 1^5$ Martha Caroline Adair. * George Humiston Lewis.
OK 2 Mary Elizabeth Adair. Colonel Johnson Harris.
$1^1 2^2 2^3 6^4 1^5$ William Penn Adair. Margaret Rogers.
2 Ella Adair. DeWitt Clinton Wilson.
$1^1 2^2 2^3 7^4 1^5$ Edward Henry Adair. Martha M. Leatherwood.
2 James Warren Adair.
OK 3 Mary Louella Adair. *
4 Timothy Meigs Adair. Martha Sanders and ——
$1^1 2^2 2^3 8^4 1^5$ Sarah Elizabeth Lindsley. Nathan Baron Danenburg.

Ross

1^1 Ghi-goo-ie. William Shorey. A50
$1^1 1^2$ Annie Shorey. John McDonald.
2 Elizabeth Shorey. John Lowrey.
$1^1 1^2 1^3$ Mary McDonald. Daniel Ross. A51
$1^1 2^2 1^3$ Elizabeth Lowrey. William Shorey Pack.
$1^1 1^2 1^3 1^4$ Jennie Ross. Joseph Coody.
2 Elizabeth Ross. John Golden Ross.
OK 3 John Ross. Quatie and Mary Bryan Stapler.
4 Lewis Ross. Fannie Holt.
5 Susannah Ross. Henry Nave.
6 Andrew Ross. Susan Lowrey.
7 Annie Ross. William Nave.
8 Margaret Ross. Elijah Hicks.
9 Maria Ross. Jonathan Mulkey.
$1^1 2^2 1^3 1^4$ Thomas Jefferson Pack. Jennie Taylor.
OK 2 Cynthia Pack. John Cowart.
$1^1 1^2 1^3 1^4 1^5$ William Shorey Coody. Susan Henley and Elizabeth Pack Fields.
2 Mary Coody. Nicholas Dalton Scales.
OK 3 Daniel Ross Coody. Amanda Drew, Sarah Ross and Eliza Levisa Bennett.
4 Elizabeth Coody. * Greenwood LeFlore.

5 Letitia Coody. Looney Price.
6 Maria Ross Coody. John Gabriel Madison Hawkins.
7 Louisa Jane Coody. Frederick Augustus Kerr.
8 Flora Coody. General Daniel Henry Rucker.
9 Joseph McDonald Coody. Mary Rebecca Harris nee Thornberry and Mary Muskogee Hardage.
$1^1 1^2 1^3 2^4 1^5$ William Potter Ross. Mary Jane Ross.
2 Daniel Hicks Ross. Catherine Gunter.
OK 3 Eliza Jane Ross. *
4 John Andrew Ross. Eliza Wilkerson.
5 Elnora Ross. *
6 Lewis Anderson Ross. Nellie Potts.
$1^1 1^2 1^3 3^4 1^5$ James Ross. Sallie Mannion.
2 Allen Ross. Jennie Fields.
OK 3 Jennie Ross. Return Johnathan Meigs and Andrew Ross Nave.
4 Silas Dean Ross. * Nannie Rhoda Stiff, Jennie Sanders and Elizabeth Raper.
5 George Washington Ross. Nannie Otterlifter.

---

6 John Ross. Elizabeth Chouteau and Louisa Catherine Means.

---

7 Annie Bryan Ross. * Leonidas Dobson.
8 John Ross. Caroline Cornelison Lazalear and Christine Foreman nee Haglund.
$1^1 1^2 1^3 4^4 1^5$ Minerva A. Ross. * George Michael Murrell.
2 John McDonald Ross. *
3 Araminta Ross. James Springston Vann.
4 Robert Daniel Ross. Caroline Todd.
5 Mary Jane Ross. William Potter Ross.
6 Amanda Melvina Ross. George Michael Murrell.

---

7 Henry Clay Ross. Elizabeth Campbell and Josephine Pettit.

---

8 Sarah Ross. Daniel Ross Coody.

---

9 Helen Ross. Lewis Rogers.

---

10 Jack Spears Ross. Elizabeth Feelin.
$1^1 1^2 1^3 5^4 1^5$ Eliza Nave. George Washington Gunter.
2 Mary Nave. Anderson Pierce Lowrey.
3 John Nave. Rachel Looney.
4 Daniel R. Nave. Jennie Carey.
5 Andrew Ross Nave. Jennie Meigs nee Ross.
6 Elvira Nave. Charles Clayborn Price, Joseph M. Gilbert and Samuel McDaniel.
7 George Washington Nave. * Sarah Josephine Vaught.

8 Minerva Nave. Riley Keys.

9 Frances M. Nave. John Carroll Cunningham.

10 Susie Nave. Watie Robertson.

11 Henry Nave. Charlotte Reese.

$1^{1}1^{2}1^{3}6^{4}1^{5}$ Oliver Perry Ross. Susan Vann, Elzina Hair nee Goonan.

2 Daniel H. Ross. Naomi Chisholm and Sarah Halfbreed.

OK 3 Andrew J. Ross. Nannie Otterlifter and Nannie Halfbreed.

4 Samuel Houston Ross. Sarah Grimmett.

5 William Coody Ross. Mary Ann Spears.

6 Joseph Miller Ross. Ruth Drew.

7 Joshua Ross. Muskogee Yargee.

8 Richard Johnson Ross. Elizabeth Stidham.

9 Jennie Pocahontas Ross. John D. Murrell.

$1^{1}1^{2}1^{3}7^{4}1^{5}$ Mary Ann Nave. John Clark and Flea Smith.

2 Nannie Nave. Samuel Riley.

$1^{1}1^{2}1^{3}8^{4}1^{5}$ Senora Hicks. Susan.

2 Jennie Hicks. John Wardell Stapller.

OK 3 Daniel Ross Hicks. Nancy Jane Rider, Esther Pritchett and Nancy Evaline Green nee Linder.

4 Mary Hicks. Joseph Rogers McCoy.

5 Charles Renatus Hicks. * Lucinda Ross.

6 John Ross Hicks. Catherine Beavert,* Sabra Buffington McCoy,* Mary A. Chambers and Mary Elizabeth Rockwell.

7 Victoria Susan Hicks. DeWitt Clinton Lipe.

$1^{1}1^{2}1^{3}9^{4}1^{5}$ James Daniel Mulkey. Elizabeth Cleveland Joy.

2 Lewis Andrew Mulkey. Adeline Goins.

OK 3 William Ross Mulkey. Margaret Rebecca Hudson.

$1^{1}2^{2}1^{3}1^{4}1^{5}$ Lowrey Vann Pack. *

2 William Shorey Pack. Jennie Starr and Araminta Ragsdale nee Gunter.

OK 3 Cynthia Pack. Daniel Harmon.

4 Amanda Pack. Thomas Cordery.

$1^{1}2^{2}1^{3}2^{4}1^{5}$ Lemuel Cowart. Mary Ann Dameron.

2 Jennie Cowart. Matthew Williams.

OK 3 Thomas Cowart. Jennie Day.

4 John Cowart. Fannie Huey.

5 Slater Cowart. Nannie King.

$1^{1}1^{2}1^{3}1^{4}1^{5}1^{6}$ Henrietta Jane Coody. *

---

2 William Shorey Coody *

3 Ella Flora Coody. Joseph Madison Robinson.

$1^{1}1^{2}1^{3}1^{4}2^{5}1^{6}$ Nancy Jane Scales. Abner Sayers.

2 Charlotte Gordon Scales. John Thompson Drew.

OK 3 Eliza Scales. * William Ratliff.

4 Joseph Absalom Scales. Rose Tally and Amanda Patience Fowler nee Morgan.

$1^1 1^2 1^3 1^4 3^5 1^6$ Alice Coody. William Wilson.

2 Lewis R. Coody. Mary Susan Cordery, Elizabeth Collier, Nannie Hanks and Martha Lavina Hill.

OK 3 Mary Coody. *

4 Sarah Coody. *

5 Martha Coody. *

6 Joseph Coody.

7 Margaret Coody. John Stringer Scott.

8 Daniel Ross Coody. Julia Griffin.

9 Letitia Coody. Edward Smith.

$1^1 1^2 1^3 1^4 5^5 1^6$ William Shorey Price. *

2 Daniel Coody Price. Mary Ann Jones.

OK 3 Montezuma Price. Alice Johnson.

4 Millard Filmore Price. *

5 George Murrell Price. Eliza Jane Vinyard nee Roach.

6 Annie F. Price. Otis Saladin Skidmore.

7 Caroline Walker Price. James Lee Floyd.

$1^1 1^2 1^3 1^4 6^5 1^6$ Martha Jane Hawkins. Hamilton Alexander Starkweather.

2 Henry Clay Hawkins.

OK 3 Samuel Frelinghyson Hawkins.

4 Maria Louisa Hawkins. Henry Graham Wood.

5 John Gabriel Hawkins. Flora Madeline Thorne.

6 Nannie Ross Hawkins. *

7 Sarah Stapler Hawkins. Dennis Wesley Smith.

$1^1 1^2 1^3 1^4 7^5 1^6$ Frank Kerr. Margaret Taylor, Jennie McIva Ross, Elizabeth Clyne and Fannie Lowrey nee Hendricks.

2 Flora McIva Kerr. Henry Lisenbe.

OK 3 Minerva Murrell Kerr. George Washington Hendricks.

4 William Wirt Kerr. *

5 Neville Craig Kerr. Lucinda Lowrey.

6 Annie Eliza Kerr. George Washington Elliott.

7 John Ross Kerr. *

8 Frederick Augustus Kerr. Eva Scott.

9 Mary Elizabeth Kerr. Conrad Koehler and Moses Anspach.

10 Charles Ross Coody Kerr. *

$1^1 1^2 1^3 1^4 8^5 1^6$ Ross Rucker. *

2 Louisa Rucker.

$1^1 1^2 1^3 1^4 9^5 1^6$ Sarah Jane Coody.

2 Flora Rucker Coody. Richard Young Audd.

OK 4 William Shorey Coody. Louvenia Gaylor.

3 Eula Muskogee Coody. Edward Hendricks Walker.

5 Minnie Vann Coody. David Washington.

6 Amanda Ella Coody. Laurel Pittman.

$1^1 1^2 1^3 2^4 1^5 1^6$ William Dayton Ross. *

2 Emma Lincoln Ross.

OK 3 Cora Ross. Dr. Robert B. Howard.

4 Mary Ross. William R. Badgett.

5 Hubbard Ross. Harriette Babb.
6 Phillips Ross. *
$1^1 1^2 1^3 2^4 2^5 1^6$ Edward Gunter Ross.
2 William Potter Ross. Maude Walker.
OK 3 Catherine E. Ross. George Oliver Butler.
$1^1 1^2 1^3 2^4 4^5 1^6$ John Houston Ross. Lillian M. Glasglow.
2 Flora Lee Ross. Charles Walter Phillips.
OK 3 Dannie Hughes Ross. Bates B. Burnett.
4 Eliza Jane Ross. William Finley Blakemore.
$1^1 1^2 1^3 2^4 6^5 1^6$ McDonald Ross. *
2 Shorey W. Ross.
OK 3 Eliza Ross.
4 William Potter Ross. Annie May Balentine.
5 Lewis Anderson Ross.
6 Wirt Ross.
7 Daniel Hughes Ross.
$1^1 1^2 1^3 3^4 1^5 1^6$ Susannah Coody Ross. Isaac Alexander Wilson.
OK 2 Gilbert Russell Ross. Emeline Parris and Mary J. Christian.
$1^1 1^2 1^3 3^4 2^5 1^6$ Lucinda Ross. * Charles Renatus Hicks.
2 Victoria Ross. *
OK 3 Susan H. Ross. Osceola Powell Daniel.
4 Rufus O. Ross. Elizabeth Grace Meigs.
5 Robert Bruce Ross. Fannie Thornton.
6 Emma Ross. Osceola Powell Daniel.
7 William Wallace Ross. Delilah Jane Daniel.
8 Elizabeth Ross. * John Ross Vann.
$1^1 1^2 1^3 3^4 3^5 1^6$ John Ross Meigs. Mary Elizabeth Freeman.
2 Henry Clay Meigs. Josephine L. Bigelow.
OK 3 Elizabeth Grace Meigs. Rufus O. Ross.
4 Return Robert Meigs. Jennie Ross, Helen Chrissie Blevins.
5 Submit Meigs. John Francis Lyons.

———

6 Andrew Ross Nave. Julia Eagle.
7 Henrietta Jane Nave. William Henry Hinton.
$1^1 1^2 1^3 3^4 5^5 1^6$ Jennie Melvie Ross. * Frank Kerr.
2 Silas Dinsmore Ross. Susie Backbone and Sarah Osborn.
OK 3 Sarah Stapler Ross. Samuel Houston Adair.

———

4 Mary Jones Ross. James Franklin Petty.
$1^1 1^2 1^3 3^4 6^5 1^6$ Emily Jane Ross. Clement Denoya.
2 Mary Ellen Ross. Thomas Joseph Rogers and Oscar C. Hadden.

———

3 Ida Ross.
4 Floyd Freeman Ross.
$1^1 1^2 1^3 3^4 8^5 1^6$ Addie Roche Ross. William Henry Norrid.

2 Leonidas Cookman Ross. Grace Keam.
OK 3 Mary Ross. *
$1^1 1^2 1^3 4^4 3^5 1^6$ Fannie Vann. Florian Haradin Nash.
$1^1 1^2 1^3 4^4 4^5 1^6$ Lewis Ross. Laura Augusta French.
2 Edward Pope Ross. *
OK 3 Belle Ross.
4 Alice Ross. Dr. Robert B. Howard.
5 Fannie M. Ross. Herbert Kneeland.
$1^1 1^2 1^3 4^4 5^5 1^6$ William Dayton Ross. *
2 Emma Lincoln Ross.
OK 3 Cora Ross. Dr. Robert B. Howard.
4 Mary Ross. William R. Badgett.
5 Hubbard Ross. Harriette Babb.
6 Phillips Ross. *
$1^1 1^2 1^3 4^4 6^5 1^6$ George Ross Murrell. Margaret Gavin.
2 Fannie Elizabeth Murrell. Frank Alexander and J. Emory Hughes.
OK 3 Rosanna E. Murrell. William Archer Chambers.
4 Louis Edward Murrell.
$1^1 1^2 1^3 4^4 7^5 1^6$ Frank Ross. Ella Fisher.

---

2 Margaret Jane Ross. Joel Mayes Bryan.
OK 3 Joseph Miller Ross.
4 Felix Henry Ross.
5 Mary J. Ross.
$1^1 1^2 1^3 4^4 8^5 1^6$ Alice Coody. William Wilson.
2 Lewis Ross Coody. Mary Susan Cordery, Elizabeth Collier, Nannie Hanks and Martha Lavenia Hill.
OK 3 Mary Coody. *
4 Sarah Coody. *
5 Martha Coody. *
6 Joseph Coody. Eliza Swett and Margaret A. King nee Lindsey.
7 Margaret Coody. John Stringer Scott.
8 Daniel Ross Coody. Julia Griffin.
$1^1 1^2 1^3 4^4 9^5 1^6$ Rosalie Rogers. Benjamin Franklin Avant.
OK 2 Lewis Rogers.
$1^1 1^2 1^3 4^4 10^5 1^6$ Jackson Ross. Jessie E. Vann.
2 Lewis Ross. Sarah Hosey.
3 John Ross. Anna Hosey.
4 Nannie Ross. Lewis Mouse.
$1^1 1^2 1^3 5^4 1^5 1^6$ Mary Gunter. Ezekial Jack and Jonathan Riley.
2 Susie Gunter. George R. Johnson and James Choate.
OK 3 Samuel Gunter. Fannie Daniel.
4 Araminta Gunter. John Ragsdale, William Shorey Pack.
5 John Edward Gunter. Mary Lee.

6 George Washington Gunter. Catherine Benge, Mary Davis and Ella Spradling.
7 Elizabeth Gunter. *
8 Jeanette Gunter. Jacob Edward Barrow.
$1^{1}1^{2}1^{3}5^{4}2^{5}1^{6}$ Daniel Webster Lowrey. *
2 Henry Lowrey. Mary Parris and Emeline Evans nee Russell.
3 Lucy Ann Lowrey. Charles Hicks Campbell.
4 Dollie Eunice Lowrey. James Fields,* Thomas Starr and Charles Galloway.
5 George Lowrey. *
6 Susie Lowrey. Richard Robertson and Thomas Jefferson Carter.
7 Eliza Lowrey. William Henry Davis.
8 James Monroe Lowrey. Susie Vickery.
9 Andrew Lowrey. Dora Pinckney nee Bruton.
$1^{1}1^{2}1^{3}5^{4}3^{5}1^{6}$ Silas Nave.
OK 2 Mary Alice Nave. William Penn Payne.
$1^{1}1^{2}1^{3}5^{4}4^{5}1^{6}$ Joseph Coody Nave. Sarah Downing, Rachel Pauline Starr nee Henry and
2 Walter Duncan Nave. Sarah Josephine Fane.
OK 3 Samuel Nave. * Annie Cochran nee Coats.
4 Jennie Nave. Walker Russell.
$1^{1}1^{2}1^{3}5^{4}5^{5}1^{6}$ Andrew Ross Nave. Julia Eagle.
OK 2 Henrietta Jane Nave. William Henry Hinton.
$1^{1}1^{2}1^{3}5^{4}6^{5}1^{6}$ John H. Price. Ruth Ann Starr.
2 Mary Jane Price. Henry James, Winfield Gray and Rev. David Nathaniel Allen.
OK 3 Susie Ann Price. Alexander Gibson Murray.
4 Charles Cintoola Price. *

---

5 Joanna Gillis. Frank Alexander Billingslea.

---

6 Martin McDaniel. Della Moore.
$1^{1}1^{2}1^{3}5^{4}8^{5}1^{6}$ Fannie N. Keys. William Henry Balentine.
OK 2 Riley Keys. Julia Turner.
$1^{1}1^{2}1^{3}5^{4}9^{5}1^{6}$ Alfred Carroll Cunningham. Laura Lombard.
2 William Ross Cunningham.
OK 3 Minnie Ross Cunningham. Richard Fields Vann and Sidney Elllsworth Bell.
$1^{1}1^{2}1^{3}5^{4}11^{5}1^{6}$ John McDonald Nave. *
2 Susie Ellen Nave. Wilson Walkingstick.
3 Henry Dobson Nave.
$1^{1}1^{2}1^{3}6^{4}1^{5}1^{6}$ Elizabeth Ross. * Frank Nash.
2 George Lowrey Ross. Ruth B. Springston.
OK 3 Juliette Ross. William Roberson.

---

4 Mary Ann Bishop Ross. Andrew Hair and William Thomas Jones.

5 Minnie Ross. George A. Walden.

6 Andrew Enoli Ross. Catherine Cooper.

7 Susie Ross. Charles Nicholas Mitchell.

8 Jennie Ross. Joseph Sixkiller.

$1^{1}1^{2}1^{3}6^{4}2^{5}1^{6}$ James L. Ross.

2 Jennie Ross. Return Robert Meigs.

OK 3 McDuff Ross. Catherine Nave nee Reese and

4 Alexander Ross. Mary Armstrong.

5 Christopher Ross.

$1^{1}1^{2}1^{3}6^{4}3^{5}1^{6}$ Daniel L. Ross. Ruth Caroline Holland.

---

2 Houston Ross.

OK 3 Lydia Ross. Rufus William Twitty.

$1^{1}1^{2}1^{3}6^{4}4^{5}1^{6}$ Susan Ross. Jesse Cochran.

2 John Henry Ross. Fannie Downing.

OK 3 Catherine Ross. Silas Grayson Wills.

$1^{1}1^{2}1^{3}6^{4}5^{5}1^{6}$ Rosa Lee Ross. William Samuel Miles.

2 Susie Lowrey Ross.

OK 3 Joshua Ewing Ross. Nellie Banks.

4 John Yargee Ross.

5 Jennie Pocahontas Ross.

$1^{1}1^{2}1^{3}6^{4}8^{5}1^{6}$ Catherine Ross. Samuel Grayson.

OK 2 Jennie Ross.

$1^{1}1^{2}1^{3}7^{4}1^{5}1^{6}$ Emily Jane Clark. Thomas Ross, John Blackwell and Willis Battles.

2 Sarah Cynthia Clark. Allen Lynch.

OK 3 Ruth Elizabeth Downing. Alexander Buffington and Anderson Lynch.

---

4 William A. Smith. Sarah Huff.

$1^{1}1^{2}1^{3}7^{4}2^{5}1^{6}$ William Riley.

2 Sarah Riley.

$1^{1}1^{2}1^{3}8^{4}1^{5}1^{6}$ Jennie Hicks. * William Penn Crowder.

2 Hannah Hicks.

OK 3 Mary Hicks.

4 Charles Hicks.

5 Edward Hicks.

6 Jesse Hicks.

7 John Hicks.

8 Susannah Hicks.

$1^{1}1^{2}1^{3}8^{4}2^{5}1^{6}$ James Senora Stapler. Lelia Wilson Breedlove

2 Mary Louise Stapler. *

OK 3 John Brian Stapler. Ella Zaphora Morgan.

4 Margaret Hicks. *

$1^1 1^2 1^3 8^4 3^5 1^6$ Edward Daniel Hicks. Elizabeth Henrietta Musgrove.
$1^1 1^2 1^3 8^4 4^5 1^6$ Margaret McCoy. * John B. Brown.
2 Jennie Diana McCoy. Vann Chambers.
OK 3 Charles Renatus McCoy.
4 Daniel Homer. *
5 Nannie Rider McCoy. Walter Adair Mayes.
$1^1 1^2 1^3 8^4 6^5 1^6$ Henry Chambers Hicks. *
2 Nancy Jane Hicks. Alexander Frederick Parsley.
3 Cora Archer Hicks. Dr. John Otto Rogers.

---

4 Eugene Ross Hicks.
$1^1 1^2 1^3 8^4 7^5 1^6$ John Gunter Lipe. Sarah Lulu Foreman.
$1^1 1^2 1^3 9^4 1^5 1^6$ Wiley R. Mulkey. Martha Mahala Paul.
2 Annie C. Mulkey. Thomas J. Cowan.
3 Alonzo S. Mulkey.
4 Charles Alva Mulkey. Mabel Dell Bomberger.
5 Lewis W. Mulkey.
6 Jonathan Daniel Mulkey. Sallie Vann.
7 Jennie Mulkey.
8 Rose E. C. Mulkey.
$1^1 1^2 1^3 9^4 2^5 1^6$ Lucinda Mulkey. William Askins.
2 Louisa A. Mulkey. Alfred Cox and James B. Kay.
OK 3 Jonathan Mulkey.
4 Isabella Mulkey. Ferdinand Farmer.
5 Julia Mulkey.
6 James Mulkey.
7 Vida Mulkey. William M. Carr.
8 John Ross Mulkey.
$1^1 1^2 1^3 9^4 3^5 1^6$ James Daniel Mulkey. Mary Priscilla Wilson.
2 Mary Brooks Mulkey. Walter Willis.
OK 3 Amanda Avis Mulkey. John Rankin Amos.
4 Eliza Maria Mulkey. John Thomas Miller.
6 John Ross Mulkey.

CHAPTER XIX

Continuation of Old Families

Gosaduisga

1^1 Go-sa-du-i-sga.

$1^1 1^2$ Nannie. John Thornton.

2 Elizabeth. James Vann, William Springston, John Shepherd and Edward Adair.

$1^1 1^2 1^3$ William Thornton. Nannie McPherson, Ge-yo-hi Porter and Elizabeth Bean nee Phillips.

2 James Thornton. *

OK 3 Charles Thornton. Maria McIntosh and Mary Crossland.

4 Amos Thornton. Elizabeth Holt, Elizabeth McAdams, Minerva Foreman and Mary Souiekiller.

5 John Thornton. Pinkie Blagg and Frances Alberty.

6 Riley Thornton. Rebecca Mitchell and Eliza Maw.

7 Wiley Glover Thornton.. Nannie Brimmer and Avery Meanman.

8 Delilah Thornton. William Harlin, Alexander Shook, James Taylor and Joseph Dawson.

9 Smith Thornton. Caroline Daniel and Lucy Crittenden.

10 Elizabeth Thornton. *

$1^1 2^2 1^3$ Delilah Amelia Vann. David McNair.

---

2 Jennie Springston. Joseph Vann and Thomas Mitchell. A52

3 Edley Springston. Elizabeth Foreman.

---

4 John Shepherd. Sallie Daniel, Ruth Fawling and Josephine Killian.

---

5 Edward Adair. Nannie Shields and Mary Harnage.

$1^1 1^2 1^3 1^4$ Elizabeth Thornton. Samuel Walkingstick.

---

2 Walter Thornton. Elizabeth Jones.

---

3 Jolly Thornton. Mary Riley.

---

4 Ruth Ann Thornton. Cornelius Alberty and Walter Adair Starr.

$1^1 1^2 3^3 1^4$ Shepherd Thornton.

---

2 John Thornton.

$1^1 1^2 4^3 1^4$ Elizabeth Thornton. Richard Thompson.

2 Thomas Jefferson Thornton. *

OK 3 Lewis Ross Thornton. Ellen Stetson Cooley.

4 John Thornton. *

5 William Harrison Thornton. *

---

6 Thomas Jefferson Thornton. Mary L. Rogers.
7 Mary Ellen Thornton. Charles Cochran.
8 Nicholas McNair Thornton. Clara Hicks and Flora Ingram.
9 John Shepherd Thornton. * Cynthia Pettit.
10 William Glover Thornton. *
$1^1 1^2 5^3 1^4$ Wiliam Thornton. Minerva Jane Foreman.
2 Calvin Thornton. * Malinda Sutton.

OK 3 Martha Thornton. Robert Williams.
4 John T. Thornton.*
5 Walter King Thornton. *
$1^1 1^2 5^3 1^4$ Mary Ann Thornton. * Benjamin E. Gump and George W. Boles.

---

2 Thomas Thornton. Hettie Dennis.
3 Osceola Thornton. *
$1^1 1^2 7^3 1^4$ Amos Thornton. Clara Phillips and Rachel Boards.
2 William Thornton. Mary Sanders.
OK 3 John Thornton. Lucinda Sanders.
4 Elizabeth Thornton. * Clausine.
5 Mary Thornton. John Goodwin and Austin B. Hosler.
6 Nancy Jane Thornton. Johnson Robbins.
7 Sallie Thornton. Abraham Sixkiller and Dick Duck.
8 Joseph Thornton. Margaret Wilson.

---

9 Ruth Thornton. Taylor Sixkiller and Archilla Scraper.
10 James Thornton. Nancy Jane Sanders and Margaret Clyffton Starr.
$1^1 1^2 8^3 1^4$ William Harlin. *

---

2 James Shook. Eliza Justice nee Vann and Sarah Elizabeth Sears.

OK 3 Martha Taylor. Ensley Lacey.
4 Creed Taylor.
5 Lewis Taylor. *

---

6 Mary Dawson. Robert Barnes Mitchell and John H. Welty.
7 Joseph Dawson. * Mary Ragsdale.
8 Elizabeth Dawson. *
9 Thomas Dawson. *
$1^1 1^2 9^3 1^4$ Nannie Thornton. Moses Parris and John Parris.
2 William Thornton. *
OK 3 Fannie Thornton. Robert Bruce Ross.

---

4 Elizabeth Thornton. George Sanders.
5 Jacob Thornton. *
6 Marion Thornton. Lucy Goodwin.
$1^1 2^2 1^3 1^4$ James Vann McNair. Eliza Childers.
2 Nicholas Byers McNair. Mary Rogers.
OK 3 Mary Vann McNair. Clement Neely and William Rogers.
4 Elizabeth McNair. Jesse Bean and John Weir.
5 Martha McNair. David Vann.
6 Clement Vann McNair. Susannah Martin and Martha Ann Smith nee Childers.
$1^1 2^2 2^3 1^4$ James Springton Vann. Araminta Ross.
2 Mary Vann. *
OK 3 John Shepherd Vann. Elizabeth Pack Coody nee Fields.
4 Delilah Amelia Vann. Oliver Hazard Perry Brewer.
5 Henry Clay Vann. *
$1^1 2^2 3^3 1^4$ Delilah Springston. John Ferguson, Henry Hill and Frank Marrs.
2 John Springston.
3 Mary Springston. John Henry and George Beamer.
4 Miles Springston. *
5 Edward Springston. *
6 Nannie Springston. *
7 George Springston. *
$1^1 2^2 4^3 1^4$ Elizabeth Shepherd. John Brown.
2 Clement Shepherd. *
3 Joseph Shepherd. Nannie Thompson.
4 Fane Shepherd. *
5 David Shepherd. *

6 William Shepherd. Mary Ann Wilson and Mary F. James.
7 Albert Shepherd. Lucy Jones.
8 Augustus Shepherd. *
9 Ruth Shepherd. John Martin, Thomas Franks and Lemuel Wickett.
10 Clementine Shepherd. William McConkle and Sterling Colston.
11 George W. Shepherd. Stella Stegall.
12 John Shepherd. *
$1^1 2^2 5^3 1^4$ Delilah Adair. Joseph McMimm Starr.
2 Susie Adair. *

OK 3 Jennie Adair. John Peter Oliver Clyne.
4 Edley Adair. Emily Rogers.
5 Elizabeth Adair. John Hildebrand Cookson.
$1^1 1^2 1^3 1^4 1^5$ Wilson Walkingstick. Susie Ellen Nave.
$1^1 1^2 1^3 2^4 1^5$ Wallace Thornton. Mary Louvenia Garrison.
2 Smith Thornton. Ella Cox.

OK 3 William Thornton. Sallie Yahola nee

$1^1 1^2 1^3 3^4 1^5$ William Thonton. Nancy Anna Lee Barnes.

$1^1 1^2 1^3 4^4 1^5$ Emmet Starr.

2 George Colbert Starr. *

OK 3 Mary Bell Starr. Dr. Wade Hampton Vann.

4 Lettie Boyd Starr.

5 Joseph McCracken Starr.

$1^1 1^2 4^3 1^4 1^5$ Margaret Emma Thompson. Clark Charlesworth Lipe.

2 Sue Elizabeth Thompson. Henry Eiffort.

OK 3 Tookah Thompson. William Smelser Nash.

4 Caroline Harriette Thompson. David Albert Mounts.

5 John Lanigan Thompson. *

$1^1 1^2 4^3 3^4 1^5$ Mary Louisa Thornton. John B. Edwards and H. P. Davis.

2 Charles Amos Thornton. Sadie E. Larned.

3 Guy Earl Thornton. Nannie Proctor.

4 Clement Vann Thornton.

$1^1 1^2 4^3 6^4 1^5$ Murrell Thornton.

OK 2 Mary Gladys Thornton.

$1^1 1^2 4^3 7^4 1^5$ Sarah Cochran.

OK 2 Maude Beulah Cochran. Thomas A. Hathcock.

3 Hoolie Bell Cochran.

4 Ada Cochran.

---

5 Jesse Edward Cochran.

$1^1 1^2 4^3 8^4 1^5$ Percy M. Thornton. Agnes Holden.

---

2 Owen Thornton.

$1^1 1^2 5^3 1^4 1^5$ Eliza Jane Thornton. Charles Oliver Frye.

$1^1 1^2 5^3 3^4 1^5$ Mary Frances Williams. *

2 John Henry Wiliams. *

3 Charles McClellan Williams.

4 William Walter Williams. Elizabeth Leona Alberty.

5 Robert Benjamin Williams.

6 Ada Elizabeth Williams. George William Christie.

7 Lee Williams. Maude Leslie Adair.

8 Ellis Bluford Williams.

9 Ellen Williams.

10 Frederick Williams.

$1^1 1^2 6^3 2^4 1^5$ Delilah Thornton. Charles Hanes.

$1^1 1^2 7^3 1^4 1^5$ Elizabeth Thornton. James N. Palone.

---

2 Susie Thornton. Goback Christy.

3 William Henry Thornton.

4 Richard Foreman Thornton.

5 Nannie J. Thornton. Leo M. White.

$1^1 1^2 7^3 2^4 1^5$ Nannie J. Thornton. Simeon Eldridge.

$1^1 1^2 7^3 3^4 1^5$ Reese Thornton.

$1^1 1^2 7^3 5^4 1^5$ Lucy Goodwin. Marion Thornton.

2 John Goodwin. Margie Elnora Pyeatt.

$1^1 1^2 7^3 6^4 1^5$ Levi Robbins. *

2 Timothy Robbins.

3 Alexander Robbins. *

4 John Robbins. *

5 Glover Robbins. *

6 Josephine Robbins.

$1^1 1^2 7^3 7^4 1^5$ Henry Sixkiller.

OK 2 Charles Watts.

$1^1 1^2 7^3 8^4 1^5$ Delilah Mary Thornton.

2 Jesse Thornton.

OK 3 Wiley Thornton.

4 William Thornton.

$1^1 1^2 7^3 9^4 1^5$ Mary Etta Scraper.

OK 2 John Scraper.

$1^1 1^2 7^3 10^4 1^5$ Susan Elizabeth Thornton.

---

2 Jesse Jackson Thornton.

3 Rogers Thornton.

4 Nicholas Thornton.

$1^1 1^2 8^3 2^4 1^5$ Nellie Shook. James Walker.

2 Elizabeth Shook. Andrew Jackson Harris.

OK 3 William Tucker Shook. Evretta Summerhill.

4 John B. Shook.

5 Amos Shook.

6 Lillie May Shook.

$1^1 1^2 8^3 3^4 1^5$ Miles Lacey. * Alice Barnes.

2 John Drew Lacey. Mary Doherty nee Pettit and Lucy Frances Prunty.

OK 3 Delilah Lacey. *

$1^1 1^2 8^3 4^4 1^5$ James Taylor.

$1^1 1^2 8^3 6^4 1^5$ Mary Mitchell. James Shell.

2 Frank Reed Mitchell.

OK 3 Margaret Mitchell. Wiliam Penn Crowder.

4 Joseph Mitchell. Mary Hayes.

---

5 Lydia F. Welty. John Hayes.

6 Roscoe H. Welty.

$1^1 1^2 9^3 1^4 1^5$ Emeline Rarris. Gilbert Russell Ross and Thomas Johnson Parris.

2 Caroline Parris. David Ridge.

OK 3 Samantha Parris. Rufus Daniel Ross.

4 Edward Parris. Esther Elva Ingram.

5 Triphena Parris. Robert Bruce Bean.

$1^1 1^2 9^3 3^4 1^5$ Charles McClellan Ross. Sarah Thomas Scruggs and Susie Ellen Morris.

2 William Wallace Ross. Mary Henrietta Moore.

OK 3 Rufus Daniel Ross. Emma Tooka Sixkiller and Samantha Parris.

4 Lulu Victoria Ross. James Henderson.

5 Fannie Vann Ross. Walter Ellis Duncan.

6 Jennie Fields Ross. Jesse Clifton Cobb.

7 Sue Mary Ross. Samuel Victor Eubanks.

8 Robert Bruce Ross.

9 Anna Phillips Ross. Lieutenant Edwin William Piburn.

$1^1 1^2 9^3 4^4 1^5$ Charles Sanders. Mary Ann Talbert.

$1^1 1^2 9^3 6^4 1^5$ Elizabeth Thornton.

2 Mary Thornton. *

3 Henry Joseph Thornton.

$1^1 2^2 1^3 1^4 1^5$ Felix Hurd McNair. Louisa Jane Vann and Nannie Sarah Bushyhead.

2 Delilah McNair. * Frank Shafer.

OK 3 Martha McNair. William Henry Mayes.

$1^1 2^2 1^3 2^4 1^5$ Sarah McNair. Brice Martin Adair.

2 Martha McNair. * Joel Bryan Mayes.

OK 3 William Lucullus McNair. Rachel Mayes.

4 John R. McNair. Cynthia Huffaker and Elizabeth Parrott.

5 Clement McNair. *

6 Mary Delilah McNair. Benjamin Franklin Adair.

7 Talbert McNair. * Nellie Carter.

8 Oscar McNair. *

9 Nicholas Benjamin McNair. Rachel Sanders and Martha E. Jones.

$1^1 2^2 1^3 3^4 1^5$ Albina McNair Rogers. Anderson Smith Bell.

2 Henry Rogers. Martha McNair.

3 David M. Rogers. Mary Strickland.

4 Robert Nicholas Rogers. Sarah Jones.

$1^1 2^2 1^3 4^4 1^5$ Amelia Bean. John Chambers.

2 David Bean. *

3 Talbert Bean. *

4 Augustus Bean. *

5 William E. Bean. Nancy Ann nee Blythe.

6 Almira Neely Bean. * John Chambers.

---

7 Susan Virginia Weir. * William Henry Mayes.

8 Clementine Weir. Augustus A. Shutt.

$1^1 2^2 1^3 5^4 1^5$ Clement Neely Vann. Isadora V. Mackey.

2 Nicholas Byers Vann. *

3 David Lucullus Vann. *

4 Mary Delilah Vann. George Washington Drew and Joel Bryan Mayes.

5 Charles Avoy Vann. *
6 Joseph Lewis Vann. Caroline Elizabeth Sixkiller.
7 Martha Elizabeth Vann. Samuel Houston Mayes.
$1^1 2^2 1^3 6^4 1^5$ Martha McNair. Henry Rogers and John Martin Thompson.
2 John Martin McNair. Mary Jane Hale.

OK 3 Clement Alexander McNair.
4 Nicholas George McNair.
5 Amelia Delilah McNair. William Archibald Henry.
6 Ezra Almon McNair.
7 Leoda Tennessee McNair. John Fischer.
8 Mary Elizabeth McNair. John Carley.
$1^1 2^2 2^3 1^4 1^5$ Fannie Vann. Florian Haraden Nash.
$1^1 2^2 2^3 3^4 1^5$ Jennie Vann. William Wilson Harnage.
2 John Vann. *
3 Richard Fields Vann. Minnie Ross Cunningham.
4 Charles Edward Vann. Ada Raymond.
$1^1 2^2 2^3 4^4 1^5$ Mary Vann Brewer. *
2 John Duncan Brewer. *
OK 3 Thomas Henry Brewer. *
4 Cherokee Juliette Brewer. Walter Hampton Jackson.
5 Oliver Hazard Perry Brewer.
$1^1 2^2 3^3 1^4 1^5$ Martha Jane Ferguson. William Henry Land.
2 Elizabeth Ferguson. Houston Smith.

---

3 Napoleon Marrs.
$1^1 2^2 3^3 3^4 1^5$ John Henry.
2 Margaret Henry.

---

3 Lewis Beamer. Alice Towie.
4 John Beamer. Alice Bigdollar.
$1^1 2^2 4^3 1^4 1^5$ William Brown. Frances Silverheels and Amanda Black.
$1^1 2^2 4^3 3^4 1^5$ John Shepherd. Roxie Evans.
2 Mary Shepherd.
3 Emma Shepherd. Jesse Thompson.
4 James Shepherd. *
$1^1 2^2 4^3 6^4 1^5$ Annie Shepherd. William Smith and U. K. Vasbinda.

---

2 Charles H. Shepherd. *

---

3 William Ernest Shepherd.
4 Elizabeth Shepherd.
$1^1 2^2 4^3 7^4 1^5$ Fane Shepherd. *
2 Eliza Shepherd. Henry Brazeel.
3 Malinda L. Shepherd. John W. Thompson.
4 Richard Shepherd.
$1^1 2^2 4^3 9^4 1^5$ Alpha O. Wickett.

$1^1 2^2 4^3 11^4 1^5$ Augustus Shepherd.

2 Charles Shepherd.

OK 3 Edward Shepherd.

4 Pearl Shepherd.

5 Jackson Shepherd.

$1^1 2^2 5^3 1^4 1^5$ Nancy Ann Starr. William Duncan and Young Charles Gordon Duncan.

2 George Harlan Starr. *

OK 3 Martha Jane Starr. George Washington Crittenden.

4 Joseph McMinn Starr. Sarah Crittenden and Susie Shell.

5 Walter Adair Starr. Ruth Ann Alberty nee Thornton, Ella Elizabeth Christie and Saphronia Barnett nee Crutchfield.

6 Sallie Elizabeth Starr. Frank Howard.

7 Edward Bruce Starr. Rachel Pauline Henry.

8 Clement Vann Starr. *

9 Caleb Wilson Starr.

$1^1 2^2 5^3 2^4 1^5$ Emily Clyne. Frank Howard.

2 Edward Adair Clyne. Nannie J. Whitmire.

OK 3 Elizabeth Clyne. Martin Jackson Bradford.

4 Sallie Clyne.

5 Timothy Walker Clyne. Nora Alice Smith.

6 Ella Clyne. Frank Stapler Howard.

$1^1 2^2 5^3 4^4 1^5$ Ruth Adair. *

2 James Adair. *

$1^1 2^2 5^3 5^4 1^5$ Andrew Griffin Cookson. Mary Jane Carlile.

2 Edley Levi Cookson. Agnes Pettit.

OK 3 Joseph J. Cookson. Eliza Pettit.

4 Delilah Cookson. Michael K. Patrick.

Conrad.

1^1 Onai. Hamilton Conrad.

$1^1 1^2$ Rattlinggourd Conrad. Mary Toney.

2 Hair Conrad. Ollie Candy and Melvina McGee.

OK 3 Youngwolf Conrad. Jennie Taylor.

4 Quatie Conrad. Alexander Brown, Archibald Fields and John Benge.

$1^1 1^2 1^3$ Dorcas Rattlinggourd. Richard Foreman.

2 Tony Rattlinggourd. Lucretia Tiger.

OK 3 Jackson Rattlinggourd. Elsie Wilson. A54

4 Sallie Rattlinggourd. Samuel Foreman and Peacheater Sixkiller.

5 Catherine Rattlinggourd. George Washington Campbell.

6 Daniel Rattlinggourd. Eliza Abigal Looney.

7 John Rattlinggourd. Nannie Mannion.

8 Margaret aRttlinggourd. Benjamin Downing.

9 David Rattlinggourd. * Nannie Jennings nee.

10 Charles Rattlinggourd. Lucy McIntosh *, Levisa McIntosh *, Elizabeth Campbell*, —— Benge and Susie Hair.

$1^{1}2^{2}1^{3}$ Elizabeth Hair. Daniel Hopkins.

2 Susie Hair. Charles Rattlinggourd.

3 Jefferson Hair. Chinosa O'Fields, Mary Tyner nee Sanders and Eliza Ramsey nee Tyner.

4 Diana Hair. Wade Hampton Robertson.

5 John Hair. Lucy Robertson, Annie Sanders, Mary Butler and Lucy Justice.

6 Nannie Hair. *

7 Mary Hair. John Ramsey.

---

8 James Hair. Sarah Davis, Susie Reese and Nellie Robertson.

9 Elizabeth Hair. Ashhopper.

10 Ollie Hair. Wallace Vann.

---

11 Eliza Hair. Starr Deerinthewater, Johnson Blythe and George Roberts.

$1^{1}3^{2}1^{3}$ Susie Wolf. Samuel Ballard and Michael Bridgemaker.

---

2 Nannie Wolf. Thomas Starr.

OK 3 Margaret Wolf. Daniel McCoy.

4 Annie Wolf. William Williams and James Sterling Price.

5 Dennis Wolf. Isabel Fields and Peggy McDaniel.

$1^{1}4^{2}1^{3}$ John Lucien Brown. Elizabeth Coody nee Meade, Minerva Coker nee Foster and Mary Lowrey nee Simpson.

---

2 Jennie Fields. Allen Ross.

OK 3 Anderson Benge. Elizabeth Busky and Susan Henrietta Foreman.

$1^{1}5^{2}1^{3}$ John Terrapin. Ga-ho-ka Ratliff and Nannie Blalock nee Bark.

2 Jennie Terrapin. So-sa and Edward Foreman. A53

OK 3 James Terrapin. *

4 Thomas Fox Conrad. Caroline Wheeler.

$1^{1}1^{2}1^{3}1^{4}$ Anthony Foreman. Nellie Buffington and Eliza Toney.

2 Lucinda Foreman. John Foster.

3 John Foreman. Susie Leach.

4 Lewis Foreman.

5 Amos Foreman. * Eliza Gunter.

6 William H. Foreman. Letitia Woodward.

7 Thomas Foreman. *

8 Ruth Foreman. Patrick Lyman.

9 Edward Foreman. *

10 Emily Foreman. Wallace Ratliff.

11 George Foreman. Mary Lowrey.

$1^1 1^2 2^3 1^4$ Polly Gourd. Wickliffe.
2 Rider Gourd. Catherine Wolf.
$1^1 1^2 3^3 1^4$ Joseph Gourd. *
2 Nannie Gourd. Joshua Roach.
OK 3 Charlotte Gourd. Llachlan Beavert and William Pinckney McCay.
4 Susie Gourd. Wiliam H. Turner.
5 Looney Gourd. Julia Cliffner and Lydia Humphreys.
6 Archibald Gourd. *
7 Richard Gourd. * Nannie R. Gourd nee
8 Ellis Gourd. Susie Hendricks.
9 James Gourd. Elizabeth Hendricks, Nancy Jane Lillard nee Patrick and Adeline Johnson nee Payne.
10 Thomas Gourd. *
11 Jennie Gourd. Wilkerson Hubbard Parris.
12 Elizabeth Gourd. James G. Mehlin.
13 Mary Gourd. Asa Guinn.
11 Alice Gourd. * Andrew Henderson Norwood.
$1^1 1^2 4^3 1^4$ Nannie Foreman. John T. Foster and Redbird Sixkiller.
2 Sarah Foreman. Benjamin Foster and Elijah Mayfield *
OK 3 Elias Gourd Foreman. Jennie Alberty and Mary Sanders nee Smith.
4 Catherine Foreman. Aaron Crittenden, George Tiesky, Scudders Downing and Nelson Terrapin.
5 Ellis Foreman. Elizabeth Crittenden and Sarah Kelly nee Phillips.
$1^1 1^2 5^3 1^4$ Samuel Campbell. Polly Starr and Elizabeth Cramp nee Hildebrand.
$1^1 1^2 6^3 1^4$ Looney Gourd. Sallie F. Carter and Dorothy Theresa Meeker.
2 Charles Gourd. * Samantha Miller.
OK 3 Sarah Gourd. *
4 John Gourd. Artemissa Beavert.
5 Timothy Gourd. Julia Roberson.
6 Thomas Gourd. Paralee McPherson.
7 Alexander Gourd. Elizabeth Daugherty.
$1^1 1^2 7^3 1^4$ Jesse Gourd. Susie Benge.
2 Sarah Gourd. Stephen Vann.
OK 3 Thomas Gourd. Maria Smith.
4 Caroline Gourd.
5 Nannie Gourd.
6 Charles Gourd. Nannie Christy.
7 Maude Gourd. John Downing and Wesley Lester Carroll.
$1^1 1^2 8^3 1^4$ William Downing. Susan J. Reese.
2 Charles Downing. Susan Downing nee Reese.
3 Cynthia Downing. Henry Lowrey.
4 Catherine Downing. * William Steele.

5 Sarah Downing. —— Glass, —— Raven, David A. Martin, Perry Hysel and Johnson Riley.
6 Elizabeth Downing. Ellis Lowrey.
7 Clarinda Downing. James Lowrey and David A. Martin.
$1^1 1^2 10^3 1^4$ Thomas Gourd. Rebecca Smith and Nannie Beaver.

---

2 Mary Gourd. Joseph Herberger.
OK 3 Martin Gourd. *
$1^1 2^2 1^3 1^4$ Rebecca Hopkins. Simpson Foster Monroe and Dr. Peter Tabler.
2 Electa Hopkins. Henry Crittenden.
OK 3 Martha Hopkins. George Smith.
4 Belle Hopkins. John Marcus Countryman.
5 Sarah Abigal Hapkins. Stephen Gray Garbarini.
$1^1 2^2 2^3 1^4$ Nellie Gourd. * Cherokee Manning.
$1^1 2^2 3^3 1^4$ Nancy Ann Hair. William Campbell and Joseph Seabolt.

---

2 Elizabeth Hair. * Samuel Cloud.
OK 3 Diana Hair. * Ahleecher.
4 Charlotte Hair. *
5 Clay Hair. Martha Fox.
6 John Hair. *

---

7 Abigal Hair. James McDaniel and Ahleecher.

---

8 David Hair. Sallie Wickliffe.
9 Joseph Hair.
10 George Hair. *

---

11 Francis Marion Hair. Sarah Watkins.
$1^1 2^2 4^3 1^4$ Richard Robertson. Susan Lowrey and Susan Wilkerson.
2 Maria Louisa Robertson. Stephen Spears.
OK 3 Jefferson Allen Robertson. Lou Rountree and Annie O'Riley.
4 Emiline McCoy Robertson. Bluford West Foreman.
5 Evans Price Robertson. Sarah Ellen Spears.
$1^1 2^2 5^3 1^4$ Ezekial Hair. Catherine Fishhawk, Amanda Kanoska and

---

2 Amanda Hair. Mitchell Hildebrand and Stephen Hildebrand.

---

3 Elizabeth Hair. George Benge.
4 John Hair. Mary Elizabeth Davis.

---

5 Thomas Candy Hair. *
6 Medley Tyner Hair. *
7 George Candy Hair. Mary Levi and Jennie Lind Starr nee Starr.

$1^{1}2^{2}7^{3}1^{4}$ Martha Ramsey. John Mosley.

2 Susie Ramsey. Maxwell Chambers.

$1^{1}2^{2}8^{3}1^{4}$ Catherine Hair. Soldier Sixkiller.

2 Nicholas Hair. Lucinda Robinson.

---

3 Samuel Hair. Jennie Still.

4 John Hair. Mary McPherson.

5 Elizabeth Hair. Hulburt Bean.

6 Margaret Hair. Deerinthewater.

7 Araminta Hair. George Ross.

8 James Hair. Elizabeth Gibbs nee Holt and Sarah Cox.

9 Jesse Hair. Fannie Tyner.

10 Solomon Hair. Beatrice Brown.

$1^{1}2^{2}9^{3}1^{4}$ Annie Hopper.

2 Joseph Hopper. *

OK 3 George Hopper. *

4 Sallie Hopper. John French.

5 Susie Hopper. David Sanders.

6 Martin Hopper. Mary Frisley, Annie Bolin and Nellie Christy.

7 Jennie Hopper. Charles Pritchett.

$1^{1}2^{2}11^{3}1^{4}$ Jackson Blythe.

2 Elizabeth Blythe. Richard H. Bowles.

---

3 Joseph Roberts.

$1^{1}3^{2}1^{3}1^{4}$ Ruth May. James Grigsby.

---

2 Alexander Ballard. Catherine Whitecatcher, Lucy Swimmer and Rachel Patrick.

OK 3 Annie Ballard. * Levi Rogers and Daniel Ballou.

---

4 Downy Ballard. *

5 Thomas Ballard. Mariammne Catherine Lillard.

6 Susie Ballard. *

$1^{1}3^{2}2^{3}1^{4}$ James Starr. Lettie Boyd Chambers.

2 Ellis Harlan Starr.

OK 3 Richard Taylor Starr.*

4 Nancy Jane Starr. Joseph Chambers.

5 Bluford West Starr. Margaret Ann McDaniel.

$1^{1}3^{2}3^{3}1^{4}$ Joseph Rogers McCoy. Mary Hicks.

2 Sallie McCoy. Andrew Miller and Charles Bushyhead.

3 James Christopher McCoy. Jennie Adair, Margaret Foreman and Malinda Carey nee Downing.

---

4 Rory McCoy. *

5 Ruth Emeline McCoy. George Washington Hause and Jerome Newton Kepheart.
6 Samuel Worcester McCoy. Elizabeth Foreman.
7 Mary McCoy. Wiley Vann.
8 Amanda McCoy. * Daniel Bushyhead.
9 Margaret McCoy. * Surry Eaton Beck.
10 Daniel Hicks McCoy. * Nannie Davis and Rebecca Fowler.
11 Sabra Buffington McCoy. *John Ross Hicks.
12 John Alexander McCoy. Elizabeth Keys, Jennie Dennis, Annie Coker, Annie Chooie and Margaret Hogan.
$1^1 3^2 4^3 1^4$ Maria Jane Williams. *
2 Emma Lowrey Williams. * Daniel McCoy Gunter.

OK 3 John Price. Catherine McDaniel.
4 Sarah Robidet Price. *
$1^1 3^2 5^3 1^4$ Thomas Wolf. Sarah Nix.
2 Nancy E. Wolf. * Thomas Jefferson Monroe.
3 Margaret Ann Wolf. Richard M. Fields and George Ewers.
4 James Wolf. *
5 Martha Wolf. *

---

6 Hawk Wolf. Catherine Alexander.
7 Louisa Jane Wolf. Samuel Chambers and John Horn.

---

8 Araminta Wolf. Wilson Girty.
$1^1 4^2 1^3 1^4$ John B. Brown. Margaret McCoy * and Susan Frances Colbert.
OK 3 Joseph C. Brown. Elizabeth Cox.
4 Susan Elizabeth Brown. David Martin.
5 Ebenezer Brown. Elsie Wilson nee Colbert.

---

2 Julia Brown. James McGilton Chaney.

---

6 Louis Laforce Brown. Matilda Goodtraveler.
$1^1 4^2 2^3 1^4$ Lucinda Ross. * Charles Renatus Hicks.
2 Victoria Ross. *
OK 3 Susan Ross. Osceola Powell Daniel.
4 Rufus O. Ross. Elizabeth Grace Meigs.
5 Robert Bruce Ross. Fannie Thornton.
6 Emma Ross. Osceola Powell Daniel.
7 William Wallace Ross. Delilah Jane Daniel.
8 Elizabeth Ross. * John Ross Vann.
$1^1 4^2 3^3 1^4$ Susie Benge. Jesse Gourd.

---

2 George Benge. Elizabeth Hair.

---

3 James Franklin Benge. Ruth Ellen Martin.

4 Richard Fields Benge. Martha Adair Brewer.

$1^15^211^31^4$ Charles Terrapin. Catherine E. Bark.

2 Lydia Terrapin.

$1^15^22^31^4$ John Wade Johnson. Sallie Mayes and

2 Mary Johnson. Stephen Foreman.

3 Eliza Johnson. *

---

4 Joseph Anthony Foreman. Rachel Hampton.

5 Susan Frances Foreman. * George Washington Smith.

6 Thomas Fox Foreman. Ada Vann nee Chandler.

$1^15^24^31^4$ Alice V. Conrad.

2 Myrtle Conrad.

Riley.

1^1 Samuel Riley. Gu-lu-sti-yu and Ni-go-di-ge-yu. A55

1^11^2 Nannie Riley. John McNary.

2 Richard Riley. Diana Campbell.

3 Mary Riley. Samuel Keys.

4 Elizabeth Riley. Isaac Keys.

5 John Riley. Susan Walker.

6 Nellie Riley. Charles Coody.

7 Sallie Riley. William Keys.

8 Lucy Riley. Owen Brady.

9 Louisa Riley. Dennis Biggs.

10 Loony Riley. Rachel Stuart.

11 Rachel Riley. Daniel Milton and James McDaniel.

---

12 James Riley. Jennie Shields and

13 Catherine Riley. Andrew Lacey.

14 Martha Riley. John Hall.

15 Madison Riley. *

16 Nelson Riley. Elizabeth Thompson and Mary Cordell nee

$1^11^21^3$ Margaret McNary. James Thompson.

$1^12^21^3$ Jennie Riley. David Carter. A45

OK 2 Elizabeth Riley. Wright Romine and Jacob Bushyhead.

$1^13^21^3$ Anariah Keys. Benjamin Price.

2 Richard Keys. Mary A. Hayes.

OK 5 Evaline Keys. Theodore McCoy.

4 Samuel Riley Keys. Mary Easter Hanna.

5 James Madison Keys. Mary Etta Smith.

6 Mary Keys. Stephen Bruner.

$1^14^21^3$ Nannie Keys. Thomas Bertholf.

2 Riley Keys. Eliza Gunter, Esther Lee and Minerva Nave.

OK 3 Leroy Keys. Jennie Gunter and Nannie Melton.

4 Letitia Keys. Edward Gunter and Jackson Tyner.

5 Lydia Keys. * John King.

| 6 George Washington Keys. *

| 7 Thomas Jefferson Keys. *

8 Sallie Keys. John Spears.

9 Richard R. Keys. Amanda Walker.

10 Electa Bosworth Keys. Marcus O. Bertholf.

11 Rachel Keys. Pinckney McCay.

12 Samuel Houston Keys. Cherokee Melton and Sarah McIntosh.

13 Martha J. Keys. Edward Wright, Andrew Tyner and James Atkins.

14 Isaac William Keys. Jennie Ramsey, Cynthia Irving and Martha E. Holland nee Miller.

15 Susan Keys. Edward Melton.

16 Elizabeth Keys. George Harlan.

$1^{1}5^{2}1^{3}$ Felix Riley. Mary Stewart, Susie Bigby, Annie Peacheater nee Hendricks and Naomi Vickery.

2 Nannie Riley. *

3 Sallie W. Riley. Rev. Stephen Foreman.

4 Jennie C. Riley. William R. Bean and Nicholas Woods.

5 Perloney Riley. *

6 Susan Riley.Sanders Choate.

7 Samuel Riley. Nannie Nave.

8 Malinda Riley. Levi Jordan.

9 Rebecca McNair Riley. Alexander Drumgool Wilson and Archibald M. Wilson.

10 Laura Riley. * John Lowrey McCoy.

11 John McNary Riley. Nannie Ivey.

$1^{1}6^{2}1^{3}$ Archibald Coody. Elizabeth Meade.

2 Engevine Coody. Elizabeth McPherson.

OK 3 Richard Coody. Belinda George Riley.

4 Rufus Coody. * Margaret Gunter.

5 Madison Coody. Margaret Coody nee Gunter.

6 Charles Coody. * Susie Fields.

7 Sallie Coody. * Hugh Montgomery McPherson.

8 Elizabeth Coody. Wiley Forrester.

9 Nannie Coody. Richard Carter.

10 Samuel Coody. * Sallie Riley.

$1^{1}7^{2}1^{3}$ Lewis Keys. Catherine McDaniel.

2 Diana Keys. * Joseph Spears.

OK 3 Levi Keys. * Lucinda Jane Sanders.

4 Mary Keys. *

5 Monroe Calvin Keys. Lucy Lowrey Hoyt.

6 Elizabeth A. Keys. Johnson Riley.

7 Looney Keys. *

$1^{1}8^{2}1^{3}$ Samuel Riley Brady. Sallie Prince and Mary Wilkerson.

2 Eliza Brady. David Webber and Daniel Perdue.

OK 3 Malinda Brady. William Freshower. and McKenzie Coats.

4 Charles Brady. *

5 Earl Brady.

6 James Monroe Brady. Elizabeth Gore, Nellie McIntosh and Elizabeth Whitman.
7 Isaac Lewis Brady. * Sarah Hale.
8 Lucinda Brady.
9 Rachel Brady. * Pinson England.
10 Sallie Brady. Wiley McNair Guilliams.

$1^19^21^3$ Napoleon Bonaparte Biggs. *
2 Sallie Biggs. *
OK 3 Minerva Biggs. * John Thompson.
4 Eliza Biggs. *
5 John Biggs. *

$1^110^21^3$ Eliza Riley. George Harlan.
2 Belinda George Riley. Richard Coody.
OK 3 Samuel King Riley. Sallie A. Rider.
4 John Riley. Minerva Porter.
5 Mary Jane Riley. Watson Walker.
6 Rufus Riley. Elizabeth Risner.
7 Lucy Riley. Andrew Jackson Greenway.
8 Sallie Riley. * Samuel Coody.
9 Ellen Riley. William Roach.
10 Randolph Riley. Eliza Coody and Missouri Ellen Harlow.

$1^111^21^3$ John Melton. *

---

2 Elias McDaniel. *
OK 3 Charles McDaniel. *
4 Joseph McDaniel. *

$1^112^21^3$ Lewis Riley. Nicey Maxfield, Nancy Tassell, Elizabeth Rogers, Sarah Childers and Mary Martin nee McLaughlin.
2 Susan Riley. James Madison Payne.
OK 3 Malinda Riley. — Applegate, John Hall and — Crockett.
4 Nannie Riley.

---

5 Jonathan Riley. Mary Jack nee Gunter.

$1^113^21^3$ Ensley Lacey. Martha Taylor and Mary Bolin.
2 Amanda Lacey. Robert Wilkins.
3 Eliza Lacey. Richard Rogers.
4 Mary Lacey. * —— Hill, —— Haynes and Jesse Lee.
5 Alexander Lacey. * Elizabeth Thornton.
6 Catherine Lacey. *

$1^114^21^3$ Elizabeth Hall. Eli Spears.
2 Ellen Hall. *
OK 3 Martha Hall. *

$1^116^21^3$ Ellen Riley. *
2 Margaret Riley. *
OK 3 Julius Riley. Amanda Cordell.
4 Joseph Riley. Matilda Maxfield and Lucy Ore nee Lusk.

5 Mary Ann Riley. Thomas Maxfield and William M. Triplett.

6 Perry Andre Riley. Eliza Colston.

7 Charles Riley. *

---

8 Martha Jane Riley. * William Freeman.

9 Louisa Riley. *

$1^1 1^2 1^3 1^4$ Mary Ann Thompson. William Smith Terrell.

2 Angerona Thompson. * William Choate.

3 William U. Thompson. Sallie B. Johnson.

4 Lurena Thompson. James Frazier.

$1^1 2^2 1^3 1^4$ Richard Carter. Nannie Coody.

2 Alexander Carter. *

OK 3 John Ross Carter. * Sarah Rogers.

4 Benjamin Wisner Carter. Nannie Elliott and Serena Josephine Guy.

5 Diana Carter. William Parrott.

6 Sallie F. Carter. Looney Gourd.

7 Thomas Jefferson Carter. Susie Robertson nee Lowrey.

8 Nannie Carter. *James Brower.

9 David Tecumseh Carter. Emma Williams Chambers.

10 Osceola Carter. *

$1^1 2^2 2^3 1^4$ Sarah Jane Romine. *

2 Caroline Eliza Romine. Thomas Ballard and David Edward Sanders.

OK 3 Joseph Bushyhead. Delilah Sixkiller.

4 Lovely Ann Bushyhead. John Beard.

$1^1 3^2 1^3 1^4$ Samuel Joseph Price. Sarah Williams.

2 Catherine Price.

$1^1 3^2 2^3 1^4$ Willamson Roland Winston Cobb Keys. Mary E. Booth.

2 Mary Ann Keys. Julian F. Hickle.

3 Charles Lewis Keys. Martha Jane McIntyre.

4 Sarah Keys. —— Fawnberg.

5 Eliza Keys. Hugh O'Neill.

6 Theodore S. Keys. Margaret J. Kesterson.

7 Linnie Jane Keys. George William Batson and Daniel Crail.

8 Rebecca Alice Keys. Frances Marion Booth.

$1^1 3^2 3^3 1^4$ James Christopher McCoy. *

2 Leander McCoy. *

3 Eliza McCoy. Richard Chastain.

4 Musidora McCoy. *

5 James McCoy. Lonie Martin.

$1^1 3^2 4^3 1^4$ Mary Elizabeth Keys. * Lemuel Saunders.

2 Polina Jane Keys. George Washington Patrick.

OK 3 William Campbell Mason Keys. Fannie Mullins.

4 Levi Rogers Keys. Levannah Elizabeth Carlile nee Catron.

5 Samuel Joseph Keys. Mary Theresa Thomas.

$1^1 3^2 5^3 1^4$ William Samuel Keys. Texas Cox.

2 Hulda Keys. Joseph Lusk and Matthew James Whitfield.

OK 3 James Theodore Keys. Margaret Elizabeth Spears nee Carlile.

4 Lorenzo Dow Keys.

5 Virginia Caperton Keys. Benjamin Duff.

6 Dudley Columbus Keys. Amanda Catherine Langley.

7 Mitchell Graham Keys. Sarah Jane Leadford.

8 Mary Olivia Keys.

9 Martha Keys. John S. Hyatt.

10 Ophelia Warren Keys. William Franklin Langley.

$1^1 3^2 6^3 1^4$ Letitia Ann Williams.

---

2 John R. Bruner. Letha Harrison.

3 Isaac Norris Bruner. Martha Margaret Harrison.

4 George Samuel Bruner. Maude Amanda America Holloway.

5 Theodore Syphian Bruner. Martha Caroline Gamblin.

$1^1 4^2 1^3 1^4$ Elizabeth Letitia Bertholf. William F. McIntosh.

2 Jennie Bertholf. Charles Bray.

OK 3 Isaac Wesley Bertholf. *

4 Thomas Bertholf. *

5 Cornelia L. Bertholf. * Daniel Fields Smith.

6 William Henry Bertholf. Amanda Jane McLemore.

7 Electa Victoria Bertholf. Stand Watie Gray.

8 Richard Riley Bertholf. Octavia Maxfield.

$1^1 4^2 2^3 1^4$ Elsie Keys. *

2 George Keys. *

3 Alice Keys. * John Gonzales.

---

4 Lewis Keys. * Nancy Wheeler Watie.

5 Elizabeth Keys. * John Alexander McCoy.

---

6 Nancy Jane Keys. James Monroe Wilkerson and John Lyman.

7 Louisa Keys. *

8 Mary Ellen Keys. William Bentz and Pleasant Porter.

---

9 Fannie Keys. William Henry Balentine.

10 Riley Keys. Julia Turner.

$1^1 4^2 3^3 1^4$ Riley J. Keys. * Nancy Perloney Harlan.

2 Letitia Keys. Mitchell Harlan, Johnson Riley and Joseph Asbury Denbo.

---

3 Oceola Keys. Nannie Ashcraft.

---

2 Nannie Tyner. William Pettit.

OK 3 Lydia Tyner. Bluford West Rider.

4 George Washington Tyner. Mary Shaw and Mary Ann Elder.

5 Fannie Tyner. *

$1^14^28^31^4$ Minerva Spears. *

2 Araminta Spears. *

OK 3 Mary Spears. Edward Campbell.

$1^14^29^31^4$ Samuel H. Keys. Mary E. Tarrents.

2 Elizabeth Keys. *

OK 3 Nellie Walker Keys. Albert P. Litto.

4 George Edward Keys. *

$1^14^210^31^4$ John Riley Bertholf.

2 Nancy Jane Bertholf. Otto Zufall.

OK 3 Martha Leonora Bertholf. Pleasant Porter.

4 Letitia Ann Bertholf. William Arthur Madden.

5 Thomas Edward Bertholf. Ada Bird Barton.

$1^14^212^31^4$ Victoria Keys. Lewis Keys.

---

2 Samuel Keys.

OK 3 Edward Keys.

4 Eliza Keys. Frederick Dyer.

5 Richard Keys.

6 James H. Keys.

7 Leroy Keys.

8 Ella Keys.

9 Ada Keys.

$1^14^214^31^4$ Leroy Hammond Keys. Isabelle Thomas.

---

2 Jessie Lena Keys. Samuel Jordan.

OK 3 Nellie Grace Keys.

4 Ida Myrtle Keys.

$1^15^21^31^4$ Richard Riley. Mary A. Simpkins.

---

2 Jennie Riley. Looney Seabolt, James Roberts, Eugene Triplett and Jasper Newton Scrimsher.

3 Sarah Riley. David Seabolt and Walter Scott Agnew.

4 Harrison Riley. *

---

5 Susan Riley. Ellis Gourd.

---

6 John Riley. Mary Harden.

7 Sarah Riley. *

---

8 Nancy Jane Riley. William Rider, Fredrick Mayes and Charles Wallace.

9 Samuel Riley. *

$1^15^23^31^4$ Austin Worcester Foreman. *

2 Ermina Nash Foreman. *

3 Jeremiah Everett Foreman. Celeste Stidham.

4 Susie Elizabeth Foreman. *

5 John Anthony Foreman. Eliza Mary Blythe and Nancy Amanda Smith.

6 Stephen Taylor Foreman. Ada Carter McClellan.

7 Jennie Lind Foreman. Charles McClure McClellan.

8 Archibald Alexander Foreman. * Annie Rucks.

9 Austin Worcester Foreman. Emma Josephine Ridenhour and Margaret Edith George.

$1^{1}5^{2}4^{3}1^{4}$ Sarah Bean. Samuel Childers and ———Lucas.

2 Robert Bruce Bean. Emily Ophelia Walker.

OK 3 Albert Bean. *

4 DeWitt Anderson Bean. Lucy ——— and Emily Ophelia Bean nee Walker.

5 Josephus Bean. Martha McDonald, Eveline Ward and Sarah Evans.

6 Mary Pauline Bean. William Blythe, John Friend and Samuel G. Heffington.

7 Edward Russell Bean. Ruby Romain McGath.

$1^{1}5^{2}6^{3}1^{4}$ George Washington Choate. Caroline Elizabeth Sanders and Elizabeth Sanders.

$1^{1}5^{2}7^{3}1^{4}$ William Riley.

2 Sarah Riley.

$1^{1}5^{2}8^{3}1^{4}$ John W. Jordan. Sallie B. Thompson nee Bean, Martha Rowland and Tennessee Jane Riley.

$1^{1}5^{2}9^{3}1^{4}$ Susan Rebecca Wilson. Joseph Polston, Thomas Washington Lindsey and William Thomas Huitt.

2 Isabel Brandon Wilson. Henry Parish and Benjamin A. Rush.

OK 3 Laura Alice Wilson. John Raymond and Thomas Henry.

4 James Madison Wilson. Araminta Pharris.

5 Anise Femister Wilson. James Alexander Rice.

$1^{1}5^{2}11^{3}1^{4}$ Sallie Riley. Joseph Mason French.

2 Susan Elizabeth Riley. John Bean Gott.

OK 3 Alice Riley. James Sneed Vann.

4 Laura Bertha Riley. William Henry Marker.

$1^{1}6^{2}1^{3}1^{4}$ Delilah Coody. *

2 Ellen Coody. Thomas Lewis Rogers.

3 Archibald Coody. Hannah Jane Foreman.

4 Charles Edward Coody. Laura Wilson nee Haff.

$1^{1}6^{2}2^{3}1^{4}$ Elizabeth Coody. Rufus Coody.

2 Engevine Coody. Nannie ———.

$1^{1}6^{2}3^{3}1^{4}$ Charles Coody.

2 John Henry Coody. Mary Ellen Rogers and Mary Ann Wilkerson.

$1^{1}6^{2}5^{3}1^{4}$ Jennie Coody. *

$1\,1^16^29^31^4$ Alice Forrester. N. A. Mallery and John Hohenstein.
2 Annie Elizabeth Forrester. Levi Parish.
$1^16^29^81^4$ James Madison Carter. *
2 Jennie Carter. *
3 Nellie Carter. * Talbert McNair.
4 Richard R. Carter. *
$1^17^21^81^4$ William Keys. Martha Brewster.
2 James McDaniel Keys. Nancy Jane Mayes.
3 John Keys. *
4 Ellen Keys. *
5 Lewis Shell Keys. Elizabeth Haseltine Taylor.

---

6 Joanna Keys. Moses Benona Hunley and William Patrick Heffernan.
$1^17^25^31^4$ Mary Eunice Keys. Hamilton Balentine.
2 Lydia Emma Keys. Charles Johnson Kavanaugh Taylor.
OK 3 Fannie Myrtle Keys. James Andrew Leforce.
4 Sarah Ann Keys. Samuel Leforce.

---

5 Elizabeth Riley Keys. Orin Giteau Althy and John M. Chumley.
6 Monroe Amory Keys. Martha Donnelly.
7 Lucy Keys. John B. Miles.
$1^17^26^31^4$ Martha Belle Riley. John Porter Thurman.
$1^18^21^81^4$ Charles Brady. * Nannie Roberson.

---

2 Adelaide Brady. William Wallace Freshower, Thomas Fox Brewer, Wiley McNair Guilliams and Richard Lafayette Sutherlin.

OK 3 William Brady. Caroline Smith* and Martha Hensley.
$1^18^22^81^4$ Owen Webber. *

---

2 Elizabeth Perdue. Jack Risner.
OK 3 Nannie Perdue. John Robison.
4 Caroline Perdue. * Jack Risner.
5 Eliza Perdue. * John Allen.
$1^18^23^31^4$ Joseph Freshower. Mary Clark.
2 William Wallace Freshower. Adelaide Brady.
OK 3 Henry Clay Freshower. *
4 Lucy Jane Freshower. *

---

5 Malinda Coats. * James Case.
6 Samuel Coats. Cora Wattenberger and Alice Craig.
$1^18^26^31^4$ Margaret Brady. William Henry Allison.

---

2 William Wallace Brady.

3 Rosella Brady.

$1^1 8^2 10^3 1^4$ Lucy Malinda Guilliams. *

$1^1 10^2 2^3 1^4$ Charles Coody. *

OK 2 John Henry Coody. Mary Ellen Rogers and Mary Ann Wilkerson.*

$1^1 10^2 3^3 1^4$ Victoria Ellen Riley. Marion Walker Couch.

2 Laura Sigison Riley. A. Frank Johnson.

OK 3 Clara C. Riley. Samuel Parks.

4 Mary Jane Riley. William Emory Roberts.

5 John Randolph Riley. Irene Kating.

6 George Washington Riley. Mary Ellen Smith.

$1^1 10^2 4^3 1^4$ Lewis Porter Riley. Elizabeth Compston.

2 Eliza Ellen Riley. * James Milton Holley.

OK 3 James Riley. Jennie May Paxton.

4 Sallie Lucinda Riley. Albert Melvin McMain.

$1^1 10^2 5^3 1^4$ Wiliam J. Walker. Georgia A. Harlow.

$1^1 10^2 6^3 1^4$ Samuel R. Riley. Nannie B. Seabolt.

2 Rufus Randolph Riley.

3 Atwood Riley. Effie Mattox.

$1^1 10^2 7^3 1^4$ Alonzo Greenway. Rose Anna Glenn.

2 Minnie Greenway. *

$1^1 10^2 10^3 1^4$ Ida May Riley. Martin Clarkson Woody.

$1^1 12^2 1^3 1^4$ Eliza Riley. John Lovett.

2 Ruth Riley. Reese Candy and Rev. Stephen Foreman.

OK 3 Jennie Riley. *

---

4 Johnson Riley. Letitia Harlan nee Riley, Elizabeth A. Keys and Sarah Glass nee Downing.

---

5 James Riley. * Ida Gustavia Dance.

6 Flora Riley. Osceola Powell Daniel.

$1^1 12^2 2^3 1^4$ William Penn Payne. Amanda Scott and Alice Nave.

2 Cicero Payne. Caroline Foster.

3 James Madison Payne. *

4 John Jolly Payne. Mary Elizabeth Israel.

5 Lewis Albert Payne. Ella Bullfrog.

$1^1 12^2 3^3 1^4$ James Applegate.

---

2 Jennie Thornton. *

---

3 Arthur Crockett. *

4 Ann Crockett. Andrew Jackson Jeremiah.

5 Abigal Crockett.

$1^1 12^2 4^3 1^4$ Jennie Payne. *

---

2 Flora Malinda Thorne. John Gabriel Hawkins.

$1^1 13^2 1^3 1^4$ Larry Miles Lacey. * Alice Barnes.

2 John Drew Lacey. Mary Doherty nee Pettit and Lucy Frances Prunty.

OK 3 Delilah Lacey. *

---

4 Sarah Belle Lacey. Robert T. Thornton, George J. Salley.

$1^{1}13^{2}2^{3}1^{4}$ Georgia Ann Wilkins. John Osborn Walker and William Scott.

2 Josephine Wilkins. Alfred Forsette and Joseph Marchand.

$1^{1}13^{2}3^{3}1^{4}$ James Rogers. Mary Sanders.

$1^{1}14^{2}1^{3}1^{4}$ John Albion Spears. Josephine Turner and Belle Langley.

2 Sarah Ellen Spears. Evans Price Robertson.

3 Lorenzo Delano Spears. Jennie Columbia Beavert.

$1^{1}16^{2}3^{3}1^{4}$ Elizabeth Riley. * McCoy Smith.

$1^{1}16^{2}4^{3}1^{4}$ Addie Riley. James Kyle.

2 Nelson Riley. *

---

3 Charles Riley. *

$1^{1}16^{2}5^{3}1^{4}$ Octavia Maxfield. Richard Riley Bertholf.

2 Ida Verona Maxfield. James Harvey Lindsey.

OK 3 Lillie Riley. Claude Hanks McDaniel.

$1^{1}16^{2}6^{3}1^{4}$ Nancy Amanda Riley. John Lee Lamb.

Duncan

1^{1} Dorcas. ———Benge and Young Charles Gordon Duncan. A47

$1^{1}1^{2}$ Edmond Benge. Mary Rains.

---

2 John Duncan. Elizabeth Abercrombie.

3 Rebecca Duncan. James Landrum.

4 Emily Duncan. Alexander Kell.

5 Elizabeth Duncan. *

6 Lewis Duncan. *

7 Charles Duncan. Mahala Abercrombie.

$1^{1}1^{2}1^{3}$ Charles R. Duncan. Judith Roach.

2 Martha Duncan. David Jones.

OK 3 John R. Duncan. *

4 Jennie Duncan. Thomas Carey.

5 Edmond Duncan. Maria Richey and Barbara Ashley.

6 William B. Duncan. Narcissa Reeves Foreman nee Carey.

7 Lewis Duncan. Mary Spears.

8 George Washington Duncan. * Martha Carey and Margaret Scrimsher.

9 Nathaniel Green Duncan. Ellen Martin.

10 James R. Duncan. Elizabeth Dennis and Susan Bryant.

11 Mary Duncan. James Martin, Samuel K. Weir, Thomas Hickox and George W. Moore.

12 Ross Cherokee Duncan. Mary Goddard and Susie McLain.

$1^{1}2^{2}1^{3}$ Hannah Duncan. Ezekial Buffington McLaughlin.

2 Emily Duncan. John Beck and Thomas Winchester Measles.
OK 3 Mahala Duncan. James Smith West.
4 Walter Adair Duncan. Martha Bell, Martha Wilson and Catherine Ann Caleb nee Larzalere.
5 James Abercrombie Duncan. Eliza Denton and Lucy Ann Duncan nee Clark.
6 Young Charles Gordon Duncan. Sinia Eaton and Nancy Ann Duncan nee Starr.
7 John Tommason Duncan. Elizabeth Sanders.
8 DeWitt Clinton Duncan. * Helen Rosencrantz.
9 William Wirt Duncan. Nancy Ann Starr.
10 Elizabeth Ann Duncan. Isaac Brown Hitchcock.
11 Joshua Bertholf Duncan. Elizabeth Ray and Lucy Ann Thompson nee Clark.
$1^13^21^3$ Nannie Landrum. Samuel Thomas.
2 Elizabeth Landrum. Andrew McLaughlin.
OK 3 Hiram Terrell Landrum. Mary Muskrat.
4 Charles Landrum. Ruth Proctor.
5 James Landrum Susan Muskrat.
6 Rebecca Landrum. * Thomas Davis.
7 Benjamin Franklin Landrum. Mary Berry and Elizabeth Woodall.
8 David Dixon Landrum. Susie Crutchfield.
9 Jemima Landrum. Elijah Moore and Wiley Earbob.
10 John Landrum. Nellie Otterlifter.
11 Aaron Landrum. Easter Muskrat.
12 Dorcas Landrum. Elowie Butler. A61
13 Rachel Landrum. George Buffington.
$1^14^21^3$ James Kell. Elizabeth Edgington, Julia Rogers and Nancy Edgington.
2 Andrew Kell. Annie Hawkins and Mary Huss.
OK 3 David Kell. Dorcas Corban nee Duncan.
4 John Kell. *
5 Elizabeth Kell. Lewis Rolston.
6 Rebecca Kell. Samuel Simons.
7 Nannie Kell. George Murray and William Lilly.
$1^17^21^3$ John Adair Duncan. * Mary McWilliams nee Fields.
2 Young Charles Duncan. *
OK 3 Dorcas Duncan. John Manuel Corban, David Kell and John McMurtry.
4 Caleb Duncan. Mary Elizabeth Hudson.
5 James Burr Duncan. Annie Jane Woodall.
6 Jonathan Gordon Duncan. *
7 Elizabeth Harriette Duncan. Henry Lewis Smith.
8 Thomas Washington Duncan. Edith Chapman Wright.
9 Robert Lewis Duncan. Sophia Neeley.

10 Rebecca Jane Duncan. John W. Carter.
11 Leonidas Philip Duncan. Mary Fleming.

$1^11^21^31^4$ Andrew Jackson Duncan.
2 Martha Duncan. Douglas Bryson.
3 William Duncan.
4 Francis Duncan.
5 Marion Duncan.

$1^11^22^31^4$ Elizabeth Jones. John Rattlinggourd, Risingfawn and Henry Blalock.
2 Frank Jones. *
3 George Jones. *

$1^11^24^31^4$ Edmond Duncan Carey. Lucy Pigeon and Lydia Ann Pigeon.
2 Mary Ann Carey. Caleb Willis Conner.
OK 3 Ross Thomas Carey. Rebecca Conner, Josephine Blevins and Nannie Henrietta Nidiffer.

$1^11^25^31^4$ Jennie Duncan. *
2 Sarah Elizabeth Duncan. *

---

3 Margaret Duncan. Otis J. Wing and Henry Odell.
4 Barbara Catherine Duncan. William Ferdinand Goodman.

$1^11^26^31^4$ Narcissa Jane Duncan. Henry Harrison Scraper.
OK 2 John Hamilton Duncan.

$1^11^27^31^4$ Alice Duncan.

$1^11^29^31^4$ Bluford Alberty Duncan. Samantha Carter nee Lane.
2 Rebecca Jane Duncan. Francis Marion Conner.

$1^11^210^31^4$ Daniel Duncan. * Angeline Daniel.

---

2 Dorcas Duncan. Theodore Thomas Kelly.
3 Rebecca Duncan. Zeno Cox and John B. Lawrence.

$1^11^211^31^4$ William Martin. *
2 Charlotte Martin. *

OK 3 Nathaniel Breckenridge Weir. Mary Elvina Pitcher.

---

4 Henry Hickox. Mariammne Connelly.
5 Annie Hickox. Dr. Albert Harvey Collins.

$1^11^212^31^4$ William Duncan. *
2 Laura Duncan. Job Beaver Parker.

$1^12^21^31^4$ Mary McLaughlin. Samuel Martin and George W. Hughes.
2 John McLaughlin.
OK 3 Ezekial Collin McLaughlin. Susie Harkins and Ellen J. Harkins.
4 Jennie McLaughlin. Ellis McDaniel.
5 David McLaughlin. Frances Reynolds.

$1^1 2^2 2^3 1^4$ William Wilburn Beck *

2 David McLaughlin Beck. Mary Elizabeth Vickery, Julia— and Amanda New nee Hillen.

OK 3 Louisa Beck. John Pinkney Chandler.

4 Martha Beck. *

5 Tabitha Beck. Andrew Freeny.

6 Mary Beck. John Talbert and Henry Clay Freeny.

7 Aaron Beck. *

8 Elizabeth Beck. Daniel Foreman and Rider Cloud.

9 Joseph Beck. *

10 Sinia Beck. Jeremiah Horn and James Murphy.

11 Susie W. Beck. *

12 Sallie B. Beck. Seabron G. Mabry.

13 Emily Beck. John Alexander Sevier and Thomas Dyer.

14 John Walter Beck. Cynthia Ragsdale.

$1^1 2^2 3^3 1^4$ Walter Adair West. Sallie Elizabeth Wright.

2 William North West. Eliza Rogers and Clementine Shadles.

OK 3 Laura Ann West. William Pinkston Gray, Amos D. Haymaker and Frank Rogers.

4 DeWitt Clinton West. *

5 Marcellus Lilburn West. Delilah Scraper.

6 John Duncan West. Nannie Brown.

7 Sarah Jane West. *

8 James Bell West. Josephine Smith

9 Tabitha Louisa West. John Rogers Martin and Vet Thompson.

$1^1 2^2 4^3 1^4$ Mariammne Celeste Duncan. * Thomas Everidge Oaks.

2 Anacrion Bell Duncan. *

OK 3 Jarrette Merini Duncan. Nannie Buffington.

---

4. John Ellis Duncan. Susie Elizabeth Carselowry.

5 Mary Ann Elizabeth Duncan. Harvey Wirt Courtland Shelton.

6 Emma Duncan. Frank McFerran Berry.

7 Jennie Duncan. *

$1^1 2^2 5^3 1^4$ Jimmie Abercrombie Duncan. Frederick Lafayette Langley and Dr. Alonzo Clarence Render.

2 Lucy Elizabeth Duncan. George Fergerson.

OK 3 Charles DeWitt Duncan. Rosa Lunday.

$1^1 2^2 6^3 1^4$ Amanda Cherokee Duncan. John Tolbert Scott.

2 Temperance Duncan. *

OK 3 Millard A. Duncan. *

$1^1 2^2 7^3 1^4$ Abigal Sarah Duncan. Gabriel L. Payne.

2 Mary Elizabeth Duncan. Francis Marion Crowell.

OK 3 John Calhoun Duncan. Joanna Coody Rogers.

4 Susan Saphronia Duncan. Joseph Hall Alexander.

5 Josephine Brown Duncan. Walter Box, William Penn Chandler and

6 Ruth Etta Duncan. Jefferson Thompson Parks.

$1^{1}2^{2}9^{3}1^{4}$ Taylor Duncan. Lydia Hummingbird.

---

2 Felix Grundy Duncan. Elizabeth Shell.

OK 3 Mary Lunnie Duncan. * Alexander Wright.

4 William Wirt Duncan. Sallie Gullage.

$1^{1}2^{2}10^{3}1^{4}$ Timothy Brown Hitchcock. Annie Laura Shirley and Lucy Jane Manus.

2 Etta Smith Hitchcock. Samuel James Burns.

OK 3 Irenaes Duncan Hitchcock. Lulu Osborn.

$1^{1}2^{2}11^{3}1^{4}$ Charlotte Catherine Duncan. Rudolph Haegert and John Sheridan Martin.

2 Joshua Lafayette Duncan. Zipporah E. Truitt.

---

3 Delen Rosencrantz Duncan. Philip Donahoo and Arthur Archibald.

4 Annie Ellen Duncan. Thomas Humphries Prim.

$1^{1}3^{2}1^{3}1^{4}$ Jefferson Thomas.

$1^{1}3^{2}2^{3}1^{4}$ Rebecca Ann McLaughlin. Andrew Jackson Click.

2 James L. McLaughlin. Sarah Ann Smith.

OK 3 Andrew L. McLaughlin. *

4 Joshua Ezekial McLaughlin. Celia Davis, Etta Renfro and Margaret Caroline Inlow.

5 Mary Jane McLaughlin. Lewis Glenn and John Hendricks.

6 Joseph Frank McLaughlin. Minnie M. Price.

7 Maria C. McLaughlin. Jack Jones.

8 Rachel S. McLaughin. William H. Donelson.

9 Charles McLaughin. *

10 Benjamin Reuben McLaughin. *

$1^{1}3^{2}3^{3}1^{4}$ Joseph Landrum. Arie Beck.

2 John B. Landrum. Elizabeth Duncan* and Charlotte Jane Crickett.

OK 3 Lydia Landrum. *

$1^{1}3^{2}4^{3}1^{4}$ Thomas Landrum. Pauline Sidney nee Martin.

2 Rebecca Landrum. *

OK 3 Hiram Terrell Landrum. Arkansas Cherokee Martin.

4 Samuel Landrum. *

5 James Proctor Landrum. *

6 Rachel Landrum. Samuel Walls.

$1^{1}3^{2}5^{3}1^{4}$ Joseph Landrum. *

2 Cynthia Landrum. *

---

3 Daniel Landrum. Mary Hinton * and Annie Hoskins.

4 Nannie Landrum. Alexander Cochran.

$1^{1}3^{2}7^{3}1^{4}$ Dixon Landrum.

2 Emma Landrum. John Robert Dobkins.

OK 3 Benjamin Seth Landrum. Sallie Cavallier.
4 Cicero Martin Landrum.
5 Louisa Landrum. *
6 Charles F. Landrum.
7 William A. Landrum. *
8 Ada Landrum.
$1^13^28^31^4$ Josephine Landrum. Lewis Rogers and Frank Howard.
2 Jennie Landrum. * Anderson Landrum Crittenden Jennings.
OK 3 Mary Landrum. Joseph Vann Crutchfield.
4 Nannie Landrum. John Washington Adair.
5 Rachel Landrum. Rollin Kirk Adair.
6 Charles Dixon Landrum. *
7 Elias McLeod Landrum. Nana Woodall.
$1^13^29^31^4$ Catherine Moore. Elizur Butler Sanders.
2 James Moore. Rachel Boling and Celia Usrey.
OK 3 Keziah Camille Moore. Jeter Thompson Cunningham.
4 Cowheesit Moore. *

5 Worcester Wiley. Caroline Rogers and Elizabeth McKinney.
6 Lewis Wiley. *
$1^13^210^31^4$ Frances Delilah Landrum.*
2 Johnson Thompson Landrum. Caroline Isabelle Garbarini.
OK 3 Samuel Landrum.
4 Edward Landrum.
$1^13^211^31^4$ Derrell Landrum. *
2 Jeter Landrum. *
OK 3 Annie Landrum. *
4 Jesse Landrum.
5 David Landrum. *
$1^13^212^31^4$ Annie Butler. Joseph Box.
2 William Joel Butler.
3 Elsie Butler. John Cobb Welch.
4 Aaron Butler. Elnora Beavert and Laura Hildebrand nee
5 James Perry Butler. Nannie Muskrat.
6 John Elijah Butler. Sallie Johnson nee Cephas.
7 Elizabeth Butler. James Franklin Crittenden.
$1^13^213^31^4$ Charles Landrum Buffington.
2 John Walter Buffington. *
3 James Bufington. Ida Belle Coffelt.
$1^14^21^31^4$ Lewis Ross Kell. Sarah Chouteau nee Chambers and Sallie Matilla Poole nee Harlan.
2 John Ross Kell. * Rachel Smith.
OK 3 Nannie Kell. * Josiah Knight.
4 Frances Kell. Joseph Lynch Thompson.
5 Louisa Rolston Kell. Bevilly Bean Hickey.

7 Joseph Kell. Margaret Scott.
8 Daniel O'Connell Kell. * Susie Daniel.

---

6 William Kell. Ellen Oxier.
9 Mary Frances Kell. William F. Burchfield and John Oliver Truman.

---

10 Alice Kell. Thomas Fox French.
11 Helen Delilah Kell. Robert Mosby French.
12 James Kell. *
$1^1 4^2 2^3 1^4$ John Kell. Margaret Vickers.
2 Emily Kell. * Simpson Clark Bennett.
OK 3 Hannah Kell. * Archibald Cochran.
$1^1 4^2 3^3 1^4$ Charles Marcellus Kell.
2 Mahala Abercrombie Kell. Hebard James Tarpley.
$1^1 4^2 5^3 1^4$ Rebecca Rolston. Peter McAllister.
2 John Tate Rolston. Lena Nohle nee Schmidt.
OK 3 Frances Tate Rolston.
4 Emily Rolston. *
5 Nannie Caroline Rolston. Samuel C. Sager.
6 Lewis Rolston. Eliza Postell.
7 Eliza Rolston. *
8 Zachariah Taylor Rolston. *
9 Agnes Paschal Rolston. Adam Pfunkuche.
10 Henry Rolston.
11 Amanda Rolston. William Jones.
12 James David Rolston.
13 Martha Josephine Rolston. Jacob Hulsey.
14 Robert D. Rolston. Lulu Cunington, Vashti Eckles and Ada Alice Greer nee Atkinson.
$1^1 4^2 6^3 1^4$ William Simons. *
2 Elizabeth Adeline Simons. William Martin.
OK 3 John Ross Simons. * Martha Emeline Fields.
4 Samuel Newell Simons. *
5 Nancy Ann Simons. Jesse McCreary and Jesse Jones.
6 Martha Cherokee Simons. *
$1^1 4^2 7^3 1^4$ Cynthia Murry. *

---

2 Letitia Lilly. James Simmons.
$1^1 7^2 3^3 1^4$ John Emanuel Corban.

---

2 Charles Marcellue Kell. *
OK 3 Mahala Abercrombie Kell. Heberd James Tarpley.
$1^1 7^2 4^3 1^4$ Alfred Buffington Duncan. Lucy Ann Murphy.
2 Charles Selden Duncan.
OK 3 Catherine Elizabeth Duncan.
4 Julia Ann Duncan. James Alonzo Matthews.

6 John Adair Duncan.
7 Robert Lee Duncan.
8 Louisa Rebecca Duncan. George Henry Shock.
9 Emily Jane Duncan. Edwin Hartley Bragdon.
$1^17^25^31^4$ Charles Burr Duncan.
2 Elizabeth Duncan. * John B. Landrum.
$1^17^27^31^4$ Alice Rebecca Smith. John Martin Daniel.
$1^17^28^31^4$ Joel Marion Duncan.
2 Martha Jane Duncan. Theodore Garvin.
OK 3 Annie Alice Duncan.
$1^17^210^31^4$ Millard Filmore Carted.
2 George Walter Carter. Effie C. Roberson.
OK 3 Robert Lee Carter. Cassie Delilah Marshall.
4 Florence Eveline Carter.
5 Mary Elizabeth Carter. Thomas Jefferson Montgomery.
6 Clement Adair Carter. Edith Dora Drinkwater.
$1^17^211^31^4$ Louisa Duncan.
2 Leonidas Philip Duncan.
OK 3 Mary Rebecca Duncan.
4 Jennie Duncan.
5 Maude Adair Duncan.
6 Robert Fleming Duncan.
7 Thomas Washington Duncan.
8 Stephen Duncan.

Halfbreed.

1^1 Gu-u-li-si.
1^11^2 Lydia Halfbreed. Charles Renatus Hicks.
2 Pigeon Halfbreed. Neki Fields.
3 Chinosa Halfbreed. Joseph Crutchfield. A59
4 Susannah Halfbreed. John Wickett Fields.
5 Jennie Halfbreed. * A46
6 Elizabeth Halfbreed. Squirrel.
7 Jesse Halfbreed. Jennie Fields.
$1^11^21^3$ Catherine Hicks. Andrew Miller and Thomas Gann.
2 George Hicks. Aky Rogers and Lucy Fields.
$1^12^21^3$ Catherine Pigeon.
2 Sulteesga Pigeon. Oo-ye-ki.
OK 3 Jack Pigeon. Elsie Buzzard.
4 Lydia Pigeon. Lewis Cunnigan.
5 Alfred Pigeon. Rachel Ketcher, Serena Frazier and Susie McGhee nee Beck.
$1^13^21^3$ George Hunter.

---

2 John Crutchfield. Mary Etta Ladd and Emma Gibbs. A58
3 Susie Crutchfield. David Dixon Landurum.
4. Richard McLeod Crutchfield. Susan Ware and Susan Moore.
$1^14^21^3$ Elizabeth Fields. * Stand Watie.

2 Mary Fields. * Rufus McGuilliams, John Adair Duncan, Thomas Fleming and Daniel Pinson.

OK 3 John McFerran Fields. Elizabeth Smith.

4 Eliza Fields. John Alexander Watie and Samuel Smith.

5 Timothy Fields. Eliza McIntosh, Polly Fields and Elmira Rogers.

6 Rachel Fields.

7 James Fields. * Dollie Eunice Lowrey.

$1^{1}6^{2}1^{3}$ Joseph Squirrel. *

2 Nannie Squirrel. George Fields.

3 Walker Squirrel. *

4 William Squirrel. ——— Walker.

---

5 Tiana Fields.

$1^{1}7^{2}1^{3}$ Margaret Halfbreed. Ezekial Daniel and William Taylor.

2 Sarah Halfbreed. Daniel H. Ross.

OK 3 Stand Halfbreed. Sarah Carey.

4 Tiana Halfbreed. George Downing.

5 Melvina Halfbreed. Blackhaw.

6 Mary Halfbreed. Edward Downing.

7 Eliza Halfbreed. James Bowles.

8 Richard Halfbreed. *

9 Elizabeth Halfbreed. John Bigby.

---

10 James Halfbreed. Martha Duck.

$1^{1}1^{2}1^{3}1^{4}$ Avery Vann Miller. Nannie Ward and Susie Spaniard.

2 Elizabeth Miller. James Fields and Philip Inlow.

OK 3 Alfred Miller. Elizabeth Seabolt nee Levi.

4 Isabelle Miller. Stand Watie, —— Hicks and Kinch Hargroves.

5 Elmira Miller. Benjamin Paden.

6 Lucinda Miller. Calvin Adair.

7 Andrew Miller. Sallie McCoy.

---

8 George Gann. Mary Ann Starr nee McCoy.

9 Elias Gann. *

10 Isaac Gann.*

11 Ruth Gann. William Edwin Brown.

$1^{1}1^{2}2^{3}1^{4}$ Aaron Hicks. Nannie Riley.

2 Nannie Hicks. * John Bickles.

OK 3 Delilah Hicks. * Bryan Ward.

4 Jefferson Hicks. Nannie Lowrey and Margaret Lowrey.

5 Eleanor Ophelia Hicks. Gilbert Wilsan.

6 Henry Hicks. Annie.

7 David Hicks. * Elzina Wilson.

8 Frank Hicks. *Celia Baldridge.

9 William Hicks. Priscilla Thompson.

10 Mary Hicks. W. A. Coleman.

OK $1^1 2^2 1^3 1^4$ Lucy Pigeon. Edmond Duncan Carey.

OK $1^1 2^2 2^3 1^4$ Mary Pigeon. Peter Dennis.

$1^1 2^2 3^3 1^4$ Takie Pigeon. John Choo-hoo-sti.

OK 2 Lucy Pigeon. Philip Daniel and William P. Ross Buzzard.

$1^1 2^2 4^3 1^4$ George Cunnigan. Sarah Ballard.

2 Johnson Cunnigan.

3 Elizabeth Cunnigan.

4 Easter Cunnigan. Richard Hummingbird.

$1^1 2^2 5^3 1^4$ Lydia Ann Pigeon. Edmond Duncan Carey.

$1^1 3^2 2^3 1^4$ Joseph Vann Crutchfield. Mary Maria Landrum.

2 Leroy Ladd Cruachfield. Elizabeth Horton.

OK 3 James Madison Crutchfield. Libbie Hunt, Fannie Holt nee Daniel and Josephine Amber Newlon.

4 Saphronia Winn Crutchfield. Flavius Joseuhus Barrett, Walter Adair Starr, Dr. Newlon and Flavius Josephus Barrett.

5 Mary Alice Crutchfield. William Electra Halsell.

6 Richard Crutchfield. Fannie Earp.

7 Laura Emma Crutchfield. Harvey C. Cooper.

8 William Crutchfield. Caroline Houts.

9 Dona Belle Crutchfield. John Berry Stevens.

10 John King Crutchfield. Maud Flippin.

---

11 Minnie A. Crutchfield. Joseph A. Mobley.

12 Allie Crutchfield. Walter Watkins.

13 Orah G. Crutchfield.

$1^1 3^2 3^3 1^4$ Josephine Landrum. Lewis Rogers and Frank Howard.

2 Martha Jane Landrum. * Anderson Crittenden Jennings.

OK 3 Mary Maria Landrum. Joseph Vann Crutchfield.

4 Nannie Landrum. John Washington Adair.

5 Rachel Landrum. Rollin Kirk Adair.

6 Charles Dixon Landrum. *

7 Elias McLeod Landrum. Nana Woodall.

$1^1 3^2 4^3 1^4$ Ida Crutchfield. John T. Milholand.

$1^1 4^2 3^3 1^4$ Richard Sosa Fields. *

2 Kiowa Ratliff Fields. Martha Kellar Mackey.

OK 3 Elizabeth Fields. Israel Duval and George Starr.

---

4 Ellen Fields. Lewis Wolf.

5 Moses Fields. *

$1^1 4^2 4^3 1^4$ Susannah Watie. Thomas Jefferson Bean.

2 Nannie Wheeler Watie. *Lewis Keys.

OK 3 Famous Smith. Mary Maude Vann and Maude Brooks.

4 John Smith. Martha Elizabeth Simmons.

5 Louisa Smith. John Barnett.

$1^14^25^31^4$ Sirissa Iowa Fields. John Candy and Richard Rogers.

2 John Johnson Fields. Elizabeth Boudinot nee Starr.

OK 3 Mary Fields. John Hood.

4 Eliza Fields. John McCoy.

$1^14^26^31^4$ Mary Rogers. John Brimage.

$1^16^22^31^4$ Mary Fields. Oceola Powell Daniel.

$1^17^22^31^4$ Daniel L. Ross. Ruth Caroline Holland.

$1^17^23^31^4$ Nannie Halfbreed. Gent Gibson.

OK 2 Lucinda Halfbreed. Thomas Leader.

$1^17^24^31^4$ Elizabeth Downing. William Riddle.

OK 2 Thomas Downing. Maria Love and Hattie E. Abner.

$1^17^25^31^4$ Mary Blackhaw. Duncan Leader.

OK 2 Jennie Blackhawk. Eli Wilkerson.

$1^17^26^31^4$ Lucy Downing. William Edwin Johnson.

$1^17^27^31^4$ Minnie Bowles. Elijah Hermogene Lerblance and Orlando Shay.

OK 2 Richard H. Bowles. Elizabeth Blythe and Nannie Downing.

$1^17^210^31^4$ Louvenia Halfbreed. *

Reese.

1^1 Nancy. Charles Reese and Alexander McPherson.

1^11^2 Susannah Reese. Oo-wa-tie. A37

2 Charles Reese. Nellie McCoy.

---

3 John McPherson. Susie McCoy.

4 Andrew McPhersan.

5 Alexander McPherson.

Smith.

1^1 ——— Smith.

1^11^2 Cabin Smith.

2 McCoy Smith. *

$1^11^21^3$ Hominy Simth. Aky Fields and Peggy.

2 Oo-du-ski Smith. Tiger.

3 Tiania Smith. Scraper.

4 Go-li-si Smith. Turtle.

5 Gu-er-tsa Smith. Sixkiller.

6 Archilla Smith. Agnes Fields.

$1^11^21^31^4$ Ta-cha-gi-si Smith. *

$1^11^22^31^4$ Ta-chi-chi Tiger.

2 Redbird Tiger.

3 Messenger Tiger. Celia Love.

4 Pelican Tiger.

5 Mark Tiger. Mary Thompson and Stidham nee Trott.

6 Ti-ca-no-hi-la Tiger.

7 Dirtthower Tiger.

8 Ka-hi-ta Tiger.

9 Wa-li-a Tiger

10 Lucretia Tiger. Tony R. Gourd.

$1^{1}1^{2}3^{3}1^{4}$ George W. Scraper. Louisa McIntosh.

2 Archibald Scraper. Malinda McIntosh.

3 Charles Scraper.

4 Otter Scraper.

5 Sallie Scraper. Watie Cummings.

$1^{1}1^{2}5^{3}1^{4}$ Cricket Sixkliler. Deborah Whaley and Elizabeth Foreman.

2 Redbird Sixkiller. Pamelia Whaley, Nannie Foster nee Foreman and Elizabeth Proctor nee Foreman *

3 Tail Sixkiller. Alie Keath.

4 Soldier Sixkiller. Katie.

5 Frog Sixkiller.

6 Delaware Sixkiller. Jennie Walker.

7 Blackhaw Sixkiller.

8 Susan Sixkiller. * Yellowhammer.

9 Peacheater Sixkiller. Sallie Foreman nee Rattlinggourd.

10 Lucinda Sixkiller. Samuel Cloud.

$1^{1}1^{2}6^{3}1^{4}$ John Smith. * Margaret Hendricks.

2 Rachel Smith. John Rider.

OK 3 Charles Smith. *

4 Elizabeth Smith. John McFerran Fields, Thomas Adkins and George Drum.

5 Samuel Houston Smith. *

6 Eliza Smith. David Grayson, Jackson Cozens and Francis Marion Seabolt.

Hildebrand.

1^{1} John Hildebrand. —— andSusannah Womancatcher A60

$1^{1}1^{2}$ Michael Hildebrand. Nannie Martin.

2 Peter Hildebrand. Elizabeth Harlan. A25

OK 3 George Hildebrand. Susannah Graves.

4 John Hildebrand. Micatiah Terrapin.

5 Sarah Hildebrand. Blackcoat and Youngwolf. A62

6 Nannie Hildebrand. Hiram McCreary.

7 David Hildebrand. Elizabeth McCarty.

8 Mary Hildebrand. —— Hambright and Daniel Hafer.

9 Elizabeth Hildebrand. —— Coody.

$1^{2}1^{1}1^{8}$ Elizabeth Hildebrand. James Pettit and Robert Armstrong.

2 John Hildebrand. Nicey and Annie Wasp.

OK 3 Jennie Hildebrand. Joseph Cooksan.

4 Margaret Hildebrand. John Catron.

5 Delilah Hildebrand. Jesse McLain.

6 Elizabeth Hildebrand. Joshua Kilpatrick.

7 Stephen Hildebrand. Mary Potts and Mary Beck.

8 Rachel Hildebrand. Reese T. Mitchell.

9 Nannie Hildebrand. Thomas Horn, George Lovett, Frederick Irving, Charles Poe and —— Hoskins.

10 Joseph Martin Hildebrand. Lucy Starr, Louvinia Patterson, Elizabeth Gentry, Mary King, Martha Wofford and Mary E. Coyne.

11 Brice Hildebrand. Mary Sturdivant nee Beck and Mary Swimmer.

12 Mary Hildebrand. Isaac Mayfield.

$1^22^11^3$ Barbara Hildebrand. Hiram Linder.

2 James V. Hildebrand. Sarah Elizabeth Fields.

OK 3 Jennie Hildebrand. John Williams.

4 Catherine Hildebrand. Levi Bailey.

5 John Walker Hildebrand. Eliza Jane White.

6 Ellis Harlan Hildebrand. Sallie Stover * and Josephine —.

7 Lewis W. Hildebrand. Lucy Ratliff.

8 Isaac Newton Hildebrand. Jennie Ratliff.

9 Mary Elizabeth Hildebrand. Daniel Jones Frazier.

10 Minerva Hildebrand. Charles Ratliff and Anderson Reynolds.

$1^13^21^3$ Moses Hildebrand. Noo-ca-ti.

2 Mary Hildebrand. Hoyt.

3 Catherine Hildebrand. Teehee.

4 John Hildebrand.

5 Michael Hildebrand. Sarah Hicks.

6 Peter Hildebrand. Annie Fawling.

7 Samuel Hildebrand. Susannah Rogers.

8 Barbara Hildebrand. William Longknife and ———

9 George Hildebrand.

10 Martha Hildebrand.

$1^14^21^3$ Elizabeth Hildebrand.

$1^15^21^3$ Jesse Culstee. * Eliza Turtle.

---

2 Thomas Blackcoat. Minerva Carr.

OK 3 John Wolf.

4 Rachel Wolf. * Henry Dobson Reese.

5 Mary Wolf. * ——— Collins.

$1^16^21^8$ Amanda J. McCreary. * Alfred Clark Raymond.

2 Mary McCreary. James Alcorn.

OK 3 Napoleon McCreary. Jennie Harper.

$1^17^21^3$ John Hildebrand. Ellen Pettit.

2 Maria Hildebrand. John Wright-Alberty.

OK 3 Mary Hildebrand. Simon Lewis.

4 Arie Hildebrand. Calvin Parks and James Lewis Puskett.

$1^18^21^3$ Napoleon Bonaparte Hambright. *

2 Hiram Hambright. *

3 James Monroe Hambright. *

$1^{1}9^{2}1^{3}$ Felix Grundy Coody. *
OK 2 Archibald Coody. *

England.

1^{1} David England. Susan A. Conner.
$1^{1}1^{2}$ Martin England.
2 Louisa England. Robert Blackstone.
3 Irene England. Lee Scrimsher.
4 Pinson England. *
5 Carlton England. *
6 Arminda England. William England, Isaac Scrimsher and Elias Jenkins.
7 Mitchell England. Lucinda Jones.
8 Saphronia England. Thomas Monroe.
9 Sabra E. England. * Peter Clark and Andrew Kelly.
10 Martha England. *
$1^{1}2^{2}1^{3}$ Josephine Blackstone. Stephen Carlisle.
2 Pleasant Napoleon Blackstone. Jennie Catherine Lipe.
OK 3 Robert E. Blackstone. Sallie Jennings.
4 Eliza Blackstone. James McMurry.
5 Thomas Blackstone. Rosa Vaught.
6 Laura L. Blackstone.
$1^{1}3^{2}1^{3}$ Eliza Scrimsher. Lewis Fields and William Williamson.
2 Laura Scrimsher. James Pryor and Harry Kelly.
3 Margaret Scrimsher. Joseph Green and Trueman Tanner.
$1^{1}6^{2}1^{3}$ Mary Scrimsher.
2 Berilla Scrimsher. Abram Meeks.
3 Arabella Scrimsher. Enoch Sutherland.
4 Saphronia Scrimsher. Zan Main, Lewis Rogers and Dr. J. A. Nolen.
5 Ruth Scrimsher. Charles Tyler.

---

6 Ida Josephine Jenkins. John Wesley Harris.
7 Henry Jenkins. Delilah Arms.
$1^{1}8^{2}1^{3}$ Saphronia Monroe. James H. Hereford.

Thompson.

1^{1} ———. ———Thompson.
$1^{1}1^{2}$ Jack Thompson. Jennie Vann, Nana and Elizabeth Merrell

---

2 Laugh at mush.
3 Ne-coo-ie.
$1^{1}1^{2}1^{3}$ William Thompson. Nannie Merrell and Elizabeth Fields.

---

2 Alexander Thompson. Elizabeth Tipton.
3 Sallie Thompson. Samuel Mackey.
4 Charles Thompson. *
5 Nannie Thompson. Benjamin Merrell.
6 Elizabeth Thompson. Nelson Riley.

---

7 Margaret Thompson. Elijah Lynch and ——— Barker.
8 Betsey Thompson. Robert Runyan.
9 John Thompson. *
10 Richard Thompson. Caroline Simpson and Elizabeth Thornton.
11 James Thompson. *
12 Jennie Thompson. Samuel Crossland.
$1^1 1^2 1^3 1^4$ Jennie Thompson. * Dr. Yarnall.

---

2 John Thompson. Margaret Fields, Minerva Biggs * and Elizabeth Griffin.
OK 3 Charles Thompson. Susie Taylor.
4 Alexander Thompson. Ruth Phillips and Elmira McLain.
$1^1 1^2 2^3 1^4$ Ruth Thompson. *
2 Jack Thompson. *
3 Maria Thompson. Archibald Lee.
4 Calvin Thompson. *
5 "Major Thompson. *
$1^1 1^2 3^3 1^4$ Nannie Mackey. Joseph Tally and David Vann.
2 Preston Meckey. * Nannie Vann.
3 William Mackey. Nannie Drew.
4 George Mackey. *
5 Corinne Mackey. *
6 James Mackey. Polly Tally and Louisa Fields
$1^1 1^2 5^3 1^4$ Elizabeth Merrell. David Ivey.
2 Eliza Merrell. William Polson.
OK 3 William Merrell. Nannie Walker.
4 Sallie Merrell. Cornelius Parris.
5 Nannie Merrell. Rufus West.
6 Mary Merrell. James Starnes.
7 Benjamin Merrell.
8 Margaret Merrell. —— Williamson and Thomas Brackett.
$1^1 1^2 6^3 1^4$ Ellen Riley. *
2 Margaret Riley. *
OK 3 Julius Riley. Amanda Cordell.
4 Joseph Riley. Matilda Maxfield and Lucy Ore nee Lusk.
5 Mary Ann Riley. Thomas Maxfield and Thomas M. Triplett.
6 Perry Andre Riley. Eliza Colson.
7 Charles Riley. *
$1^1 1^2 7^3 1^4$ John Lynch. *
2 Catherine Lynch.

---

3 Charles Barker.
$1^1 1^2 8^3 1^4$ Maria Whitney. Goree.

---

2 Joseph Runyan. *
3 Ruth Runyan. *

4 Sarah Runyan. * Lemuel Parris.
5 Lawson Runyon. Mary Jane Merrell and Elsie Martin.
$1^{1}1^{2}10^{3}1^{4}$ Margaret Emma Thompson. Clark Charlesworth Lipe.
2 Sue Elizabeth Thompson. Washington Henry Eiffort.
OK 3 Tooka Thompson. William Smelser Nash.
4 Caroline Harriette Thompson. David Albert Mounts. •
5 John Lanigan Thompson.
$1^{1}1^{2}12^{3}1^{4}$ Samuel Crossland.
2 Martha Crossland. William Ratliff and Lafayette Buchanan.

---

3 Richard Scott. Susan Foreman Choate.
$1^{1}1^{2}1^{3}2^{4}1^{5}$ William Thompson. Catherine Lynch.
2 Mary Thompson. Henry Ross.
3 Louisa Josephine Thompson. John Henry Crane.
$1^{1}1^{2}1^{3}3^{4}1^{5}$ Naomi Victoria Thompson. Michael Fields.
2 Perry Thompson. Henriette Vann and Diana Pigeon.
$1^{1}1^{2}1^{3}4^{4}1^{5}$ Charles Thompson. *
2 Jennie Thompson. *
OK 3 Lucinda Thompson. *
$1^{1}1^{2}3^{3}1^{4}1^{5}$ Samuel Tally. Nellie Drum.
2 Rose Tally. Joseph Absalom Scales.
3 Jennie Tally. Charles Watts and John Q. Hayes.

---

4 William Vann. Charlotte McLaughlin.
5 Joseph Vann. * Emma Drew.
6 George B. Vann. Mary.
7 Robert P. Vann. Ermina Cooie Foreman.
8 Maude M. Vann. Famous Smith.
$1^{1}1^{2}3^{3}2^{4}1^{5}$ Mary Mackey. James D. Willison.
OK 2 Anna Dorothy Mackey. William Harvison.
$1^{1}1^{2}3^{3}6^{4}1^{5}$ John Drew Mackey. * Margaret Moore.
2 Sallie Georgianna Mackey. John Lafayette Brown.
OK 3 Martha Kellar Mackey. Kiowa Ratliff Fields.
4 Nannie Laura Mackey.
5 Lugie Watts Mackey. Charles Washington Starr.
$1^{1}1^{2}5^{3}1^{4}1^{5}$ Nancy Ann Ivey. John Riley.
$1^{1}1^{2}5^{3}2^{4}1^{5}$ Nannie Polston.
2 Elizabeth Polston. James Tally.
3 Sarah Polston.
4 Margaret Polston. Teacher and Albert Shepherd.
5 Joseph Polston. Susan Riley.
$1^{1}1^{2}5^{3}3^{4}1^{5}$ James Merrell. Rachel Hicks.
2 Mary Jane Merrell. Lawson Runyon.
$1^{1}1^{2}5^{3}4^{4}1^{5}$ Henry Parris. Rachel Parker or Wolf.
$1^{1}1^{2}5^{3}5^{4}1^{5}$ James West. *
2 Sarah S. West. Joseph Antoine.
3 Mary Ann West. William Perkins.

4 Morgan West. Finley.
5 Charles West. *
$1^1 1^2 5^3 6^4 1^5$ Jefferson Starnes. Ruth Gott and Margaret Sevenstar.
2 John Starnes. Nettie Jeffries, Elizabeth Duffey and Almira Johnson.
3 Lillie Starnes. Lindsey Wallace.
4 Margaret Starnes. Ira Creach.
$1^1 1^2 5^3 8^4 1^5$ Mary Williamson. William E. Greenleaf.
$1^1 1^2 6^3 3^4 1^5$ Elizabeth Riley. * McCoy Smith.
$1^1 1^2 6^3 4^4 1^5$ Addie Riley. James Kyle.
2 Nelson Riley. *

---

3 Charles Riley. *
$1^1 1^2 6^3 5^4 1^5$ Octavia Maxfield. Richard Riley Bertholf.
2 Ida Verona Maxfield. James Harvey Lindsey.
3 Lillie Maxfield. Claude Hanks McDaniel.
$1^1 1^2 6^3 6^4 1^5$ Nannie Amanda Riley. John Lee Lamb.

Seabolt.

1^1 Henry Seabolt. Celia Timberlake and
$1^1 1^2$ John Seabolt. Jennie Benge.
2 Thomas Seabolt. Hicks.
3 Catherine Seabolt. John Chambers.
4 Nannie Seabolt. * A-li-cha.
5 Susie Seabolt. Ned Fields.
6 Joseph Seabolt. Nannie Campbell nee Hair.

---

7 King Seabolt. Betsey Downing.
8 Henry Seabolt. Eliza Benge.
9 Elsie Seabolt.
10 Margaret Seabolt. Mack Benge.
11 Annie Seabolt. Charles Foreman.
12 Richard Seabolt.

Wilkerson.

1^1 Coo-ta-ya. Edward Wilkerson and John Wilkerson.
$1^1 1^2$ Eliza Wilkerson. Jesse Bushyhead.

---

2 Aaron Wilkerson.
3 Richard Wilkerson. *
4 James Wilkersan. *
5 George Wilkerson. Susan Poorbear.
6 John Wilkerson. Annie Woods.
151 John Wilkerson. Rebecca Oglesby.
2 Riley Wilkerson. *
3 James Monroe Wilkerson. Nancy Jane Keys.
4 George Wilkerson.
5 Laura Wells Wilkerson. Wilson Sanders.
6 Eliza Wilkerson. John Ross.

7 Leonard Worcester Wilkerson. Ellen Bible.
8 Mary Wilkerson. John Henry Coody.
$1^1 6^2 1^3$ Martha Wilkerson. *John Groom.
2 Nannie Wilkerson. *Solomon Ray.
3 Mary Wilkerson. Charles Jones.
4 Elizabeth Wilkerson. Mack Messer.
5 John Wilkerson. Jennie Campbell.
6 Ace Wilkerson. Margaret Jones.
7 Caroline Wilkerson. * Joseph Wickett.
8 Whidby Wilkerson. Elnora Winpiegler nee Jones.

Blair.

1^1 Quatie. Jonathan Blythe.
$1^1 1^2$ Sarah George Blair.

---

2 Nannie Blythe. George Blair.
3 James Blythe. *
$1^1 1^2 1^3$ James Blair. *
2 Elizabeth Blair. John Lowrey.
3 Lewis Blair. Polly Benge * and
4 Catherine Blair. ———McCuen.
5 Lucy Blair. Samuel Houston Benge.
6 Amy Blair. *
7 Margaret Blair. Obediah Benge.
8 Jonathan Blair. *
9 Charles Blair. *
10 Thomas Blair. Margaret Sanders.
11 Sallie Blair. *
12 Susannah Blair. *
13 Eliza Blair. George Washington Baldridge.
14 Mary Blair. Albert Johnson.
15 Bettie Blair. Robert E. Sutton.

Ratliff.

1^1 Richard Ratliff.
$1^1 1^2$ Annie Ratliff. John Coker.
2 Richard Ratliff. Chiuke and
$1^1 2^2 1^3$ Alexander Ratliff.
2 Abraham Ratliff. Lydia.
OK 3 William Ratliff. *
4 Robin Ratliff. Aky Webber.
5 Daniel Ratliff. Eliza Wickett and Annie Ballard.
6 Lydia Ratliff. Matthew Jones.
7 Annie Ratliff. Charles Wickett.
8 Charlotte Ratliff. *

---

9 Archibald Ratliff.
10 Thompson Ratliff. *

$1^{1}2^{2}2^{3}1^{4}$ Susannah Ratliff. *

2 Samuel Ratliff. *

3 John Ratliff. *

4 Eliza Ratliff. *

$1^{1}2^{2}6^{3}1^{4}$ Nannie Jones. * Jesse Wickett.

2 Elizabeth Jones. *

3 Lucy Jones. Albert Shepherd.

4 Charles Jones. Mary Wilkerson.

5 Andrew Jones. Belle Heaton.

6 Margaret Jones. Ace Wilkerson.

7 Elnora Jones. George Winpiegler and Whidby Wilkerson.

8 Hester Jones Joseph Wickett and Thomas Heaton.

9 Richard Jones. *

10 Malinda Jones. *

Timpson.

1^{1} Benjamin Timpson. Sarah.

$1^{1}1^{2}$ Jennie Timpson. Jacob Harnage.

2 Benjamin Timpson. Lucy Smith and Harriette Mingus.

3 Mary Ann Timpson. *

4 John Timpson.

$1^{1}1^{2}1^{3}$ Nellie Harnage. John Ragsdale.

2 Elizabeth Harnage. Robert Rogers.

3 Ezekial Harnage. Jennie Skit.

4 Jacob Harnage. Sallie Harlan and Mary Rowe. *

5 Mary Harnage. Edward Adair.

$1^{1}2^{2}1^{3}$ Sarah Timpson. Jonas Phillips.

2 Mary Ann Timpson. John Hilary Clark.

OK 3 John Calvin Timpson. *

4 Eliza Timpson. Aaron Burr.

5 Henry Clay Timpson. *

6 Martha Jane Timpson. Jesse Arnold.

7 Lydia Timpson. Archibald Cochran.

8 Nannie Timpson. Crane.

9 Caroline Timpson. Benjamin Pettit.

---

10 Melvina Timpson. Levi Silk.

11 Susan Timpson. Richard Terrell.

12 Alfred Timpson. *

13 Hannah Timpson. *

14 James Timpson. Etheline Carroll.

15 Drucilla Timpson. *

16 Posey Humphreys Timpson.

$1^{1}1^{2}1^{3}1^{4}$ Elizabeth Ragsdale. *

2 Isaac Ragsdale. Mary Sanders.

3 Thomas Ragsdale. Nannie Stop.

4 Susie Ragsdale. Ignacious Few.

5 John Ragsdale. Nannie Harnage.

6 William Ragsdale. *
7 Ezekial Ragsdale. Nannie Edwards.
$1^11^22^31^4$ Jennie Rogers. Benjamin West.
$1^11^23^31^4$ Nannie Harnage. John Ragsdale.
2 Lydia Harnage. William Bean.
$1^11^24^31^4$ George Harlan Harnage. *
$1^11^25^31^4$ John Stansel. Martha McDaniel.

---

2 Jennie Adair. John Perry Oliver Clyne.
OK 3 Edley Adair. Emily Rogers.
4 Elizabeth Adair. John Hildebrand Cookson.
$1^12^31^21^4$ William P. Phillips. Lucinda Quinton.
2 Mary Ann Phillips. Benjamin Pettit.
3 Eliza Phillips. John Poorbear.
4 Nannie Phillips. Wilson Weely.
5 Margaret Phillips. Archibald Lovett.
$1^12^22^31^4$ Jay Clark.
2 Silas Dean Clark. Elizabeth Griffin.
3 Taylor Clark.
4 Margaret Clark.
$1^12^26^31^4$ Thomas Arnold. *
2 William Arnold.
$1^12^27^31^4$ Mary Cochran. *
2 Caroline Cochran. Ras Akin.
$1^12^29^31^4$ Nicholas Pettit. Annie Gustin.
$1^12^210^31^4$ Nannie Silk. *
2 William Silk.
$1^11^21^32^41^5$ Margaret Ragsdale. *
2 John Ragsdale. Aramina Gunter.
OK 3 Polly Ragsdale. Joseph Dawson and J. V. McPherson.
4 Ellen Ragsdale. Jasper Chaney.
5 Lucy Ragsdale. Charles England.
6 Isaac Harvey Ragsdale. Johnanna Johnson.
7 Cynthia Ragsdale. Joseph Hines.
$1^11^21^33^41^5$ Jennie Ragsdale. * ——Simco.
2 Pamelia Ragsdale.
$1^11^21^34^41^5$ Amanda Few. John Shell.
2 Hannah Few. Eli Clyne.
3 John Few. *
4 Eliza Few. *
$1^11^21^35^41^5$ William Riley Ragsdale.
$1^11^21^37^41^5$ John Ragsdale. * Elizabeth.
$1^11^22^31^41^5$ Jonathan West. *
2 Laura West. Joseph Raper.
3 Robert West.
4 Jennie West.
5 James West. *

$1^1 1^2 3^3 1^4 1^5$ Ezekial Taylor. * Ruth Ramsey nee Mosley and Ada Foreman.

OK 2 William Riley Ragsdale.

$1^1 1^2 3^3 2^4 1^5$ Delilah Bean. David Tucker.

2 Nancy Jane Bean. Flint Walkingstick.

OK 3 Sallie Bean. Edward Walkingstick.

4 William Tooyah Bean.

$1^1 1^2 5^3 1^4 1^5$ Lewis Stansel. Mary Tooy.

2 Elizabeth Stansel. John Wolf and Walter Sanders.

3 John Stansel. Sarah Sanders.

Springston

1^1 Nancy. William Springston.

$1^1 1^2$ Ruth Springston. John Foreman and George Wilson

$1^1 1^2 1^3$ Johnson Foreman. Elizabeth B. Mann.

---

2 William Wilson. Malinda Chisholm nee Wharton, Mary Thornton nee Sanders and Eliza Hyles nee

OK 3 Mary Wilson. James Audrain.

4 Elizabeth Wilson. Austin Copeland, Thomas C. Thomas and Gilbert Holcomb.

5 Archibald M. Wilson. Delilah Starr nee Johnson and Rebecca McNair Wilson nee Riley.

6 Rebecca Wilson. ———Wilharm, Samuel McKinney and Andrew McKinney.

7 Alexander Drumgool Wilson. Rebecca McNair Riley.

8 George W. Wilson. Carmalita —— and Elsie Davis.

9 Ruth Wilson. Walter Copeland, ——Bennett, ——Webb and George Myers.

10 Anderson Springston Wilson. Nannie Catherine Daniel.

11 John Wilson.

12 Malinda Wilson. Miles Collins, James Young and James Adams.

$1^1 1^2 1^3$ Martha J. Foreman. * Jenkins Maxfield.

2 William Archibald Foreman. Susie Chisholm nee Pindar.

OK 3 Naomi Ruth Foreman. Joseph T. Garrison.

4 Mary Louvenia Foreman. *

5 Return Jonathan Foreman. * Eliza J. Brewer and Harriette E. Colbert.

6 Jesse Bushyhead Foreman. Emma Vore.

7 Susan Frances Foreman. John Raymond and Joseph Martin Lynch.

$1^1 1^2 2^3 1^4$ Emily Wilson. Napoleon Bonaparte Breedlove.

2 William Wilson. Alice Coody.

OK 3 Rory McCoy Wilson. Laura Bruce.

4 Finney Chisholm Wilson. Amanda Broyles.

5 Eliza Wilson. Lorenzo Williams.

$1^1 1^2 3^3 1^4$ Jennie Audrain. John Wills and I. N. Smith.

2 Mary Mahana Audrain. Percy L. Walker.

3 Winfield Scott Andrain. Eliza Williams.

4 Lucy Audrain. James McGannon.

5 Frank G. Audrain. Malissa Williams.

$1^1 1^2 4^3 1^4$ Mary Copeland. William Melton.

2 Martha Copeland. Ellis Buffington, Toliver Thomas, Ezekial Buffington* and James Cohee*.

3 George Copeland.

4 Alexander Copeland. Catherine Thomas, Sarah McNair nee Miller, Nannie S. Allen nee West and Nannie Cowels nee Conner.

5 Jerusha Copeland. Robert Audrain.

6 Austin Copeland.

7 Pamelia Copeland. Christopher Columbus Isbell.

8 Rebecca Copeland. George Cox and Stephen Cox.

---

9 Archibald Wilson Thomas. Jennie Reppeto.

10 William Wirt Thomas.

11 Charles Delano Thomas.

$1^1 1^2 5^3 1^4$ Anise Femister Wilson. James Alexander Rice.

$1^1 1^2 6^3 1^4$ Alexander F. McKinney. Nannie Redding, Minnie Wheeler.

---

2 Dennie Bushyhead McKinney. Delia Crawford and Belle Johnson.

3 Andrew Jackson McKinney. Mary Wells.

4 Johnson Perry McKinney. Hortense Baptiste.

$1^1 1^2 7^3 1^4$ Susan Rebecca Wilson. Joseph Polson, Thomas Washington Lindsay and William Thomas Hewitt.

2 Isabel Brandon Wilson. Henry Parris, Benjamin A. Rush.

OK 3 Laura Adair Wilson. John Raymond and Thomas Henry.

4 James Madison Wilson. Araminta Pharris.

$1^1 1^2 8^3 1^4$ Henry Wilson. Laura

---

2 Ora Wilson. Bruton.

$1^1 1^2 9^3 1^4$ William Copeland.

---

2 Julia Bennett. Robert Mann.

---

3 John Webb.

---

4 George Myers. Talitha Dunaway.

$1^1 1^2 10^3 1^4$ DeWitt Clinton Wilson. Ella Adair.

2 James Daniel Wilson. Letitia M. Fields.

OK 3 Mary Emma Wilson.

$1^11^212^31^4$ Mike Collins.

---

2 John Young.
3 Robert Young.
4 Nannie Young. Rollin Hill.

Woodall.

1^1 Ellen Moore. George Caruth Woodall.
1^11^2 Charles Woodall. Susannah Watie.
2 Annie Jane Woodall. James Duncan.
OK 3 Elizabeth Woodall. Benjamin Fránklin Landrum.
4 William Coffee Woodall. Margaret A. Reese and
5 James Tuck Woodall. Elizabeth Perdue.
6 Thomas Jefferson Woodall. *
7 John Peter Woodall. Mary Thorn and Maver M. Cecil nee Saunders.
8 Louisa Woodall. Isaac Shouse.
9 Nannie Woodall. *
10 George Washington Woodall. Susannah Muskrat.
11 Stan Goney Woodall. *

Butler

1^1 Edward Butler. Elizabeth Jane Nivens, Elizabeth Keys nee
1^11^2 Jennie Elizabeth Butler. McCoy Smith.

---

2 Mannie Garrett Butler. Anna Carter.
OK 3 Sarah Butler. Benjamin Porter and John W. Sanders.
4 Tooka Butler. Clarence William Turner.
5 Robert Lee Butler. Caroline Lindsey.
$1^11^21^3$ Edward Butler Smith. Etta Word.
2 Walter Duncan Smith.
OK 3 Juliette Taylor Smith.
4 Wilson Nevins Smith.
5 Mannie Garrett Smith. Jessie Watson.
6 May Smith.
7 Junie Smith.
8 Jennie Elizabeth Smith.
$1^12^21^3$ Elizabeth Butler.
2 Fountain Crabtree Butler.
OK 3 Sammie Butler.
$1^13^21^3$ Nina Porter. * Eck E. Brook.
2 Edward Porter.
OK 3 Benjamin Porter.

---

4 Edna Sanders. ——Mooney and Chester Klick.
5 Elizabeth Sanders.
6 Maude Sanders. Howell Scott.
7 Mildred Sanders.
$1^14^21^3$ Tooka K. Turner. Charles Bagg.

2 Charence William Turner.

OK 3 Marian Turner.

$1^1 5^2 1^3$ Robert Lee Butler.

$1^1 1^2 1^3 1^4$ Edward Butler Smith.

2 Jennie May Smith.

OK 3 Juliette Elizabeth Smith.

$1^1 1^2 5^3 1^4$ Clayton Smith.

$1^1 3^2 4^3 1^4$ Mooney.

$1^1 3^2 6^3 1^4$ Scott.

2 Scott.

Rogers

1^1 John Rogers. Tiana Foster.

$1^1 1^2$ Hilliard Rogers. Martha Fields.

2 James Rogers. *

OK 3 Thomas Rogers. Susan Cochran.

4 Lewis Rogers. Elizabeth J. Lisenbe, Sarah Fields and Saphronia Main nee Scrimsher.

5 Mary Rogers. Thomas Childers.

6 Sallie Rogers. Larkin McGhee.

7 Martha Rogers. Joseph A. Henry.

8 Susan Rogers. *

9 Rachel Rogers. George Washington Walker.

10 Elizabeth Rogers. Jesse Cochran.

Raper

1^1 Jesse Raper. Mary McDaniel.

$1^1 1^2$ Martin Raper.

2 Catherine Raper. Isaac Johnson.

3 Charles Raper. Sarah Franklin.

4 Patsy Raper. * Dr. Fane.

5 Eliza Raper. James Brown.

6 Lewis Raper.

7 Gabriel Raper. *

8 Nannie Raper. James Holland.

9 John A. Raper. Mary Ann Tillotson.

10 Alonzo Raper. *

11 Rachel A. Raper.

$1^1 8^2 1^3$ Pleasant Holland. Nannie Horn.

2 Ruth Caroline Holland. Daniel Ross.

OK 3 Martha Holland. Samuel Johnson.

4 John Wesley Holland. Hettie Hern.

5 Jesse Holland.

6 Louisa Holland. Matthew Sanders.

7 Nancy Jane Holland. Moses Alberty.

8 James Lafayette Holland. Harriette Thompson.

9 William Grant Holland. Elizabeth Alberty.

10 Henry Sherman Holland.

11 Richard Spencer Holland. Laura Harmon.

12 Dora Belle Holland.

Hendricks

1^{1} Susannah. William Hendricks.
$1^{1}1^{2}$ James R. Hendricks. Nannie Woodall.
2 Annie Hendricks. George Peacheater and Felix Riley.
OK 3 Jane Hendricks. John Terrell and Green Parris.
4 Margaret Hendricks. Andrew Woodall.
5 John Hendricks. Pretia Tiesky and Mary Jane Brogan nee McLaughlin.
6 Nancy Hendricks. Henry Chambers.
7 Susannah Hendricks. Abraham Woodall.
8 Catherine Hendricks. James Chambers.
9 William H. Hendricks. Narcissa Crittenden and Ann Eliza Benge nee Linder.*
10 Willis Hendricks. Araminta Fish.
11 Franklin Hendricks. Annie Terrell nee Woodall.
12 Elizabeth Hendricks. James R. Gourd.
13 Thomas Hendricks. Nellie Ragsdale.
$1^{1}1^{2}1^{3}$ Jennie Hendricks. John Ragsdale.
2 Jonas Hendricks.
3 Dennis Hendricks. Eliza Jane Fish.
4 Minerva Hendricks. Joseph Poorboy and George Craft.
5 Cornelia Hendricks.
6 Louisa Hendricks. ———Miles.
$1^{1}2^{2}1^{3}$ Susan Riley. Ellis R. Gourd.

---

2 William Beatty. Louisa Parris.
3 Sallie Beatty.

---

4 Looney Price. Sarah Wofford.
$1^{1}3^{2}1^{3}$ Rebecca Terrell. Coleman Roberson.
2 Nannie Terrell. Green Terrell.
3 Elizabeth Terrell. George Bolin.

---

4 Sallie Parris.
5 Henry Parris. Barbara Marshall.
6 Emma Parris. Stephen Spears.
7 John Parris. Catherine Terrell.
$1^{1}4^{2}1^{3}$ Daniel Woodall. Emeline Ragsdale.
2 William Woodall. Potts.
3 Annie Woodall. Aaron Terrell.
4 Caroline Woodall. John Beaver Post.
$1^{1}5^{2}1^{3}$ Elnora Hendricks. George R. Gourd.
$1^{1}6^{2}1^{3}$ Ann Eliza Chambers. *
2 Mary A. Chambers. John Ross Hicks.
OK 3 Vann Chambers. Jennie Diana McCoy.
4 Elizabeth Chambers. Lippman Rosenthal and Charles Lamb.*

5 Jefferson Parks Chambers. Melissa Parris and Emma Wilcox.
6 Amelia Delilah Chambers. * David Lair Denny.
7 William Maxwell Chambers. Belle Bray.
8 Lettie Boyd Chambers. * David Lair Denny.
9 Nancy Jane Chambers. *
$1^17^21^3$ Thomas Fox Woodall. Mary Fields and Emma Fields nee Howland.
$1^18^21^3$ Elsie Jane Chambers. William Walkley, George Nipper and David Lair Denny.
2 George Sanders Chambers. Belle Chouteau nee Smith.
OK 3 David Chambers.
4 Robert Emory Chambers. Charlotte Ann Diedrich.
5 James Chambers. *
6 William A. Chambers. Minnie Brown and Emma Chambers nee Wilcox.
7 Mary Ella Chambers. * John Phillips.
8 Maxwell Chambers. Nellie White.
$1^19^21^3$ Fannie Hendricks. Frank Kerr.
$1^110^21^3$ Fannie E. Hendricks. Montgomery Canada.
2 Rachel Hendricks. Daniel Turner.
3 Charles Hendricks. *
4 White Hendricks. Rose Case and Mary Fossett.
5 Oscar Hendricks. *
6 Robert M. Hendricks. Gay Howard.
$1^112^21^3$ Eliza R. Gourd. Robert Watson Hicks and Lewis C. Cordery.
2 Elizabeth Gourd. William L. Cordrey.
3 Ellen Gourd. Daniel Webster Lowrey.
4 Thomas Gourd. Sallie Buse.
5 Jeanette Gourd. William L. Cordrey and George W. Griffin.
$1^113^21^3$ Rufus Hendricks. Susie Stanley.
2 Thomas Hendricks. Stanley and Bessie Bagley.
3 Susie Hendricks.
4 Janana Hendricks.

A 1. Ludovic Grant, who was said to have been a Scotchman, in a statement recorded on page 301 of the Charlestown, South Carolina probate court in the book of "1754-1758' in a sworn statement of January 12, 1756, says "It is about thirty years since I went into the Cherokee Country where I have resided ever since" "I speak their language". He married a full blood Cherokee woman of the Long Hair clan. He was among the Cherokees at the same time that Christian Priber and James Adair was in the nation. Grant's half breed daughter married William Emory, an Englishman.

A2. Rim Fawling, Ezekial Buffington, Robert Due and John Rogers were Englishmen.

A3. John Stuart was stationed at Fort Loudon as the Captain of a British company in 1757. The fort was besieged and captured by the war chief O-go-no-sto-ta on August 7, 1760. Nearly all of the garrison was killed, but Captain Stuart was rescued and taken to Virginia by the civil chief, Atacullaculla. Stuart was later appointed Superintendent of Indian Affairs, South of Ohio River and married Susannah Emory and their only child was always known as Oo-no-du-tu or Bushyhead and this name has clung to his descendants. Captain Stuart himself was known to his Cherokee acquaintances as Oo-no-du-tu on account of his shock of blond hair. He died at Pensacola, Fla., February 21, 1779. Susannah's second husband was Richard Fields, an Englishman and her third husband was Brigadier General Joseph Martin, who had the rare distinction of simultaneously bearing commissions to this rank in the militia service of Virginia and North Carolina.

A4. John Fawling's wife was a half breed Cherokee. Fawling was killed by James Vann, his wife's brother.

A5. David Gentry, a blacksmith was also the first husband of Tiana Rogers.

A6. John Rogers' first wife was Elizabeth Due nee Emory and his second wife was his step-daughter Jennie Due.

A7. Captain John Rogers settled at Dardanelle, Arkansas in 1821. He was the last chief of the "Old Settler" Cherokees. He died at Washington in 1846 and is buried in the National Cemetery. The wives of John and James Rogers were sisters.

A8. Richard Fields emigrated to Texas in 1821 and was killed in 1827.

A9. George Fields was a captain of Cherokee auxillaries to Gen. Andrew Jacksons army in the Creek war of 1814.

A10. Turtle Fields served with the Cherokee allies of the American forces in the Creek war of 1814 and later became a Methodist minister.

A11. John Martin, born October 20, 1781. He was a member of the Cherokee Constitutional convention of 1827, was the first Treasurer and first Chief Justice of the Cherokee Nation. He died on October 17, 1740 and is buried at Fort Gibson.

A12. Jeter Lynch was of Irish descent.

A13. Daniel Davis was born in North Carolina in 1785 and died in Georgia in June 1866.

A14. Major Downing, said to have been a Major in the British army married a full blood Cherokee woman of the Wolf clan.

A15. Tradition says that after a violent storm on the coast of South Carolina a baby was found on the beach, leashed to a spar. He was well clothed and the only word that he could articulate was "Jack" and upon being adopted by a family known as Wright, he was known as Jack Wright. He married Jennie Crittenden.

A16. Moses Alberty, born April 18, 1788. Died May 3, 1877.

A17. Clarissa Wright, born October 25, 1803, married Elijah Phillips.

A18. Rebecca Wright born January 1, 1814, married Joel Mayes Bryan born October 22, 1809. She died April 5, 1882. He died August 7, 1899.

A19. Joseph Vann, whose Cherokee name was Teaultle, was born on February 11, 1798. He was a member of the constitutional convention

1827 from Hightower District and of that of 1839. He was president of the Senate from 1841 to 1843. Elected Assistant Chief in 1839 and 1859. He died May 3, 1877.

A20. David Vann born January 1, 1800. He was elected Treasurer of the Cherokee Nation in 1839, 1843, 1847 and 1851. He was killed by the "Pin'" Indians on December 23, 1863.

A21. Andrew M. Vann was a resident of the Texas Cherokee Nation on July 20, 1833. He was elected Assistant Chief of the Cherokee Nation on June 28, 1840 vice (his brother) Joseph Vann, resigned.

A22. A full blood Cherokee of the Wolf clan, whose name may have been Na-ni. Her first husband, Kingfisher, of the Deer clan, was the father of her first two children; Catherine and Fivekiller. In a battle with the Muskogees, Kingfisher was killed and his wife, who had been laying behind a log, chewing the bullets so that they would lacerate the more; picked up his rifle and fought as a warrior throughout the rest of the skirmish. The Muskogees were defeated and according to custom the captured spoils were divided among the victors. Kingfisher's widow was given a negro that had been captured from the vanquished and in this manner became the first slave owner among the Cherokees and by common consent she became the Ghi-ga-u, or Beloved Woman of the Cherokees, this life time distinction was only granted as an extreme mark of valorious merit and carried with it the right to speak, vote and act in all of the peace and war councils of the tribe, it also vested her with the supreme pardoning power of the tribe, a prerogative that was not granted to any other, not even the powerful peace or war chiefs.

She was described even after she was an old woman as a person of remarkable beauty, poise "with a queenly and commanding presence." Her second husband was Bryan Ward, a White man, a widower, who had located in the Cherokee country as a trader. Ward had brought his son John, whose deceased mother was a White woman, and John subsequently married Catherine McDaniel, a half breed Cherokee woman and is the ancestor of the numerous Ward family, among the Cherokees. Bryan Ward had one daughter; Elizabeth, by the Ghi-ga-u; whose first husband was Brigadier General Joseph Martin and her second husband was ———Hughes, a trader. Bryan Ward lived only a few years after his marriage to The Ghi-ga-u.

In June 1776, Dragging Canoe, Abraham and Raven; war chiefs of the Cherokees, with about two hundred and fifty warriors each, at the instigation of the British, planned to attack the western settlements. But the effect of these raids were greatly modified by the Ghi-ga-u's timely warning to the settlers. On July 20, 1776, Abraham marching to attack Watauga, in East Tennessee, captured Mrs. Bean, wife of William Bean, the mother of the first White child born in Tennessee. On the return of the war party to the Cherokee country, Mrs. Bean was condemned by her captors to be burned at the stake. She was conducted to the top of the mound that stood in the center of Tuskeegee,[1] which was located just above the mouth of Tellico or Little Tennessee River, where she was bound to the stake, the fagots were piled around her, but just as the torch was about to be applied, the Ghigau appeared, cut the thongs that bound her and took the captive to her home.

where the grateful Mrs. Bean taught her how to keep house and make butter.

As soon as it was safe to do so, the Ghigau sent Mrs. Bean under the escort of her brother, Tuskeegeeteehee or Longfellow of Chistatoa and her son Hiskyteehee, or Fivekiller, sometimes known as Little Fellow, to her husband and family.

Tuskeegee is the town name of one of the original eight subdivisions of the Cusetah, the primal peace town of the Coosas, the primordial mother tribe of the Muskogees, Choctaws, Chickasaws and Seminoles. The suffix tee-hee, means killer and therefore the Ghigau's brother's name was Tuskeegee killer, although he was known to the English by the descriptive name of Longfellow on account of his stature. Hisky is the Cherokee rendering of the number, five.

At the beginning of September 1780 Gates had been defeated at Camden. Savannah and Charlestown were in the hands of the British; Georgia and South Carolina were conquered; the enemy exultantly moved northwest to the conquest of North Carolina and Virginia. This was the critical moment of the Revolution. Alexander Cameron of Lochabar, the British agent among the Cherokees and an intermarried citizen of that nation had been able to sustain the alliance of the Chickamaugas and many other Cherokees as well as other tribesmen with the British interests. Brave and resourceful pioneer soldiers, dressed in homespun and buckskin, coon skinned capped with the peculiar rifle with which they were wont to shoot the head off of a squirrel in the tallest tree or cut the neck of the turkey at an incredible distance, held back the equally dangerous Indians and Tories while others of their kind destroyed Ferguson's crack troops at Kings Mountain on October 7, 1780 and turned the tide in favor of the Americans.

While a portion of the patriots won in the Kings Mountain campaign, that part that were rearguarding the frontier became short of rations. "Nancy Ward agreed to furnish beef and had some cattle driven in."[1] She and her family had been consistent Americans since she had sent William Fawling[2] and Isaac Thomas on a hundred and twenty mile trip to warn the settlers of the proposed attack of Dragging Canoe, Abraham and Raven with their pro British Cherokee commands in July 1776.[3]

"When the Revolutionary War came, the British Government determined to employ the Indians against the southern and western frontiers. The organization of the southern tribes was intrusted to Superintendent Stuart. Their general plan which was only partially successful, was to land an army in west Florida, march them through the country of the Creeks and Chickasaws, who were each to furnish five hundred warriors and thence to Echota, the capital of the Cherokee nation. Being reinforced by the Cherokees, they were to invade the whole of the southern frontier, while the attention of the colonies was diverted by formidable naval and military demonstrations on the sea coast. Circular letters outlining the plan, intended for the information of the Tories who were expected to repair to the royal standards, were issued May 9, and reached the Watauga settlement May 18, 1776.

The Cherokees, when the plan was first submitted to them, were not prepared to take sides in the contest. A civil war was unknown to their nation, and they could hardly believe that the British government would make war against a part of its own people. Moreover, they had been at peace with the Americans since their treaty with Governor Bell, had no new complaint against them and were living heedless, happy lives in their own towns.

The campaign was planned with the utmost secrecy. It was agreed that North Carolina and Virginia, South Carolina and Georgia should be attacked simultaneously; the Overhill towns were to fall upon the back settlements of North Carolina and Virginia; the Middle towns were to invade the outlying districts of South Carolina; and the Lower towns were to strike the frontiers of Georgia.

The Overhill towns which mustered about seven hundred warriors were to move in three divisions; the first, commanded by Chuconsene or Dragging Canoe, who has been called a savage Napoleon, was to march against the Holston settlements; the second under Ooskiah or Abraham of Chilhowie, a half breed chief who had fought under Washington on the frontiers of Virginia, was to attack Watauga; and the third led by Colonah or the Raven of Echota was to scour Carters Valley.

At this time there lived in Echota a famous Indian woman named Nancy Ward. She held the office of Ghigau or Beloved Woman, which not only gave her the right to speak in council, but conferred such great power that she might, by the wave of a swan's wing, deliver a prisoner condemned by the council, though already tied to the stake. She was of queenly and commanding presence and manners and her house was furnished in a style suitable to her high dignity. She was a successful cattle raiser and is said to have been the first to introduce that industry among the Cherokees.

When Nancy Ward found that her people had fallen in with the plans of Stuart and Cameron, she communicated the intelligence to a trader named Isaac Thomas and provided him with the means of setting out as an express to warn the back settlers of their danger. Thomas was a man of character and a true American, who has left distinguished descendants in the State of Louisiana. Accompanied by William Fawling, he lost no time in conveying the alarming intelligence to the people on the Watauga and Holston. His services were afterwards recognized and rewarded by the State of Virginia.

The information conveyed by Thomas produced great consternation on the border. Couriers were dispatched in every direction. They had not had an Indian war since the settlement was begun, some seven years before. There was not a fort or block house from Wolf Hills westward. But preparations for defense now became nervously active; the people rushed together in every neighborhood and hurriedly cnstructed forts and stockades. Dragging Canoe was met at Long Island on the Holston on July 20, 1776 and defeated. Fort Watauga was attacked at sunrise next morning by Abraham who was driven away after having captured Mrs. William Bean and Samuel Moore, a boy Raven upon finding the Carter's Valley in forts and prepared and having heard of the repulses of Dragging Canoe and Abraham retired without doing any damage.

Upon the whole, the Indian invasion was a failure, owing to the timely warning of Nancy Ward, and the concentration of the inhabitants in forts built in consequence of the information she conveyed. If the well guarded secret of the Indian campaign had not been disclosed and they had been permitted to steal upon the defenseles backwoodsmen, who, in fancied security, had remained scattered over the extensive frontiers, every soul of them would probably have been swept from the borders of Tennessee. As it was, only slight injury was inflicted on the Whites; a few were killed, some were wounded and two were taken prisoners. The boy, Samuel Moore, was burned at the stake. The Tassel, afterwards asserted that he was the only White person burned by the Indians in Tennessee."

Ghigau for many years conducted an inn at Womankiller ford of the Ocowee River and became quite wealthy, her property consisting of live stock slaves and money. The traveling public called her "Granny Ward" on account of her age and the fact that she was the widow of Bryan Ward. After she got so old that she could not attend the councils, she sent her walking cane and vote on all important questions and in this manner voted at Amoah, on May 6, 1817, the renounciation of her delegated rights and in favor of the first constitutional enactment of the Cherokees.

She died at her home at the Womankiller Ford of Ocowee River in the spring of 1824.

A23. Ellis Harlan's direct line of descent was:

1^{1}. James Harlan, born about 1625 near Durham, England.

$1^{1}1^{2}$. George Harlan, married in County Armaugh, Ireland on September 17, 1678, Elizabeth Duck. Came to America and settled in Chester Co., Pennsylvania in 1687.

$1^{1}1^{2}1^{3}$. Ezekial Harlan, born in County of Down, Ireland on June 16, 1679. Married Rachel Buffington.

$1^{1}1^{2}1^{3}1^{4}$ Ezekial Harlan, born in Chester Co., Pennsylvania on May 19, 1707. Married October 23, 1724 Hannah Osborn, born February 21, 1707 in Delaware Co., Pennsylvania. Both lived and died in Chester Co., Pennsylvania.

$1^{1}1^{2}1^{3}1^{4}1^{5}$. Ellis Harlan born about 1731. Married Mrs. Catherine Walker.

A24. Caleb Starr's direct line of descent was:

1^{1}. John Starr of Oldcastle, County of Meath, Ireland, was according to tradition a son of an English captain of infantry in Cromwell's army, who settled in Ireland at the close of the civil war. John and many of his descendants were members of the Society of Friends.

$1^{1}1^{2}$. John Starr born in July 1674 at Oldcastle. He married at Ballyhaes Meeting on June 11, 1706 Sarah Martin. They came to Chester County, Pennsylvania, prior to 1717, but returned to Ireland and settled at Coote Hill, County of Cavan.

$1^{1}1^{2}1^{3}$ John Starr lived in West Nantuel Township, Chester Country, Pennsylvania. He probably died between 1771 and 1774 and his third wife; Annie probably died some ten years later, as their names were dropped from the tax rolls during these years.

$1^{1}1^{2}1^{3}1^{4}$ Alexander Starr, son of John and Annie, married Deborah

Bryant. They lived and died in Chester County, Pennsylvania. The death of the latter occurring in 1830.

$1^{1}1^{2}1^{3}1^{4}1^{5}$. Caleb Starr born in Chester County, Pennsylvania about 1758. He together with Joseph McMinn, emigrated to Tennessee in about 1775. He married Nannie Harlan. He owned and lived on section 9 of FTIS, Range 1, East on Conasauga Creek, in McMinn County, Tennessee. Mrs. Starr died in 1841 and he died in 1843.

A25. Peter Hildebrand, born May 10, 1782 in Germany. Married Elizabeth Harlan, born August 15, 1793. She died September 19, 1826. He was one of the Captains of Emigrant detachments in 1838-39 and located on Flint Creek where he operated a saw, turning and grist mill. He died on December 11, 1851.

A26. Anthony Foreman was a Scotchman. His second wife, Elizabeth was a niece of his first wife.

A27. Archibald Foreman was born on January 1, 1801 and died on May 28, 1838.

A28. Mary Ann Bigby was born on August 9, 1802. She married David Taylor, born December 16, 1791 in Orange County, Virginia.

A29. Teesee Guess was born in 1789. This second wife Rebecca Bowles was born in 1816. She died on October 12, 1866 and he died on September 17, 1867.

A30. John Gunter was a Welchman and operated a powder mill in the Cherokee country in 1814.

A31. George Lowrey was born about 1770. He and his son in law David Brown had finished a Cherokee spelling book in English characters at the time that Sequoyah announced his invention. Lucy Lowrey nee Benge was born about 1786. She died on October 10, 1846 and he died on October 20, 1852.

A32. Tahlonteeskee was a prominent Chicamauga warrior in 1792. In the United States—Cherokee October 25, 1805 Doublehead, who had hitherto been an implacable war chief was granted three separate tracts of one square mile each and Tahlonteeskee received a square mile of land on the north bank, of the Tennessee River, for their influence in negotiating the treaty. This action becoming unpopular, Tahlonteeskee emigrated to the Western Cherokee country where he was elected Principal Chief in 1818.

A33. John Bowles was the son of a Scotch trader and a full blood Cherokee woman. His father was killed and robbed by two North Carolinans while on his way home from Charlestown with goods for his establishment This murder was in 1768 when the son was only twelve years of age, but within the next two years the fair complexioned, auburn haired boy had killed both of his father's slayers. Bowles settled at Runningwater Town, one of the Chicamauga settlements near Lookout Mountain and at this place he became involved in an altercation with some pioneers who were floating down the Tennessee River and killed all the boatmen in June 1794. Bowles and his followers now manned the boats and navigated them down to the mouth of St. Francis River in the Spanish province of Louisiana.

On arriving at their destination they placed all of the White women and children in a boat, relinquished to them all of the furniture which they claimed and allowed them to descend the Mississippi River to New Orleans.

Bowles and his followers joined the Cherokees that had lived in that locality for many years and he became their Chief in 1795 a position he held until 1813. On account of the earthquake that centered in their settlement in the winter of 1811-12, the Cherokees moved enmass to the country between Arkansas and White Rivers and a few of them settled south of the former stream. In accordance with the United States Cherokee treaties the limits of the Cherokee country was marked in the spring of 1819 by William Rector, Surveyor General of Arkansas and because it was not extended to include his town on Petit Jean Creek, on the south side of Arkansas River, Bowles with some sixty townsmen and their families emigrated in the winter of 1819-20 to the Spanish colony of Texas and settled between the Trinity and Angelina Rivers. They staid in Texas until July 16, 1839 when Bowles was killed and his colony evicted.

A34. Michael Sanders, an Englishman from Virginia married Susie, a full blood Cherokee of the Bird clan.

A35. Alexander Sanders killed Chief Doublehead in a drunken brawl at Hiwassee Ferry in the summer of 1807. He was a Captain of the Cherokee allies of General Andrew Jackson in 1814. It is said his name is on the military rolls as Jeremiah.

A36. Nancy Sanders born in 1782. Married George Harlan and Ambrose Harnage. The latter was a White man, who died October 20, 1842. She died July 11, 1834.

A37. Major Ridge and Oo-wa-tie, or The Ancient, were full blood Cherokees of the Deer clan. They were full brothers and born in Hiwassee town. Susie Wickett was a half blood English Cherokee and Susannah Reese was a half blood Welch-Cherokee. Ridge was a Major of the Cherokee allies of the United States soldiers in the war of 1814. He was killed at about ten o'clock a. m. on June 22, 1839. All of Oo-wa-tie's children were known as Watie's the first Oo, being dropped, except in the case of his second son Killikeenah or Buck, who out of gratitude for benefactions, adopted the name of Elias Boudinot and his descent have always been known as Boudinots instead of Waties.

A38. Stand Watie was born December 12, 1806 and died September 9, 1871.

A39. George Ward, born March 17, 1787. Married December 15, 1805. Lucy Mayes, a White woman and sister of Samuel Mayes. He was assassinated during the civil war by Pin Indians and Mrs. Ward died on November 11, 1867.

A40. Thomas Cordery married Susannah, a full blood Cherokee of the Blind Savannah clan.

A41. John Rogers, born in 1779 in Burke County, Georgia of Scotch and English descent, married Sarah Cordery. He was known as "Nolachucky Jack" Rogers. Mrs. Rogers died on July 14, 1842 and he died on July 30, 1851.

A42. Jackson Rogers born October 12, 1816. Married February 7, 1844 Sarah G. Blackburn, born June 3, 1821. He enlisted in Company B, First Georgia Infantry under Colonel William Dabney. He was captured in July 1864 and held at Camp Douglas, in Chicago, until he was parolled on June 16, 1865. He was elected a member of the Georgia legislature in 1875. He died May 14, 1899.

A43. Mary Daniel, born October 15, 1787. Married Thomas Buffington and on his decease she married Lewis Blackburn, a White man, born July 17, 1778 in Stokes County, North Carolina.

A44. Malinda Wharton was born December 25, 1803 in Virginia. She married Thomas Chisholm, born in 1790. He was elected Third Chief of the Western Cherokees on July 16, 1834. The Principal Chief at that time was John Jolly and the Second Chief, was Blackcoat. Thomas Chisholm was attacked with typhoid fever at the council at Tahlonteeskee and on being taken to his home on Beatty's Prairie, he died on November 12, 1834. Mrs. Chisholm's second husband was William Wilson, born October 14, 1811. She died on February 19, 1864 and he died on June 20, 1897.

A45. David Carter born in 1807. Married Jennie Riley, born in 1817. He was elected Judge of Tahlequah District in 1841. Elected Senator from the same district in 1842. He was a Justice of the Supreme Court and also Superintendent of Education from 1836 to 1845. Resigned these to become Editor of the Cherokee Advocate, was Chief Justice of the Cherokee Nation from 1851 to 1854 and was later a Justice of the Supreme Court. He died on February 1, 1867 and his wife died on March 1, 1867.

A46. Jennie Halfbreed, her brothers and sisters belonged to the Blind Savannah clan.

A47. John Adair, a Scotchman, married Mrs. Ge-ho-ga Foster, a full blood Cherokee of the Deer clan. She was a sister of Mrs. Dorcas Duncan, wife of Young Charles Gordon Duncan who was also a Scotchman. Adair had five children that lived to be grown and after her death he married Jennie Kilgore, a White woman, by whom he had ten children.

A48. Walter Adair was born on December 11, 1783. He married on May 15, 1804 Rachel Thompson, a White woman, born December 24, 1786. He died on January 12, 1835 and his wife died on April 22, 1876.

A49. Walter Scott Adair was born on January 28, 1791. He married on November 16, 1824 Nancy Harris, born in 1807. He was the first master of the second masonic lodge in Oklahoma. He died September 26, 1854. She died March 9, 1884.

A50. William Shorey, a Scotchman married Ghigooie a full blood Cherokee of the Bird clan.

A51. Mollie McDonald, born November 1, 1770. She married Daniel Ross, a Scotchman, born in 1760 in Sutherlandshire, Scotland. She died October 5, 1808 and he died on May 22, 1830.

A52. Jennie Springston born December 23, 1804. Married Joseph Vann born in 1800. He died or October 26, 1844. She died August 4, 1863.

A53. Tradition avers that Jennie Taylor, a Scotch woman married a member of the English aristocracy named Fox. That they had two sons and then separated, the father retaining the elder, on whom the right of primogeniture would vest the estates and she kept the younger brother, who was thence forward known as Charles Fox-Taylor. The widow later married a Hollander named Conrad and emigrated to America, settling in the vicinity of the Cherokees. Charles Fox-Taylor married Jennie Walker, a grand daughter of the Ghi-ga-u, and his half brother; Hamilton Conrad married Onai, a full blood Cherokee woman of the Bird clan. The descendants Charles Fox-Taylor were known as Taylors.

Hamilton and Onai Conrad had five children; Rattlinggourd, Hair, Youngwolf, Quatie and Terrapinhead Conrad. Although Hair Conrad was the only one except a grandson of Terrepinhead who retained his full patronymic. Rattlinggourd and his descent were always known as Rattlinggourds. Youngwolf's generation were known by the family name of Wolf and Terrapinhead's children and descendants were known as Terrapins, with the exception of his youngest son, who although a full brother to the other children was known as Thomas Fox Conrad.

Terrapinhead's only daughter, Jennie, married a half blood Spanish-Cherokee whose only name was So-sa or Goose but he became locally known as Dick Spaniard, on acount of his extraction. Upon his enlistment in the confederate service he gave the name So-sa and upon the adjutants query for a christian name, he said Johnson or as the Cherokees pronounced it, Jonson would do. He was killed in a skirmish at Tahlequah and Jennie named their posthumous son; John Johnson using the father's assumed christian name for his surname.

A54. Jackson Rattlinggourd was born in 1809. Married Elsie Wilson born in 1808. She died October 4, 1884. He died on April 10, 1885.

A55. Samuel Riley, a White man, married Gu-lu-sti-yu and Ni-go-di-ge-yu. They were sisters and belonged to the Long Hair clan.

A56. Loony Riley born November 12, 1800, married in 1818 Rachel Stuart, a White woman, born December 21, 1800. He died February 28, 1883. She died April 15, 1883.

A57. Edmond Benge, who was most probably a three quarter blood Cherokee was born in 1784. He married on July 25, 1810 Mary Rains, a White woman born December 8, 1792. She died in Georgia prior to 1839 and he died on September 12, 1844.

A58. John Crutchfield, born July 29, 1822 and died in September 1886.

A59. Joseph and Rock Crutchfield were the sons of a full blood Cherokee mother and a White trader whose trading station was near James Vann's residence at Spring Place. Vann and Crutchfield became mixed up in a broil in which the latter was killed. Vann at once adopted the orphan boys and raised them as if they were his own and when they were grown equipped them with well improved plantations and gave several slaves to each.

A60. John Hildebrand was a native of Germany and his first five children were full blooded Germans. His last four children were half breed Cherokee-Germans.

A61. Elowie or Elijah Butler was born in 1817. He was converted and joined the Methodist church when quite young. He was admitted to the ministry on trial in October 1853 and was assigned to the Spring Creek circuit, transferred to the Senica and Delaware circuit in 1854 and to the Big Bend of Arkansas river with Reverend Wiliam McIntosh in 1855. A large colony of Cherokee had for many years lived in this far western location residing on both sides of the river, where they stayed until this section was sold to the Osages and Pawnees and then most of them returned to the Cherokee Nation east of the ninety sixth meridian. It was several years after Reverend Elowie or Elijah had been in the ministry before he commenced to be known as Butler. He was ordained a deacon in October 1858 by Bishop Early at Skullyville. During 1860 and 1861 he was again filling the station at Big Bend. He served in the confederate army under Captain Thompson Mayes. From 1866 to 1871 he worked on the Grand River circuit with Reverend D. B. Cummings. He was elected Judge of Delaware District in 1867 and 1869. His wife, Dorcas Landrum was born in 1829. Reverend "Butler was of that type of the Indian preacher of which we have had many during the years of our missionary work. Solid, full of purpose and fidelity, he was devoted to his work and stuck to it under all possible circumstances."[1] Reverend Butler died April 27, 1873 and Mrs. Dorcas Butler died on January 13, 1898.

A62. Sarah Hildebrand was born on November 26, 1788. She married Blackcoat. By an act of the council at Piney on Piney Creek, Arkansas Cherokee Nation, on September 11, 1824, it was provided that "the Executive Department of the Cherokee Government shall consist of three persons, that is, a First Chief, a Second Chief, and a Third or minor Chief, which chiefs shall serve for a term of four years from the date of their appointment, and the First and Second Chiefs shall receive a salary of one hundred dollars annually, and the Third or minor Chief, sixty dollars."[2] At that time the Cherokees were often at war with neighboring tribes and their country was not healthy and one or two of the chiefs might die or be killed within a few days of each other and for that reason three chiefs were elected.

Redbird Smith

STOKE SMITH
6TH SON
KIAH SMITH
7TH SON
JOHN SMITH
OLDEST SON
RED BIRD SMITH
SAM SMITH
2ND SON
RICHARD SMITH
3RD SON
THOMAS SMITH
4TH SON

CHAPTER XX

The Full Blood Cherokees' Progress. Political, Business and Social Activities

Redbird Smith, who was the moving spirit of the Nighthawk branch of the Keetoowah organization of Full-blood Cherokees, was born July 19th, 1850, somewhere near the city of Ft. Smith, Ark. His father and mother, together with other Cherokees being enroute to Indian Territory from Georgia.

Pig Redbird Smith, (the name Smith being added by the white people in Georgia because he was a blacksmith by trade), was an old and ardent adherent of the ancient rituals, customs and practices of the "Long House" group of eastern Indians of which the Cherokees were the head band or tribe.

The wife of Pig Redbird Smith and mother of Redbird Smith was Lizzie Hildebrand Smith, a woman who carried the best blood-lines of the Cherokees.

At an early date in the boyhood life of Redbird Smith, his father dedicated him to the services and cause of the Cherokee people in accordance with ancient customs and usages. At the early age of ten years, Redbird received instruction at the council fires. At this time, the latter part of 1859, Pig Redbird Smith, Budd Gritts and Vann, all being impressed with the virtues of the religious and moral codes of the ancient Keetoowah order, concluded to reorganize.

REDBIRD SMITH'S HOME

On the porch are Redbird Smith, his Councilmen and his 5th son, George. On the ground are his wife, 2 daughters, 8 sons, their wives and grandchildren.

Budd Gritts, who was a Baptist Minister, was prevailed upon to draft a Constitution and Laws of government for the use of the people in their group, which was compatible with the changing conditions religiously and politically. The constitution and Laws of Government was formally adopted and the Keetoowahs prospered and lived in peace under it for many years.

During the period from 1859 to 1889, the Keetoowahs flourished and were strongly united. Almost without exception the Keetoowahs went with the North in the Civil War. In all this period the Keetoowahs were either Baptists, Methodists, Presbyterians, a few Quakers, and a part of them worshipped according to the rituals of the ancient Keetoowah, but all got along harmoniously. Dissentions came only after the white Missionaries objected to and condemned what they termed "the Pagan Form of worship" of the ancient Keetowahs, and designated as "The work of the Devil."

Influenced by these white teachers, who were conscientious and sincere in their efforts of Christian work, the members of the diferent denominations became strictly sectarian in their practice, but there was still no enmity existing.

The Keetoowah Constitution and Laws of Government was amended in 1889, making it rather a political organization in character. From this period the differences between the Christian Keetoowahs and the Ancient Keetoowahs became more marked, and there was lack of harmony even in their policies of political effort.

In 1895 when the question of the allotment of lands to the members of the Five Civilized Tribes was being agitated, the ancient Keetoowahs became very active in opposing the proposed change. In this, however, all the Keetoowah element were united in their opposition to any speedy change. From this time to 1900 the following of Redbird Smith were designated universally as the "Nighthawk Keetoowahs" because of their vigilence in their activities.

On January 31st, 1899, a general election was held for the purpose of determining on what is known as the Dawes Commission Treaty. The Full-bloods lost by two thousand fifteen votes. The Keetoowahs were united in their opposition to the allotment of lands and dissolution of their government, but a part of them saw that the change was inevitably coming and adjusted themselves accordingly.

Redbird Smith, however, took the position that it was grossly unjust for the United States Government, their Trustee, to precipitately plunge a large number of his people into so radically changed conditions, he accordingly advised his following (about 5789 according to the roll of their number at that time) that he reposed confidence in the integrity of the intentions of the Government of the United States to uphold its Treaty Stipulations; that sooner or later the Government would see the injustice to the Full-bloods and would take active measures to make amends. He therefore counselled his people not to participate further in the deliberations of what he termed the majority of the advocates of the change. He and his group stood steadfast in this recalcitrant attitude until about 1910 when he became convinced that it was useless.

In 1908 his position as Chairman was officially changed by the Nighthawk Keetoowah Council to that of Chief. An election was held for this purpose and he was unanimously elected in that caapcity for life, which he held and ably filled until his death, November 8th, 1918, after a short illness of forty-eight hours.

Redbird Smith was a man endowed with a great native ability and great enough to admit his own mistakes. In this matter he said: "After my selection as a Chief, I awakened to the grave and great responsibilities of a leader of men. I looked about and saw that I had led my people down a long and steep mountain side, now it was my duty to turn and lead them back upward and save them. The unfortunate thing in the mistakes and errors of leaders or of governments is the penalty the innocent and loyal followers have to pay. My greatest ambition has always been to think right and do right. It is my belief that this is the fulfilling of the law of the Great Creator. In the upbuilding of my people it is my purpose that we shall be spiritually right and industrially strong."

"I have always believed that the Great Creator had a great design for my people, the Cherokees. I have been taught that from my childhood up and now in my mature manhood I recognize it as a great truth. Our forces have been dissipated by the external forces, perhaps it has been just a training, but we must now get together as a race and render our contribution to mankind."

Redbird Smith (left), and Bluford Sixkiller, Asst. Chief (right), instructing children in the Ketoowah Ritual.

"We are endowed with intelligence, we are industrious, we are loyal, and we are spiritual but we are overlooking the particular Cherokee mission on earth, for no man nor race is endowed with these qualifications without a designed purpose. Work and right training is the solution of my follwing. We as a group are still groping in darkness in many things, but this we know, we must work. A kindly man cannot help his neighbor in need unless he have a surplus and he cannot have a surplus unles he works. It is so simple and yet we have to continually remind our people of this."

"Our Mixed-bloods should not be overlooked in this program of a racial awakening. Our pride in our ancestral heritage is our great incentive for handing something worth while to our posterity. It is this pride in ancestry that makes men strong and loyal for their principle in life. It is this same pride that makes men give up their all for their Government."

In the last few years of his life Redbird Smith became obsessed with his ambition for his people. He insisted in securing the services of one who was willing to co-operate with him in working some industrial plan for the Nighthawk Keetoowah Group, and he did not give up his program until he secured an agreement with this party to serve with his people for seven years, beginning with January 1st, 1918.

His program covered not only the Nighthawks, but all people of Cherokee blood. His great ambition was to accomplish a united spirit of co-operation among all the factors of the Cherokee people. It was distinctly not his idea to reestablish the old and discarded regime of the Cherokee Government, but to awaken a racial pride, so that the more fortunate of the race may become great factors in helping their less fortunate brethren.

It is this spirit and ambition of his that has prevailed even after his death, and that which his survivors in Office are carrying out in the selection of Levi Gritts as Chief of the Cherokees. It should be understood that it is purely a purpose of unifying the Cherokee people to a grand effort of agrandizing the race that it may acquit itself as a contributor to a grand race of men in America, as Redbird called it "The Mother of the New World."

To fulfill these purposes the Cherokee Executive Council was organized, with the following members:

Cherokee Executive Council

W. Tate Brady, Chairman of Executive Counsel, Secretary W. M. Gulager.

Ketoowahs Incorporated:

John B. Smith, Tahlequah, Oklahoma — Robert Meigs, Parkhill, Oklahoma.
Rider Ratler, Lyons, Oklahoma. — Peter Cramp, Porum, Oklahoma.
Isaac Greece, Tahlequah, Oklahaoma.

For the Eastern and Western:

Watt Mayes, Pryor, Oklahoma. — E. N. Washbourne, Jay, Oklahoma.
James Hilderbrand, Bernice, Oklahoma. — J. R. McIntosh, Claremore, Okla.
Geo. Mayes, Pryor, Oklahoma.

Cherokee Personal Committee:

S. R. Lewis, Tulsa, Oklahoma. — W. T. Brady, Tulsa, Oklahoma.
W. M. Gulager, Muskogee, Oklahoma. — J. G. Sanders, Tulsa, Oklahoma.
S. G. Maxfield, Tulsa, Oklahoma.

Nighthawk Keetoowahs:

Sam Smith, Gore, Oklahoma. — Sam R. Smith, Gore, Oklahoma.
John R. Smith, Gore, Oklahoma. — Osie Hogshooter, Tahlequah, Oklahoma.
Alex Deerinwater Tahlequah, Oklahoma. — Lincoln Towie, Tahlequah, Okla.

Delaware Cherokees:

Joe A. Barles, Dewey, Oklahoma. Geo. Bullett, Tulsa, Oklahoma.
A. H. Norwood, Dewey, Oklahoma. Solomon Ketchum, Vinita, Oklahoma.
C. Wilson, Nowata, Oklahoma.

Bluford Sixkiller, who was Redbird's asistant from 1908 until Sept. 12th, 1920, which he resigned on account of poor health. William Rogers succeeded to his place by election on the same date. William Rogers is 51 years of age and a faithful follower of Redbird Smith. He is a man of sterling qualities and has rendered invaluable service to his people.

Bluford Sixkiller died November 23rd, 1921, aged 73 years.

Sam Smith, the son of Redbird Smith succeeded to his father's place as Chief of the Nighthawk Keetoowahs, April 7th, 1919. He is successfully carrying out his father's program. Makes a wise and conservative leader and yet very progressive.

Oce Hogshooter, the secretary of the organization has served in that capacity since 1908. A man fifty years of age and an active worker and a wise counsellor to his people.

John Redbird Smith, the official Interpreter of the Organization since 1900 and a steadfast assistant of his revered father. A man of strong convictions, conscientious, fearless and a very strong factor in the work of bringing the Nighthawks out of the wilderness.

All of Redbird's ten living children are ardent followers of their father. Redbird left surviving him, his wife, two daughters, eight sons and thirty-five grandchildren.

Lucy Fields Smith, the surviving wife of Redbird's, was born near Braggs, Oklahoma, in 1852. Her father was Richard Fields, who at the time of his death in Washington, D. C., was the attorney general of the Cherokee Nation. Her mother was Eliza Brewer Fields, who survived until Jan. 1890.

This noble and loyal wife of Redbird Smith was largely responsible for his sucess in life. She is a wonderful mother. When her two youngest boys departed for the Army encampment, Kian and Stokes, she calmly gave her boys up and bade them to be courageous and acquit themselves as men.

It is a noteworthy fact that Chief Redbird, issued an edict to all the fires of the Nighthawk Keetoowahs, calling upon all members of draft age to offer themselves without reserve and to take no advantage of the exemption provided for. This was carried except in two cases.

The following named were all great factors in the work of the Keetoowah organization: Anderson Gritts, Ned Ten Killer, Nagada Seweegbe, Joe Chewy, Lacy Hawkins, Daniel Redbird, George Benge, Stool Jackson, George Hughes, Ned Bullfrog, Sanee Goo-yah, Sand, Wilson Girty, Tom Horn, Charley Ketcher, John Wycliff, Jim Wycliff, Charley Scott, Alex McCoy, Paul Glass, Joshua Glass, Jim Alex, Alex Deerinwater, Jim Hogshooter, Will Sand and George Smith.

The following notice of election of Levi Gritts, Chief of the Cherokees, is a splendid written document and fully explains the necessity and importance of the election:

Box, Oklahoma, December 9th, 1920.

Mr. Levi Gritts,
Muskogee, Oklahoma.
My dear Mr. Gritts:—Pursuant to a well defined plan and program of the Nighthawk Keetoowahs of Full-blood Cherokee Indians, you have seen designated by the Council of said Society to serve our suffering cause in the capacity of CHIEF OF THE CHEROKEES.

With the death of the late Chief Rogers, terminated the officially recognized position of Cherokee Chief. The elimination of this office seemed at the time to be natural and it was the concensus of opinion on the part of the Cherokees themselves as well as the Departmental administrators of our affairs that there was no further need of the office of a Chief in our changed conditions.

Your attention is respectfully invited to the following analysis as we have. in our humble way, been able to reach:

(1) Chief Redbird Smith. (2) Lucy Smith, his wife. (3) Mrs Ella McLain, daughter. (4) John Redbird Smith. (5) Sam Smith. (6) Mrs. Susie Starr, daughter. (8) Thomas Smith. (9) George Smith. (10) Mose Smith. (11) Kiah Smith. (12) Stoke Smith.

Taking the Full-blood, particularly the Nighthawk Keetoowahs, as a basis of this analysis, we find, first; That beginning with the trying times of the year Nineteen Hundred, these people were overwhelmed with what seemed to them an attempt on the part of the United States government to divest them of what they considered their vested rights; they were all too suddenly divested of the rights and prerogatives of self determination in their National governmental affairs, with the result that they eventually crystalized into a recalcitrant attitude. They looked askance upon every movement of the government, taking the position that every move now, meant exploitation of what little they may have left of a once vast holdings.

This unfortunate position was largely justified and amplified by the fact that a large number of their own blood, who had been fortunate enough to have received the advantages of literary training, now became the allies of the unscrupulous and exploiting hordes, who infested the country during the said "trying times," an element, who seem to destiny itself to have designed to always precede the wholesome citizenry, who eventually supercede and predominate, and held full sway for a number of years.

A further elaboration of this particular phase of our analysis is unnecessary with you, who lived and survived through a period of bitter and trying experiences. The incarceration of an educated Full-blood Indian in a Penal Institution of our new state was not beyond the intelligence of our Full-bloods. They recognized the brazen rebuke and the NOTICE TO THEM of their futile and hopeless position as a group and kind.

Proceeding now to the SECOND and final analysis, we submit the following deductions: The advance and gradual increase numerically of the substantial class of citizens, home builders and hence nation builders, and the two decades of close contact and living in the atmosphere of intensive constructive effort, of which our young state stands without a precedent; and last but not least, the loyal and unequivocal response of not only our Full-blood Nighthawks but of all the American Indians, to the Nation's call to Arms and Service in our recent World Struggle; all contribute to rehabilitate the Indians' self respect and confidence in themselves, as well as confidence in the integrity of purpose in their behalf on the part of the Government of the Unitd States.

It is gratifying to note, that with all the effusive commendations and extravagant expressions of appreciation on the part of the American people, for the creditable manner in which our people acquitted themselves in the War with Germany, the Indians have not become imbued with the idea of self-importance. In fact, the Indians of America merely had a chance to show what is inherently in them as a race. In their own estimation they did no more than any loyal citizen should have done. It was a spontaneous reciprocal response to a Great Government, who by virtue of being entangled in a World crisis, called upon its whole people to a united effort.

There is carried with this, a new psychological angle so far as the Full-blood Indian is concerned. For the first time in history he realizes through the attitude of the United States Government, that his material effects and his manhood are a National asset; that he is a part and parcel of the body politic of a great Commonwealth. He is alert to the responsibilities of his new position. He is expecting participation in the administration of his affairs. He is keenly cognizant and sensible of the new responsibilities with which he is about to be endowed. Within a decade the restricted period shall terminate and during that same space of time all our Claims against our Government may be adjudicated and finally settled.

Now, confidently and sincerely these Ful-lblood Cherokees point out that by virtue of their new position and relatlons they must come into closer touch and cooperation with the supervisory and administrative agencies of the Government, and of their number many have no other means of communcation except through the medium of the Cherokee language. These conditions demand and require more than a mere Official Interpreter at the Departmental offices.

From now on for the next few years the Cherokees must have a real REPRESENTATIVE at the headquarters of the Five Civilized Tribes' agency, for the following potent reasons: First, the unrestricted intermarried and mixed-blood Cherokee citizens, while to all intents and purposes are like any white American citizens, they are interested and have equitable rights in all matters pertaining to our unadjusted claims against the United States, it is of imperative importance that their efforts should co-ordinate with our efforts in the accomplishment of said adjustments. This can be achieved by uniting all forces through the one proposed REPRESENTATIVE. Secondly, the restricted full-bloods, who are still possessed of restricted landed assets as well as restricted funds, are most vitally ineterested in the administerial agencies of the Government, particularly at this time of anticipated important changes in the personnel as well as policies in the Departments directly affecting them. This group being largely composed of non-English speaking people, and being by custom and practice trained to do their business through a Chief, it is but natural and logical that now, when a united Cherokee effort is so apparently necessary to accomplish anything for the good of all, they should demand and designate a CHIEF.

Our determination on you for the place is not because of our desire to confer an HONORARY position upon you, as a recognition of your former positions in our behalf, but because we know your DEPENDABILITY AND EFFICIENT QUALIFICATIONS for such responsibility. You are a Full-blood Cherokee, reared and developed under Full-blood life conditions. You understand and sympathize with the thought and life of the Full-blood. You have had the advantages of an academic training. You are master of both the Cherokee and the English languages. You have survived the crucial test of the transition period of the last decade in our country. You have reached the age of calm and conservative discernment. Those enumerated experiences and advantages of your life, together with your native-born ambitions for your people, commend you as a safe and sane leader and counsellor for us all.

We, of the Nighthawk Keetoowah contingent of the Cherokee Indians repose implicit confidence in the integrity of your thought and regard for the various groups and interests of our people and sincerely feel that you are capable and will render us most valuable service.

In accepting the arduous task we are thrusting upon you, we desire to urg ethe necessity of immedite action and co-operation of the other factors and groups to the end that we may be properly and effectively organized for a united effort in the prosecution of our various interests. We believe that now is the opportune time to make our representations to the dispensers of patronage of the incoming administration. If the Indian manhood and his material assets were of so vital a part to the United States in time of trouble, it is certainly no more than just and right that we participate in a careful selection of men of recognized calibre coupled with unimpeachable character for administrators of our material possessions of millions of dollars in value, as well as the more momentous question of our moral and intellectual development.

THE KEETOOWAH COUNCIL, 1916.

The office of COMMISSIONER OF INDIAN AFFAIRS is one of paramount interest to every Indian of the United States. Next in importance, particularly insofar as we are concerned, is the office of Superintendent of tion in this matter be immediately submitted to the proper sources of authortion in this matter be immediately submitted to the proper sourecs of authority, to the end that the demands of our INTERESTS may receive a satisfactory degree of consideration.

You are therefore, by virtue hereof, and the urgent immediate demands of our interests, and the interests of all the Cherokees, made and constituted the CHEROKEE CHIEF.

With sincere regard and respect,
(Signed) SAM SMITH,
Chief of the Nighthawk Keetoowahs.

(SEAL)

Attest.
(Signed) Oce Hogshooter,
Secretary Nighthawk Keetoowahs.

Cobb, Dr. Isabel (See Grant)—Martha Blythe, born Jan. 31, 1812. Married in May 1828 Alexander Clingan, born Feb. 20, 1801 in Hawkins County, Tennessee. He died February 1, 1964 and she died August 7, 1868. They were the parents of: Evaline Clingan, born in Bradley County, Tennessee, April 13, 1835. Married December 15, 1857, Joseph Benson Cobb, born in Blount County, Tennessee, July 26, 1828. He died March 22, 1896, and she died November 17, 1918. They were the parents of Isabel, born October 25, 1858; William Cowan, born April 1, 1860 and was murdered July 27, 1880; Martha, born December 28, 1861; Joseph Benson, born February 21, 1863; Alexander Clingan, born September 15, 1864; Samuel Sylvester, born December 12, 1865, and Addie Malinda Cobb, born September 9, 1870.

Isabel Cobb, graduated from Female Seminary, January 27, 1879, Glendale Female College, Glendale, Ohio, June 8, 1881 and the Womans Medical- College of Pennsyl vania May 5,1892. Since that date she has been a regular practitioner at Wagoner. Martha Cobb graduated from Female Seminary, June 30, 1888 and Kansas Agriculture College June 6, 1888. Married June 11, 1891, Clement George Clarke, born Febru- He graduated from Kansas Agricultural College, June 6, 1888, Yale Academy in 1895, and the Theological Course in Yale in 1900. A Congregationalist minister, he was lecturer on social hygiene with the American Army in France. They are the parents of Helen Isabel, born November 13, 1894, educated at Smith College North Hampton, Massachusetts and Columbia College, New York City; Dana Cobb, born January 27, 1898, graduated from Yale, June 21, 1821 and Clement Cobb Clarke, born January 29, 1904.

O. LONZO CONNER

Conner (See Duncan and Grant) O. Lonzo Conner, born Feb. 12, 1877 at Fairland, Okla. son of Francis Marion, (born Mar 29, 1852, in Jasper Co., Missouri, married December 24, 1873) and Rebecca Jane (Duncan) Conner, born October 29, 1858 and died at Fairland March 12, 1911. He was educated in the Cherokee public schools, Male Seminary and graduated from Robbin's Business College, Sedalia, Missouri; he married December 30, 1896 at Beattie's Prairie, Kate Eugenia Yeargain, born March 31, 1878; she was the daughter of James Chambers, born February 27, 1842 in Lebanon, Tenn. and married March 4, 1866, and Mary Jane (Kinney) Yeargain, born June 25, 1848 at Ft. Smith, Arkansas, and died December 25, 1912 at Southwest City, Missouri. Mrs. Kate E. Conner was educated in the Cherokee public schools and the Female Seminary. Mr. and Mrs. O. Lonzo Conner are the parents of Nevada Maude, born Oct. 24, 1897, graduated from the University of Okla. in 1919, is an Easter Star and Gamma Phi Beta; O. Lonzo J., born July 18, 1900; Clifton Sidney, born July 16, 1902; James Marion born December 26, 1910 and Ramey Eugene Conner born September 24, 1914.'

The steps in O. Lonzo Conner's Masonic history is as follows: Initiation July 7, 1898, passed August 7, and raised September 24, 1898 in Frisco Lodge No. 24 at Fairland. Received Royal Arch Degree at Vinita Chapter No. 18 September 24, 1899; Commandery Degree at Muskogee Commandery No. 2 September 20, 1900; Council Degree from Muskogee Council No. 2 May 26, 1915; Consistory Degree in India Consistory McAlester April 1907; Honorary Degree K. C. H. Washington D. C. October 1911. Royal Order of Scotland, Washington D. C. October 1911; received the 33rd. Degree Honorary October 28, 1915 at Washington D. C.; elected Knight of the Red Cross Constantine in October 1914, by St. Louis Conclave No. 19; elected Junior Grand Warden of the Grand Lodge A. F. and A. M. of the state of Oklahoma in February 1916, Senior Grand Warden February 1917; Deputy Grand Master February 1918 and Grand Master April 1919. He was also the first Exalted Ruler of Vinita Lodge 1162 B. P. O. E.

CHIEF LEVI GRITTS

WILLIAM LITTLE

Flippin, Mrs. J. F. (See Grant)—Mary Lane Little, born June 24, 1875 in Walker Co., Ga., educated at Vinita. Married September 30, 1894 James Fugett Flippin, born January 8, 1870 in Denton County, Texas. They are the parents of Mary Theresa, born June 29, 1896; Ruth Aline, born January 1, 1902 and Rebecca Lane Flippin, born May 16, 1905. Mr. Flippin has been prominently identified with the Farmers Bank and Trust Co. from its inception.

Joseph Martin, born in Charlottsville, Virginia in 1840, as a fur trader and planter he became quite wealthy. He held the following military offices in the revolutionary army: Captain of the Transylvania Militia, elected in March 1776, became Mayor February 17, 1779 and Lieutenant Colonel in March 1781. His daughter Rachel married Daniel Davis and the oldest son, Martin Davis, born August 27, 1809, married April 29, 1980 Julia Ann Tate, born January 5, 1822 in Habersham County, Georgia. Martin Davis died November 11, 1859 and his widow died September 28, 1882.

Martin and Julia Anna Davis were the parents of Jane, who married William C. Patton; Rachel, married George W. Hill; Martin and Theresa Lane Davis, born September 11, 1853, married February 29, 1872 William Little, born July 8, 1840 in Walker County, Georgia. Theresan Lane Little died March 21, 1888, and William Little died April 23, 1911. William and Theresa Lane Little were the parents of Mrs. Mary Lane Flippin.

Agnew, Walter S. (See Grant, Foreman and Cordery)—Walter Scott Agnew was born May 16, 1842. Served the Confederacy in Company B, First Cherokee Mounted Rifles and Company E, Second Cherokee Mounted Volunteers. He married in December, 1866, Sarah Seabolt nee Riley, daughter of Felix and Susie (Bigby) Riley. Mr. and Mrs. Agnew had one child, Laura Agnew, who married William H. Robinson. Mrs. Sarah Agnew died and Mr. Agnew married in July, 1870, Mary Elizabeth, daughter of Andrew Jackson and Lucy (Vickory) Cobb, born May 19, 1849. Mr. and Mrs. Agnew are residents of Muskogee. They are the parents of: Ellen, John Lowrey, Robert Miller, Walter Lee and Josephus E. Agnew.

Walter Scott Agnew was elected a member of Council from Canadian District in 187, Senator in 1889 and District Judge of the same District in 1895.

LULU M. HEFNER

Hefner, Mrs. Lulu M. (See Ward)—Lula May, daughter of James Marion and Annie Henrietta (Prather) Tittle was born August 9, 1874, educated at Vinita and the Female Seminary; married at Lenapah December 29, 1892 John Emory Heffner. They are the parents of: Roy Emory, born March 13, 1903, and married Fredda Vinyard; Edith Lena, born December 18, 1905; Helen K., born October 2, 1905 and Ruby L., born January 20, 1907.

Handsome attractive and resourcesful, she has been more than ordinarily successful in business. At the time Nowata was beginning to be one of the busy oil town of Oklahoma, Mrs. Heffner opened and conducted the first millinery store in the city, run on a regular metropolitan basis. She disposed of this business and drilled a producing oil well on her own property. This stimulus to the first lady oil operator in Oklahoma was followed by more oil wells, and so keen was her discernment and judgment that she had ahd the rare honor of never having some of her surplus in Nowata realty, she is the largest lady property owner in the city. Mrs. Heffner finds time to take part in the social affairs of the community, and is a favorite member of different clubs. She is also active in all movements for public welfare.

MRS. DR. LOU G. HOWELL

Howell, Mrs. Lou G. (See Cordery, Grant, Ghigau and Oolootsa)—Lou Gott Harris, born at Ft. Gibson July 31, 1886, educated at Nowata High school and Oswego, Kansas, graduated from the former; she was married January 7, 1905 to Dr. Dumont D. Howell, born January 14, 1874 in Murphy, North Carolina, graduated from the Nashville Medical College in 1903. Died December 6, 1919; he was a Mason and Elk. They are the parents of: Sue Catherine, born April 25, 1906. Alfred Dumont, born April, 30, 1908; Lucile Genevieve, born December 2, 1912 and Margaret Imogene, born December 2, 1914.

Charles Joseph Harris, born April 6, 1848, married Emma J. Walker. He died January 30, 1892. They were the parents of Mrs. Lou Howell.

D. W. LIPE

Lipe, Nannie E. (See Oolootsa and Downing)—Major Downing of the British Army married in the early part of the eighteenth century a full blood Cherokee of the Wolf Clan. Their only daughter Nancy was the mother of Margaret McSwain who married Avery Vann and their eldest child; Joseph Vann whose Cherokee name was Teaultle, was born on February 11, 1798. He married Catherine Rowe. Joseph Vann was a signer of the constitution of 1827 from Cooweescoowee Dist,, elected assistant Chief of the Cherokee Nation September 9, 1839 and August 1859. Joseph and Catherine Vann were the parents of Mary Francis who married Edwin Archer. Mr. and Mrs. Archer's daughter, Mary Elizabeth, born October 19, 1847 married Mar. 1, 1871 DeWitt Clinton Lipe, born February 17, 1840 in Tahlequah District. Mary E. Lipe died March 18, 1914. D. W Lipe died December 6, 1916. They were the parents of; Nannie E. born June 14, 1872; Victoria Susie born February 1, 1874 and Lola Vann Lipe born January 28, 1877. By a previous marriage Mr. Lipe had a son, John Gunter Lipe born December 16, 1864 and died May 19, 1913.

Misses Nannie E. and Lola V. Lipe belong to the Wolf Clan the Cherokee name of the former is, Conaluga and that of the latter is Ahniwake. They are both graduates of the Oswego Female College of Oswego, Kansas, and University Preparatory School, Claremore. DeWitt Clinton Lipe attended the Male Seminary from 1852 to 1854. Handsome, efficient, gracious with the soul of integrity, Mr. Lipe was often called upon to serve his people. Elected clerk of Cooweescoowee District January 21, 1874 and August 2, 1875; Senator August 5, 1877, National Treasurer November 11, 1879, Senator August 3, 1885 from which he resigned and was elected for another four year term as National Treasurer on November 14, 1895. On the coming of Statehood he was elected County Clerk of Rogers County for the first two terms.

Walter A. Mayes

Mayes, Walter A. (See Grant, Foreman, Adair, Ross and Conrad)—Charlette, daughter of Reverend Jesse and Eliza (Wilkerson) Bushyhead, was born March 16, 1830. Married May 21, 1846, George Washington, son of Samuel and Nannie (Adair) Mayes, born November 5, 1824. He was a member of Captain M. Adair's Company, Second Cherokee ounted Rifles. He was a member of the Committee representing Going Snake District in the Confederate Cherokee Council, from 1862 to 1865. He was elected a member of the Cherokee Citizenship Commission on December 4, 1879; and elected High Sheriff of the Cherokee Nation in November 1891. Mrs. Charlette Mayes died January 23, 1878, and he died October 28, 1894. They were the parents of Jesse Bushyhead, George Washington, Nancy Jane, Elizabeth, Edward, Walter Adair, John Thompson, and Samuel Houston Mayes.

Walter Adair Mayes was born December 9, 1860, and married in December 1890, Nannie Wright, daughter of Joseph Rogers and Mary (Hicks) McCoy, born March 25, 1866. They are the parents of: Hall, George Washington, Mary Diana, Jesse Lamar, and Joseph Mayes.

R. L. FARRAR

Farrar, Richard L. (See Cordery)—Sallie Martin, daughter of Henry Hawkins and Mary Savannah (Harris) Oliver, was born June 24, 1876. She married December 21, 1890, Richard Lee Farrar, born February 18, 1866, in Gibson County, Tennessee. They are the parents of Jessie May, born February 11, 1896; and Bruce Farrar, born Sept. 5, 1898.

Mary Savannah, daughter of James S. Harris, born January 12, 1858, married December 8, 1874, Henry Hawkins Oliver, who was born November 28, 1856, in Milton County, Georgia. They were the parents of Mrs. Richard L. Farrar.

GEORGE W. FIELDS

Fields, George W.—Born in the same room, on July 10, 1882, in which the sterling old patriot, Stand Watie died on September 9, 1871, Senator George W. Fields seems to have in some mystical way been imbued with a similar character of reticent perseverance. Reared in a community of earnest honest integrity, where the mass was willing to receive limited educations and settle to lives of arduous husbandry, thus contributing to the sane thinking and deliberate backbone of the glorious republic. George Fields, as others of his mould have done since the dawn of civilization, by steady pertinacity, gained by frugal care and close application on a common school education and while working on the farm and closing his days in the public schools came to him the listless longing for a Male Seminary education, the acme of solicitude of the patriotic Cherokee. The quiet, gentlemanly and agreeable country lad, stintingly saved small sums that gained the coveted goal of an entrance into the Seminary, where he graduated on May 28, 1902, using as the subject of his oration, Sequoyah. The best indication of the regard that the instructors and fellow pupils had of him could be gained by their soft inflection of speech when they spoke of him.

Of generous physical proportions, manager of the Seminary baseball and football teams, an athlete of more than ordinary acquirements, he listened not to the call of the plaudits of the diamond and roped arena, but sought the quieter vocations, the teacher and farmer.

On April 3, 1904, Mr. Fields married at Southwest City, Missouri, Miss Jennie, the accomplished and talented daughter of Mr. and Mrs. John Glass of Chelsea, Oklahoma.

Mr. Fields like all of the prominent Cherokees, transferred to the State of Oklahoma an equal mead of patriotic love and fealty that they had evinced for their Nation, as they felt that it was a natural fruition.

A democrat, he was nominated and elected as the first register of deeds of Delaware, his native county, in the first state election. The approval of his course in this office was bestowed in reelection by his fellow citizens, the people that had known him from boyhood. Five years were encompassed in these two terms and he was then elected State Senator from the thirtieth district in 1912. In the senate he never missed a roll call, was seldom heard on the floor but had the reputation of being one of the most eifficent workers of that body of able men.

In 1913, he was admitted to the bar and opened an office early in 1920, when he became established in Oklahoma City where his volume of business, within two years would bear favorable comparison with any in the state. His reticence is that of the anglist and omniverous student. As Attorney in the Texas-Cherokee suit for reparations for one and one-half million acres of land, he has developed and is forwarding the largest civil case of the Cherokees.

Fraternally Mr. Fields is a Mason of the 32nd degree, an Elk and Shriner; also a member of the American Legion, Oklahoma State Bar Association and of the Christian church.

CHAS. W. POOLE

Poole, Emma G. (See Ghigau and Sanders).—Emma Gazelle, daughter of William W. and Julia (Van Olhausen) Musick, born in St. Louis, Missouri, March 20, 1864, educated in that city and graduated from the Kndergarden Instruction School, taught in that branch in St. Louis and in Worcester Academy at Vinita, married January 11, 1888 in St. Louis Mission Charles Walton Poole, born in the Cherokee Nation, October 25, 1859, son of John and Sarah Myra (Harlan) Poole. He was the pioneer merchant of Chelsea, and postmaster of that place for nine years. He was a 32nd degree Mason and Shriner. He died May 14, 1910. Mrs. Poole is an Eeastern Star and White Shriner, a Methodist and belongs to the Dephian Club.

Charles W. and Emma G. Poole were the parents of Charles Walton, born September 25, 1889; Carlisle A., born April 21, 1894; Scott O., born October 2, 1889, enlisted in the Navy in 1917, was a yoeman on the Minnesota, and honorably discharged in January 1920; Gladys C., born August 29, 1901 member Senior class Chelsea High School 1921 .

The parents of Emma G. Poole were natives of Virginia; her father was born September 2, 1862, and her mother, October 25, 1829.

JOHN E. DeLOZIER

DeLozier, Mrs. Georgia (See Adair)—Georgia Virginia Adair was born in Whitfield County, Georgia, January 29, 1869, educated in Flint and and Cooweescoowee District, Indian Territory. Married near Adair January 8, 1888 to Reuben E. DeLozier, born June 20th, 1855 at Osceola, Mo. He died at Adair, Okla., April 23, 1921. They were the parents of Fountain G. born Sept. 19, 1888; Manford E. born Sept. 25, 1891; John Edward, born July 16th, 1893; Ralph Adair, born April 4th, 1896; Hazel M. born August 18, 1898 and Vivian V. DeLozier born September 3, 1901.

John Edward DeLozier was a Master Mason. John Edward enlisted in the World War September 23, 1917 at Camp Travis, Texas. Assigned to Company A 344th Machine Gun Batallion, 90th Division. Sailed for France June 21, 1918 and arrived July 7. Corporal DeLozier was carrying ammunition for his platoon in the St. Mihiel drive, when an officer asked for volunteers to go forward and get military information and he offered his services. In crossing the battlefield he was struck on the helmet by a machine gun bullet which severely wounded him in the head, from which he died the following day, Sept 15, 1918. Te body of the young hero was returned to Adair and buried with military honors May 29, 1921.

Edward Alexander, son of John and Ann Berry (Graham) Adair was born at Dalton, Georgia, February 25, 1847, was a member of Company C, Edmondson's Batallion, Georgia Confederate service. Married in October 1867 to Narcissa M. Harrison, born December 25, 1846, in Murray County, Georgia. He was elected sheriff of Cooweescoowee District August 5, 1889 and was elected Councilor from the same District August 7, 1899. He was killed by runaway team December 3, 1901 and Mrs. Adair lives at Adair, Oklahoma.

DARIUS E. WARD

Ward, Darius E. (See Ward and Ooloötsa) —Darius Edwin, son of James and Esther Susan (Hoyt) Ward was born on Beatties Prairie, Delaware District, November 23, 1854. Educated in Nazareth Hall, Northampton County, Pennsylvania. Married at Bethlehem, Pennsylvania November 20, 1875 Sarah Caroline, daughter of Mrs. John Ritter, born September 27, 1857 in Bucks County, Penn. She died February 29, 1896. They were the parents of Minnie Esther, born September 2, 1876, married Boone Forst Gray; Jay Herbert, born February 10, 1879, James Darius, born October 20, 1880, Hindman Hoyt, born December 14, 1885 and died June 13, 1906; Sidney Rueds, born January 19, 1888; Gertrude Irene, born July 31, 1889; Ruth Edna born June 22, 1893; Sarah Ruby, born February 3, 1896. Mr. Ward married August 9, 1897 Mary Murphy nee Hester, born July 1, 1870 in Davidson County, Tennessee. They were the parents of Martha Ann born Nov. 14, 1898. Mr. Ward is a cabinet maker. He belongs to the Holly clan and his Cherokee name is Kee-too-wha-gi. Is P. S. R. of Knights of Pythias, a member of the Moravian church, was Secretary of the "Old Settlers Commissioners, elected a member of the Cherokee Board of Education November 15, 1900 having previously been the Inspector of the building of the Female Seminary on the part of the Nation. Was County Commissioner of Cherokee County 1910-1912.

S. R. LEWIS

Lewis, S. R.—One of this nation's oldest families at Jamestown in 1607 together with those other pioneers they began hewing this great nation from a Virginia wilderness.

This family has direct lines of descendency through the Randolphs, Washingtons, Carters and Lees each of which bears many pages of historical importance. Each epoch of the nation's history has brought forward a Lewis to fulfill his destiny in lending his effort to the up-building of the country. For the purpose of this family's connection with the Cherokee Nation the line will begin of record when Thomas Jefferson sent his young kinsman Merriweather Lewis to join Clark in the eventful exploration of the great Northwest. From the landing of the cavaliers in Virginia to the present day the

Lewis family has been conspicuous in the affairs of this great Republic.

Alexander S. Lewis was born November 25, 1842 at Blountsville, Alabama and is the son of Rev. Stephen M. Lewis born in 1819 also in the state of Alabama an ordained minister in the Presbyterian church, removed to the State of Texas in 1850 was a Chaplain in Col. George Baylors regiment of Texas Cavalry Confederate Army and served throughout the Civil War in such capacity. Rev. Stephen M. Lewis was a direct male relative of the family of Merriwether Lewis, the great explorer above mentioned. He died in 1907 at the age of 88 years. Alexander S. Lewis settled at Dawson, Tulsa County, Oklahoma, in the early eighties of the nineteenth century, having moved from Texas, where his parents had lived since their removal from Alabama, and in common with the best families of the old South they had been reduced from affluence to poverty by the Civil War. Mr. Lewis married Elizabeth P. Dawson, related to the well known Dawson famliy of the Cherokee Nation, whose members were admitted to Cherokee citizenship after the Civil War. With their arrival at Dawson the family had again acquired a small competence, but through all their vicissitudes they had retained and cherished the priceless inheritance of gentility and integrity. The children were given the best educatonal advantages the parents could afford, which was the equipment with which Stephen Riley Lewis entered business life. From his beginning in the small town he has through honest enterprise arrived at the point of success which rehabilitates the old family name in financial prominence, while it always held the social position that the family standard at all times required.

Stephen Riley Lewis was born December 27, 1873 in Hill County, Texas. He was educated in the Dawson neighborhood and in the Quaker Mission at Skiatook, Oklahoma. He was admitted to the practice of law by the United States Interior Department in January 1902, admitted to practice in the Supreme Courtof Oklahoma June 10, 1910 and the United States Supreme Court March 20, 1916. He married on March 23, 1898, Minnie Carter born in Cooweescoowee District of the Cherokee Nation September 16, 1876. She was the daughter of David Tecumseh and Emma Williams (Chambers) Carter, and first cousin to Congressman Charles D. Carter. Mrs. Minnie Lewis died December 20, 1898. Stephen Riley Lewis married June 12, 1907, Elizabeth Belle Scrimsher, born September 3, 1873. She is the daughter of John Gunter Scrimsher, born August 17, 1835 who was educated in the schools of Tahlequah and at the Male Seminary, taught at Green Leaf school in 1859 and married on Septembr 15th of that Juliette Melvin Candy, born August 7, 1841. John Gunter Scrimsher enlisted in the Confederate service at the beginning of the Civil war and was a captain in Colonel Stand Watie's regiment. At the close of the war he settled on Dog Creek in Cooweescoowee District, and was honored by that district in the following elections: Sheriff, 1877; Senator 1883, 1887 and 1897; District Judge 1893 and he was elected by ouncil a delegate to Washington in November 1883. Judge Scrimsher was killed on his farm by lightning July 5, 1905. Judge and Mrs. Scrimsher were the parents of Sarah Catherine born July 27, 1866 and married William E. Sanders; Elizabeth Bell; Ernest Vivian, born July 24, 1875, and Juliette born January 12, 1878, married Abraham Vandyke Robinson.

Mrs. Lewis' paternal grand-parents were Martin Matthew Scrimsher, born in 1806 in Blount County, Tennessee; married September 22, 1831 at Creek Path, Alabama to Elizabeth Hunt Gunter, born in September 1804.

Martin Scrimsher was one of the argonauts of 1849 that made the trip to California. He died in 1865, and Mrs. Elizabeth Hunt Scrimsher died a sudden death at the residence of Judge Scrimsher in Claremore on February 14, 1877. She was the daughter of John Gunter an Englishman, who came to the Cherokee Country East of the Mississippi in 1760. He was a powder maker and owned and operated a mill at Nicojack. His wife was Catherine, a full blood Cherokee of the Paint Clan. She died August 11, 1835, and he died the 28th of the same month and year.

Mrs. Elizabeth Lewis' maternal grandparents were George Washington, and Elizabeth Hughes (Bell) Candy. George Washington Candy was District Judge of Flint District in 1845-7.

WILLIAM PENN ADAIR

Adair, William P. (See Grant, Ghigau, and Adair)—William Penn, son of Dr. Walter Thompson and Mary B. Adair was born January 10, 1861, educated at Male Seminary. Married at Salina, April 12, 1891 Margaret, daughter of Virgil and Eliza Rogers, born May 25, 1875. They are the parents of DeWitt Jacob, born January 14, 1892, married Josephine Hume; Walter Thompson, born June 2, 1894, married Lina B. Reagan; Mary Ellen, September 18, 1897 and William Commodore Adair, born October 17, 1905.

Mr. Adair belongs to the Deer Clan and his Cherokee name is Augona. He is the owner of the telephone exchange at Adair.

John and Edward Adair, Scotchman and brothers, married into the Cherokee Nation in about 1770. John was the father of Walter Adair, called "Black Watt' and Edward had a son, Walter Scott Adair, called "Red Watt' Adair. Dr. Walter Thompson Adair, son of Geo. Washington and grandson of "Black Watt' married Mary Buffington Adair the daughter of "Red Watt" Adair and they were the parents of William Penn Adair, the subject of sketch.

Mary Buffington Adair graduated from the Female Seminary in the first class in February, 1855. While the parents of Mrs. Adair were both Rogers' before their marriage, they were not blood relatives.

E. R. GOURD

Gourd, Ellis R. (See Conrad and Riley)—Ellis R., son of Ellis R. and Susan (Riley) Gourd was born April 22, 1864. Educated in the Cherokee national schools. Married October 10, 1886 Martha Miller, born September 15, 1865. They are the parents of John Ellis, William Penn, Bonnielynn and Lucinda R. Gourd.

Rattlinggourd Conrad married Polly Toney and their son Jackson Rattlinggourd was born in 1809. Married Elsie Wilson, born in 1808. He was judge of Tahlequah District from 1862 until 1873. Mrs. Elsie R. Gourd died October 4, 1884 and he died April 10, 1885. Their son Ellis R. Gourd married Susan, daughter of Felix and Annie (Hendricks) Riley. Ellis R. Gourd Sr. died March 22, 1864.

JOHN GUNTER SANDERS

Sanders, John Gunter (See Ghigau, Sanders, Oolootsa and Adair)—John Gunter, son of William Edward and Sarah Catherine (Scrimsher) Sanders was born at the Sanders homestead, southwest of Claremore Mound on April 23, 1891. He was educated at Claremore Public Schools, A. and M. College, Stillwater, Okla, and Henry Kendall College, Tulsa, Okla. Gentlemanly and reserved Mr. Sanders is one of the foremost and most progressive members of his tribe. Of distinguished lineage it is but naturel that he should take a leaders place in the councils of the Cherokee.

His father was born in Going Snake District April 2, 1861, just as the calamitous war clouds spread desolation over the happy homes of the Cherokees. Four years later the impoverished tribe returned to their desolate land, when during the next several years not only was the educational advantages inadequate but stark poverty was general in the entire border land. During these years of privations William Edward Sanders passed through the ordinary school years with scant educational advantages. He did not despair but worked and applied himself until it would have been hard to imagine that Halsell's genial and polished young ranch boss had not had the advantages of a university. His party in seeking a strong man for sheriff of Cooweescoowee District chose him in 1885. He was elected and gave such general satisfaction that he was easily reelected. He refused to run in 1889 and devoted himself to improving his farm on Verdigris River. This farm site had in the first quarter of the eighteenth century, been the location of a peach orchard that was owned and maintained by Claremore's band of Osages and for that reason it had been known locally as the "Osage Peach Orchard."

Mr. Sanders was married at the residence of his friend, Judge Walter Adair Starr, on March 2, 1890 to Sarah Catherine, the popular and gracious daughter of Judge and Mrs. John Gunter Scrimsher, born July 27, 1866. Two happy years sped by for them, John Gunter was born and at the succeeding August election the suffrages of a satisfied constituency recalled the father to the office of sheriff. But on January 28, 1892 the dark angel of death called the blessed mother, after a few days of pneumonia. So well had Sheriff Sanders served his people that they elected him to the Senate at the elction of 1893. As sheriff and county commissioner, Mr. Sanders is at present one of the most popular and respected citizens of Rogers County. Adair, Gunter, Sanders and Candy, a noble heritage to represent and defend by life's actions.

John G. Sanders, the subject of this sketch, is a member of the Cherokee Executive Council (The business committee designated to attend to Cherokee tribal affairs.) He has devoted a good part of his time during the past two years to tribal matters and is one of the delegates appointed to represent the Cherokee Executive Council before the Congress at Washington D. C. at the present Session. Mr. Sanders lives in the City of Tulsa with his uncle, Mr. S. R. Lewis, and is a very popular and highly respected young man.

BUENA VISTA WHITE

Buena Vista White—Daughter of Jackson and Harriett White, Talala, Okla., born October 22, 1891. Graduated from Henry Kendall College June 9, 1909; Hardin College, Mexico, Mo., degree of L. B. and Voice, May 28, 1912. Did special work in voice with Composer Daniel Prothero, Chicago; special work in Pedagogy at University of Chicago; was special instructor in city schools of Collinsville, Claremore, Tulsa, Bartlesville and Muskogee; at present Musical Supervisor in Central High School, Muskogee.

White, Mrs. J. C. (See Grant and Duncan) —Helen Duncan, daughter of George W. and Mary (McLaughlin) Hughes, born at St. Gibson April 21, 1874. Educated at Tahlequah and the Female Seminary. Married at Ft. Gibson December 25, 1890, Jackson Calhoun, son of Joseph and Harriett White born February 17, 1862 in Calhoun county, Mississippi. They are the parents of Buena Vista White, born October 22, 1891. Graduated from the Henry Kendall college June 9, 1901; graduated from Hardin College, Mexico, Missouri, May 28, 1912 with B. L. degree and Voice. Has done much special work in voice with composer Daniel Prothero of Chicago; also special work in Pedagogy at the University of Chicago. Was special instructor in the city schools of Collinsville 1913-14, Claremore 1915, Tulsa, Bartlesville and Muskogee; was special instructor in music at the Northeastern Normal at Tahlequah, summer of 1915. Is at present musical supervisor at Central High School Muskogee.

Mr. White conducts a grain business at Talala. He is a member of the W. O. W. and Modern Woodmen Fraternities.

The royal families of Melaghlins of the Hy-Nial race of Meath are so named because they are the descendants of Maelseachlain II, king of Ireland who died in 1022 A. D. In the mutations of time the name has been changed to McLaughlin, or the sons of Laughlin.

MRS. EMMA CAREY

Carey, Mrs. Emma. (See Downing and Thompson).—Emma McDonald was born at Fort Gibson, August 13, 1871, educated at Western Female Seminary, Oxford, Ohio, and Presbyterian Mission, Muskogee, from which she graduated. She taught five years in the public schools of the Cherokee Nation, and married at Fort Gibson January 27, 1894, William Vann Carey, educated in the Cherokee public schools and Male Seminary. He was a handsome man of charming personality, had the inherent polish of a scholar and wrote an excellent hand. He was elected Clerk of the Cooweescoowee District August 3, 1885, and August 1, 1887, and was President of the Cherokee Board of Education from 1893 to 1897. He died June 19, 1900.

Mr. and Mrs. Carey were the parents of: Fiona Vann, born October 28, 1895, graduated from Stevens College, Columbia, Missouri, and is a commercial artist in Chicago. Sansa Vera Pann, born April 5, 1897, educated at Stevens College Conservatory of Music, and is one the Lyceum and Chautauqua circuit; Majora Bartles, born November 27, 1898, graduated from Stevens College and is instructor in Domestic Science in Nowata City Schools; and William Vann Carey is a member of the 1922 class at Westminster, Fulton, Missouri.

William Vann Carey was the son of Rev. Walker and Malinda (Downing) Carey and Mrs. Emma Carey is the daugter of Jack and Jane (Scott) McDonald.

GEORGE ADAIR

Adair, George (See Adair and Grant)—George Adair, born at Braggs May 24, 1887, educated in the Cherokee Public Schools. Married at Nowata in 1907 Edna F., daughter of Mr. and Mrs. Adolphus McCoy. He enlisted for the World War on September 19, 1917 and was assigned to the 36th Division, was taken from the firing line in France and placed with other full blood Cherokees in the telephone service, where they foiled the German "listeners in" by repeating, receiving, and transmitting the military orders in the Cherokee language Young Adair, who like all full blood Cherokees, is intensely patriotic and counts this service among the proudest days of his life, for was he not fighting shoulder to shoulder with his kilted kinsmen of Scotland.

Henry Ganoe, son of George M. and Catherine (Fields) Adair married Caroline Bunch and they were the parents of George Adair (See sketch of his brother, Levi Adair)

DAVIS HILL

Hill, (See Grant and Ghigau)—Davis Hill, born Sept. 21, 1863 at Lafayette, Georgia was educated at Ringold and Cedar Grove, Ga. He married at Vinita on November 29, 1888 Fannie Elizabeth Parks, born January 9, 1871 at Elk Mills, Missouri. She was educated at the Orphan Asylum and Howard Payne College, Fayette, Missouri. Mr. and Mrs. Davis Hill are the parents of: George Robert born Oct. 26, 1890; James Julian, born Sept. 20, 1892; Wm. Thompson, born February 22, 1895; Rachel born August 23, 1897; John Ruskin born May 18, 1899; Maria Anna born April 6, 1901; Francis Elizabeth born July 5, 1903; Mary Davis born January 25, 1906; Orval Hall, born Feb. 12, 1908 and Josephine Almira born Sept. 16, 1911.

Mrs. Davis Hill is the daughter of Thomas Jefferson Parks, born Oct. 18, 1821 and married Anna Thompson born Sept. 11, 1830. He died May 6, 1883.

Joseph Martin born about 1740 in Albermarle County Virginia; he was elected Capt. of Transylvania Militia of the Revolutionary army in 1776; became Major on Feb. 17, 1779 and Lieut. Col. in March 1781. His daughter Nannie married Jeter Lynch and was the great grand-mother of Mrs. Davis Hill. Sabra the daughter of Joseph Martin and the sister of Mrs. Nannie Lynch married Daniel Davis and was the great gand-mother of Davis Hill.

Davis Hill has an enviable record as an ex-member of the state School Board which was an unsolicited appointment. Three of the sons of Mr. and Mrs. Hill saw service in the World War, James J. Capt. William T. and John R., while their brother George was rejected on account of being underweight.

LUCIEN W. BUFFINGTON

Buffington, Nancy G. (See Grant, Ghigau, Oolootsa, Adair and Ross)—Nancy G. Gunter was born February 19, 1867 in Ft. Smith, Arkansas. She was educated in the Public Schools of the Cherokee Nation and at the Female Seminary. She married at Vinita on April 4, 1886, Lucien Webster Buffington, born August 15, 1857 on Beatties Prairie, Deleware District. He was educated in the Public Schools of that vicinity. He came as a boy to Vinita, shortly after it was established and lived there until his death, which occurred on December 3, 1919. Quiet, unostentatious and gentlemanly he accumulated an extra competence and for several years preceding his death had been president of the Vinita National Bank. He was elected Town Lot Commissioner in 1886 and 1888. He was the son of William Wirt and Josephine (Bell) Buffington and his parental grand-parents were John Adair and Jennie (Martin) Bell.

Nancy G. Buffington is the daughter of Samuel and Fannie (Daniel) Gunter. Samuel Gunter was born March 16, 1840 in Skin Bayou District. He was the most intrepid and daring of Watie's Captains. He married in 1864 at Spencer Academy, Choctaw Nation, Fannie, the daughter of Robert Buffington and Ann (Taylor) Daniel. Robert B. Daniel was elected Senator from Deleware District in 1847, Clerk of the Senate in 1849 and Assistant Chief of the Cherokee Nation in 1871. He died January 16, 1873.

Captain Samuel and Fannie Gunter were the parents of Nannie E, John Edward, born November 12, 1869 and Samie, born July 31, 1873 and married Andrew Bell Cunningham.

GEORGE McCOY

McCoy, George (See Downing)—Major Downing, an officer in the British army, married a full blood Cherokee woman of the Wolf Clan and their daughter, Nannie, married —— McSwain. Their daughter, Elizabeth McSwain, married David Welch and they were the parents of Elizabeth, George Washington and Sidney Welch. Elizabeth Welch, born November 11, 1811, married Joshua Buffington, Isaac Ragsdale, —— Nix and Moses Alberty. George Washington Welch married Margaret Jones. He died March 20, 1840, and she died July 26, 1851.

Elizabeth Welch had no children by her marriage with Nix and her children by her other three marriages were: Nannie Buffington, David Welch and Winnie Jane Ragsdale; Eli Snow and George Washington Alberty.

George Washington and Margaret (Jones) Welch's children were: David, born September 15, 1819; Lemuel Bruenton, born September 15, 1824; Sidney, born July 9, 1827; Diana, born June 9, 1831; Margaret Ann, born December 17, 1832; George, born July 2, 1837, and Rosanna Welch, born in May, 1840. David Welch married Harriette Elizabeth Smithwick. Lemuel Bruenton Welch married Mary Ann Harris; Sidney Welch married Prince Albert Carnes, and John Wilkey. Diana Welch married Joseph Henry Carnes. Margaret Ann Welch married William Green Ward. George Welch married Nannie Jones. Rosanna Welch married McCoy and their children were: Julia Ann, George, John William, James Willis, Elizabeth, Lucinda, Sallie and Ida McCoy. Julia McCoy married William Oscar Ames. George McCoy married Victoria Fuller. John William McCoy married Isabelle King. James Willis McCoy married Martha Thomason. Lucinda McCoy married Irving Ward. Sallie McCoy married James Odle.

George and Victoria (Fuller) McCoy were the parents of William B., Ida R. V., and Elsie McCoy.

HOUSTON B. TEEHEE

Tehee, Houston Benge (See Oolootsa)—Houston Benge Tehee, whose activity has spelled success, is well known as the Register of the Treasury of the United States, whose name appears on all of the Government bonds issued during the world war period and is now a Vice-President and the Treasurer and General Manager of the Continental Asphalt and Petroleum Company, with headquarters in Oklahoma City. In various ways he has been closely identified with the development and upbuilding of this section of the country, his efforts being at all times a tangible element in the growth and progress that has wrought a most wonderful transformation in Oklahoma within the past few decades. Mr. Tehee was born in the Cherokee Nation, now Sequoyah County, Oklahoma, October 31, 1874, and is a representative of two of the old prominent Cherokee families ,the Teehee and Benge families. On the rolls of the Cherokee Nation his father is listed as seven-eighths Cherokee, Houston B. Teehee as five-eighths. His mother was a one-half Cherokee, her death occurring prior to the enrollment. The father, Stephen Teehee, was born in the Cherokee Nation of Georgia, December 25, 1837, and died in the Cherokee Nation of the Indian Territory in 1907. The mother, who bore the maiden name of Rhoda Benge, was born in the Cherokee Nation of the Indian Territory and passed away in 1886 at the comparatively early age of thirty-nine years. The father had come to the Indian Territory in young manhood. He had obtained a common school education in the Indian schools and afterward engaged in farming. Throughout his life he remained a student of men and events and became one of the most prominent citizens of the future State of Oklahoma. From 1867 until 1896 he was closely identified with public affairs of the Cherokee Nation ,serving as district clerk, as district solicitor and as circuit judge and his decisions in the last named office were noted for justice and impartiality. He served likewise as a member o fthe council and of the senate and was a member of the Executive Council. He likewise was made a member of the grand council and was assistant chief of the Nation. He also did most effective religious work, being a minister of the Baptist church and preaching extensively to his people. He spoke entirely in the Cherokee tongue and was universally honored and loved. His life was an example to the younger generation and an inspiration to all with whom he came in contact. He made his home near Sallisaw, Oklahoma. His was a large family, there being two sets of children, but only two of the first set survive; Houston B. and Stephen B., the latter now connected with the United States Merchant Marine. The name was originally Tehee but on the Indian rolls the spelling was changed to the present form. The name has figured prominently upon the pages of history of the Indian Territory and later in connection with the development of the State of Oklahoma and the work instituted by the father has been carried on by the son, for Houston B. Teehee Is today one of the prominent and influential residents of Oklahoma City.

His boyhood days were spent on the home farm, and imbued by the example of his father, his boyhood ambition was to become as good and upright a man as was his sire. He attended the common schools and afterward the Male Seminary at Tahlequah, while for one year he was a student in the Fort Worth University. He afterward returned to Tahlequah, where he engaged in mervchandising as a clerk for a period of ten years. He afterward spent two years as cashier in the Cherokee National Bank of Tahlequah. While thus engaged he studied law under the direction of the Hon. John H. Pitchford, who is now a Justice of the Supreme Court of Oklahoma, and in March, 1907, was admitted to the bar. He resigned his position as bank cashier in June, 1908, and entered upon the practice of his profession in Tahlequah, devoting his attention to probate oil and gas law. His practice soon became extensive and of a very important character, connecting him with much of the notable litigations heard in the courts of the district. He likewise became very prominent in connection with public affairs there, serving as Alderman of Tahlequah from 1902 until 1906. In 1908 he was elected to the office of Mayor and remained the chief executive of the city for two years. He also filled out an unexpired term as County Attorney, succeeding his law partner W. L. Johns. In 1911 and 1913 he was elected to represent his district in the third and fourth general assembly of Oklahoma, where he was noted as an authority on constitutional law, and in 1914 he was appointed United States probate attorney. In 1915 he went to Washington, D. C., as Register of the United States Treasury. His entire career has been marked by steady progress. The money which he obtained from the Cherokee strip was used in paying his tuition in the Fort Worth University. He thus early displayed his ambition and the elementary strength of his character. Step by step he has advanced, each forward step bringing him into a field of wider opportunities and broader usefulness. In 1919 he became Treasurer of the Seamans Oil Company and The R. E. Seamans Company, Inc., of New York City and Oklahoma City, and in 1921 he was made Treasurer and General Manager of all of the Seamans Oil Company interests under the name of the Continental Asphalt and Petroleum Company and was elected as one of its Vice-Presidents. While in Washington he was very active in promoting Indian matters generally, as well as in performing the duties of his position in connection with the United States Treasury. He now devotes the major part of his attention to his oil business. He makes his legal home in Cherokee County where he has a beautiful residence of the bungalow type, the house being surrounded by spacious grounds and being one of the show places of Cherokee County.

Mr. Teehee was married in Tahlequah, December 11, 1898, to Miss Mayme Hagelund, who was born in Marion, Alabama. Her parents were natives of Sweden and in their youth came to the United States, settling in Alabama, the father's death occurring in Marion. They were parents of two children. Mrs. Hagelund went to Chattanooga, Tennessee, and later became the wife of Dr. Stephen Foreman, one of the foremost physicians and leading citizens of the Cherokees. In 1893 they removed to Tahlequah. Mrs. Teehee occupies a very prominent social position. While they have no children, they have reared the children of Dr. Stephen and Mrs. Foreman since the latter's death. These are: Sue, now the wife of Roy J. Wiggins, an officer of the First State Bank of Tahlequah; John D. R. Foreman of Chattanooga, and Frank Foreman living in Sapulpa.

Mr. Teehee acts as counselor and adviser to many representatives of the Cherokee Nation. He greatly enjoys the out-of-doors and is a lover of nature and all that is beautiful. He also finds keenest pleasure in literature and his constant reading keeps him in touch with the trend of modern thought and progress. He belongs to Cherokee Lodge A. F. & A. M., the oldest Masonic lodge of Oklahoma, and he likewise has a membership with the Knights of Pythias and the Woodmen of the World, while his religious faith is indicated by his membership in the Presbyterian Church.

RICHARD FIELD

HON. JOHN GUNTER SCHRIMSHER

Schrimsher, John Gunter (See Ghigau, Oolootsa and Adair)—Katie, a fullblood Cherokee woman of the "Paint" clan, married John Gunter who in 1814 was a powder maker. He died August 28, 1835. And Mrs. Katie Gunter died August 11, 1835. Their daughter Elizabeth Hunt Gunter, born in September 1804, married September 22, 1831, Martin Matthew Schrimsher, born in 1806, in Blount County, Tennessee. Mr. Schrimsher was one of the emigrants to California in 1849, but only stayed in that section for a short time, returning to the Cherokee Nation. He died in 1856. Mrs. Schrimsher died at John G. Schrimsher's home near Claremore, February 14, 1877. Their son, John Gunter Schrimsher was born August 17, 1835. He was educated at the Male Seminary, and married on September 15th, 1859, Juliette Melisno, daughter of George Washington and Elizabeth Hughes (Bell) Candy, born August 7, 1841.

John G. Schrimsher settled in Cooweescoowee District before the Civil war, and represented that district in the Confederate Council from 1862 to 1866. He was a Captain in the Confederate service and at the close of the Civil war in 1867, was Sheriff of Cooweescoowee District; and was elected to the same office in 1877. He was elected Senator of Cooweescoowee District in 1879 and 1883; and was elected a delegate to Washington in 1883 and 1885. Was elected Judge of Cooweescoowee District in 1893, and Senator from the same District in 1897. He was killed by lightning on the morning of July 5, 1905.

Mr. and Mrs. Scrimsher were the parents of Sarah Catherine, who married William Edward Sanders; Elizabeth Bell who married Stephen Riley Lewis; Ernest Vivian, who married Susan Phillips; Juliette Melvina Schrimsher who married Abraham Vandyke Robinson.

Mrs. Schrimsher makes her home with her daughter, Mrs. Stephen Riley Lewis in Tulsa.

Mr. Schrimsher was a man of rare judgment and discernment. He was exceedingly popular as was evidenced by the number of offices to which he was elected. He was a member of the Masonic fraternity.

JOHN C. STARR

Starr, J. C. (See Ghigau and Grant)—James, son of Ezekial and Mary (Upshaw) Starr, was born in Tennessee on February 13, 1883. He served the Confederacy in Captain George Harlan Starr's company. His first wife was Sarah Byers and they were the parents of: Mary, who married James Manuel Price; Charlotte Elizabeth, who married Richard Welch, John Stocker and Henry Harrison Sanders. George Washington Starr was the third and youngest child of James and Sarah Starr. After the death of Mrs. Sarah Starr, James Starr married on December 28, 1869, Mrs. Emma Jane Evans, daughter of John and Rachel (Smith) Rider, born September 8, 1842. Mrs. Emma Jane Starr had by her first husband, one daughter: Minnie Louisa Evans, who married Teesee Chambers.

James and Emma Jane Starr were the parents of: John Caleb, Lulu, Jessie, Emma, Ezekial and Susan Starr. John Caleb Starr was born October 15, 1870. Graduated from the Male Seminary December 12, 1890 and received the following diplomas from the Fort Smith Business College: Bookkeeping, May 28, 1891; Penmanship, May 26, 1892; and Stenography May 29, 1893. He married October 16, 1894, Miss Elizabeth Belle Zimmerman, born March 9, 1870, in Clinton, Missouri. They are the parents of: Jessie Belle, James Clarence, Martha E. and Charles J. Starr. Jessie Belle Starr married John Turner Dameron.

John Caleb Starr, who was one of the best, if not the best, stenographers and penmen among the Cherokees, was the secretary to the Cherokee Commissioners that made the final roll of the tribe. When this task was finished he was admitted to the bar and became actively interested in oil production. He is at present one of the largest land owners in Oklahoma and his oil interests are so large that he requires a large office to house his records and employs a stenographer and bookkeeper, besides doing an immense amount of the executive and clerical work himself. His hobby is farming. An omniverous worker, a tireless student and an analytical thinker, Mr. Starr is always a man of the people and progressive citizen. His son, James Clarence Starr, has won laurels as an orator in the eastern colleges.

T. J. McGHEE Q. P. McGHEE

McGhee, Quilliki P.—Quilliki Phillips, son of Thomas Jefferson and Martha (Hanna) McGhee, is a native of Delaware District in which District he was educated. He married Miss Letitia Hanna and they were the parents of two children. Mrs. Letitia McGhee died and he married her sister.

Thomas Jefferson, son of Ambrose and Judith (Cochran) McGhee, married Martha Hanna and they were the parents of: Samuel Albert, James M., Thomas Jefferson, Viola, Clero, Saladin C., Joseph Fox and Quilliki P. McGhee. Thomas Jefferson McGhee, Sr. was First Lieutenant of Company E of the First Cherokee Mounted Volunteers in the Confederate service. He was elected Shriff of Delaware District in 1867 and was elected Clerk of the same District in 1880, 1881, 1883, 1885 and 1889. A brilliant interpreter and orator, he was one of the most popular and progressive citizens of Delaware District. Reared by such a father it was but natural that the talented and forceful son, Quilliki P. should be endowed with a logical and analytical mind that would render him one of the most successful attorneys and jurists of northeastern Oklahoma. He was admitted to the bar in December 1914 and his large legal practice has rendered him a wealthy one. While active in the councils of the republican party he never allowed his name to be used in connection with any office until 1920, when he was elected County Judge of Ottawa County by an immense majority.

OCE HOGSHOOTER
Secretary of the Nighthawk Katoowah

JANANNA BALLARD

W. H. BALLARD

Ballard, W. H. (See Grant, Ghigua, and Ward)—William, son of Archibald and Annie (Fields) Ballard, was born May 29, 1852. Married December 26, 1871 Charlotte Mayes and they were the parents of: Janana, Anna, Ruth May, Ethel Savilla and Zoe Wyly Ballard.

This family furnished the largest number of graduates from the Seminaries, they being as follows: Janana in 1896, Anna in 1897, Lucinda in 1899, Sarah Eleanor in 1902, William Houston in 1904 and Ruth May in 1906. Miss Janana is and has been a teacher in the Northeastern State Normal since its inception. Anna married Crawford Conner. Lucinda married William Lee Harlan. Sarah Eleanor married Roy Woods. Ruth May married Frank Fleming. Ethel Savilla married Robert Hall. Zoe Wyly married Harold Bunch. William Houston, born May 29, 1884, married Anna Buchanan, born December 25, 1889. They were the parents of Tesquantnee Swimmer Ballard, born February 14, 1906. Mrs. Anna Ballard is now deceased. William Houston Ballard was elected District Clerk of Delaware County in 1910 and 1912. He is at present Deputy Clerk of Muskogee County.

MARY RILEY ROBERTS

Roberts, Mrs. W. A. (See Reily and Ghigau)—Mary, daughter of Samuel King and Sallie A. (Rider) Riley was born at Doaksville, Choctaw Nation, February 2, 1866, educated at the Cherokee Orphan Asylum. Married July 29, 1885 William Emory Roberts, born September 24, 1861 near Parkerburg, Indiana. They are the parents of: James Thomas, born November 20, 1886, married Mabel N. Howard and has one son, James Thomas Roberts, a soldier in the World War. Charles Arthur, born September 19, 1891, served with the 20th Engineers in the Wohdr War, married Ethel Shufeldt; William Edward born November 5, 1888, was a Second Lieutenant in the World War; Floyd Bryan Roberts, born October 29, 1896.

Of reserved, gracious presence, Mrs. Roberts has always been a social favorite. She is a Methodist, Eastern Star, White Shriner and Historian of the United Daughters of the Confederacy.

DR. JAMES GRADY HARRIS

Harris, Dr. James Grady (See Cordery)—Parker Collins born November 9, 1845, married Angeline Davis born July 19, 1859, in DeKalb Co., Ala. They are the parents of Robert Harris, born Dec. 19, 1882; Colonel Parker Harris, born July 3, 1885; Emily Harris, born April 29, 1887; Dr. James Grady Harris, born February 18, 1889; Susie Ella Harris, born September 4, 1890; Mary Vann Harris, born October 10, 1893; George Harris, born November 14, 1895; Martha Harris, born June 2, 1899; Ida Harris, born Marhc 1, 1901, and Catherine Harris.

Dr. James Grady Harris was educated in the Male Seminary, Northeastern State Normal, and the Medical Department of the University of Tennessee, graduating from the latter institution. He is a 32nd degree Mason, Shriner and Elk. He is also a member of the Kappa Psi Medical Fraternity. He served in the U. S. Army during the World War as Captain, and served at the Base Hospital at Camp Bowie, Texas, from September 1917 to September 1918; and Assistant to Camp Surgeon, Camp Shelby, Mississippi from September 1918 to April 1919. He is a member of the Muskogee County and State Medical Societies, and of the Southern Medical Association.

MRS. EMILY W. BREEDLOVE

WILLIAM T. WILSON
OF
WILSON'S ROCK, ARK.

Breedlove—Malinda, daughter of William and Jamima (Bryant) Wharton, was born in Virginia December 25, 1803. Married in 1819 Thomas, son of John D. and Martha (Holmes) Chisholm, born in 1793 and died November 12, 1834. They were the parents of: Jane Elizabeth, Alfred Finney, William Wharton, and Narcissa Clerk Chisholm. Mrs. Malinda Chisholm married in January 1836 William, son of George and Ruth (Springston) Wilson, born October 14, 1911. She died February 19, 1864 and he died June 30, 1897. They were the parents of Emily Walker and William Wilson. Jane Elizabeth Chisholm married Joseph Blagne Lynde and Caswell Wright Bruton. Alfred Finney Chisholm married Margaret Harper. William Wharton Chisholm married Susie Pindar; they had two children: Alice, who married James Henry Cobb and Narcissa Chisholm, married Matthew Archer and Frank Taylor.

Narcissa Clark Chisholm married Robert Latham Owen; they were the parents of Major William Otway Owen, M. D. and United States Senator Robert Latham Owen. Emily Walker Wilson born October 5, 1836 married October 1, 1875 Napoleon Bonaparte, son of James W. and Maria (Winchester) Breedlove, born August 11, 1825 in Sumner County, Tennessee. He was successively regimental, brigade, division and departmental quartermaster of the Trans-Mississippi Confederate Units. He died November 9, 1911. They were the parents of: Lelia Wilson, Waller Winchester, Emma Maria, Florence and Jennie Breedlove. Lelia Wilson Breedlove, born April 13, 1859 in New Orleans. Married September 27, 1881 James Senora Stapler, born September 27, 1856. She died April 16, 1898, and he died in July 1906. They were the parents of: Lorena Oklahoma, born March 26, 1885; Anna Bryan, born November 13, 1887; Otway Hicks, born September 13, 1890 and John Wharton Stapler, born July 25, 1897. Waller Winchester Breedlove was born January 13, 1861. Married June 1, 1887 Priscilla Williams, born July 10, 1866 in Shawnee, Kansas. He was elected a member of Council from Delaware District, August 3, 1903. Emma Maria Breedlove was born September 16, 1863. Graduated from the Female Seminary June 28, 1883, and was drowned May 24, 1888. Florence Breedlove, born December 28, 1869, married September 6, 1893 Othie Andres Smith, born April 21, 1868. They are the parents of: Lee Breedlove, born July 28, 1894 and died October 16, 1918; Lelia Lucile, born February 15, 1896; Ruth Emily, born December 4, 1897, and Owen Philip Smith, born February 4, 1906. Jennie Breedlove was born April 1, 1873 and died January 30, 1895. William Wilson born January 9, 1843 married Alice Coody and they died without descent.

Thomas Wharton was created Marquis of Wharton, by King George I, in 1715 and his son Philip Wharton, born in 1698 was, on account of his brilliant attainments as an orator and leader in parliament, made Duke of Wharton on January 20, 1718. He died at Catalona, Spain May 31, 1731. His son. Sir William Wharton was the father of Samuel Wharton. Jesse son of Samuel Wharton was the father of Jesse Wharton, Jr. William, the son of Jesse Wharton, Jr. married Jamima Bryant of Abingdon, Virginia and they were the parents of Malinda, Margaret, Mary and Violet Wharton. Malinda daughter of William and Jamima (Bryant) Wharton married Thomas Chisholm and William Wilson.

CHAPTER XXI

The references appearing in parenthesis at the beginning of each paragraph following the name refers to the connection among the foregoing old families.

Alberty, Judge B. W. (See Downing)—Bluford West Alberty, born February 17, 1853. He married September 7, 1884 Louvinia Jane Adair nee Lewis, born May 13, 1862 in Washington County, Arkansas having previously been elected as a member of the Supreme Court. He was elected Chief Justice on November 15, 1892. On the coming of statehood he was elected the first Judge of Adair County in 1907.

Alberty, John Wright—Born July 26, 1834. Married April 15, 1852 Clara West nee Buffington, born 1825. She died July 1864 and he died August 29, 1905. They were the parents of Bluford West Alberty and Ellis B. Alberty, May 1854, died Dec. 1, 1880, Mose Alberty, April 1857, died Nov. 14, 1891, Joseph Vann Alberty, July 1860, living, Elizabeth Jane, April 1863—April 1867. John Wright Alberty was a member of Captain George H. Starr's company in the Confederate Cherokee Mounted Rilfe Regiment. He was elected Chief Justice of the Cherokee Nation in 1883.

Adair, John M.—(Ooloottsa and Adair)—John Martin Adair, born at Fort Gibson, June 3, 1858. Attended Shurtleff College. Served in Troop L. First United States Volunteer Cavalry in the Spanish American War. This regiment was known as the "Rough Riders" and his commander was Colonel Theodore Roosevelt. Captain Allyn Capron, Captain of Troop L was in the battles of that war that was fought in Cuba. John M. Adair married at Tahlequah in 1903 Triphena Terrell, born in 1871.

Adair, Robert E. (See Grant, Adair, Mc Nair and Ross—Robert Emmett, son of Brice Martin and Sarah (McNair) Adair was born in Salina District, December 16, 1861, educated at the Cherokee Orphan Asylum and Male Seminary. Married November 8, 1893 Ida Lavinia Elliott, born at Muskogee, March 30, 1874, educated at Harrell Institute, Muskogee. They are the parents of Rollin Elliott, born September 4, 1894, George Washington, born March 27, 1896, Fredrick Burl, born October 3, 1897, John William, born December 22, 1899, Emmett Ray, born April 4, 1908 and Arthur Allen Adair, born September 7, 1911. Mr. Adair was elected District Clerk of Salina District, August 5, 1889.

In the first quarter of the eighteenth century, William Martin, a wealthy merchant of Bristol, bought the ship, "Brice" gave it to his son Joseph and sent him to Virginia to keep him from marrying a girl that the father objected to. Joseph married Susannah Childs and settled on a large estaate near Charlottsville in Albernarle County, Virginia. Their son Joseph was elected Captain of Transylvania Militia in the American service in 1776, became Major February 17, 1779 and Lieutenant Colonel in March 1781. Elected Brigadier General of North Carolina December 15, 1787 and appointed Brigadier General of Virginia by Governor "Light Horse Harry" Lee on December 11, 1893. The name Brice has always been used in the Martin descent both in and out of the Cherokee Nation. General Martin's grand-daughter; Martha or "Patsy" married George Washington Adair and they were the grand parents of Robert Emmett Adair. Mrs Ida L. Adair is the daughter of George Washington and Ann Eliza (Kerr) Elliott and grand-daugter of Fredrick A. and Louise Jane (Coody) Kerr. Mr. Adair belongs to the Wolf Clan and Mrs. Adair belangs to the Bird Clan.

Arnold, E. B. (See Grant, Ghigau and Adair)—Ernest Brigham Arnold, born May 2, 1884. Educated at Cumberland University, Lebanon, Tennessee from which he graduated with the LLB. degree in 1905. He married Clyde Horn, born Aug. 23, 1888. She graduated fro Female Seminary May 31, 1906. They are the parents of: Hamilton Laverne born June 28, 1912 and Thomas Brigham Arnold, born Jan. 11, 1914. Ernest Brigham Arnold was elected County Attorney of Adair Co. in 1907 and District Judge of the First District in 1918 and resigned from that position on August 1st, 1921 in order that he might reassume his law practice.

James Warren Adair married Susanah Deborah Bean and their daughter Minerva Cornelia, married Thomas H. Horn and they were the parents of Mrs. E. B. Arnold.

Armstrong, Mrs. A. W. (See Cordery and McNair)—Mary Elizabeth, daughter of David McNair and ary J. (Strickland) Rogers, born

Bristol, England in order to break up a love match, furnished his youngest son, Joseph with a ship named the "Brice" and sent him to Virginia, where Joseph married Susannah Childs, member of a prominent Colonial family, and settled near Charlottesville Albermarle county in that state. Their third son Joseph, was born in 1840. He became a fur trader and amassed a fortune. He held the following military positions: Captain of the Transylvania Militia, elected in 1776 became Major February 17, 1779 and Lieut. Col. in 1781. He was elected Brig. Genl. of North Carolina by the Legislature Dec. 15, 1787 and was commissioned Brig. Gen. of the 20th. Brigade of Virginia Militia by Gov. Henry Lee Dec. 11, 1793. He was the father of Martha called "Patsy" Martin, who married George Washington, the son of John and Gahoka Adair. George Washington and Martha Adair were the parents of Brice Martin Adair who married Sarah McNair. They were the parents of Rolllin K. Adair, Townsite Commissioner 1888 and Superintendent of the Male Seminary 1895-99.
(See Ross).

Adair, Mrs. Joseph W. (See Ross)—Cora AnnSayers, born near Pryor, February 28, 1896. Married at Big Cabin, July 2, 1916, Joseph William, son of Allen and Kittie Adair, born September 8th, 1891, in Harrison County, Kentucky. They are the parents of Virginia Elizabeth, born August 22, 1918 and Allen Sayers Adair, born March 26, 1919. Mr. Adair is a farmer near Pryor.

Henry Drew, son of Abner and Nancy Jane (Coody) Sayers was born March 9, 1862 Married October 5, 1892,, Dora Thompson. born March 11, 1869 in Macom County, Missouri. Henry Drew died March 28, 1899.

Allton, Mrs. Joseph M. (See Cordery and Carter)—Thomas Cordery, an Irishman married Susannah, a full blood Cherokee of the Blind Savannah Clan. Their daughter Susie married John Mosley and they were the parents of Sarah Ruth Mosley, born in 1841 married October 16, 1864 Lewis Clark Ramsey, who served in the civil war in Captain Benjamin Wisner Carter's company. After his death Mrs. Ramsey married January 5, 1877 Ezekial Taylor.
married Jannuary 5, 1877 Ezekial Taylor.

Lewis Clark and Sarah Ruth Ramsey were the parents of Susan Elizabeth Ramsey, born December 7, 1866, educated in the Cherokee Orphan Asylum and Female Seminary. Married at Oowala July 31, 1888 Joseph Morgan, son of David and Eliza (Billingsley) Allton, born July 31, 1856 in Virginia. They are the parents of: David Clark, Percy Samuel and Charles Joseph Allton. David Clark Alton born June 30, 1889 married Maude Mamie Vincent, their children are: Frances Russell, born January 4, 1910; Dick Vincent. born January 2, 1911; David C., born July 13, 1912; Buford Kedrick, born May 15, 1915 and Maurine Allton, born September 6, 1917. Percy Samuel Allton born May 25, 1893. Married Cherokee Jones and his one son, Joseph Jones Allton, born September 7, 1920. Charles Joseph Allton born December 29, 1897. Married August 2, 1919 Pearl Jane Hanson, born in August 1898. They are the parents of Martha Sue Alton, born November 20, 1920.

Alberty, William T. (See Grant and Downing)—William Towers Alberty, born November 25, 1888. Enlisted in the world war in September 1917. Assigned to the Nintieth Division, 358th Infantry as teamster. Sailed for France June 20, 1918, was in the offensive operations at St. Mihiel and Argonne Forest and after the Armistice was with the Army of Occupation, returned to the United Statse in June 1919 and was discharged at Camp Paike on the twenty-second of that month. Married at Claremore, June 28, 1920, Elizabeth, daughter of Grant and Nannie Barker, born May 11, 1902 in Minifee County, Kentucky. They are the parents of Udolphus Grant Alberty, born June 28, 1921.

Jacob Udolphus, son of John D. and Jennie (Buffington) Alberty married Annie Charlotte, daughter of Ellis and Charlotte (Eaton) Towers, were the parents of William Towers Alberty.

Adair, E. E. (See Adair and Ghigau)—Edward Everett, son of John Thompson and Penelope (Mayfield) Adair, born They are the parents of: Jessie Alice Adair born May 20, 1880 married Moses Frye Sanders, they had one daughter, Mary Louvenia Sanders, born November 16, 1904. Mrs. Sanders died and the daughter has been reared by Mr. and Mrs. Adair; Cherokee April 15, 1853, married June 29, 1879 Rachel Louvenia Twist, born May 25, 1859. Cornelia Adair, born September 26, 1883, married Hoolie Sanders. She died September 11, 1907. The third and fourth daughters of Mr. and Mrs. E. E. Adair were Sarah Ruth, born August 23, 1886, died May 21, 1894 and Elizabeth M. Adair, born September 18, 1891 ,died August 3, 1893.

Edward Everette Adair was elected Clerk of Sequoyah District August 3, 1885. Elected Councilor from the same district August 1, 1887 and August 5, 1895. During the former incumbency he was one of the "Immortal fourteen" that sustained Chief Joel B. Mayes in his effort to get a better rental price for the Outlet. Mr. Adair is engaged in farming and stockraising, takes an active part in movements of public welfare and ranks among the leaders of his community.

Bass, Josie Gertrude, (See Foreman, Cordery, Grant and Riley)—Josephine Gertrude daughter of John Anthony and Eliza Mary Blythe Foreman was born Tuesday November 19, 1872. Educated at Oowala and Female Seminary. Married at Talala, September 30, 1897 Willim Robert Bass, born September 15, 1872 in Wilson county, Tennesee. He died February 3, 1912. They were the parents of: Robert Morris. Educated at Ramona and Oklahoma University, born July 20, 1898 and Harold E. Bass, born May 16. 1903.

John Anthony, son of Reverend Stephen and Sallie W. (Riley) Foreman was born at Park Hill, June 10, 1844. Educated at Park Hill and served the Confederacy in the Cherokee Mounted Volunteers. Married July 8, 1869 Eliza Mary, daughter of James Chastain and Sarah Jamima (Rogers) Blythe, born February 10, 1850. She died April 13, 1879. He was elected Judge of Cooweescoowee District August 6, 1883. Judge Foreman's second wife was Nancy Amanda Smith. She was at that time in "young ladies school" as Matron, Las Vegas, New Mexico. She died December 12, 1920.

Blake, Samuel C. (See Downing, Gore)—Samuel Coke Blake, born at Cane Hill, Washington, Washington Co. Ark. April 10, 1862, educated in that county, married at Wagoner, June 10, 1888, Georgia Anna Pharris, born Oct. 5, 1867 at Petaluma, Calif. They are the parents of: Jennie Agnes, born August 23, 1889, married Charles E. Stamps; Nita Emory, born February 11, 1892, married Charles Alonzo Spencer and has two children, Myrtle Caroline, born February 5, 1911 and Alonzo Blake Spencer, born March 24, 1919; John Fenlon, born September 4, 1894; Albert Watts, born May 17, 1897; Georgia Kezzie, born April 18, 1900, married October 24, 1919, Clifford Moore and has one son, Samuel Marion Moore, born December 17, 1920; Mabel Heber, born November 23, 1903; Hester Keep, born January 30, 1906 and Ruby Opal Blake, born November 2, 1909.

Samuel Blake, born January 5, 1818, in Ryde, Isle of Wright, England, and married Martha Jane Pyratt who was born in 1824. She died in 1914 and Samuel Blake died in 1878. They were the parents of Samuel Coke Blake. James and Kate (Finley) Pyratt, natives of North Carolina, settled thirteen miles west of Little Rock, Arkansas, in 1812, and moved to Cane Hill, Washington County, Arkansas, 1827. Since that time the Pyratt's have been socially prominent in Arkansas.

Margaret Downing, a Cherokee, married Bledsoe Gore, a white man, and their daughter, Agnes Gore, born April 10, 1829, married April 1, 1850, Pleasant Holloman Pharris, born July 11, 1826, in Tennessee. He served in the sixth Missouri Cavalry in the Mexican War. He died January 1893 and Mrs. Agnes Pharris died in 1913. They were the parents of Mrs. Samuel Coke Blake. Samuel Coke Blake is the founder and breeder of the Famous Blake Horse, near Pryor,

Brown, Mrs. N. R. (See Grant)—Jennie E. Cole born in Cooweescoowee District, Jan. 16, 1887, married at Pryor Dec. 24, 1902, N. R., son of John W. and Catherine Brown, born Nov. 8, 1881, in Hickman County, Kentucky.

They are the parents of Herbert Reed, born March 27, 1904, Virgie D. born June 6, 1906; Owen, born August 2, 1911; Elmer Jackson, born March 7, 1917 and John Wesley Brown, born June 13, 1919.

Mary L., daughter of Henry C. and Amanda Jane (Rogers) Fields was born Sept. 10, 1866. Married January 20, 1884, John Cole, born June 12, 1858 in Kentucky. They are the parents of Mrs. N. R. Brown. Mrs. Brown is the great great great granddaughter of Richard Fields, Chief of the Texas Cherokees.

Blount, Mrs. Oscar (See England) Eulalah Sophronia, daughter of John Wesley and Ida Josephine (Jenkins) Harris was born near Vinita, Sept. 5, 1890, educated at Female Seminary and Willie Halsell College. Married at Vinita, Nov. 6, 1909 Oscar, son of Webster W. and Anise Blount, born April 7, 1884 in Carroll County, Missouri. They are the parents of Beulah Ethel, born November 2, 1910; Flora Cornelia, born March 4, 1921 and Oscar Harris Blount, born December 15, 1913. Mr. Blount is a farmer near Vinita.

Ida Josephine, daughter of Elias H. and Arminda (England) Jenkins married John Wesley Harris and they are the parents of Mrs. Eulah Sophronia Blount who was named for her parental aunt Mrs. Eulalah May Lukenbill, who died in 1889.

The Blounts are of ancient Norman blood, the first Blount in England accompanied William ,the Conquorer, in October 1066. The head of the family was created Lord Blount by the King on December 3, 1326. A branch of the family came to America, settled in Tennessee where members became Governors and United States Senators. Blount County in that state is named for them.

Brown, Mrs. C. W. (See Grant and Sanders)—Delores Cole, born January 24, 1880, educated at the Presbyterian College at Tahlequah. Married at Pryor January 23, 1900, Charles Wesley Brown, born May 15th, 1873, in Hickman County, Clinton, Kentucky. They are the parents of Delores Ethylene, born April 10, 1902 and Gordon Wesley, born October 23, 1919. Mr. Brown is a farmer. Mr. and Mrs. Brown are members of the Methodist church. She is an Eastern Star and a Rebecca.

Nannie, daughter of Johnson and Margaret (Winters) Vann, married Daniel Boone Cole and they were the parents of Mrs. Charles Wesley Brown.

Belcher, Mrs. A. M. (See Cordery and Grant)—Cora Mary, daughter of William Davidson, and Mary Jane (Baumgarner) Clingan was born at Gibson station, Cherokee Nation May 12, 1878, educated at the Female Seminary, and Cottey College, Nevada, Missouri; married at Wagoner November 21, 1911, Rev. A. M. Belcher, born February 22, 1867 in Bluntsville, Ala. They are the parents of Bruce Clingan Belcher, born June 14, 1912 at Henryetta, Okla.

Reverend Belcher is a South Methodist and built the first church to be erected in Wagoner. Mrs. Belcher is a member of the Home Missionary Society and the Eastern Star.

Bird, William (See Cochran)—Emily, daughter of Price and Lucy (Keener) Cochran, born August 17, 1869. Married Dec. 27, 1884, Jerry Watts. Married Dec. 25, 1891 William, son of James and Elizabeth Bird. She is the mother of Edward Watts, born Jan. 5, 1887. Served in France in Co. "C" 358th Infantry from June 20, 1918 to June 27, 1919. Tessie Bird, born March 4, 1898; Lucinda Bird, born June 10, 1901; Mary Bird, born October 23, 1904; William Bird, born November 5, 1908 and Ona Bird born August 27, 1910. Mrs. Bird's Cherokee name is Ai-tsi.

Bates, Mrs. Dr. S. R. (See Downing)—Hattie Lindsey, born Jan. 3, 1872, educated at Chouteau and Female Seminary. Married January 20, 1900, Dr. Samuel Ralston Bates, born Jan. 2, 1870 in Winchester, Tenn. He graduated from the Medical Department of Vanderbilt University in May 1897.

The heads of the Scottish house of Lindsay at different dates were Sir Walter Lindsay in 1116 A. D., David Lindsay who was created first Earl of Crawford in 1398 and Alexander Lindsay who became Earl of Balcarres, January 9, 1651. Mrs. Bates' mother was the daughter of Joel Mayes Bryan. The first Bryan to become a citizen of England was Richard Fitz Gilbert Bryan, who accompanied his cousin, William the Conqueror to England in October 1066. He was the son of Gilbert, Count of Brione in Normandy, whose father was Richard III, Duke of Normandy, who was the uncle of William the Conqueror. Richard III was the son of Richard the Good, Duke of Normandy by his wife; Judith of Rennes. Richard the Good, was the son of Richard I, Duke of Normandy and he was the son of William "Longsword" Duke of Normandy from 927 to 943. Duke William was the son of Robert, the king who overrun northern France, married in 912 Gisele, daughter of Charles IV, King of France and became the first Duke of Normandy in 911. Duke Robert was the son of Regvald the Rich, Jarl of Norway.

Baugh, Mr. J. L. (See Grant, Downing, Ghigau, Foreman, Ross and Conrad)—Joel Lindsey Baugh, born Jan. 8, 1858. Educated in Male Seminary. Married Aug. 19, 1888

Sue Adair, daughter of Jacob West and Charlotte (West) Markham, born July 25, 1872. She died March 15, 1899 and he married at Locust Grove, May 30, 1901, Nannie Scales, daughter of John Taylor and Mary Elizabeth

Bachtel, Mrs. Mary Jane (See England, Ghigau and Hildebrand)—Mary Jane, daughter of William and Arminda (England) England was born on Honey Creek, Delaware District, Cherokee Nation, December 30, 1848. Her first husband was James Franklin Williams, born July 30, 1844 and died November 8, 1873. They were the parents of: Joseph Lowrey Williams, born November 30, 1866; Genevieve Shanahan, born December 28, 1868 and Martha Jane Sanders, born April 9, 1871. Mrs. Williams second husband was William Habish, who died October 3, 1883. Their daughter, Louise, born June 23, 1878, married George T. Harrell. Mrs. Habish's third husband, Daniel Bachtel, was born August 14, 1845 and died March 22, 1897. They were the parents of: Daniel Lorenzo, born May 28, 1887; Otis, born September 9, 1889 and Elza Bachtel, born March 2, 1891. Daniel Lorenzo Bachtel was a member of Headquarters Co. 332, Quarter Masters Corps having entered service June 27, 1918 was in service overseas from July 26, 1918 to July 18, 1919 as sergeant. Discharged at Camp Pike, July 30, 1919. Elza Bachtel entered service June 27, 1918. Member A. E. F. August 22, 1918 to June 22, 1919. Assigned to Company 165 Depot Brigade July 2, 1918. Appointed Corporal March 14, 1919. Discharged at Camp Pike, July 5, 1919.

Baker, Mrs. Margaret. (See Ward)—Margaret M. Ward, born January 10, 1886, educated at Female Seminary. Married at Bryan's Chapel, January 17, 1886, Joseph Franklin Baker. He died October 9, 1915. They were the parents of: Ollie Jane, born December 4, 1886, married Claude Cullison; John Oscar, born April 17, 1888, married Nannie McNair; Joseph Franklin, born September 24, 1890; Odessa Margaret, born July 25, 1898; Vera, born June 22, 1905; and Frank, born April 15, 1908. Mrs. Baker is engaged in farming, dairying and poultry raising.

John S., son of Bryan and Temperance (Stansil) Ward, was born October 7, 1920. Married July 27, 1857, Jane Loveless, born May 1, 1842. She died January 16, 1890, and he died June 15, 1896. They were the parents of Mrs. Margaret H. Baker.

Beamer, William. (See Foreman and Gusoduesga.)—William Beamer, born in 1853, educated in Kansas City. Married in 1872, Alice Towie. They are the parents of: Samuel, born August 14, 1873; Nannie, born July 3, 1875; Elizabeth, born March 21, 1878, married Charles Teehee; Louanna, born September 1, 1880; Emeline, born March 15, 1882; Ida, born March 1, 1891; and George Beamer, born May 26, 1894. Mr. Beamer is an ordained minister of the Baptist church and a member of the order of I. O. O. F.

Elizabeth, a half blood Cherokee, married William Springston, an English trader and their son Edley Springston, married Elizabeth Foreman, and their daughter, Mary, married John Henry and George Beamer. George and Mary (Foreman) Beamer were the parents of Rev. William Beamer, the subject of this sketch.

Billingslea (See Oolootsa, Ross, Sanders and Ghigau.)—Jeannette Starr was born February 16, 1862, in Tahlequah. She was educated in the Cherokee public schools and graduated from Female Seminary July 2, 1880. Married at Vinita April 1, 1885. Frank Alexander Billingslea, born August 9, 1851, in Crawfordville, Taliaferro County, Ga. He died May 9, 1913. They were the parents of Dollie Willie, born at Vinita, August 21, 1887, and Joseph Billingslea, born July 17, 1891 in Vinita.

Thomas, son of James and Lettie Boyd (Chambers) Starr, was born March 12, 1840, married August 20, 1860, Dollie Eunice, daughter of Anderson and Mary (Nave) Lowrey, born February 10, 1840. Thomas Starr died December 25, 1862. Jeannette Starr was their only child.

Frank Alexander Billingslea's first wife, Joanna Gillis, a second cousin of Mrs. Jeannette Billingslea. Frank A. and Joanna (Gillis) Billingslea had three children; McLeod Edward, born October 25, 1875; Frank Daley, born November 3, 1887; and Helen Estella Billingslea, born January, 1880, and married William Frank Pierce.

Frank Alexander Billingslea was elected a member of the Council on August 3, 1890, without the solicitation of a single vote.

Mrs. Billingslea belongs to the Methodist church and was very active as a special worker in the Red Cross service during the World war. Her son, Joseph, was in active service.

(McCoy) Drew, born October 24, 1877. Mr. Baugh's children by his first wife are: Charlotte, born July 21, 1889; Joel Lindsey, born April 27, 1893; Roscoe Randall, born January 14, 1895; on war being declared against Germany he volunteered and was on the offensive line until the armistice was signed; and Edgar Baugh, born May 5, 1897, married August 3rd, 1917, Mary Sixkiller, born August 21, 1899, and they are the parents of Dollie Belle and Margie Jane Baugh. Joel Lindsey Baugh is a man of striking personality, his democracy of spirit renders him very popular. He was elected Senator from Cooweescoowee District, August 3, 1891 and Clerk of the Senate in 1903. He was associated with his grandfather Bryan in winning the "Old Settlers" Cherokee claim and is at present postmaster at Choteau. In 1901 he was appointed by the Principal Chief of the Cherokee Nation as an attorney with W. W. Hastings before the Dawes Commission in making the final rolls of citizenship of the Cherokee Nation.

Joel Mayes Bryan, born October 22, 1809, and died August 7, 1898, was the father of Charlotte Bryan, born September 21, 1833, married July 19, 1854, John H. Baugh, born March 3, 1825, in Alabama. They were the parents of Joel Lindsey Baugh. The first known Bryan in English history was Gilbert, Count of Brionne, who accompanied his cousin, William the Conqueror, in October, 1066; he was France, the grandson of Richard III, Duke of Normandy, uncle of William the Conqueror, and descendent in the twelfth generation from Charlemagne.

Benge, Oce (See Grant, Ghigau, Foreman and Conrad)—Richard Fields Benge, commonly called "Oce" Benge, was born in Tahlequah District, September 9, 1851. Married at Locust Grove, February 18, 1883, Martha Adair, daughter of George Washington and Cherokee (Ratliff) Brewer, born July 7, 1861, and educated in Female Seminary. They are the parents of Georgia Alma, born April 30, 1885, married William C. Johnston April 4, 1919; Eleanor Osceola, born January 18, 1887, married C. A. Dunham October 3, 1913, parents of Roy Mills, born September 1, 1915, and Beatrice Eleanore Durham, born July 28, 1919; Lelia Leone, born December 16, 1892, married Wm. Cecil McLaughlin, March 28, 1919. They are the parents of Cecil Benge McLaughlin, born May 10, 1921; Dora Elizabeth, born September 4, 1896, and Senora Benge, born July 2, 1902. Mr. Benge is a farmer near Adair. He was elected Sheriff of Saline District August 6, 1883 and August 3, 1885. Elected a member of Council from the same District August 1, 1887.

Delilah, daughter of Richard Fields, Chief of the Texas Cherokees, married James Foreman and they were the parents of Susan Henrietta Foreman, born December 18, 1827, married Anderson Benge. He died January 4, 1868, aged about fifty years and Mrs. Benge died September 12, 1883. They were the parents of James Foreman and Richard Fields Benge.

George Fields, a brother of Chief Richard Fields, was a captain in the United States service in the Creek war of 1814. His daughter Nannie, born June 10, 1810, married Richard Ratliff, born 1804 and their daughter Cherokee, born July 10, 1839 married May 13, 1854, George Washington Brewer, born June 12,, 1831. He died February 14, 1868. Mrs. Brewer died October 12, 1916.

Bledsoe, Mrs. I. P. (See Grant, Downing and Daniel)—Belle, daughter of Henry and Nancy (Buffington) Hightman was born December 6, 1869 in Cooweescoowee District. Married May 1, 1887, Isaac Pipkins, son of Watt and Martha Ann Bledsoe, born January 28, 1847, in DeSota County, Mississippi. They are the parents of Henry Watts, born September 28, 1889; Sallie Martha, born June 28, 1892, graduated from Female Seminary May 27 1919, married L. C, Freeman; Joel Clement, born February 20, 1895, telegraph operator at Choteau; William Alberty, born August 15, 1898; Edna, born June 18, 1901, stenographer in M. O. & G. R. office at Muskogee; Fannie Gray, born December 18, 1903; Ruth, born September 2, 1906, and Pearl Elizabeth Bledsoe, born March 29, 1909. Mrs. Bledsoe is a Presbyterian and a member of the Woodmen Circle and Degree of Honor.

Captain William W., son of Moses and Sallie (Wright) Alberty, was born July 2, 1824, married Musidora, daughter of William and Nellie (May) Rogers his first wife and were the parents of Mrs. Henry Hightman. Moses Alberty was a native of Surrey County, North Carolina and married about 1810 Sallie Wright. William Rogers was the elder brother of Tiana Rogers, who married General Samuel Houston. Captain Alberty was an opulent and influential merchant at Flat Rock, near Grand River, in Cooweescoowee District, before the Civil war.

Brown, Charles G. (See Ward)—Charles G. Brown, born in Texas ,March 12, 1854, educated at Tullahassee Mission in the Creek Nation. Married at Salina, Cherokee Nation July 30, 1880, Mary, daughter of William and Lenora Coker, born in Boone County, Ark. January 25, 1865. They are the parents of: Lulu, born December 10, 1881; Quatie, born December 21, 1890; Etta Beatrice, born November 23, 1896; Nannie Lenora, born July 21, 1899 and Delora D., born April 19, 1905. Mr. Brown is farming near Pryor.

John Ward, a white man, married Catherine McDaniel of Scotch-Cherokee descent and they were the parents of Charles Ward who married Ruth Hollingsworth and they were the parents of Nancy Adeline Ward, who married Joseph Brown and they were the parents of Charles G. Brown, the subject of this sketch.

Bowers (See Grant and Daniels)—Lola Garrett, born November 29, 1887, educated in the Cherokee public schools and the Female Seminary from which she graduated June 1, 1905. She was an instructor in the Pryor schools in 1905-6 and in the Female Seminary in 1907-08; married at Muldrow Dec. 9, 1909, E. M. Bowers, born April 10, 1875. They are the parents of Genevieve Elizabeth, born July 13, 1911; Jane Rhea, born August 28, 1914 and Mary Ann Bowers, born Oct. 4, 1918. Mrs. Bowers is a member of the Baptist church. Mr. Bowers is prominently connected with the banking interests of the Citizens Bank and Trust Company of Pryor and of the state.

Ellis Buffington, an eighth blood Cherokee, married Catherine Daniel, a quarter blook Cherokee. He died in June 1858, and she died November 20, 1867. They were the parents of Ezekial Buffington, born August 7, 1811, married September 19, 1868 Louisa Newman, born May 14, 1817, in Tennessee. He died January 4, 1864, and she died February 15, 1898. Their daughter Mary, married Jerome Lorenzo Greer, and they were the parents of Elizabeth Ann Greer, born August 30, 1856, married March 17, 1875, James Robert Garrett, born June 29, 1850, in Carroll County, Tennessee. She died May 15, 1902, and he died January 9, 1918. They were the parents of Mrs. Lola Bowers.

Buffington, Joel W. (See Downing, Grant and Daniel)—Joel Webster Buffington, born near Pryor, October 12, 1898, educated at Pryor and Male Seminary. Married at Pryor November 28, 1918, Eva, daughter of Grant and Josephine Teter, born November 12, 1895. They are the parents of: Harry Webster, born August 27, 1919, and Gordon Warren Buffington, born Dec. 11, 1920. Mr. Buffington is a farmer near Pryor.

Joel Mayes Bryan married Rebecca Wright, their daughter Nancy Jane married John Ross Buffington, and they were the parents of John Ross Buffington, who married Sadie Highland, and they are the parents of Joel Webster Buffington.

Buffington, John Ross (See Grant, Downing and Daniel)—John Ross, son of John Ross and Nancy Jane (Bryan) Buffington, was born at Doaksville, Choctaw Nation June 2, 1864, educated in the Cherokee National Schools, Male Seminary, Tahlequah, Oklahoma. Married at Pryor, July 6, 1891, Sadie, daughter of Robert and Susan Highland, born October 28, 1865, in Denver, Colorado. They are the parents of Nancy Jane, born April 15, 1892, educated at Female Seminary; Carrie Rebecca, born May 17, 1893, educated at Female Seminary; Charles Ross, born May 29, 1894; Hallie Hazel, born August 2, 1897; Joel Webster, born October 12, 1900, and Cherokee Georgia Buffington, born December 16, 1901. Mr. Buffington's Cherokee name is Cooweescoowee.

Buffington, Charles Ross (See Grant, Downing and Daniel)—Charles Ross Buffington was born at Bryan's chapel May 29, 1894, educated in the Cherokee public schools, Male Seminary and North Eastern State Normal. Was assigned to Co. C., 360th Inf. Reg. 90th Div., sailed for France June 14 1918, at Hampton Roads Dec. 30, 1910; discharged as Corp. at Ft. Sill Jan. 23, 1919. He is a member of the Pryor Post American Legion and the A. H. T. A. Returned to his home, took up school teaching and later became connected with the post office.

John Ross Buffington, born April 11,

1833, married Nancy Jane Bryan, born October 8, 1835. He died August 22, 1870 and she died December 12, 1888. They were the parents of John Buffington, born June 2, 1864, married July 6, 1891 Sadie Highland, born October 7, 1865 in Denver, Colorado. They are the parents of the subject of this sketch.

Burns, Mrs. S. J. (Etta) (See Duncan)—Etta Hitchcock born December 14, 1860 at Park Hill, Cherokee Nation. Educated at home. She married December 30, 1880 Samuel James Burns born March 15, 1851 in Lindsey, Canada. Samuel J. and Ettta Burns have one daughter, Lily Dimple Burns, born September 30, 1881. She graduated from Worchester Academy, Vinita on May 20, 1898. Married Marshall Crutchfield Stevens, born December 1, 1879.

Samuel J. and Etta Burns located in Vinita in 1884 and opened a merchantile establishment which is still in existence.

Mrs. Burns, whose Cherokee name is Sihs-sli, affiliated with the Methodist church, the Delphian and Premier Worth While clubs and is a charter member of the Eastern Star Chapter and Past Matron of the same, a member of the White Shrine and Daughters of the American Revolution. She was President of the local cemetery association at the time it was named Fairview.

Etta H. Burns is the daughter of Isaac Brown Hitchcock, born, February 28, 1825 at Dwight Mission, Arkansas Cherokee Nation. He married February 8, 1857 Elizabeth Ann Duncan, born July 10, 1833. She graduated from Female Seminary in February 1856. She died October 4, 1886 and he died January 16, 1911. They were the parents of Timothy Brown, born May 19, 1858, Etta Smith and Irenaeus Duncan Hitchcock, born September 6, 1864 in Tabor, Iowa.

Jacob Hitchcock, the grandfather of Mrs. Burns arrived at Dwight, Site as a missionary in July 1820 and helped to construct the Mission.

Blake, John F.—John Fenlon Blake, born September 4, 1894, educated at Pryor. Enlisted in the World War at Camp Travis, Texas, September 22, 1917. Assigned to the 90th Division, 344th Machine Gun Battery, was in the St. Mihiel and Argonne Forest offensives and after the Armistice was in the Army of Occupation. He was discharged at Camp Pike, June 23, 1919. He married at Pryor August 30, 1917, Badgie, daughter of Joseph and Elizabeth Coppinger, born June 27, 1894. They are the parents of: Mozelle Edna, born May 27, 1918 and Coke J. Born June 3, 1920. Mr. Blake is a farmer near Pryor.

Brown, Mrs. Jay Paul (See Grant and Foreman)—Alma Ramona Taylor born in Hanford, California, July 16, 1884, educated in Missouri Valley College, Marshall, Missouri and Fairmont Seminary, Weatherford, Texas, graduating from the latter in 1905, specialized in instrumental music. She married at Chouteau November 27, 1917, Jay Paul, son of Paul Jay and Martha A. Brown, born October 15, 1874 in Wood County, Ohio. They are the parents of Martha Sue Brown, born at Muskogee, December 28, 1919. Mr. Brown is a merchant at Chouteau.

Ann Olivia, daughter of Isaac and Catherine (Ratliff) Bushyhead was born in Georgia, November 27, 1830, educated at Dwight Mission. Married October 4, 1846, John Brown Choate, born March 5, 1824. She died April 29, 1877 and he died February 16, 1893. They were the parents of Susie Jane Choate, born November 29, 1853. Married December 14, 1882 Robert Stewart Taylor, born November 27, 1830 in Washington County, Pennsylvania and graduated from Jefferson College, Pennsylvania. He died September 1897 and she married January 1, 1902, Valentine Gray. She died February 10, 1919.

Barton, (See Grant, Downing, Oolootsa, Foreman and Ghigau)—Edwin Harley Barton, born Aug. 8, 1890 at Baptist in Going Snake District, educated at Pryor, Chelsea and Tahlequah; graduated from Sweeney's Automobile School in Kansas City, Mo.; married November 4, 1911 Bonnie E. daughter of John B. and Rachael F. Heflin. Edwin H. and Bonnie E. Barton are the parents of Frances Mae Barton, born November 12, 1912.

Mary Van Lasley, born in 1862, married September 6, 1888 Frederick Spencer Barton, born September 8, 1851 in Piqua Miami county, Ohio. He died April 2, 1921. They were the parents of Edwin Harley Barton, whose Cherokee name is Oonodet. He is an expert automobile mechanic and owns a Battery Service Station in Pryor where he is a member of the Commercial Club; in religion he is a Baptist, and is a member of the I. O. O. F., Woodmen of the World and a Yeoman.

Caudill, Mrs. James W. (See Grant, Ghigau and Adair)—Lou, daughter of Alfred Estis and Margaret Elizabeth (Adair) Holland was born at Stillwell, May 8, 1887 and educated at Grove. Married at Bentonville, Arkansas, May 19, 1905, James Watson, son of James A. and Eliza Caudill, born April 16 1879 in Rowen County, Kentucky. They are the parents of. J. Holland, born October 11, 1906; Alton Estis, born July 7, 1908; Ruby Mozelle, born February 2, 1911; Ruth Lorene born December 2, 1913 and James Paul, born July 9, 1918.

Mr. Caudill is a farmer near Adair.

James Warren, son of Walter Scott and Nancy (Harris) Adair married Deborah Bean and they were the parents of Margaret Elizabeth (Adair) Holland.

Caywood, Mrs. J. E. (See Grant and Foreman)—Mary Elizabeth, daughter of William and Eliza Jane (Proctor) Horn, born July 21, 1882, educated in Delaware District and Female Seminary. Married at Vinita July 4, 1900, John Edward son of Stephen M. and Nancy Ann Caywood, born Aug. 30, 1872 in Hickory Co., Mo. They are the parents of William Marion, born June 30, 1901; Walter, born Aug. 1, 1903; and Thelma Emma born November 3, 1909. Mr. Caywood is a farmer near Big Cabin. Mrs. Caywood is a member of the United Brethren church.

Jeremiah Horn, a white man, married Elsie, daughter of Chief Charles R. Hicks and their son, John Horn, born August 3, 1823 married Jane July and they were the parents of William Horn, born December 24, 1855, married March, 1878, Eliza Jane Proctor and they were the parents of Mrs. Mary Elizabeth Caywood.

Campbell, John R. (See Grant and Ghigau)—John Randolph Campbell, born Aug. 8, 1877, educated in Orphan Asylum. Married at Oscola, Mo., May 28, 1903, Maude, daughter of Albert and Lucinda Bell, born Nov. 25 1876 in Douglas Co., Kas. They are the parents of Clarence Ray, born January 22, 1905; Edna May, born October 18, 1906; Clinton Albert, born October 11, 1912; Delora, born April 24, 1915; Glenn ,born September 26, 1917, Otis Ralph Campbell, born March 13, 1921.

Sarah, daughter of Nelson and Rosa (West) Rogers, married Alfred Eugene Campbell and they were the parents of John Randolph Campbell, the subject of this sketch.

Croker, Bula D. (See Grant and Ghigau) —Bula D. Edmondson, born on Beatties Prairie, Feb. 17, 1884 educated in the Cherokee National schools and graduated from Female Seminary May 29, 1902. Being possessed of superior histrionic talents she specialized in music and expression in Boston and in New York City. Having a brilliant personality and much of the impelling magnetic qualities of her distinguished Uncle, Wm. W. Hastings she soon rose to an eminent rank in her chosen profession. She married in New York City, Richard Croker, a native of Black Rock, Ireland and Chieftain of Tammany Hall. Mr. and Mrs. Croker divide their time between their home in New York City, Miami, Florida and their castle in Ireland.

Joseph Martin, born about 1740 on his father's plantation near Charlotteville, Virginia. He became a fur trader and planter. amassing a great deal of wealth. His place in the revolutionary army was: elected Captain of the Transylvania Militia in 1776, became Major February 17, 1779, Lieutenant Colonel in March 1781. Elected Brigadier General of the North Carolina Militia by legislature on December 15, 1787, and was commissioned Brigadier General of the Twentieth Brigade of Virginia Militia by Governor Henry Lee on December 11, 1793.

Martinsville, county seat of Henry County, Virginia and the place of his residence was named for him. He died at his home in Virginia on December 18, 1808, was buried with military and Masonic honors.

General Joseph Martin married Susannah Fields Nee Emory and their children were; John, born October 20, 1781, was the first Treasurer and first Supreme Judge of the Cherokee Nation. He was a member of the Cherokee Constitutional Convention of 1817 from Coosawaytee District, he emigrated to the Western Cherokee Nation in the spring of 1828 and located at Grand Salina on Grand River. His death occured on October 17, 1840, and he is buried at Fort Gibson. His two younger sisters were Nancy, married Jeter Lynch and Rachel, who married Daniel Davis. Jeter and Rachel (Martin) Lynch were the parents of Mary Lynch who married John Williams and their son Joseph Lynch Williams born August 1, 1837, married October 2, 1859, Louisa J. Stooer, born April 8, 1840, in Delaware District. Joseph Lynch Williams died November 5, 1860. Joseph Lynch and Louisa J (Stooer) Williams were the parents of Florence Eugenia Williams, born August 3, 1860, she married February 7, 1878, Michael Smith Edmondson, born September 9, 1853, in Georgia and they are the parents of Cherokee Dora, who married Robert Bruce Garrett; Gonia L., who married G. B. Finnin and Bula D., the subject of this sketch.

Crittenden, Richard H. (See Sanders and Downing)—Richard Henry Crittenden of the Deer Clan, whose Cherokee name si Wa-hala or Bold Eagle, was born in Going Snake District April 9, 1877, educated in the Male Seminary. He married January 17, 1897, Nannie, daughter of Jesse and Frances (Wright) Wright, born 1872. They were the parents of: Fannie Alice, born March 8, 1898; Rogert Lee, born January 4, 1900 and Mary Susan Crittenden, born June 8, 1906. Mrs. Nannie Crittenden died September 8, 1913, and he married on October 20, 1917, Hettie, daughter of Simon and Emma Rogers, born January 15, 1898. They are the parents of Harriett Juanita, born October 6, 1918, and Nellle Catherine Crittenden, born Janury 7, 1921.

John Ross, son of Harry and Susie (Wolf) Crittenden, was born in Georgia, June 30, 1839, educated in Going Snake District. Married January 12, 1862, Alice Harlan, born March 12, 1841. He was elected District Judge of Going Snake District, August 5, 1895, and died June 5, 1896. They were the parents of Richard Henry Crittenden.

Carman, William A. (See Ward)—William Andrew Carman, born July 30, 1896. Enrolled in the World war service at Camp Logan, Tex., Sept. 3, 1918. Assigned to the Fifteenth Sanitary Train. Discharged at Camp Logan, February 2, 1919. Married December 1, 1919, Virginia, daughter of John and Bettie Ford, born December 11, 1901, in Mayes County, Oklahoma. They are the parents of J. T. Carman, born January 31, 1921. Mr. Carman is farming near Adair.

George Ward, born in the old Cherokee Nation, east of the Mississippi River, March 17, 1878, married Lucy Mayes, an aunt of Chiefs Joel Bryan and Samuel Houston Mayes. Their daughter, Mary, married Joseph Henry Clark and they were the parents of Louisa Maria Clark, who married Daniel Young and was the mother of Catherine Jane Young, the wife of Joshua T. Carman and the mother of William Andrew Carman, the subject of this sketch.

Clark, William A.—William Andrew Clark, born near Tahlequah June 2nd, 1861, educated at the Cherokee Orphan Asylum, married at Pryor, June 17, 1891, Lillie Berry, born October 29, 1872, in Athens, McMinn county, Tennessee. They are the parents of: Joseph James, born November 12th 1893, graduated from the Naval Academy at Annapolis, Maryland, June 28th, 1917; served through the World war as Lieutenant on U. S. S. North Carolina and is at present (1921) on the U. S. S. Brooks in Asiatic waters; Lucy Jane, born February 21, 1895, graduated with A. B. from the University of Oklahoma June 4, 1918; Mary Louise, born September 22, 1897, graduated in a business course and is connected with the First National Bank of Chelsea; Clarinda Stella, born March 31, 1900, married June 17, 1918, L. C. Olinger; Virginia Mae Olinger, born July 31st, 1921; William Andrew, born July 10, 1903; John D., born November 1, 1906; George W., born November 10, 1913, and Virginia Elizabeth, born Feb. 1, 1917.

Mr. Clark is one of the substantial citizens of his community, having amassed more than a competency by close and intelligent application as a farmer and stock raiser. He is a Master Mason; he has paid especial attention to raising his family to a good and useful life, the results being seen in Lieutenant Clark and his sisters.

Countryman, James T. (See Ward)—James Thomas, son of George Washington and Minerva (Ballard) Countryman was born in Delaware District July 26, 1874, and educated in the Cherokee National Schools. Married at Fairland, September 6, 1894, Eve, daughter of Newton and Mary Lauderback, born June 26 1875, in Lafayette County, Mo. They are the parents of: Eliza, born August 31, 1895; Lafayette, born September 8, 1897; Henry, born February 18, 1899; Samuel, born December 28, 1900, married Anna daughter of Hudson and Belle Layton, who have a daughter, Ruby Juanita, born January 5, 1921; Oliver, born September 8,

1903, and Elmer, born January 10, 1909.

Martha Ward, born February 22, 1819, married John Countryman, a white man. They were the parents of George Washington Countryman, who married Minerva Ballard.

Chandler, Van S. (See Ward)—Van S., son of Burgess Gaither and Annie Eliza (Gunter) Chandler, born Aug. 20, 1882, educated at Willie Halsell College, Vinita. Married at Vinita, June 12, 1912, Maude A. daughter of L. A. and Sadie A. Williams, born July 25, 1890, in Linn Co., Kas. They are the parents of: Orin Stuart, born April 20, 1913; Wilmer Gawain, born July 25, 1915 and Stacy Burgess Chandler, born February 12, 1920. Mr. Chandler, who is the younger brother of Hon. Thomas A. Chandler, Congressman from the First District of Oklahoma, is a dealer in hay, grain and farm machinery.

Cobb, Gilbert Benson (See Grant)—Alexander Clingan, son of Joseph Benson and Evelyn (Clingan) Cobb, was born September, 15, 1864. Married at Carthage, Illinois, August 23, 1887, Lucy Van Zile, born January 10, 1863, in Ripley County, Indiana. She died March 31, 1893, and Mr. Cobb married June 29, 1898, Lillie May Pharr, born December 7, 1867, in Lincoln County, Missouri. Mr. Cobb is the father of: Gilbert Benson, born June 11, 1889 at Carthage, Illinois, educated at Wagoner. Married at Wagoner, December, 1910, Annette, daughter of Alfred and Adilee Sullivan, born October 20, 1874, in Wayne County, Missouri. They are the parents of Mary Evaline, born December 5, 1911; Naomi, born January 5, 1913; Alfred Alexander, born February 24, 1914; Joseph Benson, born November 14, 1915; Sylvester Van Zile, born December 22, 1917, and John Sullivan, born October 11, 1919; Isabel J. B., born September 28, 1921; Mary Isabel, born August 12, 1891, at Wagoner, graduated from Wagoner High School in 1910, and Oklahoma Agricultural College in 1913. Married at Wagoner June, 1914, Loyal Frederick. They are the parents of Ellen Isabel, born January 30, 1915; Kenyon Thomas, born January 3, 1917; Loyal Cobb, born April 23, 1919, and Martha Marie Payne, born May 7, 1920; William Alexander, born July 10, 1899. Married June 28, 1919, Marie G. daughter of Albert W. and Mary Brown. They are the parents of William Alexander Cobb, born June 14, 1920; Irene, born November 21, 1901; Harry Franklin, born October 13, 1902; Kedzie Pharr, born April 22, 1904 and MaZelle Cobb, born February 21, 1908.

Crittenden, George W. (See Sanders and Grant)—George W. Crittenden, born in Going Snake District, March 25, 1875, educated at Male Seminary. Married February 2, 1896, Jessie Beatrice Lamb nee Martin, born at Greenbrier April 20, 1874, educated at Hogans Institute. They are the parents of Ross Hillis, born Feb. 22, 1909; Jennie Alice born March 10, 1911 and Ruth Marie, born Jan. 14, 1916. Besides their own children they have reared Barbara and Christiana Bell, the two orphan daughters of Mr. Crittenden's brother, John H. George W. Crittenden belongs to the Deer Clan and his Cherokee name is Sequoyah. He is a farmer and a member of the Odd Fellow lodge.

Mrs. Crittenden is the daughter of Joseph Lynch Martin who is known throughout the Cherokee Nation as "Greenbrier Joe" and noted for his shrewd philosophical sayings. Mr. Crittenden is the son of Judge John Ross and Alice (Harlin) Crittenden. His Cherokee name is Tickanooly, meaning bean bread.

Carselowey, James R. (See Grant, Downing and Daniel)—James Robert Carselowey, born at Vinita, February 15, 1875, educated in public schools, Willie Halsell College, Vinita; married at Adair Nov. 28, 1900, Annie B., daughter of Alonzo B. and Lavenia A. Fishback, born February 27, 1882, in Tarrant County, Texas. They are the parents of: James Manford, born November 28, 1901; Lavenia Gertrude, born February 27, 1905; Elsie Roberta, born December 24, 1906; Raymond Russell, born September 23, 1908; Lahoma, born April 7, 1911 and Pauline Carselowey, born February 2, 1913. Mr. Carselowey is a man of pleasing personality, more than ordinary information and ability, but is modest and honest almost to a fault. He has been a telegraph operator and newspaper correspondent and is at present the owner and editor of the Adair Citizen.

James Madison, son of George and Mary (Daniel) Carselowey was born November 29, 1848. Married November 7, 1870, Catherine, daughter of Joseph and Celia (Woodall) Emory, born August 8, 1853. He died November 7, 1900. They were the parents of

Arthur Andrew Carselowey and Stella Evelyn Carselowey.

Couch, Mrs. Irving (See Grant)—Anna K., daughter of Joseph Lynch and Miranda (Young) Thompson, was born near Pensacola, August 14, 1900, educated in Mayes and Craig County. Married at Vinita, Jan. 10, 1920 to Ervin, son of James Monroe and Mollie Couch. Mr. and Mrs. Couch are farming near Pensacola.

Cole, John M. (See Grant and Sanders)—John M., son of Daniel Boone and Nannie (Vann) Cole was born in Cooweescoowee District, February 26, 1882. Married at Pryor, October 19, 1901, Letitia, daughter of John and Catherine Brown, born December 23, 1885, in Ballard County, Kentucky. They were the parents of Henry Mitchell, born November 28, 1905; Mayomma born November 23, 1909; Shirley Brooks, born November 26, 1910. Charlie Milburn, born August 22, 1913; Anna Belle, born December 18, 1915 and John Junior Cole, born December 29, 1918. Mr. Cole is a farmer, a Mason and Odd Fellow.

Johnson Vann, the grandson of John and Elizabeth (Wickett) Fields, married Margaret Winters and they were the parents of Mrs. Nannie Cole. Margaret or Peggy Winters was the daughter of John and Jennie (Sanders) Winters and the grand-daughter of Alexander and Peggy (Sonicooie) Sanders. Alexander Sanders was a captain of the Cherokee allies of the Americans in the Creek War of 1814. Mrs. Peggie (Sonicooie) Sanders was the daughter of Susannah and step-daughter of Thomas Cordery.

Carlile, Mrs. Stephen (See Ghigau and Hildebrand)—Sadie, daughter of S. P. Luna and Sarah (Butler) Luna, born July 10, 1888 in the Ozark County, Missouri. Married at Tahlequah, September 29, 1909 Stephen Foreman, son of Thomas Holmes and Levannah Elizabeth (Catron) Carlile. born January 5, 1873 in Tahlequah District, educated in Tahlequah District and Male Seminary. They are the parents of: Hazel, born August 1, 1910; Helen, born May 25, 1912; Stephen, born January 12, 1918; and Leo, born February 22, 1920. Stephen Foreman Carlile died September 5, 1919, Carlile is farming near Park Hill.

Carlile, William A. (See Ghigau and Hildebrand) — William Andrew, son of Stephen Foreman and Emma (Carter) Carlile, born October 1, 1893, educated in Tahlequah District and Male Seminary. Married at Tahlequah, April 2, 1912, Alma daughter of S. P. Luna and Sarah (Butler). Luna, born November 4, 1894 in Ozark County, Missouri. They are the parents of Jewell Carlile, born September 25, 1912.

Thomas Holmes Carlile married Elizabeth, daughter of John and Margaret (Hildebrand) Catron and they were the parents of Stephen Foreman Carlile.

Carman, Daniel (See Ward)—Daniel Young Carman, born Aug. 11, 1895, educated at Adair. Married at Pryor, Oct. 9, 1914, Grace, daughter of James Madison and Jessie Floyd, born October 12, 1896 in Scotland County, Missouri. They are the parents of Ermel, born September 28, 1915; Revis Goodwin, born March 5, 1917 and Loyce Carmen, born May 24, 1919. Mr. Carmen is a farmer near Adair and is a member of the I. O. O. F.

Louisa Maria Clark, born March 18, 1845. Married April 8, 1869 Daniel Young, born June 14, 1844 in Waldmore, Bavaria. He served in Company K. 107 Ohio Volunteer Infantry during the Civil War. They were the parents of Catherine Jane Young, born February 15, 1873. Married July 19, 1891, Joshua Thomas Carman, born March 25th, 1855 in Dade County, Missouri. He died April 15, 1918. They were the parents of Daniel Young Carman, the subject of this sketch.

Coats, Mrs. Susie D. (See Grant and Hildebrand) — Susie Dora, daughter of James and Emily (Harlin) Sunday was born in Cooweescoowee District, September 12, 1876, educated in Female Seminary Married September 11, 1893 James, son of James McKenzie and Annie C. (Spears) Coats, born April 1, 1866. They are the parents of: Jennie Bessie, born January 25, 1894; James McKenzie, born September 20, 1896; Elmer Earl, born September 4, 1901; Capitola Wyly, born February 15, 1903; Lulu May, born January 20, 1906; Eugene ,born October 15, 1908; Belva Lockwood, born June 8, 1910 and David Coats, born March 3, 1912. Mr. Coats died December 15, 1915. Mrs. Coats manages a farm near Pryor. Miss Jennie Bessie Coats was elected Court Clerk of Mayes County November 5, 1918 and November 2. 1920. James McKenzie was educated in Pryor and Agricultural College at Stillwater and served in the World War over seas 15 months. Capitola Wyly is a member of the 1922 High School class at Pryor.

Lucinda, daughter of Samuel and Catherine (Hildebrand) Martin married Joseph Spears and they were the parents of Annie C. Spears wife of James McKenzie Coats.

Cochran, Mrs. Ned A. (See Grant)—William Penn Adair Martin, born at Greenbriar, Aug. 1, 1879, educated locally and Female Seminary. Married at Pryor, July 24, 1915, Ned Adair Cochran, son of Richard and Mary Cochran, born August 20, 1880, educated at Orphan Asylum. They are the parents of Mary Virginia, born July 26, 1910; Cherokee Adair, born January 5, 1912; Joseph Martin, born February 28, 1915 and Robert Edward, born March 4, 1917. Mrs. Cocharn belongs to the Deer Clan.

Joseph Lynch Martin, born in Georgia, August 20, 1820. Married July 21, 1870 Jennie Harlin, born April 8, 1849 at Tahlequah. He died November 9, 1891. They were the parents of Mrs. Ned A Cochran

Cornatzer—Cyrus Cicero Cornatzer, whose Shawne name is See-tah-way-see-cah, and who belongs to the Rabbit Clan, was born February 11, 1853 on One Hundred and Ten Mile Creek in Kansas Territory. He is the son of Samuel M. and Caroline Cornatzer. the former was born May 6, 1824 in Oxford, North Carolina, and the latter was born in December 1834. Cyrus C. Cornatzer married Lydia J. Boggan March 23, 1871. Several years after her death he married on October 11, 1911 Miss Kate, daughter of Joseph Tyson and Martha Jane Zimmerman.

Cyrus C. Cornatzer was educated in the Johnson county Kansas schools; is a master Mason, and ,elected Solicitor of the Delaware District August 4, 1879, and a member of the Council from Cooweescoowee District August 5, 1895 and August 7, 1899 Four were born to the first marriage: Cornelia B. born February 18, 1872; Ninia Jane, born May 22, 1873; one boy, early deceased, Walter Cyrus, born April 24, 1878. Ninia Jane married R. L Madison, Big Cabin, Oklahoma; Caroline B. married Earl Galbreath, Big Cabin, Oklahoma. Mrs. Kate Cornatzer is a sister of Mrs. J. C. Starr, Vinita, Oklahoma. Has two brothers H. Zimmerman, Salt Lake City, Utah, and Joseph Clarence Zimmerman, St. Joseph, Missouri.

Chamberlain. (See Oo-loot-sa)—William Clifford Chamberlain was born April 23, in Flint Dist. He was educated at Neosho, Mo. He settled in Vinita and married Sept. 10, 1875, Lydia Ann Ward, born August 1. 1856. Se died June 28, 1882, and he married September 24, 1885 Madge, daughter of Hamilton W. and Margaret Goodykoontz, born August 7, 1859. Mrs. Madge Chamberlain taught school for seven years before her marriage, the last two being at Worcester Academy at Vinita.

William C. Chamberlain's children by his first marriage were: Flora Hoyt, born March 6, 1877 and died August 13, 1896; Edith Ursa deceased; Clara Emily Chamberlain, born August 2, 1881. By his second marriage his children were: Winfred Clark, born April 3, 1888, married October 20, 1897 Ethel O'Neil; Lois Margaret born February 27, 1893; Milo Reu born March 8, 1895, married October 8, 1916 Lulu Scarborough; Cline Lowry born May 30, 1897; Quatie Eulalia born May 13, 1899. Two sons, William Clifford and Lucian B. died in infancy.

William C. Chamberlain's Cherokee name is Su-Sen-Kee and he belongs to the Holly Clan. He is a member of the Congregational church and has been twice elected Mayor of Vinita.

Amory Nelson, son of William and Flora (Hoyt) Chamberlain was born November 29, 1821 at Brainard Mission. He married December 2, 1846 Eunice Dolly, daughter of Milo and Lydia (Lowry) Hoyt, born December 14, 1820. Rev. Amory Chamberlain was one of the best Cherokee interpreters for the Council and he was also Superintendent of both the male and female Seminary. Rev. A. N. Chamberlain died July 4, 1894 and his wife died seventeen days later. William C. was his second son.

Duncan, Mrs. John O. (See Grant, Duncan and Sanders)—Joanna Coody Rogers daughter of Charles Rogers Coody and Nancy (Patton) Rogers was born in Cooweescoowee District in 1861. Educated in the Cherokee Nation Schools, graduating from the Female Seminary, June 30, 1881. Taught school and in 1885 she married at Fort Gibson, John Clinton, son of John Thompson and Elizabeth Ann (Sanders) Duncan, born in 1859 in Flint District, Cherokee Nation. He was educated in the Cherokee Public Schools and Male Seminary. Fortunate in having splendid educations. discriminative and appreciative minds, Mr and Mrs. Duncan have always been unobtrusive leaders in their community. Mrs. Duncan is the grand-daughter of Captain John Rogers, last chief of the Western Cherokees and a sister of William Charles Rogers, the last chief of the Cherokees. While the Duncan family has furnished many of the finest minds and characters, one of their peculiarities is the fact that they generally refused public offices.

Dannenberg, Robert C. (See Grant and Oolootsa)—Robert Carter, son of John Henry and Annie E. (Ferguson) Dannenberg, was born in Missouri, April 12, 1877, educated in Flint District and Male Seminary. Married at Tahlequah June 16, 1902, Mary, daughter of John and Jennie (Lowrey) Hubbard, born in Tahlequah District, November 28, 1878, and educated at Tahlequah and Muskogee. They are the parents of John Henry Dannenburg, born October 16, 1908, and Genie Dannenberg, born Mar. 5, 1915. Mr. Dannenberg is a farmer and stock raiser near Tahlequah.

Henry, son of Anderson Pierce and Mary (Nave) Lowrey, married Mary Parris and they were the parents of Jennie Lowrey who married John Hubbard.

Christine, daughter of John and Susie (McCoy) McPherson, married Nathan Baron Dannenberg, and they were the parents of John Henry Dannenberg, who married Annie E. Ferguson.

Dykes, Mrs. Julius C. (See Foreman)—Cora Evelyn Mizer, born at Chelsea, Nov. 28, 1895, educated at Chelsea and Female Seminary. Married at Galena, Kas., April 16, 1918, Julius Otto Dykes, born February 11, 1896. They are the parents of: Julius Otto, born Jan. 14, 1919, and Evelyn Jane Dykes, born March 31, 1921. Mr. Dykes, who is the maternal grandson of Julius and Jennie (Bigby) Henchoz, saw service in the World war in Company C, 49th Infantry, which he joined August 26, 1918, sailed for France, October 31, 1918, returned January 16, 1919 and was discharged at Ft. Leavenworth, February 11, 1919.

DeLozier, Manford E. (See Adair)—Manford E. DeLozier, born Sept. 25, 1891, at Adair, educated locally. Married at Muskogee, October 4, 1914, Amanda F., daughter of John B. and Bettie J. Gibson, born January 5th, 1895, in Missouri. They are the parents of Vivian Marie, born February 20, 1916, and Reuben Edward DeLozier, Jr., born August 18, 1819. After clerking in the Bank of Adair for some time, Mr. DeLozier gave up that place to assume the more congenial occupation of farming and stock raising.

Edward, the son of John and Gahoga Adair, was born February 7, 1789. Married June 17, 1809, Martha Richie, born February 10, 1790. She died July 7, 1857, and he died December 21, 1864. They were the parents of John Adair, born May 1, 1812. Married March 20, 1832, Anna Berry Graham, born October 12, 1816. He died March 15, 1877, and she died November 1, 1900. Their son, Edward Alexander Adair, was born February 25, 1847. Married October 1867, Narcissa Malissa Harrison, born December 25, 1846, in Murray County, Georgia. He died December 3, 1901, and she is still living. They were the parents of: Georgia Virginia Adair, born at Dalton, Georgia, January 29, 1869. Married January 8, 1888, Reuben Edward DeLozier, born June 20, 1855, at Osceola, Missouri. Elected County Commissioner of Mayes County September 17, 1907. He died April 23, 1921. They were the parents of Manford E. DeLozier, the subject of this sketch.

Dobkins (See Duncan)—Benjamin Dustin Dobkins, born Aug. 6, 1879, was educated at Vinita, the Male Seminary, and graduated from the Ontario, Canada, Veterinary College. He married June 3, 1903, Gertrude, daughter of J. M. and Gertrude Ragland of Lebanon, Mo. Dr. Benjamin D. and Mrs. Dobkins, have one daughter, Miss Jaunita Cherokee, born July 5, 1904.

Dr. Dobkins has been State Veterinary for ten consecutive years, is the author of the Oklahoma State Veterinary Laws and was President of the State Veterinary Association in 1912-13-14 and 15. He is a Mason. Odd Fellow and is President of the State Bank at Welch, Oklahoma.

Emma, daughter of Benjamin Franklin and Mary (Berry) Landrum, was born June 15. 1852, at Beattie's Prairie in Delaware District. She married October 6, 1875, John Robert Dobkins, born May 8, 1857, in Texas. Mrs. Emma Dobkins died August 17. 1886. John Robert Dobkins died August 15, 1914. They were the parents of: Dr. Benjamin D. and his twin sister, Ada Bertha who married B. H. Duvall and lives at Welch. Nora, born October 1, 1881 and married is now Mrs. Hampton of Welch, and Hugh C. Dobkins, born October 23, 1884, and died August 6, 1911.

Benjamin Franklin, son of James and Rebecca (Duncan) Landrum, was born in 1822. He was elected Senator from Delaware District August 4, 1873, August 2, 1875, and August 5, 1877. He died February 19, 1879. It was one of his educated slaves that composed and played the celebrated violin piece, "I'll Tell You, Marsa Ben, Yo Niggers Gwine to Leave Yo," just previous to the wholesale escape of Landrum's and other slaves in 1842.

Deitrick, Mrs. J. R. (See Grant and Downing)—Lillie Belle Beck, born September 16, 1883, educated at Delaware District. Married Dec. 7, 1902, J. R., son of Jacob and Eliza Deitrick. They are the parents of: Beula Elizabeth, born Oct. 6, 1903; Addie Eveline, born August 10, 1905; Annie Lucile, born June 23, 1907; Aubrey Haskell, born January 26, 1910; Loil Wilson, born January 23, 1913; Robert Willard, born April 5, 1915, and Jaunita May Detrick, born September 1, 1920. Mr. Deitrick is a farmer near Ketchum.

Jeffrey Beck, an Englishman, married Sallie Downing, a Cherokee. Their son, Ezekial, married Martha Sturdivant, and they were the parents of Geoge W. Beck, who married Sarah Elizabeth Davis. They were the parents of Mrs. Lillie Belle (Beck) Deitrick.

Drew, George E.—George E., son of Charles and Martha (Lee) Drew, was born at Webber Falls, Dec. 12, 1872, educated at the Orphan Asylum. Married near Pryor Nov. 8, 1894, Susie, daughter of Zachariah and Eunice (Bledsoe) Putnam. They are the parents of Eugene H., born April 30, 1896, married Billie Coats; Richard E., born Oct. 18, 1899; Eunice P., born May 23, 1902; Paula E., born Feb. 14, 1910, and Howard L. Drew, born Nov. 22, 1912.

Elliott, Hiram T. (See Foreman)—Hiram Thomas, son of Hiram Thomas, and Callie (Whatenberger) Elliott, born in Delaware Dist., Nov. 26, 1892, educated locally and in Male Seminary. Married at Vinita, April 1, 1914, Minnie J., daughter of Drewey and Margaret Trickey. They are the parents of: Rella, born May 17, 1915; Eugen, born Mar. 20, 1917, and Maxine, born Feb. 10, 1918; Leroy Elliott, born Oct. 2, 1920. Mr. Elliott is a farmer near Big Cabin.

Elliott, James E. (See Foreman)—James E., son of George and Rachel (Henson) Elliott, was born in Vinita, Mar. 16, 1875, educated in Delaware Dist. Married at Adair Apr. 4, 1889, Eva, daughter of Joseph S. and Nancy Wickham, born Dec. 8, 1875, Schuyler County, Missouri. They are the parents of Sadie Marie, born April 1, 1903; Juanita Josephine, born October 28, 1913, James Howard Elliott, born November 22, 1916. Mr. Elliott is a farmer and stock raiser, and is a member of the Independent Order of I. O. O. F His Cherokee name is Oo-ch-la-ta.

Elliott, Mrs. Callie (See Foreman)—Callie, daughter of Samuel and Annie (Edwards) Whatenberger, born March 15, 1868, in Springfield, Mo. Educated in Texas. Married at Vinita Jan. 7, 1892, Hiram Thompson Elliott, son of Archibald and Rachel (Smith) Elliott, born May 22, 1858. They were the parents of Hiram Thompson Elliott, Jr., born November 26, 1892; Samuel Talbert, born July 5th, 1894, married Genevieve Blackford, Vera May, born February 26, 1896, married Guy L. Jones, and has one son, Raymond Jones, born April 4, 1914; Lucullus, born August 25, 1899, is in the United States Marine Corps in Haiti; Lucien Bell, born July 27, 1901; Flossie, born Jan. 2, 1904; Ruth, born May 24, 1905; Robert, born August 21, 1910, and Glenn, born March 6, 1913. Mr. Elliott died July 1, 1915.

Edmondson, Mrs. Jefferson D. (See Grant and Ward)—Lulu Eugenia, daughter of Samuel Taylor and Catherine Jane (Lear) Ward was born in Ark. Feb 28, 1864, educated in Delaware District. Married on Beattie's Prairie October 6, 1887, Jefferson Davis, son of Augusta Van and Laura Edmonson, born April 21, 1861, in Washington County, Arkansas. They are the parents of: Olive Estella, born April 3, 1889, graduated from Female Seminary, May 29, 1907, married Cicero J. Howard; Laura Helen, born June 8, 1893, and Doda Kate Edmondson, born January 16, 1896, married Peter Ware. Mr. Edmondson is farming near Pryor.

George Ward, born March 17, 1787, married December 15, 1805, Lucy Mayes, born March 5, 1879. She was the aunt of Chiefs Joel B. and Samuel H. Mayes. George Ward was assassinated, and his widow died November 1, 1867. They were the parents of: James Ward, born Jan. 17, 1815, married Louisa M. Williams, born June 30,

1825. He died July 20, 1868 and she died October 16, 1894. Their son Samuel Taylor Ward, born June 13, 1847, married in 1862 Catherine Jane Lear, born in 1844 in Morgan County, Mo. He died February 25, 1864 and she is still living.

Epperson, Benjamin F. (See Grant and Foreman)—Benjamin F., son of William H. and Margaret Epperson was born Oct. 3, 1878 in Bradley Co., Tenn. Married at Pryor July 12, 1904, Dora May, daughter of William and Eliza Jane (Proctor) Horn, born June 1, 1880 and educated in Delaware Dist. They were the parents of: Arthur R. born Feb. 2, 1905; Louisa, born July 8, 1907; Robert L., born Feb. 5, 1910; Nannie Ruth, born Sept. 16, 1912 and Maggie May Epperson, born November 9, 1917. Mrs. Dora May Epperson died August 18, 1920. Mr. Epperson is a farmer near Big Cabin and is a member of the Independent Order of Odd Fellows.

Anthony Foreman, a Scotchman, married Susie, a full Cherokee. Their son Thomas married Susannah Brown nee Fields and they were the parents of Elizabeth Foreman who married Johnson Proctor. They were the parents of Mrs. Eliza Jane (Proctor) Horn.

Epperson, Mrs. Joseph (See Grant and Downing)—Bettie, daughter of Columbus and Amanda (Ross) Phipps was born July 6, 1882. Married at Wagoner, July 29, 1902 Joseph Epperson, born in 1882 In Cleaburn County Arkansas. They are the parents of: William C., born December 11, 1903; Columbus P., born March 8, 1908; Lela Pearl, born April 7, 1911; Zulma Inez, born March 27, 1913, and Garrett Epperson, born September 16, 1915.

Epperson, Mrs. J. O. (See Grant and Downing)—Mary, daughter of John and Susan (Gentry) Wood was born in Tahlequah District, June 16, 1883, educated in Female Seminary. Married at Tahlequah January 16, 1899, J. O., son of William H. and Margaret Epperson. They are the parents of: Oscar L., born December 31, 1900; Benjamin F., born August 13, 1902; Lola May, born November 29, 1905; Hendietta, born April 17, 1907; Eugene, born December 12, 1908; Bessie Marie, born June 10, 1911; Susie, born July 30, 1912; Walter Floyd, born May 21, 1914 and Mattie M., born December 30, 1918. Mr. and Mrs. Epperson are farming near Big Cabin.

Eaton, Ellis M. (See Grant and Downing)—Ellis Menchell, son of Richard and Elizabeth (Alberty) Eaton born Jan. 18, 1861, married Jan. 3, 1886, Mary, daughter of Moses and Elizabeth (Buffington Alberty) born Dec. 19, 1865. They are the parents of: Lelia, born Apr. 7, 1887 and graduated from Female Seminary May 29, 1907; Richard, born Oct. 7, 1890, married Esther Gardner; William M,. born March 25, 1898 married Corn Thompson and Edgar W. Eaton born Aug. 29, 1899. Mr. and Mrs. Ellis M. Eaton are members of the Methodist church and he belongs to both of the Woodmen Orders.

Ellis Menchall Eaton was elected to the Council from Cooweescoowee District on August 7, 1899, and August 5, 1901. Moses Alberty, father of Mrs. Eaton was born April 22, 1820. He was Justice of the Middle Circuit of the Cherokee Nation from 1855 to 1859 and was elected Executive Councilor in 1867. He was the chief attorney for Ezekial Proctor who was charged with the murder at the time of the Going Snake court house fight in 1872 and during the fight he was shot and killed by what was supposed to have been an accidental stray shot.

Fields, Henry F. (See Grant)—Henry Franklin, son of Henry Clay and Amanda Jane (Rogers) Fields was born Aug. 31. 1876 at Pryor July 15, 1900, Nettie B. daughter of Richard Watson and Mary Stokes born Nov. 4, 1880 in Ky. They are the parents of: Mabel, born December 4, 1901 Graduated from Pryor High School 1920 and is teaching at Bristow; Owen G., born May 6, 1904 and Haward Franklin Fields, born April 6, 1910. Mr. Fields is a farmer near Pryor. He is a member of the Masonic lodge in Pryor, himself, wife and daughter Miss Mabel are Eastern Stars.

Richard Fields, Chief of the Texas Cherokees was the father of George Fields who married Sallie Daniel. Their son, Henry Clay Fields, born October 21, 1844, married February 1861 Amanda Jane Rogers, born July 17, 1847 in Johnson County, Missouri. They were the parents of Henry Franklin Fields.

Faulkner, Benjamin F. (See Grant, Downing and Halfbreed)—Benjamin Faulkner, born Oct. 14, 1874, educated at the Male Seminary; married in Sept. 1893, Susie J. Humphrey, born in 1877 in Tenn. They are the parents of: Lelia Beatrice, born June 18. 1894; John Shafter, born March 1, 1899; Robert, born August 12, 1901. Beulah B., born September 20, 1907; Owen born August 26, 1910 and Beulah Clarice born January 25, 1913.

Benjamin F. Faulkner was elected Sheriff of Sequoyah county in Nov. 1918. Robert Faulkner was appointed Sheriff of Sequoyah District in May 1882, Franklin Faulkner was elected Judge of Sequoyah District in 1871-77-79-81 and 1883.

James T. Stewart was elected Solicitor of Sequoyah District in 1891. Alexander McCoy was Secretary of the Council May 6, 1817; clerk of the Senate from 1819 to May 1827, excepting 1822, and he was secretary of the Constitutional Convention of May, 1827.

Faulkner, Mrs. D. J. (See Foreman, Riley, Adair, Grant and Ghigau)—David Jesse, son of assistant Chief David McNair and Rachel Louvenia (Adair) Faulkner was born Jan. 2, 1874, educated in the Cherokee public schools and Male Seminary, married October 31, 1900 Jennie McClellan Foreman, born at Oowala November 12, 1878, she was educated at Oowala and graduated from Female Seminary June 1, 1898. They are the parents of Tiana, born September 11, 1901; Ooloötsa, born July 12, 1903; Frank Foreman born December 23, 1905; Ada McClellen, born March 2, 1910; David Famlyn, born January 30, 1912; Taylor Adair, born February 8, 1915 and Ahniwake, born December 23, 1920. David L. Faulkner's Cherokee name is Te-quen-yoste, he belongs to the Odd Fellow and Knights of Pythias lodges and is engaged in stock raising north of Claremore. He was elected a member of Council from Sequoyah District August 7, 1899 and elected County Commissioner of Rogers county November 5, 1812.

Mrs. David J. Faulkner is the daughter of Stephen Taylor Foreman born at Park Hill, September 24, 1848 married at Cane Hill Arkansas April 28, 1874 Ada Carter McClellan, born October 23, 1853. Stephen Taylor Foreman died January 30, 1891.

John Thompson Adair, born December 22, 1812, married January 30, 1840 Penelope Mayfield, born May 12, 1824. He was delegate to Washington, Chairman of the Citizenship Court and Chief Justice of the Cherokee Nation. Their daughter Rachel Louvinia Adair, born January 6, 1844, married April 28, 1867, David McNair Faulkner, born May 12, 1841. He was First Lieutenant in Captain Bluford West Alberty's company of the Second Cherokee Mounted Volunteers. Elected Councilor from Sequoyah District in 1869 and 1877, senator from the same district 1879, 1881, 1889, 1895 and 1901; Delegate to Washington and Assistant Chief of the Cherokee Nation on August 3, 1903 retaining his office until June 30, 1914. He died on August 2, 1914.

Foreman, Mrs. Nannie (See Grant, Downing, Foreman, Watie, Conrad and Halfbreed) —Return, son of Ellis and Sarah (Phillips) Foreman was educated in the Cherokee National Schools. Married at Muskogee, Nannie, daughter of Thomas Jefferson and Susannah (Watie) Bean, born March 25, 1881. They are the parents of Joseph, born October 16, 1917 and Samuel Foreman, born February 6, 1911.

John Alexander Watie married Eliza Fields and they were the parents of Mrs. Susannah (Watie) Bean.

Ellis (commonly called "Tyler") son of Samuel and Sallie (Gourd) Foreman married Sarah, daughter of Elijah and Sidney Crittenden) Phillips and they were the parents of Return Foreman.

Flournoy, Mrs. Anna (See Grant)—Anna Wilson, born June 3, 1855, married in Wood Co., Texas Sept. 12, 1871, De Hardiman Flournoy, born Mar. 1, 1848 in Nacodoches Co. Tex. He served the confederacy in Company G. Texas Portison Rangers, under Captain John Thompson and Colonel Walter P. Lane. He died March 7, 1908. Mr. and Mrs. Flournoy were the parents of Ellen Minerva, born August 9, 1872; Lillie John, born April 5, 1874; Raleigh De, born July 15, 1876; Walter Gray, born February 2, 1881 and Clara May Llournoy, born September 2, 1884

John W. Wilson, born September 15, 1824, in Jasper, Marion County, Tennessee, married July 6, 1854 in Rusk County, Tex., Ellen E. Thompson born April 12, 1838. He died January 28, 1867 and she died June 25, 1867. They were the parents of Anna (Wilson) Flournoy.

Grant, G. O. (See Grant, Halfbreed and Duncan)—George Owen, son of Edward and Susannah (Paden) Grant born December 25, 1883, graduated from Male Seminary May 28, 1902. Married Dec. 30, 1906, Lillie May, daughter of Jeter Lynch and Keziah (Moore) Cunningham, born May 23, 1879. They are the parents of: Owen C. Grant, born September 25, 1910; Kezia Elizabeth Grant, born September 28, 1914;

Victor Monnet Grant, born Feb. 26, 1917.

George Owen Grant was elected Register of Deeds of Adair County in 1910. Graduated from the Law Department of the University of Oklahoma in June, 1914. Elected County Attorney of Adair County 1918 and 1920. Delegate to Republican National Convention at Chicago 1916 and 1920.

Ghormley, William H. (See Foreman and Conrad)—William Charles, son of Michael Orlando and Nancy (David) Ghormley, born Jan. 22, 1876, educated in the Cherokee Public Schools and Male Seminary, from which he graduated June 25, 1897. He married at Tahlequah, Sept. 19, 1899, Elizabeth Emily, daughter of William H. and Letitia (Woodward) Foreman, born Dec. 27, 1897. They are the parents of: Stella, born April 24, 1901; Maurice, born Jan. 13, 1903; Connell Rogers, born Sept. 23, 1904; Dwight, born Dec. 21, 1907; Roberta, born April 29, 1909; Ima Jane, born January 9, 1912, and Pauline Irma Ghormley, born July 11, 1915. Mr. Ghormley is a member of the Methodist church and belongs to the Masonic, Odd Fellow, Woodmen of the World, Modern Woodmen and Anti-Horsethief fraternities.

Gibbs, Mrs. Andrew J.—Caroline, daughter of Pleas and Martha (Carnes) Tidwell, was born in Georgia, Dec. 25, 1853, and educated in that state. Married February 1884, Andrew J., son of William and Elizabeth Gibbs. They are the parents of Lillie O., born December 23, 1887, married Ernest McLaughlin, and died in October 1907; William P., born August 22, 1889; Hattie E., born March 3, 1892; Allen D., born March 30, 1894; Louanna, born February 3, 1895, married Hosea Chidester, and has one daughter, Nona, born January 21, 1915; Mary G., born December 9, 1897, married Owen Washam; Leonard Andrew, born October 15, 1902; Ezra F., born November 28, 1903 and Samuel B. Gibbs, born October 28, 1908. Mr. and Mrs. Gibbs have reared Everett McLaughlin, their grandson, born May 8, 1907.

Gwartney, Walter E. (See Ward)—Walter Edward Gwartney, born near Pryor, Aug. 20, 1895, educated at Pryor. Married at Pryor, May 30, 1913, Bessie, daughter of Joseph and Sallie McWaters, born April 7, 1896, in Gainsville, Cook County, Texas. They are the parents of: Walter Eugene, born September 5, 1914; Muriel Marguerite, born June 2, 1916; Edward Russell, born August 13, 1917, and Susie Irene Gwartney, born November 21, 1919.

Bryan Ward married Temerance Stansil. Their son, John S. Ward, married Jennie Loveless, and they were the parents of Susie Ward, wife of Edward Gwartney, and mother of Walter Edward Gwartney.

Garvin, Ben F. (See Ooloctsa and Blair)—Benjamin Franklin Garvin, born May 1, 1861. Married August 8, 1882, Sarah Benge, born September 15, 1862. She died. He married Eliza J. Baldridge, born June 6, 1864. He is the father of Margaret Nannie, married Nov. 8, 1901; Walter Agnew; Ada Cornelia, married James Hail; Benjamin Franklin, married Goode; Mary Ellen, married Benjamin Franklin Bradley. Elizabeth Caroline, married James McCullough; Edward Frye, married Jessie Amos, and Elmer C. Garvin. Benjamin Franklin Garvin, Sr., is a Mason, Odd Fellow and Woodman of the World.

Gunter (See Grant, Ooloctsa, Adair, Ghigau and Ross)—Nancy E. Gunter was born Feb. 19, 1867, in Ft. Smith, Arkansas. She was educated in the public schools of the Cherokee Nation and at the Female Seminary. She married at Vinita on April 4, 1886, Lucien Webster Buffington, born April 15, 1857, on Beattie's Prairie, Delaware District. He was educated in the Public Schools of that vicinity. He came as a boy to Vinita, shortly after it was established and lived there until his death, which occurred on December 3, 1919. Quite unostentatious and gentlemanly, he accumulated an extra compensation and for several years preceding his death had been president of the Vinita National bank. He was elected Town Lot Commissioner in 1886 and 1888. He was the son of William Wirt and Josephine (Bell) Buffington and his paternal grandparents were John Adair and Jennie (Martin) Bell.

Nancy E. Buffington is the daughter of Samuel and Fannie (Daniel) Gunter. Samuel Gunter was born March 16, 1840, in Skin Bayou District. He was the most intrepid and daring of Watie's captains. He married in 1864 at Spencer Academy, Choctaw Nation, Fannie, the daughter of Robert Buffington and Ann (Taylor) Daniel. Robert B. Daniel was elected Senator from Deleware District in 1847, Clerk of the Senate in 1849 and Assistant Chief of the Cherokee

Nation in 1871. He died January 16, 1872. Captain Samuel and Fannie Gunter were the parents of Nannie E., John Edward, born November 12, 1869, and Sammie, born July 31, 1873, and married Andrew Bell Cunningham.

Galbreath, Mrs. Earl.—Carrie Choteau Cornatzer was born in Delaware District, February 18, 1872, educated at Vinita and Lawrence, Kansas. Married November 27, 1900, Benjamin F. Choteau, born February 18, 1861, in Johnson County, Kansas. He died January 20, 1903, and she married January 20, 1914, Earl, son of Edward and Anna Galbreath, born July 23, 1890, in Boone County, Missouri. Her son by her first marriage, Walter Choteau, was born August 4, 1902. Mr. Galbreath is a farmer near Big Cabin.

Marie Therese Bourgeois, an orphan Creole of New Orleans, married Auguste Rene Choteau, a native of Southeastern France. Her son, Jean Pierre Choteau, founded St. Louis, Missouri, when he was less than fifteen years of age. His second wife was Bridget Sancier and their youngest son, Frederick Bates Choteau, together with his elder brother, founded Kansas City, Missouri. Frederick Bates Choteau married Elizabeth Tooley, a Shawnee, and they were the parents of William Myers Choteau who married Mary Silverheel and they were the parents of Benjamin F. Choteau, who married Caroline Cornatzer and is the father of Walter Choteau.

Gentry, Mrs. William M. (See Hicks)—Margaret, daughter of Robert Ray and Cynthia Jane (Horn) Taylor, was born Nov. 10, 1873, educated at Worcester Academy, and Willie Halsell College, Vinita. Married at Weston, Texas, April 18, 1891, William M. son of W. J. and Nancy A. Gentry, born August 10, 1871, in Ray County, Missouri. They are the parents of: Ralph Ray, born July 7, 1893; Blanche Sunbeam, born Oct. 15, 1896; Christopher Robert, born March 23, 1900; Winnie Gertrude, born April 7, 1902; Hearst T., born May 6, 1904; William Lee, born April 30, 1908; Annie Audrey, born January 28, 1910; Ruth, born Dec. 28, 1912, and Juna Gentry, born March 2, 1916. True to the family custom, William M. Gentry is a farmer and raiser of thoroughbred saddle stock at his splendidly equipped Rose Valley Farm.

Jeremiah Horn, a white man, married Elsie, the daughter of Chief Charles R. Hicks and their son, William Horn, married Margaret Leadbetter, and they were the parents of Cynthia J. Horn, born in Texas, November 29, 1847. Married in March, 1871, Robert Ray Taylor, born in Tennessee, November 20, 1847.

Chief Charles R. Hiçks, on whom an extended sketch is given in the historical text was the son of Nathan and Elizabeth (Broom) Hicks, his mother being a daughter of Chief Broom of Broomtown, where his first printed Cherokee law was enacted on September 11, 1808.

Goss, Benjamin F. (See Grant, Downing, Ghigau, Oolootsa and Adair)—Benjamin Franklin, son of George Washington and Mary Alice (Mayes) Goss, born May 14, 1884, married Jan. 10, 1906, Flora Etta, daughter of Jacob Udolphus and Annie Charlotte (Towers) Alberty, born April 4, 1885. They are the parents of John Thompson, born Jan. 27, 1907; William Clarence, born September 22, 1909; George Washington, born January 3, 1912, and Mary Charlotte Goss, born May 4, 1915.

George Washington Goss is the son of Benjamin F. and Sarah Emily (Bean) Goss.

Jacob Udolphus Alberty is the son of John D. and Jennie (Buffington) Alberty.

Gott, A. M. (See Cordery)—Sue T., daughter of Charles, a native of Spartenberg Dist., S. Car., and Jane (Collins) Harris, was born July 6, 1846, and married Nov. 8, 1869, Alfred Mason Gott, born Sept. 28, 1844, in Logan County, Illinois. He was a member of Company A, Terry's Texas Rangers before and during the Civil war. Mrs. Gott died March 30, 1916.

George, Mrs. Estelle (See Grant)—Ada, daughter of Joseph Lynch and Alice (Tucker) Thompson, born Jan. 26, 1881, educated at Vinita and Female Seminary. Married at Vinita, December 8, 1909, to Estel E. George, born Nov. 26, 1881, in Cooper County, Missouri. They are the parents of Mary Ellen George born November 12, 1911. Mr. and Mrs. George are farming near Big Cabin.

Graham, Mrs. T. O. (See Grant)—Ludovic Grant was a trader among the Cherokees in 1735. He married a member of the Wolf Clan. Their only a child, a daughter, married William Emory, an Englishman. From this union there were three daughters, the youngest of whom was Susannah whose third husband was General Joseph Martin of the Revolutionary army and later U. S. agent for the Cherokees. General and Susannah Martin's daughter Nannie married Jeter Lynch an Irishman. Maria, daughter of Jeter and Susannah Lynch married Johnson Thompson and later Andrew Brown Cunningham. From this union were born the following children: James Franklin Thompson who married Caroline Elizabeth McCord; Joseph Lynch Thompson, married Frances Kell; Alice Tucker; and Miranda King, nee Riley; Sabra Anne Cunningham married Lucien Burr Bell and Jeter Thompson Cunningham, born Dec. 1, 1843, was 1st Lieut. of Co. A, First Cherokee Mounted Volunteers in the Confederate service, under Captain Hugh Tinnon and Colonel Stand Watie. He married on June 13, 1886 Camille Moore, born Feb. 12, 1849. He was elected to the Council from Delaware District August 2, 1869 and August 4, 1873; Elected Clerk of the same district August 2, 1875. Mrs. Keziah Camille Cunningham was the daughter of Elijah and Jamima (Landrum) Moore, and the grand-daughter of James and Rebecca (Duncan) Landrum.

Jeter Thompson and Keziah Camille Cunningham were parents of Andrew Bell Cunningham, Principal Chief of the Cherokee Nation; Catherine Aurora born February 17, 1871, married Connell Rogers; Jeter Thompson born January 12, 1873, married Margaret Ellis; Keziah Elizabeth, born January 14, 1875, married Oliver Lynch Wyly, and Hugh Morgan Rogers. Lily May, born May 23, 1879, married George Owen Grant; Belle, born April 26, 1881, graduated from the Female Seminary May 25, 1900, married Dec. 21, 1910; Thomas Oscar Graham, born December 4, 1875. Albert Sidney Johnson born February 19, 1883, married Margaret Daugherty; Roxana born March 8, 1885 married Dr. E. B. Reed.

Humphreys, Margaret nee Woodall (See Hendricks)—Margaret Woodall, born July 18, 1866. Married at Tahlequah Nov. 24, 1909. James Humphreys, born in Monroe County, Tennessee in 1867. They are the parents of Roxis, born August 30, 1910; Harrison, born March 16, 1912; Eula, born June 10, 1914; and Virgil, born May 3, 1916. James Humphreys is a Mason and an Odd Fellow.

Hendricks, Thomas Sr. (See Hendricks)—Thomas Hendricks was born Aug. 29, 1839. He served during the Civil War in the Indian Home Guards under Captain Blunt. Married at Park Hill in 1869, Nellie Ragsdale, born September 22, 1839. They were the parents of Rufus, Thomas, Susie and Janana Hendricks. Thomas Hendricks was elected Councilor from Tahlequah District August 3, 1885.

Hendricks, Thomas Jr. (See Hendricks)—Thomas Hendricks, Jr. born at Tahlequah Jan. 14, 1877. Educated at Tahlequah. Married at Tahlequah Jan. 11, 1899, Maud Stanley, born April 25, 1888. She died Mar. 6, 1910. They were the parents of: Robert E. born Dec. 9, 1899; Clara M. born May 2, 1900; Viola, born October 21, 1902; Thelma G. born October 16, 1904; Wirt, born April 4, 1906 ;and Maude Hendricks, born February 25, 1908. Mrs Hendricks died March 6, 1910 and he married at Muskogee September 29, 1910, Bessie Bagley born February 19, 1895 in Missouri. They are the parents of Hazel, born September 16, 1912; Ross, born February 2, 1915; Pauline, born June 9, 1918. and Thomas Franklin Hendricks born March 13, 1921. Mr. Hendricks Cherokee name is Teeseeyauke, he is a member of the A. H. T. A.

Heflin, D. G. (See Grant and Ghigau)—Elizabeth Christine, daughter of Dr. Jeter Lynch and Mary Jane (Taylor) Thompson, born Jan. 28, 1854, in Delaware Dist. Married Oct. 17, 1871, William, son of William and (Timberlake) Eubanks, born in Going Snake District, Dec. 3, 1841. He enlisted in 1861 in Captain George Harlan Starr's Co. of the First Cherokee Mounted Rifles. Was First Lieutenant of Captain William Taylor's Company and upon the decease of Taylor he became Captain. He was elected Executive Councilor in November 1887. Mrs. Eubanks died March 29, 1912. They were the parents of Ada Archer Eubanks, born at Tahlequah June 25, 1884, educated at Tahlequah and Female Seminary. Married at Tahlequah July 30, 1905, Dessis Garfield, son of Rachel and J. Barto Heflin, born February 10, 1882 in Harrison, Boon County, Arkansas. She died February 21, 1913. They were the parents of Dennis Garfield born at Tahlequah May 24, 1906 and Rachel Elizabeth Heflin, born at Tahlequah April 18, 1909.

Harlan, William Lee (See Ghigau and Grant)—William Lee, son of George Washington and Sarah Jane (Cecil) Harlan was born in Delaware District, September 12, 1874. Married March 29, 1904 Lucinda, daughter of William and Charlotte (Mayes) Ballard, born near Carey's Ferry on Grand River June 11, 1879. She graduated from the Female Seminary June 29, 1899. They are the parents of: Grace Leota, born July 4, 1905; Vanney, born July 27, 1907; Jewell Bernice, born March 12, 1913 and William Lee Harlan, born July 20, 1920.

Mr. and Mrs. Harlan are members of the Methodist Church. He is a farmer and stockraiser near White Oak.

William, son of Archibald and Annie (Fields) Ballard born in Delaware District May 29, 1852 and educated in that District. Married December 26, 1871 Charlotte Mayes, born August 6, 1851. They are the parents of Mrs. Lucinda (Ballard) Harlan.

Hawkins, Roswell Drake (See Ghigau)—Roswell Drake, son of Adison Gregory and Ruth (Parks) Hawkins was born in Vinita March 27, 1891. Educated at Vinita and Kemper Military College. Married at Los Angeles, Calif. Aug. 21, 1911 La Donne Helen, daughter of Joseph and Mabel Paulet, born Aug. 15, in Centralia, Cook Co. Ill. They are the parents of Roswell Drake, Jr., born March 5, 1918 and Beverly Joyce Hawkins, born March 18, 1921. Mr. Hawkins is one of the prosperous young cattlemen of Craig County.

Mrs. Ruth Hawkins is the daughter of Supreme Judge George Washington and Louise (Spriggs) Parks.

Hayes, Mrs. Eliza (See Griffin)—Eliza, daughter of William and Eliza Griffin was born Sept. 25, 1861. Educated in the Cherokee public schools and Female Seminary. Taught school for some time and married at Webbers Falls on Jan. 11, 1883 Richard, son of John and Rebecca Hayes, born Sept. 3, 1859 in Cherokee Nation, Indian Territory. They are the parents of Emma Hays, born Dec. 13, 1884.

Mrs. Hayes is a member of the Methodist church. Her Cherokee name is Lesi Saluaya and she belongs to the Holly clan

Horrell, Mrs. Louise H. (See England)—Louisa H. daughter of William and Mary Jane (England) Habish, born June 23, 1878. Educated in the Cherokee Public Schools and Worchester Academy, Vinita. Married at Oswego, Kansas March 8, 1905, George T., son of Benjamin and Mary Frances Horrel. They are the parents of: Mary Thelma, born February 9, 1906 and Allen C. Horrell, born October 31, 1908.

Mr. Horrell is a stillman with the St. Clair Refining Company.

Hickey, George H. (See Grant, Adair and Ghigau)—George Henry, son of Thomas Preston and Lucinda (Gott) Hickey, born November 24, 1880, educated in Coowuscoowee District. Married at Pryor January 5, 1904, Sallie, daughter of James Allen and Annie (Foster) Mayes, born May 10, 1879. They are the parents of Benjamin Martin, born April 6, 1900; Lulu Myrtle, born September 29, 1904; Susie Alice, born January 6, 1907; Georgia Margueritta, born September 13, 1910 and Thomas Preston Hickey, born November 20, 1911.

Hickey, John Walter. (See Grant, Ghigau, and Adair)—John Walter, son of Thomas Preston and Lucinda (Gott) Hickey, born May 22, 1892. Married at Independence, Kansas, March 15, 1916, Maude Alma, daughter of William and Mary Lucinda (Adair) Gott, born March 4, 1899 in Flint District. They are the parents of Yvonne, born August 5, 1917 and William Bryant Hickey, born August 25, 1920.

Ludovic Grant, a Scotch trader married a full blood Cherokee woman of the Wolf Clan. Their daughter married William Emory an Englishman and they were the parents of Susannah who married Richard Fields, a white man. Their son Thomas Fields, married Nancy Rogers nee Downing and they were the parents of Rachel Jane Fields, born in 1813, married Henry Hickey, born March 15, 1815 in Tennessee. Their son, Thomas Preston Hickey, born September 15, 1853. Married May 26, 1874 Lucinda Gott, born August 12, 1854. They are the parents of John Walter Hickey, the subject of this sketch.

Harris, Mrs. J. W. (See England)—Ida Josephine, daughter of Elias H. and Arminda (England) Jenkins was born in Cooweescoowee District, July 4, 1870 and educated at the Cherokee National schools. Married at Siloam Spring, Arkansas, July 10, 1886, John Wesley Harris, born June 23, 1867, in Winebago County, Illinois. They are the parents of: Flora May, born July 25, 1887; Gertrude N., born January 13, 1889; Ulalah S., born September 5, 1890; Roy C., born April 20, 1892, and John Wesley Harris, born June 3, 1897. Mr. Harris is a farmer and stock raiser near Vinita. He was elected County Commissioner of Craig County, September 17, 1907.

Joseph Roswell Harris was born in Durant, Illinois, Nov. 17, 1837. Served in the Civil war in Company H, 74th Illinois Infantry; married Aug. 27, 1866, Rachel Putney. She died November 23, 1911, and he died May 23, 1921. They were the parents of: John Wesley and Ulalah Harris.

Arminda England was born November 25, 1831; married William England, Isaac Schrimsher and Elias H. Jenkins. She died December 27, 1879.

Harris, Colonel Johnson (See Grant, Cordery and Adair)—Colonel Johnson Harris, named for his father's friend, Colonel Johnson, was born April 19, 1856, in Georgia; died at Muskogee, Sept. 25, 1921. Educated in Canadian District and Male Seminary. Married August 12, 1877, Nannie E., daughter of Richard F., and Rachel Elizabeth (Goss) Fields, born October 7, 1849. She died November 14, 1887, and he married March 4, 1891, Mary Elizábeth, daughter of William Penn and Sarah Ann (Adair) Adair, born June 12, 1864. She died Nov. 11, 1902, and he married Caroline Alice Collins nee Hall. Colonel Johnson Harris is the father of: Beuna Vista, born October 26, 1877; William Richard, born January 23, 1880. Graduated from Male Seminary, May 24, 1900. Died October 24, 1917; Colonel Johnson, born March 22, 1882, married February 22, 1910, Caroline Elizabeth Ghormley, born June 3, 1888. Graduated from Female Seminary June 1, 1905. They are the parents of Ewing Johnson, born December 14, 1910; Russell Fields, born July 27, 1912; Buena W., born May 6, 1914; Jocarey, born October 6, 1916; Nannie, born September 6, 1918, and William Richard Harris, born April 12, 1921. Joel Adair, born June 22, 1894 and died June 30, 1915, Caroline Ellen, born November 8, 1896. Married September 24, 1919, W. A. Robertson; and Charles Hasting Harris, born August 15, 1899. Colonel Johnson Harris was elected Senator from Canadian District in 1881, 1883 and 1885. He was President of the Senate from 1883 to 1885. Elected delegate to Washington in 1886 and 1895. Elected Treasurer November 6, 1891, and on the 23rd of the succeeding month was elected Principal Chief. Elected Senator from Tahlequah District in 1899.

Hendricks, Rufus—(See Hendricks)—Rufus, son of Thomas and Nellie Hendricks was born October 25, 1869, educated in the Cherokee National schools. Married at Tahlequah December 22, 1895 to Susie, daughter of Joseph and Almeda Stanley, born March 22, 1876 in Jasper County, Missouri. They are the parents of: Joseph born September 29, 1896; James, born November 12, 1897; Willdie, born January 6, 1899; Marcus A. born July 26, 1901; Harvey, born March 29, 1903; Edna, born August 2, 1906; Herchell, born July 13, 1908; Herbert, born April 17, 1910; Ethel, born November 4, 1911; Iva, born May 16, 1913; Elva born November 3, 1915, and Dolora, born January 4, 917. Mr. Hendricks is one of the representative farmers of his community and has been a member of the district school board for seven years.

Henry, Mrs. W. G.—(See Downing, Daniel and Foreman)—Nannie Catherine Daniel, born January 12, 1835, married December 23, 1857 Anderson Springton Wilson, born in 1830. They were the parents of DeWitt, born January 7, 1860; James Daniel born February 2, 1861 and May Wilson, born May 1, 1862. Anderson Springston Wilson died December 26, 1865 and his widow married Henry Clay Barnes in 1872; Henry Clay Barnes was born at Dwight Mission, Cherokee Nation, August 29, 1845. They were the parents of Myrtle, born July 25, 1874, educated at Tahlequah Female Seminary, married May 14, 1891 Wallace Gibbs Henry, born April 6, 1872.

W. G. and Myrtle Henry are the parents of DeWitt Clinton, born April 11, 1892; Roy Wilson, born July 22, 1897 and Myra May born Dec. 8, 1903. Nancy Catherine Barnes died Dec. 10, 1889.

Hammett, James W.—(See Mills and Grant)—Mary Mills, Cherokee name Gaule-tsa, born December 25, 1875 near Sallisaw, is the daughter of Charles and Margaret (Johnson) Mills. Educated at Cherokee public schools and Female Seminary. Married James W. Hammett. They are the parents of: Richard L., born January 3, 1895, married Ruby Landrum; Mary Elizabeth, born August 3, 1869 Ethel Christine, born December 25, 1898 and James E. Hammett, born September 8, 1901.

Hallum, Mrs| William O.—Mary Ella daughter of R. L. and Eliza Jane (Morris) England, born in Delaware District, February 11, 1882, educated in the Cherokee National Schools. Married February 12, 1900 William O., son of Wm. B. born October 17, 1821, died October 25, 1895, and Micca (England) Hallum, born June 8, 1825, died November 14, 1887 in Georgia. They are the parents of Maude Evelyn, born January 10, 1901, married Marion B. Carico and has one son, Jock Carico, born September 5, 1919; Eliza May, born April 9, 1903; Susie Leona, born October 3, 1907 and Sadie Floris Hallum, born January 2, 1914.

Houston, Mrs. Lee—(See Ward)—Stella Lenora, daughter of Lovell Peabody and Johnanna (Powell) Ballard, born in Delaware District, August 23, 1900. Educated at Ketchum. Married at Siloam Springs, Arkansas, September 2, 1916, Lee, son of A. P. and Mary Houston, born July 26, 1892 in Berry County, Missouri. They are the parents of: Lillie May, born July 15, 1917 and Mary Ann Houston, born March 31, 1920. Mr. Houston is a farmer near Ketchum.

Nancy, daughter of James and Sidney (Redding) Ward was born Jan. 29, 1830. Married Sept. 21, 1845, Cal Dean Gunter, born March 30, 1818. He died March 27, 1898. They were the parents of Anna Eliza Gunter, born May 4, 1848 and married John Powell. Their daughter, Johnanna Powell was born February 15, 1869 and married February 28, 1899, Lovell Peabody Ballard, born January 27, 1879 in Benton County, Arkansas. She died August 20, 1920.

Howell, Mrs. C. W.—(See Hildebrand)—Sena B., daughter of John T. and Laura (Hildebrand) Davis was born in Delaware District, September 20, 1887, educated in the Cherokee National Schools. Married at Vinita, February 11, 1906, C. W., son of Lemuel and Elizabeth Howell. They are the parents of Nora May, born May 31, 1913; Woodrow Wilson, born November 5, 1916; and Louis C. Howell, born September 8, 1919. Mr. Howell is a farmer near Ketchum.

Hendricks, Mrs. James B.—Eleanor E. J., daughter of James A. and Mary A. (Tyner) Hibbs, was born in the Cherokee Nation March 18, 1882, educated in the Cherokee National Schools. Married Nov. 4, 1900, James B., son of Elkanah and Margaret Hendricks. They are the parents of: Zilph, born Nov. 2, 1901; Lonnie, born June 11, 1903, is at present in the U. S. Coast Artillery in California; Mamie, born August 25, 1904, married Harry Cook; Ray, born July 31, 1906; Jessie, born February 26, 1908; Jay born April 25, 1909; Marie, born May 1, 1910; Lawrence, born January 26, 1912; Nina, born May 1, 1914; Cecil born September 9, 1915; Elkana, born September 11, 1917, and Margaret Hendricks, born February 1, 1919.

Hogue, Mrs. Joseph S.—(See Oolootsa and Ghigau)—Mary Erskine Clark, born December 12, 1880, educated at Jackson, Tennessee. Married at Chelsea June 5, 1898 Joseph Sterling Hogue, born January 28, 1867 in Granger County, Tennessee. They are the parents of Joseph Clarke, born January 7, 1900; Condroy Lea, born June 20, 1903 and Sarah Erskine Hogue, born April 7, 1906.

Mr. Hogue is a live stock dealer at Chelsea. Mrs. Hogue is the daughter of Richard and Emma (Lea) Clark and the granddaughter of Armstrong and Minerva Jane (Walker) Lea.

Jones, Mrs. George W.—Annie Odette, daughter of L. Baxter and Frances P. (McGee) Prather was born in Cowskin Prairie, Delaware District, November 17, 1887, and educated in Female Seminary. Married at Vinita September 25, 1905, George W. son of Winfield Scott and Lillie D. (Fisher) Jones, born December 19, 1881, in Seneca, Missouri. They are the parents of: Fannie Lillie, born August 5, 1906; Sylvia Clovis, born February 9, 1908; Tracy Edwin, born May 29, 1909; Opal Ethel, born June 10, 1911; Othoe Harold, born April 13, 1913; Bertha Evelyn, born February 1, 1915 and George Henry Jones, born February 25, 1920. Mr. Jones is a farmer near Big Cabin.

Journeycake, Mrs. Eliza A.—See Downing)—Eliza Ann, daughter of Carter and Catherine (Benge) Daniel was born July 16,

1860, educated at the Cherokee Orphan Asylum, married December 23, 1881 Isaac Newton Journeycake, born February, 1859 and died in 1916. They were the parents of: Robert Joseph, born October 26, 1882 and died April 14, 1903; Jesse Daniel, born March 21, 1890 ,married Georgia Shamblin; Isaac Newton, born October 23, 1892, married Tanna Crisp, and Bender Journeycake, born May 23, 1895.

Mrs. Journeycake's Cherokee name is Chiouke.

Jones, Mrs. Dr. J. S.—(See Foreman).—Mary Elizabeth Dege, born in Atlanta, Georgia, October 30, 1881, educated at Pryor and Female Seminary. Married October 5, 1907, J. S. Jones, D. D. S. They are the parents of James Staunton, born January 5, 1909; Mary Pauline, born July 7, 1911 and Helen Mercedes Jones, born September 13, 1913.

Dr. Jones is a graduate of the Southern Dental College of Atlanta, Georgia. He was a volunteer in the World War and was stationed at Camp Greenleaf, was commissioned a First Lieutenant and transferred to Camp Mills, N. Y. Received his discharge on January 21, 1919. He is at present the Commander of the American Legion camp at Pryor. Mrs. Dr. Jones belongs to the Baptist church, is an Eastern Star and White Shriner.

Anthony Foreman, a Scotchman married Susie, a full blood Cherokee of the Savannah Clan and their daughter Catherine married James Bigby. They were the parents of Mary Anna Bigby, born August 9, 1802, she married David Taylor, born in Orange County, Virginia, December 16, 1791. Their son James Taylor was the father of Laura Alice Taylor, born June 10, 1846, in North Carolina, married at Walhalla, South Carolina, October 13, 1867, John Henry Dege born February 4, 1845 in Bassum, Hanover Germany and they were the parents of Mrs. Mary Elizabeth Jones.

Johnston, John Edward.—(See Ross, Oolotsa and Wilson)—John Edward Johnston, born March 21, 1881. Married December 25, 1906 at Muldrow, Oklahoma, Ida, daughter of Alexander F. and Nannie (Ridding) McKinney, born June 10, 1887. Mrs. Johnston died April 21, 1915. They were the parents of Albert Sidney, born December 23, 1907; John Edward, born August 2, 1909; William Alexander, born November 28, 1910; and Joseph Franklin Johnston, born January 28, 1913. Mr. Johnston married Mrs. Anne Bruton Levy, February 25, 1921 .

John Edward Johnston was elected Sheriff of Sequoyah County, September 17, 1907; November 8, 1910 and Navember 5, 1912

Catherine, a full blood Cherokee married John Gunter, said to have been a Welshman. Their son, Samuel, married Ayoka and their son, George Washington Gunter, married Eliza Nave. He was elected Senator from Sequoyah District, August 6, 1849. Their daughter Susan Catherine Gunter married Robert Johnston and James Choate and was the mother of Albert Main Johnson who married Delilah Baldridge and they are the parents of John E. Johnston, the subject of this sketch. Albert M. Johnston was elected Sheriff of Sequoyah District August 4, 1879 and August 1, 1881.

Riggs, William G.—(See Sanders, Grant and Ross).—Juliette Scrimsher Chambers. born November 25, 1873 near Claremore, educated in the Cherokee National schools and graduated from the Fort Worth Business College, married at Claremore June 22, 1902 William Grant Riggs, born January 14, 1869 in Missouri . They are the parents of: Lee Grant, born June 21, 1908 and Joseph Vann Riggs born November 27, 1914. Mr. Riggs is a substantial stockholder in the Farmers Bank and Trust Co., of Claremore. By a former marriage Mr. Riggs has three thildren; Martha Mary, born June 14, 1896; William Edgar, born November 8, 1898 and Rolla L. Riggs, born August 31, 1900. Mrs. Juliette S. Riggs' Cherokee name is, Wuti and she belongs to the Bird Clan.

Henry Chambers, son of Maxwell and Elsie (Sanders) Chambers, was born April 21, 1823, married Nancy Hendricks, born September 4, 1825. He was elected Senator from Cooweescoowee District August 2, 1875 and August 5, 1877. Mrs. Nancy Chambers died November 26, 1879. He was elected Treasurer of the Cherokee Nation in 1883 and Assistant Chief on August 3. 1891. He died of infuenza at Tahlequah on December 10, 1891. His son Vann Chambers was born on February 15, 1850 married July 28, 1871 Jennie D. McCoy, born April 25, 1854. They are the parents of: Juliette Schrimsher, Elizabeth, Louis R.,

Vann Sanders, Clarence, Cora and Joanna Rogers Chambers.

Keith, James G.—James G., son of Joel M. and Susan Ann (McClure) Keith was born in Georgia, March 4, 1874, and educated in that State. He married at Claremore, March 4, 1900, Lottie, daughter of A. L. and Abigal Knox, born April 2, 1880 in Concordia, Kansas and was educated in that state. They are the parents of: Joel A., born May 27, 1901; Viola R., born January 7, 1903; James R., born October 27, 1905; Mary A., born August 2, 1907; Susan E., born November 7, 1916; Sarah Charlotte born February 25, 1919; and LaVaughn Keith, born July 26, 1921. Mr. Keith is a member of the A. H. T. A. and of the Baptist church.

Kerr, Mrs. Robert.—Anna Marie, daughter of John and Jane (Daugherty) Greenfeather was born in Delaware District, February 3, 1885. Educated at Ketchum. Married at Vinita, in January 1905. Robert, son of Alexander and Tilda Kerr, born August 30, 1890. They are the parents of: Cora, born August 30, 1901 married Clyde Bosley: Tilda, born June 30, 1904; Robert, born July 23, 1906; Lee Allen, born September 17, 1910; Lora May, born October 28, 1912 and Irene Elizabeth Kerr, born January 16, 1917. Mr. Kerr is a farmer near Ketchum.

Keys, Elizabeth (See Grant, Ghigau, Foreman, Adair and Riley)—James McIntosh Keys, born near the mouth of Fourteen Mile Creek in Tahlequah District, March 25, 1843. Educated in that District. He enlisted at the beginning of the war under his cousin Captain O. H. P. Brewer and served four years in the Confederacy. Naturally kind, considerate and of much more than ordinary native ability. He married in March 16, 1869 Nancy Jane Mayes, born April 29, 1850 near Baptist, Going Snake District. She was educated at Baptist Mission. He was elected Solicitor of Cooweescoowee District August 4, 1879 and August 6, 1883. Elected senator from the same District August 3, 1891. Elected a member of the townsite commission in 1881 and Chief Justice of the Cherokee Nation in November 1885. On the inception of statehood he was elected Senator from the twenty-ninth District.

James McDaniel and Nancy Jane (Mayes) Keys were the parents of; Dennis Bushyhead, born July 15, 1878; Bluford Alberty, born February 12, 1882 and Elizabeth Covel Keys, born September 12, 1885 and she graduated from Female Seminary June 3, 1904.

Mrs. Nancy Jane Keys is the daughter of George Washington and Charlotte (Bushyhead) Mayes.

Kelley, Mrs. W. P.—Fannie Viola, daughter of George and Lucinda (Jones) Wingfield, born December 8, 1871. Married at Vinita, November 25, 1889, William P. son of John and Elizabeth Kelley, born June 26, 1864 in Texas Co. Mo. They are the parents of Lizzie Lucinda Kelley, born August 5, 1886. Married 1919 Stephen Edward Landrum, born July 18, 1895. He served in the World War from November 1917 to February 27, 1919. They are the parents of Willie Steve (girl) Landrum, born May 12, 1920. The Kelleys and Landrums are farmers near Big Cabin in Craig County.

King, Richard W. (Ward)—Richard Willey, son of Judge Benjamin Cooper and Abbie (Kadle) King was born August 1, 1871, educated at Tahlequah and Male Seminary. Married July 20, 1890 Melvin Holland, born May 26, 1871. They were the parents of· Benjamin Cooper born December 23, 1892, married at Tahlequah August 30, 1912 to Peggy Balleau born in 1894. Has one son, Richard Chester King, born Nov. 15, 1913. Clifford Willey, born Dec. 27, 1902 and John King, born April 1, 1910.

Benjamin Cooper King was elected Judge of Tahlequah District, August 5, 1889. Richard Willey King was elected County Commissioner of the Third District of Cherokee County on November 5, 1912. He is an Odd Fellow and Knight of Pythias. Benjamin Cooper King, Jr., is a Mason and Odd Fellow.

Letteer, Mrs. Roy (See Grant)—Lahoma Lucile, daughter of Chief William Charles and Nannie (Haynie) Rogers, was born at Skiatook, May 4, 1900. Educated at Skiatook and married in Oklahoma City, Oct. 19, 1920, Roy, son of Mr. and Mrs. W. H. Letteer. They are the parents of Jane E. Letteer, born September 11, 1921.

Mrs. Letteer is the daughter of William Charels Rogers the last chief of the Cherokees and the great grand-daughter of Captain John Rogers, the last chief of the Old Settler Cherokees.

Lightle, James (See Thompson)—James, son of Edward and Sarah Lightle was born

Tuesday, August 22, 1889 in Scammon, Cherokee County, Kansas. Educated at Talala. Married at Talala, November 6th, 1910, Nettie, daughter of Lawson and Mary Jane (Merrill) Runyar, born Nov. 6, 1886. They are the parents of Elsie Florence Lightle, born April 23, 1913.

Mr. Lightle is a pharmacist at Talala.

Little, Mrs. Joseph (See Grant)—Joseph Carter, son of William and Theresa Lane (Davis) Little was born at Vinita, Monday May 19, 1879. Educated in Worchester Academy, Vinita. Married at Chelsea Oct. 23, 1904, Myrtle, daughter of E. M. and Victoria (Powell) Arnold, born Oct. 23, 1884, and educated at Chelsea, Cherokee Nation. They are the parents of: Joseph, born April 5, 1907; William, born Sept. 30, 1909; Robert, born Aug. 31, 1911; Mary, born Nov. 12, 1913; Ruth, born March 9, 1918; James, born March 3, 1920. Mr. Little is one of the largest range and feeding cattle men in Oklahoma owning and leasing an extensive acreage for that purpose west of Ramona.

Lane, Rosa Gazelle—Rosa Gazelle, daughter of Dr. Andrew Jackson Lane born March 27, 1851 in Giles County, Tennessee graduated from the University of Louisiana in 1874, married December 25, 1877, Lucinda E. Journeycake nee Elliott, born April 14, 1852 at Leavenworth Kas. He died Oct. 31, 1896; Lane born Jan. 31, 1882 near Oowala, Cherokee Nation. She was educated at the Oowala public school, Female Seminary, graduating June 9, 1903, Lexington, Mo. and Petersburg, Virginia. Taught school several years and elected City Clerk of Claremore in 1921. She is a member of the Claremore Eastern Star Chapter and P. E. O. Sisterhood, chapter K. at Tulsa.

Lee, David M. (See Downing)—David Marshall, son of John and Mary (Faulkner) Lee, was born in Sequoyah District July 9, 1861, educated in Male Seminary. Married March 12, 1881, Mary Elmira, daughter of James Franklin and Elmire (Simcoe) Bethel, born September 10, 1858 in Sebastian County, Arkansas. They are the parents of Florence Ada, deceased; Lizzie May, born Jan. 16, 1883, married W. F. Wasson; Lou Emma, born December 15, 1886, married James A. Jackson and died July 28, 1920; Flossie Edna, born February 13, 1889, married James B. Galloway and Frank Emmett Lee, born October 23, 1891 and married Mary Daugherty. David Marshall Lee is a Mason, Odd Fellow and Knight of Pythias. He was elected to council from Sequoyah District, August 1, 1887. Mr. and Mrs. Lee have gratuitously adopted and reared the following orphans: James Sanderrs, Florence Emma Lackey, Mary Jane Lee, Wash Lee, Maudie May Lee, Carnell Overtaker, Alfred Andrews, David Bates Jackson, Flossie May Jackson and James P. Jackson, Jr.

Benjamin, son of Thomas and Catherine Pettit, married Peggy Cunningan and their daughter Nannie married Franklin Faulkner and they were the parents of Mary Faulkner who married John Lee.

Lipe, John Casper (See Grant, Thornton, Thompson, Oolootsa and Ross)—John Casper, son of Clark Charlesworth and Margaret Emma (Thompson) Lipe was born November 27, 1878, educated at the Cherokee public school, graduated from Male Seminary June 30, 1899 and from Spauldings Commercial College of Kansas City in July 13, 1906 Anna Belle Price, born Jan. 2, 1887 in Gonzales, Texas. She was educated at Oolagah and graduated from Female Seminary June 1, 1905. They have one daughter; Muriel Joy Lipe born March 21, 1908. Mr. Lipe's Cherokee name is Tauaneesie, he is an Elk, Woodman of the World, Knight Templar and Shriner.

Looney Price was born in February 1799, married December 28, 1837 Lititia Coady. This talented and cultivated family moved to Texas before the Civil War. Their son Daniel Coady Price, born January 31, 1844 was a member of Co. A., Terry's Texas Ranger regiment during the Civil War, elected sheriff of Gonzales Co., Texas November 4, 1882 he married Mary Anna Jones and they were the parents of: Anna Belle (Price) Lipe.

Oliver Wack Lipe born January 20, 1914 at Fort Plains, N. Y., he was elected Captain in the New York State Guards in 1833. He married in 1839, Catherine Vaught nee Gunter, born at Gunter's Landing in Alabama in May 1811. He was Commissary in Stand Watie's regiment. His son Clark Charlesworth Lipe was Adjutant in Captain John Scrimsher's company in the Confederate Cherokee service. Adjutant Lipe always ended up his roll call with the names of three of the full blood Cherokee soldiers: "Runabout, Turnover and Kickup." John

Casper Lipe has served one year in the Missouri National Guards and was Captain of the first Home Guard company organized in the state of Oklahoma receiving his commission from Gov. Robert L. Williams.

Lamon, Mrs. William A. (See Grant and Cordery)—Martha Evaline Clingan, born at Gibson Station Cherokee Nation, March 21, 1874, educated at the Female Seminary and Sedalia, Missouri, taught at Harrell Institute at Muskogee, and married at Gibson Station February 1, 1899 William Archibald, son of Robert A. and Melvina Lamon, born March 15, 1869 in Granada, Miss. They are the parents of: Mary E., born October 29, 1899; Melvina, born April 17, 1901; Catherine Wise, born October 27, 1902; Helen Martha, April 22, 1904; William Archibald, born February 4, 1910; Robert Edward, born February 4, 1912, and John Clingan Lamon, born May 3, 1913.

William Archibald Lamon is engaged in the realty and cotton business and owns the Farmers and Merchants gin at Wagoner. Mrs. Lamon is a Methodist, Eastern Star and White Shriner, a member of the Twentieth Century Club and the Home Mission Society.

William Davidson, son of Alexander and Martha (Blythe) Clingan was born November 25, 1833 in Bradley county Tennessee; served the Confederate army as First Lieutenant Company K, 15th Texas Cavalry Married at Perryville, Choctaw Nation February 6, 1870 Mary Jane, daughter of Samuel and Margaret (Vickery) Bumgarner, born January 18, 1845 on the Grand river Going Snake District. William Davidson Clingan died March 31, 1912. They were the parents of Mrs. Martha Lamon. The name Baumgarner is derived from the Ger-

Lipe, Lulu (See Oolootsa, Ross, Foreman and Riley)—Sarah Lulu Foreman, born March 15, 1875, educated at Oowala public school and the Female Seminary, from which she graduated in 1895. Married January 4, 1899 John Gunter Lipe, born December 16, 1864. He was educated at the Male Seminary and the University of Arkansas; engaged in the farming and cattle business; was a Mason, Elk, and Woodman of the World; he died May 20, 1913. Mr. and Mrs. Lipe were the parents of: Flora Foreman, born November 14, 1899; Ada Catherine, born August 27, 1901; Dewitt, born January 26, 1904; Lucy Campbell, born March 28, 1908 and Lulu Victoria Lipe, born August 27, 1912.

Stephen Taylor Foreman, born at Park Hill, Tahlequah District, September 24, 1849, married April 28, 1874 Ada Carter McClellan, born at Cane Hill, Arkansas, October 25, 1854. They were the parents of Mrs. Sarah Lipe.

Landrum, Johnson (See Duncan, Ghigau, and Conrad)—Johnson Landrum, born 1860. Married April 2, 1889, Catherine Isabel, daughter of Stephen Gray and Sarah Abigal (Hopkins) Garbarini, born June 23, 1868. They were the parents of: Nellie Jesephine, born May 6, 1890; Clifton Lawrence, born May 12, 1893; Stephen Edward, born July 18, 1895; Mary Isabel, born January 21, 1898; Ada M., Jaunita T., and Helena B. Landrum died November 19, 1906.

James Landrum, a white man, married Rebecca Duncan, a half-blood Scotch-Cherokee. Their son, John, married Nellie Otterlifter and they were the parents of Johnson Landrum.

Lowry, Andrew Nave (Ross and Oolootst)—Andrew Nave Lowry, born March 6, 1853, married March 26, 1882 Dora Pinkney nee Bruton, born February 16, 1863 in Barry County, Missouri. They are the parents of James Bruton, Mary, married Levi Clark; Daniel Valentine; Charles Anderson; Jeanette Starr; Andrew; George Henry; Lucy and Silas C. Lowry. Andrew N. Lowry belongs to the Wolf Clan and his Cherokee name is Wahyaneet.

Lawrence, (See Grant, Adair and Go-sa-du-i-sga)—Sarah Jane Adair, born March 10, 1875 at Salina; educated in the Cherokee National schools; Female Seminary, from which she graduated June 23, 1892, and Howard Payne College, Fayette, Missouri June 9, 1896. She married December 29, 1899, James Augustus Lawrence, born Oct. 18, 1856 in Texas. They are the parents of two sons: Augustus Adair, born April 21, 1901 and Gilbert Shelton, born Nov. 3, 1903.

Mr. Lawrence is the principal merchant of Tahlequah, and they have a beautiful home just east of the city.

Mrs. Lawrence is a descendant of the Martin family of Virginia. William Martin, the first known member of this family was a wealthy merchant of Bristol, England. He was the father of three children: George, Nannie and Joseph. He furnished Joseph with a ship, the Brice, and sent him to Virginia in the first quarter of the eighteenth century to keep him from contracting a marriage in England to which the father objected. Joseph married in Virginia, Susannah Childs, a member of a prominent Colonial family. They settled near Charlotteville, Albermarle county in that state where their third son Joseph Jr., was born in 1740. Joseph Jr. became a fur trader and planter, amassing a great deal of wealth. He was elected Captain of the Transylvania Militia in 1776, became Major February 17, 1779, Lieutenant Colonel in March 1781. His activities were directed against the loyalist (Tory) English, Cherokees and others of the allies in the country west of the Alleghany Mountains, they having been stirred to violence by a letter of May 9, 1776, from the British Superintendent of Southern Indian Affairs, calling on them for concerted action in killing men, women and children of the Revolutionists and their sympathizers. The South had been practically subjugated by the summer of 1780, and it was only by the efforts of such transmountain patriots as Colonel Joseph Martin that it was possible for a part of the soldiers to strike and destroy Ferguson at King's Mountain October 7, 1780 and thereby turn the tide in favor of the Americans. Colonel Martin was not at King's Mountain, as he was busy holding the British allies of the West at bay. He was elected Brigadier General of the North Carolina Militia by legislature on December 15, 1787 and was commissioned Brigadier General of the Twentieth Brigade of Virginia Militia by Governor Henry Lee of Virginia on December 11, 1793.

Martinsville, county seat of Henry county Virginia, and the place of his residence was named for him. He visited the Cherokee Nation in 1808, shortly after his visit and return home died on December 18, 1808, and was buried with military and Masonic honors. His brother Brice, named for his father's ship, was a Major in the Creek War. His nephew Brice Hammack was a resident of Warren county, Missouri.

General Joseph Martin married Susannah Fields, nee Emory, and their children were: John, born October 20, 1781, first Treasurer of the Cherokee Nation 1819, and the first Supreme Judge 1821. His wives Nellie and Lucy McDaniel were sisters. John Martin was elected Town Site Commissioner of New Echota November 12, 1825. He was a member of the Constitutional Convention of 1827 from Coosweescoowee District. He came west in the spring of 1838 and located on Grand River, near the Grand Saline. He died October 17, 1840 and is buried at Ft. Gibson. Nancy Martin, second child of General Joseph and Susannah Martin, married Jeter Lynch, and Sabra, the third daughter of General and Mrs. Martin married Daniel Davis who was born in 1785 in North Carolina, and he died in June 1866.

Judge John, and Nellie (McDaniel) Martin's oldest child was Martha, called "Patsy" born April 7, 1815, married June 25, 1829 George Washington Adair, born December 11, 1806. He was one of the leaders of the Treaty party and died April 22, 1862. Mrs. Martha Adair died January 24, 1825. George Washington and Martha Adair were the parents of: William Penn, born April 15, 1830; Brice Martin, named for his maternal uncle, born November 5, 1830; Dr. Walter Thompson, born March 13, 1838, married Rev. Joseph Franklin Thompson; Benjamin Franklin, born September 22, 1842, served four years in the Confederate service, married April 4, 1869 Mary Delilah McNair, died April 1885; Benjamin Franklin Adair died September 21, 1894; Rachael Jane, born December 20, 1845 and married Milton Howard McCullough; Cherokee Cornelia Adair, born June 16, 1848, married Jesse Bushyhead Mayes.

Benjamin Franklin and Mary Delilah (McNair) Adair were the parents of: Brice Martin, born February 17, 1870, and died May 27, 1898; Sarah Jane (Bluie) and Cherokee Cornelia, born January 11, 1881; graduated from the Female Seminary, 1899, graduated from Howard Payne College, Fayette, Mo., 1901. Married Junius Brutus Moore, January 10, 1904.

Lipe, Clarke Charlesworth, (See Thornton, Oolootsa and Thompson)—Clarke Charlesworth Lipe was born November 15, 1887, married at Tulsa July 19, 1914 Lucy V. daughter of John and Sarah Sellers born Nov. 22, 1888 near Stilwell, Cherokee Nation. They are the parents of Clarke Charlesworth Lipe born January 4, 1916. Mr. Lipe's Cherokee name is, Oolasanti. Mrs. Lipe is a member of the Baptist church.

John Gunter married Catherine a full

blood Cherokee of the Paint Clan and they settled on the Tennessee River in north Alabama, where he made powder and operated a ferry. Their daughter Catherine married as her second husband Oliver Wack Lipe born January 20, 1814 at Fort Plains, New York. He was a merchant at Fort Gibson and the first mayor of that town. He had five children of whom Clarke Charlesworth was the youngest. One of Clark Charlesworth's older brothers was John Gunter Lipe, born January 1, 1844. Though ordinarily happy and pleasant he wrote the following lines in the autograph album of Miss Victoria Susan Hicks on February 27, 1861:

"I stand at the portal and knock,
And tearfully, prayerfully wait,
O! who will unfasten the lock,
And open the beautiful gate?

Forever and ever and ever,
Must I linger and suffer alone?
Are there none that are able to sever,
The fetters that keep me from home?

My spirit is lonely and weary,
I long for the beautiful streets.
The world is so chilly and dreary,
And bleeding and torn are my feet."
John Gunter Lipe.

He was killed in a skirmish on Bayou Monard on July 27, 1862.

McSpadden, Oscar Lyle, (See Grant and Oolootsa)—Oscar Lyle McSpadden, born November 2, 1892 educated at Chelsea; married September 1920, Georgia Craig.

Mr. McSpadden is engaged in stock raising for the firm of Milam & McSpadden near Magdalena New Mexico, where he has taken active part in the upbuilding of the community; he is a 32nd degree Mason and Shriner. Attended Business College in Coffeyville, Kas. Was in the stock business prior to going to New Mexico.

McIntosh, Mrs. John R.—Maria L. Seguichy, born in Salina District of the Cherokee Nation, educated at the Female Seminary and Bacone University; taught school in Cooweescoowee and Delaware Districts; married at Chelsea, January 25, 1891 John Ross McIntosh, born Feb. 26, 1866. They are the parents of. Beatrice N., born December 14 ,1891, married Paul W. Fry, and Ethel R., born December 21, 1902, married Roy Johnson.

The proper name of Segulchys is Cummings. But as is often the case, the Cherokee name was universally used. Mrs. McIntosh's maternal grandfather was Joseph Powell, brother of Captain William Powell of the United States Army (1839). Her brother Joseph R. Sequichy was editor of The Cherokee Advocate 1897-8. He died August 4, 1920. Mrs. McIntosh's name is Waleeah.

John Ross McIntosh was elected member of the Council from Cooweescoowee District August 2, 1897 and was elected by that body as Speaker. He was elected Treasurer of Rogers county in November 1920. His Father, John McIntosh, who died July 17, 1916 was the last Chief Justice of the Cherokee Nation.

Mr. and Mrs. McIntosh speak both the English and Cherokee language with more than ordinary proficiency.

McSpadden, J. T. (See Oolootsa, Downing and Cordery)—Sallie Clementine Rogers, born in Bonham, Texas, December 16, 1863. Educated in the Cherokee public schools, and Cherokee Orphan Asylum; married December 16, 1885 John Thomas McSpadden, born March 15, 1852 in DeKalb county Alabama. They are the parents of: Clement Mayes, born December 20, 1886, graduated from Kemper Military School, Boonville, Missouri May 29, 1902, died in California August 20, 1912; May, born July 21, 1891, graduated from the Female Seminary May 29, 1907, married Charles Walton Poole; Herbert Thomas, born October 1. 1893, graduated from the Male Seminary May 31, 1910, served during the World War in the Rainbow Division; Maude Irene, born April 5, 1896, graduated from Chelsea High School 1916, married William Walker Milam; Helen, born April 11, 1899, graduated from the Chelsea high school class of 1917; Pauline Elizabeth, born September 13, 1901, Graduate Chelsea High School class of 1922 and Maurice Rogers McSpadden, born April 10, 1905.

John Thomas McSpadden, a successful stockman and farmer is the son of Reverend T. K. B. and Elizabeth (Green) McSpadden. Mrs. Sallie Clementine McSpadden is the daughter of Clement Vann and Mary America (Scrimsher) Rogers. Clement Rogers was a Captain in the Confederate Cherokee service, senator and District Judge of Coowescoowee District and a member of the Oklahoma Constitutional convention which named Rogers county in his honor.

McLaughlin, Mrs. William C. (See Grant, Ghigau, Foreman, Conrad, Duncan and Half breed)—William Cecil McLaughlin, born September 22, 1893, educated at Grove Stilwell and Muskogee, graduating in a business course from the latter. Married at Vinita, March 28, 1919, Lelia Leone, daughter of Richard Fields and Martha Adair (Brewer) Benge, born on Lynch's Prairie December 16, 1892. They are the parents of Cecil Benge McLaughlin, born May 10, 1921. Mr. McLaughlin is farming near Adair.

Elizabeth, daughter of Andrew and Catherine (Hicks) Miller married Philip Inlow a native of South Carolina and their son, Sylvester Inlow, born June 24, 1837, married December 28, 1861 Susannah Paden, born November 1, 1844. He died June 13, 1878 and she died February 13, 1889. Their daughter Margaret Caroline Inlow, born August 6, 1879 married September 20, 1890 Joshua Ezekial McLaughlin, born February 14, 1853.

Samuel, Mrs. P. W. (See Grant and Ghigau)—Florence Wilson McSpadden, born June 26, 1873 at Tahlequah. Educated at the Tahlequah City Schools and graduated from Female Seminary, June 23, 1892. Married at Tahlequah in January 1895 Philip Wharton Samuel born September 19, 1867 in Calloway County, Missouri and graduated from Spaulding's Business College May 2, 1888. They are the parents of Vance Ray, born November 21, 1897 and Maurine Samuel born October 22, 1902.

Philip Wharton Samuel is very prominent in the banking circles of the State, having been Cashier of the First National Bank at Pryor, President of First State Bank of Vinita for seven years, Cashier and late President of the Oklahoma State of Muskogee, which was changed under his management to the Exchange National Bank.

Mrs. Samuel is a member of the Methodist Church and was a tireless worker in World War Auxiliary activities.

James Walker, son of Reverend J. K. B. McSpadden, was born October 25, 1848 in Alabama, married April 18, 1872 Annie, daughter of Dr. Jeter Lynch and Mary Jane (Taylor) Thompson born May 4, 1852 in Delaware District, Cherokee Nation. They were the parents of Florence Wilson; Richard Vance, Mary Jane, who married Thomas R. Crookshank and James Walker McSpadden, Jr.

Mrs. Samuel's grandfather, Rev. Thomas K. B. McSpadden joined the Methodist Indian Conference October 30, 1879. He was from the Van Buren circuit of north Alabama. The rest of life work of this truly consecrated Missionary was among the Cherokees. He died in 1878 while in charge of the Fort Gibson Circuit.

McKisick, Mrs. J. H. (See Ghigau, Conrad and Duncan)—Nellie Josephine, daughter of Johnson Thompson and Catherine Isabel (Garbarine) Landrum, was born in Delaware District, May 6, 1890 and educated locally. Married at Vinita, August 8, 1910, James Houston, son of Charles D. and Lydia Elizabeth McKisick, born May 30, 1882 in Benton County, Ark. They are the parents of Stephen Dean, born June 14, 1912 and Clark Douglas McKisick, born August 6, 1919. Mr. McKisick is a mill owner and operator at Big Cabin. Mrs. Kisick is a member of the United Brethren Church.

John, son of James and Rebecca (Duncan) Landrum married Nellie Otterlefter and they were the parents of Johnson Thompson Landrum.

Samuel Candy, a white man, married Catherine, a full blood of the Wolf Clan. Their son, Samuel Candy, married Elizabeth West, a white woman. They were the parents of Ollie Candy who married Hair Conrad and their daughter Elizabeth married Daniel Hopkins. Daniel Hopkins and Elizabeth Hopkins were the parents of Sarah Abigal Hopkins, born Jan. 7, 1839 married September 9, 1860, Stephen Gray Garbarini, born September 8, 1827 in Tureila, Italy. They were the parents of Catherine Isabel, born June 23, 1868, married April 1889, Johnson Thompson Landrum, born in 1860. The word Garbarine in Italian, is, one who pleases by graciousness.

McLain, Mrs. Pleas L. (See Mayes)—Martha A., daughter of W. R. Wayburn born August 14, 1835 in North Carolina married in Rusk County, Texas November 23, 1854, Mary Ann Gage, born Nov. 7, 1835 in Georgia. Mrs. Wayburn died October 4, 1878 and Mr. Wayburn died July

29, 1879; born in Montague, Texas January 27, 1873, married near Pryor, August 23, 1891 Pleas L. son of Levi and Rebecca McLain. Mr. and Mrs. McLain are the parents of: Floy R. born October 5, 1892 and died Oct. 27, 1891; Lloyd L. born January 11, 1894; Cora N. born December 12, 1896; Nannie R. born September 4, 1899; Cherry born November 8, 1903 and died January 19, 1904 and Watt Mayes McLain, born April 16, 1905.

Mayturn, Mrs. Walter, (See Gosaduesga)—Minnie Eveline daughter of Charles A. and Minerva (Nelms) Roberson, was born Monday September 22, 1884. Educated in the Cherokee Public Schools. Married at Chelsea Oct. 15, 1901 Walter M., son of John and Esther Mayturn, born Nov. 7, 1874 in Iowa. They are the parents of Amos, born August 28, 1902; Minerva C., born October 28, 1904; Zona Belle, born October 1, 1906; Florence, born Sept. 1, 1909; Glenn, born Feb. 19 1913 and Alto, born June 8, 1915. Mr. Mayturn who is a progressive farmer near Bushyhead, is a member of the Woodmen of the World and has been a member of the District School Board for over seven years.

Minerva, daughter of Lewis and Mary (Denton) Nelms was born in the Cherokee Nation in July 1858. Married May 6, 1878 Charles A., son of Samuel and Elizabeth Roberson, born May 27, 1859 in Muscatine, Iowa.

Mayes, Hall, (See Grant, Downing, Foreman, Oolootsa, Adair, Ross, Conrad and Duncan)—Hall, son of Walter Adair and Nannie Riley (McCoy) Mayes was born near Pryor September 26, 1891, educated at Male Seminary, Bacone University and Agricultural College at Stillwater. Married at Muskogee, September 1, 1915, Sallie Pearl, daughter of Henry Clay and Nannie Vinita (West) Cochran, born October 18, 1893. Educated at Female Seminary and Northeastern State Normal, Tahlequah. They are the parents of Virginia Lee, born September 26, 1916; Mary Hall, born July 22, 1918 and Lucile Cochran Mayes, born July 19, 1920.

Samuel Mayes, born April 11, 1803, in Tennessee. Married January 27, 1824 Nancy Adair, born October 7, 1808. He died December 30, 1858 and she died March 18, 1876. They were the parents of George Washington Mayes born November 5, 1824. Married May 21, 1846, Charlotte Bushyhead born March 16, 1830. She died January 23, 1878 and he died October 28, 1894. They were the parents of Walter Adair Mayes born December 9, 1860. Married December 25, 1890 Nannie Rider McCoy born March 25, 1868. They were the parents of Hall Mayes.

John Rogers married Tiana Foster. They were the parents of Elizabeth Rogers who married Jesse Cochran and their son Jesse the parents of Henry Clay Cochran who married Nannie Vinita West and they were the parents of Sallie Pearl (Cochran) Mayes.

Mounts, Mrs. John T. (See Thompson and Thornton)—Evaline, daughter of Lawson and Elsie Jane Martin Runyan, born near Fort Gibson in 1882. Educated in the Cherokee Public Schools and Female Seminary. Married at Fort Gibson in 1912, John Thompson, son of David Albert and Caroline Harriette (Thompson) Mounts, born Thursday February 26, 1880. They are the parents of Thelma J. Mounts.

Mitchell, William D. (See Hildebrand and Ghigau)—William D., son of Reese T. and Rachel (Hildebrand) Mitchell was born October 5, 1854. Educated in the Cherokee Public Schools and is a blacksmith. He married in Delaware District March 7, 1875, Elizabeth, daughter of George and Elizabeth Newton, born June 1, 1855 in Marion Counthe masonic fraternity. He was elected a ty, Missouri. Mr. Mitchell is a member of member of council from Going Snake District, August 1, 1887 and August 5, 1889 and was one of the "Immortal fourteen" that sustained Chief Joel B. Mayes in his fight against the cattle men of the Cherokee outlet for a higher grazing lease rental.

Merritt, L. L.—Lucas Leslie, son of Timothy Carpenter and Rosella (Holloway) Merritt, was born in Indiana May 10, 1888 and educated in that State. Married at Talala Nov. 6, 1910, Mary Jane, daughter of Charles and Cynthia (Bible) Robinson, born October 4, 1890. Mr. Merritt is the Ford agent at Talala.

Mayes, Dr. Joseph F. (See Adair McNair and Downing)—Dr. Joseph F. Mayes, born December 21, 1877, educated at Male Seminary, Central College, Fayette, Missouri and the Medical Department of Washington University, St. Louis, Missouri. He graduated from the two latter institutions. He located in St. Louis in his profession and rapidly built up a large practice. He married there on June 14, 1909 Miss Esmeralda Berry, born November 4, 1887. They are the parents of Esmeralda Mary, born January 21, 1913 and Samuel Houston Mayes, born August 11, 1917. Dr. Mayes is a thirty-second degree Mason and a Shriner.

John Adair, a Scotchman married Gahoga, a full blood Cherkoee of the Deer Clan. They were the parents of: Walter Adair, called "Black Watt" born December 11, 1783, married May 15, 1804 Rachel Thompson born December 24, 1786. He died January 20, 1835 and she died April 22, 1876. They were the parents of: Nancy Adair, born October 7, 1808, married January 22, 1824 Samuel Mayes born April 11, 1803, in Tennessee. He died December 30, 1858 and she died March 18, 1876. They were the parents of: George Washington, John Thompson, Frank A., James Allen, Joel Bryan, Rachel, William Henry, Samuel Houston, and Wiley B. Mayes. John Thompson Mayes was a Captain in the Confederate service. Joel Bryan and Samuel Houston Mayes were Principal Chiefs of the Cherokee Nation the latter was born May 11, 1845, married November 9, 1871 Martha Elizabeth Vann, born October 4, 1852 and she died December 27, 1907. They were the parents of the subject of this sketch.

Mayes, Mrs. Tip C.—(See Grant, Foreman, England, and Adair).—Flora May, daughter of John Wesley and Ida Josephine (Jenkins) Harris, born at Vinita, July 25, 1887, married at Vinita March 3, 1908, Tip Cicero, son of George Washington and Susie E. (Martin) Mayes, born June 1, 1874. Educated at Male Seminary and Bacone University, Muskogee. He is a member of the Masonic lodge at Pryor.

George Washington, son of Samuel and Nancy (Adair) Mayes, born November 5, 1824, married May 21, 1846 Charlotte Bushyhead, born March 16, 1830. She died January 23, 1878 and he died October 28, 1894. They were the parents of George Washington Mayes, the father of Tip Cicero.

Joseph Boswell Harris, born in Durand, Winnebago County, Iillinois, November 17, 1837, served during the civil war in Co. H, Seventy-fourth Illinois Infantry. Married August 27, 1866, Rachel Putney. She died November 23, 1911 and he died May 23, 1921. They were the parents of John Wesley and Ulalah May (Harris) Lukenbill, who died in 1889. John Wesley Harris was elected County Commissioner of Craig County, September 17, 1907.

Manifee, Mrs. Victoria Belle—Victoria Belle Manifee, born August 14, 1881, educated at Chelsea, married July 29, 1900 John L. Manifee. Mr. Manifee died Feb. 13, 1905. From this union was born the following children: Leah, born May 20, 1901 and George, born September 2, 1904.

Mrs. Manifee's father John G. McIntosh, last executive chief of the Cherokee Nation died July 17, 1916. Her brother John R. McIntosh is the Treasurer of Rogers county.

Moore, Cora A.—(See Grant and Downing—Francis Milton Musgrove born December 6, 1847 at Baptist Mission, Going Snake Disctrict, educated at Baptist Mission. Married June 2, 1865 Clara Elizabeth Alberty, born June 11, 1845 near Baptist Mission. Frank M. who was always known as Frank was elected a member of Council from Cooweescoowee District August 1, 1881; Senator May 5, 1887 and Councilor January 24, 1888. He died January 17, 1895.

Francis M. and Clara E. Musgrove were the parents of: Elizabeth H., born November 21, 1867, and married Edward D. Hicks; James Tandy ,born August 5, 1869 graduated from Male Seminary June 28, 1888 elected sheriff of Cooweescoowee District August 1, 1893. He was killed June 3, 1895 while in performance of the duties of his office. Sallie S., born January 9, 1871, married Charles M. Cox and J. A. Martin; William Alberty, born September 13, 1873; Margaret May, born January 4, 1876 married Walter R. Eaton and died October 7, 1916; Cora Archer, born February 26, 1879, graduated from Female Seminary June 25, 1897, married February 22, 1899 James Herbert Moore, born Jan. 14, 1876. Clement Rogers born February 14, 1882, appointed County Clerk of Rogers County in 1919 and elected to the same office in 1920; Frank F., born January 18, 1885 and Andrew Lane Musgrove, born August 19, 1889.

James Herbert and Cora Archer Moore are the parents of: William, born January 13, 1900; Foreman, born Sept. 13, 1902; Veta Clara, born April 20, 1905, Nellie, born January 6, 1907; Marjorie born November 25, 1913, died January 23, 1914; James Herbert Jr., born February 26 1914; Linn Ross, born November 21, 1918; Joseph and Samuel, twins, born July 31, 1920.

Moore, Mrs. Henry W. (See Adair, Ghigau and Sanders).—Ina Lee, daughter of John Harrell and Emma (Choate) Adair, was born July 13, 1884, educated at Dwight Mission and the Female Seminary. Married at Sallisaw, July 20, 1902 Henry W. Moore, born in 1878. They are the parents of: Horace Adair, born September 8, 1903; Emmet Togo, born June 6, 1905; Alma, born May 21, 1907; John Alonzo, born April 21, 1911; Samuel A. Hartman, born October 25, 1914; Henry W. Jr., born December 9, 1916, Edward McDonald, born March 26, 1919 and Billy Wood Moore, born August 29, 1921.

Moore, Mrs. J. G.—(See Cordery and Daniel).—Stonewall Jackson Rogers, born March 21, 1867, married in July 1890 Mary Kelly, born June 30, 1870 in Tennessee. She died in February 1907, and he died September 13, 1907. They were the parents of Frances Leeper, born in Cleveland, Tennessee, September 1, 1892, educated at Chelsea, Northeastern State Normal, and the University of Tennessee; married at Sapulpa, Oklahoma, November 4, 1916 Joseph Garland Moore; Robert Kelly, born January 26, 1895; Mary Louisa, graduate of Chelsea High School, 1919; Henry Curtis, born January 30, 1903, graduate of the Chelsea High School May 1921, and Rebecca McNally Rogers born June 19, 1904.

Joseph Garland and Frances Leeper Moore are the parents of Eugenia Graeme, born August 4, 1918 and Joseph Garland Moore, born September 4, 1920.

Milam, J. B.—(See Oolootsa and Grant)—Elizabeth Peach McSpadden, born August 27, 1883 at Chelsea, Cherokee Nation, educated at Chelsea and the Female Seminary at Tahlequah, from which she graduated June 9, 1903. Married April 6, 1904 Jesse Bartley Milam, born March 10, 1884, graduated from the Metropolitan Business College, Dallas, Texas, May 24, 1902; President of the Bank of Chelsea, and was appointed as one of the three members of the State Banking Board in 1920.

Mr. and Mrs. Milam are the parents of: Hindman Stuart, born April 16, 1907; Mildred Elizabeth, born May 10, 1910, and Mary Ellen, born May 16, 1916. Mrs. Milam belongs to the Methodist church, is an Eastern Star, and a member of the Delphian Club.

Florence Ellen Hoyt, born November 2, 1858 in Pennsylvania, married April 8, 1879 Joel Cowan McSpadden born April 6, 1850 in DeKalb county, Ala. He died at Alberquerque, N. M., June 16, 1898, interment at Chelsea cemetery June 24, 1898. They are the parents of Elizabeth Peach (McSpadden) Milam.

Joel Cowan McSpadden was the son of Reverend T. K. B. and Elizabeth (Green) McSpadden.

Jesse Bartley is the son of William Guinn Milan and Sarah E. (Couch) Milan.

Milam, Mrs. G. W.—(See Grant)—Sarah Ellen Couch, born near Italy, Texas, October 17, 1863, educated in Texas and at the Female Seminary of the Cherokee Nation, married October 20, 1881, William Guinn Milam, born March 12, 1860 in Moulton, Lawrence county, Alabama. He is the son of J. B. and Sallie J. Milam. William Guinn and Sarah E. Milam are the parents of: Jesse Bartley, born March 10, 1884; Allie, born November 26, 1885; Noolie, born November 16, 1888; Viola, born February 17, 1891; Charles, born July 23, 1894, enlisted in the 90th Division Headquarters Signal Corpse, 358th. Infantry; was killed in action at Argonne, France, October 24, 1918, paying the supreme sacrifice that the world might live; William Walker, born July 26, 1896; Annie Wheeler, born September 15, 1898, and Gladys May, born October 14, 1901.

Nancy Ellen Adair, born October 18, 1839, married June 15, 1856 Samuel Mitchell Couch, born January 3, 1838 in Alabama. She died November 1, 1873, and he died September 25, 1877. They were the parents of Sarah E. (Couch) Milam.

William Guinn Milam was elected County Commissioner of Rogers county in 1907-10. He is an active and broadminded citizen, taking interest in every movement for public welfare, supporting the various civic movements, and rounding out the life of a useful citizen.

Milam, Walker Mrs. (See Oolootsa, Cordery, Downing and Grant)—Maude Irene McSpadden, born April 5, 1896, educated at Chelsea, and A. & M. College at Stillwater, graduated from the Chelsea High School in 1916, married at Chelsea May 19, 1917 William Walker Milam, born July 26, 1896, educated at Chelsea, Kemper Military School,

Boonville, Missouri and Oklahoma University. He served in the army during the World War; he is president of the Milam Oil ompany, is a 32nd degree Mason and Shriner. Mr. and Mrs. Milam are the parents of: William Thomas, born June 19, 1918, and Walker Mortlock, born January 24, 1921.

Robert Rogers, a quarter-blood Cherokee married Sallie Vann, an eighth-blood Cherokee, born January 28, 1818. He died July 4, 1842 and she died May 28, 1882. They were the parents of Clement Vann Rogers, born January 11, 1839, married Mary America Schrimsher, born October 9, 1839. She died May 28, 1890 and he died October 28, 1911. He was the oldest member of the Oklahoma State Constitutional Convention, and Rogers county was named in his honor.

Clement Vann, and Mary America Rogers were the parents of: Sally Clementine, married John Thomas McSpadden; Robert Martin, died aged seventeen; Maude Ethel, married Captain Lane Lane; May, married John Matthews Yocan, and Frank Stine; William Penn Rogers, the celebrated comedian and movie actor.

John Thomas and Sallie Clementine McSpadden are the parents of the subject of this sketch.

Musgrove, Clem R. (See Grant and Downing)—Clement Rogers, son of Francis and Clara Elizabeth (Alberty) Musgrove, born February 14, 1882 near Oowala. Educated at Oowala and Male Seminary, married at Claremore December 25, 1905 Veta L., daughter of Jonas R. and Rosa L. Harris. They are the parents of: Dorothy L., born July 1, 1909 and Edwin H. Musgrove born September 16, 1912. Clement R. Musgrove is an Elk. He was appointed County Clerk of Rogers County, May 3, 1920, and elected to the same position in November 1920.

Matheson, Mrs. A. R.—(See Thompson, Thornton and Oolootsa)—Maudie, daughter of Henry and Susan E. (Thompson) Eiffert was born January 1, 1872 at Ft. Gibson, educated at Vinita and in the Female Seminary; married at Muskogee, October 1, 1889 Alexander Ross Mathewson, born March 28, 1867 in St. Louis, Missouri. From this union the following children were born: Floyd, born October 9, 1894, married Lola Beaubean; Richard Thomson, born January 13, 1897, married Erin Forsyth; Ross, born May 24, 1899, married Grace Parrish and Helen Matheson, born October 24, 1902, married LaFayette Parrish.

Martin, Mrs. Granville—(See Grant and Adair)—Granville, son of Joseph Lynch and Jennie (Harlin) Martin born at Greenbrier, January 14, 1876. Married November 2, 1902, Lala, daughter of Wiley and Margaret (McLaughlin) Mayes, born January 11, 1880, educated in Female Seminary. They are the parents of: Clarence Markham, born August 19, 1903; Alice Marie, born December 12, 1904; Joseph, born June 7, 1907; Mayes, born September 23, 1909; Marguerite, born November 6, 1912; Cunnie Jr., born March 16, 1915 and Jennie Louise Martin, born April 30, 1920. Mr. Martin is a farmer and stockman. Mrs. Martin is a niece of the Chiefs, Joel M. and Samuel H. Mayes.

Miller, Mrs. Robert—Nellie Anderson, born Feb. 9, 1884, educated locally. Married at Pryor April 21, 1903 Robert Miller, born January 18, 1879 in Mayes County, Oklahoma. They are the parents of: Tip Bluford, born December 31, 1905; Martha LaVaughn, born April 29, 1908, and Roberta M. Miller, born June 2, 1912.

Rufus Anderson, born February 27, 1853, in Illinois. Married in 1877, Melvina Wayburn, born January 27, 1859.

Mayes, George W.—(See Adair, Gant and Foreman)—George Washington Mayes, born in Going Snake District, November 21, 1848 educated in the Cherokee National schools, married April 18, 1872 Susie Emory Martin, born July 25, 1854. They were the parents of: Tip Cicero, born June 1, 1873; Carrie B., born June 16, 1875; Pixie A., born January 31, 1879; Edward T., born July 15, 1884 and Richard C. Mayes, born April 20, 1887. Mr. Mayes is a successful farmer and stockman. He lives on the location of the Captain Nathaniel Pryor farm which was settled before 1820 and is the oldest farm in Oklahoma. George W. Mayes is a sturdy representative citizen and an ideal American. He was elected Councilor from Cooweescoowee District August 3, 1893 and 5, 1901. He was elected sheriff of Mayes County November 8, 1910 and November 5, 1912. Mr. Mayes Cheroke name is, Touneetor Youngbeaver. He is a Baptist and belongs to the Odd Fellows and is a Scottish Rite of the eighteenth degree.

George Washington Mayes, born November 5, 1824, married May 21, 1846 Charlotte, daughter of Rev. Jesse and Elizabeth (Wilkerson) Bushyhead, born March 16, 1830. She died January 23, 1878 and he died October 28, 1894. They were the parents of: Jesse Bushyhead, born February 13, 1847; George Washington, subject of this sketch; Nancy Jane, wife of Judge James M. Keys; Elizabeth, wife of John Henry Covel; Edward Bushyhead, born June 8, 1853 and died in March 1874; Walter Adair, born December 10, 1860; John Thompson, born June 6, 1863 and Samuel Houston, born October 1, 1866.

Murphy, Looney—Looney Murphy, born April 16, 1893. Married at Tahlequah, March 15, 1918 Stella Stevens, born March 22, 1897. They are the parents of Thomas Murphy, born January 5, 1919. Looney was in service in France for four months during the World War.

Murphy, Mrs. Amanda.—Amanda Terrell, born June 14, 1871. Married at Tahlequah, June 23, 1888 Thomas Murphy, born September 13, 1863, died October 17, 1920. They were the parents of Sallie, married Benjamin Riggs and has four children: Theodora, Ruby, Madeline and Jewell Riggs; Looney; Thomas and Herbert.

Mayes, S. H. Jr.—(See Grant, Foreman and Adair).—Samuel Houston, son of George Washington and Charlotte (Bushyhead) Mayes was born in the Choctaw Nation, October 11, 1866, educated in Saline District and Male Seminary, from which he graduated May 14, 1886. Married on Markhams Prairie, August 2, 1892, Florence, daughter of Frank and Sarah Nicodemus, born at Tahlequah, November 29, 1871. They are the parents of Charlotte E., born May 6, 1893, married Robert Sanders; Pearl Christine, born November 19, 1894, married Robert Langston; Ruth, born July 15, 1896, and Sarah, born June 19, 1901. Mr. Mayes is a farmer near Pryor. His Cherokee name is Sa-moo-sti. He was elected to Council from Coowuscoowee District, August 5, 1901. He is the nephew of Principal Chiefs: Dennis W. Bushyhead, Joel B. and Samuel H. Mayes.

John Stuart was born in Scotland during the first quarter of the eighteenth century and was sent to Fort London on the Tennessee River as a Captain of a British Company of highland Scotch in 1754 . He married Susannah Emory a quarterblood Cherokee and was known on account of his mop of hair as Oo-no-dut or Bushyhead. He and Susannah had one son, who never had any other name than Oo-no-dut and from that time forward the Stuarts in the Cherokee Nation have invariably been known as Bushyhead.

Madison, Mrs. Robert L.—Ninya Jane, daughter of Cyrus and Lydia (Boggan) Cornatzer was born in Deleware District May 22, 1874 and educated in Kansas. Married at Vinita, November 16, 1892, Robert L., son of Isaac Gray and Elizabeth Madison, born October 8, 1861 in Hickory County, Missouri. They are the parents of Lydia, born April 6, 1894; Dabny Lee, born April 28, 1902 and Joseph Farris Madison, born May 22, 1904. Mr. Madison is a farmer and orchardist near Big Cabin.

Cyrus Cornatzer, born in Johnson County, Kansas, February 10, 1852, married in March 1870, Lydia Boggan, born in Wadesborough, North Carolina, December 12, 1852. She died September 4, 1899.

Cyrus C. Cornatzer lives in Vinita. He was the last Chief the Shawnee Tribe had before allotment.

Merritt, Mrs. Leon C.—(See Grant and Halfbreed).—Hope Eva Bowman, born December 20, 1887, educated at Pryor and Female Seminary. Married July 8, 1906 Leon C. Merritt. They are the parents of Fern Aileen, born September 20, 1907; Naomi Leon, born June 11, 1910; Timothy Clarence, born October 20, 1913 and Alice Inez Merritt, born December 13, 1919.

Leon C. Merritt is an automobile dealer at Chelsea. Mrs. Merritt is a member of the Christian church and the Woodmen's Circle, Eastern Star and Rebecca orders. Her parents were James Earl and Jane Ida (Wilson) Bowman, the latter is the daughter of Gilbert and Eleanor Ophelia (Hicks) Wilson.

Mitchell, Robert Lee (See Ghigau and Rogers)—Robert Lee Mitchell, born April 10, 1876 in Cherokee Nation. His Cherokee name is Quaqua. Educated in the Cherokee Public Schools and Male Seminary from which he graduated June 28, 1895 He was an instructor at the Cherokee Orphan Asylum from 1895 to 1899 and at the Male Seminary from 1900 to 1902. Graduated from the Medical Department of the University of Ark. in 1904. He located at his present home in Vinita in the practice of medicine. He is an Episcopalian and has advanced as far as the shrine in Masonry. He has been a member of the city school board. He married at Muskogee, Okla., on June 1, 1915 Josephine G. Barker, born September 19, 1881 in Cooweescoowee District. She is the daughter of Artemus Andrew and Mary A. (Rogers) Barker. Artemus A. Barker was born December 4, 1851 in Morton, Scott County, Mississippi, married February 20, 1878 Mary A. Rogers, born February 7, 1860 in Chico, Butte County, California. Mary A. Rogers was the daughter of Thomas and Susan (Cochran) Rogers. Josephine G. Barker graduated from the Female Seminary May 25, 1900 and did post graduate work at Forest Park University, St. Louis, Missouri. She belongs to the Episcopal church and is a member of the Sachem Club. Dr. and Mrs. Robert Lee Mitchell are the parents of one son, Robert Thurston Mitchell, born at Vinita, May 28, 1916. They were very active in world war work, Mrs. Mitchell in the Red Cross and allied services and Dr. Mitchell entered the service on May 18, 1918 in the Medical Corps, was in France and Germany for 18 months, during which time he was advanced to a Captaincy, and is now a member of the medical reserve corps with rank of Major.

Matney, Mrs. D. B.—Mamie, daughter of Barney and Susie Tucker was born March 8, 1868, in Johnson County, Kansas, educated in that county. Married in Kansas City, Kansas, May 1, 1887, David B., son of John R. and Missouri Matney, born October 8, 1862 in Jackson County, Missouri. They are the parents of Albert J., born March 4, 1888, married Jennie Connel, had two children, Albert Eugene, born November 1, 1911 and Geneva Matney, born December 14, 1913. Albert J. died at Roswell, New Mexico, January 21, 1915 and Lewis Franklin Matney, born August 27, 1889 Mr. Matney is a farmer near Vinita.

Lewis Franklin Matney married Bessie Roberts nee Hale at Vinita, Craig County, Oklahoma, August 30, 1919. Served in World War from July 1918 to December 21, 1918.

Moore, Mrs. A. J.—(See Ga-sa-du-e-sge) —Bessie Shutt, born at Springfield, Missouri February 4, 1874, educated at Springfield and the Female Seminary. She married at Wagoner, December 12, 1900, A. J., son of J. W. and Elizabeth Moore. A. J. and Bessie (Shutt) Moore are the parents of: Howard W., born October 17, 1901 and Malcolm, born January 2, 1904. Mr. Moore is a pharmacist and Mrs. Moore is a member of the Christian Scientist church and is a Rebecca.

Delilah Amelia, daughter of James and Elizabeth Vann was born in 1795, married David McNair, born 1774. He died August 15, 1836 and she died November 30, 1838. Their daughter Elizabeth married John Bean and John Weir. Her children were: Amelia, David, Talbert, Augustus, William E. and Almira Neely Bean; Susan Virginia and Clementine Weir. The latter was born May 15, 1848 and married at Springfield, Missouri, February 9, 1865 Augustus A. Shutt, a native of Virginia. He died April 8, 1875. They were the parents of Ella Virginia, John Weir and Bessie Shutt. The latter the subject of this sketch.

Benjamin Gold of Litchfield, Connecticut, the father-in-law of Elias Boudinot stopped at the home of David and Delilah Amelia McNair in October 1829 and in a letter to his brother Hezekiah wrote. "He had a beautiful white house, and about six or seven hundred acres of the best land you ever saw and negroes enough to tend it and clear as much more as he pleased. He raised this year about five thousand bushels of corn and it would make you feel small to see his situation."

Patterson, M. L.—(See Berry and Ghigau) —M. L., son of Thomas and Adeline (Berry) Patterson, was born December 21,1856, in South Carolina. Married July 14, 1890 Zona, daughter of Albert and Sarah Dawson, born February 5, 1870 in Tarrant County, Texas. They are the parents of Sarah, born April 21, 1891; Martha, born January 1, 1893; Claude A., born March 6, 1895, served in the A. E. F. for two years in France as sniper; Edgar Dawson, born July 3, 1897, served for two years and six months on the battleship South Carolina in the navy; Thomas, born June 9, 1899; Roscoe, born December 24, 1893; Ola born July 17, 1907 Fredrick, born October 12, 1909, and Virgil V. born August 29, 1901.

Mr. Patterson is a farmer near Talala.

Post, Mrs. Caroline—(See Hendricks).—Caroline Woodall born November 29, 1855. Married at Tahlequah, July 30, 1881, John

Beaver Post, born July 16, 1849. They are the parents of: William, Margaret, Andrew, Addielee, Charles and Daniel Post. Charles Post served through the World War.

Padgett, Mrs. T. R.—Rena Anderson, born near Pryor, November 5, 1887. Educated locally. Married August 29, 1906 T. R. Padgett, born November 2, 1885 in Morgan County, Missouri. They are the parents of: Jessie Bluford, born June 21, 1907; Nolan Floyd, born December 29, 1915; Nellie Edith, born July 5, 1917 and Alma Rena Padgett, born September 7, 1920.

Mrs. Padgett is the daughter of Rufus Anderson, born February 27, 1853 in Illinois and Melvina (Wayburn) Anderson born January 17, 1859 in Texas.

Poplin, Mrs. George W.—(See Ward)—Catherine O. Chandler, born at Siloam, Arkansas, January 26, 1873 and educated at Vinita. Married at Vinita, January 18, 1891 George Washington, son of William H. and Sarah Jane Poplin, born December 10, 1872 in Stodard County, Missouri. They are the parents of Anna Jane, born November 28, 1891; Ora Adelia, born March 18, 1893; Gaithor Oliver, born July 23, 1895; Marguerite, born October 9, 1897; Rosebud, born September 24, 1899; Nellie, born March 29, 1902; Van and Nan, twins, born April 16, 1906; Loren Ross, born June 11, 1908 and Ray Poplin, born December 20, 1910.

Gaithor Oliver Poplin enlisted in the World War at Pryor, September 22, 1917. Was made Corporal Company A, 344th M. G. B. N. Promoted to Sergeant October 1, 1918. Was in the offensive at Villa en Haye August 24 to September 11, 1918 and St. Mihiel, Preverenville, Meuse, Argonne and Breussey from Sept 12 to November 11, 1918. He was gassed on September 17, 1918 at St. Mihiel. Was in the Army of Occupation at Gillenfeld, Germany from December 19, 1918 to May 19, 1919. Sailed for America May 28,1918 and was discharged at Camp Pike, Arkansas, June 23, 1919.

George W. Poplin is a bridge carpenter for the M. K. & T. R. R. with headquarters at Adair. Mrs. Poplin is a sister of Congressman Chandler of the First District of Oklahoma

Anna Eliza, daughter of Caldean and Nancy (Ward) Gunter married Burgess Gaithor Chandler and they are the parents of Mrs. Catherine O. (Chandler) Poplin.

Parkinson, Mary Terry.—(See Grant)—Addie Malinda Cobb, born September 9, 1870, educated in the Cherokee National schools and Female Seminary, married at Wagoner, June 4, 1891 Terry A. Parkinson, born May 12, 1866 in Coffey county, Kansas. They are the parents of Rachel May, born May 1, 1892 who married James L. Williamson, and they have three daughters, Mary June, Helen Isabel and Bettie Rhea; Ruth, born August 28, 1893, married H. Roy Cunningham; Joseph Terry, born February 9, 1895, married Leotis Pelsue; Isabel Jane, born October 20, 1896, married James David Garrison and had one daughter, Lotta Jane, born September 5, 1916. Mrs. Garrison died December 13, 1918; Addie Florence, born January 16, 1900, married March 6, 1919 Alexander Cowan, and have one child, Alex Parkman, born February 6, 1920; Bruce Cobb, born April 30, 1901; Evie, born July 19, 1902 and James Parkinson, born July 27, 1904.

Terry A. Parkinson is engaged in farming, stock raising and has extensive oil and realty holdings. Mrs. Parkinson is a home woman, a Presbyterian, Eastern Star, and President of the Arts and Crafts Club. Mr. Parkinson is a Democrat and was elected County Clerk of Wagoner county in 1915-16, from which office he resigned in October 1917 and was elected to the lower house of the Legisuature from Wagoner county in 1918.

Evaline, daughter of Alexander and Martha (Blythe) Clingan, was born in Bradley county Tennessee April 13, 1835, married December 15, 1857 Joseph Benson Cobb, born July 26, 1828 in Blount county, Tennessee. He died March 22, 1896, and she died November 17, 1918. They were the parents of Mrs. Addie M. Parkinson.

Prater, Mrs. Henry L. D.—(See Downing, Ghigau and Hildebrand)—Henry Laurens Dawes, son of Henry Sheridan and Mattie Celeste (Thompson) Prater, born February 25, 1900. Married December 30, 1919 Martha, daughter of John and Bettie (Lucas) Ham, born April 27, 1900. They are the parents of William Eugene Prater, born April 23, 1920. Mr. and Mrs. Prater are farming near Adair.

Clara, daughter of Thomas Lewis and

Amelia (Alberty) Rider married David George Thompson and they were the parents of Mattie Celeste (Thompson) Prater.

Jennie, daughter of Stephen and Mary (Potts) Hildebrand married William Lucas and they were the parents of Bettie (Lucas) Ham.

Prater, David George.—(See Downing and Ghigau)—David George Prater, born August 10, 1889. Married December 18, 1907 Clennie B., daughter of Thomas and Susan C. Jackson, born in 1890 in Carroll County, Arkansas. They are the parents of: Leland Stanford, born March 7, 1909; George Sheridan, born April 18, 1911; Guy Thomas, born February 1, 1913; William Granville, born February 4, 1915; Beatrice, born October 2, 1917 and Celeste Prater born February 6, 1920. Mr. Prater is a farmer near Adair. He is an Odd Fellow and Ancient Order of United Workman. Mrs. Prater belongs to the Rebeccas.

Moses Alberty, born April 18, 1788 in Surry County, North Carolina. Married Sallie Wright. Their daughter Amelia, born January 2,. 1839 married Thomas Lewis Rider and they were the parents of Clarissa Caroline who married David George Thompson and their daughter Martha Celeste married Henry Sheridan Prater and they were the parents of David George Prater.

Propp, Mrs. F. W. (See Ghigau)—Mary Eleanor, daughter of David and Lucinda Ann (Harlan) Archer, born in Kansas, May 2, 1867, and educated in Cherokee County, Kansas. Married at Baxter Springs in that state, January 2, 1888 Frederick William, son of Carl and Henrietta (Stabnow) Propp, born July 22, 1859 in Germany. They are the parents of: Carl Williard, born August 21, 1906 and Elva Carlene Propp, born December 30, 1910. Mr. Propp is a farmer and stock raiser near Adair. Mrs. Propp is a Presbyterian and a member of the Grange and Rebeccas.

David M., son of Ezekial and Hannah (Lewis) Harlan married Lucinda Tucker and they were the parents of Lucinda Ann (Harlan) Archer.

William Harlan of Durham County, England was the father of James Harlan of Monkwearmouth, England and he was the father of George Harlan born about 1649, who together with his wife Elizabeth came to American in 1887 and settled in Chester County, Pennsylvania. Their son, Ezekial Harlan, married Mary Beyer and they were the parents of Ezekial Harlan who married Hannah Obern. All of the above named were Quakers and from George forward they lived in Chester County, where also was born Ellis, born about 1733, the son of Ezekial and Hannah (Obern) Harlan who married Catherine, a full blood Cherokee and they were the parents of Ezekial Harlan who married Hannah Lewis.

Roberts, Charles D.— (See Grant, Downing, Foreman and Sanders).—Essie Elizabeth Foreman, whose Cherokee name is Chiuka, was born at Chelsea, December 1, 1886. Graduated from Cottey College, Nevada, Missouri in 1908. Was Art teacher in Chelsea, Oklahoma. Married at Tulsa, July 29, 1916 Charles D. Robarts. He is a thirty-second degree Mason and entered the marine service in the World War on August 3, 1918 and was awarded a medal of honor. Mrs. Robarts is an Episcopalian and Eastern Star.

Nelson B., son of Ellis and Margaret (Richardson) Foreman was born in Going Snake District, November 20, 1860. Married November 8, 1882 Nannie C. Williams, born November 26, 1862 in Texas.

Robertson, Judge A. E. (See Ghigau, Foreman, Riley and Conrad).—Arthur Evans son of Evans Price and Sarah Ellen (Spears) Robertson was born at Hulbert, Cherokee Nation, Tuesday, September 18, 1888. He was educated in the Cherokee National Schools, Henry Kendall College of Muskogee, graduating from the preparatory department; St. Charles Military College, St. Charles, Missouri; University of Tulsa, from which he graduated; University of Oklahoma, Norman, Oklahoma and University of Paris, Paris, France. He served in the A. E. F. in France with the 143rd Infantry, 36th Division. His Cherokee name is Wah-la-see and he belongs to the Bird Clan. He is a member of the Presbyterian church and the Knights of Pythias fraternity.

Reverend Evans Price, son of Wade Hampton, and Diana (Hair) Robertson was born at Tahlequah, October 10, 1855. Married at Tahlequah, June 24, 1883 Sarah Ellen, daughter of Eli and Elizabeth (Hall) Spears, born at Catchertown, Tahlequah District. April 3, 1855. Wade Hampton Robertson a native of McMinn County, Tennessee. A member of Company E. Second Indian Home

Guards. He was killed in a skirmish at Tahlequah on March 28, 1863, originally buried in the Cherokee Capitol square but later removed to the city cemetery.

Arthur Evans Robertson was elected County Judge of Cherokee County, November 2, 1920.

Odle, Mrs. Marvin—(See Ward).—Lulu Brown, born near Pryor, December 10, 1881, educated at Pryor. Married at Adair, January 22, 1900 George Southerland. They were the parents of Sequoyah Vann, born June 16, 1901; Mary Helen, born January 27, 1904, and Maurine Southerland, born August 3, 1908. Mrs. Lulu Southerland married July 21, 1908 Marvin, son of John and Mary Odle, born April 5, 1885 in Henry County, Missouri. They are the parents of: Alma Beatrice, born March 11, 1911; Charles Eugene, born June 18, 1913 and Virginia Lee Odle, born October 25, 1917. Mr. Odle is farming near Pryor.

Charles Ward married Rutt Hollingsworth Their daughter Mary Adeline Ward married Joseph Brown and they were the parents of Charles Brown, born in Texas, March 12, 1854. He married at Salina, Cherokee Nation, July 30, 1880 Mary Coker, born in Boone County, Arkansas, January 25, 1865

Reagan, Austin.—(See Foreman)—Austin Greely, son of Meriweather G. and Lydia A. (Hicks) Reagan, born September 25, 1888, educated in Male Seminary from which he graduated May 29, 1907. He married at Tahlequah, September 17, 1917, Grace, daughter of John Robert and Nancy J. Wade, born May 18, 1896. They are the parents of: Knowlton, born March 30, 1918; Ruthben, born December 30, 1919, and the twins Woodrow and Warren Reagan, born March 4, 1921. Mr. Regan is a farmer and school teacher in Cherokee Ccounty, Oklahoma.

Renfro, Mrs. William D.—(See Riley).—Betty Sutherlin, born September 19, 1897, educated at the Cherokee Orphan Asylum. Married December 28, 1897 William David, son of Dave K. and Alef (Tillman) Renfro, born August 29, 1870 in Brown County, Texas. They are the parents of: William David, born January 26, 1900 and is at present in tthe 1922 class in the University of Oklahoma, where he is a member of the Alpha Kappa Psi fraternity; Elza Tillman, born April 3, 1902, is a student in Tulsa University and a Phi Delta Theta; Alef Adelaide, born February 23, 1904, and Ima Jean Renfro, born October 30, 1907.

Adelaide McGuilliams nee Brady married in November 1878 Richard Lafayette Southerlin, born May 2, 1841, in Bryan County, Kentucky. He served during the Civil War in the First Tennessee Cavalry, Confederate Army. Mrs. Southerlin died February 17, 1887, and he died in 1889. They were the parents of Mrs. William D. Renfro. Mr. Renfro is a retired ranchman.

Reed, Mary Theresa—(See Grant)—Mary Theresa Flippin daughter of, J. F. and Mary Lane (Little) Flippin and grand-daughter of William and Theresa Lane (Davis) Little was born at Verdigris, June 29, 1896, married at Claremore September 3, 1915 A. F. Reed born April 10, 1893 in Arkansas. They are the parents of: Elizabeth Ann, born October 26, 1916 and James Franklin Reed, born November 24, 1919. Mr. Reed is assistant cashier of the Farmers Bank and Trust Co. of Claremore.

Ross, Nellie K.—(See Grant, Sanders, Ross and Ghigau)—Nellie Katherine McLeod, born February 8, 1872 at Tahlequah. Educated in the Cherokee Public Schools, Female Seminary and Drury College, Springfield, Missouri. She married April 26, 1891 George Starr Ross, born June 27, 1865. He was educated in the Cherokee National Schools and Male Seminary. He died November 24, 1894. They were the parents of Wayne McLeod born February 27, 1892 and Roy Vivian Ross, born January 15, 1894 and died October 9, 1920. Mrs. Ross' Cherokee name is Iyuka. She is a Presbyterian and a member of the Quest Club. Wayne McLeod Ross is a book-keeper in the Farmers Bank and Trust Company at Claremore.

Mrs. Ross' parents were: Murdock McLeod, born January 28, 1834 at Cape John, Picton County, Nova Scotia, he married February 10, 1868 Annie Henry Brown, born August 5, 1851 at Tahlequah. She died December 31, 1873 and he died May 18, 1917.

Ross, Sborry W.—Among the collection of papers and charters of the reign of Alexander II, King of Scotland is a "Charter of Ferquhard Ross, of the Earldom of Ross." It is dated 1220. This grantee was called Macan-t Sagairt ,or the Priest's son, and was supposed to be the son of Gills Anrias from whom the Highland Clan Aindreas took its name. Firquhard, Earl of Ross founded the abbey of Fearn in Rosshire. His son William was one of the Scottish nobles who, under Alexander III, bound themselves to make no peace with England in which the Prince and chiefs of Wales were not included.

John, Earl of Ross was also Earl of Buchan and later Hugh became Laird of Balnagowan. His grandson Hugh, the third Laird of Balnagowan married Lady Janet, the daughter of the Earl of Sutherland, suzereign of Sutherlandshire.

The Ross coat of arms, granted in 1681, bears the motto; "Floret Qui Laborat."

Daniel Ross was born in 1760 in Sutherlandshire, Scotland. He married at Chickamauga in 1786 Mollie McDonald born November 1, 1770. She died October 5, 1808 and Daniel Ross died May 22, 1830. Eliza Ross was born May 25, 1789, married John Golden Ross, born Dec. 22, 1878, died June 2, 1858.

Daniel and Mollie Ross were the parents of: Jennie, born March 25, 1789 and married Joseph Cordey, born Feb. 19, 1779. Died Oct. 11, 1859. John Ross, Principal chief of the Cherokee Nation from 1828 to 1866; Susannah, born December 10, 1793 and married Henry Nave; Lewis, born February 20, 1795; Andrew, born December 19, 1798; Annie, born November 15, 1800 and married William Nave; Margaret, born July 5, 1803 and married Elijah Hicks; Marie, born January 13, 1806 and married Jonathan Mulkey.

John Golden and Elizabeth Ross were the parents of: William Potter, Principal Chief of the Cherokee Nation; Daniel Hughes, Miss E. Jane, John Andrew, Miss Elnora, and Lewis Anderson Ross. The latter was born July 2, 1834. Elected Senator from Tahlequah District in 1867, 1869 and 1873. He married on January 29, 1868 Miss Nellie Potts. He was elected auditor of the Cherokee Nation in 1869 and 1884. He died April 12, 1885.

Lewis Anderson and Nellie Ross were the parents of: McDonald, born August 19, 1869; Shorey W., born March 9, 1871; Eliza, born December 15, 1872; William, born January 5, 1875; Lewis, Wirt, born March 7, 1880 and Daniel Ross, February 17, 1882.

Shorey W. Ross is the ablest literary individual of the Cherokee Nation and an unconscious follower of the old Ross motto of "He prospers who labors." He depends for most of his material on the legend and folklore indigenous to his locality and the only instances of errors in his articles are attributable to some few of the stories that are told to him, but with a true Scotch canniness he is generally able to sift the true from the false. The literature of the Cherokees and the State lose many gems because of the natural reticence of one of Nature's noblemen; Shorey W. Ross.

Robinson, Juliette M. (See Oolootsa, Ghegau, Adair and Grant)—John Gunter Scrimsher, born August 17, 1835 in Alabama. Fducated in the Cherokee public schools and Male Seminary. Taught school one term at Greenleaf and married September 15, 1859 Juliette Melvina Scrimsher, born August 7, 1841. He was a Captain in the Confederate Service and a Senator in the Southern Cherokee Council during the Civil war. He was elected sheriff of Cooweescoowee District August 5, 1867 and August 5, 1877; Senator August 4, 1879 and August 6, 1883; Delagate to Washington 1883 and 1885, Senator August 1, 1877; District Judge August 1, 1893 and Senator August 2, 1897. He was killed by a lightning stroke on July 5, 1905.

John Gunter and Juliette Melvina (Candy) Scrimsher were the parents of Sarah Catherine, born July 27, 1866 married March 2, 1890 William Edward Sanders and died January 28, 1892; Elizabeth Bell born September 3, 1873 and married Stephen Riley Lewis; Ernest Vivian born July 24, 1875 and married Susie Philips and Juliette Melvina born January 12, 1878. Graduated from Female Seminary June 1, 1898. Married May 10, 1902 Abraham Vandyke Robinson born April 18, 1878.

A. V. and Juliette Melvina Robinson are the parents of: Hubert Spencer, born April 2,1903; Lulu Elizabeth born March 18, 1906 Abraham Vandyke born August 9, 1911 and Juliette Melvina Robinson born January 26, 1914. Abraham Vandyke Robinson was elected Court Clerk of Rogers County, Oklahoma in 1918 and 1920. Mrs. Robinson's Cherokee name is, Cowana and she belongs to the Deer Clan.

Smith, George W.—George Washington Smith, born in Flint District, July 18, 1878. educated locally and in Male Seminary. Married Nov. 24, 1904. Jennie May Paden, born Sept. 24, 1885. They are the parents of Grover Paden, born Aug. 30th, 1905; and George Washington Smith, Jr. born April 14. 1907. George Washington is a Royal Arch Mason. He was a member of the legislature from Adair County in 1910 and 1911.

Chief Charles R. Hicks married Nancy Broom and their daughter Elsie married Jeremiah Horn, they are the parents of John Horn who married Nellie Miller and their daughter, Elizabeth, married Charles Smith and they were the parents of George Washington Smith, the subject of the sketch. Mrs. Smith is the daughter of Benjamni F. and Lucy Paden and the grand-daughter of Benjamin and Elmire (Miller) Paden.

Sanders, Mrs. Benjamin F. (See England, Hildebrand and Ghigau)—Martha Jane, daughter of James Franklin and Mary Jane (England) Williams was born in Cherokee Nation, April 9, 1870. Educated in the Cherokee Nation. Married at Vinita, August 7, 1887, Benjamin Franklin Sanders, born June 30, 1861 in Clay County, Texas. They are the parents of Martha Leoma Sanders, born August 18, 1890. Educated in Female Seminary, Hardin College, Mexico, Missouri and the Southern Seminary, Beuna Vista, Virginia, graduating from the latter institution. She married James H. Thigpin, a graduate of the Alabama State Agricultural College. They are now living at Fort Worth Texas, where he is the Superintendent of the Refrigerating Department of the Swift Packing Plant. He is a thirty second degree Mason and Shriner.

Mr. Sanders is one of the most successful farmers and stockraisers of Craig County.

Sanders, Mrs. Bryan E. (See Grant and Ward)—Adda LaDayle, daughter of John Lowrey and Laura Ann (Edmondson) Ward was born Wednesday August 8, 1895. Educated in the Cherokee public schools and Female Seminary. Married at Tulsa Nov 29, 1917 Bryan Elton son of William Henry and Rose Mary Sanders, born July 25, 189[illegible] in Benton County, Ark. They are the parents of Mariann Josephine Sanders, born July 6, 1921. Mrs. Sanders is a member of the Christian church. Mr. Sanders served six months in the World's War as secretary to Captain Martin R. Rohn at Camp Pike. He is a member of the American Legion.

John Lowrey, son of James and Louisa M. (Williams) Ward was born July 20, 1851, married January 3, 1878 Laura Ann, daughter of Augustus Van and Laura Ann (Denman) (Edmondson, born December 18, 1858 in Gordon County, Georgia.

Laura Ann (Edmondson) Ward was born near Atlanta, Georgia, Dec. 18, 1858. She was the daughter of Augustus Vann Edmondson and Laura Ann Denman who belonged to two of the most prominent families in North Georgia. Her grandfather Col. Felix G. Denman was one of the wealthiest planters and slave holders prior to the Civil War. Her father Augustus Vann Edmondson came to this country from Texas in the early seventies. Locating in what is now Delaware County and was a power in the community in which he lived. On account of his powerful and sterling character the Cherokees named him Kluntutchy meaning in English a "Lion". She was married to John Lowrey Ward at Baties Prairie Jan. 3, 1878. To this union there were seven children born. Mrs. Dora Olive Cunningham, Tahlequah, Okla., Mrs. Lura Loux, Maysville, Ark., Mrs Leola Faye Newton, Maysville, Ark., Mrs. Cornelia Josephine Taylor, Wichita Falls, Texas, Mrs. Adda LaDayle Sanders, Tulsa, Okla., John Denman Ward, Tulsa, Okla., and Winnie Davis who died while attending school at Cherokee National Female Seminary March 21, 1908.

Mrs. Ward passed away in the Morning Side hospital at Tulsa, Okla., Dec. 8, 1919 and was laid to rest in Edmondson cemetery near her home. The passing away of Mrs. Ward has been the removal of one of the landmarks in Delaware County. She had lived in this community for nearly half century. She was a member of the Christian church, a good neighbor, wife and mother. A woman who loved her home and one who considered no crown higher than to be queen of that home, looking upon its preservation as the greatest ambition of womanhood. She was Aunt to Mrs. Richard Croker (Beulah Benton Edmondson) known as the Indian princess.

Samuel, Mrs Clarence L. (See Adair, McNair and Downing)—Carrie M. Mayes born January 27, 1880. Graduated from Howard Payne College. Fayette, Missouri, in 189[illegible]. Married January 29, 1909 Clarence L. Samuel, born arch 23, 1876. They are the parents of: Clarence L born December 26, 1909; Martha Elizabeth born March 10,

1914 and Samuel Charles Samuel, born Feb. 22, 1916 and died May 9, 1917.

David Vann, born January 1, 1800, married Martha McNair, born September 1. 1812. He was murdered on December 23, 1863 and his widow died in March 1875. They were the parents of: Clement Neeley brilliant attorney, Lieutenant Colonel in the Confederate service and Treasurer of the Cherokee Nation; Nicholas Byers; David Lucullus; Mary Delilah graduated in the second class (1856) from Female Seminary, married George W. Drew and Joel Bryan Mayes twice elected Principal Chief of the Cherokee Nation; Charles Avoy; Joseph Lewis and Martha Elizabeth Vann born at New Hope October 4, 1852, married Nov., 9, 1871 Samuel Houston Mayes, born May 11, 1845. She died Dec. 27, 1907. Samuel Houston the youngest brother of Chief Joel Bryan Mayes was elected Principal Chief of the Cherokee Nation August 5, 1895.

Chief Samuel Houston and Martha Elizabeth (Vann) Mayes were the parents of William Lucullus, Dr. Joseph F. and Carrie M. Mayes, the subject of this sketch.

Snodgrass, Mrs. T. L. (See Grant, Downing and Ghigau)—Lydia Beatrice Wilder, born Jan. 28, 1883, in Choteau, educated at Harrell Institute, Muskogee. Married at Choteau November 4, 1900, Thomas Leonard, son of E. C. and Nora Snodgrass, born Nov. 16, 1873 in Washington County, Va They are the parents of: Carlotta Marie Snodgrass, born May 17, 1912.

Charlotte Belle, daughter of Ellis and Clara (Buffington) West, born August 10, 1847, married March 1870 Jacob West Markham, born July 2, 1843. He died April 27, 1877 and she married March 1878, William Lavesque Wilder, born March 24, 1839 in Lafayette County, Tennessee, served during the Civil War in Co. "A" Twelfth Arkansas Infantry, Confederate army. He died Aug. 6, 1916. Mr. and Mrs. Wilder were the parents of Mrs. Thomas L. Snodgrass. Mr. Snodgrass is in the hardware business in Choteau.

Sleeper, Mrs. Minnie, (See Cordery)—Minnie Lucile Jackson, born at Tanglewood, the country home of her parents, August 7, 1871, educated in the public schools and Female Seminary, married June 27, 1894, Gideon Daniels Sleeper, born October 5. 1858 in Liberty, Miss. He died August 7, 1916. They are parents of the following children: Julia Virginia, born April 22, 1895; Gideon Daniels, born June 10, 1897; Walter Jackson, born March 17, 1899; Martha Elizabeth, born January 19, 1901, married A. J. Rawlins; Minnie Louisa, born August 23, 1906. Gideon Daniels Sleeper Sr. was appointed Commissioner in 1909 and elected to the same office in 1910-12.

Martha Elizabeth Harris an eighth blood Cherokee of the Blind Savannah Clan was born January 31, 1844 in Georgia. She married in November 1862 William Jackson, born May 4, 1835 in Mortonhamstead, Devonshire, England. He was Captain of Company B Scantling's Squadron, Texas Confederate Cavalry. He was elected a member of the council from Cooweescowee District on August 5, 1889.

Mrs. Jackson died March 17, 1902 and Captain Jackson died March 2, 1911. They were the parents of Walter Hampton, Andrew and Minnie Lucile Jackson the subject of this sketch.

Mrs. Sleeper is in the fifth generation from Thomas Cordery, who married Susannah, a full blood Cherokee of the Blind Savannah Clan. The first known Cordery was Souchville-Cordery who came across from Normandy to England with William, The Conqueror in 1066.

Smith, Mrs. Richard Lafayette, (See Grant and Ward)—Richard Lafayette, son of Frederick David and Charlotte Elizabeth (Fields) Smith, born September 7, 1899, educated at Big Cabin. Married at Big Cabin May 31, 1919, Minnie Carrie, daughter of Robert Louis and Caroline Emma (Schmidt) Steigleder, born March 11, 1900, in Booneville, Missouri. They are the parents of Louis Richard Smith, born March 2, 1920 and Milton Eldo Smith born Nov. 5, 1921. Mr. Smith is a farmer and breeder of Purebreed Hereford cattle and is a member of the I. O. O. F. Fraternity. Mr. Steigleder was born July 10, 1862, in Iowa. Mrs. Steigleder was born in Missouri April 2, 1871 and they were married in Booneville, Missouri, September 9, 1888.

Sunday, Andrew, (See Conrad)—Andrew Sunday, born Aug. 13, 1877, educated in Cherokee Public Schools and Male Seminary. Married Sept. 27, 1897, Sallie Davis, born Feb. 23, 1879, in Cumberland County. Ky.

They are the parents of: Mary, born April 4, 1898; Elva, born May 11; 1900; Lois, born Dec. 29, 1902; Jessie, born April 11, 1907; Clarence, born April 15, 1911; Robert Owen, born Feb. 6, 1914; Alice, born July 31, 1916; and Percy Sunday, born May 28, 1919. Mr. Sunday is a Baptist and Mason.

Hair Conrad was a half breed Cherokee, one quarter Scotch and one quarter Hollander. He was Captain of a company of the Cherokee allies to the United States in 1814, was a member of the Constitutional convention of 1827, was captain of the first detachment of emigrants to leave the Old Nation for the west in 1838, was elected a member of council from Tahlequah District August 7, 1843. He died November 2, 1844. He married Melvina McGhee and they were the parents of James, who as well as all of the descendents of Hair Conrad was called Hair instead of Conrad. This James Hair was the father of Nicholas Hair who married Lucinda Roberson and they were the parents of Andrew Sunday, the subject of this sketch.

Stiles, Chas. W. (See Adair)—Charlotte Elizabeth Vann, born February 7, 1868, married September 10, 1885 Charles William Stiles, born December 4, 1866 in Iroquois county, Illinois. They are the parents of: William, born June 5, 1894; Emma Jessie, born July 17, 1895, graduated from the Law Department University, Oklahoma, and married Gordon Fryer; Clarinda Ermina, born June 25, 1897, and married J. F. Sullivan; Elsie Josephine Stiles was born November 17, 1902.

Mr. Stiles is Roadmaster on the M. K. & T. railroad, is a thirty second degree Mason and Shriner; Mrs. Stiles is an Eastern Star and White Shriner.

Rev. James Jenkins Trott, a Methodist missionary married Rachel Ponds Adair, a quarter-blood Cherokee and their daughter Nancy A. Trott, born March 10, 1835, married October 20, 1860 Joseph George Washington Vann born February 15, 1832. She died January 29, 1876 and he died February 15, 1888. They were the parents of: James, born August 15, 1861; Joseph Webster, born April 13, 1865; Charlotte Elizabeth, born February 7, 1868; Joseph Harding, born December 15, 1869, and Emma Ann Vann, born October 7, 1873.

Stewart, James O.—James O. son of William and Marion (Dougherty) Stewart born December 3, 1878. Married at Adair August 29, 1899 Maude, daughter of H. C. and Lean Hieronymus, born May 4, 1879. They are the parents of Ralph M. born January 17, 1901, married November 4, 1920, Myrtle Martin; Pauline born October 4, 1902; Grace Oneida, born December 31 1903; Ruth, born December 31, 1905; and James Carl Stewart, born April 18, 1914. Mr. Stewart is a farmer and a member of the Modern Woodman of America.

Shade, Henry (See Grant and Oolootsa)—Henry, son of Isaac and Lucy (Smith) Shade was born in Tahlequah District, July 15, 1875, married Feb. 19, 1902 Maggie Belt born July 19, 1880. Mr. Shade is one of the progressive farmers of Cherokee County and is a firm believer in good citizenship.

Susie, the daughter of Edmond and Nellie (Lowrey) Fawling married Thomas Smith and they were the parents of Lucy Smith, wife of Isaac Shade and mother of Henry Shade, the subject of this sketch.

Sloan, James E. (See Ghigau)—James Ellis, son of Edward E. and Naomi (Cole) Sloan, born January 7, 1894, educated in Delaware Districts and Male Seminary. Married at Claremore December 1, 1917, Gillie May, daughter of John M. and Mary C. (Roper) Carroll, born March 24, 1898 in Delaware District, educated at Big Cabin. They are the parents of: Percilla May, born August 25, 1918; Naomi Caroline, born March 1, 1920; and Dorris Louise, born June 12, 1921. Mr. Sloan enlisted in the World War September 3, 1918, and was mustered out January 7, 1919.

Thomas Martin Raper married Marcella Ferandes Townsend, their daughter Mary Caroline Raper married John M. Carroll and they were the parents of Mrs. Gillie May Sloan.

Sanders, Madison, (Raper, Sanders and Ghigau)—Madison, son of Jesse and Caroline (Catron) Sanders born in 1848. Married in 1875, Louisa, daughter of James and Nancy (Raper) Holland, born February 24, 1859. They are the parents of Caroline, married Ellis R. Alberty; Cynthia, married William Isaac Johnson; Jesse; James S.; Thomas Blair; Elizabeth; John Henry; Geneva, married Thomas Johnson and Parnett, Carl and Maggie Dee Sanders.

Madison Sanders was elected Sheriff of

Tahlequah District in 1879 and 1881. Carl D. Sanders was in the World War 7 months and 17 days, Co. K. 12th Inf.

Austin, Mrs. Sue (See Cordery)—Sue, daughter of Charles Harris and Pearl Victoria (Haas) Sisson, born December 14, 1898 at Ft. Gibson; educated at Ft. Gibson, Muskogee and Claremore. Married at Claremore June 5, 1920 Ervin F. son of Henry and Sallie Austin. Mr. Austin is engaged in the wholesale dry goods business at Claremore.

Thomas Cordery, an Irishman married Susannah, a full blood Cherokee of the Blind Savannah Clan. Their daughter Nannie married Parker Collins and they were the parents of Jennie Collins who married Charles Harris of Spartanberg district, S. Carolina Charles and Jennie Harris were the parents of Narcissa, born in 1841, married George Sisson and Jesse Wolf. She died October 18, 1898. Martha Elizabeth married Captain William Jackson; Sue F. married Alfred M. Gott; Charles Joseph and Truste Bird.

George and Narcissa Sisson were the parents of Charles Harris Sisson, born December 26, 1859, educated in the Cherokee National schools and married at Ft. Gibson, December 4, 1893 Pearl Victoria Haas, born August 29, 1879 in Tupelo, Lee county, Mississippi. They are the parents of Charles Harris, born November 5, 1894; Jessie May, born July 31, 1896; Sue, born December 14, 1898; Mary, born January 13, 1900 and Emma Pauline, born May 8, 1902.

Charles Harris Sisson was appointed Circuit Judge of the Cherokee Nation in May 1897, and was elected a member of the Council from Illinois District in Aug. 1903.

Starr, Bluford W. (See Ghigau)—Bluford West Starr, born September 1, 1858 near Fort Gibson is the son of Bluford West Starr born March 5, 1826 and died April 7, 1858 and his wife Margaret Ann (McDaniel) Starr who died July 4, 1866. Bluford W. having been left an orphan at such an early age struggled against adverse conditions and gained a creditable education. His dominant characteristics are honesty and integrity. He is a farmer, stockman and Mason. He married on November 10, 1887 Jessie Adel the daughter of Charles and Marion M. Hutchins, born Aug. 29, 1865 in Dane Co., Wisconsin. They are the parents of Charles Clarence, born October 1, 1888; Orange Walter born April 22, 1890; Glenn W. born July 6, 1892 and Jessie Marion, born December 24, 1894. Bluford W. Starr's Cherokee name is Yona and he belongs to the Wolf Clan. He was elected a member of Council from Cooweescoowee District on August 7, 1899.

Sisson, Mrs. Pearl V. (See Cordery) Pearl Victoria, daughter of J. F. and Cecilia (Gibson) Haas was born at Tupelo, Lee County Mississippi on August 29, 1879. She married at Fort Gibson, Indian Territory December 4, 1893 Charles Harris Sisson, born November 26, 1859. They are the parents of: Charles Harris born November 5, 1894; Jessie May born July 2, 1896; Sue born December 14, 1898; Mary born January 13, 1900 and Emma Pauline born May 8, 1902. Charles Harris Sisson was appointed Circuit Judge of the Cherokee Nation on May 1, 1897 and elected to Council from Illinois District on August 3, 1903.

Sandifer, Bert E., (See Sanders)—Celia Margaret Walkley born March 29, 1882 married November 30, 1902 Bert E. Sandifer, born Sept. 1, 1881. They are the parents of: William Franklin, born September 17, 1903; Robert Lee, born January 23, 1905; Owen Haskell born August 18, 1907; Alice Catherine born November 11, 1912 and Margaret Elizabeth Sandifer born August 31, 1914.

James Chambers, born June 11, 1831 married April 12, 1851 Catherine Hendricks born May 3, 1829. He was elected to Council from Cooweescoowee District August 1, 1887. He died December 16, 1897. Mrs. Catherine Chambers died Feb. 8, 1912. Their daughter Alice Jane was born June 5, 1852, she married August 18, 1872 William Walkley, born March 14, 1835 in Gloucester, England. He died October 7, 1884. William and Alice Jane (Chambers) Walkley were the parents of Mrs. Celia Margaret Sandifer.

Smith, Fred, (See Grant and Ward)—Frederick David, son of Samuel and Louisa Jane (Ward) Smith was born on Spavinaw Creek, March 24, 1865, educated in Delaware District. Married on Lynch's Prairie May 26, 1888, Charlotte Elizabeth, daughter of John Jefferson and Mary Pauline (Adair) Fields, born August 27, 1872, educated in Delaware District. They are the parents of: Frederick Eldo, born June 18, 1894, graduated from the Northeastern State

Normal at Tahlequah in 1915 and Draughons Business College and married Miss Hazel Hubbard Nov. 27, 1917; Richard Lafayette, born September 7, 1899; Charles Julian, born September 24, 1903, married Opal Pearl Long; Samuel P. Smith, born August 4, 1910. Mr. Smith is a farmer near Big Cabin and is a member of the Independent Order of Odd Fellows and Mrs. Smith is a Rebecca.

Richard, son of Ezekial and Mary Ann (Sexton) Fields married Elizabeth Blagg and they were the parents of John Jefferson Fields who married Mary Pauline Adair.

Smith, Mrs. A. J. (See Grant and Duncan) —Clearcy, daughter of Ezekial and Sabra Elizabeth (Ward) Fields, was born March 28, 1871, educated in Delaware District. Married in the Seneca Nation, Andrew Jackson, son of James and Margaret E. Smith, born in Indiana in Monroe County. They are the parents of: Cora Pearl, born September 30, 1888, married April 20, 1908 Benjamin Morris, son of John Johnson and Caroline Maria (Thompson) Caldwell born near Big Cabin August 9, 1889, two children Bertram Stanley, born June 13, 1909 and Janice Clearcy Caldwell, born April 1, 1917; Ruth Lavonia, born June 18, 1890, married McLeod Landrum Adair; Bertha Belle, born April 18, 1893 married Edward Davis. They have two sons, Preston Edward and Roger Elmo Davis; James Lafayette, born June 27, 1899; Claudius Edgar, born October 1, 1906 and Mack Andrew Smith, born June 28, 1909. Mr and Mrs. Smith belong to the Christian Church. He is a member of the I. O. O. F. and she is a Rebecca. They own and operate a fine farm near Vinita.

Richard Fields, Chief of the Texas Cherokees married Jennie Buffington and they were the parents of Ezekial who married Mary Ann Sexton. Their son Richard married Elizabeth Jane Blagg and they were the parents of Ezekial Fields who married Sabra Elizabeth Ward.

Sevier, William Penn—William Penn, son of John and Eliza (Potts) Sevier, born Aug. 7. 1874, educated at the Orphan Asylum. Married at Tahlequah, Ida E., daughter of Robin and Darky Emily Penn, born May 1, 1875. They are the parents of Alma E. Sevier, born March 25, 1903.

Mr. Sevier, who is at present a salesman, is one of the best interpreters among the Cherokees and is one of the few Cherokee typesetters. It is thought that there are not more than three in the tribe, if that many. His ancestors, his great grandfather was of Scotch descent who came to America in early days. In his line of chronology runs that of Seviers, Morgans and Kings.

Sanders, W. E. (See Sanders, Scraper, Oolootsa, Ghigau, Adair and Duncan)—William Edward Sanders, born in Going Snake District, April 2, 1861. Educated in the Cherokee Public Schools. Married March 2, 1890, Sarah Catherine Scrimsher, born July 27, 1866. She died January 28, 1892. They were the parents of John Gunter Sanders, born April 23, 1891. Mr. Sanders married at Adair in 1894 Etta Jane, daughter of Henry Harrison and Narcissa Jane (Duncan) Scraper born in 1871 in Salina District. She was educated at Worcester Academy, Vinita and Female Seminary. They are the parents of: William Edward, born October 24, 1896; Dewitt Clark, born June 30, 1898; Henry K. born October 1, 1902; Connelly, born August 16, 1906 and Owen Bates Sanders, born Sept. 25, 1914. Mr. and Mrs. Sanders are Baptists. He is a Modern Woodman and a Mason. Blessed with a splendid earnest, honest personality, he has been chosen by good majorities by his fellow citizens for the following positions Sheriff of Cooweescoowee District elected August 3, 1885, August 1, 1887, and August 3, 1891; Senator from the same district, August 1, 1893; Sheriff of Rogers County, November 8, 1910; County Commissioner of the same county, November 5, 1918 and November 2, 1920. Mrs. Sanders' father was the son of George W. Scraper and was Orderly Sergeant of Company D, Second Indian Home Guards, U. S. A.

Strange, Cicero, J. (See Grant, Ghigau, Oolootsa and Adair—Cicero James, son of William and Samantha (Boss) Strange was born February 8, 1874 in Georgia and educated in that state. Married at Chelsea December 24, 1894, Mary Bright, daughter of John Polk and Emily Jane (Walker) Drake, born January 28, 1878. They are the parents of: Mary Emma, born September 30, 1895; John Drake born February 13, 1895; Janie Anna, born April 5, 1900; Ella, born Feb. 11, 1902; Lulu Euphemia born June 26, 1904; Frank J. born February 27, 1906; Charles, born Jan. 4, 1909; Florence, born Sept. 17, 1916 and Margaret Strange born July 3, 1919.

Emily Jane, daughter of Timothy Meigs Polk Drake and they were the parents of Mary Bright (Drake) Strange.

Worsham, Mrs. Wm. A. (See Adair)—Mabel Maud Hogan born April 15, 1890, educated at Pryor and William Woods College, Fulton, Missouri. She married October 9, 1909 William A. Worsham. They are the parents of Mary Margaret, born April 1, 1911 and Gay Nell Worsham born July 20, 1913.

Vann, D. W. (See Downing)—Daniel Webster, son of James and Elizabeth (Heaton) Vann was born October 12, 1845 in Cherokee Nation. Enlisted in Company M First Cherokee Mounted Volunteers, Confederate service July 12, 1862 and on reorganization in 1863 he joined company C of the First Cherokee Mounted Rifles in which he served until the end of the war. He married Nancy Jane Riley, born Nov. 27, 1847. She died soon after their marriage and he married October 6, 1870 Clarinda Vann Rowe, born January 16, 1851. She died July 28, 1903. They were the parents of: Joseph Rowe, born June 1, 1871 and died April 13, 1890; Ada Archer born December 7, 1879 married Thomas Jackson McPherson, David Webster born January 24, 1883 married Mary Beatrice Alberty; Clarinda Alice born January 24, 1886 and William Claude Vann born August 23, 1888. Daniel Webster Vann was elected Councilor from Cooweescoowee District August 1, 1885, August 5, 1887 and August 5, 1895. His life has been characterized by fidelity to his ideals and unswerving earnest honesty.

Avery Vann a white man married Peggy McSwain a quarter blood Cherokee and their daughter Elizabeth born November 2, 1820 married David Rowe, born April 2, 1820. He was elected judge of the Northern Circuit of the Cherokee Nation, August 2, 1875. He died April 27, 1891 and she died December 11, 1896. They were the parents of: Clarinda Vann Rowe who married Daniel Webster Vann.

Wyly, Percy (See Lynch, Bufifngton, Wyly)—While yet the harp twanged in Tara's Hall and the pride and pomp of feudal Ireland vied in the jousts of their own kingdom; one of their proudest and noblest famiiles were the Lynches, and their great Castle was a salon of patriotism and pleasure. Today the castle stands an ivy covered ruin about which you will be told long before you reach its home country and the mystic legends recounted about it would fill a goodly set of quarto volumes.

But where are the Lynches, the proud and self contained race that would never bend a free born neck to prince or tyrant? They are dispersed over the world and if you could segrate them you would find them high and low in the governments of the world, earnestly, honestly doing their duties at it presented to them.

Jeter Lynch, a scion of this distinguished family married Nancy, the eldest daughter of General Joseph and Mrs. Susannah Martin in 1799.

Mr. and Mrs. Lynch's fifth child was John Adair Bell. The family of Joshua and Sabra, who married Joshua Buffington and Sabra Buffington, were: William Wirt, John Ross, Daniel Webster, Eliza and Mary Jane Buffington, the latter was born in 1840. She married February 11, 1858 Robert Fletcher Wyley born September 15, 1827 in Habersham County, Georgia. He was elected judge of Delaware District in 1877, 1879, 1881 and 1883. Elected Editor of the Cherokee Advocate in 1889 and Attorney General of the Cherokee Nation in 1897. He died November 5, 1903. Mrs. Wyly died June 4, 1902. Judge Wyly was an extraordinary handsome type of the gentlemen of the old south, standing over six feet in height with a benignant and intelligent countenance, well poised, he seemed to always have the proper courtly expression tempered by a gallant kindness of heart that commanded admiration and respect.

Judge Robert F. and Mrs. Wyly were the parents of Percy, married December 10, 1885; Ida Frances Harmon, born March 11, 1869; Robert Lee; Julia who married James Bluford Johnston; Capitola Virginia who married Mangnus Allen McSpadden; Albert Sidney who married Lillian Alexander; William Buffington who married Cora Archer McNair and Zoe Augustus who married Thomas Jefferson Watts.

Percy Wyly was born February 8, 1861. He was elected sheriff of Delaware District in 1889. He was chosen as delegate to Washington in 1890 and when the time came to negotiate for the final dissolution of their tribal rights the Nation felt the necessity of choosing some of their most trustworthy men for that duty and Percy Wyly was one of the six men honored with this trust.

Percy and Ida Frances Wyly are the parents of: James Robert, born July 26, 1886, Leah, born October 13, 1888 and Thurman Wyly born July 19, 1891.

Whisenhunt, Andrew Bell.—(See Downing—Andrew Bell, son of Noah and Nancy Jane (Phillips) Whisenhunt was born Dec. 27, 1873. Educated in the Cherokee Public Schools and Male Seminary. Married November 15, 1896, Cora Ann, daughter of John and Emily H. Cooper, born March 29, 1878 in Cook County, Texas. They are the parents of: Jefferson Bryan, born October 5, 1897. He is also a Mason; Emily Helen, born September 14, 1899; Winifred, born June 7, 1901, married December 23, 1919, Vernon Hurd and their son, Verna Lee Hurd, was born July 16, 1921; Cooper, born October 26, 1903; Ruth, born March 3, 1906; Claude, born August 3, 1908; Ross, born September 24, 1910; J. E., born November 10, 1914; Robert Bruce Whisenhunt, born June 30, 1917. Mr. and Mrs. Wisenhunt are Methodists and he is a Mason. They are farmers near Oolagah.

Sidney Crittenden married Elijah Phillips and they were the parents of Nancy Jane Phillips, born February 19, 1839. Married December 28, 1859 Noah Whisenhunt, born in Carroll County, Georgia, October 27, 1832. He served the confederacy in Co. H. 24th Arkansas Infantry. Mrs. Nancy Jane Whisenhunt died November 1911, and he died in 1914.

Emily Helen married Benjamin H. Dikeman, April 27, 1921. Their son Darrel Phillips born September 9, 1921.

Whisenhunt, Mrs. T. J.—See Downing)—Eliza, daughter of Isaac Peter and Rebecca (Woods) Howell, was born in 1869, educated in the Cherokee Public Schools. Married at Fishertown in 1886, Thomas Jefferson, son of Noah and Nancy Jane (Phillips Wisenhunt, born February 25, 1864. They are the parents of: Lilliam Audie, born in 1889, William Walter, born in 1896; Andrew Jay, born in 1897; Robert Lee, born in 1900 and Clint Whisenhunt, born in 1909. Andrew J. Whisenhunt volunteered for service in the World War, and was fifteen months in training camp but did not go over seas. Lillian Audie attended the Female Seminary during 1906-9. Thomas Jefferson Whisenhunt was elected to council from Canadian District August 5, 1895 and August 2, 1897. He was elected County Commissioner of Rogers County, November 8, 1910 and November 5, 1912. Mr. Whisenhunt is a Mason and is a farmer near Oolagah.

Sidney Crittenden married Elizabeth Phillips and they were the parents of Nancy Jane Phillips Whisenhunt.

Edith Quinton married Thomas Woods and they were the parents of Rebecca Woods who married Issac Peter Howell.

Woodward, Mrs. C. E.—(See Ross and Holland)—Florence Ella, daughter of Daniel L. and Ruth Caroline (Holland) Ross was born November 30, 1879. Educated in the Cherokee Public Schools, Female Seminary and North Eastern State Normal. Married at Parsons, Kansas, February 6, 1910, Charles Earl, son of John W. and Nancy E. Woodward, born July 15, 1880 in Dent County, Missouri. Educated in Salem High School and Draughon's Business College.

Mr. Woodward taught school four years before their marriage and Mrs. Woodward taught ten years. He was postmaster at Vera under President Wilson.

Ward.—(See Ward and Grant).—George De Shields Ward, born June 4, 1847 on Beatties Prairie, Delaware District. He belonged to Captain C. C. Waters' Company. Second Cherokee Mounted Volunteers. He married December 26, 1869, Eliza F. Phillips, born December 10, 1850 in Benton ounty, Arkansas. They are the parents of Lela Almer, born December 18, 1871; James Osman, born March 31, 1873; John Elmer, born December 7, 1876 and Ethelynn May Ward, born May 20, 1887.

Whitmire, William W. (See Ghigau and Downing)—William Walter, son of Walter Samuel and Nancy Bushyhead (Wilkerson) Whitmire was born in Going Snake District, May 28, 1877, educated in Male Seminary. Married Sept. 10, 1913, Narcissa Taylor, born April 9, 1878. They are the parents of Walter Samuel Jr., and Stand Watie Whitmire, twins, born June 19, 1920. Mr. Whitmire, whose Cherokee name is Wee-li, is a splendid interpreter of the Cherokee-English language and is a Mason.

Witz, Mrs. Harry J.—(See Daniel)—Julia Inez Scudder, born January 21, 1892, educated at Chelsea. Married October 25, 1916,

Henry J., son of Albert and May Witz. She belongs to the Methodist church and is an Eastern Star. Mr. Witz is connected with the Chelsea Oil Refinery. Mrs. Witz is the daughter of W. H. H. and Margaret Josephine Scudder.

Wallace, Sue Adair (See Adair, Grant, McNair, Halfbreed, Cordery and Duncan)—Sue Adair, born January 17, 1887 at Vinita, Cherokee Nation. Educated at Female Seminary, married December 7, 1909 Robert Wilson Wallace. They are the parents of: Helen Adair Wallace born June 7, 1914. Mrs. Wallace's Cherokee name is Susonia. Mr. Wallace is an oil producer in the West Verginia and Texas oil fields.

Hutchins, Lew Wofford (See Ghigau and Sanders)—Lew Wofford Hutchins born May 17, 1892 educated at Claremore. Married at Chelsea, June 6, 1916 Emma Lea Clarke, born July 26, 1892 in Jackson, Tennessee They are the parents of: Lew Wofford, born April 13, 1917 and Jetnette Lea Hutchins, born July 14, 1918.

Lew Wofford Hutchins is the son of Willard Edward and Nettie (Smith) Hutchins. The former born June 12, 1857 in Marion, Nebraska and married May 10, 1891 Nettie Smith, born February 15, 1872.

Emma Lea Clarke is the daughter of Richard and Emma(Lea) Clarke, the former born April 26, 1848 and married February 24, 1879 Emma Lea, born January 19, 1846. Richard Clarke is deceased and his wife died in 1920.

Walkley, William S.—(See Sanders, Ghigau and Conral)—William Spencer Walkley, born Aug. 3, 1898 married Jan. 15, 1920, Buell Shelton and they have one son, William George Walkley born February 23, 1921. Mr. Walkley's Cherokee name is Atowayne and he belongs to the Wolf Clan. He is a member of the Presbyterian church, is an Elk and Modern Woodman. He enlisted in the navy April 10, 1917, was a first class seaman on the U. S. S. Antigone and a Cockswain on the Pasadena. Mustered out July 5, 1919.

Walkley, George W.—(See Sanders, Conrad and Ghigau)—George Washington Walkley, born February 21, 1868, married January 8, 1888 Margaret O. Spencer, born October 14, 1896. They were the parents of: Mary Alice, Ruby Lucile and William Spencer Walkley

White, Mrs. Dr. L. C.—(See Ward).—Nancy Louisa, daughter of Burges Gaither and Ann Eliza (Gunter) Chandler was born in Delaware District, July 30, 1884, and was educated in Willie Halsell College, Vinita, graduating in 1900. Married at Vinita, May 22, 1907, Dr. Lee Carl, son of Dr. George W. and Georgia A. (Adair) White, born December 25, 1873 in Warren County, Kentucky. He graduated from Kentucky University in 1905 and is an alumni of the Louisville University. He is a Mason and an Odd Fellow.

They are the parents of Carl Chandler White, born March 9, 1919. Mrs. White is a member of the Methodist church and is a Rebecca. She is the youngest sister of Hon. T. A. Chandler, Congressman from the First District of Oklahoma. Dr. White enjoys a lucrative practice at Adair.

Waller, Mrs. George W.—Susie L. Hayes, born in the Salina District, Cherokee Nation, April 17, 1879, educated at Worchester Academy, Vinita, married February 26, 1895 George W. Waller, a successful farmer and stock raiser, who died August 28, 1915. They are the parents of: Goldie Jane, born September 3, 1897, married Frederick F. Taylor; William T. H., born February 5, 1899, married Della Price; Bertha M., born February 13, 1901; Bessie O. W., born September 21, 1905; Cricket Ruby, born July 4, 1907; Blynn Eldred, born September 20, 1909, and George Clifford, born February 14, 1912.

Mrs. Waller's Cherokee name is Su-saun-e. She is a member of the Methodist church.

Watts, Mrs. Charles G.—(See Downing). —Flora Elvina Lindsay, born at Chouteau, February 9, 1879, educated at Chouteau and Female Seminary from which she graduated in June 1897. She taught in the Female Seminary and the Orphan Asylum; married at Bryan's Chapel, November 4, 1905 Charles Golston, son of Jefferson and Catherine Watts, born February 8, 1875.

They are the parents of: Clyde Jefferson, born December 30, 1907, and Charles Gordon Watts, born November 10, 1911. Charles Gholson Watts was twice elected District Judge of the Third Judicial District of Oklahoma and was one of the most popular members of the bench. He resigned in the spring of 1918 to reassume his law practice

Mrs. Charles G. Watts is a Methodist, an Eastern Star, member of the Arts and Crafts Club, and the United Daughters of the Confederacy.

Rebecca Wright a quarter-blood Cherokee of the Wolf Clan married Joel Mayes Bryan. Their daughter Marie Louise married Riley Wise Lindsey, and they were the parents of Mrs. Charles Golston Watts.

The complete British peerage, which is the authority on the subject, says in Volume III, page 507 in reference to the Lindseys, as the name is spelled in Scotland, no family in Scotland "can in genealogical importance equal that of Lindsey, not only as to antiquity in the male line, but in all probability to the number of parliamentary sittings, such sittings beginning at the earliest period of which records exist.

David Lindsey of Glenesk, the Chief of that house was created Earl of Crawford between April 21, and May 2, 1398. The highlands of Crawford in Clydesdale were the ancient possessions of the Lindseys."

Weinberger, Henry.—Henry, son of Jacob and Rachel (Foreman) Weinberger, was born in the Cherokee Nation, June 12, 1895 and his sister, Susan Frances, was born October 10, 1900. They live near Big Cabin. Henry enlisted May 25, 1918, was a first class private in the Medical Department and is entitled to wear a bronze victory medal. He was discharged July 8, 1919. Their mother died December 20. 1912 and their father died November 8, 1913.

Catherine Nellie Weinberger, born September 22, 1893, is residing near Eldorado, Kansas.

Rebecca Josephine Weinberger, born March 31, 1897, died July 18, 1899.

Warner, Mrs. John L.—(See Duncan and Grant).—Dora Ella, daughter of Basil Laskin and Joella (Thompson) Nall, was born in Delaware District, December 8, 1893, educated at Pensacola. Married December 10, 1911 John Lewis, son of William T. aand Elizabeth Warner, born in Clemmons, Forsyth County, North Carolina. Educated at Blackburn and Booneville, North Carolina.

They are the parents of: Raymond, born September 5, 1912, died July 24, 1914 and Basil Bert Warner, born November 28 1914. Mr. Warner is agent at Pensacola on the M. O. & G. R. R.

Nannie, daughter of Brigadier General Joseph Martin married Jeter Lynch a member of an Irish family that traced back to royalty and they were the parents of Maria Lynch wife of Johnson Thompson and mother of Joseph Lynch Thompson who married Frances B. Kell. Their daughter Jella married Basil Laskin Nall.

Walkabout, John.—(See Conrad and Cordery)—John, son of Henry and Jennie (Hendricks) Walkabout was born October 11, 1887,. Married Jeanette Cordery, born August 6, 1889. They are the parents of: Johnnie, born August 4, 1910; Levi, born October 29, 1912, and Quinton R., born July 24, 1918. John Walkabout is the clerk of School District No. 32 of Cherokee county.

Woods, Mrs. R. C.—Lelia LeVander Mizer born at Chelsea, April 14, 1890, educated at Chelsea and Female Seminary. Married October 19, 1910, Raymond Charles Woods, born December 15, 1885, in Labette County Kansas. They are the parents of: Charles Edwin, born April 26, 1912; Lois Evelyn, born August 29, 1914 and Raymond Woods, born February 13, 1921.

Mr. Woods is the son of Oscar E. and Clara Woods, and Mrs. Lelia LeVander Woods is the daughter of John LeVander and Susan Lillie (McIntosh) Mizer; the latter, the daughter of John Ross McIntosh, the last Chief Justice of the Cherokee Nation.

Walkingstick, Simon Ralph, Jr.—Simon Ralph, son of Simon Ridge and Viola (Osborne) Walkingstick was born at Tahlequah Aug. 17, 1896. Educated at Bacone and Dartmouth Colleges, graduating from the latter with B. S .degree. Married at Syracuse, N. Y. December 15, 1917, Margaret E., daughter of C. H. McKaig. They are the parents of Syvertsen Ralph Walkingstick, born July 3, 1920.

Simon Ralph Walkingstick is a Presyterian. In Dartmouth, he was one of the eleven members of the students governing body, President of the College Y. M. C. A., President of the Collegiate Cosmopolitan Club, originator of one of the two principal College yells, Secretary of the New England College Prohibition Association, Secretary of the Army Y. M. C. A. work on the Mexican border in 1916 transferred to Egypt and then to India and later became Senior Secretary of the Y. M. C. A. activities with the

British Army of Base Area in Mesopotamia with rank of Captain and on returning to the United States he was assigned to the Oklahoma Y. M. C. A. work as Secretary of the State Indian Department.

Woodall, William C. (See Woodall and Grant)—William Coffee Woodall born in Delaware District, April 20, 1870, educated in the Cherokee National Schools. Married June 10, 1892 Sarah Ellen, daughter of John D. and Mary Jane Marker, born March 5, 1877, and educated in Delaware District. They are the parents of: Lydia Wilson, born December 14, 1895, married Everett Tipton; Stand Watie, born March 19, 1898, educated in Craig County and Haskell Institute. Married at Lawrence, Kansas June 19, 1920, Agnes, daughter of Henry Mortimer and Clara Etta Lesuer, born May 5, 1901 in Rain Bow Camp, Siskiyou County, Calif.; Vera Marguerite, born March 9, 1900; Charles Washington, born December 28, 1902; Hazel T., born February 21, 1907; and Alma Rathie, born October 25, 1909. William C. and his son Stand Watie are farmers near Vinita. William C. is a member of the Masonic order.

George Caruth Woodall, a white man, born April 27, 1804, married in December 1827 Ellen Moore, a Cherokee. He died June 1, 1880. They were the parents of William Coffee Woodall, born July 4, 1835, married April 28, 1857, Margaret A. Ruse, born March 24, 1838. She died May 30, 1889 and he died November 7, 1915. They were the parents of William Coffee Woodall who married Sarah Ellen Marker. William Coffee Woodall, Sr., was elected Councilor from Delaware District, August 2, 1875 and August 5, 1877 and elected Senator from the same district August 6, 1883. He was a man noted for his sterling integrity and honesty and was a true representative of the Woodall family.

Whitaker, W. T.—Elizabeth Taylor, daughter of David and Mary Ann (Bigby) Taylor was born in Cherokee County, North Carolina Oct. 18th, 1819, Married April 2, 1834 to Stephen Whitaker who was born in the same County and State on February 9, 1814.

They were the parents of William Thomas Whitaker, born February 14, 1854 in same County and State. William Thomas came to the Indian Territory in 1871, remaining 4 years, returned to his native state and on April 25, 1875 married Stacy L. Hood who was born in the same county and State on May 25, 1860. They removed to the Indian Territory under the supervision of the Government over the Cherokee's in 1881, living about 6 months in Muskogee, moved to Chouteau living there for 5 years and moved to Pryor, Okla. in 1887. To this Union was born James Edward, Dec. 25, 1878, William Jerry, Sept. 8, 1881, Emma D, June 11, 1883, Maggie R. June 1, 1885, J. Charles, July 4, 1888, Ella O. August 8, 1890, Claude, February 9, 1893, Clarence May 7, 1895, Edna Mae, July 26, 1901.

James E. and William J. received their education at Male Seminary, Tahlequah, Willie Halsell College, Vinita, and Henry Kendall College, Muskogee, Okla.

William J. is also a graduate of the University Medical College of Kansas City, Mo. and was First Lieutenant M. R. C. and present County Physician.

James E. was a member of Co. D, 1st Territorial Regiment in 1898 during the Spanish American War.

James E. and Wm. J. are both 32nd degree Masons and Nobles of the Mystic Shrine.

James E. married Myrtle L. Ellis on Oct. 7, 1908 and to this union was born James Ellis, Sept 1, 1909, William Thomas, May 5, 1911, Lois Mae, April 2, 1913, Fleeta Eloise, Sept. 22, 1915, George Edward and Georgia Elizabeth (twins) April 10, 1917 and Myrtle Lorine, December 12, 1920.

William J. married Lois Waldrup August 4, 1911.

Emma D. married December 13, 1904, Geo. W. Collipriest and the following children were born to this union. Gertrude Ruby, Helen, Fay and Fern (twins) and James.

Maggie D. married in 1907 to James R. Lawson and to this union a son was born namely Byron.

J. Charles married on December 10, 1902 to Curtis E. Bush and to this union a son was born, name John C.

Ella O. married June 6, 1908 Dr. L. B. Barnes.

William Thomas Whitaker founded the Whitaker Orphans Home for White Orphan children of the Indian Territory in 1897 and maintained said home and cared for hundreds of Orphan children and at the time of State hood he gave the Home to the State of Oklahoma and the Institution is now known as the East Oklahoma State School. A blessed Heritage.

Wright, E. B. (See Grant and Downing)—Ellis Buffington Wright, born in Going Snake District, October 29, 1854. Married May 29, 1881, Elizabeth, daughter of Eli West and Jennie Chinosa (Vann) Dougherty, born July 6, 1862 and graduated from Female Seminary June 27, 1879. They were the parents of: William Ellis, Francis Otto, Mayes, Bryan, Lydia, John Lindsay and Ruth Wright.

Ellis Buffington Wright is a quiet, reserved man of more than ordinary ability and he has always been noted for his unswerving integrity and reliability. He was elected Townsite Commissioner in 1892, member of Council from Cooweescoowee District August 2, 1897 and Senator from the same District on August 7, 1899. Was appointed to fill the unexpired term of Sheriff of Cooweescoowee District at the death of James Musgrove by Chief C. J. Harris.

Barrett, (See Downing, Oolootsa and Halfbreed)—John Crutchfield Barrett, born December 22, 1872 in Corsicana, Texas, educated at Willie Halsell College, Vinita; married at Claremore October 5, 1898 Victoria Lipe, born February 1, 1874 at Oowala, Cherokee Nation; educated at the Female Seminary and the Oswego Female College, Oswego, Kansas. They are the parents of Flavius, born October 7, 1900; Jack, born September 3, 1903; Mary Bessie, born October 21, 1906. Mr. and Mrs. Barrett are Presbyterians; he is a Mason and member of the Deer clan; she is a member of the Wolf Clan Cherokees.

John C. Barrett, son of Flavius Josepheus Barrett, born October 22, 1835 in Giles County Tennessee; captain Co. B. 15th Texas Cavalry in the Confederate service; he married Aug. 18, 1865 Saphronia J. Crutchfield, born November 16, 1851; he was elected to the Texas legislature from Wise county in 1866. He now lives at Vinita.

DeWitt Clinton Lipe, born February 17, 1840, attended the Male Seminary in 1854, married March 1, 1871 Mary Elizabeth Archer, born October 19, 1847. She died March 18, 1894, and he died December 6, 1916. They were the parents of Nannie E., Victoria and Lola V. Lipe. By a previous marriage Mr. Lipe had a son John Gunter Lipe. DeWitt Clinton Lipe held the following offices:; Clerk of Cooweescoowee District Senator August 5, 1877; National Treasurer Nov. 11, 1879; Senator from which he resigned and was elected member Cherokee Citizenship court Nov. 1886. He was appointed on Cherokee Outlet Bonds, 1893, National Treas. Nov. 14, 1895 and elected County Clerk Rogers county, Oklahoma for the first term of that office.

Bryan, Dr. W. W. (See Grant and Adair)—William Wear, son of Charles S. and Mildred (Wear) Bryan born September 7, 1868 in Cooper County, Missouri. Graduated from Western Dental College of Kansas City, Mo. Married at Vinita August 11, 1892, Rachel Bell, daughter of William Henry and Eliza Jane (Bell) Mayes, born September 12, 1868. They were the parents of: Charles S. born July 14, 1896, and died Nov. 9 of the same year; Frances, born May 17, 1895 and died June 21, 1895; William Mayes born July 14, 1896 and died Nov. 9, 1896; Joe Cullus, born February 10, 1903, and Mamie Alexander Bryan born October 23, 1904.

Dr. Bryan's ability in his chosen profession was recognized by his being appointed by Governor Haskell as President of the State Board of Dental Examiners, a position in which he was retained for nine years. He is the Vice-President of the First National Bank of Claremore, the oldest banking establishment in Rogers County, chartered in 1895. Dr. Bryan is the owner of a model ranch of three hundred and twenty acres, adjacent to the City of Claremore, where he maintains a splendid and commodious country seat and specializes in pedigreed live stock. His shorthorn herd is one of the best in northeastern Oklahoma. With his gracious wife and charming children he dispenses an open hospitality that renders a visit to his home a memorable occasion to the fortunate guest.

Mrs. Bryan is the neice of Chief Joel B. Mayes and Samuel Houston Mayes.

Brannon, Mrs. O. O. (See Foreman)—Lucile Sarah, daughter of Owen Henry and Ida Lorena (Stephens) Haworth was born at Tulsa, Monday, October 3, 1887. Educated in the Public Schools and Scarrett College. Married at Tulsa in 1906, Orval O. Brannon, born Oct. 28, 1883 in Martin County, Ind. They are the parents of Mary, born Nov. 3,

1907 and Thomas Brannon, born Jan 30, 1910.

Ida Lorena, daughter of Spencer Scago and Sarah (Hicks) Stephens was born March 13, 1865. Graduated from Northfield Academy, Northfield, Connecticut in 1884. Was an instructor in the first school opened in Tulsa. She married June 11, 1886 Owen Henry Haworth born April 27, 1858 in Kankakee County, Ill.

Bible, John Adam—John Adam, son of William Henry and Mary E. (Locker) Bible was born October 13, 1872. Married at Claremore July 1, 1895 Ella, daughter of Freedom E. and Louisa (Hill) Brinker, born Nov. 1, 1877 in Shelby County, Illinois. They are the parents of: Katie, born in Talala March 30, 1896 and Maude Bible, born May 8, 1900, married at Nowata, Charles A. Carter and is now living in Kansas City, Mo.

Mr. and Mrs. Bible are members of the Church of God and are progressive farmers near Talala, Oklahoma.

Boling, Mrs. Julia M. (See Grant)—Julia Matilda daughter of John and Ruth (Hall) Davis was born Tuesday June 22, 1869 in Georgia. Married at the Martin Davis homestead on the Chickamauga battle ground, Georgia, December 3, 1891 James Madison, son of Reuben and Marguerite Boling born Jan. 31, 1856.

He graduated from University of Georgia, Post Graduate of Missouri Medical College, St. Louis and University of Pennsylvania. Dr. Boling, who was a thirty second degree Mason died June 6, 1916. A pioneer physician and friend to the Cherokee and did much good. Reserved, talented and gracious; Mrs Boling being possessed of ample means maintains a home in Tulsa, but spends much of her time, traveling.

Joseph, son of Joseph and Susannah (Childs) Martin was born on his father's plantation near Charlotteville, Virginia in 1740. He was elected Captain of the Transylvania Militia in 1776 became Major, February 17, 1779 and Lieutenant Colonel in March 1781. His activities were directed against the Tories and their Indian Allies west of the Allegheny Mountains, they having been stirred to violence by a letter of May 9, 1776 from the British Superintendent of Southern Indian affairs, calling on them for concerted action in surprising and killing the men, women and children of the revolutionists and their sympathizers. The south had been practically subjugated by the summer of 1780 and it was only by the efforts of such a patriot as Major Joseph Martin that it was possible for a part of the soldiers of the Western frontier to strike and destroy Ferguson at Kings Mountain on October 7, 1780 and turn the tide in favor of the Americans. Major Martin was not at Kings Mountain, as he was busy holding the Indians of the southwest at bay. In recognition of his patriotic services he was advanced to the lieutenant colonelcy, five months later. He was elected Brigadier General of the North Carolina Militia by legislature on December 14, 1787 and was commissioned Brigadier General of the Twelfth Brigade of Virginia Militia by Governor Henry Lee on December 11, 1793.

Martinsville, county seat of Henry County, Virginia and the place of his residence was named for him. He died there on December 18, 1808 and was buried with Military and Masonic honors.

He married Susannah Fields near Emory and their third and youngest child was Sabra Martin who married Daniel Davis, born in 1785 in North Carolina and died in June 1866. Their son Martin Davis was born August 27, 1809. Married April 29, 1840 Julia Ann Fate, born January 5, 1823 in Georgia. He died November 11, 1850 and she died September 28, 1882. They were the parents of John Davis born September 8, 1846. Married September 5, 1868 Ruth Hall born in Walker County, Georgia. They were the parents of Mrs. Julia M. Boling.

Martine was one of the Norman Knights who accompanied William the Conqueror in the conquest of England in October 1066 and the family later changed the name to Martin.

Garrett, R. B. (See Grant and Ward)—Robert Bruce Garrett, born December 2, 1876 near Baptist Mission, Going Snake District educated in the Cherokee Public Schools and graduated from Male Seminary May 31, 1901. Appointed principal of the Cherokee Orphan Asylum in 1902. Married October 3, 1903, Cherokee Dora Edmondson, born October 23, 1879 in Delaware District, educated in the National Schools and graduated from Female Seminary June 23, 1897. They are the parents of Kathleen Butler Garrett, born January 22. 1906.

James Robert Garrett, born June 29, 1850 in Carroll County, Tennessee married March 17, 1875, Elizabeth Greer, born August 30, 1854. He was appointed Clerk of Going Snake District, July 29, 1890 and elected to the same office, August 3, 1891. Mrs. J. R. Garrett died in 1903 and he died in January 1918. They were the parents of Robert Bruce, born Dec. 2, 1876; Simeon, born January 24, 1878 and died Oct. 1902; Mary E. born May 30, 1881; Allie R. born March 3, 1885; Lola born November 29, 1889; Captain J. W. born January 20, 1890 and Thomas B. Garrett, born April 16, 1892.

Robert Bruce Garrett's Cherokee name is Oochalata and that of his wife is Cherokee. They are members of the Methodist church. He is a Mason and Knight of Pythias and she is an Eastern Star.

Carroll, Mrs. John M. (See Raper, Townsend)—Mary C. daughter of Thomas Martin and Marcella Fernandas (Townsend) Raper, was born in Georgia June 5, 1876, educated in Georgia, Indian Territory and North Carolina. Married January 8, 1893, John M. son of Jesse R. and Mary Jane Carroll, born Nov. 24, 1870 in Cherokee County, N. Carolina. They are the parents of: Myrtle J. born March 31, 1894. Married J. L. Nall, has one daughter Ella Clementine Nall, born April 20, 1914; Clem, born February 13, 1896; Gillie May, born March 24, 1898, married to James Ellis Sloan, Dec. 1, 1917; Jesse L. born July 11, 1900; Julia,, born February 2, 1904; Edith, born February 11, 1907; Olive Marie, born March 7, 1909; Thomas Grant, born August 23, 1911; Clinton Hoolie, born March 5, 1914; Leona, born January 22, 1919; and Warren G., born March 31, 1921. Mr. and Mrs. Carrol are farmers and belong to the Church of God.

Clem Carrol 1st. Sgt. of 358 Inf. 90 Div. was married to Nina Bryant May 7, 1921 at Muskogee, Okla. He was educated in Okla. and Missouri. Graduated from Rude's Business College in Carthage, Missouri.

Thomas M. Raper and family also his grandmother and grandfather, Polly and Jessie Raper immigrated from the state of Georgia to this country in 1881 and were admitted to citizenship in the same year. The daughter Mary went back to Georgia and North Carolina for a short time and later returned to the territory in 1893.

Bard, Thomas D. Jr., (See Cordery, Foreman and Blackburn)—Thomas Dunn, son of Thomas Dunn and Laura (Rogers) Bard, was born Oct. 4, 1880 in Dalton, Georgia. Educated in the Cherokee National Schools and Willie Halsell College. Joined the "Rough Riders" but mustered out on account of defective vision. Married at Claremore January 2, 1910, Elizabeth Belle, daughter of Joseph and Elizabeth Cherokee (Wisner) Prather, born July 29, 1889. They are the parents of: Jennie May, born Nov. 29, 1910; Jackson Rogers, born June 21, 1912 and Thomas Dunn Bard III, born May 24, 1915.

Elizabeth Belle was educated at the Female Seminary and was a member of the graduating class of the last term of school at the old Male Seminary which burned April 12, 1910.

James Holmes, son of Thomas Bard of Maryland, married Elizabeth Holiday Dunn and they were the parents of Thomas Dunn Bard who married Laura Rogers.

Benjamin B. Wisner married Jennie, daughter of John and Elizabeth (Foreman) Elliott and they were the parents of Elizabeth Cherokee Wisner, born April 24, 1856. Married Joseph Prather in 1881 and she died September 12, 1894.

Mr. and Mrs. Bard are Presbyterians. He is an Elk and an Eagle.

Cook, Mrs. Henry N. (See Grant)—Alice, daughter of Joseph Lynch and Alice (Tucker) Thompson was born Jan. 26, 1881, educated at Vinita and Female Seminary. Married at Vinita September 18, 1906 Henry N. born Dec. 21, 1863, son of Henry and Margaret Cook, born Aug. 17, 1836 in Missouri.

They are the parents of: Evelyn Louise and Lucille Marie, twins, born December 16, 1907; Ellen Jaunita, born December 22, 1908; Joseph Lewis, born April 25, 1911; Henry Ernest, born August 20, 1913; George Robert, born July 28, 1916; and Alice Vivian, born July 4, 1919. Mr. Cook's first wife was Lila N. Foreman, a Cherokee whom he married Nov. 20, 1898, died Dec. 6, 1905. Mr. Cook is a farmer near Pensacola.

Conner, Mrs. Crawford (See Grant, Ghigau and Duncan)—Anna, daughter of William Charlotte (Mayes) Ballard was born July 4, 1877. Educated in the Cherokee public schools and Female Seminary, from which she graduated June 25, 1897. She married at Fairland July 10, 1901 Crawford, son of Francis Marion and Rebecca (Duncan) Conner, born October 31, 1881. Educated in the Cherokee public schools and Bacone Indian University. They are the parents of: Francis William born June 16, 1902 now deceased; Marvin Rogers, born July 24, 1903; Millard, born May 9, 1905; Ruth, born Feb. 17, 1907; Lois, born August 13th, 1908 and Rebecca Conner, born April 26, 1914. Miss Conner's Cherokee name is Ahniwake. Mr. Conner is a carpenter at Miami. They are members of the Latter Day Saints church.

William, son of Archibald and Annie (Fields) Ballard married Charlotte Mayes and they are the parents of Mrs. Anna Conner

Curtsinger, Mrs. Richard N. (See Hicks)—Louise Fannie Horn, born in Texas June 8, 1868 and educated in that State. She married December 15, 1886, Richard N., son of Sanford and Mary Ann Curtsinger, born Sept. 22, 1860, in Kentucky. He died October 16, 1918. They were the parents of: Frederick, born October 10, 1889, enlisted in the World War September 22, 1917, assigned to Co. A. 11th Battalion, United States Guards and was honorably discharged December 12, 1918; Etta, born June 1, 1892 married Gilbert West. They have one child Sylvia Etta, born March 1, 1912; Eva Lena, born June 1, 1918. Married Ben Head. She died Sept. 1900; they were the parents of twins Etta and Gilbert West; Clifford, born March 16, 1901 and Millard Curtsinger was born March 5, 1907.

Broom of Broomtown, where the first printed law of the Cherokee Nation was enacted on September 11, 1808, was a subchief of the tribe. His daughter Nancy married Nathan Hicks and they were the parents of Charles R. Hicks, second chief of this nation. Charles R. Hicks was one of the most talented and remarkable characters of the extreme frontier from 1790 to 1827 and during this period conducted practically all of the business of the nation with the United States. His daughter, Elsie married Jeremiah Horn, a white man and they were the parents of William Horn, who married Margaret Ledbetter and they were the parents of Mrs. Louise Fannie Curtsinger.

Copeland, Mrs. Walter (See Ghigau)—Tennessee Almyra, daughter of Garrett and Jane (Harlan) Lane was born February 16, 1849 in Tennessee. Married October 16, 1866 David Solon James, born January 5, 1842 in Stone County, Missouri. He served the union in Co. E, 14th Kansas Cavalry. They are the parents of Clara Della James, born in the Cherokee Nation, near Miami June 16 ,1875. Educated in the Female Seminary and Worcester Academy, Vinita, graduating from the latter institution in 1893. Taught school in the Cherokee Nation for twenty years and married at Miami, May 12, 1915 Walter, son of George O., born in 1841 and Amanda Copeland born in 1842 in Indiana.

Mrs. Copeland is a member of the Methodist Church and Eastern Star Chaper. Mr. Copeland is a merchant at Welch.

Cearley, John G. (See Ghigau and England)—John Gordon, son of Edmond Jeptha and Sarah Letitia (Thompson) Cearley, born in Georgia May 19, 1880, educated in that State and in the Cherokee Nation. Married at Neosho, Missouri, January 15, 1908. Gertrude N., daughter of John Wesley and Ida Josephine (Jenkins) Harris, born near Vinita, January 13, 1899. They are the parents of Howard Luther, born October 8, 1908; Kenneth Raymond, born November 16, 1910 and John Gordon Cearley, born June 28, 1914. Mr. Cearley is a farmer near Big Cabin.

Nannie Rider married David Thompson. Their son, Caleb Starr Thompson, married Matilda Cordill and they were the parents of Sarah Letitia Thompson who married Edmond Jeptha Cearley.

Arminda England married Elias H. Jenkins and they were the parents of Ida Josephine Jenkins who married John Wesley Harris.

Donnelly, James H. (See Grant and Daniel)—James Henry, son of Henry and Emma Jane (Daniel) was born August 29, 1871. Educated in William Halsell College, Vinita. Married at Vinita January 5, 1896 Bertha Alice, daughter of Jasper and Lucy Claussen, born March 18, 1880, Christian County, Ill.

They are the parents of: Mattie Agnes, born November 2, 1896, married William Beeman and has one son, William Stanton Beeman, born March 20, 1920; James Orville, born August 20, 1899; Ray Edgar, born February 20, 1903 and Bernice Mildred Donnelly, born March 6, 1906. Mr. and Mrs. Donnelly are members of the Presbyterian Church. He is a farmer, near Vinita. Educated at Willie Halsell College and Worcester Academy.

Fields, William Lee (See Grant)—William Lee Fields, born in Cooweescoowee District, November 29, 1875, educated at Willie Halsell College and Male Seminary. Married in June 1902 Dora E. Johnson. They were the parents of Bertha Helena, born August 29, 1903, married Jesse McCreary June 8, 1921; Violet Fern, born October 17, 1908; Apple Dorothy Fields, born June 20, 1910; William Lee, born March 20, 1913; Jesse Thomas, born April 17, 1915; Franklin Chester born August 15, 1917 and Fredonia Ellen Fields, born December 22, 1920.

Henry Clay, son of Richard and Mary (Wilds) Fields born October 21, 1844 Married in February 1861 Amanda Jane Rogers, born July 17, 1847, in Johnson County, Missouri. They were the parents of William Lee Fields, who is also the great great grandson of Richard Fields, Chief of Texas Cherokees.

Foreman, Thomas Watie (See Grant, Foreman, Hildebrand, Seabolt anad Duncan)—Thomas Watie, son of Thomas Leroy and Susan M. (Wolf) Foreman was born at Tahlequah January 12, 1860. Educated at Tahlequah. Married at Tahlequah, March 28, 1886. Cherokee Duncan daughter of George Washington and Mary (McLaughlin) Hughes, born February 11, 1870. They are the parents of: William Evarts, born Dec. 18, 1886, was in officers training camp during World War and is practicing law at Tulsa; Watie Cornelius, born Feb. 3, 1891 was in railroad service during the war and is the auditor of an oil company in Rogers, Arkansas, and Thomas Hughie Foreman, the youngest son was born May 9, 1894 was in the aerial service during the war and is a deputy sheriff in Miami, Florida. In Nov. 1921 was commissioned U. S. Prohibition agent for Miami Dist. Mr. Foreman's Cherokee name is Takatoka. He has been a member of the Masonic fraternity since 1884. Has been a law enforcement officer since statehood. He entered the Cherokee Advocate office at the age of fifteen and served on its staff until its discontinuance, being for a quarter of a century its business manager and for a good part of the time actual but not nominal Editor.

Thomas Leroy was the son of Charles and Annie (Seabolt) Foreman.

Susan (Wolfe) Foreman mother of T. W Foreman was a daughter of Thomas B. Wolfe the first settler of Tahlequah, built first house in 1835 before removal of Cherokees from Georgia. Was an old settler or Western Cherokee. When Cherokees in general council met and adopted the constitution and Act of Union and selected the location for the Cherokee capital T. B. Wolfe donated the ground which was called Tahlequah and ever afterward was known as the capital of the Cherokees.

Graves, Clarence—Clarence, son of Charles and Abbie (Guthrie) Grave, was born in Wyandotte, Kas., Sept. 20, 1872. He married at Talala, Effie, daughter of Mr. and Mrs. W. A. Griffith. Mr. Graves has a splendid education especially along commercial lines. He has been prominent in the mercantile activities of Talala since almost the beginning of the town. His father was a native of Hancock, Washington Co., Mo., he being the son of a prominent attorney who died while on legal business in Washington, D. C.

Mrs. Abbie (Guthrie) Graves was of Wyandotte and Shawnee extraction.

Harnage, C. L. (See Ghigau and Sanders)—Custis Lee, son of John Griffith and Emily Walker (Mayfield) Harnage was born June 30, 1867. Educated in Texas. Married at Vinita Jan. 29, 1899 Frances Catherine, daughter of Joseph Henry and Ruth Jane (Harlan) Hunt, born August 3, 1874. She was educated in Vinita. They were the parents of: Emma Ruth, born March 25, 1900; James Hall, born Jan. 10, 1902; Nannie Pauline, born Dec. 4, 1904, died Dec. 26, 1918; Lucile Dixie, born July 18, 1909; and Curtis Le Harnage, born Jan. 18, 1913.

Mr. Harnage is a farmer and stockraiser at Talala. He is a member of the Masonic, I. O. O. F. and Knights of Pythias fraternities.

Henry, Jesse (See Grant)—Ghigovi married Love and Muskrat. All were full blood Cherokees. Her children by the first marriage were: Celia, married Messenger Tiger; Lucy, married Jesse, son of William Henry; Tahnee, married Thomas Henry Alexander: Nannie, married Rock Crutchfield and Annie Love married Whirlwind. Her three daughters, Olkiney, Ailsey and Alee Muskrat, died without descent.

Jesse and Lucy (Love) Henry were the parents of Josiah Henry, born January 1,

1850 married December 26, 1871, Laura Alice, daughter of Ellis and Martha (Copeland) Buffington, born September 22, 1852. They were the parents of Jesse Henry, born July 16, 1875, educated in the Cherokee National Schools. Married Margaret Jeanette Allen nee Toole and they had two sons: Josiah, born Jan. 3, 1898 and William E. Henry born Feb. 3, 1901. Mr. Henry's second wife Vernie Ream Crittenden is now deceased and they had no children. Mr. Henry is a farmer near Claremore.

Highland, James (See Ghigau)—James Highland born February 19, 1877 is the son of Michael and Nellie (Smith) Highland, the former a native of Dublin, Ireland and the latter born at Webber's Falls, Cherokee Nation. James Highland was educated in the Cherokee public schools and Willie Halsell College, Vinita, he married at Vinita, September 8, 1910 Belle, daughter of William and Alma Robbins. Mr. Highland was a member of Battery D, Heavy Artillery in the Spanish-American war. He is a Knight of Pythias. He has been in the meat business in Vinita as cutter since 1894.

Henry, Laura Alice (See Grant)—Laura Alice, daughter of Ellis and Martha (Copeland) Buffington was born September 22, 1852. Married December 26, 1871, Josiah, son of Jesse and Lucy (Love) Henry, born January 1, 1850. He was elected in November 1869, Solicitor of Cooweescoowee District and appointed to the same office in 1876 by the Chief. Elected Councilor from Cooweescoowee District August 1, 1881 and August 2, 1897. He died Oct. 4, 1904 and she died Nov. 12, 1906. They were the parents of Rosa Jane Henry, born August 10, 1883, educated in the Cherokee Public Schools and Female Seminary and E. E. Rector, born Feb. 27, 1873 Butler County, Kansas. They are the parents of Edna May, born Dec. 19, 1899; James Emmett, born Oct. 29 1906; Josiah, born June 28, 1908 and Frances Rector born July 5, 1910. They are farmers near Claremore. They belong to the Methodist Church and he is a Mason. Mrs. Rector's Cherokee name is Ay-ni. Josiah Henry son of Jess Henry was married May 19, 1918 to Marie Potts and there was born to them two children, Frances N. Henry born March 11, 1919 and Beman L. Henry born Oct. 22, 1920.

Haddan, Mrs. Barney D. (See Grant)—Elizabeth Jane Fields, born February 13, 1880, educated at Hogan Institute. Married August 9, 1894, David Barney Haddan, born Jan. 28, 1866, in Neoshoe County, Mo. They are the parents of Thomas Elmer Franklin, born Jan. 19, 1898. Married Sept. 7, 1919, Lena May Williams, born Jan. 7, 1897 in Colon County, Texas and Marie Susan Haddan, born January 2, 1903, graduated from Pryor High Schol 1921 and married at Miami, Okla., June 29, 1921 Orum R. Garner born May 1, 1899 in Benton Co. Arkansas. Thos. E. F. Hadden, Jr., son of Thomas E. F and Lena Mae was born Aug. 1, 1921 at Pryor, Okla. Mrs. Haddan is a member of the Eastern Star Chapter No. 50 of Pryor. Mrs. Garner is a member of this chapter also.

David Barney Haddan is a successful farmer and stock raiser, a member of the Masonic lodge and I. O. O. F. of Pryor. He was elected County Commissioner of Mayes County, November 8, 1910.

Henry Clay, son of Richard and Mary (Wilds) Fields was born October 21, 1844. Married in February 1861, Amanda Jane Rogers, born July 17, 1847 in Johnson County, Missouri. They were the parents of Mrs. David Barney Haddan, who is also the great, great grand-daughter of Richard Fields, Chief of the Texas Cherokees.

Carrie R. Fields born March 31, 1886, educated at Pryor, Indian Territory. Married to Joseph S. Butler Sept. 27, 1903, born Nov. 13, 1881. Mr. Butler is a farmer and stockman, member of A. O. U. W of Pryor and Mrs. Butler is a member of Eastern Star chapter No. 50 of Pryor.

Roland F. Butler, born Oct. 31, 1904 at Pryor a Pryor High School Student.

Margaret Marie Butler born March 21, 1912 .

Hail, Mrs. Cleo (See Ghigau and Sanders) —Margaret, daughter of John Bell and Delilah (Roach) Smith was born at Tahlequah Oct. 4, 1895, educated in Tahlequah District and Haskell Institute, Lawrence, Kansas. Married at Tahlequah March 9, 1918, A. Cleo, son of John and Mary Hall, born near Tahlequah in 1897. They are the parents of Morris Hail, born Jan. 26,1920. Mr. Hail is a farmer near Tahlequah.

George ,son of Joshua and Almira (Harlan) Roach married Nannie Pritchett and they were the parents of Delilah (Roach) Smith. George Roach was elected Sheriff of Tahlequah District August 1, 1887. Reverend Samuel Smith, the paternal grandfather of Mrs. Margaret Hail was elected Executive Councilor in 1867; Delegate to Washington, 1867, 1868, 1869 and 1870; Senator from Saline District August 5, 1877, August 1, 1881, August 6, 1883; Assistant Chief August 1, 1887, Senator from Saline District August 1, 1893 and August 5, 1895. He was President of the Senate during the latter term.

Hicks, E. D—If you were fortunate enough to be able to see a copy of the Laws of the Cherokee Nation published in 1852 you could find on pages three and four, the first printed law of the Cherokee Tribe, promulgated on Sept. 11, 1808 at Broom's Town. It has the approval of Enola or Blackfox as Principal Chief and Pathkiller as Second Chief. It bears the signature of Charles Hicks as "Sec'y. to Council."

Broom's Town was the home of Chief Broom whose daughter Nancy, a member of the Wolf clan marrried Nathan Hicks, a white man. Nathan and Nancy Hicks were the parents of Charles, William and Elizabeth Hicks who married James Vann, Richard Fields, Eliphas Holt and William Campbell. There were possibly other brothers and sisters, but their names are unknown. Charles Hicks was probably born in the decade between 1760 and 1770. It is not known when he was educated as there were no schools among the Cherokees during his boyhood. He joined the Church of the United Brethren at Spring Place and was baptized on April 10, 1813, at which time the missionaries, as was their wont, conferred upon him the middle name of Renatus, or the Renewed; Charles Renatus Hicks.

When the constitutional act of May 6, 1817 was passed at Amoch it was signed by Second Chief Charles Hicks, but he failed as he did in practically every instance to append his official title.[1]

In October 1817 he was described as follows: "He is a half-breed Cherokee, about fifty years of age. He has very pleasant features and an intelligent countenance. He speaks the English language with utmost facility and with great propriety—I was exceedingly surprised that a Cherokee should be able to obtain so extensive a knowledge of English as he possessed: He reads better than one-half of the white people and writes an easy hand, For thirty years he has been, as occasions required, an interpreter for the United States. As a man of integrity, temperance and intelligence he has long sustained a most reputable character."[1]

He was Treasurer[2] of the Cherokee Nation in 1825 as well as Second Chief. His residence was in Chickamauga District on October 12, 1826[3].

His last known signature was attached to a Council Bill of November 28, 1826 and he probably died shortly after this date and during 1827 his brother William Hicks became Principal Chief, which office he held until October 1828.

Chief Charles R. Hicks was the father of Elijah Hicks who was born June 20, 1796. He was Clerk of Council in 1822 and shortly afterward married Miss Margaret Ross, born July 5, 1803. He was living in Coosawatee District in October 1826[4]. He was President of the National Committee during the year of 1827. He was appointed editor of the Cherokee Phoenix on August 1, 1832[5] and retained that position until May 31, 1834. The press was confiscated and destroyed after that date.

Elijah Hicks was a Captain of one of the Emigrant Cherokee detachments. His detachment, according to Chief Ross' statement embraced eight hundred fifty eight individuals, fifty four of whom died enroute. They were the second contingent to start, the date of same being September 9, 1838 and arrived in the Western Cherokee Nation in advance of the other trains on January 4. 1839.

He was a signer of the Constitution of 1839 and settled on the California at the present site of Claremore, where he conducted a general store and called his home Echota or as he spelled it and as it is pronounced "Sauty." He was elected a delegate to Washington in 1839 and 1843. Elected Clerk of the Cherokee Senate in 1845 and having been chosen as Senator from Saline District which at that time embraced over ten million acres of land and extended west to the one hundredth meridian, he was elected president of the Senate. He died on August 6, 1856 and is buried in the cemetery at Claremore. His wife died in 1862.

The children of Elijah and Margaret Hicks were: Senora; Jane who married John

HOME OF CHIEF LEVI GRITTS, MUSKOGEE

Wardell Stapler; Daniel Ross who married Nancy Jane Rider and Evaline Linder; Mary A. Chambers and Mary Elizabeth Rockwell; and Victoria Susan who married DeWitt Clinton Lipe.

Daniel Ross Hicks was born August 26, 1827 in Chickamauga District, Cherokee District and Cherokee Nation. He married Nancy Jane Rider born June 6, 1839. She was the daughter of Amelia (Alberty) Rider and the grand daughter of Austin and Mary Pauline (Starr) Rider. She was also the grand daughter of Moses and Sallie (Wright) Alberty. She graduated from the Female Seminary in February 1855. She was teaching the National school near Claremore Mound in 1858 and 1859 and at the expiration of the latter term she married Mr. Hicks, who was at that time sheriff of Cooweescoowee District with a jurisdiction extending west to the hundredth meridian. She died January 9, 1866. He was elected judge of Cooweescoowee District in 1867 and 1869. Executive Councilor on November 13, 1872, Clerk of Tahlequah District in 1875, Clerk of Council in 1878 and 1879 and Clerk of the Senate in 1881. He died February 12, 1883.

Daniel Ross and Nancy Jane Hicks were the parents of Edward Daniel Hicks, born January 1, 1866. He was educated in the National school and at the University of Arkansas. Was bookkeeper for Stapler and Sons at Tahlequah for several years and later purchased this business. While at Oowala he married on September 27, 1885 Miss Elizabeth Henrietta born November 21, 1867, daughter of Hon. Frank Musgrove, a wealthy farmer of that neighborhood. They are the parents of a family that does credit to their community, namely; Janie Stapler, born September 10, 1886, graduated from the Female Seminary June 9, 1903 and married John Griffith Harnage, now deceased; Joseph Daniel, born March 27, 1888, married Francis J. Lindsey who graduated from the Female Seminary May 27, 1908; Clara Eva born February 10, 1890 and married John Reed Alley; William Pendleton, born Sept. 2, 1896 and married Margaret Kay Roll; Edward, born March 29, 1898 and Margaret Enola Hicks. The latter a beautiful and popular young lady is now deceased.

Teter, Mrs. Lewis (See Grant)—Alice Fields, born February 20, 1869, educated at Bryan's Chapel on Grand River, she married January 18, 1888, Lewis Teter, born February 22, 1854 in W. Va. They are the parents of: Clara Jane, born April 23, 1891, married T. J. Kinion; Myrtle, born Feb. 10, 1894, married John L. V. Thomas; Walter, born Feb. 12, 1896, married Mabel Giles; Edna, born September 21, 1898, married Bryan Jones; Goldie E. born March 12, 1902, graduated from Pryor High School 1921, and Lewis Leon Teter, born April 14, 1906.

Mrs. Teter is the great great grand-daughter of Richard Fields, Chief of the Texas Cherokees. The Fields' have for the last hundred years been one of the most illustrious families of the Cherokees.

Tyner, Thomas J. (See Tyner)—Thomas Jefferson son of Carter Blackstone and Esther Jane (Piblow) Tyner was born March 1, 1878. Educated in the Cherokee Public Schools and Friends Mission at Skiatook. Married April 27, 1914 Carrie, daughter of Geo. W. Willits and Rachel (Connor) Willits born Dec. 23, 1883 in Wise County, Texas.

Thompson, Lewis Kell (See Grant and Duncan)—Lewis Kell, son of Joseph Lynch and Frances (Kell) Thompson, was born in Delaware District October 10, 1873, educated in the Cherokee National Schools and at Vinita. Married December 25, 1898 to Nellie H. Stilley, daughter of Samuel and Lucy F .Stilley, born Nov. 16, 1880 in Delaware District now Mayes County, Oklahoma. They are the parents of: James Robert, born October 24, 1901; Lewis Leroy, born May 11, 1905; Nellie Glennis, born January 4, 1913 and Dainie Jaunita Thompson, born December 12, 1916. Mr. Thompson is a farmer near Pensacola, Okla.

Emily Duncan married Alexander Kell and their son, James, married Elizabeth Edgington and they were the parents of Frances Kell who married Joseph Lynch Thompson.

Tuton, Mrs. Thomas Henry (See Grant and Cordery)—Ethel M. Rogers, born March 23, 1899 educated at Pryor, Okla., and Boulder University, Colorado, graduating from the Pryor High School in 1920. She married at Guthrie March 30, 1921, Thomas Henry Tuton, a druggist at Arcadia, Okla., Mrs. Tuton is a member of the Methodist Church and is an Eastern Star.

Samuel Martin married Catherine Hildebrand and their son William A. Martin married Nannie Lucas nee Guinn. They were the parents of Almon Martin, born November 14, 1842. He was a member of Company M, First Cherokee Mounted Volunteers, Confederate Service. After the war he married Sarah Jane Cordery, both are now deceased. They were the parents of Sallie Martin, born January 30, 1869, educated in the Cherokee National Schools and Female Seminary. She married August 22, 1888, John Cicero Rogers, born September 9, 1861 in Washington County, Arkansas and they are the parents of Mrs. Ethel M. Tuton.

Thomas Cordery, an Irishman married Susannah, a full blood Cherokee of the Blind Savannah Clan. They were the parents of David Cordery who married Charlotte Goss and they in turn were the parents of Thomas Cordery who married his first cousin Sallie Vickery and they were the parents of Jane Cordery who married Almon Martin.

Thompson, Robert J. (See Grant and Ghigau)—Robert Jefferson, son of Johnson and Eliza Christine (Taylor) Thompson was born October 29, 1860, educated at Tahlequah, Male Seminary and Bacone College, graduating from the latter. Married in 1892, Rosa Gritts, born July 16, 1863 and died Feb. 25, 1910. They were the parents of: Eloise, born June 9, 1897; Ida Frances, born Nov 29, 1899; Susie Taylor, born Feb. 19, 1902; Thomas Fox, born Oct. 4, 1905 and Sammie Cunningham Thompson, born May 6, 1908. James J. Thompson born 1893, died in 1897. Rose Jessie Thompson, born Aug 16, 1895, died in 1897. Mr. Thompson is a member of the Knights of Pythias.

Trout, Mrs. Isaac (See Ghigau and Ward)—Eva Lena, daughter of Edward Estel and Naomi Ann (Cole) Sloan was born near Big Cabin, May 7, 1890, was educated in Delaware District and Female Seminary. Married at Big Cabin April 16, 1908, Isaac Day, son of George Washington and Martha Ann (Parks) Trout, born at Big Cabin, February 16, 1888, educated locally and at Male Seminary. They were the parents of: Eugene Albert, born May 11, 1909; Sue Gale, born October 27, 1914; Gay Nell Groves, born January 7, 1917 and Creed Pershing, born October 16, 1918. Mr. Trout is a prosperous live stock dealer at Big Cabin.

Louisa Jane, daughter of George Howard and Mary (Carroll) Ward married Samuel Trout and they were the parents of George Washington Trout.

Taylor, Richard L. (Halfbreed and Ghigau)—Richard Lee, son of William and Elizabeth (Grimmett) Taylor was born in 1854. Married in 1880 Margaret Elmira Paden, born in 1856. They are the parents of: Nannie C. married Felix N. Holland; Annie Almira, married W. A. Corley; Mary Amelia, married Thomas E. Holland; Susie Bunch, married Claude Doherty; Richard Lee; William Benjamin, deceased, and Martha Catherine living, married Tiny Hill, deceased. Richard Lee Taylor was elected Sheriff of Flint District August 1, 1887; August 5, 1889 and August 1, 1893. Elected Senator from the same district August 3, 1903. Elected County Commissioner of Adair County November 3, 1914.

Taylor, James L. (See Foreman)—James Lincoln Taylor, born on the Cherokee reservation in North Carolina, September 7, 1860. educated locally. Married at Pryor April 21, 1895, Dora B. Carty, daughter of Charles and Marie Carty, born Feb. 21, 1872, in Benton County, Ark. They are the parents of: Nellie B., born Feb. 10, 1896, married C. F. Conner; Alice, born March 9, 1899, Marguerite, born Oct. 5, 1902, married L. N. Logsden; William, born August 1, 1905 and Charles Henry, born August 7, 1915. Mr. Taylor is a member of the Independent Order of Odd Fellows and Knights of Pythias. He was postmaster of Pryor from 1894 to 1898 and was elected Solicitor of Cooweescoowee District August 2, 1897.

James Madison, son of David and Mary Ann (Bigby) Taylor married Addie Manchester and they were the parents of James Lincoln Taylor.

Tadpole, Eli—Dorcas, daughter of William and Amanda (Fish) Foreman was born in Tahlequah District, January 9, 1871, educated at Eureka in above named District. Married January 1885, Eli, son of John and Lucinda Tadpole, born in Tahlequah District, March 18, 1865 and educated in the Cherokee National Schools. They are the parents of. Lelia, born Apr. 10, 1890, married Emmet Shewbart and J. A. Wilson; they are the parents of Belle Christine born in 1921; Emma born May 15, 1892 married W. T. Gardner; they are the parents of Herbert, born Mar. 12, 1911, Wilford, born Apr. 5, 1917, Percy born Feb. 15, 1920; Wm. H.

born July 6, 1897; Anna B., born Jan. 11, 1900, married Feb. 3, 1908 Albert Merry; and Herman Tadpole born Oct. 10, 1906; they have two daughters, Doris Catherine, born in 1920 and Nellie Wanda born Aug. 2, 1921. Mr. Tadpole is a farmer near Pryor. Mrs. Tadpole belongs to the Wolf Clan and her Cherokee name is Dar-ki.

Terrell, Samuel (See Grant, Conrad and Hendricks)—Samuel, son of John and Samantha (Gourd) Terrell, was born in Tahlequah District No. 17, 1878, educated at Eureka and Male Seminary. Married Sept. 4, 1910, Rachel, daughter of Benjamin and Cynthia (Lillard) Talley, born March 7, 1886 and educated in Tahlequah District. They are the parents of: Susie, born June 20, 1921 and Samuel Terrell, born Sept 1, 1913. Mr. Terrell is a farmer near Tahlequah and Mrs. Terrell is a vocal music teacher.

Susie Martin married Noah Lillard and their daughter Cynthia married Benjamin Talley.

Jackson R. Gourd married Elsie Wilson and their son, Ellis, married Susan Riley. They were the parents of Samantha Gourd who married John and was the mother of Samuel Terrell.

Tanner, Robert T. (See Adair and Grant) —Mary Elizabeth daughter of William Peters and Rachel Louisa (Adair) McClellan, born April 7, 1879. Educated in the Cherokee public schools and Female Seminary. Married December 26, 1906 Robert Tanner son of Benjamin N. born in Boone County, Ky., Jan 6, 1842 and Nannie V. Tanner, born March 10, 1848 in Chariton County, Missouri. They are the parents of Pearl Edith, born September 28, 1910; Mary Louisa born May 15, 1912 and Robert Turner Tanner born January 14, 1917. Mr. and Mrs. Tanner are members of the Presbyterian Church and she is an Eastern Star. Mr. Tanner is a furniture dealer and conducts a splendid farm.

Ludovic Grant a Scotchman married a full blood Cherokee woman. Their daughter married William Emory, an Englishman and they in turn were the parents of Susannah Emory, whose third husband was Joseph Martin, born about 1740 near Charlotteville, Albermarle County, Virginia. He held the following revolutionary offices: elected Captain of the Transylvania Militia in 1776, became Major February 17, 1779 and Lieutenant Colonel in March 1781. He was elected Brigadier General of the North Carolina militia by legislature on December 15, 1787 and was commissioned Brigadier General of the Twentieth Brigade of Virginia Militia by Governor Henry Lee of Virginia on Dec. 11, 1793. Martinsville the county seat of Henry County, Virginia was named for him. His daughter Nancy married Jeter Lynch and they were the parents of Rachel Lynch who married Thomas Benjamin Adair and their only son John Lynch Adair married Mary Jane Jeffreys, a native of Virginia, and their daughter Rachel Louisa Adair married William Peters McClellan of Cane Hill, Arkansas and they were the parents of Mrs. Mary Elizabeth Tanner.

Thompson, Thomas Fox (See Grant and Ghigau)—Thomas Fox Thompson, born in Tahlequah District, May 3, 1848 and educated at Pea Ridge, Ark. Married Dec. 18, 1870 Susan C. Parks and after her death married on May 19, 1914 Lillie McBride, nee Schaer; his Cherokee name is Chisgua-kyah and he belongs to the Deer Clan. He is a Methodist and had retired after having been in the dry goods and grocery business in Vinita for twenty years. Mr. Thompson was elected member of the Council from Delaware District in 1879.

Tinker, Mrs. Minnie—Minnie, the daughter of Henry and Mary (Walker) Spybuck was born in Bird Creek, a few miles south of Skiatook. She was educated at the Quaker Mission, two miles north of Skiatook and is a member of that church. She married at Hill Side, Okla. in 1903 Richard Tinker who is a member of one of the most prominent Osage families. They are the parents of Henry Franklin, born Feb. 25, 1907; George Edward, born Aug. 6, 1912 and Thomas Jefferson Tinker, born Aug. 15, 1917.

Mr. Tinker is a farmer and a member of the Modern Woodman of America. Mrs Tinker is a Shawnee, a member of two of the most prominent families of that tribe, as the Walkers have been as noted in the history and councils of the tribe as were the Spybucks.

Thompson, Mrs. Vet. (See Duncan and

Grant)—Louisa Tabitha West, born March 8 1862, educated in Female Seminary. Married September 28, 1880, John Rogers Martin, born February 25, 1885. They were the parents of Hernando, born August 14, 1882; Birdie May, born March 26, 1884; Johanna R, born July 18, 1886, and DeWitt T .Martin, born May 12, 1888. John Rogers Martin died November 10, 1887, and she married January 27, 1890, Vet Thompson, born September 8, 1861, in Macon County, Missouri. They are the parents of James W., born April 11, 1891; Lewis, born February 2, 1893, and Carrie, born November 13, 1898. Mr. Thompson is a farmer. Mrs. Thompson's Cherokee name is Takie. She is a member of the Methodist church.

Charles Duncan, a Scotchman, married about 1784 Dorcas, a full blood Cherokee of the Derr Clan. Their son, John, married Elizabeth Abercromby, a native of Ten-essee. The Abercrombys belong to the ancient nobility of Stirling County in Great Britain. Airthey Castle was their ancestral county seat. As late as 1883 the family owned 15,264 acres. The head of the family in 1916 was Lord George Abercromby. John and Elizabeth (Abercromby) Duncan were the parents of Mahala Duncan, born June 21, 1821. Married July 18, 1838 James Smith West, born May 24, 1817, in Alabama. He died Sept. 22, 1865, and she died November 27, 1879. They were the parents of Mrs. Louisa Tabitha Thompson.

Trout, Logan. (See Ward)—Logan, son of George Washington and Mary (Eaton) Trout, was born in Delaware District, April 8, 1876. and educated at Big Cabin and Male Seminary. Married near Grove October 8, 1894, Jennie, daughter of William and Sallie Walls, born March 22, 1879, in Berry County, Missouri. They are the parents of: George Washington, born January 1, 1898; Buford Lee, born April 2, 1899; Edith M., born September 23, 1902, married J. F. Daniel; Thomas L., born Nov. 8, 1904; Veachel, born Dec. 25, 1907; Clinton, born May 6, 1909; Samuel, born February 16, 1916, and Warren Harding Trout, born May 6, 1921 Mr. Trout has conducted a mill and elevator at Big Cabin for fourteen years. He belongs to the Christian church and is a Woodman of the World.

George Howard, son of Samuel and Sallie (Earwood) Ward, was born in January, 1801, married Mary Carroll, born in 1792 in Burke County, North Carolina. He died March 15, 1866. They were the parents of Louisa Ward, who married Samuel Trout and she was the mother of George Washington Trout, who married Mary Eaton.

Trout, Mrs. Samuel L. (See Duncan, Ward and Downing)—Samuel Lee, son of Andrew M. and Sarah A. (Reed) Trout, born January 27, 1878, educated in Delaware District and Male Seminary. Married June 29, 1898, Cornelia Eliza, daughter of Walter Adair and Sallie Elizabeth (Wright) West, born September 5, 1879, at Spavinaw and educated in Female Seminary. They are the parents of Viola Velena, born July 13, 1899; Mary Irene, born September 2, 1901; Veda Jessie, born May 1, 1905; Loyd Newton, born December 27, 1908; Lovise Velma, born September 13, 1913, and Pearl LeVonne Trout, born August 1, 1916; Samuel L. Trout, Jr., born August 15, 1921. Mr. Trout is a farmer and stockraiser near Adair. Mrs. Trout is a Baptist.

Andrew M., son of Samuel and Louisa Jane (Ward) Trout, was born November 5. 1855. Married March 1877, Sarah A. Reed, born in Towns County, Georgia.

Taylor, John M. (See Foreman) —John Manchester, son of James Madison, born April 18, 1818, and died January 7, 1907, and Addie (Manchester) Taylor was born Aug. 14, 1860, in Cherokee County, North Carolina, and was educated in the Cumberland Presbyterian College, Louden, Tennessee, and at Atlanta, Georgia. Married at Claremore, Thursday, February 23, 1893, Bertha E. McCutchan, daughter of Samuel and Margaret McCutchan, born November 29, 1872, at Redoak, Charlotte County, Virginia and was educated in Missouri. They are the parents of Blaine Samuel, born June 25, 1894; Robert Clinton, born July 24, 1897; served during the World war in the Medical Corps; Florence Thelma, born August 17, 1902; McCutchan, born November 28, 1904; Oklahoma, born November 6, 1906, and John Manchester Taylor, born November 8, 1909.

David Taylor, born December 16, 1791, in Orange County, Virginia, married Mary Ann Bigby, born August 9, 1802, and they were the parents of James Madison Taylor, who married Addie Manchester, a native of Providence, R. I.

John Manchester Taylor, whose Cherokee name is Katahya, is a thirty-second degree Mason, Shriner and Elk. Attorney for the Cherokees, Creeks and Seminoles. Was U. S. Deputy Marshal for the Fort Smith Court for twenty-three years; Indian Police twelve years; Deputy Sheriff five years; Postal Inspector three years; Assistant Solicitor of Cooweescoowee District eight years; United States Commissioner 4 years and Master in Chancery.

Thompson, Mrs. Bert F. (See England) —Maggie L., daughter of William Garrett and Eliza (Scrimsher) Williamson, was born May 1, 1880. Educated in Worcester Academy, Vinita, and Female Seminary. Married near White Oak June 13, 1898, Bert F., son of Nathaniel and Zerilda Thompson. They are the parents of: Albert Louis, born Aug. 13, 1900; Harley C., born Nov. 22, 1904; Mabel Aline, born Oct. 15, 1908; Velma Viola, born Jan. 13, 1911, and Jaunita Thompson, born Sept. 2, 1913. Mr. Thompson is a farmer and stockman, near Centralia.

Maurice, born February 19, 1918. Baby, born Nov. 8, 1921.

Taylor, Mrs. Louisa J. Taylor. (See Foreman)—Louisa Jane, daughter of William and Elizabeth (Moon) Dinsmore, was born In Tenn. in 1863. Married in 1878, James Elbert, son of Thomas Jefferson and Martha Ann (Bradley) Taylor, born Sept. 10, 1855. He died in 1918. They were the parents of. Lenora May, born May 17, 1883, married Robert F. Auten; Dora Jessie, born November 17, 1884, married John Julian Buster; Samuel Cornelius, born December 25, 1886, married Beulah Wynatt; Clyde Elizabeth, born September 13, 1888, married Robert J. Rogers; Xenaphon Elbert, born February 13, 1890; Bertha Belle, born November 3, 1891; Emma Iola, born August 18, 1893, married Daniel Henry Bell; Walter A., born August 19, 1897; Mary Imo, born January 4, 1900, and Bernard Dinsmore Taylor, born March 3, 1904.

Mary Ann, daughter of James and Catherine (Foreman) Bigby, was born August 9, 1802. Married David Taylor, born in Orange County, Virginia, December 16, 1791. They were the parents of Thomas Jefferson Taylor, who married Martha Ann Bradley.

Tell, Mrs. W. W. (See Adair and Ghigau)—William Warren, son of Charles W. and Jennie E. Tell, was born April 1, 1860, in the Province of New Brunswick, Canada. Married June 1, 1899, Sarah Emily, daughter of Richard and Susannah Deborah (Goss) Welch, born February 25, 1874, educated at the Orphan Asylum. They are the parents of: Alice Carey, born March 10, 1901; Benjamin Goss, born May 17, 1904; Ruth Marguerite, born November 3, 1906; Daisy Oklahoma, born January 17, 1909, and Wilson Owen Tell born October 7, 1915. Mrs. Tell's Cherokee name is Cha-ka-wa. She is a member of the Baptist Church.

Without pretentions, William W. Tell is a rarely gifted and useful citizen, his stock of general and exact information would not suffer in comparison with that of many University Professors and degree men. He was elected County Commissioner of Mayes County, November 5, 1912, and November 2, 1920, and was appointed to that office in 1915. He is a farmer.

Trott, W. L. (See Adair)—John Adair, a Scotchman, married Gahoka, a full blood Cherokee woman of the Deer Clan. Their son, Samuel, married Edith, a white woman, and they were the parents of Rachel Pounds Adair, who married Reverend James Jenkins Trott, who, as early as 1828, was the "general missionary" of the Methodist church among the Cherokees in Georgia, Tennesse, Alabama and North Carolina. Their son, William Lafayette Trott, born March 10, 1844, married Malinda Stover, born September 20, 1848, and died September 20, 1868, He then married Louisa J. Moore in 1869. She died July 9, 1918. They were the parents of: William Henry and Dot Fanny, born Dec. 4, 1877. He married Doney Crumby and has one son, Henry Moore Trott, born April 27, 1904.

Dot Fay Trott, daughter of W. L. and Louisa Trott, was born March 13, 1885, and never married.

James J. Trott was arrested by Georgia authorities because he refused to take the oath of allegiance to the State of Georgia, as he already had taken the oath of allegiance to the Cherokee Nation. They released him on condition that he leave the state. He moved to Tennessee, where he remained until 1857, when he moved to the Cherokee Nation.

Adair, Arthur (See Adair)—Arthur, son

of William Penn and Julia (Allison) Adair was born August 13, 1882, educated locally. Married July 23, 1905, Ida, daughter of W. C. and Nancy Jane Freeman, born in Missouri. They are the parents of: Selena Marie, born January 21, 1908; Beulah Belle, born September 12, 1909; Norman Lee, born June 29, 1914; Edith Mae, born September 15, 1917 and Wilma Adele Adair, born February 24, 1919.

Allcott, A. B. (See Ward and Ghigau)—Henrietta Evaline Nidiffer, born January 10, 1883 near Nudmore, Delaware District. She was educated in the Cherokee National schools, and graduated from St. Johns Training School of Nursing in 1915. Married July 26, 1920 A. B. Allcott son of Jonathan P. and Anna Allcott, A. B. Allcott was born May 27th, 1886, in McDowell, Barry County, Missouri. He is an expert electrician and has been Superintendent of the electric light plant at Afton and has recently accepted a like position at at Pauls Valley.

George Ward was born March 17, 1787. Had a splendid education and his handwriting was extraordinarily good. He married December 15, 1805, Lucy Mayes, born Mar. 5, 1789 in Tennessee. Lucy was a sister of Samuel Mayes and aunt of Chiefs Joel B. and Samuel H. Mayes. She died November 11, 1867 and George Ward was killed by "Pin" Indians in 1863. George and Lucy (Mayes), Ward's eldest child, Savina, was born May 1807 in Warren County, Tennessee. She married Felix Arthur and her death occurred on April 16, 1883. Felix and Savina Arthur's daughter, Lucy, born April 6, 1828, married Isaac Nidiffer born July 18, 1818. She died April 2, 1886 and he died February 2, 1890. They were the parents of Samuel, Freeman, Sabrina, married Robert K. Nix; Sarah, married Isaac Mode; Felix Grundy, born Mrch 16, 1853, married April 23, 1876 Joanna Ruth Linder, born February 8, 1861. He died October 16, 1896 and she died July 2, 1919; Martha Jane, married George Monroe Ward; Nancy married Ross T. Carey and John F. Miller; George; Rachel, married John S. Thomason and Lucy Nidiffer married Joseph Kelly.

Felix Grundy and Joanna Ruth Nidiffer were the parents of Emma Josephine, Anna Lulu, Henrietta Evaline (Subject of this sketch)Martha Minnie, John Ross, George William, Freeman Edward and Mary Lucile Nidiffer. George W. and Freeman E. are deceased.

Adair, Timothy M. (See Grant, Adair, Saunders, Downing and Ghigau)—Timothy Meigs, son of Hugh Montgomery and Martha L. (Johnson) Adair was born at Stillwell September 2, 1882. Educated in the Cherokee Public Schools. Married at Nowata April 16, 1906. Martha daughter of Thomas Didymas and Joanna (Pitt) Saunders, born at Braggs December 28, 1885. She died Feb. 10, 1913. They were the parents of: Cleburne, born Feb. 17, 1908. Thereon, born June 30, 1921 and Velma Adair, born Jan. 11, 1913. Mr. Adair married June 22, 1917 Katie E., daughter of John and Mary Nunallee born at Bragg, Okla. 1891. Their children are Warren, born Dec. 26, 1919 and Eugene Adair, born Aug. 6, 1921. Mr. Adair's Cherokee name is Skiya and he belongs to the Long Hair Clan. He is a farmer near Centralia, and is a member of the Independent Order of Odd Fellows Fraternity. He was elected County Commissioner of Nowata County November 7, 1916.

Frank Pettie married Mary Beck and they were the parents of Mrs. Joanna Saunders.

Boudinot, Frank J. (See Watie, Grant and Ross)—Frank Josiah, son of William Penn and Caroline (Fields) Boudinot, was born August 20, 1866, in the Cherokee Nation. Educated in Bacone College or Indian University (near Muskogee), Flint High School (Michigan) and University of Michigan. He took a course in law at the University of Michigan in 1894-5-6. He is a member of the Knights of Pythias fraternity. His Cherokee name is Kaw-la-nah (Raven) and he belongs to the Cherokee Holly clan. He has been the attorney, counselor and adviser of the Kee-too-wah Society of Cherokees since 1899 and was elected Principal Chief of the Cherokee Nation by a Joint session of the National Council on November 21, 1895. He was one of Chief Bushyhead's Executive Secretaries in 1887, clerk of the Cherokee Supreme Court 1887-89 and was one of the attorneys for the Cherokee Nation before the Dawes Commission in 1896. Under his advice and direction the Eastern Cherokees were organized in 1900 by the Keetoowah Society, which resulted ultimately in the collection of the five million dollar Emigrant Cherokee claim—paid in 1910. Was, by act of Congress, Mar. 3, 1919, made special attorney for the Cherokee Nation to prosecute a claim against the United States for interest on the funds which arose out of the judgment in the Emigrant case, the amount claimed being about four million dollars. He married at Fort Gibson, July 23, 1897, Annie Stapler, daughter of Judge Henry Clay and Josephine (Bigelow) Meigs and great-great-grand daughter of Colonel Return Jonathan Meigs, personal friend and aide to General George Washington; she is also a great-grand daughter of Chief John Ross. They are the parents of: Frank Josiah, Jr., born January 16, 1899 (2nd. Lieutenant Air Service Aeronautics in the World War) and Henry Meigs Boudinot, born July 27, 1907.

Gul-la-gee-nah (Buck Deer), son of Oo-wa-tie, was born in the old Cherokee Nation in Georgia in 1802. Out of gratitude for favors he adopted the name of his benefactor, Elias Boudinot. Having received a splendid classical education he devoted his entire life and energies for the Cherokees and at his death on June 21, 1839, he was a poor man, regardless of the fact that at that time he was one of the best known, ablest and greatest citizens the Cherokee Nation had.

Billings, Mrs. E. C. (See Ward and Cordery)—Jessie Lee, daughter of James Lovely and Charlotte (Ward) Bumgarner, born July 2, 1884, educated at Female Seminary and Lawrence, Kansas. Married at Spavinaw March 30, 1902, K. C. Billings, son of John C. and America Billings; born Aug. 10, 1818 in Texas. They are the parents of Beatrice T., born April 16, 1906; Love, born August 17, 1908; Charlotte America, born August 31, 1910; Edith Belle, born April 22, 1912; Myrtle Ceaphine, born November 10, 1916 and Iva Dell Billings, born October 25, 1918.

Cobb, Phil. H. (See Grent)—Alexander Adam Clingan, born February 20, 1801. Married in May 1828 Martha Jane Blythe, born January 31, 1812 in Tennessee. Their daughter Evaline Clingan, born April 13, 1835 married December 15, 1857, Joseph Benson Cobb, born July 26, 1828 in Blount County, Tennessee. He died March 22, 1896 and she died Nov. 17, 1918. Their son, Samuel Sylvester Cobb married Carrie Kennedy Hunter and they are the parents of Phil Hunter Cobb, born May 31, 1895. Educated in Wagoner, where he married October 1, 1918 Hazel Ruth, daughter of S. A. and Naomi Best, born June 27, 1901. They are the parents of Dorothy Louise Cobb, born Oct. 23 ,1920. Mr. Cobb is a farmer, near Wagoner.

Ellis, Mrs. Thomas J. (See Adair and Grant—Mary May, daughter of Robert Taylor and Sue Krebs (McCoy) Morrison born April 12, 1884 in Sequoyah District. Educated in the Cherokee National Schools. Married in Bartlesville Jan. 28, 1901 Thomas Jefferson, son of Thomas Jefferson and V. Ellis, born Dec. 16, 1881 in Sedan, Chautauqua County, Kansas. They are the parents of Gladys, born May 10, 1905; Evelyn, born June 23, 1907 and Judson Ellis, born Oct. 29, 1909. Thomas Jefferson Ellis is a member of the Masonic fraternity and is one of the substantial cattlemen and bankers of Washington County. One of the leading democrats of Washington County, he was appointed as the first county assessor in 1911 and elected to the same office in 1912.

Ellen, daughter of Andrew and Mary (Miller) Adair married Richard Martin, son of Alexander and Sarah Elizabeth (Hicks) McCoy and they were the parents of Mrs. Sue Krebs (McCoy) Morrison.

Edmondson, Mrs. Florence E. (See Ward and Grant)—Florence Eugenia Williams, born Aug. 3, 1860 in Delaware Dist., educated in the Cherokee Public Schools and Female Seminary. She married Feb. 7, 1878 on Beatties Prairie, Michael Smith Edmondson, born September 9, 1853 in Georgia. They are the parents of: Cherry D. born October 23, 1879; Gonia L. born January 1, 1882 and Bula B. born February 17, 1884. Mrs. Edmondson's Cherokee name is Galela, she is a member of the Methodist church, is an Eastern Star and belongs to the W. C. T. U.

George Ward, born March 17, 1787 married December 15, 1805 Lucy Mayes, the Aunt of Chiefs Joel Bryan and Samuel Houston Mayes. She was born March 5, 1789. George Ward was killed during the civil war and his widow died November 1, 1867. Their daughter Charlotte was born July 18, 1809 in Tennessee, she married January 13, 1821, John H. Stover, born June 2, 1802. Mrs. Stover died August 13, 1857 and he died March 31, 1865. Louisa J. daughter of John and Charlotte (Ward) Stover was born August 8, 1840. She married October 2, 1859 Joseph Lynch Williams (whose Cherokee name was Osceola) born August 1, 1837. They were the parents of Florence Eugenia, Joseph L. Williams, died November 5, 1860. Mrs. Louisa J. (Stover) Williams married February 2, 1864, William Archibald Yell Hastings, born March 8, 1842 in Benton County, Arkansas, and they were the parents of: John Rogers, William, Writ and Charlotte Delilah Hastings. Mrs. Louisa J. Hastings died February 7, 1918 and W. A. Y. Hastings, died at the residence of his son, John Rogers.

Evans, Mrs. Lester (See Ghigau, Adair, Cordery and Halfbreed)—Susannah Deborah, daughter of Ephriam Martin and Sallie (Starr) Adair was born in Flint District September 4, 1860. Educated in the Cherokee Public schools and Female Seminary. Married Alexander, son of Andrew Vann and Sallie Ann (Williams) Jordan. He died April 1884. They were the parents of: Belle Leslie, Myrtle and the twins, Alexander and Vannie Jordan. Mrs. Jordan married March 16, 1886, Lester, son of Benoni and Mary E. Evans, born January 3, 1860 in Michigan. They are the parents of Minnie Evans who married Harry Stanley. Mrs. Evans is a member of the Wolf Clan and her Cherokee name is Susanie. Mr. Evans is a member of the Masonic fraternity. They are members of the Methodist Church and are farmers, near Centralia.

Fite, Mrs. F. B. (See Grant)—Julia Theresa, daughter of William Columbus and Jane (Davis) Patton was born December 29, 1867 in Walker County, Georgia. Educated at Drury College, Springfield, Missouri, and Vassar College. She married at Vinita November 13, 1889 Francis Bartow, son of Dr. H. W. and Sarah (Denman) Fite, born October 17, 1861 in Bartow County, Georgia. He graduated in 1886 from the Southern Medical College at Atlanta, Georgia, having received the medal for highest efficiency in his class. He is a leader in Oklahoma in surgery and civic progress. Dr. and Mrs. Fite, whose home is in Muskogee, are the parents of William aPtton, born August 31, 1890; Frances, born September 24, 1893; Francis Bartow, born December 20, 1895: Edward Halsell, born December 27, 1898 and Julian Bixby Fite, born September 30, 1906. William Patton Fite graduated from Shattuck Military School, Faribault, Minnesota, from University of Virginia in 1913 with the A. B. degree and in 1915 from the Medical Department. He married June 1, 1918 Miss Maurine Mitchell of Fort Worth, Texas. Their daughter Jane Fite was born October 7. 1920. He served in the World War as Captain in the Medical Corps 36th Division. Is now practicing surgery in partnership with his father at Muskogee. Francis Fite graduated from Vassar College in 1916. Married July 7, 1920, Hubert Ambrister, an attorney in Oklahoma City. Francis Bartow Fite Jr. graduated from Shattuck Military School, from University of Virginia in 1920 with honors in the A. B. degree and is in the 1922 law class of that institution. He served on the staff of Aide de camp to Major General Sturgis, 80th Division rank as First Lieutenant. Edward Halsell Fite graduated from Shattuck Military School, entered the University of Virginia and enlisted for service in the world war. was assigned to the officers Training Camp at Camp Lee, Virginia. At the signing of the armistice he returned to the University where he is now a member of the Medical Class of 1923. Julian Bixby Fite is a student in Shattuck Military School.

Ludovic Grant, a Scotch trader settled at Tellico, on the Tennessee River in 1720 and married a full blood Cherokee of the Wolf Clan. Their daughter married William Emory, an Englishman and their daughter, Susannah Emory married Captain John Stuart of the British army. Her second husband was Brigadier General Joseph and Susannah (Childs) Martin, born in 1740 near Charlotteville, Virginia. He was elected Captain of the Transylvania Militia in 1776, became Major on February 17, 1779 and was promoted to the lieutenant colonelcy in March 1781. He was elected Brigadier General of the North Carolina Militia by legislature on December 15, 1787, and was commissioned Brigadier General of the Twelfth Brigadier of Virginia Militia by Governor "Light Horse Harry" Lee on December 11, 1783. He died at Martinsville, County seat of Henry county, Virginia, which had been named for him, on December 18, 1808. He was buried with military and masonic honors. His daughter. Rachel married Daniel Davis and their son Martin Davis married Julia Tate. Their daughter Jane married William Columbus Patton.

Joseph, the father of Brigadier General

Joseph Martin, was a son of William Martin, a wealthy merchant of Bristol, England, who gave his son a ship and sent him to Virginia, sometime in the first quarter of the eighteenth century to keep him from marrying a girl to whom the father objected. Martin was one of the Norman Knights who accompanied William the Conqueror in the battle of Hastings and conquest of England in 1066. The family later dropped the terminal and spelled the name, Martain.

Foreman, William W. (See Grant, Ghigau, Foreman, Cordery, Adair, Duncan and Half-breed)—William Wilburn, son of Daniel C. and Elizabeth (Beck) Foreman was born March 17, 1871. Educated in the Cherokee Public Schools. Married in Canadian District March 11, 1896 Belle Leslie, daughter of Alexander and Susan Deborah (Adair) Jordan, born in Canadian District June 27, 1881. They are the parents of: James Andrew, born July 28, 1898; married Edna Richardson; Bessie J. born April 3, 1900; Jesse, born March 21, 1903; Samuel, born Dec. 4, 1907; Perry born Oct. 12, 1911 and Hooley Foreman, born Feb. 28, 1915. Mr. Foreman is a farmer, near Centralia.

Fry, Cullie (See Sanders and Seabolt)—Lettie, daughter of John and Catherine (Seabolt) Chambers, was born in January 1843. Educated in the Cherokee National Schools. Married William Fry, born September 15, 1834. He was a stone mason, having served his apprenticeship in England, of which he was a native. Mrs. Lettie Fry died June 3, 1883 and he died Feb. 7, 1915. They were the parents of Cullie Fry, born Sept. 3, 1878, educated in the Cherokee Public Schools and Male Seminary. Married at Independence, Kansas October 12. 1897, Irene, daughter of Edward and Nancy Trout, born Nov. 22, 1874 in Barton County, Missouri. They are the parents of: Gertrude, born Dec. 18, 1898; Cecil Raymond, born Aug. 3, 1900; Lettie Marie, born May 12, 1902; and Wahneta Fry, born Sept. 3, 1908.

Mr. Fry is one of the farmers and stockmen of Rogers County. He is a member of the Woodmen of the World and Masonic fraternities at Claremore. Is a member of Oklahoma Consistory No. 1 Guthrie, Okla.

Glass, John (See Grant)—John Drake, son of John and Samantha Glass was born June 16, 1891. Educated in the Cherokee Public Schools and Male Seminary. Married at Grove, Okla., 1910, Pearl I. daughter of George Washington and Fanny Goad, born Sept. 20, 1892 in Morgan County. Kentucky. They are the parents of John Kenneth Glass, born Sept. 9, 1911. Mr. and Mrs. Glass are farmers and school teachers. He belongs to the Wolf Clan. John Kenneth Glass' Cherokee name is Da-ga-Do-goh.

Harlan, George W. (See Ghigau)—George Washington, son of David M. and Rebecca (Vannoy) Harlan was born in the Cherokee Nation August 10, 1856 and educated in the Cherokee Public Schools. Married in Delaware District May 30, 1873, Sarah Jane, daughter of Whitten and Nannie Cecil, (the former a native of Kentucky and the latter of Virginia) born July 3, 1855, in Crawford County, Illinois. They are the parents of: William Lee, born September 12, 1874, married Lucinda Ballard and Minnie Belle, born September 1, 1877 and married W. A. J. Trotter.

Mr. Harlan is a farmer near White Oak.

The Harlans, who in the seventh and eighth centuries were known in the Bard's sons as Herelingas and Harlungi were located in Brisach Castle in Alsatia.

Harris, Mrs. Reuben (See Foreman)—Andrew Taylor, a native of Orange County, Virginia married Jennie Bigby and they were the parents of Minerva Jane Taylor who married Robert Wesley Walker, a native of North Carolina. Their daughter Senora Adelaide Walker born December 23, 1859, in Tennessee, married June 16, 1878 Morgan Lemuel Pyeatt born in Washington County, Arkansas December 29, 1851. He died April 29, 1889. Their daughter, Bessie Lee Pyeatt was born at Tahlequah in 1883. Educated in the Female Seminary. Married at Collinsville in 1901 Reuben, son of Mr. and Mrs. Anderson Harris. They are the parents of: George, born Dec. 1911; Violet, born April 6, 1903; Beunah, born Aug. 1, 1912 and Arthur Harris, born March 28, 1919. Mr. and Mrs. Harris are members of the Methodist Church. He is an Odd Fellow and Knight of Pythias. They are farmers, near Ramona, Okla.

Judge Walker, Mrs. Harris' grandfather was Supreme Judge of Indian Territory.

Hutchins, Nettie (See Ghigau and Sanders)—Nettie, daughter of Robin and Nancy

Jane (Starr) Smith was born February 15, 1872 near Claremore. She was educated at West Point public school on Dog Creek and Female Seminary. She married May 10, 1891, Willard Edward Hutchins, born June 12, 1857 in Marion, Nebraska. They were the parents of: Lew Wofford, born May 17, 1892, Blueford Ralph, born Nov. 25th, 1893: Ual Ross, born October 11, 1895: Ethel Dane, born October 14, 1897: Willard Beatrice Hutchins, born October 19, 1902. Nettie Hutchins Cherokee name is Chauouke and she belongs to the Wolf Clan. Her father Robin Smith was elected Councilor from Cooweescoowee District on August 5, 1867 and August 2, 1869. He died December 6, 1872.

Holloway, Mrs. Allen D. (See Rogers)—Eva, daughter of Artemus Andrews and Mary A. (Rogers) Barker, born near Kinnison, June 20, 1886. Educated in Female Seminary, St. Teresa Academy, Kansas City and Forest Park University, St. Louis, Missouri. Married at Vinita May 10, 1906 Allen D. Holloway, son of William and Cordelia Holloway, born 1879 in Cass County, Mo.

They are the parents of: Mary Dee, born May 1, 1910 and William Andrew Holloway, born July 11, 1917. Mrs. Holloway is a member of the Methodist Church and the Eastern Star Chapter. Mr. Holloway is the cashier of the Oklahoma State Bank at Welch, Okla.

McSpadden, Mrs. W. F. (See Carter and Riley)—Serena Carter Parrott, born at Silverlake in Cooweescoowee District March 25, 1870, educated at the Cherokee Orphan Asylum from which she graduated June 17, 1886. Married February 17, 1889 William Fair (son of Rev. T. K. B. and Elizabeth (Green) McSpadden) born December 25, 1856 in Dalton, Georgia. They are the parents of: Zoe, born November 15, 1889, educated at Chelsea and Female Seminary, from which she graduated May 29, 1907, married December 26, 1911 Earl Preston Whitehill; Floyd Carter, born August 19, 1891; Roscoe Conklin, born September 19, 1893; Zella Christine, born September 21, 1897; Alma, born March 8, 1900; William Fair, born December 9, 1902; Clinton, born June 10, 1905; Roger, born June 26, 1907 and Clarence Allen McSpadden, born December 11, 1913.

Earl Preston and Zoe Whitehill are the parents of Christine May, born September 18, 1915 and Earl Preston Whitehill born March 14, 1920.

William Fair McSpadden is a farmer and Vice-President of the Bank of Chelsea. Earl Preston Whitehill is the Field Superintendent of the Lyons Petroleum Company. Mrs. William Fair McSpadden is the daughter of William P. and Diana (Carter) Parrott and first cousin to Congressman Charles D. Carter.

McSpadden, R. V. (See Foreman, Riley, Grant and Ghigau)—Richard Vance McSpadden born July 30, 1879 at Tahlequah. Educated at Tahlequah Public School and graduated from Male Seminary June 29, 1898. He married April 27, 1904 Ermina Essie Foreman, born February 23, 1879 in Vinita. She was educated in Vinita, Jackson, Tenn. and Cincinnati, Ohio. They are both members of the Methodist Church but do not belong to any fraternal orders or clubs. Mr. McSpadden is an oil producer and his wife was very energetic in World War work, especially in Red Cross work and as the directing officer of the Surgical Dressing rooms.

James Walker McSpadden, the son of Reverend T. K. B. McSpadden, was born October 25, 1848 in Alabama. Married April 18, 1872 Annie Thompson, born May 4, 1852. He was for many years one of the stable business men of Tahlequah, as merchant and miller. Mrs. McSpadden died Sept. 20, 1891. Mr. McSpadden died April 19, 1905. Mr. and Mrs. McSpadden were the parents of Florence Wilson, married Philip Wharton Samuel; Richard Vance; Mary Jane, married Thomas R. Crookshank, and James Walker McSpadden, Jr.

Ermina Essie Foreman was the only child of Dr. Austin Worcester Foreman, born at Park Hill, August 18, 1855. Graduated from the Louisville Medical College and located at Vinita, where he married on February 23, Emma Josephine Ridenhour, born May 18, 1858, in Vienna, Mo. Mrs. Foreman died January 23, 1899. He died December 18, 1910.

Mrs. Ermina E. McSpadden's paternal Grandfather was Rev. Stephen Foreman, born February 22, 1807. He graduated from Princeton University. Was elected assistant Editor of the Cherokee Phoenix November 4, 1829. Married Sallie W. Riley. March 27, 1834. Ordained as a Presbyterian Minister, September 25, 1835. He was elected as the first superintendent of Cherokee National Schools in 1841. Elected to the Supreme Court Bench on October 11, 1844, Executive Councilor in 1847 and 1855 and Clerk of the Senate in 1867. He died December 8, 1881. He also, with the Rev. Dr. Worcester, translated the Bible into Cherokee and established the first Presbyterian Church in Tahlequah.

Mayes, Wiley B. (See Adair and Downing) Wiley B. Mayes, born April 15, 1848, in Flint District, married in May 1872 Emma Bombrake, born in 1854. They were the parents of Thompson, born July 6, 1873 and Sinie B. Mayes, born Oct. 20, 1876. Mrs. Emma Mayes died April 18, 1877. Mr. Mayes married February 11, 1879, Margaret Gillis nee McLaughlin born July 13, 1859. They were the parents of Lola Mayes, born January 11, 1880. Mrs. Margaret Mayes died January 19, 1883 and Mr. Mayes married July 22, 1885 Ermina Cherokee Vann born February 26, 1856.

James Vann married September 17, 1829 Elizabeth Heaton, a native of Georgia. He died January 20, 1857 and she died May 6, 1860. They were the parents of Ermina Cherokee (Vann) Mayes.

Walter Adair, called "Black Watt' to distinguish him from his cousin, Walter Scott Adair, who was called "Red Watt' was born December 11, 1783, married May 13, 1804 Rachel Thompson, born December 24, 1786. He died January 20, 1835 and she died April 22, 1876. They were the parents of Nancy Adair, born October 7, 1808, married January 22, 1824, Samuel Mayes, born November 11, 1803 in Tennessee. He died December 30, 1858 and she died March 18, 1876. They were the parents of Wiley B. Mayes.

Martin, Mrs. William H. (See Ross and Oolootsa)—Jennie, daughter of Henry and Mary (Parris) Lowrey was born August 1, 1858, educated in the Cherokee National Schools. Married in 1855 John Hubbard. They were the parents of: Joanna, born November 26, 1876 and Mary Hubbard, born November 28, 1878. Mrs. Jennie Hubbard married Sept. 9, 1883, William Hercules, son of Hercules T. and Permelia Martin. They are the parents of: Frank Garland, born August 9, 1884; Eugene Warren, born January 30, 1886; William Henry, born January 28, 1888; Susie Lowrey, born December 1, 1889; Teresa Josephine born March 1, 1892;Ellen Cordelia born December 22, 1893; Jennie, born December 2, 1895, and Sequoyah Raymond Martin born January 18, 1899 and died May 16, 1917. Frank Garland (in world war).

Anderson Pierce, son of Assistant Chief George and Lucy (Benge) Lowrey, born in 1811 married Mary Nave, born October 16, 1813. He died July 12, 1853 and she died July 3, 1896. They were the parents of Henry Lowrey, born December 28, 1835 and married Mary Parris.

Henry Lowrey and Mary were the parents of George Guess born Feb. 3, 1854; Jennie born Aug. 1, 1858; Daniel born October 2, 1860 Dollie Eunice born Dec. 3 1862. Anderson born 1866; Matilda born April 24, 1870 and Henry Beecher born July 9, 1873.

McNair, Nicholas B. (See Sanders, Cordery and McNair)—Nicholas B. McNair, born May 1, 1859, educated in the schools of the Cherokee Nation, married in December 1877 Rachel, daughter of Thomas and Nannie (Sonicooie) Sanders, born in 1849. They were the parents of: Oscar, born October 12, 1878; Clement, born January 28, 1880 and Etta McNair, born August 12, 1882. Mrs. Rachel McNair died December 22, 1884. He married December 25, 1894, Martha, daughter of William McDonald and Nancy Jones, born March 12, 1866 in Union County, Georgia. They are the parents of: Nannie, born August 28, 1895; William Gunter, born July 15, 1897; Benjamin Franklin, born September 9, 1899; James Porter, born December 30, 1901 and Phillp Pinckney, born October 23, 1905. Mr. McNair belongs to the Wolf Clan, is a farmer and a member of the Masonic and Odd Fellows fraternities.

David McNair, of Scotch decent, born in 1744, married Delilah Amelia, daughter of "Rich" Joseph and Elizabeth Vann, born in 1795. He died August 15, 1836 and she died November 30, 1838. Their son, Nicholas Byers McNair, married Mary, the daughter of John and Sarah (Cordery) Rogers. John Rogers, of English and Scotch descent, was born in 1779 in Burke County, Georgia. He was called "Nolichucky Jack" to differentiate him from another intermarried citizen of the Nation at that period, the other one was called "Hell Fire Jack" Rogers. Nicholas Byers and Mary (Rogers) McNair were the parents of Nicholas B. McNair, the subject of this sketch.

Moore, Mrs. J. B. (See Grant, Daniel, Adair and Gusoduesga)—Cherokee Cornelia, daughter of Benjamin Franklin and Mary Delilah (McNair) Adair, was born at Salina, January 11, 1881. Graduated from the Cherokee Female Seminary. She married Jan. 10, 1904 James Brutus, son of Alexander Moore, born Nov. 8, 1874. They are the parents of: William Adair, born Dec. 25, 1904; James, B. born March 15, 1907; Lawrence, born June 9, 1910; Mary Eleanor, born May 1, 1913 and Cherokee Adair Moore, born June 1, 1915.

On account of a love affair, to which his father objected, Joseph the son of William Martin, a wealthy merchant of Bristol, was given a ship, the Brice, during the first quarter of the eighteenth century and sent to Virginia, when shortly after his arrival he married Susannah Childs, a member of a prominent family and established a plantation near Charlotteville. Their son, Joseph was born there in 1740. The blood of the pioneer, Norman Knight, Martine, who was with William the Conqueror at the fateful battle of Hastings in October 1066, impelled young Joseph to cross the southern Alleghenys where he became a prosperous fur trader and planter. In 1776, one year after the battle of Lexington, John Martin was elected captain of the Transylvania Militia, the almost unknown but indispensable guard of the revolution that enabled the Americans to send Ferguson back and turned the tide against the hitherto successful Britons. Martin had already, on February 17, 1779 been made a Major and five months after the battle of Kings Mountain, he was promoted to a lieutenant colonelcy. He died at Martinsville, Henry County, Virginia on December 18, 1808 where he was buried with military and masonic honors.

His son John Martin was born October 20, 1781. Was the first Chief Justice and first Treasurer of the Cherokee Nation. He died in 1836 and was buried at Ft. Gibson. He marrier Nellie McDaniel, and their eldest child Martha, called "Patsy" Martin married George Washington Adair, and they were the parents of Benjamin Franklin Adair, who married Delilah McNair.

Mayes, Hall (See Grant, Downing, Foreman, Ooolootsa, Adair, Ross, Conrad and Duncan)—Hall, son of Walter and Nannie Riley (McCoy) Mayes was born near Pryor September 26, 1891, educated at Male Seminary, Bacone University and Agricultural College at Stillwater. Married at Muskogee, September 1, 1915, Sallie Pearl, daughter of Henry Clay and Nannie Vinita (West) Cochran Mayes, born July 19, 1920.

Samuel Mayes, born April 11, 1803, in Tennessee. Married January 27, 1824 Nancy Adair, born October 7, 1808. He died December 30, 1858 and she died March 18, 1876. They were the parents of George Washington Mayes born November 5, 1824. Married May 21, 1846, Charlotte Bushyhead born March 16, 1830. She died January 23, 1878 and he died October 28, 1894 They were the parents of Walter Adair Mayes born December 9, 1860. Married December 25, 1890 Nannie Rider McCoy born March 25, 1866. They were the parents of Hall Mayes.

John Rogers married Tiana Foster. They were the parents of Elizabeth Rogers who married Jesse Cochran and their son Jesse Cochran married Susie Ross. They were the parents of Henry Clay Cochran who married Nannie Vinita West and they were the parents of Sallie Pearl (Cochran) Mayes.

Nall, Mrs. Basil (See Grant and Dnucan) —Joella, daughter of Joseph Lynch Thompson and Frances B. Kell was born in Texas November 27, 1866, educated at Vinita. Married February 1, 1893, Basil Laskin Nall, son of Larkin and Rebecca Nall, born in Washington County, Arkansas. February 1, 1857. They are the parents of Dora Ella, born December 8, 1893; Josie Esther, born December 22, 1895, married at Vinita, September 22, 1915 N. B. Kerr; Georgia A. born February 14, 1902, and Mary Alice Nall, born April 3, 1906. The Nalls and Kerrs are farmers and live near Pensacola.

Nannie, the daughter of Brigadier General Joseph Martin married Jeter Lynch a member of the Irish nobility and they were the parents of Maria Lynch who married Jeter Thompson and they were the parents of Joseph Lynch Thompson who married Frances B. Kell.

Basil L. and Joella Noll's oldest daughter, Dora Ella was married to John Lewis Warner December 10, 1911 and had two children, Herchel Ray, born Sept. 5, 1912 and Basil Bert was born Nov. 28, 1914.

Odle, Mrs. Grover C. (See Ward)—Caroline Jane Gwatney, born Nov. 23, 1884, educated at Pryor and Female Seminary. Married March 18, 1906, Grover Cleveland, son of John and Mary Odle, born March 29, 1879 in Henry County, Mo. They are the parents of: Burdette, born November 8, 1906; John Edward, born August 4, 1911; Ruth, born June 20, 1914 and Mary Odle, born October 31, 1916. Mr. Odle is a farmer near Pryor.

Edward Gwartney, born in Indiana March 16, 1860. Married December 29, 1881 Susie, daughter of John S. and Jane (Loveless) Ward, born July 29, 1865. She died Jan. 21, 1898. They were the parents of Mrs. Caroline Jane Odle.

Pace, Mrs. William H. (See Downing and Adair)—Annie Lydia, daughter of John and Rosella (Adair) Downing was born in Saline District September 10, 1871. Educated in Female Seminary and Harrell Institute, Muskogee. Married at Locust Grove December 22, 1898, William Hayden, son of William and Loretta Pace, born in 1868 in Benton County, Ark. They are the parents of: Elbert Edward, born November 21, 1899 was in the S. A. T. C. at Oklahoma University and is at present attending the A. and M. College at Stillwater; Hayden Adair, born February 19, 1901; Clyde Lewis, born November 30, 1902; Joe Sheldon, born June 14, 1904; Loretta Lucile, born January 15, 1906; Howard, born October 5, 1907 and Alfred Collins Pace born August 7, 1909.

Mr. and Mrs. Pace are members of the Methodist Church. He is a farmer and stockraiser, near Welch; specializing in pure bred Short Horn cattle and Poland China Hogs.

Sparlin, Benjamin F. (See Grant, Palmour)—Benjamin, son of Oliver and Mattie Sparlin was born in Oklahoma Nov. 17, 1885. Married at Claremore, Okla. November 9, 1914, Mary L. Sparlin, daughter of B. F. and Amandie Palmour born Oct. 23, 1887 in Georgia. They are the parents of Amy Gazelle, born March 12, 1917 and William Sparlin, born June 10, 1920. Mr. Sparlin is a farmer near Chelsea.

Rogers, James F. (See Rogers)—James Foster, son of Lewis and Elizabeth J. (Lisenbe) Rogers was born in September 1881. Educated in the Cherokee public schools and Male Seminary. Married at Vinita 1893 Josephine, daughter of John D. and Jennie Marker, born June 9, 1877. They are the parents of: Flora E. born February 16, 1894; James Foster, born July 13, 1899; Nellie Bell, born June 9, 1900; Mary J. born April 5, 1902; Annie L., born March 12, 1904 and Lewis T. born August 8, 1907. Mr. and Mrs. Rogers have adopted and are raising Talala Buchanan Rogers, born Oct. 18, 1912, a Cherokee girl. Mr. Rogers is a prosperous farmer and stockman.

Phillips, Mrs. Woodley, (See Grant and Oolootsa)—Maude Hoyt McSpadden, born at Chelsea, Cherokee Nation, March 15, 1885, educated at Chelsea and the Female Seminary, from which she graduated June 9, 1903. She married April 3, 1905 Woodley Gail Phillips, born in Crawford Co. Penn. May 15, 1877. They are the parents of Joel Arthur, born February 6, 1906 who died Dec. 13, 1914; Donald Mortimer, born Oct. 12, 1908; Ross Marvin, born Apr. 15, 1912; Lawrence Gail, born Mar. 22, 1916; Paul McSpadden, born March 25, 1918.

Woodley Gail Phillips of English descent was among oil operators coming into Oklahoma from Pennsylvania in September, 1902.. Connected with Cherokee Oil and Gas Co., one of the pioneer companies of the state.

Phillips, Mrs. W. P. (See Grant, Daniel, Ghigau and Adair)—Jane Anna, daughter of James Allen and Johnanna Bell (Buffington) Thompson was born November 17, 1873. Educated in the Cherokee National schools and Female Seminary, from which she graduated June 29, 1893. She married at Tahlequah January 9, 1895 William Penn, son of M. H. and Josephine Phillips born December 14, 1869. Educated in Delaware District and Male Seminary. They are the parents of: Lulu Bell, born October 14, 1895. Educated in Kendall College, Chicago and New York, graduating from the former; Dewey, born March 27, 1898 and had the same educational advantages as did her sister, and William Penn Phillips, Jr. born Aug. 5, 1900, served six months in the United States Marines, receiving a medal for meritorious conduct. The Phillips' are members of the Methodist church. He is an Elk and she belongs to the Daughters of the American Revolution.

Joseph, the son of William Martin, a wealthy merchant of Bristol, England settled near Charlotteville, Virginia in the first quarter of the eighteenth century. His son Joseph was born on this plantation in 1740. Joseph Jr. became a fur trader and planter, amassing wealth. He was elected Captain of the Transylvania Militia in 1776 became Major, February 17, 1779 and Lieutenant Colonel in March 1781. His services were incited against the Tories and their Indian allies west of the Allegheny Mountains, they having been stirred to violence by a letter from the British Superintendent of Southern Indian affairs, dated May 9, 1776 calling on them for concerted action in surprising and killing the men, women and children of the revolutionists and their sympathizers. The south had been practically subjugated by the summer of 1780 and it was only by the efforts of such transmontane patriots as Major Joseph Martin that it was possible for a part of the soldiers of the Mustmer fountain to strike and destroy Ferguson at Kings Mountain on October 7, 1780 and thereby turn the tide in favor of the Americans. Major Martin was not at Kings Mountain as he was busy holding the British allies of the southwest at bay. In further recognition of his patriotic services, he was advanced to the lieutenant colonelcy, five months later. He was elected Brigadier General of the North Carolina Militia by legislature on December 15, 1787 and was commissioned Brigadier General of the Twelfth Brigade of Virginia Militia by Governor "Light Horse Harry" Lee on December 11, 1793.

He died at Martinsville, Henry County, Virginia on December 8, 1808 and was buried with military and masonic honors. He married Susan Fields nee Emory and their second child was Nancy Martin who married Peter Lynch. The eldest of their eight children was Martha Lynch born in March 1801. Married in 1816, James Allen Thompson born July 4, 1795 in Pendleton District, South Carolina. She died September 19, 1861 and he died February, 10, Johnson Thompson married January 5, 1843 Eliza Christine Taylor born October 6, 1826. He died April 7, 1900 and she died February 16, 1902. Their son James Allen Thompson born in 1851, married Johnanna Bell Buffington, born February 13, 1854. She died October 12, 1881 and he died in October 1915. They were the parents of Mrs. William Penn Phillips.

Fletcher, C. L.—C. L. Fletcher, son of B. G. and M. H. (Guthrie) Fletcher was born Jan. 25, 1885. Educated at the Male Seminary and Commercial College, Ft. Smith, Ark.; married Dec. 23, 1906 to Margaret M. daughter of Alford B. and America (Johnson) Holland. Born July 24, 1886, died Nov. 21, 1911. Two children were born to this union, Loren born Feb. 23, 1909 and Maggie H. born Nov. 7, 1911, died Aug. 27. 1912.

Married Lillian Blake Dec. 6, 1913, daughter of B. W. and Sarah H. Blake, born in the state of West Virginia March 24, 1894. Two children were born to this union Jack, born Mar. 12, 1916 and Joe R. born April 13, 1920. Mr. Fletcher was elected County Commissioner of Adair County in 1918.

Griffin, George W. (See Conrad and Hendricks)—George W., son of Isaiah and Katie (Rich) Griffin was born in Rutherford County, Tennessee March 4, 1861; married at Tahlequah Aug. 8, 1899 Jenetta, daughter of James R. and Elizabeth (Hendricks) Gourd, born Jan. 24, 1868. They are the parents of Alice, born Oct. 15, 1901; Ira, born Oct. 3, 1908, and Blanche Griffin born Oct. 25, 1911. Mr. Griffin is a farmer near Hulbert, Oklahoma.

Harris, Mrs. J. W. Jr. (See England)—Lydia, daughter of Robert L. and Nynia Jane (Cornatzer) Madison was born in Craig County, April 6, 1894 and graduated in 1917 from the Vinita High School. Married at Vinita May 10, 1919, John Wesley, son of John Wesley and Ida Josephine Harris, born near Vinita, June 3, 1897. They are the parents of Grace Cornelia Harris, born March 19, 1920.

Mr. Harris enlisted for the World War at Vinita, August 29, 1917. Sent to Camp Pike ,Arkansas where he was assigned to Co. K. 166 Reg., 83rd Division. Sailed for France September 1, 1917. Transferred to Co. 1, 152 Regiment 40th Divisions.

Hildebrand, Mrs. Samuel (See Hildebrand) —Fannie, daughter of Frank and Agnes (Foster) Fritz was born in Cooweescoowee District October 8, 1879. Educated at Carlyle and Haskell Institutes. Married at Vinita February 24, 1900 Samuel, son of Benjamin and Delilah (O'Fields) Hildebrand, born February 14, 1880. Educated in the Male

Seminary. They are the parents of Agnes, born February 25, 1902; Lura, born March 27, 1904; Edward, born May 3, 1906; Aaron born April 19, 1908; Glenn, born October 23, 1911; Floyd, born January 17, 1914; Georgia, born February 22, 1918 and Melvin Hildebrand, born January 31, 1920. Mrs. Hildebrand is a Methodist and a Rebekah. Mr. Hildebrand is a member of the Independent Order of Odd Fellows. They are farmers near Vinita.

Pennel, Mrs. Henry C. (See Grant and Duncan)—Dora Fannie, daughter of Thomas Fox and Helen Alice (Kell) French, born July 17, 1874. Educated at Fort Gibson and Female Seminary. Married December 6, 1893 Henry Camillius son of William and Caroline Pennel, born January 18, 1873 in Washington County, Ark. They are the parents of: Thomas William born October 5, 1895; Charles Columbus, born December 9, 1897; James Kell, born January 19, 1900; Bernice, born Feb. 27, 1904 and Thelda Pennel, born March 3, 1915. Mr. and Mrs. Pennel are member of the Holiness Church. They are farmers, near Hulbert, Okla.

Rogers, Miss Mary K. (See Cordery and Daniel)—Henry Curtis Rogers, born in 1825. Married Louisa Jane Thompson nee Blackburn, born in 1823. She died November 30, 1883 and he died February 3, 1896. They were the parents of: Mary Kinney; Catherine who married Isaac Newton Strickland; Lucy P. who married William Ridge Rogers; Eugene Overby who married William Rufus Greer; William Henry, elected Treasurer of Rogers County 1907 and 1910 and County Commissioner of the same county; and Stonewall Jackson Rogers.

Miss Mary Kinney Rogers is a graduate from the Moravian School of Salem, N. C. Mrs. Eugenia Oglesby Greer was President of the East Oklahoma Woman's Missionary Society for three years. She is still actively engaged in missionary work.

McCullough, Mrs. Peter (See Grant and Adair)—Sarah Penelope Fields, born April 2, 1842. Married October 20, 1859. John Jackson Smith, born December 22, 1836 in McMinn County, Tennessee. They were the parents of Magenia Jane Smith, born October 24, 1871. Educated in the Cherokee Public Schools and Female Seminary. Married March 4, 1895 Peter, son of Milton Howard and Rachel Jane (Adair) McCullough, born May 29, 1872. They are the parents of: Winnie Davis, born in 1899; Rex J. born in 1901; Gladys M. born in 1904; William Penn, born in 1907 and Joy M. born in 1910. Mr. and Mrs. McCullough are members of the Christian Church. He is a merchant in Miami where he has been City Treasurer.

Rex J. McCullough served in the marines during the World War, was honorably discharged with meritorious citation.

Minnie Davis McCullough graduated from the Miami High School in 1917. Assigned to special stenographic work in the war and Treasury Departments at Washington. Mrs. McCullough is a composer and writer of verse.

Smith, Fred, (See Grant and Ward)—Frederick David, son of Samuel and Louisa Jane (Ward) Smith was born on Spavinaw Creek, March 24, 1865, educated in Delaware District. Married on Lynch's Prairie May 26, 1888, Charlotte Elizabeth, daughter of John Jefferson and Mary Pauline (Adair) Fields, born August 27, 1872, educated in Delaware District. They are the parents of. Frederick Eldo, born June 19, 1894, graduated from the Northeastern State Normal at Tahlequah in 1915 and Draughons Business College; Richard Lafayette, born September 7, 1899; Charles Julian, born September 24, 1903, married Opal Pearl Young; Samuel P. Smith, born August 4, 1910. Mr. Smith is a farmer near Big Cabin and is a member of the Independent Order of Odd Fellows and Mrs. Smith is a Rebecca.

Richard, son of Ezekial and Mary Ann (Sexton) Fields married Elizabeth Blagg and they were the parents of John Jefferson Fields who married Mary Pauline Adair.

Snider, (See Grant and Duncan)—Elbert Jacob, son of Andrew Johnson (born May 1, 1867 in Davis County, Mo.) and Cynthia (Muskrat) Snider, born May 4, 1867, in Delaware District and married November 28, 1886 and died July 2, 1902, was born September 29, 1888 at Grove, Delaware District. He was educated at Grove and Male Seminary. He married September 26, 1912, Martha Elizabeth, daughter of John Martin Daniel (born October 2, 1843 married August 31, 1876 and died October 10, 1913) and Alice R. (Smith) Daniels (born June 10, 1854 at Fayetteville, Arkansas and died November 10, 1905), born April 13, 1888 and married September 26, 1912 at Vinita. Elbert J. and Martha E. Snider are the parents of Genevieve M. born October 27, 1913 and Elbert Jacob Snider, born November 22. 1915.

John Martin Daniel was elected Sheriff of Delaware District August 4, 1873 and member of council from same district August 6, 1883 and his son, James Henry, the eldest brother of Mrs. Martha E. Snider was elected a member of the Council in 1902.

Elbert Jacob Snider is the grandson of Jacob and Martha (Fields) Muskrat; great grandson of Ezekial and Polly Ann (Sexton) Fields and the great great grandson of Richard Fields, Chief of the Texas Cherokee from 1822 until his death in 1827. Elbert J. Snider, has three brothers, James Floyd, born January 1, 1890; Roy Clinton, born May 3, 1892 and Cecil Freeman Snider born May 3, 1897.

Mrs. Martha E. Snider's brothers and sisters are Marmaduke, born October 9, 1877; James Henry, born April 9, 1879 and died May 5, Robert John born May 9, 1881; Lulu May, born January 21, 1884; Eliza J. born March 25, 1886; Emma E. born February 19, 1880; William A. born August 26, 1892; Edgar Jackson, born February 14, 1895 and Walter Scott Daniel, born Dec. 12, 1898. Elbert J. Snider had one sister, born Nov. 16, 1900 and died July 7, 1902.

Thompson, John F. (See Ghigau)—John Franklin, son of Caleb Starr and Matilda (Cordill) Thompson, was born November 20, 1853 in Union County, Georgia and educated in that State. Married in Georgia Aug. 13, 1876, Amanda C., daughter of Lewis and Catherine Little born Sept. 12, 1813 in N. C. They are the parents of: Lewis Caleb, born June 13, 1877 and died Dec. 4, 1899; David Elihu, born Aug. 4, 1878 and died Nov. 7, 1920; William Lafayette, born Nov. 13, 1879; Annie M. born July 19, 1881, died Jan. 30, 1903; John Nelson, born April 10, 1883; Mary S. born Oct. 29, 1884 and married James G. Trapp; Nellie, born Aug. 1, 1886 and married L. F. Johnson; Margaret Latitia, born Aug. 24, 1889 and married E. B. Edwards; Pearly, born April 2, 1891, died April 26, 1891; Jesse Clayborn, born June 5, 1895. Mr. Thompson is a farmer near Tahlequah. He affiliated with Cherokee Lodge No. 10 of Tahlequah on November 9, 1883 and was Master of the Masonic Lodge from 1896 to 1900 and was again chosen for that position in 1902. He was elected County Commissioner of Cherokee County, November 7, 1916.

Reid, James Walker (See Thompson)—A minister of the Presbyterian Church does not draw a large salary. Ordinarily he can by careful saving give his children a common school, high school or more rarely a university education, but it requires rare ability for a man to stay in the ministry through a long and useful life, generally stationed in the smaller cities, to give not only one but several of his sons and daughter extra American and European university educations, such as are generally at the behest of families of opulence, but this was one of the distinguished abilities of Reverend and Mrs. Gilbert Taylor Thompson.

Gilbert Taylor Thompson, son of Matthew and Sallie Turner (Denman) Thompson, was born April 15, 1847. Graduated from Sonora Masonic Institute in 1868. Married February 2, 1865 Josephine Amanda King, born April 10, 1847 in Cass County Georgia. He was ordained a minister in the Presbyterian Church in April 1874, at Resaca, Georgia. He died at Tahlequah April 20, 1901.

The sons and daughters of Reverend and Mrs. Thompson are the most highly educated family among the Cherokees, several of them having been educated abroad. They are: Allison Denman, Ernest, Milton King, James Kidd, Cleo, Gilbert Taylor and Matthew Aster.

Cleo Thompson graduated from the Presbyterian College of Upper Missouri in 1893 and Ward Seminary, Nashville in 1896, married on Dec. 25, 1899 to James Walker Reid, born May 31, 1870 in Mecklinburg Co., N. Car. Mr. Reid is a graduate of Erskine College, Due West, S. C. Mr. and Mrs. Reid live at Tahlequah, where he has been in business for several years.

They are the parents of children of whom they will ever have reason to be proud: Thompson Reid, born January 26, 1901; Mary Cleo born April 6, 1904; James Walker, Jr., born Aug 30, 1906 and Marjorie, born July 14, 1910.

Sullivan, Frank R. (See Grant and Cordery)—Frank Robert, son of James and Mary Ann, (McPherson) Sullivan was born near

Claremore April 5, 1878. Educated at Yellow Springs, Cooweescoowee District. Married Daisy Bishop. They were the parents of James Bradshaw Sullivan, born June 10, 1897. Mr. Sullivan married June 2, 1900, Peggy Stop born in 1875 and educated at Catoosa. They are the parents of: Andrew Leerskov, born February 8, 1914, and Mary Belle Sullivan, born June 24, 1916. Mr. Sullivan is a farmer near Claremore.

James, son of George and Elizabeth Ann (Rogers) Sullivan was born in Georgia April 23, 1849. Married Mary Ann, daughter of George Washington and Elmira (Gardinhier) McPherson, born November 19, 1846. She died in 1883 and he died June 25, 1901.

Susan, daughter of John and Nannie (Fields) Crutchfield married James Stopp and they were the parents of Mrs. Frank Sullivan.

Smith, Richard M. (See Grant)—Ella, daughter of Wirt and Sarah (Woodward) Fields, born April 17, 1853, married at Fort Gibson Frank N. Smith, born in 1845. Mrs. Smith died November 6, 1891. They were the parents of Richard Martin Smith, born Jan. 28, 1881, educated in the Cherokee Public School, and Male Seminary. Married at Wagoner Aug. 10, 1903, Carrie, daughter of Columbus and Amanda Phipps, born March 4, 1887. They are the parents of Gideon, born Sept. 25, 1906 and Theron Smith, born Feb. 3, 1910. Mr. and Mrs. Smith are members of the Methodist Church. He is a member of the I. O. O. F. and is a farmer, near Wagoner.

Susannah Wolf married Henry Woodard and their son Thomas Woodard married Nannie Morning. They were the parents of Sarah Woodard who married Wirt Fields.

Thornton, Orville E. (See Ward)—Orville Elihu, son of George Washington and Emily Jane (Austin) Thornton was born May 29, 1876, in Iowa and educated in that state; married in Iowa April 2, 1898 Drucilla A., daughter of Reuben and Elizabeth Ann Conley, Their adopted daughter Georgia Myrtle Martin was born at Centralia February 22,1910 and has been with them since she was 5 days old. She is generally known as Georgia Myrtle Thornton. Mr. Thornton is Justice of the Peace at Centralia and is engaged in farming.

George Washington Thornton was born on Beatties Prairie on February 2, 1856.

Adair, Samuel (See Adair)—Samuel, the son of Rufus and Jennie (Fields) Adair, was born in the Cherokee Nation August 12, 1869; was educated at the Cherokee Orphan Asylum. He married March 6, 1892, Mary the daughter of Dick Welch, born May 30, 1877. They were the parents of Jennie, born November 28, 1892; Edna, born April 27, 1897; Levi, born December 15, 1898; Griffin born April 3rd, 1905; Sue, born December 8, 1900; and Benjamin Adair, born December 15, 1910. Mr. and Mrs. Adair are members of the Presbyterian Church. He was a deputy U. S. Marshal and special officer for the Frisco Railway Company. Their son Levi, enlisted and was on the firing line in France during the recent war.

Adair, A. Frank (See Grant)—Arthur Frank, son of John Lynch and Mary Jane (Jeffreys) Adair was born August 28, 1858, educated in Male Seminary. Married at Tahlequah September 1, 1886 Mollie Elizabeth Miller, born February 22, 1868. They were the parents of: Arthur Lynch, born May 11, 1891 and Owen Lewis Adair, born March 18, 1893.

Rachel, daughter of Jeter and Nancy (Martin) Lynch married Thomas Benjamin Adair and they were the parents of John Lynch Adair who married Mary Jane Jeffreys a native of Virginia.

Burgess, Mrs. T. H. (See Ward)—Mary Ann Gwartney born December 10, 1887 educated at Pryor and Female Seminary. Married at Pryor, December 17, 1905, T. H., son of Robert and Sarah Burgess, born Sept. 26, 1880 in Washington County, Ark. They are the parents of Bryant L. born March 14, 1908; Lucille, born January 15, 1910; Thomas Henry, born September 19, 1911; Jack, born November 15, 1915 and Leonard Burgess, born June 17, 1920. Mr. Burgess is farming near Pryor.

John S. Ward, born October 7, 1820. Married July 27, 1857 Jennie Loveless, born May 1, 1842. She died January 16, 1890 and he died June 15, 1896. Their daughter Susie married Edward Gwartney and they are the parents of Mrs. T. H. Burgess.

Downing, George B. (See Downing)—George Brewer, son of David and Catherine (Faught) Downing, born May 8, 1858, educated in Going Snake District. Married February 30, 1877 Arabella Wagoner, born in 1860 in Washington County, Arkansas. They are the parents of: David Monroe, born December 2, 1877; Timmie Jane, born October 28, 1879; Catherine Mahala, James Lewis, Effie Ola, born September 20, 1893; William Alexander; and Jessie Downing, born August 22, 1902. George Brewer is a Mason. He was appointed Sheriff of Saline District, September 23, 1897.

Dupree, William E. (See Adair)—Dr. William J. Dupree, born December 25, 1824, in Alabama, married in 1851 Charlotte, daughter of John and Charlotte (Adair) Bell. They were the parents of William E. Dupree, born November 9, 1857 in Wood Co. Texas and he was educated at Jamestown, 5 miles north of Overton, Texas. He married at Quitman, Tex. on Jan. 11, 1883, Fannie L., daughter of Dr. W. E. H. and Fannie (Aycok) Wright, born Jan. 14, 1861, in Wood County, Texas. They are the parents of Elmer, born October 24, 1883; Herbert, born April 2, 1887, died April 2, 1918; Emma, born December 13, 1888; Wright, born October 8, 1890; Bessie, born May 29, 1892; Fred, born August 20, 1895; Annie, born July 4, 1899; Eleanor Dupree, born August 2, 1904.

Bessie Dupree married Dorsey E. Hall, and they are the parents of Dorsey E. Hall, Jr., born April 30, 1916; Wright Dupree and Eleanor Elizabeth, twins, born July 20, 1917. Wright Dupree Hall died January 16, 1920; Alonzo Carter Hall, born July 19, 1920. Mr. and Mrs. Hall are living in Fort Collins, Colorado.

Mr. and Mrs. Dupree are members of the Baptist Church, and he is a successful farmer near Vinita.

Jamestown, Smith Co. Texas was noted for its good school. In the fall of 1866 Dr. Dupree moved there from his farm in Wood Co., Tex. to educate his children. In 1877 he moved back to his farm in Wood Co.

Mitchell, Clay Albion (See Oolootsa and Foreman)—George W. Mitchell, born December 26, 1852 at Bloomfield, Arkansas; married June 13, 1886, in Going Snake District, Martha J. Horn, who was born March 17, 1862. They are the parents of Clay Albion Mitchell, born April 1, 1894, who was educated at Vinita, Oklahoma, and married at Vinita on December 23, 1916, Martha Eunice, daughter of Sarah (Nazworthy) Chamberlain, born February 5, 1899, and was educated at Vinita, Oklahoma. They are the parents of Robert Clay, born October 30, 1917 and Hazel Maurine Mitchell, born February 14, 1919.

Mr. and Mrs. Mitchell are members of the Christian Church, and he is a farmer near Bluejacket, Oklahoma.

John Horn married Susan Louella Foreman, and they were the parents of Mrs. Martha J. (Horn) Mitchell.

Reverend Amory Nelson Chamberlain married Dollie Eunice Hoyt, and they were the parents of Edward Warner Chamberlain.

Meek, William A. (See England, Grant and Daniels)—David England married Susan A. Conner. Their daughter Arminda England married William England, Isaac Scrimsher and Elias H. Jenkins. Her daughter, Alta Berilla Scrimsher, born November 24, 1855, died Sept. 8, 1885; married January 20, 1873 Abram Meek born September 27, 1851 in Vandalia, Illinois. Died April 15, 1907. Their son William Alvin Meek was born November 7, 1880. Educated in Male Seminary at Tahlequah and Draughon's Business College, Oklahoma City, graduating from the latter July 21, 1904. Married August 8, 1909, Ada, daughter of Henry and Emma Jane Donelly, born June 24, 1890, educated in Willie Halsell College and Sacred Heart Academy at Vinita. They are the parents of Ada Fay Meek, born April 29, 1912. Mr. and Mrs. Meek are members of the Methodist Church. He is a merchant and is postmaster at Miles.

Merrell, Mrs. William—Corintha C. daughter of Pleas and Sarah Cheek was born March 2, 1875. Educated at Grove. Married at Vinita October 15, 1893 William, son of Asa C. and Emeline Merrell, born May 9, 1865 in Saline County, Mo. They are the parents of Luvena, born May 5, 1897, married July 20, 1918, John Robinson and has one daughter Audra May, born May 7, 1920. Lola, born March 2, 1900, married July 5, 1920 Bee Garrison; Pleasant Chandler, born February 17, 1904; Jewell, born February 15, 1909 and Euphaetta Merrell, born February 24, 1912. Mr. and Mrs. Merrell are residents of Welch.

Mitchell, Mrs. George W. (See Grant, Downing, and Foreman)—George W., son of George W. and Mary A. Mitchell, was born in Bloomfield, Arkansas, December 26, 1852; married Susan Cherokee, daughter of Stephen and Polly C. (Beck) Hildebrand. They were the parents of Dr. Robert L., born April 10, 1876; Levia L., born July 7, 1878; Savola L., born April 5, 1881; Claud S., born May 16, 1883. After the death of Mrs. Susan Cherokee Mitchell, Mr. Mitchell married, on June 13, 1886, Martha J. Horn, born March 17, 1862. They are the parents of Lee R. Mitchell, born December 11, 1888; Joseph F. Mitchell, born February 10, 1891; Clay A. Mitchell, born April 1, 1895; Beulah V. Mitchell, born October 7, 1897; George W. Mitchell, Jr., born June 25, 1899; Ross B. Mitchell, born January 10, 1902; and Foreman Drew Mitchell, born September 7, 1904.

Mrs. Martha J. Mitchell is the daughter of John Horn, born August 3, 1823, and died in 1888. Her maternal grandmother, Elsie Hicks, who married Jeremiah Horn, a white man, was the daughter of "Chief" Charles R. Hicks.

George W. Mitchell was a member of the Cherokee National Board of Education from 1895 to 1897.

Stephen Hildebrand married Mary, daughter of Jeffrey and Sallie (Downing) Beck and they were the parents of Mrs. Susan Cherokee (Hildebrand) Mitchell.

Martha J. Mitchell was a grand daughter of Dr. Bark and Rachel Foreman and a daughter of Susan Horn.

Rambo, Mrs. Lola M. (See Grant, Ooloootsa and Adair)—Lola M., daughter of Marshall and Pauline (McCoy) Mann, was born September 6, 1885 at Vinita, Oklahoma. She was educated at Kidd-Key College at Sherman, Texas, and Willie Halsell College at Vinita, Oklahoma. She graduated from the latter institution; and also took a stenographic course at this school. She was married at Muskogee December 4, 1907, to Walter A., son of James J. and Mary A. Rambo. They are the parents of Alma Elsine, born Sept. 12, 1908; Marshall J., born Oct. 31, 1910; Kenneth, born Aug. 17, 1913 and Pauline Louise Rambo, born January 6, 1916.

Mrs. Rambo is private secretary to the Superintendent for the Five Civilized Tribes at Muskogee. She is a member of the Saint Paul Methodist Church of Muskogee; Eastern Star and Knights and Ladies of Security fraternities. Mrs. Rambo has held the positions of Secretary for James C. Davis Asst. Creek National Attorney under R. C. Allen, Creek National Attorney and the same office under William M. Harrison, Government Probate Attorney.

Marshall Mann, born March 9, 1850 in Ohio, married, at Webbers Falls on March 24, 1873, Pauline J. McCoy, who was born July 24, 1853, in the Cherokee Nation.

Pauline Jane, daughter of John Lowrey and Lucy Jane (Adair) McCoy married Marshall Mann, March 24, 1873.

Swain, Mrs. Rebecca M. (See Thompson and Riley)—Joseph Polstrom, born February 11, 1834, in Birmingham, Alabama; married November 16, 1863 in Bayou Menârd, Susan Rebecca Wilson, who was born July 19, 1846, at Fort Gibson. They were the parents of Rebecca McNair Polstrom, born August 19, 1864 on Bayou Menard, and was educated in the Female Seminary at Tahlequah. She married December 27, 1879, John, son of George and Nancy (Cramer) Swain, born October 5, 1833 in Westmoreland County, Pennsylvania. He served in the Union Army during the Civil War in Company E, Fourth California Infantry. He died April 6, 1920. Mr. Swain was a charter member of the Vinita Lodge No 5, A. F. & A. M. and a 32nd degree Mason. Mrs. Swain is a member of the Congregational Church; and Grand Matron of the Order of the Eastern Star of the Indian Territory, having held that position in 1895-6. She is also a member of the Womans Civic League, Delphian and Premier Worthwhile Clubs.

Mrs. Swain's Cherokee name is Quaitsla, and she is a member of the "Long Hair" clan.

Skinner, Mrs. Ray N. (See Downing and Duncan)—Jemima Winnie Davis, daughter of Robert Ray and Cynthia Jane (Horn) Taylor was born Tuesday, February 12, 1898. Educated at Willie Halsell College and Sacred Heart Institute, Vinita. Married at Carthage, Missouri, August 25, 1913, Ray Nathaniel, son of Nathaniel and Nannie (Kell) Skinner, born September 28, 1884, in Vinita. They are the parents of Gay Nell Skinner, born March 1, 1914 in Phoenix, Arizona.

Nannie, daughter of Lewis Ross and Sarah (Chambers) Kell was born January 28,

1861. Married in March 1879 Nathanial Skinner, born April 8, 1851 in Harrison County, Kentucky. She died January 28, 1889.

Nancy Elizabeth, daughter of Broom, Chief of Broomstown, a full blood Cherokee of the Wolf Clan married Nathan Hicks, a white man. They were the parents of Charles R. Hicks, born in 1760 and died in 1826. Elsie, daughter of Charles R. Hicks, born in 1760 and died in 1826. Elsie, daughter of Charles R. Hicks, married Jeremiah Horn, a white man and they were the parents of William Horn who married Margaret Ledbetter. Their daughter Cynthia Jane Horn was born November 29, 1847 in Collin County, Texas. Married in Collin County, March 14, 1871, Robert Ray Taylor, born November 25, 1832 in Wilson County, Tennessee. He died February 12, 1920. Mr. Skinner is a farmer and stockraiser near Vinita. Mrs. Skinner's Cherokee name is Walleah.

Weir, Joseph Harris (See Ward)—Joseph Harris, son of Webster Wayne and Sabra (England) Weir was born January 7, 1889, educated at Vinita. Married near Ketchum, April 10, 1910, Leona, daughter of John and Jessie Williams June 25, 1893. They are the parents of Jessie Lucile born May 6, 1913; Joe Lee Wayne, born May 14, 1916 and Billie J. born February 18, 1921.

Joseph, son of William and Susie (Ward) England married Sabra Cooper and they were the parents of Sabra England who married Webster Wayne Weir.

Smith, Mrs. Ford (See Ghigau and Hildebrand)—Eliza, daughter of Henry and Margaret (Patrick) Fry, born February 15, 1866. Educated in the Cherokee Public Schools and Female Seminary. Married at Tahlequah February 15, 1882 to Warren Alonzo, son of Alonzo and Sarah Westover, born March 22, 1844 in Illinois. He died November 28, 1896. They were the parents of: Willard W. born February 14, 1883; Thomas H. born December 11, 1885; Lelia Etta, born August 23, 1887; Josephine M. born January 27, 1890; Warren Ferdinand, born May 28, 1892 and died Feb. 28, 1913. Mrs. Eliza Westover married at Oolagah August 6, 1897 to Ford Clement, son of James G. and Amelia Smith born April 10, 1866, in Armstrong County, Pennsylvania. They are the parents of: Lewis Clement, born May 4, 1898 and James Reagar Smith, born February 12, 1901. Mr. and Mrs. Smith are farmers near Wann, Okla. Their three sons were in service in the World War.

Andrews, Mrs. Homer A. (See England)—Sarah Caldonia, daughter of Abram and Alta Berilla (Scrimsher) Meek, born October 26, 1876. Married near Vinita August 10, 1892 Homer A. son of Homer Francis and Mary E. Andrews, born Jan. 10, 1874 in Cherokee County, Kan. They are the parents of: Mary, born September 17, 1893; Alvin Franklin born March 27, 1896; Clyde Edward, born March 14, 1900; Bethel Loraine, born October 5, 1902, graduated from Bacone College, Muskogee, May 23, 1921; Mable Clare, born September 23, 1904; Alice Jaunita born October 13, 1906; Zenobia Ruth, born April 18, 1910; Homer Allen born December 18, 1914 and George Wayne Andrews born Sept. 12, 1917. Alvin Franklin Andrews enlisted for World War September 26, 1916 at Oklahoma City was assigned to Coast Artillery, Battery 6, 62nd Regiment, was in France from August 1918 to February 1919, advanced to corporal and sergeant. Discharged in September, 1920.

Campbell, Mrs. H. B. (See Ghigau)—Laura Craig born at Welch December 16, 1889. Graduated from the Welch High School. Married at Welch December 23, 1912 to Harvey Brooks, son of Jacob A. and Anna Campbell, born Nov. 13, 1875 in Saline County, Mo. They are the parents of: Harvey Craig born December 17, 1915; Laura Kathryn, born September 27, 1918 and Mary Eugenia Campbell, born March 8, 1921. Mrs.Campbell is a member of the Christian Church. He is a wholesale hay and grain dealer and President of the Oklahoma State Bank of Welch.

Mrs. Campbell is the daughter of Franklin Wallace and Catherine (Tetrick) Craig. Craig County was named for her Uncle, Granville C. Craig.

Cox, Mrs. Zeno M. (See Grant, Cordery and Duncan)—Emma J., daughter of David McLaughlin and Mary J. (Vickery) Beck was born August 17, 1874. Educated in the Cherokee Public Schools. Married in 1893 W. J. Elledge. They were the parents of Roy P. born November 4, 1894 and Cena Belle Elledge, born June 20, 1896. Mrs. Elledge married in December 1899 Zeno M. son of Aaron and Sarah Cox, born January

6, 1852. They were the parents of: Zeno M., born November 24, 1901, Sarah Vinita, born February 8, 1906; Cherokee Juanita, born September 27, 1911; Melvin, born September 12, 1912 and Clinton Clark Cox born October 4, 1916. Mr. Cox is a farmer near Estella Okla., Craig County.

Hill, Mrs. Henry J. (See Adair)—Emma, the daughter of William E. and Fannie L. (Wright) Dupree, was born in Tex., Dec. 13, 1888; educated at Willie Halsell College at Vinita, and the Northeastern State Normal at Tahlequah, Okla. She married at Vinita on Dec. 22, 1915, Henry J., son of Frederick W. and Catherine Hill. He was born May 5, 1885, in Asherville, Mitchell County, Kansas. They are the parents of Frederick William, born October 2, 1916, in Birmingham, Alabama; Anna Catherine, born December 25, 1917, in Memphis, Tennessee, and Henry Marion Hill, born January 28, 1920, in Vinita, Oklahoma.

Mr. and Mrs. Hill are members of the Presbyterian church. He is a boilermaker, and is officiated with the Masonic fraternity.

Klaus, William H. (See Sanders and Ward) —William Henry, son of Robert and Polly (Sanders) Klaus, was born on Grand River, opposite the mouth of Horse Creek, on February 28, 1874. Educated in Worcester Academy, Vinita. Married at Vinita November 17, 1895, Charlotte, daughter of Isaac Marshall and Sarah Elizabeth (Nidiffer) Mode, born March 18, 1877, in Delaware District, and educated at Willie Halsell College, Vinita. They are the parents of: Jesse Henry, born Oct. 4, 1896, and Anna Mae Klaus, born September 12, 1905.

Mr. and Mrs. Klaus are farmers, near Vinita. Isaac Nidiffer married Lucy Arthur and they were the parents of Mrs. Elizabeth Mode.

Le Force, Mrs. James A. (See Riley and Oolootsa)—Fannie Myrtle, daughter of Monroe Calvin and Lucy Lowrey (Hoyt) Keys, was born in the Choctaw Nation, November 5, 1862. Educated in the Female Seminary and Northfield Seminary in Massachusetts. Married at Vinita September 11, 1892, James Andy, son of John B. and Amanda (Blankenship) LeForce, born December 26, 1859. They are the parents of Flossie Mae, born October 14, 1893, graduated from Vinita High School, 1914, University of Oklahoma, with an A B. degree in 1920; James Lowrey, born January 31, 1895, enlisted for the World war September 28, 1917, assigned to a machine gun company in 358 Machine Gun Co., 90th Division, and was in the offensive line from September 12, 1918, until the signing of the armistice, and was then with the army of occupation, was discharged at Camp Pike June 21, 1919. Married June 19, 1920, Lois Rachel Britton; their daughter was born March 3, 1921. Sarah Lottie, born November 21, 1897, graduated from Vinita High School in 1917, and is attending the University of Oklahoma; and Charles William Leforce, born November 9, 1905.

Mr. and Mrs. LeForce are members of the Presbyterian church, her Cherokee name is Au-nah-hee. Mr. LeForce is a successful farmer and stockman.

Roberts, Mrs. Walter E. (See Oolootsa). —Edward Warner, son of Amory E. and Dollie Eunicia (Hoyt) Chamberlin, born October 10, 1853. Married August 2, 1883, Sarah E. Nazworthy, born May 20, 1863, in Illinois. He died March 21, 1899. They were the parents of Laura Hoyt Chamberlin, born at Vinita, March 11, 1886, educated in Female Seminary. Married at Vinita November 25, 1906, Walton E., son of William F. and Nancy Francis Roberts, born Sept. 19, 1887. They are the parents of Louis Walton, born October 1907; Donald Edward, born October 30, 1913, and Eva Juanita Roberts, born November 22, 1916. Mr. Roberts is with the St. Clair Refinery at Vinita.

Wimer, Mrs. J. H. (See Grant)—Herbert, son of John Martin, and Corinne E. (Washburn) Thompson, married Clarkie. A. Lee, and they were the parents of Hallie C. Thompson, born August 28, 1873, at Coodie's Bluff in Cooweescoowee District. She was educated at Little Rock, Arkansas, and taught six years in the public schools at Vinita, and two years in Willie Halsell College of the same place, and was associate reporter of the Vinita Daily Chieftain for seven years. She married at Vinita July 17, 1905, J. H., son of Henry and Rebecca Wimer. Mr. and Mrs. Wimer are members of the Christian church. He is a prominent farmer and stockman near Vinita, and owner of the Cabin Valley farm.

Mrs. Wimer's half sister, Ethel Thompson, married J. F. Nolan, and lives in New Mexico.

Mr. Wimer's first wife was Ella Franklin and their three children were as follows: Rebecca D., born March 5, 1895, and married Clyde C. Thompson; Jacob F., born March 15, 1897, and married Bettie Lomax; Parmelia Ellen Wimer, born September 5, 1900, and makes her home with her parents.

French, Joseph M. (See Grant and Riley)—Joseph Mason, son of Robert Mosby and Margaret (Fields) French, was born near Stillwell Sept. 22, 1856, and was educated in the Cherokee National schools. He married at Fort Gibson on July 19, 1876, Sallie, daughter of John McNary and Nancy (Ivy) Riley, born Oct. 9, 1860. Mrs. French died Nov. 11, 1901. They were the parents of Frances Abigail born July 27, 1879, Jennie Myrtle, born February 7, 1881; Lewis, born July 28, 1883; Gypsy, born November 24, 1886; George Yarborough, born March 12, 1889; Beulah, born July 8, 1891; Cabal Vaughan, born Dec. 6, 1893; Joseph Mason, born July 24, 1898; and John Foreman, born October 22, 1901.

Mr. French's second wife, E. May (Elliott) French, is the mother of Nina, (born Feb. 12, 1904, and Walter French, born Feb. 8, 1906. Mr. French is a member of the Methodist church, Knights of Pythias, and the Redman fraternities. He was elected superintendent of the Female Seminary in 1895.

Russell, Connie—Martha Ann Shinn, born June 12, 1870, married February 5, 1890, Campbell Russell, born October 22, 1863, in Morgan County, Alabama.

Mrs. Russell died October 9, 1894. They were the parents of Connie, born November 24, 1890; Carl, born June 8, 1892, and Christopher Russell, born November 25, 1893.

Campbell Russell has represented his district in the Oklahoma senate, and is at present a member of the State Corporation Commission.

Martin, Robert Lee, (See Grant and Woodall).—John Peter, the son of George Caruth and Ellen (Moore) Woodall, was born January 11, 1841. He married January 1, 1871, Maver M. Cecil, nee Saunders, born May 9, 1842. They were the parents of Maver Woodall, Born Feb. 7, 1881; educated in the public schools of the Cherokee Nation, and married at Adair on July 25, 1897, Robert Lee, the son of Richard Lewis and Nancy Ellen (Rogers) Martin born Aug. 23, 1876. They were the parents of Dane, born July 9, 1898; Edgar, born August 12, 1901; Linnie, born June 25, 1904 and Aena, born July 11, 1907.

Mr. Martin, who is an oil man, and one of the most prominent men of the Osage tribe of Indians, is a member of the Masonic fraternity. Mrs. Martin is a Presbyterian, and a member of the United Daughters of the Confederacy.

Garrett, Susan Frances (See Foreman)—Rachel Catherine, daughter of John and Susan Louella (Foreman) Horn, was born June 7, 1860, was educated in the Female Seminary. She married Oct. 21, 1883, Joseph Monroe Garett, who was born Oct. 23, 1859 in Green Co., Ark. He died April 8, 1899. They were the parents of Mattie Bell, born Sept. 27, 1884; Robert Monroe, born February 7, 1886; Frank Pierson, born September 16, 1889; Susan Frances, born July 8, 1891; Eva, born February 13, 1896; and Joseph Bruce Garrett, born March 28, 1899.

Miss Susan Frances, whose Cherokee name is Khawk, is a member of the Methodist church. She was educated in the Cherokee Female Seminary, and the Northeastern Oklahoma State Normal School, and has been teaching in the schools of Oklahoma since 1911.

The children of Rachel Katherine and Joe M. Garrett are Claude Stephen Garrett, born Aug. 29, 1887, and Henry Edgar Garrett, born Jan. 21, 1893.

Hurst, Mrs. John R. (See Grant)—John Randolph, son of Christopher Columbus and Mary Ann (Blythe) Hurst was born Monday, April 18, 1853. Educated in the Cherokee National Schools. Married December 5, 1879, Sarah Elizabeth, daughter of John and Elizabeth (Hogan) Brown, born November 14, 1854 in Newton County, Missouri. They were the parents of Christopher Columbus, born September 30, 1880; Mary Ellen, born May 24, 1885; Winema Rachel, born September 30, 1891 and Albert J. Hurst, born January 7, 1894.

John, son of William and Nannie (Fields) Blythe married Justin Cadle and they were the parents of Mrs. Mary Ann (Blythe) Hurst.

Meeker, George Weigand (See Ghigau and Foreman)—Josephine, the daughter of Joseph Martin and Lucy (Starr) Hildebrand, married John Meeker, and they were the parents of George Weigand Meeker, born March 1, 1877. He was educated in the Cherokee public schools and the Male Seminary. He married on Nov. 26, 1906, Bertha Bell, daughter of John J. Patrick, born August 2, 1843. They are the parents of Foster born November 4, 1907, and Robert Lee Meeker, born September 28, 1912.

Mr. Meeker served from July 29, 1899 to May 8, 1901 in Co. H, 32nd U. S. Vol. Inf. of which 18 months was spent in actual field service on Luzon Island.

Meigs, Henry C. (See Grant and Ross)—Henry Clay Meigs, born at Park Hill, Tahlequah District November 16, 1841, married January 11, 1868, Josephine L. Bigelow, born August 27, 1843, in Flint District. Mrs. Meigs died January 15, 1895. They were the parents of Caroline Few, Annie Stapler, Robert Henry, James McDonald, Alice Maud, and Josephine L. Meigs.

Mr. Meigs who served in the Confederate Service in 1861-2, is a grandson of Chief John Ross, has many of the amiable traits of his distinguished ancestor. He was elected clerk of Illinois District August 1, 1893, and Judge of the same District on August 5, 1895. Mr. Meigs has for the last fifty years lived at Fort Gibson.

Cochran, Jessie E. (See Foreman and Go-sa-du-i-sga)—Jesse Edward Cochran was born March 28, 1895. Educated in the Cherokee Public Schools. Married at Tahlequah May 15, 1915 Carrie, daughter of George and Addie Dawson, born Aug. 9, 1895. They are the parents of Maurice, born March 3, 1916; Frances born Oct. 5, 1918 and Willard Cochran, born May 9, 1921. Mr. Cochran is a farmer near Grand River. Amos Thornton married Minerva Foreman and they were the parents of Mary Ellen (Thornton) Cochran born February 14, 1857. She died February 16, 1899. She was the mother of Jesse Edward Cochran.

Davidson, Mrs. Ermine Josephine (See Ward and Ghigau)—Felix Grundy, son of Isaac and Lucy (Arthur) Nidiffer, was born March 16, 1853. Married April 23, 1876, Joanna Ruth, daughter of John Ross and Annie (Hildebrand) Lender, born February 8, 1861. Felix Grundy Nidiffer died October 16, 1896. She died July 2, 1911. They were the parents of Ermina Josephine Nidiffer, born September 2, 1877. Educated in the Female Seminary. Married at Afton March 21, 1899, Thomas David son of William and Jane Davidson, born April 27, 1871, in Bates County, Missouri. They are the parents of Anna Laura, born December 21, 1899, married Everett Holt; Ruth Jane, born June 23, 1902, married Clyde E. Andrews; Athelene, born July 22, 1904, married Hallet Peace; Cecil Kornegay, born November 9, 1906; Thomas Eugene, born June 26, 1910; Freeman Edward, born June 23, 1912; Mary Elizabeth, born November 18, 1914 and Olive Louise Davidson, born June 24, 1918.

Everett and Anna Lura Holt are the parents of: Kenneth Eugene, born February 20, 1918; Evelyn Marie, boron September 9, 1919 and Maurice Clyde Hereford Holt, born May 21, 1921.

Balentine, Mary Eunice, (See Oolootsa and Riley)—Monroe Calvin Keys, born September 15, 1826. Married at Park Hill, May 31, 1855 Lucy Lowrey Hoyt, born September 16, 1831. She graduated from the Female Seminary in 1854. He was a member of Captain Benjamin Wisner Carter's Company in the confederate service. He died March 3, 1881 and she died Aug. 24, 1912. They were the parents of Mary Eunice, born May 31, 1856; Lydia Emma, born September 16, 1858; Fannie Myrtle, born November 5, 1862; Sarah Ann born October 6, 1865; Elizabeth Riley, born January 13, 1868; Monroe Amory, born February 21, 1870 and Lucy D. Keys, born March 31, 1872. Mary Eunice married December 28, 1875, Hamilton Balentine, son of Rev. Hamilton Balentine and Anna Hoyt Balentine, born April 18, 1850. He died February 22, 1900. She died April 25, 1920. They were the parents of Mary Eunice, born May 4, 1899 and Ellen Stella Balentine, born May 5, 1892. Mary Eunice Balentine was educated in Vinita and the Northeastern State Normal and is a teacher. Ellen Stella Balentine was educated in Vinita (Valentine's Business College Graduate) and is a stenographer. Both of the sisters live with their maternal Aunt: Sarah Ann, who married on October 26, 1887 John Samuel, son of John Bradley and Amanda (Blankenship) LeForce, born Jan. 27, 1864 in Indiana. Mrs. LeForce, was educated in Worcester Academy and Female Seminary. Mr. and Mrs. LeForce are Methodists. He is a prosperous farmer and stockman at Vinita.

Glenn, Franklin C. (See Foreman and Saunders)—Franklin Clyde, son of Jesse Edward and Margaret (Cowan) Glenn, born July 17, 1890, educated in the Cherokee Public Schools and Male Seminary. Married at Vinita June 22, 1913 Marcella Carrie, daughter of Jefferson and Nannie E. (Saunders) Tyner, born September 23, 1893 educated in Female Seminary and Northeastern Oklahoma State Normal. They are the parents of: Kenneth Edward, born July 3, 1914 and Lavance Arnold Glenn born May 29, 1916. Mr. and Mrs. Glenn are farmers near Miles.

Jesse Edward Glenn was the son of Henry Glenn and Jennie Foreman.

Nannie E. Saunders was the daughter of George O. Saunders and Jennie Lale.

McCorkle, David (See Ross)—Emma, daughter of John Thompson and Charlotte Gordon (Scales) Drew, was born October 29, 1856, and married May, 1876, William Green Robinson, born Jan. 1856 and died Nov. 8, 1886.

Mrs. Emma Robinson married April 28, 1891, Joseph Loren McCorkle, born Sept. 19, 1837, in Louisa County, Virginia. She died Jan. 8, 1906, and Mr. McCorkle died Jan 3, 1916.

William G. and Emma Robinson were the parents of Mary Charlotte Robinson, born August 7, 1877, and married January 28, 1898, David Wisel, son of Joseph Loren McCorkle, born March 17, 1867, in Muskogee County, Okla. They were the parents of Joseph Loren, born October 28, 1899, and James Milton McCorkle, born May 18, 1902; Catherine Elizabeth born August 4, 1906; David Wisel born July 12, 1909; Mary Louisa, born Nov. 27, 1911; Drew Holt, born Dec. 31, 1913 and William Thomas born Sept. 23, 1916, on day first troop train left Muskogee to world's war.

Lewis, Mrs. Albert (See Hendricks)—Hettie, daughter of Henry and Mary (Hendricks) Walkabout was born at Tahlequah Oct. 19, 1879. Educated at Park Hill Mission. Married at Inola May 29, 1902, Albert, son of Ira H. and Sarah E. Lewis, born Aug. 14, 1879 in Washington County, Ark.

They are the parents of Grace E. Lewis born Aug. 21, 1903; Ira A. born June 2, 1905; Beatrice, born Oct. 17, 1906; Velma, born April 28, 1909; Mildred born Feb. 18, 1913; Edgarita, born Jan. 3, 1916; Hilda, born Sept. 13, 1916; and Vernon, born April 10, 1919.

Mrs. Lewis' Cherokee name is Ahniwake. They are Methodists and Mr. Lewis is an oil producer and farmer and a member of the Yeoman fraternity.

Thomas, Mrs. James H. (See Foreman and Riley)—Eugenia, the daughter of Eugene and Jane (Riley) Triplett, was born at Fort Gibson in 1844; was educated in the Cherokee public schools, and the Cherokee National Female Seminary. She married at Wagoner on Dec. 25, 1892; James H. Thomas, born in Oklahoma in 1874. They are the parents of George H., born April 5, 1897; Arvol V., born June 10, 1899; Theron T., born July 8, 1901; Gladys M., born January 16, 1905; Helen, born January 3, 1909; Celia and Lewis Thomas, born June 20, 1911.

Mr. Thomas is a member of the Knights of Pythias; and is a prominent business man in Tulsa, Oklahoma.

Crowell, Mrs. Francis M. (See Sanders and Duncan)—John Thomason Duncan married Elizabeth S. Sanders, and they were the parents of Mary Elizabeth Duncan, born February 8, 1858; and was educated in the Cherokee Nation and at the University of Arkansas. She taught school for six years among the full-bloods; and married at Van Buren, Arkansas, January 15, 1883, Francis Marion, son of Dr. M. and Nancy A. Crowell, born March 14, 1859 in Tallapoosa County, Alabama. They are the parents of Erda Victor, born December 25, 1884; Alvin Byron, born September 1, 1886; Frank M. born September 7, 1890, and Hunter K. Crowell, born April 17, 1893.

Mr. and Mrs. Crowell are members of the

Methodist church. He is the proprietor of a flourishing mercantile business at Afton, Oklahoma. Mrs. Crowell is a member of the Eastern Star Sisterhood. Her Cherokee name is Ka-ha-yu-ka.

Alvin B. Crowell saw service in France in the Rainbow Division, being at the front at Chateau Thierry, Argonne Forest and other offensives, during which time he was promoted to the rank of sergeant and was retained in the Army of Occupation in Germany. H. K. Crowell was in the Commissary Department at Camp Travis at the time of the signing of the Armistice. Frank M. Crowell married Miss Evelyn Dooley and has two boys Frank Marion Jr., the 3rd and 12 years old and Master Ted Crowell 4 years. They live in Tulsa. E. V. and A. B. Crowell are now located in Los Angeles, Cal. in the magazine business. H. Kent Crowell located in New York, being a professional designer in ladies headware, making trips to Paris to study the styles.

George, Mrs. Earnest (See Grant)—Ada, daughter of Joseph Lynch and Alice (Tucker) Thompson, born January 26, 1881, educated at Vinita and Female Seminary. Married at Vinita, December 8, 1909, Earnest George, born Nov. 26, 1881, in Cooper Co., Missouri. They are the parents of Mary Ellen George, born Novembr 12, 1911. Mr. and Mrs. George are farming near Big Cabin.

Mrs. Harriet M. Thompson wife of Joseph Lynch Thompson died Nov. 27, 1921. Stepmother of Ada Thompson, wife of Earnest E .George.

Gonzales, Frank (See Downing and Adair) —Andrew Franklin, son of Dennis and Rachel (Pettit) Gonzales, was born January 26, 1874. His first wife, Catherine Young, died April 22, 1892. He married again on August 23, 1897, Bessie Stewart, born February 22, 1889 in Scott County, Arkansas. He was elected a member of the Cherokee Council from Illinois District in 1903.

Rachel, daughter of Charles and Charlotte (Adair) Pettit, married Dennis Gonzales, and was the mother of Andrew Franklin Gonzales.

Rogers, Mrs. Andrew L. (See Oolootsa, Duncan and Halfbreed.)—Andrew Lewis, son of Andrew Lewis and Cherokee America (Morgan) Rogers, was born July 3, 1860; and was educated in the Cherokee Public schools and the Male Seminary. He married May 19, 1909, Josephine Landrum, daughter of Frank and Josephine (Landrum) Howard, born November 23, 1879. She graduated from the Female Seminary May 30, 1901. They are the parents of the following children: Andrew Lewis, born June 7, 1910; Paul Sevier, born Sept. 20, 1912 (died June 27, 1915); Patricia, born March 17, 1915; Josephine Landrum, born April 18, 1917 and Kenneth Howard, born Nov. 19, 1919.

Elliott, Mrs. Emerson (See England)—Nelle Blackwell, daughter of Abram and Alta Berrilla (Schrimsher) Meek was born August 10, 1884. Educated in Female Seminary from which she graduated in 1904. Married at Vinita October 9, 1906 Emerson, son of Silas and Belle Elliott, born 1887, in Dubois County, Ind. They are the parents of: Cleeta Rhea, born May 30, 1908; Howard Wayne, born July 30, 1910; Clifford Charles born August 13, 1912; Ralph Homer, born June 15, 1914, and Carl Vincent Emerson, born July 21, 1916. Mr. and Mrs. Elliott are members of the Christian church and his business interests are in Vinita.

Hicks, Herbert W. (See Foreman)—Abijah Hicks, born March 2, 1819, married Jan. 30, 1852, Hannah Worcester, born January 29, 1834 in New Echota, Georgia. He died June 4, 1862. Mrs. Hannah Hicks died Feb. 3, 1917. They were the parents of Percy W., Emma I., Edith H., Clara A. and Herbert Worcester Hicks. Percy W. married Elma Garrett and lives at Fort Gibson. Edith married Charles W. Smith and Richard M. Walker. Clara A. married Nicholas McNair Thornton and George I. Hopson.

Herbert Worcester Hicks was born at Park Hill May 18, 1861; and married at Fayetteville, Arkansas, on December 23, 1886, Rachel, the daughter of James and Sarah Cardwell, who was born July 20, 1869, in Washington County, Arkansas. They are the parents of Ethel Inez, born December 24, 1889; Homer Wilton, born October 22, 1891; Clifton A., born November 16, 1894; Vera Clare, born Oct. 14, 1896 died Nov. 28, 1900; Ralph Connor, born March 30, 1903, and Herbert Morris, born June 3, 1907. Ethel Inez married A. M.

Buster, and Homer Wilton married Ferrel Thompson.

Mr. Hicks Cherokee name is E-no-li. His mother was a daughter of Reverend Samuel A. Worcester, one of the first Missionaries to the Cherokees, coming with them from Tennessee and Georgia, in 1838; his father was a descendant of Charles Hicks, a Cherokee Chief in the old Cherokee Nation.

Chumley, Elizabeth K. (See Oolootsa and Riley)—Elizabeth Riley Keys was born January 13, 1869. Educated at Worcester Academy and Female Seminary. Married at Centralia Sept. 12, 1912, John M., son of Robert and Fannie Chumley. Mr. and Mrs. Chumley are members of the Presbyterian church.

Lydia Emma Keys, a sister of Mrs. Chumley's married Charles J. Taylor, now deceased. Their daughter Alma Lane Taylor, born January 26, 1900, married March 24, 1918 J. E. Bennett. They have one daughter, Bettie Bennett, born February 8, 1919.

Monroe Calvin Keys married Lucy Lowrey Hoyt and they were the parents of Lydia Emma and Elizabeth Riley Keys.

Hastings, John R. (See Grant, Foreman and Ward)—William Archibald Yell Hastings was born March 8, 1842 in Benton County, Arkansas. He served in Company H, First Cherokee Mounted Rifles, under Captain John Thompson Mayes, during the Civil War. He married February 2, 1864, Louisa J. Williams, nee Stover, born April 8, 1840. Mrs. Hastings died Feb. 7, 1918. Mr. Hastings died April 28, 1919. They were the parents of John Rogers, William Wert, and Charlotte Delilah Hastings. Charlotte Delilah Hastings married Samuel Grant Victor, and is now deceased. John Rogers Hastings was born on Beattys Prairie August 1, 1865, and was educated in the Cherokee Public Schools, and the Male Seminary, from which he graduated May 4, 1886. He married at Tahlequah Feb. 20 1901 Elizabeth Victoria, daughter of Spencer and Margarette (Proctor) Shelton, born Dec. 9, 1872, at Tahlequah. Mrs. Elizabeth V. Hastings died Jan. 23, 1916. They were the parents of William Wert Hastings, born January 20, 1902; Suwayne Hastings, born September 9, 1903; John Rogers Hastings, born February 24, 1905 and Robert Owen Hastings was born Jan. 27, 1909. Edgar Hastings was born October 27, 1910. Mr. Hastings was elected Clerk of Delaware District in 1891, and again in 1895, and Senator from the same District in 1897-99 and 1901.

Pete Hastings, as he is generally known, is one of nature's noblemen, rugged, honest and a true friend.

Johnson Proctor married Elizabeth Foreman, and they were the parents of Margarette, who married Spencer Shelton.

Adair, T. J.—Though not of the royal line, Harold, the son of the great Earl Godwin, had been elected and served for forty weeks as King of England, until on the fated fourteenth of October 1066 he was overthrown by the victorious legions of William, Duke of Normandy. Thenceforward known as William I, King of England and popularly called The Conqueror. The polish and elegance of the world at that time was best exemplified by the Norman Knights and Nobles, many of whom accompanied Arlotta's son, settled in and directed the destinies of England.

Among the proud cavaliers was d'Heanage. Hundreds of years later his more democratic descendants dismantled the orthography and pronunciation and called themselves Harnage; became roundheads, ironsides, nonconformists, presbyterians and emigrated to America to swell the tide of hardy pioneers that was sweeping to and over the southern Appalachians, to make the world safer for civilization.

They came, to another race of people, they saw a pride and energy equal to their own and many of them married among the Cherokees. Ambrose Harnage, one of these Englishmen, married in about 1810 Nancy Harlan nee Sanders, born in 1782, the daughter of Mitchell Sanders, an English trader from Virginia and his wife Susie, a full blood Cherokee of the Long Hair clan.

Ambrose and Nancy Harnage's children were: William, born June 5, 1811 and married Patsy Snow; George married Nancy Mayfield; John Griffith born January 16, 1817, married February 20, 1837 Ruth Starr born December 25, 1820, she died July 5, 1843. He married January 12, 1844 Emily Walker Mayfield born August 20, 1830. He died January 12, 1891. She died March 29,

1899; Andrew Jackson, born June 20, 1818 and died May 27, 1847! Elizabeth Harnage born August 20, 1820 and married John Adair Bell. She died May 27, 1847.

Emily Mayfield was the daughter of Jesse and Sallie (Starr) Mayfield.

John Griffith and Emily Walker Harnage were the parents of: William Thomas born July 27, 1847; Mary Victoria, born October 23, 1851, married William Lucullus Carr; Ida Eugenia, born October 18, 1853, married John Taylor Ewers and John M. Morse; Loretta Beldora, born October 10, 1855, married John Stringer Scott; Nannie Ethel, born September 19, 1858, married William Boone; John Custis Lee, born June 30, 1867, married Francis Catherine Hunt and Lena born November 1, 1869, Graduate from Alexander Institute, Kilgore, Texas, June 7, 1887, married January 1, 1893 Thomas James Adair, born January 4, 1856.

Thomas James Adair is the son of John Lynch Adair, born April 12, 1828 and Mary Jane Jeffries, born September 9, 1831 in Virginia, married February 22, 1855. John Lynch Adair served four years in the confederate army, was clerk of the Cherokee senate in 1869-70. Elected Editor of the Cherokee Advocate in 1873 and elected as one of the committee to superintend the erection of the Cherokee national jail in the same year. Elected member of the Board of Education in 1875. Elected Town lot Commissioner in 1878. Elected delegate to Washington November 28, 1879. Appointed a member of the Board of Education June 6, 1881. He was for several years executive secretary to the Principal Chief and died at Tahlequah on October 21, 1896. Mrs. Mary J. Adai died May 8, 1897

Andrews, Mrs. George P. (See Grant, Foreman and Riley)—Susie Catherine, daughter of Jasper Newton and Mary Jane (Riley) Schrimsher, was born in 1878; educated at Wagoner and the Cherokee Female Seminary. She married at Wagoner in 1899, George P. Andrews. They are the parents of Howard and Hazel.

Mr. and Mrs. Andrews are members of the Presbyterian Church, and he is a Mason and a prominent oil producer.

Alton, Chas. J. (See Cordery and Carter) —Thomas Cordery, an Irishman, married Susannah, a full blood Cherokee of the Blind Savannah Clan. Their daughter, Susie, married John Mosley. John and Susie Mosley were the parents of Sarah Ruth Mosely, born in 1841, married October 16, 1864 Lewis Clark Ramsey, who served during the Civil War in Captain Benjamin Wisner Carter's company. After his death Mrs. Ramsey married January 5, 1877 Ezekial Taylor.

Lewis Clark and Sarah Ruth Ramsey were the parents of Susan Elizabeth Ramsey, born December 7, 1866. She was educated at the Cherokee Orphan Asylum and Female Seminary. Married at Oowala July 31, 1888 Joseph Morgan Alton, son of David and Eliza (Billingsley) Alton, born July 31, 1856 in West Virginia. They are the parents of: Percy Samuel, born May 25, 1893, married Cherokee Jones; Percy Charles Joseph Alton born Dec. 29, 1897. Married Aug. 2, 1919, Pearl Jane Hansen born in 1898.

Abbott, Mrs. John H. (See Word and Foreman)—Martha Alice, daughter of John Wesley and Mary Elvira (Ward) Holland, was born January 28, 1862; married at Stilwell June 21, 1884; Robert Early, born February 16, 1858, in Gilmer County, Georgia. He died August 27, 1906. They were the parents of Dora, born March 16, 1886; John William, born June 22, 1887; Mary Angeline, born February 1, 1889; Martha Lou, born September 17, 1893, and died November 7, 1911; Robert Ross, born October 14, 1895; Ida Belle, born February 3, 1898, and died September 23, 1920; Mollie Elmira, born October 24, 1900, and Dovie Early, born November 3, 1904.

Ida Belle Early married Herbert Line and they had two children: John Wesley, born May 1, 1918, and Martha Line, born July 3, 1919.

Mrs. Martha Alice Early married John H. Abbott, born in 1847 in Florida. His first wife was Ellen Isabel, daughter of Robert Early and Minerva Jane (Taylor) Walker, born in 1867, and died in 1898. John H. and Ellen Isabel Abbott were the parents of Ethel Louisa, born October 5, 1875; Eugene Michael, born November 25, 1877; John Wesley, born September 28, 1879; Caroline Minerva, born December 23, 1880; Senora Julia, born November 20, 1882; Fannie Edith, born February 15, 1885; Mae Lillian, born September 20, 1887; Butler Lafayette, born July 24, 1889; William Ghormley, born

October 20, 1893, and Jennie Ellen Abbott, born November 13, 1895.

Adkirson, Jasper (See Hendricks and Ghigau)—Jasper Newton, son of Jasper and Susan Jane (Schrimsher) Adkirson, was born in Tahlequah District in 1869, educated at Menard and Male Seminary. Married Susie Hendricks. They were the parents of: Clarence, Thomas, Catherine, Paralee, Pollie, Susie and Nellie Adkirson. Mr. Adkirson married Nancy Jane Phillips nee Stephens. They are the parents of Jasper Adkirson. Mr. Adkirson is a farmer, an A. H. T. A. and a justice of the peace.

Allen, John Randolph — John Randolph Allen a pioneer of Tennessee was the father of John Randolph Allen, born in 1836, who married in 1876, Nora Martin, born in 1858, both were natives of Tennessee. John Randolph and Nora (Martin) Allen were the parents of John Randolph Allen, born February 17, 1877 in Chicago, Illinois. Married at Fort Smith, Arkansas December 25, 1916, Lulu, daughter of George and Mary Vaughn, born May 8, 1892 in Arkansas City, Kansas.

Mr. Allen organized and directed the first exclusively Indian agricultural and art fair among the Seminole and Creek Indians at Wetumka, Hughes County.

Ambrister, Mrs. Hubert (See Grant)—Julia Theresa daughter of William Columbus and Jane (Davis) Patton, married Dr. Francis Bartow Fite; and they were the parents of Frances Fite, born Sept. 24, 1893, in Muskogee. She was educated in National Cathedral School, Washington, D. C., and graduated from Vassar College. She married at Muskogee July 7, 1920, Hubert, son of Samuel A. Ambrister, born Feb. 1891, in Norman County, Oklahoma. Mr. Ambrister was educated in Norman High School and is a graduate of University of Okla. He is practicing law in Oklahoma City. He served two years in the Aviation Corps during the World War.

Thomas James Adair is the grand son of Thomas Benjamin Adair was a native of Thomas Benjamin and Rachel (Lynch) Adair Georgia and the son of John and Jennie (Kilgore) Adair. Jennie Kilgore was said to have been a paternal aunt of Congressman "Buck" Kilgore of Texas.

Thomas James Adair was elected a member of the Board of Education in 1883 and chosen as Secretary of that body. He has for many years been one of the leading merchants of Tahlequah.

Mr. and Mrs. Adair have only one daughter; Miss Emily, a talented and accomplished young lady who is a graduate from the Northeastern Oklahoma State Normal. She was born December 9, 1893.

Adair, Virgil H. (See Adair)—Virgil Harvey Adair, born April 15, 1869, married October 2, 1892, Dorinda, daughter of Jesse and Hariette Calloway, born April 9, 1874 in Missouri. They are the parents of: Viola, born June 15, 1893, married A. B. Jordan; Millard Herron, born July 16, 1898, married Minnie Thompson; Winnie, born December 23, 1900; Virgil, born March 27, 1903; Velma born November 15, 1904; Delphia, born February 28, 1907; Gladys, born December 23, 1909; Francis, born June 27, 1913 and Neva Marie, born July 31, 1915. Mr. Adair belongs to the Wolf Clan and is a Mason. He was elected a member of Council from Cooweescoowee District, August 3, 1903.

Edward Alexander, son of John and Ann Berry (Graham) Adair was born August 25, 1847, was a member of Company C of Edmondson's Georgia Batallion, Confederate service. Married in October 1867 Narcissa Malissa Harrison, born December 25, 1846 in Murray County Georgia. He died December 3, 1901. They were the parents of Virgil Harvey Adair, the subject of this sketch.

Addington, Cicero W. (See Foreman, Ghigau and Adair)—Cicero White Addington, born in Goingsnake District June 7, 1875, educated at the Male Seminary; married September 13, 1899 Mary Lowenia, daughter of Oscar F. and Mary Catherine (Rider) Adair, born December 19, 1875. They are the parents of: Clarence Grady, born April 24, 1901; Frederick Earl, born April 13, 1902; and Jennings Mayes. Mr. Addington was elected Clerk of Adair county in 1918.

Minerva Isabel, daughter of Abijah and Isabelle (Taylor) Akin was born June 7, 1852; married September 3, 1874, Henry Newton Addington. They were the parents of Cicero White Addington.

Adair, Mrs. Joseph W. (See Ross)—Cora Ann Sayers, born near Pryor, February 28, 1896. Married at Big Cabin, July 2, 1916, Joseph William, son of Allen and Kittie

Adair. They are the parents of Virginia Elizabeth, born August 22, 1918 and Allen Sayers Adair, born March 26, 1919. Mr. Adair is a farmer near Pryor.

Henry Drew, son of Abner and Nancy Jane (Coody) Sayers was born March 9, 1862. Married October 5, 1892, Dora Thompson, born March 11, 1869 in Macon County, Missouri.

Archer, Edwin (See Downing)—Edwin Archer, born September 19, 1817 in New York City. Married February 26, 1845 Mary Francis Vann, born September 21, 1825 in Georgia. He died May 15, 1893.

They were the parents of: Mary Elizabeth, married DeWitt Clinton Lipe; Louisa Catherine, married Freeland McIntosh; Ada, born March 16, 1860, educated in the Cherokee public schools and the Kirkwood (Missouri) Seminary, from which she graduated June 8, 1882, married February 28, 1888, Daniel Vincent Jones, born December 28, 1858 in Grayson county, Texas; Cora, married William Ross Shackelford; Carlotta Archer, graduated from the Cherokee Female Seminary June 28, 1883, appointed member of the Cherokee Board of Education; appointed County Superintendent of Public Instruction of Mayes county in July 1908, elected to that office in 1910-12-16-18 and 1920.

Daniel Vincent and Ada (Archer) Jones were the parents of: Vera, born December 10, 1895, graduated from the Female Seminary May 29, 1907; Jean, born December 2, 1895, and Mary Jones, born July 15, 1899.

Joseph Vann, born February 11, 1798, married Catherine Rowe. He was elected a member of the Cherokee Constitutional Convention of 1827 from Coosawatee District; elected Senator from the Salina District August 20, 1841, and elected President of the Senate; elected again to the same office August 6, 1849; elected Associate Justice of the Supreme court in 1847, Delegate to Washington 1851, Executive Councilor 1853-55-57; Assistant Chief of the Cherokee Nation August 1, 1859. He was the father of Mrs. Mary Francis Vann. He died May 3, 1877.

Aldrich, Mrs. Augustus W.—Ara, daughter of Goren and Eliza (Wheatley) Thomas was born in Kentucky, June 23, 1886 and educated in that State. Married at Muskogee, October 22, 1905 Augustus William, son of Ferdinand and Pauline Aldrich. They are the parents of John Harley, born November 10, 1906 and Roger Arthur Aldrich born August 2, 1909. Mr. and Mrs. Aldrich are members of the Apostolic church. Mr. Aldrich is a farmer, near Ketchum.

Andrews, Mrs. Homer A. (See England) Sarah Caldonia, daughter of Abram and Alta Bernilla (Scrimsher) Meek, born October 26, 1876. Married near Vinita August 10, 1892 Homer A., son of Homer Francis and Mary E. Andrews. They are the parents of. Mary, born September 17, 1893; Alvin Franklin born March 27, 1896; Clyde Edward, born March 14, 1900; Bethel Loraine, born October 5, 1902; Mable Clare, born September 23, 1904; Alice Juanita, born October 13, 1906; Zenobia Ruth, born April 18, 1910; Homer Allen born December 18, 1910; Homer Allen born December 18, 1914 and George Wayne Andrews graduated from Bacone College, Muskogee, Okla., May 23, 1921. Alvin Franklin Andrews enlisted for World War September 26, 1916 at Oklahoma City was assigned to Coast Artillery, Battery 6, 62nd Regiment, was in France from August 1918 to February 1919, advanced to corporal and sergeant. Discharged in September, 1920.

Samuel, Mrs. William R. (See Downing)—Minnie L., daughter of Clement and Rebecca Caroline (Bryan) Hayden, was born at Chouteau April 5, 1879. She was educated in Liberty, Mo and married on April 21, 1901, William Ruben Samuel, born February 2, 1869 in Calloway County, Missouri. He graduated May 28, 1902, from Stephens College, Columbia, Missouri. They are the parents of Rebecca Ann Samuel, born Oct. 3, 1917. Mr. Samuel is Secretary of the State Bankers Association, and is a Mason and Odd Fellow. He was for four years State Insurance Commissioner. Mr. and Mrs. Samuel are members of the Methodist church, and residents of Oklahoma City.

Rebecca Wright, born January 1, 1814, married Joel Mayes Bryan, born October 22, 1809. She died April 5, 1882, and he died August 7, 1899. They were the parents of Rebecca Caroline Bryan, born January 30, 1850, who married March 7, 1869, Clement Hayden, born March 20, 1846 in Benton County, Arkansas. Mrs. Hayden died July 11, 1916 and Mr. Hayden died May 2, 1916.

Beamer, Samuel. (See Gusoduesga and Foreman).—Samuel Beamer, born August 14, 1873. Educated locally. Married Mary Nelson.

Nancy, a full-blood Cherokee, married a Mr. Drumgoole, and their daughter, Ruth, married John Foreman. They were the parents of Elizabeth Foreman, who married Eddy Springston, and they were the parents of Mary Springston, who married John Henry and George Beamer, and was the mother of Rev. William Beamer, who married Alice Towie, and they are the parents of Samuel Beamer, the subject of this sketch.

Blake, Mrs. J. K. (See Grant and Ross).—Henry Clay, son of Return Jonathan and Jennie (Ross) Meigs, was born November 16, 1841. He married January 11, 1868, Josephine L. Bigelow, born August 27, 1843. Mrs. Meigs is deceased. They were the parents of Caroline F., who married Richard C. Adams; Anna Stapler, who married Frank J. Boudinot; Robert Henry; James McDonald; Alice Maude, who married E. A. Hill; and Josephine L., who married James K. Blake.

Mrs. James K. Blake graduated from the Female Seminary May 31, 1906. Henry Clay Meigs, father of Mrs. Blake, was elected clerk of Illinois District in 1893, and Judge of the same District in 1895.

Brown, Albert.—Albert, son of John T. and Lou (Griggs) Brown, was born in Muskogee in 1887. Educated in the public schools. Married at Claremore in 1908. Mary, daughter of Mr. and Mrs. Frederick Carter.

They are the parents of : Juanita and Gabriel. Mr. Brown is a farmer and a member of the A. H. T. A.

Burr, Mrs. Margaret (See Gardner)—Margaret Bumgarner, born November 7, 1857, married May 12, 1877, Dr. Rollin A. Burr, born August 29, 1854. He died October 3, 1895. Their children were: James Walter, John William, Jesse E., Margaret Etta, Nina Alice, Harris E., and Robert Emmett Burr. Mrs. Burr is the daughter of Samuel and Margaret (Vickery) Bumgarner.

Boudinot, Richard F. (See Grant, Watie and Adiar.)—Richard Fields, son of William Penn and Caroline M. (Fields) Boudinot, was born June 7, 1856. He married June 8, 1896, Mary Catherine, daughter of James Roe and Rachel Ann (Adair) Treppard, born August 28, 1873. They are the parents of Caroline Mary, born March 22, 1891; Elinor Margaret, born October 25, 1893; Harriet Gold, born November 25, 1897; William Penn, born Nov. 23, 1900; and Rachel Catharine, born Sept. 24, 1903.

Mr. and Mrs. Boudinot are residents of Braggs, Okla.

Benge, Mrs. Samuel, Jr. (See Hildebrand, Ghigan, Oolootsa and Grant.)—Samuel Houston, son of Samuel Houston and Josephine J. (Walker) Benge, was born at Fort Gibson in 1898. Educated at Fort Gobson. Married in 1918, Margaret, daughter of Mr. and Mrs. John Hildebrand. They are the parents of Samuel Houston Benge. Mr. Benge is a farmer near Fort Gibson.

Samuel Houston, son of Martin and Eliza (Lowrey) Benge was born January 28, 1832. Elected Councilor from Sequoyah District Aug. 3, 1857, and elected solicitor of the same District in 1859. He was First Lieutenant of Company A, Third Indian Home Guards, and a signer of the treaty of 1866. He married October 15, 1866, Nannie, daughter of Theodore Brewster, born in October, 1845. He was elected senator from Illinois District in 1869, 1871, 1873, 1875, 1879 and 1883. Elected delegate to Washington December 16, 1869, and November 25, 1871. Samuel Houston and Nannie (Brewster) Benge were the parents of Samuel Houston Benge, who married Josephine J. Walker.

Cochran, Jesse. (See Foreman and Gosa-du-i-sga.)—Jesse Edward Cochran was born March 28, 1895. Educated in the Cherokee public schools. Married at Tahlequah in 1915, Carrie, daughter of George Dawson. They are the parents of Morris, Francis, and Willard Cachran. Mr. Cochran is a farmer.

Amos Thornton married Minerva Foreman and they were the parents of Mary Ellen (Thornton) Cochran, born February 14. 1857. She died February 16, 1899. She was the mother of Jesse Edward Cochran.

Canadel, Mrs. Arthur E. (See Ghigau and Rogers)—Sarah, daughter of George Washington and Rachel (Rogers) Walker, born April 13, 1858. Married March 13, 1873, William Martin, born June 17, 1830, in Frankfort, Kentucky. Their daughter, Armanda Nelia, was born August 28, 1882. She was educated in the Cherokee public schools, married at Nowata, 1899, Daniel, son of Mr. and Mrs. Thomas Anderson. They were the parents of: Nevin Thomas, Stanley Quay, and Lucille Dannie Anderson. Mrs. Anderson's second husband is Arthur Ellsmere Cansdell. They are the parents of: Gay Marguerite and Jewell Cansdell.

Chamberlin, Arthur F. (See Oolootsa)—Arthur Fanshaw, son of Rev. Armory N. and Eunice Dolly (Hoyt) Chamberlain, was born October 9, 1857 in Flint District. He was educated in the public schools and Male Seminary, and married June 9, 1883, at Neosho, Missouri, Letitia, daughter of Hamilton W., and Margaret Goodykoontz, born March 18, 1861, in Newton County, Missouri. They located in Vinita, and are the parents of: Dolly Edith (Cherokee name Oo-loo-tsa) born August 19, 1887; educatea in the schools of Vinita, and Henry Kendall College; married June 22, 1907, William Robinson; Catherine Brown, born December 25, 1893; educated at Vinita and Miami University, Oxford, Ohio; married December 22, 1916, James W. Dunnington, son of W. G. and India Knight Dunnington; Arthur Fanshaw Chamberlain, born March 8, 1900. He was in school in Hampton Sidney College in Virginia at the beginning of the war; he enlisted and was mustered out of service at the close of the war. He is superintendent of a tobacco factory at Danville, Virginia.

Reverend Armory Nelson, son of Rev. William and Fern (Hoyt) Chamberlain, was born Nov. 29, 1821, at Brainard Mission. He married December 3, 1846, Eunice Dolly, daughter of Milo and Lydia (Lowry) Hoyt, born Dec. 14, 1820, on Chickamaugua river. Rev. A. N. Chamberlain, although a white man, spoke the Cherokee language perfectly. He died July 4. 1894, and his widow died on the 21st of the same month. Their children were. Abijal Eunice, born May 18, 1849; Nelson Bucher, born Sept. 9, 1850; William Clifford, born April 23, 1852; Edward Warren, born October 10, 1853; Arthur Fanshaw, born Oct. 9, 1857; Henru Eugene, born Feb. 24, 1860; Robt. Lee Chamberlain, born Oct. 28, 1865.

Arthur F. Chamberlain is a Mason. He belongs to the Holly Clan of the Cherokees. His Indian name is Sequoyah.

Chamberlain, Nelson B. (See Oolootsa). —Nelson Beecher, son of Reverend Armory Nelson and Dollie (Hoyt)Chamberlain, was born at Park Hill September 9, 1850. Educated in the Cherokee Nation. Married June 12, 1877, Emma Marie Meeks. June 9, 1858. She died January 31, 1888. They were the parents of: Emma Grace, born April 7, 1881, married Clarence William LeForce, born December 31, 1879, in Labitte County, Kansas. They have five children, Ora B., born April 21, 1904; John D., born October 6, 1910; Marie Dewdrop, born January 22, 1913; Loreone Lorene, born January 19, 1917, and Grace Eunice, born December 26, 1918; Marie Eunice, born September 29, 1882, married Frank Edward Nix; and William Nelson Chamberlain, born November 22, 1883. Mr. Chamberlain married March 26, 1886, Sarah Viola, daughter of John Lee and Amanda (Blankenship) LeForce, born December 4, 1866, in Indiana. They are the parents of: Abigal Otelia, born October 18, 1890, married Thomas Cogni; Erastus Donald, born November 7, 1892 Mary Ellen, born April 23, 1894, married William A. Parker; and Clarence Eugene Chamberlain, born August 25, 1896. Mr. Chamberlain is a member of the Deer Clan and his Cherokee name is See-yah. He is a farmer near Estella.

Clark, Lucy. (See Ward and Duncan)—Lucy A. Clark, born February 7, 1848, on Beattie's Prairie, Delaware District, married December 25, 1869, Joshua Bertholf Duncan, born December 13, 1835. He died December 14, 1875. She married August 30, 1877, James Abercrombie Duncan, born June 3, 1825, and died December 26, 1898. Mrs. Duncan's children are: Deden Rosecrans, born March 25, 1874; Annie, born April 7, 1876; Jimmie A., born October 30, 1879; Lucy Elizabeth, born March 14, 1884; and Charles DeWitt Duncan, born April 10, 1886.

Clark, Wm. N. (See Scraper, Ward and Grant)—William N., son of Judge George Washington and Lydia A. (Scraper) Clark, was born April 3, 1866, educated in the public schools of the Cherokee Nation, and graduated from Male Seminary June 25, 1885. He married September 26, 1894, Lilla John, daughter of De Hardiman and Anna (Wilson) Flournoy, born April 15, 1874. W. H. Clark's Cherokee name is Oo-law-hut. He is a Methodist and a Mason. W. H. and Lillar J. Flournoy are the parents of: James Wilson, born February 28, 1896;

Mabel Clyde, born December 18, 1898; Raleigh Phillips, born January 5, 1900; Rosa Blanche, born January 5, 1902; William Henry, born May 4, 1904; E. W.., born August 15, 1906; C. F., born February 22, 1908; L. B. Clark, born September 9, 1913, and Clifford Clark, born March 12, 1916.

Coast, Mrs. Frank (See Grant)—Alice May, daughter of Andrew Elijah and Clarinda (Baggett) Tucker, was born in 1880. Educated at the Friends Mission at Skiatook. Married at Nowata, Frank Croft Coast.

They are the parents of Waller, Clara, Albert, Margaret and Verna Coast. Mr. Coast is a farmer and stockman and is a member of the Masonic fraternity. Mrs. Coast is a member of the Friends church.

Andrew Elijah, the son of Andrew Jackson and Mary (Blythe) Tucker, was born in the Neutral Land, now Cherokee County, Kansas, in 1857. Married April 16, 1878, Clarinda Baggett, a native of Illinois. He died April 16, 1897.

Couch, Herbert F. (See Grant)—Herbert Franklin, son of James C., and Elizabeth (Collier) Couch, was born February 7, 1875, in Italy, Texas. Received a collegiate education in his native town. Married at Coody's Bluff, March 1, 1896, Ida May, daughter of Calvin and Elizabeth (Bullette) Coker, born April 28, 1879, at Coody's Bluff. Educated in the Cherokee National Schools. They are the parents of: Victor Clark, born January 15, 1897; Elmer, born August 31st, 1900 Leola, born December 29, 1902; Curtis Foreman, born November 24, 1905; Herbert Franklin, born January 23, 1908; Randolph Penn, born February 22, 1910, Wanda Wanette, born Feb. 14, 1912 and, Vivian Lane Couch, born October 6, 1916. Mr. Couch is a member of the Knights of Pythias fraternity. He is a wealthy oil and gas producer, living at present in Nowata.

Calvin Coker was the son of John Rogers and Annie (Hogan) Coker.

Cook, Mrs. Lee.—Nannie, daughter of Clark and Lydia (Smith) Swimmer, was born in the Cherokee Nation. Educated in the Cherokee National schools. Married at Webbers Falls in 1898 Lee Cook.

They are the parents of: Andrew, who served three months in the World war; Glenn, and Evaline Cook. Mr. Cook is a farmer.

Coyn, Jeter J. (See Grant)—Peter Joseph Coyn, born of Irish parentage, in England October 19, 1869, married at Vinita March 11, 1893 Margaret Shanahan, born May 31, 1874. They are the parents of: Mary Ellen, born March 27, 1894, married F. M. Gleason; Agnes Mary, born January 5, 1896; Patrick William, born March 16, 1898, served in the World war overseas fourteen months in the Aerial Corps; Peter Joseph, born March 12, 1900; Caroline, born March 9, 1904; Emmett Charles, born January 5, 1907; Joseph L., born June 8, 1910; Woodrow Riley, born February 10, 1913, and Marguerite Ambrosia Coyne, born November 13, 1916. Mr. and Mrs. Coyne are members of the Catholic church and are successful farmers near Estella. Straightforward, honest and logical Peter J. Coyne has been chosen by his fellow citizens as flotorial representative of Craig and Rogers Counties on November 3, 1908; representative of Craig County on November 8, 1910, and November 5, 1912, and state senator from the twenty-ninth district on November 7, 1916.

Patrick Shanahan, born Mar. 11, 1833, in Tipperary, Ireland, and married Charlotte daughter of Nelson and Margaret (Scrimsher) Rogers, born January 27, 1858.

Cowan, Felix G.—Richard Cowan was born October 9, 1839, in Georgia, and married in April, 1865, in Illinois, Elzada Allen, born November 22, 1840, in Tennessee. They were the parents of Felix G. Cowan, born July 22, 1866, in Illinois; and Sarah Cowan, who married James A. Thompson, and is now deceased. Mr. Cowan was educated in the Cherokee Nation, and married on June 1, 1886, Lulu Murry, and on March 22, 1909, he married at Indianoola, Iowa, Rebecca Blair, daughter of Calvin C., and Cinthia Blair.

Mrs. Cowan had three brothers and one sister as follows: William E., Jane A., Almus C., and Joel O., Blair. Only the latter is now living.

Mr. Cowan was in the mercantile business in Vinita for twenty-seven years. He was elected County Commissioner of Craig County on November 5, 1918, but resigned from this office and was appointed steward of the State Hospital at Vinita. Pleasant, urbane and gentlemanly, Mr. Cowan has a host of friends. He is a member of the

Methodist church, Hill Crest Club, Masons, Shriners, Odd Fellows, Modern Woodmen of America, Fraternal Aid, and Elks fraternities. He was a member of the City Council of Vinita for twelve years, part of the time of which he acted as mayor.

Countryman, John A. (See Ward and Hildebrand)—John Anderson, son of George Washington and Minerva (Ballard) Countryman, was born in Delaware District March 14, 1872, and educated in the Cherokee National schools. Married at Afton August 1, 1900, Jane O., daughter of Dennis and Lucy Hildebrand, born May 7, 1882. They are the parents of W. T., born July 14, 1901 Velva Irene, born June 23, 1903, married B. F. Frisbie and has one daughter, Ethel Irene Frisbie, born September 24, 1920; Ned, born March 14, 1907, and Houston, Countryman, born August 18, 1910.

Crowell, Mrs. Francis M. (See Sanders and Duncan)—John Tomason Duncan married Elizabeth S. Sanders, and they were the parents of Mary Elizabeth Duncan, born February 8, 1858; and was educated in the Cherokee Nation and at the University of Arkansas. She taught school for six years among the full-bloods, and married at Van Buren, Arkansas, January 15, 1883, Francis Marion, son of Dr. M. and Nancy A. Crowell, born March 15, 1859, in Tallapoosa County, Alabama. They are the parents of Erda Victor, born December 24, 1884; Alvin Byron, born September 1, 1886; Frank M., born September 7, 1890, and Hunter K. Crowell, born April 17, 1893.

Mr. and Mrs. Crowell are members of the Methodist church. He is the proprietor of a flourishing mercantile business at Afton, Oklahoma. Mrs. Crowell is a member of the Eastern Star Sisterhood. Her Cherokee name is Ka-ha-yu-ka.

Alvin B. Crowell saw service in France in the Rainbow Division, being at the front at Chateau Thierry, Argonne Forest and other offensives, during which time he was promoted to the rank of sergeant and was retained in the Army of Occupation in Germany. H. K. Crowell was in the Commissary Department at Camp Travis at the time of the signing of the armistice. Frank M. Crowell married Miss Evelyn Dooley and has two boys, Frank Marion Jr. the 3rd, 12 years old and Master Ted Crowell, 4 years old. E. V. and A. B. Crowell are now located in Los Angeles, Calif. in the manufacturing business. H. Kent Crowell located in New York, being a professional designer in ladies headwear, making trips to Paris to study the styles.

Calvert, Mrs. Sarah (See Crittenden)—Sarah A. Crittenden was born in the Cherokee Nation March 25, 1868 and educated in the Cherokee National schools. Married near Alluwee January 1, 1889 Samuel N. son of Lowrey and Amanda Calvert born March 11, 1863 in Dearborn County, Indiana. They are the parents of: Amanda Alice, born August 9, 1890; Charles Elmer, born January 2, 1893, married at Tucumcari, N. M. September 28, 1911, Minnie May Conant; their children are Charles Richard born Nov. 24, 1913; Vivian May, born May 1, 1915, Anna Mildred born Nov. 16, 1916, Lela Captola born Apr. 10, 1919 and Lucile Leona Calvert born Feb. 3, 1920; Lela Delvia, born May 13, 1901 married at Vinita September 24, 1916 W. F. son of John and Lucinda Lay born May 10, 1889. Their children are Jaunita Fern, born August 16, 1918 and Clara Marie Lay, born July 12, 1920; Mildred Loree, born November 20, 1908 In Quay Co. N. M. and Clara Myrtle Calvert, born January 27, 1911.

The Calverts and Lays are farmers, near Estella.

Cunningham, Thomas F. (See Ross, Sanders and Ghigau)—Thomas Francis, son of William Ross Cunningham and Eliza Colston, was born at Fort Gibson on April 21, 1880. He was educated at Fort Gibson and Bacone University. He married January 29, 1902, Emily Harnage, daughter of John Stringer Scott and Loretta Beldora Harnage, born August 16, 1882, and was educated in Fort Gibson anad Bacone University. They are the parents of John Calhoun, born June 2, 1904, and Frances Marion Cunningham, born October 28, 1908.

Mr. and Mrs. Cunningham are residents of Fort Gibson, Oklahoma.

Alley, Mrs. John R. (See Grant, Downing, Ghigau and Ross) Clara Eva, daughter of Edward Daniel and Elizabeth Henryetta (Musgrove) Hicks, was born in Tahlequah on February 10, 1890. She was educated in the Female Seminary, from which she graduated. She married at Claremore Aug. 15, 1908, John Reed, son of Frederick and Sarah Dameron Alley, born Sept. 26, 1873, in Yell County, Ark. They are the parents of Lawrence Alley, born May 21, 1910.

Mr. Alley is a contractor in Oklahoma City, and a member of the Masonic fraternity. They are members of the Presbyterian church.

Francis Marion Mushgrove married Clara Eva Alberty, and they were the parents of Mrs. Edward Daniel Hicks.

Daniel Ross Hicks married Nancy Jane Rider, and they were the parents of Edward Daniel Hicks.

Mrs. James K. Blake graduated from the Female Seminary May 31, 1906. Henry Clay Meigs, father of Mrs. Blake, was elected clerk of Illinois District in 1893, and Judge of the same District in 1895.

Donnelly, Thomas A. (See Grant, Daniel and Foreman)—Thomas Austin, son of Henry and Emma Jane (Daniel) Donnelly, born in Delaware District March 18, 1878, educated in Vinita. Married at Vinita November 1, 1900 Mary Ella, daughter of Jesse Edward and Margaret L. (Cowan) Glenn, born December 13, 1877, educated in the Cherokee Public Schools and Female Seminary. They are the parents of: Gladys Austin born November 10, 1901; Glessie Ada, born October 29, 1906, Thomas Winton, born December 26, 1909. Fleeta Avis, born September 11, 1911 and Betty Jean Donnelly, born July 26, 1921. Mr. and Mrs. Donnelly are farmers, near Vinita. They are members of the Baptist Church and he is a member of the I. O. O. F. fraternity. They are always active in all social and welfare activities in their community, and were local leaders in Red Cross and war work.

Henry and Jennie (Foreman) Glenn were the parents of Jesse Edward Glenn.

Duncan, Mrs. Lucy (See Grant, Ward and Duncan)—Lucy A., daughter of Joseph H. and Polly (Ward) Clark, was born February 7, 1848 on Beatty's Prairie in Delaware District. She was educated in the Cherokee National Schools, and married December 25, 1869 Joshua B. Duncan, born December 13, 1835; and he died December 14, 1875. They were the parents of Helen Rosencrantz, born March 25, 1874, and Annie Ellen Duncan, born April 7, 1876. Mrs. Lucy A. Duncan on August 30, 1877, married James A. Duncan, the brother of her first husband, and he was born June 3, 1825. He died December 26, 1898. They were the parents of Jimmie Abercrombie, born October 30, 1879; Lucy Elizabeth, born March 14, 1884, and Charles DeWitt Duncan, born April 10, 1886.

Delen R. Duncan is a very accomplished artist and makes her home in Columbia, Mo.

Mrs. Duncan is the owner and proprietor of large farming interests near Afton. She is a member of the Methodist church.

Dupree, Fred Lee (See Adair)—William E. Dupree was born November 9, 1857, in Texas; married January 11, 1883, at Whitman, Texas, to Fannie L. Wright, who was born January 14, 1860 in Texas. They are the parents of Emma Dupree, born December 13, 1888; and Fred Lee Dupree, born August 20, 1895 at Vinita. Emma Dupree was educated at Willie Halsell College at Vinita, and the Northeastern State Normal at Tahlequah, Oklahoma. She married on December 22, 1915, at Vinita, Henry J., the son of Frederick W. and Catherine Hill. They are the parents of Frederick William, born October 2, 1916; Anna Catherine, born December 25, 1917; Henry Marion Hill, born January 28, 1920.

Mr. and Mrs. Hill are members of the Baptist Church. He is a Mason and employed as a boilermaker at Tulsa, Oklahoma.

Fred Lee Dupree married at Vinita November 26, 1917, Winnie M., daughter of Lilburn P. and Helena (Marrs) Scott. They are the parents of Robert Morris Dupree, born October 24, 1918, at Vinita. Mr. and Mrs. Dupree are members of the Baptist Church, and he is a successful farmer near Vinita. Mrs. Dupree is a member of the Ward family of Cherokees.

Dupree, Wright (See Adair)—Wright Dupree, born August 8, 1890 in Texas, was educated at Vinita, Oklahoma, and Sedalia, Missouri Business College. He married at Centralia, Oklahoma, July 12, 1914, Rosa, daughter of I. J. and Emma Wright, born January 12, 1894. They are the parents of Louis Wright Dupree, born June 9, 1915, and Francis Elizabeth Dupree, born April 1, 1917. Mr. Dupree is the son of William E. Dupree, born November 9, 1857 in Texas, who married Anna L. Wright on January 11, 1883. They are members of the talented Bell and Adair families. Mr. and Mrs. Dupree are members of the Baptist Church, and he is a rural mail carrier at Vinita, Oklahoma.

Durall, Mrs. Benoni H. (See Duncan)—Ada Bertha, daughter of John Robert and Emma (Landrum) Dobkins was born August 6, 1879. Educated at Chetopa, Kansas. Married at Welch, August 25, 1897 Benona H., son of B. S. and Anna Durall, born March 9, 1873 in Neosho County, Kansas. They are the parents of Harold Robert, born June 23, 1898. Enlisted in the navy during the World War assigned to the reserves force stationed at Pelham Bay, N. Y. from May 29, 1918 to February 1, 1919. Married May 15, 1921 Florence L. Rodant; Hugh Allen, born November 16, 1902; George Marvin, born March 2, 1905; Ada Leah, born May 5, 1907, and Charles Ivan Durall, born March 10, 1913. Mrs. Benona H. Durall is a member of the Methodist Church, Rebecca and Eastern Star orders. Mr. Durall is engaged in the insurance and loan business in Welch.

Durall, Mrs. George W. (See Ghigau)—Franklin Wallace. son of Samuel and Eliza (Harlan) Craig born in Missouri, March 15, 1854. Married November 8, 1878 Catherine Fetrick, born January 13, 1854 in Shelby County, Missouri. He died February 23, 1894. They were the parents of Edna Earl Craig, born June 8, 1880, educated in Female Seminary. Married at Claremore August 5, 1897 George Wesbroford, son of Benoni S. and Anna Durall, born October 23, 1878. They are the parents of: Benoni Franklin, born June 3, 1898, married October 6, 1918 Georgia Ann Brown, has one daughter, Mary Joe Durall, born June 20, 1920; George Raymond born July 14, 1900 married October 4, 1918 Corna Cass and their daughter, Marjorie Ann was born October 13, 1920; Jack Leroy, born January 15, 1910; Harvey Robert, born September 11, 1915 and Edna Virginia Durall, born July 14, 1918. Benoni Franklin Durall enlisted and was at the officers training camp. Mr. and Mrs. Durall are members of the Methodist Church. He is a Mason and she is an Eastern Star. Mr. Durall is in the loan and insurance business at Welch.

Elliott, Samuel T. (See Foreman)—Samuel Talbert, son of Hiram and Callie (Whatenberger) Elliott was born in Delaware District July 5, 1894 and was educated in that district. Married at Big Cabin September 25, 1916 Geneva, daughter of A. W. and Minnie Blackford. They are the parents of: Magdelene Lenox, born March 17, 1918 and Garth Dalmond Elliott, born September 10, 1920. Mr. Elliott is a farmer near Big Cabin. Elizabeth, daughter of John Foreman married John Elliott, a White man. They were the parents of Archibald Elliott who married Rachel Smith and they were the parents of Hiram Thomas Elliott, born May 22, 1854 married January 7, 1882 Callie Whatenberger.

England, Mrs. John—Susan Maude, daughter of Joseph Wesley and Martha (Perry) Davis was born February 5, 1879 in Georgia and educated in that State. She married in Georgia May 12, 1897 John, son of Joseph and Susan England. They are the parents of. Frederick Price, born November 6, 1898; Pauline, born February 9, 1901, married July 16, 1919 David C. Smith and has one daughter, Ruby Lee Smith, born April 19, 1920; Doc Herron, born April 18, 1904; Willie May, born July 18, 1906; Susan Maude, born January 20, 1909; Joseph Preston, born May 18, 1911 and Martha Lou, born February 26, 1915. Mr. England is an employee of the M. K. and T. R. R. and lives at Adair.

Gibbs, Joseph L. (See Conrad)—Joseph Lewis Gibbs born April 29, 1864 in Mattoon, Illinois and married August 20, 1891 Eliza Gourd born December 28, 1873 near Claremore. They are the parents of: Charles A. born January 9, 1894 and Joseph Scott Gibbs born May 6, 1896. Joseph L. Gibbs is the proprietor of one of the best curio stores of the southwest, with his ability he specializes in American made articles, coins and Navajo blankets.

Mrs. Joseph L. Gibbs is the daughter of John R. and Artemissa (Beavert) Gourd. The former now deceased was born August 5, 1850 married in 1872 Artemassa Beavert born January 4, 1857. John R. Gourd was elected August 5, 1895.

Onai a full blood Cherokee of the Bird Clan married Hamilton Conrad whose father was a Hollander and his mother a Scotch woman. Their oldest son was Rattlinggourd Conrad, but all of his descent in the male line was always known as Rattlinggourd's or Gourds, instead of Conrad. Rattlinggourd and Polly (Toney) Conrad were the parents of: Jackson and Daniel Rattlinggourd. The former was born in 1809, married Elsie Wilson, born in 1808. He died April 10, 1885 and his wife had died on the fourth day of October of the previous year. He was elected Judge of Tahlequah District August 5, 1867 and August 7, 1871. Their daughter Charlotte born July 3, 1829 married Larkin Beavert and they were the parents of: Artemissa Beavert who married John Rattlinggourd the son of the above mentioned Daniel Rattlinggourd whose wife was Eliza Lacey.

Chas. A. Gibbs married April 22, 1920 to Sylvia Augusta Griswold born February 21, 1896, the daughter of Mr. and Mrs. F. G. Griswold of Claremore, Okla.

Lauchner, Mrs. Clarence M.—Mary A. daughter of Chester and Etta (Nair) Taylor was born January 31, 1896 in the Cherokee Nation. Educated in the Cherokee national schools. Married at Claremore April 22, 1912 Clarence M. son of William and Mary Lauchner, born Nov. 11, 1890 in Craig County, Okla. They are the parents of Chester Francis, born August 26, 1915; and Evelyn Talita Lauchner, born May 10, 1919. Mr. and Mrs. Lauchner are farmers, near Vinita. They are members of the Baptist church. Mrs. Lauchner has one sister: Miss Emma Cynthia Taylor, born December 2, 1898.

Jones, Mrs. George L. (See Sanders and Grant)—Lorena, daughter of Daniel Boone and Nannie (Vann) Cole, was born near Pryor, July 24, 1881, educated at Pryor and the Female Seminary. Married Dec. 16 1901, George L. born April 15, 1877 in Texas, son of Mack, born July 29, 1844 and Nannie Jones, born Jan. 9, 1842. They are the parents of: Mabel Lee, born November 30, 1902; Otta May, born March 26, 1904; Cornelius, born September 17, 1905; Haskell born September 19, 1907; Willie, born October 9, 1912 and Carl Jones, born February 23, 1915.

Johnson Vann, the grandson of John and Elizabeth (Wickett) Fields, married Margaret Winters and was the father of Mrs. Nannie Cole. Margaret or "Peggy" Winters was the daughter of John and Jennie (Sanders) Winters and the granddaughter of Captain Alexander and Peggy (Sonicooie) Sanders.

Lipe, Mrs. Margaret (See Thompson, Thornton and Ooolootsa)—Margaret Emma, daughter of Richard and Elizabeth (Thornton) Thompson was born at Fort Gibson, January 2, 1849. Married at Fort Gibson August 29, 1873, to Clark Charlesworth, son of Oliver Wack and Catherine (Gunter) Lipe, born near Tahlequah, March 10, 1847. He died May 25, 1901. They were the the parents of Howard, born May 19, 1873. Died September 19, 1875. Herman Vann, born February 19, 1876, married Mary Iris Smith. John Caspar, born November 2?, 1878 ,married Annabel Price. DeWitt Clinton born November 22, 1881 and died August 19, 1901; Beulah, born May 25, 1884 married George Smith. Clark Charlesworth, Jr., born November 15, 1887, married Lucy Sellers; Clarence Lipe born July 9, 1891.

Clark Charlesworth Sr. was a member of Captain Benjamin Weisner Carter's Company. He was elected Clerk of Cooweescoowee District, August 6, 1877 and August 4, 1879. Elected Clerk of the Council in November 1885. Mrs. Lipe conducts a successful stock farm near Sageeyah, on the old Homestead settled in 1876.

Morgan, Gideon (See Oolootsa)—Gideon Morgan, born April 3, 1851. Married June 25, 1874 Mary Llewellyn Payne, born October 1, 1855 in Sebastian County, Arkansas. They are the parents of: Houston Mayo, born May 4, 1875; Mary Llewellyn born June 23, 1877; Martha Lelia, born November 13, 1879; Margaret Elizabeth, born October 25, 1882; Amanda Payne, born Aug. 25, 1885; Sallie Mayo born April 15, 1888 and Ellen Payne Morris Morgan, born March 4, 1896. Gideon Morgan was elected Senator from Tahlequah District, Aug. 5, 1901. Elected a member of the legislature from Mayes County, November 5, 1912 and November 5, 1918.

Joseph, the son of General John Sevier married Elizabeth Lowry, a half blood Cherokee and their daughter Margaret, born October 8, 1799. Married October 27, 1815, Gideon Morgan, born at Ramorga, Connecticut, August 6, 1776. He died September 18, 1851 and was buried at Calhoun, Tenneesee. Mrs. Morgan died March 25, 1862. Gideon Morgan organized and was Major of the Cherokee batallion that were allies of the Americans in the Creek war of 1814. Gideon and Margaret (Sevier) Morgan were the parents of George Morgan, born December 1, 1817. Married October 26, 1848

Martha Keziah Mayo, born in Washington, Ray County, Tennessee June 16, 1826. He was a Captain in the Mexican war and Major of the Third Tennessee Volunteer Infantry C. S. A. 1861 to May 1862 and Major of 2nd Kentucky Cavalry (Morgan's regiment) until his death, Oct. 28,1862. He was mortally wounded at Ashland Ky. Oct. 18, 1862 and died Oct. 27, 1862. He is buried in Lexington, Ky. Mrs. Morgan died June 7, 1871. They were the parents of Gideon Morgan, the subject of this sketch.

Foreman, Mrs. Ada C. (See Foreman and Riley)—Reverend Stephen Foreman was born October 22, 1807, married March 27, 1834, Sallie W. Riley. He was ordained a Presbyterian Minister September 25, 1835; and was elected Justice of the Supreme Court of the Cherokee Nation, October 11, 1844; Executive Councilor in 1847 and 1855 and was clerk of the Senate in 1867. Mrs. Foreman died August 6, 1861; and he died December 8, 1881. They were the parents of Stephen Taylor Foreman, born at Park Hill September 24, 1848; and married April 28, 1874 Ada Carter, daughter of Sarah and White McClellan, born at Cane Hill, Arkansas on October 25, 1853. He died January 1, 1891. Mrs. Foreman is now a resident of Claremore, Oklahoma.

Mr. and Mrs. Taylor Foreman were the parents of Sarah Lula, who married John Gunter Lipe; Jennie McClelland, who married David Jesse Faulkner; Ada Laura; Victoria Lipe, who married Stephenson Kennedy; Taylor Worcester and Perry Ashbrook Foreman. Ada Laura and Perry Ashbrook Foreman are now deceased. Taylor Worcester Foreman was born near Oowala, Cooweescoowee District on July 6, 1888; was educated at Oowala and the Male Seminary. He enlisted in the U. S. Army as a private in 1909; was commissioned Captain of Infantry August 15, 1917 and assigned to the 327th Field Artillery, detailed as Instructor in Infantry School of Arms of the 84th Division; assigned to the 301st Division in July 1918, with which he went to France, commanding Company E; was promoted August 26, 1918, to Major and assigned to the command of the 2nd Battalion of the 301st Division, and was commander of this regifent from November 10, 1918 to the latter part of the succeeding month. Was detailed for duty with the Inspector Generals department as investigating officer at Camp Pontanezan, France, which position he held until his return to America in the following September. Was commissioned a Captain in the Regular Army on July 1, 1920, and assigned to Camp Benning, Georgia; and is at present an instructor in that school. Captain Foreman married at Indianapolis, Indiana May 23, 1915 Ethel Irene Tobin. Their son, Taylor Worcester Foreman was born at Indianapolis on July 1, 1918.

Gamble, James M. F.—James Madison Fletcher, son of William and Elizabeth (Plunkett) Gamble, was born in Indiana May 31, 1856. Married May 31, 1882 Julia Ann, daughter of Samuel and Mary Ann (Fish) Wheeler. They are the parents of Verdie Ansell, born April 12, 1883, is a Mason and Woodman of the World, married Ethel Sutton; Bernice Gordon, born April 5, 1885; Dudley Martin, born October 18, 1888, married Flo Waybrigh and Otto Erick Gamble, born March 11, 1901.

Goforth, Mrs. Albert P. (See Foreman)—Elizabeth, daughter of Andrew and Jennie (Bigby) Taylor was born in the Cherokee Nation, east of the Mississippi. She married William Covington Ghormley, born March 25, 1817. He died September 10, 1896. Their daughter Isabel Jane Ghormley married Felix Nelson Witt.

Rachel Matilda, daughter of Felix Nelson and Isabel Jane Witt was born in Going Snake District September 24, 1874 and educated in that District. She married on July 24, 1890 Albert Perry, son of Jefferson and Catherine Goforth, born February 14, 1864 in Georgia. They are the parents of: Eulelma Pearl, born January 5, 1892, married Philander B. Day; Eulelia Catherine, born January 20, 1893; Lula Belle, born May 26, 1897 married July 17, 1921 Joseph C. Melton; Alta, born June 6, 1899; Marietta, born January 4, 1905; Albert, born September 21, 1907; Bessie Jaunita, born September 15, 1910 and Elizabeth Lee Goforth, born April 2, 1912. Mr. Goforth is a farmer, near Viinta.

Goddard, William P. (See Grant, England, Ghigau and Ward)—Catherine, daughter of William and Elizabeth (Harlin) England was born November 11, 1855. Married December 23, 1869 Larkin, son of Ira and Elizabeth (Blythe) Goddard. He died May 28th, 1873 and she died February 21, 1921. They were the parents of William Penn Goddard, born November 3, 1870. Educated in the Male Seminary. Married at Bluejacket, April 15, 1894 Nora, daughter of Gabriel and Cynthia Endicott born March 8, 1875 in Bourbon County, Kansas. They are the parents of Fleming Larkin Goddard, born June 17, 1896. Married May 4, 1918 Ethel Pennington. They are the parents of Erma Gine Goddard born at Welch, July 14, 1920.

Greece, Thomas—Thomas, son of George Greece, was born in the Cherokee Nation, educated in Male Seminary. Married at Welling in 1907 Nannie Walker. Mr. Grease is a farmer and belongs to the Presbyterian church.

Grimes, Ethel Ray Green—Ethel Ray Green, born near Vinita, November 25, 1892, was a daughter of Joseph and Margarette A. (Scrimsher) Green. She was educated at the Female Seminary at Tahlequah; married at McAlester, Oklahoma December 23, 1917, Grady L. Grimes. They are now members of the Methodist Church. Mr. Grimes is a Mason, and is an automobile mechanic.

Gulager, Mary (See Oolootsa)—Martha Lucretia Scrimsher was born December 9, 1845, and married January 27, 1869, Frederick William Gulager, who was born March 14, 1844, in Washington, District of Columbia. They are the parents of William Martin Christian; Mary Elizabeth; Henry Gunter; and John Delaney Gulager.

Mary Elizabeth Gulager was born April 27, 1880, and graduated from the Cherokee National Female Seminary May 25, 1900.

Gatlin, Mrs. Emma Nora (See Grant and Oolootsa)—Emma Nora, daughter of Frank and May (Hanks) Rhomer, was born February 2, 1889, and educated at Webbers Falls, and the Cherokee National Female Seminary. She married Samuel Bell Maxey, son of James and Matilda (Yearby) Gatlin, born May 25, 1887. Mr. and Mrs. Gatlin are residents of Webbers Falls.

James, son of James and Lucy (McCoy) Gatlin, married Matilda Yearby and they were the parents of Samuel Bell Maxey Gatlin.

Calvin Jones Hanks married Emma Walker the daughter of John Lowery and Charlotte (Ratliff) McCoy, and they were the parents of Mrs. May Rhomer.

Fair, Jake (See Grant and Ghigau)—Jake Fair, born July 3, 1896. Married at Pryor May 1913 Hazel, daughter of James and Flora Stamper. They are the parents of: James Louis, born June 3, 1916; Flora Ellen, born July 23, 1918 and Junior David Fair, born August 3, 1919.

Ellen Wilkerson, born February 18, 1870. Married Lewis Kelly Fair, born January 25, 1864. They are the parents of Jake Fair.

Fields, Ezekial (See Grant and Ward)—Ezekial, son of Richard and Elizabeth Jane (Blagg) Fields was born in Delaware District November 16, 1859, educated in the Cherokee National schools. Married Sabra Elizabeth, daughter of George Howard and Mary Carroll Ward. Their children are: Clarissa Eliza, born Mar 28, 1870; Richard, born Nov. 17, 1873; Belle, born in 1875; Luvonia born in 1877; and Cora Fields born in 1884. Mr. and Mrs. Ezekial Fields separated and he married December 6, 1899 Lennie Marshall born July 30, 1877 in McDonald County, Missouri. They are the parents of: Inez L., born September 18, 1900; Edna Ann, born January 18, 1902; James E., born August 21, 1905 and John J. Fields, born March 21, 1907.

Ezekial, son of Richard Fields, Chief of the Texas Cherokees married Mary Ann Sexton and they were the parents of Richard who married Elizabeth Jane Blagg.

Franklin, Mrs. Oscar (See Adair and Ghigau)—Frankie May Adair, born February 25, 1874. Married at Chouteau, December 18, 1912 Oscar, son of Marion and Jennie Franklin. They are the parents of Hogan Christopher, born September 4, 1913; Oscar George, born December 4, 1917 and Owen Adair Franklin born June 15, 1920. Mr. Franklin is a farmer and their residence is six miles north east of Chouteau.

Benjamin Franklin Goss married Sarah Emily Bean. Their daughter Susannah Deborah married Richard Welch and they were the parents of Sarah Emily who is the mother of Mrs. Frankie May Franklin.

Frazier, Mrs. Samuel (See Ward)—Sarah Ann, daughter of Cal Dean and Nancy (Ward) Gunter was born at Siloam Springs, Arkansas January 31, 1867 and was educated in the Cherokee national schools. Married April 10, 1888 Samuel, son of William Thomas and Nancy Frazier, born October 29, 1864 in Texas. They are the parents of: Cal Dean, born February 26, 1889; Lela Jessie born July 13, 1892; Grace, born November 6, 1897; Lillian born March 6, 1904 and, William Thomas Frazier, born June 12, 1909. Mr. Frazier is a farmer and stock raiser near Adair.

James, son of John and Catherine (McDaniel) Ward was born October 22, 1785 married Lucy Haynie born October 30, 1787. He died May 20, 1859 and she died September 26, 1869. They were the parents of Nancy Ward, born January 29, 1830, married September 21, 1845 Cal. Dean Gunter, born March 30, 1818 in Warren County, Tennessee. He died March 27, 1898.

Freeman, Mrs. George H. (See Grant)—Ruth Jane, daughter of Ellis and Mary (Fields) Dick was born in Delaware District January 8, 1870, and was educated in the Cherokee National Schools. Married October 17, 1884, Charles Henry, Hawkins, born in Lewis County, Missouri, October 16, 1860. They are the parents of Emma Lee Hawkins, born near Catale, February 18, 1898. Married at Claremore, September 12, 1919, George H. son of John and Martha Freeman, born February 15, 1896.

They are the parents of Paul Lawrence Freeman, born August 2, 1920.

Mr. Freeman served in the World War in Company H, 56th Infantry. Honorably discharged at Fort Sheridan, February 28, 1919.

Hall, Frederick—Frederick, son of William and Martha (Childers) Hall, born in the Cherokee Nation in 1873. Married in 1896 Katie Burgin. They are the parents of: Martha May, Arthur, Iva Jane and Alvina Hall. Mr. and Mrs. Hall are members of the Baptist church and are farmers.

Hamilton, Mrs. Henry J.—Neppie, daughter of Pleasant Napoleon Blackstone and Mary Barr was born at Muskogee July 9, 1881, educated in Bacone College, Muskogee. She married March 8, 1906, Henry J. Hamilton. They are the parents of Ollie, born October 24, 1906; Maude, born January 17, 1908; Lillian, born May 20, 1909; Henry J. born June 27, 1911; Nellie, born November 13, 1912; George, born August 4, 1914; Jacob Clark, born January 12, 1916 and Neppie Leona Hamilton, born August 15, 1918. Mrs. Hamilton's Cherokee name is Utiya.

Harnage, William Custis (See Ghigau and Sanders)—William Curtis Harnage was born April 15, 1884, and was educated in the Male Seminary and Henry Kendall College in Muskogee, graduating from the latter institution. He married at Tahlequah in 1905, Rose B., daughter of H. L. Nye. They are the parents of William Halleck, born in 1906 Griffith Scott, born in 1909 and Lawrence Nye Harnage born in 1912.

Mr. and Mrs. Harnage are members of the Presbyterian Church, and he is affiliated with the Knights of Pythias organization.

William Thomas Harnage was born July 27, 1847, and married December 25, 1870, 1850 in Marshall County, Mississippi. He was elected Senator from Tahlequah District August 7, 1899. They were the parents of William Custis Harnage.

Hawkins, Pearl D. (See Grant and Harlan)—Ruth Jane, daughter of Ellis and Mary (Fields) Dick was born in Delaware District January 8, 1870. Married October 17, 1884, Charles Henry Hawkins, born in Lewis County, Missouri, October 16, 1860. They are the parents of Pearl D. Hawkins born near Catale, July 31, 1894. Married at Vinita October 27, 1917, Myrtle B., daughter of Andrew Oliver and Cora Pearl (Richards) Harlan, born July 26, 1894. He enlisted for the World War at Vinita May 26, 1918. Was Sergeant of Base Hospital No. 82. Sailed for France August 31, 1918. Was on the Toul front nine months. Landed in the United States June 8, 1919 and was discharged at Camp Pike on June 23.

Mr. Hawkins is a farmer near Big Cabin. He is a member of the Modern Woodmen of America.

Heady, Mrs. Frankie F. (See Ghigau)—Frankie Folsom, daughter of John H. and Lulu (Boynton) Kendall was born at Chelsea August 11, 1886. Educated in Nowata High and Cincinnati C. C. M. graduating from the former in 1906 and the latter in 1908. Married at Independence, Kansas March 17, 1911 Frank son of J. B. Heady, born at Watova. They are the parents of J. B., born February 4, 1912; Byron Leroy, born October 2, 1914; Mildred Marie, born February 4, 1917 and died October 23, 1918; James Ewing, born September 17, 1918 and Jeanne Eileen Heady, born November 23, 1920. Mrs. Heady is a member of the Presbyterian church. Mr. Heady is the foreman of the St. Vlair Oil Refinery at Vinita.

Henry, Mrs. W. G. (See Downing, Daniel and Foreman)—Nannie Catherine Daniel, born January 12, 1835, married December 23, 1857 Anderson Springston Wilson born in 1830. They were the parents of DeWitt, born January 7, 1859; James Daniel, born February 2, 1861 and May Wilson, born May 1, 1862. Anderson Springston Wilson died December 26, 1865 and his widow married December 14, 1872 Henry Clay Barnes, born August 29, 1845 at Dwight Mission, Cherokee Nation and they were the parents of Myrtle Barnes, born in Flint District July 25, 1874, educated at Tahlequah and Female Seminary. Married May 14, 1891 Wallace Gibbs Henry, born April 6, 1872. W. G. and Myrtle Henry are the parents of DeWitt Cllinton, born April 4, 1892; Roy Wilson, born July 22, 1897 and Myra May Henry, born December 8, 1903. Nancy Catherine Barnes died December 10, 1889.

Holland, Richard S. (See Raper, Ghigau and Oolootsa)—Richard Spencer Holland, born November 2, 1872. Married Laura, daughter of Daniel and Cynthia (Pack) Harmon. They are the parents of: Flora L. and Grace Holland. Richard Spencer Holland was elected Court Clerk of Adair County in 1918 and 1920.

Howard, Frank S. (See Adair and Ghigau) —Frank Stapler, son of Frank and Sallie (Starr) Howard, was born January 30, 1873. Married Caroline Allen, born May 30, 1873, and died February 8, 1899. He married Ella Clyne, born April 26, 1870. His children are: Catherine, born November 7, 1896; Dewey, born April 22, 1898; Sallie Emma; Ella May; Grover Franklin and Edgar Starr Howard.

Frank S. Howard was elected County Commissioner of Adair in 1910 and 1912.

Hubbard, Thomas — Thomas, son of Wilkerson and Harriette (Thomas) Hubbard, was born in the Cherokee Nation in 1852. Mr. Hubbard, who is a successful farmer near Tahlequah, has never married.

Jordan, Mrs. Luther—Victoria, daughter of Robert and Ivy Ann (Taylor) Powell, born in North Carolina, September 17, 1880. Married at Adair, November 6, 1902, Luther, son of John and Mary Jordan. They are the parents of. Myrtle Marie, born September 25, 1903; William L., born October 4, 1904, and Florence Jordan, born December 14, 1910. Mr. Jordan is a farmer and lives near Adair. They are members of the Methodist church.

Jordan, Mrs. Arthur R. (See Adair)—Viola Adair, born June 15, 1893, educated at Adair. Married at Adair October 28, 1911, Arthur Basil Jordan. They are the parents of: Anna Mae, born Aug. 17, 1912; Basil Franklin, born February 4, 1914; Ruby La Von, born October 30, 1915; Carl Hubert, born March 4, 1918, and Virgil Lawrence Jordan, born December 23, 1919. Mrs. Jordan belongs to the Deer Clan. Mr. Jordan is farming near Adair.

Virgil Harry Adair married Dorinda Calloway and they are the parents of Mrs. Arthur B. Jordan.

Jones, Mrs. Thomas P. (See Downing) —Rachel, daughter of Nicholas and Martha (Shirley) Byers, was born August 24, 1875. Married at Tahlequah March 1, 1896, Thomas Pinckney, son of William M. and Nancy Jones. They are the parents of: Bryan, born May 22, 1897; Polk, born October 30, 1898; Granville, born December 31, 1900; Nannie, born September 9, 1902; Margaret, born August 22, 1904; Ruth, born March 22, 1906; Cherokee, born March 18, 1908; Buena, born February 18, 1911; Lucullus, born August 31, 1913; Eldee, born October 15, 1915; and Mary Joe Jones, born July 13, 1918.

Elizabeth, daughter of James and Ka-ta-ka-ya Crittenden, married Lord Wellington Shirley, born May 27, 1825. He was elected Judge of Tahlequah District August 1, 1881, and August 3, 1891. He died June 9, 1894. They were the parents of Martha Shirley.

Johnson, Isaac—Isaac, son of Milo and Adeline (Payne) Johnson, was born in 1883, educated at Tahlequah. Married at Muskogee in 1913. His children are Jessie, Maxine and Willard Johnson. Mr. Johnson is an efficient state enforcement officer.

Jackson, Mrs. Fred L.—Rosa A., daughter of John H. and Mary Malisson (Frantz) Morris, born February 24, 1893, near Welch. Educated in the Cherokee National schools. Married at Centralia, June 2, 1912, Fred L., son of Robert Lee and Lulu Jackson.

They are the parents of: Carwel Lee, born April 21, 1914, and Norma Jennie, born Mar. 3, 1919. Mrs. Jackson is a Methodist and a member of the Eastern Star. Mr. Jackson has been a banker in Welch for nine years and is at present interested in oil production.

Mrs. Jackson is the great-great granddaughter of Pathkiller, who was Principal Chief of the Cherokees at the beginning of the nineteenth century. His daughter, Elsie, married Eldrige, and their eldest child, Margaret, generally called Peggy, married Jesse Morris, and they were the great grandparents of Mrs. Rosa A. Jackson.

Jordan, Robert Lee. (See Riley)—Robert E. Lee, son of John W. and Sallie (Bean) Jordan, born in 1867 in Texas. Educated in the Male Seminary. Married in the Cherokee Outlet in 1890, Harriette A., daughter of Richard A. and Mary A. (Simkins) Riley. They are the parents of: Lee Owen, born February 8, 1891; William Penn Adair, born December 15, 1892, and Dennis Bushyhead Jordan, born November 24, 1894, who was in the navy for two years during the war, during which time he crossed the ocean thirty-four times and was on watch twice when German submarines were sighted and sunk.

Mr. Jordan is a member of the Knights of Pythias fraternity and is a farmer, near Collinsville.

Kelley, Lulu N. (See Sanders and Ghigau)—Lulu Nannie, daughter of John and Sallie Matilla (Harlan) Poole, was born March 22, 1862, in Delaware District, Cherokee Nation. She was educated in the Cherokee public schools and Female Seminary. She married at Vinita, August 27, 1887, Frederick Lincoln Kelley. He died at Vinita November 2, 1911. Mr. Kelley was one of the best posted and successful hay and grain dealers in northeast Oklahoma. Frederick L. and Lulu N. Kelley were the parents of Pauline Gazelle, born February 16, 1889, and married Charles W. Flint; Frederick Lincoln, born July 31, 1893, and George Samuel Kelley, born August 21, 1895.

Lulu N. Kelley's Cherokee name is Salala. She is a member of the Methodist church and belongs to the Eastern Star Chapter in Vinita. She was deeply interested in the World war work and did efficient service in the Red Cross and other activities.

John and Sallie Matilla (Harlan) Poole were the parents of Fannie, who married James Henry Akin; Charles Walton, and Lulu Nannie Poole.

Lulu N. Poole's maternal grandparents were Ellis Sanders, son of George and Nancy (Sanders) Harlan, born March 4, 1804, married 1828 Nancy Barnett, born September 18, 1800, in Onslow County, North Carolina. Ellis Sanders Harlan was a clerk of election at the Court House Precinct in Hickory Log District, Cherokee Nation, for the selection of delegates to the Cherokee Constitutional Convention of July, 1827. He was elected to Council from Flint District in 1855. He died December 7, 1866.

Kerr, Mrs. Thomas. (See Duncan and Grant).—Susan Tolbert, daughter of John Tolbert and Amanda Cherokee (Duncan) Scott, was born in Delaware District May 11, 1873, educated in that District. Married at Seneca, Missouri, May 20, 1892, Thomas son of Alexander and Matilda Kerr. They are the parents of Ollie May Kerr, born November 22, 1894, married November 27, 1912, J. C. Carr, and has one daughter, Lena May Carr, born September 23, 1919. Mr. Kerr is a farmer, near Vinita.

Charles Duncan, a Scotchman, married about 1784, Dorcas, a full-blood Cherokee, of the Deer Clan. Their son, John, married Elizabeth Abercromby, and they were the parents of Charles Gordan Duncan, born June 3, 1825, and married Sinia Eaton, born February 7, 1825. They were the parents of Amanda Cherokee Duncan, born in Going Snake District, July 26, 1850. Married December 16, 1869, John Tolbert Scott.

Keys, Monroe A. (See Grant, Oolootsa, Daniel and Riley.)—Monroe Amory, son of Monroe Calvin and Lucy Lowrey (Hoyt) Keys, was born February 21, 1870. Educated in the Male Seminary. Married March 25, 1905, Martha Ann daughter of Henry and Emma Jane (Daniel) Donnelly, born March 11, 1874, educated in the Cherokee public schools and Worcester Academy. They are the parents of: Wahnie, born March 7, 1908; Emma, born December 17, 1909; Amory, born January 16, 1912; Jane, born December 5, 1914, and Clun Keys, born February 10, 1917. Mr. Keys is a member of the Holly Clan. His Cherokee name is Clun-tee-sta. He is a farmer near Vinita.

Kincaid, Edward C. (See Adair)—Edward C. Kincaid, born January 28, 1875. Married at Pryor March 31, 1906, Mary L., daughter of David and Lydia Givins. They are the parents of: Julia Pearl Kincaid, born April 29, 1908. Mr. Kincaid is a farmer, belongs to the Baptist church, is a member of the Ancient Order of United Workmen and Mutual Aid Society.

Collins McDonald, born December 23, 1807. Married March 20, 1832, Naroena Adair born September 8, 1815. She died April 28, 1862, and he died November 5,

1895. Their daughter, Nancy Missouri McDonald, born November 31, 1849, married Joseph Kincaid, a native of Georgia and they were the parents of Edward C. Kincaid, the subject of this sketch.

Lane, Mrs. C. L. (See Downing, Corduroy and Oolootsa.)—Maude Ethel Rogers, born November 28, 1869, educated at Female Seminary, and Howard Payne College, Fayette, Missouri. Married October 4, 1891, Captain Lane Lane, born November 26, 1867, in Red River County, Texas. He graduated from "Kemper Family School," Booneville, Missouri, June 8, 1887, and conducted a drug store in Chelsea for thirty years. They were the parents of: Estelle, born September 20, 1892; Ethel Lindsay, born October 19, 1894, graduate of Chelsea High School and Northwestern State Normal at Tahlequah in 1918; James Gunter, born May 12, 1897; and Lasca Gazelle Lane, born June 19, 1905.

Clement Vann Rogers, born in the Western Cherokee Nation, January 11, 1839, educated at Baptist Mission, Going Snake District, and Male Seminary. Married in 1858 Mary America Scrimsher, born October 9, 1839, and settled on Caney River in Cooweescoowee District. Was Captain of Co. C First Cherokee Mounted Volunteers and senator from Cooweescoowee District in the Confederate Cherokee Council from 1862 to 1865. Settled on the Verdigris River after the Civil war. Elected Judge of Cooweescoowee Dist. Aug. 5, 1877; senator from the same District August 4, 1879, August 1, 1883, August 7, 1899, and August 3, 1903. Elected as a member of the Cherokee Commission to negotiate with the "Dawes" Commission for the final disposition of the Cherokee Nation. Elected a member of the Oklahoma Constitutional Convention from the Sixty-fourth District on November 6, 1906. Rogers County, Oklahoma, was named for him. Mrs. Mary America (Scrimsher) Rogers died May 28, 1890, and he died October 28, 1911. They were the parents of: Sallie Clemantin, Robert Martin, Maude Ethel, subject of this sketch, May and William Penn Rogers.

Leafer, Mrs. John. (See Conrad and Foreman)—Floren Frances, daughter of William H. and Letitia (Woodard) Foreman, born April 2, 1881, educated in the Cherokee National schools in Tahlequah District. Married at Tahlequah in 1903 John Leafer. They are the parents of John and Lawrence Leafer. Mr. Leafer is a farmer near Tahlequah.

Lowrey, Daniel W. (See Oolootsa, Ross, Conrad and Hildebrand.)—Daniel Webster, son of Henry and Mary (Parris) Lowrey, born October 2, 1860. Educated in the Cherokee National Schools; married July 19, 1885, Ellen, daughter of James and Elizabeth (Hendricks) Gourd, born May 1, 1862, educated in the Cherokee Public Schools and Female Seminary. They are the parents of: Florence, born May 23, 1886; George, born August 15, 1887; Richard Walker, born September 8, 1890; James, born October 13, 1892; John, born September 4, 1894, and Dora Lowrey, born August 21, 1898. James and John Lowrey each served a year in the American Expeditionary Forces in France. Mr. and Mrs. Lowrey are members of the Methodist Church and he is a Modern Woodman of America. They are farmers, near Wann.

Lynch, Joseph Martin. (See Grant and Adair)—Joseph Martin Lynch, born July 30, 1881, educated in Male Seminary and Cumberland University, Lebanon, Tennessee, graduating from the Law Department of the latter, but refused to take the Tenneessee bar examination because negroes were included in the class. Elected Register of Deeds of Adair County, September 17, 1807. He married Hazel Capitola Mason. He served for several years as attorney for the Interior Department and on November 8, 1919, refused the appointment of Register of the United States Treasury, because it would be impossible for him to take his aged father from his home and friends and he would not leave him.

Mr. Lynch's great-great-grandfather, Joseph Martin, a native of Albermarle County, Virginia, was elected Major in the Revolutionary Army, February 17, 1779, and promoted to a Lieutenant Colonelcy in March, 1781. He was elected Brigadier General of the North Carolina militia, December 15, 1787, and was commissioned Brigadier General of the 20th Brigade of Virginia militia by Governor "Light Horse Harry" Lee on December 11, 1793. His son John Martin, was a member of the Constitutional Convention of 1827, and was the first Chief Justice and first treasurer of the Cherokee Nation. Mr. Lynch's grandfather, Joseph Martin Lynch, was a delegate from the

Cherokee Nation to Washington in 1839, and was elected Senator from Delaware District August 2, 1842. Mr. Lynch's father, Cicero Leonidas Lynch, was elected sheriff of Flint District August 2, 1875, and August 5, 1877, elected senator from the same district August 1, 1881. Elected Circuit Judge August 6, 1883, and August 1, 1887, the terms being for four years. He was elected Associate Justice of the Cherokee Nation, November 13, 1897.

Lynch, Mrs. Georgia. (See Grant and Foreman)—Joseph Vann generally called Joe) married Polly Black, and they were the parents of William, David, Sofia, Johnson Sallie and Delilah Vann. David Vann married Nancy Tally, nee Mackey, and they were the parents of William, Joseph, George B., Robert P., and Maud May Vann.

William Vann was the father of Georgia Eulalia Vann, born September 17, 1876. She was educated in Canadian District and the Female Seminary. She married March 20, 1T98, Joseph Johnson, son of Joseph Martin and Susan Francis (Foreman) Lynch, born September 29, 1875. He graduated from the Male Seminary in 1896, and died June 1, 1921. They were the parents of Cherokee Rose Lynch, and Jess Vann Lynch.

Lowrey, Mrs. Myrtle (See Ghigau, Grant, Adair and Oolootsa)—Luther Martin, son of Captain Ephriam Martin, and Sallie (Starr) Adair, married Lillie M. Waldrop and their daughter, Myrtle Lucinda Adair, born in 1891, was educated in the Cherokee Public Schools. Married in 1910, Randolph, son of Austin and Sallie (Choker) Lowrey, born February 6, 1889. They were the parents of Wesley Lowrey. Mrs. Lowrey is a member of the Baptist church.

McKisick, Mrs. J. H. (See Ghigau, Conrad and Duncan)—Nellie Josephine, daughter of Johnson Thompson and Catherine Isabel (Garbarine) Landrum, was born in Delaware District, May 6, 1890, and educated locally. Married at Vinita, August 8, 1910, James Houston, son of Charles D., and Lydia Elizabeth McKisick. They are the parents of Stephen Dean, born July 14, 1912, and Clark Douglas McKisick, born August 6, 1919. Mr. McKisick is a mill owner and operator at Big Cabin. Mrs. McKisick is a member of the United Brethren Church.

John, son of James and Rebecca (Duncan) Landrum married Nellie Otterlefter, and they were the parents of Johnson Thompson Landrum.

Samuel Candy, a white man, married Catherine, a full-blood Cherokee of the Wolf Clan. Their son, Samuel Candy, married Elizabeth West, a white woman. They were the parents of Ollie Candy, who married Hair Conrad and their daughter, Elizabeth, married Daniel Hopkins. Daniel and Elizabeth Hopkins were the parents of Sarah Abigal Hopkins, born January 27, 1839, married September 9, 1860, Stephen Gray Garbarini, born September 8, 1827, in Turelia, Italy. They were the parents of Catherine Isabel, born June 23, 1868, married April 2, 1889, Johnson Thompson Landrum, born 1860.

McLaughlin, William C. (See Grant, Ghigau, Foreman, Conrad, Duncan, and Halfbreed).—William Cecil McLaughlin, born September 22, 1893, educated at Grove, Stilwell and Muskogee, graduating in a business course from the latter. Married at Vinita, March 28, 1919, Lelia Leone, daughter of Richard Fields and Martha Adair (Brewer) Benge, born on Lynch's Prairie December 16, 1892. They are the parents of Cecil Benge McLaughlin, born May 10, 1921. Mr. McLaughlin is farming near Adair.

Elizabeth, daughter of Andrew and Catherine (Hicks) Miller, married Philip Inlow, a native of South Carolina, and their son, Sylvester Inlow, born June 24, 1837, married December 28, 1861, Susannah Paden, born November 1, 1844. He died June 13, 1878, and she died February 13, 1889. Their daughter, Margaret Caroline Inlow, born August 6, 1879, married September 20, 1890, Joshua Ezekial McLaughlin, born February 14, 1853. They were the parents of William Cecil McLaughlin.

McLain, Mrs. Jesse. (See Oolootsa and Ghigau)—Margaret, daughter of Samuel Houston and Nannie (Brewster) Benge, born Wednesday, March 2, 1870. Educated at Fort Gibson and Female Seminary. Married July 17, 1885, Jesse, son of Calvin and Charlotte (Martin) McLain, born in February, 1855, educated in the Cherokee Public Schools and Male Seminary. They are the parents of: Nannie Lee, Samuel Houston, Calvin Cross, Eliza Jane, George Washington and Charlotte Benge. Calvin C. was in the A. E. F. in France for seven months and his younger brother, George W., was preparing to embark at the time the Armistice was signed.

McLain, James (See Ghigau)—James, son of Calvin and Charlotte (Martin) McLain married Elizabeth J. Kennedy, born June 22, 1875, and Lulu Breeden. By the first marriage there was born: Henriette J. and Sarah Vivian McLain, and by the second marriage, Haskell, Etta, Cora, Woodrow, Calvin, Charlotte and Lucy McLain.

Mr. McLain was educated at the Orphan Asylum. He is a member of the A. F. T. A., which is one of the best indications of a man's respectability and responsibility. He is a farmer near Claremore.

Martin, Mrs. DeWitt (See Grant and Duncan)—DeWitt T. Martin, born May 12, 1888 Enlisted in the World war Nov. 22, 1917. Assigned to the 17th Co. of the 2nd Regiment as an air service mechanic January 27, 1918. Sailed for France March 14, 1918, where his service entitled him to two gold chevrons. Returned to the United States May 29, 1919. Honorably discharged at Camp Pike June 13, 1919. Married at Carthage, Missouri, May 1, 1920, Mary Ethel daughter of I. D. and Rachel A. Boston. They are the parents of Caroline Louise Martin, born March 24, 1821.

Joseph Martin of Bristol, England, settled on a plantation near Charlotteville, Albermarle County, Virginia, in the first quarter of the eighteenth century. He married Susannah Childs and they were the parents of Joseph Martin, born about 1740. He was a Lieutenant Colonel in the American service in the Revolutionary war. He married Susannah Fields, nee Emory, a quarter-blood Cherokee, and they were the parents of John Martin, who was the first Chief Justice and first Treasurer of the Cherokee Nation. Judge John Martin was the father of Joseph Lynch Martin, whose son, John Rogers Martin was the father of DeWitt T. Martin.

Martin, Joel T. (See Ghigau and Rogers) —Joel Thomas, son of William and Sarah Martin, born August 21, 1876, educated in the Cherokee Public Schools. Married October 26, 1896, Myrtle Stephens, nee Stephenson, born April 19, 1878, in Nodaway County, Missouri. One son, William A. Martin, married in 1899, Stella, daughter of Mr. and Mrs. Argentine Causdell. They are the parents of: Pauline, May and George Martin.

Mr. Martin is a member of the Owls fraternity. He is a farmer near Ruby.

George Washington Walker married Rachel Rogers and they were the parents of Mrs. Sarah Marlins.

Mayes, Watt A. (See Adair, Foreman, Ross and Grant)—Walter Adair Mayes, born December 10, 1860, educated in the Cherokee public schools and Male Seminary, married December 31, 1890, Nannie Rider McCoy, born March 25, 1865. She was educated in the National schools and Female Seminary. They are the parents of: Hall, born September, 23, 1891; Washington E., born September 8, 1893; Clarence, born October 23, 1895; Mayme Lucile, born November 14, 1897; Jesse Lamar, born May 1, 1900; and Joseph McCoy Mayes, born June 9, 1903.

Walter Adair Mayes is the son of George Washington Mayes, born November 11, 1824, married May 21, 1846, Charlotte Bushyhead, born March 16, 1830. She died January 23, 1878, and he died October 28, 1894. George Washington was the son of Samuel and Nancy (Adair) Mayes. Charlotte was the daughter of Rev. Jesse and Eliza (Wilkerson) Bushyhead. Walter Adair Mayes is the nephew of Chiefs Dennis Wolf Bushyhead, Joel Bryan and Samuel Houston Mayes and Miss Nannie Mayes is the grandniece of Chief John Ross and great granddaughter of Chief Charles Renatus Hicks.

Mrs Walter Adair Mayes is the daughter of Joseph Rogers McCoy, who married on December 16, 1851, Nancy Hicks, born September 16, 1830. He died July 4, 1866.

Walter A. Mayes' Cherokee name is Oganostota and he belongs to the Deer Clan. Mrs. Mayes' Cherokee name is Walllah and she belongs to the bird clan.

Meeks, William—William, son of George and Minerva (Fleetwood) Meeks, was born March 5, 1880 in Sequoyah District, educated in Cherokee public schools and Male Seminary, married September 11, 1905 Goldie May Perry. They are the parents of Sylvia Pauline, born September 7, 1906; Mary Louise, born June 3, 1909; Della Ruth, born September 19, 1912 and Wyllie Burtis, born June 1, 1919. William Meeks was left an orphan while a small child and through adverse circumstances has struggled to a competence and the respect of his community. A Methodist in church affiliation he has ascended in masonry to the Thirty second degree and Shriner. He served in Company K, First Infantry for two and a half years in the Phillipines during the Spanish-American war and was very active in World War work. His brother Lewis Samuel was a member of the Thirteenth Marines in the World War.

Mitchell, Mrs. Claud W. (See Grant and Duncan)—Emma E., daughter of John Martin and Alice R. (Smith) Daniel, was born at Vinita, February 19, 1892; was educated at the Female Seminary at Tahlequah. She married at Vinita July 31, 1911, Claud W., son of William W. and Emma Mitchell. Mr. Mitchell died October 23, 1918. They were the parents of Mary Nadine, born March 3, July 8, 1918.

John Martin Daniel was born October 2, 1843, and married August 1, 1876, Alice R. Smith, born June 10, 1855. They were the parents of Marma D., James Henry, Robert John, Lula May, Eliza E., Martha J., Emma E., William, Edgar Jackson and Walter Scott Daniel.

Lula May Daniel married R. F. Parker, and lives at Welch, Oklahoma. Eliza E. Daniel married Samuel Nidiffer and Jeff Blevins. Martha J. Daniel married Elbert Snider and lives at Vinita, Oklahoma.

Miller, Mrs. James (See Ward)—Mary, daughter of Robert and Martha Alice (Holland) Early, was born in 1889 at Stilwell. Educated in the Cherokee public schools, Female Seminary and Hill's Business College, Oklahoma City, graduating from the latter institution. Married at Joplin, Missouri in 1912 James, son of Mr. and Mrs. James C. Miller. She taught in the public schools for ten years prior to her marriage. Mr. and Mrs. Miller are members of the Baptist church. He is a farmer, near Foyil and she is a member of the Ladies Home Demonstration Club.

Milton, Annie Leola (See Adair)—Annie Leola, daughter of William Penn and Julia (Allison) Adair, was born June 1, 1883, at Stilwell. She married December 17, 1899, Alvin Hendrex, and they were the parents of Virgil Felix, born September 7, 1901; William Harrison, born July 27, 1904; Orvill Lee, born August 5, 1906; Paul Lyman, born February 18, 1909, and Ralph Herald Hendrex, born January 29, 1913. Her second and present husband is Curt Milton. They are the parents of Carl Dale, born July 24, 1918; Harvey Haskell Milton, born June 10, 1921. Mrs. Milton is a member of the Christian Church.

Miles, Mrs. John B. (See Oolootsa and Riley)—Lucy D., daughter of Monroe Calvin and Lucy Lowrey (Hoyt) Kyes was born March 31, 1872. Educated in Female Seminary. Married at Pleasant Hill, December 26, 1894 John Benedict, son of Mr. and Mrs. Benedict Miles. They are the parents of: Benedict Franklin, born October 3, 1895; Elizabeth, born January 16, 1897; Guy, born ay 31, 1904 and Lydia Esther Miles, born May 12, 1906.

Benedict Franklin Miles was in the A. E. F. He is a prosperous farmer near Miles.

James Herbert and Cora Archer Moore are the parents of: William, born January 13, 1900; Foreman, born September 13, 1902; Veta Clara, born April 20, 1905; Nellie, born January 6, 1907; James Herbert, born February 26, 1914; Len Ross, born November 21, 1918; Joseph and Samuel, born July 31, 1920.

Morris, Mrs. Evans—Eliza, daughter of Richard and Polly (Hogshooter) O'Field was born in 1864. Educated in the Cherokee National Schools. Married Mr. Colston. They were the parents of Bettie, born January 10, 1883; Cynthia, married Charles Heard.

Mrs. Cynthia Heard died October 21, 1918 and Charles Heard died October 23, 1918. Their children Louise, born February 2, 1912; Helen born December 2, 1914 and Laura Maxine Heard born March 18, 1917, were adopted and are being reared by Mr. and Mrs. Morris, as is also, Ernest Hildebrand, born March 8, 1907. Fannie Colston, the third daughter of Mrs. Evan Morris was born August 29, 1896. Mrs. Eliza Colston married March 23, 1899 Evan, son of William and Eleanor Morris.

They are the parents of William R. Morris, born April 9, 1900. Blessed are they that gratuitously care for orphans.

Mounts, Mrs. Ted R. (See Thompson and Gusoduesga)—Ada, daughter of William and Elizabeth (Cobb) Brown was born in 1887. Educated in the Cherokee Public Schools and Female Seminary. Married at Fort Gibson in 1911, Ted Ray, son of David Albert and Caroline Harriette (Thompson) Mounts born at Fort Gibson, Saturday March 29,

1884. They are the parents of Mary, Cherokee, Okla.; Billie Brown, Louise Ramona and Ted Ray Mounts.

Mr. and Mrs. Mounts are representative citizens of Fort Gibson and are well known for their public spirited citizenship.

Muskrat, Joseph D.—Joseph D. Muskrat, born October 30, 1850, near Mayesville, In Delaware District. Elected Sheriff of Delaware District in 1883. Married August 10, 1884 Florence Roseborough. They are the parents of: Nina Pearl, born May 27, 1885; Ira D., born April 20, 1887; Ruby E., born December 26, 1898 and Frank B. Muskrat, born June 11, 1902. Joseph D. Muskrat was elected Solicitor in 1893.

Muskrat, Jacob J. (See Duncan)—Jacob Jackson Muskrat, born in Delaware District September 30, 1885 and educated in Saline District. Married at Southwest City, Missouri August 8, 1908 Perry Lee, daughter of Mosley and Ellen Stratton.

They are the parents of: Howard M., born November 20, 1909 and Lottie T Muskrat, born October 30, 1919. Mr. Muskrat is a farmer, near Bernice.

Jacob Jackson Muskrat is the son of Jacob Muskrat born in 1838 and died October 5, 1888 and Elizabeth Emily, daughter of Peter and Rebecca (Rolston) McAllister.

Martin, Eugene Warren (See Oolootsa and Ross)—Eugene Warren, son of William Henry and Sarah Jane (Lowrey) Martin, born January 30, 1886, was educated in Tahlequah District and the Male Seminary. He married at Oklahoma City, April 1, 1915 Neva, daughter of Hosea Claude and Alice I. Frizielle, born Dec. 19, 1889 in Polk County Missouri. She was educated in the Public schools in Oklahoma City. They are the parents of Pauline Mae, born Dec. 22, 1917 and Harold Leroy Martin, born May 24, 1919. Mr. Martin is a business man in Oklahoma City.

William Henry Martin is a grand son of Hercules Martin a fullblood Cherokee, and his Cherokee name was Clogase. Hercules Martin was one of the best known and most proficient interpreters and clerical man of his day in the Cherokee Nation.

Nichols, Mr. Charles—Fannie, daughter of David and Sarah (Easley) Humphrey was born May 1, 1886 in the Cherokee Nation. Educated at Vinita and married at Vinita May 4, 1918 Charles, son of Mr. and Mrs. Nichols. They are members of the Methodist church and are farmers near Vinita.

Nidiffer, John R. (See Ward and Ghigau)—John Ross Nidiffer, born November 22, 1886, educated in Cherokee Public Schools and Male Seminary. He is a railroader and entered the Navy on September 7, 1917, served on the U. S. S. St. Louis, discharged August 8, 1919. Married June 28, 1920, Ethel Cora Culley nee Courtney.

Newman, Mrs. Charles N. (See Downing)—Thomas, son of Joel and Nellie (Quinton) Kelly was born in Polk County, Arkansas December 26, 1845. Married in November 1867 Valera Arkansas Britton, born in 1847 in Sebastian County, Arkansas. They were the parents of Bessie Kelly born at Westville, December 23, 1891. Educated at Centralia. Married at Centralia December 24, 1912, Charles N. son of William and Nancy Newman. They are the parents of Howard Lee, born February 22, 1914; Dellas Wayne, born June 12, 1916 and Charles Kelly Newman, born March 13, 1920. Mr. and Mrs. Newman are farmers, near Centralia.

Nicholson, Richard E. (See Oolootsa)—Rory McCoy, son of John R. and Sarah (Gunter) Nicholson, was born March 14, 1848, and married Margaret Elizabeth Bibles, born December 15, 1857, and died April 1, 1890. He died January 8, 1891. They were the parents of Richard Edward Nicholson, born August 11, 1878, and married November 4, 1900, Annie Pearson, born January 20, 1881, in Schuyler County, Illinois.

Mr. and Mrs. Richard E. Nicholson are the parents of Roy Preston born July 18, 1903; Edgar Russel born December 7, 1905, and Hattie Nicholson born September 15, 1907.

Parks—Jennie Taylor, a Scotch girl married an Englishman named Charles Fox. Two sons were born of this union. In later years the parents were divorced. The father kept the eldest son, who according to the English law of primogeniture was to succeed to his titles and estate, but allowed his wife to keep Charles, the younger son who had no vested prospects and his mother added her maiden name to his, and thenceforward he was known as Charles Fox-Taylor. Charles Fox-Taylor married Jennie Walker, the granddaughter of the Ghigau, or Beloved Woman of the Cherokees. This was the supreme title and was granted only on account of extreme merit and was so rarely conferred that no other instance of its invokement was known.

Charles and Jennie Fox-Taylor's third child and only daughter, Susan was born in February 1798 and married in April 1814 Samuel Parks, born January 12, 1789. He was fiscal agent for John Ross in 1838-9, securing wagons and teams for him. Parks died on June 3, 1841 and his widow died December 12, 1876. Samuel and Susan Parks children were, consecutively: Ruth married Dickson Price; Almira married James Price; Jennie married John Langdon and Joseph Collyr; George W. married Louisa Spriggs; Thomas Jefferson born Nov. 18, 1821 married Maria Annie Thompson, born September 11, 1830; Thomas Jefferson Parks died May 6, 1883; Calvin, William, Mary Ann married William C. Day; Lieutenant Colonel Robert C., John Ross and Samuel.

Maria Annie Parks nee Thompson was the daughter of James Allen and Martha (Lynch) Thompson; the granddaughter of Jeter and Nannie (Martin) Lynch; the great granddaughter of General and Susannah (Emory) Martin.

Thomas Jefferson Parks was born in the Eastern Cherokee Nation on October 18, 1821. Emigrated with his parents to the Western Cherokee Nation in 1838-9. He married February 10, 1848 Miss Thompson and settled in Delaware District where he was a prosperous farmer and merchant until the civil war. Returning in poverty to his desolated home after the war, he by hard work and close application, soon acquired another competence. He was a master mason and while always having a wholesome interest in politics, he on account of his business interests never allowed his name to be used as an aspirant for office. He died on May 6, 1883.

Thomas Jefferson and Maria Annie Parks were the parents of Susan Martha born December 1, 1848, married Edwin E. Carr; Johnson Calvin, born December 2. 1851, married Minerva Williams; Mary Jane, born March 28, 1856, married Robert Franklin Browning; Emma Josephine born May 8, 1858, married Robert Samuels; Anna Medora born March 5, 1860 married James Bonaparte Woodall; Jefferson Thompson born March 13, 1862, married Ruth Etta Duncan; Nancy Almira born May 20, 1865, married Henry Clay Ballard; Rev. James Allen, born March 20, 1867 married Florence Youngblood and Fannie born January 9, 1871, married Davis Hill.

Ruth Etta (Duncan) Parks is the daughter of John Tommason and Eliza Annie (Sanders) Duncan; the grand daughter of John and Elizabeth (Abercrombie) Duncan, and Robert and Mary (McCreary) Sanders; the great grand daughter of Charles Gordon Duncan, a Scotchman and his wife Dorcas a full blood Cherokee of the Deer clan. Dorcas was a full sister to Ge-ho-ga who married John Adair.

Jefferson Thompson Parks was born on January 13, 1862. He graduated from the Cherokee National Male Seminary June 26, 1884. Was elected a member of the Board of Education in 1898. After having conducted a large merchantile establishment at Tahlequah he closed out that business and commenced practicing law. Being an ardent democrat, he at the advent of statehood was elected judge of Cheroke County and was reelected.

The home life of Judge and Mrs. Parks is ideal, pleasant and cultured, they have been blessed with five children: Clarena the eldest is deceased, Ruth Anna is the wife of Frederick Hathaway; Mildred Josephine is Mrs. Thomas L. Ballinger of Park Hill; Miss Wahlelle, and Jefferson Thompson Jr. are a part of the pleasures and attractions of the Park's home.

Parker, Mrs. William A. (See Oolootsa)—Mary Ellen Chamberlin born at Vinita, April 23, 1893, educated in Vinita. Married at Nowata July 5, 1910 William A. Parker. They are the parents of Norman Eugene, born April 1, 1912; Billie born January 23, 1914; Viola May, born May 15, 1916 and Mary Jane Parker, born November 1, 1919. Mrs. Mary Ellen Parker is the daughter of Nelson Bucher and Sarah Viola (LeForce) Chamberlin.

Pierce, Mrs. James M. (See Cordery)—Nancy Jane, daughter of Albert and Louisa (Cordery) Anderson, was born January 1, 1882; and married August 23, 1896, James Madison Pierce, born December 13, 1877, in Hall County, Georgia. They were the parents of Gertrude; James Clayton and Earl B. Pierce.

Mr. Pierce is one of the wealthiest cotton

farmers of the Muskogee-Fort Gibson section, owning and operating hundreds of acres of valuable land, and several cotton gins.

Peterson, Mrs. Chris B. (See Hildebrand)—Lucinda, daughter of Benjamin J. and Delilah (O'Field) Hildebrand was born September 9, 1882. Educated in the Cherokee public schools and Female Seminary. Married at Vinita July 23, 1909 Pigeon Hanson and her present husband is Christ B. son of Peter and Anna Mary Peterson.

Her children by her first husband, are: John, born June 23, 1910, Woodrow, born June 2, 1913 and Loretta Hanson born July 2, 1916. By the present husband she has one daughter, Anna Laura Peterson, born May 12, 1920. Mrs. Peterson belongs to the Wolf Clan and her Cherokee name is Luski. Mr. Peterson is a farmer, near White Oak.

Prater, Mrs. Henry S. (See Downing and Ghigau)—Martha Celeste Thompson, born March 16, 1868, married February 1, 1887, Henry Sheridan, son of Thomas D. and Mary Elizabeth Prater, born June 13, 1866 in Camden County, Tennessee. They are the parents of David George, born August 10, 1891, and married Nancy May Youngblood, born in March 1895, and their three children are John F., born September 8, 1911, Benjamin Hester Prater, born March 28, 1913, and Pansy May Prater, born May 16, 1915; Mary Caroline Prater, born September 30, 1896, married September 23, 1915, Guy P. Holmes. She died November 26, 1918, and left two children: Mary Lorena, born October 19, 1916, and Helen Pauline Holmes born May 17, 1918; Henry L. Dawes, born February 25, 1900; Mable Clara, born August 26, 1902; Robbie, born September 1, 1904; Nellie Maude, born September 27, 1906, and Rollie Austin Prater, born February 7, 1909.

Clara Rider, born June 20, 1842, married July 5, 1865, David George Thompson, born November 10, 1840, in Newton County, Georgia. He served during the Civil War in Captain Jonathan Nail's company of the First Chickasaw Cavalry, Confederate service. Mrs. Thompson died August 6, 1916. They were the parents of Mrs. Mattie Celeste Prater.

Pointer, Mrs. Patsy (See Grant, Adair and Foreman)—Martha Adair, daughter of Jesse Bushyhead and Cherokee Cornelia (Adair) Mayes was born January 10, 1875 and educated in the Female Seminary, from which she graduated in 1892. She married December 16, 1900, Edwin Mooring Pointer, born June 17, 1868, in Monroe County, Arkansas. He graduated from Cumberland University at Lebanon, Tennessee, and in Law Course in the same institution in 1897; was appointed District Clerk of Sequoyah County after Statehood. He died January 5, 1910.

The following children were born from this union: Samuel Jesse, born November 15, 1901, and James David Pointer, born January 11, 1909.

Pettitt, Mrs. William P. (See Grant, Tyner, Adair and Riley)—William Percival, son of William and Nannie (Tyner) Pettitt, was born Sept. 20, 1867; educated at Fort Gibson and the Male Seminary. He married March 18, 1894, Mary Jane, daughter of Benjamin and Sallie (Guerin) Adair, born Thursday, January 1, 1874, in Illinois District. She was educated in the Female Seminary. They moved on April 17, 1894, from Illinois District to Cooweescoowee District, settling three-fourths of a mile north of the Cherokee and Creek line, where they lived until January 19, 1903, when they moved to their present residence at Inola. Mr. and Mrs. Pettitt are the parents of Pearl Olive born Oct. 7, 1895; Bertha Talala, born October 27, 1897; Floyd Henry, born March 1, 1900; William Percival, born November 15, 1902; Mazie Opal, born April 15, 1905; Mary Elizabeth, born November 1, 1907, and Elnora Cherokee Pettitt, born October 16, 1913.

Puryear, Mrs. Lucy (See Riley)—Lucy, daughter of John and Nannie (Perdue) Robinson, was born February 8th, 876, and married in the year 1894, Homer Puryear, who was born August 16, 1862, in Lawrence County, Alabama. They were the parents of Ernest Homer Puryear, who was born December 18, 1896.

Robinson, Mrs. Leroy S. (See Grant)—George Ella, daughter of R. A. and Edith Caroline (Rogers) Prather, was born on Beatties Prairie, January 15, 1869; was educated in Delaware District and the Female Seminary, graduating June 28, 1894. She married at Vinita October 29, 1895, Leroy S., son of William and Malinda Robinson. They are the parents of LeElla, born in April 1900; Carleton, born February 15, 1902, and Leroy Prather Rogers, born April 5,

1905. Leroy S. Robinson died April 26, 1911. Mrs. Robinson is a member of the Methodist church.

LeElla Robinson graduated from the Vinita High School and the Northeastern State Normal at Tahlequah. She attended the Collins Agricultural College at Fort Collins, Colorado, where she was a member of the Kappa Delta Sorority. She married on December 24, 1919, Chesley H. Harris.

Nancy Downing married Charles Rogers and they had two children; Pleasant and Eliza Rogers who married John Seabolt. Nancy's second husband was Thomas Fields and their seven children were, consecutively: Sallie Elizabeth, who married James Hildebrand; Rachel Jane, married William Stiff and Henry Richard Fields married Rachel Goss; Margaret Wilson married Robert Mosby French; Josiah Foreman died in California, December 13, 1852, and Caroline Matilda Rogers Fields married William Penn Boudinot. Pleasant Rogers was the father of Mrs. Edith Caroline (Rogers) Prather.

Rector, Mrs. Ed. (See Grant)—Laura Alice, daughter of Ellis and Martha (Copeland) Buffington was born September 22, 1852. Married December 26, 1871 Josiah, son of Jesse and Lucy (Love) Henry, born January 1, 1850. He was elected in November 1869 Solicitor of Cooweescoowee District and appointed to the same office in 1876 by the Chief. Elected Councilor from Cooweescoowee District August 1, 1881 and August 2, 1897. They were the parents of Rosa Jane Henry, born August 10, 1883, educated in the Cherokee public schools and Female Seminary. Married at Claremore in 1905 Edward, son of Mr. and Mrs. Sylvanus Rector. They are the parents of Edna May, James Emmet, born October 29, 1906 and Frances Rector. Mr. and Mrs. Rector are farmers, near Claremore, they belong to the Methodist church and he is a Mason. Mrs. Rector's Cherokee name is Ay-ni.

Rhomer, Mrs. May (See Grant and Ooolootsa)—May, the daughter of Calvin Jones and Emma Walker (McCoy) Hanks, was born at Webbers Falls March 2, 1869; was educated at Webbers Falls and the Female Seminary. She married April 15, 1887, Frank Rhomer.

Thev are the parents of Emma Nora, born February 2, 1889; May Frances, born November 17, 1891; Margaret Bell, born April 2, 1894; and Fannie Charlotte Rhomer, born March 20, 1896. The Rhomers are farmers near Webbers Falls.

Calvin Jones, son of Robert Taylor and Margaret Ann Ward (Morgan) Hanks, was born February 8, 1836 and married April 11, 1861, Emma Walker McCoy, who was born April 3, 1841. He was a private in Captain John S. Vann's Company, and in Captain Samuel Gunter's Company in the Confederate Army. He was elected Counselor from Canadian District August 5, 1867; and Senator from the same District August 6, 1877. He died May 16, 1879.

Mrs. Emma Hanks, nee McCoy died February 8, 1900. They were the parents of Mrs. May Rhomer.

Riley, Mrs. Stella (See Riley)—Stella, daughter of Milton and Jemima (Scott) Moore born in 1873 in Missouri. Married in 1894 John H., son of Richard and Mary A. (Simkins) Riley. They were the parents of: Ruth Pearl, born February 6, 1896; Mamie A., born June 23, 1900; Mabel, born May 13, 1902 and Prentice Riley, born February 22, 1904. Mrs. Riley who is a member of the Latter Day Saints Church, is a farmer, near Vera.

Roach, Thomas S. (See Ghigau and Sanders) — George Roach married Nannie Pritchett, and they were the parents of Thomas Suake Roach who married Wycie McDaniel.

Mr. Roach who has been for several years Special Field Man for the U. S. Indian Agency at Muskogee, is one of the most prominent fullbloods of the tribe. Besides being cautious and diplomatic, he speaks both the English and Cherokee languages fluently, and is of inestimable value to his employers.

Rogers, Connell (See Grant, Ooolootsa and Duncan)—Connell, son of Andrew Lewis and Cherokee America (Morgan) Rogers, born September 19, 1850 in Tennessee. Married February 5, 1878 Florence Nash born August 29, 1848. She died February 21, 1886. They were the parents of: Gertrude Whitman, born July 11, 1879 and Ella Coffin Rogers, born March 13, 1883 Mr. Rogers married June 17, 1891 Kathleen Aurora daughter of Jeter Thompson and Keziat (Moore) Cunningham, born February 17, 1871. Educated in Worcester Academy, Vinita and Female Seminary. They are the parents of Marion Sevier, born July 8, 1892; Lewis Byrne, born December 27,

1895 served in France during the World War; Howard Cunningham, born December 31, 1899 and Connell, born June 22, 1909. Mr. and Mrs. Rogers are members of the Presbyterian church. She belongs to the Eastern Star, American Legion Auxilliary, Adelphian and Women's Democratic clubs. Her Cherokee name is Walleat.

Reliable, agreeable and efficient Mr. Rogers has been the preference by his constituency as Auditor of the Cherokee Nation in 1879; Senator from Illinois Dist. in 1885 and 1897; Secretary of the Cherokee National Board of Education 1898; Treasurer of Muskogee County 1907, 1913 and 1914. He is a planter and banker at Fort Gibson.

Rogers, William P. A. (See Downing, Cordery and Oolootsa)—William Penn Adair, son of Clement Vann and Mary America (Scrimsher) Rogers was born at the Rogers homestead near Oolagah November 4, 1879. Educated at Kemper Military School, Booneville, Missouri. Married at Rogers, Arkansas November 25, 1908 Betty, daughter of Mr. and Mrs. J. W. Blake. They are the parents of: William Vann, born October 20, 1911; Mary Amelia, born May 18, 1913 and James Blake Rogers, born July 25, 1915. Mr. Rogers is a member of the Shrine and Elk fraternities. He is a member of two clubs, the Lambs and Friars. Commencing in the theatrical profession as an expert roper, while traveling in South Africa, he has had a remarkably successful career as a comedian, monologist and scenario artist.

Rogers, Mrs. J. C. (See Grant and Cordery)—Sallie Martin, born January 30, 1869, educated in the Cherokee public schools and Female Seminary. Married August 22, 1888 John Cicero Rogers, born September 9, 1861 in Washington County, , Arkansas. They are the parents of. Pearl Lottie, born July 18, 1889, Frank, born April 27, 1892; Hugh E. born June 5, 1894; Terry P., born January 14, 1897. Ethel M., born March 23, 1899; Eula May, born September 30, 1901 and Ruth Martin, born June 25, 1914.

Samuel Martin married Catherine Hildebrand and their son William A. Martin married Nannie Lucas nee Guinn. They were the parents of: John Brice, who married Lucinda Still; Sarah Jane, married Samuel Bryant; Almon born November 4, 1842. He was a member of Company M, First Cherokee Mounted Volunteers Confederate service under Captain O. H. P. Brewer. He married Sarah Jane Cordery. She died February 23, 1874.

They were the parents of: Andrew Jackson, married Anna Belle Morrow; Sallie, the subject of this sketch; Nannie, married Riley Barnett and Mary Ann Martin, married William E. Curtis.

Rogers, Lewis (See Grant, Ghigau, Duncan and Halfbreed)—Lewis, the son of Nelson and Rosa (West) Rogers, was born in Saline District Novxember 14, 1840. His first wife was Josephine Landrum, and the second was Helen Ross. Lewis and Helen Rogers were the parents of Rosa, who married Benjamin Avant; and of Lewis Rogers, Junior.

Mr. Rogers is a wealthy retired business man and a member of the Methodist church.

Rogers, Thomas (See Grant and Downing)—Thomas Lewis, son of Thomas Lewis and Nancy C. (Martin) Rogers, was born near Pawhuska, September 2, 1885. He was educated in that city. He married in 1917 at Joplin, Missouri, Bessie Barrett. He is the father of Thomas Lewis, born July 28. 1911; and Nancy Rogers, born April 24, 1914.

Mr. Rogers is a member of the Christian church, and a merchant at Pawhuska.

Rogers, Jasper (See Grant)—Jasper, the son of Joseph and Elizabeth (Carpenter) Rogers, was born January 13, 1871, in Saline District. He married November 4, 1900, Rosa Bell, daughter of David and Mary Ellen (Chouteau) Fronkier, and she was born July 11, 1880, in the Osage Nation. Mr. and Mrs. Rogers are the parents of Cecilia M., Emmet Jasper, Maud, Flora Thadine, and Josephine Rogers.

Mr. Rogers is in business at Pawhuska; and he and his wife are both members of the Osage Nation.

Jean Pierre Chouteau, the founder of the City of Saint Louis, Missouri, married Pelegie Kiersereau, and they were the parents of Colonel August Pierre Chouteau who lived at Grand Saline on Grand River, and he was the father of Gesseau Chouteau, born in 1822.

Gesseau Chouteau served four years in the Confederate Army, and was a brilliant interpreter and an eloquent orator. Gesseau and Mary Ann Chouteau were the parents of Mary Ellen Chouteau who married David Fronkier.

Ross, Mrs. Lila J. (See Grant, Downing, Ross and Conrad)—Delila L. Jane, daughter of Carter and Katie (Benge) Daniel, was born December 8, 1857, and educated in the Female Seminary at Tahlequah. She married December 23, 1875 at Tahlequah, William Wallace, son of Allen and Jennie (Fields) Ross, who was born July 23, 1851, at Tahlequah. Mr. Ross was educated in the Male Seminary at Tahlequah, and was a grandson of Chief John Ross. Mr. and Mrs. Ross were the parents of Allen C., born June 27, 1882; and was educated at the Male Seminary; Elizabeth Vann born Apr. 11, 1884; Jane Stapler, born June 20, 1887, and Wallace Carter Ross, born October 2, 1893. William Wallace Ross died October 11, 1915. He had been Superintendent of the Male Seminary and of the Orphan Asylum for terms of four years each.

Mrs. Lila Ross' Cherokee name is Ki-na-lu-ga. Elizabeth Vann Ross married Carl E. Mills, and lives at Okmulgee. Mr. and Mrs. Mills were the parents of Arnetah Elizabeth born June 25, 1908; Mary Alice, born Aug. 22, 1910 and Wahleah Jane, born Jan. 12, 1915. Janie Stapler Ross married William David, the son of Rollin K. and Rachel (Landrum) Adair, and they are living at Drumright, Okla. Wallace Carter Ross was a member of the A. E. F. from May 29, 1918 until June 18, 1919, having served on the offensive at Meuse Argonne and other front lines.

Sanders, Mrs. Benjamin (See England, Hildebrand and Ghigau)—Martha Jane, daughter of James Franklin and Mary Jane (England) Williams was born in Cherokee Nation, Apr. 7, 1870. Educated in the Cherokee Nation. Married at Vinita, Aug. 1887, Benjamin Franklin Sanders, born June 30, 1861 in Clay County, Texas. They are the parents of Martha Leona Sanders, born August 18, 1890. Educated in Female Seminary, Hardin College, Mexico, Missouri and the Southern Seminary, Beuna Vista, Virginia, graduating from the latter institution. She married James H. Thigpin, a graduate of the Alabama State Agricultural College. They are now living at Fort Worth, Texas, where he is the Superintendent of Refrigerating Department of the Swift Packing Plant. He is a thirty second degree Mason and Shriner.

Mr. Sanders is one of the most successful farmers and stockraisers of Craig County.

Sortore, Mrs. John—Jennie, daughter of Pink and Susie Allen was born near Claremore March 1, 1888 educated at Justice public school. Married Oct. 28, 1902 John, son of John and Mary P. (Herd) Sortore. They are the parents of: Mabel Clair, born March 14, 1904 and Minnie Carmel Sortore, born September 4, 1907.

Mr. and Mrs. Sortore are members of the Christian Church and are farmers, near Claremore. Mr. Sortore who is by profession an engineer is a member of the Woodmen of the World fraternity.

Schrimsher, Ernest V. (See Ghigau, Oolootsa and Adair)—Ernest Vivian, son of John Gunter and Juliette Melvina (Candy) Schrimsher was born July 24, 1875 near Claremore. Educated in the Cherokee public schools and Male Seminary. Married at Nowata in 1902, Susie, daughter of Mr. and Mrs. Hugh Phillips.

Educated in the Cherokee public schools and Female Seminary, from which she graduated June 27, 1895. They are the parents of: Maxine and Oleta, twins; John Gunter, Grace, Stephen and Virginia.

Mr. Schrimsher is a Mason. He served as postmaster of Collinsville during the incumbency of President Wilson.

Schuth, Mrs. William J. (See Ghigau)—Eva Stella, daughter of Franklin Wallace and Catherine (Fetrick) Craig was born January 7, 1883 and educated at Welch. Married at Welch March 28, 1900 William J. son of Mr. and Mrs. Frank Schuth.

They are the parents of: Walter J., born July 1, 1903; William Craig, born September 6, 1910. Elzy Ivan, born June 16, 1917 and Gyneth Wayne Schuth, born July 24, 1920. Mr. and Mrs. Schuth are members of the Christian Church. He is a state highway supervisor. She is a Rebecca and during the war, was President of the Pleasant Valley Red Cross Association at Welch.

Scott, Richard J. (See Thompson and Sanders)—Richard John, son of Starling and Jennie (Thompson) Scott, was born at Fort Gibson March 20, 1852; educated in the Cherokee National Schools, and married at Vian July 26, 1893, Susie Florence, daughter of George Wesley and Caroline Elizabeth (Sanders) Choate, born November 21,

1872. They are the parents of Caroline Early, born July 12, 1896; Susie J., born August 3, 1899, Arthur Lee, born April 21, 1903; George Sanders, born December 20, 1906; Perry Owen, born May 8, 1909, and Richard John Scott, Jr., born October 26, 1915.

Mr. Scott's Cherokee name is Noxie, and he belongs to the Bird Clan. He is a farmer near Sallisaw. He has the peculiar quality of being able to acquire any ordinary piece of property and by living on it for a short time, transform it into the semblance of a park. He is a member of the Methodist Church, South; the Ancient Order of United Workmen, and Woodmen of the World fraternities. He organized the Eastern Emigrant and Western Cherokees, and is their attorney in fact in their suit for the removal of restrictions and other incumbrances upon the allotted lands of the tribe, and is still prosecuting this case. He is a teetotaler in regard to the non-use of intoxicants and tobacco.

Scudder, Nellie V. (See Daniel)—William Henry Harrison Scudder, born in Georgia March 8, 1841. Served the confederacy in Co. B, Cobb's Legion, Georgia Cavalry. He married February 16, 1869 Margaret Josephine Garmany born in Forsythe County, Georgia September 25, 1850. He died August 2, 1911. They were the parents of Ida Josephine, deceased; Addie Elizabeth married Thomas McKinney Price; Laura Kinney, married Dr. Oliver W. Farrar and James Jasper Gaskey; Mary Emma married David Clinton Hall and William Sherman Moore; Gordon Hampton; Newton Garmany; Margaret Lillian married J. W. Bishop; Nellie Vinita; Annie Clark married C. Earl Woodward; William Henry Harrison; Julia Inez, married Henry J. Witz and Lewis Blackburn Scudder.

Shoemake, Mrs. Nannie B. (See Grant and Foreman)—Nannie B., daughter of Joseph Martin and Susan Francis (Foreman) Lynch, was born at Webbers Falls, and in the Female Seminary at Tahlequah, Oklahoma. She married Thomas H. Shoemake.

Susan Francis, daughter of Johnson and Elizabeth B. (Mann) Foreman, was born August 26, 1847; married May 23, 1866 John Raymond, a native of Cuyahoga County, Ohio. He died November 27, 1873. She married December 23, 1874, Joseph Martin Lynch, born February 2, 1839. He was first lieutenant of Company "D", First Cherokee Mounted Rifles, under Captain James M. Bell and Colonel Stand Watie. He was afterwards first lieutenant in Captain Clement Vann Roger's Company. He was elected Senator from Canadian District on August 6, 1877, and again on August 1, 1887; and was elected Circuit Judge of the Southern Judicial Circuit of the Cherokee Nation August 6, 1883. And in 1889 he was elected to the Supreme Bench. He died January 14, 1890. He was the father of Mrs. Nannie B. Shoemake.

Shanahan, Mrs. Jennie (See Ghigau, England and Hildebrand)—Genevieve, daughter of James Franklin and Mary Jane (England) Williams was born in Delaware District December 18, 1868. Educated in the Cherokee Public Schools and Female Seminary. She married February 17, 1885 Timothy Deneen, son of Patrick and Margaret (Deneen) Shanahan, born April 21, 1863 in Minnesota. Mr. Shanahan is a well to do farmer in Craig County, his post office being Vinita. He is a first cousin to Governor Deneen of Illinois.

Mrs. Shanahan has one full brother, Joseph Lowrey Williams; one full sister, Mrs. Martha Jane Sanders. Mr. and Mrs. Shanahan have six living children: Margaret Christine Johnson, born May 26, 1888; Jennie Josephine Couch, born May 16, 1896; Timothy Lloyd, born March 27, 1902, Lenora Catherine, born September 1, 1907; Benjamin Tillman, born November 24, 1910 and John Doran Shanahan, born October 21, 1912.

Sharp, Mary Elizabeth (See Grant)—Mary Elizabeth Sharp, born at Chelsea April 2, 1892. Educated at Chelsea and Female Seminary.

Calvin Coker, born July 16, 1850. Married Elizabeth Bullett. She died May 14, 1891 and he married November 22, 1891 Mary Eliza Wimley nee Couch, born January 30, 1861. Calvin and Elizabeth (Bullette) Coker were the parents of Nancy Ann Coker, born at Coody Bluff April 16, 1873, educated in that vicinity. She married September 30, 1888 John M. Sharp, born January 13, 1862 in Ellis County, Texas. She died January 26, 1917. They were the parents of Mary Elizabeth, Burr Wilson and William Calvin Sharp.

Miss Mary Elizabeth Sharp is the great great granddaughter of John Rogers, last Principal Chief of the Western Cherokees.

Skinner, Mrs. Heber (See Grant and and Ghigau)—John Brewer married Elizabeth Taylor, and their son George Washington Brewer married Cherokee Ratliff, and they were the parents of Nannie Ethel Brewer, born February 20, 1859. She married February 18, 1883, John Martin, son of Joseph and Martha (Fields) Riley, born January 16, 1851. Mrs. Riley died April 22, 1909. They were the parents of Mattie Riley, born July 25, 1880, at Tahlequah and she was educated at the Female Seminary and Howard Payne College, of Fayette, Missouri, graduating from the latter institution. She married at Vinita March 11, 1902, Heber Skinner, and they are the parents of Mary Pauline, born October 5, 1905; and Louis Farley Skinner born July 23, 1907. Mary Pauline Skinner is attending Lenox Hall School in St. Louis, Missouri.

Mr .and Mrs. Skinner are members of the Methodist church, and he is one of the most prominent of cattle men in northeastern Oklahoma.

Sloan, James E. (See Ghigau)—James Ellis, son of Edward E. and Naomi (Cole) Sloan born January 7, 1894, educated in Delaware District and Male Seminary. Married at Claremore December 1, 1917 Gillie May, daughter of John M. and Mary C. (Roper) Carroll, born March 24, 1898 in Delaware District, educated at Big Cabin. They are the parents of: Percilla May, born August 25, 1918; Naomi Caroline, born March 1, 1920 and Dorris Louise, born June 12, 1921. Mr. Sloan enlisted in the world war September 3, 1918 and was mustered out January 7, 1919.

Thomas Martin Roper married Marcella Fernandes Townsend, their daughter. Mary Caroline Roper married John M. Carroll and they were the parents of Mrs. Gillie May Sloan.

Sloan, Samuel J. (See Ghigau)—Samuel John, son of Edward Estel and Naomi Ann (Cole) Sloan, born March 1, 1889, educated at Vinita. Married at Vinita October 13, 1908 Ruth, daughter of Charles and Elizabeth McKissick. They are the parents of: Samuel Floyd, born July 3, 1909 and Charles Herbert Sloan, born March 3, 1916. Mr. Sloan is an electrician, but is at present farming near Big Cabin.

Deborah Starr, married Richard Newland and William Harvey Sloan. Her son Edward Estel Sloan married Naomi Ann Cole and they are the parents of Samuel John Sloan.

Smith, Mr. W. F.—Lucy, daughter of Louis and Harriette(Thorpe) Daugherty, born in Johnson County, Kansas August 27, 1859. Married Febraury 22, 1876 W. F. son of J. J. and Jane Smith.

They are the parents of: Hattie Jane, born July 23, 1877; Lucy F., born December 23, 1882; William L., born July 8, 1887; Louis E., born December 1, 1895. He was a private in Co. K, 56th Infantry from July 19, 1918 to July 4, 1919. Discharged at Camp Pike July 9, 1919 and David C, born February 25, 1901. Mr. and Mrs. Smith are farmers, near Adair.

Smith, Mrs. R. A. (See Duncan, Ross and Downing)—Nannie Vinita West, born September 20, 1871, was educated in the Female Seminary. She married January 1, 1891, Henry Clay Cochran, born December 12, 1872. They were the parents of Sallie Pearl Cochran, born September 18, 1892, and Henry Clay Cochran, born September 21, 1901; he married on April 24, 1920, Willie Louise Ross, born January 25, 1902. They are the parents of Keller Mozelle Cochran, born August 16, 1921.

Mr. and Mrs. Henry C. Cochran were divorced and Mrs. Cochran married on December 24, 1904, R. A., son of James and Rachel Smith, born May 10, 1872, in Scotch County, Indiana. They are the parents of Luvenia N., born May 13, 1907; Robert West, born April 3, 1909, and Max Carlton Smith, born April 18, 1911. Mrs. Smith's Cherokee name is Waty. She is a member of the Baptist church. R. A. Smith was elected County Commissioner of Mayes County on November 5, 1918, and on November 2, 1920.

Charles Duncan, a Scotchman, married, about 1874, Dorcas, a full blood Cherokee woman of the Deer Clan. Their son, John, married Elizabeth Abercromby a native of Tennessee. The Abercrombys belonged to the ancient nobility of Stirling County, Great Britain, where their county seat was Airthy Castle, and even as late as 1883, the family owned 15,265 acres of land in England. The head of the family in 1916 was Lord George Abercromby. John and Elizabeth (Abercromby) Duncan were the parents of

Mahala Duncan, born June 21, 1821; and married July 18, 1838 James Smith West, born May 24, 1817 in Alabama. He died in 1865, and she died November 27, 1879. Their son, Walter Adair West, born April 29, 1841, married August 15, 1863 Sallie Elizabeth Wright, born April 1, 1844. She died February 5, 1890. They were the parents of Mrs. Nannie Vinita (West) Smith.

Southerland, Arabella (See England)—David England married Susan A. Conner, and they were the parents of Arminda England, born November 25, 1831. She married William England, Isaac Scrimsher, and Elias Jenkins. She died December 27, 1879. Her children by her first husband were as follows: Mary Arabella and Abram Meek. Arabella was born September 9, 1857 in Delaware District; educated in the Cherokee National schools; and married in March 1874 on Beatty's Prairie. Enoch S. Southerland

Their children all died in infancy. Her sister, Sophronia, married Zan Main, Lewis Rogers, and Dr. J. A. Nolan. Her half sister, Ida J. Jenkins, married John Wesley Harris and her half brother Henry, married Delilah Arms. Mrs. Southerland's father, Isaac Schrimsher, was first married to Ruth Fields.

Mrs. Southerland is a member of the Presbyterian Church. Her Cherokee name is Okewat.

Sunday, Edward—Edward, son of William and Mary Sunday, was born in 1856 and on account of the Civil war he was not able to attend school but being a man of more than ordinary natural intelligence he has not only made a splendid citizen but has accumulated a comfortable competency. He married in 1872 Nancy, daughter of Mr. and Mrs. Thomas Wilkerson. They were the parents of: Jennie, born September 5, 1875; William E., Lulu, married John Asa Polson; Edward A., married Rebecca Bible. Edward Sunday's second wife was Margaret Sanders nee Garner and their daughter Ellen Sunday was born October 2, 1888 and married Charles P. Morgan. Not having had the opportunity of gaining an education himself, Mr. Sunday has given each of his children a splendid education; all being graduates. His son, William E., is one of the most substantial business men in Rogers County. Edward Sunday was elected a member of the Cherokee National Council, August 1, 1887 and was later the first Mayor of Oolagah in which town he now resides.

Stokes, Elizabeth Thatcher (See Foreman) Herschael Vetran, son of Jeremiah Young and Mary Malinda (Walker) Stokes, born Sept. 21, 1882 educated in Cooweeescoowee District. Married at Muskogee June 28, 1909 Elizabeth, daughter of Joel T. and Mary L. (Kitchum) Thatcher, born in Delaware District November 12, 1883 and educated at Vinita. They are the parents of: Herschael Owen, born April 2, 1910 and Darwin Clark Stokes, born September 13, 1911.

Minerva Jane Taylor married Robert Wesley Walker and they were the parents of Mary Malinda (Walker) Stokes. Robert Wesley Walker was elected Judge of Going Snake District March 24, 1879, appointed Attorney General of Cherokee Nation December 20, 1892 and elected Chief Justice of Cherokee Nation in November 1893.

Joel Mayes Thatcher, brother of Mrs. H. V. Stokes was a soldier in the world war.

Starr, Mrs. Fannie (See Grant and Ghigau)—Ellis Bean, son of Thomas and Catherine (Reese) Starr, was born May 10, 1843. He served the Confederacy in Captain John Porum Davis' company, and later in Captain Ephriam Martin Adair's company. He married February 28, 1877, Fannie Griffin, born January 1, 1855. He died April 24, 1896. They were the parents of Thomas Bruce, born September 15, 1885; Mary Bunch, born November 3, 1888; Eliza Cherokee, born December 15, 1890, and Margaret Bird Starr, born February 5, 1895.

Mr. Starr was at the time of his death, credited with being one of the wealthiest cattle men among the Cherokees. One of his odd habits was that if he met and stopped to talk with anyone for any length of time, he invariably got off his horse, often saying that the horse needed rest.

Sixkiller, Samuel (See Grant, Foreman and Sixkiller)—Gu-o-tsa Smith, a half breed Cherokee woman of the Paint Clan, married Sixkiller, a full blooded Cherokee. Their son, Red Bird Sixkiller, married Pamelia Whaley, a White woman, and they in turn were the parents of Samuel Sixkiller who married Fannie Foreman; and Lucas Sixkiller who married Emma Blythe.

Samuel and Fannie (Foreman) Sixkiller were the parents of Samuel Rasmus Sixkiller, born February 13, 1877, and graduated from Carlisle University in 1895.

Lucas and Emma (Blythe) Sixkiller were the parents of Mattie B. Sixkiller, born December 14, 1874, in Delaware District; and she married on June 26, 1911, Samuel Sixkiller.

Absalom Blythe married Mary J. Millsap, and they were the parents of Emma Blythe who married Lucas Sixkiller.

Thomas Foreman married Elizabeth Chicken and they were the parents of Fannie Foreman, who married Samuel Sixkiller.

Red Bird Sixkiller was a man of sterling personality; he was born in the old Cherokee Nation. When he was about eleven years old he attended a school some seven miles from his home and had to go over a point of Lookout Mountain to get to school. It was necessary for him to start before daylight to get to school before it opened. One morning he was going over this point of Lookout Mountain when he heard a panther scream in a nearby thicket; no habitation was near and having heard that panthers would not come near fire, he gathered some pine knots and struck a fire with a piece of flint and steel, made a fire and stood around it until daylight when he deemed that he would be secure from the panther. He was a First Lieutenant, and generally commander of Troop L of the Third Indian Home Guard, in which his son Samuel was also a member. After the Civil War Red Bird Sixkiller became, on June 6, 1872, Judge of Saline District and on the succeeding November was promoted to the Supreme Bench of the State.

Samuel Sixkiller partook of many of the traits of his father, was pleasant, agreeable and fearless. He was elected High Sheriff of the Cherokee Nation in November 1875, and again in November 1877. After the expiration of this office he was chosen on account of his capability, Captain of the Indian Police for the Indian Territory, and served in this capacity until his death.

Starr, Eldee (See Ghigau and Adair)—George Harlan Starr married Nannie Bell and they were the parents of Ezekial Eugene Starr who married Margaret, the daughter of Caleb and Lucinda (Griffin) Starr. Ezekial E. and Margaret Starr were the parents of Charles Lucien, Eldee, Mary Bell, Joel Mayes, Caroline Lucinda, Trixie, and Ezekial Blake Starr. Charles Lucien Starr married Amy Benge; Mary Bell Starr married Albert Moore Campbell; Joel Mayes Starr married Caroline Ferguson; and Caroline Lucinda Starr married James Robert Wyly. Eldee Starr was educated in the Female Seminary and the Forest Park University in St. Louis, Missouri, graduating from both institutions. She is a member of the South Methodist Church, and the Eastern Star Chapter. Her Cherokee name is Se-hah-yah Noxie. She is a clerk in the office of the Superintendent for the Five Civilized Tribes, doing extra work at Tahlequah.

The Starrs of Oklahoma are descendants from those of Chester County, Pennsylvania, formerly of Oldcastle, Ireland, and a little earlier from England. The name is derived from the Norman word Starri, which means hawk.

George Harlan Starr, the grandfather of Miss Eldee, had a peculiar habit of filling a corn crib that stood in the woods back of his farm, and giving general notice to the neighborhood that they might use this corn gratis, in case of necessity; and when the crib became depleted he refilled it.

Ezekial Starr, the father of Miss Eldee, was elected Senator from Flint District in August, 1883; and elected Treasurer of the Cherokee Nation December 23, 1891. He made the Strip Payment of over seven million dollars to the Cherokee Nation; and one of the proud heritages of the family is the fact that no one ever accused him of appropriating a dollar of this or any other fund placed in his trust.

Starr, Trixie (See Adair and Ghigau)—Trixie, daughter of Ezekial Eugene and Margaret E. Starr, was born at Tahlequah June 24, 1892; and was educated in Tahlequah, Oklahoma. Her Cherokee name is Ah-na-hi Noxie. She is a member of the Methodist, church and the Eastern Star order. She is a clerk in the office of the Commissioner of the Five Civilized Tribes.

Ezekial Eugene Starr was the son of George Harlan and Nannie (Bell) Starr. George Harlan Starr, the Grandfather of Miss Trixie was the son of Kaleb and Nannie (Harlan) Starr.

Ezekial Eugene Starr was treasurer of the Cherokee Nation and Senator from Flint District, as will be shown in the official lists of this volume.

Springston, John L. (See Foreman)—Anderson Springston was born October 13, 1814, and married Sallie Elliott. He died March 15, 1866, and Mrs. Sallie Elliott died in December 1876. Their son John Leah Springston was born October 13, 1844, he served in Company I, Third Indian Home Guard during the Civil War. He married March 8, 1885 Alice Carey Springston nee Gray, who was born December 31, 1861 in Georgia. Their son William Boudinot Springston was born October 28, 1886 in Tahlequah; was educated in the National schools of the Cherokee Nation. He married at Fort Smith, Arkansas, December 25, 1915, Lula, daughter of R. M. and Mary Ida Osborn, and was born September 29, 1886, in Johnson County, Arkansas.

Mr. and Mrs. William B. Springston have one son, William B. Junior, born October 15, 1918. Mr. Springston is a banker and a member of the Presbyterian church. He is affiliated with the Masonic fraternity.

Render, Mrs. Doctor Alonzo C. (See Ward and Downing)—Jimmie Abercrombie, daughter of James Abercrombie and Lucy Ann (Clerk) Duncan, was born near Afton October 30, 1879. She married in Kansas City October 22, 1919, Dr. Alonzo C., son of Joshawa and Martha Forsythe Render, born August 8, 1876 in Louisville, Logansport Co., Ky. He was educated in Louisville Ky. and is a graduate from Northwestern University, Chicago. Dr. and Mrs. Render are members of the South Methodist church, and he belongs to the Masonic fraternity.

Parlette, Mrs. Snowden (See Oolootsa)—James Columbus Morris married Ellen F. McElrath, and they were the parents of Mary Trimble Morris, born at Fort Gibson October 5, 1882, and was educated at Tahlequah and the Female Seminary. She married at Tahlequah May 15, 1898, Snowden, son of Franklin and Alice Parlette, born Jan. 29, 1880 in Wamego, Kansas. He was educated in Baker University and graduated from Harvard University. They are the parents of John, born April 17, 1911, and Snowden Parlette, born Jan 16, 1918. Mr. Parlette is in the wholesale book and stationery business in Oklahoma City. He is a thirty-second degree Mason and one of the most substantial business men of Oklahoma City. Mrs. Parlette is a member of the Daughters of Revolution and Daughters of the Confederacy.

Ellen F. McElrath was born March 18, 1846 in Knoxville County, Tennessee. She married in 1865, Major James Columbus Morris born July 13, 1843. Major Morris was an officer of the Confederacy in his native State. He died in 1895.

Caldwell, B. M. (See Grant and Duncan)—Benjamin Morris, son of John Johnson and Caroline Maria (Thompson) Caldwell, was born August 9, 1889. Educated in the Cherokee Public schools, and married Cora Bell Smith.

Caroline Maria Caldwell, nee Thompson, was born July 18, 1860. She married January 12, 1879 John Johnson Caldwell, born February 27, 1849, in Pendleton County, Kentucky. She died February 2, 1894. They were the parents of Benjamin Morris Caldwell.

Barbre, Mrs. Jesse A. (See Ghigau, Foreman and Adair.)—Phoeba Montana, daughter of Thomas Lafayette and Josephine (Pace) Rider, was born December 28, 1885, and educated at the Female Seminary. She married Jesse Albert Barbre, and they are the parents of William Albert Barbre. Mr. Barbre is one of the most prominent contractors and insurance men of the State, his office being at Muskogee. He was the campaign manager for Governor J. B. A. Robertson and helped to pile up the largest majority that had ever been secured for any Governor in the State of Oklahoma.

Ackley, Mrs. Levi (See Grant and Ghigau)—Mary Jane, daughter of John Joshua and Minerva Elizabeth (Lillard) Patrick, was born March 12, 1868. Educated in the Cherokee National school, and married January 20, 1887 Levi Ackley, born June 28, 1861, in Bruce County, Ontario, Canada. They are the parents of Oliver Frederick, Madge Elizabeth, Lee Etta, and Edna Almira Ackley. Mr. and Mrs. Ackley are residents of Muskogee.

Barker, William Henry (See Ghigau)—Elvira, daughter of Jesse and Sallie (Starr) Mayfield, married William Henry Barker; and they were the parents of Sallie Belle Barker who married Henry Forney Nicholson. Mr. Barker was elected a member of Council from Canadian District in 1889, and was chosen by that body as their speaker. He was elected Circuit Judge of the Southern Judicial Circuit of the Cherokee Nation in 1891, serving for a four-year term. He is at present a retired farmer at Muskogee.

Starr, A. N. (See Ghigau, Sanders, Adair and Gosaduisga)—Edward Bruce, son of Joseph McMinn and Delilah (Adair) Starr, was born April 2, 1850, and married Rachel Pauline Henry. His death occurred on May 18, 1882. They were the parents of: Ida Martha, born October 6, 1874; Archibald Noon, born June 3, 1877, and Susan Delilah Starr, born April 3, 1880. The middle name, Noon, in Mr| Starr's name is from the Cherokee name "noona", meaning potato. He married in July, 1897, Mary Pauline Terrell, born April 13, 1880; and they were the parents of: Thomas Andrew, Toney Bryan, and Edward Bruce Starr. Mrs. Mary Pauline Terrell, born April 13, 1880; and they were the parents of Thomas Andrew, Toney Bryan, and Edward Bruce Starr. Mrs. Mary Pauline Starr died, and Mr. Starr married Margaret Lelia Coffee, and they were the parents of Henry Lane, Samuel Boyd, and Eliza Pauline Starr. Mrs. Margaret Lelia Starr is now deceased, and Mr. Starr and his children live near Claremore where they conduct a farm.

Crittenden, Walter S. (See Ghigau, Sanders, Adair and Gosaduisga)—Walter Starr, son of George Washington and Martha Jane (Starr) Crittenden, was born in May, 1868; educated in the Male Seminary. He married Rachel P. Vann, nee Henry, daughter of Archibald and Polly (Sanders) Henry. Her first husband was Edward Bruce Starr, born April 2, 1850, and died April 18, 1882. Mr. and Mrs. Crittenden are members of the Methodist church and are farmers near Claremore, Oklahoma.

Craig, A. H. (See Ghigau and Conrad)—Nancy Jane, daughter of Daniel and Annie (Ballard) Ratliff, born February 21, 1874, married September 3, 1891 Amon Hale Craig, born February 15, 1858 in Jackson County, Tennessee. They are the parents of Ada Starr, born August 15, 1893; Amon Hale, born June 6, 1896; Clifford Cravens, born August 2, 1898, and Warren Reed Craig, born October 22, 1899.

Evans, Marie (See Grant)—Susan Ola, daughter of William H. and Hannah (Davis) Corn, was born July 24, 1876, and married William E. Evans. They were the parents of Marie, born August 5, 1894, and Leander Keys Evans, born April 6, 1897.

Dunham, Mrs. Elleanor O. (See Grant, Ghigau, Foreman and Conrad)—Martha Adair, daughter of George Washington and Cherokee (Ratliff) Brewer, married Richard Fields Benge, and they were the parents of Georgia Alma, Elleanor Osceola, Lelia Leon, Dora, and Senora Sammie Benge.

Eleanor Osceola Benge, born January 18, 1889, married Cleveland Bunham and lives near Adair, Oklahoma.

Keys, Dennis B. (See Grant, Ghigau, Foreman, Adair and Riley)—Dennis Bushyhead, son of James McDaniel and Nancy Jane (Mayes) Keys, was born July 15, 1878, and married Nannie Ethel, daughter of John Martin and Nannie Ethel (Brewer) Riley, born October 15, 1883. They are the parents of Gordon Lindsay Keys.

Charlotte, daughter of Reverend Jesse and Eliza (Wilkerson) Bushyhead, married George Washington Mayes, and they were the parents of Nancy Jane Mayes who married James McDaniel Keys.

George Washington, son of John and Elizabeth (Taylor) Brewer, married Cherokee (Ratliff) and they were the parents of Mrs. Nannie Ethel Riley.

Gulager, F. W. (See Oolootsa)—Martha Lucretia, daughter of Martin Mathew and Elizabeth Hunt (Gunter) Scrimsher, was born December 9, 1845. Educated in the Cherokee Nation, and married January 27, 1869, Frederick William Gulager, born March 14, 1844 in Washington, District of Columbia. They are the parents of William Martin, Christian, Mary Elizabeth, Henry Gunter, and John Delancy Gulager.

Mary Elizabeth Gulager was born April 27, 1880 and graduated from the Female Seminary May 25, 1900.

Gaines, Dr. J. H. (See Ghigau and Oolootsa)—Cynthia, daughter of Thomas Jefferson and Jennie (Taylor) Pack, married Daniel Harmon and they were the parents of Emma Henrietta, Jennie, Laura, Elizabeth, McGilbra, Benjamin Franklin, and Lena Modesta Harmon.

Lena Modesta Harmon was born October 23, 1885, and married Dr. John Harris Gaines, born April 29, 1870 in Washington County, Arkansas. He graduated from the Memphis Hospital Medical College in 1906, and is at present practicing medicine at Warner, Oklahoma. They are the parents of Daniel Benjamin, born September 26, 1910; Helen Elizabeth, born September 8, 1912 and Dorothy Gaines, born April 28, 1916.

Dr. Gaines was Court Clerk of Muskogee County from 1917 to 1919.

Duncan, John E. (See Grant, Downing, Ghigau and Duncan)—John Ellis, son of Reverend Walter Adair and Martha (Wilson) Duncan, was born March 26, 1861; educated in the Cherokee Nation and married January 1, 1890, Susan Elizabeth, daughter of James and Catherine (Emory) Carselowry, born July 30, 1873. They are the parents of: Ellis Crowell, Robert Stewart, Kathleen Nana, Albert Carselowry, Walter Abercrombie, Johnnie May, and Charles D. Duncan.

Mr. Duncan was elected Clerk of Tahlequah District in 1893 and was the last elected High Sheriff of the Cherokee Nation.

Cunningham, A. B. (See Grant, Ghigau, Ooloötsa, Adair and Duncan)—Andrew Bell, son of Jeter Thompson and Keziah Camille (Moore) Cunningham, was elected Sheriff of Tahlequah District in 1897, and upon the death of Chief William C. Rogers, he was appointed by the Interior Department as Chief of the Cherokee Nation.

Jeter Thompson, son of Andrew Brown and Mariah (Lynch) Cunningham, was born December 1, 1843. He was First Lieutenant of Company A, First Cherokee Mounted Volunteers, under Captain Hugh Tinnin and Colonel Stand Watie. He married on June 13, 1866, Keziah Camille, daughter of Elijah and Jamima (Landrum) Moore, born February 12, 1849. He was elected Councilor from Delaware District August 2, 1869, and August 4, 1873; elected Clerk of the same District August 2, 1875. He moved to Tahlequah where he was for several years Executive Secretary to the Chief.

Croom, Elmer C. (See Grant and Ooloötsa)—Lorella Coleman, born March 14, 1858, married September 17, 1874 Joseph Thomas Smith, born December 10, 1846 were the parents of Jessie Morton Smith, born June 22, 1875. She married December 27, 1894, Isaac Newton Croom, born August 12, 1867 in Madison County, Tennessee. They were the parents of Joseph Newton, Marvin Earl, William Lee, Elmer Clement, and Lula Irene Croom. The Crooms are residents of Muskogee.

Cowan, Alex, Jr. (See Grant)—Alexander Clingan, son of Andrew Finis and Elizabeth Jeanette (Clingan) Sowan, was born October 7, 1861, and married December 30, 1886, Lillie Bone Crawford, born April 24, 1871 in Ellis County, Texas. They were the parents of Stella Cherry, Terry Crawford, Louie Alexa, Georgia Hardy, Alexander Finie, and Andrew Jasper Cowan.

Martha Jane, daughter of William and (Fields) Blythe, married Alexander Adam Clingan, and they were the parents of Elizabeth Jeanette Clingan who married Andrew Finis Cowan.

Martin, Frank G. (See Ooloötsa and Ross)—Frank Garland, son of William Hercules and Jennie (Lowrey) Martin, was born in Tahlequah District on August 9, 1884.

Jennie, daughter of Henry and Mary (Parris) Lowrey, married August 6, 1875 John Hubbard, born May 24, 1849. He died March 11, 1880. She married on September 9, 1883, William Hercules Martin, born March 9, 1855. By her first marriage she had two children, Joanna and Mary Hubbard; and by the second marriage her children were, consecutively: Frank Garland, Eugene Warren, William Henry, Susie Lowrey, Teresa Josephine, Ellen Cordelia, Jennie, and Sequoyah Raymond Martin.

Horn Mrs. Eliza (See Grant and Foreman)—Eliza Jane, daughter of Johnson and Elizabeth (Foreman) Proctor, was born April 8, 1851, and married March 18, 1878 William H. Horn, born December 24, 1854. He died March 6, 1897. They were the parents of Dora May, Mary Elizabeth, Margaret, Charles Thomas, and George Hoolie Horn. Mrs. Horn owns and conducts a farm near Big Cabin, Oklahoma.

Rider, Thomas L. (See Ghigau, Foreman and Adair)—Thomas Lafayette, son of Charles Austin Augustus and Mary Ann (Bigby) Rider, was born April 12, 1856; and married September 29, 1878 Josephine Pace, born March 22 ,1861, in Cherokee County, Georgia. They are the parents of Ola, Mary Angeline, Ruth Belle, Phoeba Montana, Mittie Earl, Roscoe Conklin, Milton Clark, Iva Josephine, Cherokee Augusta, and Anna Monetta Rider.

Mary Ann, daughter of Thomas Wilson and Margaret Catherine (Adair) Bigby, was born November 6, 1834, married Charles Austin Augustus Rider, born November 28, 1830. She died in 1861; and he died December 24, 1901. They were the parents of Thomas Lafayette Rider.

Mr. Rider was elected Representative from Adair County in the first, second ,and fourth Legislatures; and was elected Senator from the 28th District for the seventh and eighth Legislatures.

Richards, R. D. (See Grant)—Mary, daughter of John W. and Ellen (Thompson) Wilson, was born January 2, 1857, and married July 1, 1875 Willis Taylor Richards, born June 6, 1847 in Lauderdale County, Mississippi. He served in Company B, 46th Texas Infantry in the Confederate Service. He was elected a member of Council from Tahlequah District in 1903. They are the parents of Roderick Dhu Richards, born July 5, 1884, and graduated from the Male Seminary June 10, 1903. He married Grace Roper Wallace who graduated from the Female Seminary on June 9, 1903.

Rogers, Mrs. Bertha (See Ooloootsa, Ross and Gosaduisga)—Lewis Ross, son of Florian Haraden and Fannie (Vann) Nash, was born April 15, 1864, married May 15, 1890 Emma Beck, born January 21, 1871. She died May 5, 1896. They were the parents of Fairy Fawn and Edgar Ross Nash. Mr. Nash married November 24, 1897 Bertha McSpadden, born January 16, 1877, and they were the parents of Dorothy Margaret and Clarence E. Nash. Mr. Nash died and Mrs. Nash married Hugh Morgan Rogers, born Sept. 16, 1864. They were the parents of one child and Mr. Rogers is now deceased. Mrs. Rogers is a resident of Fort Gibson, Oklahoma.

Scott, Mrs. Walter (See Grant and Ross)—Nannie Ratliff born December 29, 1856, married Thomas Fox French, and they were the parents of Bernice Martha French who married James Milner Howard; Margaret French who married Charles McDonald, and Nannie French who married Lewis G. Girtley Sleeper. Thomas Fox French died and Mrs. French married Rufus Wyatt McCracken and they were the parents of Walter Scott McCracken. Mr. and Mrs. McCracken were divorced and she married Walter Scott. Mr. and Mrs. Scott are well-to-do farmers near Fort Gibson, Oklahoma.

Hickey, Thomas P. (See Grant and Ghigau)—Lucinda, daughter of John and Margaret (Bean) Gott, was born August 12, 1854. Married Thomas Preston, son of Henry H. and Rachel Jane (Fields) Hickey, born September 15, 1853. They were the parents of Nannie Belle, Edna Earl, George Henry, Nellie Myrtle, Rachel Cherokee, William Bevelly, John Walter, Richard Carter, and Mary Lucinda Hickey.

Head, W. F. (See Ward)—Mary Ward, daughter of Robert Andrew and Frances M. (Ward) Hosey, was born September 4, 1882; married Walter Ford Head. Mr. Head is an experienced linotype operator, living at Muskogee.

Harnage, C. D. (See Grant, Ghigau, Sanders and Gosaduisga)—William Wilson, son of George and Nannie (Mayfield) Harnage, married Jennie, daughter of John Shepherd and Elizabeth P. (Fields) Vann, and they are the parents of Richard Vann and Charles Dana Harnage.

Hanks, Mrs. Mary E. (See Downing, Oolootsa)—Robert Taylor, son of Robert Taylor and Margaret Ann Ward (Morgan) Hanks, was born January 9, 1840. He married December 22, 1890 Mary Elizabeth, daughter of Robert and Jennie (Wright) Wafford, born September 7, 1864, and they were the parents of Roberta Inez Hanks.

Mr. Hanks was appointed Circuit Judge for the Southern Circuit of the Cherokee Nation, May 3, 1878, and was elected to this position on August 5, succeeding. He was elected a member of Council from Canadian District in 1879 and 1881; and was elected Clerk of the Council in 1885.

Sanders, Lewis J. (See Sanders)—Samuel D., son of Andrew Sanders, married Nancy Jane Gafford and Martha Ann Harris. Samuel D. and Nancy Jane Sanders were the parents of Lewis Johnson Sanders, born December 12, 1872, and married March 3, 1891 Mary Ellen Parson, born April 30, 1875. They were the parents of Thomas Johnson, Charlotte Mable, William F., and Ora E. Sanders.

Peck, A. D. (See Foreman)—Rachel Barnes, born November 27, 1834, married Jenkins Whiteside Maxfield. She died in 1861, and he died in 1877. They were the parents of Mary Maxfield, born September 1, 1856, and married October 12, 1873 James M. Milner, born December 11, 1847, in Greencastle, Indiana. They were the parents of William Jenkins, Florence Elizabeth, John Gage, Josephine Elmira Milner. Mr. Milner died, and Mrs. Milner married on March 4, 1894 Adolpha D. Peck, born Jan. 25, 1863 in Mohaska County, Iowa. They are the parents of Charles Everett, born January 25, 1896, and Jesse Bushyhead Peck, born June 23, 1901.

Floreain H. Nash, (See Oolootsa)—Lucy Morgan, daughter of Andrew Lewis and Cherokee America (Morgan) Rogers, was born June 6, 1857 and married November 11, 1874, Floreain Haraden Nash, born November 28, 1837 in New Orleans, Louisiana. She died December 28, 1890.

Mr. Nash was Grand Master of the Indian Territory Grand Lodge A. F. A. M. in 1885, 86 and 87. Mr. and Mrs. Nash were the parents of Fannie Elizabeth, Floreain Haraden, Frank Ayer, Lucy Morgan, Corinne, Hilda, and Edwin Otto Nash.

Mayes, W. L. (See Downing, Oolootsa, Adair and Ghigoneli)—William Lucullus, son of Samuel Houston and Martha Elizabeth (Vann) Mayes, was born February 6, 1874; educated in the Male Seminary. He married January 8, 1901, Mary Llewellyn, daughter of Gideon and Mary Llewellyn (Payne) Morgan, born June 23, 1877 and graduated from the Female Seminary June 28, 1894. They are the parents of Martha Llewellyn Mayes, born August 24, 1902. Mr. Mayes is prominently identified with real estate and oil activities in Muskogee, Oklahoma.

Morgan, Lelia (See Oolootsa)—Gideon Morgan, born April 3, 1851, married June 25, 1874, Mary Llewellyn Payne, born Oct. 1, 1855 in Sebastian County, Arkansas. Mr. Morgan was elected Senator from Tahlequah District August 5, 1901; and was elected a member of the State Legislature from Mayes County in the fourth and seventh Legislatures. Mr. and Mrs. Morgan were the parents of Houston Mayo, Mary Llewellyn, Martha Lelia, Margaret Elizabeth, Amanda Payne, Sallie Mayo, and Nellie Payne Morgan.

Miller, William W. (See Grant and Halfbreed)—Joseph Gambold, son of Avery Vann and Nannie (Ward) Miller, was born July 16, 1828. Married March 1, 1850, Jennie, daughter of James and Matilda (Benge) Buffington, born February 10, 1833. He was a member of Company E, First Cherokee Mounted Rifles, under Captain Joseph F. Thompson. Mr. Miller died February 26, 1897. They were the parents of William Walter Miller, born July 20, 1853. He married March 16, 1884 Mary Francis Bishop, born April 7, 1863 in Decater County, Indiana; and they were the parents of Charles William, Henry Mayes, Joseph Gambold, David Andrew, Matilda Ann, and John Buffington Miller.

Tyner, Mrs. George M. (See Sanders)—Nancy, daughter of George O. Saunders and Jennie Tail married Jefferson Tyner and their son George Marion Tyner was born April 10, 1883. Graduated from Male Seminary May 29, 1907. Married at Vinita June 16, 1916 Ethel, daughter of John Pleasant and Martha J. Marshall, born March 5, 1889 in Texas. They are the parents of George Marion Tyner, Jr. born August 24, 1917.

Mr. and Mrs. Tyner are members of the Methodist Church. They taught school several years before their marriage.

Shimoon, Dr. George (See Oolootsa)—Gertrude Whitman, daughter of Connell and Florence (Nash) Rogers, was born July 11, 1879. Educated in the Cherokee public schools and Female Seminary, graduating from the latter on June 24, 1897. Marmried at Fort Gibson March 24, 1908, Dr. George Shimoon, D. D. S., born Dec. 18, 1878, in Burmia, Persia. Educated in Missionary College and Knox College, Gilesbeury, Illinois and graduated from Indiana Dental College. They are the parents of Miriam Shimoon, born August 14, 1918. Mrs. Gertrude W. Shimoon died April 11, 1906.

Alberty, Mrs. Charlotte (See Grant and Downing)—Charlotte Ann, daughter of Ellis B. and Charlotte (Eaton) Towers, was born September 30, 1854. She married January 1, 1872, Jacob U., son of John D. and Jennie (Dougherty) Alberty, who was born March 20, 1854. Mr. Alberty died October 27, 1906. They were the parents of John Henry, born February 20, 1874; Nancy Jane, born March 17, 1876, and died August 25, 1893; Joshua Homer, born April 24, 1878; Flora Etta born April 4, 1885; William Towers, born November 25, 1887; Arthur Burr, born January 19, 1891. Joshua Homer Alberty married Eva Henry, and he died August 28, 1907. They were the parents of Gladys May Alberty, born November 20, 1905. Mrs. Eva Alberty lives in Colorado.

Mrs. Charlotte A. Alberty's Cherokee name is Ah-ni-wake, and she is a member of the Presbyterian church.

One daughter, Lola Beatrice Alberty born April 18, 1882, died Oct. 24, 1883. John Henry Alberty died July 13, 1914. Joshua Homer died Aug. 28, 1907.

Brown, Mrs. W. L. (See Downing)—Leona Deen, daughter of Clement and Rebecca Caroline (Bryan) Hayden, was born August 18, 1886, at Chouteau. She was educated in her native village and Stephens College, Columbia, Mo. She married at Chouteau March 5, 1905, William L., son of Wifford C. Brown and Sarah Francis Brown, born July 7, 1883, in Anderson County, Ky. He was educated in his native county and Danville, Ind., and graduated from Waddy College, Waddy, Ky. They are the parents of Eloise Caroline, born Feb. 8, 1906, Charles Hayden, born Aug 5, 1907 and William L. Jr. born Sept. 1, 1909,. Mr. Brown is a business man in Oklahoma City and they are members of the Methodist church.

Clement Hayden, born March 20, 1846, in Benton County, Arkansas. Married March 7, 1869, Rebecca Caroline Bryan, born Jan. 30, 1850. She died July 9, 1917. They were the parents of Mrs. Leona D. Brown. Clement Hayden died May 2nd, 1917.

Gilliland, Mrs. Homer F. (See Turner)—Anna Laura, daughter of William and Annie Laurie Turner, was born October 14, 1890. She graduated from the Female Seminary May 27, 1909; and married Jan. 18, 1918, Homer F. Gilliland, born Jan. 12, 1885, in Johnson County, Ark. He was educated in Ft. Smith Public Schools and University of Arkansas. Mr. Gilliland is a banker in Ft. Gibson, Okla.

William Hendricks, born August 25, 1795 in North Carolina. Married in September 1816 Susannah, born in 1798. He died January 21, 1868 and she died January 25, 1868. They were the parents of Hendricks, born May 24, 1819. Married George Peacheater and Felix Riley and they were the parents of Mrs. Susan R. Gourd.

Rhomer, Mrs. May (See Grant and Oolootsa)—May, the daughter of Calvin Jones and Emma Walker (McCoy) Hanks, was born at Webbers Falls July 19, 1872; was educated at Webbers Falls and the Female Seminary. She married April 15, 1888, Frank Rhomer, born Jan. 6, 1863 in New Orleans, La. They are the parents of Emma Nora, born February 2, 1889; May Frances, born November 17, 1891; Margaret Bell, born April 2, 1894; and Fannie Charlotte Rhomer, born March 20, 1896. The Rhomers are farmers near Webbers Falls.

Margaret Belle Rhomer married Robert Preston Vann, Jr. of Webbers Falls. Mr. Vann was killed in action Sept. 12, 1918 in France. His body was sent back home to his wife Margaret Belle and was buried by her in the National Cemetery at Ft. Gibson, Aug. 10, 1921.

May Frances Rhomer married Charles F. Ross, grandson of Andrew Ross. Their children are Charles Rhomer Ross, born at Webbers Falls; Beulah May Ross, born at Webbers Falls February 5, 1918 and Robbie Belle Ross born at Webbers April 6, 1919. They now live in Sapulpa, Okla.

Calvin Jones, son of Robert Taylor and Margaret Ann Ward (Morgan) Hanks, was born February 8, 1836, and married April 11, 1861 Emma Walker McCoy, who was born April 3, 1841. He was a private in Captain John S. Vann's Company, and in Captain Samuel Gunter's Company in the Confederate army. He was elected Councilor from Canadian District August 5, 1867; and Senator from the same District August 6, 1887. He died May 1, 1879.

Mrs. Emma Hanks, nee McCoy died February 8, 1900. They were the parents of Mrs. May Rhomer.

Shaw, Mrs. Walter W.—Mary, daughter of John and Nellie (Conkle) Bullette, was born at Claremore October 24, 1886. She was educated in Lexington, Missouri Baptist Female College and Lindenwood Seminary, St. Louis, Missouri, graduating from the latter institution. She married in 1906 at Claremore, Walter W., son of Charles and Ida (White) Shaw, born November 21, 1880 in Owego, New York. They are the parents of Walter W., Jr. born April 17, 1907, and Martha Helen Shaw, born August 7, 1908. Mr. and Mrs. Shaw are members of the Presbyterian church. He is a Mason. He was elected County Judge of Rogers County, November 5, 1912 and is at present interested in the Exchange Trust Company of Tulsa.

John Bullette, the father of Mrs. Shaw was elected a member of the Cherokee National Council on February 28, 1876; was elected Clerk of Cooweescoowee District August 1, 1881, and Solicitor of the same District on August 5, 1895.

Captain White Eyes, Head War Chief of the Delawares and personal friend of George Washington was an ally of the Americans in the revolutionary war. He was the father of Nee-what-wes, who married Ah-ke-che-lung-un-a-qua and their daughter Elizabeth married William Connor of Noblesville, Indiana, and they in turn were the parents of Eliza Connor who married Pendoxey or George Bullette, a renowned and intrepid trader whose operations extended as far west as the Rocky Mountains. In the first decade of the eighteenth century he established and was chief of Delawaretown on Spavinaw Creek, from which Delaware County, Oklahoma, derived its name. Chief Bullette commanded the Delawares at the battle of Claremore Mound in 1818. John, the son of George and Eliza (Connor) Bullette, was the father of John and George Bullette, the latter and surviving brother is the present Chief of the Delawares.

Adair, Oscar F. (See Adair, Ghigau and Foreman)—Oscar Fitzaland, son of John Thompson and Penelope (Mayfield) Adair, was born March 8, 1848. Married February 3, 1875 Mary Catherine, daughter of Augustus and Mary Ann (Bigby) Rider, born April 20, 1859. They were the parents of Mary Louvenia; Wenona; William Penn; Sarah Ruth; John Lafayette; Rose Ada; and Walthal Corrigan Adair.

John Adair, a Scotchman, married Gahoka's full-blood Cherokee of the Deer Clan. Their son, Walter, commonly called "Black Watt" Adair, was born December 11, 1783, and married May 15, 1804 Rachel Thompson, born December 24, 1776. He died January 20, 1835; and she died April 22, 1876. Their son John Thompson Adair was born December 22, 1812, and married January 30, 1840, Penelope Mayfield, born May 12, 1824. He died December 23, 1891. They were the parents of Oscar Fitzaland, who was elected Judge of Sequoyah District in 1885 and 1887; and Commissioner of Sequoyah County in 1907.

Trout, George W. (See Ward and Ghigau) —George Washington, son of Samuel and Louisa (Ward) Trout was born in Georgia, September 15, 1847. He served the Confederacy during the Civil War under Cap- and Joseph Franklin Thompscon. He is at present (1921) one, of not over twenty survivors, of the Confederate Cherokee Brigade of over three thousand veterans. He married in December 1868 Mary Eaton, born in 1847. They were the parents of: Sallie Emma, born May 4, 1870, married William Baker; Elizabeth, born December 1872; married Charles S. McComb; Logan John, born April 8, 1876; and James Morton, born April 21, 1883. Mrs. Mary Trout died April 25, 1883. He married July 29, 1884, Martha Ann, daughter of Richard Taylor and Sarah Elizabeth (Day) Parks, born March 26, 1885 In Bradley County, Tennessee. They are the parents of: Henry Ward, born July 29, 1886 Isaac Day, born February 16, 1888; Georgia Ann, born December 24, 1890, and Creed B. Trout, born September 27, 1892; he enlisted in the World War at Vinita, September 22, 1917; was assigned to Battery A, 319th Field Artillery, 82nd Division. Was in the actions of Toul Sector, August 16 to 28; St. Mihiel, September 12 to 16; Meuse-Argonne, September 26 to November 11, 1918; Army of Occupation to May 12, 1919. Was discharged at Camp Pike, Arkansas, May 24, 1919. He is entitled to wear a gold service chevron.

Henry Ward Trout married Stella Lauchner and they were the parents of Leta B. Trout. Mr. Trout's second wife was Eva Ketchum, and they are the parents of Lucile and Argyle Woodrow Trout.

George W. Trout is an Odd Fellow and Mason, and has been for many years a merchant at Big Cabin.

Pierce, Mrs. James M. (See Cordery)—Nancy Jane, daughter of Albert and Louisa (Cordery) Anderson, was born January 1, 1882; and married August 23, 1896, James Madison Pierce, born December 13, 1877, in Hall County, Georgia. They were the parents of Gertrude, born June 3, 1897; Mark, born November 7, 1898; James Clayton, born February 7, 1902 and Earl B. Pierce, born February 8, 1905.

Mr. Pierce is one of the wealthiest cotton farmers of the Muskogee-Fort Gibson section, owning and operating hundreds of acres of valuable land, and several cotton gins.

Abbott, Mrs. John H. (See Ward and Foreman)—Martha Alice, daughter of John Wesley and Mary Elvira (Ward) Holland. was born January 28, 1862; married at Stilwell June 21, 1884; Robert Early, born February 16, 1858, in Gilmer County, Georgia. He died August 27, 1906. They were the parents of Dora, born March 16, 1886; John William, born June 22, 1887 Mary Angeline, born February 1, 1889; Martha Lou. born September 17, 1893, and died November 7, 1911; Robert Ross, born October 14, 1895; Ida Belle. born February 3, 1898, and died September 23, 1920; Mollie Elmira.

born October 24, 1900, and Dovie Early, born November 3, 1904.

Ida Belle Early married Herbert Line and they had two children: John Wesley, born May 1, 1918, and Martha Line, born July 3, 1919.

Mrs. Martha Alice Early married John H. Abbott, born in 1847 in Florida. His first wife was Ellen Isabel, daughter of Robert Early and Minerva Jane (Taylor) Walker, born in 1867, and died in 1898. John H. and Ellen Isabel Abbott were the parents of Ethel Louisa, born October 5, 1875; Eugene Michael, born November 25, 1877; John Wesley, born September 28, 1879; Caroline Minerva, born December 23, 1880; Senora Julia, born November 20, 1882; Fannie Edith, born February 15, 1885; Mae Lillian, born September 20, 1887; Butler Lafayette, born July 24, 1889; William Ghormley, born October 20, 1893, and Jennie Ellen Abbott, born November 13, 1895.

Woodall, Leander (See Woodall)—Leander, son of James Tuck and Elizabeth (Perdue) Woodall, was born in Delaware District February 8, 1876, educated at Ketchum. Married in Arkansas, February 22, 1906 Jessie, daughter of John L. and Malinda Berry. Mr. Woodall is a farmer near Ketchum, he is a member of the A. H. T. A. which means that he is a supporter of good citizenship.

Peebles, Mrs. James L. (See Grant and Foreman)—Nannie, daughter of Spencer and Margaret (Proctor) Shelton was educated in Tahlequah District and Female Seminary. Married at Tahlequah, James L., son of Mr. and Mrs. Peebles.

They are the parents of: Joseph Lawrence, James Shelton, Charlotte May, Edgar Vann, Vera E., Robert, Virginia and Spencer Peebles. Mr. Peebles is farmer near Tahlequah, is a member of the Woodmen of the World. He was elected County Commissioner of Cherokee County September 17, 1907.

Margaret, daughter of Johnson and Elizabeth (Foreman) Proctor was born May 1, 1846 and married Spencer Shelton. She died April 14, 1885.

Cochran, Mrs. Ned A. (See Grant)—Willie Penn Adair Martin, born at Greenbriar, August 1, 1879, educated locally and at Female Seminary. Married at Pryor, July 24, 1905 Ned Adair, son of Richard and Mary Cochran, born August 20, 1880, educated at Orphan Asylum. They are the parents of Mary Virginia, born July 26, 1910 Cherry Adair, born January 5, 1912; Joseph Martin born February 28, 1915 and Robert Edward born March 4, 1917. Mrs. Cochran belongs to the Deer clan and her Cherokee name is Coluna.

Joseph Lynch Martin, born in Georgia, August 20, 1820. Married July 21, 1870 Jennie Harlin, born April 8, 1849 at Tahlequah. He died November 9, 1891. They were the parents of Mrs. Ned A. Cochran.

LaHay, Margaret Russell (See Grant)—Joseph Martin, son of John and Helen Marr (Martin) La Hay, was born August 27, 1864 at Boggy Depot in the Choctaw Nation. He married November 10, 1886 at Richmond, Missouri, Annie Russell, born December 12, 1864, at Wishaw, Scotland. They were the parents of Margaret Russell La Hay, born July 26, 1890, at Claremore. She was educated in the Claremore public schools, Drury College, Springfield, Missouri, and Mary Baldwin Seminary, Staunton, Virginia. Mrs. La Hay is a member of the Presbyterian church and is at present a clerk in the Union Agency at Muskogee.

Joseph Martin La Hay, the Father of Miss Margaret, was a man of splendid intellect, pleasing personality, and genial character. He held at different times the highest offices in both the Masonic and Knights of Pythias fraternities. He was Clerk and Senator of Cooweescoowee District.

Williams, Sarah B. (See Cordery)—Sarah, daughter of William and Susan (Vance) Burgess, was born near Pryor, Saturday December 19, 1857. Educated in the Cherokee Public Schools. Her first husband was John McPherson and her second husband, whom she married in 1893 was William, son of Edward Williams. Mr. and Mrs. Williams are the parents of Willie Jane, and Annie Gladys Williams.

John, son of William and Mary (Vann) Burgess married Mary Smith and they were the parents of William Burgess who married Susan Vance.

Cox, J. D. (See Duncan)—James Duncan, son of Zeno and Rebecca (Duncan) Cox born August 7, 1886, educated in the Cherokee national schools. Married at Vinita September 27, 1913 May C., daughter of William and Minerva Shockey. They are the parents of: Riley, born March 11,

1914; Cora, born June 14, 1915; James Duncan, born June 17, 1917 and Lucile Cox, born March 3, 1919. Mr. Cox is a farmer.

Sanders, Sequoyah (See Grant, Downing, Ghigau and Sanders)—Sequoyah, the son of Thomas Didymus and Joanna (Pettit) Sanders, was born at Braggs in 1888. He was educated in the public schools of the Cherokee Nation; married at Independence, Kansas Cora Wyatt. They are the parents of Coaone and Georgia Sanders.

Mr. and Mrs. Sanders are members of the Nazarene Church.

Wahyah, brother of Mr. Sanders, married Willie Hawkins; and his brother Joseph Emmet Sanders married Jennie Riley. The latter couple are the parents of Thomas Didymus, Anna May and Emeline Sanders.

Frank Pettit married Mary Beck and they were the parents of Mrs. Joanna (Pettit) Sanders.

Chandler, Vann S. (See Ward)—Vann S., son of Burgess Gaithor and Annie Eliza (Gunter) Chandler, born August 20, 1882, educated at William Halsell College, Vinita. Married at Vinita, June 1, 1912, Maude A. daughter of L. A. and Annie E. Williams. They are the parents of: Lawrence Stuart, born April 20, 1913; Wilma Gawdin, born July 25, 1915 and Burgess Chandler, born February 12, 1920. Mr. Chandler who is a younger brother of Hon. Thomas A. Chandler, Congressman from the First District of Oklahoma, is a dealer in hay, grain and farm machinery.

Sanders, Mrs. Dollie (See Foreman and Go-oo-du-i-sga)—Dollie, daughter of Charles and Mary Ellen (Thornton) Cochran, born August 23, 1877. Married at Tahlequah in 1897, S. L. Sanders. They are the parents of: Murrell, Charles, Haskell, and Ross Saunders.

Mary Ellen, daughter of Amos and Minerva (Foreman) Thornton was born February 14, 1857. Married June 15, 1876 Charles Cochran, born in 1845. He died March 16, 1889 and she died February 16, 1899. They were the parents of Mrs. Dollie Saunders.

Coats, Mrs. Susie D. (See Grant and Hildebrand)—Susie Dora, daughter of James and Emily (Harlin) Sunday was born in Cooweescoowee District September 12, 1876, educated in Female Seminary. Married September 11, 1893 James, son of James McKenzie and Annie C. (Spears) Coats, born April 1, 1866. They are the parents of: Jennie Bessie, born January 25, 1894; James McKenzie, born September 20, 1896; Elmer Earl, born September 4, 1901; Capitola Wyly, born February 15, 1903; Lulu May, born January 20, 1906 Eugene, born October 15, 1908; Belva Lockwood, born June 8, 1910 and David Coats, born March 3, 1912. Mr. Coats died December 15, 1915. Mrs. Coats manages a farm near Pryor. Miss Jennie Bessie Coats was elected Court Clerk of Mayes County November 5, 1918 and November 2, 1920. James McKenzie was educated in Pryor and Agricultural College at Stillwater. Capitola Wyly is a member of the 1922 High School class at Pryor.

Lucinda, daughter of Samuel and Catherine (Hildebrand) Martin married Joseph Spears and they were the parents of Annie C. Spears wife of James McKenzie Coats.

Alberty, Arthur (See Downing and Grant) —Arthur Burr, son of Jacob U. and Annie Charlotte (Towers) Alberty was born January 19, 1894.

Sallie Wright married Moses Alberty and their son John D. Alberty married Jennie Buffington. They were the parents of Jacob U. Alberty, who was the father of Arthur Burr Alberty.

Wilson, Mrs. DeWitt (See Grant, Downing, Adair, Daniel and Wilson)—DeWitt Clinton, son of Anderson Springston and Nancy Catherine (Daniel) Wilson was born January 7, 1859. Educated in the Cherokee National schools. Married June 25, 1885 Mary Ellen, daughter of Dr. Walter Thompson and Mary Buffington (Adair) Adair, born November 1, 1864. She graduated from the Cherokee National Female Seminary June 29, 1881 and Kirkwood 1883. They are the parents of: Lelia Stapler, born September 26, 1889, and Clinton Wilson, born January 5, 1893. Lelia Stapler Wilson, who is an accomplished musician, is the wife of Leon L. Leslie.

Nannie Catherine Daniel, born January 12, 1835, married December 23, 1858 Anderson Springston Wilson, born in 1830. They were the parents of DeWitt Clinton Wilson. Anderson Springston Wilson died December 26, 1865. Mrs. Nannie Catherine Wilson married December 14, 1872 Henry Clay Barnes. She died December 10, 1889.

Joseph Martin, born near Charlotteville, Virginia in 1740, married Susannah Fields nee Emory, and they were the parents of John Martin, who married Nannie McDaniel. Martha, commonly called "Patsy" the eldest daughter of John and Nellie Martin, married George Washington, son of Walter, called "Black Watt" and Rachel Thompson Adair. Dr. Walter Thompson Adair, son of Walter and Rachel Adair, married Mary Buffington, daughter of Walter Scott, commonly called "Red Watt" and Nannie (Harris) Adair and they were the parents of Mrs. DeWitt Clinton Wilson.

Carden, William T. (See Hildebrand)—Barbara Hildebrand born in Tennessee January 13, 1828. Married Robert Woodard from whom she was divorced and then married William Longknife. Both her husbands were Cherokees. William and Barbara Longknife who had been living on Honey Creek in Delaware District joined the California argonauts in 1850. The caravan in which they embarked consisted of about seventy-five persons, one-third of whom were Cherokees, among whom were: O. H. P. and George W. Brewer, James S. Vann, Martin Matthew Scrimsher, John Hildebrand, John Wolf, John W. Candy, Buffalo, Richard R. Keys, Thomas Fox Taylor, Return Jonathan Meigs, Mr. and Mrs. Longknife. They started from the mouth of Verdigris, going northwest over the old California trail until they intercepted the Evans route which extended westward from Westport. They traveled six months before reaching their destination. R. J. Meigs who was a son-in-law of Chief John Ross died near Salt Lake, Utah on August 6, 1850. Mary Jane, the eldest daughter of William and Barbara Longknife was born while enroute on September 18, 1850. She is now living in Honolulu. The second daughter, Anna Diane Longknife was born in California June 23, 1859. She was educated in and graduated from the Sacred Heart Convent in Honolulu, Hawaii, in 1875. Married in Honolulu June 24, 1884 John Joseph Carden. He died September 15, 1915. They were the parents of: William Thomas, born March 3, 1888; John Joseph, born February 25, 1890; Edward Walter, born October 21, 1892, and Mae Mary Anna Carden, born December 19, 1895. William Thomas Carden graduated from the University of California with the B. L. degree and from Harvard as a L. L. B., and is an attorney. 10 and 11 Brewer Bldg., Honolulu, Hawaii. He married March 23, 1916 Florence Gavin Cassidy; their daughter, Florence Aline Carden was born March 12, 1917. John Joseph Carden graduated from the University of California with the B. S. degree and from John Hopkins University Medical Department. He is a Captain in the Medical Corps of the United States Army and is stationed at Carlisle Barracks, Pennsylvania. Edward Walter Carden graduated from the University of California. Married August 10, 1918 Hazel Hunt Vinton and their daughter, Barbara Vinton Carden was born March 28, 1921. Mae Mary Anna Carden graduated with the A. B. degree from Vassar and is living with her mother in Honolulu.

Barbara (Hildebrand) Longknife's mother was named Diane Graves instead of Susannah Graves, as given in the Hildebrand family.

Tyner, Aaron (See Carter)—James Fields, son of Lewis and Sallie (Parris) Tyner, married Quatie Charley and they were the parents of Delilah, born June 3, 1883; Aaron, born December 22, 1886; James, born March 26, 1888; Ralph, born February 19, 1891 and Minnie Christine Tyner. Aaron Tyner was educated in the Male Seminary. He married Susie Fields. He is a member of the Independent Order of Odd Fellows fraternity and is a substantial farmer near Sperry.

Lewis Tyner was born in 1837. Married Sallie, daughter of Moses and Mary (Langley) Parris, born in 1883. She died March 15, 1868 and he died October 10, 1894. They were the parents of James Fields Tyner.

Markham, B. H. (See Ghigau)—Bettie Ann, daughter of James Walker and Lucy Cordelia Skinner, was born April 12, 1888. Married at Clarksville, Arkansas, December 23, 1909 Baird Hackett Markham, born March 28, 1887, in Decatur, Texas. They are the parents of Jewell Marie, born August 17, 1911 and Baird Hackett, son of Winston Baird and Ada Hackett Markham, born April 12, 1916. Mr. Markham was educated in the Denison High School and the Texas Christian University of Waco, graduating from both. He is the owner of the Markham Motor Company of Oklahoma City. Mr. and Mrs. Markham are members of the Presbyterian church. He is affiliated with the Elks, Odd Fellows, Woodmen and Knights of Pythias. Is a member of the Kiwanee, Golf, Automobile, Lakeside Country, Add Centarian, National Guard, National Highway, Oklahoma City Chamber of Commerce, Clubs. He has been President of the Oklahoma Automobile Dealers Association, President of the National Guard Club and Colonel of the Oklahoma National Guards by virtue of which he was acting Adjutant General of Oklahoma.

Lucy Cordelia, daughter of Judge George Washington and Louisa (Spriggs) Parks, was born June 12, 1852. Married September 26, 1876 James Walker Skinner, born June 15, 1844 in Kentucky. He was Captain of Company A, 2nd Kentucky Cavalry under Colonel Basil Duke. Mrs. Skinner died July 29, 1896 and he died July 11, 1921. They were the parents of: Rosa Louisa, Willie, Thomas Fox, Morgan Desha, Galooga Theresa, Bettie Ann and Mary Ann Skinner. Rosa Louisa Skinner married Elizur B. Neville. Willie Skinner married Silas M. Meeks. Galooga Theresa Skinner married Seth Reed. Bettie Ann Skinner married B. H. Markham and lives in Oklahoma City.

Archer, Mrs. Thomas B. (See England)—Anna Bell daughter of Abram and Alta Berilla (Schrimsher) Meeks was born near Vinita November 20, 1878. Educated in Worcester Academy. Married April 22, 1897 Thomas B. Archer son of Thomas and Fannie Archer, born Aug. 29, 1873 in Vernon County, Navada, Mo. They are the parents of Irra, born July 10, 1898; Otto B., born July 9, 1900, Fannie B., born February 13, 1902; Thomas B., born November 15, 1903; Abram born November 4, 1905 and Morrill Archer, born March 22, 1908. Mr. and Mrs. Archer are members of the Baptist Church. He is a produce merchant at Vinita. Ina, Otto B. and Fannie B. Archer are graduates from Vinita High School. Ima married at Vinita January 17, 1920 Harold E. Boggs. Otto Archer married at Vinita July 19, 1921 Gertrude Braden.

Owen, Mrs. Thomas H. (See Grant)—Louise Scott, daughter of James Orval and Mary E. (Davis) Hall, was born near Vinita, August 23, 1877. She was educated at Vinita and Harrell Institute, and is a graduate from the latter institution. She married November 2, 1898, Luman Franklin Parker, born August 23, 1872, in Phelps County, Missouri. He died Aug. 14, 1912. Mrs. Parker married Thos. H. Owen March 12, 1916. They are residents of Oklahoma City.

Eaton, Mrs. Rachel Caroline (See Ward)—Nannie Elizabeth Williams was born April 8, 1851. Married May 17, 1868 George Washington Eaton. He had served the confederacy in Company B, Morgan's Battalion, Texas cavalry under Captain Boggs and Lieutenant Charles Morgan. Mrs. Eaton died September 21, 1896.

Mr. and Mrs. Eaton were the parents of: Rachel Caroline, James Calvin, Martha Pauline and John Merrit Eaton. Rachel Caroline Eaton graduated from the Female Seminary in 1888 and from several other institutions of higher education and is the possessor of the degree of Mistress of Arts. She married James Alexander Burns, from whom she was divorced. She was the author of the scholarly "John Ross and the Cherokee Indians". She was elected Superintendent of Public Instruction of Rogers County in 1920. James Calvin Eaton is a prosperous farmer near Oolagah. Martha Pauline Eaton graduated from the Female Seminary in 1897 and married James Morning York who was elected Assessor of Rogers County in 1918. John Merrit Eaton graduated from the Male Seminary in 1899.

Payne, Marble Lewis—Marble Lewis, son of William and Nancy Payne was born in 1850 in North Carolina. He married at Tahlequah in 1904 Mahala Wilson. They were the parents of Emma, Lula, Charles and William Payne. Mr. Payne's children by his second marriage are Frank, Albert and Mary Payne.

Mr. Payne is one of the progressive farmers of the Tahlequah vicinity, is a member of the Independent Order of Odd Fellows and has been a member of the local school board several times. His Cherokee name is Lu-ie-us-te-na and he belongs to the Wolf Clan.

William Payne, the son, is a Spanish-American war veteran.

Carter, Charles D. (See Carter and Riley)—Charles D., son of Captain Benjamin Wisner and Serena J. (Guy) Carter, was born August 6, 1868. Married December 29, 1891 Ada Gertrude Wilson. She died January 19, 1901. They were the parents of:

Estella LeFlore, Lena Cecil, Julia Josephine and Benjamin Wisner Carter. Mr. Carter's second wife was Mrs. Cecil Jones, nee Whittington.

Nathaniel Carter, a Virginian, came to the Cherokee Nation and married a Cherokee. Their son David was born in 1802. He married in 1829 Jennie, daughter of Richard and Diana (Campbell) Riley, born in 1807. He was clerk of the Council in 1839. Elected Associate Justice of the Supreme Court in 1842; he resigned that post and was elected Superintendent of Schools in 1843. Elected Editor of the Cherokee Advocate in 1849 and Chief Justice of the Cherokee Nation in 1851, also a member of the board of directors of the Cherokee Seminaries in the same year. Elected a member of the Cherokee Senate (Committee) from Tahlequah District August 6, 1855. Elected Associate Justice of the Supreme Court in 1857. He died February 1, 1867 and Mrs. Carter died March 1, 1867.

Benjamin Wisner, son of David and Jennie (Riley) Carter was born January 5, 1837. Graduated from the Male Seminary in October 1856. He married Nannie Elliott and they had one son, John Elliott Carter. Mrs. Carter died and when the civil war began he joined Brewer's company and later raised and was elected captain of a company. He married in 1865 Serena Josephine Guy, a member of one of the most distinguished Chickasaw families. After the civil war he made his home in the Chickasaw Nation where he was honored with practically every office except Chief, which could only be held by a native Chickasaw.

Charles D. Carter, son of Benjamin Wisner and Serena Josephine Carter has been a representative in Congress from Oklahoma since statehood.

Gatlin, Mrs. Emma Nora (See Grant and Oolootsa)—Emma Nora, daughter of Frank and May (Hanks) Rhomer was born February 2, 1889 and educated at Webbers Falls and Female Seminary. She married August 1, 1907 Samuel Bell Maxey, son of James and Matilda (Yearby) Gatlin, born May 26, 1887. They are the parents of: Frank Rhomer, born August 19, 1908; Helen Charlotta, born January 23, 1910; John McCoy, born September 20, 1911 and died in infancy; Calvin James, born July 16, 1913; Virginia May, born June 13, 1915; the twins, Maxine and Allene, born May 11, 1920. Allene died in infancy and Willie Patricia Gatlin, born November 20, 1917. Mr. and Mrs. Gatlin are residents of Webbers Falls.

James, son of James and Lucy (McCoy) Gatlin married Matilda Yearby and they are the parents of Samuel Bell Maxey Gatlin.

Calvin Jones Hanks married Emma Walker, daughter of John Lowrey and Charlotte (Ratliff) McCoy and they were the parents of Mrs. May Rhomar, Mrs. Maggie McEachen, Mrs. Emma Branan, Miss Daisy Hanks and Calvin Jones Hanks, Jr.

Adair, Mrs. Luther H. (See Ghigau and Adair)—Lillie M. daughter of Allen and Lou (Fisher) Waldrop was born in Texas Friday Dec 8, 1865. Married Nov. 17, 1883 Luther Martin, son of Captain Ephriam Martin and Sallie (Starr) Adair, born in Flint District April 30, 1859. He died January 3, 1908. They were the parents of. Sarah Leola, born June 3, 1885; William Luther, born Feb. 16, 1887; Mary, born Aug. 5, 1889; Myrtle Lucinda, born December 11, 1891; Altie, born Nov. 4, 1894; Collie Bessie, born Jan. 1, 1897; Emmet Marshall born July 11, 1899; Nona Bertha, born Sept. 17, 1901; Arnie C., born Feb. 23, 1904 and Howard Ugean Adair, born Jan. 31, 1908. Sarah and Mary attended the Female Seminary. William L. was educated in Male Seminary and spent nine months in the service of the World War. Mrs. Adair is a member of the Church of God.

Hefflefinger, Mrs. Eliza C. (See Rogers)—Eliza, daughter of Jesse and Elizabeth Cochran was born in the Cherokee Nation in 1853. At the time that she would be in school the Civil War with all of its malevolence broke over the Cherokee Nation and it is only due to her native ability that she is now widely known for her general intelligence and information. She married in 1872 Greenville Pace Hefflefinger. He was one of the most progressive farmers of his community and always kept thoroughly abreast with the period. They were the parents of Joseph and Fannie Hefflefinger. Mrs. Hefflefinger is a member of the Presbyterian church.

Adair, Levi (See Grant and Adair)—George M. Adair married Catherine Fields and their son Henry Ganoe Adair was born August 10, 1865. Married in May 1884 Caroline Bunch, born April 13, 1863. He was elected sheriff of Illinois District August 5, 1895. He died. They were the parents of: Araminta, born May 10, 1885; George, born May 24, 1887; John Bell, born June 12, 1894; Catherine, born August 9, 1897; Levi, born June 9, 1900 and Zola B. Adair, born June 10, 1905.

John Adair, a Scotchman married in 1789 Ga-ho-ka, a full blood Cherokee of the Deer Clan. Their son Samuel Adair married Mary Hughes. He was elected sheriff of Flint District in 1857 and 1859. Elected judge of the same District 1867, 1873, and 1877. He died February 17, 1879. His wife had died in 1874. They were the parents of George M. Adair who married Catherine Fields. (See sketch of his brother, George Adair)

Ogden, Mrs. D. T. (See Ward and Adair) —Jessie Curtis Abney, born July 24, 1900 in Afton Delaware District; educated at Afton and took a business course at Coffeyville Kansas; graduate of the Afton High School. Married Sept. 14, 1919 at Independence, Kansas, D. T. Ogden, son of W. A. and Julia Ogden. Mr. Ogden is assistant cashier of the First National Bank of Afton.

John Adair, a Scotchman, married Gahoga, a full blood Cherokee of the Deer Clan. Their son Samuel married Edith Pounds; they were the parents of: Rachael Pounds Adair, who married Rev. James Jenkins Trott, a Methodist minister. Rev. and Mrs. Trott were the parents of: James Cicero Trott, who was generally known by his Indian name of Osceola, born April 6, 1839 in Woodbury, Tennessee, married March 1, 1886 Madora Stover, born Jan. 25, 1852 In Delaware District. She is the daughter of John Henry Stover, died March 31, 1865.

James C. and Medora Trott are the parents of: Birdie Adair, born Nov. 25, 1871; educated in Vinita public schools and Worcester Academy, from which she graduated; she taught school several years and married Sept. 6, 1895 Robert A. Abney, born Aug. 15, 1869 in Saline county, Illinois. Until his death he was in the mercantile business at Afton; he died July 16, 1906 and Mrs. Birdie A. Abney died Sept. 3, 1919; Eugene Homer and Willie A. Trott.

Jennings, Landrum Crittenden (See Grant, Foreman and Conrad)—Caroline, daughter of John and Nellie (Martin) Agnew, married Anderson Landrum Crittenden Jennings, and they were the parents of Landrum Crittenden Jennings, born in 1876; he was educated in Worcester Academy and the Male Seminary, being a graduate from the latter institution. He married in 1899 Jananna, daughter of James Franklin and Ruth Ellen (Martin) Benge, born in 1880. She was educated in Vinita. They are the parents of Clara May Jennings, born June 21, 1900, at Chelsea. She graduated from the Muskogee Central High School in 1919, and is at present a stenographer in the office of the Superintendent of the Five Civilized Tribes. Miss Jennings, as well as her parents, brothers and sisters, are members of the Methodist Church.

Susan Henrietta, daughter of James and Delilah (Fields) Foreman, married Anderson Benge, and they were the parents of James Franklin Benge who married Ruth Ellen Martin.

Arning, Mrs. Susan E. (See Ghigau)—Susan Ellen, daughter of James and Amanda Walker (Martin) was born June 17, 1876. Educated in the Cherokee Public Schools and Female Seminary. Married January 13, 1894, William Ulyssus Hill, born October 22, 1866 in Douglas County, Kansas. They were the parents of Harrietta Ruth Hill, born October 8, 1897. Mrs. Hill secured a divorce and married on January 13, 1906, Mr. Arning. They are the parents of Floyd born August 22, 1912 and Ancel Arning, born September 29, 1914.

Mr. and Mrs. Arning are farmers and are members of the Holiness Church.

Woodward, John S.—John S. Woodward, son of Jackson and Lizzie (Smith) Woodward, was born in Oklahoma in 1861; married in Oklahoma in 1875, Mary Fondren. They have one son, David 22 years old, who spent two years in France in the World War, where he was wounded and also gassed. John S. Woodward is a member of the Wolf Clan, a member of the Methodist church and a farmer near Tahlequah.

Whiteaker, Grace E.—Grace Elizabeth Barks, daughter of Edward and Victoria (Fields) Barks was born January 17, 1900 at Vinita, and educated in the Cherokee schools; she married at Vinita, May 25, 1917 Robert Whiteaker, son of William and Dorothy Whiteaker. Mrs. Whiteaker has one sister and one brother living. The sister Hazel Willie married Floyd Edward

Smith and is living in Roswell, N. M. They have three children, Levina, Nanetta and Nedowa; her brother is Miles Mathew Barks.

Wright, Jesse E.—Son of John R. and Charlotte C. (Whitmire) Wright was born Jan. 22, 1871 in Going Snake District; married in June 1892 in Adair county Mary E., daughter of Walter and Sally West. They are the parents of. Willie Cornelia, born April 3, 1898, and Sally born July 30, 1903. Mr. Wright was educated in the Cherokee schools, and spent two years at the Male Seminary. He is a farmer, successful and takes part in all movements for public welfare.

Wormington, Mrs. Minerva (See Ross)—Minerva, daughter of Isaac Alexander and Susannah Coody (Ross) Wilson was born at Tahlequah on Tuesday June 1, 1886. Educated in the Cherokee Public Schools and Female Seminary. She married in 1914 at Tulsa, Frederick Wormington and they are the parents of Lorine Wormington, age six. Mrs. Wormington's father was a gentleman of more than ordinary intelligence and her mother was a member of the distinguished Ross family.

Williams, Sarah Burgess—Daughter of William and Susan (Vance) Burgess was born at Pryor Creek, in 1857, married in the Indian Nation in 1893, William Williams, son of Elwood Williams. They are the parents of: Willie J. 26 years, and Annie Gladys age twenty two years. Mr. and Mrs. Williams are members of the Baptist church, and he is a member of the W. O. W.

Washam, Mrs. Rufus O.—Gertrude M., daughter of A. J. and Caroline (Tidwell) Gibbs, was born Dec. 9, 1898; educated in the Oklahoma Public schools; married February 19, 1914 at Pryor Rufus O. Washam, son of John T. and Alice Washam. They are the parents of: Mabel Evaline born May 18, 1915; Walsie Lorene, born Dec. 11, 1918. Mr. and Mrs. Washam are engaged in farming.

Boone, William Cecil (See Oolootsa)—Cecil William, the son of Alexander and Ora Cherokee (Nicholson) Boone, was born on Spencer Creek September 6, 1900; was educated in the public schools of the State. He is a member of Latter Day Saints Church, and belongs to the Independent Order of Odd Fellows.

Ora Cherokee, daughter of Richard Lee and Bidipher (Foulger) Nicholson, was born on Spencer Creek July 6, 1880; married December 22, 1897, Alexander Boone who was born March 22, 1875.

Maxfield, Stephen G.—Stephen G., the son of Jenkins Whiteside and Kate (Hastings) Maxfield, was born in 1873; was educated in the public schools of the Cherokee Nation. He married at Claremore in 1894, Ada, the daughter of Joseph Shockey. They are the parents of Grace, Cora, Pauline, Almeda, and Woodrow Maxfield.

Mr. and Mrs. Maxfield are members of the Methodist Church. He is affiliated with the Independent Order of Odd Fellows, and the Knights of Pythias.

Eddings, Americus—Americus, son of Jasper and Gertrude (Ross) Eddings was born in 1869 in Arkansas. Educated at Mountain Home, Arkansas. Married in Baxter County, Arkansas. Mary, daughter of Mr. and Mrs. Charles Meumer. They are the parents of Charles, Lawrence, Andrew, served twelve months in the World War and Jasper Eddings. Mr. and Mrs. Eddings follow the general Cherokee vocation of farming.

Ware, Mrs. David A.—Nancy (Martin) Rogers was born in the Saline District in 1848; married in 1869, David A. Ware. She is the mother of Bertha born in 1875, Martha born in 1877 and Thomas Rogers. Thomas L. Rogers was the first Judge of the Osages. Mrs. Ware is a member of the Christian church and a ceaseless welfare worker.

Webb, Maude Ella (See Cordery)—James Forrest Webb, born August 24, 1862, in Gwinnett County, Georgia, married January 21, 1882 Elizabeth Parker, daughter of Parker Collins and Elizabeth (Little) Harris, and they were the parents of Maude Ella Webb, born May 25, 1890. Miss Webb was educated at the Female Seminary; and is at present cashier in a drug store in Oklahoma City.

Smith, Mrs. Jasper E. (See Cordery)—Catherine Ann, daughter of John Parker and Sarah Elizabeth (Davis) Collins was born in Delaware District November 20, 1889, educated in the Cherokee National Schools. Married at Vinita, December 24, 1908, Jasper E. son of Charles and Levonia Smith. They are the parents of: Watie Dufferin, born October 18, 1909; Don Tate, born September 20, 1911; Pauline Ruth, born August 9, 1914; and Betty Imogene Smith, born July 15, 1920. Mr. Smith is a farmer and dealer in cattle and hogs near Ketchum.

Thomas Cordery married Susannah a full blood Cherokee of the Savannah Clan. Their son, Early, married Charlotte Berryhill and they were the parents of Nancy Angeline Cordrey who married Joseph Collins, a white man and they were the parents of John Parker Collins, born March 17, 1855, married November 4, 1888, Sarah Elizabeth Beck nee Davis, born in Kansas March 10, 1867.

Tucker, Levi—Levi, son of William Tucker, was married at Tahlequah in 1894 to Annie McKay, daughter of Alfred and Lucinda (Ketcher) McKay. They are the parents of: William, Ollie, Susie, Sallie, Eliza, Madison, Levi, and Mary Tucker. Mr. and Mrs. Tucker were educated in Tahlequah District and are representative citizens of Cherokee County.

Walkabout, Joseph—Joseph, son of Jennie (Hendricks) Walkabout was born near Tahlequah in 1880 and educated in that city. He married in Tahlequah in 1904 Mary Cordery, and they are the parents of: Jennie, Eliza and Josephine Walkabout. Mr. Walkabout is a splendid representative citizen, and has been Deputy Sheriff of Cherokee County.

Gritts, Ned—One of the prominent men of Northeastern Oklahoma is Ned, the son of John B. and Charlotte (Allen) Gritts, who was born in 1877 near Stilwell. He married Nannie Chooie, and they were the parents of Genevieve, born August 23, 1899; Nicholas born February 10, 1903, and Nancy born in 1905. Mrs. Nannie Gritts died and Mr. Gritts married at Fort Worth, Texas in 1907, Miss Leah, the daughter of Wallace Haney. Mr. Gritts was educated at the Male Seminary and Presbyterian Mission, graduating from the latter institution. He is a member of the Knights of Pythias and Independent Order of Odd Fellows fraternities. He was chief of police of Tahlequah from 1917 to 1919, and was deputy Marshall of Eastern Oklahoma from 1913 to 1919. He is a member of the Wolf Clan.

19'9. He is a member of the Wolf Clan.

Gish, Mrs. E. W. (See Oolootsa, Cordery, Adair and Gosaduisga)—Martin R. Brown, born February 27, 1858 at Fort Gibson. married May 9, 1888 Nannie C. McNair, born in 1866. They were the parents of Catherine Brown born in 1891 at Tahlequah, married in Oklahoma City in 1915, Emmett W. Gish. They are the parents of Dorothy Louise Gish, age five years. Mr. Gish is a merchant in Oklahoma City. Mr and Mrs. Gish are members of the Presbyterian church. Martin R. Brown, commonly called by his Cherokee name Tuxie, was a very prominent citizen of the Cherokee Nation. Elected clerk of the Illinois District in 1881; elected a member of the Board of Education of the Cherokee Nation in November 1886, and Superintendent of the Male Seminary in 1894. Mr. and Mrs. Brown are now deceased.

Swift, Frank T. (See Carter and Sanders) —Martha, daughter of LeRoy and Mary (Sanders) Tyner, married Frank Boyd Swift and they were the parents of Frank Tyner Switf, Benjamin W. Swift, and James French Swift.

Frank Tyner Swift was born March 5, 1867. Educated in Kansas; married December 30, 1890 Nellie Butler, born February 27, 1871, in Bourbon County, Kansas. They were the parents of Chrystal, born December 25, 1891; Frank Butler born June 20, 1894; and Mable Swift born July 6, 1896.

Frank Boyd Swift was a Captain in the Federal Army in Kansas, and was a pioneer newspaper man in that State. Frank Tyner Swift is the principal dealer in coal and ice in Muskogee.

Trott, Mrs. James Campbell (See Ward and Adair)—James Campbell Trott, born Apr. 6, at Woodburt, Tenn., educated there, married March 1, 1868 Madora Stover, born Jan. 25, 1852 on Beattie's Prairie, Delaware District. They are the parents of Birdie Adair, born Nov. 25, 1869; Eugene Homer, born March 18, 1873 and Willie Trott, born September 29, 1881. James Trott's Cherokee name is Osceola. He is retired from business and he and his wife are members of the Christian church.

Armstrong, Mrs. A. W. (See Cordery and McNair)—Mary Elizabeth, daughter of David McNair and Mary J. (Strickland) Rogers born July 9, 1870. Married August 3, 1896. Alexandder Watson, son of J. W. and Elizabeth Armstrong, born November 8, 1850, in

Sangamon County, Illinois. They are the parents of Harold Strickland born near Adair May 21, 1897. He enlisted in the World War and was at Camp Logan when the armistice was signed.

Austin (See Cordery)—Sue, daughter of Charles Harris and Pearl Victoria (Haat) Sisson, born December 14, 1898, at Ft. Gibson; educated at Ft. Gibson, Muskogee and Claremore. Married at Claremore June 5, 1920, Ervin, son of Henry and Sallie Austin. Mr. Austin is engaged in the wholesale dry goods business at Claremore.

Thomas Cordery, an Irishman, married Susannah, a full blood Cherokee of the Blind Savannah Clan. Their daughter Nannie married Parker Collins and they were the parents of Jennie Collins who married Charles Harris of Spartanburg district, South Carolina. Charles and Jennie Harris were the parents of Narcissa, born in 1841, married George Sisson and Jesse Wolf, she died October 18, 1898. Martha Elizabeth married Captain William Jackson; Sue F. married Alfred M. Gott; Charles Joseph and Trustle Bird.

George and Narcissa Sisson were the parents of Charles Harris Sisson, born December 26, 1859, educated in the Cherokee national schools and married at Ft. Gibson, December 4, 1893, Pearl Victoria Haas, born August 29, 1879, in Tupelo, Lee County, Mississippi. They are the parents of Charles Harris, born November 5, 1894; Charles Harris Sisson, Jr., married September 26, 1921, to Josephine Reed, born in Ardmore, Oklahoma, 1895. Jessie May, born July 31, 1896, married to John S. Matthews, April 18, 1917. John S. Matthews, born October 17, 1894. Sue, born December 14, 1898; Mary, born January 13, 1900 and Emma Pauline, born May 8, 1902.

Charles Harris Sisson was appointed Circuit Judge of the Cherokee Nation in May 1897, and was elected a member of the Council from Illinois District in August, 1903.

Archer, Carlotta (See Downing)—Edwin Archer, born September 19, 1817, in New York City. Married February 26, 1845, Mary Francis Vann, born September 21, 1825, in Georgia. He died May 15, 1893, and she died in 1921.

They were the parents of: Mary Elizabeth, married DeWitt Clinton Lipe; Louisa Catherine, married Freeland McIntosh; Ada, born March 16, 1860, educated in the Cherokee public schools and the Kirkwood (Mis souri) Seminary from which she graduated June 8, 1882, married February 28, 1888, Daniel Vincent Jones, born December 28, 1858 in Grayson county, Texas; Cora, married William Ross Shackelford; Charlotta Archer graduated from the Cherokee Female Seminary June 28, 1883, appointed member of the Cherokee board of education November 11, 1905; appointed County Superintendent of Public Instruction of Mayes county in July, 1908, elected to that office in 1910-12-16-18 and 1920.

Daniel Vincent and Ada (Archer) Jones were the parents of: Vera, born December 10, 1895, graduated from the Female Seminary May 29, 1907; Jean, born December 2, 1895, and Mary Jones, born July 15, 1899, and died May 11, 1917.

Joseph Vann, born February 1, 1789, married Catherine Rowe. He was elected a member of the Cherokee Constitutional Convention of 1827 from Coosawatee District elected Senator from the Salina District August 2, 1844, and elected President of the Senate, elected again to the same office August 6, 1849; elected Associate Justice of the Supreme ourt in 1847, Delegate to Washington, 1851, Executive Councilor 1853-55-57; Assistant Chief of the Cherokee Nation on August 1, 1859. He was the father of Mrs. Mary Francis Vann. He died May 3, 1877.

Adair, Rollin K. (See Adair, Grant, McNair, Halfbreed, Cordery and Duncan)—Rollin K. Adair, whose Cherokee name is Takatoka, of the Blind Savannah Clan, was born March 17, 1855, at Locust Grove in Salina District. Educated in the Cherokee Nation and at Dartmouth College. He married August 25, 1881, Rachel Landrum, born November 18, 1859. She died December 5, 1919. They were the parents of: Charles Bertram, born February 15, 1882; Robert McLeod, born July 5, 1884; William David, November 8, 1885; Sue M., born January 17, 1887; Sadie K., born July 6, 1889, and Rachel L., born December 24, 1897.

William Martin, a wealthy merchant of Bristol, England in order to break up a love match, furnished his youngest son, Joseph with a ship named the "Brice" and sent him to Virginia, where Joseph married Susannah Childs, member of a prominent Colonial family, and settled near Charlotteville Albermarle county in that state. Their third son Joseph, was born in 1840. He became a fur trader and amassed a fortune. He held the following military positions: Captain of the Transylvania Militia, elected in 1776 became Major February 17, 1779 and Lieut. Col. in 1781. He was elected Brig. Genl. of North Carolina by the Legislature Dec. 15, 1787 and was commissioned Brig. Gen. of the 20th Brigade of Virginia Militia by Gov. Henry Lee Dec. 11, 1793. He was the father of Martha called "Patsy" Martin, who married George Washington, the son of John and Gahoka Adair. George Washington and Martha Adair were the parents of Brice Martin Adair who married Sarah McNair. They were the parents of Rollin K. Adair, Townsite Commissioner 1888 and Superintendent of the Male Seminary 1895-99.

Index

OLD FAMILIES

The letter and number on the right side of page refer to descriptions beginning on page 446

PORTRAITS

GENERAL INDEX

A

B

References

38—1. Spanish Regime in Missouri Volume 2.
39—1. State Papers Indian Affairs, Vol. 2, page 11.
2. Ibid, page 31.
41—1 Tennessee Historical Magazine, Vol. 4, page 271-2.
100—1. H. R. Doc. No. 288, page 5.
2. Ibid, page 6.
101—1. H. R. Doc. No. 288, page 10.
103—2. H. R. Doc. No. 288, page 3.
4. Ibid, pages 57 to 69.
2. Ibid, page 46.
116—1. Doc No. 129, pages 59 and 60.
143—1. Lt. Col. Thomas Fox Taylor was killed on Bayou Menard July 27, 1862.
2. Quartermaster George W. Adair died April 22, 1862 and was succeeded by his son, Brice Martin Adair.
3. George West was killed at Ft. Gibson, May 20, 1863.
152—2. Rebellion Records, Series 1, Vol XIII, page 491.
3. Ibid, page 492.
4. Rebellion Records Vol. III, page 591.
5. Ibid, Vol. XIII, pages 595 and 598.
6. Ibid, page 489.
7. Ibid, Vol III, page 673.
8. Ibid, page 675.
159—1. Ibid Vol. XIII, pages 821, 842, 847, 849 and 861.
2. Ibid, page 431.
1. Ibid, page 473.
160—2. Rebellion Records, Vol. XIII, page 488.
3. Commissioner of Indian Affairs Report for 1865, page 286.
1. ebellion Records, Vol. XIII, page 552.
2. Ibid, page 565.
177—1. J. Harlan, Oct. 1, 1865 in Annual Report of the Commissioner of Indian Affairs, 1865, page 288.
225—1. Early History of the Cherokees, page 71.
2. Ibid, page 81.
3. Ibid, page 75.
4. Ibid page 75.
5. Ibid, page 45.
6. United States--Cherokee Treaty of December 29, 1835, article 10.
226—1. Laws of the Cherokee Nation, 1852, page 45.
2. Ibid, page 33.
4. Ibid, page 76.
1. Ibid, page 77.
2. Ibid, page 90.
3. Ibid, page 101.
227—1. Cherokee Advocate, January 29, 1846.
1. Laws of the Cherokee Nation, 18852, page 90.
2. Ibid, page 134.
3. Cherokee Advocate March 1846.
4. Cherokee Advocate, June 1845.
5. Laws of the Cherokee Nation 1852, page 141.
6. Ibid, page 165.
7. Ibid, page 136.
8. Ibid, page 186.
228—1. Annual Report of the Commissioner of Indian Affairs 1858, page 142.
2. Annual Report of the Commissioner of Indian Affairs 1859, page 177.
1. Laws o the Cherokee Nation, 1868, page 611.
229—2. Ibid, page 71.
3. Ibid, page 84.
4. Commissioner of Indian Affairs Report for 1877.
2. Act of Council November 17, 1843.
3. Act of Council November 18, 1846 and November 3, 1847.
4. Acts of Council November 11, 148 and November 19 1849.
5. Acts of Council November 6, 1851.
1. Laws of the Cherokee Nation 1875, page 188.
231—1. Treaty of December 25, 1835, article 10.
2. Laws of the Cherokee Nation 1852, page 146.
3. Annual Catalogues of the Seminaries.
1. Acts of Council, November 12, 1847.
1. "The Cherokee Nation is not excelled by any country in the inducements offered the youth." Annual Catalogues of the Seminaries.
232—1. Commissioner of Indian Affairs Report for 1855, page 451.
2. Catherine Hastings was a full blood Cherokee girl who was given that name by the Missionaries at Dwight Mission.
233—1. Martha Whiting was a full blood Cherokee girl who was given that name by the Missionaries at Dwight Mission.
233—2. Emma Lowrey Williams received as a graduation gift from her grandmother Wolf, a thousand dollar mahogany piano. Miss Williams, who was accounted a very brilliant girl, was dressed at her graduation in a gown which she had spun, wove and made.
3. Some of the extracts from an autograph album of Victoria Susan Hicks are appended.
234—1. Isabel Cobb graduated Glendale Female College, Glendale, Ohio, June 8 1881 and from the Woman's Medical College of Pennsylvania May 5, 1892.
235—1. Carlotta Archer was appointed Superintendent of Instruction of Mayes County in July 1908 and was elected to the same office in 1910, 1912, 1916, 1918 and 1920.

2. Author of the Life of General Stand Watie.
3. John Carlton Anderson was elected district clerk of Mayes County in 1907, 1910 and 1912.
4. H. W. C. Shelton was elected Suprintendent of Public Instruction of Craig County in 1907 and 1910.
5. Miss Oregonia Bell was the daughter of Dr. Moses Bell.
6. Miss Caleb was a white girl and the stepdaughter of Reverend Walter Adair Duncan.
235—1. This was the class of 1887. Graduation excercises were had at the Male Seminary.
2. Author of "John Ross and the Cherokee Indians." She was elected Superintendent of Public Instruction of Rogers County in 1920.
3. Edwin Mooring Pointer was appointed District Clark of Sequoyah county in 1907.
236—4. James Turner Edmondson was elected a member of the Oklahoma Constitutional Convention from District No. 66.
1. Charles Golston Watts was twice elected Judge of the Third District of Oklahoma.
2. James Morning York was elected Assessor of Rogers County in 1918.
3. William Pugh Cunningham was elected Register of Deeds of Delaware County in 1912.
1. Abraham Vandyke Robinson was elected County Clerk of Rogers County in 1918 and 1920.
2. Ella Mae Covel was elected City Clerk of Tahlequah in 1919 and 1921.
3. Eugene Nixon Williamson was elected Register of Deeds of Craig County in 1907 and 1910.
237—1. Aneliza Eulalia Sevier was born July 7, 1881 and elected Worthy Grand Motron of the Indian Territory Grand Chapter of Eastern Star on August 16, 1907.
2. Minnie Benge was elected Superintendent of Public Instruction of Cherokee County in 1920.
237—1. Sallie Pauline Parris was elected Superintendent of Public Instruction of Cherokee County in 1912.
238—1. Amanda Payne Morgan was elected Superintendent of Public Instruction of Washington County in 1907, 1910 and 1912.
1. Edmond Brigham Arnold was elected Attorney of Adair County in 1907 and Judge of the First District of Oklahoma in 1918.
2. Edwin Bentley Hunt was elected Attorney of Deleware County in 1912.
1. Cicero Johnson Howard was appointed County Clerk of Mayes County in June 1918.
239—1. E. R. Bell was elected Superintendent of Public Instruction of Nowata County in 1916, 1918 and 1920.
1. Commissioner of Indian Affairs Report for 1856.
241—1. Albert Sidney Wyly was elected a member of the Oklahoma Constitutional Convention from District No. 72.
2. James Turner Edmondson was elected a member of Oklahoma Constitutional Convention from District No. 66.
3. Samuel Frazier Parks was elected Judge of Craig County in 1910 and 1912.
242—1. John J. Lovett was appointed County Clerk of Cherokee County in 1913.
2. William Henry Ballentine was elected County Clerk of Cherokee County in 1916 and 1918.
242—1. George Washington Fields was elected Register of Deeds of Delaware County in 1907 and 1910. Elected Senator from the Thirteenth District of Oklahoma in 1912.
2. George Owen Grant was elected County Attorney of Adair County in 1918 and 1920.
3. James Bascom Johnson was elected Superintendent of Public Instruction of Adair County in 1907 and 1910.
4. James S. Sanders was elected Sheriff of Cherokee County in 1907 and Treasurer of the same county in 1916 and 1918.
1. William Houston Ballard was elected District Clerk of Delaware County in 1910 and 1912.
2. Wilson Nivens Smith was elected Judge of Delaware County in 1907.
3. Samuel Jesse Starr was elected County Clerk of Adair County in 1912 and 1914.
1. Jarrette Bell Harlan was elected Surveyor of Delaware County in 1907.
243—2. Henry Wood was elected County Commissioner of Muskogee County in 1916, resigned and was elected City Commissioner of Muskogee, resigned and was appointed Private Secretary to Governor Robertson, resigned and was appointed State Highway Commissioner.
243—1. John Grover Scales was elected Superintendent of Public Instruction of Delaware County in 1910 and 1912 Treasurer in 1916 and County Judge in 1918 and 1920.
2. Lee Roy Mitchell was elected District Clerk of Craig County in 1912.
1. Laws of the Cherokee Nation 1852, page 77.
2. Acts of Council December 23, 1843 and January 8, 1844.
3. Laws of the Cherokee Nation 1875, page 262.
4. Ibid, page 260.
5. Laws of the Cherokee Nation 1852, page 75.
6. Ibid, page 182.
246—1. Ibid, page 191.
2. Ibid, page 193.
3. Laws of the Cherokee Nation 1875, page 258.
4. Ibid, page 263.
1. Cherokee Advocate, February 2, 1887.
2. Tahlequah Arrow, Vol. 17, No. 11 of November 21 1903.
254—1. Letters written by Mrs. Cassandra Lockwood, edited but unpublished manuscript by Joseph B. Thoburn, page 32.
257—2. Poor Lo, by Walter N. Wyeth, page 54.
1. Ibid, page 38.
259—1. Nicholas Dalton Scales was born in 1802 in Rockingham County, North Carolina.
261—1. The constitution of the Cherokee Nation was concluded on September 6, 1839.
2. The Cherokee government ceased on June 30, 1898.
265—1. Laws of the Cherokee Nation 1852, page 54.
2. Ibid, page 35.
1: Ibid, pages 82 and 97.
2. Ibid, page 155.
3. Ibid, page 167.
4. Ibid page 171.
1. Letter of Colonel Watie in Chronicles of Oklahoma, Vol. I, No. 1, Page 42.

2. Constitution of 1839, article 3, section 4.
3. William Thornton was appointed but refused to qualify and his brother Charles
266—1. Elias McLeod Landrum was elected State Senator from the Thirtieth District in 1907 and 1911.
267—1. Eli H. Whitmire was elected County Commissioner of Adair County in 1918.
269—2. Gideon Morgan was elected a member of Legislature from Mayes County in the Fourth and Seventh Legislatures.
207—1. Connell Rogers was elected Treasurer of Muskogee County in 1907 and 1914 and was appointed to the same office in 1913.
270—1. Porum, Oklahoma was named for John Porum Davis.
271—2. Charles Edward Vann was elected County Commissioner of Muskogee County in 1907.
1. Charles Oliver Frye was elected a member of Oklahoma Constitutional Convention from District No. 84.
2. Isaac Abraham Jacobs was elected a representative from Sequoyah County in the Second Legislature.
272—1. Richard Lee Taylor was elected a County Commissioner in Adair County in 1918.
2. DeWitt Clinton Lipe was elected County Clerk of Rogers County in 1907 and 1910.
3. Clement Vann ogers was elected a member of the Oklahoma Constitutional Convention from District No. 61 and Rogers County was named for him.
273—4. Riley Wise Lindsey was elected to legislature from Mayes County in the Third Legislature.
1. James McDaniel Keys was elected Senator from the Twenty-ninth District in 1907.
2. William Edward Sanders was elected Sheriff of Rogers County in 1910, Commissioner of the same county in 1918 and 1920.
273—3. George Washington Mayes was elected Sheriff of Mayes County in 1910 and 1912.
4. John Franklin was elected Commissioner of Craig County in 1918.
1. Edward Northrup Washburn was elected Court Clerk of Delaware County in 1920.
274—1. Peter's Prairie in Delaware County was named for Peter.
1. Reverend Charles Bluejacket, a Methodist, was born in Michigan in 1816. He was the paternal grandson of Marmaduke Van Swerangen, born in Virginia in 1761. captured by the Shawnees in 1778 and adopted into the tribe under the name of Bluejacket. Kansas Historical Collections. Vol. X, page 397.
2. Thomas Bluejacket is the nephew of Reverand Chorles Bluejacket.
1. Weatherford Beck was generally called "Did" Beck.
2. James Proctor Butler was elected to Legislature from Delaware District in 1920.
3. James Riley Copeland was elected a member of the Oklahoma Constitutional Convention from District No. 62.
275—4. T. Wyman Thompson was elected County Commissioner of Mayes County in 1918.
5. John Hamilton Gibson was elected a member of legislature from Delaware County in 1916 and 1918.
6. Lee Bell Smith was elected a member of legislature from Delaware County in 1907.
7. George Alexander Cox was elected District Clerk of Delaware County in 1907.
276—1. Cicero Johnson Howard was appointed County Clerk of Mayes County in June 1918. vice, his brother, Lewis Anderson Howard, who resigned to enter the army.
1. Francis Clark Adair was elected Sheriff of Adair County in 1907.
277—2. Edward Adair Clyne was elected Treasurer of Adair County in 1907.
279—1. John Benge was generally known as "Riddle" Benge.
1. Leggings killed Chief Richard Fields in Texas in January, 1827.
208—1. John Dimar Jordan was elected Sheriff of Washington County, Oklahoma in 1907 1910 and 1912. De died in office.
208—2. Thomas Jefferson Whsenhunt was elected County Commissioner of Rogers County in 1910 and 1912.
3. William Billingslea Beck was elected Representative from McIntosh County in 1907.
281—2. William Charles Dumont Patton was appointed District Clerk of Sequoyah County in 1909 and was elected to that office in 1910.
3. David Jesse Faulkner was elected County Commissioner of Rogers County in 1912.
4. James Willoughby Breedlove was elected a Representative from Sequoyah County in 1912.
5. William Nucholls Littlejohn was a member of the Constitutional Convention form District No. 78, he was elected judge of Sequoyah County in 1907 and 1910.
283—2. Joseph Benson Cobb was elected County Commissioner of Wagoner County in 1918.
1. John Ross McIntosh was elected Treasurer of Rogers County in 1920.
2. James Sanford Davenport was elected Congressman from Oklahoma for four terms.
283—3. Henry Cirkham Walkley was elected Register of Deeds of Tulsa County in 1907 and 1910.
4. William Lafayette Trott was elected Register of Deeds of Craig County in 1912.
285—1. The same individual, although a prominent man, was known as either: Wilson, Osceola or Oce Hair. He did not belong to the Conrad family.
286—1. Oscar Fitzaland Adair was elected County Commissioner of Sequoyah County in 1907.
287—1. John W. Brown was generally called "Scoy" Brown.
2. John Benge was generally known as "Riddle" Benge.
289—1. It was Lome Seven, who thinking that he had his opposing counsel, Lucien Burr Bell (generally called by his Cherokee name, Hoolie, the Cherokee word for bell) in a close place, said: "O, Mr. Hoolie, I've got you by the tight place."
290—1. Andrew Jackson Jeremiah was elected County Commissioner of Sequoyah County in 1907.
291—1. William Walter Wright was elected Treasurer of Adair Coounty in 1918 and 1920.
293—1. Bluford West Alberty was elected County Judge of Adair County in 1907.
295—1. John T. Beamer was also known as Jack Doubletooth. He was killed near the mouth of Pryor Creek on December 30, 1874.
1. Reverend Evan Jones was not a citizen of the Cherokee Nation at that time.
297—1. Pilling's Bibliography of the Iroquoian Lenguages, page 41.
1. Richard Halfbreed was generally known as Richard H. Fields.
298—1. Thomas Albert Chandler was elected to Congress from the First District of Oklahoma in 1916 and 1920.

INDEX

TO THE

HISTORY

OF THE

CHEROKEE INDIANS

AND

Their Legends and Folk Lore.

With a

New Added Index

By

JEFF BOWEN

JANAWAY PUBLISHING
Santa Maria, California

www.ingramcontent.com/pod-product-compliance
Lightning Source LLC
Chambersburg PA
CBHW030634150426
42811CB00048B/102